OCEAN AND COASTAL LAW AND POLICY

DONALD C. BAUR, TIM EICHENBERG, AND MICHAEL SUTTON

For updates: www.ababooks.org/coastallaw/

Section of Environment, Energy, and Resources
American Bar Association

Cover design by Laurie McDonald.

Photography for cover copyright © 2007 Chuck Davis/Tidal Flats, Ltd. All Right Reserved.

Printed in the United States of America.

Printed on paper that contains 30% recycled fiber.

17 16 15 14 13 5 4 3 2

Library of Congress Cataloging-in-Publication Data

Ocean and coastal law and policy/edited by Donald C. Baur, Tim Eichenberg, and Michael Sutton.—1st ed.
   p. cm.
Includes index.
ISBN-13: 978-1-59031-982-6
ISBN-10: 1-59031-982-6
  1. Coastal zone management—Law and legislation—United States. 2. Law of the sea—United States. I. Baur, Donald C. II. Eichenberg, Tim. III. Sutton, Michael.

KF5627.O24 2008
346.7304'6917—dc22

                                 2008005472

Acknowledgments

The editors acknowledge and greatly appreciate the hard work and editorial assistance of Rebecca Brezenoff of Perkins Coie for her efforts to coordinate this book over its three-year preparation period. They also are grateful for the research and review assistance of Emily Merolli of Perkins Coie, Aimee David and Kathleen Hills of the Monterey Bay Aquarium, and law students Melissa Locke of Vermont Law School and Darcy Vaugh of University of California, Hastings College of Law. Thanks also to the reviewers of this book on the ABA Book Publications Committee of the Section of Environment, Energy, and Resources: Kim Diana Connolly, Robin Kundis Craig, and Sam Kalen; and ABA Publishing's Deputy Director, Rick Paszkiet. Finally, the editors thank Laurie McDonald and Tim Robertson for their technical assistance in the preparation of this book.

Summary Table of Contents

Contents

Chapter Seven

Coastal Water Quality Protection 205
Robin Kundis Craig

Chapter Fifteen

The Law of Marine Mammal Conservation **477**

Donald C. Baur, Michael L. Gosliner, and Nina M. Young

Chapter Sixteen

The Endangered Species Act and Marine Species **519**

Wm. Robert Irvin and Michael J. Bean

Chapter Twenty
**Ocean Commissions Issue an Urgent Call for Action to Reform
U.S. Ocean Policy and Law**. 655
Sarah Chasis

About the Editors

Donald C. Baur is a partner in the Washington, D.C., office of Perkins Coie LLP. He previously has served as General Counsel of the U.S. Marine Mammal Commission and as an attorney advisor in the Office of the Solicitor for the U.S. Department of the Interior, where he served in the Office's Honors Program. He graduated with highest honors from Trinity College and from the University of Pennsylvania School of Law. Mr. Baur is on the summer faculty of the Vermont Law School, where he teaches Ocean and Coastal Law. He also taught Federal Wildlife Law at the Golden Gate School of Law, and serves as Co-Chair of the ALI-ABA Environmental Institute Conference on Species Protection and the Law and as an instructor in the Environmental Law Institute's Environmental Boot Camp. He is Vice Chair of the Book Publications Committee of the ABA Section of Environment, Energy, and Resources, and he has served with Wm. Robert Irvin as coeditor of the ABA's *Endangered Species Act: Law, Policy, and Perspectives* (2002). Mr. Baur has published over twenty law review and related articles, many of which concern marine environment. He received grants from the Turner Foundation to prepare a legal analysis, through the World Wildlife Fund, of marine protected areas (published with Wm. Robert Irvin and Darren Misenko in the *Vermont Law Review*) and the Packard Foundation, for a legal analysis of marine ecosystem-based management (Chapter 19 of this book).

Tim Eichenberg is Chief Counsel of the San Francisco Bay Conservation and Development Commission and teaches Ocean and Coastal Law at the Vermont Law School. He has served as legal counsel for the Ocean Conservancy, California Coastal Commission, Oceana, and the Environmental Defense Center. He chaired the Clean Water Network in Washington, D.C., helped found the Casco Baykeeper Program in Maine, and taught courses in environmental law at the University of Maine School of Law, Golden Gate University School of Law, and the Environmental Law Institute. Mr. Eichenberg is a graduate of Earlham College and the Washington University School of Law, and was awarded a post-doctoral fellowship in marine policy at the Woods Hole Oceanographic Institution. He is a member of the Bar in California and the District of Columbia, and has published more than 30 articles and reports on environmental issues.

Michael Sutton serves as Vice President of the Monterey Bay Aquarium and directs a new program known as the Center for the Future of the Oceans. The mission of the Center is to inspire action for conservation of the oceans. Previously, Mr. Sutton headed the Marine Fisheries Program at the David & Lucile Packard Foundation in Los Altos, California, the largest private funder of ocean conservation efforts in North America. Earlier, Mr. Sutton founded and directed the World Wildlife Fund's Endangered Seas Campaign, a global effort to promote the conservation and sustainable use of marine fisheries. Before joining the WWF staff, Mr. Sutton served as a special agent with the U.S. Fish and Wildlife Service and as a park ranger with the National Park Service in Yosemite, Yellowstone, Biscayne, and Virgin Islands National Parks and Death Valley National Monument. He received a bachelor's degree in wildlife biology from Utah State University in 1978 and pursued graduate studies in marine biology at the University of Sydney, Australia. His research involved the behavioral ecology of coral reef fishes on the Great Barrier Reef. In 1992, he received a law degree in international and natural resources law from the George Washington University's National Law Center in Washington, D.C. Mr. Sutton has served as a senior advisor to the Secretary of Commerce and the Secretary of State on marine fishery issues, sitting on two Federal Advisory Committees. He was a founding member of the national steering committees of both the Marine Fish Conservation Network and the Ocean Wildlife Campaign, the latter an international coalition working to conserve large pelagic fishes such as sharks, tuna, and swordfish. He has lectured at graduate seminars on ocean conservation at Harvard, Yale, Columbia, Stanford, Tufts, the George Washington University, and the University of Rhode Island.

About the Contributors

Michael J. Bean has headed the Wildlife Program of Environmental Defense since 1977. In 2003 he became codirector of its Center for Conservation Incentives. A 1973 graduate of the Yale Law School, he serves on the board of Resources for the Future and is a past member of Board on Environmental Studies and Toxicology of the National Research Council of the National Academy of Sciences, and the board of directors of the Environmental Law Institute. He was appointed by former Interior Secretary Gale Norton to be one of the ten members of the National Wildlife Refuge Centennial Commission and until recently served as the director of the Pew Fellows Program in Marine Conservation. His book, *The Evolution of National Wildlife Law,* the third edition of which was written with Melanie J. Rowland in 1997, is generally regarded as the leading text on the subject of wildlife conservation law. Mr. Bean pioneered the use of "safe harbor agreements" as an incentive-based strategy to gain the cooperation of private landowners in conserving endangered species. Mr. Bean's work with safe harbor agreements is part of a larger effort to address the importance of incentives—both financial and regulatory—in accomplishing conservation goals, and was instrumental in Environmental Defense's creation in 2003 of a Center for Conservation Incentives, which is dedicated to exploring, testing, and implementing incentive-based strategies for conserving biodiversity.

Sarah Chasis is a senior attorney at the Natural Resources Defense Council, Inc. She has been with the NRDC for more than thirty years and serves as the Director of NRDC's Ocean Initiative. Her advocacy for oceans and coastal waters has been wide-ranging: She has sued to protect sensitive ocean areas from offshore oil drilling, promoted the clean-up of coastal pollution, protected the public from swimming in polluted waters at the nation's beaches, and worked for better domestic and international fisheries management. She recently helped convince Congress to pass legislation requiring an end to unsustainable harvest of ocean fisheries and has successfully promoted state legislation and initiatives to strengthen protection for coastal and ocean resources. In recognition of her work on behalf of coastal protection, Ms. Chasis was selected as the first Coastal Steward of the Year by the National Oceanic and Atmospheric Administration. Ms. Chasis has participated in a wide variety of commissions and coalitions including three years staffing NRDC's president while he served on the Pew Oceans Commission. She is an Adjunct Professor of Clinical Law at the New York University School of Law, where she teaches an Environmental Law Clinic. Last year she received the Smith College Medal, awarded to women who have risen to the top of their fields while contributing their talent and expertise to the improvement of others' lives.

Kim Diana Connolly is an Associate Professor of Law at the University of South Carolina School of Law. Professor Connolly received her undergraduate degree in chemistry from the University of North Carolina at Chapel Hill, where she was a Morehead Scholar. She received her J.D. from Georgetown University Law Center in 1993. Before joining the law faculty in 1999, Professor Connolly worked at a number of Washington, D.C., law firms specializing in environmental law. Prior to law school, Professor Connolly was the Director of the North Carolina Rural Communities Assistance Project, Inc., and also served as a VISTA Volunteer. Professor Connolly teaches a variety of environmental law courses. She is also a member of the summer faculty at Vermont Law School, where she teaches Wetlands Law and Policy. Her areas of academic interest include wetlands and other natural resources and public lands law, and her scholarly works have appeared in a number of journals and other publications. Professor Connolly served as coeditor of the ABA's *Wetlands Law and Policy: Understanding Section 404*. She speaks regularly at national and international conferences on wetlands, coastal, and other environmental matters. Professor Connolly is also an associate faculty member of the University of South Carolina School of the Environment.

John Costenbader received his J.D. in May 2008 from The George Washington University Law School. While at GW, John clerked with the USAID General Counsel's Office, Environment and Natural Resources Division of the Department of Justice, and the Environmental Section of the Attorney General's Office of Rio de Janeiro, Brazil. John also earned a Master of Public Affairs from Indiana University's School of Public and Environmental Affairs in 2003, where he concentrated in Environmental Policy and Natural Resource Management. Prior to law school, John managed U.S. government research contracts in Sub-Saharan Africa and Latin America. In addition, John served as a forestry volunteer with the Peace Corps in Mali, West Africa from 1995 to 1997.

Aaron C. Courtney practices natural resource and environmental law with a focus on Clean Water Act (CWA), Endangered Species Act (ESA), and National Environmental Policy Act compliance, and hazardous and solid waste issues. He assists clients in federal and state environmental permitting and other compliance matters, with an emphasis on Section 7 consultations and dredge and fill and water quality permits. Mr. Courtney also represents clients on litigation related to the ESA, CWA, and hazardous waste cleanup and cost recovery. He has lectured on numerous environmental legal matters, including the ESA, invasive species, the CWA, and environmental regulatory compliance issues. Mr. Courtney recently spent several years on the faculty at Lewis & Clark Law School in Portland, Oregon, where he taught courses on the ESA, Environmental Issues in Business Transactions, and Environmental Litigation, and helped run the law school's environmental litigation clinic. Mr. Courtney's current practice is based in Stoel Rives LLP's Portland, Oregon, office, and he continues to teach at Lewis & Clark Law School as an Adjunct Professor. He earned both a B.A. (1989) and an M.S. (1993) in Biology and Environmental Sciences at the University of Virginia and his J.D. at the University of Virginia School of Law (1992).

Robin Kundis Craig is the Attorneys' Title Insurance Fund Professor of Law at the Florida State University College of Law, Tallahassee, Florida. Her scholarship focuses on all things water, particularly the Clean Water Act, ocean and coastal law, the intersection of land and sea, and the intersection of environmental and constitutional law. Professor Craig's work with the Clean Water Act was recently recognized through her 2005–2007 appointment to the National Research Council, National Academy of Sciences' Committee on the Clean Water Act and the Mississippi River, which reviewed the role of the Clean Water Act in improving water quality along the Mississippi River and in the Gulf of Mexico. Among other positions with the American Bar Association, she is a past Chair and current Vice Chair of the ABA Section of Environment, Energy, and Resources' Marine Resources Committee. Professor Craig has published two books, *The Clean Water Act and the Constitution* (Environmental Law Institute 2004; second edition forthcoming 2008/2009) and *Environmental Law in Context* (Thomson/West 2005; second edition forthcoming June 2008), an environmental law textbook. She authored the "Oceans and Estuaries" chapter of *Stumbling Toward Sustainability* (Environmental Law Institute 2002), and has published more than thirty law review articles, book chapters, and other significant writings. Professor Craig earned her J.D. summa cum laude in 1996 from Lewis & Clark Law School, graduating first in her class and earning that school's Environmental Law Certificate; her Ph.D. in 1993 from the University of California; her M.A. in 1986 from the Johns Hopkins University; and her B.A. cum laude in 1985 from Pomona College. She has been admitted to the Oregon State Bar and the federal bar for the U.S. District Court for the District of Oregon.

Josh Eagle is an Assistant Professor of Law at the University of South Carolina School of Law, where he teaches property, natural resources, and ocean and coastal law. Prior to arriving in South Carolina, Professor Eagle was co-founder and director of the Stanford Fisheries Policy Project at Stanford Law School. He has served as a Trial Attorney for the U.S. Justice Department and as wildlife counsel for the National Audubon Society. He is a graduate of Johns Hopkins (B.A.), Colorado State University (M.S., Forest Sciences), and Georgetown University Law Center (J.D.).

Kristen M. Fletcher is the Executive Director of the Coastal States Organization (CSO), which represents the interests of the governors from the thirty-five coastal states and territories on federal, legislative, and policy issues relating to sound coastal, Great Lakes, and ocean management. Ms. Fletcher's current work includes reauthorization of the Coastal Zone Management Act, serving on the MMS Subcommittee on Alternative Energy, and legislative efforts toward adapting to climate change. Prior to joining CSO, Ms. Fletcher directed the Marine Affairs Institute and Rhode Island Sea Grant Legal Program at Roger Williams University, where she advised university researchers, federal and state agencies, and other Sea Grant constituents on ocean and coastal law issues and directed research and outreach projects. While at RWU, she taught Ocean and Coastal Law, Natural Resources Law, and Fisheries Law. Previously, she directed the Mississippi-Alabama Sea Grant Legal Program and was founding director of the National Sea Grant Law Center at the University of Mississippi School of Law. Ms. Fletcher earned her B.A. in Political Science and Spanish from Auburn University, J.D. from the University of Notre Dame School of Law, and

Masters of Law in Environmental and Natural Resources Law from Lewis & Clark Law School. She is President of The Coastal Society and a Senior Fellow with the Environmental Leadership Program.

Michael Goo is Climate Legislative Director for the Natural Resources Defense Council, a non-profit environmental group. Mr. Goo joined NRDC in September of 2007. Prior to joining NRDC, he served as Majority Counsel to the United States Senate Environment and Public Works Committee, under Chairman Barbara Boxer, with responsibility for all clean air and climate change issues. He also served as Minority Counsel to the Senate Environment Committee working for ranking member Jim Jeffords. Between 2001 and 2005, Mr. Goo served as Minority Counsel to the House Energy and Commerce Committee, under Ranking Member John Dingell, responsible for clean air and climate change issues. Prior to his work on Capitol Hill, he worked in the Office of General Counsel at EPA between 1993 and 2001, serving in a variety of positions, including Special Assistant to the General Counsel for three EPA General Counsels and an air attorney in numerous rulemakings and litigation. Mr. Goo's work at EPA included serving as the lead agency attorney in the *American Trucking Associations v. Whitman* case, which was eventually resolved in favor of EPA by the United States Supreme Court in a unanimous opinion, upholding EPA'S National Ambient Air Quality Standards for ozone and particulate matter. He also worked as an environmental attorney in private practice for the law firm Perkins Coie between 1988 and 1993. Mr. Goo is a cum laude graduate of Vassar College and The Washington University School of Law and a member of the District of Columbia Bar.

Michael L. Gosliner is General Counsel of the Marine Mammal Commission, a position he has held since 1987. Prior to that, he served as an attorney with the National Oceanic and Atmospheric Administration, specializing in Endangered Species Act and Marine Mammal Protection Act issues. In these capacities, he has been personally involved in most of the legal issues related to marine mammal conservation that have developed over the past twenty-five years. He received his J.D. from Hastings College of the Law and holds an undergraduate degree in biology from the University of California at Berkeley. He is a member of the California Bar.

Wm. Robert Irvin is Senior Vice President for Conservation Programs at Defenders of Wildlife in Washington, D.C., where he manages conservation policy, litigation, field conservation, and international conservation programs, supervising a staff of policy advocates, scientists, and lawyers in the United States, Mexico, and Canada. Prior to joining Defenders of Wildlife, Mr. Irvin served as Director of U.S. Conservation for World Wildlife Fund; Vice President for Marine Wildlife Conservation and General Counsel for the Center for Marine Conservation; Senior Counsel for Fish and Wildlife on the Majority Staff of the U.S. Senate Committee on Environment and Public Works; Counsel and Director of the Fisheries and Wildlife Division, National Wildlife Federation; Trial Attorney in the Civil Division of the U.S. Department of Justice; and was in private legal practice in Portland, Oregon. Mr. Irvin has written and lectured extensively on biodiversity conservation issues. He is the coeditor, with Donald C. Baur, of the American Bar Association's deskbook on the Endangered Species Act, *Endangered Species Act: Law, Policy, and Perspectives* (2002). He was a member of the World Conservation Union's (IUCN) Red List Criteria Review Working Group, which revised the standards for listing threatened species globally. Mr. Irvin has taught Biodiversity Protection at Vermont Law School and the University of Maryland School of Law. Mr. Irvin graduated magna cum laude with a B.S. degree in Forest Science from Utah State University in 1980. He earned a J.D., Order of the Coif, in 1983 from the University of Oregon School of Law. He has served as cochair of the Environment, Energy, and Natural Resources Section of the District of Columbia Bar and is on the board of directors of the Environmental Law Institute.

Suzanne Iudicello is an independent consultant and writer on marine conservation and fisheries issues. She served as Vice President and General Counsel of the Center for Marine Conservation (now the Ocean Conservancy) and worked for the Alaska legislature and Alaska Governor's Washington, D.C. office. In both those capacities, she worked with national advocacy groups on reauthorizations of the Marine Mammal Protection Act, Magnuson-Stevens Fishery Conservation and Management Act, Clean Water Act, Clean Air Act, and Oil Pollution Act. She serves on the design committee for the Report on the State of the Nation's Ecosystems at the Heinz Center for Science, Economics, and the Environment. Ms. Iudicello has authored and coauthored numerous articles and four books. She received her J.D. from the National Law Center at the George Washington University.

Michael A. Mantell works on strategic conservation philanthropy, habitat planning, and conservation finance with the Resources Law Group, a unique law and consulting firm in Sacramento, California. He has worked with the David and Lucile Packard Foundation, the independent nonprofit Resources Legacy Fund, and others in designing and participating in the investment of private philanthropic funds and loans in programs and projects that have yielded extensive conservation outcomes for land and marine conservation. From 1991 to 1997, he served as Undersecretary for Resources for the State of California, where he oversaw the Resources Agency, was a principal architect of California's Natural Community Conservation Planning program, and helped develop a new oceans strategy for the state. Prior to that, he was the General Counsel of the World Wildlife Fund, where he oversaw legal and congressional matters and worked on international debt-for-nature deals; and served as a Deputy City Attorney for Los Angeles. Mr. Mantell served as Campaign Chair for the Yes on Proposition 84 campaign, a $5.4 billion bond measure providing critical investments in California's coastal, water, and land resources, approved by California voters in November 2006.

Milo C. Mason is an attorney assigned to offshore minerals management matters at the U.S. Department of the Interior. He joined DOI's Solicitor's Office as a Regional Solicitor's Office law clerk. He came to Washington, D.C., as an Honor's Program Attorney. He joined the Offshore Minerals and International Law Branch in 1981 and worked on OCS regulations, lease sales, litigation, boundary, and Coastal Zone Management Act implementation issues. In 1983, he was asked to be the career staff attorney overseeing the federal court litigation on surface coal mining regulations. In

1990, he was appointed Assistant Solicitor–Offshore Minerals. Mr. Mason has served as a member of the U.S. Delegation to the 7th Law of the Sea Convention Meeting, a member of the delegation that successfully negotiated the Mexican/U.S. submerged lands boundary treaty of 2000 for the Western Gap of the Gulf of Mexico, and a member of various interagency committees at the State Department. He serves on the U.S. Baseline Committee and the Interagency Marine Boundary Working Group. He has been an Adjunct Professor at the George Washington University Law School, teaching courses on environmental enforcement and, for twenty years, an editorial board member of the American Bar Association magazine *Natural Resources & Environment*, serving now as its Interview Editor. He has published various articles, most notably "A Tax Code We Can Understand and Live With," *The National Law Journal*, December 22, 1997; "Preventing Accidents and Anarchy: Toward a Science of Compliance," *Natural Resources & Environment*, Spring 2000; "Toward Fully Understood Compliance: Knowing Enforcement Mechanisms," *Natural Resources & Environment*, Spring 1994 (with coauthor Paul Smyth); and "Making Tough Choices Easier: Compliance and Enforcement 102," *Natural Resources & Environment*, Spring 2004 (with coauthor Paul Smyth). Mr. Mason is a graduate of Cornell University (B.A.), Stanford University (M.A.), and Harvard Law School (J.D.).

Emily K. Merolli is an associate in the Washington, D.C., office of Perkins Coie LLP, where she practices environmental and natural resources law. Her practice includes wide-ranging experience with ocean and coastal resources, species protection, water quality, offshore energy development, and national environmental review. She has contributed numerous articles in the Sea Grant legal reporters *The Sandbar* and *Waterlog*. Ms. Merolli is a graduate of Vermont Law School (J.D. 2006, cum laude; M.S.E.L. 2006, cum laude) and the University of California, Davis (B.S. 2002 in Environmental Policy Analysis and Planning). She is a member of the Bar in California.

Darren Misenko has a solo practice in Duxbury, Vermont, focusing on environmental and natural resource law. He formerly served as Federal Consistency Specialist for the Office of Ocean and Coastal Management, National Oceanic and Atmospheric Administration, United States Department of Commerce. His experience includes extensive work on environmental and natural resource law matters including coastal zone management and marine protected areas. Darren also coauthored the law review article "Putting 'Protection' into Marine Protected Areas," presented at the Changing Tides in Ocean Management symposium, *Vermont Law Review,* Spring 2004. He is a graduate of Vermont Law School (J.D. 2003, M.S.E.L. 2003, cum laude) and the State University of New York at Potsdam (B.A. 1996, cum laude) and is a member of the Bar in New York and Vermont.

Patrick A. Parenteau is Professor of Law and Director of the Environmental and Natural Resources Law Clinic at Vermont Law School. He previously served as Director of the Environmental Law Center at Vermont Law School from 1993 to 1999. Professor Parenteau also teaches in the Environmental Studies Program at Dartmouth College. Professor Parenteau has an extensive background in environmental and natural resources law. His previous positions include Vice President for Conservation with the National Wildlife Federation in Washington, D.C. (1976–1984); General Counsel to the New England Regional Office of the EPA in Boston (1984–1987); Commissioner of the Vermont Department of Environmental Conservation (1987–1989); and Of Counsel with the Perkins Coie law firm in Portland, Oregon (1989–1993). Professor Parenteau is a nationally recognized expert on the Endangered Species Act, the Clean Water Act, the National Environmental Policy Act, and other environmental laws. He has been involved in drafting, litigating, implementing, teaching, and writing about these laws for over thirty years. He is a recipient of the National Wildlife Federation's Conservation Achievement Award for 2006 in recognition of his contributions to wildlife conservation and environmental education. He holds a B.S. from Regis University, a J.D. from Creighton University, and an LL.M. in Environmental Law from the George Washington University.

Ann Powers is a faculty member of the Center for Environmental Legal Studies, where her teaching and scholarship focus on water quality, wetland protection, water pollution trading programs, and coastal and ocean issues. Until joining the Center in 1995, she was Vice President and General Counsel of the Chesapeake Bay Foundation, where she supervised the Foundation's pollution control advocacy program. Professor Powers also served as a senior trial attorney in the Environmental Enforcement Section of the U.S. Department of Justice, handling both civil and criminal cases, and as an Assistant United States Attorney for the District of Columbia. Professor Powers has testified on numerous occasions before the United States Senate and House of Representatives and state legislatures and commissions, and has served on many national and international boards and panels. She is a member of the World Conservation Union's (IUCN) Commission on Environmental Law, and chairs the Land-Based Pollution Subcommittee of the Commission's Oceans, Coasts & Coral Reefs Specialist Group. She is a director of the Pace Environmental Litigation Clinic. Professor Powers is a graduate of Indiana University and Georgetown University Law Center.

Sylvia Quast the Chief of Civil Defensive Litigation for the United States Attorney's Office in the Eastern District of California. She was previously with the Resources Law Group in Sacramento, California, where her practice focused on complex environmental and natural resource planning and management issues, including legal counseling for conservation philanthropy program and helping to manage a $5.4 billion voter-approved bond campaign for clean water, parks, and coastal protection. She also served as Senior Counsel in the Policy Section of the United States Department of Justice's Environment and Natural Resources Division. In that capacity, she represented the United States in several major cases, including enforcement actions such as a United States Supreme Court case upholding protections for wetlands in California's Central Valley, and challenges to federal programs such as the federal-state CALFED Bay-Delta Program and the operation of the lower Snake River dams in Washington State. Her responsibilities included nonlitigation activities as well, such as preparation for congressional hearings and representing the Justice Department on the United States Coral Reef Task Force's Steering Committee. Ms. Quast received her B.A. (summa cum laude) from the University of Minnesota and her J.D. (cum laude) from Harvard Law School.

Michael W. Reed's legal career has focused on questions of maritime boundaries and jurisdiction. His introduction to the subject came as a Coast Guard officer involved in the enforcement of United States fisheries laws against foreign distant-water fleets operating off our coasts. Upon completion of his Coast Guard service Mr. Reed moved to the Department of Justice where he continued to concentrate on coastal and offshore boundaries and jurisdictional questions. His Justice Department practice included litigating eleven Supreme Court original actions between the federal government and its coastal states over the limits of state and federal maritime jurisdiction. Other maritime cases involved marine mammal protection, natural resource production, and claims to sunken treasure. Throughout his federal career Mr. Reed served as a member of the Interagency Committee on the Delimitation of the United States Baseline, a group charged with producing, and keeping up to date, a set of nautical charts depicting our various zones of maritime jurisdiction. Those charts are relied on by enforcement agencies and foreign governments as the official United States statement of its maritime claims. Mr. Reed is a graduate of the University of Washington School of Law and has done postgraduate study in public international law at the George Washington University. He has recently retired from the Department of Justice and lives in Southern California, where he teaches occasional courses in public lands and environmental law at the University of San Diego School of Law and consults on maritime jurisdiction and boundaries. His most recent publication, *Shore and Sea Boundaries*, vol. 3, covers United States Supreme Court law on the subject.

Stephen E. Roady is an attorney with Earthjustice (formerly the Sierra Club Legal Defense Fund), where he works on ocean conservation, ecosystem protection, and other environmental issues. He has been closely involved with ocean issues since 1998, when he joined Earthjustice as the director of the Ocean Law Project (OLP) and led a team of lawyers working to protect United States ocean resources. During 2001 and 2002, Mr. Roady served as the first president of Oceana, a nonprofit, international ocean conservation organization. During 1989 and 1990, he served as legal advisor to U.S. Senator John H. Chafee (R.-R.I.) on a wide range of environmental issues. A graduate of Duke Law School and Davidson College, Mr. Roady is an adjunct faculty member at the American University Washington College of Law. He is a visiting scholar at Duke University, where he teaches Ocean and Coastal Law and Policy. Harvard Law School named Mr. Roady a Wasserstein Public Interest Fellow for 2007–2008.

David K. Schorr is an independent consultant based in Washington, D.C., with expertise in fisheries and in issues surrounding globalization and the environment. From 1993 until 2002, Mr. Schorr directed the World Wildlife Fund's Sustainable Commerce Program, with its focus on the environmental aspects of international trade and investment policies. Since 2002, Mr. Schorr has served as a Senior Fellow to

WWF, guiding WWF's participation in WTO negotiations aimed at curbing harmful fisheries subsidies. Prior to joining WWF, Mr. Schorr practiced law in Washington, D.C., representing developing-country governmental clients on international legal and political matters. In the 1980s, he lived and worked in Europe as a nuclear weapons policy analyst, and coauthored *How Nuclear Weapons Decisions Are Made* (MacMillan 1986). A graduate of the Yale Law School and of Oberlin College, Mr. Schorr has taught courses on basic trade law and on trade and environment as a member of the adjunct faculties of the Georgetown University Law Center and the American University Washington College of Law.

Jennifer L. Schorr is an Assistant Attorney General for the State of Alaska in the Environmental Section. Ms. Schorr was previously an associate in the Seattle office of Perkins Coie LLP, where she practiced environmental, natural resources, and land use law, including oceans and coastal law. She is a graduate of the University of Washington School of Law and has a Master of Marine Affairs from the School of Marine Affairs at the University of Washington, and a B.A. from Colorado College. Ms. Schorr is the author of "The Australian National Representative System of Marine Protected Areas and the Marine Zoning System: A Model for the United States?," *Pacific Rim Law & Policy Journal* (University of Washington 2004), and a report for the National Marine Fisheries Service regarding comanagement of marine mammals under the Marine Mammal Protection Act (1998).

Janis Searles is a lawyer and activist with broad experience in ocean conservation, public lands, fisheries, and other environmental issues. Ms. Searles is Vice President for legal affairs for Ocean Conservancy, a nonprofit organization that promotes healthy and diverse ocean ecosystems and opposes practices that threaten ocean life and human life. Ms. Searles also serves as an adjunct faculty member of the Northwestern School of Law. Prior to Ocean Conservancy, Ms. Searles was Senior Counsel for Oceana, focused on marine conservation and habitat protection in Alaska, Washington, Oregon, and California, and was a staff attorney in the Alaska office of Earthjustice, where she practiced federal environmental law. Ms. Searles graduated summa cum laude from the Northwestern School of Law of Lewis and Clark College, after graduating from Reed College.

Odin Smith is an attorney with the National Oceanic and Atmospheric Administration, where he advises primarily on ocean and coastal resource management issues. Mr. Smith previously coordinated an environmental compliance program in the National Park Service, and practiced environmental, natural resources, and federal Indian law in the Washington, D.C., office of Perkins Coie LLP. Mr. Smith holds a B.S. (summa cum laude) in geosciences from the University of Arizona, an M.S. in geology from the Massachusetts Institute of Technology, and a J.D. (magna cum laude) from the George Washington University Law School.

Christophe A. G. Tulou is a consultant on environmental, natural resource, and ocean policy issues, based in Washington, D.C., and is currently serving as Director of the H. John Heinz III Center's program on Sustainable Oceans, Coasts, and Waterways (SOCW). In that capacity, he is directing the Heinz Center's initiative on coastal resilience, The Nation's Coasts: A Vision and Action Agenda for the Future. Mr. Tulou also serves on the Heinz Center's SOCW Advisory Committee. Mr. Tulou previously served as president of the nonprofit Center for SeaChange, which he established to advance substantial reform of U.S. ocean laws and policies. He also helped guide the Pew Oceans Commission, as its executive director, to the publication of *America's Living Oceans: Charting a Course for Sea Change,* a compilation of policy recommendations to restore and protect living marine resources in U.S. waters. Mr. Tulou served as Cabinet Secretary for Delaware's Department of Natural Resources and Environmental Control, and served over a decade in Congress. Mr. Tulou was born in Geneva, Switzerland. He earned his B.S. in Biology at the College of William and Mary, and received two master's degrees—one in Zoology and the other in Marine Affairs—from the University of Rhode Island. He also received a law degree from Georgetown University while working on Capitol Hill. He is a member of the Virginia and District of Columbia Bars.

Jon M. Van Dyke has been Professor of Law at the William S. Richardson School of Law, University of Hawaii, since 1976, where he teaches Constitutional Law, International Law, International Ocean Law, and International Human Rights. Previously he taught at the Hastings College of the Law (University of California) in San Francisco (1971–76) and Catholic University Law School (1967–69) in Washington, D.C. He has served as Associate Dean at the University of Hawaii's Law School (1980–82) and as Director of the University's Spark M. Matsunaga Institute of Peace (1988–90). He earned his J.D. degree at Harvard (1967) and his B.A. degree at Yale (1964), both cum laude. He was a law clerk for Roger L. Traynor, Chief Justice of the California Supreme Court, in 1969–70. Professor Van Dyke has written or edited ten books and has authored many articles on constitutional law and international law topics. His latest book is *Who Owns the Crown Lands of Hawaii?*, published by the University of Hawaii Press in 2008. He has engaged in important litigation on constitutional rights in the state and federal courts of Hawaii as well as the U.S. Court of Appeals for the Ninth Circuit and several Asian and South Pacific courts. He has served as a consultant for the South Pacific Regional Environmental Programme; the Permanent South Pacific Commission; the Association of Pacific Island Legislatures; the governments of Turkey, Vanuatu, and Nauru; the Office of Hawaiian Affairs; the State Council of Hawaiian Homestead Associations; the City and County of Honolulu; the County Council and Charter Commission of Maui; and the Planning Departments or Commissions of the Counties of Kauai, Maui, and Hawaii. He is a member of the editorial boards of *Marine Policy* and *The International Journal of Marine and Coastal Law,* and is on the advisory board of the Center for International Environmental Law and the Law of the Sea Institute. In 1987, he received the University of Hawaii Presidential Citation for Excellence in Teaching; and in 1984, 1993, 1996, and 2002 he was selected as the "Outstanding Professor" at the Law School.

Sloane A. Wildman is a partner in the Washington, D.C., office of Perkins Coie LLP. Ms. Wildman counsels clients in all aspects of environmental and natural resources law and regulation, including the Resource Conservation and Recovery Act; Comprehensive Environmental Response, Compensation, and Liability Act/Emergency Planning and Community Right-to-Know Act release reporting; CERCLA cleanups and Natural Resource Damages claims; Clean Water Act (including Wetlands); Ocean Dumping Act; Wildlife and Marine Resources; International Convention for the Prevention of Pollution from Ships (MARPOL); Safe Drinking Water Act; Toxic Substances Control Act; and Clean Air Act. She represents clients in administrative, civil judicial, and criminal enforcement cases and conducts environmental due diligence in connection with corporate and real estate transactions.

Nina M. Young is President of Ocean Research, Conservation, and Solutions (ORCAS) Consulting. She drafts positions statements, policy papers, legislation, comment letters, and scientific reports for clients such as the Consortium for Oceanographic Research and Education, the Office of International Affairs in the National Oceanic and Atmospheric Administration, the Friends of the Sea Otter, and Alliance to Protect Nantucket Sound. Formerly the Director of Marine Wildlife Conservation at The Ocean Conservancy (TOC), she led TOC's efforts to conserve marine mammals. She has been instrumental in negotiating and drafting amendments to the Marine Mammal Protection Act and international treaties to eliminate the accidental entanglement and death of dolphins, whales, and other marine mammals in commercial fishing operations. Ms. Young has participated in government research cruises to assess marine mammal populations along the Atlantic coast and to develop field protocols and techniques to autopsy dead marine mammals and rescue live stranded marine mammals. Before joining TOC, she was a Researcher at Battelle Ocean Sciences and the field task leader for NOAA's Mussel Watch Program. At Battelle, Ms. Young organized and participated in over twenty-five research expeditions and logged over 2,500 hours at sea. Her work in marine mammalogy includes population assessment and physiological, anatomical, and behavioral studies. Her publications include papers on whales, dolphins, and sea lions, and reports on organic and trace element contaminants found in bivalves in U.S. coastal areas. Ms. Young is a member of the Society for Marine Mammalogy and a past president of the International Association for Aquatic Animal Medicine, and she holds an M.S. degree (Major: Physiology; Minor: Zoology and Veterinary Science) from the University of Florida.

Foreword

The Earth's oceans and coasts are severely threatened. To formulate responses to these threats, we each had the honor of chairing a major national ocean commission. These commissions, the congressionally created and presidentially appointed U.S. Commission on Ocean Policy and the privately funded Pew Oceans Commission, identified remarkably similar core priorities and made complementary recommendations for improvements needed in the way our nation currently addresses a number of critical ocean and coastal issues. As a follow-up to the work of the two commissions, we are continuing to seek implementation of the solutions they identified as we work together as the Joint Ocean Commission Initiative.

In many ways, ocean and coastal law and policy mirror the resources they were created to manage, restore, and protect: They are complex, intertwined, and fluid. As the chairs of our respective commissions, we each had the opportunity to learn a great deal about ocean and coastal issues and the laws that govern them. Over the course of our investigations and discussions with hundreds of individuals, we heard sobering accounts of the severe threats to our nation's oceans, coasts, and Great Lakes that continue to plague us, including

- Changes in ocean chemistry, wind circulation, arctic ice coverage, and other impacts associated with global climate change
- Poor water quality that impacts human health and forces numerous beach closures
- Enormous human, environmental, and economic impacts associated with hurricanes and other coastal hazards
- Fishery stock failures
- Increasing frequency and size of red tides and other harmful algal blooms
- Massive and growing dead zones in the Chesapeake Bay, Gulf of Mexico, and most recently off the coast of Oregon
- Continuing coral reef loss
- Economic and ecologic losses associated with the increasing prevalence of invasive species

Many of the reasons for declining ocean and coastal ecosystem health are due to failures in our governance approaches and structures, including fragmented laws, confusing and overlapping jurisdictions, and lack of a clear national ocean policy. Our two commissions came to strikingly similar conclusions: We must overhaul our ocean governance system and unify our nation with a common goal of protecting and restoring our ocean and coastal ecosystems so that they will continue to be healthy and resilient and able to provide the goods and services that people want and need.

As this volume explains, there is a significant body of law governing most ocean and coastal uses and activities, including fisheries management, protection of habitat and of living marine resources, coastal development, pollution, offshore development, and our nation's role within the international community. All of these are important, and, as we now understand, all are interconnected. That is why both commissions strongly endorsed a transition toward ecosystem-based management as a system for both governing and managing human activities. It recognizes and is responsive to the needs of the natural ecosystem and human activities, balancing the needs of different living and nonliving components of the land, sea, and atmosphere with the health of human communities.

One of the difficulties with implementing ecosystem-based management is that our legal and regulatory structures are not currently designed to manage that way. Laws governing ocean and coastal uses most often focus on a single use or issue, are often disconnected, and at times are inconsistent with each other. This is a reflection of existing institutional processes and legislative mandates that focus largely on single issues or respond to specific and immediate needs and problems as they arise, rather than within an ecosystem-based approach, and it is for this reason that both of our commissions concluded that a major overhaul in our governance structure is needed.

Another difficulty comes from the failure of the United States Senate to provide its advice and consent for U.S. accession to the United Nations Convention on the Law of the Sea. The Convention provides essential protections to our nation's economic and security interests. It also includes environmental safeguards and protects the right to conduct research in international waters. Moreover, becoming a party to the Convention would allow us to participate in international processes that mediate conflicts over maritime resources. Major U.S. industries and environmental organizations, the President, the Joint Chiefs of Staff, and high-ranking officials in the Departments of State and Defense have all expressed their support for the Convention. As one of the few remaining nations that is not a party to the Convention, we jeopardize our ability to protect our national interests with regard to the use and protection of the seas.

The laws and policies governing ocean and coastal resources are necessarily complex because of the vast and interconnected nature of the resources themselves, and this will always be the case. However, improvements in the integration and coordination of these laws is essential if our nation is to make significant progress dealing with the next generation of ocean-related issues that cut across political, social, economic, geographic, and scientific boundaries.

Increased appreciation of the need for a governance system that will allow us to more effectively bridge and connect these diverse areas, led by institutions that have the organizational and fiscal capacity and legislative mandate to implement such a regime, will result in a system that anticipates problems before they arise, addresses them when they do, and provides for the balanced use, protection, and stewardship of our ocean and coastal resources.

This will require a thoughtful and deliberative process and will build upon the current legal framework. Thus, the only way to improve our existing governance system is to understand how it currently works. This book represents the thoughts of an excellent collection of scholars and practitioners in the field of ocean and coastal law and policy and provides a significant contribution to that understanding. It is an excellent resource for the practitioner, government official, or scholar, one that will help all of these professionals in their efforts to facilitate the transition toward an ecosystem-based management approach.

Admiral James D. Watkins, U.S. Navy (Ret.)
The Honorable Leon E. Panetta
Co-Chairs, Joint Ocean Commission Initiative
March 2008

chapter one

National and International Jurisdictions and Boundaries

Michael W. Reed

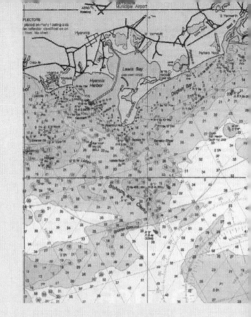

I. Introduction

A survey of ocean and coastal law begins with an understanding of national jurisdiction offshore. The extent of a sovereign's right to assert authority beyond its uplands to the adjacent seas is a matter of public international law and has been heatedly debated for centuries. National positions on the issue are derived from national interests. Maritime powers have traditionally advocated a maximum freedom of the seas, allowing their naval and commercial vessels to ply the oceans with a minimum of interference. Such nations have opposed extended claims of maritime jurisdiction. The maritime interests of other States may be concentrated near their own coasts. These nations have been more likely to make extensive maritime claims, to fisheries resources for example, in order to protect their own interests from foreign competition.

> **The extent of a sovereign's right to assert authority beyond its uplands to the adjacent seas is a matter of public international law and has been heatedly debated for centuries.**

Maritime boundaries today are significant for two primary purposes. First, they define the limits of the coastal sovereign's right to offshore resources. Second, they define the limits of the coastal sovereign's right to control activities that may adversely affect its interests. The coast of Massachusetts provides an example. The bay on the northeast coast of Martha's Vineyard is inland water, subject to the complete jurisdiction of the United States and the State of Massachusetts (see Figure 1.3, page 14). Resources within a bay belong to the state. The three-mile belt seaward of the Massachusetts coast is the original territorial sea of the United States and Massachusetts's state boundary. The state may control resource exploitation and generally assert its authority within that line. Activities seaward of the state boundary are subject to federal jurisdiction. These include: the exploitation of seabed resources; other seabed activities; the management of living resources; protection of the marine environment; and customs, fiscal, and immigration control. But the reach of the United States' jurisdiction varies depending on the activity. A specific federal statute may apply in the inland waters, the three-mile zone, the modern twelve-mile territorial sea, the additional twelve-mile contiguous zone, or the two hundred–mile exclusive economic zone. Compliance with state and federal laws, and enforcement of those laws, requires an understanding of the various zones of maritime jurisdiction and an ability to determine their boundaries.

Compliance with state and federal laws, and enforcement of those laws, requires an understanding of the various zones of maritime jurisdiction and an ability to determine their boundaries.

Throughout history perceived national interests have resulted in a wide variety of maritime claims, ranging from assertions of sovereignty over vast ocean areas not even adjacent to the claimants' uplands to contentions that the open seas are never subject to national jurisdiction but always open to the free use of all comers. The most notable of the extensive claims was based on a fifteenth-century papal bull of Alexander VI. The Pope's purpose was to divide Spanish and Portuguese interests in the New World, but his proclamation was later relied on to support claims to vast areas of the oceans.[1] Portugal, in an effort to monopolize trade in the Far East, cited the bull in support of its claimed authority to prohibit competitors from sailing the waters of the western Pacific.

The Portuguese assertion led to the most famous chapter in the debate over sovereignty of the seas. In 1609, Hugo Grotius published his famous work *Mare Liberum* to refute the Portuguese claim and support the Dutch East India Company's right to navigate and trade in the Far East. In 1635, John Selden published his equally famous *Mar Clausum* in rebuttal. Selden, an Englishman, had no particular interest in the Far East question but felt compelled to respond to Grotius's premise that the oceans are open to all because, at the time, England was claiming sovereignty over the seas adjacent to its coasts.[2]

Within little more than a century, the Grotius position had prevailed. All major powers recognized that a coastal state's sovereignty over the adjacent sea, if ever legitimate, was limited to a narrow band of water that has become known as the "territorial sea." At the time of American independence, there was no international consensus on the existence or width of that band.[3] Soon thereafter, however, diplomatic notes from Secretary of State Jefferson to Britain and France referred to an American territorial sea of three nautical miles.[4] For most of American history, that remained the internationally recognized limit of maritime sovereignty.

Today the Grotius-Selden controversy is only of historic interest. But it provides a useful point from which to understand modern ocean and coastal law. In the seventeenth century, national jurisdiction over the seas was seen as an all-or-nothing proposition. If such jurisdiction existed, it was as extensive as a sovereign's jurisdiction over its uplands, including the right to prohibit transit by foreign vessels. If it did not exist, the oceans lay beyond the protection of any sovereign, an international "common," and their resources subject to misuse and destruction.[5]

Modern law of the sea is more flexible, no longer limiting its jurisdictional options to total sovereignty or no protection at all. It has evolved to accommodate numerous interests in the use and resources of the seas. Nor is the law of maritime jurisdiction any longer a hodgepodge of competing national claims. The twentieth century brought a number of international efforts to codify the law of the sea. Those efforts produced wide consensus on four conventions that clarified maritime law in 1958.[6] Subsequent negotiations produced a single, comprehensive codification of principles governing the law of the sea in 1982 (hereinafter, 1982 Convention, or Convention).[7]

The 1982 Convention provides the international law framework for the domestic ocean and coastal law which is the subject of this volume. This chapter reviews the Convention's relevant provisions briefly before proceeding to discussions of their application in American practice.

II. The Current State of the Law—Jurisdictions and Boundaries

A. Zones of Maritime Jurisdiction

International law, as codified in the 1982 Convention on the Law of the Sea, recognizes the right of sovereigns to assert jurisdiction in maritime zones adjacent to their coasts. The Convention identifies a number of such zones and permits the coastal State to establish such zones and, within them, assert jurisdiction over specific resources and activities.[8] Typically a coastal State's authority is more comprehensive nearer its uplands and diminishes with the distance offshore. See Figure 1.1, page 7.

There are seven zones of maritime jurisdiction, and each has its own degree of coastal State jurisdiction.

International law . . . recognizes the right of sovereigns to assert jurisdiction in maritime zones adjacent to their coasts.

1. Internal Waters

"Waters on the landward side of the baseline of the territorial sea form part of the internal waters of the State." Convention, Article 8(1).

Internal waters, often referred to as "inland waters" in American practice, are waters which lie landward of the coast.[9] For purposes of our discussion of ocean and coastal law, relevant internal waters are: rivers which flow into the sea, bays, ports, and tidal waters along the open coast at any stage of the tide above mean low-water.[10]

Identifying the limits of inland waters is important for at least three reasons. First, they are the only zone of maritime jurisdiction over which the coastal State has complete control. For international purposes, the coastal nation has jurisdiction over its internal waters similar to its jurisdiction over uplands. Most significant for maritime purposes, foreign vessels may not enter internal waters without the coastal State's permission and pursuant to its conditions for admission.[11] Second, domestic law of the United States may apply differently in the inland waters than it does in the adjacent territorial sea, requiring identification of the boundary between the two. Finally, the seaward limit of inland waters is the baseline for determining the outer limits of the offshore maritime zones, including the territorial sea, contiguous zone, exclusive economic zone, and, generally, the continental shelf.

The limits of inland waters are identified as follows.

a. Bays

Bays that meet specific geographic criteria are inland waters. The 1982 Convention defines a bay as "a well-marked indentation whose penetration is in such proportion to the width of its mouth as to contain landlocked waters and constitute more than a mere curvature of the coast." Convention, Article 10(2).[12]

Chesapeake Bay, Delaware Bay, and San Francisco Bay are good examples of juridical bays. The waters landward of the mouth of each are clearly inland. But many "indentations into the coast" are not so obviously landlocked. The United States Supreme Court has adjudicated numerous disputes between the federal and state governments to determine whether a particular indentation meets the international law requirements for inland water status.[13] Although each case presents novel legal issues, the following basic principles can be identified.

To qualify as inland water, the indentation, in normal circumstances, should be "landlocked" by the mainland, not by adjacent islands.[14] The area of the indentation must, at a minimum, be that of a semicircle whose diameter is the mouth of the bay. The mouth of a bay is a straight line between the headlands which give the indentation its landlocked nature.[15] The termini of that line are the points on each headland at which the coast of the indentation ceases to face the landlocked waters and looks out upon the open sea.[16] If the bay's mouth is twenty-four nautical miles in length, or less, that mouth is the limit of inland waters. If the geographic mouth is more than twenty-four miles wide, a twenty-four-mile line is constructed within the bay to enclose the maximum possible water area, and that line is the limit of inland waters.[17]

b. Rivers

Rivers are also inland waters. "If a river flows directly into the sea, the baseline [coastline or limit of inland waters] shall be a straight line across the mouth of the river between points on the low-water line of its banks." Convention, Article 9. Although many rivers flow directly into the sea, they have created few jurisdictional issues. The inland waters of the river end at its mouth. The limits of inland waters of rivers can be determined through application of geometric tests, as they are for bays.[18]

However, problems can arise when a river flows into an estuary or a bay. The Geographer of the Department of State once defined a river, in a Supreme Court proceeding, as a body of freshwater, naturally flowing from a region of higher elevation to a region of lower elevation, which is contained between parallel or nearly parallel banks.[19] A river ceases to be a river when it broadens into an estuary or bay. The mouth of the river is the point at which the definition is not met. The rules for bays are separately applied to the estuary or bay to determine whether its water is inland.

A river may be extended into the sea by artificial works. It is not unusual, for hydrological reasons, to continue the natural riverbanks offshore with parallel jetties. In such cases the limit of inland waters is a line joining the seawardmost points of the jetties.[20]

Unlike its approach to bays, the Convention places no maximum limit on the width of a river's mouth.

c. Ports

Harbors and ports are inland waters. Article 11 of the Convention provides that "[f]or purposes of delimiting the territorial sea, the outermost permanent harbour works which form an integral part of the harbour system are regarded as forming part of the coast." The Article does not specifically say that the waters of the port are inland, but the history of the provision, going back to the 1930 Hague Conference for the Codification of International Law, makes clear that they are. The United States has adopted that interpretation.[21]

Delimitation of the limits of inland waters in ports and harbors does not follow the approach taken with bays and rivers. The mouths of bays and rivers are identified through the application of objective mathematical tests to the relevant geography. By contrast, in the only adjudicated example of which we are aware, the limit of inland waters in a port was determined by function. In defining the Port of San Pedro, serving Los Angeles, the Supreme Court's Special Master declined to apply the objective criteria employed for bays and looked instead for the area which formed a single, integrated harbor.[22]

The inland waters of a port must, to some extent, be enclosed by natural or artificial structures. In one sense roadsteads, where vessels can anchor to load or off-load when piers are unnecessary or not available, are often part of a functioning port. Nevertheless, they do not become part of the inland waters of the coastal State.[23]

d. The Low-Water Tidal Datum

Article 5 of the Convention provides that "the normal baseline for measuring the breadth of the territorial sea is the low-water line along the coast as marked on large-scale charts officially recognized by the coastal State." Article 8 provides that "waters on the landward side of the baseline of the territorial sea form part of the internal waters of the State." Taken together, these two provisions make clear that internal waters are not just landlocked water bodies protected in some sense by the mainland. They also include that narrow band of open sea which covers the beach at any stage of the tide above mean low-water.

One matter must be clarified at this point. The United States and many other countries publish official nautical charts of their coastlines. Typically those charts depict a low-water line. Article 5 is sometimes incorrectly read to mean that the baseline, or seaward limit of inland waters, is—by operation of law—established by such charts. That is not the intent of the Convention's provision. The somewhat awkward wording of Article 5 is necessary because there is no single low-water datum. Hydrographers can identify a number of datums that fit the description. The language of Article 5 was chosen because no single low-water datum had been generally accepted for charting purposes around the world, and charts were being produced using a number of datums.

Article 5 means that the particular low-water line adopted by each country for its charting purposes is to be its "normal baseline." For the United States that is a datum generally referred to as "mean low-water." The critical point for our purposes is that if the chart does not accurately depict the low-water line, the baseline, or seaward limit of inland waters, is the *actual* mean low-water line, not the charted line.[24]

Both nature and human intervention are constantly changing our coastlines. It is impossible to maintain a chart that depicts the mean low-water line exactly as it is from day to day. The Supreme Court has deferred to the National Oceanic and Atmospheric Administration (NOAA) in its choice of datums to be charted as the United States' baseline.[25] At the same time, the Court has recognized that the charts themselves may not, at any given time, precisely reflect that baseline. The official charts are presumed to accurately reflect the present location of the low-water line, but that presumption is subject to attack.

From the foregoing it is possible to identify internal, or inland, waters.[26] The question is, however, why is such a delineation significant?

Numerous federal and state statutes apply to activities in our internal waters. Those discussed in following chapters are the most important but are by no means an exhaustive list. Statutes, however, present a common problem that should be noted here: rarely do they use the term "internal waters." More typical are references to "waters of the United States," "territorial waters," or "navigable waters." None of these terms has a consistent international definition. In American practice "navigable waters" are those that are subject to the ebb and flow of the tide or are navigable in fact.[27] "Territorial waters" usually means internal waters together with the territorial sea.[28] "Waters of the United States" is a term used in recent environmental legislation and has been interpreted to include waters which are hydrologically tied to navigable waters although not necessarily navigable themselves.[29] Each of the foregoing examples includes inland waters. The practitioner must be careful when dealing with these terms.

Identifying inland waters may also be important in determining title to submerged lands. The beds of navigable, internal waters generally belong to the state in which they lie. Each of the original thirteen states owned title to the beds of its navigable waterways, and the federal government has been determined, pursuant to the equal footing doctrine, to have held such beds in territories in trust for future states and transferred them at statehood.[30] Title to the beds of non-navigable internal waters, on the other hand, is usually held by the adjacent upland landowner.

Finally, and probably most important for our discussion of ocean and coastal law, the seaward limits of internal waters provide the baseline from which more seaward zones of maritime jurisdiction are delimited, as we see in the remaining discussions in this Part. We deal with the problems of locating this baseline in Part III.A.

. . . the seaward limits of internal waters provide the baseline from which more seaward zones of maritime jurisdiction are delimited . . .

2. Territorial Sea

"The sovereignty of a coastal State extends, beyond its land territory and internal waters . . . to an adjacent belt of sea, described as the territorial sea." Convention, Article 2(1).

The territorial sea is a narrow belt of ocean immediately seaward of the coast. Article 3 of the Convention provides that "[e]very State has the right to establish the breadth of its territorial sea up to a limit not exceeding 12 nautical miles, measured from [its] baselines." The outer limit of the territorial sea is a line "every point of which is at a distance from the nearest point of the baseline equal to the breadth of the territorial sea." Convention, Article 4.[31] By definition there is only one possible outer limit of the territorial sea once its breadth is known and the baseline is established. Controversies over the seaward limits of the territorial sea, and most other offshore boundaries, are actually baseline controversies.

Within the territorial sea the coastal State may exercise jurisdiction that is almost as comprehensive as that asserted over its internal waters. The two significant differences are the internationally recognized right of vessels to transit a foreign State's territorial sea in what is called "innocent passage,"[32] and the understanding that, as

Figure 1.1
Zones of Maritime Jurisdiction

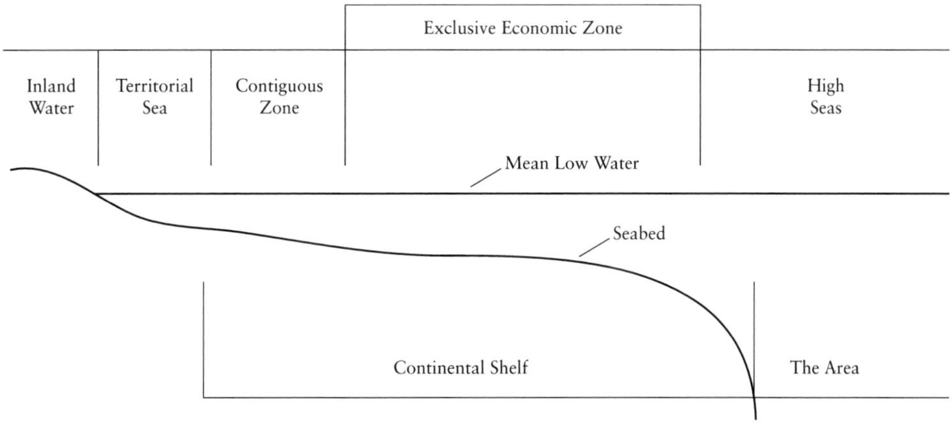

Source: Michael W. Reed

a general principle, the coastal State will not exercise its criminal jurisdiction over activities occurring on a vessel in innocent passage unless those activities affect the coastal State.[33] With these exceptions, the coastal State may extend the reach of its domestic legislation to the limits of its territorial sea and enforce the provisions of that legislation against its own citizens and foreigners.

3. Contiguous Zone

"In a zone contiguous to its territorial sea . . . the coastal State may exercise the control to" prevent and punish violations of its customs, fiscal, immigration, or sanitary laws and regulations within its territorial sea. Article 33(1).

The boundaries of the contiguous zone are the seaward limit of the territorial sea (a maximum of twelve nautical miles from the coast), and a line up to twenty-four miles from the coast. The difference between coastal State jurisdiction in the territorial sea and the contiguous zone is best described as follows: The territorial sea is subject to sovereignty of the upland State.

The international community's sole interest, the right to navigate in innocent passage, is protected through an exception to that sovereign control. In contrast, the coastal State's jurisdiction in the contiguous zone is limited to specifically identified exceptions to the international community's primary interests. Foreign vessels need not assert a right of innocent passage, and carefully meet definitions of "innocence" and "passage," as they must in the territorial sea. Nor are foreign aircraft prohibited from overflying the contiguous zone without the permission of the coastal State.[34]

The contiguous zone concept has carried over from the 1958 Convention on the Territorial Sea and the Contiguous Zone,[35] predecessor to the 1982 Law of the Sea Convention. But protections provided by a contiguous zone may now be less important with the 1982 Convention's addition of an Exclusive Economic Zone. Nevertheless, the United States presently claims both a contiguous zone and an exclusive economic zone.[36]

4. Exclusive Economic Zone

"The exclusive economic zone is an area beyond and adjacent to the territorial sea. Convention, Article 55. "In the exclusive economic zone the coastal State has sovereign [exclusive] rights for the purpose of exploring and exploiting, conserving and managing the natural resources." Article 56. In addition, the coastal State has jurisdiction with regard to artificial islands, marine scientific research, and protection of the marine environment. Article 60.

"The exclusive economic zone is an area beyond and adjacent to the territorial sea."

The Exclusive Economic Zone (EEZ) is a creature of the 1982 Convention. As Prescott and Schofield explain, the EEZ "represents a compromise between competing coastal state resource interests and interests of those states concerned to preserve freedom of navigation."[37] Prior to 1982 some coastal sovereigns interested in protecting offshore resources sought to do so by making extreme territorial sea claims, sometimes extending as much as two hundred miles from their coastlines.[38] As previously discussed, territorial seas are zones of complete sovereignty, subject only to the limited right of innocent passage. Other States, whose primary interest was freedom of navigation for their naval and commercial fleets, felt threatened by such extended claims.[39]

The EEZ concept is an interesting solution. Coastal State control over natural resources is recognized, but navigation and overflight not inconsistent with resource interests are not restricted.[40]

The EEZ is defined as a zone lying seaward of the territorial sea to a distance of no more than two hundred nautical miles from the coast.[41] As with the outer limits of the territorial sea and contiguous zone, constructing the outer limit of the EEZ is a relatively simple task, now accomplished by computer programs, once the baseline, or coastline, is determined.

The EEZ compromise does not simply recognize a coastal State's right to offshore resources, it imposes significant obligations on the claimant State to manage and conserve those resources. For example, the coastal State must "ensure through proper conservation and management measures that maintenance of the living resources . . . is not endangered by over-exploitation" and manage species to produce "the maximum sustainable yield."[42] If the coastal State will not take the total allowable catch, foreign vessels must be allowed to fish the excess, pursuant to regulations of the coastal State.[43]

The United States has claimed an exclusive fishery zone extending two hundred miles from its coasts since 1976.[44] That legislation was later adopted as our primary domestic implementing legislation for the EEZ.[45] The Magnuson-Stevens Act focuses on the protection and management of commercial species in the EEZ.[46] Other federal statutes protect additional interests. The Marine Sanctuaries Act extends federal protection to other living and nonliving objects of national significance in specifically designated portions of the EEZ.[47] The Marine Mammal Protection Act prohibits "taking" marine mammals within two hundred miles of our coast.[48]

5. Continental Shelf

"The continental shelf of a coastal State comprises the sea-bed and subsoil of the submarine areas that extend beyond its territorial sea throughout the natural prolongation of its land territory to [the greater of] the outer edge of the continental margin or . . . 200 miles from . . . [its coast]." Article 76(1).

As a geologic matter, the continental shelf is that gently sloping, subsea feature which extends the uplands offshore before dropping precipitously to the ocean depths.[49] It may extend a short distance from the coast or hundreds of miles seaward. But under the 1982 Convention's definition, a coastal State's continental shelf rights extend to a minimum of 200, and maximum of 350, nautical miles from the coast.[50]

The coastal State has the exclusive right to explore and exploit the natural resources of its continental shelf.[51] But, these rights differ significantly from those in the EEZ.

In contrast to its approach in the EEZ, which provides that foreign interests may harvest resources not fully utilized by the coastal State, no other State may explore for, or exploit, the natural resources of the coastal State's continental shelf without the latter's consent.[52]

The Convention does recognize two important international rights on and above the continental shelf. The first is the right to navigate the waters and airspace above the continental shelf.[53] The second is the right of all States to lay submarine pipelines and cables on the continental shelf of another State.[54]

For at least sixty years coastal States have asserted special rights over resources of their continental shelves, without necessarily claiming jurisdiction over resources or activities in the water column above.[55] In 1953, Congress enacted two pieces of legislation governing the development of offshore mineral resources. First it granted the coastal states the exclusive right to develop seabed resources for specific distances off their shores.[56] Then it set up a comprehensive scheme for the federal development of mineral resources seaward of the state grants to the edge of the continental shelf.[57] Production from the continental shelf has been a significant source of energy, as well as income, for both the federal government and the states.

Potential problems concerning American jurisdiction over the continental shelf are looming, as discussed in Part III.B.2.

6. High Seas

"All parts of the sea that are not included in the exclusive economic zone, in the territorial sea or in the internal waters of a State, or in the archipelagic waters of an archipelagic State" are high seas.[58] Article 86.

Waters seaward of the zones of coastal State jurisdiction just discussed are open to the use of all nations. Among the freedoms recognized on the high seas are: navigation, overflight, laying submarine cables and pipelines, constructing artificial islands and installations, fishing,[59] and scientific research.[60]

However, those who enjoy the high seas freedoms must keep in mind that they are not beyond the reach of all authority. Every State may control its own nationals, and flag vessels, wherever found. Much federal law extends to Americans and American vessels on the high seas. For example, the prohibitions of the Endangered Species Act apply to "any person subject to the jurisdiction of the United States,"[61] and prohibit, among many other things, "taking" an endangered species on the high seas.[62] Likewise, the Marine Mammal Protection Act makes it illegal for any person or vessel subject to the jurisdiction of the United States to take any marine mammal on the high seas.[63]

Articles 86–120 of the 1982 Convention set out specific rights and obligations of individuals and sovereigns on the high seas.

7. The "Area"

The seabed beyond the limits of national jurisdiction is described as the "Area." The Convention recognizes the Area and its resources as "the common heritage of mankind." Article 136. These resources may be developed under the supervision of the International Sea-bed Authority, as provided in the Convention.[64]

The seabed beyond the limits of national jurisdiction is described as the "Area." The Convention recognizes the Area and its resources as "the common heritage of mankind."

8. Overlapping Maritime Boundaries

A substantial difficulty in delimiting the boundaries of the previously described zones occurs in areas of potentially overlapping maritime jurisdiction between adjacent coastal States, such as the United States and Mexico, or of opposite States, such as the United States and the Bahamas. The Convention does not provide a formula for constructing common boundaries in such circumstances. Its general approach is to encourage agreement between the sovereigns. In the absence of agreement, the Convention's approach differs slightly depending on the zone of jurisdiction at issue.

When the territorial seas of neighboring sovereigns abut, neither State may unilaterally extend its jurisdiction beyond a median (equidistant) line measured from the coastline of each, unless "historic title or other special circumstances" require a variation.[65] Conflicts over the boundaries of EEZs are to be resolved "on the basis of international law . . . in order to achieve an equitable solution."[66] If there is no agreement "within a reasonable period," the matter is to be resolved through procedures set out in the dispute resolution process provided in Articles 279–299 of the Convention.[67] Overlapping continental shelf claims are to be resolved in the same way.[68]

Some, but not all, of these international boundaries have been resolved between the United States and its neighbors.[69]

9. State Boundaries

State boundaries can also create complications. Our discussion of maritime zones has, to this point, dealt only with federal and international law. However, the various states of the Union may have concurrent jurisdiction within two of the zones discussed.

Inland waters are entirely within the boundaries of the states. State laws apply in those waters unless preempted by federal law. In addition, the states play a major role in implementing and enforcing some federal legislation in their inland waters. The Clean Water Act is a prime example. It establishes goals for restoring and maintaining the quality of the waters of the United States. At a national level, water quality guidelines are set by the Environmental Protection Agency.[70] However, authority for implementing programs to achieve those goals can then be delegated to the individual states.[71]

Inland waters are not limited to those that form part of the coastline. Boundary lakes and rivers are inland, lie within both state and national boundaries, and are subject to both federal and state jurisdiction.[72]

State boundaries also extend offshore. In most cases they are described by state constitution or statute as extending three miles from the coast, the limit of the territorial sea of the United States from 1793 until 1988. The states are sovereign within this maritime belt and, as a general proposition, may apply state laws as they do on land.[73] It is common, for example, for the states to regulate fisheries in their offshore waters.[74] They may also implement federal legislation, such as the just-mentioned Clean Water Act, in state offshore waters.[75]

The exact location of a state's offshore boundaries can raise difficult issues. Traditionally, state offshore boundaries have coincided with the federal territorial sea limit. However, the territorial sea was extended to twelve miles in 1988, and state boundaries remained where they were.[76] Even more confusing, state offshore boundaries which were typically ambulatory have been fixed for some purposes. Thus, some coastal states now have two offshore boundaries. Which boundary is applicable for which purpose may be a difficult question. A discussion of that point is one of the unresolved questions included in Part III.B.

Wherever a state's seaward boundary is located, there is always the additional problem of how the upland boundary separating it from a neighboring state is to be extended offshore to divide their areas of maritime jurisdiction, the same problem discussed above with respect to international boundaries. These "lateral boundaries" are typically not set out in technical terms in a state's boundary description. Nor are there any principles in domestic law to help resolve the problem.

The preferable solution is agreement between the states. A number of lateral boundaries have been resolved through compacts negotiated by the states involved.[77] Three have been litigated. The first, *New Hampshire v. Maine,* extends the boundary that separates the two states through the Piscataqua River to its mouth.[78] The Texas/Louisiana and Georgia/South Carolina lateral offshore boundaries have also been contested in Supreme Court Original actions. It happens that each of these lateral boundaries begins at the mouth of an inland water body. In *Texas v. Louisiana* the offshore lateral boundary was found to begin at the midpoint of the mouth of the Sabine River and continue offshore on a line which ran at all times equidistant from the coasts of the two states.[79] The upland boundary between Georgia and South Carolina lies in the Savannah River. The Supreme Court's Special Master determined that equity required that a lateral boundary dividing the states' offshore jurisdiction begin on the mouth of a bay into which the Savannah River flows and continue seaward on a line perpendicular to the bay closing line on which it began. The Court agreed.[80]

A few principles come from these litigated cases which may be useful in future controversies. First, international law may be useful in resolving domestic offshore boundary issues. Second, absent agreement, "equity" is the goal in dividing offshore interests. Third, all else being equal, an equidistant boundary will do equity. Finally, special circumstances will justify deviations from the equidistance line.

III. Emerging and Unresolved Issues

A number of unresolved issues exist with respect to the just discussed zones of maritime jurisdiction. First are difficulties in precisely delimiting the boundaries of those zones. Equally important are questions of just what jurisdiction the United States has purported to assert in each zone, and whether those assertions are consistent with international law. We will look at each of those subjects in turn.

A. Boundaries of the Maritime Zones

Central to delimiting the boundaries of each zone of maritime jurisdiction is accurately locating the baseline, generally referred to as the "coastline" in American practice. As noted above, the coastline is a composite of the mean low-water line along the open coast and closing lines across the mouths of inland water bodies that open on the sea.

Mean low-water is usually depicted as a dotted line enclosing green tint on official National Ocean Service nautical charts. See Figure 1.2.[81] Inland water closing lines that affect the limits of the territorial sea are constructed using the Convention's legal criteria and are also depicted on the charts. See Figure 1.3. Maritime zones of jurisdiction are measured from both.[82]

Figure 1.2
South Coast of Cape Cod, Massachusetts

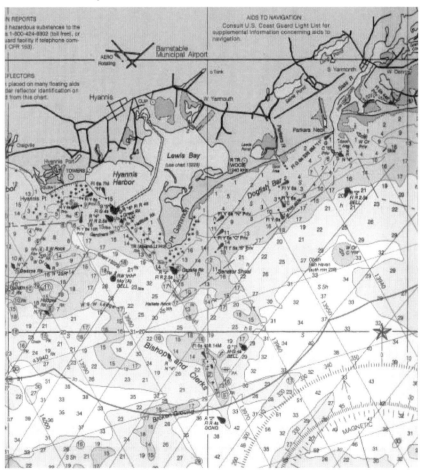

Source: NOAA chart 13237, *Nantucket Sound and Approaches*, 39th Edition, May 2003.

Figure 1.3
Southeast Portion of Martha's Vineyard, Massachusetts

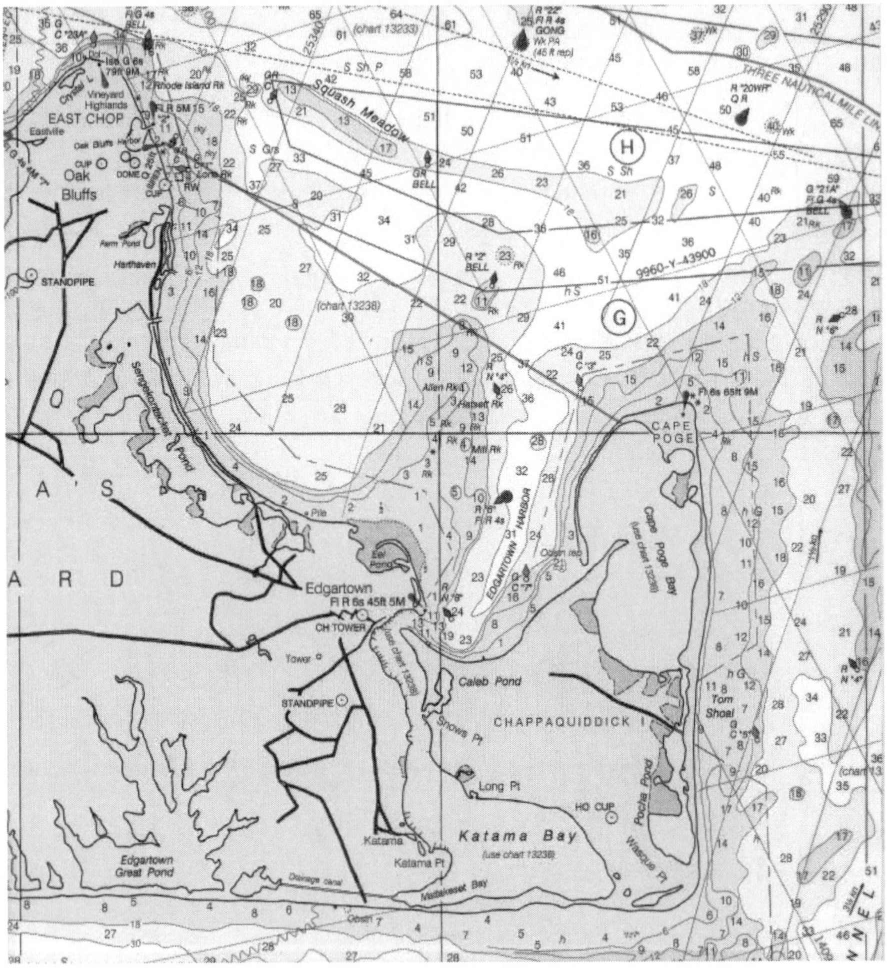

Source: NOAA chart 13237, *Nantucket Sound and Approaches*, 39th Edition, May 2003.

What then are the unresolved issues associated with locating the zones of maritime jurisdiction?

The first, and constantly recurring, coastline issue results from the fact that the coastline is ambulatory. The low-water line depicted on nautical charts accurately reflects the land/water interface, at mean low-water, as of the time of the survey upon which the chart was based. But accretion and erosion may alter that line, and it is the actual land-water interface at mean low-water which is the coastline, not the charted line.[83] Without evidence to the contrary, the official charts are given deference in locating the coastline, but the courts will permit a party, including the federal government, to prove that the coastline has moved from its charted position.[84] The best and most recent evidence will be admitted to prove the present location of the coast.[85]

Changes in the low-water line can also affect inland water closing lines in a number of ways. Kotzebue Sound in Alaska met all the tests for inland water status until erosion along one of its headlands caused the mouth to exceed the twenty-four-mile maximum. Thereafter, a twenty-four-mile fallback line was constructed within the Sound, as permitted under Article 10(5), but a substantial area of the Sound which had been inland water now lies beyond Alaska's three-mile boundary. Accretion or erosion within an indentation might also affect its ability to meet the minimum area measurement of Article 10(2).

In short, an interested party may challenge the accuracy of the nautical chart on which the federal government has constructed its zones of maritime jurisdiction. But challenges may also be based on incorrect assumptions as to what is a proper coastal base point. Such assumptions may occur for a number of reasons.

Insufficient information on the chart sometimes leads to problems with boundary determinations. Even a completely accurate chart may contain insufficient information to make baseline determinations. For example, in three common instances it is not possible to determine from the chart whether a particular feature qualifies as part of the coastline.

The first such feature is a "rock awash," shown on NOAA charts as an asterisk or an asterisk surrounded by dots.[86] See Figure 1.4. By definition the height of a rock awash, with respect to a tidal datum, is unknown. Yet, if the feature is a naturally formed area of land which rises above mean high-water, it is an island under international law and is part of the coastline for measuring the territorial sea and contiguous zone. If it is capable of sustaining human habitation or economic life, it will also have an exclusive economic zone and continental shelf.[87]

If the feature is above water only at low-tide, it is part of the coastline for measuring the territorial sea if, and only if, it is "at a distance not exceeding the breadth of the territorial sea from the mainland or an island."[88]

Such offshore features can have a significant effect on maritime boundaries, yet it is impossible to tell from the chart whether they are proper base points. The Coastline Committee, which constructs our maritime zones on official charts, often goes to great lengths to determine whether a particular point qualifies as part of the coast.[89] But definitive information may not be available. In those cases, the government may be persuaded to conduct the necessary surveys to make that determination and may accept evidence supplied by states or private parties.

That situation arose recently in Nantucket Sound. Small features are known to lie in the Sound approximately two nautical miles south of Pt. Gammon on Cape Cod. They are depicted on official charts as rocks awash, warning the mariner of danger even though they might not be visible at all stages of the tide (see Figure 1.2). There

Figure 1.4
Official Nautical Chart Symbol for "Rock Awash (Height Unknown)"

a	*	⁛		Rock awash (height unknown)

Source: Chart No. 1, *United States of America Nautical Symbols, Abbreviations and Terms*, 10th Edition, November 1997, page 46.

is no way, however, to determine from the chart whether they are islands, low-tide elevations, or submerged. As a consequence, they were not originally used to delimit the maritime boundaries of Massachusetts south of Cape Cod.

A proposal to conduct activities seaward of the charted state boundary that might violate Massachusetts law brought new interest in the status of these features, and subsequent surveys determined that they do qualify as part of the "coastline" of Massachusetts and base points for delimiting the state boundary and other zones of maritime jurisdiction.[90]

Features charted as rocks awash appear at many places along our coasts. They often create a potential boundary controversy. Other offshore features may be charted above mean low-water yet raise doubt as to whether they are proper baseline points. International law requires that an island or low-tide elevation be "naturally formed" and composed of "land" to constitute part of the coastline.[91] Either of these requirements can raise questions that are unanswered by the nautical charts.

> **Features charted as rocks awash appear at many places along our coasts. They often create a potential boundary controversy.**

"Naturally formed" suggests that any feature that owes its existence to direct human intervention does not qualify as part of the coast. Examples of features not qualifying as base points on this ground have included a navigation beacon built on a permanently submerged reef,[92] an artificial island used for petroleum drilling,[93] and spoil banks resulting from dredging channels.[94] It is not always easy to determine whether a particular feature was created by man or nature. For example, low-tide elevations near the mouth of the Bass River, as seen on Figure 1.2, may have been formed through the natural deposit of silt at the river's mouth or as a result of dredging the channel. The chart does not identify their source. The Coastline Committee has treated similar features as "natural," and used them as part of the coastline, if there is no reasonable basis for assuming that they are manmade.[95]

The requirement that a feature be composed of "land" has prompted some expert discussion. Commentators seem to be in agreement that "land" means dirt, rock, sand, gravel, organic matter, or combinations of these materials.[96] The federal government argued in *United States v. Alaska*, Supreme Court No. 84 Original, that ice could not be treated as land so as to raise a feature above mean high-water when its gravel content alone would be insufficient to do so.[97]

> **The requirement that a feature be composed of "land" has prompted some expert discussion.**

Presumably a court would hear evidence as to whether a given feature is naturally formed and made of land. Official charts do not, usually, answer those questions.

Nor do charts alone tell us whether artificial structures attached to the natural coast are part of the legal coastline. Article 11 of the Convention provides that "the outermost permanent harbour works . . . are regarded as forming part of the coast." The Convention does not define "harbour works," but American practice provides some help. One commentator, Aaron Shalowitz, has defined them as "structures erected along the seacoast at inlets or rivers for protective purposes, or for enclosing sea areas adjacent to the coast to provide anchorage and shelter."[98] The Supreme Court has quoted that definition with favor.[99]

Examples are solid structures, such as the breakwaters which form the port of San Pedro,[100] and the jetties at the mouth of the Sabine River between Texas and Louisiana.[101] Accepted harborworks have provided some coast protective function and possessed a continuous low-water line which could be treated as the coastline. In contrast, subsurface "harborworks," such as dredged channels, have been rejected as base points for zones of maritime jurisdiction,[102] as have open pile piers.[103]

The various types of artificial coastline construction often cannot be easily distinguished on nautical charts. For example, jetties (which are usually solid and treated as harborworks) may be represented on charts with the same symbol as piers (which are usually constructed on piles and are not base points).[104] See Figure 1.5. Both the Coastline Committee and the courts will accept evidence of a structure's actual construction in determining whether it serves as a harborwork and part of the baseline for zones of maritime jurisdiction.

The foregoing unresolved issues arise from questions of fact which may affect the location of the baseline from which maritime zones are measured. However, disputes may also arise when facts are agreed upon but the proper application of the law is at issue. We now turn to examples of such unresolved issues.

> **. . . disputes may also arise when facts are agreed upon but the proper application of the law is at issue.**

Another source of confusion over boundaries arises from disagreement as to the proper application of legal criteria to particular geographic examples. Although the boundary principles with which we are concerned come from international law, the United States Supreme Court has been more involved in their interpretation than has any international tribunal. This has happened because the international principles have been adopted by the Supreme Court for purposes of implementing the Submerged Lands Act, domestic legislation which has been the subject of extensive litigation for the last fifty years. During that time, the Court has resolved many legal questions raised by the principles, but a number remain unanswered. Most of these questions involve setting the limits of inland waters.

Juridical bays seem to create the greatest difficulty. Juridical bays are those indentations into the mainland which meet the criteria of Article 10 of the 1982 Convention.[105] Their waters are inland, and closing lines across their entrances form part of the coastline from which more seaward zones of maritime jurisdiction are measured. Although

Figure 1.5
Official Nautical Chart Symbol for "Pier, Jetty"

Source: Chart No. 1, *United States of America Nautical Symbols, Abbreviations and Terms,* 10th Edition, November 1997, page 27.

the Court, and its Special Masters, have adjudicated the status of innumerable alleged juridical bays, no two geographic formations are identical. For that reason, today's juridical bay controversy can always be distinguished, in some way, from yesterday's.

A popular recent issue has been to what extent an island, or islands, can be said to form a bay. The Supreme Court has recognized that "the general understanding has been—and under the Convention certainly remains—that bays are indentations in the mainland, and that islands off the shore" do not create bays.[106] Nevertheless, the Court has said that in unusual circumstances an island may be so closely associated with the mainland that it must be treated as mainland and, as such, becomes available as the potential headland of a bay.

The Court has set out criteria to help determine when an island is legally part of the mainland, including: size, distance from the mainland, depth and utility of intervening waters, shape, and the island's relationship to the configuration or curvature of the coast.[107] It has also produced two useful examples. The first found Long Island to be assimilated to the mainland of New York, through Manhattan, making Long Island Sound a juridical bay.[108] The second found Kuiu, Kupreanof, and Mitkof Islands, in the Alexander Archipelago of southeast Alaska, not to be assimilated to one another and the mainland to create juridical bays to their north and south.[109]

Island assimilation questions may arise in the future. The Court's opinions in the Louisiana, Long Island, and Alaska cases, along with the extensive reports of its Special Masters in each, will provide the starting point for the resolution of any new controversy.

How exactly to make the mathematical calculations implicit in Article 10's juridical bay tests is also, to some extent, an unanswered question. The Article provides two objective requirements for juridical bay status. The first is that a bay's "penetration [into the mainland] is in such proportion to the width of its mouth as to contain land-locked waters."[110] Unfortunately, the Article says no more about how the depth measurement is to be made nor what ratio of width to depth is required for juridical bay status. Many international geographers have discussed alternatives and offered preferred methods.[111] The federal government has suggested that a closing line constructed across the mouth of the embayment be compared to the longest straight line running from any point on that mouth to the deepest point of penetration in the water body. It then contends that if the width of mouth is no greater than the depth of penetration, the water body is landlocked.[112] The Supreme Court has not yet endorsed this, or any other, specific method for testing this initial requirement of Article 10, and the issue remains open for future litigants.[113]

The second requirement of Article 10 is that an indentation's area be "as large as, or larger than, that of the semi-circle whose diameter is a line drawn across the mouth of that indentation." The minimum area requirement is easy enough to calculate once the mouth is established. The unresolved issue is how adjacent water bodies, if any exist, are to be dealt with in measuring the area of the indentation in question. The issue was first raised in *United States v. Louisiana* where the state took an expansive view, arguing that any connected waterways should be included for semicircle measurement, and the federal government contended that no two distinct water bodies should be treated as one for this purpose.[114] The Court gave some guidance, but much room is left for imaginative counsel in future litigation. In most cases, state interests will be fostered by including the greatest water area for semicircle measurement purposes.

A separate category of inland waters may also present unresolved issues, not because the law isn't clear but because each claim will have to be resolved on its particular facts. Referred to as historic inland water claims, these are areas which have acquired their inland water status through a form of prescription rather than geography. The Supreme Court has described historic bays as waters over which the "coastal nation has traditionally asserted and maintained dominion with the acquiescence of foreign nations."[115] It has recognized that an historic claim requires proof of three elements. "The coastal nation must have effectively exercised sovereignty over the area continuously during a time sufficient to create a usage and have done so under the general toleration of the community of States."[116] If historic inland waters are proven, their seaward limits are part of the coastline of the United States from which more seaward zones of maritime jurisdiction are measured.[117]

A number of states have alleged that waters off their coasts, which do not qualify as inland under the geographic tests, have nevertheless been treated as such, over a substantial period of time with the acquiescence of foreign States. Additional state claims are possible, but the lack of success in prior historic water claims may discourage them.[118]

Finally, with respect to baseline questions, a new and interesting issue has been introduced by the 1982 Convention.

Article 121 of the Convention defines an island as "a naturally formed area of land, surrounded by water, which is above water at high tide."[119] The Article then provides, as had prior international law, that an island shall have a territorial sea and contiguous zone. However, Article 121(3) specifically provides that the more extensive EEZ and continental shelf are not generated by "rocks which cannot sustain human habitation or economic life of their own" even though they otherwise qualify as islands.

The purpose of the provision seems clear. "Article 121(3) was to prevent tiny, insular features called 'rocks' from significantly reducing the international areas of seabed and sea that belong to all the states in the world."[120] The point is well made when commentators Prescott and Schofield note that a de minimus rock could produce an Exclusive Economic Zone of 125,600 square nautical miles.[121]

Unlike baseline provisions carried over from the 1958 to the 1982 Conventions, the language of Article 121(3) has not been the subject of litigation in the American courts. It has, however, "been the source of an extensive and unresolved legal and scholarly debate."[122] That debate has identified a substantial number of issues regarding the definition of the word "rock" and the meaning of the phrase "which cannot sustain human habitation or economic life of their own."

With respect to the definition of "rocks" the debate raises, but does not necessarily resolve, the following questions. Must a "rock" be consolidated material, or does it include sand? By using the term "rock" did the drafters intend to include only some of the features which qualify as islands? Is the term "rock" used to refer to size rather than composition?

The separate requirement that an island be able to sustain human habitation or economic life raises even more unresolved issues, including the following. Must the feature actually be supporting a stable community of people, or is the capacity to support all that is required? Does the fact that the feature once supported communities prove its status? Might the ability of a feature to support habitation change over time, either because of changes to the feature or to economics?[123] Is the future capacity to support human habitation, assuming unlimited financial support, enough? Must the "economic life" referred to in Article 121(3) be self-supporting? Are radio stations, weather observation posts, or lighthouses "economic life"?

The unresolved issues arising from Article 121(3) are numerous and interesting. We can imagine their arising in American practice if a restriction is enforced in a portion of our EEZ that is only within two hundred miles of a naturally formed area of land, which is above high tide, but which is arguably just a rock and unable to sustain human habitation or economic life.

Yet another area of dispute in defining coastal jurisdiction involves fixed boundaries and the unusual issues associated with them. Until now we have discussed maritime zones whose boundaries are ambulatory because they are measured from ambulatory baselines. However, all, or portions of, the seaward boundary of one important maritime zone, each state's Submerged Lands Act grant, may be fixed—unaffected by the ambulatory low-water line. Submerged Lands Act boundaries may become fixed in three circumstances.

The first circumstance applies only to the extraordinary nine-mile grants to Texas and Florida in the Gulf of Mexico.[124] These grants do not necessarily extend nine nautical miles from the present coastline. Instead, they are measured to a maximum of nine miles from the coastline as it existed at the time of Texas's admission and Florida's readmission to the Union. In effect, the grants are the lesser of a line nine miles from the historic coastline and a line nine miles from the present coastline. The actual limit of the states' Submerged Lands Act grant is, therefore, a composite of those two lines, adopting the segment of each which is less seaward.[125]

Any state's Submerged Lands Act grant may also be fixed by operation of law. As originally enacted, the Submerged Lands Act provided an ambulatory seaward boundary because it was measured from an ambulatory baseline. These ambulatory boundaries created continuous title questions between the federal government and the coastal states and also raised security of interest concerns for their lessees. To ease the administration of offshore leasing, Congress amended the Act in 1986 to provide that "any boundary between a State and the United States under this subchapter or subchapter II of this chapter which has been or is hereafter fixed by coordinates under a final decree of the United States Supreme Court shall remain immobilized at the coordinates provided under such decree and shall not be ambulatory."[126]

A number of federal/state Submerged Lands Act boundaries have been permanently fixed through this means, simplifying lease administration, protecting contract rights, and eliminating the need for litigation with every coastline change. Some of these boundaries have been described for the entire coast of a state by Supreme Court decree.[127] Others deal only with portions of a state's coastline.[128] Unlike the Texas and Florida historic boundaries, boundaries fixed by law subsequent to a Supreme Court decree may work to the advantage of either party. If the coastline from which a fixed boundary is measured moves seaward by accretion, the federal government gains by the fixing. If the coastline moves landward by erosion, the fixed boundary is now more than three miles offshore and the state benefits.

States that do not have fixed Submerged Lands Act boundaries, and are interested in having them, can reach an agreement with the federal government on a precise line and incorporate the line's description in a proposed decree for the Court. All coastal states except Washington, Oregon, and Hawaii have been involved in submerged lands litigation with the United States in which the Supreme Court has retained jurisdiction to enter further decrees. No new litigation would have to be filed in those instances. Presumably new Original actions would have to be filed in the Supreme Court to deal with the Washington, Oregon, and Hawaii boundaries, but the Court has been helpful in resolving such issues.

Fixed Submerged Lands Act boundaries create at least three issues that have not been resolved in litigation. The first is whether the "coastline" or "baseline" of a state is a "boundary" for purposes of 43 U.S.C. Section 1301(b). The Supreme Court's tidelands decisions, which have produced most of the domestic law with which we are concerned here, involve disputes over the location of the coastline, not the Submerged Lands Act "boundary," which is usually three miles seaward. The Court's decisions in those cases typically contain only the answers to the legal and factual issues involved, without defining the coastline by coordinates.[129] Subsequent decrees may describe the coastline by coordinates but not the three-mile extension which is the boundary between state and federal mineral interests.[130] Still others have included a description, by coordinates, of the three-mile boundary.[131]

A coastline description is clearly not a "boundary between a State and the United States." The coastline separates state inland submerged lands from state offshore submerged lands. However, the coastline does dictate the location of the boundary referred to in the Submerged Lands Act. Once the coast is described, only one three-mile line can be constructed from it. It could be argued that the coastline description "constructively" includes the boundary description.

The better reading of the statutory provision is that only the three-mile line is the "boundary" between the state and the United States. Parties who want a fixed federal/state boundary should assure that the three-mile line is described by coordinates in a Supreme Court decree.

State Submerged Lands Act baselines may also differ from those being used for measuring other zones of maritime jurisdiction for another reason. As discussed above, the legal coastline includes some artificial structures such as jetties and other harbor-works. All else being equal, these structures form part of the baseline for measuring the states' Submerged Lands Act grant. The United States argued in *United States v. California* that such a rule was unfair to the federal government because a state could expand its Submerged Lands Act grant, and cut into the federal seabed beyond, by constructing harborworks along its coast and measuring its three-mile grant from the tips of those structures.[132] The Supreme Court showed little sympathy, reminding the federal government that the harborworks of concern would be in the navigable waters of the United States, in which the government "had power to protect its interests from encroachment by unwarranted artificial structures, and that the effect of any future changes could thus be the subject of agreement between the parties."[133]

The government has done just that. Before the Corps of Engineers will issue the permit required to construct harborworks, it will consider the Submerged Lands Act consequence of the proposed structure.[134] The federal government is then given an opportunity to negotiate a waiver with the state concerned. Typically, the state will waive any claim to a Submerged Lands Act extension from the proposed structure and, if it otherwise meets the Corps' requirements, a permit will be issued. Thereafter, the structure will form part of the coastline for all but Submerged Lands Act purposes, and the state's Submerged Lands Act grant will continue to be measured from the natural coastline.

The Supreme Court has upheld the federal government's right to condition Corps of Engineers permits on such waivers.[135] If the United States fails to get a waiver, the structure extends the state's Submerged Lands Act grant.[136]

Submerged Lands Act boundaries that do not coincide with traditional state boundaries measured from the ambulatory coastline create another unresolved issue worthy of consideration here. That is "whether state boundaries, and the reach of federal statutes other than the Submerged Lands Act, are affected by fixing the Submerged Lands Act boundary."

It could be argued that state boundaries, which typically run three miles seaward of their ambulatory coastlines, become fixed when the Submerged Lands Act boundaries are fixed. But we believe that would be the improper conclusion.

Neither the original tidelands decisions nor the Submerged Lands Act which reversed them had anything to do with state offshore boundaries. In the first tidelands case, the Supreme Court recognized the federal government's paramount right to mineral resources seaward of the California coastline.[137] But at the same time it recognized the existence of state offshore boundaries and the states' continued authority within those boundaries.[138] Three years later, in the first Louisiana tidelands decision, it made clear that "[t]he matter of state boundaries has no bearing on the present problem."[139] The Supreme Court had long recognized the existence of state boundaries offshore, and state jurisdiction within those boundaries, and continued to do so in the tidelands decisions.

Congress did the same. In 1953 it enacted the Submerged Lands Act, granting coastal states the offshore mineral interests that they had been denied in the early tidelands cases. It defined state boundaries for purposes of the Act, limiting most states to three-mile grants, but specifically provided that "[n]othing in this section is to be construed as questioning or in any manner prejudicing the existence of any State's seaward boundary beyond three geographic miles."[140] The 1986 amendment to the Act did not provide that Submerged Lands Act boundaries described in a Supreme Court decree would fix state boundaries for all purposes. The amendment fixed boundaries which had been established under the Act, not state boundaries generally. Only Section 2 of the Act, 43 U.S.C. 1301, which defines boundaries for purposes of the grant, was amended. Section 4, 43 U.S.C. 1312, which disclaims any intent of Congress to alter other state boundaries, was not amended.

In short, the Submerged Lands Act does not limit traditional state boundaries.

Additional confusion arises because Congress has referred to Submerged Lands Act boundaries in subsequent federal legislation, sometimes appearing to adopt the Submerged Lands Act boundaries for other federal purposes. Those statutes prompt a separate question: Is their jurisdiction limited by boundaries fixed under the Submerged Lands Act? Although the question has not been considered by the courts, the best response can be constructed based on the apparent congressional intent.

The Magnuson Fishery Conservation and Management Act of 1976, 16 U.S.C. Sections 1801 *et seq.*, is the first example. The Act asserts federal fisheries jurisdiction in "a 197-mile zone contiguous to the territorial sea of the United States. . . . [T]he inner boundary of the zone is a line coterminous with the seaward boundary of each of the coastal States."[141] The Act says nothing more about how to determine the location of a state's seaward boundary. However, the Senate Committee Report explains that "seaward boundaries of the coastal States are defined in section 2 of the Submerged Lands Act (43 U.S.C. 1301)."[142] In 1976, the Submerged Lands Act boundary was ambulatory. Ten years later Congress amended that Act to provide for fixing boundaries by Supreme Court decree.[143]

That amendment raises the question whether the landward boundary of our 197-mile Fishery Conservation Zone, now the EEZ, is an ambulatory boundary measured from the coastline employed for international purposes or, where it is the subject of a Supreme Court decree, it is the fixed boundary used for Submerged Lands Act purposes. The courts have not considered the issue.

Arguments may be made on either side, but we believe the better interpretation to be that Congress intended the inner limit of the Fishery Conservation Zone to be an ambulatory line.

First, there can be no doubt that to fix the inner boundary of the Fishery Conservation Zone merely by operation of the 1986 amendment to the Submerged Lands Act would be inconsistent with the intent of Congress in 1976 and 1986. When Congress adopted Submerged Lands Act boundaries for purposes of the Magnuson Act, those boundaries were ambulatory. The Senate Committee Report consistently uses terms which indicate an intent to employ ambulatory boundaries for the Fishery Conservation Zone. State boundaries are described in the Magnuson Act as extending three miles from the "coast." Unless otherwise limited, "coasts" are understood to be ambulatory as are any boundaries measured from them.[144] To emphasize that point, the Senate noted that "the shore or coastline is the baseline from which the territorial sea is measured as set forth in the Convention on the Territorial Sea and the Contiguous Zone." The Convention's "coast" is an ambulatory line.[145]

Second, the purposes of the Magnuson Act would be violated by an interpretation that the inner boundary of the Fishery Conservation Zone had been immobilized by operation of the 1986 amendment to the Submerged Lands Act. Congress adopted the then ambulatory Submerged Lands Act boundary for purposes of the Magnuson Act specifically because it "preserves the domestic breakdown of management authority between States and the Federal Government which has prevailed since the founding of the republic."[146] That authority was based upon ambulatory boundaries, measured from ambulatory baselines. Supreme Court decisions from early in our history, through and following the tidelands controversies, recognize traditional state jurisdiction over fisheries off their coasts.[147] This traditional authority included the measurement of maritime zones from ambulatory boundaries.

Finally, Congress itself has clearly indicated that Submerged Lands Act and Magnuson Act boundaries need not be identical. The Magnuson Act, as amended, extends state fisheries management authority "to any pocket of waters that is adjacent to the State and totally enclosed by lines delimiting the territorial sea."[148] Areas of Nantucket Sound and the Alexander Archipelago of southeast Alaska were specifically made subject to state fishery jurisdiction.[149] The Supreme Court has found that the center of Nantucket Sound is not within Massachusetts's Submerged Lands Act boundaries.[150] Nor are all waters of the Alexander Archipelago within Alaska's Submerged Lands Act grant.[151] Clearly, Congress does not believe that Submerged Lands Act and Magnuson Act boundaries must coincide. The better interpretation would seem to be that state fisheries boundaries remain ambulatory when Submerged Lands Act boundaries are fixed.

The Coastal Zone Management Act of 1972, 16 U.S.C. Section 1451, raises a related question. It describes the coastal zone, an area of state jurisdiction, as extending "seaward to the outer limit of State title and ownership under the Submerged Lands Act."[152] Like the Magnuson Act, the Coastal Zone Management Act became law prior to the Submerged Lands Act amendment which provides for fixed boundaries. Nonetheless, the two laws do not raise the same question. The reach of the Coastal Zone legislation is not to a "boundary," a term whose definition has changed in subsequent years, but to "title" to seabed resources. Congressional intent is clear; the coastal zone extends to the limit of state submerged lands rights. In most cases, those rights will extend three miles seaward of an ambulatory coastline. However, where the Supreme Court has entered a final decree describing the seaward limit of a state's Submerged Lands Act grant, that line will be fixed. In the former case, the seaward limit of the state's coastal zone will be ambulatory. In the latter it will be fixed. The coastal zone ends where the state's title to submerged lands ends.

This conclusion is consistent with the jurisdictional scheme adopted by Congress in the Coastal Zone Management Act. By statutory definition, the "coastal zone" includes all area between its landward and seaward boundaries *except* "lands the use of which is by law subject solely to the discretion of or which is held in trust by the Federal Government, its officers or agents."[153] That provision includes the submerged lands of the outer continental shelf which are managed by the federal government.[154]

Congressional intent and logic seem to support the conclusion that the coastal zone ends where state title to submerged lands ends.

The foregoing are examples of emerging and unresolved issues associated with the location of our various zones of maritime jurisdiction. Additional unresolved issues exist concerning the jurisdiction presently claimed, or not claimed, in those zones.

B. Unresolved Issues Involving Jurisdiction in Each of the Zones of Maritime Jurisdiction

1. Within the Territorial Sea

Confusion may arise as to the scope of authority claimed by the United States over its original territorial sea, the three-mile belt lying immediately seaward of our coastline. This confusion should be easily resolved. Each of a number of terms includes this maritime zone. A statute which applies within the navigable waters, navigable waters of the United States, seaward boundary of a state, territorial limits of the United States, territorial sea, territorial waters, territory and waters, United States, waters of the United States, or waters subject to the jurisdiction of the United States can be presumed to apply within three miles of the coast.

The more difficult question is which of those statutes extends farther, to the limits of our twelve-mile territorial sea. President Reagan extended the territorial sea to twelve nautical miles on December 27, 1988. He did so under the constitutional authority of the President over international affairs. He did not, however, believe that he had authority to unilaterally extend the reach of existing federal legislation and specifically provided that "[n]othing in this Proclamation: (a) extends or otherwise alters existing Federal or State law or any jurisdiction, rights, legal interests, or obligations derived therefrom."[155] So the extension of domestic legislation, to the full distance permitted by international law, awaited congressional action.

Congress has since extended a few of the federal statutes which govern offshore activities.[156] Many others have not been extended.[157] Two problems can be identified. First, legal practitioners must be especially careful when dealing with any federal assertion of maritime jurisdiction to ascertain whether the reach of the statute in question has been extended to include the modern twelve-mile territorial sea. The numerous statutory terms which, until 1988, were understood to include the territorial sea no longer answer the question. It is necessary to look farther to determine whether Congress has expanded the reach of each statute. Second, the list of unextended statutes should be reviewed to determine whether it is in the best interest of the United States to claim the internationally recognized maximum of coastal State jurisdiction.

2. The Continental Shelf

Two questions have recently arisen over the extent of federal jurisdiction on the outer continental shelf, the submerged lands seaward of the states' Submerged Lands Act grant. These two issues involve the United States Army Corps of Engineers' assertion of authority to regulate the placement of structures and laying of cables on the seabed.[158]

The first unresolved issue concerns the extent of the Corps's authority to prevent obstructions to navigation by artificial islands and fixed structures on the outer continental shelf. International law clearly provides such authority to the coastal sovereign.[159] So did federal law until 1978.[160] But in that year the Outer Continental Shelf Lands Act, 43 U.S.C. Sections 1331 *et seq.*, was amended and the Corps's authority has, thereafter, been described as extending only to "installations ... which may be erected thereon for the purpose of exploring for, developing, or producing resources therefrom."[161]

The change might seem, on its face, to limit the Corps's traditional authority. However, one federal court of appeals has ruled that that was not the congressional intent. The litigation was a challenge to a Corps permit for the construction of a data tower preliminary to a proposed wind project for the production of electricity in the middle of Nantucket Sound. Finding the amendment itself ambiguous, the United States Court of Appeals for the First Circuit looked to its legislative history. The House Conference Report on the bill declares that "all artificial islands and fixed structures on the [OCS], whether or not they are erected for the purpose of exploring for, developing, removing and transporting resources therefrom," are subject to Corps authority,[162] and the Court adopted that reading.[163]

Under the circumstances, we believe that this might be considered an unresolved issue. The statute, it seems to us, may be considered clear on its face, limiting Corps jurisdiction to installations to be used in resource exploration, development, or production. In that circumstance, many jurists would refuse to look beyond the statute itself, reasoning that Congress knows how to delegate the necessary authority to the Corps if that is its intent.

The data tower litigation raises a second question which, we believe, should also be considered unresolved. That is: What is the authority of the Corps to grant interests in federal property on the outer continental shelf? The court of appeals recognized that although the Corps can prevent construction on the outer continental shelf, it does not follow that the Corps alone may authorize such construction.[164] The right to occupy land is a property interest.[165] Congress is the custodian of federal lands.[166] The Supreme Court does not easily recognize authority in the executive branch to surrender federal property interests on offshore submerged lands without clear congressional delegation.[167]

In the data tower case, the Corps relied upon authority found in the Outer Continental Shelf Lands Act, 43 U.S.C. Sections 1331 *et seq.*, to grant the right to occupy federal lands. Yet the Act specifically provides a means for acquiring property interests on the outer continental shelf. Such grants are to be made by the Department of the Interior, not the United States Army.[168]

Corps regulations governing permit issuance require the applicant to affirm that he has, or will acquire, the necessary property interest to occupy the land involved.[169] The applicant here made that affirmation, yet all agree that he had no such interest at that time and would not be able to acquire it because no authority existed for the federal government to convey an interest for such purpose.[170] As the Corps is aware, the United States holds title to the bed of Nantucket Sound more than three miles from the coast.[171]

As a result of the Energy Policy Act of 2005, Public Law 109-58, this question has been at least partially resolved. In provisions of that law amending the Outer Continental Shelf Lands Act, Congress expressly granted to the Secretary of the Interior the authority to convey interests in federal lands on the outer continental shelf for alternative energy purposes. There remain, however, other potential uses of such areas (large-scale aquaculture, floating casinos, etc.) that do not have an express source of authorization and raise the same question presented by the data power case.

Corps of Engineers authority over laying cables on the outer continental shelf also raises unresolved issues. In recent years the demand for international telecommunications capacity has mushroomed. A substantial portion of that demand is met with the use of transoceanic submarine cables. The extent to which a coastal sovereign may regulate the placement of such cables on its continental shelf is a matter of some dispute between the cable industry and the Corps.

International law has a long history in dealing with this issue. Transatlantic cables have existed for almost 150 years. The first international agreement governing submarine cables was negotiated more than 120 years ago.[172] The 1982 United Nations Convention on the Law of the Sea continues to recognize the international right to lay cables on the continental shelf, and within the Exclusive Economic Zone, of other sovereigns.[173] When Presidents Reagan and Clinton established our EEZ and modern contiguous zone, they specifically recognized the continuing international right to lay and repair submarine cables in those zones.[174]

The Corps of Engineers issues permits for laying cables on our continental shelf, but that permit program raises a number of unresolved issues.

First, it is not clear where the Corps finds the statutory authority for its assertions of jurisdiction. Various Corps of Engineers districts seem to take different approaches. Some cite Section 404 of the Clean Water Act and Section 10 of the Rivers and Harbors Act as authority,[175] but Corps jurisdiction under these statutes applies only in the navigable waters of the United States, which are limited by those Acts to three miles from the coast.[176] Other Corps districts cite the Outer Continental Shelf Lands Act, 43 U.S.C. Section 1333(e). As noted above, questions remain regarding that section's use to regulate nonextractive structures on the continental shelf.

The United States Court of Appeals for the First Circuit recognized Corps authority over the data tower in Nantucket Sound because it is an "artificial island" and the legislative history of 43 U.S.C. Section 1333(e) indicates congressional intent to retain Corps authority over such structures.[177] Seabed cables are not artificial islands or structures. The two categories are clearly distinguished in international law.[178] What is more, international law recognizes coastal State authority over cable installation only as necessary to protect the exploration and exploitation of natural resources from its shelf.[179] There is no indication that the Corps of Engineers limits its asserted control of subsea cables to the protection of those interests.

President Reagan's EEZ Proclamation made clear that the United States did not infringe on the internationally recognized freedom to lay and repair cables. Giving the Corps every benefit of the doubt, it still must be said that there are unresolved issues associated with its regulation of cables on the outer continental shelf.[180]

IV. Conclusion

Several potential resolutions are available for some of the unresolved issues just discussed. Others may be those kinds of legal problems which can only be resolved case by case. These resolutions and issues are summarized as follows:

1. Coastal states and the federal government should strongly consider fixing their mutual Submerged Lands Act/Outer Continental Shelf Lands Act boundary in any area where mineral production is now being conducted or is likely to be in the foreseeable future.[181]

2. Congress should consider clarifying the Magnuson-Stevens and Coastal Zone Management Acts to make clear whether the seaward reach of either is intended to be fixed when a state's Submerged Lands Act grant becomes fixed.[182]

3. If the Magnuson-Stevens and Coastal Zone Management Acts are not clarified regarding fixed boundaries, future proposed Supreme Court decrees might incorporate the parties' understanding as to the effect of their proposal on non-Submerged Lands Act boundaries.

The United States should ratify the 1982 United Nations Convention on the Law of the Sea.

4. The United States should ratify the 1982 United Nations Convention on the Law of the Sea.[183]

5. The 1982 Convention sets out rights and obligations of sovereigns and individuals. A comprehensive survey should be done to ensure that federal law takes advantage of all rights provided by the Convention and meets all obligations.

6. A separate survey should be conducted to determine which federal laws presently apply in which zones of maritime jurisdiction.[184]

7. Following the survey just proposed, Congress should, with respect to each such statute, determine whether it is in the best interest of the United States to extend its reach to the greatest extent permitted by international law.

8. Following the determination just proposed, Congress should amend each statute that involves maritime jurisdiction to make clear its intended geographic reach.

9. Congress should clarify agency authority over activities on the outer continental shelf, assuring that federal agency actions are consistent with clearly stated congressional intent and international law.[185]

Many of the issues discussed above could be resolved through these recommendations. Others, mostly arising by the nature of ambulatory coastlines, would not. They will have to be resolved case by case as they have been in the past.[186]

Notes

1. A bull is an edict of the Pope of Rome, issued in this instance to resolve conflicting jurisdictional claims of Portugal and Spain in the New World. I. D. P. O'CONNELL, THE INTERNATIONAL LAW OF THE SEA 2 (I.A. Shearer ed., 1982).

2. That claim was not only minuscule in comparison to that being made by Portugal, but it was also short-lived. PHILIP C. JESSUP, THE LAW OF TERRITORIAL WATERS AND MARITIME JURISDICTION 4 (1927).

3. United States v. California, 332 U.S. 19, 32 (1947).

4. Note to British Minister. Reprinted in H. Ex. Doc. No. 324, 42nd Cong., 2d Sess. (1872) 553–554. Note to French Minister. American State Papers, 1 Foreign Relations 183–184 (183–184).

5. For an interesting discussion of the threat to commonly held resources, *see* G. Hardin, *The Tragedy of the Commons*, 162 SCIENCE 1243 (1968).

6. Convention on the Territorial Sea and the Contiguous Zone, 15 U.S.T. 1607, T.I.A.S. 5638; Convention on the Continental Shelf, 15 U.S.T. 473, T.I.A.S. 5578; Convention on Fishing and Conservation of the Living Resources of the High Seas, 17 U.S.T. 140, T.I.A.S. 5969; and Convention on the High Seas, 13 U.S.T. 231, T.I.A.S. 5200.

7. United Nations Convention on the Law of the Sea, U.N. Doc. A/CONF.62/122 (1982), reprinted in 21 ILM 1261–1354 (1982).

8. The term "State," when it appears in this chapter, is used in the international sense, referring to a nation-state, unless the context indicates that one of the political subdivisions of the United States is intended. The word "state" refers to one of the fifty states.

9. As will be discussed below, that "coast" is also known as the "baseline" of the upland State.

10. "[T]he normal baseline . . . is the low-water line along the coast." Convention, Article 5.

11. The single exception to this rule does not apply to the United States. Article 7 of the Convention provides that where a coast is deeply indented, fringed by islands, or unstable (as in the case of a river delta) the sovereign *may* construct an artificial coastline with a series of straight lines. The waters landward of that line then become internal but remain open to innocent passage of foreign vessels if they would not otherwise be inland. Convention, Article 8(2). The United States does not employ this "straight baseline" method for delimiting its inland waters. United States v. Louisiana, 394 U.S. 11, 67 (1969).

12. A "mere curvature," as used in Article 10(2), is a stretch of coast which, although concave, is not sufficiently enclosed to be considered landlocked. That is to say, it does not meet the geometric requirements of the Article. Centerville Harbor, on the south coast of Cape Cod, is an excellent example.

13. These disputes have generally arisen in controversies over the application of the Submerged Lands Act, 43 U.S.C. § 1301 *et seq.*, federal legislation granting the coastal states mineral rights to submerged lands within, generally, three nautical miles of their coasts. For purposes of defining the coasts the Supreme Court has adopted the definitions of the 1958 Convention on the Territorial Sea and the Contiguous Zone, United States v. California, 381 U.S. 139, 165 (1965), but the relevant coastline provisions of that Convention are identical to those of the 1982 Convention.

14. United States v. Louisiana, 394 U.S. 11, 62 (1969). However, islands may be so closely associated with the mainland as to be "constructively" part of it and help in forming a bay. Long Island is an example. United States v. Maine (New York/Rhode Island), 469 U.S. 504 (1985).

15. Although islands intersected by, or in the vicinity of, that line may dictate the construction of multiple mouths to the bay using headlands on the islands as well as the mainland. United States v. Louisiana, 394 U.S. 11, 56 (1969).

16. The preferred method for determining these entrance points is a geometric analysis developed by Drs. Robert Hodgson and Lewis Alexander and described by them as "the 45 degree test." The method was discussed by the Supreme Court, with approval, in United States v. Maine (Rhode Island and New York Boundary Case, 469 U.S. 504, at 522 (1985).

17. Convention, Article 10(5). Cook Inlet, Alaska is a good example.
18. *See supra* note 15.
19. Testimony of Dr. Robert Hodgson before the Special Master in Texas v. Louisiana, Number 36 Original, Transcript at 522–529.
20. Jetties extend the Sabine River, between Louisiana and Texas, more than two miles offshore. Texas v. Louisiana, 406 U.S. 465 (1976).
21. 1 Aaron L. Shalowitz, Shore and Sea Boundaries 61 (1962), quoting from a brief for the United States in United States v. California, Number 6 Original, October Term, 1951.
22. United States v. California, Number 5 Original, Report of the Special Master of August 20, 1979, at 8–13.
23. A substantial roadstead lies seaward of, and adjacent to, the breakwater which forms the Port of San Pedro, but it was not included within its inland waters by the Supreme Court. United States v. California, 449 U.S. 408 (1981). Article 12 of the 1982 Convention deals separately with roadsteads, providing only that if they are "wholly or partly outside the outer limit of the territorial sea" they are included in the territorial sea. The United States has no roadsteads which extend beyond our twelve-mile territorial sea.
24. In fact, some charts will not show a low-water line at all because at the chart's scale the low- and high-water lines merge, or because that portion of the coastline is unsurveyed. *See* NOAA Chart 1, Nautical Chart Symbols, Abbreviations and Terms 14 (10th ed. 1997).
25. United States v. California, 381 U.S. 175, 176 (1965).
26. A separate category of inland waters is recognized in international law and in the 1982 Convention but not described by the Convention. So-called historic waters can be thought of as customary international law exceptions to the Convention's requirements for inland water status. Article 10(6). Mississippi Sound and Vineyard Sound are the only historic inland water bodies in the United States that would not otherwise qualify as inland waters under principles of the Convention. Historic waters are discussed further in Part III.A, *infra*.
27. Phillips Petroleum Co. v. Mississippi, 484 U.S. 469 (1988).
28. Shalowitz, *supra* note 21, at 317.
29. United States v. Riverside Bayview Homes, 474 U.S. 121, 133 (1985); 40 C.F.R. § 122.2.
30. Pollard's Lessee v. Hagan, 44 U.S. (3 How.) 212 (1845). Congress may, however, reserve those submerged lands at the time of statehood, retaining title for the federal government. Utah Div. of State Lands v. United States, 482 U.S. 193 (1987); Idaho v. United States, 533 U.S. 262 (2001); United States v. Alaska, 521 U.S. 1 (1997); Alaska v. United States, 545 U.S. 75 (2005).
31. Originally these lines were produced manually by constructing arcs of circles from points on the baseline. Today computers do that work.
32. Definitions of "innocent" and "passage," along with associated rights and obligations of the coastal state and foreign vessels engaged in such passage, are set out in Articles 17–32 of the Convention. Two provisions worth noting are that submarines are required to transit a foreign territorial sea on the surface and fly their flags (Article 20), and only ships, not airplanes, enjoy a right of innocent passage (Article 17).
33. Article 27. Civil jurisdiction over the foreign vessel is also limited (Article 28).
34. Article 58(1).
35. Article 24, 15 U.S.T. (Pt. 2) 1607, T.I.A.S. 5639.
36. Presidential Proclamation No. 7219, 64 F.R. 48,701 (1999) (contiguous zone); Presidential Proclamation No. 5039, 48 F.R. 10,605 (1983) (exclusive economic zone).
37. Victor Prescott & Clive Schofield, The Maritime Political Boundaries of the World 19 (2d ed. 2005). This volume is highly recommended to those interested in worldwide maritime boundaries.
38. J. Ashley Roach & Robert W. Smith, United States Responses to Excessive Maritime Claims 151–153 (2d ed. 1996).

39. This conflict created a major international problem for the United States through the latter half of the twentieth century. *Id.* at 36.
40. Article 58.
41. Article 57. The EEZ is often referred to, in shorthand, as a 200-mile zone. In fact, of course, it is actually only 188 miles wide when the coastal State claims the maximum allowed 12-mile territorial sea. Note that the previously described contiguous zone is subsumed into the EEZ.
42. Article 61(1).
43. Article 62.
44. Magnuson Fishery Conservation and Management Act, later amended and retitled Magnuson-Stevens Fishery Conservation and Management Act, 16 U.S.C. §§ 1801 *et seq.*
45. A stated purpose of the Act is to "conserve and manage the fishery resources found off the coasts of the United States . . . by exercising: (A) sovereign rights for the purposes of exploring, exploiting, conserving, and managing all fish within the exclusive economic zone established by Presidential Proclamation 5030, dated March 10, 1983." That proclamation can be found at 48 Fed. Reg. 10605 (1983).
46. The Act also protects anadromous species and living resources of the continental shelf beyond the two-hundred-mile EEZ. 16 U.S.C. § 1801(b)(1).
47. 16 U.S.C. §§ 1431 *et seq.*, particularly 1432(3) and 1437(k).
48. 16 U.S.C. §§ 1362 *et seq.*, particularly §§ 1372(a)(2) and 1362(15)(B).
49. Continental shelves may extend significant distances offshore, as do the United States' continental shelves in the Gulf of Mexico and Bering Sea, or they may be narrow, as is the shelf off the coast of California.
50. Article 76(6).
51. Article 77(1). These resources include not only minerals and other nonliving resources, which may be on or beneath the seabed, but also "living organisms . . . which, at the harvestable stage, either are immobile on or under the sea-bed or are unable to move except in constant physical contact with the sea-bed or the subsoil." Article 77(4).
52. Article 77(2).
53. Article 78.
54. Article 79. Article 79 provides, by way of limitation, that the coastal State may impose "reasonable measures" for the exploration of its shelf resources and to control pollution from pipelines. The coastal State may also dictate the route of a pipeline on its continental shelf and impose conditions for cables and pipelines "entering its territory or territorial sea." *Id.*
55. The first such formal claim was made by President Truman. Proclamation No. 2267, 10 Fed. Reg. 12303 (1945). The right to make such claims was later recognized by the international community. Convention on the Continental Shelf, April 23, 1958, 15 U.S.T. 471, T.I.A.S. 5578.
56. Submerged Lands Act, 43 U.S.C. §§ 1301 *et seq.* The grants generally extend three nautical miles from the coast. States bordering on the Gulf of Mexico, however, were given an opportunity to prove that they entered the Union with more extensive boundaries and, if able to do so, were granted up to nine miles of submerged lands within those boundaries. Texas and Florida, on its Gulf coast, have established such boundaries. United States v. Louisiana, 363 U.S. 1, 29 (1960).
57. Outer Continental Shelf Lands Act, 43 U.S.C. §§ 1331 *et seq.*
58. An "archipelagic State" is a State composed entirely of a group or groups of islands. The United States is not an archipelagic State, and the Convention's special treatment of such States is not covered in this discussion.
59. Subject to conservation and management obligations imposed on flag States by the Convention and treaties and implemented through flag state legislation. Articles 116–120.
60. Article 87.
61. 16 U.S.C. § 1538(a)(1).
62. 16 U.S.C. § 1538(a)(1)(C).

63. 16 U.S.C. § 1372(a). (The statute provides for limited exceptions to the takings prohibition.)
64. Articles 156–191.
65. Article 15.
66. Article 74(1).
67. Article 74(2).
68. Article 83.
69. PRESCOTT, *supra* note 37, at 579, 598, 599, 606, 619, and 651.
70. 33 U.S.C. § 1314.
71. 33 U.S.C. § 1342(b).
72. Boundary rivers include the Rio Grande and a short stretch of the St. Lawrence. The four Great Lakes that are shared with Canada are boundary lakes. In each case the international boundary has been established by treaty within the waterway, and all waters on the American side of that boundary are inland and within the boundary of a state. For a thorough description of all state boundaries, *see* Franklin K. Van Zandt, *Boundaries of the United States and the Several States,* GEOLOGICAL SURVEY PROFESSIONAL PAPER 909 (1976).
73. Because this maritime zone is part of the "navigable waters of the United States," it is also subject to federal jurisdiction. Conflicts may result in a preemption of state law.
74. Toomer v. Witsell, 334 U.S. 385, 393 (1948).
75. Interesting questions arise regarding the extent of state jurisdiction offshore under particular statutes, a subject that will be broached in Part III.B.
76. Presidential Proclamation 5928 provides, in relevant part, that "[n]othing in this Proclamation (a) extends or otherwise alters existing Federal or State law or any jurisdiction, rights, legal interests, or obligations derived therefrom." Proclamation No. 5928, 54 Fed. Reg. 777 (1988).
77. *See, e.g.,* the compact resolving Florida and Georgia's mutual offshore boundary. Pub. L. 91-498, 84 Stat. 1094 (1970).
78. New Hampshire v. Maine, 426 U.S. 363 (1976).
79. Texas v. Louisiana, 426 U.S. 465 (1976).
80. Georgia v. South Carolina, 497 U.S. 376 (1990).
81. In normal circumstances the low-water line will extend from the mainland or an island, defined as a naturally formed area of land which extends above high-water. Article 121(1). However, a naturally formed feature that is not connected to the mainland or an island but extends above mean low-water is part of the coastline if, and only if, it lies within the territorial sea of the mainland or an island. Article 13. Such a feature is shown at the mouth of the Bass River on Figure 1.2.
82. The inland water closing lines and offshore boundaries are constructed on official NOAA charts by a federal interagency group known as the Committee on Delimitation of the United States Coastline. Rhode Island and New York Boundary Case, 469 U.S. 504, 522 (1985). Those closing lines and boundaries represent the federal position on the limits of the zones depicted but are subject to correction with changes in the coastline. The Committee's charter is reproduced at 3 MICHAEL W. REED, SHORE AND SEA BOUNDARIES, 415–418 (2000).
83. United States v. Louisiana, Report of the Special Master of July 31, 1974, at 25; United States v. Louisiana, 394 U.S. 11, 40-41 n.48 (1969).
84. United States v. Louisiana, 394 U.S. 11, 40-41 n.48 (1969).
85. United States v. Louisiana, Report of the Special Master of July 31, 1974, at 25 and 43; United States v. Alaska, 521 U.S. 1, 22–32 (1997).
86. CHART 1, *supra* note 24, at 46.
87. Article 121(3).
88. Article 13. This conditional significance of a mere low-tide elevation is carried over from Article 11 of the 1958 Convention on the Territorial Sea and the Contiguous Zone, *supra* note 6. It reflects a compromise in the definition of "island" in that Convention and the weight to be given various offshore features for boundary delimitation purposes.

89. *See supra* note 82.

90. 70 Fed. Reg. 9104-01 (2005).

91. Articles 13 and 121.

92. United States v. Henning, 7 F.2d 488 (S.D. Ala. 1925).

93. United States v. California, 447 U.S. 1, 5 (1980).

94. United States v. Louisiana, 394 U.S. 11, 41 n.48 (1969).

95. Minutes of August 3, 1970.

96. Robert D. Hodgson, Islands: Special and Normal Circumstances (Gambell & Pontecorvo eds., 1974); Law of the Sea: Emerging Regime; Lumb, The Law of the Sea and Australian Off-Shore Areas 14 (2d ed., 1978); Johnson, *Artificial Islands*, 4 Int'l L.Q. 203, 213–14 (1951); and Clive R. Symmons, United States v. Alaska, Number 84 Original, transcript of proceedings before the Special Master, at 1099.

97. As it turned out the Court resolved the island question in the federal government's favor without having to determine whether ice qualified as land. United States v. Alaska, 521 U.S. 1, 22–32 (1997).

98. Shalowitz, *supra* note 21, at 292.

99. United States v. Louisiana, 394 U.S. 11, 37 n.42 (1960).

100. United States v. California, 381 U.S. 448, 451 (1966).

101. "[U]nder Article 8 [of the 1958 Convention on the Territorial Sea and the Contiguous Zone] the 'outermost permanent harbour works' in this case are the jetties at the entrance of the Sabine River into the Gulf of Mexico." Texas v. Louisiana, Report of Special Master Van Pelt of October Term 1974, at 29.

102. United States v. Louisiana, 394 U.S. 11, 402–03 (1969).

103. United States v. California, 447 U.S. 1, 4–6 (1980).

104. Chart 1, *supra* note 24, at 27.

105. References in Supreme Court decisions are to Article 7 of the 1958 Convention on the Territorial Sea and the Contiguous Zone because that is the Convention specifically adopted by the Court to provide the principles for interpreting the Submerged Lands Act. However, Article 7 of the 1958 Convention and Article 10 of the 1982 Convention are identical.

106. United States v. Louisiana, 394 U.S. 11, 62 (1969).

107. United States v. Louisiana, 394 U.S. 11, 64 (1969); United States v. Maine et al., 469 U.S. 504, 517 (1985).

108. United States v. Maine et al., 469 U.S. 504 (1985).

109. Alaska v. United States, 545 U.S. 75 (2005).

110. Article 10(2).

111. 3 Reed, Shore and Sea Boundaries 223–36 (2000).

112. Using Figure 1.3 as an example, the gray line between East Chop and Cape Poge is the mouth of a juridical bay to its southwest. The maximum depth of that bay's penetration can be measured on a line from a point on the mouth near its northwestern terminus to a point on the western shore of Chappaquiddick Island three-quarters of a mile southwest of the entrance to Cape Poge Bay. The depth of penetration exceeds the width of mouth, meeting the primary requirement of Article 10.

113. The Court has said that this primary test must be met before the more objective semicircle test is made, the latter being a minimum requirement. United States v. Louisiana, 394 U.S. 11, 54 (1969). For more thorough discussions of the alternative proposal for calculating a width-to-depth ratio, *see* United States v. Alaska, Report of the Special Master of March 1996, at 182–226; and Alaska v. United States, Report of the Special Master of March 2004, at 201–26.

114. Swinging an arc from the midpoint of the gray closing line in Figure 1.3, we find that the water area of the enclosed indentation meets the semicircle test without including the adjacent, but distinctly separate, Sengekontacket Pond, Katama Bay, or Cape Poge Bay.

115. United States v. California, 381 U.S. 139, 172 (1965).

116. Alabama and Mississippi Boundary Cases, 470 U.S. 93, 102 (1985).

117. Not all historic waters qualify as "inland." They may be inland, territorial, or, presumably, historic contiguous zones or exclusive fisheries zones depending on the type of jurisdiction asserted and accepted by the international community. "If the claimant State exercised sovereignty as over internal waters, the area claimed would be internal waters, and if the sovereignty exercised was sovereignty as over the territorial sea, the areas would be territorial sea." United States v. Louisiana, 394 U.S. 11, 24 n.28, quoting *Juridical Regime of Historic Waters, Including Historic Bays,* [1962] 2 Y.B. Int'l L. Comm'n, 1, 24, U.N. Doc. A/CN.4/143 (1962).

118. Only Mississippi Sound and Vineyard Sound have been adjudicated historic waters. Alabama and Mississippi Boundary Cases, 470 U.S. 93 (1985); and United States v. Maine (Massachusetts), 475 U.S. 89 (1986). States which unsuccessfully asserted historic inland water claims include: California, 381 U.S. 139 (1965); Louisiana, 394 U.S. 11 (1969); Alaska, 422 U.S. 184 (1975) and 545 U.S. 75 (2005); Florida, 420 U.S. 531 (1975); Massachusetts (Nantucket Sound), 475 U.S. 89 (1986); and Rhode Island, 469 U.S. 504 (1985).

119. The definition is identical to that in Article 10 of the 1958 Convention on the Territorial Sea and the Contiguous Zone.

120. Prescott, *supra* note 37, at 81–82.

121. *Id.* at 82.

122. *Id.* at 58.

123. For example, guano islands might once have sustained human economic life but be no longer able to. Prescott, *supra* note 37, at 77, quoting Jonathan I. Charney, *Rocks That Cannot Sustain Human Habitation,* 93 Am. J. Int'l L. 867 (1999).

124. Florida and Texas qualified for these nine-mile grants because their historic boundaries extended nine miles into the Gulf and were approved by Congress at the time of Texas's original admission to the Union in 1845 and Florida's readmission in 1868. 43 U.S.C. § 1301(b); United States v. Louisiana, 363 U.S. 1, 64 (1960); United States v. Florida, 363 U.S. 121, 129 (1960).

125. Texas Boundary Case, 394 U.S. 1, 5 (1969).

126. Pub. L. 99-272, 100 Stat. 151 (1986); codified at 43 U.S.C. § 1301(b).

127. United States v. Louisiana, 452 U.S. 726 (1981).

128. United States v. California, 449 U.S. 408 (1981).

129. United States v. Louisiana, 394 U.S. 11 (1969).

130. United States v. Louisiana, 422 U.S. 13 (1975).

131. United States v. Louisiana, 452 U.S. 726 (1981).

132. The jetties at the mouth of the Sabine River, for example, extend Louisiana's Submerged Lands Act rights by almost three nautical miles.

133. United States v. California, 381 U.S. 139, 176 (1965).

134. "Structures or work affecting coastal waters may modify the coast line or base line from which the territorial sea is measured for purposes of the Submerged Lands Act and international law. Application for structures or work affecting coastal waters will therefore be reviewed specifically to determine whether the coast line might be altered. If it is determined that such a change might occur, coordination with the Attorney General and the Solicitor of the Department of the Interior is required before final action is taken." 33 C.F.R. § 320.4.

135. The Supreme Court described the Corps' authority under Section 10 of the Rivers and Harbors Act, 33 U.S.C. § 403, as apparent "unlimited discretion to grant or deny a permit for construction of a structure such as the one at issue in this case." United States v. Alaska, 503 U.S. 567, 576 (1992).

136. United States v. Alaska, Report of the Special Master of March 1996, 311-37; United States v. Alaska, 521 U.S. 1, 62 (1997).

137. United States v. California, 332 U.S. 19 (1947).

138. United States v. California, 332 U.S. 19, 38 (1947), quoting from Skiriotes v. Florida, 313 U.S. 69, 75 (1941).

139. United States v. Louisiana, 339 U.S. 699, 705 (1950). The Court also explained that it was making no determination "on the power of a State to extend, define, or establish its external territorial limits or on the consequences of any such extension *vis a vis* persons other than the United States or those acting on behalf of or pursuant to its authority." *Id.*

140. 43 U.S.C. § 1312.

141. 16 U.S.C. § 1811.

142. S. Rep. No. 94-416, 94th Cong., 1st Sess., at 22 (1976). The House Conference Committee Report contains similar language. "The term 'seaward boundary' when used in reference to a coastal state has the same meaning as . . . in the Submerged Lands Act of 1953 (43 U.S.C. 1301(b))." H. Rep. No. 94-948, at 41 (1976).

143. Pub. L. 92-272, § 8005 (1986).

144. Texas Boundary Case, 394 U.S. 1, 5 (1969).

145. *Id.*

146. S. Rep. No. 94-416, 94th Cong., 1st Sess. on S. 961, at 22 (1976).

147. Manchester v. Massachusetts, 139 U.S. 240 (1891); Skiriotes v. Florida, 313 U.S. 69 (1941); Toomer v. Witsell, 334 U.S. 385 (1947).

148. 16 U.S.C. § 1856(a)(2)(A).

149. 16 U.S.C. § 1856(a)(2)(B) and (C).

150. United States v. Maine (Massachusetts), 475 U.S. 89 (1987).

151. Alaska v. United States, 545 U.S. 75 (2005).

152. 16 U.S.C. § 1453(1).

153. 16 U.S.C. § 1453(1). *See also* S. Rep. No. 92-753, April 19, 1972, regarding Pub. L. 92-583, 1972 U.S.C.C.A.N. 4776, at 4783 describing the seaward boundary of the coastal zone as "the outer limit of State title and ownership under the Submerged Lands Act."

154. Outer Continental Shelf Lands Act, 43 U.S.C. §§ 1331 *et seq.*

155. Presidential Proclamation No. 5928, 54 Fed. Reg. 777 (1988).

156. Examples include federal statutes concerning: port and waterway safety, 46 U.S.C. § 2101(17)(a); vessel radiotelephone communications, 33 U.S.C. § 1203(b); vessel movement and anchorage in time of conflict, 50 U.S.C. § 195(2); and marine sanctuary protection, 16 U.S.C. § 1437(k).

157. Examples include statutes concerning: ocean dumping, 33 U.S.C. §§ 1401(b) and 1902(a)(2); and clean water, 33 U.S.C. §§ 1311(f) and 1362(8).

158. The author gratefully acknowledges contributions to this section from the following unpublished papers: LCDR Rock C. De Tolve, U.S.N. JAG, "The Fight over 'Non-Extractive' Activity on the United States' Outer Continental Shelf," May 2005; and Nicholas A. Fromherz, "The Answer Is Blowing in the Wind: Corps Authority to Regulate Offshore Wind Farms," May 2005.

159. Article 60(1) of the 1982 Convention on the Law of the Sea provides that "[i]n the exclusive economic zone, the coastal State shall have the exclusive right to construct and authorize and regulate the construction, operation and use of: (a) artificial islands; (b) installations and structures for the purposes provided for in article 56 and other economic purposes; (c) installations and structures which may interfere with the exercise of the rights of the coastal State in the zone." Apropos of the point to be made here, Article 56 includes "the production of energy from the water, currents and winds" among its purposes.

160. Until the Outer Continental Shelf Lands Act was amended in 1978, it expressly provided the Corps with jurisdiction over "all artificial islands and fixed structures" erected on the outer continental shelf.

161. 43 U.S.C. §§ 1333(e) and 1333(a)(1).

162. H.R. Conf. Rep. No. 95-1474 at 82 (1978), reprinted in 1978 U.S.C.C.A.N. 1674, 1681.

163. Alliance to Protect Nantucket Sound, Inc. v. U.S. Dep't of the Army, 398 F.3d 105 (1st Cir. 2005).

164. "Whether, and under what circumstances, additional authorization is necessary before a developer infringes on the federal government's rights in the OCS is a thorny issue." Alliance to Protect Nantucket Sound, Inc. v. U.S. Dep't of the Army, 398 F.3d 105, 114 (1st Cir. 2005).

165. "Present estates in land carry with them, as their single most salient characteristic, the present right to exclusive possession." WILLIAM B. STOEBUCK & DALE A. WHITMAN, THE LAW OF PROPERTY 25 (3d ed. 2000). "In the main . . . it is true that the right physically to exclude others is the most nearly absolute of the many property rights that flow from the ownership and rightful possession of land. A recent decision of the Supreme Court reminds us anew that the owner may generally insist strictly upon excluding others, without their competing claims being balanced in, as is often done with other property rights." Id. at 411, citing Loretto v. Teleprompter Manhattan CATV Corp., 458 U.S. 419 (1982).

166. U.S. CONST. art. IV, § 3; United States v. City and County of San Francisco, 112 F. Supp. 451 (N.D. Cal. 1953), aff'd, 223 F.2d 737 (9th Cir. 1955), cert. denied, 350 U.S. 903 (1955).

167. United States v. California, 332 U.S. 19, 39–40 (1947).

168. 43 U.S.C. § 1334.

169. 33 C.F.R. § 320.4(g)(6) provides that a Corps permit "does not convey any property rights . . . or any exclusive privileges . . . [nor does it] authorize any injury to property or invasion of rights or any infringement of Federal, state or local laws or regulations. The applicant's signature application is an affirmation that the applicant possesses or will possess the requisite property interest to undertake the activity proposed in the application."

170. The United States Court of Appeals gave no substantive significance to this misstatement, apparently holding that the property owner's permission is not required because the construction of a tower constitutes "no real infringement on federal interests" in the lands involved. Alliance to Protect Nantucket Sound, Inc. v. U.S. Dep't of the Army, 398 F.3d 105, 114 (1st Cir. 2005).

171. United States v. Maine (Massachusetts), 475 U.S. 89 (1986) (decision), 516 U.S. 365 (1996), "affirming the title of the United States to the seabed more than three geographic miles seaward of the coastline" of Massachusetts.

172. International Convention for the Protection of Submarine Cables (1885), 24 Stat. 989.

173. With respect to the continental shelf, the 1982 Convention provides, in relevant part, that "[a]ll States are entitled to lay submarine cables and pipelines on the continental shelf." Article 79(1). But for its limited right to protect the exploration and exploitation of shelf resources, "the coastal State may not impede the laying or maintenance of such cables." Article 79(2). With respect to the Exclusive Economic Zone, the Convention provides, in relevant part, that "all States . . . enjoy . . . the freedoms . . . of the laying of submarine cables . . . and other internationally lawful uses of the sea related to those freedoms." Article 58(1).

174. Presidential Proclamation No. 5030, 48 Fed. Reg. 10,605 (1983) (establishing EEZ); and Presidential Proclamation No. 7210, 48 Fed. Reg. 48,701 (1999) (establishing contiguous zone).

175. Now codified at 33 U.S.C. § 1344.

176. 1362 U.S.C. §§ (7) and (8).

177. Alliance to Protect Nantucket Sound, Inc. v. U.S. Dep't of the Army, 398 F.3d 105, 108–11 (1st Cir. 2005).

178. Compare Articles 60 and 80, which recognize the coastal State's "exclusive right to authorize and regulate" artificial islands, with Article 79, which recognizes the right of the international community to lay submarine cables, with minimum coastal state regulation.

179. Article 79(2).

180. The commercial and security interests of the United States weigh in favor of preserving the international right to lay and repair cables on continental shelves worldwide.

181. Fixing Submerged Lands Act boundaries creates a minor problem in interpreting the consequence on Magnuson-Stevens and Coastal Zone Management Act boundaries, but we

believe that that problem is easily resolved and, in any case, is outweighed by the value of a fixed line for the administration of offshore leases. The federal/state boundaries can be fixed by agreeing on a line and incorporating its description in a Supreme Court decree. Most coastal states have been parties to Original actions over which the Court has retained jurisdiction to enter further decrees. New actions might be filed for the remaining states.

182. We believe that state boundaries remain ambulatory for most other purposes, including fisheries jurisdiction, and that it would make sense not to fix the Magnuson-Stevens Act boundary. In contrast, because the reach of the Coastal Zone Management Act is specifically tied to seabed ownership, and because the CZMA specifically excludes federal lands from the coastal zone in any case, it makes sense to fix the limits of the coastal zone when Submerged Lands Act boundaries are fixed. We believe that these suggestions maximize state jurisdiction and are consistent with Congressional intent.

183. The United States was actively involved in the negotiations which resulted in the 1982 Convention. On balance, we believe, the U.S. delegation did an extraordinary job of protecting America's critical interests. A vast majority, if not all, of the Convention's provisions must now be understood to reflect customary international law. We believe that the time has come for the United States to ratify the Convention.

184. When Presidential Proclamations extended the three-mile territorial sea to twelve nautical miles and the seaward boundary of the contiguous zone from twelve to twenty-four miles, the actions had only international consequences. The reach of domestic legislation was not affected. Since that time Congress has approached the matter piecemeal. Some statutes were amended to apply in the new zones. Others were amended to make clear that they apply only where they always did. And most have not been dealt with at all. We believe that a systematic review should be made of all legislation which applies to "navigable waters of the United States," "territorial waters," "territorial sea," "territory and waters of the United States," and similar terms and a determination made as to the geographic reach of each within our modern zones of maritime jurisdiction.

185. Here we think it particularly important that a federal agency be given congressional direction and authority to grant rights to occupy federal submerged lands of the outer continental shelf for purposes not envisioned in existing legislation. There is also an apparent need for separate legislation governing federal jurisdiction over subsea cables on the outer continental shelf.

186. That, we think, is inevitable. Coastlines, by their nature, are ambulatory, as are the boundaries measured from them. International law on the point is not likely to change. The primary purpose of nautical charts is to maximize maritime safety, as it should be.

chapter two

The Public Trust Doctrine

Stephen E. Roady

I. Introduction: The Origins and Significance of the Public Trust Doctrine

The Public Trust Doctrine springs from ancient law concepts that treated certain lands and waters as belonging to the public for public benefit—and therefore guaranteed public access and use. As currently defined, "public trust lands" include coastal lands located seaward of the high-water mark, lands and waters subject to the ebb and flow of the tide, and the beds of navigable rivers and streams. These lands and waters are protected by the Doctrine, which, broadly speaking, requires the sovereign to manage them for the benefit of the citizenry.

The Public Trust Doctrine is controversial, and its contours are not sharply defined. It is controversial because it has the potential to pit the public interest in access to certain lands and waters against property owners asserting a competing interest. Moreover, from its origins that tied it to navigable waters and the seashore, its reach has evolved to include other natural resources, with its outer boundaries not yet fully plumbed.

This chapter focuses on the implications of the Public Trust Doctrine for three critical coastal issues: managing coastal development, controlling beach access and use, and protecting natural resources in coastal and ocean waters.

The author gratefully acknowledges the thoughtful assistance of Mary Turnipseed, Ph.D. candidate at Duke University, and Janet Moon, J.D. candidate at Syracuse University, in the preparation of this chapter.

The origins of the Public Trust Doctrine can be traced formally to the Romans, who likely derived the concept initially from the Greeks.

The origins of the Public Trust Doctrine can be traced formally to the Romans, who likely derived the concept initially from the Greeks. The Doctrine was absorbed and modified by the common law of England and later inherited by the American colonies.

An early description of the concept on which the Public Trust Doctrine is based appears in the Institutes of Justinian (AD 533), which describes the "law of nature" to include things common to humankind such as the sea and the seashore:

> By the law of nature these things are common to all mankind—the air, running water, the sea, and consequently the shores of the sea. No one, therefore, is forbidden to approach the seashore, provided that he respects habitations, monuments, and the buildings, which are not, like the sea, subject only to the law of nations.[1]

The Institutes of Justinian copied many concepts, perhaps including this "common ownership and access" notion, from the second-century Institutes and Journal of Gaius—which in turn adopted many natural law concepts from the Greek philosophers, especially the Stoics. The Institutes further specified certain public rights to these common areas, including the right to place a cottage on the seashore and the right to fish in the sea from the shore.[2]

A natural consequence of treating certain lands and waters as open to the public for public benefit is to charge the sovereign with both the authority and the duty to protect that benefit. That is, if certain lands are held in trust for the public, there must logically be a trustee with the task of protecting the corpus of the trust. Scholars are in disagreement over whether the Roman system included any method for enforcing the duties of the state as a trustee. In his seminal article on the Public Trust Doctrine, Professor Joseph Sax noted that "[a]lthough the state apparently did protect public uses, no evidence is available that public rights could be legally asserted against a recalcitrant government."[3]

Moreover, whether the sovereign had a duty to reserve the seashore and the sea for public use fell into question during the Middle Ages, when it appears various English sovereigns granted private rights to coastal areas and waters. The Magna Carta (1215), however, arguably reined in the alleged authority of the King to make such grants.[4] Also in the thirteenth century, Bracton reiterated the Justinian notion that certain resources were common to the public: "By natural law, these are common to all: running water, the air, the sea, and the shores of the sea. No one is forbidden access to the seashore."[5]

In the 1600s, Matthew Hale's *De Jure Maris* (1667) reinvigorated the concept of public rights of access and use with respect to coastal waters. Common law courts in England expanded the Doctrine to reach all "navigable waters," which—in England—came to mean all those waters that were subject to the ebb and flow of the tide.[6] The process by which this came to be the accepted law in England was fraught with controversy. According to Professor Richard Lazarus, Queen Elizabeth's lawyer originally developed the theory that the Crown was the owner of the seashore to the high-water mark, absent a specific grant of the shore itself in a royal deed.[7] This theory met strong resistance from property owners, but successive sovereigns persisted in order to "enhance the royal purse, and in time the courts fell in line."[8]

In the 1600s, Matthew Hale's *De Jure Maris* (1667) reinvigorated the concept of public rights of access and use with respect to coastal waters.

Under the common law, there were two aspects of ownership with respect to public trust lands: (1) the public right to use the lands (the *jus publicum*) and (2) the private right of possession of the lands (the *jus privatum*). The sovereign held both of these aspects of ownership. In theory, the sovereign had the duty to protect the *jus publicum*, even though it was possible for a private owner to demonstrate that the King had conveyed the *jus privatum* to him.[9]

When the American colonies imported the common law from England, they fell heir to the general outline of the public trust concept as it was then in force under the Common Law.[10] In broad terms, then, the original colonies carried the basic elements of the Public Trust Doctrine concept forward when they established the United States.[11] And under the equal footing doctrine, states entering the Union after the Revolution were deemed to have inherited the same "public trust" principles as did the original colonies.[12]

The original colonies carried the basic elements of the Public Trust Doctrine concept forward when they established the United States.

Some commentators believe that there exists a "federal" public trust doctrine in addition to the fifty separate "state" public trust doctrines. One legal scholar has opined that there is a separate federal public trust, that there are certain minimum requirements for the trust set by the Constitution, and that the states are not free to completely abrogate this trust.[13]

Putting aside for the moment the nature of the "federal" public trust, certain "core principles" of the Public Trust Doctrine now prevail in each state. Thus, each state:

- Has public trust interests, rights, and responsibilities in its navigable waters, the lands beneath these waters, and the living resources therein;
- Has the authority to define the boundary limits of the lands and waters held in public trust;
- Has the authority to recognize and convey private proprietary rights (the *jus privatum*) in its trust lands, and thus diminish the public's rights therein, with the corollary responsibility not to substantially impair the public's use and enjoyment of the remaining trust lands, waters, and living resources;
- Has a trustee's duty and responsibility to preserve and continuously assure the public's ability to fully use and enjoy public trust lands and waters for certain trust uses; and

- Does not have the power to abdicate its role of trustee of the public's *jus publicum* rights, although in certain limited cases the State can terminate the *jus publicum* in small parcels of trust land.[14]

As with other aspects of the common law, however, each state has remained free to adapt the specific outlines of the Public Trust Doctrine to its own uses.[15] Accordingly, various states have defined the reach and scope of the doctrine differently.[16] For example, although most coastal states deem title to all coastal property seaward of the mean high-water line to be held by the states, some states—including Delaware, Massachusetts, and Virginia—historically have granted private title holdings that run to the low-water line.[17] Notwithstanding these grants, both Delaware and Virginia have also allowed the public a right of access to and use of the tidelands.[18]

II. The Current State of the Public Trust Doctrine

This section examines the evolution and current state of the Public Trust Doctrine with respect to coastal lands and waters under U.S. law. Because the Doctrine requires the government to protect public trust lands,[19] it imposes a range of duties on the government in its role as trustee.[20] These trustee duties can often clash with the rights asserted by coastal property owners,[21] with respect to beach use and access and the protection of coastal resources.

Scholars differ on the proper role and scope of the Public Trust Doctrine. One view, traceable to Professor Sax and echoed by others, holds that the Doctrine sweeps broadly and is capable of expansion to protect a wide range of resources in the name of the public.[22] Another, contrary view is that the Doctrine is limited in scope and that it should be subservient to constitutional rights such as those pertaining to property.[23] Opportunities for this debate to focus on coastal and ocean resource management are likely to grow as demand for those resources increases.

A. The Evolution and Scope of the Doctrine Under U.S. Law

The first U.S. case to address the Public Trust Doctrine in some detail was *Arnold v. Mundy*.[24] In a ruling that largely outlined the Doctrine as it would apply in this country, the Supreme Court of New Jersey ruled that a property owner who traced his title to a pre-statehood conveyance from the King could not prevent the public from oystering on his tidelands.[25] The court ruled that the sovereign holds the beds and waters of the seacoast in trust for the people, and that the states—as sovereigns—had succeeded to that trust previously held by the King.[26] Interestingly, the court described the nature of the public's interest in these lands in exceedingly broad language, to include "fishing, fowling, sustenance and all other uses of the water and its products."[27] Moreover, the court held that any grant purporting to divest citizens of these common rights was void: "[the sovereign] cannot . . . make a direct and absolute grant of the waters of the state, divesting all the citizens of their common right."[28]

Although it noted in *Martin v. Waddell's Lessee* that the "absolute right" to navigable waters and the soils thereunder were held by the states for the "common use" of the people,[29] the Supreme Court of the United States did not fully explore the Public Trust Doctrine until the 1890s. Ruling that Illinois could not grant control of the Chicago harbor and adjacent lands to a private company, the Court described the Doctrine in sweeping terms in *Illinois Central Railroad Co. v. Illinois*.[30] In so doing, it emphasized that public trust lands are held forever by the state for the people:

> [T]he State holds the title to lands under navigable waters . . . [b]ut it is a title different in character from that which the State holds in lands intended for sale. . . . It is a title held in trust for the people of the State that they may enjoy the navigation of the waters, carry on commerce over them, and have liberty of fishing therein freed from the obstruction or interference of private parties. . . . The trust devolving upon the State for the public . . . cannot be relinquished by a transfer of the property. The control of the State for the purposes of the trust can never be lost, except as to such parcels as are used in promoting the interests of the public therein, or can be disposed of without any substantial impairment of the public interest in the lands and waters remaining. . . . The State can no more abdicate its trust over property in which the whole people are interested, like navigable waters and soils under them, so as to leave them entirely under the use and control of private parties, except in the instance of [navigation and other acts that do not impair the public interest] than it can abdicate its police powers.[31]

In analyzing *Illinois Central*, Professor Charles Wilkinson concludes that the Supreme Court was articulating a federal public trust "servitude" that burdens public trust lands with the duty to allow public access.[32] Wilkinson argues that the ruling in *Illinois Central* makes clear that the Court viewed the doctrine as one of general applicability to all states and that by its nature it included certain minimum requirements.[33] Other commentators agree that the public trust described in *Illinois Central* has federal overtones.[34]

In the years following *Illinois Central*, which analogizes the sovereign's duty to protect public trust lands to its constitutional duty to protect citizens under the police power, some coastal state courts have expressed the view that the Public Trust Doctrine is more a creature of the common law than of the Constitution. For example, the North Carolina Supreme Court has held that "[t]he public trust doctrine is a common law doctrine. In the absence of a constitutional basis for the public trust doctrine, it cannot be used to invalidate acts of the legislature which are not proscribed by our [North Carolina's] Constitution."[35] Rhode Island has reached a similar conclusion.[36]

By contrast, courts in other coastal states have issued rulings that elevate the Public Trust Doctrine to something akin to constitutional status. For example, in *Orion Corp. v. State*, the Supreme Court of Washington ruled that the trust applied to tidelands could not be abrogated even by express legislation and that the legislature lacked authority to abdicate state sovereignty over those lands.[37]

Several states have enacted constitutional provisions that effectively adopt the public trust concept. For example, article IX, section 1 of the Louisiana Constitution states:

> The natural resources of the state, including air and water, and the healthful, scenic, historic, and aesthetic quality of the environment shall be protected, conserved, and replenished insofar as possible and consistent with the health, safety and welfare of the people. The legislature shall enact laws to implement this policy.

The Louisiana Supreme Court emphasized that the State constitution imposes an affirmative duty on the State as trustee to protect public trust resources.[38] Consistent with this approach and with the explicit directive of article IX, section 1 of the State constitution, the Louisiana legislature has enacted legislation declaring that the marine fishery resources of the State "are managed by the state in trust for the benefit of all its citizens" under "the public trust doctrine."[39]

The Hawaii Constitution contains a similarly strong affirmation of the Public Trust Doctrine in article XI, section 1:

> For the benefit of present and future generations, the State and its political subdivisions shall conserve and protect Hawaii's natural beauty and all natural resources, including land, water, air, minerals and energy sources, and shall promote the development and utilization of these resources in a manner consistent with their conservation and in furtherance of the self-sufficiency of the State.

The Alaska Constitution contains several provisions that have been interpreted to embody the Public Trust Doctrine. Article VIII, section 2 of that constitution states that "the legislature shall provide for the utilization, development, and conservation of all natural resources belonging to the State, including land and waters, for the maximum benefit of its people." Article VIII, section 3 states further that "wherever occurring in their natural state, fish, wildlife, and waters are reserved to the people for common use."

The Alaska Supreme Court has ruled that the provisions of article VIII impose certain public trust duties on the State and prevented an effort to allocate certain alleged rights in the salmon fishery to specified subgroups of the public.[40] The Alaska Supreme Court has also ruled that any grant by the legislature of public trust lands will be presumed to preserve the trust unless explicitly stated otherwise.[41]

The Public Trust Doctrine that came to the United States from England limited the reach of the Doctrine to "navigable" waters, and the Supreme Court took the view early on that this term was defined in England as those waters subject to the ebb and flow of the tide. Nevertheless, the Supreme Court eventually expanded the definition of "navigable waters" inland to include rivers and lakes that were "navigable in fact" even though they were not subject to tidal influence.[42] As a result, in this country the Doctrine came to apply to lands beneath navigable—but nontidal—freshwater rivers and streams.

In *Phillips Petroleum Co. v. Mississippi* the Supreme Court further expanded the scope of lands covered by the Doctrine, ruling that the extension of the Doctrine to nontidal waters in cases such as *Genessee Chief* did not have the effect of requiring that only lands under navigable waters could qualify as trust lands.[43] Thus, the Court held that lands located under nonnavigable waters that were influenced by the tide qualified as Public Trust Doctrine lands.[44] Following that ruling, public trust lands in this country consist of (1) all lands located under navigable waters, (2) all coastal lands seaward of the high-water mark, and (3) all lands subject to tidal influence.[45]

B. The Public Trust, Takings, and Coastal Development

The coastal population of the United States has increased steadily during the past three decades. According to the United States Commission on Ocean Policy, "[b]etween 1970 and 2000, the population of coastal watershed counties grew by 37 million people . . . and is projected to increase by another 21 million by 2015."[46] In light of increasing pressure to develop the coasts, the obligation of coastal states to protect public trust lands is being tested. Commonly, this test takes the form of a challenge by property owners when states assert authority to prohibit or limit coastal building projects; the owners invoke the Fifth Amendment to the Constitution and claim that the states cannot restrict the use of their property without compensation.

The Fifth Amendment provides that "[n]o person shall be . . . deprived of life, liberty, or property without due process of law, nor shall private property be taken for public use, without just compensation." The Fifth Amendment applies to the states through the Fourteenth Amendment:

> No State shall make or enforce any law which shall abridge the privileges or immunities of citizens of the United States; nor shall any State deprive any person of life, liberty, or property, without due process of law; nor deny to any person within its jurisdiction the equal protection of the laws.

In *Pennsylvania Coal Co. v. Mahon,*[47] the Supreme Court ruled that "while property may be regulated to a certain extent, if regulation goes too far it will be recognized as a taking." [48] In the decades since *Pennsylvania Coal*, the Court tended to "engag[e] in . . . essentially ad hoc, factual inquiries" in determining whether a particular regulation constitutes a taking.[49] Indeed, the Court's decisions on whether a particular action constitutes a "regulatory taking" had become sufficiently muddled by the end of the 1980s that Justice Stevens characterized them as "open-ended and standardless."[50]

However, in 1992 the Supreme Court proffered a more general rule, holding in a coastal property setting that "regulations that compel the property owner to suffer a physical 'invasion' of his property," and regulations that deny "all economically beneficial or productive use of land" are compensable as "takings" under the Fifth Amendment.[51]

In *Lucas v. South Carolina*, the property owner purchased two oceanfront lots on a particularly precarious stretch of beach that was nonetheless zoned and considered suitable for the construction of single-family residences.[52] Two years later, South Carolina enacted a beachfront management law that resulted in the establishment of a "baseline" along the beach: because the beach in question was located in an "inlet erosion zone" that was subject to fluctuation, no residences could be constructed seaward of a line drawn twenty feet landward of that baseline.[53] These actions by the State prevented the property owner from constructing anything more than a walkway or a small deck on his two properties. The property owner claimed that this law had deprived him of "all economically viable use" of his lots and that he was therefore entitled to compensation. The South Carolina Supreme Court rejected his claim, ruling that the law did not amount to a "regulatory taking" because it sought to prevent serious public harm that results from unwise beachfront development.[54]

On appeal, the Supreme Court reversed. Disagreeing with the South Carolina court that states can avoid compensating landowners simply by alleging that the challenged restrictions are based on an effort to prevent public harm, the Court held that:

> [w]here the State seeks to sustain regulation that deprives land of all economically beneficial use, we think it may resist compensation only if the logically antecedent inquiry into the nature of the owner's estate shows that the proscribed use interests were not part of his title to begin with. . . . Any limitation [depriving land of all economically beneficial use] cannot be newly legislated or decreed (without compensation) but must inhere in the title itself, in the restrictions that background principles of the State's law of property and nuisance already place upon land ownership.[55]

Accordingly, the Supreme Court remanded the case to South Carolina. Noting that "[i]t seems unlikely that common-law principles would have prevented the erection of any habitable or productive improvements on petitioner's land," the Court emphasized that the State could prevail in resisting compensation to the landowner only if it could "identify background principles of nuisance and property law that prohibit the uses he now intends in the circumstances in which the property is presently found."[56]

On remand, the South Carolina Supreme Court concluded that the State was required to demonstrate that the property owner's "intended use of his land was not part of the bundle of rights inhering in his title."[57] Finding that the State had been unable to show that "any common law basis exists by which it could restrain Lucas's desired use of his land," the South Carolina Supreme Court directed the parties to present evidence of the actual damages sustained by the property owner as a result of a "temporary nonacquisitory" taking of his property.[58]

Almost a decade after *Lucas*, in *Palazzolo v. Rhode Island*,[59] the Supreme Court determined that there was not a "total taking" of the property owner's interests where the state had allowed him to develop an upland portion of his coastal property while denying him the ability to develop adjacent coastal wetlands on that property. The property in *Palazzolo* encompassed roughly twenty acres located on a narrow spit of land adjacent to an intertidal inlet near the Atlantic Ocean.[60] Most of the acreage—about eighteen acres—consisted of "salt marsh subject to tidal flooding."[61] However, a portion of the eastern side of the property was located upland of the marsh and capable of being developed; uncontested testimony established that this portion of the property would be worth approximately $200,000 if developed.[62]

After several unsuccessful efforts to secure a permit to fill and develop the marshes on his property, the owner ultimately filed a takings challenge to the State's denial of his request for a permit to fill eleven acres of the marsh with gravel to build a private beach club.[63] The U.S. Supreme Court affirmed the decision of the Rhode Island Supreme Court that the State had not deprived the property owner of "all economically beneficial use" of his property "because the uplands portion of the property can still be improved."[64] By concluding that there had been no "taking" compensable under the Fifth Amendment, the Court in *Palazzolo* avoided the need to examine the question framed by the *Lucas* analysis—whether any "background principles" in the law of Rhode Island had already placed restrictions on the ability of the coastal property owner to develop his land.

Although both cases involved public trust coastal lands, neither *Lucas* nor *Palazzolo* mentioned the Public Trust Doctrine.[65] However, the Doctrine has been relied upon as a "background principle" by two subsequent courts to defeat takings claims involving coastal property.

First, in *Esplanade Properties v. City of Seattle*,[66] the Ninth Circuit invoked the Public Trust Doctrine to reject a takings claim by a development company that had been denied a permit to build homes on platforms and pilings in a Seattle tidal bay. The property was located below a bluff near a city park and marina; it is submerged by the tide roughly half the time.[67] The court found that the Public Trust Doctrine of the State of Washington "ran with the title to the tideland properties and alone precluded the shoreline residential development proposed by Esplanade."[68] The U.S. Supreme Court denied review of the developer's petition for certiorari.[69]

Similarly, in *McQueen v. South Carolina Coastal Council*,[70] the South Carolina Supreme Court held that a property owner could not fill his partially inundated beachfront land because the Public Trust Doctrine acted as an inherent limitation on his title.[71] The property in question had been "highland" beach at the time of its purchase, but had been partly converted to marsh over the course of thirty years of natural erosion along the beach. The South Carolina Supreme Court ruled that: (1) the State holds presumptive title to lands below the high-water mark both in *jus privatum* and in *jus publicum*; (2) the State has "the exclusive right to control land below the high-water mark for the public benefit, and cannot permit activity that substantially impairs the public interest in marine life, water quality, or public access"; (3) the State's presumptive title to lands below the high-water mark applies to tidelands; (4) "wetlands created by the encroachment of navigable tidal water belong to the State"; (5) "[p]roof that land was highland at the time of grant and tidelands were subsequently created by the rising of tidal water cannot defeat the State's presumptive title to tidelands"; (6) the reversion of the property owner's lands from highlands to tidelands "effected a restriction on McQueen's property rights inherent in the owner-ship of property bordering tidal water"; (7) "the tidelands included on McQueen's lots are public trust property subject to the control of the State."[72]

Accordingly, citing *Esplanade Properties*, the South Carolina Supreme Court held that "McQueen's ownership rights do not include the right to backfill or place bulk-heads on public trust land and the State need not compensate him for the denial of permits to do what he cannot otherwise do."[73] Thus, the South Carolina court reasoned that the Doctrine constituted a "background principle" under the *Lucas* analysis and that, as such, it defeated the owner's claim that the denial of his ability to develop his land triggered compensation as a Fifth Amendment "taking." Notably, as with *Esplanade Properties*, the U.S. Supreme Court did not grant review of *McQueen*. Instead, it denied certiorari.[74]

In the wake of *Lucas* and *Palazzolo*, and given the refusal of the Supreme Court to review either *McQueen* or *Esplanade*, numerous commentators have noted that the Public Trust Doctrine can be considered a "background principle" that can defeat a takings claim.[75] In sum, coastal states can invoke the Public Trust Doctrine to manage the development of beachfront and other coastal property with some confidence that they will be protected against a successful takings claim.

C. The Public Trust Doctrine and Beach Access and Uses

Distinct from the question of constructing homes, condominiums, cottages, and other buildings in coastal areas is the question of general public access to, and use of, the beaches of this country. The Public Trust Doctrine is based on the Justinian concept that the seashore is "common to all mankind" and that "[n]o one, therefore, is forbid-den to approach the seashore."[76] Justinian also espoused the public right to fish in the sea from the shore.[77] With these public trust principles in mind, this section examines the differing ways in which the Supreme Court and the states have approached the question of beach access and use.

In order to appreciate the question of public access to beaches, it is important to understand the beachfront property ownership situation. In most coastal states the state asserts ownership of the beach up to the mean high-water mark. In four coastal states (Maine, Massachusetts, Delaware, and Virginia), the state asserts ownership only up to the low-water mark. In either case, beachfront property owners claim title to the so-called dry-sand portion of the beach—that is, they claim ownership of all beachfront land adjoining their property that lies landward of the mean high-water mark. Under the traditional Public Trust Doctrine, trust lands do not include the dry-sand beach. These facts give rise to two kinds of access issues: (1) public rights to so-called perpendicular access—that is, the right to proceed from an upland position toward the ocean across the property owner's private property (including the dry-sand beach) to a point on the wet-sand beach (the area of the beach that lies seaward of the mean high tide line); and (2) public rights to so-called lateral access—that is, once on the beach, the right to proceed up and down the beach by use of the dry-sand portion and to use that portion of the beach for recreational activities such as sunbathing.

1. Supreme Court Intimations on Beach Access

The Supreme Court has never ruled directly on the question whether the Public Trust Doctrine guarantees the public certain rights of access to and use of the beaches. Two Supreme Court cases, however, shed light on this question.

In *Nollan v. California Coastal Commission*,[78] the Court ruled that California could not condition the rebuilding of a beach home on the grant by the homeowners of an easement allowing the public lateral access across their beach (which was located between two public beaches) without compensating the homeowners for the easement. The specific easement imposed by the California Coastal Commission would have required the property owners to allow the public "to pass across a portion of their property bounded by the mean high tide line on one side, and their seawall on the other side."[79] In justifying the easement, the Coastal Commission found that construction of the new house would "increase blockage of the view of the ocean" and thereby contribute to "a 'wall' of residential structures that would prevent the public 'psychologically . . . from realizing a stretch of coastline exists nearby that they have every right to visit.'"[80] The Commission also determined that construction of the house, when added to other beach construction in the area, would "cumulatively 'burden the public's ability to traverse to and along the shorefront.'"[81]

The Supreme Court began its analysis by observing (by way of dictum) that "the appropriation of a public easement across a landowner's premises" constitutes the taking of a property interest.[82] Thus, in further dictum, it observed that "we have no doubt there would have been a taking" had the easement in question not been conditioned on the building of the new house.[83] It then held that the easement was not a proper exercise of the state police power, even conditioned as it was, because the easement failed to further the ends advanced as reasons for its imposition.[84] Specifically, it concluded that the easement lacked an "essential nexus" because it would not reduce "any obstacles to viewing the beach created by the new house" and it would not lower any "'psychological barrier' to using the public beaches, or . . . help to remedy any additional congestion on them caused by construction."[85]

The facts of *Nollan*, and the dissents of Justices Brennan and Blackmun, establish that the case does not speak directly to the question of public beach access under the Public Trust Doctrine. First, the land across which the easement would lie was allegedly to be located above the mean high tide line; thus it presumably was not considered public trust land in California.[86] Second, as Justice Blackmun explicitly stated, "I do not understand the Court's opinion in this case to implicate in any way the public-trust doctrine."[87] The majority did not contest this statement in its opinion; thus presumably it is correct.[88] However, by requiring states to closely link the condition imposed on the beachfront property owner to the problem the condition seeks to resolve, the case arguably raises the bar for states seeking to invoke the Doctrine to impose easements allowing lateral access across beach property.[89]

One year following *Nollan*, the Supreme Court recognized that states traditionally deem public trust lands to be available for a wide range of issues—including not only the traditional uses of navigation and fishing but also other recreational uses. In

Phillips Petroleum Co. v. Mississippi,[90] the Court pointed out that cases which have discussed state public trust interests in nonnavigable tidelands have described those interests to encompass hunting, as well as "bathing, swimming, recreation, fishing, and mineral development."[91] Thus, although *Phillips Petroleum* does not address the question of public access to public trust lands such as beaches, it suggests that there might be grounds for relying on the Public Trust Doctrine to justify the access needed to engage in recreational and other activities that traditionally are protected by that Doctrine. As noted later in this chapter, states such as New Jersey and Washington have gone in this direction.

2. State Court Interpretations Concerning Beach Access

Few states approach the issue of beach access as a matter of anything other than common law. Nonetheless, two state constitutions (Alaska and California) expressly grant the public a right of access to navigable waters, and therefore can be construed as providing a certain right of both perpendicular and lateral access to beachfront property.[92] North Carolina also has a constitutional provision that can be interpreted to support a public right to beach access.[93]

Some states have enacted legislation that provides public rights of access to the beach. For example, a Texas statute guarantees the public the right of access to the dry-sand beach.[94] Similarly, both Washington and North Carolina have statutory provisions that support a right of public beach access.[95] The California Coastal Act establishes as a basic goal the effort to "[m]aximize public access to and along the coast and maximize public recreational opportunities in the coastal zone consistent with sound resource conservation principles and constitutionally protected rights of private property owners."[96]

A few state courts have adopted the view that the Public Trust Doctrine provides a basis for allowing the public a reasonable right of access to the beach—a so-called perpendicular right of access.[97] Other state courts have relied on the Doctrine to allow both lateral access along the beach and access to and use of the "dry-sand" portion of the beach by the public under certain conditions. The states with expansive judicial views include New Jersey, North Carolina, California, Washington, and Hawaii. Other states, such as Maine, New Hampshire, Massachusetts, and Maryland, have taken a more constrained view of the potential uses of the Doctrine. The expansive and restrictive views of these state courts are discussed below.

a. States Advancing an Expansive View of Access Under the Doctrine

The courts of New Jersey have relied upon the Public Trust Doctrine to provide the public a significant degree of beach access—including access to the dry-sand portion of the beach. In *Borough of Neptune City v. Borough of Avon-by-the-Sea*,[98] the New Jersey Supreme Court ruled that the Public Trust Doctrine protects recreational uses, including bathing, swimming, and other shore activities, and concluded that this protection included allowing activities on a municipally owned dry-sand beach located immediately landward of the high-water mark.[99]

Roughly a decade later, in *Matthews v. Bay Head Improvement Ass'n*, the same court expanded this right of public access to dry-sand beaches owned not by a municipality but by a partially private organization. In both *Neptune City* and *Matthews*, the court took the view that the Public Trust Doctrine should not be perceived as "fixed or static" but that it is a doctrine that can be "molded and extended to meet changing conditions and needs of the public it was created to benefit."[100] In *Matthews*, the court specifically held that the public enjoys a public trust right to cross over dry-sand beaches to gain access to the shore and also enjoys recreational rights on those same dry-sand beaches.[101] At the same time, the court emphasized that both of these access rights should not be completely unfettered; both are subject to reasonable restrictions by the property owner.[102]

The New Jersey Supreme Court continues to expand the scope of public access to beaches that are, in its view, protected under the Public Trust Doctrine. It applied the *Matthews* reasoning recently to hold that the Public Trust Doctrine requires the dry-sand area of a private beachfront property to be open to the public, subject to a reasonable fee for services provided by the property owner.[103]

Notwithstanding the *Nollan* ruling that restricted the power of the California Coastal Commission to impose a public right of passage upon a beachfront property owner, a number of earlier California cases recognize public beach access rights.[104] Additionally, in *Marks v. Whitney* the court determined that the Public Trust Doctrine empowers the state to make public trust tidelands available to the public for a variety of uses.[105]

Both North Carolina and Washington courts have concluded that the Public Trust Doctrine protects the right of the public to gain access to tidelands and shorelands for the purpose of fishing and recreation.[106]

In a trio of cases, *County of Hawaii v. Sotomura*,[107] *In re Ashford*,[108] and *State of Hawaii v. Zimring*,[109] the Supreme Court of Hawaii emphasized that the State holds lands up to the vegetation line on the beach in trust for the public and that customary uses of the public on those lands, including access for fishing and recreation, are protected.

b. States Advancing a Restrictive View of Access Under the Doctrine

Courts located in several East Coast states have adopted the view that the Public Trust Doctrine does not provide a right of public access to tidelands and the shore. In *Opinion of the Justices*,[110] the Supreme Court of Massachusetts issued an opinion declaring unconstitutional a bill that would have included a public right of passage along the beach "between the mean high water line and the extreme low water line." In so doing, the court refused to expand the public trust rights of navigation and fishing to include a right of passage, stating that "[w]e are unable to find any authority that the rights of the public include a right to walk on the beach."[111] The court also specifically rejected the approach taken by the Supreme Court of New Jersey in *Borough of Neptune City v. Borough of Avon-by-the-Sea*.[112]

Fifteen years later, the Supreme Court of Maine arrived at a similar result in *Bell v. Town of Wells*.[113] There the court reviewed a state statute (the Public Trust in Intertidal Land Act) that declared (1) "the intertidal lands of the State are impressed with a public trust" and (2) the rights of the public in intertidal lands under that public trust included a right to use that land for recreation.[114] The court first found that, in Maine, "the owner of shoreland above the mean high water mark presumptively held title in fee to intertidal land subject only to the public's right to fish, fowl, and navigate."[115] The court then concluded that the statute "takes for public use much greater rights in the intertidal zone than are reserved by the common law and therefore on its face constitutes an unconstitutional taking of private property."[116]

Finally, in an intriguing case that required the court to interpret the Charter of Maryland, the Maryland Court of Appeals rejected an assertion of public trust rights to recreate on the dry-sand beach in Ocean City.[117] The court concluded that the assertion of such public trust rights would damage the property owner who was endeavoring to construct a condominium on that part of the beach, and declared that such damage was of a kind "specifically proscribed" by the Charter.[118]

D. The Public Trust Doctrine and Ocean and Coastal Natural Resources

The Public Trust Doctrine imposes a duty on the sovereign to act as a steward of public trust lands.[119] Thus, the Doctrine often is invoked in an effort to protect coastal natural resources. This section examines how the courts have viewed the Doctrine in the context of disputes over several categories of those resources: marshes, fisheries, and energy reserves.

1. The Public Trust Doctrine and Coastal Marsh Management

Coastal marshes are now recognized as essential to the proper functioning of coastal and ocean ecosystems.[120] However, many states did not place much value on coastal marshes until fairly recently. Several cases have addressed whether the Public Trust Doctrine can be employed to protect these marshes from being destroyed in the course of coastal development.

In *Gwathmey v. North Carolina*,[121] the North Carolina Supreme Court ruled that marshes deemed navigable in fact could be protected by the Public Trust Doctrine.[122] Similarly, in *McQueen v. South Carolina Coastal Council*,[123] the court concluded that the State's public trust interest in wetlands justified denying the ability of the property owner to fill in and destroy those wetlands. In that case, as noted earlier in this chapter, the Public Trust Doctrine protected the State from the owner's takings claim.[124]

2. The Public Trust Doctrine and Fisheries Management

The Institutes of Justinian mentioned the right to fish as a right common to all.[125] And the common law handed down to the United States protected the right to fish as part of the public trust. Not surprisingly, then, the earliest cases examining the meaning of the Public Trust Doctrine in this country found that the Doctrine protected the rights of the public to fish in waters owned by the states.[126] This trend has continued unbroken, with states granting the public the right to fish while maintaining their public trust duties to protect and preserve fish stocks and aquatic resources.[127]

3. The Public Trust Doctrine and Energy Resource Management

Courts in California and Florida have relied upon the Public Trust Doctrine to restrict oil and gas development. In California, a trial court has held that the Public Trust Doctrine can be a basis for denying permission to commence development and operation of an offshore oil well.[128] The court rejected the oil company's argument that it had a vested right to proceed with constructing drilling platforms in state tidelands following nearly twenty years of exploration and environmental analysis, noting:

> This is the beauty of the California doctrine that all public lands are forever held in the public use until irrevocably, physically and actually used. Thus, in conformity with such doctrine, thousands of acres of California offshore tideland are always subject to the public trust doctrine until so developed.[129]

In Florida, a court of appeals has ruled that the State could rely upon the Public Trust Doctrine to prevent the sale or execution of any oil or gas lease in State waters, and rejected the claim of an oil company that enactment of legislation that cut off its ability to pursue such leases amounted to an unconstitutional taking of property.[130]

III. Emerging and Unresolved Issues Under the Public Trust Doctrine

As this chapter demonstrates, in many coastal states—perhaps most coastal states outside the Northeast—the Public Trust Doctrine is viewed as flexible and subject to expansion beyond its traditional core protections for fishing and navigation. Against this backdrop, several emerging issues could trigger efforts to invoke the Doctrine. These issues include beach restoration and protection, fishery management, prosecution of aquaculture projects, and exploration and development of energy resources. With the possible exception of beach restoration, each of these issues raises the question whether there is a federal public trust doctrine applicable to ocean waters that lie in the federal Exclusive Economic Zone seaward of state-controlled waters.

A. The Public Trust Doctrine and Beach Management

Beaches on barrier islands from Maine to Texas tend to migrate in response to natural forces exerted by tides, rivers, currents, storms, and other natural phenomena. Beachfront communities and property owners have responded to this fact with intense efforts to stabilize, restore, and "nourish" beaches. These efforts fall into two categories: (1) efforts by private property owners to armor their beachfront in the hope of halting erosion, and (2) efforts by both private property owners and the government to deposit sand directly onto eroded beaches in an effort to restore the shape of the beaches themselves. These efforts are quite expensive and have met with mixed success.

The Public Trust Doctrine has both defensive application to these actions that affect the shape of the beach. First, the state (along with affected communities) could argue that the Doctrine imposes an affirmative duty on the government to restore beaches that are eroded by natural events or by the actions of beachfront property owners. Second, the state could argue that the Doctrine prevents beachfront owners from erecting

The Public Trust Doctrine has both offensive and defensive application to . . . actions that affect the shape of the beach.

hardened structures (jetties, etc.) that have the effect of altering the shape of the beach both up-current and down-current.

One commentator has advocated relying on the Public Trust Doctrine to protect "sand rights" and thereby to protect the shape of the beach.[131] Under this theory, the Doctrine would impose on the state the duty to ensure that beaches enjoy a continuing ability to receive and deposit sand from all natural sand sources, including rivers.[132] The ramifications of this application of the Public Trust Doctrine could be significant; under it states could be required to restrict the construction of dams that store sediment otherwise bound for beaches. In addition, states could restrict local or private efforts to armor the shoreline.

North Carolina has enacted legislation that vests title in the State to publicly financed re-nourished beaches.[133] Once the State assumes title to these re-nourished beaches, it assumes the duty of a trustee of those beaches for the public. It remains to be seen whether this duty will be deemed to include a continuing obligation to re-nourish the beaches if they are subject to erosion.

B. The Public Trust Doctrine and Fisheries Management

From the Magna Carta in 1215, it has been clear that both the sovereign and the elected government are charged with the duty to protect fishing. The Magna Carta promised that the King would remove any enclosures that he had hitherto placed on riverbanks.[134] Numerous ancient acts of Parliament demonstrate that this duty has included the duty to prohibit the use of destructive fishing gear and gear that kills an excessive number of fish.[135]

Both the state and federal governments regulate marine fishery resources in the United States. Each state relies upon its own statutes and regulations to manage fisheries located in state waters. For fish species that are found in the waters of several states, regulation also takes place under interstate management organizations such as the Atlantic States Marine Fisheries Commission. The federal government exercises fishery management authority under the Magnuson-Stevens Fishery Conservation and Management Act (MSA) for fish located in the Exclusive Economic Zone (EEZ)—those ocean waters seaward of the state waters boundary out to two hundred miles offshore.[136]

States have the duty under the Public Trust Doctrine to manage fisheries in their waters in the fashion of a prudent trustee; they must avoid the waste of the resource.[137] Therefore, the states must take reasonable and effective measures to protect fish populations from being overfished. These measures include limiting the number of fish landed each fishing season in a manner sufficient to ensure that the fishery can be prosecuted in a sustainable way from year to year. They also include preventing the use of destructive fishing gear, such as trawl nets that sweep the ocean floor and destroy fish habitat. And, as noted by legal scholar Professor Ralph Johnson, the duty to protect fishing includes the duty to protect water quality sufficient to ensure that the fish are healthy:

[P]rotection of fisheries implicitly includes protection of water quality. . . . Regardless of where the right of a fishery is recognized, it is meaningless unless fish are there to be caught. If the water is polluted, the fish die. Thus the right of fishery necessarily includes an implied right to water quality sufficient to support the fishery.[138]

Louisiana has enacted a statute that explicitly acknowledges its duty under the Public Trust Doctrine to manage its marine fishery resources "in trust for the benefit of all its citizens."[139] This statute further provides that "the state's marine fishery resources require proper management in order to be sustained biologically and to continually produce a maximum yield of social and economic benefits."[140] This legislative statement of the public trust could be invoked to require the State to pursue specific measures in State waters that reduce or eliminate destructive fishing gear and fishing practices.

Likewise, some commentators have suggested that the federal government should be deemed to be under a duty as trustee of the fishery resources in the EEZ to protect those resources for the public.[141] Other authorities have suggested that the federal government is under a statutory duty to protect fishery resources as well.[142]

The Public Trust Doctrine could help shape the approach to one controversial method for addressing the protection of fishery resources—the creation of marine protected areas in the ocean. The government can seek to restrict or eliminate fishing in these areas in an effort to protect fish populations. Some conservation groups and scientists believe that marine protected areas are vital in protecting ocean resources.[143] Some fishing groups, particularly those representing recreational fishermen, question the efficacy of marine protected areas and oppose their use in various parts of the country.[144]

As trustee for the natural resources in the ocean, the government is charged with the duty to prevent those resources from being wasted. Thus, where the government concludes that restricting fishing in certain areas of the ocean is required in order to protect a healthy fishery (for example, limiting fishing in a spawning area or an area that contains vital habitat), the Public Trust Doctrine would support fishing restrictions. It is likely, however, that—as was the case with the Channel Islands controversy in California—some fishermen will argue that they can fish the ocean without significant restrictions. One recent student commentator has suggested that the Doctrine supports reasonable access restrictions designed for a conservation purpose and that courts are likely to uphold creation of marine protected areas against challenges by fishermen seeking unrestricted access.[145]

C. The Public Trust Doctrine and Management of Aquaculture

The federal government is promoting aquaculture as a way of helping to compensate for chronic depletion of marine fishery resources.[146] Aquaculture is on the increase in state waters, primarily based on farmed Atlantic salmon in the states of Maine and Washington.[147] Although it holds the promise of enhancing the public good by making more seafood available, aquaculture also portends several potential infringements on public interests in the oceans. Specifically, salmon farming runs the risk of biological contamination of local fish stocks.[148] In addition, the release of wastes from salmon farming "can lead to nutrient loading, toxic algae blooms, oxygen depletion, and the subsequent death of marine organisms."[149] Moreover, because fish farming necessitates blocking the farmed areas off from public access, it raises the potential of adversely affecting local fishing interests.[150]

The Public Trust Doctrine imposes a duty on both the states and the federal government to ensure that aquaculture develops in a way that protects existing marine resources and ensures that public access to the oceans is not unreasonably restricted.[151]

D. The Public Trust Doctrine and Management of Energy Resources

Coastal states have taken different approaches to regulating the development of energy resources in their trust lands and waters. On one end of the spectrum, Louisiana and Texas have allowed a significant amount of oil and gas exploration and development to take place both onshore and offshore. On the other end of the spectrum, California and North Carolina have resisted such development. Nor is the energy issue limited to oil and gas development. At present, much controversy attends a proposal to develop a wind farm in Nantucket Sound in coastal waters of Massachusetts. In addition, the effort to establish liquefied natural gas facilities in the Gulf of Mexico and elsewhere is generating much public interest and concern.

The Public Trust Doctrine can play an important role in energy resource management where the resources are located in public trust lands or waters. Professor Sax noted that the Doctrine has application whenever "diffuse public interests need protection against tightly organized groups with clear and immediate goals."[152] This phrase aptly describes the situation when energy companies seek to exploit natural resources in coastal and ocean lands and waters. As noted earlier in this chapter, courts in California and Florida have relied upon the Doctrine to limit offshore oil and gas development.[153]

As this country looks more closely at ways to exploit its energy resources and as interest increases in developing those resources in trust lands and waters, the question will arise whether the Public Trust Doctrine can provide useful standards for evaluating specific energy proposals. Legal scholars have suggested that the Doctrine is well suited for this role and provides a basis for balancing the need for energy with the need to protect the public interest. Professor Ralph Johnson has suggested the following approach:

> [A]ny time public trust resources are to be committed to some alternate public or private use, the legislature or the courts could require under the public trust doctrine (1) a full examination of all realistic alternatives, and (2) that the best conventional or best available technology be applied so as to minimize the risk to public trust resources. Alternatively, the doctrine could be used to require oil companies and others to develop new technologies where existing ones are inadequate.[154]

Professor Johnson also suggests that the Doctrine justifies the state legislature "adopting any level of water quality control that is politically acceptable" in addressing such activities as transport of oil in trust waters: "[n]o polluter can claim a vested property right to continue depositing wastes . . . because all such rights are subject to the pre-existing burden of the public trust doctrine."[155] He suggests further that the Doctrine would support a state legislature in adopting any number of measures to protect the public resources it holds in trust, including: (1) higher standards for oil transportation safety; (2) zoning that prohibited oil transportation facilities in ecologically sensitive areas; (3) state oversight of federal activities that adversely affect public trust resources; and (4) requirements that federal projects be modified in order to be deemed in compliance with the consistency provisions of the Coastal Zone Management Act.[156] In addition, he suggests that state administrative agencies carry the responsibility to protect the public interests in trust lands.[157] In his view, administrative agencies have the duty to consider the effects of their actions upon public trust resources and to protect those resources in a manner that is consistent with state law.[158]

This line of reasoning, which relies upon the protections guaranteed the public in trust lands and waters and the concomitant duty of the state as trustee of those lands and waters, could apply to situations such as the effort to locate certain liquefied natural gas facilities in the Gulf of Mexico. Members of the public concerned about the possible effects on the natural resources of the Gulf occasioned by such facilities could invoke the Doctrine and ask the legislatures and administrative agencies of affected states to adopt an array of protective measures. In addition, they could ask courts to rule that certain restrictions are appropriate in the event the states do not act in a manner that protects the public trust.

E. A Federal Public Trust Doctrine in the Exclusive Economic Zone

The federal government has long maintained an interest in asserting its authority over ocean waters. Beginning with navigation and national security issues that attended the founding of this country, this interest has expanded to include the protection of fishing rights and the right to control use of other natural resources located in the ocean bed.

In two proclamations issued in 1945, President Truman asserted federal authority over fishing activity in areas of the high seas contiguous to the coasts of the United States and also over marine minerals to the edge of the continental shelf.[159] In 1972, the Congress enacted the Marine Protection, Research, and Sanctuaries Act, which, inter alia, established a procedure for creating marine sanctuaries to the edge of the continental shelf.[160] In 1976 and in subsequent reauthorizations, the Fishery Conservation and Management Act asserted United States authority to regulate all fishing (both domestic and foreign) to two hundred miles off the coasts.[161] Finally, in 1983 President Reagan proclaimed the "sovereign rights and jurisdiction" of the United States—in the form of an "Exclusive Economic Zone" (EEZ)—over the living and nonliving natural resources of the "seabed and subsoil and the superadjacent waters" from the point where jurisdiction under the territorial sea ends out to two hundred nautical miles offshore.[162]

Shortly after creation of the United States EEZ, one legal scholar suggested that applying the Public Trust Doctrine there would be an appropriate means for protecting EEZ resources.[163] According to Professor Casey Jarman, "Resources claimed under the Proclamation [establishing the EEZ] are public resources which the government holds in trust for the people of the United States. The formal establishment of sovereign rights arguably carries with it an increased role of public stewardship over these resources."[164] Other scholars similarly concluded that the assertion of United States sovereignty provided grounds for a federal government stewardship role in the EEZ:

> [I]mplicit in the notion of sovereign rights is a higher level of government authority over and greater responsibility for marine resources than existed before. . . . [I]t appears that the EEZ notion of sovereign rights brings with it the idea of more responsibility for the common property resources found in the ocean—an increased role of public or common stewardship.[165]

Looking back to its origins, there are sound reasons for applying the Public Trust Doctrine in the federal EEZ. The Institutes of Justinian declares that the sea is one of the things that is "common to all mankind."[166] And the underlying principle of preserving public access to the federally controlled part of the sea for public benefit is consonant with the theory upon which the doctrine has been developed with respect to coastal lands and waters.

Moreover, the doctrine has come to include the imposition of trust duties on whatever government is asserting authority and control over the lands and waters in question. Thus, the states were given duties as trustees over tidelands because title to those lands was vested in them when they joined the Union.[167] In similar fashion, it is arguable that the federal government should be given trustee duties with respect to the lands and waters of the EEZ; the federal government asserts control over the EEZ,[168] and the sea is one of those common areas protected by the original concept set out in the Institutes of Justinian.

An underlying theoretical question, however, is whether the federal government inherited a separate federal public trust duty from England when this country was founded. Stated differently, the question is whether the central concept underlying the Public Trust Doctrine—the right of the public to access and use certain "common" areas—imposes an overarching duty upon the United States government to protect such areas, a duty that could be applied to "federal" lands or waters not controlled by the states but controlled instead by the federal government. This question has never been resolved.

There are both constitutional and case-based theories upon which such a "federal public trust doctrine" for the EEZ could be constructed. Some writers have argued that the powers reserved to the people by the Ninth and Tenth Amendments to the Constitution should be interpreted to include common rights such as those protected by the Public Trust Doctrine.[169] The Tenth Amendment provides that "[t]he powers not delegated to the United States by the Constitution, nor prohibited by it to the

States, are reserved to the States respectively, or to the people." Under this Amendment, the people of this country could assert that the federal government must act as a responsible steward of all EEZ resources: either the Constitution delegated authority over the EEZ to the federal government, in which case the federal government holds EEZ resources as a sovereign entity with concomitant trust responsibilities or—because the EEZ lies outside state boundaries—that authority resides in the people, in which case they could demand that the federal government act as a trustee and protect their interests there.

The case law theory for a "federal public trust doctrine" is based upon two nineteenth-century Supreme Court rulings. In *Pollard's Lessee v. Hagan*,[170] the Court made clear that the federal government held the lands under navigable waters in the Territories that had not yet become states "in trust" for those future states.[171] In *Shively v. Bowlby*,[172] the Court noted that title to all lands underlying navigable waters was vested in the sovereign for the benefit of the people, but also observed that the United States enjoyed authority (under the Property Clause) to convey the "trust" lands located in the Territories to third parties—so long as the conveyance was for a public purpose appropriate to the Territory.[173] Reading *Pollard's Lessee* (which talks of the federal duty to hold lands in trust) together with *Shively* (which continues to impart some duty on the federal government to honor a public purpose even if it conveys the lands) leaves room for the inference that the federal government inherited separate public trust duties when this country was formed.[174] As noted earlier in this chapter, a leading authority on the Public Trust Doctrine, Professor Charles Wilkinson, argues that such a separate "federal public trust" exists.[175] However, as the D.C. Circuit has noted, Professor Wilkinson has also observed that, because "[n]o case has struck down a federal transfer of lands under navigable waterways before statehood . . . there is no *holding* that the classic public trust doctrine applied to the United States."[176]

Two federal district courts have suggested that public trust duties apply to the federal government. In *United States v. 1.58 Acres of Land*,[177] the federal government sought to condemn tideland property lying adjacent to the docks in Boston. The Commonwealth of Massachusetts resisted, arguing that the federal government could gain title and transfer to a third party, thereby unlawfully extinguishing the state's public trust rights and duties in that land. The court rejected the Commonwealth's objection, but observed in dictum that the federal government and the state government share public trust duties and that neither "sovereign" can abdicate its public trust duties with respect to trust lands.[178]

In *In re Steuart Transportation Co.*,[179] the question was whether the State of Virginia and the United States could sue an oil carrier for damages to wildlife resulting from an oil spill. The court held that the Public Trust Doctrine vests both the State of Virginia and the United States with "the right and the duty to protect and preserve the public's interest in natural wildlife resources."[180]

As the federal government becomes involved on a larger scale with regulating efforts to exploit resources in the EEZ—including not only fisheries but also energy resources and offshore aquaculture—opportunities will arise to raise the Public Trust

Doctrine as an important consideration.[181] Everyone with a stake in our oceans—from the general public to local and state governments—should consider invoking that Doctrine and working to ensure that it is included at all levels of federal planning and management in the EEZ.

IV. Conclusion

This chapter has provided an overview of the Public Trust Doctrine in the context of ocean and coastal resource management. The Doctrine has the potential to play a significant role in various aspects of that management. First, it can be used to protect from takings challenges the management of coastal property development. Second, it can be used to grant the public both perpendicular and horizontal use of the beach, including the dry-sand beach. Third, it can be used to protect coastal and estuarine wetlands and marshes. Fourth, it can be invoked to ensure responsible development of energy and natural resources. Finally, the Doctrine holds the promise of protecting ocean resources not only in state waters but also in federal waters to the full extent of this nation's Exclusive Economic Zone.

Notes

1. J. INST. 2.1.1.
2. *Id.* § 5.
3. Joseph L. Sax, *The Public Trust Doctrine in Natural Resource Law: Effective Judicial Intervention*, 68 MICH. L. REV. 471, 475 (1970) [hereinafter *The Public Trust Doctrine*]; *see also* Richard J. Lazarus, *Changing Conceptions of Property and Sovereignty in Natural Resources: Questioning the Public Trust Doctrine*, 71 IOWA L. REV. 631, 633–35 and n.12 (1986) [hereinafter *Changing Conceptions*] (noting questions whether the Roman system actually included a public trust doctrine in any meaningful sense).
4. Martin v. Waddell's Lessee, 41 U.S. (16 Pet.) 367, 410 (1842) (it "must be regarded as settled in England, against the right of the King, since the Magna Carta, to make a private grant in such lands and waters"); Idaho v. Coeur d'Alene Tribe of Idaho, 521 U.S. 261, 284 (1997); *but cf. Changing Conceptions*, *supra* note 3, at 635 n.18 (questioning the scope of the Magna Carta language).
5. 2 H. BRACTON, ON THE LAWS AND CUSTOMS OF ENGLAND 39–40 (S. Thorne trans., 1968) quoted in Susan Morath Horner, *Embryo, Not Fossil: Breathing Life into the Public Trust in Wildlife*, 35 LAND & WATER L. REV. 23, 33 n.43 (2000) [hereinafter *Embryo*]. Much ink has been spilled in an effort to trace the evolution of the Public Trust Doctrine from its ancient origins through the Middle Ages and into the common law that was transmitted to the American colonies. *See Changing Conceptions*, *supra* note 3, at 633–35; *Embryo*, at 31–36. Ms. Horner concludes that development of the Doctrine during this period was "complex and multi-faceted, making it difficult to draw reliable conclusions." *Embryo*, at 33.
6. *See* Shively v. Bowlby, 152 U.S. 1, 57 (1894); *see also* Ralph W. Johnson et al., *The Public Trust Doctrine and Coastal Zone Management in Washington State*, 67 WASH. L. REV. 521, 529 (1992) [hereinafter *Public Trust in Washington State*] (courts in England "recognized that the Crown held the beds of navigable waters in trust for the people for navigation, commerce, and fisheries. Even the Crown could not destroy this trust.").
7. *Changing Conceptions*, *supra* note 3, at 635 n.19.
8. *Id.* The intensity of the resistance to this theory is illustrated by the fact that one of the specific reasons invoked for the beheading of King Charles I was the "taking away of men's rights under colour of the King's title to land between high and low water marks." Article 26 of the Grand Remonstrance presented to Charles I on December 1, 1641, quoted

in *Changing Conceptions.* As it happened, the unfortunate King Charles had decided the first case formally adopting the novel theory advanced by Queen Elizabeth's lawyer.

9. *Id.* at 635 n.20.

10. *See* Shively v. Bowlby, 152 U.S. 1, 14–15 (1894).

11. *See* Martin v. Waddell's Lessee, 41 U.S. (16 Pet.) 367, 410 (1842) ("when the revolution took place, the people of each state became themselves sovereign; and in that character hold the absolute right to all their navigable waters, and the soils under them, for their own common use, subject only to the rights since surrendered by the constitution to the general government").

12. Pollard's Lessee v. Hagan, 44 U.S. (3 How.) 212, 228–30 (1845) ("[t]he shores of navigable waters, and the soils under them, were not granted by the Constitution to the United States, but were reserved to the states respectively . . . [t]he new states have the same rights, sovereignty, and jurisdiction over this subject as the original states").

13. Charles F. Wilkinson, *The Headwaters of the Public Trust: Some Thoughts on the Source and Scope of the Traditional Doctrine,* 19 ENVT'L L. 425, 453–64 (1989) [hereinafter *Headwaters*]; *see also* George P. Smith II & Michael W. Sweeney, *The Public Trust Doctrine and Natural Law: Emanations Within a Penumbra,* 33 B.C. ENVT'L AFF. L. REV. 307, 314–21 (2006) (invoking the reservations of powers and rights in the people under the Ninth and Tenth Amendments as Constitutional sources for the Doctrine).

14. Coastal States Organization, "Putting the Public Trust Doctrine to Work: The Application of the Public Trust Doctrine to the Management of Lands, Waters, and Living Resources of the Coastal States" (2d ed. 1997) [hereinafter "Putting the Doctrine to Work")] at 17–18.

15. *Shively* at 14, 26; Phillips Petroleum Co. v. Mississippi, 484 U.S. 469, 475 (1988).

16. "Putting the Doctrine to Work," *supra* note 14, at 17–18.

17. *Id.* at 483 n.12.

18. *Id.*

19. *See* Illinois Central Railroad Co. v. Illinois, 146 U.S. 387, 453 (1892).

20. *See Embryo, supra* note 5, at 27–30, 43.

21. In Professor Charles Wilkinson's famous phrase: "[T]he debate [over the trust] evidences, at its quick, a collision between two treasured sets of expectancy interests: those of private landowners who expect their titles to land and water to remain secure, and those of the general public, which expects that most of its rivers will remain rivers, its lakes lakes, its bays bays." *Headwaters, supra* note 13, at 426.

22. *See The Public Trust Doctrine, supra* note 3; *Headwaters, supra* note 13; Hope M. Babcock, *Has the Supreme Court Finally Drained the Swamp of Takings Jurisprudence? The Impact of* Lucas v. South Carolina Coastal Council *on Wetlands and Coastal Barrier Beaches,* 19 HARV. ENVTL. L. REV. 1, (1995).

23. *See* Smith & Sweeney, *supra* note 13; James R. Rasband, *The Public Trust Doctrine: A Tragedy of the Common Law,* 77 TEX. L. REV. 1335 (1999); James L. Huffman, *A Fish out of Water: The Public Trust Doctrine in a Constitutional Democracy,* 19 ENVTL. L. 527, 566–67 (1989).

24. 10 Am. Dec. 356 (N.J. 1821).

25. *Id.* at 368.

26. *Id.*

27. *Id.*

28. *Id.*

29. *Martin, supra* note 11.

30. 146 U.S. 387 (1892).

31. *Id.* at 453–54.

32. *Headwaters, supra* note 13, at 450–460.

33. *Id.*

34. Joseph D. Kearney & Thomas W. Merrill, *The Origins of the American Public Trust Doctrine: What Really Happened in Illinois Central,* 71 U. CHI. L. REV. 799, 928–29 (2004); *see also Public Trust in Washington State, supra* note 6, at 549 (summarizing Professor Wilkinson's arguments).

35. Gwathmey v. State of North Carolina, 464 S.E.2d 674, 682–84 (N.C. 1995).

36. *See* Providence Chamber of Commerce v. State, 657 A.2d 1038, 1041–43 (R.I. 1995) (public trust doctrine based on common law).

37. Orion Corp. v. State, 747 P.2d 1067 (Wash. 1987), *cert. denied*, 486 U.S. 1022 (1988). *See* Ralph W. Johnson, *Oil and the Public Trust Doctrine in Washington*, 14 U. Puget Sound L. Rev. 671, 684 [hereinafter *Oil and the Public Trust*] (the ruling in *Orion* "seems to give the public trust doctrine Constitution-like power"); *see also Public Trust in Washington State*, *supra* note 6, at 527 (the Doctrine is "quasi-constitutional").

38. Save Ourselves, Inc. v. Louisiana Environmental Control Commission, 452 So. 2d 1152, 1156 (La. 1984).

39. La. Rev. Stat. § 56:640.3.

40. Pullen v. Ulmer, 923 P.2d 54, 59 (Alaska 1996).

41. CWC Fisheries, Inc. v. Bunker, 755 P.2d 1115, 1118–19 (1988).

42. The Propeller Genessee Chief v. Fitzhugh, 12 How. 443, 454–57 (1852); and *Barney v. Keokuk*, 94 U.S. 324, 338 (1877). *See also* Oregon *ex rel.* State Land Board v. Corvallis Sand & Gravel Co., 429 U.S. 363, 374 (1977).

43. *Phillips Petroleum Co. v. Mississippi*, 484 U.S. 469 (1988).

44. *Id.* at 484–85.

45. Thus, coastal wetlands that are subject to tidal influence are considered public trust lands. However, in what the Coastal States Organization terms a "paradox," freshwater bottomlands are not considered public trust lands. As the Organization explains, navigability is "the sole measure of the geographic scope of the Public Trust Doctrine for freshwaters, when it has been specifically rejected for tidewaters [in *Phillips Petroleum*]." "Putting the Doctrine to Work," *supra* note 14, at 29.

46. U.S. Commission on Ocean Policy, An Ocean Blueprint for the 21st Century, 13 (2004).

47. 260 U.S. 393 (1922).

48. *Id.* at 415.

49. Penn Central Transportation Co. v. New York City, 438 U.S. 104, 124 (1978).

50. First English Evangelical Lutheran Church v. County of Los Angeles, 482 U.S. 304, 340 n.17 (1987) (Stevens, J., dissenting).

51. Lucas v. South Carolina Coastal Council, 505 U.S. 1003, 1019 (1992).

52. *Id.*

53. *Id.* at 1008–09.

54. Lucas v. South Carolina Coastal Council, 404 S.E.2d 895, 896 (S.C. 1991).

55. *Lucas*, *supra* note 51, at 1029.

56. *Id.* at 1031.

57. Lucas v. South Carolina Coastal Council, 424 S.E.2d 484, 485 (S.C. 1992).

58. The South Carolina court deemed the taking "temporary" because an amendment to the beach management act allowed the property owner to apply for a special permit that would allow construction seaward of the baseline. *Lucas* 505 U.S. at 1010–13; *see also Lucas*, 424 S.E.2d at 485.

59. 533 U.S. 606 (2001).

60. *Id.* at 613.

61. *Id.; and see id.* at 647 (Ginsburg, J., dissenting).

62. *Id.* at 621.

63. *Id.* at 615.

64. *Id.* at 630.

65. The South Carolina Supreme Court referred to the Doctrine in a footnote in its initial *Lucas* opinion, but expressly rested its ruling solely on another ground. *Lucas* 404 S.E.2d 896 and n.1 (S.C. 1991).

66. 307 F.3d 978, 985 (9th Cir. 2002), *cert. denied*, 123 S. Ct. 2574 (2003).

67. *Id.* at 980.

68. *Id.* at 986.

69. Esplanade Properties, LLC v. City of Seattle, Washington, 123 S. Ct. 2574 (June 16, 2003).

70. 580 S.E.2d 116 (S.C. 2003), *cert. denied*, 540 U.S. 982 (2003).

71. *Id.* at 119–20.

72. *Id.*

73. *Id.* at 120.

74. McQueen v. South Carolina Dep't of Health and Envtl. Control, Office of Ocean and Coastal Resource Mgmt., aka South Carolina Coastal Council, 124 S. Ct. 466 (2003).

75. *See* Michael C. Blumm & Lucas Ritchie, *Lucas's Unlikely Legacy: The Rise of Background Principles as Categorical Takings Defenses*, 29 Harv. Envtl L. Rev. 321, 341–44 (2005) (citing takings cases where the doctrine has been successfully invoked); Babcock, *supra* note 22, at 38–49 (the Doctrine should qualify as a background principle "in the many jurisdictions in which it has long been used for a variety of environmentally protective purposes").

76. J. Inst. 2.1.1.

77. *Id.* § 5.

78. 483 U.S. 825 (1987).

79. *Id.* at 828.

80. *Id.* at 828–29 (quoting Commission findings).

81. *Id.* at 829 (quoting Commission findings).

82. *Id.* at 831.

83. *Id.* at 831.

84. *Id.* at 837–39.

85. *Id.* at 838–39.

86. Interestingly, Justice Brennan noted in his dissent that the land was likely, as a matter of fact, located below the mean high tide line. *Id.* at 862 and n.11.

87. *Id.* at 865.

88. *See id.* at 832–33. Indeed, one legal scholar has offered the view that the case might have been decided the other way if the State of California had relied upon the Public Trust Doctrine. *Public Trust in Washington State, supra* note 6, at 595–96.

89. *See* "Putting the Doctrine to Work," *supra* note 14, at 367.

90. 484 U.S. 469 (1988).

91. *Id.* at 482–83 and n.12 (referring to the States of Virginia and Mississippi).

92. *See* Alaska Const. art. VIII, § 14 ("Free access to the navigable or public waters of the State . . . can not be denied any citizen of the United States or resident of the State."); Cal. Const. art. X, § 4 (preventing any owner of property fronting tidal lands "or other navigable water in this State" from excluding "the right of way to such water whenever it is required for any public purpose" and instructing the State legislature "to enact such laws as will give the most liberal construction to this provision, so that access to the navigable waters of this State shall always be attainable for the people thereof."). Justice Brennan invoked this provision in his dissent in *Nollan,* but Justice Scalia retorted with a citation to an opinion from the California Attorney General that raised the question whether the provision had been given much effect. *See Nollan, supra* note 78, at 832–33.

93. *See* N.C. Const. art. XIV, § 5 ("It shall be the policy of this State to conserve and protect its lands and waters for the benefit of all its citizenry, and to this end it shall be a proper function of the State of North Carolina and its political subdivisions to acquire and preserve park, recreational, and scenic areas, to control and limit the pollution of our air and water, to control excessive noise, and in every other appropriate way to preserve as a part of the common heritage of this State its forests, wetlands, estuaries, beaches, historical sites, openlands, and places of beauty.").

94. Tex. Nat. Res. Code Ann., § 61.011 (Vernon Supp. 1996) ("The public shall have the free and unrestricted right of ingress and egress to the larger area extending from the line of mean low tide to the line of vegetation.").

95. *See* Wash. Admin. Code 332-30-144(4)(d) (2007); N.C. Gen. Stat. § 146-6(f) and 1-45.1 (2007) ("[Public trust rights] include . . . public access to the beaches."); and N.C. Gen. Stat. § 77-20 (2007).

96. Cal. Coastal Act § 30001.5.

97. Several states have invoked other doctrines such as custom, implied dedication, prescription, and easement as alternative ways to support access to beaches. *See, e.g.,* Concerned Citizens v. Holden Beach Enterprises, 404 S.E.2d 677 (N.C. 1991) (finding a prescriptive easement that allowed public beach access); Public Access Shoreline Hawaii v. Hawaii County Planning Commission, 903 P.2d 1246, 1268–69 (Haw. 1995), *cert. denied,* 517 U.S. 1163 (1996) (recognizing customary Hawaiian rights to access); State *ex rel.* Thornton v. Hay, 462 P.2d 671, 676–78 (Or. 1969) (invoking law of custom to allow public use of dry-sand beach); Seaway Co. v. Attorney General, 375 S.W.2d 923, 935–37 (Tex. Civ. App. 1964) (finding public beach easement by implied dedication).

98. 294 A.2d 47 (N.J. 1972).

99. *Id.* at 54–55.

100. *Borough of Neptune City,* 294 A.2d at 54–55.

101. *Matthews,* 471 A.2d 355 (N.J. 1984).

102. *Id.* at 364.

103. Raleigh Ave. Beach Ass'n v. Atlantis Beach Club, Inc., 879 A.2d 112 (N.J. 2005).

104. *See, e.g.,* Dietz v. King, 465 P.2d 50 (Cal. Feb. 19, 1970) (members of the public authorized to bring an action to use a beach access route); Morse v. E.A. Robey and Co., 29 Cal. Rptr. 734 (Cal. 1963) (public can bring quiet title action to easements in a public beach).

105. 6 Cal. 3d 251, 491 P.2d 374 (Cal. 1971).

106. *See* Weeks v. North Carolina Dep't of Natural Res. & Cmty. Dev., 388 S.E.2d 228, 234–35 (N.C. Ct. App. 1990) (upholding denial of request to construct pier as a reasonable exercise of state public trust duty to ensure tidelands are accessible to the public); Caminiti v. Boyle, 732 P.2d 989, 996 (Wash. 1987) (observing in dictum that public access to tidelands and shorelands must be preserved).

107. 517 P.2d 57 (Haw. 1973).

108. 440 P.2d 76 (Haw. 1968).

109. 479 P.2d 202 (Haw. 1970).

110. 313 N.E.2d 561 (Mass. 1974).

111. *Id.* at 566–67.

112. *Id.* at 567.

113. 557 A.2d 168 (Me. 1989).

114. *Id.* at 176.

115. *Id.* at 171.

116. *Id.* at 176–77.

117. Department of Natural Res. v. Mayor and Council of Ocean City, 332 A.2d 630 (Md. Ct. App. 1975).

118. *Id.* at 637.

119. *See Illinois Central, supra* note 19, at 453 (the state cannot abdicate its trust over public trust property because "such abdication is not consistent with the exercise of that trust which requires the government of the State to preserve such waters for the use of the public"); New Jersey Dep't of Envtl. Protection v. Jersey Central Power & Light Co., 308 A.2d 671, 674 (N.J. Super. Ct. Law Div. 1973) (state has "affirmative fiduciary obligation to ensure that the rights of the public to a viable marine environment are protected, and to seek compensation for any diminution in that trust corpus"), *aff'd,* 336 A.2d 750 (N.J. Super. Ct. App. Div. 1975), *rev'd on other grounds,* 351 A.2d 337 (N.J. 1976).

120. U.S. Commission on Ocean Policy, *supra* note 46, at 125–33.

121. 464 S.E.2d 674, 682–84 (N.C. 1995).

122. *See also The Battle to Preserve North Carolina's Estuarine Marshes: The 1985 Legislation, Private Claims to Estuarine Marshes, Denial of Permits to Fill, and the Public Trust,* 64 N.C. L. Rev. 565, 611–22 (concluding that the state has authority to deny permits to fill marshes on public trust grounds where the original sale of the marsh from the state remained subject to the public trust).

123. 580 S.E. 2d 116 (S.C. 2003).

124. 580 S.E.2d 116, 120 (S.C. 2003).

125. J. Inst. 2.1.1, 2.1.2, 2.1.5.

126. *See, e.g.,* Arnold v. Mundy, 6 N.J. L. 1 (N.J. 1821) (property owner precluded from preventing oystering on his tidelands); *Martin supra* note 4, at 410.

127. *See* People v. Zankich, 20 Cal. App. 3d 971, 980–81 (1971) (state may close fishing areas); Ventura County Commercial Fishermen's Ass'n v. California Fish & Game Comm'n, 2004 WL 293565 (Cal. Ct. App. 2d Div., Feb. 17, 2004) (state may establish marine reserves to protect fish stocks).

128. Atlantic Richfield Co. v. State Lands Comm'n, 21 ELR 21320 (Cal. Super. Ct. Los Angeles County, Jan. 24, 1990).

129. *Id.* at 21321.

130. Coastal Petroleum v. Chiles, 701 So. 2d 619, 624–25 (Fla. 1st Dist. Ct. App. 1997) (noting that the Public Trust Doctrine is embodied in article X, section 11 of the Florida constitution, and quoting with approval the trial court finding that the Doctrine imposes upon the State "an affirmative obligation to restrict or eliminate private activity on sovereign lands when such activity becomes contrary to the public interest").

131. Katherine E. Stone, *Sand Rights: A Legal System to Protect the "Shores of the Sea,"* 29 STETSON L. REV. 709 (2000).

132. *Id.* at 727–32.

133. *See* N.C. GEN. STAT. § 146-6(f).

134. Magna Carta provision 47 (1215) ("All forests that have been created in our reign shall at once be disafforested. River-banks that have been enclosed in our reign shall be treated similarly.").

135. *See, e.g.,* No Man Shall Fasten Nets to Any Thing over Rivers, 2 Hen. 6, c.15 (1423); An Act for the Preservation of Fishing in the River Severn, 30 Car. 2, c.9 (1678).

136. Pursuant to the MSA, the federal government exercises management control of EEZ fisheries via a system of regional fishery management councils. The National Marine Fisheries Service, a federal agency housed within the National Oceanic and Atmospheric Administration of the Commerce Department, holds ultimate authority to approve or disapprove fisheries management decisions recommended by these regional councils. 16 U.S.C. § 1854.

137. "Putting the Doctrine to Work," *supra* note 14, at 17–18 (noting the duty to preserve public trust resources).

138. *Oil and the Public Trust, supra* note 37, at 678 and n.50.

139. LA. REV. STAT. 56:640.3.

140. *Id.*

141. *See* Casey Jarman, *The Public Trust Doctrine in the Exclusive Economic Zone,* 65 OR. L. REV. 1 (1986), and discussion *infra* Part III.E.

142. *See* National Research Council, *Improving the Use of the "Best Scientific Information Available" Standard in Fisheries Management,* National Academies Press 19–20 (2004) (discussing uncertainty in fisheries science and noting that "[a] management decision that allows a fishery to continue at a rate that ultimately forces its closure is undesirable for many biological, economic, and social reasons. Recognizing this situation, Congress added the mandate to avoid overfishing to the 1996 reauthorization of the Magnuson-Stevens Act. This objective is consistent with the precautionary approach of 'acting before there is strong proof of harm particularly if the harm may be delayed and irreversible.'").

143. *See* Kate Wing, *Keeping Oceans Wild: How Marine Reserves Protect Our Living Seas,* Natural Resources Defense Council (2001); Callum M. Roberts et al., *Effects of Marine Reserves on Adjacent Fisheries,* 294 SCIENCE 1920–23 (November 30, 2001) (arguing that these areas improve fishing).

144. *See Ventura County, supra* note 127 (unsuccessful challenge to the establishment of marine protected areas at the Channel Islands in California).

145. Katryna D. Bevis, Note, *Stopping the Silver Bullet: How Recreational Fishermen Can Use the Public Trust Doctrine to Prevent the Creation of Marine Reserves,* 13 SOUTHEASTERN ENVTL. L.J. 171, 201 (2005).

146. *See* National Marine Fisheries Office, "NOAA's Aquaculture Policy" (1998) ("If the current estimates for world per capita consumption of seafood are accurate, the projected demand for seafood will not be met without growth and technological advancement in

aquaculture to supplement the harvest of wild stocks.") *quoted in* Melissa Schatzberg, Note, *Salmon Aquaculture in Federal Waters: Shaping Offshore Aquaculture Through the Coastal Zone Management Act*, 55 STAN. L. REV. 249, 252 n.10 (2002).

147. According to a report prepared by the Pew Oceans Commission in 2001, the production of farmed Atlantic salmon in the United States increased by 468% between 1989 and 1998. *Id.* at 253 n.19.

148. *Id.* at 255–56.

149. *Id.* at 257.

150. *See* Andrea Marston, Note, *Aquaculture and the Public Trust Doctrine: Accommodating Competing Uses of Coastal Waters in New England*, 21 VT. L. REV. 335, 358–59 and nn.174–75 (1996).

151. *See, e.g.*, Hope M. Babcock, *Grotius, Ocean Fish Ranching and the Public Trust Doctrine: Ride 'Em Charlie Tuna*, 26 STANFORD ENVT'L L.J. 3 (2007).

152. *The Public Trust Doctrine*, *supra* note 3, at 556.

153. *See Atlantic Richfield*, *supra* note 128; and *Coastal Petroleum*, *supra* note 130.

154. *Oil and the Public Trust*, *supra* note 37, at 704.

155. *Id.* at 705–06.

156. *Id.* at 706.

157. *Id.* at 706–07.

158. *Id.*

159. *See Policy of the United States with Respect to Coastal Fisheries in Certain Areas of the High Seas*, Proclamation No. 2668, 10 Fed. Reg. 12,303 (Sept. 28, 1945) *and Policy of the United States with Respect to the Natural Resources of the Subsoil and Seabed of the Continental Shelf*, Proclamation No. 2667, 10 Fed. Reg. 12,303 (Sept. 28, 1945).

160. 33 U.S.C. §§ 1431–34.

161. 16 U.S.C. § 1801(b)(1).

162. *See Exclusive Economic Zone of the United States of America*, Proclamation No. 5030, 48 Fed. Reg. 10,605 (Mar. 10, 1983), codified at 3 C.F.R. § 5030. For a detailed overview of steps taken by the United States to expand its authority offshore, *see* Jarman, *supra* note 141, at 3–7 (1986).

163. Jarman, *supra* note 141, at 1.

164. *Id.* at 2.

165. Biliana Cicin-Sain & Robert W. Knecht, *The Problem of Governance of U.S. Ocean Resources and the New Exclusive Economic Zone*, 15 OCEAN DEV. & INT'L L. 289, 306–07 (1985).

166. J. INST. 2.1.1.

167. *Phillips Petroleum*, *supra* note 43.

168. International law also cedes a large measure of control over the EEZ to the United States, granting this country sovereign rights there for the purposes, inter alia, of conserving and managing living and nonliving resources.

169. *See* Smith & Sweeney, *supra* note 13, at 314–17 (2006).

170. 3 How. 212 (1845).

171. *Id.* at 228–30.

172. 152 U.S. 1, 11–14 (1894).

173. *Id. See also* Utah Div. of State Lands v. United States, 482 U.S. 193, 195–97 (1987).

174. *Cf.* District of Columbia v. Air Florida, Inc., 750 F.2d 1077, 1083 n.33 (D.C. Cir. 1984) (*Shively* "may be read to suggest that the United States was bound by the classic public trust doctrine in dealing with beds of navigable waters before statehood.").

175. *Headwaters*, *supra* note 13, at 453–64.

176. *Id., quoting* Wilkinson, *The Public Trust Doctrine in Public Land Law*, 14 U.C. DAVIS L. REV. 269 at 301 n.146 (emphasis added).

177. 523 F. Supp. 120 (D. Mass. 1981).

178. *Id.* at 124–25.

179. 495 F. Supp. 38 (E.D. Va. 1980).

180. *Id.* at 40.

181. *See, e.g.*, Babcock, *supra* note 151.

chapter three

Role of the States

Sylvia Quast
Michael A. Mantell

Map prepared by the Massachusetts Office of Coastal Zone Management, 2007. Used by permission.

I. Introduction

Since the founding of the United States, the individual states have been on the frontlines of overseeing and managing their coastal resources and neighboring ocean areas. Although the Constitution gave the federal government significant authority with regard to maritime affairs by giving the federal courts jurisdiction over "all Cases of admiralty and maritime jurisdiction" and Congress the power to regulate interstate commerce (which was primarily maritime at that time), most decisions about use and management of coastal and ocean resources were left to the states.[1] Only within the last fifty years has the federal government become more active in this area, and even now, most federal programs affecting these resources rely heavily on state implementation and enforcement.

Given their place on the frontlines, the states have historically served as leaders in ocean and coastal protection. Washington State enacted its Shoreline Management Act a year before the Congress enacted the Federal Coastal Zone Management Act, and California and Florida were already establishing marine protected areas over a decade before the national Marine Protection, Research, and Sanctuaries Act was signed into law. Perhaps most impressive in this regard are the states' forays into protecting their fisheries, which in some cases began while they were still British colonies, centuries

The authors would like to thank Jenna Settino and Sydney Carrillo for their assistance in preparing this chapter.

before passage of what is now the best-known fishery management law in the United States, the Magnuson-Stevens Fishery Conservation and Management Act of 1976.

As the federal government became more involved in regulation of coastal and marine resources, the states also had to bridge the gap between Washington, D.C., and local communities. Some of the federal programs most relevant to the lives of coastal communities, such as the Coastal Zone Management Act and the Clean Water Act, place the onus of achieving federal policy goals on the states. These laws require participating states to develop, implement, and enforce rules and programs at a local level. This can be challenging at times because different states can have very different issues—the specific problems facing Louisiana with regard to coastal protection and water quality are not the same as those of Florida or Maine—and the best response to such issues may not fit readily into a one-size-fits-all federal program.

However, the bridge that the states provide between the federal government and local communities operates both ways. The states' responses to local concerns, such as Washington State's Shoreline Management Act or California's and Florida's creation of marine reserves, can set an example for nationwide legislation. The states can also collect the concerns of local communities about issues such as offshore oil drilling, fish farming, or beach erosion and, by bringing them together, amplify those concerns so that they may be better heard and addressed by the federal government.

the states play a multifaceted role in developing and implementing ocean and coastal policy

As this brief discussion indicates, the states play a multifaceted role in developing and implementing ocean and coastal policy. Rather than trying to describe every state program, every regional program, or even every federal program that is carried out by the states and that affects our coasts and oceans, this chapter gives an overview of some of the programs that have the most impact on the lives of coastal residents and their environment. It first looks at the foundation for state oversight and management of coastal lands and the neighboring marine environment, which is the state's ownership in trust of tidelands and nearshore submerged lands. It then discusses the means by which states exercise their authority over these areas, namely under state-originated laws and programs, federal programs which the states implement, and regional programs. The chapter closes by discussing some of the challenges that the states face with regard to fisheries, water quality, and marine protected areas and gives examples of innovative state programs intended to confront those challenges.

II. The Current State of the Law

A. State Jurisdiction over the Coast and Nearshore Waters

the Supreme Court determined as early as 1842 that the states had primary responsibility for their coastal areas

Although the Constitution carved out a significant role for the otherwise limited national government in regulating and adjudicating maritime matters, the Supreme Court determined as early as 1842 that the states had primary responsibility for their coastal areas. In a dispute over whether private citizens or the public held the rights to a New Jersey oyster fishery, the Court held that it was the State that took over the British Crown's rights in the navigable waters and the soils under those waters.[2] The State held these rights in trust for the public, subject only to the provisions of the Constitution.[3] As a corollary to this, subsequent cases held that if there was no federal legislation regarding an activity in the bays, inlets, harbors, and ports of the United States, the right to control such activities remained with the states.[4]

More than one hundred years later in *United States v. California*,[5] the Court limited the reach of these cases when it held that they only applied to inland waters and the area between the high- and low-water marks. It further held that the federal government owned all submerged land seaward of the ordinary low-water mark.[5]

This curtailment of the states' authority was brief. Congress responded to *United States v. California* by passing the Submerged Lands Act of 1953,[6] which relinquished to the states all lands lying beneath navigable waters within the boundaries of the states, including the improvements and natural resources on those lands.[7] Thus, as a rule, the states and territories have jurisdiction over coastal waters extending out to three geographical miles of the coastline, where the coastline is defined as "the line of ordinary low water along that portion of the coast which is in direct contact with the open sea and the line marking the seaward limit of inland waters."[8] The states also have title to lands shoreward of the low-water line, such as periodically submerged tidelands and inland navigable waters, under the equal footing doctrine of the Constitution as well as the Submerged Lands Act.[9]

The primary exceptions to the three-mile rule are Texas, Florida, Puerto Rico, the Great Lakes States, and the Commonwealth of the Northern Mariana Islands (CNMI). Due to historical circumstances, Texas, Florida (with respect to its Gulf Coast), and Puerto Rico hold title to the three marine leagues, or approximately nine miles, seaward of their coastlines.[10] Also, the boundaries of states bordering the Great Lakes extend to the international boundary of the United States.[11] On the other hand, the United States has "paramount rights" seaward of the ordinary low-water mark in the CNMI, leaving the CNMI with effectively no jurisdiction over the sea around it.[12]

The Submerged Lands Act also gives the states title over "inland waters."[13] The Act does not define this term, and much Supreme Court ink has been spilled over its meaning with regard to a variety of coastal areas. For purposes of determining whether a particular coastal area belongs to a state or to the federal government, the Court typically adopts terms and definitions provided in the Convention on the Territorial Sea and the Contiguous Zone, [1964] 15 U.S.T. (pt. 2) 1607, T.I.A.S. No. 5639 (the Convention).[14] For example, the Court has held that Long Island Sound and Block Island Sound, west of the line between Montauk Point on Long Island and Watch Hill Point in Rhode Island, are juridical bays under article 7 of the Convention and that they are internal state waters as a result.[15] Similarly, it concluded that the Mississippi Sound qualifies as a historic bay and that the waters of the Sound, therefore, are inland waters.[16] On the other hand, although the Court determined that Monterey Bay belongs to the State of California, most of California's major bays and areas such as the Santa Barbara Channel are not "inland waters."[17]

Although the states have the authority to manage, develop, and lease resources throughout the water column and the land beneath it,[18] their jurisdiction over the three-mile belt of waters is not unlimited. The Submerged Lands Act reserved to the federal government the right to use, improve, and regulate such lands and the accompanying waters for the purposes of navigation, flood control, or production of power.[19] The United States also retained all its navigational servitude and rights, as well as its regulatory powers and control over, these waters "for the constitutional purposes of commerce, navigation, national defense, and international affairs."[20] Thus, for example, the Army Corps of Engineers asserts regulatory jurisdiction over dredge and fill activities and the Marine Mammal Protection Act preempts state law regarding take of marine mammals in the three-mile zone.[21] The Supreme Court has also held state laws to be preempted when they prohibit fishing by nonresidents with federal commercial fishing licenses.[22]

In some circumstances, states have successfully asserted jurisdiction over activities in waters beyond the three-mile limit. For example, states have occasionally prohibited the landing of certain fish species even though they were legally taken in federal waters offshore. Thus, the California Supreme Court upheld the conviction of two commercial fishermen holding state licenses who had caught swordfish in violation of California regulations off the coast of California beyond the three-mile limit.[23] The Alaska Supreme Court reached a similar conclusion about a commercial fishing boat registered in Alaska and catching king crab beyond the three-mile limit in Alaska.[24]

B. State Oversight and Management of Coastal Resources

Given the states' ownership of and jurisdiction over the submerged lands and waters within three miles of their coastlines and the economic importance of coastal areas and seas both historically and in the present, it is not surprising that the coastal states generally have myriad laws and programs that address their coastal and ocean resources. This section will begin by focusing on two substantive areas in which state-generated laws and programs affect how those resources are used—taking of ocean life and marine protected areas.

Coastal and ocean wildlife and other resources tend not to recognize political boundaries

Coastal and ocean wildlife and other resources tend not to recognize political boundaries, so states often need to operate within other governmental structures to protect those resources and to respond to the issues they present. For example, under the Federal Clean Water Act and the Coastal Zone Management Act, it falls primarily to the states to find ways to implement and enforce the federal policies and goals established in these laws. Many states also participate in multi-state regional entities such as the Chesapeake Bay Program to deal with problems that are not obviously national in scope, but which cannot be adequately addressed by any one state without coordination and collaboration with other states or entities. Several types of regional entities will be discussed at the end of this section.

1. State Laws and Programs

It is almost a constitutional cliché to refer to the states as laboratories for policy making, but there is a considerable degree of validity to the cliché in the area of ocean and coastal protection. A review of the coastal states' legal regimes and programs shows considerable diversity in their approaches to balancing protection of coastal and marine resources with mounting population and development pressures. To give an overview of each coastal state's legal and regulatory schemes would require an entire book on its own, so this chapter will instead give a snapshot of what various states are doing in two of the most important areas.

a. Taking of Marine Life

The states have exerted control over the fisheries off their coasts since the founding of the Republic, and in the case of the original thirteen colonies, even before that time. As early as the period between 1678 and 1680, for instance, a colonial Virginia county court sought to protect fisheries by enjoining the spearing of fish.[25] Oyster fisheries in particular were a subject of early regulation, with fights over ownership of oyster beds and state laws regarding fishing reaching the highest courts in the land.[26] This history of state fisheries regulation continues to the present day, with every coastal state having licensing programs for commercial and recreational fishing. These programs cover a wide variety of species, including finfish, shellfish, crustaceans, invertebrates such as octopus and worms, seaweed, algae, and coral.[27]

With the enactment of the Magnuson-Stevens Fishery Conservation and Management Act in 1976 (MSA),[28] the federal government asserted greater control over fishing activities in federal waters of the Exclusive Economic Zone.[29] The Act explicitly excepted the Dungeness crab fishery on the Pacific Coast, which continues to be regulated by California, Oregon, and Washington.[30] The federal government may also regulate fisheries within the boundary of a state (except for "internal waters") under a fishery management plan if the Secretary finds that fishing for the species primarily occurs beyond the state's waters and that the state has taken or has failed to take an action that will adversely affect the fishery management plan.[31] However, the MSA states that as a general matter, nothing in the Act "shall be construed as extending or diminishing the jurisdiction or authority of any State within its boundaries."[32] Moreover, the states may regulate fishing vessels outside of their boundaries in certain defined circumstances.[33] Accordingly, the states still retain control of fisheries within their waters.

The MSA also creates a significant role for the input of states into the fisheries off their coasts. As will be discussed in greater detail in another chapter, the Act establishes seven regional fishery management councils and requires that each state have at least one seat on the council in their region.[34] This gives the states significant input into fisheries management plans and other fisheries policy issues decided by the councils. At a practical level, the states also bear a considerable degree of responsibility for enforcement of the Act because the enforcement resources of the National Oceanic and Atmospheric Administration (NOAA) are limited. Indeed, in almost every coastal state and territory, NOAA has cooperative enforcement agreements that deputize state fishery enforcement officials to enforce federal law.[35]

The states also play a leading role in regulating fish farming and aquaculture, with most coastal states having a regulatory program for finfish, shellfish, and, in some cases, algal species.[36] Indeed, California last year recently enacted aquaculture legislation that may serve as a model for other states and the federal government.

b. Marine Protected Areas

The states have been leaders nationally and internationally in establishing marine protected areas. In 1959, Florida established John Pennekamp Coral Reef State Park in the Florida Keys, which protects over one hundred square miles of coral reef, mangroves, and sea grass flats.[37] A year later, California established Point Lobos State Reserve, which protects endangered archeological sites, unique geological formations, and an area of incredibly rich flora and fauna of both land and sea on the central coast of the state.[38] Over a decade passed before the federal government enacted the Marine Protection, Research, and Sanctuaries Act of 1972,[39] and another two years elapsed before it created the first marine sanctuary to preserve the USS *Monitor*, a Civil War ironclad wrecked off the North Carolina coast.[40] (Queensland, Australia, appears to have established the first marine park in the world in 1937 but did not designate any more such parks until 1974.)[41]

Almost a half-century after the establishment of Florida's Pennekamp State Park, most of the coastal states now have marine protected areas of one form or another. Much like terrestrial protected areas such as wildlife refuges, parks, forests, and grasslands, these areas operate under a wide range of legal protections and include areas designated for a wide variety of purposes, such as the protection of shellfish, or marine flora and fauna more generally, and areas containing archaeological resources.

Some protected areas are designated for very specific purposes. For example, some states have designated areas as "shellfish preserves." Oregon's Department of Fish and Wildlife has closed certain areas of its coast to commercial and personal shellfish fishing to protect experimental clam and oyster cultivation.[42] Also, in 2001, Maine's legislature established the Great Salt Bay Marine Shellfish Preserve, which prohibits taking of shellfish or other activity disturbing the bottom of the tidal portion of the Damariscotta River.[43] However, finfishing may occur in the preserve, as well as authorized research activities.[44]

Another increasingly common form of special purpose marine protected area is the historical or archaeological preserve. In 1987, Florida began to develop a statewide system of underwater parks featuring shipwrecks and other historical sites that are open to the public year-round free of charge.[45] There are now nine parks in that system.[46] Maryland has created the U-1105 *Black Panther* Shipwreck Preserve, which protects a German World War II–era submarine at the bottom of the Potomac River.[47] North Carolina also has the USS *Huron* Historic Shipwreck Preserve off Nags Head.[48]

In addition to these preserves and parks dedicated to underwater archaeology, many other marine protected areas in other states have historical and archaeological components, such as Point Lobos Reserve in California.[49]

However, the most common type of marine protected area is a general purpose reserve that regulates extraction of natural resources. Several states have legislation that establishes a system of such reserves or parks. Although intensive resource extraction activities such as drilling, dredging, and filling are generally not allowed in these areas, a relatively wide range of activities is permissible, including fishing and aquaculture. Examples include the following.

- Massachusetts, which has enacted the Ocean Sanctuaries Act (OSA).[50] The OSA established five ocean sanctuaries, which includes most state waters from the mean low-water mark seaward, with the exception of those in Boston Harbor and east.[51] It provides the State Department of Conservation and Recreation with jurisdiction over any activity that would significantly alter[52] or otherwise endanger the ecology or appearance of the ocean, seabed, subsoil, or the Cape Cod National Seashore.[53] It generally prohibits: building any structure on the seabed or under the subsoil; constructing or operating offshore or floating electric generating stations; drilling for or removing any sand, gravel, or other minerals, gases, or oils; dumping or discharging any commercial, municipal, domestic, or industrial wastes; doing commercial advertising; and incinerating solid waste or refuse on or in vessels moored or afloat within an ocean sanctuary.[54] Many other activities are statutorily allowed, however, including propagating and harvesting shellfish.[55] The Act does not establish a separate permitting procedure, but does require other state departments and agencies to "confer and consult" with the Department to ensure compliance with the Act.[56] The Ocean Sanctuaries program is to be consistent with and form a part of the Massachusetts Coastal Zone Management Program.[57]
- The North Carolina legislature has established the North Carolina Coastal Reserve System,[58] which is to be used primarily for research and education, but other public uses, such as hunting, fishing, navigation, and recreation, are allowed to the extent they are consistent with these primary uses.[59]
- Florida has also developed a system of forty-one aquatic parks, pursuant to the Aquatic Preserve Act of 1975.[60] Almost all of these parks are located on the coastline. Aquaculture may be authorized in the reserves,[61] but only limited dredging or filling,[62] and no drilling for oil or gas or mineral excavation may occur.[63] Lawful and traditional public uses such as fishing, boating, and swimming may not be interfered with unreasonably.[64]
- The Washington State Parks and Recreation Commission is authorized by statute to establish underwater parks to provide for diverse recreational diving opportunities and to conserve and protect unique marine resources of the State.[65]
- The Alaska legislature has established a marine parks system, in which hunting, fishing, and aquaculture are allowed.[66]

Other states have established marine protected areas with more stringent protections. For example, Oregon has administratively established a variety of areas including:

- Marine gardens—areas that are targeted for educational programs that allow visitors to enjoy and learn about intertidal resources and that are off-limits to collection of any marine invertebrate (except single mussels for bait);[67]
- Habitat refuges—areas that are needed to maintain the health of the rocky shore ecosystem and that are closed to the taking of marine fish, shellfish, and all marine invertebrates;[68] and
- Research reserves—subtidal and intertidal areas that have been designated for scientists to reliably obtain rocky shore information over time on natural variations and changes in the marine environment. These areas are used for scientific study or research including baseline studies, monitoring, or applied research. Different levels of take are allowed for different reserves.[69]

Hawaii also has established numerous marine protected areas. Marine Life Conservation Districts (MLCDs) are designed to conserve and replenish marine resources.[70] MLCDs were introduced to Hawaii in the fall of 1967 with Hanauma Bay on Oahu.[71] The resulting increase in fish populations was substantial, and the bay has become world famous. Now, there are eleven MLCDs statewide, and other sites are being considered as well.[72] Because the purpose of MLCDs is to protect marine life to the greatest extent possible, the taking of any type of living material (fishes, eggs, shells, corals, algae, etc.) and nonliving habitat material (sand, rocks, coral skeletons, etc.) is generally restricted, if it is allowed at all.[73] This fosters nonconsumptive uses of the area, such as swimming, snorkeling, and diving. Fishing may be allowed subject to certain types of gear restrictions, which result from input received during the public meeting process.[74]

More recently, Hawaii created the nation's largest marine refuge, the Northwestern Hawaiian Islands Marine Refuge.[75] This marine refuge limits entry to those who have obtained permits.[76] On June 15, 2006, it was incorporated into the Papahanaumokuakea Marine National Monument, the world's largest protected area of any kind under active management, by presidential proclamation.

2. Implementation of Federal Programs

Many of the major federal environmental laws establish a regulatory regime in which states serve on the frontlines in the battle to achieve the statute's goals. For example, the Clean Air Act requires the states to adopt implementation plans for national ambient air quality standards, with detailed requirements for what such plans must include.[77] The states may also seek authorization from the U.S. Environmental Protection Agency (EPA) to administer and enforce their own hazardous waste program in lieu of the federal program established by the Resource Conservation and Recovery Act.[78]

In this regard, the two preeminent federal laws concerning coastal and ocean protection are the Clean Water Act, 33 U.S.C. § 101 *et seq.*, and the Coastal Zone Management Act, 16 U.S.C. § 1451 *et seq.*

a. Clean Water Act

The Federal Clean Water Act (CWA) offers the states and territories the option of administering their own permit program for discharges into waters within the state's jurisdiction.[79] Although most states and territories have sought and received authorization to issue permits under section 402 of the Act,[80] which concerns discharge of pollutants by factories and the like, very few have sought this authorization under section 404 of the Act,[81] which primarily concerns dredging and filling of wetlands and other water bodies. Accordingly and because coastal wetlands are the subject of another chapter, this section will focus on state administration of Section 402 programs.

A state that wishes to oversee permitting under section 402, also known as the National Pollutant Discharge Elimination System (NPDES) program, may do so by submitting "a full and complete description" of its proposed permitting program, supported by a statement that the state has adequate legal authority to carry out the program.[82] The proposed program must meet certain minimum requirements regarding, for example, monitoring, reporting, public notice of permit applications, and the ability to abate violations and assess penalties.[83]

If EPA determines that the state's proposed program meets all these statutory requirements, it must approve the program and suspend all federal permitting of discharges covered by the state program.[84] EPA may withdraw its approval of a state program if it determines that the state is not administering the program in accordance with the CWA's standards, but can do so only after a public hearing and an opportunity for the state to correct the problems.[85] A state may also voluntarily relinquish its permitting authority to EPA.[86] Although EPA-authorized state programs have primary permitting responsibility, EPA retains the authority to veto state-issued permits under certain conditions.[87]

b. Coastal Zone Management Act

The Coastal Zone Management Act (CZMA) strives to preserve and protect the resources of the United States' coastal zone.[88] The CZMA defines the "coastal zone" to mean "the coastal waters . . . and the adjacent shorelands . . . strongly influenced by each other and in proximity to the shorelines of the several coastal states, and includes islands, transition and intertidal areas, salt marshes, wetlands, and beaches."[89] The "coastal waters" include the Great Lakes and those waters that contain a "measurable quantity" of seawater, including bayous, ponds, and estuaries.[90]

The CZMA encourages the states to develop and implement Coastal Zone Management Programs (CZMP) that balance natural resource protection with compatible coastal development.[91] The Secretary of Commerce, through NOAA, oversees programs that provide the coastal states with grants and technical assistance for program development and implementation.[92] To qualify for federal approval, the state's management program must, *inter alia*, identify the boundaries of the coastal zone subject to the program, define what constitutes permissible land and water uses within the coastal zone, inventory and designate areas of particular concern within the coastal zone, and describe how the state plans to implement the program.[93] Thirty-four of thirty-five coastal states and territories have coastal programs in place, covering ninety-nine percent of the nation's marine and Great Lake coastlines.[94]

The CZMA gives the states some flexibility in determining how their management programs will control land and water uses. They may establish criteria and standards for local implementation, directly plan and regulate land and water use in the coastal zone, or establish an administrative review process to determine whether proposed projects or regulations in the coastal zone are consistent with the CZMP and, accordingly, whether to approve the project or regulation.[95] Several state programs, such as Washington's Shoreline Management Act and California's Coastal Commission, have gone beyond the minima established in the CZMA and have rigorous coastal protection measures in place. However, if the Secretary of Commerce determines that a coastal state is failing to adhere to its CZMP, or the terms of a CZMA grant or cooperative agreement, the Secretary can suspend financial assistance and ultimately withdraw approval of the CZMP.[96]

In states with federally approved CZMPs, an applicant for a federal permit to conduct activities in the coastal zone, or affecting any land or water use or natural resource of the coastal zone, must certify to the federal permitting agency that its activity is consistent with the CZMP.[97] It must also provide the state with a copy of the certification and the relevant information and data.[98] The state then must notify the federal agency at the earliest practicable time whether it concurs with the certification.[99] If it does not notify the federal agency within six months of receipt of the certification, its concurrence is conclusively presumed.[100] The Secretary of Commerce can override a state's objection to a certification if it finds that the activities in question are consistent with the CZMA or are otherwise necessary for national security.[101] Federal agency actions in the coastal zone or affecting any land or water use or natural resource of the coastal zone must also be consistent with the CZMP to the maximum extent practicable.[102]

States with approved CZMAs must prepare and submit a Coastal Nonpoint Source Pollution Control Program to both the Secretary of Commerce and the EPA.[103] The program should provide for management measures for nonpoint source pollution to restore and protect coastal waters, and shall be closely coordinated with other state and local authorities.[104] In particular, states should implement management measures based on the best available, economically achievable technology to address the impacts of: agricultural, silvicultural, and urban runoff; dams and shoreline erosion controls; and marinas and recreational boating.

3. Regional Programs

States also participate in a variety of regional programs to respond to issues transcending political boundaries. Some of these programs are focused on managing a shared water body or ecosystem, while others are more focused on managing highly mobile marine resources, such as fisheries. Some of these programs were created at the initiative of the federal government, the best-known example being the fishery management councils established under the Magnuson-Stevens Fishery Conservation and Management Act.[105] Others are created at the initiative of one or more states or through a convergence of state and federal agencies.

The Chesapeake Bay Program is an example of states banding together to respond to a shared problem. In the late 1970s and early 1980s, the states ringing the Chesapeake recognized that the Bay was in decline. Thus, in 1983 Maryland, Pennsylvania, Virginia, and the District of Columbia entered into an agreement with one another and the Federal EPA to halt that decline and create a regional partnership to restore the Bay.[106] These states and the EPA also formed a regional partnership known as the Chesapeake Bay Program to oversee and coordinate restoration efforts.[107] The Bay Program includes as a member the Chesapeake Bay Commission, which comprises legislators and cabinet secretaries from three states—Maryland, Virginia, and Pennsylvania—and advises the three states on legislative issues of Bay-wide concern.[108] The Program has also sought to increase involvement of the headwaters states of New York, West Virginia, and Delaware to assist in reducing nutrient and sediment flows into the Bay.[109] The Bay Program can issue guidelines and policies to ensure a consistent approach to water protection in the Bay, and has used a facilitated consensus-based approach that created nutrient trading fundamental principles and guidelines.[110] Completed in 2001, these guidelines will ensure nutrient trading approaches in the watershed are consistent, compatible, and fully supportive of Chesapeake Bay Program goals.[111]

More recently, the states bordering the Gulf of Mexico formed the Gulf of Mexico Alliance, with federal agency participation, to address similar issues in the Gulf.[112] In March 2006, the Alliance released an ambitious action plan signed by the Governors of each state that spells out what they will do both individually and together to protect and conserve the Gulf.[113]

The Great Lakes Commission is also an example of a regional organization formed by states surrounding a water body (or, in this case, connected water bodies) to promote an integrated management approach.[114] The Commission has conferred associate member status on two Canadian provinces that border the Great Lakes and the St. Lawrence River, Ontario and Quebec.[115] Each jurisdiction appoints a delegation of senior agency officials and/or legislators to the Commission to address resource management, environmental protection, transportation, and sustainable development issues in connection with the Great Lakes system.[116] The Gulf of Maine Council on the Marine Environment is another U.S.-Canadian partnership of governmental and non-governmental organizations working to maintain and enhance environmental quality, in this case in the Gulf of Maine.[117]

In addition to the regional fisheries management councils, virtually all of the coastal states also participate in regional fisheries commissions, of which there are four: the Atlantic States Marine Fisheries Commission,[118] the Gulf States Marine Fisheries

Commission,[119] the Pacific States Marine Fisheries Commission,[120] and the Great Lakes Fishery Commission.[121] The responsibilities vary somewhat between the commissions, as each was created separately, some through charters among the relevant states and some through act of the federal government. For example, the Atlantic and Gulf States Commissions have developed management plans for nearshore fisheries, just as the regional councils created under the Magnuson-Stevens Act develop fishery management plans for fisheries in federal waters.[122] The Pacific States Commission, in contrast, does not have regulatory or management authority, and instead serves as a contractor for grants, coordinates research projects, and provides a forum for the Pacific States (with the exception of Hawaii) to discuss mutual concerns.[123] These Fishery Commissions pre-date the Magnuson-Stevens Act by two to three decades, and each has a charter that has been approved by the federal government, except for the Great Lakes Commission, which was created by an international agreement, the Convention on Great Lakes Fisheries Between the United States of America and Canada.[124]

III. Emerging and Unresolved Issues

A. Fisheries and Other Taking of Marine Life

Many of the United States' fisheries are in decline. According to the National Marine Fisheries Service (NMFS), by the end of 2006, more than one-quarter of the nation's commercially and recreationally important fish stocks whose status is known were overfished or experiencing overfishing.[125] In the same report, NMFS noted that there was inadequate information to determine whether another one-third of the stocks was overfished.[126]

Collapse of fisheries can result in substantial social and economic consequences as well as environmental harm. For example, decreasing salmon populations in the Northwest have cost 72,000 jobs and more than a half billion dollars.[127] To address overfishing and the problems it causes, the states have adopted and are implementing various programs. Examples include California's Marine Life Management Act, various programs to promote aquaculture, and North Carolina's Coastal Habitat Protection Plan.

Like the Magnuson-Stevens Act at the national level and similar statutes in other countries, California's Marine Life Management Act (MLMA) enacted in 1998 adopts the use of fishery management plans to protect its marine fishery resources. Rather than focusing on a single species in developing fishery management plans, however, the MLMA protects the habitat and ecosystem, including nonfish species, that a fishery may affect as well.[128] The MLMA establishes sustainability as the primary goal in managing fisheries, rather than treating it as one consideration among others in making management decisions.[129] It also regulates sport fishermen as well as commercial fishermen.[130] As a result, the MLMA is considerably more protective of fishery and other marine life resources than either the Magnuson-Stevens Act or fishery management laws in other states. California has already developed six plans under the MLMA.

Several states have developed programs to promote oyster fisheries in particular. States from Maryland to Florida have oyster reef rebuilding programs, which some have combined with shell recycling programs. For example, in 1996, North Carolina began implementing an oyster sanctuary program, in which it builds reefs of oyster shells and riprap in previously viable oyster producing sites—no taking of oysters or use of bottom disturbing gear is permitted in these sanctuaries. South Carolina has a similar program, which includes an oyster shell recycling component. The hope is that these reef rebuilding and protection programs will rebuild severely decimated stocks of native Eastern oysters.

North Carolina launched an even more ambitious effort to protect its fisheries and their habitats in 1997, when its legislature passed the Fisheries Reform Act.[133] The law contains the directive to protect and enhance habitats supporting coastal fisheries and requires cooperation among three state rule-making Commissions that have jurisdiction over the areas that affect fisheries: Environmental Management Commission, Coastal Resources Commission, and Marine Fisheries Commission. The Commissions were required to work together to develop, adopt, and implement plans to protect and restore fisheries' habitats.

The product of this effort was the North Carolina Coastal Habitat Protection Plan (CHPP), released at the end of 2004. The CHPP identifies six types of habitats that produce North Carolina's coastal fisheries resources (shell bottom, sea grasses, wetlands, hard bottoms, soft bottoms, and the water column). It provides information on the habitats' distribution and abundance, ecological functions and importance to fish production, status and trends, threats to the habitats, and recommendations to deal with the threats. Although the CHPP is impressive because of the breadth of its examination of the State's marine environment, what is most striking about this effort is that the three state agencies have actually started carrying out its recommendations.

B. Water Quality

Water quality is a fundamental factor affecting fisheries and marine ecosystems more generally. The United States has made great strides in improving the health of its water bodies since the passage of the Clean Water Act, which the states have played a fundamental role in implementing, as described above. However, poor coastal water quality is a continuing source of concern. The EPA's most recent National Coastal Condition Report states that 37% of the major estuarine areas in the United States are in poor condition.[131]

One way that coastal states are responding to the challenge of coastal water quality is through the creation of Coastal Nonpoint Source Pollution Control Programs pursuant to the CZMA, as described earlier in this chapter. Other programs that occur in the context of state-federal partnerships include the following:

- "Clean marina" programs that offer information, guidance, and technical assistance to marina operators, local governments, and recreational boaters on best management practices that can be used to prevent or reduce pollution;

- "Clean vessel" programs to help vessel operators dispose of sewage properly; and
- Marine debris programs, such as Washington State's Derelict Fishing Gear Removal Project or the Gulf States Commission's derelict trap and trap removal programs.

Several regional programs, such as the Chesapeake Bay Program described earlier, are also focused on improving water quality.

Although not historically considered a water quality issue, the introduction of aquatic invasive species via the discharge of ballast water from ships has become an issue that the states are dealing with in the absence of strong federal leadership. Ships take on water to aid their stability and structural integrity on voyages and then discharge the water after their voyage is complete.[132] This water can contain numerous species that are native to the area in which the ship takes on the water but quickly become pests in the area in which the ship ultimately releases the water.[133] One example of such a species is the European green crab, first seen in San Francisco Bay in 1989 and now widespread on both coasts.[134] The introduction of this crab has significantly altered ecosystems, competing with native fish and bird species for food, and may threaten Dungeness crab, clam, and oyster fisheries.[135]

The United States Coast Guard developed rules requiring vessels entering the United States' Exclusive Economic Zone to engage in ballast water exchange in the middle of the ocean, but this does not address domestic port-to-port contamination.[136] As a result, the West Coast states adopted laws or rules to make ballast water exchange mandatory for ships entering their state waters as well.[137] The Great Lakes states of Minnesota and Michigan have also adopted rules to deal with this problem. Meanwhile, the EPA is defending itself in litigation charging that it improperly failed to develop rules under the Clean Water Act for ballast water discharges.

C. Marine Protected Areas

States have long been in the forefront of developing programs to set aside marine and coastal areas. As noted earlier in this chapter, however, these areas often have only limited protections. They also tend to be established in a scattershot fashion.

California has embarked upon an ambitious program to take a more systematic view of its marine protected areas (MPAs). In 1999, the California legislature determined that the State's system of MPAs needed to be redesigned to increase its coherence and its effectiveness at protecting the state's marine life, habitat, and ecosystems.[138] It noted that California's existing MPAs were established on a piecemeal basis and often lacked clearly defined purposes, effective management measures, and enforcement, resulting in the appearance of protection but in fact failing to protect and conserve marine life and habitat.[139] As a result, it enacted the Marine Life Protection Act (MLPA).[140]

The MLPA requires California's Fish and Game Commission to adopt a Marine Life Protection Program that will, among other goals, protect the natural diversity and abundance of marine life, the structure, function, and integrity of marine ecosystems, and generally ensure that the State's MPAs are designed and managed as a network.[141] The program may include areas with different levels of protection, but must include an improved marine life reserve component, where the term "marine life reserve" refers to an MPA in which all extractive activities, including the taking of marine life species, is prohibited.[142] Further, the MLPA requires public and scientific input at every phase of this process and contemplates the use of adaptive management of the MPAs once they have been established.[143]

In 2005, the Commission adopted a master plan that will guide implementation of the MLPA and the siting of new MPAs, as well as major modifications to existing MPAs.[144] In April 2007, the Commission approved regulations establishing a new network of MPAs that would protect approximately eighteen percent of State waters on California's central coast in a complex system of fully protected marine reserves, marine conservation areas where some fishing is allowed, and marine parks where only sportfishing is permitted. California's goal is to have in place a statewide network of MPAs by 2011.

IV. Conclusion

States play key and diverse roles in creating and implementing programs to manage coastal and marine resources. States will continue to experiment and innovate with new approaches to coastal and marine management, even as political and budgeting constraints make leadership on these issues at the federal level difficult, if not impossible. This is already apparent on issues regarding global warming, use of desalination, and siting of energy facilities.

One area of emerging interest to states is new governance structures for the management of ocean resource programs. Building on the recommendations of the Pew Oceans Commission and the U.S. Commission on Ocean Policy, for example, California has enacted the California Ocean Protection Act (COPA). COPA creates a new cabinet-level Ocean Protection Council to oversee ocean programs for the state, provide funding for key programs through an Ocean Protection Fund, and make recommendations on needed legislative changes.

Advances in science and technologies and expanding use of ecosystem-based management will require the development of new approaches by states to foster more integration, coordination, and comprehensive strategies for managing coastal and marine resources. In this way, states will likely continue to innovate and help inform discussion for future federal policies, as well as make genuine, measurable improvement in coastal and marine environments.

Notes

1. U.S. Const. art. I, § 8, cl. 3; art. III, § 2, cl. 1.
2. Martin v. Waddell, 41 U.S. (16 Pet.) 367, 411–14 (1842) (regarding the original thirteen colonies); Pollard v. Hagan, 44 U.S. (3 How.) 212, 228–29 (1845) (regarding subsequently admitted states).

3. This subsequently became known as the public trust doctrine. Illinois Central R.R. v. Illinois, 146 U.S. 387 (1892) (invalidating Illinois' conveyance of Chicago's waterfront to railroad).

4. Manchester v. Massachusetts, 139 U.S. 240, 266 (1891) (menhaden fishing); Cooley v. Board of Wardens, 53 U.S. 299 (1851) (pilotage of vessels).

5. *Id.*

6. 43 U.S.C. § 1301 *et seq.*

7. United States v. California, 447 U.S. 1 (1980).

8. United States v. Maine, 469 U.S. 504, 512–13 (1980); 43 U.S.C. §§ 1301(c), 1311, 1312 (2000). The coastline is based on the "natural coast" and is not extended by piers, which are attached to the mainland and under which water flows freely, nor by an artificial island complex projecting into the sea, which is connected to shore by a causeway. United States v. California, 447 U.S. 1 (1980).

9. California *ex rel.* State Lands Comm'n v. United States, 457 U.S. 273, 283 (1982).

10. 48 U.S.C. § 749; United States v. Louisiana, 389 U.S. 155, 160 n.2 (1967); United States v. Florida, 363 U.S. 121, 129 (1960).

11. 43 U.S.C. § 1312.

12. Commonwealth of the Northern Mariana Islands v. United States, 399 F.3d 1057 (2005).

13. 43 U.S.C. § 1301(c).

14. United States v. Louisiana, 470 U.S. 93, 98 (1985); United States v. Maine, 469 U.S. 504, 512–13 (1980). *See also* Alaska v. United States, 545 U.S. 75 (2005).

15. United States v. Maine, 469 U.S. 504, 526 (1980). The Convention's Article 7(2) defines a "juridical bay" as "[a] well-marked indentation whose penetration is in such proportion to the width of its mouth as to contain landlocked waters and constitute more than a mere curvature of the coast. An indentation shall not, however, be regarded as a bay unless its area is as large as, or larger than, that of the semi-circle whose diameter is a line drawn across the mouth of that indentation." Convention on the Territorial Sea and the Contiguous Zone [1964], 15 U.S.T. (pt. 2) 1607, T.I.A.S. No. 5639. *See also* United States v. Maine, 469 U.S. at 519.

16. United States v. Louisiana, 470 U.S. 93, 94 (1985).

17. United States v. California, 381 U.S. 139 (1965).

18. 43 U.S.C. § 1311(a).

19. 43 U.S.C. § 1311(d).

20. 43 U.S.C. § 1314; Douglas v. Seacoast Products, Inc., 431 U.S. 265, 284 (1977); United States v. Louisiana, 363 U.S. 1, 10 (1960).

21. 33 C.F.R. § 329.12 (2005); 16 U.S.C. § 1379(a).

22. *Douglas, supra* note 21.

23. People v. Weeren, 26 Cal. 3d 654, 607 P.2d 1279 (1980).

24. State v. F/V Baranof, 677 P.2d 1245 (Alaska 1984).

25. *See* John C. Pearson, *The Fish and Fisheries of Colonial Virginia*, 23 WM. & MARY Q.2D 278, 280 (1943). *See also* Thomas Lund, *Early American Wildlife Law*, 51 N.Y.U. L. REV. 703, 719–21 (1976) (discussing colonial and early state statutes establishing closing periods for taking waterfowl, fish, and oysters); Commonwealth v. Wentworth, 15 Mass. 188 (1818) (discussing laws regulating fishing in Penobscot Bay and the rivers leading into it).

26. Trustees of Brookhaven v. Strong, 60 N.Y. 56, 68–69 (1875) (discussing disputes in colonial New York over oyster fisheries); Smith v. Maryland, 59 U.S. 71 (1855) (upholding seizure of vessel for violation of 1833 state law prohibiting harvest of oysters except by specified means); Hayden v. Noyes, 5 Conn. 391 (1824) (take limited to no more than six bushels of oysters per week and requiring fishing licenses for such activity).

27. *See, e.g.*, ME. REV. STAT. tit. 12, §§ 6421–6823 (2005); HAW. REV. STAT. ANN. §§ 190-1, 190-3 (Michie 2005); HAW. CODE R. § 13-95 (Weil 2006).

28. Magnuson-Stevens Fisheries Conservation and Management Act, 16 U.S.C. § 1801 *et seq.* (2005).

29. The Exclusive Economic Zone is an area beyond and adjacent to the territorial sea, generally extending about two hundred nautical miles out from the coast. *See, e.g.,* United Nations Convention on the Law of the Sea, Dec. 10, 1982, 1833 U.N.T.S. 43–44; Magnuson-Stevens Fishery Conservation and Management Act, 16 U.S.C. § 1801 *et seq.* (2005).

30. 16 U.S.C. § 1856 Other provisions (authority of States of Washington, Oregon, and California to manage Dungeness crab fishery).

31. 16 U.S.C. § 1856(b).

32. 16 U.S.C. § 1856(a).

33. 16 U.S.C. § 1856(a)(3).

34. 16 U.S.C. § 1852.

35. NOAA Fisheries: Office for Law Enforcement, State Partners, http://www.nmfs.noaa.gov/ole/part_state.html.

36. *See, e.g.,* ME. CODE R. § 133-88 (1998); FLA. ADMIN. CODE ANN. r. 5L-3 (2000); WASH. ADMIN. CODE § 220-76 (2005).

37. FLA. STAT. § 258.083 (2005); *see also* About John Pennekamp Coral Reef State Park, http://www.pennekamppark.com/about_history.html.

38. 14 C.F.R § 4752; *see also* California State Parks, Point Lobos State Reserve, http://www.parks.ca.gov/default.asp?page_id=571.

39. Marine Protection, Research, and Sanctuaries Act of 1972, 16 U.S.C. §§ 1431 *et seq.*

40. 15 C.F.R. § 922. *See also* NOAA *Monitor* National Marine Sanctuary, http://monitor.noaa.gov/.

41. Queensland Government, Environmental Protection Agency, Queensland Parks and Wildlife Service, http://www.epa.qld.gov.au/parks_and_forests/marine_parks/.

42. OR. ADMIN. R. 635-005-0015 (2006).

43. ME. REV. STAT. ANN. tit. 12, § 6961 (2005).

44. *Id.*

45. Florida Office of Cultural and Historic Programs, Underwater Archeology, http://dhr.dos.state.fl.us/archaeology/underwater/preserves/.

46. *Id.*

47. Maryland Historic Trust, U-1105 Shipwreck Preserve, http://www.marylandhistoricaltrust.net/u1105.html.

48. North Carolina Office of State Archaeology, http://www.arch.dcr.state.nc.us/ncarch/underwater/huron.htm.

49. Point Lobos State Reserve, http://pt-lobos.parks.state.ca.us/.

50. MASS. GEN. LAWS ch. 132A, §§ 12A–16F, 18 (2005); corresponding regulations at 302 MASS. CODE REGS. 5.00.

51. MASS. GEN. LAWS ch. 132A, § 13.

52. "Seriously [sic] alter includes, but is not limited to, one or more of the following actions: removing, excavating, or dredging any soil, sand, gravel, or other minerals or aggregate material of any kind in any significant amounts; changing drainage or flushing characteristics, salinity distribution, sedimentation or flow patterns, flood storage areas or the water table, to more than a negligible extent; dumping, discharging, or filling with any material of any kind that could significantly degrade water quality; driving pilings or erecting buildings, structures or obstructions of any kind of any significant size or quantity, whether or not they interfere with the flow of water; destroying or adversely affecting in more than a negligible way any plant or animal life, including shellfish and fisheries; changing the temperature, biochemical oxygen demand (BOD) or other natural characteristics of the water so that there is a more than negligible adverse effect on the marine environment; significantly increasing the development of already developed areas; and developing any previously undeveloped or natural areas." 302 MASS. CODE REGS. 5.04.

53. MASS. GEN. LAWS ch. 132A, § 14.

54. MASS. GEN. LAWS ch. 132A, § 15.

55. *Id.* § 16.

56. *Id.* § 18.

57. 302 Mass. Code Regs. 5.02 (2).

58. N.C. Gen. Stat. §§ 113A-129.1–.3 (2005).

59. *Id.* § 113A-129.2(e).

60. Fla. Stat. § 258.35 *et seq.* (2005).

61. *Id.* § 258.42(b).

62. *Id.* § 258.42(3)(a).

63. *Id.* § 258.42(3)(c) and (d).

64. *Id.* § 258.43(1).

65. Wash. Rev. Code § 79A.05.355 *et seq.* (2005).

66. Alaska Stat. § 41.21.300, .306 (2006).

67. Or. Admin. R. 635-039 *et seq.* (2004), *available at* http://www.dfw.state.or.us/ODF Whtml/Regulations/2004_commercial.pdf ; *see also* Oregon Ocean Policy Advisory Council (OPAC), Oregon Territorial Sea Plan (2001), *available at* http://www.oregon.gov/LCD/ OCMP/Ocean_Intro.shtml (follow "Oregon Territorial Sea Plan" hyperlink).

68. *Id.*

69. *Id.*

70. Haw. Code R. §§ 13-28 through 13-38 (2005); *see also* http://www.hawaii.gov/dlnr/dar/ mlcd/index.htm.

71. Haw. Code R. § 13-28.

72. *Id.* §§ 13-28 through 13-38 (2005); *see also* http://www.hawaii.gov/dlnr/dar/mlcd/index .htm.

73. Haw. Rev. Stat § 190-3.

74. Haw. Code R. § 13-75.

75. Haw. Rev. Stat. § 188-37; Haw. Code R. § 13-74; *see also* State of Hawaii, Department of Land and Natural Resources, Division of Aquatic Resources *available at* http://www .hawaii.gov/dlnr/dar/fish_regs/nwhi.htm.

76. Haw. Code R. § 13-60.5.

77. 42 U.S.C. § 7410.

78. 42 U.S.C. § 6926(b).

79. 33 U.S.C. §§ 1342(b), 1344(g). Of the coastal states, only two—Alaska and New Hampshire—do not have authorized NPDES programs.

80. *Id.* § 1342.

81. *Id.* § 1344.

82. *Id.* § 1342(b).

83. *Id.*

84. *Id.* §§ 1342(b) and (c)(1); National Ass'n of Homebuilders v. Defenders of Wildlife, 127 U.S. 2518 (decided June 25, 2007).

85. 33 U.S.C. § 1342(c)(3); 40 C.F.R. § 123.63.

86. *Id.* § 1342(c)(4); 40 C.F.R. § 123.64.

87. 33 U.S.C. § 1342(d)(2); 40 C.F.R. § 123.44(c). *See also National Ass'n of Homebuilders, supra* note 84.

88. 16 U.S.C. § 1452(1).

89. *Id.* § 1453(1).

90. *Id.* § 1453(3).

91. *Id.* § 1452(2).

92. *Id.* §§ 1454, 1455, 1456(c).

93. *Id.* § 1455(d)(2).

94. U.S. Commission on Ocean Policy, An Ocean Blueprint for the 21st Century Final Report, 153 (September 20, 2004), *available at* http://www.oceancommission .gov/documents/full_color_rpt/welcome.html#final. Illinois does not have an approved program.

95. 16 U.S.C. § 1455(d)(11).

96. *Id.* §§ 1458(c) and (d).

97. *Id.* § 1456(c)(3)(A).

98. *Id.*

99. *Id.*

100. *Id.*

101. *Id.*

102. *Id.* § 1456(c)(1)(A).

103. *Id.* § 1455(b)(a).

104. *Id.*

105. *Id.* § 1852.

106. Chesapeake Bay Agreement (1983), *available at* http://www.chesapeakebay.net/pubs/ 1983ChesapeakeBayAgreement.pdf; *see also* Chesapeake Bay Agreement (1987), *available at* http://www.chesapeakebay.net/pubs/199.pdf; and Chesapeake 2000, available at http://www.chesapeakebay.net/agreement.htm.

107. *See* The Chesapeake Bay Program, http://www.chesapeakebay.net/program.htm.

108. *Id.*

109. *Id.*

110. The Chesapeake Bay Program Nutrient Trading Negotiation Team, Chesapeake Bay Program Nutrient Trading Fundamental Principles and Guidelines (March 2001) *available at* http://www.chesapeakebay.net (follow "publications" hyperlink; then follow "Bay Restoration—Nutrient Trading" hyperlink; then follow "Principles and Guidelines" hyperlink).

111. *Id.*

112. Gulf of Mexico Alliance, http://www.dep.state.fl.us/gulf/.

113. *See id.*

114. P.L. 90-419, *available at* Great Lakes Basin Compact, http://www.glc.org/about/glbc.html; *see also* Great Lakes Commission, http://www.glc.org/.

115. Great Lakes Commission Declaration of Partnership, http://www.glc.org/about/pdf/ declarations.pdf.

116. About the Great Lakes Commission, http://www.glc.org/about/.

117. Gulf of Maine Council on the Marine Environment, http://www.gulfofmaine.org/.

118. Atlantic States Marine Fisheries Commission, Interstate Fisheries Management Program Charter, Washington, DC (2003), *available at* http://www.asmfc.org/.

119. Gulf States Marine Fisheries Commission Compact, http://www.gsmfc.org/.

120. Pacific States Marine Fisheries Commission Compact, http://www.psmfc.org/index.php (follow "Publications and Maps" hyperlink; then follow "PSMFC Compact" hyperlink).

121. Convention on Great Lakes Fisheries Between the United States of America and Canada, http://www.glfc.org/pubs/conv.htm.

122. Atlantic States Commission, Interstate Fisheries Management Program (ISFMP) http:// www.asmfc.org/.

123. *See generally* Pacific States Marine Fisheries Commission website at http://www.psmfc .org.

124. Convention on Great Lakes Fisheries, *supra* note 121.

125. National Marine Fisheries Service Annual Report to Congress on the Status of U.S. Fisheries (2004), *available at* http://www.nmfs.noaa.gov (follow "Sustaining Fisheries" hyperlink; then follow "2006 Status of U.S. Fisheries Report to Congress"; then follow "2006 Report of Status of U.S. Fisheries" hyperlink).

126. *Id.*

127. U.S. Commission on Ocean Policy, *supra* note 94.

128. *Id.* §§ 7056(b), 7080, 7084.

129. *Id.* § 7056.

130. *Id.* §§ 7056, 7072(a).

131. EPA National Estuary Coastal Condition Report Executive Summary at ES.8 (June 2007).

132. U.S. Commission on Ocean Policy, *supra* note 94.

133. *Id.* at 256.

134. *Id.* at 253.

135. *Id.*

136. *Id.* at 257.
137. *Id.*
138. Cal. Fish & Game Code § 2853(a).
139. *Id.* § 2851(a).
140. *Id.* §§ 2850–2863.
141. *Id.* § 2853(b).
142. Cal. Fish & Game Code §§ 2852(d), 2853(c); Cal. Pub. Res. Code § 26710(a). To improve the State's ability to manage its MPAs, it also enacted the Marine Managed Areas Improvement Act, Pub. Res. Code § 36600 *et seq.,* which required that the existing array of eighteen classes and subclasses of marine managed areas be reduced to six, each of which has clearly stated parameters and prohibitions. Pub. Res. Code §§ at 36601(a)(4), 36700, 36710. This Act also required that whenever a marine managed area is located next to a terrestrial protected area, the managing agencies for both areas are to "coordinate their activities to the greatest extent possible to achieve the objectives of both areas." Pub. Res. Code § 36601(c).
143. *See, e.g.,* Cal. Fish & Game Code § 2856(a)(2).
144. *Id.* § 2855.

chapter four

Regulation of Coastal Wetlands and Other Waters in the United States

Kim Diana Connolly

I. Introduction

The wetlands along our nation's coastline provide valuable resources that support large sections of the U.S. economy.[1] Wetlands can be found in every state[2] and differ depending on soil differences, topography, climate, hydrology, water chemistry, vegetation, and human impact.[3] All wetlands provide various "functions and values" important to our nation, including water quality improvement through the trapping and filtering of pollutants, flood water retention and storage, habitat for endangered and other species, recreational and educational activities, and aesthetic values.[4] Situated at the boundaries of land and ocean, coastal wetlands (such as tidal marshes and mangrove forests) provide many of these functions and values, including vital ecosystem services such as water storage and habitat for economically important species.[5] These crucial coastal resources are in decline.[6]

The author gratefully acknowledges very helpful comments on an earlier draft from Lance D. Wood, Assistant Chief Counsel for Environmental Law and Regulatory Programs at the U.S. Army Corps of Engineers and Professorial Lecturer in Law, George Washington University School of Law.

Wetlands are defined scientifically as those lands where water saturation is the dominant factor in determining the nature of soil development and the types of animal and plant communities living in the soil and on its surface.[7] The U.S. Environmental Protection Agency (EPA) and the U.S. Army Corps of Engineers (Corps) define wetlands as "those areas that are inundated or saturated by surface or ground water at a frequency and duration sufficient to support, and that under normal circumstances do support, a prevalence of vegetation typically adapted for life in saturated soil conditions. Wetlands generally include swamps, marshes, bogs and similar areas."[8]

> **Wetlands are defined scientifically as those lands where water saturation is the dominant factor in determining the nature of soil development and the types of animal and plant communities living in the soil and on its surface.**

Coastal wetlands (and other coastal waters) throughout the United States are subject to regulation by local,[9] state,[10] and federal authorities.[11] The federal government has taken an interest in coastal wetlands for quite some time, but only in recent decades has it begun to regulate activities in coastal wetlands.[12] The Federal Water Pollution Control Act[13] (commonly known as the Clean Water Act, or CWA)[14] Section 404 program[15] and the Rivers and Harbors Act of 1899 Section 10 program[16] form the foundation of the federal government's coastal wetlands regulatory efforts.[17]

In addition to the Section 404 and Section 10 regulatory programs, other federal programs encourage preservation of wetlands through direct regulation, financial incentives, outright acquisition, or other management techniques.[18] International cooperative efforts through the Convention on Wetlands of International Importance Especially as Waterfowl Habitat, often referred to as the Ramsar Convention on Wetlands or the Ramsar Convention,[19] also encourage wetland preservation.[20]

The Section 404 and Section 10 programs are implemented primarily by the Corps.[21] EPA also plays a role in Section 404 implementation.[22] Through these statutes, the Corps (and EPA in some contexts) has permitting authority for many activities, including construction and dredging, in the nation's "navigable waters."[23] The Clean Water Act provides that states may administer the Section 404 permit program for waters, including wetlands, that are not subject to Section 10 jurisdiction,[24] but only Michigan and New Jersey have assumed that authority.[25]

Since the 1980s, the federal government has embraced a national goal of no overall net loss of the nation's wetland resources,[26] and on Earth Day 2004 reiterated a goal of achieving a net gain in wetland resources throughout the United States.[27] Despite the federal government's long-term experience and recent renewed commitments, wetlands have been and remain the subject of considerable controversy.[28] Accordingly, when it comes to wetlands and related coastal resources, the regulatory arena is in a state of semi-constant flux.[29]

To fully understand the following discussion, it is important to know the key players in coastal wetlands regulation. As the frontline regulator, the Corps delegates most day-to-day responsibilities to district engineers and more than one thousand regulatory personnel nationwide.[30] On rare occasions, the decisions of district engineers may be "elevated" for review by Corps headquarters.[31] The EPA also has an important regulatory and oversight role.[32] Furthermore, states have a crucial role in certifying water quality pursuant to Section 401 of the Clean Water Act,[33] and, for coastal areas, making a consistency determination[34] with the Coastal Zone Management Act (CZMA).[35] Other federal agencies with particular experience also play important parts in permit review.[36]

This chapter gives an overview of the regulatory requirements associated with coastal wetlands and other coastal waters. It first summarizes the current state of the law, beginning with the obligations imposed by the Rivers and Harbors Act of 1899 Section 10 and continuing with an overview of Clean Water Act Section 404 requirements. It then discusses regulatory program permitting requirements and enforcement matters. The chapter closes by offering insight into emerging trends and unresolved issues.

At this point it is important to note that the Corps also influences coastal and ocean areas through its Civil Works water resource development activities.[37] The Corps's traditional role is to advance water resource development projects.[38] In fact, the Corps has been called the world's largest civil engineering firm.[39] In recent years, the effectiveness of the Corps's Civil Works activities has been called into question.[40] Following Hurricanes Katrina and Rita in 2005[41] and the failure of the Louisiana levees,[42] Corps nonregulatory activities were increasingly attacked and scrutinized.[43] This chapter, however, will focus on regulatory roles of the Corps and other federal agencies.

II. The Current State of the Law

The U.S. offices of the United States Army Corps of Engineers (Corps) are divided into eight regional divisions and thirty-eight districts.[44] Division and district boundaries, for the most part, are determined by watersheds[45] and often cross state lines.[46] The districts[47] are the "operational level" of the Corps, implementing day-to-day activities in all areas.[48] Thus, the following discussion represents general principles and approaches that may vary in actual practice depending on the district in question.[49]

Part II.A of this chapter will explore the Rivers and Harbors Act of 1899 Section 10 framework. Part II.B will delve into Clean Water Act Section 404 requirements. Part II.C will cover permitting requirements that apply to both programs, and Part II.D will discuss appeal and enforcement options.

A. Section 10 of the Rivers and Harbors Act of 1899: Jurisdiction and Authority

Early in our nation's history,[50] the U.S. Supreme Court determined that traditionally navigable waters were subject to federal control, development, and regulation under the Commerce Clause of the Constitution.[51] Accordingly, to reflect a "national focus on the use and development of national waterways,"[52] Congress considered and enacted a series of Rivers and Harbors Acts,[53] including the Rivers and Harbors Act of

1899,[54] many provisions of which are still in force. Section 10 of the 1899 Act makes it unlawful "to excavate or fill, or in any manner to alter or modify the course, location, condition, or capacity of, any port, roadstead, haven, harbor, canal, lake, harbor of refuge, or inclosure [sic] within the limits of any breakwater, or of the channel of any navigable water" without the appropriate permit.[55] The Corps[56] was charged with implementing the Act, including its regulatory provisions.[57] Today, many coastal activities will require a Rivers and Harbors Act Section 10 permit from the Corps.[58]

The substance of the regulatory provisions of the Rivers and Harbors Act of 1899 has been unchanged since enactment. The Supreme Court has had only a few occasions to construe those regulatory provisions and has interpreted the authority granted to the Corps very broadly.[59] Many coastal activities involve construction, excavation, or deposition of materials in jurisdictional waters, and thus appropriately fall within Section 10 permitting requirements.[60]

The process for issuing standard individual Section 10 permits is almost the same as that for Section 404 of the Clean Water Act[61] and will only be covered briefly here. The Section 404 permit process will be discussed in depth in Part II.B of this chapter.[62] Basically, a completed individual permit application[63] triggers a public notice soliciting comments,[64] followed by a detailed review of the proposal.[65] This review by the appropriate district office[66] usually involves an environmental assessment[67] and a determination as to whether a public hearing is necessary.[68]

Whether a permit is issued by the Corps depends on evaluation of the proposed activity[69] and of the potential impact of that activity on the public interest.[70] After considering all relevant factors, the District Engineer will issue, deny, or condition permits for Section 10 activities.[71] In addition to an administrative appeal of a permit decision with which an applicant is dissatisfied,[72] applicants may challenge permit decisions in the appropriate U.S. District Court under the Administrative Procedure Act.[73] The Corps, acting through the U.S. Department of Justice, may enforce failure to comply with the Rivers and Harbors Act as a criminal violation or by means of civil enforcement.[74] After investigation of a particular failure to comply, the Corps can take legal action[75] or grant an after-the-fact permit.[76]

B. Section 404 of the Clean Water Act: Jurisdiction and Authority

The Clean Water Act[77] Section 404[78] program was one of a number of new environmental laws evolving in the late 1960s through the early 1980s.[79] Through that new law, Congress sought to "restore and maintain the chemical, physical and biological integrity of our nation's waters."[80] Section 404 was entitled "Permits for Dredged or Fill Material."[81]

Under Section 404, "[t]he Secretary [of the Army] may issue permits, after notice and opportunity for public hearings[,] for the discharge of dredged or fill material into the navigable waters at specified disposal sites."[82] Without a Section 404 permit, someone discharging dredged or fill materials would, in most cases, be in violation of Clean Water Act Section 301, which directs that "[e]xcept as in compliance with this section and [various sections including 404] of this Act, the discharge of any pollutant by any person shall be unlawful."[83]

Unfortunately, the scope of federal jurisdiction is not entirely clear in the language of Section 404. Consequently, it is vital to understand the implementing regulations and other guidance documents issued by the Corps and the EPA, as well as myriad judicial decisions, to apply Section 404's requirements.[84] Even these sources often fail to provide clear answers. Through the years, stakeholders—including the agencies, the permitted community, the conservation community, and the courts—have disagreed about the program's coverage.[85]

Nevertheless, the initial source for those seeking to undertake activities in coastal wetlands is almost certainly the regulations promulgated by the Corps and the EPA to implement their Section 404 program responsibilities.[86] To supplement and clarify these regulations, the Corps occasionally issues Regulatory Guidance Letters (RGLs)[87] and other guidance documents.[88] Furthermore, various Memoranda of Agreement govern interactions among federal agencies.[89] These additional sources of regulatory information often provide useful and important details about particular issues under the Section 404 program.[90]

The EPA's role in the Section 404 program is significant.[91] The CWA requires the application of guidelines promulgated by the EPA in conjunction with the Corps when issuing permits.[92] Commonly referred to as the 404(b)(1) Guidelines, they are actually formal, binding regulations.[93] Additionally, the EPA may "veto" any Corps decision to issue a Section 404 permit.[94] The EPA also has certain enforcement responsibilities for Section 404[95] and has authority to review and approve applications by states that want to assume some of the Corps's permitting responsibilities.[96] The statutory division of authority between the EPA and the Corps has sometimes generated confusion about program responsibilities, much of which has been clarified through Memoranda of Agreement between the agencies and by one Opinion of the Attorney General of the United States.[97]

Section 404 only applies when the federal government has jurisdiction over both the property proposed for development and the activity proposed to be undertaken. Determining whether jurisdiction over the property exists necessitates (1) that the property can be delineated as a water of the United States, such as a wetland,[98] and (2) that it can be considered jurisdictional "navigable waters" for purposes of the CWA.[99] Even if geographic jurisdiction exists, the Corps must also have jurisdiction over the activity, which necessitates (1) that there be no applicable exemption[100] and (2) that the proposed activity involves a discharge of dredged or fill material.[101]

1. Wetland Delineations

Determining whether an area is subject to Section 404 regulation typically involves review by a Corps district office[102] and can involve a wetland "delineation."[103] Wetland delineations are based on a scientific assessment of the particular property.[104] As discussed in Part I, both the EPA and the Corps have identical definitions of wetlands.[105]

To ascertain whether the three parameters in this legal definition (hydrophytic vegetation, hydric soil, and hydrology) are met, field personnel use a wetland delineation manual.[106] Following a controversy in the early 1990s,[107] Congress directed the National Academy of Sciences to develop a new way to delineate wetlands;[108] however, the Corps 1987 wetland delineation manual remains the guiding force.[109] A delineation is part of a "jurisdictional determination" (JD), the formal process of determining whether Section 404 applies to a particular piece of property.[110] Jurisdictional determinations generally expire after five years.[111]

2. Section 404 Geographic Jurisdiction

The second step in determining whether the federal government has jurisdiction over a piece of property requires analysis of whether a delineated wetland is a "navigable water" as required by the statutory language in Section 404.[112] "Navigable waters" are defined in the CWA as "waters of the United States."[113] Early judicial decisions,[114] supported by later interpretations,[115] have concluded that this definition signaled Congress's intent[116] to provide a more expansive jurisdiction under Section 404 than is provided by the Corps' jurisdiction over activities in "navigable waters" under the Rivers and Harbors Act of 1899.[117] On this basis, federal regulatory jurisdiction has evolved over the years to include areas that fall well beyond traditional definitions of "navigable waters." Yet how far this jurisdiction can and should reach is an area of fervent debate.[118]

In an effort to "restore and maintain the chemical, physical, and biological integrity of the Nation's waters,"[119] Congress prohibited "the discharge of any pollutant by any person" without a permit issued in compliance with the Clean Water Act.[120] Section 404 of the Act authorized permits from the Corps "for the discharge of dredged or fill material into the navigable waters at specified disposal sites."[121] The fact that the term "navigable waters" was defined by Congress only as "waters of the United States, including the territorial seas,"[122] however, has spawned much litigation and confusion. The most recent statement by the Supreme Court on that issue was delivered in 2006.[123] But that fractured opinion[124] left this hotly contested area of law with increased confusion[125] and guaranteed continued combat.[126]

To understand how this confusion developed, it is helpful to start with the early interpretations of the term "navigable waters" in CWA Section 404, as originally enacted in 1972. The Corps initially construed its jurisdictional authority very narrowly,[127] leading to a 1975 district court challenge.[128] Unlike the more narrow definition of navigable waters appropriate to jurisdiction under the Rivers and Harbors Act,[129] the court held that through Section 404 Congress had "asserted federal jurisdiction over the nation's waters to the maximum extent permissible under the Commerce Clause of the Constitution."[130] Given that directive, the Corps of Engineers shortly thereafter issued broad regulations[131] (which are essentially the same today) that asserted jurisdiction beyond traditionally navigable waters to interstate waters, other waters for which commerce connections can be found, and impoundments and tributaries of same.[132]

This 1975 regulatory interpretation led to significant controversy[133] and caused Congress to reexamine the intended breadth of the program in its 1977 reauthorization of the Clean Water Act.[134] An amendment proposing to narrow jurisdiction was defeated, with a statement from the Senate Committee on Environment and Public Works trying to "dispel the widespread fears that the program is regulating activities that were not intended to be regulated."[135] The Supreme Court subsequently held in 1985 through its unanimous *Riverside Bayview Homes* decision that Congress's actions and statements indicated it intended the phrase "navigable waters" to include wetlands, without regard to artificial geographic limitations, when it passed the 1977 amendments.[136]

That unanimous Court decision led the Corps (and EPA) to reconsider the breadth of appropriate federal regulatory reach and issue slightly revised regulations with preamble language that came to be known as the "Migratory Bird Rule," which asserted jurisdiction over certain intrastate waters based on their actual or potential use as a habitat for migratory birds.[137] Upheld by a number of circuit courts,[138] this Corps and EPA interpretation ultimately was ruled overbroad by a 5-4 Supreme Court decision in *Solid Waste Agency of Northern Cook County v. U.S. Army Corps of Engineers* (SWANCC).[139] The decision concluded that an abandoned sand and gravel pit without any surface connections to other waters that provided habitat for migratory birds was beyond the regulatory authority granted by Congress through the Clean Water Act.[140] Despite extensive briefing on the issue, the Court did not reach a constitutional question.[141]

Almost all subsequent interpretations of the SWANCC decision as it applied to adjacent waters and tributaries found it to be very narrow.[142] However, post-SWANCC decisions were not in universal agreement.[143] Furthermore, the agencies gave mixed signals as to how they were going to proceed in dealing with the issue of jurisdiction,[144] to the annoyance of many potential permit applicants.[145] It therefore was greeted by some as good news when the Supreme Court accepted for review two Sixth Circuit decisions interpreting SWANCC with respect to jurisdiction over adjacent wetlands and tributaries.[146]

What resulted, however, was not increased clarity. Instead, in *Rapanos v. United States*,[147] the Supreme Court issued a fractured opinion of a plurality, two concurrences, and two dissents, that has led to even less certainty.[148] Justice Scalia's plurality opinion in *Rapanos*, relying on a 1954 edition of *Webster's New International Dictionary* to define "waters,"[149] called for a significant narrowing of Clean Water Act jurisdiction.[150] Justice Scalia and three other Justices concluded that "waters of the United States" include "only those relatively permanent, standing or continuously flowing bodies of water 'forming geographic features' that are described in ordinary parlance as streams . . . oceans, rivers [and] lakes. The phrase does not include channels through which water flows intermittently or ephemerally, or channels that periodically provide drainage for rainfall."[151] Likewise, the plurality indicated that "only those wetlands with a continuous surface connection to bodies that are 'waters of the United States' in their own right, so that there is no clear demarcation between 'waters' and wetlands 'adjacent to' such waters, are covered by the Act."[152]

By contrast, Justice Stevens and three other Justices in dissent would have upheld the lower court jurisdictional findings and deferred to agency interpretations supporting the jurisdiction over the waters at issue as reflecting congressional intent.[153] The swing vote was Justice Kennedy, who agreed with the plurality as to the remand decision but disagreed vehemently as to its reasoning.[154] Justice Kennedy would find jurisdiction supported only where there is a "significant nexus between the wetlands in question and navigable waters in the traditional sense . . . assessed in terms of the statute's goals and purposes."[155] Justice Kennedy's significant nexus can be found "if the wetlands, either alone or in combination with similarly situated lands in the region, significantly affect the chemical, physical, and biological integrity of other covered waters more readily understood as 'navigable.'"[156]

As Chief Justice Roberts noted in a separate concurring opinion in *Rapanos*, "[N]o opinion commands a majority of the Court on precisely how to read Congress'[s] limits on the reach of the Clean Water Act. Lower courts and regulated entities will now have to feel their way on a case-by-case basis."[157] Justice Stevens's opinion concluded that because all four Justices who joined the dissenting opinion would uphold the Corps's jurisdiction in tests set forth by either the plurality (by a showing of a continuous surface connection between the wetlands and a relatively permanent body of water connected to a traditional navigable in fact water, even though there may be no significant nexus between the wetlands and the traditional navigable in fact water) or the concurrence (regulate wetlands adjacent to nonnavigable waters if the wetlands have a significant nexus to a navigable in fact water), "on remand each of the judgments should be reinstated if *either* of those tests is met."[158]

Post-SWANCC guidance[159] took almost two years to produce[160] and was considered by many to be less than guiding.[161] It similarly took almost a year to issue post-*Rapanos* guidance,[162] and, like the SWANCC guidance, it too has received mixed reviews.[163] This guidance document states that, following *Rapanos*, federal jurisdiction will routinely be asserted over traditional navigable waters, wetlands adjacent to traditional navigable waters, non-navigable tributaries of traditional navigable waters that are relatively permanent where the tributaries typically flow year-round or have continuous flow at least seasonally (e.g., typically three months), and wetlands that directly abut such tributaries.[164] However, fact-specific jurisdictional analysis to assess whether there is a significant nexus with traditional navigable waters will be required under the guidance for non-navigable tributaries that are not relatively permanent, wetlands adjacent to non-navigable tributaries that are not relatively permanent, and wetlands adjacent to but that do not directly abut a relatively permanent non-navigable tributary.[165] Finally, jurisdiction will generally will not be asserted over swales or erosional features (e.g., gullies, small washes characterized by low volume, infrequent, or short duration flow) and ditches (including roadside ditches) excavated wholly in and draining only uplands and that do not carry a relatively permanent flow of water.[166] A comment period expired in early 2008 regarding this guidance,[167] and future developments in the area will depend on many variables.

In the *Rapanos* decision, a number of the Justices called for a rulemaking to redefine "waters of the United States." The Chief Justice, in his separate concurring opinion, chastised the government for abandoning the previous rulemaking proceeding that would have defined "waters of the United States."[168] Had the government proceeded by regulation, Chief Justice Roberts asserted, it would have been "afforded generous leeway by the courts in interpreting" the Clean Water Act under *Chevron*.[169] Justice Kennedy also suggested that the agency could use rulemaking to identify categories of tributaries that could be regulated as "waters of the United States" in order to avoid making "significant nexus" decisions on a case-by-case basis in adjudication.[170] Finally, Justice Breyer wrote a separate dissenting opinion arguing that congressional intent dictated that scientific questions associated with determining the jurisdictional scope of "waters of the United States" should be resolved by agencies through rulemaking, rather than by courts on an ad hoc basis.[171] Whether a rulemaking is forthcoming remains unclear at this time.

Judicial response to the *Rapanos* decision has been mixed. In the Ninth[172] and Seventh[173] Circuits, analyses have been based on Justice Kennedy's test.[174] Yet the First Circuit expressed some doubts about these other circuits' approaches.[175] A later Ninth Circuit analysis struggled to apply the various *Rapanos* jurisdictional tests to an isolated salt-processing pond.[176] A district court in Texas declined to apply *Rapanos*.[177] Litigation developments post-*Rapanos* are occurring almost weekly—one good summary is maintained by the National Wildlife Federation entitled *Summary of Post*-Rapanos *and Post*-SWANCC *Court Decisions*.[178] Many more cases are pending, and geographic jurisdiction under Section 404 remains in disarray.[179]

3. Section 404(f) Exemptions

Congress exempted certain activities from regulation by CWA Section 404(f).[180] The section exempts the following activities:

(A) normal farming, silviculture, and ranching activities such as plowing, seeding, cultivating, minor drainage, harvesting for the production of food, fiber, and forest products, or upland soil and water conservation projects;

(B) maintenance, including emergency reconstruction of recently damaged parts, of currently serviceable structures such as dikes, dams, levees, groins, riprap, breakwaters, causeways, and bridge abutments or approaches, and transportation structures;

(C) construction or maintenance of farm or stock ponds or irrigation ditches, or the maintenance of drainage ditches;

(D) construction of temporary sedimentation basins on a construction site which does not include placement of fill material into the navigable waters;

(E) construction or maintenance of farm roads or forest roads, or temporary roads for mining equipment, where such roads are constructed in accordance with best management practices, to assure that flow and circulation patterns and chemical and biological characteristics of the navigable waters is [sic] not reduced, and that any adverse effect on the aquatic environment will be otherwise minimized;

(F) activities where a State has an approved nonpoint source management program.[181]

Various statutory and regulatory conditions limit these exemptions,[182] which have been interpreted narrowly by the courts.[183] These exemptions are also restricted by Section 404(f)(2)'s "recapture" provision, which directs that

[a]ny discharge of dredged or fill material into the navigable waters incidental to any activity having as its purpose bringing an area of the navigable waters into a use to which it was not previously subject, where the flow or circulation of navigable waters may be impaired or the reach of such waters be reduced, shall be required to have a permit under this section.[184]

The first 404(f) exemption, for "normal farming, silviculture and ranching activities," has been narrowly construed by Corps regulations and regulatory guidance.[185] Likewise, the exemption for maintenance of currently serviceable structures does not include activities that "change[] the character, scope, or size of the original fill design."[186] Exempted emergency reconstructions of recently damaged structures must proceed "within a reasonable time after the damage occurs."[187] Farm or stock pond construction must consider "the relative size of a proposed pond in relation to the size of the farming/ranching operation"[188] and "must actually be used in [established] farming/ranching operations" to qualify for an exemption.[189] "Construction site" is defined in the Corps regulations for purposes of an exemption to encompass "any site involving the erection of buildings, roads, and other discrete structures and the installation of support facilities necessary for construction and utilization of such structures" as well as "any other land areas which involve land-disturbing excavation activities . . . where an increase in the runoff of sediment is controlled through the use of sedimentation basins."[190] Construction or maintenance of farm roads or forest roads is only exempt if best management practices (BMPs) are used that meet certain "baseline provisions"[191] and if such maintenance or construction is related to farming and silviculture and part of an established, ongoing farming or silvicultural operation.[192]

4. Regulated Discharges of Dredged or Fill Material

CWA Section 404 is only authorized to regulate "the discharge of dredged or fill material . . . ."[193] Thus, the draining of wetlands is not explicitly listed as a regulated activity under Section 404,[194] although many drainage activities, such as constructing a ditch in a wetland, may well involve discharges of dredged or fill material requiring a Section 404 permit. Excavation and/or clearing wetlands of vegetation may or may not be regulated, depending on the particular situation.[195] The extent to which specific activities in jurisdictional waters[196] are regulated is, in fact, a tumultuous subject.[197]

CWA Section 301 prohibits the "discharge of any pollutant by any person" that does not comply with conditions set forth in a permit.[198] The debate regarding regulated activities thus revolves around the interpretation of the term "discharge." The CWA provides that "[t]he term 'discharge' when used without qualification includes a discharge of a pollutant, and a discharge of pollutants."[199] It also defines "discharge" as: "(A) any addition of any pollutant to navigable waters from any point source, (B) any addition of any pollutant to the waters of the contiguous zone or the ocean from any point source other than a vessel or other floating craft."[200] Therefore, Section 404 regulation is triggered only when a discharge involves (1) the addition to "navigable waters"[201] of (2) dredged or fill material that is a (3) pollutant (4) from a point source. As elaborated on later in this section, Congress defined two of these terms ("point source" and "pollutant") in the statute itself, and the Corps later defined the terms "dredged material" and "fill material" via regulation.

Congress defined "pollutant" (in the definitions section applicable to the entire CWA) to include a wide array of materials, including "dredged spoil," "sewage," "biological material," "rock," and "sand."[202] In the context of Section 404, courts have construed the definition of "pollutant" broadly to include a wide range of diverse materials, including "fill material";[203] "dredged materials, including native soils excavated by ditching activities";[204] "rock fill, dirt, organic debris, and biological materials";[205] and other matter.[206] Congress defined "point source" as "any discernible, confined and discrete conveyance, including but not limited to any pipe, ditch, channel, tunnel, conduit, well, discrete fissure, container, rolling stock, concentrated animal feeding operation, or vessel . . . from which pollutants are or may be discharged."[207] In the context of wetlands and other waters, equipment routinely used to clear or alter wetlands (such as backhoes, bulldozers, and dump trucks) has been held to fall within the "point source" definition when such equipment is used to place or move pollutants.[208] The major disputes about regulated discharges involve interpreting the term "addition" when referring to a pollutant in the CWA Section 404 context; this term was left undefined by Congress.

Regulation of discharges of fill material[209] is straightforward in terms of interpreting "addition." In the past, the Corps defined "fill" based on a so-called primary purpose test through which it only regulated materials "used for the primary purpose of replacing aquatic area with dry land or changing the bottom elevation of a water body."[210] By contrast, EPA historically used an "effects" test, regulating materials that had the effect of replacing "waters of the United States" with dry land or that changed the bottom elevation of a water body for any purpose.[211] In 2002, the Corps and EPA reconciled their previously differing "fill material" definitions by amending both Corps and EPA regulations to provide a single consistent definition following EPA's original approach, thus defining fill material as those discharges that have the effect of changing the elevation of a water body.[212] Thus, addition of any fill material[213] is regulated under Section 404 unless an exemption applies.[214]

Significantly more controversial, however, is regulation of "dredged" material, which may involve analysis of whether, and the extent to which, the redeposit of materials into the same waters from which they were removed, excavated, cleared, or otherwise disturbed can properly be regarded as a regulated "addition" of a pollutant. The formal definition of "dredged material" is straightforward: it is material "excavated or dredged from waters of the United States."[215] The issue becomes trickier, however, when regulation involves dredged material that is discharged or "redeposited" in the same general area from which it is excavated or dredged.

The Fourth Circuit recently explained the redeposit phenomenon as follows:

[T]he statute does not prohibit the addition of material; it prohibits "the addition of any pollutant." The idea that there could be an addition of a pollutant without an addition of material seems to us entirely unremarkable, at least when an activity transforms some material from a nonpollutant into a pollutant, as occurred here. In the course of digging a ditch across the [particular] property, the contractor removed earth and vegetable matter from the wetland. Once it was removed, that material became "dredged spoil," a statutory pollutant and a type of material that up until then was not present on the [] property. It is of no consequence that what is now dredged spoil was previously present on the same property in the less threatening form of dirt and vegetation in an undisturbed state. What is important is that once that material was excavated from the wetland, its redeposit in that same wetland added a pollutant where none had been before.[216]

This debate about discharge and excavated material has become more heated in recent years because of so-called "incidental fallback." In its 1998 *National Mining Association v. U.S. Army Corps of Engineers* decision, the Circuit Court for the District of Columbia held that Congress did not intend to regulate purely incidental fallback under Section 404.[217] *National Mining Association* involved a facial challenge to a 1993 Corps regulation that claimed as jurisdictional "any addition, including any redeposit, of dredged material, including excavated material, into waters of the United States which is incidental to any activity,"[218] unless it "does not have or would not have the effect of destroying or degrading an area of waters of the United States."[219]

This 1993 rule, which came to be called the Excavation Rule or the Tulloch Rule after Corps District Engineer Colonel Tulloch,[220] was a response to an earlier interpretation of the concept of "redeposit" in a 1986 Corps regulation.[221] This narrow interpretation of one aspect of "redeposit" was stated as follows: "[t]he term ('discharge of dredged material') does not include de minimis incidental soil movement occurring during normal dredging operations."[222] That concept was challenged by environmental interests in *North Carolina Wildlife Federation v. Tulloch*[223] and a settlement agreement led to a revised rule interpreting regulable discharges of dredged material issued in 1993.[224] The so-called Tulloch Rule clarified that the Corps intended to require a Section 404 permit for any incidental addition of dredged or excavated material associated with any activity that has or would have the effect of destroying or degrading an area of water of the United States.[225] To accomplish that goal, the Corps redefined "discharge of dredged material" to include "any addition, including any redeposit, of dredged material" within the waters of the United States.[226]

The facial challenge resulted in a 1998 holding by the D.C. Circuit that the Tulloch Rule was invalid, concluding that incidental fallback during excavation activities cannot properly be regarded as the "addition of a pollutant."[227] The court distinguished earlier "redeposit" cases, concluding that none of those decisions specifically addressed whether incidental fallback from excavation activities constitutes a discharge.[228] On that question, the court concluded that the "term 'addition' cannot reasonably be said to encompass the situation in which material is removed from the waters of the United States and a small portion of it happens to fall back."[229]

The *National Mining Association* opinion nevertheless indicated that the Corps would not be precluded from regulating "some forms of redeposit"[230] and acknowledged that requiring all regulated pollutants to "come from outside sources would effectively remove the dredge-and-fill provision from the statute."[231] Accordingly, it limited its holding to the Corps's attempt, under the Tulloch Rule, to regulate "a wide range of activities that cannot remotely be said to 'add' anything to the waters of the United States."[232]

Subsequent to that decision, addition has also been explored in the context of "deep ripping."[233] In *Borden Ranch Partnership v. U.S. Army Corps of Engineers,*[234] the Ninth Circuit held, and the Supreme Court affirmed,[235] that this practice was subject to Corps jurisdiction under Section 404.[236]

In response to *National Mining Association,* in 1999 the Corps and EPA jointly issued direct amendments clarifying that not all redeposits of dredged material were to be considered "discharges" subject to Section 404 regulation and excluding "incidental fallback" from the definition of "discharge of dredged materials."[237] Then in January 2001, following notice and comment, the agencies issued a new final rule redefining "discharge of dredged material."[238] That 2001 rule provided, in part:

(d)(1) Except as provided below in paragraph (d)(3), the term discharge of dredged material means any addition of dredged material into, including any redeposit of dredged material other than incidental fallback within, the waters of the United States. The term includes, but is not limited to, the following:

(i) The addition of dredged material to a specified discharge site located in waters of the United States;

(ii) The runoff or overflow from a contained land or water disposal area; and

(iii) Any addition, including redeposit other than incidental fallback, of dredged material, including excavated material, into waters of the United States which is incidental to any activity, including mechanized landclearing, ditching, channelization, or other excavation.[239]

The rule also provided a definition of "incidental fallback" as "the redeposit of small volumes of dredged material that is incidental to excavation activity in waters of the United States when such material falls back to substantially the same place as the initial removal."[240] It also indicated that "[t]he Corps and EPA regard the use of mechanized earth-moving equipment to conduct landclearing, ditching, channelization, in-stream mining or other earth-moving activity in waters of the United States as resulting in a discharge of dredged material unless project-specific evidence shows that the activity results in only incidental fallback."[241]

Shortly after the Corps finalized the 2001 rule redefining "discharge of dredged materials," the National Association of Home Builders filed a facial challenge.[242] The district court initially dismissed the challenge as not ripe for review,[243] but the D.C. Circuit Court ruled in 2006 that the lawsuit could proceed.[244] Reconsideration by the D.C. District Court resulted in a 2007 summary judgment ruling,[245] dubbed "Tulloch II,"[246] that the new definition was invalid.[247] The 2007 holding concluded that the definition of "incidental fallback" erroneously included a volume requirement.[248] The court indicated that incidental fallback instead should be distinguished from regulable redeposit by (1) the time the material is held before being dropped to earth; and (2) the distance between the place where material is collected and the place where it is dropped.[249] The D.C. District Court also directed reconsideration of the statement that the Corps and EPA will regard the use of mechanized earthmoving equipment as resulting in a discharge of dredged material unless project-specific evidence shows otherwise, noting that the agencies cannot require project-specific evidence from projects over which they have no regulatory authority.[250]

The Corps and EPA thus will have to issue a yet-again revised definition of "discharge" in light of this ruling. The politics of that revision process will be interesting to watch.[251]

C. The Corps Regulatory Permit Process

Assuming, as covered previously, that the Corps has geographic[252] and activity[253] jurisdiction over a proposed undertaking and no exemption applies, a permit will be required. As discussed at length in the following sections, the permit requirement can be met by general permits in most cases,[254] but some activities will require an individual permit application.[255] Most Corps regulatory permits will require mitigation of some sort.[256]

1. General Permits

The vast majority of Corps regulatory permit actions involve authorization by general permits.[257] In fact, in FY2005, of the 89,516 federal permit authorizations made by the Corps, 78,336[258] were authorized by the general permitting program, most under CWA Section 404(e).[259] Of those general permit authorizations, 34,114, or thirty-eight percent, were made by nationwide general permits (NWPs).[260] By statute, the Corps's general permits are limited to categories of activities involving discharges of dredged or fill material into waters of the United States that are similar in nature and cause only minimal adverse environmental effects when performed separately and considered cumulatively.[261]

General permits involve a programmatic review when they are issued, meaning that practicable alternatives analyses,[262] public interest review,[263] compliance with the National Environmental Policy Act,[264] and other matters are not undertaken on a permit-by-permit basis.[265] This procedure significantly reduces the processing time for such permits.[266] General permits include state, regional, programmatic, and nationwide general permits.[267]

Those who may not qualify for a general permit may nevertheless be able to get a streamlined individual permit through a "letter of permission," which the Corps defines as "a type of permit issued through an abbreviated processing procedure which includes coordination with Federal and state fish and wildlife agencies . . . and a public interest evaluation, but without the publishing of an individual public notice."[268] Activities that do not qualify for any streamlined permitting must proceed through the individual permitting process.[269]

Issued by the various Corps district and division offices, state and regional general permits vary in different areas of the country.[270] To determine what permits might be available in a particular area, contact district or regional offices of the Corps.[271] Likewise, programmatic permits "founded on an existing state, local or other Federal agency program [are] designed to avoid duplication with that program"[272] and vary across the country.

The nationwide permit program has been the subject of much discord over the years.[273] Most recently, in September 2006, the U.S. District Court for the District of Columbia issued a long-awaited ruling[274] regarding the 2000/2002 NWP issuance.[275] Members of the permitted community[276] had sued the Corps, asserting that the NWPs as issued exceeded the Corps's authority.[277] The court held that the Corps "adequately explained its reasoning behind its issuance of the NWPs and [general conditions] and clearly acted within its authority."[278]

The Corps recently issued revised NWPs (which it must do every five years).[279] The 2007 issuance includes forty-nine total available NWPs, which comprise forty-three reissued and six new NWPs.[280] The types of activities governed by NWPs vary, but include a variety of minor development, maintenance, and other activities.[281] Corps Headquarters has general information about NWP,[282] and some districts post information on the Internet about particular general permit applications,[283] but many do not. Most NWPs have acreage and linear feet limitations as well as other conditions which should be carefully reviewed, and may require preconstruction notification.[284]

The new 2007 NWPs cover Emergency Repair Activities, Discharges into Ditches and Canals, Pipeline Safety Program Designated Time Sensitive Inspections and Repairs, Commercial Shellfish Aquaculture Activities, Coal Remining Activities, and Underground Coal Mining Activities.[285] The final issuance of the 2007 NWPs stated that they were immediately effective after obtaining a project-specific water quality certification under Clean Water Act Section 401,[286] or, where applicable, Coastal Zone Management certification.[287] During the sixty days after issuance of the new NWPs, every state had the opportunity to issue, deny, or condition generic Section 401 certifications or CZMA concurrences, along with state conditions to the NWPs.[288]

Corps division engineers were allowed to add, after public review and consultation, regional conditions to protect local aquatic ecosystems, such as fens or bottomland hardwoods, or minimize adverse effects on fish or shellfish spawning, wildlife nesting, or other ecologically critical events.[289] Given the contentious nature of the Corps regulatory program and the history of discord associated with the nationwide permit program, it is possible the 2007 permits will be challenged.

2. Individual Permits

On average, approximately five percent of permit actions undertaken annually by the Corps proceed through an individual permit process.[290] If an individual permit is required, the Corps encourages, but does not require, a pre-application consultation.[291] The application itself[292] requires a variety of relevant information, including a complete description of the proposed activity (including necessary drawings, sketches, or plans sufficient for public notice);[293] location, purpose, and need for the proposed activity; scheduling information regarding the proposed activity; the names and addresses of adjoining property owners and the location and dimensions of adjacent structures; and a list of authorizations required by other federal, interstate, or local agencies for the work, including all approvals or denials already made.[294] Section 404 permit applications must also describe the purpose of the discharge, explain the type, composition, and quantity of the material and the method of its transportation and disposal, and provide details about the location of the disposal site.[295] Permit applications may be completed online.[296]

The receiving Corps district office has fifteen days to review a submitted application and determine whether it is complete.[297] Once an application is deemed complete, a public notice including specifics about the applicant and the activity must be issued.[298] Appropriate opportunities to comment on the proposed action must be provided to other federal agencies, including EPA;[299] the U.S. Fish and Wildlife Service (FWS);[300] the National Marine Fisheries Service (NMFS);[301] state wildlife, historic preservation,[302] and environmental agencies;[303] and other federal and state agencies.[304] The Corps must inform the applicant about substantive comments that the agency received and provide an opportunity to supply additional information or supplement the application.[305] The Corps may also require the applicant to submit additional information to address specific issues raised during the public comment period.[306] The applicant must respond to the Corps's request for information within thirty days, unless the applicant requests additional time to respond and the Corps grants the request.[307] If the applicant does not respond to the Corps's request for additional information, the agency will consider the application withdrawn or will make a final decision on the application as is.[308] The Corps may also hold a public hearing on any permit application prior to review unless the agency determines "that the issues raised are insubstantial or there is otherwise no valid interest to be served by a hearing."[309] Public hearings are rare.[310]

Permits are reviewed based on particular criteria. The CWA requires the Corps to evaluate every wetland permit application under Section 404(b)(1) Guidelines that EPA promulgated in consultation with the Corps.[311] These guidelines prohibit the

Corps from issuing a wetland permit if there is a "practicable alternative" to the proposed activity that would have a less adverse impact on the aquatic ecosystem.[312] In addition, the guidelines create a presumption that there are practicable alternatives to discharges of dredged or fill material into wetlands when the proposed activity is not water-dependent.[313]

The 404(b)(1) Guidelines also prohibit the issuance of a permit when the proposed activity causes or contributes to significant degradation of waters of the United States,[314] causes or contributes to a violation of state water quality standards, violates federal toxic pollution standards, jeopardizes endangered species or destroys or adversely modifies their critical habitat, or violates federal marine sanctuary protection requirements.[315] Further, the 404(b)(1) Guidelines form the basis for the mitigation requirements, discussed further in Part II.C.3.[316]

The Corps also undertakes a separate "public interest" review[317] that evaluates probable impacts, including cumulative impacts, of the proposed activity and its use.[318] The required public interest review considers many factors, including conservation, economics, aesthetics, general environmental concerns, wetlands, historic properties, fish and wildlife values, floodplain values, land use, navigation, shore erosion and accretion, recreation, water supply and conservation, water quality, energy needs, safety, food and fiber production, mineral needs, considerations of property ownership, and the needs and welfare of the people.[319] The modern Corps public interest review standard is not whether a proposed activity is in the public interest but whether granting the permit would be "contrary to" the public interest.[320]

A variety of other laws may come into play in any individual Corps permit decision process. These laws include the National Environmental Policy Act (NEPA), the Endangered Species Act (ESA), the National Historic Preservation Act (NHPA), CWA Section 401, and the Coastal Zone Management Act (CZMA).[321]

NEPA requires preparation of an environmental impact statement (EIS) for any "major federal action significantly affecting the quality of the human environment,"[322] and consideration of environmental impacts of proposed actions and their alternatives.[323] Both the Corps and the Council on Environmental Quality (CEQ)[324] have established procedures that the Corps must follow to comply with NEPA when it reviews a wetland permit application.[325]Most Corps permit decisions comply with NEPA through completion of an Environmental Assessment (EA).[326]

The ESA requires that permits do not jeopardize an endangered or threatened species, or destroy or adversely modify designated critical habitat.[327] When the Corps receives a wetland permit application, it complies with the ESA by determining whether the proposed activities meet the Act's requirements.[328] The public notice for each individual permit application will indicate whether the Corps has concluded that the proposal will not affect endangered or threatened species or designated critical habitat.[329] A conclusion that the proposed activity may affect an endangered or threatened species or designated critical habitat will trigger formal consultation procedures[330] with either the Fish and Wildlife Service[331] or the National Marine Fisheries Service,[332] depending on the species.[333] If it is determined that the activity will jeopardize an endangered or threatened species or destroy or adversely affect designated critical habitat, unless reasonable and prudent alternatives can be developed, the Corps must deny the permit.[334] A separate analysis may be triggered if animals protected under the Marine Mammal Protection Act[335] might be impacted by a project.

The National Historic Preservation Act (NHPA)[336] requires federal agencies undertaking or licensing activities that may affect properties listed on the National Register of Historic Places to consider the effect of the project on those properties and to provide the Advisory Council on Historic Preservation (ACHP) an opportunity to comment on the project.[337] Corps NHPA regulations[338] set forth additional permit review procedures for a proposed activity that would involve property listed or eligible for listing on the National Register of Historic Places.[339] If historic properties may be affected by a proposed activity, the Corps must send a notice to the state historic preservation officer (SHPO)[340] or the tribal historic preservation officer (THPO),[341] the ACHP, the regional office of the National Park Service,[342] and other parties for their comments.[343] This is a pure consultation requirement, because the NHPA does not require the Corps to avoid or minimize the effects of a proposed activity on historic properties.[344] The Corps's "public interest" review[345] also allows the addition of permit conditions to minimize or avoid harm to historic properties if deemed necessary to protect the public interest.[346]

Finally, CWA Section 401 provides a mechanism for state certification that proposed activities will not violate various state water quality laws.[347] The Corps cannot issue a permit under Section 404 unless the state issues (or waives its right to issue) a Section 401 certification.[348] Waiver occurs if the state does not act on the Corps's request for certification within sixty days.[349] Likewise, for states with an approved program under the Coastal Zone Management Act,[350] the Corps cannot issue a wetland permit for an activity that affects the coastal zone unless the state certifies that the proposed activity complies with the state's Coastal Zone Management Program.[351]

The Corps's review of a wetland permit application generally proceeds concurrently with the review of relevant federal, state, and local agencies.[352] Accordingly, the Corps may establish joint review procedures with expert agencies on a state or local level.[353] The Corps must fully consider the comments of those agencies regarding their areas of expertise on relevant statutes, regulations, and policies.[354] This consideration of expert agency comments can come into play when the Corps determines whether issuance of the permit is contrary to the public interest.[355] The Corps or other agencies may complete their reviews first.[356] However, the Corps retains full authority to decide whether to issue or deny a permit, or to include specific conditions.[357] Permits are sometimes issued pending final review by other expert agencies.[358]

The district engineer is charged with the final decision on permit applications,[359] which is generally an issuance, often with conditions, or a denial supported by a written statement of findings (SOF).[360] To accept a proffered permit, the applicant must sign the permit to indicate understanding of and intent to comply with conditions included in the permit.[361] The issuance of the permit does not convey any property rights or exclusive privileges to the applicant.[362]

Permits usually authorize that the discharged material can remain indefinitely.[363] Permits also usually require that the permittee start and finish construction work or other work associated with the permitted activity on specific dates.[364] Corps approval for such work will automatically expire on the date specified in the permit unless the permittee requests and receives an extension from the district engineer,[365] which generally must comply with the normal permit issuance procedures.[366] Such extensions are usually granted unless the district engineer determines that an extension would be contrary to the public interest.[367]

On its own or at the request of the permittee or a third party, the Corps has authority to reevaluate a valid permit and consider the circumstances or conditions of any permit.[368] Such a reevaluation may result in a Corps decision to modify, suspend, or revoke the permit as necessary based on considerations of the public interest.[369] In deciding whether to modify, suspend, or revoke a permit, the Corps will consider such factors as (1) the permittee's compliance with the permit, (2) changes in circumstances relating to the permitted activity, and whether the permit conditions are adequate to address those changes; (3) significant objections to the permitted activity that were not considered earlier; (4) changes in the law; and (5) whether modification, suspension, or revocation would adversely affect the permittee's reasonable plans and investments.[370] Such reevaluations are unusual.

In the rare instance that the Corps denies an application for an individual permit,[371] or, more commonly, includes terms and conditions in an individual permit that lead an applicant to decline the permit, the applicant can appeal the Corps's action through an administrative appeal.[372] There are also opportunities for judicial review of agency actions that will be further discussed in a later section of this chapter.

Although the Corps has the lead role,[373] Congress gave EPA an important role throughout the Section 404 permitting process, beyond enacting the Section 404(b)(1) Guidelines discussed earlier.[374] Section 404(c) grants EPA the authority to "veto" Corps decisions to permit discharges of dredged or fill material in a defined area.[375] An EPA veto requires a determination that the proposed discharge "will have an unacceptable adverse effect on municipal water supplies, shellfish beds and fishery areas (including spawning and breeding areas), wildlife, or recreational areas. . . ."[376] This veto power has been rarely exercised.[377] EPA, like other agencies discussed later in this chapter, also has review authority for areas in which it possesses particular expertise.

The Corps is, as discussed earlier, required to consult other agencies as appropriate during the permitting process, and necessary review procedures should be completed in a coordinated manner.[378] The FWS,[379] the NMFS,[380] and the Natural Resources Conservation Service (NRCS) within the Department of Agriculture[381] have less prominent but important advisory and regulatory roles. The FWS and NMFS must be granted the opportunity to comment on all individual and some general Section 404 permits.[382] The NRCS administers the "Swampbuster" program, which is designed to discourage the conversion of wetlands for agricultural purposes.[383] Pursuant to Section 404(q) mandates, the Corps has entered into Memoranda of Agreement with various federal agencies regarding efficient processing of permit applications and allowing for headquarters-level review of particular permit authorizations under certain conditions.[384]

3. Mitigation Requirements

Assuming that the United States has jurisdiction over both a particular wetland or other water[385] and the proposed activity,[386] issuance of a permit would, in most cases, require mitigation to alleviate the damage to the aquatic environment by regulated activities.[387] Called "a central premise of Federal wetland regulatory programs,"[388] mitigation typically includes three key steps: avoidance, minimization, and compensation.[389] Underlying the requirement of mitigation is the attempt to ensure "no net loss" of wetland functions and values,[390] a concept that the George W. Bush Administration has publicly embraced as recently as August 2006.[391] However, because EPA and the Corps believe compensatory mitigation may not be practicable and appropriate in every permit action, this "no net loss" goal is not translated into limits on each permit decision.[392] Yet where practicable and appropriate, compensatory mitigation "should provide, at a minimum, one for one functional replacement (i.e., no net loss of values), with an adequate margin of safety to reflect the expected degree of success associated with the mitigation plan."[393]

Section 404[394] does not expressly require mitigation for every permit granted. Section 404(b)(1),[395] which authorizes EPA to promulgate guidelines (in conjunction with the Corps), to regulate the discharge of dredged or fill material into waters of the United States, has, however, been interpreted to support the modern mitigation framework.[396] Thus EPA, through its Section 404(b)(1) Guidelines,[397] provides the primary regulatory basis for requiring permit applicants to avoid, minimize, and compensate for adverse impacts on waters of the United States.[398] The Corps has a separate mitigation regulation that applies to permits that it processes, including CWA Section 404 as well as Rivers and Harbors Act of 1899 Section 10.[399]

Day-to-day implementation of mitigation requirements is directed through guidance documents.[400] The most important of these current guidance documents is a 1990 Memorandum of Agreement between EPA and the Corps entitled *Concerning the Determination of Mitigation Under the Clean Water Act Section 404(b)(1) Guidelines*. New mitigation regulations, however, are currently in the drafting and review stage.[401]

Mitigation is supposed to proceed in the sequence described earlier: avoid, minimize, and compensate. The first step, avoidance, involves searching for an alternative to the discharge.[402] In the case of an individual permit, this step is often coupled with the Section 404(b)(1) Guidelines requirement that permit applicants demonstrate there is no "practicable alternative to the proposed discharge which would have less adverse impact on the aquatic ecosystem."[403] The second step is minimization, whereby a permit applicant must take appropriate and practicable steps to minimize unavoidable impacts.[404] As described in the Section 404(b)(1) Guidelines, minimization can occur through a variety of means, including: location choice for the discharge (such as using a space that is confined or has been previously used);[405] actions that affect the discharged material itself[406] or control the material after discharge (such as using cover vegetation to prevent erosion or using lined containment areas to prevent leaching);[407]

actions that affect the method of dispersion (such as silt screens)[408] or employ technology to limit impacts (such as mats under heavy equipment to reduce wetland surface compaction and rutting);[409] or actions that limit impacts to plant and animal populations (such as timing discharges to avoid spawning, migration, or nesting seasons).[410]

The last step of the mitigation sequence, compensation, is undertaken only if impacts cannot be avoided and minimized.[411] Compensatory mitigation involves site-specific efforts designed to restore, enhance, create, or preserve wetland functions. Recent Corps guidance adopts a watershed approach to mitigation, which focuses on entire water systems and their constituent parts rather than just the specific site at issue.[412] Increased focus on watersheds is found in the new proposed regulations.[413]

Increased focus on watersheds is found in the new proposed regulations.

Types of compensation vary.[414] Restoration may include reestablishing former wetlands or rehabilitating degraded wetlands or both.[415] Enhancement requires improving the functional value (such as by replanting native plant species or altering hydrology) of a degraded wetland.[416] Restoration differs from enhancement because enhancement always involves a site that still holds some wetland functions. Creation requires wetland construction, by excavating and using berms and dikes, in an upland area where no wetland previously existed. It is considered an "uncertain" practice[417] and thus is less preferable than restoration and enhancement.[418] Preservation, allowed only in "exceptional circumstances,"[419] requires land-use restrictions, such as conservation easements, on a wetland site or title transfer to the government or private conservation entity such as a land trust that is dedicated to protecting the area. Disfavored because it yields a net loss of wetland functions, preservation may be allowed for highly functional areas or rare wetland types threatened with development.[420]

The location of compensatory mitigation can also vary.[421] On-site, rather than off-site, compensatory mitigation is generally preferred.[422] On-site compensatory mitigation involves a project in an area "adjacent or contiguous to the discharge site."[423] Off-site compensatory mitigation, preferably in proximity to the discharge, may be allowed if on-site compensatory mitigation is impracticable or off-site compensatory mitigation "provides more watershed benefit than on-site mitigation, e.g., is of greater ecological importance to the region of impact."[424] A project's likelihood of success, its ecological sustainability, the practicability of long-term monitoring and maintenance, and relative costs of compensatory mitigation alternatives are taken into account in approving location.[425]

The approach to functions in compensatory mitigation can vary as well.[426] In-kind, rather than out-of-kind, compensatory mitigation is generally preferred.[427] In-kind compensatory mitigation replaces the functions and values lost as a result of the proposed project for which a permit is sought.[428] Out-of-kind compensation may be "appropriate when it is practicable and provides more environmental or watershed benefit than in-kind compensation (e.g., of greater ecological importance to the region of impact)."[429] In general, the Corps prefers that the construction of mitigation projects proceed concurrently with authorized impacts to wetlands. In this way, temporal functional losses can be minimized and compliance with compensatory mitigation conditions can be better monitored.[430]

Mitigation banks may provide compensatory mitigation options for some permit applicants.[431] A mitigation bank is "a site where wetlands and/or other aquatic resources are restored, created, enhanced, or in exceptional circumstances, preserved expressly for the purpose of providing compensatory mitigation in advance of authorized impacts to similar resources."[432] Mitigation bank sponsors can be public or private[433] and either may implement mitigation activities to offset wetland impacts caused by their own development projects or may provide mitigation credits to others.[434] Because banks often preexist and are thus functioning in advance of project impacts,[435] credits obtained from the bank can reduce the temporal loss of wetland functions associated with requirements for future mitigation. Functioning wetlands in banks also allow permit applicants to reduce the time that the Corps and resource agencies devote to reviewing proposed (and speculative) compensatory mitigation proposals.[436] When mitigation credits are for sale, many factors weigh into the price.[437]

To create a mitigation banking instrument,[438] a Mitigation Bank Review Team (MBRT) made up of representatives from the Corps, the EPA, the FWS, the NMFS, the NRCS, and state, tribal, and local regulatory and resource agencies works together and "strive(s) to obtain consensus on its actions."[439] Each bank's service area is geographically restricted to an area that "can reasonably be expected to provide appropriate compensation" for wetland impacts,[440] such as a county or a watershed.[441] Management of a mitigation bank during its operational life, and thereafter, is left to a sponsor,[442] and the banking instrument specifies protections, such as conservation easements and restrictive deeds, intended to secure the replaced functions and values over the long term[443] as well as formal financial assurances.[444]

Another compensatory mitigation option is in-lieu fees.[445] In addition to banks, in-lieu fees may be used to provide "funds to an in-lieu-fee sponsor instead of either completing project-specific mitigation."[446] Guidance issued in 2000 by multiple agencies states that such agreements are to be "consistent with the Banking Guidance," which suggests that the in-lieu-fee arrangement should produce advance mitigation, as mitigation banks are required to do. The proposed new mitigation regulations would limit in-lieu-fee opportunities.[447]

Streamlined general permits often require mitigation.[448] Even though the permits are streamlined, sequencing is required.[449] Appropriate compensatory mitigation for nationwide permits "at a minimum one-for-one ratio will be required for all wetland losses that exceed 1/10 acre and require preconstruction notification."[450] Such mitigation may require buffers or other approaches best for the resource[451] and can be accomplished through mitigation banks and in-lieu-fee programs if deemed appropriate by the District Engineer.[452] Compensatory mitigation is intended only to reduce impacts overall and may not "be used to increase the acreage losses allowed by the acreage limits" of the general permits.[453]

In light of criticism[454] and debate in recent years, various federal agencies came together in 2002 to form a National Wetlands Mitigation Action Plan[455] to address mitigation issues.[456] This Plan included the development of various guidance documents and other concrete action items to assist in better implementation of mitigation goals.[457] Progress on many aspects of the National Wetlands Mitigation Action Plan stalled, however, when Congress, in the National Defense Authorization Act for 2004,[458] called on the Corps to promulgate new mitigation regulations. Although the legislation required the new regulations to be finalized by November 2005, the Corps and the EPA did not issue a proposed rule until March 2006. This proposal, entitled *Compensatory Mitigation for Losses of Aquatic Resources,*[459] would provide a revised approach to governing compensatory mitigation for authorized impacts to wetlands, streams, and other waters.[460] After a thirty-day extension of the comment period,[461] hundreds of comments were submitted regarding the regulation.[462] A final rule revising mitigation requirements was expected in late 2007 but was not issued. It is unclear whether new mitigation regulations will be issued in the near future.[463]

Failure to comply with compensatory mitigation required as a condition of a Section 404 permit may result in an enforcement action[464] or revocation of the permit.[465] In the case of a mitigation bank, the bank's sponsor and not the permittee will likely be held responsible for any failures.[466]

D. Appeals and Enforcement

Applicants dissatisfied with a Corps district office decision have various options to challenge the result. Applicants may bring an administrative appeal, mount a substantive challenge in federal court, or bring a takings claim.

1. Administrative Appeals

A regulatory permit applicant unhappy with a Corps district decision on either a permit application or a jurisdictional determination may appeal[467] to one of eight regional Corps offices.[468] In some circumstances, such an appeal may be a necessary prerequisite to a legal challenge in federal court.[469] Following required written notification by the Corps,[470] the permit applicant has sixty days to submit an appeal.[471] The administrative appeal process is informal, and the Corps must make a final decision on the appeal within ninety days after receiving a complete request for appeal from the permit applicant.[472] Although Corps regulations allow permit applicants to administratively appeal individual permit denials or declined permits, the regulations do not allow third parties to administratively appeal any Corps permit decisions.[473]

Despite some advantages,[474] one obvious disadvantage of the Corps's model of decentralized decision making is potential inconsistencies.[475] Affected parties[476] have thus been provided with this opportunity to appeal "approved jurisdictional determinations (JDs), permit applications denied with prejudice, and declined permits"[477] to a higher level within the Corps. A flow chart explaining the administrative appeals process is available on the Corps's website.[478] Strict timing and paperwork requirements apply to the administrative appeals process.[479]

2. Judicial Challenges

A dissatisfied permit applicant also may bring a suit in federal court challenging a final substantive decision of the Corps or EPA, provided that certain requirements are met.[480] Final Corps decisions are defined as "the initial decision to issue or deny a permit," unless the applicant submits an accepted request for appeal.[481] For cases against the Corps or EPA, typical litigative requirements of standing, exhaustion of administrative remedies, ripeness, and mootness apply to such challenges.[482] The CWA does not provide a specific statute of limitations, but some courts have applied the six-year general statute of limitations for civil actions commenced against the United States.[483] Agency decisions challenged by permit applicants will be set aside only if they are found to be "arbitrary, capricious, an abuse of discretion, or otherwise not in accordance with law."[484]

3. Enforcement

For enforcement cases[485] against violators, the government and citizens have a number of options. The Corps and EPA have the authority to issue either cease and desist letters or administrative orders to require compliance with Section 404 program requirements.[486] Likewise, either agency may assess administrative penalties.[487] With the assistance of the Department of Justice (DOJ), the agencies are authorized to commence civil actions for injunctive relief, including restoration of damaged wetlands, and/or civil penalties.[488] The CWA also authorizes the Corps[489] and EPA[490] to commence civil actions to enforce the requirements of the Section 404 program in certain circumstances with the assistance of the DOJ and its U.S. Attorneys across the country.[491] The DOJ, including its U.S. Attorneys, is responsible for prosecuting persons who engage in activities prohibited and made criminal by Section 309(c).[492] Finally, Section 505 of the CWA provides for citizen suits.[493] Citizen suits[494] may be brought (1) against "any person . . . who is alleged to be in violation of . . . an effluent standard or limitation under [the CWA],"[495] and (2) against EPA or the Corps alleging that the agency has failed to perform a nondiscretionary act or duty.[496]

4. Takings

Finally, sometimes a claim may be brought asserting that a Corps or EPA decision so restricts the use of private property that the agency action amounts to a "taking" in violation of the Fifth Amendment to the Constitution of the United States.[497] Because most of the nation's wetlands are in private ownership and because the Section 404 program can impose significant costs on landowners and developers, wetland protection measures often collide with the rights and economic expectations of property owners.[498] Wetland cases have figured prominently in the development of takings jurisprudence in federal courts.[499]

III. Emerging and Unresolved Issues

Why are wetlands such a controversial topic? Opinions vary. Some believe that the program at its beginnings was flawed due to congressional imprecision in enacting Section 404, perhaps exacerbated by agency overreaching.[500] Others believe that the high percentage of wetlands held as private property contributes to the discord.[501] Still others believe that the nature of the resource makes it difficult to manage[502] or that there is insufficient respect for these irreplaceable resources.[503] Regardless of the reason, it is certain that thirty-five years after the enactment of what we now call the Clean Water Act, wetland regulation is in a state of surprising flux.

Some current areas of conflict include geographic jurisdiction, activity jurisdiction, streamlined permitting and other permitting matters, mitigation, and implementing the goal of "no net loss." Furthermore, emerging issues such as the national climate change debate offer further challenges with respect to coastal wetland regulation. Each of these issues will be discussed briefly here.

A. Geographic Jurisdiction

As discussed earlier,[504] the recent U.S. Supreme Court decision in *Rapanos v. United States*[505] has left the ongoing debate about the geographic jurisdiction of the Section 404 program adrift. The 2007 guidance has not alleviated—and in fact has contributed to—the confusion.[506] Revised regulations do not seem imminent.[507] One potential response to the *Rapanos* litigation is a legislative clarification of the scope of "waters of the United States" under the Clean Water Act.[508] In other words, Congress could amend the Clean Water Act to explicitly authorize regulation of those waters. Shortly after the Court issued its opinions in the *Rapanos* litigation, several environmental groups began campaigning heavily for passage of the Clean Water Authority Restoration Act,[509] which would redefine "waters of the United States" using the long-standing regulatory definition[510] as

> all waters subject to the ebb and flow of the tide, the territorial seas, and all interstate and intrastate waters and their tributaries, including lakes, rivers, streams (including intermittent streams), mudflats, sandflats, wetlands, sloughs, prairie potholes, wet meadows, playa lakes, natural ponds, and all impoundments of the foregoing, to the fullest extent that these waters, or activities affecting these waters, are subject to the legislative power of Congress under the Constitution.[511]

Such an approach has met with stiff resistance.[512] The future of geographic jurisdiction thus remains murky.

B. Activity Jurisdiction

In light of the 2007 Tulloch II decision,[513] the scope of activities subject to Section 404 jurisdiction is once again unclear. This decision reopens the debate about regulation of mechanized earthmoving equipment and other activities in jurisdictional waters, in terms of what is defined as dredged material and what discharge involves.[514] The difference between incidental fallback, which cannot be regulated, and other regulable redeposits[515] will be the subject of much debate.

C. Streamlined Permits

A perpetual controversy surrounds the Section 404(e)[516] authorized general permits, particularly the Nationwide General Permits.[517] The dispute as to the latest round of these permits is heating up,[518] and litigation from stakeholders on either side may well ensue.

D. Mitigation

New mitigation regulations may be issued shortly.[519] The debate on mitigation has been heated through the years[520] and promises to be even more controversial in the event of a new regulatory framework.

E. Climate Change

Global climate change, also known as global warming,[521] presents particular challenges to the nation's coastal wetlands. As the United Nations–sanctioned report recently concluded, global warming is a serious problem.[522] The 2003 Pew Commission likewise report indicates that

> scientists expect . . . climate change will result [in] . . . serious, if not catastrophic, damage to some ecosystems. Important coastal and ocean habitats, including coral reefs, coastal wetlands, estuaries, and mangrove forests will be particularly vulnerable to the effects of climate change. These systems are essential nurseries for commercial fisheries and support tourism and recreation.[523]

Like other environmental treasures, wetlands are seriously endangered by the changing climate.[524] Coastal wetlands are certain to be negatively impacted by global climate change,[525] most imminently through rising sea levels.[526] Whether regulatory or legislative fixes focus on (or even indirectly impact) the wetlands regulatory program is yet to be seen.

IV. Conclusion

The regulation of coastal wetlands, like the regulation of other wetlands nationwide, continues to be a controversial area of law.[527] Some want to undertake what they consider to be economically beneficial activities in these areas with minimal oversight, while others want to preserve these areas and preclude many human activities. Still others are in between.[528] The regulators are charged with striking a balance.

In the midst of this debate, our nation's oceans and coasts are in trouble,[529] and in 2003 national commissions pointed to measures tied up with the Corps regulatory program as recommendations for improvement.[530] Although success in designing a functional ocean and coastal regulatory program may depend on including protections for these vital resources, the reality is that any modifications to the Corps regulatory program implementing Section 10 of the Rivers and Harbors Act of 1899 and Section 404 of the Clean Water Act will be politically charged and subject to spirited debate. Yet the threats facing our coastal wetlands are too important to shy away from attempting to increase protections in a way that the regulated community (and the general public) can support.

Notes

1. *See* T.E. DAHL, U.S. FISH & WILDLIFE SERV., STATUS AND TRENDS OF WETLANDS IN THE CONTERMINOUS UNITED STATES 1998 TO 2004 (2005) 48, *available at* http://wetlandsfws

.er.usgs.gov/status_trends/national_reports/trends_2005_report.pdf ("vegetated components of the estuarine and marine systems are among the most biologically productive aquatic ecosystems in the world. Wetlands along the nation's coastline have provided valuable resources and supported large sections of the nation's economy. Wetlands have also provided opportunities for recreation and supported commercially valuable fish and crustacean populations. Composition of marine and estuarine intertidal wetlands, fish and shellfish species accounted for about 75 percent of the total annual seafood harvest in the United States. In the Gulf of Mexico, coastal waters attracted millions of sport fishermen and beach users as tourism in the Gulf coast states contributed over $20 billion to the nation's economy. The importance of both estuarine and freshwater wetlands to fish populations, and sport and commercial fishing cannot be overemphasized. This link between wetlands and aquatic species includes ecological processes that are important for maintaining food webs, land and water interactions, and environmental quality. Wetland loss and its effect on fish populations are among the many issues forcing a re-evaluation of activities on the landscape." *Id.*, citations omitted.).

2. *See* NatureServe, Biodiversity Values of Geographically Isolated Wetlands in the United States (2005), *available at* http://www.natureserve.org/publications/isolated wetlands.jsp. For locations of wetlands of international importance throughout the world, see *The Ramsar Convention on Wetlands*, www.ramsar.org, and Wetlands International, *Ramsar Sites Information Service*, http://www.wetlands.org/RSDB/default.htm.

3. U.S. Environmental Prot. Agency, *Wetlands Definitions*, http://www.epa.gov/owow/ wetlands/what/definitions.html.

4. *See generally* Nat'l Acad. of Sciences, Nat'l Research Council, Wetlands: Characteristics and Boundaries (1995), *available at* http://www.nap.edu/books/0309051347/ html/index.html; U.S. Army Corps of Eng'rs, *Technical and Biological Information*, *available at* http://www.usace.army.mil/inet/functions/cw/cecwo/reg/techbio.htm; U.S. Envtl. Prot. Agency, *Functions and Values*, *available at* http://www.epa.gov/owow/wetlands/ functions.html 07. *See also* Brief of Ecological Society of America, Society of Wetland Scientists, American Society of Limnology and Oceanography, and Estuarine Research Federation As *Amici Curiae* in Support of Respondents, Rapanos v. United States, Carabell v. U.S. Army Corps of Eng'rs, 126 S. Ct. 2208 (2006) (Nos. 04-1034, 04-1384), Supreme Court of the United States, Jan. 13, 2006, *available at* http://www.eswr.com/1105/rapanos/ rapamicesa.pdf.

5. Donald R. Cahoon, U.S. Geological Services, *Response of Coastal Ecosystems to Sea-Level Rise: Assessing Wetland Elevation Changes, Potential for Submergence, and Management Options* (2004), *available at* http://www.nrel.colostate.edu/projects/brd_global_ change/proj_43_wetland_elev.html.

6. Dahl, *supra* note 1, at 48–49. Note that generally, the George W. Bush Administration's data show that other wetland resources are increasing. *Id.* at 16. *See also* Pew Oceans Comm'n, America's Living Oceans: Charting a Course for Sea Change (2003), *available at* http://www.pewtrusts.com/pdf/env_pew_oceans_final_report.pdf ("Coastal development and associated sprawl destroy and endanger coastal wetlands and estuaries that serve as nurseries for many valuable fishery species. More than 20,000 acres of these sensitive habitats disappear each year." *Id.* at vi.).

7. Lewis M. Cowardin et al., Classification of Wetlands and Deepwater Habitats of the United States 1-2 (U.S. Fish & Wildlife Serv. 1979)|*available at* http://www.fws .gov/nwi/Pubs_Reports/Class_Manual/class_titlepg.htm.

8. 40 C.F.R. 230.3(t) (2006); 33 C.F.R. 328.3 (2006). For additional official definitions of wetlands, *see* Commission on Geosciences, Environment and Resources, Nat'l Research Council, Toward a Coordinated Spatial Data Infrastructure for the Nation 77 (Nat'l Academies Press 1993), *available at* http://www.nap.edu/openbook/ 0309048990/html/77.html.

9. *See generally* Jon Kusler, Ass'n of State Wetland Managers, A Guide for Local Governments: Wetlands and Watershed Management (2003), *available at* http:// www.aswm.org/propub/pubs/aswm/wetlandswatershed.pdf; Kim Diana Connolly, *Looking to Local Law: Can Local Ordinances Help Protect Isolated Wetlands?* 27 Nat'l

WETLANDS NEWSLETTER 21 (May–June 2005); John R. Nolon, *In Praise of Parochialism: The Advent of Local Environmental Law*, 26 HARV. ENVTL. L. REV. 365 (2002).

10. *See* Association of State Wetlands Managers, *State Wetland Programs*, *available at* http://aswm.org/swp/statemainpage9.htm.

11. *See generally* KIM DIANA CONNOLLY, STEPHEN M. JOHNSON & DOUGLAS R. WILLIAMS, WETLANDS LAW AND POLICY: UNDERSTANDING SECTION 404 (Am. Bar Ass'n, 2005). *See also* WILLIAM L. WANT, LAW OF WETLANDS REGULATION (Westlaw 1989 and Supp. 2006); Environmental Law Institute, *Wetlands Program*, *available at* http://www2.eli.org/research/wetlands.htm.

12. *See* CONNOLLY ET AL., *supra* note 11, at 2–7.

13. Pub. L. No. 92-500, 86 Stat. 816 (1972), *as codified in* 33 U.S.C. §§ 1251–1387 (2000).

14. The Federal Water Pollution Control Act (FWPCA) is commonly referred to as the Clean Water Act following the 1977 amendments to the FWPCA. Pub. L. No. 95-217, 91 Stat. 1566 (1977) ("SEC. 518. This Act may be cited as the 'Federal Water Pollution Control Act' commonly referred to as the Clean Water Act.").

15. *See* U.S. Army Corps of Eng'rs, *Regulatory Program Overview*, *available at* http://www.usace.army.mil/cw/cecwo/reg/oceover.htm; U.S. Environmental Prot. Agency, *Section 404 of Clean Water Act: Program Questions and Overview*, *available at* http://www.epa.gov/owow/wetlands/facts/fact12.html. *See also infra* Section II.B.

16. *See infra* Section II.A.

17. Many scholars have pointed out the failures of the permitting process. *See, e.g.*, Michael C. Blumm & D. Bernard Zaleha, *Federal Wetlands Protection Under the Clean Water Act: Regulatory Ambivalence, Intergovernmental Tension, and a Call for Reform*, 60 U. COLO. L. REV. 695 (1989); Oliver A. Houck, *Hard Choices: The Analysis of Alternatives Under Section 404 of the Clean Water Act and Similar Environmental Laws*, 60 U. COLO. L. REV. 773 (1989); Hope Babcock, *Federal Wetlands Regulatory Policy: Up to Its Ears in Alligators*, 8 PACE ENVTL. L. REV. 307 (1991); and Alyson C. Flournoy, *Section 404 at Thirty-Something: A Program in Search of a Policy*, 55 ALA. L. REV. 607 (2004).

18. *See, e.g.*, the Coastal Wetlands Planning, Protection, and Restoration Act, 104 Stat. 4779, Title III of Pub. L. 101-646, 16 U.S.C. §§ 3951–56 (2000), which established the National Coastal Wetlands Conservation Grant Program to acquire, restore, and enhance wetlands of coastal states and the Trust Territories. *See also* North American Wetlands Conservation Act, 103 Stat. 1968; Pub. L. 101-233, 16 U.S.C. §§ 4401–12 (2000), which provides funding and administrative direction for implementation of the North American Waterfowl Management Plan and a Tripartite Agreement on wetlands between Canada, the U.S., and Mexico.

19. Convention on Wetlands of International Importance Especially as Waterfowl Habitat, *opened for signature* Feb. 2, 1971, T.I.A.S. No. 1084, 996 U.N.T.S. 245 (amended 1982 & 1987).

20. *See generally The Ramsar Convention on Wetlands*, www.ramsar.org; *United States National Ramsar Committee*, http://www.ramsarcommittee.us/index.asp. *See also* Royal C. Gardner and Kim Diana Connolly, *The Ramsar Convention on Wetlands: The Benefits of International Designation Within the United States*, 37 ENVTL L. REP. 10089 (Feb. 2007).

21. The website for the U.S. Army Corps of Engineers Regulatory Program can be found at http://www.usace.army.mil/inet/functions/cw/cecwo/reg/.

22. *See infra* notes 373–377 and accompanying text.

23. Interpretation of "navigable waters" has been and remains the subject of serious debate. *See infra* Section II.B.2.

24. 33 U.S.C. § 1344(h)(2)(A); *see also* 33 C.F.R. § 323.5. States cannot obtain authority to issue permits for discharges of dredged or fill material into "waters which are presently used, or are susceptible to use in their natural condition or by reasonable improvement as a means to transport interstate or foreign commerce shoreward to their ordinary high water mark, including all waters which are subject to the ebb and flow of the tide shoreward to

their mean high water mark, or mean higher high water mark on the west coast, including wetlands adjacent thereto." 33 U.S.C. § 1344(g)(1); 33 C.F.R. § 323.5.

25. *See* 59 Fed. Reg. 9933 (1994) (final approval of New Jersey's program); 49 Fed. Reg. 38,947 (1984) (final approval of Michigan's program).

26. *See* Environmental Protection Agency, the U.S. Army Corps of Eng'rs, and the U.S. Departments of Agriculture, Commerce, Interior, and Transportation, *National Wetlands Mitigation Action Plan* (Dec. 24, 2002), *available at* http://www.mitigationactionplan .gov/map1226withsign.pdf. *See also* U.S. Army Corps of Engineers, Regulatory Guidance Letter (RGL) 02-02, *Guidance on Compensatory Mitigation Projects for Aquatic Resource Impacts Under the Corps Regulatory Program Pursuant to Section 404 of the Clean Water Act and Section 10 of the Rivers and Harbors Act of 1899*, at 1 (Dec. 24, 2002), *available at* http://www.usace.army.mil/inet/functions/cw/cecwo/reg/RGL2-02.pdf.

27. *See* The White House, *Fact Sheet: President Announces Wetlands Initiative on Earth Day* (Apr. 22, 2004), *available at* http://www.whitehouse.gov/news/releases/2004/04/20040 -4221.html (setting forth information about President George W. Bush's announcement that his administration was "moving beyond a policy of 'no net loss' of wetlands to have an overall increase of wetlands in America each year."). *See also Norton and Johanns Commend Gains in U.S. Wetlands*, Southwest Farm Press, May 9, 2006, *available at* http://southwestfarmpress.com/news/06-05-00-norton-johanns-wetlands/ ("The net gain was achieved because increases in shallow-pond-type wetlands offset the continued, but smaller, losses in swamp and marshland type wetlands. This report shows a loss of 523,500 acres of swamp and marsh wetlands and a gain of 715,300 acres of shallow-water wetlands. . . . 'In 2004 President Bush directed that the nation move beyond the "no net-loss" of wetlands in America to having an overall increase of wetlands over the next five years. We are certainly on the way to meeting that goal.'") *Cf.* Julie Sibbing, Nat'l Wildlife Fed'n, *Nowhere Near No Net Loss*, *available at* http://www.nwf.org/ wildlife/pdfs/Nowhere NearNoNetLoss.pdf.

28. A partial list of the parties who weighed in on the most recent U.S. Supreme Court decision on wetlands in *Rapanos v. United States*, 547 U.S. ___ (2006), 126 S. Ct. 2208 (2006), demonstrates the great interest in this topic. Those submitting amicus curiae briefs in support of the government's position included Macomb County; New York, Michigan, Arizona, Arkansas, California, Connecticut, Delaware, Florida, Hawaii, Illinois, Iowa, Kentucky, Louisiana, Maine, Maryland, Massachusetts, Minnesota, Mississippi, Missouri, Montana, New Hampshire, New Jersey, New Mexico, North Carolina, Ohio, Oklahoma, Oregon, Rhode Island, South Carolina, Tennessee, Vermont, Washington, and Wisconsin; the District of Columbia, the Pennsylvania Dep't of Envtl Prot., and the International Ass'n of Fish & Wildlife Agencies; Chesapeake Bay Foundation; New York City; Ecological Society of Am., Society of Wetland Scientists, American Society of Limnology and Oceanography, and Estuarine Research Fed'n; National Mitigation Banking Ass'n; Members of Congress (Reps. John D. Dingell [D-Mich.], John Conyers, Jr. [D-Mich.], Charles B. Rangel [D-N.Y.], Robert F. Drinan, Gary W. Hart, Kenneth W. Hechler, Charles McC. Mathias, Jr., Paul N. McCloskey, Jr., and Richard Schultz Schweiker; American Rivers, Environmental Defense, National Audubon Soc'y, NRDC, Physicians for Soc. Responsibility, Sierra Club, Tip of the Mitt Watershed Council, and Waterkeeper Alliance; Environmental Law Inst.; American Planning Ass'n; Former EPA administrators (Carol Browner, William K. Reilly, Douglas Costle, Russell Train); Ducks Unlimited, NWF, American Fisheries Society, American Sportfishing Ass'n, Bass Pro Shops, Boone & Crocket Club, Izaak Walton League of Am., Michigan United Conservation Clubs, The Orvis Co., Pheasants Forever, Theodore Roosevelt Conservation Partnership, Trout Unlimited, Wildlife Management Inst., and The Wildlife Soc'y; Western Org. of Res. Councils, Idaho Rural Council, Northern Plains Res. Council, Powder River Basin Council, Dakota Res. Council, Oregon Rural Action, Western Colo. Congress, Community Ass'n for Restoration of the Env't, Concerned Citizens for Clean Water, Rios Bravos, New Mexico Acequia Ass'n, Headwaters, Oregon Natural Res. Council, Snake Valley Citizens'

Alliance, Northern Cal. River Watch, Arizona Wildlife Fed'n, Walker Lake Working Group, Wyoming Outdoor Council, Iowa Farmers Union, and Mineral County; Scientists Jared Diamond, Paul Ehrlich, Harold Mooney, Gordon Orians, Stuart Pimm, Sandra Postel, Peter Raven, John Terborgh, David Wilcove, and Edward O. Wilson; Ass'n of State Wetland Managers, Ass'n of State Floodplain Managers, and New England Interstate Water Pollution Control Comm'n; Association of State and Interstate Water Pollution Control Adm'rs; Calvin Johnson. Those submitting briefs in support of the petitioners' positions included Claremont Inst., Center for Constitutional Jurisprudence; NationalAss'n of Home Builders; National Fed'n of Indep. Bus. Legal Found.; National Stone, Sand and Gravel Ass'n, American Rd. and Transp. Builders Ass'n, City of Victorville, Calif., and Nationwide Pub. Projects Coal.; CropLife Am., National Cattlemen's Beef Ass'n, National Corn Growers Ass'n, National Council of Farmer Coops., National Pork Producers Council, Dairy Producers of New Mexico, Kansas Livestock Ass'n, and Texas Cattle Feeders Ass'n; American Farm Bureau Fed'n; International Council of Shopping Ctrs., National Multi Housing Council, National Ass'n of Indus. and Office Props., Real Estate Roundtable, Associated Gen. Contractors of Am., American Resort Dev. Ass'n, and National Ass'n of Real Estate Inv. Trusts; Foundation for Envtl. and Econ. Progress, National Ass'n of Realtors, Utility Water Act Group, and U.S. Chamber of Commerce; Home Builders Ass'n of Cent. Ariz.; American Petroleum Inst.; Alaska, Utah, Western Urban Water Coal., National Water Res. Ass'n, Association of Cal. Water Agencies, Central Ariz. Water Conservation Dist., State Water Contractors, Metropolitan Water Dist. of S. Cal., Westlands Water Dist., San Diego County Water Auth., and California Farm Bureau Fed'n; Cato Inst., New England Legal Found. and Charles Johnson, Mountain States Legal Found., Washington Legal Found., Allied Educ. Found., Laurence A. Peterson, and Edmond C. Packee, Jr.; Mackinac Ctr, for Public Policy; National Ass'n of Waterfront Employers; Western Coal. of Arid States; Attainable Housing Alliance; Pulte Homes, Centex Homes, Hovnanian Enter., KB Home, Lennar Corp., and M.D.C. Holdings Inc.; Rep. John Duncan (R-Tenn.). *See* Endangered Species and Wetlands Report, *Rapanos/Carabell page*, *available at* http://www.eswr.com/1105/rapanos/ for copies of various briefs.

29. *See, e.g.,* Flournoy, *Section 404 at Thirty-Something, supra* note 17; Gregory T. Broderick, *From Migratory Birds to Migratory Molecules: The Continuing Battle over the Scope of Federal Jurisdiction Under the Clean Water Act*, 2005, 30 COLUM. J. ENVTL. L. 473 (2005); Bradford C. Mank, *The Murky Future of the Clean Water Act After SWANCC: Using a Hydrological Connection Approach to Saving the Clean Water Act*, 30 ECOLOGY L.Q. 811 (2003); Michael J. Gerhardt, *On Revolution and Wetland Regulations*, 90 GEO. L.J. 2143 (2002); Anjali Kharod, *Wetlands Regulatory Morass: The Missing Tulloch Rule*, 15 VILL. ENVTL. L.J. 67 (2004).

30. According to its FY2008 Budget Documentation, the Corps' Regulatory Program has approximately 1200 regulatory staff (including biologists, engineers, archaeologists, sociologists, etc.) in eight division and thirty-eight district offices nationwide. These staff provide approximately 100,000 written authorizations and more than 100,000 jurisdictional determinations (JDs) annually, and are involved annually in approximately 4000 unauthorized activities (enforcement cases), 7000 permit compliance inspections, and 60 appeals (involving denied or conditioned permits or JDs). E-mail from Russell L. Kaiser, U.S. Army Corps of Eng'rs, "RE: Help with More Data (UNCLASSIFIED)" (Mar. 9, 2007).

31. Elevations are pursuant to 33 U.S.C. § 1344(q) (2000). For an example of a Memorandum of Agreement implementing this subsection, see Clean Water Act Section 404(q) Memorandum of Agreement Between the Environmental Protection Agency and the Department of the Army (Aug. 11, 1992), *available at* http://www.usace.army.mil/inet/functions/cw/cecwo/reg/epa404q.htm.

32. *See infra* notes 365–69 and accompanying text.

33. 33 U.S.C. § 1341 (2000). *See generally* U.S. Envtl. Prot. Agency, *Water Quality and 401 Certification*, *available at* http://www.epa.gov/owow/wetlands/waterquality/.

34. *See* U.S. Dep't of Commerce, National Oceanic and Atmospheric Administration, Ocean and Coastal Res. Management, *Federal Consistency Resources, available at* http://coastalmanagement.noaa.gov/consistency/resources.html.

35. 16 U.S.C. §§ 1451–65 (2000). For general information on coastal regulation, see U.S. Dep't of Commerce, Nat'l Oceanic and Atmospheric Administration, Ocean and Coastal Res. Management, *Who We Are, available at* http://coastalmanagement.noaa.gov/.

36. 33 C.F.R. § 325.3 (2006) (directing public notices be sent "to the U.S. Senators and Representatives for the area where the work is to be performed, the field representative of the Secretary of the Interior, the Regional Director of the Fish and Wildlife Service, the Regional Director of the National Park Service, the Regional Administrator of the Environmental Protection Agency (EPA), the Regional Director of the National Marine Fisheries Service of the National Oceanic and Atmospheric Administration (NOAA), the head of the state agency responsible for fish and wildlife resources, the State Historic Preservation Officer, and the District Commander, U.S. Coast Guard.").

37. U.S. Army Corps of Eng'rs, *Civil Works, available at* http://www.usace.army.mil/cw/index.html. *See also* Nicole T. Carter & Betsy A. Cody, Congressional Research Service, *The Civil Works Program of the Army Corps of Engineers: A Primer, available at* http://www.fas.org/sgp/crs/natsec/RS20866.pdf. Although Corps Civil Works activities do not require formal regulatory program permits, its own regulations state that the Corps must apply the guidelines and substantive requirements of the Clean Water Act and other environmental laws to Corps activities. 33 C.F.R. pt. 335.

38. The Corps' general website specifies its role in "[p]lanning, designing, building and operating water resources and other civil works projects (Navigation, Flood Control, Environmental Protection, Disaster Response, etc.)," U.S. Army Corps of Eng'rs, *Who We Are, available at* http://www.usace.army.mil/who/. *See also* W. Christian Hoyer, *Corps of Engineers Dredge and Fill Jurisdiction: Buttressing a Citadel Under Siege*, 26 U. FLA. L. REV. 19, 20 (1973).

39. *See* Garrett Power, *The Fox in the Chicken Coop: The Regulatory Program of the U.S. Army Corps of Engineers*, 63 VA. L. REV. 503, 504 (1977).

40. *See* Nicole T. Carter, Congressional Research Service, *"Corps of Engineers Reform" in WRDA 2005, available at* http://www.ncseonline.org/NLE/CRSreports/05aug/RS22129.pdf ("Support for changing the Corps' practices gained momentum in 2000 in the wake of a series of critical articles in the Washington Post, whistleblower allegations, and ensuing investigations. Many of the supporters of these changes, primarily environmental groups, sought to modify Corps project planning (e.g., by changing the benefit-cost analysis and consideration of environmental impacts and benefits) to require additional review of Corps projects (e.g., through external review of Corps feasibility reports), and to strengthen environmental protection (e.g., through modifications to fish and wildlife mitigation requirements). These kinds of changes often were referred to as 'Corps reform.' Although Corps reforms were discussed in the 106th, 107th, and 108th Congresses, no significant changes were enacted." *Id*. at 2).

41. *See generally* Richard D. Knabb, Jamie R. Rhome & Daniel P. Brown, National Hurricane Center, *Tropical Cyclone Report—Hurricane Katrina, 23–30 August 2005* (Dec. 20, 2005), *available at* http://www.nhc.noaa.gov/pdf/TCR-AL122005_Katrina.pdf; Richard D. Knabb, Daniel P. Brown & Jamie R. Rhome, National Hurricane Center, *Tropical Cyclone Report—Hurricane Rita, 18–26 September 2005* (Mar. 17, 2006), *available at* http://www.nhc.noaa.gov/pdf/TCR-AL182005_Rita.pdf.

42. U.S. Army Corps of Eng'rs, *Performance Evaluation of the New Orleans and Southeast Louisiana Hurricane Protection System Draft Final Report of the Interagency Performance Evaluation Task Force* (June 1, 2006), *available at* https://ipet.wes.army.mil/. *See* John Schwarz, *Army Corps Admits Flaws in New Orleans Levees*, N.Y. TIMES, June 1, 2006, at A-19.

43. *See supra* Carter, note 40, at 3.

44. *See* U.S. Army Corps of Eng'rs, *Where We Are, available at* http://www.usace.army.mil/howdoi/where.html#State.

45. *See* U.S. Army Corps of Eng'rs, *COE Division and District Regulatory Boundaries, available at* http://www.usace.army.mil/cw/cecwo/reg/boundmap.pdf.

46. See U.S. Army Corps of Eng'rs, *Districts by State, available at* http://www.usace.army.mil/howdoi/where.html#States.

47. Direct links to Corps district offices can be found at U.S. Army Corps of Engineers Regulatory Program, *District Offices, available at* http://www.usace.army.mil/cw/cecwo/reg/district.htm.

48. *See* U.S. Army Corps of Eng'rs, *Where We Are, supra* note 44.

49. 33 C.F.R. § 320.1(a)(2) (2006) ("The Corps is a highly decentralized organization. Most of the authority for administering the regulatory program has been delegated to the [thirty-eight] district engineers and [eight] division engineers.")

50. Gibbons v. Ogden, 22 U.S. 1 (1824); The Daniel Ball, 77 U.S. 557 (1871); United States v. The Montello, 87 U.S. 430 (1874). For a more recent discussion of constitutional authority underlying the Rivers and Harbors Act, 33 U.S.C. §§ 401–18 (2000), see Wyandotte Transp. Co. v. United States, 389 U.S. 191, 201 (1967). *See generally* William Andreen, *The Evolution of Water Pollution Control in the United States: State, Local and Federal Efforts, 1789–1972: Part I*, 21 STAN. ENVTL. L.J. 145–200 (2003); William Andreen, *The Evolution of Water Pollution Control in the United States: State, Local and Federal Efforts, 1789–1972: Part II*, 21 STAN. ENVTL. L.J. 215–94 (2003).

51. U.S. CONST. art. I, § 8, cl. 3 (empowers the U.S. Congress "[t]o regulate Commerce with foreign Nations, and among the several States, and with the Indian Tribes").

52. Sam Kalen, *Commerce to Conservation: The Call for a National Water Policy and the Evolution of Federal Jurisdiction over Wetlands*, 69 N.D. L. REV. 873, 879 (1993).

53. Rivers and Harbors Act of 1899, ch. 425, 30 Stat. 1121 (1899) (codified as amended at 33 U.S.C. §§ 401–18 (2000)). *See also* Rivers and Harbors Appropriations Act of 1886, ch. 929, 24 Stat. 310, 329 (1886); Rivers and Harbors Appropriations Act of 1890, ch. 907, 26 Stat. 426 (1890); River and Harbor Act of 1894, ch. 299, 28 Stat. 338, 363 (1894); River and Harbor Appropriations Act of 1896, ch. 314, 29 Stat. 202, 234 (1896). *See generally* Neil J. Barker, *Sections 9 and 10 of the Rivers and Harbors Act of 1899: Potent Tools for Environmental Protection*, 6 ECOLOGY L.Q. 109, 111–15 (1976) for an excellent overview of the evolution of the Rivers and Harbors Act of 1899 and its precursors. *See also* G. Koonce, *Federal Laws Affecting Rivers and Harbors Works* (1926), *reprinted in Water Pollution Control Legislation—1971 (Oversight of Existing Program): Hearings Before the House Comm. on Public Works*, 92d Cong., 1st Sess. 284, 287 (1971).

54. 33 U.S.C. §§ 401–18 (2000).

55. The full text of Section 10 of the Rivers and Harbors Act reads: "That the creation of any obstruction not affirmatively authorized by Congress, to the navigable capacity of any of the waters of the United States is hereby prohibited; and it shall not be lawful to build or commence the building of any wharf, pier, dolphin, boom, weir, breakwater, bulkhead, jetty, or other structures in any port, roadstead, haven, harbor, canal, navigable river, or other water of the United States, outside established harbor lines, or where no harbor lines have been established, except on plans recommended by the Chief of Engineers and authorized by the Secretary of War; and it shall not be lawful to excavate or fill, or in any manner to alter or modify the course, location, condition, or capacity of, any port, roadstead, haven, harbor, canal, lake, harbor of refuge, or inclosure [sic] within the limits of any breakwater, or of the channel of any navigable water of the United States, unless the work has been recommended by the Chief of Engineers and authorized by the Secretary of War prior to beginning the same." 33 U.S.C. § 403 (2000). The Corps' current regulations state in relevant part that "[t]he U.S. Army Corps of Engineers has been involved in regulating certain activities in the nation's waters since 1890." 33 C.F.R. § 320.1(a)(1) (2007).

56. Congress created the U.S. Army Corps of Engineers in 1802. Act of Mar. 16, 1802, ch. 9, § 26, 2 Stat. 132, 137. Its duties eventually expanded to include regulatory functions. *See generally* Garrett Power, *The Fox in the Chicken Coop: The Regulatory Program of the U.S. Army Corps of Engineers*, 63 VA. L. REV. 503 (1977).

57. *See* U.S. Army Corps of Eng'rs, *Summary of History, available at* http://www.usace.army
.mil/cw/cecwo/reg/reghist.pdf.

58. Several other sections of the Rivers and Harbors Act of 1899 may be relevant to coastal
activities. For example, Section 9 (*codified at* 33 U.S.C. § 401 (2000)) sets forth requirements for approval of dams, dikes, bridges, or causeways to be constructed over or in
navigable waters. Likewise, Section 11 (*codified at* 33 U.S.C. § 404 (2000)) gives the Secretary of the Army the power to establish harbor lines beyond which no structures may
extend. Section 12 (*codified at* 33 U.S.C. § 406 (2000)) makes violations of sections 9, 10,
and 11 criminal acts and imposes fines or imprisonment or both, and also provides for
the removal or treatment of offending structures. Finally, Section 13, commonly known
as "The Refuse Act" (*codified at* 33 U.S.C. § 407 (2000)) prohibits the discharge of "any
refuse matter of any kind or description" into navigable waters.

59. United States v. Alaska, 503 U.S. 569 (1992) (upholding the Corps' interpretation of the
Rivers and Harbors Act to require a permit to build an artificial addition to the Alaska
coastline). Other courts have approved similarly broad interpretations, such as a court upholding a Corps determination that houseboats were structures requiring Section 10 permits, *United States v. Hernandez*, 979 F. Supp. 70 (D.P.R. 1997), and a court approving
jurisdiction over salmon farm aquaculture pen sites, *United States Pub. Interest Research
Group v. Atl. Salmon of Maine*, 257 F. Supp. 2d 407 (D. Me. 2003).

60. *See generally* U.S. Army Corps of Eng'rs, *Regulatory Program Overview, available at*
http://www.usace.army.mil/cw/cecwo/reg/oceover.htm.

61. 33 C.F.R. pt. 325 (2007). "The processing procedures of this Part apply to any Department of the Army (DA) permit. Special procedures and additional information are contained in 33 CFR Parts 320 through 324, 327 and Part 330." *Id.* § 325.1(a).

62. *See infra* Section II.C.

63. The Corps will not process a permit application until it has been deemed "complete,"
which means that it includes all relevant documentation. 33 C.F.R. § 325.2 (2006).

64. 33 C.F.R. § 325.3 (2007).

65. For an excellent overview of the Section 10 permit process, see Michael G. Proctor, *Section 10 of the Rivers and Harbors Act and Western Water Allocations—Are the Western
States Up a Creek Without a Permit?* 10 B.C. Envtl. Aff. L. Rev. 111 (1982).

66. Locations and contact information for the thirty-eight Corps district offices nationwide
can be found at U.S. Army Corps of Engineers, *District Offices, available at* http://www
.usace.army.mil/cw/cecwo/reg/district.htm.

67. 33 C.F.R. pt. 325, *Appendix B—NEPA Implementation, available at* http://www.usace
.army.mil/cw/cecwo/reg/33cfr325.htm#appendixB.

68. *Id.* pt. 327 (2007).

69. *Id.* pt. 322 (2007).

70. *Id.* § 320.4(a)(2) (2007).

71. *Id.* § 325.5 (2007).

72. *Id.* pt. 331. *See* U.S. Army Corps of Eng'rs, *Administrative Appeals, available at* http://
www.usace.army.mil/cw/cecwo/reg/appeals.htm. *See also* notes 467–479 and accompanying text.

73. 5 U.S.C. § 702 (2000). In order to prevail, the applicant must meet certain criteria, such as
showing that the administrative decision was "arbitrary, capricious, an abuse of discretion
or otherwise not in accordance with law." *Id.* § 706(2)(A). *See, e.g.*, DiVosta Rentals, Inc.
v. Lee, 488 F.2d 674 (5th Cir. 1973), *cert. denied*, 416 U.S. 984 (1974).

74. 33 C.F.R. pt. 326 (2007). Private parties may not bring suit to enforce Rivers and Harbors
Act provisions. California v. Sierra Club, 451 U.S. 287 (1981).

75. 33 C.F.R. § 326.5 (2007).

76. *Id.* § 326.3(e).

77. Pub. L. No. 92-500, 86 Stat. 816 (1972), *as codified in* 33 U.S.C. §§ 1251–1387 (2000),
further amended in Pub. L. No. 95-217, 91 Stat. 1567 (1977); Pub. L. No. 100-4, 101
Stat. 45 (1987).

78. 33 U.S.C. § 1344 (2000).

79. *See generally* RICHARD J. LAZARUS, THE MAKING OF ENVIRONMENTAL LAW (Univ. Chicago 2004). *See also* Natural Res. Def. Council, *E-law: What Started It All? available at* http://www.nrdc.org/legislation/helaw.asp; William Andreen, *The Evolving Law of Environmental Protection in the United States: 1970–1991,* 9 ENVTL. & PLANNING L.J. 96 (1992). For information on the first Earth Day, *see* Senator Gaylord Nelson, *How the First Earth Day Came About, available at* http://earthday.envirolink.org/history.html (noting that during the early and mid-1960s in nationwide speeches, he determined that "[a]ll across the country, evidence of environmental degradation was appearing everywhere, and everyone noticed except the political establishment. The environmental issue simply was not to be found on the nation's political agenda. The people were concerned, but the politicians were not."); and U.S. Envtl. Prot. Agency, *History—Earth Day, available at* http://epa.gov/history/topics/earthday/index.htm. *See also* ROBERT W. ADLER, JESSICA C. LANDMAN & DIANE M. CAMERON, THE CLEAN WATER ACT 20 YEARS LATER (1993).

80. 33 U.S.C. § 1251(a) (2000). To achieve this objective, Congress listed seven goals, each of which indicates concern for values other than navigability. *Id.* § 1251(a)(1)–(6). These broad goals of the law include "protection and propagation of fish, shellfish, and wildlife," "recreation in and on the water," elimination of "the discharge of toxic pollutants in toxic amounts," and "programs for the control of nonpoint source pollution." *Id.*

81. *Id.* § 1344 (2000).

82. *Id.*

83. 33 U.S.C. § 1311(a) (2000).

84. For a detailed overview of these requirements, *see* CONNOLLY ET AL., WETLANDS LAW AND POLICY, *supra* note 11.

85. One scholar recently summarized the tensions related to Section 404 regulation as follows: "These tensions can be traced in large measure to four structural flaws in section 404's design: the lack of a clear goal, the conflicts inherent in the Corps-EPA-section 404 relationship, reliance on a water statute to protect wetlands, and the regulation of activities in wetlands under a pollution control approach." Flournoy, *Section 404 at Thirty-Something, supra* note 17, at 608. *See also* Michael C. Blumm, *The Clean Water Act's Section 404 Permit Program Enters Its Adolescence: An Institutional and Programmatic Perspective,* 8 ECOLOGY L.Q. 409 (1980); Blumm & Zaleha, *Federal Wetlands Protection Under the Clean Water Act, supra* note 17; Houck, *Hard Choices, supra* note 17; and Kalen, *Commerce to Conservation, supra* note 52.

86. The Corps regulations are located in 33 C.F.R. pts. 320–31, *available at* http://www.usace.army.mil/inet/functions/cw/cecwo/reg/sadmin3.htm; EPA's primary regulations can be found in 40 C.F.R. pts. 230–33, *available at* http://www.epa.gov/owow/wetlands/regs/. Separate enforcement regulations can be found in U.S. Envtl. Prot. Agency, *Consolidated Rules of Practice Governing the Administrative Assessment of Civil Penalties and the Revocation or Suspension of Permits,* 40 C.F.R. pt. 22, *available at* http://www.epa.gov/owow/wetlands/pdf/40cfrPart22.pdf.

87. *See* U.S. Army Corps of Eng'rs, *Regulatory Guidance Letters, available at* http://www.usace.army.mil/inet/functions/cw/cecwo/reg/rglsindx.htm ("Regulatory Guidance Letters (RGL's) were developed by the Corps as a system to organize and track written guidance issued to its field agencies. RGL's are normally issued as a result of evolving policy; judicial decisions and changes to the Corps regulations or another agency's regulations which affect the permit program. RGL's are used only to interpret or clarify existing Regulatory Program policy, but do provide mandatory guidance to the Corps district offices.").

88. For examples of such memoranda "to the field," *see* U.S. Army Corps of Engineers, Memorandum to the Field, Application of Best Management Practices to Mechanical Silvicultural Site Preparation Activities for the Establishment of Pine Plantations in the Southeast (1995), *available at* http://www.usace.army.mil/cw/cecwo/reg/mou/silvicul.htm, and U.S. Environmental Prot. Agency and U.S. Army Corps of Engineers, Guidance for Corps and EPA Field Offices Regarding Clean Water Act Section 404 Jurisdiction Over Isolated Waters in Light of United States v. James J. Wilson (May 29, 1998), *available at* http://www.epa.gov/region6/6en/w/wilguid.pdf.

89. U.S. Army Corps of Eng'rs, *Memorandum of Understanding/Agreement, available at* http://www.usace.army.mil/cw/cecwo/reg/mou/moumoas.htm.

90. Note that these additional sources are not considered laws but interpretations of the law. "Interpretive rules simply state what the administrative agency thinks the statute means, and only 'remind' affected parties of existing duties." Jerri's Ceramic Arts, Inc. v. Consumer Product Safety Comm'n, 874 F.2d 205, 207 (4th Cir. 1989).

91. *See generally* U.S. Envtl. Prot. Agency, *Wetland Regulatory Authority, available at* http://www.epa.gov/owow/wetlands/pdf/reg_authority_pr.pdf (identifying EPA's role and responsibility as follows: "Develops and interprets policy, guidance and environmental criteria used in evaluating permit applications; Determines scope of geographic jurisdiction and applicability of exemptions; Approves and oversees State and Tribal assumption; Reviews and comments on individual permit applications; Has authority to prohibit, deny, or restrict the use of any defined area as a disposal site (Section 404(c)); Can elevate specific cases (Section 404(q)); Enforces Section 404 provisions.")

92. 33 U.S.C. § 1344(b)(2000).

93. 40 C.F.R. pt. 230 (2007), *available at* http://www.usace.army.mil/inet/functions/cw/cecwo/reg/40cfr230.htm. *See* Mark T. Pifher, *The Section 404(b)(1) Guidelines and Practicable Alternatives Analysis, in* CONNOLLY ET AL., WETLANDS LAW AND POLICY, *supra* note 11 for a detailed overview of the Section 404(b)(1) Guidelines.

94. 33 U.S.C. § 1344(c) (2000). *See* William B. Ellis, *The EPA Veto and Related Matters* in CONNOLLY ET AL., WETLANDS LAW AND POLICY, *supra* note 11, for a detailed overview of the EPA veto process.

95. *See* 33 U.S.C. § 1319. *See also* Memorandum Between the Department of the Army and the Environmental Protection Agency entitled *Federal Enforcement for the Section 404 Program of the Clean Water Act (1989), available at* http://www.epa.gov/owow/wetlands/regs/enfmoa.html.

96. Section 404(g) provides authority for and criteria regarding state assumption of permitting authority. 33 U.S.C. § 1344(g).

97. *See, e.g.,* Memorandum of Agreement Concerning the Determination of the Geographic Jurisdiction of the Section 404 Program, *reprinted in* 58 Fed. Reg. 4995 (Jan.19, 1993); Memorandum of Agreement Between the Environmental Protection Agency and the Department of the Army Concerning the Determination of Mitigation Under the Clean Water Act Section 404(b)(1) Guidelines, *reprinted in* 55 Fed. Reg. 9210 (Mar. 12, 1990); Opinion of Attorney General Benjamin Civiletti, 43 Op. Att'y Gen.15; Clean Water Section 404(q) Memorandum of Agreement Between the Environmental Protection Agency and the Department of the Army, *available at* http://www.epa.gov/OWOW/wetlands/regs/dispmoa.html; Memorandum of Agreement Between the Department of the Army and the Environmental Protection Agency Concerning Federal Enforcement for the Section 404 Program of the Clean Water Act, *available at* http://www.epa.gov/OWOW/wetlands/regs/enfmoa.html; 1986 Memorandum of Agreement Between the Assistant Administrator for External Affairs and Water, U.S. Environmental Protection Agency, and the Assistant Secretary of the Army for Civil Works Concerning Regulation of Discharges of Solid Waste Under the Clean Water Act, *available at* http://www.epa.gov/owow/wetlands/guidance/solwaste.html. The Corps and EPA have also jointly issued field guidance concerning the Section 404 program. *See, e.g., Memorandum: Individual Permit Flexibility for Small Landowners, available at* http://www.epa.gov/owow/wetlands/guidance/landowne.html; *Memorandum: Appropriate Level of Analysis Required for Evaluating Compliance with the Section 404(b)(1) Guidelines Alternatives Requirements, available at* http://www.usace.army.mil/inet/functions/cw/cecwo/reg/flexible.htm.

98. *See infra* notes 102–09 and accompanying text.

99. *See infra* Section II.B.2.

100. *See infra* notes 178–193 and accompanying text.

101. *See infra* notes 191–251 and accompanying text.

102. 33 C.F.R. § 320.1(a)(6) ("The Corps has authorized its district engineers to issue formal determinations concerning the applicability of the Clean Water Act or the Rivers and

Harbors Act of 1899 to activities or tracts of land and the applicability of general permits or statutory exemptions to proposed activities. A determination pursuant to this authorization shall constitute a Corps final agency action. Nothing contained in this section is intended to affect any authority EPA has under the Clean Water Act.")

103. U.S. Army Engineer Waterways Experiment Station, *Corps of Engineers Wetlands Delineation Manual*, Technical Report Y-87-1 (1987), *available at* http://el.erdc.usace.army.mil/wetlands/pdfs/wlman87.pdf. Regional supplementation may be appropriate depending on the location of the property at issue. *See* U.S. Army Corps of Eng'rs, *Regional Supplements to Corps Delineation Manual, available at* http://www.usace.army.mil/cw/cecwo/reg/reg_supp.htm.

104. To get a sense of the analysis required in delineating a particular site, *see* Soc'y of Wetland Scientists, *Wetland-Related Training Courses & Workshops, available at* http://www.sws.org/training/ (including courses in, among other things, Wetland Delineation Training; Ecological Risk Assessment; Wetland Plant Identification; Hydric Soil Identification: Basic Processes; Hydric Soil Identification: Advanced Problems; and Planning Hydrology for Constructed Wetlands).

105. 33 C.F.R. § 328.3(b) (Corps); 40 C.F.R. § 230.3(t) (EPA).

106. U.S. Army Corps of Eng'rs, *Wetlands Delineation Manual, supra* note 103.

107. *See generally* United States v. Ellen, 961 F.2d 462, 464–66 (4th Cir. 1992), *cert. denied*, 506 U.S. 875 (1992). *See also* J.B. Ruhl, *Biodiversity Conservation and the Ever-Expanding Web of Federal Laws Regulating Nonfederal Lands: Time for Something Completely Different?* 66 U. Colo. L. Rev. 555 n.142 (1995).

108. Energy and Water Development Appropriations Act of 1992, Title 1, Pub. L. 102-104, 105 Stat. 518 (1991), *continued in* Pub. L. No. 102-377, 106 Stat. 1315 (1992); Department of Veterans Affairs and Housing and Urban Development, and Independent Agencies Appropriations Act, 1993, Pub. L. No. 102-389, 106 Stat. 1571 (1992).

109. Environmental Protection Agency and Department of the Army, *Memorandum of Agreement Concerning the Determination of the Geographic Jurisdiction of the Section 404 Program*, 58 Fed. Reg. 4995 (1993).

110. Following issuance of the *Rapanos* Guidance, see *supra* note 103 and accompanying text, the U.S. Army Corps of Engineers issued a new jurisdictional determination form, *available at* http://www.usace.army.mil/cw/cecwo/reg/cwa_guide/app_b_approved_jd_form.pdf.

111. RGL 05-02, *Expiration of Geographic Jurisdictional Determinations of Waters of the United States, available at* http://www.usace.army.mil/cw/cecwo/reg/rgls/RGL05-02.pdf.

112. 33 U.S.C. § 1344(a) (2000).

113. *Id.* § 1362(7).

114. *See, e.g.*, Natural Res. Defense Council, Inc. v. Callaway, 392 F. Supp. 685 (D.C. Cir. 1975); United States v. Riverside Bayview Homes, 474 U.S. 121 (1985).

115. *See infra* note 142.

116. *See* Brief of The Honorable John D. Dingell, The Honorable John Conyers, Jr., The Honorable Robert F. Drinan, The Honorable Gary W. Hart, The Honorable Kenneth W. Hechler, The Honorable Charles McCurdy Mathias, Jr., The Honorable Paul N. McCloskey, Jr., The Honorable Charles B. Rangel, and The Honorable Richard Schultz Schweiker, as *Amici Curiae* in Support of The Respondent, 126 S. Ct. 2208 (2006) (Nos. 04-1034, 04-1384), Supreme Court of The United States, Jan. 13, 2006, *available at* http://www.eswr.com/1105/rapanos/rapamicongress.pdf.

117. 33 C.F.R. § 321.2(a) ("The term 'navigable waters of the United States' means those waters of the United States that are subject to the ebb and flow of the tide shoreward to the mean high water mark and/or are presently used, or have been used in the past, or may be susceptible to use to transport interstate or foreign commerce.")

118. *See generally* Robert Meltz & Claudia Copeland, Congressional Research Service, *The Wetlands Coverage of the Clean Water Act Is Revisited by the Supreme Court*: Rapanos v. United States (Sept. 12, 2006), *available at* http://www.ncseonline.org/NLE/CRSreports/06Oct/RL33263.pdf.

119. *See supra* note 80.
120. *Id.* § 1311(a).
121. *Id.* § 1344(a).
122. *Id.* § 1362(7).
123. Rapanos v. United States, 126 S. Ct. 2208 (2006). *See generally* Meltz & Copeland, *The Wetlands Coverage of the Clean Water Act Is Revisited, supra* note 118. For background materials on the cases, including the original Carabell permit application and associated documentation as well as the *Rapanos* enforcement documents, *see* Kim Diana Connolly, *U.S. Supreme Court* Rapanos *and* Carabell *Wetlands Cases, available at* http://www.law.sc.edu/wetlands/rapanos-carabell/. *See also* James Murphy, *Muddying the Waters of the Clean Water Act:* Rapanos v. United States *and the Future of America's Water Resources*, 31 Vermont L.R. 355 (2007).
124. *See infra* notes 147–58 and accompanying text.
125. *See* compiled initial press coverage at Kim Diana Connolly, *U.S. Supreme Court* Rapanos *and* Carabell *Wetlands Cases, available at* http://www.law.sc.edu/wetlands/rapanos-carabell/carabell.shtml#press_coverage. *See also* Ass'n of State Wetland Managers, Rapanos/ Carabell, *available at* http://www.aswm.org/fwp/rapanos_state2006.htm; Jon A. Mueller, *Adjacent Wetlands: Is Your Nexus Significant?* Rapanos v. United States, *Daily Env't Rep. Analysis and Perspective*, Mar. 12, 2007, *available at* http://pubs.bna.com/NWSSTND/IP/BNA/DEN.NSF/SearchAllView/35AF1F7BA69BB2088525729A000BF59A?Open&highlight=RAPANOS,GUIDANCE#%3C~A0B4D2N5D7~%3E.
126. *Compare* Pacific Legal Found., Rapanos Blog, http://rapanos.typepad.com *with* Clean Water Network, *Supreme Court Delivers Murky Ruling on* Carabell *and* Rapanos, http://www.cleanwaternetwork.org//issues/scope/getengaged/displaycontent.cfm?ContentID=388&ContentTypeID=4&PageFormat=DisplayContent&ConfigID=146. *See also* Georgetown Univ. Law Ctr., *The Clean Water Act in the Supreme Court: The* Rapanos *and* Carabell *Decisions, available at* http://www.podcastdirectory.com/podshows/626338; and Akin Gump, *SCOTUS Blog, available at* http://www.scotusblog.com/wp/uncategorized/decisions-clean-water-act-search-limited.
127. Initial Corps regulations defined Section 404 navigable waters as "those waters of the United States which are subject to the ebb and flow of the tide, and/or are presently, or have been in the past, or may be in the future susceptible for use for purposes of interstate or foreign commerce." 39 Fed. Reg. 12,115, 12,119 (1974).
128. Natural Res. Defense Council v. Callaway, 392 F. Supp. 685 (D.D.C. 1975).
129. *See supra* Section II.A.
130. *Callaway*, 392 F. Supp. at 686. *See also* United States v. Ashland Oil & Transp. Co., 504 F.2d 1317 (6th Cir. 1974) (holding that to interpret the Conference Report's reference to "the broadest possible constitutional interpretation unencumbered by agency determinations which have been made or may be made for administrative purposes" otherwise than to mean that Congress intended that the Act reach any activity that substantially affects commerce would "turn a great legislative enactment into a meaningless jumble of words." *Id.* at 1325).
131. 40 Fed. Reg. 31,320 (1975).
132. The definition as it appears in full in the regulations reads as follows:

> The term "waters of the United States" means:
>
> (1) All waters which are currently used, or were used in the past, or may be susceptible to use in interstate or foreign commerce, including all waters which are subject to the ebb and flow of the tide;
>
> (2) All interstate waters including interstate wetlands;
>
> (3) All other waters such as intrastate lakes, rivers, streams (including intermittent streams), mudflats, sandflats, wetlands, sloughs, prairie potholes, wet meadows, playa lakes, or natural ponds, the use, degradation or destruction of which could affect interstate or foreign commerce including any such waters:

(i) Which are or could be used by interstate or foreign travelers for recreational or other purposes; or

(ii) From which fish or shellfish are or could be taken and sold in interstate or foreign commerce; or

(iii) Which are used or could be used for industrial purpose by industries in interstate commerce;

(4) All impoundments of waters otherwise defined as waters of the United States under the definition;

(5) Tributaries of waters identified in paragraphs (a)(1)–(4) of this section;

(6) The territorial seas;

(7) Wetlands adjacent to waters (other than waters that are themselves wetlands) identified in paragraphs (a)(1)–(6) of this section.

(8) Waters of the United States do not include prior converted cropland. Notwithstanding the determination of an area's status as prior converted cropland by any other Federal Agency, for the purposes of the Clean Water Act, the final authority regarding Clean Water Act jurisdiction remains with EPA. Waste treatment systems, including treatment ponds or lagoons designed to meet the requirements of CWA (other than cooling ponds as defined in 40 CFR 423.11(m) which also meet the criteria of this definition) are not waters of the United States. 33 C.F.R. § 328.3(a)(2007).

133. James R. Curtiss, Note, *The Clean Water Act of 1977: Midcourse Corrections in the Section 404 Program*, 57 NEB. L. REV. 1092, 1103–07 (1978).

134. *See generally id.* 1107–12; Blumm, *The Clean Water Act's Section 404 Permit Program Enters Its Adolescence, supra* note 85.

135. S. Rep. No. 95-370, 95th Cong., 1st Sess. (1977), at 74–75. During the Senate's floor debate on the 1977 amendments, Senator Lloyd Bentsen of Texas offered an amendment to the Environment and Public Works Committee's bill that would have amended the Act to limit the scope of Section 404 to only traditionally navigable waters and their adjacent wetlands, but the resulting negative vote caused Senator Bentsen himself to state: "[t]he committee has failed to recommend any reduction in the scope of the § 404 permit program. . . . The program would still cover all waters of the United States, including small streams, ponds, isolated marshes, and intermittently flowing gullies." 123 Cong. Rec. 26,711 (Aug. 4, 1977).

136. *See Riverside Bayview*, 474 U.S. at 137 ("Although we are chary of attributing significance to Congress' failure to act[,] a refusal by Congress to overrule an agency's construction of legislation is at least some evidence of the reasonableness of that construction, particularly where the administrative construction has been brought to Congress' attention through legislation specifically designed to supplant it."); *see also* Minnehaha Creek Watershed Dist. v. Hoffman, 597 F.2d 617, 626 (8th Cir. 1979) (relying on 1977 legislative history to determine regulatory scope of Section 404 as originally passed).

137. Final Rule for Regulatory Programs of the Corps of Engineers, 51 Fed. Reg. 41,217 (1986) (codified at 33 C.F.R. §§ 320–30); Clean Water Act Section 404 Program Definitions and Permit Exemptions; Section 404 State Program Regulations, 53 Fed. Reg. 20,765 (1988) (codified at 40 C.F.R. §§ 232–33).

138. *See, e.g.*, Leslie Salt Co. v. United States, 896 F.2d 354 (9th Cir. 1990), *cert. denied*, 498 U.S. 1126 (1991) (upheld the Migratory Bird Rule); Hoffman Homes v. EPA, 999 F.2d 256 (7th Cir. 1993) (likewise upheld the rule); Tabb Lakes v. United States, 715 F. Supp. 726 (E.D. Va. 1988), *aff'd without opinion*, 885 F.2d 866 (4th Cir. 1989) (Migratory Bird Rule held invalid in the Fourth Circuit in 1989 for failure to follow the Administrative Procedure Act required notice and comment procedures); United States v. Wilson, 133

F.3d 251 (4th Cir. 1997). *See also* Dennis J. Priolo, *Section 404 of the Clean Water Act: The Case for Expansion of Federal Jurisdiction Over Isolated Wetlands,* 30 Land & Water L. Rev. 91 (1995).

139. 531 U.S. 159, 174 (2001). For a scholarly examination of the post-SWANCC jurisdiction issues, from differing perspectives, *see* Lance D. Wood, *Don't Be Misled: CWA Jurisdiction Extends to All Non-Navigable Tributaries of the Traditional Navigable Waters and to Their Adjacent Wetlands,* 34 Envtl. L. Rep. 10187 (Feb. 2004); Virginia Albrecht and Stephen Nickelsburg, *Could SWANCC Be Right? A New Look at the Legislative History of the Clean Water Act,* 32 Envtl. L. Rep. (Sept. 2002).

140. SWANCC, 531 U.S. at 174 ("Permitting respondents to claim federal jurisdiction over ponds and mudflats falling within the 'Migratory Bird Rule' would result in a significant impingement of the States' traditional and primary power over land and water use. *See, e.g.,* Hess v. Port Authority Trans-Hudson Corporation, 513 U.S. 30, 44 (1994) ("[R]egulation of land use [is] a function traditionally performed by local governments."). Rather than expressing a desire to readjust the federal-state balance in this manner, Congress chose to 'recognize, preserve, and protect the primary responsibilities and rights of States . . . to plan the development and use . . . of land and water resources. . . .' 33 U.S.C. § 1251(b). We thus read the statute as written to avoid the significant constitutional and federalism questions raised by respondents' interpretation, and therefore reject the request for administrative deference." *Id.*). The Association of State Wetland Managers has an informative website about post-SWANCC developments. Ass'n of State Wetland Managers, *SWANCC v. USACOE Special, available at* http://www.aswm.org/fwp/swancc/index .htm. *See also* Edward A. Fitzgerald, *Solid Waste Agency of Northern Cook County v. U.S. Army Corps of Engineers: Isolated Waters, Migratory Birds, Statutory and Constitutional Interpretation,* 43 Nat. Resources J. 11 (2003).

141. SWANCC, 531 U.S. at 173.

142. *See, e.g.,* Save Our Sonoran, Inc. v. Flowers, 408 F.3d 1113 (9th Cir. 2005); Treacy v. Newdunn Assocs. LLP, 344 F.3d 407 (4th Cir. 2003); United States v. Deaton, 332 F.3d 698 (4th Cir. 2003), *cert. denied,* 541 U.S. 972 (2004); Community Ass'n for Restoration of Env't v. Henry Bosma Dairy, 305 F.3d 943 (9th Cir. 2002); Headwaters, Inc. v. Talent Irrigation Dist., 243 F.3d 526 (9th Cir. 2001).

143. *See In re* Needham, 354 F.3d 340 (5th Cir. 2003); Rice v. Harken Exploration Co., 250 F.3d 264 (5th Cir. 2001).

144. In 2003, EPA and the Corps issued a post-SWANCC Advance Notice of Proposed Rule Making suggesting it may be appropriate to revise the regulatory definition of "waters of the United States." *Advance Notice of Proposed Rulemaking ("ANPRM") on the Clean Water Act Regulatory Definition of "Waters of the United States,"* 68 Fed. Reg. 1991 (Jan. 15, 2003), *available at* http://www.epa.gov/owow/wetlands/pdf/ ANPRM-FR.pdf. The agencies sought comment on issues associated with the scope of waters subject to the CWA in light of SWANCC, and solicited input from the general public, scientific community, and federal and state resource agencies on the implications of SWANCC on jurisdictional decisions and other changes stakeholders might consider appropriate. *Id.* Over 135,000 comments were submitted, many in opposition to the proposal. Natural Res. Defense Council, *Bush Administration Plans to Limit Scope of Clean Water Act, available at* http://www.nrdcdev.org/media/pressreleases/030203.asp. The proposed rule subsequently was withdrawn. *EPA and Army Corps Issue Wetlands Decision, available at* http://yosemite.epa.gov/opa/admpress.nsf/b1ab9f485b098972852562e7004dc686/ 540f28acf38d7f9b85256dfe00714ab0?OpenDocument.

145. A February 2004 General Accounting Office report discussed how EPA's and the Corps' regulations defining waters of the United States leave room for interpretation by Corps districts when considering (1) adjacent wetlands, (2) tributaries, and (3) ditches and other human-made conveyances. General Accounting Office (now the Government Accountability Office), GAO-04-297, *Waters and Wetlands: Corps of Engineers Needs to Evaluate Its District Office Practices in Determining Jurisdiction, available at* http://www.gao .gov/new.items/d04297.pdf. The 2004 report studied various Corps district office practices

and concluded that Corps districts differ in how they interpret and apply the federal regulations when determining which waters and wetlands are subject to federal jurisdiction. "For example, one district generally regulates wetlands located within 200 feet of other jurisdictional waters, while other districts consider the proximity of wetlands to other jurisdictional waters without any reference to a specific linear distance. Additionally, some districts assert jurisdiction over all wetlands located in the 100-year floodplain, while others do not consider floodplains as a factor." *Id.* The GAO Report recommended that "the Corps, in consultation with the Environmental Protection Agency (EPA): (1) survey district office practices in making jurisdictional determinations to determine if significant differences exist, (2) evaluate whether and how these differences need to be resolved, and (3) require districts to document their practices and make this information publicly available." *Id. See also* U.S. Government Accountability Office, *Waters and Wetlands: Corps of Engineers Needs to Better Support Its Decisions for Not Asserting Jurisdiction* (Sept. 2005), *available at* http://www.gao.gov/new.items/d05870.pdf.

146. United States v. Rapanos, 376 F.3d 629 (6th Cir. 2004); and Carabell v. U.S. Army Corps of Eng'rs, 391 F.3d 704 (6th Cir. 2004). Both cases involved regulation of wetlands that were adjacent to nonnavigable tributaries of traditional navigable waters, and the *Carabell* case involved regulation of a wetland that was separated from a tributary by a berm.

147. 126 S. Ct. 2208 (2006).

148. *See* Stephen M. Johnson, Kim Diana Connolly & Mark A. Ryan, Supplements to N4, é) <,? éV N, Ké4 ?+(AA; , Second Edition and V ,N<?+L {é<V é?+ él A<5)X {éP? — +,KLN?+5?3 él)N5A? é´3´ (Jan. 2007), *available at* http://www.abanet.org/abastore/front_ end/static/nosearch/watersuppp001-017.pdf.

149. 126 S. Ct. at 2255.

150. *Id.* at 2221.

151. *Id.* at 2225.

152. *Id.*

153. *Id.* at 2264 (Stevens, J., dissenting).

154. *Id.* at 2246 ("the plurality's opinion is inconsistent with the Act's text, structure, and purpose").

155. *Id.* at 2248.

156. *Id.*

157. *Id.* at 2236.

158. *Id.* at 2265. The dissenters note that it would be unusual, but not impossible, for wetlands to meet the plurality's surface connection test but not meet Kennedy's significant nexus test. *Id.* (emphasis in original).

159. Following issuance of a "legal interpretation" (Gary S. Guzy, EPA, Robert M. Andersen, Corps, *Supreme Court Ruling Concerning CWA Jurisdiction over Isolated Waters*, Jan. 19, 2001, *available at* http://www.aswm.org/fwp/swancc/legal.pdf), almost two years passed before a formal response was produced following SWANCC. *See* Advanced Notice of Proposed Rulemaking on the Clean Water Act Regulatory Definition of "Waters of the United States," Appendix A, Joint Memorandum, 68 Fed. Reg. 1995 (Jan. 15, 2003).

160. Joint Memorandum, *supra* note 159.

161. *See* Susan Bruninga, *EPA, Corps Guidance Could Be Modified as Part of Bigger Effort to Improve Program*, BNA Daily Env't, Apr. 29, 2004, at A6 ("The guidance issued in 2003 has been criticized by environmental advocates who say it does not provide enough protections to isolated wetlands and that up to 20 million acres of wetlands could be at risk. Industry groups said the guidance does not do enough to clarify which wetlands are covered by the Clean Water Act, especially after recent conflicting court decisions on jurisdictional issues.").

162. U.S. Army Corps of Eng'rs & U.S. Environ. Protection Agency, *Clean Water Act Jurisdiction Following the U.S. Supreme Court's Decision in Rapanos v. United States & Carabell v. United States* (June 5, 2007), *available at* http://www.usace.army.mil/cw/ cecwo/reg/cwa_guide/rapanos_guide_memo.pdf (hereinafter Rapanos Guidance). *See also* Memorandum for Director of Civil Works and US EPA Regional Administrators: U.S.

Environmental Protection Agency (EPA) and U.S. Army Corps of Engineers (Corps) Co-ordination on Jurisdictional Determinations (JDs) under Clean Water Act (CWA) Section 404 in Light of the SWANCC and Rapanos Supreme Court Decisions, *available at* http://www.usace.army.mil/cw/cecwo/reg/cwa_guide/rapanos_moa_06-05-07.pdf; U.S. Army Corps of Eng'rs and the U.S. Environ. Protection Agency. *U.S. Army Corps of Engineers Jurisdictional Determination Form Instructional Guidebook, available at* http://www.usace.army.mil/cw/cecwo/reg/cwa_guide/jd_guidebook_051207final.pdf (a 60 page set of "instructions to aid field staff in completing the Approved Jurisdictional Determination Form ('JD form')").

163. *Compare* Pacific Legal Foundation, *Rapanos Guidance—Docket Number EPA-HQ-OW-2007-0282, (Jan 15, 2008) available at* http://rapanos.typepad.com/PLFcomments RapanosGuidance.pdf *with Long-Awaited Guidance Further Jeopardizes Protection of Our Waters, Congress Must Act to Protect the Nation's Waters available at* http://www.nwf.org/news/story.cfm?pageId=FD79890E-15C5-5FE8-B0CA9F1BD523DFED

164. *Rapanos Guidance, supra* note 162, at 1.

165. *Id.*

166. *Id.*

167. U.S. Army Corps of Eng'rs, U.S. Environmental Protection Agency, *EPA and Army Corps of Engineers Guidance Regarding Clean Water Act Jurisdiction after Rapanos*, 72 Fed. Reg. 31,824 (2007).

168. 126 S. Ct. at 2236.

169. *Id.* Chief Justice Roberts's statement in his concurrence is interesting, because statutory interpretations receive deference under *Chevron* only when a statute is ambiguous, and the Chief Justice joined the plurality opinion which concluded that the "only plausible interpretation of 'waters of the United States' was 'relatively permanent, standing or con-tinuously flowing bodies of water forming geographic features' that are described in ordi-nary parlance as streams, . . . oceans, rivers, [and] lakes." 126 S. Ct. at 2225.

170. *Id.* at 2248.

171. *Id.* at 2266.

172. Northern Cal. River Watch v. City of Healdsburg, 457 F.3d 1023 (9th Cir. 2006).

173. United States v. Gerke Excavating, Inc., 464 F.3d 723 (7th Cir. 2006).

174. *See, e.g., Gerke*, 464 F.3d at 725 ("[A]s a practical matter the Kennedy concurrence is the least common denominator (always, when his view favors federal authority).")

175. United States v. Johnson, 467 F.3d 56 (1st Cir. 2006) ("Curiously, without explanation, the [*Gerke*] court equates the 'narrowest opinion' with the one least restrictive of federal authority to regulate." *Id.* at 61.).

176. San Francisco Baykeeper v. Cargill Salt Div., 481 F.3d 700 (9th Cir. 2007).

177. United States v. Chevron Pipe Line Co., 437 F. Supp. 2d 605 (N.D. Tex. 2006) ("Because Justice Kennedy failed to elaborate on the 'significant nexus' required, this Court will look to the prior reasoning in this circuit. The Fifth Circuit . . . has interpreted 'the waters of the United States' narrowly under the OPA. Without any clear direction on determining a significant nexus, this Court will do exactly as Chief Justice Roberts declared—'feel [its] way on a case-by-case basis.' (Roberts, C.J., concurring). Thus, as a matter of law in this circuit, the connection of generally dry channels and creek beds will not suffice to create a 'significant nexus' to a navigable water simply because one feeds into the next during the rare times of actual flow." *Id.* at 613.).

178. James Murphy and Janice L. Goldman-Carter, *Summary of Post-Rapanos and Post-SWANCC Court Decisions* (Oct. 2007), *available at* http://www.aswm.org/fwp/post_swancc_rapanos_1007.pdf.

179. *See, e.g.,* Statement of Kim Diana Connolly, University of South Carolina School of Law, to the United States House of Representatives Committee on Transportation and Infrastructure Hearing on "Status of the Nation's Waters, Including Wetlands, Under the Jurisdiction of the Federal Water Pollution Control Act," 17 July 2007, *available at* http://transportation.house.gov/Media/File/water/20070717/KIM%20DIANA%20CONNOLLY.pdf, Testimony by Mr. M. Reed Hopper Esq., Principal Attorney, Pacific

Legal Foundation, to the United States House of Representatives Committee on Transportation and Infrastructure Hearing on "Status of the Nation's Waters, Including Wetlands, Under the Jurisdiction of the Federal Water Pollution Control Act," 17 July 2007, *available at* http://transportation.house.gov/Media/File/water/20070717/Hopper%20Testimony .pdf.

180. 33 U.S.C. § 1344(f) (2000). The Corps' implementing regulations are found at 33 C.F.R. § 323.4 (2007), and the EPA's implementing regulations are found at 40 C.F.R. § 232.3 (2007). *See* United States v. Cumberland Farms of Connecticut, Inc., 647 F. Supp. 1166 (D. Mass. 1986) (discussing the addition of the exemptions to Section 404 in 1977. *Id.* at 1175.).

181. 33 U.S.C. § 1344(f)(1)(A)–(F) (2000). Listed exempt activities are not subject to regulation under Section 404, Section 301, *Id.* § 1311 (governing effluent limitations), or Section 402, *Id.* § 1342 (governing the National Pollutant Discharge Elimination System), but are subject to the effluent standards and prohibitions of Section 1317 governing toxic and pretreatment standards. *Id.* § 1344(f)(1).

182. 33 C.F.R. § 323.4 (2007).

183. *See, e.g.*, Greenfield Mills, Inc. v. Macklin, 361 F.3d 934, 949 (7th Cir. 2004); Borden Ranch Partnership v. U.S. Army Corps of Eng'rs, 261 F.3d 810, 815–16 (9th Cir. 2001), *aff'd by an equally divided court*, 537 U.S. 99 (2002); United States v. Larkins, 852 F.2d 189, 192 (6th Cir. 1988).

184. 33 U.S.C. § 1344(f)(2) (2000). To be "recaptured" an activity must meet both a "purpose" and an "effects" test. *See Greenfield Mills, Inc.*, at 955, *citing Borden Ranch Partnership*, 261 F.3d at 815; Avoyelles Sportsmen's League v. Marsh, 715 F.2d 897, 926 (5th Cir. 1983).

185. 33 C.F.R. § 323.4(a)(1)(iii) (2007). *Accord* United States v. Huebner, 752 F.2d 1235, 1240 (7th Cir. 1985) (exemption applies only to "'narrowly defined activities . . . that cause little or no adverse effects either individually or cumulatively [and that do not] convert more extensive areas of water to dry land or impede circulation or reduce the reach and size of the water body.").

186. 33 C.F.R. § 323.4(a)(2).

187. *Id.*

188. RGL 87-9, Section 404(f)(1)(C) *Exemption for Construction or Maintenance of Farm or Stock Ponds*, 1 (Aug. 27, 1987), *available at* http://www.usace.army.mil/inet/functions/ cw/cecwo/reg/rgls/rgl87-09.htm.

189. *Id.* The exemption may still apply if the pond was constructed, in part, for "secondary recreational use." *In re Carsten*, 211 Bank. 719, 734 (D. Mont. 1997).

190. 33 C.F.R. § 323.4(a)(4).

191. *Id.* § 323.4(a)(6).

192. RGL 86-3, Section 404(f)(1) *Exemption of Farm and Forest Roads*, 1–2 (Apr. 4, 1986), *available at* http://www.usace.army.mil/inet/functions/cw/cecwo/reg/rgls/rgl86-03.htm.

193. 33 U.S.C. § 1344(a).

194. Save Our Community v. EPA, 971 F.2d 1155 (5th Cir. 1992). Several states that have their own wetland regulatory programs do regulate beyond discharge. *See, e.g.*, Protected Waters and Wetlands Permit Program, MINN. STAT. ANN. § 103G, *available at* http://www .bwsr.state.mn.us/wetlands/wca/chapter8420.pdf ("8420.0105 SCOPE. Wetlands must not be drained, excavated, or filled wholly or partially unless replaced by restoring or creating wetland areas of at least equal public value."); Fill and Dredge in Wetlands, N.H REV. STAT. ANN. §§ 482-A:1–482-A:27, *available at* http://www.des.state.nh.us/wetlands/ pdf/482a.pdf ("No person shall excavate, remove, fill, dredge or construct any structures in or on any bank, flat, marsh, or swamp in and adjacent to any waters of the state without a permit from the department." *Id.* at § 482-A:3).

195. Excavation is specifically regulated under the more limited jurisdictional reach of Section 10 of the Rivers and Harbors Act of 1899. 33 U.S.C. § 403.

196. *See supra* Section II.B.2.

197. *See generally* H. Michael Keller, *Regulated Activities*, *in* CONNOLLY ET AL., WETLANDS LAW AND POLICY, *supra* note 11.

198. 33 U.S.C. § 1311(a)(2000).

199. *Id.* § 1362(16). The phrase "of dredged and fill material" which modifies Section 404's reference to "discharge" may make it possible to build an argument as to whether the CWA's definition of an unqualified "discharge" applies in all cases.

200. *Id.* § 1362(12).

201. *See supra* Section II.B.2.

202. 33 U.S.C. § 1362(6) (2000). The definition reads "dredged spoil, solid waste, incinerator residue, sewage, garbage, sewage, sludge, munitions, chemical wastes, biological materials, radioactive materials, heat, wrecked or discarded equipment, rock, sand, cellar dirt and industrial, municipal, and agricultural waste discharged into water." *Id.*

203. United States v. Zanger, 767 F. Supp. 1030, 1034 (N.D. Cal. 1991).

204. *See, e.g.,* United States v. Wilson, 133 F.3d 251 (4th Cir. 1997).

205. United States v. Banks, 873 F. Supp. 650, 657 (S.D. Fla. 1995), *citing* United States v. Carter, 18 Env't Rep. Cas. (BNA) 1804, 1807 (S.D. Fla. 1982); United States v. Huebner, 752 F.2d 1235, 1242 (7th Cir.), *cert. denied,* 474 U.S. 817, 106 S. Ct. 62, 88 L. Ed. 2d 50 (1985).

206. United States v. Pozsgai, 999 F.2d 719, 725 (3d Cir. 1993), *cert. denied,* 510 U.S. 1110 (pollutant includes concrete rubble and cinder block); Hanson v. United States, 710 F. Supp. 1105, 1107 (E.D. Tex. 1989) (pollutant includes bricks and sheet metal); Minnehaha Creek Watershed Dist. v. Hoffman, 597 F.2d 617, 626–27 (8th Cir. 1979) (pollutant includes "dams and riprap"); and Avoyelles Sportsmen's League v. Alexander, 473 F. Supp. 525, 532 (W.D. La. 1979) (pollutant includes "sheared trees and vegetation and scraped soil and leaf litter"). Water itself, however, has been found not to be a pollutant under the definition. Orleans Audubon Soc'y v. Lee, 742 F.2d 901, 910–11 (5th Cir. 1984).

207. 33 U.S.C. § 1362(14).

208. *See, e.g., Borden Ranch, supra* note 183, at 815; United States v. Pozsgai, 999 F.2d 719, 726 n.6 (3d Cir. 1993); Avoyelles Sportsmen's League v. Marsh, 715 F.2d 897, 922 (5th Cir. 1983); Matter of Alameda County Assessor's Parcel, 672 F. Supp. 1278, 1284–85 (N.D. Cal. 1987); United States v. Tull, 615 F. Supp. 610, 622 (E.D. Va. 1983), *aff'd,* 769 F.2d 182 (4th Cir. 1985), *rev'd on other grounds,* 481 U.S. 412 (1987); United States v. Weisman, 489 F. Supp. 1331, 1337 (M.D. Fla. 1980).

209. *See generally* U.S. Army Corps of Eng'rs, *Information on "Fill" Rule,* http://www.usace .army.mil/cw/cecwo/reg/fill.htm.

210. 33 C.F.R. § 323.3(e)(2001).

211. 40 C.F.R. § 232.2(2001).

212. Final Revisions to the Clean Water Act Regulatory Definitions of "Fill Material" and "Discharge of Fill Material," 67 Fed. Reg. 31,129 (May 9, 2002), *available at* http://www .usace.army.mil/cw/cecwo/reg/definfil.htm. This rule reconciled an issue raised in a U.S. District Court for the Southern District of West Virginia case holding mountaintop coal mining operations (in which tons of rock and earth are disposed of into valley streams) required a Section 404 permit to discharge material. Bragg v. Robertson, 72 F. Supp. 2d 642 (S.D. W. Va. 1999), *aff'd in part, vacated in part and remanded with instructions,* Bragg v. W. Va. Coal Ass'n, 248 F.3d 275 (4th Cir. 2001), *cert. denied,* 534 U.S. 1113 (2002). *See also* Kentuckians for the Commonwealth v. Rivenburgh, 204 F. Supp. 2d 927, 941 (S.D. W. Va. 2002), *rev'd,* 317 F.3d 425 (4th Cir. 2003) (lower court holding that "[w]hen overburden is dumped into valleys and streams to get rid of it, the disposal has the effect of creating dry land, but not the purpose. Because land creation or elevation is not a principle purpose of overburden disposal in streams, such a discharge would not meet the Corps's definition of 'fill material' . . . nor be permittable under § 404" reversed by the Fourth Circuit).

213. Fill material is now defined as follows: "(1) Except as specified in paragraph (3) of this definition, the term fill material means material placed in waters of the United States where the material has the effect of: (i) Replacing any portion of a water of the United States with dry land; or (ii) Changing the bottom elevation of any portion of a water of the United States. (2) Examples of such fill material include, but are not limited to: rock, sand,

soil, clay, plastics, construction debris, wood chips, overburden from mining or other excavation activities, and materials used to create any structure or infrastructure in the waters of the United States. (3) The term fill material does not include trash or garbage." 33 C.F.R. § 323.2. "Discharge of fill material" is defined in current Corps regulations to include the following activities: "[p]lacement of fill that is necessary for the construction of any structure or infrastructure in a water of the United States; the building of any structure, infrastructure, or impoundment requiring rock, sand, dirt, or other material for its construction; site-development fills for recreational, industrial, commercial, residential, or other uses; causeways or road fills; dams and dikes; artificial islands; property protection and/or reclamation devices such as riprap, groins, seawalls, breakwaters, and revetments; beach nourishment; levees; fill for structures such as sewage treatment facilities, intake and outfall pipes associated with power plants and subaqueous utility lines; placement of fill material for construction or maintenance of any liner, berm, or other infrastructure associated with solid waste landfills; placement of overburden, slurry, or tailings or similar mining-related materials; and artificial reefs." 33 C.F.R. § 323.2(f) (2007).

214. *See supra* Section II.A.3.
215. 33 C.F.R. § 323.2(c) (2007). *See* United States v. Hummel, 2003 U.S. Dist. LEXIS 5656 (2003).
216. United States v. Deaton, 209 F.3d 331 (4th Cir. 2000), *cert. denied*, 541 U.S. 972 (2004). *Accord* Avoyelles Sportsmen's League v. Marsh. 715 F.2d 897 (5th Cir. 1983) ("[t]he word 'addition,' as used in the definition of 'discharge,' may reasonably be understood to include 'redeposit,'" where such "redepositing activities would significantly alter the character of the wetlands and limit the ecological functions served by the tract." Furthermore, because "'dredged' material is by definition material that comes from the water itself," construing the term "addition" to impose a requirement that the pollutant come from outside sources "would effectively remove the dredge-and-fill provisions from the statute." *Id.* at 923–24); United States v. M.C.C. of Florida, Inc., 772 F.2d 1501, 1506 (11th Cir. 1985), *vacated and remanded on other grounds*, 481 U.S. 1034 (1987), *readopted in part and remanded on other grounds*, 848 F.2d 1133 (11th Cir. 1988), *reh'g granted in other part*, 863 F.2d 802 (11th Cir. 1989) (redepositing sediment and vegetation dredged by tugboat propellers onto adjacent sea grass beds was an "addition" of a pollutant that impacted the physical and biological integrity of the waters in question). *Cf.* United States v. Wilson, 133 F.3d 251 (4th Cir. 1997) (a divided Fourth Circuit reached no conclusion as to whether sidecasting was subject to regulation).
217. 145 F.3d 1399 (D.C. Cir. 1998).
218. 33 C.F.R. § 323.2(d)(1)(iii)(1994).
219. *Id.* § 323.2(d)(3)(i) (1994).
220. *See* Bradford C. Mank, *American Mining Congress v. Army Corps of Engineers: Ignoring Chevron and the Clean Water Act's Broad Purposes*, 25 N. Ky. L. Rev. 51 (1997).
221. In 1986, the Corps modified the definition of "discharge of dredged material" through a new regulation, effective in January 1987. 51 Fed. Reg. 41,206 (Nov. 13, 1986). This rule stated that dredging was not regulated, so long as the dredged material was not redeposited within the "waters of the United States." *See* 33 C.F.R. § 323.2 (1987); Reid v. Marsh, 20 Env't Rep. Cas. (BNA) 1336, 1341–42 (N.D. Ohio 1984). To deal with the issue of not regulating dredging itself but regulating any redeposit, the 1986 regulation directed that the "discharge of dredged material" "does not include de minimis, incidental soil movement occurring during normal dredging operations." 51 Fed. Reg. 41,206, 41,232 (Nov. 13, 1986); 33 C.F.R. § 323.2 (1987).
222. 33 C.F.R. § 323.2(d)(1994).
223. No. C90-713-CIV-5-BO (E.D.N.C. 1992).
224. 58 Fed. Reg. 45,008 (Aug. 25, 1993); 33 C.F.R. § 323.2(d) (1994).
225. *Id.*
226. 33 C.F.R. § 323.2(d)(l) (1994). Under that 1993 regulation the term "redeposit" "includes, but is not limited to, the following: (i) the addition of dredged material to a specified discharge site located in waters of the United States; (ii) the runoff or overflow from a contained land or water disposal area; and (iii) any addition, including redeposit, of

dredged material, including excavated material, into waters of the United States which is incidental to any activity, including mechanized landclearing, ditching, channelization and other excavation." *Id.*

227. *National Mining Ass'n*, 145 F.3d at 1405.

228. *Id.* at 1406.

229. *Id.* at 1404.

230. *Id.* at 1405.

231. *Id.* (quoting *Avoyelles Sportsmen's League*, 715 F.2d at 924 n.43).

232. *Id.*

233. RGL 96-2, *Applicability of Exemptions Under Section 404(f) to "Deep-Ripping" Activities in Wetlands*, 62 Fed. Reg. 31,504 (June 9, 1997), *available at* http://www.usace .army.mil/cw/cecwo/reg/rgls/rgl96-02.pdf ("the mechanical manipulation of the soil to break up or pierce highly compacted, impermeable or slowly permeable subsurface soil layers, or other similar kinds of restrictive soil layers. These practices are typically used to break up these subsoil layers (e.g., impermeable soil layer, hardpan) as part of the initial preparation of the soil to establish an agricultural or silvicultural operation.").

234. 261 F.3d 810 (9th Cir. 2001).

235. Borden Ranch Partnership v. U.S. Army Corps of Eng'rs, 537 U.S. 99 (2002). This affirmance was per curiam by an equally divided (4-4) Court in which Justice Kennedy did not participate in the consideration or decision. *Id.*

236. *See Borden Ranch*, 261 F.3d at 816 (attempt to convert, into a vineyard, property that had been used primarily as rangeland for cattle that included vernal pools, swales, and intermittent drainage areas, all of which depended on a dense layer of "clay pan" to maintain their hydrologic features).

237. 64 Fed. Reg. 25,120, 25,121 (May 10, 1999). A reviewing court upheld that rule, but cautioned the agencies not to adopt "an unduly narrow" definition of "incidental fallback." American Mining Congress v. U.S. Army Corps of Eng'rs, 120 F. Supp. 2d 23, 30 (D.D.C. 2000).

238. 66 Fed. Reg. 4550 (Jan. 17, 2001).

239. 33 C.F.R. § 323.3(d)(2).

240. *Id.* § 323.3(d)(2)(ii) (2006) ("Examples of incidental fallback include soil that is disturbed when dirt is shoveled and the back-spill that comes off a bucket when such small volume of soil or dirt falls into substantially the same place from which it was initially removed.").

241. *Id.* § 323.3(d)(2)(i).

242. National Ass'n of Home Builders v. U.S. Army Corps of Eng'rs, 311 F. Supp. 2d 91 (D.D.C. 2004).

243. *Id.* at 93.

244. National Ass'n of Home Builders v. U.S. Army Corps of Eng'rs, 440 F.3d 459 (D.C. Cir. 2006).

245. National Ass'n of Home Builders v. U.S. Army Corps of Eng'rs, 2007 U.S. Dist. LEXIS 6366 (Jan. 30, 2007).

246. *See, e.g.*, Nat'l Ass'n of Home Builders, *NAHB Applauds "Tulloch II" Clean Water Act Ruling*, *available at* http://www.nahb.org/news_details.aspx?newsID=4028 ("The Corps' Tulloch II rule was the answer to legal battles that resulted in the rejection of the first Tulloch rule, which was named after the North Carolina developer who was sued in a 1993 case filed by an environmental group. That complaint sought to have the Corps regulate "incidental fallback," or dirt that falls from the blades or buckets of construction equipment, by saying that the dirt represents an addition to the wetlands."); Van Ness Feldman, *District Court Strikes Down Clean Water Act Tulloch II Dredging Rule*, *available at* http://www.vnf.com/ content/alerts/alert020207.htm.

247. *National Ass'n of Home Builders*, slip op. at 12.

248. *Id.*

249. *Id.* at 11–12.

250. *Id.* at 13–14.

251. Patricia Ware, *Court Says Dredging Rule Invalid; Corps Should Reconsider Need for Permits*, 21 BNA Daily Env't, Feb. 1, 2007, at A15 (The National Association of Home

Builders' president said of the ruling "[w]e look forward to working with the Corps and other agencies to craft sensible regulations that allow us to provide needed housing while we continue to protect the environment." *Id.*).

252. *See supra* Section II.B.1.

253. *See supra* Section II.B.1.

254. *See infra* Section II.C.1.

255. *See infra* Section II.C.2.

256. *See infra* Section II.C.3.

257. *See generally* 33 C.F.R. pt. 330 (2007), 40 C.F.R. § 230.7 (2007); *see also* U.S. Army Corps of Eng'rs, *Nationwide Permit Program, available at* http://www.usace.army.mil/cw/cecwo/reg/nationwide_permits.htm. *See also* William E. Taylor & Kate L. Geoffroy, *General and Nationwide Permits, in* CONNOLLY ET AL., WETLANDS LAW AND POLICY, *supra* note 11, for a detailed overview of general permits, particularly the nationwide permit process.

258. U.S. Army Corps of Eng'rs, *U.S. Army Corps of Engineers Regulatory Program, ALL PERMIT DECISIONS FY 2004 & 2005* (on file with author).

259. 33 U.S.C. § 1344(e).

260. *See ALL PERMIT DECISIONS, supra* note 258.

261. 33 U.S.C. § 1344(e). *See* Alaska Ctr. for the Environment v. West, 157 F.3d 680 (9th Cir. 1998).

262. 40 C.F.R. § 230.10(a) (2007). "The NWPs authorize only those activities that result in minimal individual and cumulative adverse effects on the aquatic environment, and thus do not include a formal process for consideration of less damaging alternatives." 72 Fed. Reg. at 11,093.

263. 33 C.F.R. § 320.4(a) (2007).

264. "In order to address the requirements of the National Environmental Policy Act, the Corps prepares a decision document for each NWP along with a 404(b)(1) Guidelines analysis." 72 Fed. Reg. at 11,117. (The Corps asserts that it believes "the data in the draft decision documents comply with the requirements of NEPA. The estimates of the projected use of the NWPs, the acres impacted, and the amount of compensatory mitigation are based on available data from Corps district offices, and other sources of data, such as surveys. Those data are based on preconstruction notifications and other requests for NWP verifications for activities that do not require preconstruction notification. For those NWP activities that do not require notification, it is necessary to derive estimates. For the decision documents, we must use predictive data, since the future use of an NWP is speculative. Likewise, we cannot provide site specific information for these environmental assessments, because there are no specific sites or projects associated with the proposed issuance of an NWP." *Id.* at 11,095.).

265. *See* U.S. Army Corps of Eng'rs, *Final Documents for 2007 Nationwide Permits, available at* http://www.usace.army.mil/cw/cecwo/reg/nwp/nwp_final.htm. The decision documents each include a discussion of compliance with applicable laws, consideration of public comments, an alternatives analysis, and a general assessment of individual and cumulative impacts, including the general potential effects on public interest factors. *Id.*

266. In 1997, it was reported that the average time to evaluate projects under general permits was 15 days compared to 104 days for individual permits. *Wetlands Protection and Mitigation Banking: Hearing Before the H. Comm. on Transp. and Infrastructure Subcomm. on Water Resources and Environment*, 105th Cong. (1997) (statement of Michael L. Davis, Deputy Assistant Secretary of the Army for Civil Works, and Robert H. Wayland III, Director, Office of Wetlands, Oceans and Watersheds, Environmental Prot. Agency), *available at* http://www.usace.army.mil/cw/cecw-p/pcomp/davis120997.pdf. These numbers are similar to those reported recently. *See ALL PERMIT DECISIONS, supra* note 258.

267. Because NWPs are considered permits, and not regulations, EPA is not directly involved in the actual issuance of the proposed permits.

268. 33 C.F.R. § 325.2(e)(1). Letters of permission require that (1) the activity must fall under a district engineer–created "list of categories of activities proposed for authorization under

[letters of permission] procedures"; (2) the proposed list is subject to public notice and comment and an opportunity for public hearing; and (3) state certification pursuant to §401 of the CWA has been issued or waived and applicable Coastal Zone Management consistency determinations have been made and concurred in by affected states. 33 C.F.R. §325.2(e)(1)(ii)(A)–(C). *See also* U.S. Army Corps of Eng'rs Jacksonville District, *Letter of Permission, available at* http://www.saj.usace.army.mil/permit/permitting/lop.htm.

269. "Those activities that do not qualify for NWP authorization may be authorized by . . . individual permits." 72 Fed. Reg. at 11,094.

270. Contact information for the various district offices can be found at U.S Army Corps of Eng'rs, *Regulatory Program, District Offices, available at* http://www.usace.army.mil/cw/cecwo/reg/district.htm.

271. U.S. Army Corps of Eng'rs, *Online Permit Application Center, Guide for Permit Applicants, available at* https://epermit.usace.army.mil/forms_need.html#apply-genper ("You can contact the nearest Corps regulatory office for information on application procedures for regional general permits and programmatic general permits available in your area.").

272. 33 C.F.R. §325.5(c)(3).

273. *See* Randall S. Guttery, Stephen L. Poe & C. F. Sirmans, *Federal Wetlands Regulation: Restrictions on the Nationwide Permit Program and the Implications for Residential Property Owners*, 37 Am. Bus. L.J. 299 (2000); James L. Conner II, *Environmental Law— Nationwide Permits for Categories of Waters Issued by the Corps of Engineers Under FWPCA Section 404: A Legitimate Administrative Interpretation Ratified by Congress?* 61 N.C. L. Rev. 904 (1983); John H. Cushman, Jr., *U.S. Seeks Changes in Wetland Rules, but 2 Sides Criticize Plan*, N.Y. Times, June 24, 1998, at A-20.

274. National Ass'n of Home Builders v. U.S. Army Corps of Eng'rs, Civ. No. 00-379 (D.D.C., Sept. 29, 2006).

275. 65 Fed. Reg. 12,818 (Mar. 9, 2000); 67 Fed. Reg. 2020 (Jan. 15, 2002).

276. Suits were originally filed by the National Association of Home Builders, the National Federation of Independent Business, and the National Stone, Sand and Gravel Association.

277. National Ass'n of Home Builders, *supra* note 274, slip op. at 4–5. *See also* Amena H. Saiyid, *Corps Authority to Issue Nationwide Permits Upheld in Decision by U.S. District Court*, 190 BNA Daily Env't, Oct. 2, 2006, at A7 .

278. National Ass'n of Home Builders, *supra* note 274, slip op. at 32.

279. *Reissuance of Nationwide Permits: Notice*, 72 Fed. Reg. 11,092 (Mar. 12, 2007), *available at* http://www.usace.army.mil/cw/cecwo/reg/nwp/nwp_2007_final.pdf. *See also* Proposal to Reissue and Modify Nationwide Permits, 71 Fed. Reg. 56,258 (Sept. 26, 2006), *available at* www.regulations.gov; Amena H. Saiyid, *Corps Proposes Six New Nationwide Permits Allowing Pipeline Repair, Mining in Wetlands*, 186 BNA Daily Env't, Sept. 27, 2006, A1.

280. *Id.* The number 26 is "reserved" but no longer used for a nationwide permit due to past controversy over its coverage. *See* Bill Sapp, ABA Section on Environment, Energy and Resources, Waste Management Committee, *New and Modified Wetlands Permits Replace Nationwide Permit 26, available at* http://www.abanet.org/environ/committees/waterquality/newsletter/dec00/sapp.shtml. *See also* Claudia Copeland, Congressional Research Service, *Nationwide Permits for Wetlands Projects: Permit 26 and Other Issues and Controversies, available at* http://ncseonline.org/NLE/CRSreports/Wetlands/wet-7.cfm?&CFID=31 59399&CFTOKEN=74767317.

281. The complete list of current NWPs is as follows: 1. Aids to Navigation; 2. Structures in Artificial Canals; 3. Maintenance; 4. Fish and Wildlife Harvesting, Enhancement, and Attraction Devices and Activities; 5. Scientific Measurement Devices; 6. Survey Activities; 7. Outfall Structures and Associated Intake Structures; 8. Oil and Gas Structures on the Outer Continental Shelf; 9. Structures in Fleeting and Anchorage Areas; 10. Mooring Buoys; 11. Temporary Recreational Structures; 12. Utility Line Activities; 13. Bank Stabilization; 14. Linear Transportation Projects; 15. U.S. Coast Guard Approved Bridges; 16. Return Water from Upland Contained Disposal Areas; 17. Hydropower Projects; 18. Minor Discharges; 19. Minor Dredging; 20. Oil Spill Cleanup; 21. Surface Coal

Mining Operations; 22. Removal of Vessels; 23. Approved Categorical Exclusions; 24. Indian Tribe or State Administered Section 404 Programs; 25. Structural Discharges; 26. [Reserved]; 27. Aquatic Habitat Restoration, Establishment, and Enhancement Activities; 28. Modifications of Existing Marinas; 29. Residential Developments; 30. Moist Soil Management for Wildlife; 31. Maintenance of Existing Flood Control Facilities; 32. Completed Enforcement Actions; 33. Temporary Construction, Access, and Dewatering; 34. Cranberry Production Activities; 35. Maintenance Dredging of Existing Basins; 36. Boat Ramps; 37. Emergency Watershed Protection and Rehabilitation; 38. Cleanup of Hazardous and Toxic Waste; 39. Commercial and Institutional Developments; 40. Agricultural Activities; 41. Reshaping Existing Drainage Ditches; 42. Recreational Facilities; 43. Stormwater Management Facilities; 44. Mining Activities; 45. Repair of Uplands Damaged by Discrete Events; 46. Discharges in Ditches; 47. Pipeline Safety Program Designated Time Sensitive Inspections and Repairs; 48. Existing Commercial Shellfish Aquaculture Activities; 49. Coal Remining Activities; 50. Underground Coal Mining Activities. *Id.* at 11,180–81.

282. U.S. Army Corps of Eng'rs, *Nationwide Permit Information, available at* http://www .usace.army.mil/cw/cecwo/reg/nationwide_permits.htm.

283. *See, e.g.*, U.S. Army Corps of Eng'rs, Los Angeles District, *Pending NWP's for the Los Angeles District, available at* http://www.spl.usace.army.mil/regulatory/jdocs/readx_ pending_nwp.pl?order_by=RCVD_DT&order=cba.

284. *See* 72 Fed. Reg. at 11,181. The general conditions on NWPs are: 1. Navigation; 2. Aquatic Life Movements; 3. Spawning Areas; 4. Migratory Bird Breeding Areas; 5. Shellfish Beds; 6. Suitable Material; 7. Water Supply Intakes; 8. Adverse Effects from Impoundments; 9. Management of Water Flows; 10. Fills Within 100-Year Floodplains; 11. Equipment; 12. Soil Erosion and Sediment Controls; 13. Removal of Temporary Fills; 14. Proper Maintenance; 15. Wild and Scenic Rivers; 16. Tribal Rights; 17. Endangered Species; 18. Historic Properties; 19. Designated Critical Resource Waters; 20. Mitigation; 21. Water Quality; 22. Coastal Zone Management; 23. Regional and Case-by-Case Conditions; 24. Use of Multiple Nationwide Permits; 25. Transfer of Nationwide Permit Verifications; 26. Compliance Certification; 27. Pre-Construction Notification; and 28. Single and Complete Project. *Id.* at 11,191–96.

285. *Id.* at 56,273–76.

286. 33 U.S.C. § 1341(2000).

287. 33 C.F.R. § 320.3(b)(2007).

288. *See* 72 Fed. Reg. at 11,092.

289. *See, e.g.*, U.S. Army Corps of Eng'rs Sacramento District, *Nationwide Permit Reissuance—Request for Comments on Proposed Regional Conditions to Be Imposed by the California, Utah and Nevada Portions of the Sacramento District, available at* http:// www.spk.usace.army.mil/pub/outgoing/co/reg/pn/200650414.pdf.

290. *See ALL PERMIT DECISIONS, supra* note 258.

291. 33 C.F.R. § 325.1(b)(2007).

292. A copy of the current application can be found at U.S. Army Corps of Eng'rs, *Application for a Department of the Army Permit, available at* http://www.usace.army.mil/cw/cecwo/ reg/eng4345a.pdf. According to its upper right-hand corner, that application expired in 2004. *Id.*

293. Detailed engineering plans and specifications are not required at this stage. 33 C.F.R. § 325.1(d)(1).

294. *Id.*

295. 33 C.F.R. § 325.1(d)(4).

296. U.S. Army Corps of Eng'rs, *Online Permit Application Center, Guide for Permit Applicants, available at* https://epermit.usace.army.mil/forms_need.html#apply-genper.

297. 33 C.F.R. § 325.2(a) (2007). An application is complete when the Corps receives sufficient information to issue a public notice. *Id.* § 325.1(d)(9). The Corps can request additional information after it has determined that an application is complete if it is essential to make a public interest determination. *Id.* §§ 325.1(d)(9), 325.1(e).

298. 33 C.F.R. §§ 325.3(a), 325(c) (2007).

299. The Clean Water Act anticipates that EPA, the FWS, the NMFS, and other federal agencies will comment on wetland permit applications. *See* 33 U.S.C. § 1344(q). The Act also explicitly authorizes EPA to veto the Corps' issuance of a wetland permit. *Id.* § 1344(c).

300. The Fish and Wildlife Coordination Act, 16 U.S.C. §§ 661–66(c), requires the Corps to consult with the FWS or the NMFS, and with the head of the appropriate state agency exercising administration over the wildlife resources of the state when the Corps reviews a wetland permit application. 33 C.F.R. §§ 320.3(e), 320.4(c). In addition, the Endangered Species Act, 16 U.S.C. §§ 1531–44 (2000), may also require the Corps to consult with the FWS and the NMFS when it issues certain permits.

301. In addition to the laws cited in the previous footnote, the Magnuson-Stevens Fishery Conservation and Management Act, 16 U.S.C. § 1855(b)(2), requires the Corps to consult with the NMFS when a proposed federal activity may adversely affect identified Essential Fish Habitat (EFH). *See* 50 C.F.R. pt. 600. For general information about EFH, *see* National Oceanic and Atmospheric Administration Fisheries, *Essential Fish Habitat*, *available at* http://www.nmfs.noaa.gov/habitat/habitatprotection/efh/index.htm. *See also* Kim Diana Connolly, *An Introduction to the Essential Fish Habitat (EFH) Consultation Process for the South Atlantic Area*, 11 Se. Envtl. L.J. 1 (2003).

302. The National Historic Preservation Act of 1966, 16 U.S.C. § 470, requires the Corps to consult with state/tribal historic preservation officers and the Federal Advisory Council on Historic Preservation when it issues certain permits. *See also* 33 C.F.R. pt. 325, App. C (2007).

303. The Corps cannot issue a wetland permit unless the state in which the discharge will occur certifies that the discharge will not affect the quality of the water in the state in violation of any effluent limitations, water quality standards, or water quality requirements of that state. 33 U.S.C. § 1341; 33 C.F.R. §§ 320.3(a), 325.1(d)(4), 325.2(b)(1) (2007).

304. Federal agencies have entered into various Memoranda of Agreement pursuant to Section 404(q) of the Clean Water Act, 33 U.S.C. § 1344(q) that governs the manner in which they will comment on proposed applications and resolve any disputes regarding applications. Copies of the MOAs may be found at http://www.usace.army.mil/cw/cecwo/reg/mou/moumoas.htm.

305. 33 C.F.R. § 325.1(e) (2007). (The regulations specify that "[a] summary of the comments, the actual letters or portions thereof, or representative comment letters may be furnished to the applicant." *Id.* § 325.2(a)(3)). *See also* Mall Properties, Inc. v. Marsh, 672 F. Supp. 561, 574–75 (D. Mass. 1988) (holding that the Corps violated its regulations when it failed to inform the permit applicant that the state governor had objected to the proposed permit), *appeal dismissed on finding that remand order was nonappealable*, 881 F.2d 440 (1st Cir. 1988).

306. 33 C.F.R. § 325.2(a)(3) (2007).

307. *Id.* § 325.2(d)(5). When an applicant requests additional time to respond to the Corps' request for information, the agency may grant the request, make a final decision on the permit, or consider the application withdrawn. *Id.*

308. *Id.*

309. *Id.* § 327.4(b). A hearing request must state with particularity the reasons for the hearing. *Id.* Before the Corps grants a request for a hearing, it may attempt to resolve the issues raised by the requester informally. *Id.* Any hearing must comply with certain requirements. *Id.* § 327.11 (2007).

310. See U.S. Army Corps of Eng'rs, Baltimore District, *Regulatory Program General Information*, *available at* http://www.nab.usace.army.mil/Regulatory/gen_info.htm ("Very few applications involve a public hearing.").

311. 33 U.S.C. § 1344(b)(1). *See also* 33 C.F.R. § 320.4(a)(1) ("[A] permit will be denied if the discharge authorized by such permit would not comply with the . . . 404(b)(1) guidelines."). *Id.* § 323.6(a). Although they are referred to as guidelines, the 404(b)(1) Guidelines are binding regulations. The 404(b)(1) Guidelines do not, of course, apply to permits that are issued solely under Section 10 of the Rivers and Harbors Act.

312. 40 C.F.R. § 230.10(a). *See generally* Houck, *Hard Choices, supra* note 17.

313. 40 C.F.R. § 230.10(a)(3).

314. *Id.* §230.10(c). The guidelines identify effects deemed to be "significant," and establish tests to be used in determining significance. *Id.* In addition, the Corps has clarified that the term "significant" under the 404(b)(1) Guidelines does not have exactly the same meaning as the term "significant" under NEPA. RGL 87-02, *Use of the Word "Significant" in Permit Documentation* (Mar. 30, 1987).

315. 33 C.F.R. §230.10(b).

316. *See infra* Section II.C.3.

317. The Corps conducts a "public interest" review for all individual applications under the Rivers and Harbors Act, the Clean Water Act, or the Ocean Dumping Act. 33 C.F.R. §320.4. The Corps' website declares, "Probably the single biggest safeguard of the program is the Corps public interest review, which also forms the main framework for overall evaluation of the project. This review requires the careful weighing of all public interest factors relevant to each particular case." U.S. Army Corps of Eng'rs, *Regulatory Program Overview, available at* http://www.usace.army.mil/cw/cecwo/reg/oceover.htm.

318. 33 C.F.R. §320.4(a)(1).

319. *Id.* In every case, the Corps considers (1) the relative extent of the public and private need for the proposed activity; (2) the practicability of using reasonable alternative locations and methods to achieve the objective of the proposed activity (if there are unresolved conflicts regarding resource use); and (3) the extent and permanence of the beneficial and/or detrimental effect that the activity is likely to have on the public and private uses to which the area is suited. *Id.* §320.4(a)(2). Earlier versions of the Corps public interest review involved evaluation of fewer factors. *See* 42 Fed. Reg. 37,122 (1977). Earlier versions also involved a test as to whether the issued permit would be in the public interest. *See* 47 Fed. Reg. 31,794 (1982).

320. 33 C.F.R. §320.4(a)(1). *See* Kim Diana Connolly, *Shifting Interests: Rethinking the U.S. Army Corps of Engineers Permitting Process and Public Interest Review in Light of Hurricanes Katrina and Rita*, 32 T. Marshall L. Rev. 109 (2006).

321. For links to these and other "related laws," *see* U.S. Army Corps of Eng'rs, *Statutory, Administrative & Policy Materials, available at* http://www.usace.army.mil/cw/cecwo/reg/sadmin3.htm.

322. 42 U.S.C. §4332(2)(C).

323. *Id.* §4332(2)(E). As part of the NEPA process, cumulative effects of the proposed activity, including its indirect effects, must be considered. 40 C.F.R. §1508.8 (2007).

324. The Council on Environmental Quality (CEQ) is a federal agency created by NEPA to administer and interpret NEPA. 42 U.S.C. §4342. For more information on the CEQ, see its website at http://www.whitehouse.gov/ceq/, as well as NEPANet at http://ceq.eh.doe.gov/nepa/nepanet.htm.

325. *See* 33 C.F.R. pt. 230, pt. 325, App. B; 40 C.F.R. §§1500–08 (2007).

326. 33 C.F.R. §230.7(a) ("(a) *Regulatory Actions*. Most permits will normally require only an EA.").

327. 16 U.S.C. §1536(a)(2)(2000). *See also* 33 C.F.R. §320.3(i) (2007).

328. 33 C.F.R. §325.2(b)(5) (2007). *See also* RGL 83-06, Endangered Species Act—Regulatory Program, *available at* http://www.usace.army.mil/cw/cecwo/reg/rgls/rgl83-06.pdf.

329. *Id.*

330. *See* U.S. Fish & Wildlife Serv., Section 7 Consultation Handbook, *available at* http://www.fws.gov/endangered/consultations/s7hndbk/s7hndbk.htm.

331. *See* U.S. Fish & Wildlife Serv., *Endangered Species Related Laws, Regulations, Policies & Notices, available at* http://www.fws.gov/endangered/policies/index.html.

332. The NMFS (also known as NOAA Fisheries) has jurisdiction over marine species under the Endangered Species Act. 50 C.F.R. §402.01(b). For more information on NMFS activities with respect to endangered species, see NOAA Fisheries, *Office of Protected Resources, available at* http://www.nmfs.noaa.gov/pr/.

333. *Id.* The consultation procedures are codified in 50 C.F.R. pt. 402.

334. The consultation process involves the FWS or the NMFS preparing a "biological opinion" that evaluates whether the proposed activity will jeopardize the continued existence of a threatened or endangered species. 50 C.F.R. §402.14 (2006). That opinion may also

suggest conditions that the Corps could place on the permit to ensure that the activity will not jeopardize such species. *Id.* Even if the FWS or the NMFS concludes that the proposed activity will jeopardize a threatened or endangered species, the Corps retains the ultimate authority to determine whether the activity will jeopardize such species. Roosevelt Campobello Int'l Park Comm'n v. EPA, 684 F.2d 1041, 1049 (1st Cir. 1982); Sierra Club v. Froehlke, 534 F.2d 1289, 1303 (8th Cir. 1976). Note that the Corps is also required to consider the impacts of proposed activities on endangered or threatened species or designated critical habitat as part of the agency's "public interest" review. *See* Norfolk v. U.S. Army Corps of Eng'rs, 968 F.2d 1438, 1453 (1st Cir. 1992).

335. Marine Mammal Protection Act of 1972, 16 U.S.C. §§ 1361–1407; Regulations Governing the Taking and Importing of Marine Mammals, 50 C.F.R. pt. 216 (2006). *See also* NOAA Office of Protected Resources, *Marine Mammal Protection Act of 1972*, *available at* http://www.nmfs.noaa.gov/pr/laws/mmpa/.

336. 16 U.S.C. §§ 470, 470f (2000).

337. The ACHP has promulgated regulations that authorize state historic preservation officers (SHPOs) to consult with agencies and comment on projects in lieu of, or in addition to, the ACHP. 36 C.F.R. § 800.1(c)(ii) (2007).

338. 33 C.F.R. pt. 325, App. C (2007).

339. *Id.* § 325.2(b)(3) (2007).

340. For a list of SHPOs, see Advisory Council on Historic Preservation, *State Historic Preservation Officers*, *available at* http://www.achp.gov/shpo.html.

341. For a list of THPOs, see Advisory Council on Historic Preservation, *Tribal Historic Preservation Officers*, *available at* http://www.achp.gov/thpo.html.

342. *See* National Park Service, *History and Culture Preservation*, *available at* http://www.cr.nps.gov/preservation.htm.

343. 33 C.F.R. pt. 325, App. C, § 4a.

344. Under the NHPA, as long as the Corps consults with the ACHP and considers the impact of a project on historic properties, the Corps can issue a permit for the project even though it will adversely affect historic properties. 36 C.F.R. § 800.6(c)(2).

345. *See supra* notes 318–20 and accompanying text.

346. 33 C.F.R. pt. 325, App. C., § 10a.

347. 33 U.S.C. § 1341(a)(1). *See also* 33 C.F.R. §§ 320.3(a), 325.1(d)(4), and Regulatory Guidance Letter 87-03, Section 401 Water Quality Certification, *available at* http://www.usace.army.mil/inet/functions/cw/cecwo/reg/rgls/rgl87-03.htm. When the Corps receives a permit application, it must notify EPA that it has received the application. 33 U.S.C. § 1341(a)(2) (2000). If the EPA Administrator determines that the proposed activity may affect the water quality of any other state, the Administrator notifies the other state, the Corps, and the permit applicant. *Id.*

348. 33 C.F.R. § 325.2(b)(1)(ii) (2007).

349. *See generally* NOAA, *Federal Consistency Determination Resources*, *available at* http://coastalmanagement.noaa.gov/consistency/resources.html.

350. Coastal Zone Management Plans are reviewed and approved by the Secretary of Commerce. 16 U.S.C. § 1454 (2000).

351. *Id.* § 1456(c)(3)(A). The Act places additional constraints on federal agencies when they are the permit applicant. *See id.* § 1456(c); 33 C.F.R. § 325.2(b)(2)(i).

352. 33 C.F.R. § 320.4(j)(1).

353. *Id.* §§ 320.4(j)(5), 325.2(e)(3).

354. *See* RGL 92-01, *Federal Agencies Roles and Responsibilities*, *available at* http://www.usace.army.mil/cw/cecwo/reg/rgls/rgl92-01.pdf. *See also* 33 C.F.R. § 320.4(c); Slagle v. United States By and Through Baldwin, 809 F. Supp. 704, 712 (D. Minn. 1992) (Corps must consider the comments of local agencies); Sierra Club v. Alexander, 484 F. Supp. 455 (N.D. N.Y. 1980), *aff'd*, 633 F.2d 206 (2d Cir. 1980).

355. RGL 92-01, *supra* note 354.

356. 33 C.F.R. §§ 320.4(j)(1), 325.2(d)(4).

357. *Id.*

358. U.S. Army Corps of Eng'rs, *Provisional Permits*, RGL 93-1, *available at* http://www .usace.army.mil/cw/cecwo/reg/rgls/rgl93-01.pdf.

359. 33 C.F.R. §§ 325.2(a)(6), 325.8. District engineers refer permit applications to the division engineer for decision when (1) a referral is required by a Memorandum of Agreement with other federal agencies; (2) the recommended decision is contrary to the written position of the Governor of the state in which the permitted activity will take place; (3) there is substantial doubt as to authority, law, regulations, or policies applicable to the proposed activity; (4) a higher authority requests that the application be forwarded for decision; or (5) the district engineer is precluded by law or procedures from taking final action on the application. 33 C.F.R. § 325.8(b). The division engineer may refer the application to the Chief of Engineers in similar situations. *Id.* § 325.8(c).

360. 33 C.F.R. § 325.2(a)(6). If an EIS was prepared for the decision, the Corps must prepare a record of decision for the decision instead of a statement of findings. *Id.*

361. *Id.*

362. *Id.* § 320.4(g).

363. *Id.* § 325.6(b). "Permits for the existence of a structure or other activity of a permanent nature are usually for an indefinite duration with no expiration date cited." *Id.* However, where the permit authorizes temporary fills, it will include a definite expiration date. *Id.*

364. *Id.* § 325.6(c).

365. 33 C.F.R. § 325.6(d).

366. *Id.*

367. RGL 91-01, *Extensions of Time for Individual Permit Authorizations* (Nov. 6, 1991), *available at* http://www.usace.army.mil/cw/cecwo/reg/rgls/rgl91-01.pdf.

368. 33 C.F.R. § 325.7(a).

369. *Id.*

370. *Id.*

371. The latest posted statistics, from FY2002 and FY2003, show that in 2002, there were 128 denials of the 81,302 permits applied for (0.16%), and in 2003, there were 299 denials of the 86,177 permits applied for (0.35%). *See* U.S. Army Corps of Eng'rs, *US Army Corps of Engineers Regulatory Program* (2003), *available at* http://www.usace.army.mil/inet/ functions/cw/cecwo/reg/2003webcharts.pdf.

372. 33 C.F.R. § 320.1(a)(2).

373. 33 C.F.R. § 320.2(f)(2007).

374. *Id. See also supra* notes 311–15 and accompanying text.

375. 33 U.S.C. § 1344(c); 40 C.F.R. pt. 231.

376. 33 U.S.C. § 1344(c).

377. Only eleven vetoes have been issued pursuant to EPA § 404(c) authority. U.S. Environmental Prot. Agency, *Clean Water Act Section 404(c) "Veto Authority,"* *available at* http://www.epa .gov/owow/wetlands/pdf/404c.pdf.

378. 33 C.F.R. § 320.4(j)(1).

379. *See generally* U.S. Fish & Wildlife Serv., *available at* http://www.fws.gov/. The FWS also is responsible for keeping the National Wetlands Inventory. U.S. Fish & Wildlife Serv., *National Wetlands Inventory*, *available at* http://www.fws.gov/nwi/.

380. *See generally* NOAA Fisheries, *available at* http://www.nmfs.noaa.gov/.

381. *See generally* Natural Res. Conservation Serv., *available at* http://www.nrcs.usda.gov/.

382. 33 U.S.C. § 1344(m), (q); *see also* 33 C.F.R. § 323.4(c).

383. The Food Security Act of 1985, Pub. L. No. 99-198, 99 Stat. 1504 (1985), 16 U.S.C. §§ 3821–24 (2000), *as amended by* the Federal Agricultural Improvement and Reform Act of 1996, Pub. L. 104-127, 110 Stat. 888 (1996).

384. 33 U.S.C. § 1344(q). *See, e.g.*, Clean Water Act Section 404(q) Memorandum of Agreement Between the Environmental Protection Agency and the Department of the Army, *available at* http://www.usace.army.mil/cw/cecwo/reg/mou/epa404q.htm.

385. *See supra* Section II.B.1.

386. *See supra* Section II.B.1.

387. *See generally* Royal C. Gardner, *Mitigation*, *in* CONNOLLY ET AL., WETLANDS LAW AND POLICY, *supra* note 11.

388. White House Office on Environmental Policy, *Protecting America's Wetlands: A Fair, Flexible, and Effective Approach* (Aug. 24, 1993), *available at* http://www.usace.army .mil/inet/functions/cw/cecwo/reg/aug93wet.htm.

389. Gardner, *supra* note 387, at 260.

390. *See* Environmental Protection Agency, the U.S. Army Corps of Engineers, and the U.S. Departments of Agriculture, Commerce, Interior, and Transportation, *National Wetlands Mitigation Action Plan*, 1 (Dec. 24, 2002), *available at* http://www.mitigationactionplan .gov/map1226withsign.pdf.

391. Hearing Before the Subcommittee on Fisheries, Wildlife, and Water of the Committee on Environment and Public Works, United States Senate, 109th Cong., Aug. 1, 2006 (statements of Benjamin H. Grumbles, Assistant Administrator for Water, U.S. Environmental Protection Agency, and John Paul Woodley, Jr., Assistant Secretary of the Army for Civil Works, Department of the Army, *available at* http://www.epa.gov/water/speeches/ 060801bg.html ("President Bush established, on Earth Day 2004, a national goal to move beyond 'no net loss' of wetlands and to attain an overall increase in the quantity and quality of wetlands in America. Specifically, the President established a goal to increase, improve, and protect three million acres of wetlands by 2009. Since the President announced this objective, EPA, the Corps, the U.S. Department of Agriculture (USDA), and the Department of Interior (DOI) have restored, created, protected or improved 1,797,000 acres of wetlands. We now have 588,000 acres of wetlands that did not exist in 2004, we have improved the quality of 563,000 wetland acres that already existed, and we have protected the high quality of 646,000 acres of existing wetlands.").

392. *Memorandum of Agreement Between the Environmental Protection Agency and the Department of the Army Concerning the Determination of Mitigation Under the Clean Water Act Section 404(b)(1) Guidelines*, 55 Fed. Reg. 9210, 9212 (1990), *available at* http://www.usace.army.mil/cw/cecwo/reg/mou/mitigate.htm.

393. *Id.*; *see also* RGL 02-02, *Guidance on Compensatory Mitigation Projects*, *supra* note 26.

394. 33 U.S.C. § 1344 (2000).

395. *Id.* § 1344(b)(1).

396. Congress directed that regulations pursuant to Section 404(b)(1) "be based on criteria comparable to the criteria applicable" to ocean dumping permits and listed in CWA Section 403(c), 33 U.S.C. § 1343(c). Those criteria mandate that permits for marine discharges be issued only after considering "other possible locations and methods of disposal . . . including land-based alternatives," *id.* § 1343(c)(1)(F) and "the effect of the disposal at varying rates, of particular volumes and concentrations of pollutants," *id.* § 1343(c)(1)(E). These congressional mandates implicitly require that permits be issued only after the practicability of avoiding and minimizing wetland impacts is considered.

397. 40 C.F.R. pt. 230 (2007).

398. *Id.* § 230.10(a) (discussing avoidance and the alternatives analysis); *id.* § 230.10(d) (requiring minimization of potential impacts); *id.* §§ 230.70–.77 (further explaining measures that can minimize impacts); 40 C.F.R. § 230.75(d) (providing that applicants may be required to develop or restore habitat to compensate for damage from their proposed activities).

399. 33 C.F.R. § 320.4(r) (2007). The text of that regulation opens by noting that:

> (1) [m]itigation is an important aspect of the review and balancing process on many Department of the Army permit applications. Consideration of mitigation will occur throughout the permit application review process and includes avoiding, minimizing, rectifying, reducing, or compensating for resource losses. Losses will be avoided to the extent practicable. Compensation may occur on-site or at an off-site location. . . .

400. Corps guidance documents are not published in the *Code of Federal Regulations*, but are made available on the Corps Regulatory Program home page in the same location as the regulations. U.S. Army Corps of Eng'rs, *Statutory, Administrative & Policy Materials*, *available at* http://www.usace.army.mil/cw/cecwo/reg/sadmin3.htm.

401. *See Compensatory Mitigation for Losses of Aquatic Resources*, 71 Fed. Reg. 15,520 (Mar. 28, 2006).

402. *Memorandum of Agreement Between the Environmental Protection Agency and the Department of the Army, supra* note 392.

403. 40 C.F.R. § 230.10(a)(2007).

404. *Id.* § 230.10 (d).

405. *Id.* § 230.70.

406. *Id.* § 230.71.

407. *Id.* § 230.72.

408. *Id.* § 230.73.

409. *Id.* § 230.74.

410. *Id.* § 230.75.

411. *Memorandum of Agreement Between the Environmental Protection Agency and the Department of the Army, supra* note 392, at 9212.

412. RGL 02-02, *Guidance on Compensatory Mitigation Projects, supra* note 26, at 1, *available at* http://www.usace.army.mil/inet/functions/cw/cecwo/reg/RGL2-02.pdf. Under the watershed approach, certain circumstances may allow the Corps to provide mitigation credit for establishing and maintaining vegetated buffers or even including certain appropriate upland areas within mitigation projects. *Id.* at 5–6.

413. *Compensatory Mitigation for Losses of Aquatic Resources*, 71 Fed. Reg. 15,520, 15,523 (Mar. 28, 2006).

414. *See Multi-Agency Compensatory Mitigation Plan Checklist, available at* http://www.mitigationaction plan.gov/checklist.pdf.

415. RGL 02-02, *supra* note 412, at 4.

416. *Federal Guidance for the Establishment, Use and Operation of Mitigation Banks*, 60 Fed. Reg. 58,605, 58,613 (1995), *available at* http://www.epa.gov/owow/wetlands/guidance/mitbankn.html.

417. *Memorandum of Agreement Between the Environmental Protection Agency and the Department of the Army, supra* note 392, at 9212. *See also* NATIONAL RESEARCH COUNCIL, COMPENSATING FOR WETLAND LOSSES UNDER THE CLEAN WATER ACT (2001), *available at* http://www.nap.edu/books/0309074320/html/.

418. *Memorandum of Agreement Between the Environmental Protection Agency and the Department of the Army, supra* note 392, at 9212.

419. *Id.*

420. RGL 02-02, *supra* note 412, at 4–5.

421. National Wetlands Mitigation Action Plan, *Draft On Site/Off Site & In-kind/Out-of-kind Guidance, available at* http://www.mitigationactionplan.gov/sitekind%20guidance%20page.htm.

422. RGL 02-02, *supra* note 412, at 4–5.

423. *Id.*

424. *Id.* at 5.

425. *Id.*

426. *See Draft On Site/Off Site & In-kind/Out-of-kind Guidance, supra* note 421.

427. *Memorandum of Agreement Between the Environmental Protection Agency and the Department of the Army, supra* note 384, at 9212.

428. *See Draft On Site/Off Site & In-kind/Out-of-kind Guidance, supra* note 421.

429. RGL 02-02, *supra* note 412, at 5.

430. *Id.* at 7.

431. *See generally* National Mitigation Banking Ass'n, *What Is Mitigation Banking? available at* http://www.mitigationbanking.org/about/whatismitigationbanking.html ("Mitigation banking unites sound environmental and economic practices to restore and enhance wetlands and other natural resources. Mitigation bankers restore, enhance, create and preserve wetlands or other significant natural areas and assume responsibility for their long-term maintenance, earning mitigation credits, recognized by the regulatory agencies, for their efforts. Mitigation bankers can then sell these mitigation credits to permitees [sic]

and others who must compensate for having impacted wetlands or other natural areas. The sale of wetland credits legally transfers the liability for wetland mitigation from the permitee to the wetland banker." *Id.*).

432. *Federal Guidance for the Establishment, Use and Operation of Mitigation Banks, supra* note 416, at 58,614.

433. *Id.* at 58,613.

434. *Id.* at 58,607.

435. *Id.* at 58,612.

436. *Id.*

437. Prices range quite extensively among various banks. *See* M. Siobhan Fennessy, Associate Professor of Biology, Kenyon College, *Mitigation Banks and Credit Prices in the US, available at* http://biology.kenyon.edu/fennessy/envs93/banks.html.

438. *Id.* at 58,610.

439. *Id.*

440. *Id.*

441. *Id.*

442. *Id.* at 58,613. Sometimes a conservation organization or governmental agency can assume later management authority.

443. *Id.* at 58,612.

444. *Id.*

445. *Federal Guidance on the Use of In-Lieu-Fee Arrangements for Compensatory Mitigation Under Section 404 of the Clean Water Act and Section 10 of the Rivers and Harbors Act,* 65 Fed. Reg. 66,914 (2000), *available at* http://www.epa.gov/owow/wetlands/pdf/inlieufee.pdf. *See* Royal C. Gardner, *Money for Nothing? The Rise of Fee Mitigation,* 19 Va. Envtl. L.J. 1, 18–33 (2000).

446. *Federal Guidance on the Use of In-Lieu-Fee Arrangements, supra* note 445, at 66,915.

447. *Id.* at 15,530.

448. *Reissuance of Nationwide Permits: Notice,* 72 Fed. Reg. 11,092, 11,193 (Mar. 12, 2007), *available at* http://www.usace.army.mil/cw/cecwo/reg/nwp/nwp_2007_final.pdf ("The activity must be designed and constructed to avoid and minimize adverse effects, both temporary and permanent, to waters of the United States to the maximum extent practicable at the project site (i.e., on site). (b) Mitigation in all its forms (avoiding, minimizing, rectifying, reducing, or compensating) will be required to the extent necessary to ensure that the adverse effects to the aquatic environment are minimal.").

449. *Id.*

450. *Id.*

451. *Id.*

452. *Id.*

453. *Id.*

454. *See* Compensating for Wetland Losses Under the Clean Water Act, *supra* note 417.

455. Environmental Protection Agency, the U.S. Army Corps of Engineers, and the U.S. Departments of Agriculture, Commerce, Interior, and Transportation, *National Wetlands Mitigation Action Plan* (Dec. 24, 2002), *available at* http://www.mitigationactionplan.gov/map1226withsign.pdf.

456. A website detailing implementation of the National Wetlands Mitigation Action Plan is on hold. *See National Compensatory Mitigation Action Plan Item Tracking and Status Table, available at* http://www.mitigationactionplan.gov/actionitem.html.

457. *Id.*

458. Section 314, National Defense Authorization Act for Fiscal Year 2004, Pub. L. 108–136 (2004).

459. *Compensatory Mitigation for Losses of Aquatic Resources,* 71 Fed. Reg. 15,520 (Mar. 28, 2006). The introduction to the notice includes the following text describing the purpose of the proposal: ". . . to establish performance standards and criteria for the use of permittee responsible compensatory mitigation and mitigation banks, and to improve the quality and success of compensatory mitigation projects for activities authorized by Department

of the Army permits. The proposed regulations are also intended to account for regional variations in aquatic resource types, functions, and values, and apply equivalent standards to each type of compensatory mitigation to the maximum extent practicable. The proposed rule includes a watershed approach to improve the quality and success of compensatory mitigation projects in replacing losses of aquatic resource functions, services, and values resulting from activities authorized by Department of the Army permits."

460. *See generally* Environmental Prot. Agency, U.S. Army Corps of Eng'rs, *Proposed Wetlands Conservation Rule, available at* http://www.epa.gov/owow/wetlands/pdf/CompMit RuleFactsheet.pdf.

461. *Compensatory Mitigation for Losses of Aquatic Resources*, 71 Fed. Reg. 29,604 (May 23, 2006).

462. *See* http://www.regulations.gov/fdmspublic/component/main and search using the title of the proposed rule.

463. Memorandum from Assistant Secretary of the Army Civil Works John Paul Woodley, Jr., entitled Compensatory Mitigation for Losses of Aquatic Resources Proposed Rule, *available at* http://www.usace.army.mil/cw/cecwo/reg/news/memo_aquatic09apr07.pdf.

464. 33 U.S.C. § 1344(s) (2000). Although in very rare circumstances the EPA may become involved in enforcement matters, the Corps usually takes the enforcement lead when a permit has been issued. *Memorandum of Agreement Between the Department of the Army and the Environmental Protection Agency Concerning Federal Enforcement for the Section 404 Program of the Clean Water Act 4* (Jan. 19, 1989), *available at* http://www .usace.army.mil/inet/functions/cw/cecwo/reg/enfmoa.htm.

465. 33 C.F.R. § 325.7 (2007).

466. *Federal Guidance for the Establishment, Use and Operation of Mitigation Banks, supra* note 416, at 58,612.

467. The regulations define "appealable action" as "an approved [jurisdictional determination], a permit denial, or a declined permit." 33 C.F.R. § 331.1 (2007).

468. *Id.* pt. 331, *available at* http://www.usace.army.mil/inet/functions/cw/cecwo/reg/33cfr331 .htm.

469. *Id.* § 331.10. That regulation states that "[t]he final Corps decision on a permit application is the initial decision to issue or deny a permit, unless the applicant submits an RFA, and the division engineer accepts the RFA, pursuant to this Part." *Id.* If an action is appealed, the final Corps decision depends on the merit of the appeal: "(a) If the division engineer determines that the appeal is without merit, the final Corps decision is the district engineer's letter advising the applicant that the division engineer has decided that the appeal is without merit, confirming the district engineer's initial decision, and sending the permit denial or the proffered permit for signature to the appellant; or (b) If the division engineer determines that the appeal has merit, the final Corps decision is the district engineer's decision made pursuant to the division engineer's remand of the appealed action. These regulations provide that the Corps' initial decision to issue or deny a permit is the final decision on a permit application. For an appealed action, where the division engineer determines that the appeal has merit, the final Corps permit decision is the district engineer's decision pursuant to the division engineer's remand." *Id. See* Ozark Soc'y v. Melcher, 229 F. Supp. 2d 896 (E.D. Ark. 2002); Bay-Houston Towing Co. v. United States, 58 Fed. Cl. 462, 471 (2003).

470. 33 C.F.R. § 331.4 (2007).

471. *Id.* § 331.6. *See also* RGL 06-01, *Determining Timeliness of Requests for Appeal (RFA), available at* http://www.usace.army.mil/cw/cecwo/reg/rgls/rgl06_01.pdf.

472. 33 C.F.R. § 331.7 (2007).

473. 64 Fed. Reg. §§ 11,707, 11,711 (Mar. 9, 1999).

474. As one recent National Academy of Sciences report put it, "[o]ne advantage of this structure is that district offices may have greater flexibility to pursue innovative efforts and novel actions tailored to local conditions and preferences." National Research Council, Adaptive Management for Water Resources Project Planning (2004), *available at* http:// www.nap.edu/openbook/0309091918/html/37.html.

475. *See, e.g.,* U.S. General Accounting Office, *Waters and Wetlands—Corps of Engineers Needs to Evaluate Its District Office Practices in Determining Jurisdiction* (GAO-04-297, Feb. 2004), *available at* http://www.gao.gov/new.items/d04297.pdf ("Corps districts differ in how they interpret and apply the federal regulations when determining which waters and wetlands are subject to federal jurisdiction." *Id.* at 3.). Prior to the implementation of an administrative appeals process, dissatisfied permit applicants were forced to seek initial redress for decisions with which they disagreed through the judicial process. *Proposal to Establish an Administrative Appeal Process for the Regulatory Programs of the Corps of Engineers*, 60 Fed. Reg. 37,280 (July 19, 1995).

476. An affected party is defined as "a permit applicant, landowner, a lease, easement or option holder (i.e., an individual who has an identifiable and substantial legal interest in the property) who has received an approved JD, permit denial, or has declined a proffered individual permit." 33 C.F.R. § 331.2 (2007).

477. *Id.* § 331.1(a).

478. Available through a link at *33 CFR Part 331, Administrative Appeals Process, at* http://www.usace.army.mil/inet/functions/cw/cecwo/reg/33cfr331.htm.

479. *See* Kim Diana Connolly, *The Administrative Appeals Process, in* CONNOLLY ET AL., WETLANDS LAW AND POLICY, *supra* note 11. The process grew out of a forty-point plan developed by the 1993 White House Wetlands Working Group. White House Office on Environmental Policy, *Protecting America's Wetlands: A Fair, Flexible, and Effective Approach, available at* http://www.wetlands.com/fed/aug93wet.htm. An administrative appeals proposal was identified among the four proposals in that report to address landowner concerns, specifically designed to "allow for administrative appeals of the Corps' determination that it has regulatory jurisdiction over a particular parcel of property, permit denials, and administrative penalties."

480. *See* James G. O'Connor & Douglas R. Williams, *Enforcement and Judicial Review, in* CONNOLLY ET AL., WETLANDS LAW AND POLICY, *supra* note 11.

481. 33 C.F.R. § 331.10.

482. WANT, LAW OF WETLANDS REGULATION, *supra* note 11, §§ 9.3–9.8 (2006).

483. 28 U.S.C. § 2401 (2000).

484. 5 U.S.C. § 706(2). *See Avoyelles Sportsmen's League*, 715 F.2d at 904.

485. *See Memorandum of Agreement Between the Department of the Army and the Environmental Protection Agency Concerning Federal Enforcement for the Section 404 Program of the Clean Water Act* (Jan. 19, 1989), *available at* http://www.usace.army.mil/cw/cecwo/reg/mou/enfmoa.htm.

486. 33 U.S.C. § 1319(a) (2000) (EPA); 33 U.S.C. § 1344(s)(1) (2000) (Corps).

487. 33 U.S.C. § 1319(g) (2000).

488. 33 U.S.C. § 1319(b), (d) (2000) (EPA); 33 U.S.C. § 1344(s)(3)–(4) (2000) (Corps).

489. 33 U.S.C. § 1344(s)(1) (2000).

490. 33 U.S.C. § 1319(b) (2000).

491. Section 506 of the CWA provides:

> The Administrator [of EPA] shall request the Attorney General to appear and represent the United States in any civil or criminal action instituted under [the CWA] to which the Administrator is a party. Unless the Attorney General notifies the Administrator within a reasonable time, that he will appear in a civil action, attorneys who are officers or employees of the Environmental Protection Agency shall appear and represent the United States in such action.

33 U.S.C. § 1366 (2000).

492. 33 U.S.C. § 1319(c).

493. 33 U.S.C. § 1365 (2000).

494. *See generally* James R. May, *Now More Than Ever: Trends in Environmental Citizen Suits at 30*, Environmental Citizen Suits at Thirtysomething: A Celebration & Summit Symposium, Part I, 10 WIDENER L. REV. 1 (2003).

495. 33 U.S.C. § 1365(a)(1).

496. *Id.* § 1365(a)(2).

497. U.S. Const. amend. V: "[N]or shall private property be taken for public use, without just compensation." *See* Robert Meltz, *Wetlands and Regulatory Takings, in* Connolly et al., Wetlands Law and Policy, *supra* note 11.

498. *See generally* Robert Meltz, Congressional Research Service, *Wetlands Regulation and the Law of Property Rights "Takings," available at* http://www.ncseonline.org/nle/crsreports/wetlands/wet-6.cfm.

499. *See, e.g.*, Loveladies Harbor, 21 Cl. Ct. 153 (1990); Florida Rock, 21 Cl. Ct. 161 (1990); Forest Properties, Inc. v. United States, 177 F.3d 1360 (Fed. Cir.), *cert. denied*, 528 U.S. 951 (1999); Heck v. United States, 134 F.3d 1468 (Fed. Cir. 1998); Bayou des Familles v. United States, 130 F.3d 1034 (Fed. Cir. 1997); City Nat'l Bank v. United States, 33 Fed. Cl. 759 (1995). It has been asserted that there are more takings challenges to the federal wetlands program than to any other federal environmental program. *See* Richard C. Ausness, *Regulatory Takings and Wetlands Protection in the Post-Lucas Era*, 30 Land & Water L. Rev. 349 (1995).

500. Jeffrey A. Zinn & Claudia Copeland, Congressional Research Service, *Wetlands: An Overview of Issues, available at* http://www.ncseonline.org/NLE/CRSreports/07Jan/RL33483.pdf.

501. *Id.*

502. *See, e.g.*, Kim Diana Connolly, *Keeping Wetlands Wet: Are Existing Protections Enough?* 6 Vt. J. Envtl. L. 1 (2004/2005).

503. *See* Clean Water Network, The National Agenda, http://www.cleanwaternetwork.org/about/agenda/index.cfm.

504. *See supra* Section II.B.

505. 126 S. Ct. 2208 (2006).

506. U.S. Army Corps of Eng'rs & U.S. Environ. Protection Agency, *Clean Water Act Jurisdiction Following the U.S. Supreme Court's Decision in Rapanos v. United States & Carabell v. United States* (June 5, 2007), *available at* http://www.usace.army.mil/cw/cecwo/reg/cwa_guide/rapanos_guide_memo.pdf.

507. *See supra* notes 159–62 and accompanying text.

508. Although the plurality expressed some apprehension that the regulation of nonnavigable tributaries and adjacent wetlands could raise Commerce Clause or federalism concerns, 126 S. Ct. at 2224, neither Justice Kennedy nor the four dissenting Justices agreed that those were valid concerns. *Id.* at 2246 (Kennedy, J.); 2262 (Stevens, J., dissenting); and 2266 (Breyer, J., dissenting). Justice Kennedy asserted that "in most cases regulation of wetlands that are adjacent to tributaries and possess a significant nexus with navigable waters will raise no serious constitutional or federalism difficulty." *Id.* at 2249.

509. S. 912, 109th Cong., 1st Sess. (2005); H.R. 1356, 109th Cong., 1st Sess. (2005). There is a competing proposal pending before Congress, the Federal Wetlands Jurisdiction Act, H.R. 2658, 109th Cong., 1st Sess. (2005), which would narrow the statute's definition of federally regulated waters to those that are traditionally navigable, and their adjacent wetlands.

510. 33 C.F.R. § 328.3(a)(2007), *see supra* note 132 for the full text of the regulation.

511. *Id.*

512. *Compare* Coalition Letter on the Clean Water Restoration Act (Oct. 9, 2007) http://www.nationalcenter.org/Clean_Water_Restoration_Act_Letter_100907.pdf ("It would expand the scope of the Clean Water Act far beyond its original intent while increasing confusion over what is and isn't to be protected.") *with* Clean Water Network, *Countdown to the Clean Water Restoration Act of 2007: Everything You Wanted to Know About CWRA but Were Afraid to Ask... available at* http://www.cleanwaternetwork.org/issues/scope/newsandinfo/DisplayContent.cfm?ContentID=558&ContentTypeID=4PageFormat=DisplayContent ("Specifically, the bill reaffirms what Congress intended when it passed the Clean Water Act over 30 years ago: that all waters of the United States should be protected from pollution and destruction.").

513. *See supra* notes 242–50 and accompanying text.

514. *See supra* Section II.B.3.

515. *Id.*

516. 33 U.S.C. § 1344(e)(2000).

517. *See supra* Section II.C.1.

518. The Corps received more than 22,500 comments on the proposal. *Reissuance of Nationwide Permits: Notice*, 72 Fed. Reg. 11,092 (Mar. 12, 2007), *available at* http://www.usace.army.mil/cw/cecwo/reg/nwp/nwp_2007_final.pdf. *See also Proposal to Reissue and Modify Nationwide Permits*, 71 Fed. Reg. 56,258 (Sept. 26, 2006), *available at* www.regulations.gov.

519. *Compensatory Mitigation for Losses of Aquatic Resources*, 71 Fed. Reg. 15,520 (Mar. 28, 2006).

520. *See, e.g.*, National Wildlife Federation, Sierra Club, American Rivers, Earthjustice, Citizens to Complete the Refuge, Waterkeeper Alliance, Vermont Law School, Environmental and Natural Resources Laws Clinic, Audubon Washington, Washington Wetlands Network, Natural Resources Defense Council, Gulf Restoration Network, Appalachian Center for the Economy and the Environment, *Comments on the Proposed Rule on "Compensatory Mitigation for Losses of Aquatic Resources"* Docket Number EPA-HQ-OW-2006-0020, *available at* http://www.cwn.org/cwn/issues/wetlands/DisplayContent.cfm?ContentID=396&ContentTypeID=1PageFormat=DisplayContent.

521. *See, e.g.*, An Inconvenient Truth, *available at* http://www.climatecrisis.net/; U.S. Environmental Prot. Agency, *Climate Change*, *available at* http://www.epa.gov/climatechange/; Competitive Enterprise Institute, *Global Warming*, *available at* http://www.globalwarming.org/; Union of Concerned Scientists, *Global Warming*, *available at* http://www.ucsusa.org/global_warming/.

522. Intergovernmental Panel on Climate Change, *Climate Change 2007: The Physical Science Basis, Summary for Policy Makers*, *available at* http://www.ipcc.ch/SPM2feb07.pdf. *See generally* Intergovernmental Panel on Climate Change website *at* http://www.ipcc.ch/.

523. Pew Oceans Comm'n, America's Living Oceans: Charting a Course for Sea Change (2003) 83, *available at* http://www.pewtrusts.com/pdf/env_pew_oceans_final_report.pdf.

524. *See, e.g.*, John Kusler & Virginia Burkett, *Climate Change in Wetland Areas Part I: Potential Wetland Impacts and Interactions*, Acclimations, Newsletter of the US National Assessment of the Potential Consequences of Climate Variability and Change (May–Jun. 1999); *available at* http://www.usgcrp.gov/usgcrp/Library/national assessment/newsletter/1999.06/wet.html; James G. Titus, *Greenhouse Effect and Coastal Wetland Policy: How Americans Could Abandon an Area the Size of Massachusetts at Minimum Cost*, 15 Env't Mgmt. 39 (1991); James G. Titus, *Sea Level Rise and Wetland Loss: An Overview*, U.S. Environmental Protection Agency (1988), *available at* http://yosemite.epa.gov/oar/globalwarming.nsf/UniqueKeyLookup/SHSU5BNQKX/$File/chap1.pdf.

525. U.S. Environmental Prot. Agency, *Greenhouse Effect, Sea Level Rise and Coastal Wetlands*, *available at* http://yosemite.epa.gov/OAR%5Cglobalwarming.nsf/content/ResourceCenterPublicationsSLRCoastalWetlands.html.

526. U.S. Geological Service, *Coastal Wetlands and Global Change: Overview*, *available at* http://www.nwrc.usgs.gov/climate/fs89_97.pdf.

527. *See supra* note 17.

528. *See, e.g.*, Progressive Policy Institute, *"Hook and Bullet" Wetland Protection* (May 14, 2004), *available at* http://www.ppionline.org/ppi_ci.cfm?knlgAreaID=116&subsecID=900039&contentID=252639 ("the hook and bullet community is staking out a middle ground in the debate and becoming an important voice in the quest to protect and promote America's environmental quality." *Id.*).

529. *See* Pew Oceans Comm'n, America's Living Oceans: Charting a Course for Sea Change (2003), *available at* http://www.pewtrusts.com/pdf/env_pew_oceans_final_report.pdf ("The fundamental conclusion of the Pew Oceans Commission is that this nation needs to ensure healthy, productive, and resilient marine ecosystems for present and future generations." *Id.* at ix.); U.S. Comm'n on Ocean Policy, An Ocean Blueprint for the 21st Century: Final Report of the U.S. Commission on Ocean Policy

(2004), *available at* http://www.oceancommission.gov/documents/full_color_rpt/000_ocean_full_report.pdf; U.S. Ocean Action Plan: The Bush Administration's Response to the U.S. Commission on Ocean Policy (Dec. 17, 2004), *available at* http://ocean.ceq.gov/actionplan.pdf.

530. PEW OCEANS COMM'N, AMERICA'S LIVING OCEANS: CHARTING A COURSE FOR SEA CHANGE (2003), xi, *available at* http://www.pewtrusts.com/pdf/env_pew_oceans_final_report.pdf (Commission suggestions included the following: developing "an action plan to address nonpoint source pollution and protect water quality on a watershed basis"; identifying and protecting from development "habitat critical for the functioning of coastal ecosystems"; instituting "effective mechanisms at all levels of government to manage development and minimize its impact on coastal ecosystems"; and redirecting government programs and subsidies away from harmful coastal development and toward beneficial activities, including restoration.").

chapter five

Managing Coastal Development

Kristen M. Fletcher

I. Introduction to Coastal Management in the United States

Hurricanes Katrina and Rita brought renewed focus and criticism to the manner in which the nation manages coastal development. Making landfall in coastal Louisiana on August 29, 2005, with a storm surge of up to twenty-seven feet, Hurricane Katrina left a 90,000-square-mile disaster area. Making landfall between Texas and Louisiana just one month later, Hurricane Rita hit as one of the three strongest hurricanes ever recorded and brought along with it a ten-to-fifteen-foot storm surge. The aftermath of these storms, combined with four major storms affecting Florida in 2004, has left coastal managers fearing the worst: that the nation's coastal management tools to prevent wetland loss, the increase of erosion and impervious surfaces, and pollution from agricultural and urban runoff are not effective. Indeed, the devastation raises the question of whether the nation's primary coastal management statute, the Coastal Zone Management Act (CZMA), can prevent similar losses in other hazard-prone areas and rebuild sustainably coastal areas in Louisiana, Mississippi, and Alabama.

The term "coastal zone," the area where land meets water, was coined by the Stratton Commission in 1969, the nation's first body to take a comprehensive look at the uses and policies governing the coasts. The Stratton Commission emphasized the importance of the coastal zone to the United States:

> The coast of the United States is, in many respects, the Nation's most valuable geographic feature. It is at the juncture of the land and sea that the great part

of this Nation's trade and industry takes place. The waters off the shore are among the most biologically productive regions of the Nation.[1]

The Stratton Commission noted as early as 1969 that the coasts were threatened by increasing population concentration and commercial, recreational, and residential development.

The Commission noted as early as 1969 that the coasts were threatened by increasing population concentration and commercial, recreational, and residential development. Congress responded by enacting the Coastal Zone Management Act, establishing the framework for managing development and resource use in coastal areas with a national vision but state-led implementation. This unique federal-state partnership has garnered support over the years for encouraging a variety of tools for managing development and uses that can differ state to state and region to region.

The major goals of the CZMA are

- to encourage the states to exercise their full authority by developing land and water use programs for the coastal zone;
- to improve cooperation among federal agencies, the states, and local governments on issues affecting the coastal zone, including public participation; and
- to preserve, protect, develop, and, where possible, to restore or enhance the resources of the coastal zone for this and future generations.[2]

Despite the efforts of state coastal programs around the country, two more recent commissions, the U.S. Commission on Ocean Policy and the Pew Oceans Commission, found that pressures on the coasts have only increased.[3] Some of the most dynamic areas of the coastline—bluffs, rocky shores, beaches, dunes, and barrier islands—are also the most popular areas for recreation and development. All too obvious from Katrina and Rita, development has taken its toll: erosion from development on beaches and dunes is resulting in the loss of recreation areas, habitat, public facilities, and storm protection provided by beaches and dunes. When impervious surfaces cover more than ten percent of a watershed, the rivers, creeks, and estuaries within it become biologically degraded.[4] Projected sea level rise due to global climate change may expose shoreline development to even greater hazards. In many areas, these concerns are brought into sharp focus by Endangered Species Act listings of species dependent on coastal habitat.[5] Federal programs have also come under attack, including the Army Corps of Engineers' beach renourishment and shore armoring programs, which degrade coastal ecosystems. While providing for growing coastal economies, federal, state, and local governments have, perhaps inadvertently, encouraged growth in these sensitive areas by providing infrastructure, flood insurance, and disaster relief.

This chapter will focus on the CZMA, which provides the basic legal framework for state and federal coastal zone management while retaining most decision-making regarding the use of the coastal zone for state and local governments. It analyzes the legal regime created by the CZMA and other governing statutes including federal and state laws and doctrines that make up the canvas for managing the coasts. Finally, it examines the emerging issues of integrated coastal management, marine protected areas and other "place-based" management tools, and regional governance, as part of the comprehensive landscape of coastal management.

II. The Current State of the Law

A. Defining the Coastal Zone

The Coastal Zone Management Act defines "coastal zone" as follows:

> The term "coastal zone" means the coastal waters (including the lands therein and thereunder) and the adjacent shorelands (including the waters therein and thereunder), strongly influenced by each other and in proximity to the shorelines of the several coastal states, and includes islands, transitional and intertidal areas, salt marshes, wetlands, and beaches. The zone extends . . . seaward to the outer limit of State title and ownership under the Submerged Lands Act . . . [generally three nautical miles offshore, as discussed in the Introduction]. The zone extends inland from the shorelines only to the extent necessary to control shorelands, the uses of which have a direct and significant impact on the coastal waters, and to control those geographical areas which are likely to be affected by or vulnerable to sea level rise. Excluded from the coastal zone are lands the use of which is by law subject solely to the discretion of or which is held in trust by the Federal Government, its officers, or agents.[6]

The flexibility of the landward boundary of the coastal zone allows for major variations between states. For example, North Carolina's Coastal Area Management Act defines the inland portion of the coastal zone as the area encompassed by the twenty coastal counties influenced by tidal waters;[7] Hawaii's coastal zone includes the entire state;[8] California defines the land portion of its coastal zone as a 1,000-yard strip extending inland from its coastal waters;[9] and Massachusetts's coastal zone extends landward one hundred feet beyond the first major land transportation route encountered (e.g., a road, highway, or rail), including all of Cape Cod, Martha's Vineyard, Nantucket, and Gosnold.[10]

B. Jurisdiction in the Coastal Zone

The federal government provides funding, research, guidance, and oversight of the national coastal zone management program (the CZM program). The Department of Commerce, through the National Oceanic and Atmospheric Administration (NOAA), is delegated with the authority to administer the CZM program, working with other federal agencies with coastal resource responsibilities, including the Department of the Interior (DOI), the Environmental Protection Agency (EPA), and the Army Corps of Engineers (Corps), to identify their roles in meeting the statutory goals.

The National Ocean Service (NOS) implements the national coastal zone management program, advances partnerships, and provides science and information relevant to coastal management. Within NOS, the Office of Coastal Resource Management (OCRM) develops guidance to approve and update state coastal management programs. The OCRM oversees and negotiates the financial assistance agreements with the states, evaluates program performance, develops national coastal policy, mediates disputes, and provides other management and technical assistance to the states, federal agencies, tribes, industry, and others.[11]

The states' role is akin to that of a landowner, with some limitations related to federal authority. Generally, states hold title to the submerged lands located within three miles of their coastline (or nine miles for Texas, the Gulf coast of Florida, and Puerto Rico). While states have title and control over these resources, Congress maintains its power under the Commerce Clause to regulate state submerged lands in some circumstances.[12] Thus, the multiple uses of state submerged lands and the waters overhead are controlled by federal and state law.[13]

Even though federal lands are excluded from the definition of coastal zone, activities on federal enclaves within a state's coastal zone may still be subject to state regulation. According to the Supreme Court, "even if all federal lands are excluded from the CZMA definition of coastal zone, the CZMA does not automatically preempt all state regulation of activities on federal lands."[14] Furthermore, the Supreme Court has held that state authority to review federal actions under the CZMA's consistency provisions is intended "to reach at least some activities conducted in those federal enclaves excluded from the . . . definition of the 'coastal zone.'"[15]

Many states have managed their coastlines in some manner for the last century. Prior to 1940, most coastal states had legislation establishing offshore marine boundaries, and many state constitutions and federal acts admitting states to the Union described state boundaries as extending a marine league or more offshore.[16] However, controversies emerged in the 1930s challenging the ownership of mineral rights and oil recovered from submerged lands culminating in litigation between the federal government and California declaring that the federal government was the owner of the seabed and minerals from the mean low water line to three nautical miles seaward.[17]

Though prompted by oil and gas development, the finding that the federal government was owner of the submerged lands necessarily affected state efforts to manage other coastal resources. In response to the litigation, Congress adopted the Submerged Lands Act (SLA) in 1953 to establish state title to the submerged lands and its resources, decree the limit of state ocean boundaries, and reserve federal rights both within and beyond state territorial limits.[18] At the same time that the SLA confirmed title of the original coastal states to three geographic miles, it recognized the authority of subsequently admitted states to extend boundaries to that distance.[19]

However, Congress left it to the courts to determine whether a state could establish an historic claim beyond three miles; Texas, Florida, and Puerto Rico have established such claims. In 1960, the Supreme Court recognized the three marine league boundaries in the Gulf of Mexico of both Florida, based on congressional approval of its 1868 constitution, and Texas, based on its historic claim.[20] Furthermore, Puerto Rico's claim to three marine leagues was affirmed in federal statute.[21] In 1969, the

United States brought an action against the thirteen states bordering the Atlantic Ocean that precluded those states' claims beyond three miles.[22]

Although this dismissal of the extended jurisdiction claims in the Atlantic settled the question of the extent of coastal state boundaries, litigation has continued for decades over the exact position of the seaward boundaries of coastal states.[23] Because the SLA did not provide a legal or technical basis for delimiting boundaries, the Supreme Court adopted the provisions of the 1958 Convention on the Territorial Sea and the Contiguous Zone to address boundary delimitation questions.[24]

C. State Role in Coastal Management

The CZM program is implemented through state-level coastal programs based on the theory that state governments can most effectively manage human activities through their historical jurisdiction over land use of nonfederal property.[25] Although each state coastal management program (CMP) is unique, the programs address the broad spectrum of coastal issues identified by Congress in the CZMA. In reality, the national impact of the CZM program is the result of many thousands of state and local decisions that affect the development of the coastal area.

The CZMA requires that environmental protection, access to natural and cultural resources, and economic development be essential parts of each program.[26] It is rare to find a single state agency with the authority to address all of these activities; thus, programs often require some sort of networking among several state agencies. States develop programs that reflect priority resources and management tools including regulation, zoning, financial incentives, outreach, and education. State CMPs are submitted to the Secretary of Commerce for approval.

State CMPs have evolved over time to include best management practices for watershed and ecosystem-based management. Managing coastal watersheds requires management of the nation's estuaries, near-shore coastal waters, and ocean shorelines as the end point for creeks, rivers, and streams that drain the continental land mass. Ecosystem-based management has been seen as an alternative to costly command and control pollution regulation to a more "ecorealistic context,"[27] seeking to prevent pollution rather than merely to treat discharges.

Significantly, the CZMA focuses on the coastal zone as an important ecosystem, providing an opportunity for states to use ecosystem-based management in their coastal programs.[28] While ecosystem-based management is not specifically required in the CZMA statutory language or regulations, states have the opportunity in the coastal program development and approval process to incorporate elements of ecosystem-based management.

> **States have the opportunity in the coastal program development and approval process to incorporate elements of ecosystem-based management.**

D. Coastal Zone Management Act

The 1972 Coastal Zone Management Act[29] was passed "to preserve, protect, develop, and where possible, to restore or enhance, the resources of the Nation's coastal zone for this and succeeding generations."[30] Though it was enacted along with other major environmental legislation like the Clean Air Act and Clean Water Act, the CZMA has several key differences. First, state participation in coastal zone planning was completely voluntary; without a state-created program, federal standards or management would not apply. Second, although the statute recognized a national interest in effective coastal management, Congress also recognized that the type of land-use planning and management required was traditionally within the domain of state and local governments.

The CZMA also created the National Estuarine Research Reserve System (NERRS) to provide natural field laboratories of representative estuarine types for research and to enhance public understanding of and coastal management decisions for estuaries through education and interpretation.[31] NOAA is responsible for developing estuarine research guidelines to establish common research principles and objectives for the reserve system.

The CZMA provides federal funding for states to develop and administer coastal programs and the NERRS according to guidelines set out in the Act. While funding for program development and administration is a traditional incentive for encouraging state cooperation, the Act also provides an additional incentive for state participation—the "federal consistency" requirement. This provision assures a state that, with certain exceptions, federal agency activities or federally permitted activities will be consistent with the enforceable policies of coastal management programs.

The CZMA has been amended a number of times. The 1976 amendments facilitated energy facility siting and other energy development in direct response to the 1973 Arab oil embargo and energy crisis of the mid-1970s.[32] In 1980, Congress focused amendments on the incorporation of national interests in coastal planning, while it reduced funding and added new program goals and policies to enhance coastal management.[33] The Coastal Management Reauthorization Act of 1985 included new procedures for the review and amendment of state coastal programs.[34]

The Coastal Zone Act Reauthorization Amendments of 1990 clarified the scope and application of the federal consistency provision, and created the Coastal Zone Enhancement Grant Program to encourage states to improve their programs in one or more of eight areas of coastal concern: (1) coastal wetlands protection; (2) management of development in high hazard areas; (3) public access; (4) control of marine debris; (5) studying the cumulative and secondary impacts of coastal development; (6) special area management planning; (7) ocean resources planning; and (8) siting of coastal energy and government facilities.[35] The 1990 amendments also added the Coastal Nonpoint Pollution Control Program, a new requirement for state coastal programs to protect coastal waters from pollution from shoreline land uses.[36] The 1996 CZMA amendments did not make major substantive changes.[37]

E. State Coastal Programs

All thirty-five eligible states and territories (including Puerto Rico, the Northern Marianas, the Virgin Islands, Guam, and American Samoa) participated in the federal program during the initial program development period of the 1970s, with the Washington coastal program being the first to receive federal approval in 1976. Taking advantage of incentives in the 1990 CZMA amendments to encourage the final states to develop programs, Georgia, Minnesota, Ohio, Texas, and Indiana recently developed approved programs. Only Illinois does not have a coastal program, but renewed efforts in 2004 to establish a program. Currently, ninety-nine percent of the coasts are governed by state CMPS, indicating successful implementation of one major task of the CZMA.[38]

The approval of state CMPs has rarely been tested in the courts, possibly due to the Ninth Circuit's decision in *American Petroleum Institute v. Knecht*[39] in which the California Coastal Management Program was challenged as not specific enough to meet the statutory requirements and failing to adequately consider the national interest.[40] The Ninth Circuit Court of Appeals determined that state coastal programs did not have to amount to a zoning plan or be a predictive device for private users to rely on; instead, the program must create a framework within which the state can make rational decisions balancing competing interests and offer guidance for users.

The CZMA sanctions three techniques for state CMPs: states may establish criteria and standards for local implementation, implement direct planning and regulation at the state level, or review local project proposals on an individual basis.[41]

1. Development and Approval of State CZM Programs

The CZMA sets out the requirements for federal approval of state coastal management programs.[42] Informational and definitional requirements include identifying boundaries of the coastal zone, defining permissible land and water uses, inventorying areas of particular concern, and defining "beach." Institutionally, the program must identify the means and legal authorities by which the state can carry out the program and the organizational structure to implement the program either through existing legislation that provides the authority to create a coastal program, or new legislation to provide planning and coordination frameworks for coastal zone management.

The Secretary of Commerce, through NOAA's OCRM, determines whether a program meets the requirements for federal approval and the purposes and policies of the CZMA. Programs are generally described in environmental impact statements under the National Environmental Policy Act (NEPA) developed by NOAA and the state for program approval.[43] Program approval must include a determination that the views of federal agencies affected by the program have been "adequately considered."[44]

Procedurally, a state CMP must include procedures for intergovernmental coordination and public participation. Planning processes must be developed for prioritizing uses in the coastal zone, identifying and preserving areas of special "conservation, recreational, ecological, historical, and esthetic values," protecting and providing public access to beaches, and dealing with shoreline erosion.[45] Furthermore, the program must include a planning process for energy facilities, which "provides for adequate consideration of the national interest."[46]

It is important to note that the CZMA is but one of many federal and state programs that impact the coast. Other federal statutes that also affect coastal zone management and coastal resources include the Clean Water Act, Magnuson-Stevens

Fisheries Conservation and Management Act, Outer Continental Shelf Lands Act, Marine Mammal Protection Act, and others noted in this book.[47] Federal appropriations for dredging, beach renourishment, and other coastal zone projects can affect the coastal waters, lands, and resources. In order to better determine the effects of coastal zone management measures, states are attempting to identify indicators to assess the quality of coastal resources in relation to the specific goals of coastal management programs.[48]

2. Review of State Coastal Programs

Approved CZMA coastal programs are subject to continuing review by NOAA to determine the extent to which the state is implementing and enforcing the program. Often, NOAA will include "necessary actions" in its evaluation findings which the state may then address through subsequent grants. Also, program approval may be withdrawn or financial assistance may be suspended under certain circumstances.

For example, in the 1987 review of California's coastal program, NOAA required that the California Coastal Commission prepare and submit approval guidelines that would provide greater predictability for parties seeking consistency determinations for proposed activities affecting the Outer Continental Shelf. The Commission refused, and NOAA withheld most of the program's administrative funding. Congress enacted legislation restoring the funds, but the NOAA grant continued to be conditioned on the state adopting consistency guidelines that would be submitted to NOAA "for review and approval as a program change." California successfully challenged NOAA's authority, claiming that the agency was coercing modification of a previously approved program by conditioning further federal funding.[49]

The 1990 amendments to the CZMA clarify the procedures necessary for NOAA to withdraw funds or the approval of a state coastal management program. If a state fails to adhere to its approved program or the terms of a grant, financial assistance may not be suspended until NOAA provides the state's governor with specifications and a schedule for compliance. NOAA may not withdraw program approval unless the state fails to take the actions required for compliance.[50]

States may amend or modify an approved coastal management program by submitting the program change to the Secretary for review. In general, the Secretary must approve or disapprove the amendment within a maximum of 120 days unless additional time is necessary to meet other federal requirements. If the amendment is not disapproved within that period, it is presumed approved.[51] Until the amendment is approved, it cannot be considered an enforceable policy for purposes of federal consistency.[52] NOAA regulations distinguish between a program amendment and routine program changes.[53] An "amendment" involves "substantial changes in, or substantial changes to[,] enforceable policies or authorities related to" certain aspects of a coastal management program,[54] and requires approval under the statute.[55] "Routine program implementation" is a "[f]urther detailing of a State's program that is the result of implementing" the approved program and is not subject to the amendment approval process.[56]

3. Implementation of Coastal Program Goals

Some states, such as North Carolina and California, have passed comprehensive legislation to create their coastal management programs; other states, such as Florida, have "networked" existing legislation and regulations.[57] The CZMA provides states a great deal of flexibility in programmatic approaches.[58] However, the approval of state CMPs does not indicate congressional consent to expanded state authority, such as consent for a policy or that the policy is constitutional.[59]

The CZMA offers a state the flexibility to adopt the management approach for the coastal zone most consistent with that state's general style of land use regulation and management. For example, if the focal point of the state's general approach is local decision-making, the CMP can use that approach. States relying more on centralized controls can use that approach, either through direct state control or through state review of local and regional decisions.[60]

The CZMA also exhibits flexibility in the geographic emphasis and intensity of the regulatory program.[61] States may focus regulations on particular areas that require a greater degree of protection. Finally, the CZMA allows states to recognize that actions outside the coastal zone boundary may affect coastal resources and require attention in the coastal program.[62]

F. The CZMA Federal Consistency Requirement

Section 307 of the CZMA,[63] the federal consistency provision, is a major incentive for states to join the national coastal management program and is a powerful tool for states to manage coastal uses and resources and to facilitate cooperation and coordination with federal agencies.[64] The state coastal management agency issues federal consistency reviews for federal actions that have reasonably foreseeable effects on any land or water use or natural resource of the coastal zone. These actions must be consistent with the enforceable policies of a coastal state's federally approved CMP; failure to be "consistent" with the enforceable policies of an approved CMP halts a proposed project or action unless there is a subsequent override by the Secretary of Commerce. Federal actions include federal agency activities such as development projects performed by a federal agency, federal license or permit activities, and federal financial assistance to state and local governments.

The CZMA was amended in 1990 to

establish . . . a generally applicable rule of law that any federal agency activity (regardless of its location) is subject to [the consistency requirement] if it will affect any natural resources, land uses, or water uses in the coastal zone. No federal agency activities are categorically exempt from this requirement.[65]

The 1990 amendments replaced language requiring federal activities to "directly affect" the coastal zone. The amendments overturn *Secretary of the Interior v. California,*[66] and reflect congressional intent to

eliminate "categorical exemptions" from consistency, and instead to establish a uniform threshold standard requiring federal agencies to make a case-by-case factual determination of reasonably foreseeable effects on the coastal zone. The amendments to section 307(c)(1) were intended to leave no doubt that all federal agency activities meeting the "effects" standard are subject to the CZMA consistency requirement; that there are no exceptions or exclusions from the requirement as a matter of law; and that the new "uniform threshold standard" requires a factual determination, based on the effects of such activities on the coastal zone, to be applied on a case-by-case basis.[67]

An enforceable policy is a state policy that is legally binding under state law (e.g., through constitutional provisions, laws, regulations, land use plans, ordinances, or judicial or administrative decisions), and by which a state exerts control over private and public coastal uses and resources, and which are incorporated in the state's federally approved CMP.

Federal agencies have an affirmative duty to comply with the federal consistency requirements, complementing the requirements of the National Environmental Policy Act. Even though the CZMA effects test is different from NEPA's, and the CZMA requires federal agencies to alter projects to be consistent with state CMP policies, NOAA views NEPA as an effective delivery mechanism for federal consistency.[68] States concur with approximately ninety-three to ninety-five percent of all federal actions reviewed.[69]

1. Coastal Effects Triggering Review

While states have authority under the CZMA to review a wide range of federal actions, they only review federal actions that have reasonably foreseeable coastal effects. For federal agency activities, federal agencies make this determination of effects.[70] For federal license or permit activities and federal financial assistance activities, OCRM makes the determination of effects by approving the *lists* of federal approvals and financial assistance programs that a state includes in its CMP. If a state wishes to review an *unlisted* federal license or permit activity, it must notify the applicant and the federal agency and seek OCRM approval to review the activity. OCRM's decision is based on whether the unlisted activity will have reasonably foreseeable coastal effects, and input from the federal agency and the applicant.

Prior to the 1990 amendments changing the CZMA language from "directly affecting the coastal zone" to "affects" the coastal zone, courts disagreed about what activities triggered the federal consistency requirement. For example, one court determined that if the only significant effect of potential OCS development is the financial burden on a party, such as commercial fishermen, without evidence of environmental effects in the coastal zone, the federal consistency requirement was not triggered.[71] Another court found that the CZMA recognized economic development within the Act's purposes and that the legislative history supported the consideration of both the social and economic effects in the coastal zone.[72] However, since the 1990 amendments, the potential for conflicting interpretations has been greatly reduced, and NOAA's 2000 final rule revising the federal consistency regulations further clarified the application of consistency.[73]

2. Consistency Provisions

a. Federal Activities: Section 307(c)(1) Consistency

The CZMA section 307(c)(1) states:

> Each Federal agency activity within or outside the coastal zone that affects any land or water use or natural resource of the coastal zone shall be carried out in a manner which is consistent to the maximum extent practicable with the enforceable policies of approved State management programs. A Federal agency activity shall be subject to this paragraph unless it is subject to paragraph (2) [federal development projects] or (3) [federally licensed or permitted activities and OCS exploration and development plans].[74]

The CZMA requires federal agency activities to be fully consistent unless federal legal requirements prohibit full consistency. This ensures that federal agencies are able to meet their legally authorized mandates, even though the activity may not be consistent with a state's enforceable policy. If a federal agency has the discretion to meet a state's enforceable policy, then it must be consistent with that policy. However, federal law may limit a federal agency's discretion or an agency may deviate from full consistency due to "exigent circumstances," such as an emergency or unexpected situation requiring the agency to take immediate action. For example, there may be times that a federal legal requirement or an emergency situation requires a federal agency to act sooner than the end of the ninety-day period for a state to issue consistency.

A federal agency cannot use a lack of funds as a basis for not being consistent to the maximum extent practicable. Thus, federal agencies are encouraged to consult the CMP early to ensure that the federal agency has budgeted for meeting the state's enforceable policies. A federal agency may also proceed over a state's objection when the federal agency determines that it is *fully* consistent with the state's enforceable policies.[75]

A federal agency cannot use a lack of funds as a basis for not being consistent to the maximum extent practicable.

b. Federal Licenses and Permits: Section 307(c)(3)(A) Consistency

The CZMA section 307(c)(3)(A) provides in part:

> [A]ny applicant for a required Federal license or permit to conduct an activity, in or outside of the coastal zone, affecting any land or water use or natural resource of the coastal zone of that state shall provide in the application to the licensing or permitting agency a certification that the proposed activity complies with the enforceable policies of the state's approved program and that such activity will be conducted in a manner consistent with the program.[76]

A private individual or business, or a state or local government agency, or any other type of nonfederal entity applying to the federal government for a required permit or license or any other type of an approval or authorization must follow the requirements of CZMA section 307(c)(3)(A).[77] All federal license or permit activities occurring in the coastal zone are deemed to affect coastal uses or resources, if the state CMP has "listed" the particular federal license, permit, or approval in its federally approved CMP document. For a *listed* activity occurring *in the coastal zone,* the applicant must submit a Consistency Certification to the approving federal agency and the state CMP. In addition to the certification, the applicant must provide the state with the necessary data and information to allow the state to assess the project's effects.

c. OCS Plans: Section 307(c)(3)(B) Consistency

The CZMA section 307(c)(3)(B) provides in part:

> [A]ny person who submits to the Secretary of the Interior any plan for the exploration or development of, or production from, any area which has been leased under the Outer Continental Shelf Lands Act (43 U.S.C. 1331 *et seq.*) . . . shall, with respect to any exploration, development, or production described in such plan and affecting any land or water use or natural resource of the coastal zone of such state, attach to such plan a certification that each activity . . . complies with the enforceable policies of such state's approved management program and will be carried out in a manner consistent with such program.[78]

A private person or business applying to the U.S. Department of the Interior's Minerals Management Service (MMS) for an outer continental shelf (OCS) exploration, development, and production plan for any area leased under the Outer Continental Shelf Lands Act must certify to the relevant state CMP that any activities described in detail in such OCS plans will be conducted in a manner consistent with the enforceable policies of the state's approved CMP.[79] The process and requirements for this section generally mirror those of federal license or permit activities discussed above. The state must notify the applicant if its review will extend beyond three months; otherwise, the state's concurrence is presumed.

The section 307(c)(3)(B) consistency obligation is specifically reinforced and repeated in the Outer Continental Shelf Lands Act (OCSLA) regarding DOI approval of lessee exploration, development, and production plans.[80] The OCSLA does not require exploration, development, and production plans for OCS minerals development as it does for OCS oil and gas development. However, section 307(c)(3)(B) is not expressly limited to oil and gas exploration, development, and production plans, and DOI has considered using the exploration plan process for OCS minerals development.

A federal action that will have reasonably foreseeable coastal effects, but does not fall under the requirements for a federal license or permit,[81] OCS plans,[82] or financial assistance to state agency or local government,[83] is a federal agency activity that must follow the requirements of the CZMA and its implementing regulations.[84] For example, if a federal agency is providing funds to a private citizen for disaster relief from a hurricane, and the funds will be used for an activity with coastal effects, then the federal agency must follow the requirements for federal agency activities and provide the state CMP with a Consistency Determination.[85]

3. Secretarial Appeals

The CZMA provides two procedures for addressing disagreements concerning consistency determinations: (1) a mediation process for disagreements between federal agencies and coastal states,[86] and (2) a secretarial appeal process for federal permits and OCS exploration and development plans that are found by a state to be inconsistent with the state CMP.[87]

In the event of a disagreement between a state CMP and a federal agency, either party may request that the Secretary of Commerce mediate the dispute. Secretarial mediation is a formal process with a public hearing, submission of written briefs, and meetings between the parties. A hearing officer, appointed by the Secretary, will propose a solution. Secretarial mediation is only for states and federal agencies, and exhaustion of the mediation process is not a prerequisite to judicial review. The availability of secretarial mediation or litigation does not preclude the parties from informally mediating the dispute through OCRM or another facilitator.

In the case of a federal license or permit, an OCS oil and gas plan, or an application for federal financial assistance, the applicant may request that the Secretary override the state's consistency objection if the activity is consistent with the objectives of the CZMA (Ground I), or is otherwise necessary in the interest of national security (Ground II).[88] If the requirements of either Ground I or Ground II are met, the Secretary can override the state's objection.[89] The Secretary's inquiry into whether the grounds for an override have been met is based on an administrative record developed for the appeal. While the Secretary will review the state objection for CZMA compliance (e.g., whether the objection is based on enforceable policies), the Secretary does not review the objection for compliance with state laws and policies.

If the Secretary overrides the state's objection, the authorizing federal agency may permit or fund the activity. A secretarial override does not obviate the need for an applicant to obtain any state permits or authorizations. The secretarial appeal process is final federal agency action under the Administrative Procedure Act and is a necessary administrative action prior to litigation.[90] However, the CZMA does not create a right for private citizens or local governments to sue to enjoin developments that are inconsistent with an approved state coastal management program.[91]

4. Interstate Consistency

Interstate conflicts can occur when a state's activity, which requires a federal permit or approval, is not consistent with the coastal program policies of another state. The CZMA does not specifically address whether the consistency process applies in such situations but courts have reviewed the possibility. For example, in 1994, the state of North Carolina objected to water being drawn from Lake Gaston, on the boundary of the two states, to provide water to Virginia Beach. On the appeal of North

Carolina's determination that the activity was inconsistent with its coastal program, the Secretary of Commerce found that the plain language of the statute required that the federal government apply the consistency provision to such activities. The Secretary stated:

> While the CZMA does not give one state direct authority to control activities in another state, the CZMA does grant to states with federally approved coastal management programs the right to seek conditions on or prohibit the issuance of federal permits and licenses that would "affect" their state. Thus, Congress has, in effect, granted to states with a federally approved coastal management program, in exchange for their protecting the nation's coasts, the right to ensure that federal permittees and licensees will not further degrade those coasts. The ability to prevent the granting of federal permits and licenses is a federal authority, which has been granted to coastal states, not a state authority which has been usurped from the states. However, as a safeguard to a state's unrestrained use of this authority, an applicant can, as the City has, appeal for an override by the Secretary of Commerce.[92]

Ultimately, the Secretary of Commerce did override North Carolina's objection, thereby allowing the City of Virginia Beach to obtain federal permits to build a pipeline for the withdrawal of water from Lake Gaston.[93]

Regulations adopted in 2000 endorse such interstate use of the consistency process[94] and provide a process for a coastal state to review a federal action occurring in another state that will have coastal effects in the reviewing state.[95] The new requirements combine with the requirements under the various types of federal actions.

G. Coastal Management and Property Rights

Beachfront property is often wedged between a coastal highway and the mean high water mark, leaving little flexibility for locating structures on land. Coastal setback lines and other restrictive zones may incorporate the entire lot and coastal construction regulations, water dependency requirements, and cumulative or secondary impact analyses may affect lots in coastal areas. All of these factors make regulation of coastal construction particularly susceptible to claims that a regulation effects a taking of beachfront property. This section describes tools for regulating coastal development and the legal takings challenges that states may face in light of disproportionate effects on private landowners.

1. Regulating Coastal Development

a. Beach Management

Coastal states face unique management issues in beach areas as commercial, industrial, residential, and recreational uses of the coasts increase. The resulting development can obstruct the view of or access to the sea, eroding public trust rights and depleting coastal resources.

Since the passage of the CZMA, coastal states have attempted to protect coastlines from overdevelopment using permit systems geared toward restricting further development in fragile coastal regions, though statutes vary considerably in stringency, focus, and clarity. NOAA is charged with assisting state CMP land-use planning, construction siting, and design measures to mitigate erosion and coastal storm hazards.[96] Some states set forth explicit requirements, such as requiring a permit for certain designated activities, or for all activities within a designated coastal region.[97] Other states have detailed provisions to conserve specific resources such as fragile ecosystems or public beach access.[98] Several states have passed measures specifically addressing the problem of beach/dune erosion, including designation of "setback" zones in which all new construction is prohibited.[99] Most states, however, have stopped short of requiring the removal of existing development situated in sensitive erosion-prone areas, as an outright condemnation would likely be considered a taking. South Carolina's Beachfront Management Act provides a good example for the methods states have used in managing the resources and uses of the beach.

Coastal states face unique management issues in beach areas as commercial, industrial, residential, and recreational uses of the coasts increase.

Originally, South Carolina adopted a relatively conventional approach toward regulating beachfront development, setting out critical areas, requiring individuals to obtain a permit before developing property or engaging in a new use of property within a critical area, and regulating so-called erosion control devices such as sea walls, bulkheads, and rip-rap. The Beachfront Management Act amendments of 1988 provide additional requirements for managing beach development and protection including detailed restrictions that would, over a period of years, push back the line of development a distance of forty times the annual erosion rate and eliminate all harmful erosion control devices.[100]

The state also determined a need to gradually eliminate harmful erosion control devices. The Act provides strict guidelines under which erosion control devices may not be replaced, and must be removed at the owner's expense, if over sixty-seven percent of the "above-grade" portion of the device is destroyed. That percentage dropped to fifty percent in 2005.[101] Furthermore, the state provided specific requirements for beach renourishment. Under the original Beachfront Management Act, if any habitable structure or erosion device was replaced under the statute, the property owner was required to renourish the beach on a yearly basis. These provisions were later repealed in favor of delegating renourishment duties to local governments.

Other issues also arise in beach management including the use of more stringent regulatory regimes, the requirement of removal of existing development in dunes, and removing flood insurance options as a deterrent to development. Some states have used the refusal to pay for damaged infrastructure as a method to limit development. Because the state pays the extra cost of repairing the community's infrastructure after a storm, it could conceivably shift the expense to the affected property owners by refusing to finance repairs. Massachusetts has already adopted such a policy. An executive order, issued by then Governor Edward J. King after the blizzard of 1978, prohibits the expenditure of public funds to construct or rebuild roads, sewer lines, sea walls, and other public works on the state's barrier beaches.[102] Finally, states can assess property owners located in certain areas a higher cost to repair infrastructure or impose a tax to cover anticipated infrastructure damage.

However, landowners have brought lawsuits for erosion allegedly caused by inadequate construction or maintenance of projects. While most of these suits are aimed at the federal agencies involved (primarily the Army Corps of Engineers), states can still become implicated in the damage to private property.[103]

b. Public Access

Public access continues to be an issue for state and local governments. With increasing development on the coasts, increasing numbers of people are competing for beach access. The beach below the high tide line is part of the public trust, i.e., open to the public for swimming, recreation, and fishing. As a general rule, lateral or horizontal access along the wet sand area is a public right. While the area above the high tide line is subject to private ownership, the public may acquire the right to use perpendicular access routes or to use the dry sand area. These rights arise under common law doctrines including public easements by prescription, dedication, or customary use.

Generally, a prescriptive easement is acquired by continuous, uninterrupted, exclusive use that is open and notorious. Most states recognize that easements by prescription may arise when the public makes continual use of beach property for a certain prescriptive period, such as a set number of years. Unlike prescriptive easements, dedication of property to public use does not necessarily require a specific time period but can be shown through acquiescence of the owner in use of the land and maintenance or patrolling of a beach by municipal authorities. Finally, the doctrine of customary use relies on public use that is ancient, exercised without obligation, reasonable and not offensive to an existing law or custom.[104]

The CZMA encourages states to provide for public access for recreational purposes in their coastal programs.[105] Before the Secretary can approve a state's CMP, the program must define the term "beach" and have a planning process for access to public beaches and "other public coastal areas of environmental, recreational, historical, esthetic, ecological, or cultural value."[106] Furthermore, states may receive federal funds for the establishment of shoreline stabilization measures including the installation or rehabilitation of bulkheads for the purpose of public safety or increasing public access and use.[107]

Easements for public access are generally required by the longstanding Corps policy of providing government erosion control assistance only for beaches that are open to the public. For federally funded shore nourishment, project sponsors must

> (8) Maintain public ownership and public use of the shore upon which the amount of Federal participation is based for so long as the project remains authorized; [and]

(9) Provide and maintain necessary access roads, parking areas, and other public use facilities open and available to all on equal terms.[108]

c. Coastal Setbacks

Each CMP must include certain program elements: an identification of the boundaries of the coastal zone; a definition of permissible land uses and water users within the coastal zone which have a direct and significant impact on the coastal waters; an inventory of areas of particular concern within the coastal zone. A state also must identify the means by which it has control over the land uses and water uses in the coastal zone through its relevant constitutional provisions, laws, regulations, and judicial decisions, and provide a description of the organizational structure proposed to implement the management program, including the responsibilities of local, state, regional, and interstate agencies.[109]

The state, acting through its chosen agency, has various tools available to it for the management of the coastal zone in accordance with the management program. These tools include administering land use and water use regulations and other local planning requirements to address, among other coastal issues, urban waterfront development, building codes and construction standards, and reconstruction in the coastal zone.[110]

States use coastal setbacks to regulate coastal construction; approximately half of the coastal states have implemented a type of retreat policy by creating areas at the shoreline where development is prohibited or strictly regulated.[111] Early setback lines generally prohibited or limited construction in areas within a prescribed distance from a baseline, usually the mean high water line, the vegetation line, or a line associated with the primary dune, ranging from forty to one hundred feet. For example, Hawaii uses this type of setback line for controlling coastal development. Construction must be located a minimum of forty feet inland from the shoreline, defined as the debris or vegetation line.[112]

More recently, as understanding of beach and dune processes improved and as coastal engineering became more sophisticated, delineation of setback lines became more sophisticated and highly technical, and many states now use complicated calculations of seasonal shoreline fluctuations, vulnerability to storms and storm surges, and the rate of shoreline erosion.[113] Although this type of setback line has more scientific validity and receives deference in judicial proceedings, the complexity can be confusing to landowners who can more readily understand the impact of a fixed setback distance in conceiving their expectations of uses of the land.

South Carolina's 1988 Beachfront Management Act (the same statute that David Lucas sued under in the well-known takings case[114]) provides the authority for the state to establish a baseline on the Atlantic coast at the crest of an ideal primary oceanfront sand dune. From this baseline, a setback line was calculated at a distance of forty times the average annual erosion rate, but at a minimum distance of twenty feet landward of the baseline.[115] The area within twenty feet landward of the baseline was a "dead zone" in which major structures were not permitted. In the remaining area between the baseline and the setback line, construction is limited to habitable structures not larger than 5,000 square feet, located as far landward on a lot as possible. In the wake of Hurricane Hugo and a host of legal challenges, the Act was amended in 1990 to eliminate the twenty-foot dead zone, making all construction between the baseline and setback line subject to the same standards.[116]

States often "grandfather in" existing structures to lessen the impact of the regulation but existing structures may become subject to new regulation if they are expanded, improved, or destroyed. States may also face legal challenges about when existing structures may become subject to a new regulatory scheme.

d. Other Criteria: Water Dependency and Cumulative Impacts

The CZMA requires states to identify in their coastal management programs "a definition of what shall constitute permissible land uses and water uses within the coastal zone which have a direct and significant impact on the coastal waters."[117] The question of water dependency is important in determining permissible uses and prioritizing those uses along the coast.[118] There has been litigation involving non-water-dependent uses attached to a water-dependent use, such as an office building on the shores of Lake Union in Seattle that incorporated a rowing club. While the court found that the presence of the rowing club met the water-dependent requirement, the court left open the question of violation of the terms of the permit if the rowing club ceased to occupy the bottom floor of the building.[119]

The question of water dependency is important in determining permissible uses and prioritizing those uses along the coast.

Accounting for cumulative and secondary impacts in permitting and consistency decisions has also raised questions. States have the capacity to require review of cumulative or secondary impacts for permits issued in the coastal zone. To determine the "effect on any coastal use or resource" in applying federal consistency requirements, NOAA regulations allow states to consider "both direct effects which result from the activity and occur at the same time and place as the activity, and indirect (cumulative and secondary) effects which result from the activity and are later in time or farther removed in distance, but are still reasonably foreseeable."[120] Thus, states may review federal activities for their cumulative and secondary impacts on the coastal zone. While this authority implies a breadth of review, in cases in which federal agencies perform repeated activity "other than a development project (e.g., ongoing maintenance, waste disposal) which cumulatively has an effect upon any coastal use or resource, the Federal agency may develop a general consistency determination, thereby avoiding the necessity of issuing separate consistency determinations for each incremental action."[121]

2. Private Property Rights Challenges

While the CZMA and its implementing regulations provide guidelines for managing the coastal zone, including the regulation of private development on the coasts, states can still be challenged for taking private property for public use without just compensation under the Takings Clause of the Fifth Amendment.[122] When there has been a permanent physical invasion of land by the government, it is generally incontrovertible that there has been a taking of private property requiring compensation.[123]

In addition to instances of physical invasion or government confiscation of property, a government regulation such as a limitation on coastal development may be recognized as a taking if it "goes too far."[124] Recognizing that "government hardly could go on if to some extent values incident to property could not be diminished without paying for every such change in the general law . . . when it reaches a certain magnitude, in most if not all cases, there must be an exercise of eminent domain and compensation to sustain the act."[125] More recent U.S. Supreme Court cases have placed emphasis on the economic impact of the regulation on the property owner and the degree to which the owner's distinct investment-backed expectations have been frustrated.[126]

While no set formula exists for determining when a government regulation of private property amounts to a regulatory taking, the Supreme Court has found that when the landowner has lost all economically beneficial use of the property, generally a taking has occurred.[127] In *Lucas v. South Carolina Coastal Council*,[128] developer David Lucas sued South Carolina for denying him the right to build residential homes on two waterfront lots on a South Carolina barrier island, the Isle of Palms. The Coastal Council denied his building permit under authority of the Beachfront Management Act which limited development behind an erosion line (the "setback line" as described above), effectively prohibiting Lucas from building any structures on the property. The Court found that a taking had occurred because the legislature's actions deprived the land of all of its economic viability.[129] South Carolina bought the land from Lucas for over $1.5 million.

For those cases that fall in between a physical invasion and a total loss of property value, the Supreme Court has ruled that takings inquiries should be made on a case-by-case basis using factors such as character of the governmental action and economic impact of the regulation to determine a taking of property.[130] If a government agency has requested an exaction in exchange for the right to develop, the Supreme Court found in *Nollan v. California Coastal Commission*[131] that the state cannot condition a permit to build without showing a legitimate state purpose for the governmental mandate that is related to the exaction. If the state has both a legitimate interest, such as preventing erosion or protecting a flood plain, and the exactions bear a relationship to the impact of the proposed development, then the state's requirements will not be considered a taking.[132]

Most recently, the Supreme Court has added to its takings jurisprudence through two waterfront cases. In *Palazzolo v. Rhode Island*, the Court found that a landowner is not precluded from bringing a takings claim even though the offending statute or regulation preceded his or her acquisition of title.[133] The Supreme Court rejected the state's claim that landowner Palazzolo lacked standing because he acquired formal legal title after the enactment of the state statute forbidding filling of coastal wetlands.

The Court was unwilling "to put an expiration date on the Takings Clause" because "[f]uture generations, too, have a right to challenge unreasonable limitations on the use and value of land."[134] When the case was remanded to Rhode Island for a *Penn Central* analysis, the court found that there was no taking because the owner had an upland area that could be developed in a manner similar to surrounding properties and that the state's preclusion of coastal wetlands filling was in the public interest.[135]

In the 2005 case *Kelo v. New London,* the Supreme Court found that a municipality can use eminent domain to take property for public use even when the public use is economic development.[136] Basing its decision in part on precedent that states and municipalities are the appropriate entities for land use decisions and in part on the state's identification of economic development as a valid public purpose, the Court held that "Without exception, our cases have defined [public purpose] broadly, reflecting our longstanding policy of deference to legislative judgments in this field."[137] Ultimately, the City of New London, Connecticut, and New London Development Corporation were able to use eminent domain to implement their land use plan. The *Palazzolo* and *Kelo* decisions will likely be significant in light of redevelopment along hazard-prone areas like the Gulf Coast.

Critics argue that, at best, the Supreme Court's takings analysis is confusing, leaving in limbo many takings claims that fall between a complete loss of property value and a physical invasion. Thus, even though the CZMA grants states the authority to manage their coastal areas, they may still be vulnerable to takings claims by private landowners restricted from using their property as they wish.

H. Related Coastal Management Statutes and Programs

In addition to the CZMA, other federal laws and programs have significant coastal management implications including the National Flood Insurance Act, the Coastal Barrier Resources Act, and the National Marine Sanctuaries Program. These laws are described briefly below. Other federal laws with a fundamental relationship to coastal zone management and coastal and offshore multiple-use management also mentioned in this chapter include the National Environmental Policy Act and Outer Continental Shelf Lands Act.

1. National Flood Insurance Act

The creation of the National Flood Insurance Program by the National Flood Insurance Act of 1968[138] has led to widespread adoption of minimum federal building standards for flood-prone areas, including coastal areas. Administered by FEMA, the program is the federal government's primary tool for managing hazards through incentives and regulation. Under the program, FEMA maps the flood-prone areas throughout the nation, and provides flood insurance (or backs the private providers of flood insurance) to owners of commercial and residential structures if their communities have adopted standards for the construction of buildings in those areas. The program is intended to reduce federal flood disaster relief by supplying guaranteed flood insurance coverage to communities that adopt building standards and land use controls that minimize flood damages and property losses. State and local regulation may be stricter than federally imposed safety and building standards, and governments are encouraged to adopt land use regulations that guide development away from flood hazard areas.[139]

In addition to guaranteeing flood insurance for participating communities, the program also imposes penalties for nonparticipation. If a community with areas susceptible to flooding does not join the program, federal agencies, like the Small Business Administration and the Veterans Administration, are prohibited from providing federal assistance for development in flood-prone areas.[140] The program has been held to be neither an unconstitutional coercion, imposition of strict federal building standards on the states, nor a taking of private property as a result of diminished property values in nonparticipating communities.[141]

2. Coastal Barrier Resources Act

In 1981, the National Flood Insurance Act of 1968 was amended by the Omnibus Budget Reconciliation Act (OBRA) to prohibit the issuance of new federal flood insurance after October 1, 1983, for any new construction or for substantial improvements of structures located on undeveloped coastal barriers.[142] The Secretary of the Interior was directed by OBRA to make recommendations for the designation of coastal barriers to be included within the John Chafee Coastal Barrier Resources System (CBRS). The Coastal Barrier Resources Act[143] (CBRA) was passed in 1982 and defines coastal barriers as "a depositional geologic feature (bay barrier, tombolo, barrier spit, or barrier island) that (i) is subject to wave, tidal, and wind energies, and (ii) protects landward aquatic habitats from direct wave attack."[144] The CBRS is specifically designated on maps maintained by the Secretary of the Interior. The Secretary must review the maps every five years in order to update them to reflect the changes in size or location of any of the barriers.

CBRA restricts certain federal expenditures and financial assistance mechanisms that have the effect of encouraging development of coastal barriers. The CBRA calls for no new federal expenditures within the System relating to the construction or purchase of any structure, road, airport, boat landing facility, bridge or causeway to or on any of the habitats in the System.[145] The Act also states that no new federal flood insurance may be issued for properties that are located on System units (although existing flood insurance policies for properties located on a System unit remain in force).[146]

Despite these prohibitions, funds may be expended for the exploration, extraction, or transportation of energy resources adjacent to coastal waters, and for the construction of improvements of existing federal navigation channels. In addition, the Act authorizes expenditures for the maintenance, but not expansion, of any publicly owned or operated road or facility.[147] The Act provides several exceptions relating to the use by the military and Coast Guard of the barriers in the System and some areas are also exempted from the System by acts of Congress.[148] Additionally, the Act does not limit federal expenditures for coastal barriers that were developing or already developed at the time of the Act's passage.[149]

The CBRA and its legislative history have left federal agencies unclear as to whether the Act prohibits federal funding of projects occurring outside the boundaries of the CBRS, but whose impact would directly encourage development within the CBRS. For example, while the EPA has complied with the DOI's recommendation that it not expand a federally funded wastewater treatment plant, the Federal Highway Administration has simultaneously permitted the construction of a bridge to the non-CBRS side of a barrier island.[150]

Furthermore, the Act does not prohibit private developments within the System, nor does it prevent the issuance of federal permits necessary for development. As a result, private developments have continued despite the withdrawal of federal support under the National Flood Insurance Program.[151]

3. The National Marine Sanctuary Program

Congress created the National Marine Sanctuary Program in 1972 through the Marine Protection Reserve and Sanctuary Act.[152] The Act authorizes NOAA to create and manage marine sanctuaries in areas of national significance to protect coastal and marine resources and encourage scientific research. The thirteen existing sanctuaries are managed according to site-specific management plans developed by NOAA.[153] Generally, the management plans incorporate the concept of multiple use reflecting the multitude of pressures on these areas including recreational and commercial fishing, scuba diving, navigation, and oil exploration and drilling. Many sanctuaries include both federal and state waters, adding a layer of management and protection to part of a state's coastal zone and to waters and habitats bordering the coastal zone.

> **Implementation and enforcement are particularly challenging given that multiple agencies, both state and federal, exercise regulatory authority.**

Implementation and enforcement are particularly challenging given that multiple agencies, both state and federal, exercise regulatory authority. States are included in the selection and designation process, along with the public. Specifically, in the case of a sanctuary that is located partially or entirely within the seaward boundary of a state, the state's governor may certify to the Secretary of Commerce that the designation or any of its terms is unacceptable; in this case, the designation or the unacceptable term shall not take effect in the area of the sanctuary lying within the boundary of the state.[154]

III. Emerging Coastal Management Tools and Issues

Competing uses for the coastal zone are driving the development and implementation of new tools for coastal management including integrated coastal zone management, special area management planning and ocean zoning, marine protected or marine managed areas, and regional ecosystem-based management. This section addresses these emerging uses and the evolution of coastal zone management tools.

A. Emerging Governance: Integrated Coastal Zone Management

Integrated coastal management is based on the concept that managers identify existing and projected uses and their interactions in order to "promote compatibility and balance of uses, apply preventative and precautionary approaches, and ensure full public participation."[155] Certain states are taking the lead to integrate advanced management into their coastal waters.

In recent years, the Commonwealth of Massachusetts has conducted an assessment to produce a statewide ocean management plan to control, develop, and protect Massachusetts waters. Driven in part by proposals for offshore wind energy farms, the Ocean Management Task Force identified the shortcomings of Massachusetts's current coastal management approach as sector by sector rather than integrated. The resulting report, *Waves of Change*, called for the emergence of ocean zoning in Massachusetts and included proposed legislation to "retain and strengthen existing environmental protections associated with the ocean as a public trust resource while streamlining the array of existing statutes governing the use and protection of the Commonwealth's oceans."[156]

California joins Massachusetts on the forefront of redesigning coastal management in its state waters. California agencies completed a strategy report, *Protecting Our Ocean*, in September 2004,[157] and Governor Schwarzenegger followed with an action plan calling for the creation of comprehensive and coordinated management of the state's ocean resources.[158] California also has focused on the significant economic value of its coastal resources. The National Ocean Economic Program reported that the ocean and coast make "vital contributions to the welfare and economy of California" and that based on the importance of ocean and coastal areas to the state of California, the implementation and creation of programs require special attention.[159]

Finally, California became the first state in the nation to adopt key recommendations of the Pew Oceans Commission and the U.S. Commission on Ocean Policy to coordinate fragmented ocean management policy and shift the focus from individual species to ocean ecosystems by creating a special Ocean Protection Council and Trust Fund. The California Ocean Protection Council (OPC) consists of the Secretaries of the State Resources Agency and Environmental Protection Agency, the Chair of the State Lands Commission, a member of the State Assembly and Senate, and two public members. These governmental leaders "coordinate activities of state agencies that are related to the protection and conservation of coastal waters and ocean ecosystems"[160] and issue grants to eliminate or reduce threats to coastal and ocean ecosystems, habitats and species, foster sustainable fisheries, improve coastal water quality, and increase public access and enjoyment of ocean and coastal resources.[161] In September 2006, the OPC issued a strategic plan that identifies specific goals, objectives and strategies for protecting ocean and coastal resources in California over the next five years.[162]

While these efforts are in early stages, they represent an emerging trend toward integrated management in the form of information collection, collaborative planning, and zoning of state marine waters.

B. Marine Protected Areas and Special Area Management Planning

Though they are emerging now in many states, zoning or spatial designation and protection of waters and submerged lands are not new concepts. The CZMA directs states to provide an inventory and designation of areas that contain significant resources, and to develop standards to protect them.[163] States can accomplish this through specific laws such as coastal wetlands protection laws or through designating sites as areas of particular concern. State programs also must address issues of shoreline management, beach access and land acquisition, and ocean management.[164] In developing the program, states must strive to resolve conflicts among competing uses and, in some cases, acquire title or other interest in land or waters when necessary to achieve conformance with the management program.

Some states use Marine Protected Areas (MPAs) to preserve habitat or manage valuable marine ecosystems. In May 2000, President Clinton signed Executive Order 13158 calling for the creation of a comprehensive system of MPAs, defining an MPA as "any area of the marine environment reserved by Federal, State, territorial, tribal, or local laws or regulations to provide lasting protection for part or all of the natural and cultural resources therein" potentially including many sites in state waters.[165]

While the terms "Marine Reserves" and "Marine Protected Areas" have been used synonymously, the terms refer to marine areas that serve different functions and are governed by distinct regulations. For instance, one MPA may restrict certain types of fishing gear while marine reserves generally prohibit fishing altogether. Categories of protected areas can range from strictly protected wilderness areas to multiple-use areas. Such areas are often proposed as components of fisheries management to enhance the long-term sustainable exploitation of fishery resources or rebuild depleted stocks, and to protect particularly sensitive or previously exploited areas.

Depending on the state agency overseeing the creation of an area and the location of the area, enabling legislation may be necessary at a state level to establish the authority to create and manage an MPA. Some states have already enacted legislation that grants authority to particular agencies or subagencies to establish networks of MPAs.[166]

C. Regional Management

Political boundaries, often delineated without attention to ecosystems, create inherent hurdles for natural resource management. Not surprisingly, this fact was noted in the two Ocean Commission Reports. The Pew Oceans Commission noted that "Not a system at all, U.S. ocean policy is a hodgepodge of individual laws that has grown by accretion over the years, often in response to crisis."[167] To address this jurisdictional dilemma, both Commissions proposed regional ocean councils to "facilitate the development of regional goals and priorities and improve responses to regional issues."[168] In response, the President's Ocean Action Plan supported the creation of regional collaborations on oceans, coasts, and Great Lakes policy in partnership with states, local governments, and tribes.[169] Regional governance efforts and studies are emerging across the country,[170] but their impact on coastal zone management is unclear.

In New England, following the issuance of the Ocean Action Plan, and with federal encouragement on several levels, Rhode Island Governor Donald L. Carcieri proposed the creation of a Northeast Regional Ocean Council (NROC) comprised of stakeholders appointed by governors of each state to facilitate the development of more coordinated and collaborative regional goals and priorities and to improve responses to regional issues.[171] Governor Carcieri, as Chair of the New England Governors and Eastern Canadian Premieres Conference,[172] introduced Resolution 29–3 on the Oceans, creating an Oceans Working Committee to "foster international cooperation and collaboration on all aspects of marine and ocean related research and development . . . facilitate the exchange of information . . . seek partnerships and synergies to facilitate existing initiatives such as the Gulf of Maine Council on the Marine Environment and encourage new initiatives and partnerships . . . address related environmental issues . . . and provide a vehicle for cooperation on all aspects of ocean management."[173]

Political boundaries, often delineated without attention to ecosystems, create inherent hurdles for natural resource management.

It is likely more than coincidence that priority issues discussed for Regional Ocean Governance include several of the priority issues included in the remaining resolutions especially environmental and energy concerns.[174] While these resolutions indicate priority areas for regional and state coastal management consideration, the resolutions are only as strong as the leaders that seek to implement them. Without executive interest, leadership, and additional funding to implement regional efforts, coastal programs will likely not be able to take advantage of the benefits that regionalism may offer.

On the West Coast, the Governors of California, Washington, and Oregon announced an "Agreement of Ocean Health" on September 18, 2006. The agreement cites the two Ocean Commission Reports in forging a long-term partnership between the three states to improve beaches and coastal water quality, protect coastal habitats, promote effective ecosystem-based management, reduce impacts from offshore development, and promote ocean awareness and scientific research.[175]

IV. Conclusion: Future of Coastal Management

If the developments outlined above did not already indicate a shift toward more integrated coastal management, the hurricane seasons of 2004 and 2005 (and especially the natural and man-made tragedies following Hurricane Katrina) indicate a need for significant changes to the system for managing coastal resources in the United States. Natural systems, such as barrier islands and wetlands, are also natural defenses to storms and often are enough to withstand threats to structures and human life. Some are calling for century-long coastal plans that embrace natural systems and zoning rather than short-sighted plans decades or less "which, by their very nature, focus on short term outputs and avoid altogether the hard questions of what we can and cannot protect with the resources foreseeably available."[176]

Some argue that industry needs more predictability by weakening or replacing the federal consistency provisions of the CZMA, while others claim the CZMA should be strengthened to reflect the importance of the coastal regions and decisions affecting them. With reauthorization of the CZMA looming, new technologies and uses competing for limited space, and socioeconomic issues rising to the forefront of coastal management decisions, the time may be ripe for a paradigm shift in coastal management, or a move toward a second generation of coastal management.

Notes

1. STRATTON COMMISSION, OUR NATION AND THE SEA (1969).
2. *See generally* Coastal Zone Management Act, 16 U.S.C. §§ 1451–1466 (2000).
3. PEW OCEANS COMMISSION, AMERICA'S LIVING OCEANS 49–52 (2003); U.S. COMMISSION ON OCEAN POLICY, AN OCEAN BLUEPRINT FOR THE 21ST CENTURY 50–52 (2004) (for analysis of coastal management law, see Appendix 6 by Richard Hildreth and Kristen Fletcher).
4. *See* Dana Beach, COASTAL SPRAWL: THE EFFECTS OF URBAN DESIGN ON AQUATIC ECOSYSTEMS IN THE UNITED STATES (Pew Oceans Commission 2002).
5. For regulations related to endangered and threatened marine species, *see* 50 C.F.R. §§ 222.301–222.310.
6. 16 U.S.C. § 1453(1) (2000).
7. N.C. ADMIN. CODE §§ 113A-100–134.3 (2006).
8. HAW. REV. STAT. § 205 A (2006).
9. CAL. PUB. RES. CODE §§ 30000–30900 (2006).
10. MASS. GEN. LAWS. ch. 21A § 4A (2006); *see also* 301 MASS. CODE REGS. 20.00–26.00 (2006).
11. 15 C.F.R. § 930.3. The OCRM also administers the National Estuarine Research Reserve System (NERRS) by providing standards for designating and operating the Reserves and financial and technical assistance. See *infra* note 32 and accompanying text.
12. *See* the Submerged Lands Act, 43 U.S.C. § 1314(a) (the federal navigable servitude).
13. *See, e.g.,* Coastal Petroleum Co. v. Dep't Envtl. Prot., 672 So. 2d 574 (Fla. App. 1996) (bond requirement to protect state submerged lands during exploratory drilling imposed after the state issued offshore oil and gas leases held invalid); Fanning v. Oregon Div. of State Lands, 151 Or. App. 609, 950 P.2d 353 (1997) (forfeiture of a state lease issued for commercial kelp harvesting in state ocean waters); Gillis v. Louisiana, 294 F.3d 755 (5th Cir. 2002) (state can regulate vessel pilots beyond state's seaward boundary); James v. Alaska, 950 P.2d 1130 (Alaska 1997) (state regulation of subsistence fishing upheld); Kaneohe Bay Cruises. v. Hirata, 75 Haw. 250, 861 P.2d 1 (1993) (Hawaii statutory ban on commercial thrill craft operations in two ocean bays on weekends and holidays upheld); Oglesby v. McCoy, 255 S.E.2d 737 (N.C. Ct. App. 1979) (statute raising rent for oyster culture leases upheld); Stop the Outfall Pipe v. Mass. Water Res. Auth., 419 Mass. 1, 642 N.E.2d 568 (1994) (state agency-approved sewage outfall pipe does not violate the Massachusetts Ocean Sanctuaries Act); Vujnovich v. La. Wildlife & Fisheries Comm'n, 376 So. 2d 330 (La. App. 1979) (commission decision not to renew oyster culture leases upheld).
14. Cal. Coastal Comm'n v. Granite Rock Co., 480 U.S. 572 (1987).
15. Sec'y of the Interior v. California, 464 U.S. 312 (1984). *See* the CZMA Federal Consistency Requirement, *infra* notes 63–95 and accompanying text.
16. A marine league is a measure of distance commonly employed at sea, being equal to one-twentieth part of a degree of latitude, or three geographical or nautical miles. BLACK'S LAW DICTIONARY 967 (6th ed. 1990).
17. United States v. California, 332 U.S. 19 (1947).

18. 43 U.S.C. §§ 1301–1315 (2000).
19. 43 U.S.C. § 1312 (2000).
20. United States v. Louisiana, 363 U.S. 1 (1960).
21. 48 U.S.C. § 749 (2000).
22. United States v. Maine, 420 U.S. 515 (1975).
23. *See generally* BRUCE FLUSHMAN, WATER BOUNDARIES: DEMYSTIFYING LAND BOUNDARIES ADJACENT TO TIDAL OR NAVIGABLE WATERS (2002); Aaron L. Shalowitz, *Boundary Problems Raised by the Submerged Lands Act*, 54 COLUM. L. REV. 1021 (1954). For over thirty years, Alaska and the United States have been embroiled in boundary disputes often related to oil and gas royalties from arctic drilling. *See* Alaska v. United States, 126 S. Ct. 1014 (2006) (Court granted U.S. title to certain marine submerged lands underlying the pockets and enclaves of the Alexander Archipelago and within the exterior boundaries of Glacier Bay National Monument); United States v. Alaska, 530 U.S. 1021 (2000) (Alaska and the United States each granted some rights to Beaufort Sea mineral leasing including, with exceptions, in the National Petroleum Reserve and Arctic National Wildlife Refuge); United States v. Alaska, 521 U.S. 1 (1997) (Court granted U.S. title to submerged lands within boundaries of Petroleum Reserve and Wildlife Refuge); United States v. Alaska, 422 U.S. 184 (1975) (Court denied Alaska's claim to Cook Inlet as inland waters, granting title to United States).
24. United States v. California, 381 U.S. 139 (1965).
25. 16 U.S.C. § 1452 (2000).
26. 16 U.S.C. § 1452 (2)(a)–(k) (2000).
27. A. Dan Tarlock, *Putting Rivers Back in the Landscape: The Revival of Watershed Management in the United States*, 6 HASTINGS W.-NW. J. ENVTL. L. & POL'Y 167 (2000).
28. J. B. Ruhl, *Biodiversity Conservation and the Ever-expanding Web of Federal Laws Regulating Nonfederal Lands: Time for Something Completely Different?*, 66 U. COLO. L. REV. 555, 616 (1995).
29. 16 U.S.C. §§ 1451–1465 (2000).
30. 16 U.S.C. § 1452 (1) (2000).
31. 16 U.S.C. § 1461 (2000).
32. Pub. L. No. 94-370 (1976).
33. Pub. L. No. 96-464 (1980).
34. Pub. L. No. 99-272 (1986).
35. 16 U.S.C. § 1456b(a) (2000).
36. *Id.* § 1455b.
37. Pub. L. No. 104-150 (1996).
38. According to NOAA, over 99 percent of the 95,331 national shoreline miles currently are managed by the Program. NOAA Web site at http://www.coastalmanagement.noaa .gov/czm/oceanmanagement/waves_of_change/pdf/wavesofchange.pdf (last visited Jan. 31, 2008).
39. Am. Petroleum Inst. v. Knecht, 456 F. Supp. 889 (C.D. Cal. 1978), *aff'd*, 609 F.2d 1306 (9th Cir. 1979).
40. In Marine Forests Soc'y v. Cal. Coastal Comm'n, 128 Cal. Rptr. 2d 869 (Cal. Ct. App. 2002), a California appeals court determined that the California Coastal Act violated the separation of powers provisions of the California Constitution. The California Supreme Court reversed on appeal after the state legislature amended the California Coastal Act to address the state court's concerns. 30 Cal. Rptr. 3d 30 (2005).
41. *See* 16 U.S.C. § 1455(d)(11) (2000); 15 C.F.R. §§ 923.42, 923.44.
42. 16 U.S.C. §§ 1455–1456 (2000).
43. 42 U.S.C. §§ 4321–4370f (2000).
44. 16 U.S.C. §§ 1456(b), 1455(d)(1) (2000).
45. 16 U.S.C. § 1455(d)(2) (2000).
46. 16 U.S.C. § 1455(d)(2)(H) (2000).
47. Clean Water Act, 33 U.S.C. §§ 1251–1387 (2000); Magnuson-Stevens Fisheries Conservation and Management Act, 16 U.S.C. §§ 1801–1883 (2000); Outer Continental Shelf

Lands Act, 43 U.S.C. §§ 1331–1356a (2000); Marine Mammal Protection Act, 16 U.S.C. §§ 1361–1407 (2000).

48. H. John Heinz III Center for Sci., Econ. & Env't, The Coastal Zone Management Act: Developing a Framework for Identifying Performance Indicators (2003), *available at* http://www.heinzctr.org/NEW_WEB/PDF/CZMA.pdf (last visited Nov. 1, 2006).

49. California v. Mack, 693 F. Supp. 821 (N.D. Cal. 1988).

50. *See* 16 U.S.C. § 1458 (c)–(d) (2000).

51. *Id.* § 1455(e)(1)–(2).

52. *Id.* § 1455(e)(3)(B).

53. *See* 15 C.F.R. § 923.80–923.84.

54. 15 C.F.R. § 923.80(c).

55. 16 U.S.C. § 1455(c) (2000).

56. 15 C.F.R. § 923.84(a).

57. *See* Gilbert L. Finnell, Jr., *Coastal Land Management in Florida*, 1980 Am. B. Found. Res. J. 307 (1980).

58. (1) state establishment of criteria and standards for local implementation, subject to administrative review and enforcement; (2) direct state land and water use planning and regulation; and (3) state administrative review for consistency with the management program of all development plans, projects, or land and water use regulations, including exceptions and variances thereto, proposed by any state or local authority or private developer, with power to approve or disapprove after public notice and an opportunity for hearings. 16 U.S.C. § 1455(d)(11)(2000).

59. For example, the Third Circuit Court of Appeals has determined that although congressional consent may be a defense to a Commerce Clause challenge, neither the language of the CZMA, the legislative history, nor the case law indicates an intent in the CZMA to expand or to alter state authority in relation to the Commerce Clause. Norfolk Southern Corp. v. Oberly, 822 F.2d 388 (3d Cir. 1987).

60. 15 C.F.R. § 923.42–923.44.

61. J.B. Ruhl, *Biodiversity Conservation and the Ever-expanding Web of Federal Laws Regulating Nonfederal Lands: Time for Something Completely Different?*, 66 U. Colo. L. Rev. 555, 619 (1995).

62. This is in contrast to the Clean Water Act Section 404, for example, which would not address an activity potentially harmful to a wetlands area if the activity takes place outside the wetlands and involves no fill into the wetlands. *Id.* at 620.

63. 16 U.S.C. § 1456 (2000).

64. *See generally* NOAA, *Federal Consistency Requirements*, Sept. 20, 2004, *available at* http://coastalmanagement.noaa.gov/pdf/fedconreqmts.pdf (last visited Oct. 30, 2006).

65. Conference Report to 1990 CZMA Amendments, H.R. Conf. Rep. No. 101-964, at 970 (1990).

66. 464 U.S. 312 (1984) (holding that, inter alia, federal oil and gas lease sales did not "directly affect" the California coastal zone and therefore were not subject to federal consistency review by the State).

67. *See* Conference Report, *supra* note 65, at 970–71; 136 Cong. Rec. H 8076 (Sep. 26, 1990). The Conference Report also provides that "the term 'affecting' is to be construed broadly, including direct effects which are caused by the activity and occur at the same time and place, and indirect effects which may be caused by the activity and are later in time or farther removed in distance, but are still reasonably foreseeable." *Id.*

68. NOAA, *Federal Consistency Requirements, supra* note 64, at 4.

69. *Id.*

70. *Id.* at 10–12.

71. Kean v. Watt, 13 Envtl. L. Rep. 20,618 (D.N.J. 1982).

72. Conservation Law Found. v. Watt, 560 F. Supp. 561 (D. Mass. 1983), aff'd, 716 F.2d 946 (1st Cir. 1983).

73. *See* 65 Fed. Reg. 77,123–77,175 (Dec. 8, 2000).

74. 16 U.S.C. § 1456(c)(1)(2000).

75. 15 C.F.R. § 930.43(d).

76. 16 U.S.C. § 1456(c)(3)(A)(2000).

77. 16 U.S.C. § 1456(c)(3)(A) (2000). *See also* 15 C.F.R. pt. 930, subpts. A, B, and D, as revised by 65 Fed. Reg. 77,123–77,175 (Dec. 8, 2000).

78. 16 U.S.C. § 1456(c)(3)(B)(2000).

79. 16 U.S.C. § 1456(c)(3)(B) (2000). *See also* 15 C.F.R. pt. 930, subpts. A, B, and E, as revised by 65 Fed. Reg. 77,123–77,175 (Dec. 8, 2000).

80. 43 U.S.C. § 1351 (2000). For full language, see Appendix G.

81. 15 C.F.R. pt. 930, subpt. D.

82. *Id.* subpt. E.

83. *Id.* subpt. F.

84. *Id.* subpt. C.

85. NOAA, *Federal Consistency Requirements, supra* note 64, at 9.

86. 16 U.S.C. § 1456(h)(2000).

87. 16 U.S.C. § 1456(c)(3)(A)–(B)(20 00).

88. 16 U.S.C. § 1456(c)(3)(A), (B), (d) (2000).

89. The requirements for appeals are found at 15 C.F.R. pt. 930, subpt. H, as revised by 65 Fed. Reg. 77,123–77,175 (Dec. 8, 2000).

90. NOAA, *Federal Consistency Requirements, supra* note 64, at 9.

91. *See* Town of North Hempstead v. Village of North Hills, 482 F. Supp. 900 (E.D.N.Y. 1979) (Finding the CZMA "is neither a jurisdictional grant, nor a basis for stating a claim upon which relief can be granted," the court dismissed a CZMA claim against village by neighboring town.). *See also* Save Our Dunes v. Ala. Dep't of Envtl. Mgmt., 834 F.2d 984 (11th Cir. 1987) (holding plaintiffs had no standing to appeal a coastal permit decision); City and County of San Francisco v. United States, 443 F. Supp. 1116 (N.D. Cal. 1977), *aff'd*, 615 F.2d 498 (9th Cir. 1980); Lincoln City v. United States, No. 99-330-AS (D.C. Or. Apr. 17, 2001). *But see* California v. Watt, 683 F.2d 1253 (9th Cir. 1982), *rev'd on other grounds*, 464 U.S. 312 (1984). Citizen enforcement of the CZMA would be enhanced by congressional addition to the CZMA of a citizen suit provision like those found in the CWA, ESA, OCSLA, and other laws discussed in this chapter.

92. *See* City of Virginia Beach v. Brown, 858 F. Supp. 585 (E.D. Va. 1994).

93. In the Consistency Appeal of the Virginia Electric and Power Company from an Objection by the North Carolina Department of Environment, Health and Natural Resources, U.S. Department of Commerce, Office of the Secretary (1994).

94. *See* 15 C.F.R. § 930.150.

95. The interstate regulations are found at 15 C.F.R. pt. 930, subpt. I, as revised by 65 Fed. Reg. 77,123–77,175 (Dec. 8, 2000).

96. Nat'l Acad. Sci., The Federal Role in Beach Nourishment 61 (1995).

97. Natasha Zalkin, *Shifting Sands and Shifting Doctrines: The Supreme Court's Changing Takings Doctrine and South Carolina's Coastal Zone Statute*, 79 Calif. L. Rev. 207 n.50 (1991).

98. *Id.* nn.52–53.

99. *Id.* nn.54–56.

100. 1988 S.C. Acts 634, codified at S.C. Code Ann. §§ 48-39-10, 48-39-130, 48-39-270 to 48-39-360.

101. *Id.* § 48-39-290(B)(2)(b)(iii).

102. *See Coastal-Building Barriers*, Boston Globe, Sept. 26, 1989, at 14. But this type of approach might not be free from constitutional challenge. Most states and districts have a preexisting statutory obligation to keep existing infrastructure in good repair.

103. In general, the federal government asserts the statute of limitations defense as responses to these suits. To date, the United States Supreme Court has not ruled on the issue of whether construction of shore restoration projects may constitute continuing torts, thereby exposing the government to liability years after projects are completed.

104. *See* D. Christie & R. Hildreth, Coastal and Ocean Management Law 43–49 (2nd ed. 1999).
105. 16 U.S.C. § 1452 (2)(E) (2000).
106. 16 U.S.C. § 1455(d)(2)(G) (2000).
107. 16 U.S.C. § 1455a(b)(3), (c)(2)(C)(ii) (2000). *See also* 15 C.F.R. § 923.11 (advises states to consider public access in analysis of quality, location, distribution, and demand for the natural and man-made resources of their coastal zone); 15 C.F.R. § 923.21 (advises states to consider access when developing criteria for inventorying and designating areas of particular concern); 15 C.F.R. § 923.24 (provides guidelines for shorefront access and protection planning); 15 C.F.R. § 923.51 (advises shorefront access to be considered in federal-state consultation); and 15 C.F.R. § 923.122 (provides that the Secretary consider public access when making Coastal Zone Enhancement Grants).
108. Digest of Water Res. Policies and Auths., Pub. No. EP 1165-2-1, ch. 14-1 (U.S. Army Corps of Eng'rs, July 30, 1999) (explaining that Public Law No. 84-826 authorized federal erosion control assistance only for publicly owned shores, or for private shores if such protection would result in public benefits). *See also* 33 U.S.C. § 426 ("Shores other than public will be eligible for Federal assistance if there is benefit such as that arising from public use or from the protection of nearby public property. . . .").
109. 16 U.S.C. § 1455(d)(2) (2000).
110. *Id.*
111. John M. Houlahan, *Comparison of State Construction Setbacks to Manage Development in Coastal Hazard Areas*, 17 Coastal Mgmt. 219 (1989).
112. Haw. Rev. Stat. § 205A (2006).
113. *See* Island Harbor Beach Club. v. Dep't of Natural Res., 495 So. 2d 209 (Fla. App. 1986) (finding that because of the complexity of the technical and scientific issues and the high degree of scientific uncertainty involved, agency determinations of coastal construction control lines should be given great deference).
114. *See* Lucas v. S.C. Coastal Council, 505 U.S. 1003 (1992), *infra* notes 128–29 and accompanying text.
115. *See supra* note 100 and accompanying text.
116. S.C. Code Ann. § 48-39-290 (2006).
117. 16 U.S.C. § 1455 (d)(2)(B) (2000).
118. *Id.* § 1455 (d)(2)(E).
119. Eastlake Cmty. Council v. City of Seattle, 823 P.2d 1132 (Wash. Ct. App. 1992).
120. 15 C.F.R. § 930.11 (g).
121. 15 C.F.R. § 930.36 (c).
122. U.S. Const. amend. V. For an additional discussion of the takings issue in coastal development, see Chapter 2 on the Public Trust Doctrine.
123. Loretto v. Teleprompter Manhattan CATV Corp., 458 U.S. 419 (1982).
124. Penn. Coal Co. v. Mahon, 260 U.S. 393, 415 (1922).
125. *Id.* at 413.
126. Penn Central Transp. Co. v. City of New York, 438 U.S. 104 (1978).
127. Lucas v. S.C. Coastal Council, 505 U.S. 1003, 1019 (1992).
128. *Lucas*, 505 U.S. 1003. *See also* John Tibbetts, *Beachfront Battles over Seawalls*, 12 Coastal Heritage 3 (1997) (discussing the current issue between regulators in South Carolina and North Carolina prohibiting the building of seawalls and beachfront property owners claiming that seawalls are the only method of saving their property from falling into the sea due to extreme erosion).
129. The Court recognized an exception to the application of the *Lucas* analysis when the government bases the regulation on the "background principles of the State's law of property and nuisance." *Lucas*, 505 U.S. at 1029. The Oregon Supreme Court applied the *Lucas* analysis in Stevens v. City of Cannon Beach, in which the landowner sued the City of Cannon Beach and the state of Oregon for denials of permits to construct a seawall on

the dry sand portion of the plaintiff's beachfront lot. Stevens v. City of Cannon Beach, 845 P.2d 449 (Or. 1993), *cert. denied*, 510 U.S. 1207 (1994). The Oregon Supreme Court found that the plaintiffs had no property interest in developing the dry sand portion of their property, applying the nuisance exception of the Lucas decision and upholding the applicability of the Oregon Beach Bill. *Stevens*, 854 P.2d at 456–57; Oregon Beach Bill: 1967 Or. Laws ch. 601 (codified at Or. Rev. Stat. §§ 390.605 *et seq.* (1994)).

130. Penn Central Transp. Co., 438 U.S. at 124.

131. Nollan v. Cal. Coastal Comm'n, 483 U.S. 825 (1987).

132. Dolan v. City of Tigard, 512 U.S. 374 (1994). For a complete analysis of *Dolan*, see James H. Freis, Jr. & Stefan V. Reyniak, *Putting Takings Back into the Fifth Amendment: Land Use Planning After* Dolan v. City of Tigard, 21 Colum. J. Envtl. L. 103 (1996).

133. 533 U.S. 606 (2001).

134. *Id.* at 626. The Supreme Court also rejected the State's argument that Palazzolo's claim was not yet "ripe" for judicial resolution because he could continue to modify his proposed development plans and resubmit them to the state agency. In light of the facts, the Court held that it did not matter what form of development the landowner might propose; the state was not going to approve any major improvement of the wetlands on his land.

135. Palazzolo v. Rhode Island, R.I. Super. LEXIS 108 (2005).

136. Kelo v. New London Dev. Corp., 125 S. Ct. 2655 (2005).

137. *Id.* at 2663.

138. 42 U.S.C. §§ 4001, 4128 (2000).

139. *See, e.g.,* Fla. Stat. § 161.55(1)(d) (requiring major coastal structures to withstand wind velocities of 110 miles per hour and structures in the Florida Keys to withstand 115 mile-per-hour winds).

140. *See* 42 U.S.C. § 4106(a)(2000).

141. *See* Adolph v. Fed. Emergency Mgmt. Agency, 854 F.2d 732 (5th Cir. 1988); Tex. Landowners Rights Ass'n v. Harris, 453 F. Supp. 1025 (D.D.C. 1978).

142. 16 U.S.C. § 3505(d)(2). *See also* GAO, Coastal Barriers: Development Occurring Despite Prohibitions against Federal Assistance (July 1992).

143. 16 U.S.C. §§ 3501–3510 (2000).

144. 16 U.S.C. § 3502 (1)(A) (2000).

145. *Id.* § 3504 (A).

146. *Id.* § 3505 (d)(2).

147. *Id.* at (a)(3).

148. *See, e.g.,* Pub. L. No. 106-116, Section 1 (1999); Pub. L. No. 106-128 (1998); Pub. L. No. 105-277 (1998).

149. Rutherford H. Platt, Disasters and Democracy 30 (1999).

150. *See* 1 U.S. Dep't of Interior, Coastal Barriers Study Group, Report to Congress: Coastal Barrier Resources System with Recommendations as Required by Section 10 of the Public Law 97-348, the Coastal Barrier Resources Act of 1982, at 83 (1988); *Coastal Barrier Improvement Act of 1989: Hearings before the Subcomms. on Fisheries and Wildlife Conservation and the Environment and on Oceanography of the House Comm. on Merchant Marine and Fisheries,* 101st Cong., 66 (1989).

151. The Coastal Barrier Resources System Fact Sheet, *available at* http://www.fws.gov/cep/cbrfact.html (last visited June 22, 2003).

152. 16 U.S.C. §§ 1431–1445 (2000).

153. These sanctuaries are Stellwagen Bank (MA), *U.S.S. Monitor* (NC), Gray's Reef (GA), Florida Keys (FL), Flower Garden Banks (TX/LA), Channel Islands, Cordell Bank, Monterey Bay, and Gulf of the Farallones (CA), Olympic Coast (WA), Fagatele Bay (American Samoa), Hawaiian Islands Humpback Whale Sanctuary (HI), and Thunder Bay (Lake Huron). *See* NOAA, National Marine Sanctuaries, http://www.sanctuaries.noaa.gov/ (last visited Mar. 1, 2006).

154. 16 U.S.C. 1434 (b)(1) (2000). *See* United States v. M/V *Jacquelyn,* 100 F.3d 1520 (11th Cir. 1996) (court found that even though the Governor had filed an initial objection letter, he had not objected to final designation of the Florida Keys National Marine Sanctuary).

155. Biliana Cicin-Sain & Robert W. Knecht, The Future of US Ocean Policy 271 (Island Press 2000). Authors cite Chapter 17 of Agenda 21 and note that integrated coastal management has been embraced by numerous international agreements including the Framework Convention on Climate Change, the Convention on Biological Diversity, the Global Conference on Sustainable Development of Small Island Developing States, and the International Coral Reef Initiative.

156. Mass. Ocean Mgmt. Task Force, *Waves of Change* (Mar. 2004), governance recommendation 1, p. 29, at http://www.mass.gov/czm/oceanmanagement/waves_of_change/pdf/wavesofchange.pdf (last visited Jan. 31, 2008).

157. Cal. Res. Agency & Cal. EPA, Protecting Our Ocean: California's Action Strategy, Final Report to Governor Schwarzenegger (Sept. 2004), at http://resources.ca.gov/ocean/Cal_Ocean_Action_Strategy.pdf (last visited Nov. 1, 2006).

158. *Id.* at 2. This report focused on increasing the abundance and diversity of aquatic life in California's ocean, bays, estuaries, and coastal wetlands; improving water quality in those bodies; providing a marine and estuarine environment that Californians can productively use and safely enjoy; and supporting ocean-dependent economic activities.

159. Nat'l Ocean Econ. Program, *California's Ocean Economy,* July 2005, at http://www.resources.ca.gov/ocean/ (last visited Oct. 30, 2006).

160. The California Ocean Protection Act, Cal. Pub. Res. Code § 35615.

161. *Id* § 35650. The Council had $10 million in funds for these grants in fiscal year 2006. The Act also defines "sustainable" or "sustainability" as both of the following: "(1) Continuous replacement of resources, taking into account fluctuations in abundance and environmental variability. (2) Securing the fullest possible range of present and long-term economic, social, and ecological benefits, while maintaining biological diversity." *Id.* § 35550(d).

162. *See* California Ocean Protection Council, *A Vision for Our Ocean and Coast, Five Year Strategic Plan,* Sept. 2006, *available at* http://resources.ca.gov/copc/strategic_plan.html (last visited Nov. 1, 2006).

163. 16 U.S.C. § 1455 (d) (2000).

164. *Id.* § 1455(a).

165. Exec. Order No. 13,158, 65 Fed. Reg. 34,909 (May 26, 2000).

166. *See* California Marine Life Protection Act, Cal. Fish & Game Code §§ 2856–2863.

167. Pew Oceans Comm., America's Living Oceans at 26 (2003).

168. U.S. Comm. on Ocean Policy, An Ocean Blueprint for the 21st Century 86 (2004).

169. U.S. Ocean Action Plan 10–11 (2004), at http://ocean.ceq.gov/actionplan.pdf (last visited Jan. 5, 2006) and on file with author.

170. *See* Univ. of Wash., School of Marine Affairs, http://courses.washington.edu/oceangov/ for region-by-region details of regional ocean governance efforts (last visited Mar. 1, 2006).

171. Testimony of Governor Donald L. Carcieri to the Committee on Ocean Policy, Apr. 5, 2005 (on file with author).

172. The Conference is comprised of leaders from Connecticut, Rhode Island, Massachusetts, Vermont, New Hampshire, Maine, New Brunswick, Nova Scotia, Quebec, Prince Edward Island, and Newfoundland & Labrador. Its function is to address "issues of common interest and concern, and enact policy resolutions that call on actions by the state and provincial governments, as well as by the two national governments." More information on the Conference of New England Governors and Eastern Canadian Premieres is available at http://www.negc.org/premiers.html (last visited Jan. 5, 2006).

173. Resolution 29-3 of Aug. 29, 2005, Resolution Concerning Oceans, *available at* http://www.negc.org/documents/Resolutions.pdf (last visited Jan. 5, 2006).

174. For a sample of leading issues for regional concern, *see* Cicin-Sain & Knecht, *supra* note 155, at 7. The concerns listed include fishing habitats and stocks, conflicts between

protected marine mammals, marine transportation, land development patterns, and implications of development of new uses of the Exclusive Economic Zone, such as offshore aquaculture and wind farming.

175. *See West Coast Governors' Agreement on Ocean Health* (Sept. 18, 2006), at http://resources.ca.gov/press_documents/WCOceanAgreementp6.pdf (last visited Nov. 1, 2006).

176. Oliver A. Houck, *Environmental Protection and Sustainable Development*, at 2 (2006) (on file with author); *see also* Oliver A. Houck, *Can We Save New Orleans?*, 19 Tul. Envtl. L. J. 1 (2006).

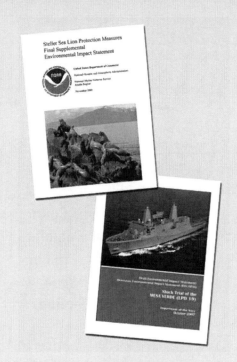

chapter six

National Environmental Policy Act

Janis Searles

I. Introduction

The National Environmental Policy Act (NEPA) passed both houses of Congress with little or no opposition in 1969,[1] and is now widely referred to as the Magna Carta of U.S. environmental laws.[2] Congress developed and embraced NEPA in part in recognition of the great damage that was being done to public resources due to ignorance about the environmental effects of actions. As noted by the Senate: "One of the major factors contributing to environmental abuse and deterioration is that actions—often actions having irreversible consequences—are undertaken without adequate consideration of, or knowledge about, their impact on the environment."[3] In enacting NEPA, Congress reframed federal agencies' approach to their statutory missions, by directing agencies to consider the environment in all of their programs and in all of their major decisions.

NEPA's enduring innovations are twofold: (1) imposing an obligation on all federal agencies to consider the environmental effects of a major federal action and alternatives to that action before taking the action; and (2) requiring disclosure of those environmental effects to the public and solicitation of the public's view on proposed actions.

NEPA is often described as a procedural, as opposed to a substantive, statute.[4] It has earned this reputation because NEPA does not prescribe a result; i.e., it does not require a federal agency to reach and implement a particular decision. Rather,

NEPA prescribes the process by which information is considered and federal decisions are made. In the classic words of the Supreme Court: "NEPA merely prohibits uninformed—rather than unwise—agency action."[5] To consider NEPA as merely a procedural statute, however, does not give due regard to Congress's purposes in enacting the statute and the effect NEPA's rigorous analytical requirements have had on decisions about public natural resources.

In the classic words of the Supreme Court: "NEPA merely prohibits uninformed—rather than unwise—agency action."

As will be described further below, because of its wide-ranging applicability to major federal actions significantly affecting the quality of the human environment, the National Environmental Policy Act plays an important role in the conservation, management, and disposition of ocean and coastal marine resources. Many if not most marine-related activities, unlike some land-based activities, occur on and affect public waters, requiring federal involvement that triggers NEPA jurisdiction. NEPA therefore can play a critical role in managing fisheries, offshore energy development, ocean dumping, and military activities, among others. Further, because of the lack of an overarching federal policy governing our oceans and the fractured jurisdiction of federal agencies responsible for different aspects of oceans management,[6] NEPA plays a unique role in injecting consideration of environmental effects in what otherwise would be single resource-driven decisions.

This chapter will describe NEPA's analytical and public processes, highlight recent trends in NEPA's applicability, and close with a discussion of the value NEPA brings to the emerging trend towards ecosystem-based management of our marine resources.

II. The Current State of the Law

When Congress passed the National Environmental Policy Act in 1969, it had in mind lofty, but eminently sensible, objectives. Congress established a new and broad-reaching national environmental policy by recognizing

> the critical importance of restoring and maintaining environmental quality to the overall welfare and development of man, [and] declar[ing] that it is the continuing policy of the Federal Government, . . . to use all practicable means and measures, . . . in a manner calculated to foster and promote the general welfare, to create and maintain conditions under which man and nature can exist in productive harmony, and fulfill the social, economic, and other requirements of present and future generations of Americans.[7]

As one noted NEPA commentator observed: "Congress intended to change federal agency decisions towards greater environmental protection."[8]

In and of itself, this new national policy represented a major shift in our approach to managing public resources by focusing on the importance of a healthy environment to a healthy populace. Prior to this point, conservation and management of most public resources was done pursuant to statutes that at best reflected multiple-use considerations, but that largely did not impose broader consideration of the environmental effects of agency actions. NEPA serves as a procedural umbrella over those substantive management statutes.

To reflect this new overarching environmental policy, in NEPA Congress announced four purposes:

1. "to declare a national policy which will encourage productive and enjoyable harmony between man and his environment;"
2. "to promote efforts which will prevent or eliminate damage to the environment and biosphere and stimulate the health and welfare of man;"
3. "to enrich the understanding of the ecological systems and natural resources important to the Nation; and"
4. "to establish a Council on Environmental Quality."[9]

To accomplish those goals, Congress created what has become known in shorthand as the environmental impact statement (EIS) process. NEPA requires all federal agencies to

(C) include in every recommendation or report on proposals for legislation and other major Federal actions significantly affecting the quality of the human environment, a detailed statement by the responsible official on—

(i) the environmental impact of the proposed action,

(ii) any adverse environmental effects which cannot be avoided should the proposal be implemented,

(iii) alternatives to the proposed action,

(iv) the relationship between local short-term uses of man's environment and the maintenance and enhancement of long-term productivity, and

(v) any irreversible and irretrievable commitments of resources which would be involved in the proposed action should it be implemented.

. . .

(E) study, develop, and describe appropriate alternatives to recommended courses of action in any proposal which involves unresolved conflicts concerning alternative uses of available resources.[10]

The description of the EIS requirement in the statute itself is limited to the language quoted above. The process for preparation and the contents of such "detailed statements" are defined more extensively by the congressionally created Council on Environmental Quality (CEQ) implementing regulations.[11]

A. Analytical Process

The primary analytical document associated with NEPA is the environmental impact statement, the "detailed statement" required by Congress. As the statute itself does not provide any definitions, the task of putting flesh on the bones of NEPA fell to the CEQ, whose regulations apply to all federal agencies.[12] In addition, each individual agency may develop procedures to supplement the CEQ regulations.[13]

The regulatory threshold for preparation of an EIS is a "major Federal action[] significantly affecting the quality of the human environment."[14] CEQ regulations define most of these terms,[15] and are entitled to "substantial deference."[16]

The CEQ regulations describe two levels of NEPA documents, the environmental assessment (EA) and the EIS.[17] Federal actions with "significant" effects must be evaluated in an EIS, whereas federal actions for which a "finding of no significant impact" may be reached may be evaluated in an EA.

1. Environmental Assessments

EAs are intended to be "concise public document(s)" that discuss the need for the proposed action, the environmental impacts of the proposed action, and alternatives to it, and that "provide sufficient evidence and analysis for determining whether to prepare an environmental impact statement or a finding of no significant impact."[18]

If, through the analysis of the effects of the proposed action in the EA, the agency can reach a "Finding of No Significant Impact" (FONSI) conclusion, then an EIS is not required.[19] The "significance" threshold is therefore an important one: actions that have significant effects must be assessed in an EIS, whereas actions that do not may be assessed in an EA.[20] Over the years, there has been a great deal of litigation over whether the significance threshold has been crossed and an EIS is required.[21]

While agencies have discretion as to how to involve the public in the EA process, courts have generally held that the public must be involved in some way in an EA's preparation.[22]

2. Environmental Impact Statements

The environmental impact statement is the main vehicle for achieving the congressional purpose and policies articulated in NEPA.[23] An EIS "is to serve as an action-forcing device to insure that the policies and goals defined in the Act are infused into the ongoing programs and actions of the Federal Government. . . . An [EIS] is more than a disclosure document. It shall be used by Federal officials in conjunction with other relevant material to plan actions and make decisions."[24]

NEPA is notable not only for its broad application—to major federal actions—but also for its broad analytical requirements. Environmental impact statements include a discussion of the purpose and need for the action, a description of the proposed action and alternative actions, a description of the environment affected by the action, and an evaluation of the environmental consequences of the proposed action and alternatives, as well as other nonanalytical sections.[25]

To determine the proper scope of an EIS, agencies are to consider connected, cumulative, and similar actions.[26] Connected actions are those that are closely related. Cumulative actions are those "which when viewed with other proposed actions have cumulatively significant impacts," and similar actions are those "which when viewed with other reasonably foreseeable or proposed agency actions, have similarities that provide a basis for evaluating their environmental consequences together."[27]

To determine the proper scope of an EIS, agencies are to consider connected, cumulative, and similar actions.

It is widely recognized that the alternatives analysis in an environmental impact statement is the "heart" of the EIS.[28] The alternatives analysis requires agencies to "[r]igorously explore and objectively evaluate all reasonable alternatives,"[29] including "reasonable alternatives not within the jurisdiction of the lead agency" and a no-action alternative.[30] Agencies must describe in detail the environmental consequences of each of the alternatives in comparative form, so that the likely benefits and tradeoffs are illustrated clearly to the public and the decision maker.

Courts have developed a "rule of reason" to determine the adequacy of alternatives to be considered in an EIS, evaluating the reasonableness of the alternatives in light of the purpose for the agency action.[31]

The environmental consequences analysis in an EIS is to include consideration of effects (discussed further below), as well as analysis of "any adverse environmental effects which cannot be avoided" and "the relationship between short-term uses of man's environment and the maintenance and enhancement of long-term productivity, and any irreversible or irretrievable commitments of resources."[32]

3. Consideration of Effects

In addition to the consideration of alternatives to a proposed action, another fundamental NEPA requirement is the obligation to consider a wide range of environmental effects of an action and its alternatives.

Agencies must consider the direct effects of the action—those effects that "are caused by the action and occur at the same time and place."[33] Agencies must consider the indirect effects of the action—those effects that "are caused by the action and are later in time or farther removed in distance, but are still reasonably foreseeable."[34] And agencies must consider cumulative impacts:[35]

> Cumulative impact is the impact on the environment which results from the incremental impact of the action when added to other past, present, and reasonably foreseeable future actions regardless of what agency (Federal or non-Federal) or person undertakes such other actions. Cumulative impacts can result from individually minor but collectively significant actions taking place over a period of time.[36]

It can be tempting to view these requirements and considerations as wearisome. But to do so would be to lose in the tangle of verbiage the very real and simple command of NEPA—think before you act.

B. Public Process Requirements

There are essentially four stages of the EIS process, each of which involves the public. First, an agency must establish "an early and open process for determining the scope of issues to be addressed and for identifying the significant issued related to a proposed action."[37] As part of this "scoping" process, the agency is obliged to publish a notice of intent in the *Federal Register* and solicit comments, including the comments of "interested persons (including those who might not be in accord with the action on environmental grounds)."[38] The scoping process is important, because agencies use it to identify and eliminate issues which are not significant or have been covered by prior environmental review,[39] and to determine "the range of actions, alternatives, and impacts to be considered in an environmental impact statement."[40] It is the public's first NEPA-based opportunity to influence the action assessed, issues analyzed, and range of alternatives and effects considered.

Second, based on the issues identified during the scoping process, the agency prepares a draft EIS.[41] The draft EIS must describe the affected environment, the proposed action and alternatives to that action, and the environmental consequences, including direct, indirect, and cumulative effects. Agencies are required to circulate draft EISs and "[r]equest comments from the public, affirmatively soliciting comments from those persons or organizations who may be interested or affected."[42] The opportunity to comment on a draft EIS is an important one—it is the first time the public gets to see the results of the analysis and a comparison between alternative courses of action.[43]

Third, the agency prepares a final EIS. The final EIS must consider and respond to comments received on the draft EIS.[44] In response to comments, an agency may make changes to alternatives or analyses, assess new alternatives, correct factual errors, and/or "[e]xplain why the comments do not warrant further agency response, citing the sources, authorities or reasons which support the agency's position."[45] The duty to respond to public comments allows members of the public some opportunity to hold an agency accountable, at least for the quality of its analysis and consideration of relevant issues.

Finally, the agency completes the EIS process by issuing a Record of Decision, which must describe not only the alternative chosen, but also identify the environmentally preferred alternative,[46] and "[s]tate whether all practicable means to avoid or minimize environmental harm from the alternative selected have been adopted, and if not, why they were not."[47]

C. Other Important NEPA Provisions

1. Limitations on Actions During NEPA Process

Importantly, during the NEPA process, agencies are prohibited from taking actions which would "[h]ave an adverse environmental impact" or would "[l]imit the choice of reasonable alternatives."[48] This limitation is an important one, intended to ensure that the NEPA process is not merely a paperwork exercise to validate a decision already made or an action already taken. Rather, agencies must complete the NEPA process before committing themselves to a course of action.

2. Categorical Exclusions

The CEQ regulations provide a mechanism for agencies to classify certain categories of actions as not having individual or cumulatively significant effects on the environment. These classifications are known as "categorical exclusions." An action that falls into a categorical exclusion may avoid environmental review under NEPA. Agencies must follow appropriate agency procedures when adopting categorical exclusions.[49] Agencies may not claim, post hoc, that an action is categorically excluded if the action does not fit into an existing category at the time of the agency decision. The public may challenge an agency's adoption of categorical exclusions.[50]

To temper the impulse to overclassify actions as categorically excluded, agencies must "provide for extraordinary circumstances in which a normally excluded action may have a significant environmental effect."[51] In such extraordinary circumstances, the NEPA analytical process applies, and the agency must prepare either an EA or an EIS.

The use of categorical exclusions has been on the rise in recent years, and efforts are increasing both administratively and legislatively to expand the universe of actions that could be categorically excluded from NEPA's requirements.[52]

3. Duty to Supplement

In NEPA, Congress imposed an ongoing duty to supplement environmental impact statements if: "(i) [t]he agency makes substantial changes in the proposed action that are relevant to environmental concerns; or (ii) [t]here are significant new circumstances or information relevant to environmental concerns and bearing on the proposed action or its impacts."[53] The process for preparing supplemental environmental impact statements is the same as the process for preparing EISs, except that there is no scoping period. This important requirement ensures that actions are taken and decisions are made based on relevant and current information.

4. Programmatic Environmental Impact Statements

As defined by CEQ, "major federal actions" include the "adoption of formal plans . . . which guide or prescribe the alternative uses of Federal resources, upon which future agency actions will be based."[54] Major federal actions may also include "proposals or parts of proposals which are related to each other closely enough to be, in effect, a single course of action,"[55] and "broad Federal actions such as the adoption of new agency programs or regulations."[56] In such cases broad-based evaluations called programmatic EISs may be prepared to eliminate the need for repetitive discussion of the same issues in action-specific EISs.[57] Thus, the EIS requirement applies not only to specific agency actions, such as the authorization of annual catch in a fishery, but also to the overall management program for that fishery.[58]

When agencies prepare broader EISs, such as EISs assessing programs, CEQ regulations allow for "tiering." Tiering permits agencies to refer back to analyses in broader EISs and thereby more narrowly frame analyses in subsequent EISs or EAs which follow.[59] The purpose of tiering is to avoid duplication of analyses and paperwork by incorporating by reference more general discussions into analyses of more specific issues.

5. Duty for Federal Coordination and Collaboration

Due to NEPA's broad application, it is not unusual for a NEPA analysis to consider a project over which multiple agencies (federal, state, tribal, or local) have some jurisdiction. In such a situation, CEQ regulations provide for designation of a lead and cooperating agencies,[60] and prescribe their respective duties.[61] The intent of the regulations is to require participation of relevant agencies as early as possible in the NEPA process, to ensure that the process and analyses incorporate all relevant expertise.

In addition, agencies are required to solicit comments from federal agencies with legal jurisdiction, and/or federal, state, and local agencies with authority to develop and enforce environmental standards, and tribes where effects may be felt on a reservation.[62]

Finally, federal agencies are authorized and encouraged to avoid duplication of federal NEPA processes and similar state and local processes.[63]

D. Little NEPAs

NEPA has spawned numerous imitators at the state level, a testament to its conceptual soundness and utility. The particulars of these so-called "little NEPAs" vary from state to state, but the statutes generally track NEPA's main provisions and include the obligation to consider the environmental consequences of state or local government activities.[64] Unlike the federal NEPA, some state NEPAs include substantive provisions, limiting actions that would be environmentally damaging.[65] Others require EIS-type analyses for any actions which may have a significant effect, rather than the federal NEPA's requirement that actions also be "major."[66]

> **NEPA has spawned numerous imitators at the state level, a testament to its conceptual soundness and utility.**

Unless there are conflicts with federal NEPA requirements, where state or local requirements include preparation of environmental impact statements, federal agencies are required to cooperate to fulfill those requirements so that one document may satisfy all applicable requirements.[67]

E. The State of NEPA

In the 1997 CEQ report on NEPA, *A Study of its Effectiveness After Twenty-Five Years*, then-CEQ Chair Kathleen A. McGinty noted:

> Overall, what we found is that NEPA is a success—it has made agencies take a hard look at the potential environmental consequences of their actions, and it has brought the public into the agency decisionmaking process like

no other statute. In a piece of legislation barely three pages long, NEPA gave both a voice to the new national consensus to protect and improve the environment, and substance to the determination by many to work together to achieve that goal.[68]

While there are many who recognize that the process mandated by NEPA has revolutionized federal decision making,[69] NEPA is not without its detractors.[70] While Ms. McGinty's assessment of NEPA is still shared by many nearly a decade later, there is an increasing trend to impose limits on NEPA. This trend is described in more detail below.

III. Emerging and Unresolved Issues

A. Narrowing NEPA's Application

In recent years NEPA's detractors have become increasingly vocal, and the statute and its implementation have been the subject of increased scrutiny. Complaints about NEPA are heard from developers and resource users who view NEPA as a barrier to their business objectives, as well as from politicians who portray NEPA as an obstacle, rather than an opportunity.

In response, federal task forces have been created to review NEPA, and there have been legislative and administrative efforts to limit the scope of actions to which NEPA applies and to constrain NEPA's analytical and public process requirements. The section below highlights some of these efforts that are either broad in application or specifically directed to the marine context.

B. Executive Branch Initiatives

There have been several efforts in recent years by the executive branch to review NEPA, improve its implementation, and limit its applicability in the marine context.

1. Council on Environmental Quality NEPA Task Force

In 2002, the Council on Environmental Quality convened a NEPA Task Force to provide the first comprehensive NEPA review in nearly a decade. The Task Force "examined the concern that the NEPA process is losing its focus to help federal agencies make better informed decisions."[71] In developing its recommendations, the Task Force met with local, state, and federal government personnel, as well as with tribes and interested members of the public. The Task Force's 2003 report, *Modernizing NEPA Implementation,* did not recommend legislative changes to NEPA. Rather, its recommendations focused on improving federal agencies' implementation of NEPA.[72] Among the many recommendations by the Task Force to "modernize NEPA implementation" are the development of a variety of handbooks to guide coordination of NEPA with other environmental consultation and coordination requirements, establishment of categorical exclusions, development of environmental assessments, and the use of programmatic analyses, among other issues.[73] As of this writing, CEQ is in the process of developing those handbooks.[74]

2. NOAA Regulatory Streamlining Process

In addition to the CEQ Task Force to modernize NEPA, the National Oceanic and Atmospheric Administration's National Marine Fisheries Service (NMFS, or NOAA Fisheries), the agency responsible for managing our nation's fisheries and other public marine resources, engaged in a Regulatory Streamlining Process designed to address perceived difficulties with NEPA implementation.

According to the Assistant Administrator for Fisheries, "NOAA Fisheries [undertook] a major regulatory streamlining project with the goal to improve the efficiency and effectiveness of regulatory operations and decrease NOAA Fisheries' vulnerability to litigation."[75] Main elements include "front-loading" the NEPA process during the early stages of fishery management action development, hiring environmental policy coordinators, delegating signature authority, and improving electronic rulemaking and permitting.[76]

Both the CEQ Task Force report and the NOAA Regulatory Streamlining Project focus on improving the implementation of NEPA without recommending legislative changes to the statute. Some of the recommendations, such as increased use of categorical exclusions, have significant potential to restrict environmental analyses and public scrutiny of agency decisions. The effect of these recommendations and streamlining efforts on NEPA's application to marine resource management and the quality of decisions will be worth watching.

3. Committee on Ocean Policy

As a final note on executive branch NEPA efforts, in response to the report by the U.S. Commission on Ocean Policy,[77] President George W. Bush signed an executive order in 2004 that established a Cabinet-level Committee on Ocean Policy "to coordinate the activities of executive branch departments and agencies regarding ocean-related matters in an integrated and effective manner to advance the environmental and economic interests of present and future generations of Americans."[78] The Committee's focus is on coordination and advice to the President. The chair of the Council on Environmental Quality serves as the chair of the new committee. Given the CEQ responsibilities with regard to NEPA, the CEQ chair's service on the new committee has the potential to improve the application of NEPA to actions affecting our oceans.

4. NEPA's Application Within and Outside the Exclusive Economic Zone

In addition to the administrative efforts outlined above, in recent years the federal government has taken the position in litigation that NEPA should not apply to federal actions in the Exclusive Economic Zone (EEZ) of the United States. Generally, there is a presumption against the extraterritorial application of U.S. statutes.[79] The premise behind this presumption is the avoidance of conflicts with other sovereign nations, or interference with foreign policy.

Courts addressing this issue in the NEPA context have, however, generally held that this presumption does not apply. The District of Columbia Circuit Court, for example, has held that NEPA applies to a federal decision to incinerate waste in Antarctica.[80] Reasoning that the purpose of NEPA is to "control the decisionmaking process of U.S. federal agencies, not the substance of agency decisions,"[81] the court concluded that the presumption against extraterritoriality did not apply "where the conduct regulated by the statute occurs primarily, if not exclusively, in the United States."[82] In cases where courts determined that NEPA does not apply, foreign policy considerations were apparent.[83]

The application of NEPA to the management of marine resources in the U.S. Exclusive Economic Zone would therefore seem to relatively noncontroversial. The majority, if not all, of the actions authorized by NOAA Fisheries/Fishery Management Council NEPA documents occur in the U.S. Exclusive Economic Zone. NOAA Fisheries and the regional Fishery Management Councils routinely prepare environmental assessments or environmental impact statements for their management decisions in the EEZ.[84]

Thus, the position taken by the U.S. government that NEPA does not apply to certain federal actions within the U.S. Exclusive Economic Zone because it is not U.S. territory is somewhat remarkable.[85] The court rejected this argument, concluding that NEPA applies in the EEZ because Congress intended for NEPA to apply in all areas under the United States' exclusive control.[86] Successful advancement of such a position has the potential to alter dramatically the management of coastal and marine resources. Given the lack of an overarching federal mandate for oceans conservation, NEPA's emphasis on analysis and disclosure of environmental impacts provides the only consistent set of considerations and procedures in the marine management context.

C. Legislative Efforts

1. Congressional Task Force

In addition to the executive branch NEPA Task Force, then-Rep. Richard Pombo (R-California), who served as the chairman and ranking member of the Committee on Resources, in the U.S. House of Representatives, convened a bipartisan task force to improve and update NEPA. "The goal is to ensure that the original intent of NEPA—that federal decisions are made in an appropriate, environmentally sound manner, rather than being focused by litigation—will become the way the statute will be implemented going forward."[87] In July 2006, the Task Force issued its Final Report.[88]

Unlike other NEPA reviews, the House Task Force report included recommendations for legislative changes to NEPA to constrain the statute's current broad application and public process opportunities. For example, one recommendation would legislate criteria to limit the use of supplemental EISs.[89] Others would amend NEPA to limit the scope of reasonable alternatives to "those supported by feasibility and engineering studies,"[90] amend NEPA to establish that an agency's assessment of current environmental conditions will serve as the methodology to account for past actions,[91] and impose time limits of eighteen and nine months for completion of EISs and EAs, respectively. Documents that are not completed within the time frames would be considered completed. [92]

Concerning public participation, the Task Force recommended that Congress require CEQ to draft regulations to give more weight to local interests than to those from others by "assess[ing] comments according to the impact on the entity submitting them."[93] The report includes recommendations to amend NEPA to limit who could prosecute a NEPA challenge.[94] The report also included a recommendation that Congress direct CEQ to draft regulations to allow existing state environmental review processes to satisfy NEPA requirements.[95]

Taken together, congressional adoption of the Task Force's recommendations would significantly limit NEPA's scope and breadth, and reduce those very benefits that make NEPA the cornerstone of environmental law—an interdisciplinary focus on the environment, subjected to broad public scrutiny. However, prospects for implementing any of the Task Force recommendations are in considerable doubt after the November 2006 elections with the defeat of Rep. Pombo and the new Democratic majority in both houses of Congress.

2. Magnuson-Stevens Act Reauthorization

Were the Task Force recommendations described above acted upon, they would apply generally to all federal agencies. Another increasing trend has been to limit the application of NEPA to certain agencies or activities via legislative or administrative means.[96] This trend was also reflected in the process leading up to the reauthorization of our nation's federal fisheries management law, the Magnuson-Stevens Fisheries Conservation and Management Act (MSA).

Another increasing trend has been to limit the application of NEPA to certain agencies or activities via legislative or administrative means.

As described in Chapter 9 on domestic fishery management, the MSA is the primary statute governing the management of federal fisheries in the Exclusive Economic Zone. In January 2007, President Bush signed the MSA reauthorization bill, H.R. 5946, into law. Early versions of the bill contained language that would exempt MSA actions from NEPA review. For example, the House Bill (H.R. 5018) provided:

> The Secretary may consider the requirements of section 102(2)(C) of the National Environmental Policy Act of 1969 . . . to have been satisfied with respect to any fishery management plan, amendment to such a plan, or regulation implementing such a plan that the Secretary determines has been prepared in accordance with applicable provisions of sections 303 and 304 of this Act.
>
> (b) LIMITATION OF APPLICATION.—This section shall not apply unless the Secretary has published a determination that sections 304 and 205 are substantially equivalent to section 102(2)(C) of the National Environmental Policy Act of 1969. . . . [97]

Congress, however, rejected this sufficiency language in favor of language from the Senate, which preserves the application of NEPA and its implementing regulations to federal fisheries management decisions.

Rather than supplant or supersede NEPA and its implementing regulations, the new law requires the Secretary of Commerce to "revise and update agency procedures for compliance with" NEPA, in consultation with the Regional Fishery Management Councils and the Council on Environmental Quality. [98]

The new procedures for MSA actions must comply with NEPA and CEQ regulations.[99] Such an approach is fully consistent with CEQ regulations, which provide for agencies to promulgate supplementary regulations to implement NEPA's statutory and regulatory requirements.[100] The congressional mandate to prepare new procedures for fishery management actions is an opportunity to improve federal fisheries management by further infusing fisheries decisions with environmental considerations. Whether the revised procedures ultimately strengthen or weaken NEPA's application to fisheries management will be fought out during the regulatory process.

Regardless of one's view as to whether NEPA is a perfect or an imperfect tool, whether it should be abolished or amended legislatively, or whether its implementation should be improved administratively, it is unlikely to be excised completely from the marine resources management arena in the near future. Given that, and given the increasingly inevitable shift to ecosystem-based management of marine resources (described further below), NEPA provides an excellent vehicle to facilitate that shift.

D. NEPA and Ecosystem-Based Management of Marine Resources

As discussed above, the U.S. and Pew Ocean Commission Reports both recognize that the current fractured policy, jurisdiction, and management of marine resources is, at best, insufficient to safeguard our public marine resources and at worst, perilous.[101] Both Commissions underscore that our oceans have reached the crisis stage and recommend that U.S. oceans policy embrace ecosystem-based management at a way to meet our marine challenges.

Both of the Commissions recognized in their own ways that the current marine resources management structure is not conducive to accomplishing a shift away from sector or single species-based management to ecosystem-based management and therefore recommended a host of changes to facilitate that transition. As of this writing, little progress has been made on the major recommendations.[102] In the absence of those major reforms, while existing marine resource management statutes provide the discretion to employ ecosystem-based management tools and techniques, a broad-scale ecosystem-based management mandate is lacking. Given this state of affairs, NEPA provides the best available path from the status quo to ecosystem-based management.[103]

Agreement as to what ecosystem-based management might mean or might look like in the marine context has been emerging. According to a Scientific Consensus Statement on Marine Ecosystem-Based Management:

Ecosystem-based management in an integrated approach to management that considers the entire ecosystem. The goal of ecosystem-based management is to maintain an ecosystem in a healthy, productive and resilient condition so that it can provide the services humans want and need. Ecosystem-based management differs from current approaches that usually focus on a single species, sector, activity or concern; it considers the cumulative impacts of different sectors. Specifically, ecosystem-based management:

- emphasizes the protection of ecosystem structure, functioning, and key processes;
- is place-based in focusing on a specific ecosystem and the range of activities affecting it;
- explicitly accounts for the interconnectedness within systems, recognizing the importance of interactions between many target species or key services and other non-target species;
- acknowledges interconnectedness among systems, such as between air, land and sea; and
- integrates ecological, social, economic, and institutional perspectives, recognizing their strong interdependences.[104]

It is widely recognized that few of the main statutes governing public lands management may be said to reflect ecological principles.[105] This is perhaps even more true in the marine public resources context, which continues to lag behind terrestrial public resources in terms of investment, the state of the science, political priority, and general public awareness. That makes NEPA's application to actions that effect the marine environment even more critical.

As described above, NEPA is unique in that it imposes an interdisciplinary approach on federal actions that are usually otherwise guided by single-use or multiple-use statutory regimes. NEPA also importantly requires consideration of direct, indirect, and cumulative impacts. NEPA has certainly been used in the terrestrial context to interject broad principles of conservation biology and ecology into public lands resource management. NEPA is beginning to serve the same function in the marine arena.[106]

Ultimately, NEPA's primary limitation is its lack of a substantive mandate.

Ultimately, however, NEPA's primary limitation is its lack of a substantive mandate. While NEPA can provide the analytical tools to consider the effects of actions on temporal and spatial scales that are relevant to ecosystem-based management and can force consideration of the broader ecological effects of proposed actions, NEPA cannot require the selection of an alternative that is considerate of the ecosystem. As such, NEPA is an important and useful analytical tool in the quest for ecosystem-based management of marine resources, but it should not be a substitute for a more far-reaching ocean policy mandate.

One illustrative example: In *Greenpeace v. NMFS,*[107] conservation plaintiffs challenged in part the continued authorization of the North Pacific groundfish fisheries without proper NEPA compliance. Specifically, the plaintiffs alleged that the Fishery Management Plans (FMPs) governing the conduct of the federal fisheries off the coast of Alaska were subject to NEPA's requirements, and that the almost two-decades-old environmental impact statements supporting the FMPs were inadequate.[108] The court agreed, and ordered the National Marine Fisheries Service to prepare a supplemental programmatic EIS.[109] This ruling is notable from both a legal and a practical perspective. From a legal perspective, it established that, as in the terrestrial context, NEPA does apply to broad federal programs—Fishery Management Plans—and requires analysis and consideration of alternatives. From a practical perspective, it provided the first real opportunity to incorporate in a systematic way ecosystem-based management principles into the single-species fishery management regime.

The programmatic EIS that resulted from the litigation is not without its flaws. It was the first of its kind for NMFS, and long overdue, leading to a fair amount of confusion over its scope and purpose, and to the inclusion of a significant amount of previously unsynthesized information.[110] Nevertheless, the EIS did accomplish a programmatic-level review of the entirety of the Fishery Management Plans and their numerous amendments, and a consideration of the effects of the prosecution of the North Pacific groundfish fisheries authorized by these plans on the marine environment. While the agency action underlying the EIS remained focused on the single sector (fisheries), species-by-species (targeted fish species) paradigm developed by the MSA, the application of NEPA to a Fishery Management Plan opened the door to consideration of ecosystem factors in a comprehensive way that had never before been done. The programmatic EIS provided the framework and analytical structure to consider the cumulative effects of decades of industrial-scale fishing on the marine environment, resulting in a significant compilation, synthesis, and analysis of data that had never before been evaluated together. Even without the selection of a paradigm-shifting management alternative, NEPA did serve its purpose of forcing consideration of the consequences of a federal action on the broader environment, and provided the vehicle for insertion of ecosystem-based management principles into that consideration.

IV. Conclusion

NEPA's passage reflected a significant change in the way our nation viewed management of public resources. While it did nothing to change the underlying management regimes governing public resources, it did require for the first time that federal managers employ an interdisciplinary approach to think about the consequences of their actions before taking them, and expose those consequences and corresponding policy trade-offs to public scrutiny.

In the view of many,[111] this author included, NEPA is under a multilayered assault that threatens to reduce and further fragment consideration of the environmental consequences of our actions on oceans at a time when two bipartisan Commissions have concluded that we need such considerations the most. Under the current statutory and regulatory regimes governing conservation, management, and disposition of public marine resources, NEPA provides the best opportunity to move oceans management from its current fractured state to one that considers the effects of single sectors on the marine ecosystem as a whole. The potential and promise of NEPA is that it "foster[s] excellent action" by forcing careful consideration.[112] The increasing trend to exempt certain agencies or types of activities from NEPA's consideration or otherwise limit the NEPA analysis or public involvement threatens to turn the clock backwards towards a highly fragmented, ecologically insensitive management approach that does not serve our nation's long-term interests.

Notes

1. 115 Cong. Rec. 19,013 (1969); 115 Cong. Rec. 26,590 (1969).
2. As one commentator noted, NEPA "has assumed quasi-constitutional status as one of the foundational laws of the modern administrative state." Bradley C. Karkkainen, *Whither NEPA*, 12 N.Y.U. Envtl. L. J. 333 (2004).
3. S. Rep. No. 91-296, at 4 (1969).
4. This is due in part to U.S. Supreme Court decisions holding that NEPA cannot "mandate particular results for only prescribe the necessary process." Robertson v. Methow Valley Citizen's Council, 490 U.S. 332, 350 (1989). *See also* Kleppe v. Sierra Club, 427 U.S. 390, 410 (1976), holding that once an agency has made a NEPA-based decision, "[t]he only role for a court is to ensure that the agency has taken a 'hard look' at the environmental consequences; it cannot 'interject itself within the area of discretion of the executive as to the choice of the action to be taken.'"
5. Robertson v. Methow Valley Citizen's Council, 490 U.S. at 352.
6. The lack of an overarching federal policy for the oceans and the gaps in federal oceans management have been noted in reports by the U.S. Commission on Ocean Policy, *An Ocean Blueprint for the 21st Century* (2004) and the Pew Oceans Commission, *American's Living Oceans* (2003), described in more detail in Chapter 20.
7. 42 U.S.C. § 4331(a).
8. Comments of Professor Oliver A. Houck to a Council on Environmental Quality Roundtable, Dec. 11, 2006, *available at* http://ceq.eh.doe.gov/ntf/inputreceived/20031212Tulane_Comments.pdf; *see also* 40 C.F.R. § 1500.6 ("Each agency shall interpret the provisions of the Act . . . as a mandate to view traditional policies and missions in light of the Act's national environmental objectives.").
9. 42 U.S.C. § 4321.
10. 42 U.S.C. § 4332.
11. For a description of the Council on Environmental Quality, *see* http://www.whitehouse.gov/ceq/aboutceq.html. In addition to the CEQ, the Environmental Protection Agency (EPA) has a unique statutorily mandated role in NEPA implementation. Section 309 of the Clear Air Act requires the EPA Administrator to review and comment in writing on the environmental impacts of major federal agency actions, among other things. As a result, the EPA reviews and has a ratings system for EISs, and files and publishes notices about NEPA documents in the Federal Register.
12. *See* 40 C.F.R. §§ 1500 *et seq.*; Exec. Order No. 11,514, 3 C.F.R. 531 (1971), reprinted as amended in 42 U.S.C. § 4321. For more on the establishment and evolution of the Council on Environmental Quality, *see* Dinah Bear, *NEPA at 19: A Primer on an "Old" Law with Solutions to New Problems*, 19 Envtl. L. Rep. (Envtl. L. Inst.) 10,060 (1989).
13. 40 C.F.R. § 1507.3(a); *see, e.g.*, NOAA Administrative Order (NAO) 216-6, *Environmental Review Procedures for Implementing the National Environmental Policy Act*, May 20, 1999; NOAA NEPA Handbook, *available at* http://www.nepa.noaa.gov/NEPA_handbook.pdf.
14. 42 U.S.C. § 4332(C). CEQ regulations require that EISs be prepared not only for specific projects, such as a timber sale or authorizing fisheries, but also for adoption of policies,

formal plans, and programs (40 C.F.R. § 1508.18), and for proposals for legislation (40 C.F.R. § 1506.8).

15. *See, e.g.,* 40 C.F.R. § 1508.18 (major federal action); *id.* § 1508.27 (significantly); *id.* § 1508.3 (affecting); *id.* § 1508.14 (human environment).

16. Andrus v. Sierra Club, 442 U.S. 347, 358 (1979); Robertson v. Methow Valley Citizens Council, 490 U.S. 332, 355 (1989).

17. *Compare* 40 C.F.R. § 1508.9 *with* 40 C.F.R. § 1508.11.

18. 40 C.F.R. § 1508.9.

19. *Id.* § 1501.4(e); *see also id.* § 1508.13.

20. "Significantly" as used in NEPA requires considerations of both context and intensity:
(a) *Context.* This means that the significance of an action must be analyzed in several contexts such as society as a whole (human, national), the affected region, the affected interests, and the locality. Significance varies with the setting of the proposed action. For instance, in the case of a site-specific action, significance would usually depend upon the effects in the locale rather than in the world as a whole. Both short- and long-term effects are relevant.
(b) *Intensity.* This refers to the severity of impact. Responsible officials must bear in mind that more than one agency may make decisions about partial aspects of a major action.
    The following should be considered in evaluating intensity:

    1. Impacts that may be both beneficial and adverse. A significant effect may exist even if the Federal agency believes that on balance the effect will be beneficial.
    2. The degree to which the proposed action affects public health or safety.
    3. Unique characteristics of the geographic area such as proximity to historic or cultural resources, park lands, prime farmlands, wetlands, wild and scenic rivers, or ecologically critical areas.
    4. The degree to which the effects on the quality of the human environment are likely to be highly controversial.
    5. The degree to which the possible effects on the human environment are highly uncertain or involve unique or unknown risks.
    6. The degree to which the action may establish a precedent for future actions with significant effects or represents a decision in principle about a future consideration.
    7. Whether the action is related to other actions with individually insignificant but cumulatively significant impacts. Significance exists if it is reasonable to anticipate a cumulatively significant impact on the environment. Significance cannot be avoided by terming an action temporary or by breaking it down into small component parts.
    8. The degree to which the action may adversely affect districts, sites, highways, structures, or objects listed in or eligible for listing in the National Register of Historic Places or may cause loss or destruction of significant scientific, cultural, or historical resources.
    9. The degree to which the action may adversely affect an endangered or threatened species or its habitat that has been determined to be critical under the Endangered Species Act of 1973.
    10. Whether the action threatens a violation of Federal, State, or local law or requirements imposed for the protection of the environment.

    40 C.F.R. § 1508.27.

21. *See, e.g.,* National Parks & Conservation Assoc. v. Babbitt, 241 F.3d 722 (9th Cir. 2001); Anderson v. Evans, 314 F.3d 1006 (9th Cir. 2002); Cabinet Mountains Wilderness v. Peterson, 685 F.2d 678 (D.C. Cir. 1982); La. Wildlife Fed'n v. York, 761 F.2d 1044 (5th Cir. 1985).

22. Citizens for Better Forestry v. U.S. Dep't. of Agriculture, 341 F.3d 961, 969–70 (9th Cir. 2003); Greater Yellowstone Coalition v. Flowers, 359 F.3d 1257, 1279 (10th Cir. 2004).

23. "Environmental impact statements shall be prepared using an inter-disciplinary approach which will insure the integrated use of the natural and social sciences and the environmental design arts (section 102(2)(A) of the Act)." 40 C.F.R. § 1502.6.

24. 40 C.F.R. § 1502.1.

25. *Id.* § 1502.10.

26. *Id.* § 1508.25(a).

27. *Id.*

28. *Id.* § 1502.14.

29. *Id.* § 1502.14(a).

30. *Id.* § 1502.14(c),(d).

31. *See, e.g.,* City of Alexandria v. Slater, 198 F.3d 862, 867 (D.C. Cir. 1999); Vermont Yankee Nuclear Power Corp. v. NRDC, 435 U.S. 519, 549–50 (1978); *see also* NRDC v. Morton, 458 F.2d 827 (D.C. Cir. 1972).

32. 40 C.F.R. § 1502.16.

33. *Id.* § 1508.8(a).

34. *Id.* § 1508.8(b).

35. For further information on the cumulative effects consideration requirement, see Council on Envtl. Quality, *Considering Cumulative Effects Under the National Environmental Policy Act,* (1997), *available at* http://ceq.eh.doe.gov/nepa/ccenepa/exec.pdf; Michael D. Smith, *Recent Trends in Cumulative Impact Caselaw,* presented at the National Association of Environmental Professionals Annual Conference (2005).

36. *Id.* § 1508.7.

37. *Id.* § 1501.7.

38. *Id.* § 1501.7(a)(1).

39. *Id.* § 1501.7(a)(3).

40. *See* 40 C.F.R. § 1508.25 (actions that should be assessed in a single EIS include connected, cumulative, and similar actions; alternatives to be evaluated in an EIS include a no-action alternative and other reasonable courses of action; and impacts include direct, indirect, and cumulative).

41. *Id.* § 1502.9(a).

42. *Id.* § 1503.1(a)(4).

43. The public must be involved in the preparation of Environmental Assessments as well. *See, e.g.,* Citizens for Better Forestry v. U.S. Dep't. of Agriculture, 341 F.3d 961, 969–70 (9th Cir. 2003); Greater Yellowstone Coalition v. Flowers, 359 F.3d 1257, 1259 (10th Cir. 2004).

44. 40 C.F.R. § 1503.4(a).

45. *Id.* § 1503.4(a)(5).

46. *Id.* § 1505.2(b).

47. *Id.* § 1505.2(c). The Record of Decision must also include a monitoring and enforcement program for any mitigation "where appropriate." *Id.*

48. *Id.* § 1506.1(a).

49. 40 C.F.R. § 1507.3.

50. Heartwood v. U.S. Forest Service, 73 F. Supp. 2d 962 (S.D. Ill. 1999), *aff'd,* 230 F.3d 947 (7th Cir. 2000).

51. 40 C.F.R. § 1508.4.

52. *See, e.g.,* 72 Fed. Reg. 7391 (Feb. 15, 2007) (Forest Service final directive describing new categorical exclusion for oil and gas project leases on National Forest System lands); 68 Fed. Reg. 33,814 (June 5, 2003) (Forest Service regulations excluding certain logging activities from NEPA review); 68 Fed. Reg. 44,598 (July 29, 2003) (Department of Interior regulations doing same); *see also* 71 Fed. Reg. 54,816 (Sept. 19, 2006) (proposed CEQ guidance on the use of categorical exclusions).

53. 40 C.F.R. § 1502.9(c)(1). CEQ also advises that EISs be reviewed every five years to assess whether a supplemental EIS is warranted. Forty Most Asked Questions Concerning CEQ's National Environmental Policy Act Regulations, 46 Fed. Reg. 18,026, 18,036 (Mar. 23, 1981), *as amended* 51 Fed. Reg. 15,618 (Apr. 25, 1986).

54. 40 C.F.R. § 1508.18(b)(2); *see also id.* at § 1506.8 (requirement for environmental impact statement for proposals for legislation significantly affecting the quality of the human environment).

55. *Id.* § 1502.4(a).

56. *Id.* § 1502.4(b).

57. *Id.* § 1500.4(i). For discussion of programmatic EISs, *see* Jon C. Cooper, *Broad Programmatic, Policy and Planning Assessments Under the National Environmental Policy Act and Similar Devices: A Quiet Revolution in an Approach to Environmental Considerations,* 11 PACE ENVTL. L. REV. 89 (1993); Beth C. Bryant, *NEPA Compliance in Fisheries Management: The Programmatic Supplemental Environmental Impact Statement on Alaskan Groundfish Fisheries and Implications for NEPA Reform,* 30 HARV. ENVTL. L. REV. 441 (2006).

58. Greenpeace v. NMFS, 55 F. Supp. 2d 1248, 1273 (W.D. Wash. 1999).

59. 40 C.F.R. § 1508.28; Forty Most Asked Questions Concerning CEQ's National Environmental Policy Act Regulations, 46 Fed. Reg. 18,026, 18,033 (Mar. 23, 1981).

60. 40 C.F.R. § 1501.5 (authorizing designation of a lead agency, describing factors to consider in determination of which agency should be the lead, and process for referral of the issue to CEQ in the event of disagreement). State or local agencies may act with a federal agency or agencies as joint lead agencies. *Id.* § 1501.5(b).

61. *Id.* § 1501.6.

62. *Id.* § 1503.1(a).

63. *Id.* § 1506.2.

64. For a description of the main aspects of these statutes, see David Sive, et al, *"Little NEPAs" and the Environmental Impact Assessment Processes,* SK094 ALI-ABA 1175 (2005).

65. *See, e.g., id.* at 1178 (describing several state NEPAs that impose substantive limitations on government action, such as preventing actions for which there are less damaging alternative courses of action).

66. *Id.* at 1181.

67. 40 C.F.R. § 1506.2(c).

68. COUNCIL ON ENVTL. QUALITY, EXECUTIVE OFFICE OF THE PRESIDENT, THE NATIONAL ENVIRONMENTAL POLICY ACT: A STUDY OF ITS EFFECTIVENESS AFTER TWENTY-FIVE YEARS at iii (1997), *available at* http://ceq.eh.doe.gov/nepa/nepa25fn.pdf.

69. *See, e.g.,* Stark Ackerman, *Observations on the Transformation of the Forest Service: The Effects of the National Environmental Policy Act on U.S. Forest Service Decision Making,* 20 ENVTL. L. 703 (1990); Robert G. Dreher, *NEPA Under Siege: The Political Assault on the National Environmental Policy Act* (Georgetown Envtl. L. & Pol'y Inst., Georgetown Univ. Law Center, 2005), *available at* http://www.law.georgetown.edu/gelpi/research_archive/nepa/NEPAUnderSeigeFinal.pdf; COUNCIL ON ENVIRONMENTAL QUALITY, EXECUTIVE OFFICE OF THE PRESIDENT, THE NATIONAL ENVIRONMENTAL POLICY ACT: A STUDY OF ITS EFFECTIVENESS AFTER TWENTY-FIVE YEARS (1997), *available at* http://ceq.eh.doe.gov/nepa/nepa25fn.pdf.

70. NEPA's detractors tend to be representatives of industries that extract public resources and some agency officials. *See, e.g.,* Bradley C. Karkkainen, *Whither NEPA,* 12 N.Y.U. ENVTL. L. J. 333 (2004).

71. CEQ Chair Memorandum on Implementing Recommendations to Modernize NEPA, May 2, 2005, *available at* http://ceq.eh.doe.gov/ntf/CEQMemo_Implementing_Recommendations.pdf.

72. The NEPA Task Force, *Report to the Council on Environmental Quality, Modernizing NEPA Implementation* (Sept. 2003), *available at* http://ceq.eh.doe.gov/ntf/report.

73. For more information see the NEPA Task Force home page at http://ceq.eh.doe.gov/ntf. CEQ hosted four Regional Roundtables following publication of the Task Force Report, and compiled the results of the discussions in a Roundtable Report at http://ceq.eh.doe.gov/ntf/roundtables.html.

74. Updates on the state of implementation efforts are posted regularly at http://ceq.eh.doe.gov/ntf/implementation.html.

75. Testimony of Dr. William T. Hogarth, Assistant Administrator for Fisheries, National Oceanic and Atmospheric Administration, before the S. Subcommittee on Oceans, Atmosphere and Fisheries, Commerce, Science, and Transportation Comm., 107th Cong. (May 9, 2002), *available at* http://www.legislative.noaa.gov/Archives/2002/hogarthtst050902.html.

76. *Id.*

77. *See* Chapter 20.

78. Exec. Order No. 13,366, 69 Fed. Reg. 76,591 (Dec. 17, 2004); Council on Environmental Quality, Committee on Ocean Policy, http://ocean.ceq.gov/welcome.html.

79. *See* EEOC v. Arabian Am. Oil Co., 499 U.S. 224 (1991).

80. Envtl. Def. Fund v. Massey, 986 F.2d 528, 529–30 (D.C. Cir. 1993).

81. *Id.* at 532.

82. *Id.* at 529; *see also* Sierra Club v. Adams, 578 F.2d 389 (D.C. Cir. 1978) (NEPA applies to South American highway construction where the United States has control over highway construction and two-thirds of the financial responsibility); People of Enewetak v. Laird, 353 F. Supp. 811 (D. Haw. 1973) (NEPA applies to United States trust territories).

83. *See, e.g.,* Natural Res. Def. Council v. Nuclear Regulatory Comm'n, 647 F.2d 1345 (D.C. Cir. 1981) (NEPA does not apply to federal issuance of an export license for nuclear power plant components based on foreign policy concerns); Greenpeace USA v. Stone, 748 F. Supp. 749 (D. Haw. 1990), *dismissed as moot,* 986 F.2d 175 (9th Cir. 1991) (NEPA does not apply to Presidential decision to transport nerve gas from West Germany to a Pacific atoll).

84. *See, e.g.,* Am. Oceans Campaign v. Daley, 183 F. Supp. 2d 1 (D.D.C. 2000) (challenging NEPA documentation for several essential fish habitat Fishery Management Plan amendments); Pac. Marine Conservation Council v. Evans, 200 F. Supp. 2d 1194 (N.D. Cal. 2002) (challenging NEPA documentation for bycatch Fishery Management Plan amendment); Conservation Law Found. v. U.S. Dep't. of Commerce, 229 F. Supp. 2d 29 (D. Mass. 2002) (challenging supplemental EIS prepared for scallop Fishery Management Plan); Natural Res. Def. Council v. NMFS, 280 F. Supp. 2d 1007 (N.D. Cal. 2003) (challenging NEPA documentation for annual catch specifications).

85. *See* Natural Res. Def. Council v. U.S. Dep't. of Navy, 2002 WL 32095131, at *10–12 (C.D. Cal. 2002), in which the U.S. Navy argued that testing active sonar technology for detecting submarines in the EEZ was not subject to environmental review under NEPA.

86. *Id.* at 12.

87. 2006 House Resources Committee Web site, on file with author.

88. Comm. on Res., U.S. House of Representatives, *Recommendations to Improve and Update the National Environmental Policy Act,* Presented to Rep. Cathy McMorris, Chair, Task Force on Improving the National Environmental Policy Act and Task Force on Updating the National Environmental Policy Act, H. Comm. on Resources, 109th Cong. (July 31, 2006) [hereinafter House Task Force Report], *available at* http://www.law.georgetown .edu/gelpi/current_research/documents/NEPATaskForce_FinalRecommendations.pdf. The Task Force received approximately 250 substantive comments on the draft report. 2006 House Resources Committee Web site, NEPA Comments Index, on file with author. A rough breakdown of the comments indicates that comments agreeing and disagreeing with the Task Force's draft recommendations were about even.

89. House Task Force Report at 17.

90. *Id.* at 19.

91. *Id.* at 21.

92. *Id.* at 17.

93. *Id.* at 18.

94. *Id.* at 18–19.

95. *Id.* at 18.

96. *See, e.g.,* Healthy Forests Restoration Act of 2003 (Pub. L. No. 108-148), which limited the NEPA process for "fuel-reduction projects" in the "wildland-urban interface." Pub. L. No. 108-148, Sec. 104(d); Vision 100—Century of Aviation Reauthorization Act (Pub. L. No. 108-176), which expedites environmental review processes for projects to increase capacity at crowded airports. For a description of various measures that exempt certain categories of federal action from NEPA review and other limitations, *see* Robert G. Dreher, *NEPA Under Siege: The Political Assault on the National Environmental Policy Act*

(Georgetown Envtl. L. & Pol'y Inst., Georgetown Univ. Law Center, 2005), *available at* http://www.law.georgetown.edu/gelpi/research_archive/nepa/NEPAUnderSeigeFinal.pdf.

97. H.R 5018 as reported. H.R. 5018 as introduced included similar language deeming any fishery management plan, plan amendment, or implementing regulations prepared pursuant to the MSA process to be in compliance with NEPA.

98. H.R. 5946, 16 U.S.C. § 1854(i)(1). The full text of the NEPA provision in the MSA reauthorization act is as follows:

SEC. 107 ENVIRONMENTAL REVIEW PROCESS.

Section 304 (16 U.S.C. 1854) is amended by adding at the end the following:

(i) ENVIRONMENTAL REVIEW PROCESS.—

(1) PROCEDURES.—The Secretary shall, in consultation with the Councils and the Council on Environmental Quality, revise and update agency procedures for compliance with the National Environmental Policy Act (42 U.S.C. 4231 et seq.). The procedures shall—

(A) conform to the time lines for review and approval of fishery management plans and plan amendments under this section; and

(B) integrate applicable environmental analysis procedures, including the time frames for public input, with the procedure for the preparation and dissemination of fishery management plans, plan amendments, and other actions taken or approved pursuant to this Act in order to provide for timely, clear and concise analysis that is useful to decision makers and the public, reduce extraneous paperwork, and effectively involve the public.

(2) USAGE.—The updated agency procedures promulgated in accordance with this section used by the Councils or the Secretary shall be the sole environmental impact assessment procedure for fishery management plans, amendments, regulations or other actions taken or approved pursuant to this Act.

(3) SCHEDULE FOR PROMULGATION OF FINAL PROCEDURES.—The Secretary shall—

(A) propose revised procedures within 6 months after the date of enactment of the Magnuson-Stevens Fishery Conservation and Management Reauthorization Act of 2006;

(B) provide 90 days for public review and comments; and

(C) promulgate final procedures no later than 12 months after the date of enactment of that Act.

(4) PUBLIC PARTICIPATION.—The Secretary is authorized and directed, in cooperation with the Council on Environmental Quality and the Councils, to involve the affected public in the development of revised procedures, including workshops or other appropriate means of public involvement.

99. *See also* S. Rep. 109-229, Apr. 4, 2006, at 8 ("The intent is not to exempt the Magnuson-Stevens Act from NEPA or any of its substantive environmental protections, including those in existing regulation."). The report is associated with an earlier version of the Senate bill, which contained the same language that was enacted, with the exception of the timeline for developing the procedures. *See also* Statement of Rep. Rahall, Dec. 8, 2006 ("Notwithstanding efforts by this Congress to undermine the National Environmental Policy Act, H.R. 5946, as amended [which Congress enacted], requires full compliance with the law. The Secretary of Commerce is directed to update the procedures for complying with

NEPA, but these new procedures will not supersede existing NEPA regulations and guidance issued by the Council on Environmental Quality.").

100. 40 C.F.R. § 1505.1, 1507.3.

101. *See supra* note 6 and accompanying text.

102. Members from both of the Commissions have created a "Joint Ocean Commission Initiative." *See* http://www.jointoceancommission.org/index.html. The Joint Ocean Commission has issued report cards for 2005 and 2006, giving the nation a D+ and C– respectively on ocean policy reform. *See* http://www.jointoceancommission.org/.

103. In fact, the U.S. Commission on Ocean Policy recommends that CEQ revise the NEPA guidelines "to state that environmental impact statements for proposed ocean- and coastal-related activities should incorporate the regional ecosystems assessments call for in Recommendation 5-5." Recommendation 5-6, *An Ocean Blueprint, supra* note 6.

104. COMPASS, *Scientific Consensus Statement on Marine Ecosystem-Based Management,* at 1, *available at* http://www.compassonline.org/pdf_files/EBM_consensus_statement_v12 .pdf.

105. *See, e.g.,* Robert B. Keiter, *Beyond the Boundary Line: Constructing a Law of Ecosystem Management,* 65 U. COLO. L. REV. 293 (1994).

106. *See, e.g., Final Environmental Impact Statement for Essential Fish Habitat Identification and Conservation in Alaska* (Apr. 2005), at http://www.fakr.noaa.gov/habitat/seis/ efheis.htm; *Alaska Groundfish Fisheries Final Programmatic Supplemental Environmental Impact Statement* (July 2004), at http://www.fakr.noaa.gov/sustainablefisheries/seis/ intro.htm; *Pacific Coast Groundfish Fishery Management Plan, Essential Fish Habitat Designation and Minimization of Adverse Impacts, Final Environmental Impact Statement* (Dec. 2005), at http://www.nwr.noaa.gov/Groundfish-Halibut/Groundfish-Fishery -Management/NEPA-Documents/EFH-Final-EIS.cfm.

107. 55 F. Supp. 2d 1248 (W.D. Wash. 1999).

108. For a discussion of Fishery Management Plans, see Chapter 9 on domestic fisheries management.

109. For a copy of the Alaska Groundfish Fisheries Final Programmatic Supplemental Environmental Impact Statement and other associated documents, see the National Marine Fisheries Service Alaska Regional Office Web site, at http://www.fakr.noaa.gov/sustainablefisheries/ seis/intro.htm.

110. The Programmatic EIS that resulted from the litigation was quite lengthy—over 7,000 pages including appendices. This length is due in large part to the fact that it was over a decade overdue. A significant portion of the EIS had to describe and assess the significant changes in the ecosystem and the fisheries that had occurred since the early 1980s and late 1990s when the last EISs were prepared. Thus, its volume was due to a long-standing lack of compliance with NEPA, rather than to NEPA's requirements. Nevertheless, the length of the EIS has been used to support arguments that NEPA should not apply to federal fisheries management measures. *See, e.g.,* Testimony by Chris Oliver, Executive Director, North Pacific Fisheries Management Council to the H. Comm. on Resources, 109th Cong. 12–13 (Oct. 27, 2005), *available at* http://www.fakr.noaa.gov/npfmc/misc_ pub/OliverTestimony_1005.pdf. For some observations concerning the PSEIS, *see* Beth C. Bryant, *NEPA Compliance in Fisheries Management: The Programmatic Supplemental Environmental Impact Statement on Alaskan Groundfish Fisheries and Implications for NEPA Reform,* 30 HARV. ENVTL. L. REV. 441 (2006).

111. *See, e.g.,* Letter from ten former Chairs and General Counsels of the President's Council on Environmental Quality to The Honorable Cathy McMorris, Chair, Task Force on Improving the National Environmental Policy Act, H. Comm. on Resources, Sept. 19, 2005, at 2–3, *available at* https://www.law.georgetown.edu/gelpi/current_research/ documents/CEQChairsLetter.pdf. The former Chairs and General Councils raised concerns that "certain recent measures and pending proposals fail to reflect, and in some instances may undermine, the basic principles served by NEPA. Measures to exempt cer-

tain agencies and programs from NEPA, to restrict or eliminate alternatives analysis, or to limit the public's right to participate in the NEPA process threaten NEPA's vital role in promoting responsible government decision-making."

112. 40 C.F.R. § 1500.1(c). "The NEPA process is intended to help public officials make decisions that are based on understanding of environmental consequences, and take actions that protect, restore, and enhance the environment." *Id.*

chapter seven

Coastal Water Quality Protection

Robin Kundis Craig

I. Introduction

In January 2005, the U.S. Environmental Protection Agency (EPA) released its second *National Coastal Condition Report*,[1] concluding, as it had in 2001, that the overall condition of the nation's coastal waters was somewhere between "fair" and "poor."[2] Of more concern was the fact that wholly "good" indicators were reported only for the marine waters off the southeastern coast of the United States[3] and that over half of the nation's assessed estuaries were impaired and unfit for fishing and swimming.

Thus, coastal water quality remains a serious environmental and economic issue for the United States. For example, major toxin-producing harmful algal blooms (HABs)—which cause fish and shellfish advisories and occasional human poisoning[4]—occur along all coasts of the United States.[5] According to the Woods Hole Oceanographic Institute, "[w]e have more toxic algal blooms, more algal toxins, more areas affected, more fisheries resources affected, and higher economic losses" compared to thirty years ago.[6] While coastal pollution is not the sole cause of the increase, "the increase of nutrients into our coastal waters will stimulate 'background' populations of microscopic and macroscopic algae (seaweeds) by fertilizing them into bloom proportions. Harmful or toxic species will thus be more abundant and more noticeable,"[7] leading not just to poisonings of shellfish and humans but also to more general hypoxic (low oxygen) conditions and more general impairments of entire marine ecosystems.[8]

Coastal water quality also affects recreation. For example, in 2006, thirty-two percent of the 3,771 monitored beaches in the United States experienced beach advisories or beach closures as a result of pollution or bacterial contamination, an increase of twenty-seven percent from 2005.[9]

Contrary to common perceptions, land-based sources of water pollution are by far the most critical to address in order to restore and protect coastal water quality. Such sources contribute seventy-seven percent of all marine pollution,[10] forty-four percent from land-based *water* pollution and thirty-three percent from land-based *air* pollution that settles back onto the ocean surface, a phenomenon known as atmospheric deposition.[11] Given the fact that most coastal and ocean pollution comes from land-based sources, regulation of onshore polluters is critical to restoring and maintaining coastal water quality. For example, urban stormwater runoff into coastal waters is a suspected cause of many beach closures and swimming-related illnesses.[12]

Land-based water pollution comes in two forms: point sources and nonpoint sources of pollution. *Point source* pollution refers to the readily identifiable discharges of pollutants into the nation's waterways. Land-based point sources that can affect coastal water quality include industrial sources, sewage treatment plants, and municipal stormwater control systems that discharge pollutants directly into coastal waters or into rivers, lakes, and streams, which then travel downstream to coastal waters. In addition, some ocean-based point sources, such as ships and oil platforms, also discharge pollutants directly into the coastal and ocean waters.

Nonpoint source pollution, in turn, refers to the more diffuse and hence less controllable sources of water pollution, especially unchanneled runoff from rain and other forms of precipitation that flows over streets, parking lots, agricultural fields, and other sources of pollutants. Atmospheric deposition is also considered nonpoint source pollution.[13] The United States indirectly regulates atmospheric deposition of pollutants through the federal Clean Air Act[14] and states' implementation of that Act.

A comprehensive program exists to regulate land-based point sources of pollution. Under the Federal Water Pollution Control Act, better known as the Clean Water Act,[15] such sources are subject to permitting, effluent limitations, monitoring, and reporting requirements that can be enforced through federal, state, or citizen action. In contrast, the U.S. Environmental Protection Agency (EPA) has consistently identified nonpoint source pollution as the most significant remaining water quality problem, with urban and agricultural runoff being two of the leading sources of water quality impairment in estuaries;[16] yet nonpoint sources of pollution are subject to a far less rigorous regulatory program than point sources. Under both the Clean Water Act and the Coastal Zone Management Act (CZMA),[17] especially as amended through the 1990 Coastal Zone Act Reauthorization Amendments (CZARA), Congress has generally left regulation of nonpoint sources to the states, which regulate such sources (if at all) through water quality management plans and "best management practices" (BMPs). Thus, the interaction between, and enforce-

The EPA has consistently identified nonpoint source pollution as the most significant remaining water quality problem.

ability of, these two federal statutes are critical in protecting and improving ocean water quality.

II. The Current State of the Law

A. Protecting Ocean Water Quality from Point Source Pollution

1. Introduction to the Clean Water Act

Congress enacted the contemporary version of the Clean Water Act through the Federal Water Pollution Control Act (FWPCA) Amendments of 1972,[18] which set out "to restore and maintain the chemical, physical, and biological integrity of the Nation's waters."[19] Specifically, the 1972 amendments established "the national goal that the discharge of pollutants into the navigable waters be eliminated by 1985,"[20] and "that wherever attainable, an interim goal of water quality which provides for the protection and propagation of fish, shellfish, and wildlife and provides for recreation in and on the water be achieved by July 1, 1983" (the so-called "fishable/swimmable" goal).[21] The 1972 amendments pursued these goals by transforming the FWPCA's previous state-focused approach to water quality regulation, based almost entirely on ambient water quality standards, into a proactive federal permitting scheme based primarily on end-of-the-pipe, technology-based effluent limitations for individual dischargers.[22]

2. The "Discharge of a Pollutant" and the Clean Water Act's Applicability to the Oceans

a. The Clean Water Act's Basic Prohibition

The Clean Water Act's central operative provision for individual dischargers, Section 301(a), states that "[e]xcept as in compliance with [the Act], the discharge of any pollutant by any person shall be unlawful."[23] Behind this seemingly simple prohibition, however, are several definitional complexities.

b. "Persons" Who Can Discharge

The Act defines "person" to be "an individual, corporation, partnership, association, State, municipality, commission, political subdivision of a State, or any interstate body."[24] Notably absent from this list is the federal government, but Section 313 of the Act requires federal facilities to comply with the Act's requirements "in the same manner, and to the same extent as any nongovernmental entity."[25]

c. "Discharge of a Pollutant"

Under the Clean Water Act, "discharge of a pollutant"

> means (A) any addition of any pollutant to *navigable waters* from any *point source*, (B) any addition of any pollutant to the waters of the *contiguous zone* or the *ocean* from any *point source other than a vessel or other floating craft.*[26]

The Act defines "point source" broadly to include "any discernible, confined, and discrete conveyance."[27] Pollutant" is also broadly defined to include "dredged spoil, solid waste, incinerator residue, sewage, garbage, sewage sludge, munitions, chemical wastes, biological materials, radioactive materials, heat, wrecked or discarded equipment, rock, sand, cellar dirt and industrial, municipal, and agricultural waste discharged into water."[28] As a practical matter, therefore, Section 301(a) prohibits all human-controlled additions of almost any material into the "navigable waters," the "contiguous zone," and the "ocean," with limited exceptions.

d. The Act's Jurisdictional Waters

The Clean Water Act segments the waters of the coastal zone and the ocean into three marine zones, and different water quality requirements apply to discharges into the ocean depending on into which zone the discharge occurs.

i. "Navigable Waters"

The Act's "navigable waters" are defined as "the waters of the United States, including the territorial seas."[29] The territorial seas, in turn, are "the belt of the seas measured from the line of ordinary low water along that portion of the coast which is in direct contact with the open sea and the line marking the seaward limit of inland waters, and extending a distance of three miles."[30] As a practical matter, the Clean Water Act's "navigable waters" designate all of the waters that are generally subject to state jurisdiction, including both the inland waters (lakes, rivers, streams, and some wetlands) and, at least roughly, the offshore coastal waters given to states by Congress in the Submerged Lands Act.[31]

The definition of "navigable waters" has become controversial regarding intrastate and apparently isolated wetlands, both statutorily and constitutionally.[32] However, the federal government's broad Commerce Clause authority over the oceans and all waters subject to the ebb and flow of the tide has left the Clean Water Act's extension to the coastal marine waters relatively uncontested.[33]

ii. "Contiguous Zone"

A more potentially ambiguous ocean zone under the Clean Water Act is the "contiguous zone," which the Act defines as "the entire zone established or to be established by the United States under Article 24 of the Convention on the Territorial Sea and the Contiguous Zone."[34] This definition references one of the four Conventions created through the 1958 United Nations Conference on the Law of the Sea (UNCLOS I), which allowed ratifying nations to claim a contiguous zone beyond their territorial seas and extending out to twelve nautical miles out to sea.[35] While international developments rendered the 1958 zones obsolete for most purposes,[36] Congress has never amended the Clean Water Act's statutory definitions. Thus, the "contiguous zone" for the Clean Water Act still refers to the zone from three to twelve nautical miles out to sea.[37]

iii. "Ocean"

The Clean Water Act defines "ocean" to be "any portion of the high seas beyond the contiguous zone."[38] Obviously, the United States cannot regulate all of the world's high seas. Instead, in concert with international law, the United States asserts jurisdiction over a two-hundred-nautical-mile-wide exclusive economic zone (EEZ)[39] and has claimed a two-hundred-nautical-mile-wide exclusive fishing zone since at least 1976.[40] Thus, while the Clean Water Act is not precise about the extent of its reach into the oceans, the most logical construction is that federal jurisdiction over point source discharges currently extends two hundred nautical miles out to sea (with certain exceptions).

iv. Regulatory Significance of the Three Marine Zones

As a practical matter, the Clean Water Act's distinction between the "contiguous zone" and the "ocean" is largely irrelevant, because almost all of the Act's provisions that apply to one of these zones will apply to the other. Instead, the critical regulatory line is three nautical miles out to sea, because the Act's "territorial sea" is part of the "navigable waters" that the Act regulates most comprehensively, while the "contiguous zone" and the "ocean" are not.[41]

3. The Clean Water Act's NPDES Permit Program and Permit Requirements for Point Source Discharges

Point sources of pollution subject to the Clean Water Act must comply with one of two permit programs. Chapter 4 describes in detail the Section 404 "dredge and fill" permit program. This chapter concentrates on the Clean Water Act's more general permit program, the Section 402 National Pollutant Discharge Elimination System (NPDES) permit program.[42] However, it is worth noting that the Section 404 permit program applies only to "discharge[s] of dredged or fill material *into the navigable waters.*"[43] As a result, the Section 404 program does not apply more than three nautical miles out to sea.[44]

The NPDES permit program governs most point source discharges of pollutants into the nation's waters. Under this program, "the Administrator [of the EPA] may, after opportunity for a public hearing, issue a permit *for the discharge of any pollutant,* or combination of pollutants, notwithstanding Section 1311(a) of this title, upon condition that such discharge will meet" a list of applicable requirements.[45] The incorporation of "discharge of a pollutant" extends the NPDES program to the full marine range of the Act's jurisdiction.

a. Technology-Based Effluent Limitations

i. Effluent Limitations in General

Of the Clean Water Act's many requirements for point source discharges, the most important are the technology-based effluent limitations,[46] which are set on the basis of the relevant industrial category or subcategory and the type of pollutant discharged[47] and then incorporated into individual NPDES permits. Originally, by July 1, 1977, the EPA Administrator was to establish effluent limitations for most pollutants for individual dischargers based on "the best practicable control technology currently available," or BPT; effluent limitations for publicly owned treatment works (POTWs, or sewage treatment facilities) were based on secondary treatment.[48] Effluent limitations for toxic pollutants, and, as of March 31, 1989, for all other pollutants discharged by non-POTWs except the conventional pollutants, are based on "the best available technology economically achievable for [each] category or class," or BAT.[49] Finally, effluent limitations for the "conventional" pollutants—pH, biological oxygen demand (BOD), fecal coliform, total suspended solids (TSS), and oil and grease—are based on "the best conventional pollutant control technology," or BCT.[50]

ii. Application of Technology-Based Effluent Limitations to Discharges into Coastal and Ocean Waters

Section 301 of the Clean Water Act emphasizes that technology-based effluent limitations shall be applied to all point source discharges of pollutants.[51] By incorporating the phrase "discharge of pollutants," Section 301 extends the technology-based effluent limitation requirement to the territorial sea, the contiguous zone, and the ocean.

Section 301 specifically prohibits the discharge of "any radiological, chemical, or biological warfare agent, any high-level radioactive waste, or any medical waste."[52] However, this absolute prohibition applies only to discharges into the *navigable waters*. Therefore, this Clean Water Act prohibition does not extend beyond the three-nautical-mile limit of the Act's territorial sea. Nevertheless, Title I of the Ocean Dumping Ban Act of 1988 made it illegal to dump sewage sludge or industrial waste into the ocean waters, while Title III specifically prohibited the dumping of infectious medical waste.[53]

iii. Modifications of Technology-Based Effluent Limitations for Discharges into Coastal and Ocean Waters

In general, the EPA sets technology-based effluent limitations for point source categories that can affect marine waters in the same way that it sets effluent limitations for all other categories of industrial polluters. Some of the most obvious examples are the technology-based effluent limitations that apply to the various categories of seafood processors and to offshore oil and gas producers.[54]

However, despite some courts' recognition that the Clean Water Act especially protects the oceanic receiving waters,[55] two provisions in Section 301 allow the EPA to modify the normal effluent limitations for discharges into the sea. First, Section 301(m) of the Act allows the EPA, with the relevant state's concurrence, to modify the BPT- and BCT-based effluent limitations and the ocean discharge criteria (see below) relating to biological oxygen demand and pH for industrial discharges of pollutants "into deep waters of the territorial seas."[56] Allowance of such modifications depends largely on a cost-benefit analysis,[57] and the EPA Administrator must terminate any permit modified under this provision "if the effluent . . . is contributing to a decline in the ambient water quality of the receiving waters."[58] However, Section 301(m) modifications have not been a significant component of the NPDES program.

Second, Section 301(h) allows the EPA to modify the standard secondary-treatment-based effluent limitations for POTWs that discharge into marine waters.[59]

In order to take advantage of the modified effluent limitations, the POTW must demonstrate to the Administrator that nine statutory requirements are met.[60] In addition, no NPDES permit issued under this provision can allow a POTW to discharge sewage sludge into the marine waters, and the receiving marine or estuarine waters must meet water quality standards before the EPA can approve modification of the standard secondary-treatment-based effluent limitations.[61]

The EPA issued its final regulations for Section 301(h) modifications in August 1996.[62] It received 208 applications for waivers, eighty-seven of which were either withdrawn or became ineligible and seventy-six of which were denied.[63] As of 2006, thirty-six communities have waivers from EPA allowing them to discharge into coastal waters sewage effluent treated to less than secondary treatment standards, while an additional nine denied communities are revising their applications.[64] "The majority of the 301(h) waivers' recipients are small POTWs that discharge less than 5 million gallons per day (MGD), although the flows from these small POTWs represent only 4 percent of the 620 MGD of wastewater under the 301(h) program."[65] Given the limited number of applications granted and the small size of the POTWs involved, Section 301(h) waivers may not have a significant effect on overall ocean water quality. Nevertheless, they have created public controversies in places like California, Puerto Rico, and Alaska.[66]

> **Thirty-six communities have EPA waivers allowing them to discharge into coastal waters sewage effluent treated to less than secondary treatment standards.**

b. Section 302 Water Quality-Based Effluent Limitations

In a typical NPDES permit, technology-based effluent limitations dictate the majority of the discharge requirements for point sources. However, if the discharge "would interfere with the attainment or maintenance of that water quality in a specific portion of the navigable waters which shall assure protection of public health, public water supplies, agricultural and industrial uses, and the protection and propagation of a balanced population of shellfish, fish, and wildlife, and allow recreational activities in and on the water," the NPDES permit must include more stringent water quality-based effluent limitations to ensure that these uses are protected.[67]

The Section 302 water quality-based effluent limitations apply only when point source discharges interfere with the water quality of the *navigable waters*.[68] Therefore, the Section 302 requirement applies to point source discharges into inland waters and the territorial sea, but *not* to discharges into the contiguous zone or the ocean.

i. The Role of Section 303 in General

An NPDES permit must include "any more stringent limitation" that is "required to implement any applicable water quality standard established pursuant to this chapter."[69] Under Section 303, the states have primary authority to set water quality standards[70] for the waters within their borders. State water quality standards establish the ambient water quality goals that discharge regulation is supposed to achieve for a particular waterbody. Designated uses specify the uses that the state wants the waterbody to be able to support and water quality criteria specify the levels of water quality necessary to support those designated uses. In addition, as part of its water quality standards program, the state must adopt an antidegradation policy to limit its ability to degrade the existing condition of its waters and protect and maintain high quality waters of exceptional recreational or ecological significance.[71]

The EPA reviews the standards submitted by states for consistency with the Act and must establish water quality standards for any state that will not do so.[72] Most states have enacted their own water quality standards. Moreover, since the 1987 amendments to the Act, federally recognized tribes can also acquire authority to set their own water quality standards,[73] and tribes increasingly have been exercising that authority.

ii. Water Quality Standards, the Territorial Sea, and "Coastal Recreation Waters"

The Clean Water Act makes it clear that the Section 303 water quality standards should define the ambient water quality goals for the first three miles of marine waters. Both the states and the EPA Administrator have a general duty to prepare water quality standards for the "navigable waters," which include the territorial sea.[74] Moreover, in 2000, Congress emphasized the role of water quality standards in the territorial sea by enacting the Beaches Environmental Assessment and Coastal Health (BEACH) Act, amending Section 303 to address the problem of disease-causing organisms—some of the causes of beach closures—in coastal waters used for recreation.[75] The BEACH Act provides state funding for water quality monitoring and for posting signs at beaches where water quality poses a threat to public health.

iii. Water Quality Standards Beyond the Three-Mile Line

The Clean Water Act's overall structure suggests that water quality standards do not apply to the marine waters beyond the territorial sea. However, the Act contains some ambiguities regarding this point. For example, to aid in the establishment of water quality standards, the EPA Administrator had to establish model water quality guidelines pursuant to Section 304.[76] Information that the EPA developed was to include "the factors necessary to restore and maintain the chemical, physical, and biological integrity of all navigable waters, ground waters, *waters of the contiguous zone, and the oceans.*"[77] In addition, as discussed above, under Section 301(h), POTWs can seek modifications of the secondary-treatment-based effluent limitations for discharges into the contiguous zone, so long as "there is an applicable water quality standard specific to the pollutant for which the modification is requested."[78]

These provisions suggest that the EPA[79] has the authority, although probably not the duty, to set water quality standards for the contiguous zone and the ocean. To date the EPA has not done so, although in 2000, in response to President Clinton's Marine Protected Area Executive Order,[80] the EPA proposed new ocean discharge criteria (see below) that would have functioned, essentially, like water quality standards for the ocean.[81] The EPA withdrew its proposed new ocean discharge criteria when President George W. Bush came into office, and they have not reappeared.

c. Section 403 Ocean Discharge Criteria

i. Section 403 in General

Point sources that "discharge into the territorial sea, the waters of the contiguous zone, or the oceans" must comply with the EPA-set ocean discharge criteria as part of their NPDES permit requirements.[82] As the EPA has noted, "because of the complexity and environmental significance of marine ecosystems," the ocean discharge criteria "specifically address[ ] impacts from . . . point sources on marine environments beyond technology- and water-quality-based effluent limitations.[83]

There are 265 NPDES discharge permits subject to the ocean discharge criteria.[84] Over half of these permits belong to POTWs.

ii. Establishing the Ocean Discharge Criteria

The Section 403(c)(1) guidelines define the allowable "degradation of waters of the territorial seas, the contiguous zone and the oceans"[85] by forcing permitting agencies to examine the effects of discharges into the marine waters. In establishing these guidelines, the EPA weighed seven statutory factors while examining how the disposal of certain pollutants would affect the ocean waters.[86] The EPA published the existing ocean discharge criteria on October 3, 1980.[87]

iii. Applying the Ocean Discharge Criteria

Under the EPA's Section 403 regulations, applicants for NPDES permits who propose to discharge into coastal or ocean waters must submit complete chemical, biochemical, and ecological analyses of their proposed discharges.[88] Based on these analyses, the EPA then determines whether the discharge will result in an "unreasonable degradation of the marine environment."[89] The EPA assesses "unreasonable degradation of the marine environment" on the basis of ten factors.[90] However, if a pollutant discharge complies with the applicable state water quality standards, the EPA will presume no unreasonable degradation of the marine environment "for any specific pollutants or conditions specified . . . in the standard."[91]

iv. Mixing Zones

The "mixing zone" provisions of the EPA's regulations regarding the ocean discharge criteria allow point source discharges to cause limited violations of the water quality standards. Under these regulations, states may allow mixing zone and other policies that affect the application and implementation of water quality standards for discharges into marine waters.[92] A "mixing zone" is "the zone extending from the sea's surface to seabed and extending laterally to a distance of 100 meters in all directions from the discharge point or to the boundary of the zone of initial dilution,"[93] which exists to allow dilution of the effluent *down to* the limits imposed by the state water quality standards. As such, water quality within the mixing zone itself may not meet the water quality standards.[94] Therefore, mixing zones are arguably a violation of congressional intent regarding the ocean discharge criteria, because Congress indicated that the EPA should keep particularly careful watch over state permitting of discharges into the ocean.[95]

v. Ocean Discharge Criteria and State-Issued NPDES Permits

Because Section 403 applies to discharges into "territorial seas," which are part of the "navigable waters," the ocean discharge criteria also apply to state-issued NPDES permits. The EPA, however, may not waive its review of state-issued NPDES permits for discharges into the territorial sea like it can for other state-issued NPDES permits.[96] Moreover, no NPDES permit for discharges into the territorial sea, the contiguous zone, or the ocean can be issued "where insufficient information exists on any proposed discharge to make a reasonable judgment on any of the guidelines."[97]

Notwithstanding the mixing zone allowance, compliance with the ocean discharge criteria is an absolute prerequisite to permitting point source discharges into any part of the ocean. If the EPA determines that the proposed discharge, either as proposed or with regulatory conditions, will not unreasonably degrade the marine environment, the NPDES permit may issue.[98] Conversely, if the discharge will unreasonably degrade the marine environment despite all possible conditions that could be imposed, the NPDES permit application must be denied.[99]

d. Other NPDES Permit Requirements

Several other requirements also apply to NPDES permits for discharges into marine waters. For example, new sources that fall within industrial categories listed in the Act or specified by the EPA[100] must comply with any applicable new source performance standards (NSPS).[101] Section 307 allows the EPA Administrator to set, for particular industrial categories or classes of dischargers, toxic effluent standards for the toxic pollutants that are more stringent than the BAT-based toxic effluent limitations, up to and including a complete prohibition on the discharge.[102] All dischargers with NPDES permits are also subject to inspection, monitoring, recordkeeping, and reporting requirements.[103]

4. Other Considerations in NPDES Permitting of Coastal- and Ocean-Related Point Sources

a. State and Tribal Assumption of the NPDES Permit Program

The Clean Water Act allows states and tribes to assume NPDES permitting authority. Most states have assumed NPDES permitting authority,[104] subject to the EPA's oversight.[105] Thus, states now issue most NPDES permits.[106] However, states lack authority to issue NPDES permit to point sources that discharge pollutants more than three miles out to sea. Thus, the EPA still issues the NPDES permits for any such discharge, regardless of the coastal state's delegated authority under the Clean Water Act. Tribes have not yet significantly acted to acquire NPDES permitting authority.

b. Stormwater Permitting

As noted, stormwater runoff—particularly agricultural and urban stormwater—can adversely affect ocean water quality. For example, twenty-eight percent of pollutants reaching estuaries and twenty percent of pollutants reaching coastal areas come from municipal separate storm sewers (MS4s) that collect and channel stormwater runoff.[107] Stormwater runoff also carries pathogens, toxics, and nutrients into coastal waters and into the streams and rivers that run to coastal waters.

Nevertheless, until 1987, stormwater was not routinely subject to NPDES permitting.[108] Because stormwater begins as runoff, a form of diffuse and uncollected water pollution, the EPA and the states have historically treated it as nonpoint source pollution.[109] However, when cities and counties collect stormwater into storm drains and stormwater systems, or when point sources otherwise collect and channel such stormwater runoff, it becomes point source pollution subject to the Clean Water Act's NPDES permit requirement[110]—including the ocean discharge criteria, effluent limitations, and, in the territorial sea, water quality standards and water-quality-based effluent limitations.

In the Water Quality Act of 1987, Congress amended Section 402 of the Clean Water Act to ensure that all industrial and municipal point sources of stormwater would be subject to NPDES permitting.[111] The amendments announced a moratorium on all NPDES permitting for stormwater discharges until October 1, 1992, subject to five exceptions: (1) stormwater discharges for which NPDES permits had already been issued; (2) industrial stormwater discharges; (3) discharges from municipal separate storm sewer systems (MS4s) serving populations of 250,000 or more (the large MS4s); (4) discharges from MS4s serving populations of 100,000 to 250,000 (the medium MS4s); and (5) stormwater discharges determined to cause significant pollution and/or violations of the water quality standards.[112]

In November 1990, the EPA issued its Phase I stormwater permitting rules, covering eleven categories of industrial activities and the large and medium MS4s.[113] Under these rules, over 100,000 industrial facilities and approximately 850 municipalities received NPDES stormwater permits.[114]

Congress extended the permit moratorium for all other stormwater point sources until October 1, 1994,[115] and the EPA did not issue its final Phase II stormwater regulations until 1999.[116] These Phase II regulations cover small MS4s serving populations of less than 100,000 and smaller scale industrial activities, such as construction activities that disturb between one and five acres of land. Many of these point source dischargers operate under general NPDES permits rather than individual permits.

c. Section 318 Aquaculture Projects versus Aquatic Animal Production Facilities

Section 318 of the Clean Water Act allows for special discharge requirements in NPDES permits for "approved aquaculture projects."[117] "Aquaculture" generally refers to "the cultivation of animals and plants in water."[118] In the coastal zone, Section 318 is particularly relevant to certain kinds of mariculture projects—aquaculture projects in the ocean—that can affect coastal water quality.[119] The EPA and the states implement

Section 318 through the normal NPDES permitting process, subject to the special allowances for "aquaculture projects."

NPDES permitting of aquaculture facilities involves a potentially complex definitional maze. "Aquaculture projects" subject to Section 318 are a rather limited category of aquaculture facility. Specifically, the EPA defines an "aquaculture project" to be "a defined managed water area which uses discharges of pollutants into that designated area for the maintenance or production of harvestable freshwater, estuarine, or marine plants or animals."[120] In other words, aquaculture projects must involve some element of recycling wastes into food.[121] Moreover, in order to get the benefits of Section 318, the aquaculture "crop" must have significant commercial value and the pollutant discharge must result in increased harvest over what would occur naturally.

Because aquaculture projects involve waste recycling, however, NPDES permitting of these projects is potentially less stringent than NPDES permitting of other kinds of point source discharges, including other kinds of aquaculture. Thus, for example, normal technology-based effluent limitations need not be applied to discharges into an approved "aquaculture project," "except with respect to toxic pollutants."[122] However, aquaculture projects located in the territorial sea, contiguous zone, or ocean still must comply with the ocean discharge criteria.[123]

Nevertheless, aquaculture project permits are a fairly limited aspect of NPDES permitting, and the EPA has expressly concluded that fish farms and fish hatcheries are *not* aquaculture projects.[124] Instead, most aquaculture facilities are treated as "aquatic animal production facilities" (AAPFs)[125]—that is, aquaculture facilities that do "not use discharges of wastes from a separate industrial or municipal point source for the maintenance, propagation and/or production of harvestable freshwater, marine, or estuarine organisms."[126] AAPFs are generally located near waters regulated under the Clean Water Act, but they are often treated as nonpoint sources of pollution.[127] However, when fish or shellfish are sufficiently concentrated, AAPFs can involve the same kind of intensive waste production as more traditional concentrated animal feeding operations (CAFOs) involving cows, pigs, or chickens.

As a result, the EPA regulates concentrated aquatic animal production facilities (CAAPFs) through the Section 402 NPDES permit program, much as it regulates CAFOs.[128] Indeed, in 2002 the EPA proposed, and in 2004 it finalized, nonnumeric effluent limitation guidelines for CAAPFs, including ocean net pen facilities producing 100,000 pounds or more of aquatic animals per year.[129] As of 2006, about 245 aquaculture facilities were subject to the CAAPF permitting requirements.[130]

d. Section 312: Discharges of Sewage from Vessels and Discharges Incidental to the Normal Operation of Vessels of the Armed Forces

The Clean Water Act defines "pollutant" explicitly to *exclude* "sewage from vessels or a discharge incidental to the normal operation of a vessel of the Armed Forces."[131] As a result, vessel discharges of sewage are not "discharges of pollutants" subject to the normal NPDES permit requirement, even though vessels *are* point sources.[132] Instead, the Act regulates these types of vessel discharges pursuant to Section 312.

i. Marine Sanitation Devices and Discharges of Sewage into the Navigable Waters

Section 312 requires the EPA Administrator, acting in conjunction with the Coast Guard, to "promulgate Federal standards of performance for marine sanitation devices . . . , which shall be designed to prevent the discharge of untreated or inadequately treated sewage into or upon the navigable waters from new vessels and existing vessels, except vessels not equipped with installed toilet facilities."[133] "Sewage" is "human body wastes and the wastes from toilets and other receptacles intended to receive or retain bodily wastes."[134] For commercial vessels on the Great Lakes only, "sewage" also includes graywater.[135]

The marine sanitation device requirement focuses on sewage discharges into the "navigable waters." As a result, it applies only to vessel discharges into inland fresh waters and the territorial sea out to three miles offshore.

ii. Sewage Discharges from Vessels of the Armed Forces

Section 312 specifies that the marine sanitation device requirements "apply to vessels owned and operated by the United States unless the Secretary of Defense finds that compliance would not be in the interest of national security."[136] "Vessels of the Armed Forces" include "any vessel owned or operated by the Department of Defense, other than a time or voyage chartered vessel," and "any vessel owned or operated by the Department of Transportation that is designated by the Secretary of the department in which the Coast Guard is operating as a vessel equivalent" to such Department of Defense vessels.[137]

iii. Discharges Incidental to the Normal Operation of Vessels of the Armed Forces

Under Section 312, the EPA Administrator and the Department of Defense, in consultation with the Coast Guard, the Secretary of Commerce, and interested states, "shall jointly determine the discharges incidental to the normal operation of a vessel of the Armed Forces for which it is reasonable and practicable to require use of a marine pollution control device to mitigate adverse impacts on the marine environment."[138] After designating the discharges to be regulated, the EPA and the Department of Defense were required to promulgate "standards of performance for each marine pollution control device required with respect to the discharge."[139]

The EPA and the Department of Defense issued joint regulations establishing the Uniform National Standards in May 1999.[140] These regulations require that vessels of the Armed Forces treat or control twenty-five different kinds of discharges, including ballast water discharges, deck runoff, graywater discharges, and discharges of submarine bilgewater.[141] However, the regulations also exempt fourteen kinds of discharge from any kind of regulation.[142]

Unlike the marine sanitation device provisions, the Armed Forces discharges provisions of Section 312 are *not* limited to the "navigable waters." These requirements thus follow the vessels of the Armed Forces wherever such vessels travel.

iv. State-Established No-Discharge Zones

Section 312 allows states to petition the EPA to establish "no discharge zones" for the waters within their borders if the enhancement of the water quality of those waters requires a complete prohibition on vessel discharges of sewage.[143] As of January 2006, twenty-six states had established "No Discharge Zone" designations for all or some of their waters: California, Nevada, Utah, Arizona, New Mexico, Texas, Missouri, Minnesota, Wisconsin, Michigan, New York, Vermont, New Hampshire, Massachusetts, Rhode Island, Tennessee, Connecticut, New Jersey, Maryland, Virginia, North Carolina, South Carolina, Georgia, Kentucky, Maine, and Florida.[144]

e. Other Discharges from Vessels and Discharges from Other Floating Craft: Territorial Sea versus Contiguous Zone and Ocean

As Section 312 suggests, discharges from vessels and other floating craft can be subject to a variety of requirements under the Clean Water Act, depending on where and what exactly the vessel or craft is discharging and, in the case of a vessel, what kind of vessel it is. As discussed, the Act's definition of "pollutant" expressly exempts "sewage from [all] vessels" and "discharges incidental to the normal operation of a vessel of the Armed Forces" from normal NPDES regulation; instead, as discussed, Section 312 governs the regulation of these discharges.

Similarly, the Clean Water Act's definition of "discharge of a pollutant" exempts from NPDES permit regulation all discharges from vessels and other floating craft that occur in the contiguous zone or the ocean[145]—that is, more than three miles out to sea. However, discharges from vessels and other floating craft *not* so exempted are still subject to the NPDES permit requirement. Thus, for example, discharges of sewage into the territorial sea from a nonvessel "other floating craft"—a collection of permanently anchored barges serving as housing—were subject to NPDES regulation under the Clean Water Act.[146]

In the same vein, vessel discharges of nonsewage pollutants into the territorial sea should be subject to the standard NPDES permit requirements, so long as the vessels involved are not part of the Armed Forces. However, the EPA, by regulation, has exempted from NPDES permit requirements "effluent from properly functioning marine engines, laundry, shower, and galley sink wastes, or any other discharge incidental to the normal operation of [any] vessel," except for ocean dumping of garbage and wastes.[147] "[T]he EPA has relied on this regulation to exempt a variety of pollutant discharges, including ballast water, from NPDES permitting requirements."[148] Nevertheless, in an unreported decision in 2005, the U.S. District Court for the Northern District of California invalidated the application of this regulation to ballast water discharges from vessels not in the Armed Forces,[149] implicitly extending the NPDES permit program to many other kinds of vessel discharges in the territorial sea.

f. Coordination with Other Statutes

The Clean Water Act's NPDES permit program dovetails with several other programs to help protect ocean water quality. Within the Clean Water Act itself, for example, the NPDES permit program dovetails with the Section 404 permit program for discharges of dredged or fill material and with the Section 312 marine sanitation device and uniform national standards requirements for various vessel discharges. Beyond the Clean Water Act, Title I of the Marine Protection, Research, and Sanctuaries Act of 1972,[150] also known as the Ocean Dumping Act (ODA), regulates the dumping of waste materials into the marine waters.[151] The ODA, which is discussed more fully in Chapter 8, most often governs vessels that haul wastes beyond the territorial sea for dumping, effectively covering the NPDES permit program's exclusion of discharges from vessels and other floating craft more than three miles out to sea and the Section 404 permit program's limitation to the territorial sea.[152]

The federal Oil Pollution Act (OPA)[153] imposes liability for cleanup and damages on "each responsible party for a vessel or a facility from which oil is discharged, or which poses the substantial threat of a discharge of oil, into or upon the navigable waters or adjoining shorelines or the exclusive economic zone."[154] The OPA thus largely displaces the Clean Water Act with respect to oil spills into the navigable waters and the oceans, seaward to the full two-hundred-mile-wide extent of the EEZ.[155] Finally,

The Clean Water Act's NPDES permit program dovetails with several other programs to help protect ocean water quality.

the federal Comprehensive Environmental Response, Compensation, and Liability Act (CERCLA)[156] renders owners, operators, transporters, and arrangers liable for cleanup costs for any release or threatened release of hazardous substances from a vessel or a facility into the environment.[157] Because CERCLA defines "[e]nvironment" to include "the navigable waters, the waters of the contiguous zone, and the ocean waters of which the natural resources are under the exclusive management authority of the United States under the Magnuson-Stevens Fishery Conservation and Management Act,"[158] it imposes cleanup and natural resources damages liability on releases of hazardous substances into the coastal waters that can be broader than the Clean Water Act's civil penalty liability, so long as the release was not a discharge that an NPDES permit allowed.[159]

5. Federal Consistency and Section 401 Certifications

a. The Section 401 Certification Requirement

Section 401 of the Clean Water Act essentially allows states to veto or condition federally permitted activities that may result in any discharge into the state's waters, including the waters of the territorial sea.[160] A federal agency cannot issue the permit if the state denies the certification,[161] and states can condition the certification on compliance with specific requirements designed to ensure compliance with the Act,[162] including both the water quality criteria and the designated uses in the relevant state water quality standards.[163] In coastal waters, therefore, Section 401 becomes one means by which states can ensure that their coastal water quality standards are met. For example, construction projects along the coast authorized through a Section 404 "dredge and fill" permit from the U.S. Army Corps of Engineers are subject to the Section 401 certification requirement.

b. The Scope of Section 401 and the Oceans

By its terms, the Section 401 applies only to discharges into the navigable waters and hence in the ocean is limited to federally permitted discharges into the territorial sea.[164] However, as Chapters 5 and 13 discuss more fully, federally regulated facilities outside the territorial sea that can affect state coastal resources under the CZMA[165] and offshore oil and gas operations regulated pursuant to the Outer Continental Shelf Lands Act[166] are subject to a similar certification requirements.

B. Protecting Ocean Water Quality from Nonpoint Source Pollution

1. Nonpoint Source Pollution and the Oceans: An Introduction

As the EPA has recognized, "[t]he United States has made tremendous advances in the past 25 years to clean up the aquatic environment by controlling pollution from industries and sewage treatment plants. Unfortunately, we did not do enough to control pollution from diffuse, or nonpoint sources. Today, nonpoint source (NPS) pollution remains the Nation's largest source of water quality problems,"[167] including ocean water quality, because "[c]oastal waters are affected by both point and nonpoint sources of pollution, with the latter a significant and, in many cases, dominant form of pollution impacting coastal water bodies."[168] Thus, addressing land-based nonpoint source pollution is the most significant remaining task in improving ocean water quality.

> **Addressing land-based nonpoint source pollution is the most significant remaining task in improving ocean water quality.**

2. Section 319 of the Clean Water Act: State Nonpoint Source Management Programs

a. Overview

The Clean Water Act does not define "nonpoint source"; instead, by implication, the term refers to any source of water pollution that is not a point source. Prior to 1987, states addressed nonpoint source pollution, if at all, only through Section 208 areawide waste treatment management plans.[169] While designed primarily to encourage states to plan for the construction of POTWs throughout the state, these Section 208 plans were also supposed to "identify, if appropriate, agriculturally and silviculturally related nonpoint sources of pollution" and "set forth procedures and methods (including land use requirements) to the extent feasible for such sources."[170]

Nevertheless, areawide waste treatment management plans were largely considered a failure with respect to effectively addressing nonpoint source pollution, because Section 208 "does not ... provide clear criteria under which EPA may determine whether a plan's provisions are adequate. As a consequence, the content of these plans is largely discretionary with the states," and "there is nothing in the CWA comparable to the Clean Air Act's mandate for federal implementation plans to substitute for such state failings."[171] "As if to punctuate the ineffectiveness of the Section 208 planning provisions, Congress ceased funding for the grants program in 1981."[172]

The ineffectiveness of Section 208 led Congress to amend the Clean Water Act in 1987 to add Section 319, which establishes the nonpoint source management program.[173] Under this program, states must "identif[y] those navigable waters within the State which, without additional action to control nonpoint sources of pollution, cannot reasonably be expected to attain or maintain applicable water quality standards or the goals and requirements" of the Act.[174] States are also required to identify the significant nonpoint sources contributing to the degradation of the listed waters, to describe a process for identifying best management practices (BMPs) and measures to control those sources, and to identify existing state and local controls on such sources.[175]

After filing initial reports with the EPA, states are required to develop, through a process of notice and comment, a state nonpoint source management program.[176] Each state program must meet six requirements, including a schedule of annual milestones for implementing BMP requirements for the various categories of nonpoint sources contributing to water quality problems within the state.[177] States that submit reports and programs that the EPA approves are eligible for federal grants, including grants to implement the nonpoint source management program[178] and grants to protect groundwater quality.[179]

b. The Geographic Scope of Section 319

Like most state-focused provisions of the Clean Water Act, the Section 319 requirements apply specifically to "navigable waters." With regard to ocean water quality, therefore, Section 319 applies to the three-mile-wide territorial sea, but not to the contiguous zone or the ocean. State Section 319 programs most often concentrate, therefore, on controlling land-based sources of runoff, a form of nonpoint source pollution that is most important to marine water quality in nearshore coastal zone. In contrast, the EPA has taken the lead in addressing a multimedia form of nonpoint source pollution—atmospheric deposition of pollutants—that can affect water quality in both the immediate coastal zone and farther out to sea.[180]

c. Federal Nonpoint Sources and Consistency

The limited case law that exists indicates that the Section 401 state certification requirement does not apply to federally permitted or licensed *nonpoint* sources of pollution.[181] However, as part of its Section 319 program, each state governor must identify "Federal financial assistance programs and Federal development projects for which the State will review individual assistance applications or development projects for their effects on water quality . . . to determine whether such assistance applications or development projects would be consistent with the" state's nonpoint source management program.[182] The EPA then notified the Office of Management and Budget of the identified assistance programs and development projects; sixty days later, each relevant federal department and agency had to "modify existing regulations to allow States to review individual development projects and assistance applications and development projects" and had to "accommodate . . . the concerns of the State regarding the consistency of such applications or projects with the State nonpoint source pollution management program."[183]

d. Implementation of Section 319

The EPA and the states began to implement Section 319 almost immediately, and the EPA began awarding grants for planning and implementation in 1990.[184] "By 1991, all 50 states and the territories had received EPA approval; by 1995, 7 tribes also had received approval. Since 1990, recipients of 319 grants have directed approximately 40 percent of awarded funds toward controlling NPS pollution from agricultural lands."[185]

The EPA's collection of "Section 319 Nonpoint Source Success Stories" from 1994, 1997, 2002, and 2005 indicates that all fifty states, as well as several territories and tribes, have (1) partially or fully restored particular waterbodies through their Section 319 programs; and/or (2) made progress toward achieving water quality goals for particular waterbodies.[186] However, the majority of assessed waterbodies still fail to achieve their water quality standards, and the EPA continues to emphasize that nonpoint source pollution remains the United States' "largest water quality problem."[187]

3. Nonpoint Source Regulation under the Coastal Zone Management Act

a. State Coastal Nonpoint Pollution Control Programs

Congressional attention to the nonpoint source water pollution problem did not end with the 1987 amendments to the Clean Water Act. In 1990, Congress enacted the Coastal Zone Act Reauthorization Amendments (CZARA), amending the federal Coastal Zone Management Act (CZMA) to address, specifically, coastal nonpoint source pollution.

b. The Purpose and Geographic Scope of the CZMA

As explained more fully in Chapter 5, Congress originally enacted the CZMA in 1972 to increase protection for the nation's coastal zone.[188] On the seaward side, state "coastal zone" jurisdiction extends to the three-mile limit established through the Submerged Lands Act, roughly the same area as the territorial sea under the Clean Water Act, except for those states with extended coastal jurisdictions.[189]

c. Implementing Coastal Nonpoint Source Control Programs

Under the CZARA, the EPA and National Oceanic and Atmospheric Administration (NOAA) had eighteen months to prepare final guidance for states regarding nonpoint source pollution control in the coastal zone.[190] Coastal states then were supposed to prepare and submit coastal nonpoint source control programs for approval by these agencies within two and one-half years;[191] in practice, many coastal states were substantially late. States were also supposed to coordinate these nonpoint source control programs both with their existing CZMA programs and with their Clean Water Act programs and water quality standards.[192]

NOAA, which jointly implements CZARA with the EPA, has emphasized that "[t]he Coastal Nonpoint Program is fundamentally about improved coordination and pollution prevention, seeking to build partnerships and networks that facilitate the implementation of appropriate methods to limit runoff pollution before problems occur."[193] Nevertheless, unlike Section 319 of the Clean Water Act, state coastal nonpoint source control programs are required to implement "enforceable" management measures to control coastal nonpoint source pollution in conformity with the EPA/ NOAA guidance.[194] Implementation of these management measures could achieve fairly stringent controls on nonpoint sources of coastal water pollution. In addition, state CZARA programs must meet seven other statutory criteria, including implementation of any additional management measures applicable to various land uses necessary to ensure that the coastal zone meets the applicable water quality standards.[195]

Unlike Section 319, CZARA has sticks as well as carrots for preparing approvable nonpoint source pollution programs. States that fail to submit approvable programs can lose federal coastal zone management assistance under the CZMA and water pollution control assistance funds under the Clean Water Act.[196] Conversely, federal grants are available to states to develop their coastal nonpoint source control programs.[197] States with approved coastal nonpoint source management programs are required to implement those programs through amendments to existing state coastal zone management plans under the CZMA and/or amendments to the state nonpoint source management program created pursuant to Section 319 of the Clean Water Act.[198]

Thirty states, including the Great Lakes states, and five territories are generally eligible to participate in CZMA programs.[199] Of those, thirty-four states and territories have approved coastal zone management plans[200] and are subject to the CZARA nonpoint source control program requirement. Nevertheless, as of July 2007, only fourteen of these coastal states and four of the territories had fully approved coastal nonpoint source control programs in place.[201] The other sixteen coastal states and territories subject to the requirement, with the exception of Indiana, have received conditional approval, with full approval pending.[202] Thus, actual implementation of CZARA is still in its early stages.[203]

d. The Federal Consistency Requirement

When states incorporate their CZARA coastal nonpoint source control programs into their existing CZMA coastal management programs, the nonpoint source requirements apply to the CZMA's federal consistency requirements,[204] discussed in Chapter 5. In contrast, when states incorporate their coastal nonpoint source control requirements into their Clean Water Act Section 319 nonpoint source management programs, Section 319's federal consistency requirement, discussed above, applies. Either way, federal agencies approving projects that can cause nonpoint source pollution within the coastal zone have responsibility to ensure that those federally approved projects comply with the nonpoint source requirements or the state water quality standards. Coastal states have aggressively asserted their rights under the CZMA's consistency provisions in a variety of factual circumstances,[205] including situations involving coastal stormwater,[206] and hence there is every reason to expect that coastal states actively seeking to protect ocean water quality will make effective use of the consistency requirement in the nonpoint source context.

III. Emerging and Unresolved Issues

A. Introduction

Point sources discharging directly into coastal and marine waters are a fairly limited category of sources that threaten coastal water quality—as noted, only 265 point sources, of the thousands of point sources regulated through NPDES permits, are subject to the ocean discharge criteria. Moreover, given that seventy-seven percent of ocean pollution comes from land-based sources, including land-based nonpoint sources, it is the regulatory mechanisms that connect land-based water pollution to ocean water quality that can be most effective in the future in improving coastal water quality. Several such mechanisms exist.

B. Clean Water Act Section 303: TMDLs

1. Overview of TMDLs

As noted, under Section 303 of the Clean Water Act, states set water quality standards to establish the ambient water quality goals for the particular waters, including the territorial sea. Moreover, the NPDES permitting agency must ensure that the effluent limitations in a particular permit are stringent enough to ensure that the receiving water achieves water quality standards. The Act's primary mechanism for connecting water quality standards, NPDES permit requirements, and nonpoint source regulation is the total maximum daily load (TMDL) program.

Under Section 303, each state must "identify those waters within its boundaries for which the [technology-based] effluent limitations . . . are not stringent enough to implement any water quality standard applicable to such waters" and then rank those water-quality-limited waters in order of priority, "taking into account the severity of the pollution and the uses to be made of such waters."[207] The state then sets TMDLs for specific pollutants for each listed waterbody "at a level necessary to implement the applicable water quality standards with seasonal variations and a margin of safety which takes into account any lack of knowledge concerning the relationship between effluent limitations and water quality."[208] The TMDL represents the total amount of a particular pollutant that can be added to the waterbody over a particular period of time without violating the applicable water quality standard.

2. Using TMDLs to Address Both Point and Nonpoint Source Pollution

Section 303 specifies that permitting agencies must modify the effluent limitations in NPDES permits to implement the established TMDL.[209] Moreover, until the waterbody attains its water quality standards, effluent limitations based on the TMDL "may be revised only if (i) the cumulative effect of all such revised effluent limitations based on the total maximum daily load or waste load allocation will assure the attainment of such water quality standard, or (ii) the designated use which is not being attained is removed in accordance with regulations established under this section."[210]

However, if a water-quality-limited waterbody is impaired as a result of nonpoint source pollution, TMDLs can also be a means for encouraging states to address both point and nonpoint sources affecting that waterbody.[211] The EPA's regulations regarding TMDLs expressly recognize that both point source loadings, termed the *waste load allocation,* and nonpoint source loading, termed the *load allocation,* are components of the total TMDL.[212] Moreover, at least one federal Court of Appeals has upheld the EPA's authority to set TMDLs for waterbodies polluted only by nonpoint sources of pollution.[213] Thus, within a given coastal state, the TMDL process can serve

The TMDL process can serve to prompt the state to regulate nonpoint sources of water pollution.

to prompt the state to regulate nonpoint sources of water pollution, especially when control of point sources is insufficient to meet water quality goals.

3. Do TMDLs Govern Upstream States?

To effectively address coastal water quality, the TMDL provisions must reach upstream to point sources and nonpoint sources of coastal pollution that may be geographically remote from the coast itself. As one extreme example, coastal water quality in the Gulf of Mexico is affected by point and nonpoint source water pollution from the entire Mississippi River drainage, which covers two-thirds of the United States.

Nevertheless, TMDLs are intrastate in focus. Section 303, for example, requires each state to identify water-quality-limited waters for "those waters within its boundaries" and to establish TMDLs for those waters.[214] Moreover, each state must then use the information generated as part of continuing planning process within the state.[215] Therefore, it is unlikely that Section 303 allows downstream coastal states to use the TMDL process to force upstream dischargers and nonpoint sources in other states to comply with coastal water quality standards.

However, both the EPA and upstream states must take account of downstream water quality standards—including coastal water quality standards—when issuing NPDES permits to point source dischargers.[216] Moreover, when upstream nonpoint sources impair downstream water quality and interfere with attainment of the downstream water quality standards, the downstream state can petition the EPA to convene a management conference of all of the relevant states, with the goal of reaching an interstate agreement to regulate the upstream nonpoint sources sufficiently to achieve downstream water quality requirements.[217] If the states reach such an agreement, moreover, they must incorporate that agreement into their respective Section 319 nonpoint source management programs.[218]

C. Clean Water Act Section 320: The National Estuary Program

In 1987, Congress established the National Estuary Program as Section 320 of the Clean Water Act.[219] Once an estuary is selected for inclusion in the program,[220] the

EPA holds a management conference in order to assess the overall water quality trends within the estuary, to "develop the relationship between the inplace loads and point and nonpoint source loadings of pollutants in the estuarine zone and the potential uses of the zone, water quality, and natural resources," and to

> develop a comprehensive conservation and management plan that recommends priority corrective actions and compliance schedules addressing point and nonpoint sources of pollution to restore and maintain the chemical, physical, and biological integrity of the estuary, including restoration and maintenance of water quality, a balanced indigenous population of shellfish, fish and wildlife, and recreational activities in the estuary, and assure that the designated uses of the estuary are protected.[221]

Once the EPA approves the management plan,[222] grants are available to state, interstate, and regional agencies, and to "other public or nonprofit private agencies, institutions, organizations, and individuals" to implement the plan, up to fifty percent of the annual aggregate costs.[223]

Section 320 thus provides states and the EPA with a mechanism for comprehensively addressing estuarine water quality, including point, nonpoint, and interstate sources of pollution.[224] Two features in particular evidence the comprehensive nature of the National Estuary Program management plans. First, many of the management plans include watershed management features, connecting maintenance of estuarine water quality to land-based sources of pollution located, often, far upstream.[225] Second, eight estuaries in the National Estuary Program and the Chesapeake Bay management project are seeking to manage air deposition of nitrogen.[226] Atmospheric deposition of pollutants, a type of nonpoint source pollution, contributes two to forty-four percent of the nitrogen pollution in these estuaries—up to 45 million tons of nitrogen per year into a single estuary system.[227]

The EPA has admitted in connection with the National Estuary Program that "environmental results are often slow in coming,"[228] and the Office of Management and Budget has suggested that the Program could be more effective in setting and working toward specific water quality goals.[229] Nevertheless, the EPA notes that "positive signs of improving environments are already emerging from the NEPs. The twenty-eight National Estuary Programs are also demonstrating success in finding effective institutional arrangements from which to manage their estuaries, securing and leveraging funds, and improving public education and citizen participation through outreach efforts."[230]

D. The EPA's Watershed Planning Program

In recognition of the geographical limitations of the Section 303 TMDL program, the EPA is developing a watershed management program to encourage states to cooperatively and comprehensively address water quality issues on a watershed basis.[231] The most active component of the EPA's watershed program thus far is the targeted watershed grant program. Since 2003, the EPA has been funding projects designed to improve the overall water quality, fish productivity, and other qualities of targeted watersheds.

While the EPA did not direct the targeted watershed program specifically at coastal water quality, several projects each year have been designed to improve the quality of coastal waters. In 2003, for example, the EPA funded three such projects. Grant recipients in Massachusetts used funds to improve stormwater management to reduce the sediment and nutrient pollution in Narragansett Bay,[232] while those in Hawaii used the funds to address agricultural runoff, bacteria pollution, and the need for sewage treatment to protect Hanalei Bay and to assess the effects of these pollutants on the Bay's coral reefs.[233] Finally, recipients in Oregon and Washington used funds to improve the Lower Columbia River estuary by replacing wetlands, reconnecting hydrology, and eradicating invasive species in part to address problems resulting from runoff of toxic and conventional pollutants.[234] Targeted watersheds in 2004 included the Kenia River estuary in Alaska and Cape Fear, North Carolina,[235] while watersheds targeted in 2005 included coastal waters in Maine, Louisiana, and California.[236]

E. Water Quality Trading Policy

In conjunction with its watershed initiative, the EPA introduced a Water Quality Trading Policy in January 2003.[237] This market-based approach to improving water quality allows point sources—especially sources of nitrogen, phosphorus, and sediment pollution—to trade discharge allowances within areas of a watershed governed by an approved TMDL.[238] Participants must already have a Clean Water Act permit and the trade must result in improvements beyond those already achievable through the technology-based effluent limitations.[239]

Like the watershed initiative, the water quality trading program is not specifically directed at coastal water quality. Nevertheless, coastal water quality restoration efforts were important to the development of this policy. In particular, the Chesapeake Bay nutrient trading program and the Long Island Sound nitrogen trading program have been important case studies.[240]

IV. Conclusion

The 2005 National Coastal Condition Report makes it clear that coastal and ocean water quality remains an issue of vital concern for the United States. As described above, the Clean Water Act's NPDES permit program does a good job of addressing ocean water pollution from point sources, especially when viewed in conjunction with other ocean- and vessel-related provisions of the Clean Water Act, the Ocean Dumping Act, the Oil Pollution Act, and CERCLA (Superfund). However, because point sources that discharge pollutants directly into the ocean are limited in number, the largest remaining marine pollution problem is land-based sources, especially land-based nonpoint sources.

While both Section 319 of the Clean Water Act and the CZARA amendments to the CZMA encourage coastal states to address nonpoint source pollution, progress in addressing these sources and improving coastal water quality has been limited. Federal statutory programs that *require* comprehensive regulation of nonpoint sources on a watershed basis are rare. The EPA's watershed initiative is a good first step toward cooperative comprehensive programs, but additional statutory reforms are likely to be necessary to fully protect and restore coastal water quality.

Notes

1. OFFICE OF RESEARCH & DEV. & OFFICE OF WATER, U.S. EPA, NATIONAL COASTAL CONDITION REPORT II, EPA-620/R-03/002 (Dec. 2004) (released Jan. 2005), *available at* http://www.epa.gov/owow/oceans/nccr/2005/index.html. In addition, in June 2007, the EPA concluded that even estuaries protected in the National Estuary Program are in poor to fair condition overall, with especially poor conditions in the Caribbean and Northeast Atlantic coastal waters. OFFICE OF WATER, U.S. EPA, NATIONAL ESTUARY PROGRAM COASTAL CONDITION REPORT ES.4, fig. ES-1 (June 2007), *available at* http://www.epa.gov/owow/oceans/nepccr/index.html.
2. OFFICE OF RESEARCH & DEV. & OFFICE OF WATER, U.S. EPA, NATIONAL COASTAL CONDITION REPORT II, EPA-620/R-03/002, at ES-2, fig. ES-1 Dec. 2004).
3. *Id.*
4. Woods Hole Oceanographic Institute, *Human Illness Associated with Harmful Algae*, http://www.whoi.edu/redtide/illness/illness.html (last visited July 14, 2007).
5. Woods Hole Oceanographic Institute, *Distribution of HABs in the US,* http://www.whoi.edu/redtide/HABdistribution/HABmap.html (last visited July 14, 2007).
6. *Id. See also* Woods Hole Oceanographic Institute, *Expansion of HAB Problems in the US,* http://www.whoi.edu/redtide/HABdistribution/habexpand.html (last visited July 14, 2007) (showing some of the expansion).
7. Woods Hole Oceanographic Institute, *Distribution of HABs in the US,* http://www.whoi.edu/redtide/HABdistribution/HABmap.html (last visited July 14, 2007).
8. Woods Hole Oceanographic Institute, *Trophic Linkages between HABs and Their Ecosystems,* http://www.whoi.edu/redtide/foodweb/HABfoodweb.html (last visited July 14, 2007).
9. Office of Water, U.S. EPA, *Beach Monitoring & Notification: National Summary: 2006 Swimming Season Update,* fig. 2, http://www.epa.gov/waterscience/beaches/seasons/2006/national.html (last visited June 5, 2007).
10. THOMAS E. SVARNEY & PATRICIA BARNES-SVARNEY, THE HANDY OCEAN ANSWER BOOK 433 (2000). *Id.*
11. *Id.* The other 23 percent of marine pollution derives from accidental spills and pollution from ships (twelve percent), ocean dumping (ten percent), and offshore oil and gas drilling and mining (one percent). *Id.* These last three sources of marine pollution are discussed in Chapters 8 and 9.
12. *See, e.g.,* Rachel T. Noble et al., *Storm Effects on Regional Beach Water Quality Along the Southern California Shoreline,* 1.1 J. WATER & HEALTH 23, 23–24 (2003) ("Land-based runoff is increasingly being recognized as a source of fecal bacteria and a public health concern at swimming beaches," and "illness rates more than double when swimming at beaches near urban runoff outlets.").
13. *See generally* OFFICE OF WETLANDS, OCEANS, & WATERSHEDS, U.S. EPA, FREQUENTLY ASKED QUESTIONS ABOUT ATMOSPHERIC DEPOSITION: A HANDBOOK FOR WATERSHED MANAGERS (EPA-453/R-01-009) (Sept. 2001), *available at* http://www.epa.gov/air/oaqps/gr8water/handbook/index.html.
14. 42 U.S.C. §§ 7401–7671q. The Clean Air Act's regulatory scheme is beyond the scope of this book, but, in general, major sources of either criteria pollutants (lead, carbon monox-

ide, sulfur dioxide, nitrogen oxides, particulates, volatile organic compounds, and ozone) or hazardous air pollutants must get a permit and comply with technology-based emissions standards. For a more detailed overview of the Clean Air Act, see generally ROY S. BELDEN, BASIC PRACTICE SERIES: CLEAN AIR ACT (ABA Section of Environment, Energy, and Resources 2001).

15. 33 U.S.C. §§ 1251–1387.
16. U.S. EPA, 2007 *Report on the Environment: Highlights of National Trends* (Peer Review and Comment Draft) 11, 14 (Aug. 2007), *available at* http://www.epa.gov/indicate/docs/roe-hd-draft-08-2007.pdf.
17. 16 U.S.C. §§ 1451–1464.
18. Pub. L. No. 92-500, 86 Stat. 816 (Oct. 18, 1972).
19. CWA § 101(a), 33 U.S.C. § 1251(a).
20. CWA § 101(a)(1), 33 U.S.C. § 1251(a)(1).
21. CWA § 101(a)(2), 33 U.S.C. § 1251(a)(2).
22. For a complete history of the evolution of the Federal Water Pollution Control Act into the contemporary Clean Water Act, see ROBIN KUNDIS CRAIG, THE CLEAN WATER ACT AND THE CONSTITUTION: LEGAL STRUCTURE AND THE PUBLIC'S RIGHT TO A CLEAN AND HEALTHY ENVIRONMENT 9–37 (2004).
23. CWA § 301(a), 33 U.S.C. § 1311(a).
24. CWA § 502(5), 33 U.S.C. § 1362(5).
25. CWA § 313(a), 33 U.S.C. § 1323(a). This provision has been subject to repeated litigation, but federal facilities *are* subject to the Act's permit requirement, even if a *state* issues the permit. *See* Pub L. No. 95-217, §§ 60, 61(a), 91 Stat. 1597, 1598 (Dec. 27, 1977) (amending Section 313 to "correct" the Supreme Court's decision that federal facilities enjoyed sovereign immunity from the state NPDES permit requirement in *Environmental Protection Agency v. California ex rel. State Water Resources Control Board*, 426 U.S. 200, 219–27 (1976)). However, federal facilities still enjoy sovereign immunity from punitive civil penalties assessed pursuant to state-delegated programs. *See generally* U.S. Dept. of Energy v. Ohio, 503 U.S. 607 (1992) (holding that neither the federal facilities provisions nor the citizen suit provisions of either the Clean Water Act nor RCRA waived the federal government's sovereign immunity from punitive civil penalties imposed under delegated state programs).
26. CWA § 502(12), 33 U.S.C. § 1362(12) (emphasis added).
27. CWA § 502(14), 33 U.S.C. § 1362(14). More specifically, "point source" "includ[es] but [is] not limited to any pipe, ditch, channel, tunnel, conduit, well, discrete fissure, container, rolling stock, concentrated animal feeding operation, or vessel or other floating craft, from which pollutants are or may be discharged. This term does not include agricultural stormwater discharges and return flows from irrigated agriculture." *Id.*
28. CWA § 502(6), 33 U.S.C. § 1362(6). However,

> The term does not mean (A) "sewage from vessels or a discharge incidental to the normal operation of a vessel of the Armed Forces" within the meaning of section 1322 of this title; or (B) water, gas, or other material which is injected into a well to facilitate production of oil or gas, or water derived in association with oil or gas production and disposed of in a well, if the well used either to facilitate production or for disposal purposes is approved by authority of the State in which the well is located, and if such State determines that such injection or disposal will not result in the degradation of ground or surface water resources.

> *Id.*

29. CWA § 502(7), 33 U.S.C. § 1352(7).
30. CWA § 502(8), 33 U.S.C. § 1352(8). Note the difference between the "territorial sea" under the Clean Water Act and the "territorial sea" for international purposes.
31. 43 U.S.C. §§ 1301–1356; *see also* the discussion of the Submerged Lands Act in Chapter 1. However, it is worth noting that the Submerged Lands Act allows states to claim more than three miles' jurisdiction offshore, and some states have succeeded in making such

claims. When such conflicts arise, the Clean Water Act's three-mile designation for the "territorial sea" controls for Clean Water Act purposes. Natural Res. Def. Council, Inc. v. EPA, 863 F.2d 1420, 1434–36 (9th Cir. 1988) (holding that the Act's definition of "territorial sea" controlled despite Florida's claim of jurisdiction over three marine leagues (approximately 10.3 miles) into the Gulf of Mexico).

32. *See generally,* United States v. Riverside Bayview Homes, Inc., 474 U.S. 121 (1985) (delineating the federal agencies' jurisdiction over wetlands adjacent to more traditionally "navigable" waters); Solid Waste Agency of N. Cook County v. U.S. Army Corps of Eng'rs, 531 U.S. 159 (2001) (refusing to decide the Commerce Clause limits of the Clean Water Act but implying that the Act cannot extend to isolated, intrastate wetlands); Rapanos v. United States (No. 04-1034)/Carabell v. U.S. Army Corps of Eng'rs (No. 04-1384), 547 U.S. ___, 126 S. Ct. 2208 (June 19, 2006) (splitting 4–1–4 on the issue of whether the Army Corps has the authority to regulate wetlands adjacent to tributaries of traditional navigable waters, with five Justices agreeing that the "any surface water connection" test was not the correct one for bringing wetlands under federal jurisdiction, but also with five Justice agreeing that wetlands with a significant nexus to traditional navigable waters are included within the scope of the Clean Water Act). This issue is discussed in greater detail in Chapter 4.

33. *See, e.g.,* United States v. Locke, 529 U.S. 89, 99 (2000) (emphasizing the strength of the federal government's interest in interstate commerce in the oceans); United States v. California, 332 U.S. 19, 36 (1947) (recognizing the United States' "paramount rights in and power over" the ocean and coastal zone).

34. CWA § 502(9), 33 U.S.C. § 1352(9).

35. Convention on the Territorial Sea and the Contiguous Zone, art. 24(2), 15 U.S.T. 1606, 1612–13, T.I.A.S. 5639, 516 U.N.T.S. 205 (1964); *see also* the discussion of UNCLOS I in Chapter 12.

36. Internationally, by 1973, a year after Congress transformed the prior Federal Water Pollution Control Act into what we now think of as the Clean Water Act, the Third United Nations Conference on the Law of the Sea began work on the third United Nations Convention on the Law of the Sea (UNCLOS III), which opened for signature in 1982 and went into effect in 1994. JOSEPH J. KALO, RICHARD G. HILDRETH, ALISON REISER, & DONNA R. CHRISTIE, COASTAL AND OCEAN LAW, 333, 337 (3rd ed. 2006); *see also* discussion of UNCLOS III in Chapter 12 of this book. Under this convention, ratifying nations could claim a twelve-nautical-mile-wide territorial sea and a twenty-four-nautical-mile-wide contiguous zone. *Id.* at 341. Domestically, in 1988 the United States claimed a twelve-nautical-mile-wide territorial sea and in 1999 claimed a contiguous zone extending from twelve nautical miles to twenty-four nautical miles out to sea. Territorial Sea of the United States of America, Proclamation No. 5928, 54 Fed. Reg. 777 (Dec. 27, 1988) (President Reagan); Contiguous Zone of the United States, Proclamation No. 7219, 64 Fed. Reg. 48,701 (Aug. 2, 1999) (President Clinton).

37. *See* Natural Res. Def. Council, Inc. v. EPA, 656 F.2d 768, 778 & n.6 (D.C. Cir. 1981) (explicitly defining the Act's "contiguous zone" as extending to twelve miles); *see also* 40 C.F.R. § 220.1(a)(3)(ii) (defining "contiguous zone" as extending beyond the territorial sea out to twelve miles for purposes of ocean dumping). Case law on this point is limited, given the relative unimportance to the "contiguous zone" to the Act's regulatory requirements. For more information about the contiguous zone see Chapters 1 and 12.

38. CWA § 502(10), 33 U.S.C. § 1362(10).

39. Exclusive Economic Zone of the United States of America, Proclamation No.5030, 48 Fed. Reg. 10605 (Mar. 10, 1983) (President Reagan). The 1982 UNCLOS III allows ratifying nations to claim such an EEZ. KALO ET AL., *supra* note 36, at 341. However, the United States has not yet ratified this Convention and hence claims its EEZ on the basis of customary international law. For more information about the EEZ see Chapter 12.

40. *See* Pub. L. No. 94-265, §§ 3(11), 101, 90 Stat. 331 (1976) (establishing this zone as part of the enactment of the Magnuson-Stevens Fishery Conservation and Management Act).

41. *See, e.g.,* Natural Res. Def. Council, Inc. v. EPA, 863 F.2d 1420, 1434–36 (9th Cir. 1988) (holding that the three-mile line of the territorial sea is the critical line for Section 401 certifications); Pac. Legal Found. v. Costle, 586 F.2d 650, 655–56 (9th Cir. 1978) (holding that beyond the three-mile limit of the territorial sea, only the EPA can issue NPDES permits for discharges into the ocean).

42. CWA § 402, 33 U.S.C. § 1342.

43. CWA § 404(a), 33 U.S.C. § 1344(a) (emphasis added). As noted above, "navigable waters" are defined as "waters of the United States, including the territorial seas." 33 U.S.C. § 1352(7).

44. In addition, discharges of dredged material, but not discharges of fill material, into the territorial sea are regulated pursuant to the Ocean Dumping Act. 40 C.F.R. § 230.2(b). For a more complete discussion of the Ocean Dumping Act, see Chapter 8.

45. CWA § 402(a)(1), 33 U.S.C. § 1342(a)(1) (emphasis added).

46. According to the Act, an "effluent limitation" is "any restriction established by a State or the Administrator on quantities, rates, and concentrations of chemical, physical, biological and other constituents which are discharged from point sources into navigable waters, the waters of the contiguous zone, or the ocean, including any schedules of compliance." CWA § 502(11), 33 U.S.C. § 1362(11). Therefore, most effluent limitations are numerical standards dictating the allowable concentrations of specific pollutants at the "end of the pipe"—that is, as effluent enters waters subject to the Act's jurisdiction.

47. CWA § 301(b), 33 U.S.C. § 1311(b).

48. CWA § 301(b)(1), 33 U.S.C. § 1311(b)(1).

49. CWA § 301(b)(2)(A), (C), (D), (F), 33 U.S.C. § 1311(b)(2)(A), (C), (D), (F).

50. CWA § 301(b)(2)(E), 33 U.S.C. § 1311(b)(2)(E).

51. CWA § 301(e), 33 U.S.C. § 1311(e).

52. CWA § 301(f), 33 U.S.C. § 1311(f).

53. U.S. EPA, *Ocean Dumping Ban Act of 1988*, http://www.epa.gov/history/topics/mprsa/02 .htm (last visited April 20, 2006).

54. 40 C.F.R. pt. 408 (effluent limitations for seafood processors); 40 C.F.R. §§ 435.12 to 435.14 (effluent limitations for offshore oil and gas operations); *see generally* Natural Res. Def. Council, Inc. v. EPA, 863 F.2d 1420 (9th Cir. 1988) (deciding a challenge to the toxic effluent limitations for oil and gas operations outside of the territorial sea); Am. Petroleum Inst. v. EPA, 858 F.2d 261 (5th Cir. 1988) (same); Ass'n of Pacific Fisheries v. EPA, 615 F.2d 794 (9th Cir. 1980) (challenging BPT- and BAT-based effluent limitations for seafood processors).

55. Weyerhaeuser Co. v. Costle, 590 F.2d 1011, 1041–44 (D.C. Cir. 1978).

56. CWA § 301(m)(1), 33 U.S.C. § 1311(m)(1).

57. Among other requirements, the permit applicant must demonstrate that "the energy and environmental costs of meeting" the standard effluent limitations and/or ocean discharge criteria "exceed by an unreasonable amount the benefits to be obtained" and that "no owner or operator of a facility comparable to that of the applicant situated in the United States has demonstrated that it would be put to a competitive disadvantage to the applicant (or the parent company or any subsidiary thereof) as a result of the issuance of a permit under this subsection." CWA § 301(m)(1)(B), (I), 33 U.S.C. § 1311(m)(1)(B), (I). In addition, the applicant must show that it qualifies for the right kind of NPDES permit, that it will engage in monitoring, that the modified requirements will not impose additional requirements on any other point or nonpoint source, that it will not increase the volume of its discharge, that the receiving waters have a strong tidal influence and other characteristics that will dilute the effluent, that the applicant will spend money on research and development of water pollution control technology, and that its exemption will not create a precedent for other dischargers. CWA § 301(m)(1)(A), (C)–(H), 33 U.S.C. § 1311(m)(1)(A), (C)–(H).

58. CWA § 301(m)(4), 33 U.S.C. § 1311(m)(4).

59. CWA § 301(h), 33 U.S.C. § 1311(h). For purposes of this provision, "the discharge of any pollutant into marine waters" means:

a discharge into deep waters of the territorial sea or the waters of the contiguous zone, or into saline estuarine waters where there is strong tidal movement and other hydrological and geological characteristics which the Administrator determines necessary to allow compliance with [water quality requirements and the Act's "fishable/swimmable" goal].

Id. Section 301(h) is thus one of the few provisions of the Clean Water Act that effectively distinguishes between the contiguous zone and the ocean: Modifications are expressly allowed for discharges into the territorial sea and contiguous zone, but implicitly *not* for discharges into the ocean.

60. CWA § 301(h), 33 U.S.C. § 1311(h). These criteria include the existence of a water quality standard for the pollutant at issue, noninterference "with the attainment and maintenance of that water quality which assures protection of public water supplies and the protection and propagation of a balanced, indigenous population of shellfish, fish and wildlife, and allows recreational activities, in and on the water," and at least primary treatment of the discharge, meaning "treatment by screening, sedimentation, and skimming adequate to remove at least 30 percent of the biological oxygen demand material and of the suspended solids in the treatment works influent, and disinfection, where appropriate." *Id.*

61. *Id.* Specifically:

In order for a permit to be issued under this subsection for the discharge of a pollutant into marine waters, such marine waters must exhibit characteristics assuring that water providing dilution does not contain significant amounts of previously discharged effluent from such treatment works. No permit issued under this subsection shall authorize the discharge of any pollutant into saline estuarine waters which at the time of application do not support a balanced indigenous population of shellfish, fish and wildlife, or allow recreation in and on the waters or which exhibit ambient water quality below applicable water quality standards adopted for the protection of public water supplies, shellfish, fish and wildlife or recreational activities or such other standards necessary to assure support and protection of such uses. The prohibition contained in the preceding sentence shall apply without regard to the presence or absence of a causal relationship between such characteristics and the applicant's current or proposed discharge.

Id. For a discussion of the Section 301(h) exemption, *see generally* Natural Res. Def. Council, Inc. v. EPA, 656 F.2d 768 (D.C. Cir. 1981).

62. *See* 69 Fed. Reg. 45,831–33 (Aug. 29, 1996). The EPA's regulations for effluent limitation modifications under this provision are found at 40 C.F.R., pt. 125, subpt. G, comprising 40 C.F.R. §§ 125.56 through 125.68 and an appendix.

63. Office of Water, U.S. EPA, *Amendments to Regulations Issued Pursuant to the Clean Water Act Section 301(h) Permit Program,* http://www.epa.gov/owow/oceans/discharges/301h.html (last visited June 22, 2006).

64. *Id.*

65. *Id.*

66. *See* Surfrider Foundation, *Coastal A–Z: 301(h) Waivers,* http://www.surfrider.org/a-z/waivers.asp (giving the history of the Section 301(h) waiver program and discussing some of its controversies).

67. CWA § 302(a), 33 U.S.C. § 1312(a).

68. *Id.*

69. CWA § 301(b)(1)(C), 33 U.S.C. § 1311(b)(1)(C).

70. According to the current Act, a

water quality standard shall consist of the designated uses of the navigable waters involved and water quality criteria for such waters based upon such uses. Such standards shall be such as to protect the public health or welfare, enhance the quality of water and serve the purposes of this chapter. Such standards shall be established taking into consideration their use and value for public water supplies,

propagation of fish and wildlife, recreational purposes, and agricultural, industrial, and other purposes, and also taking into consideration their use and value
for navigation.

CWA § 303(c)(2)(A), 33 U.S.C. § 1313(c)(2)(A).

71. 40 C.F.R. § 131.12(a)(3). For example, under these provisions and state requirements, California has prohibited the impairment of the natural water quality of 34 coastal Areas of Special Biological Significance.

72. CWA § 303(a)(3)(C), (c)(4), 33 U.S.C. § 1313(a)(3)(C), (c)(4).

73. *See* CWA § 518(e), 33 U.S.C. § 1377(e), as added by Pub. L. No. 100-4, § 506, 101 Stat. 76 (Feb. 4, 1987) (allowing the EPA "to treat an Indian tribe as a State for purposes of . . . sections . . . 303, . . . 401, 402, [and 404] . . . of this Act"). *See also* 40 C.F.R. § 131.8 (describing requirements for tribal water quality standards).

74. CWA § 303(c)(2)(A), (4), 33 U.S.C. § 1313(c)(2)(A), (4). *See also* 40 C.F.R. § 131.40 (promulgating water quality standards for Puerto Rico's territorial seas).

75. Pub. L. No. 106-284, § 2, 114 Stat. 870 (Oct. 10, 2000) (codified as CWA § 303(i), 33 U.S.C. § 1313(i)). Under these new requirements, the EPA establishes water quality criteria for various ocean-borne pathogens and pathogen indicators, and coastal states then adopt water quality criteria and water quality standards for those organisms. CWA § 303(i)(1)(A), 33 U.S.C. § 1313(i)(1)(A). The new pathogen water quality standards requirement applies to "coastal recreation waters," which are the Great Lakes and any "marine coastal waters (including coastal estuaries)" for which the state's designated uses include "swimming, bathing, surfing, or similar water contact activities." CWA § 502(21)(A), 33 U.S.C. § 1362(21)(A). Thus, application of this requirement depends on the state's designation of uses for its coastal waters.

76. CWA § 304(a), 33 U.S.C. § 1314(a).

77. CWA § 304(a)(2), 33 U.S.C. § 1314(a)(2) (emphasis added).

78. CWA § 301(h)(1), 33 U.S.C. § 1311(h)(1).

79. The EPA would set these water quality standards because waters beyond the three-mile territorial sea are federal waters. *See* Pac. Legal Found. v. Costle, 586 F.2d 650, 655–56 (9th Cir. 1978) (holding that the federal government regulates the waters beyond the territorial sea).

80. Exec. Order No. 13,158, 65 Fed. Reg. 34,909 (May 26, 2000).

81. *See generally* U.S. EPA, OCEAN DISCHARGE CRITERIA: REVISIONS TO THE OCEAN DISCHARGE CRITERIA REGULATIONS (2001); Robin Kundis Craig & Sarah Miller, *Ocean Discharge Criteria and Marine Protected Areas: Ocean Water Quality Protection Under the Clean Water Act*, 29:1 B.C. ENVTL. AFF. L. REV. 1–44 (2001).

82. CWA § 403, 33 U.S.C. § 1343.

83. U.S. EPA, *Ocean Discharge Criteria: Revision to Ocean Discharge Criteria Regulations: Notice of Public Meetings*, 65 Fed. Reg. 42936, 42937 (July 12, 2000).

84. Craig, *supra* note 81 at 1, 43 (citation omitted).

85. CWA § 403(c)(1), 33 U.S.C. § 1343(c)(1).

86. *Id.*

87. Ocean Discharge Criteria, 40 C.F.R. §§ 125.120–.124 (2001).

88. *Id.* § 125.124. The analysis must include an "[a]nalysis of the location where pollutants are sought to be discharged, including the biological community and the physical description of the discharge facility" and an "[e]valuation of the available alternatives to the discharge." *Id.*

89. *Id.* § 125.123(a), (b), (c). "Unreasonable degradation" includes "(1) Significant adverse changes in ecosystem diversity, productivity and stability of the biological community within the area of discharge and surrounding biological communities, (2) Threat to human health through direct exposure to pollutants or through consumption of exposed aquatic organisms, or (3) Loss of esthetic, recreational, scientific or economic values which is unreasonable in relation to the benefit derived from the discharge." *Id.* § 125.121(e).

90. *Id.* § 125.122(a).

91. *Id.* § 125.122(b).

92. 40 C.F.R. § 131.13.
93. 40 C.F.R. § 125.121(c).
94. U.S. EPA, Water Quality Standards handbook, 2d ed., 1993 (EPA-828-B-94-005a), at 5-2.
95. See Gershon Eliezer Cohen, *Mixing Zones: Diluting Pollution Under the Clean Water Act*, 14 Tul. Envtl. L.J. 1, 27, 81 (Winter 2000).
96. *Id.* § 403(b), 33 U.S.C. § 1343(b) (referencing CWA § 402(d), 33 U.S.C. § 1342(d)); 40 C.F.R. § 123.24(d)(1).
97. *Id.* § 403(c)(2), 33 U.S.C. § 1343(c)(2); 40 C.F.R. § 122.4(h).
98. 40 C.F.R. § 125.123(a).
99. *Id.* § 125.123(b).
100. CWA § 306(b), 33 U.S.C. § 1316(b). Congress dictated that the EPA set NSPS for "pulp and paper mills; paperboard, builders paper and board mills; meat product and rendering processing; dairy product processing; grain mills; canned and preserved fruits and vegetables processing; canned and preserved seafood processing; sugar processing; textile mills; cement manufacturing; feedlots; electroplating; organic chemicals manufacturing; inorganic chemicals manufacturing; plastic and synthetic materials manufacturing; soap and detergent manufacturing; fertilizer manufacturing; petroleum refining; iron and steel manufacturing; nonferrous metals manufacturing; phosphate manufacturing; steam electric powerplants; ferroalloy manufacturing; leather tanning and finishing; glass and asbestos manufacturing; rubber processing; and timber products processing." CWA § 306(b)(1)(A), 33 U.S.C. § 1316(b)(1)(A).
101. CWA § 306(a)(1), 33 U.S.C. § 1316(a)(1). NSPS are technology-based standards that "reflect[] the greatest degree of effluent reduction which the Administrator determines to be achievable through application of the best available demonstrated control technology [BADT], processes, operating methods, or other alternatives, including, where practicable, a standard permitting no discharge of pollutants." *Id.*
102. CWA § 307(a)(2), 33 U.S.C. § 1317(a)(2). In addition, "[a]ny effluent standard promulgated under this section shall be at least at that level which the Administrator determines provides an ample margin of safety." CWA § 307(a)(4), 33 U.S.C. § 1317(a)(4). It is also worth noting in this context that the Act itself makes it "unlawful to discharge any radiological, chemical, or biological warfare agent, any high-level radioactive waste, or any medical waste, into the navigable waters." CWA § 301(f), 33 U.S.C. § 1311(f).
103. CWA § 308, 33 U.S.C. § 1318.
104. *See* U.S. EPA, *State NPDES Permit Program Authority,* http://www.epa.gov/npdes/images/State_NPDES_Prog_Auth.pdf.
105. CWA § 402(b), (d), (i), 33 U.S.C. § 1342(b), (d), (i).
106. In contrast, only two states—Michigan and New Jersey—have assumed the authority to issue Section 404 permits. U.S. EPA, *State or Tribal Assumption of the Section 404 Permit Program,* http://www.epa.gov/owow/wetlands/facts/fact23.html (last visited Feb. 22, 2006); *see also* CWA § 404(g), 33 U.S.C. § 1344(g) (authorizing state assumption of the permit program). Thus, most Section 404 permits are federal permits issued by the Corps.
107. U.S. EPA, National Pollutant Discharge Elimination System Permit Application Regulations for Storm Water Discharges, 55 Fed. Reg. 47,990, 47,991 (Nov. 16, 1990).
108. *See, e.g.,* Natural Res. Def. Council, Inc. v. Train, 396 F. Supp. 1393, 1396–97 (D.D.C. 1975), *aff'd sub nom.* Natural Res. Def. Council, Inc. v. Costle, 568 F.2d 1369 (D.C. Cir. 1977) (overturning the EPA's 1973 regulations that would exempt stormwater point sources from NPDES permitting); Kennecott Copper Corp. v. EPA, 612 F.2d 1232, 1243 (10th Cir. 1979) (noting that the EPA lacked authority to require mining companies to collect nonpoint source storm runoff); United States v. Frezzo Bros., 642 F.2d 59, 61–62 (3d Cir. 1981) (holding that discharges of compost runoff were "not an agricultural point source" that required a permit); Natural Res. Def. Council, Inc. v. EPA, 22 F.3d 1125 (D.C. Cir. 1987) (overturning the EPA's 1984 stormwater regulations);

109. *See, e.g.*, Envtl. Def. Ctr., Inc. v. EPA, 344 F.3d 832, 841 & n.8 (9th Cir. 2003) (comparing urban storm sewers, which "are established point sources subject to NPDES permitting requirements," to "[d]iffuse runoff, such as rainwater that is not channeled through a point source," which "is considered nonpoint source pollution and is not subject to federal regulation" (citing Oregon Natural Desert Ass'n v. Dombeck, 172 F.3d 1092, 1095 (9th Cir. 1998)).

110. *See id.*

111. Pub. L. No. 100-4, §405, 101 Stat. 7, 69, codified at 33 U.S.C. §1342(p).

112. *Id.*, codified at 33 U.S.C. §1342(p)(1) (1988).

113. National Pollutant Discharge Elimination System Permit Application Regulations for Storm Water Discharges, 55 Fed. Reg. 47,990, 47,991 (Nov. 16, 1990).

114. OFFICE OF WATER, U.S. EPA, OVERVIEW OF THE STORM WATER PROGRAM (EPA 833-R-96-008) 1, 4 (1996), *available at* http://www.epa.gov/npdes/pubs/owm0195.pdf (last visited April 1, 2006).

115. Water Resources Development Act of 1992, Pub. L. No. 102-580, §364(1), 106 Stat. 4797, 4862 (1992) (codified as amended at 33 U.S.C. §1342(p)).

116. National Pollutant Discharge Elimination System—Regulations for the Revision of the Water Pollution Control Program Addressing Storm Water Discharges, 64 Fed. Reg. 68,722, 68,722 (Dec, 8, 1999).

117. CWA §318(a), 33 U.S.C. §1328(a).

118. Hubbs-SeaWorld Research Institute, *Aquaculture Quick Facts* 2 (2006).

119. For a more complete discussion of the relationship between aquaculture, mariculture, the Clean Water Act, and coastal water quality, see generally Robin Kundis Craig, *The Other Side of Sustainable Aquaculture: Mariculture and Nonpoint Source Pollution*, 9 WASH. U.J.L. & POL'Y 163 (2002); Jeremy Firestone & Robert Barber, *Fish as Pollutants: Limitations of and Crosscurrents in Law, Science, Management, and Policy*, 78 WASH. L. REV. 693–756 (2003).

120. Aquaculture Projects, 40 C.F.R. §122.25(b)(1) (2000).

121. *Id.* §125.11(a)(1)(i),(2).

122. 40 C.F.R. §125.10(c)(2000).

123. *Id.* §125.11(c). For more information on marine aquaculture, see Chapter 14 on emerging ocean uses.

124. 65 Fed. Reg. 43,586, 43,649 (July 13, 2000).

125. Revisions to the National Pollutant Discharge Elimination System Program and Federal Antidegradation Policy in Support of Revisions to the Water Quality Planning and Management Regulation, 64 Fed. Reg. 46,058, 46,074 (Aug. 23, 1999).

126. 65 Fed. Reg. 43,586, 43,649 (July 13, 2000).

127. U.S. Pub. Interest Research Group v. Atl. Salmon of Maine, 215 F. Supp. 2d 239, 249 (D. Me. 2002).

128. 64 Fed. Reg. 46,058, 46,075 (Aug. 23, 1999). The criteria for CAAPFs are codified at 40 C.F.R. §122.24 and app. C. *See also U.S. Pub. Interest Research Group*, 215 F. Supp. 2d at 246–57 (concluding that offshore salmon farms using net pens were point sources and CAAPFs subject to the standard NPDES permit requirement).

129. 67 Fed. Reg. 57,872 (Sept. 12, 2002) (proposed rules); 69 Fed. Reg. 51,891, 51,910 (Aug. 23, 2004) (final rules).

130. U.S. EPA, *Effluent Guidelines: Aquatic Animal Production Industry: Final Rule—Fact Sheet*, http://www.epa.gov/guide/aquaculture/fs-final.htm (last visited Feb. 3, 2008).

131. CWA §502(6), 33 U.S.C. §1362(6).

132. *See* CWA §502(14), 33 U.S.C. §1362(14) (defining "point source" explicitly to include "vessel or other floating craft").

133. CWA §312(b)(1), 33 U.S.C. §1322(b)(1). "New vessel," for purposes of Section 312, "includes every description of watercraft or other artificial contrivance used, or capable of being used, as a means of transportation on the navigable waters," so long as construction of the vessel begins *after* EPA promulgates the required standards. CWA §312(a)(1), 33

U.S.C. §1322(a)(1). "Existing vessels," in contrast, are vessels whose construction begins *before* EPA promulgated the standards. CWA §312(a)(2), 33 U.S.C. §1322(a)(2).

134. CWA §312(a)(6), 33 U.S.C. §1322(a)(6).

135. *Id.* "Graywater" is "galley, bath, and shower water." CWA §312(a)(11), 33 U.S.C. §1322(a)(11).

136. CWA §312(d), 33 U.S.C. §1322(d).

137. CWA §312(a)(14), 33 U.S.C. §1322(a)(14).

138. CWA §312(n)(2)(A), 33 U.S.C. §1322(n)(2)(A). A "discharge incidental to the normal operations of a vessel"

> (A) means a discharge, including—
>
> > (i) graywater, bilge water, cooling water, weather deck runoff, ballast water, oil water separator effluent, and any other pollutant discharge from the operation of a marine propulsion system, shipboard maneuvering system, crew habitability system, or installed major equipment, such as an aircraft carrier elevator or a catapult, or from a protective, preservation, or absorptive application to the hull of the vessel; and
> >
> > (ii) a discharge in connection with the testing, maintenance, and repair of a system described in clause (i) whenever the vessel is waterborne; and
>
> (B) does not include—
>
> > (i) a discharge of rubbish, trash, garbage, or other such material discharged overboard;
> >
> > (ii) an air emission resulting from the operation of a vessel propulsion system, motor driven equipment, or incinerator; or
> >
> > (iii) a discharge that is not covered by part 122.3 of title 40, Code of Federal Regulations (as in effect on February 10, 1996).

CWA §312(a)(12), 33 U.S.C. §1322(a)(12).

139. CWA §312(n)(3)(A), 33 U.S.C. §1322(n)(3)(A). A "marine pollution control device" is "any equipment or management practice" that is "designed to receive, retain, treat, control, or discharge a discharge incidental to the normal operation of a vessel." CWA §312(a)(13)(A), 33 U.S.C. §1322(a)(13)(A). When designating regulated discharges and setting the federal standards, the EPA and the Department of Defense had to consider "(i) the nature of the discharge; (ii) the environmental effects of the discharge; (iii) the practicability of using the marine pollution control device; (iv) the effect that installation or use of the marine pollution control device would have on the operation or operational capability of the vessel; (v) applicable United States law; (vi) applicable international standards; and (vii) the economic costs of the installation and use of the marine pollution control device." CWA §312(n)(2)(B), 33 U.S.C. §1322(n)(2)(B).

140. 64 Fed. Reg. 25,125 (May 10, 1999) (codified at 40 C.F.R. Part 1700).

141. *Id.* at 25,127, tbl. I.

142. *Id.* at 25,127–28, tbl. II.

143. CWA §312(f), 33 U.S.C. §1322(f).

144. Office of Water, U.S. EPA, *Vessel Sewage Discharge,* 2 (Oct. 2005), *available at* http://www.epa.gov/owow/oceans/regulatory/vesselsewage/Vessel_Sewage_DischargeFINAL.pdf.

145. CWA §502(12), 33 U.S.C. §1362(12).

146. United States v. West Indies Transp., Inc., 127 F.3d 299, 309 (3rd Cir. 1997) (holding that five fixed barges floating in Krum Bay, St. Thomas, were unusable for transportation and hence were "other floating craft," not vessels, whose discharges of sewage into the territorial sea were subject to the NPDES permit requirement).

147. 40 C.F.R. § 122.23(a).

148. Northwest Envtl. Advocates v. EPA, 2005 WL 756614, at *1 (N.D. Cal. Aug. 19, 2005).

149. *Id.* at *13. *But see* Chevron USA, Inc. v. Sheffield, 471 U.S. 1140, 1142–43 (1985) (J. White, dissenting from the denial of certiorari and apparently accepting that Section 122.23(a) "specifically exempt[s] from the NPDES permit program discharges from vessels incident to their normal operation").

150. 33 U.S.C. §§ 1401–1445.

151. MPRSA § 101(a), 33 U.S.C. § 1411(a) (stating that "no person shall transport from any location any material for the purpose of dumping it into ocean waters").

152. "Ocean waters" for purposes of the Ocean Dumping Act are "those waters of the open seas lying seaward of the base line from which the territorial sea is measured, as provided for the in the Convention on the Territorial Sea and the Contiguous Zone (15 U.S.T. 1606; T.I.A.S. 5639)." MPRSA § 3(b), 33 U.S.C. § 1402(b). The referenced Convention is one of the four conventions comprising the 1958 UNCLOS I, and it generally allowed nations to claim a territorial sea of up to three miles. Thus, the Ocean Dumping Act effectively picks up where the Clean Water Act's territorial sea leaves off. *See also* 40 C.F.R. § 230.2(b) (defining which discharges of dredged or fill material are subject to the ODA rather than the Clean Water Act); Pac. Legal Found. v. Quarles, 440 F. Supp. 316 (D. Cal. 1977) (discussing the relationship between the Clean Water Act and the ODA).

153. 33 U.S.C. §§ 2701–2761.

154. OPA § 1002, 33 U.S.C. § 2702(a).

155. *See generally* Sekco Energy, Inc. v. M/V Margaret Chouest, 820 F. Supp. 1008 (E.D. La. 1993) (discussing the relationship between the Clean Water Act and the OPA in connection with a vessel oil spill).

156. 42 U.S.C. §§ 9601–9675.

157. CERCLA § 107(a), 42 U.S.C. § 9607(a). "Vessels," for purposes of CERCLA, include "every description of watercraft or other artificial contrivance used, or capable of being used, as a means of transportation on water," CERCLA § 101(28), 42 U.S.C. § 9601(28), while a "facility" is any building, structure, site, or area where hazardous substances are found. CERCLA § 101(9), 42 U.S.C. § 9601(9). CERCLA defines "hazardous substance" broadly to include almost any hazardous or toxic substance identified pursuant to any other federal statute or by the EPA, including toxic pollutants designated under the Clean Water Act. CERCLA § 101(14), 42 U.S.C. § 9601(14).

158. CERCLA § 101(8), 42 U.S.C. § 9601(8).

159. *See* CERCLA §§ 101(10), 103(a), 42 U.S.C. §§ 9601(10), 9603(a) (exempting "federally permitted releases," including discharges allowed pursuant to an NPDES permit, from the CERCLA reporting and liability provisions).

160. Specifically, under Section 401(a), "[a]ny applicant for a Federal license or permit to conduct any activity . . . which may result in any discharge into the *navigable waters,* shall provide the licensing or permitting agency with a certification from the State in which the discharge originates or will originate . . . that such discharge will comply" with the Act's requirements. CWA § 401(a)(1), 33 U.S.C. § 1341(a)(1) (emphasis added).

161. *Id.*

162. CWA § 401(d), 33 U.S.C. § 1341(d).

163. PUD No. 1 of Jefferson County, 511 U.S. 700, 711–15 (1994). *See also* S.D. Warren Co. v. Maine Bd. of Envtl. Protection, 547 U.S. 370, 126 S. Ct. 1843 (May 15, 2006) (similarly upholding broad state authority to condition federal licenses and permits pursuant to Section 401).

164. National Res. Def. Council, Inc. v. EPA, 863 F.2d 1420, 1434–36 (9th Cir. 1988).

165. *See* CZMA § 307(c), 16 U.S.C. § 1456(c) (requiring federal agencies to carry out their activities in a manner that is consistent with the state coastal zone management program "to the maximum extent practicable").

166. 43 U.S.C. §§ 1340(c)(2), 1351(d).

167. Office of Wetlands, Oceans, & Watersheds, U.S. EPA, *Nonpoint Source Pollution: The Nation's Largest Water Quality Problem,* Pointer No. 1, EPA841-F-96-004A, http://www.epa.gov/owow/nps/facts/point1.htm (last updated Nov. 29, 2006).

168. OFFICE OF WATER, U.S. EPA, TREASURED WATERS: PROTECTING OUR COASTAL AND MARINE RESOURCES 5 (EPA/842/B-96/001) 9 (June 1996).

169. CWA § 208, 33 U.S.C. § 1288.

170. CWA § 208(b)(2)(F), 33 U.S.C. § 1288(b)(2)(F).

171. Douglas R. Williams, *When Voluntary, Incentive-Based Controls Fail: Structuring a Regulatory Response to Agricultural Nonpoint Source Water Pollution,* 9 WASH. U.J.L. & POL'Y 21, 69 (2002).

172. *Id.* at 69–70 (citations omitted).

173. Pub. L. No. 100-4, § 316(a), 101 Stat. 52 (Feb. 4, 1987), codified as 33 U.S.C. § 1329.

174. CWA § 319(a)(1)(A), 33 U.S.C. § 1329(a)(1)(A).

175. CWA § 319(a)(1)(B)–(D), 33 U.S.C. § 1329(a)(1)(B)–(D).

176. CWA § 319(b)(1), 33 U.S.C. § 1329(b)(1).

177. CWA § 319(b)(2)(C), 33 U.S.C. § 1329(b)(2)(C).

178. CWA § 319(h)(1), 33 U.S.C. § 1329(h)(1).

179. CWA § 319(i), 33 U.S.C. § 1329(i).

180. Office of Wetlands, Oceans, and Watersheds, U.S. EPA, *Air Pollution and Water Quality,* http://www.epa.gov/owow/airdeposition/ (last visited Feb. 3, 2008).

181. Oregon Natural Desert Ass'n v. Dombeck, 172 F.3d 1092 (9th Cir. 1998).

182. CWA § 319(b)(2)(F), 33 U.S.C. § 1329(b)(2)(F).

183. CWA § 319(k), 33 U.S.C. § 1329(k).

184. Office of Water, U.S. EPA, *The Nonpoint Source Management Program: Pointer No. 4* (EPA841-F-96-004D), *available at* http://www.epa.gov/owow/nps/facts/point4.htm (last updated Nov. 29, 2006).

185. *Id.*

186. *See* Office of Water, EPA, *Section 319 Nonpoint Source Success Stories,* http://www.epa.gov/owow/nps/Success319/ (last updated Feb. 22, 2006), and linked information from prior years.

187. U.S. EPA, POINTER NO. 1: NONPOINT SOURCE POLLUTION: THE NATION'S LARGEST WATER QUALITY PROBLEM (EPA 841-F-96-004A) 1 (1996), *available at* http://www.epa.gov/owow/nps/facts/point1.htm (last visited Nov. 29, 2006).

188. The "coastal zone," for purposes of this Act, is

> the coastal waters (including the lands therein and thereunder) and the adjacent shorelands (including the waters therein and thereunder), strongly influenced by each other and in proximity to the shorelines of the several coastal states, and includes islands, transitional and intertidal areas, salt marshes, wetlands, and beaches. The zone extends . . . seaward to the outer limit of State title and ownership under the Submerged Lands Act (43 U.S.C. 1301 et seq.), the Act of March 2, 1917 (48 U.S.C. 749), the Covenant to Establish a Commonwealth of the Northern Mariana Islands in Political Union with the United States of America, as approved by the Act of March 24, 1976 (48 U.S.C. 1681 note), or section 1 of the Act of November 20, 1963 (48 U.S.C. 1705), as applicable. The zone extends inland from the shorelines only to the extent necessary to control shorelands, the uses of which have a direct and significant impact on the coastal waters, and to control those geographical areas which are likely to be affected by or vulnerable to sea level rise. Excluded from the coastal zone are lands the use of which is by law subject solely to the discretion of or which is held in trust by the Federal Government, its officers or agents.

> CZMA § 304((1), 16 U.S.C. § 1453(1).

189. Some states have successfully claimed greater coastal jurisdiction under the Submerged Lands Act. Florida, for example, asserts state regulatory authority over three marine

leagues of coastal waters into the Gulf of Mexico, or approximately 10.3 miles. Therefore, Florida's "coastal zone" for purposes of the CZMA—unlike its "territorial sea" under the Clean Water Act—is also wider.

190. CZARA § 6217(g)(3)(B), 16 U.S.C. § 1455b(g)(3)(B).
191. CZARA § 6217(a)(1), 16 U.S.C. § 1455b(a)(1).
192. CZARA § 6217(a)(2), 16 U.S.C. § 1455b(a)(2).
193. Nat'l Ocean Serv., NOAA, Coastal Nonpoint Pollution Control Program 1 (2004), *available at* http://coastalmanagement.noaa.gov/nonpoint/docs/NONPOINT.pdf.
194. CZARA § 6217(b), 16 U.S.C. § 1455b(b). For purposes of this program, "management measures" are "economically achievable measures for the control of the addition of pollutants from existing and new categories and classes of nonpoint sources of pollution, which reflect the greatest degree of pollutant reduction achievable through the application of the best available nonpoint pollution control practices, technologies, processes, siting criteria, operating methods, or other alternatives." CZARA § 6217(g)(5), 16 U.S.C. § 1455b(g)(5).
195. CZARA § 6217(b)(3), 16 U.S.C. § 1455b(b)(3).
196. CZARA § 6217(c)(3), (4), 16 U.S.C. § 1455b(c)(3), (4).
197. CZARA § 6217(f), 16 U.S.C. § 1455b(f).
198. CZARA § 6217(c)(2), 16 U.S.C. § 1455b(c)(2).
199. Nat'l Ocean Serv., NOAA, *Coastal Programs: Partnering with States to Manage Our Coastline,* http://coastalmanagement.noaa.gov/programs/coast_div.html (last revised July 13, 2006).
200. *Id.* Illinois's Great Lakes coastal program is inactive.
201. Nat'l Ocean Serv., NOAA, *Coastal Nonpoint Program Approval Findings,* http://coastalmanagement.noaa.gov/nonpoint/pro_approve.html (last revised Sept. 25, 2006). The 14 states are California, Connecticut, Delaware, Maine, Maryland, Massachusetts, Minnesota, New Hampshire, New York, North Carolina, Pennsylvania, Rhode Island, Virginia, and Wisconsin, while the four territories are American Samoa, Northern Marianas Islands, Puerto Rico, and the Virgin Islands. *Id.*
202. *Id.* The 15 states are Alabama, Alaska, Florida, Georgia, Hawaii, Louisiana, Michigan, Mississippi, New Jersey, Ohio, Oregon, South Carolina, Texas, and Washington, while the remaining territory is Guam. *Id.*
203. Nat'l Ocean Serv., NOAA, Facts About the Coastal Nonpoint Pollution Control Program 2 (2004), *available at* http://coastalmanagement.noaa.gov/nonpoint/docs/NONPOINT.pdf.
204. CZMA § 307(a), 16 U.S.C. § 1456(a).
205. *See, e.g.,* Sec'y of the Interior v. California, 464 U.S. 312, 330 (1984) (involving California's assertion that the consistency requirement applies to outer continental shelf oil and gas leasing); City of Sausalito v. O'Neill, 386 F.3d 1186, 1201–02 (9th Cir. 2004) (raising the consistency requirement in the context of converting a military base into a national park); Mountain Rhythm Res. v. FERC, 302 F.3d 958, 967 (9th Cir. 2002) (discussing the consistency requirement in the context of FERC's re-licensing of hydroelectric facilities); Akiak Native Community v. U.S. Postal Service, 213 F.3d 1140, 1145 (9th Cir. 2000) (discussing the applicability of the consistency requirement to delivery of mail by hovercraft); New Jersey Dep't. of Envtl. Protection & Energy v. Long Island Power Auth., 30 F.3d 403, 419–20 (3d Cir. 1994) (seeking to demand consistency from the Nuclear Regulatory Commission in connection with shipments of partially irradiated reactor fuel); Nw. Envtl. Def. Ctr. v. Brennen, 958 F.2d 930, 936–37 (9th Cir. 1992) (discussing the consistency requirement in the context of the Pacific Fishery Management Council's regulation of salmon); Cape May Greene, Inc. v. Warren, 698 F.2d 179, 191–92 (3d Cir. 1983) (applying the consistency requirements to EPA's permitting of a sewage treatment facility); Marquez-Colon v. Reagan, 668 F.2d 611, 614–15 (1st Cir. 1981) (discussing Puerto Rico's insistence that a federal refugee detainment center comply with the consistency requirement); Save Lake Washington v. Frank, 641 F.2d 1330, 1331 (9th Cir. 1981) (discussing

Washington's insistence that NOAA's construction of dock facilities comply with the consistency requirement).

206. Knaust v. City of Kingston, 978 F. Supp. 86 (N.D.N.Y. 1997).

207. CWA § 303(d)(1)(A), 33 U.S.C. § 1313(d)(1)(A).

208. CWA § 303(d)(1)(C), 33 U.S.C. § 1313(d)(1)(C).

209. CWA § 303(d)(1), (4), 33 U.S.C. § 1313(d)(1), (4).

210. CWA § 313(d)(4)(A), 33 U.S.C. § 1313(d)(4)(A).

211. For example, according to the U.S. Department of Justice:

> In California, only 1 percent of impaired waterways fail to meet water quality standards solely because of pollution that comes from pipes, municipal waste treatment works, or other point sources. EPA shows that 54 percent of California's impaired waterways are polluted by nonpoint sources exclusively, while another 45 percent are impaired by a combination of point and nonpoint sources.

U.S. Dept. of Justice, *Federal Court Issues Landmark Clean Water Decision* 1 (April 5, 2000), *available at* http://www.usdoj.gov/opa/pr/2000/April/175enrd.htm.

212. 40 C.F.R. § 130.2(i).

213. Pronsolino v. Nastri, 291 F.3d 1123 (9th Cir. 2002).

214. CWA § 303(d)(1)(A), (C), 33 U.S.C. § 1313(d)(1)(A), (C).

215. CWA § 303(e), 33 U.S.C. § 1313(e).

216. CWA §§ 401(a)(2) (applicable to EPA-issued NPDES permits), 402(b)(5), (d) (applicable to state-issued NPDES permits), 33 U.S.C. §§ 1341(a)(2), 1342(b)(5), (d).

217. CWA § 319(g)(1), 33 U.S.C. § 1329(g)(1).

218. CWA § 319(g)(2), 33 U.S.C. § 1329(g)(2).

219. CWA § 320, 33 U.S.C. § 1330. An "estuary," for purposes of this program, is "all or part of the mouth of a river or stream or other body of water having unimpaired natural connection with the open sea and within which the sea water is measurably diluted with fresh water derived from land drainage." CWA § 104(n)(3), 33 U.S.C. § 1254(n)(3), as referenced by CWA § 320(k), 33 U.S.C. § 1330(k).

220. Under this program, state governors nominate estuaries within their borders to the EPA to be considered "an estuary of national significance," CWA § 320(a)(1), 33 U.S.C. § 1330(a)(1), or the EPA can select any estuary for inclusion in the program if that estuary "requires the control of point and nonpoint sources of pollution to supplement existing controls of pollution in more than one State." CWA § 320(a)(2)(A), 33 U.S.C. § 1330(a)(2)(A). Congress itself included a list of 17 estuaries to which the EPA was to give "priority consideration." CWA § 320(a)(2)(B), 33 U.S.C. § 1330(a)(2)(B). Currently, the National Estuary Program covers 28 estuaries, concentrated on the west, Gulf, and northeast coasts of the United States. Office of Wetlands, Oceans, and Watersheds, U.S. EPA, *Which Estuaries Are in the NEP?*, http://www.epa.gov/owow/estuaries/find.htm (last updated April 17, 2007). In addition, the Clean Water Act explicitly mandates similar management for Chesapeake Bay. CWA § 117, 33 U.S.C. § 1267. The home page for the Chesapeake Bay Program is located at http://www.chesapeakebay.net/.

221. CWA § 320(b)(1)–(4), 33 U.S.C. § 1330(b)(1)–(4).

222. *See* CWA § 320(f)(1), 33 U.S.C. § 1330(f)(1). Links to the current management plans are available at Office of Wetlands, Oceans, and Watersheds, U.S. EPA, *Comprehensive Conservation and Management Plans,* http://www.epa.gov/owow/estuaries/ccmp/index.htm (last visited April 17, 2007).

223. CWA § 320(g), 33 U.S.C. § 1330(g).

224. CWA § 117, 33 U.S.C. § 1267.

225. *See* Office of Wetlands, Oceans, and Watersheds, U.S. EPA, *Watersheds of the NEP,* http://www.epa.gov/owow/estuaries/sheds.htm (last updated April 17, 2007). The watersheds included for the Lower Columbia River, Galveston Bay, Coastal Bend Bays, and the Albemarle/Pamlico Sounds are particularly large. *Id.*

226. Office of Wetlands, Oceans, and Watersheds, U.S. EPA, *Air Pollution and Water Quality,* http://www.epa.gov/owow/airdeposition/ (last visited Feb. 3, 2008).

227. *Id.*

228. Office of Wetlands, Oceans, and Watersheds, EPA, *National Estuary Program Success Stories,* http://www.epa.gov/owow/estuaries/success.htm (last updated July 11, 2007).

229. *See* ExpectMore.gov, Office of Management and Budget, *Ocean, Coastal, and Estuary Protection Assessment,* http://www.whitehouse.gov/omb/expectmore/detail/10004370.2005.html (last visited Feb. 3, 2008).

230. Office of Wetlands, Oceans, and Watersheds, EPA, *National Estuary Program Success Stories,* http://www.epa.gov/owow/estuaries/success.htm (last visited July 11, 2007).

231. *See* Office of Wetlands, Oceans, and Watersheds, U.S. EPA, *Watershed Funding,* http://www.epa.gov/owow/funding.html (last updated May 11, 2007). "A watershed 'is the area of land where all of the water that is under it or drains off of it goes into the same place.'" Office of Wetlands, Oceans, and Watersheds, U.S. EPA, *What Is a Watershed?,* http://www.epa.gov/owow/watershed/whatis.html (last visited April 3, 2007). The EPA explains the need for such an innovation as follows:

> Over the past 20 years, substantial reductions have been achieved in the discharge of pollutants into the nation's air, lakes, rivers, wetlands, estuaries, coastal waters, and ground water. These successes have been achieved primarily by controlling point sources of pollution and, in the case of ground water, preventing contamination from hazardous waste sites. While such sources continue to be an environmental threat, it is clear that potential causes of impairment of a waterbody are as varied as human activity itself. For example, besides discharges from industrial or municipal sources, our waters may be threatened by urban, agricultural, or other forms of polluted runoff; landscape modification; depleted or contaminated ground water; changes in flow; overharvesting of fish and other organisms; introduction of exotic species; bioaccumulation of toxics; and deposition or recycling of pollutants between air, land and water.
>
> The federal laws that address these problems have tended to focus on particular sources, pollutants, or water uses and have not resulted in an integrated environmental management approach. Consequently, significant gaps exist in our efforts to protect watersheds from the cumulative impacts of a multitude of activities. Existing air, waste and pesticide management, water pollution prevention and control programs and other related natural resource programs are, however, excellent foundations on which to build a watershed approach.

Office of Wetlands, Oceans, and Watersheds, U.S. EPA, *Need for Watershed Approaches,* http://www.epa.gov/owow/watershed/framework/ch4.html (last visited May 8, 2007).

232. U.S. EPA, *Narragansett Bay,* http://www.epa.gov/owow/watershed/initiative/2003/summaries/narragansett.pdf.

233. U.S. EPA, *Hanalei Bay,* http://www.epa.gov/owow/watershed/initiative/2003/summaries/hanalei.pdf.

234. U.S. EPA, *Lower Columbia River,* http://www.epa.gov/owow/watershed/initiative/2003/summaries/lowercolumbia.pdf.

235. Office of Wetlands, Oceans, and Watersheds, U.S. EPA, *Targeted Watersheds in 2004,* http://www.epa.gov/twg/2004/2004index.html (last visited August 16, 2006).

236. Office of Wetlands, Oceans, and Watersheds, U.S. EPA, *Targeted Watersheds in 2005,* http://www.epa.gov/twg/2005/2005index.html (last visited Aug. 16, 2006).

237. Office of Water, U.S. EPA, *Water Quality Trading Policy* (Jan. 13, 2003), *available at* http://www.epa.gov/owow/watershed/trading/finalpolicy2003.pdf.

238. *Id.* at 1, 4.

239. *Id.* at 6.

240. Office of Water, U.S. EPA, *Watershed-Based NPDES Permitting,* http://cfpub.epa.gov/npdes/wqbasedpermitting/wspermitting.cfm (last visited Feb. 3, 2008).

chapter eight

Ocean Dumping and Marine Pollution

Photo by Neil J. Zammit. Used by permission.

Aaron C. Courtney
Sloane A. Wildman
Emily K. Merolli

I. Introduction

Although oceans make up more than two-thirds of the Earth's surface, scientific studies are consistently revealing the vulnerability of these immense water bodies to human influences, including pollution from land runoff and the dumping of wastes at sea. As we move into the twenty-first century, these impacts will only increase with the tremendous increase in human population and the concomitant pressure to use the oceans as an option for waste management.[1] As recently as the 1970s, tens of millions of tons of industrial and ship waste and sewage sludge were legally dumped in the world's oceans; however, ocean dumping at present is significantly restricted through several domestic and international laws.[2]

For example, ocean dumping and marine pollution from both vessels and nonvessel sources are regulated under several different federal statutes, including the Clean Water Act, the Marine Protection, Research and Sanctuaries Act, also known as the Ocean Dumping Act, and the Act to Prevent Pollution from Ships. Both the Ocean Dumping Act and Act to Prevent Pollution from Ships implement international treaties and, in coordination with the Clean Water Act, have been effective in certain ways in reducing levels of marine pollution. Nevertheless, as the condition of the earth's oceans is subject to more scientific scrutiny, and awareness about the environmental impacts of legal and illegal ocean dumping rises (e.g., growing dead zones), these laws and the regulatory programs that implement them are widely evolving in response.[3]

The regulatory response has occurred at both the international and federal level. For example, addressing pollution in the world's oceans is a priority of the United Nations Environment Programme, which recently created UN-Oceans[4] and has been hosting an increasing number of conferences worldwide to explore ocean governance issues.[5] Within the United States, the Environmental Protection Agency (EPA) and U.S. Coast Guard are developing regulations to address pollution from ballast water; in fact, over the past few years, many states have started to regulate ballast discharges in their coastal waters through locally focused measures.[6] The EPA is also beginning to evaluate whether to require Clean Water Act National Pollution Discharge Elimination System (NPDES) permits for discharges incidental to the normal operation of vessels.[7]

II. The Current State of the Law

A. Clean Water Act

Amid growing public awareness and concern for water pollution, Congress enacted the Federal Water Pollution Control Act Amendments of 1972, which, as amended in 1977, became more commonly known as the Clean Water Act.[8] The purpose of the Act is to "restore and maintain the chemical, physical, and biological integrity of the Nation's waters."[9] The Act establishes the basic structure for regulating discharges of pollutants into U.S. waters and gives the EPA authority to implement pollution control programs.

1. Jurisdiction

The main thrust of the Clean Water Act regulatory scheme is Section 301, which prohibits the discharge of any pollutant unless it is authorized by an NPDES permit.[10] The statute defines "discharge of a pollutant" as "(a) any addition of a pollutant into navigable waters from any point source, or (b) any addition of any pollutant to the waters of the contiguous zone or the ocean from any point source other than a vessel or other floating craft."[11] Thus, the applicability of the Act to marine waters depends on where the discharge occurs and whether the discharge is from a vessel or from a nonvessel point source.

"Navigable waters" means "waters of the United States including the territorial seas." The "territorial seas" extend from the coast seaward a distance of three miles.[12] The "contiguous zone" extends from three miles to twenty-four miles beyond the coastline.[13] The "ocean," as defined in the Act, means "any portion of the high seas beyond the contiguous zone" up to two hundred miles from the coast.[14]

Therefore, the Clean Water Act applies to vessel discharges up to three miles from the coast.[15] However, pollution from nonvessel sources is regulated out to two hundred miles from the shore.

2. Prohibition Against Discharge of Pollutants

As noted above, the Act generally prohibits the discharge of a pollutant without a permit. Under Section 402 of the Clean Water Act, EPA has the initial authority to issue NPDES permits for all regulated discharges of pollutants.[16] The Clean Water Act defines "pollutant" very broadly to mean "dredged spoil, solid waste, incinerator residue, sewage, garbage, sewage sludge, munitions, chemical wastes, biological materials, radioactive materials, heat, wrecked or discarded equipment, rock, sand, cellar dirt and industrial, municipal, and agricultural waste discharged into water."[17] The term "pollutant," however, does not include "sewage from vessels or a discharge incidental to the normal operation of a vessel of the Armed Forces."[18]

EPA has taken this statutory definition one step further, and by regulation has promulgated an exemption from NPDES permitting for discharges of sewage and discharges incidental to the operation of all vessels.[19] According to EPA, the following discharges do not require NPDES permits:

> Any discharge of sewage from vessels, effluent from properly functioning marine engines, laundry, shower, and galley sink wastes, or any other discharge incidental to the normal operation of a vessel.[20]

As described further below, a successful judicial challenge was recently brought against this regulation, and EPA has taken steps toward the development of an NPDES permit program framework for discharges incidental to the normal operation of vessels.[21]

3. Regulation of Pollution from Vessels Under the Clean Water Act

Pollution from commercial, recreational, and military vessels can take on a variety of forms. These include graywater, bilgewater, blackwater (sewage), ballast water, antifouling paints (and their leachate), hazardous materials, and municipal and commercial garbage and other wastes.

Pollution from commercial, recreational, and military vessels can take on a variety of forms.

a. Graywater Discharges

Graywater is wastewater from showers, sinks, laundries and kitchens, and other sources associated with the normal operation of a vessel. Both "graywater" and the phrase "discharge incidental to the normal operation of a vessel"[22] are defined in Section 312 (relating to marine sanitation devices). Because graywater meets the literal definition of a "pollutant" under the Act and vessels are "point sources," graywater discharges into navigable waters (within the three-mile limit of the territorial seas) arguably fall within the scope of Clean Water Act Section 301(a), thereby requiring an NPDES permit, unless an exclusion is provided for in the Act. However, EPA has excluded, by regulation, the components ordinarily referred to as "graywater" from the NPDES permitting requirements of the Clean Water Act.

EPA's regulatory exemption for discharges of graywater from vessels is vulnerable to the same argument advanced by the plaintiffs in a recent successful challenge to the regulatory exemption as it applies to ballast water (see discussion below).

b. Blackwater Discharges

The Clean Water Act exempts blackwater discharges (i.e., vessel sewage discharges) from NPDES permit requirements, if the blackwater is discharged through an operable marine sanitation device.[23] EPA's regulation also addresses the statutory exemption,[24] and the exemption has been noted by the courts.[25]

Section 312 of the Act requires EPA to promulgate performance standards for marine sanitation devices. The devices must be designed to prevent the discharge of untreated or inadequately treated sewage from vessels into navigable waters.[26] It is unlawful for a vessel subject to EPA's standards to operate on the navigable waters of the United States if it is not equipped with a certified *operable marine sanitation device*. The Coast Guard is charged with promulgating regulations to implement EPA's standards and for enforcing Clean Water Act Section 312.[27]

The Coast Guard regulations that implement EPA's standards generally require Type II (treatment) marine sanitation devices for most vessels.[28] A Type II device is defined in the Coast Guard regulations as

> a device that, under the test conditions described in 159.126 and 159.126a, produces an effluent having a fecal coliform bacteria count not greater than 200 per 100 milliliters and suspended solids not greater than 150 milligrams per liter.[29]

Certification of a marine sanitation device by the Coast Guard is an acknowledgment that a particular type or model of device being tested satisfies EPA's and the Coast Guard's criteria, and these include the effluent limitations for blackwater.[30] The term "operable" is undefined, but would likely be interpreted by a court as encompassing the manufacturer's suggested operation and maintenance program and operating the marine sanitation device under the conditions for which it was designed.

The Clean Water Act NPDES exemption for blackwater is only for discharges "within the meaning of" Section 312.[31] If blackwater is not discharged through an "operable" marine sanitation device, it is arguably not within the meaning of Clean Water Act Section 312. Similarly, nonroutine discharges also could be viewed as outside the scope of Section 312. Such discharges probably violate the Clean Water Act Section 301(a) absolute prohibition against unpermitted discharges.

c. Ballast Water Discharges

For nearly thirty years, EPA has exempted ballast water discharges from coverage under the Clean Water Act.[32] However, in 2006 the federal district court for the Northern District of California struck this regulation down as beyond EPA's statutory authority.[33] Recent developments regarding the regulation of ballast water discharges are discussed in Section III.A., below.

4. NPDES Permitting for Nonvessel Discharges

In addition to the typical array of terms and conditions applicable to discharges of pollutants from point sources, all NPDES permits issued for discharges into the territorial seas, the contiguous zone and the oceans must comply with EPA-issued "ocean discharge guidelines," which address "the degradation of waters of the territorial seas, the contiguous zone and the oceans."[34] EPA's ocean discharge criteria specify the ecological, social, and economic factors to be used by permit writers to evaluate the impact of a discharge on the marine environment.

The ten ocean discharge guidelines are as follows:

- The quantities, composition, and potential for bioaccumulation or persistence of the pollutants to be discharged;
- The potential transport of such pollutants by biological, physical, or chemical processes;
- The composition and vulnerability of the biological communities that may be exposed to such pollutants, including the presence of unique species or communities of species, the presence of species identified as endangered or threatened pursuant to the Endangered Species Act, or the presence of those species critical to the structure or function of the ecosystem, such as those important for the food chain;
- The importance of the receiving water area to the surrounding biological community, including the presence of spawning sites, nursery/forage areas, migratory pathways, or areas necessary for other functions or critical stages in the life cycle of an organism;
- The existence of special aquatic sites, including, but not limited to marine sanctuaries and refuges, parks, national and historic monuments, national seashores, wilderness areas, and coral reefs;
- The potential impacts on human health through direct and indirect pathways;
- Existing or potential recreational and commercial fishing, including finfishing and shellfishing;
- Any applicable requirements of an approved Coastal Zone Management plan;
- Such other factors relating to the effects of the discharge as may be appropriate; and
- Marine water quality criteria developed pursuant to Section 304(a)(1).[35]

In the absence of sufficient information to support a "no unreasonable degradation" finding, EPA may still issue a permit, but only if it determines that the discharge will not cause irreparable harm. In such a case, a permit may be issued while data on ecosystem health is collected and evaluated prior to reissuance of the permit. These data are collected as part of a monitoring program to assess the impact of the discharge, as well as an assessment of alternative sites for the discharge or disposal of the wastewater. Data are also gathered through monitoring compliance with all other conditions in the permit.[36]

5. Enforcement

The Clean Water Act contains extensive enforcement provisions, and violations of the Act are subject to administrative, civil judicial (including citizen suits), and criminal enforcement.

a. Civil Liability

EPA may issue a compliance order or bring a civil suit in U.S. district court against persons who violate the terms of a permit, with penalties as high as $32,500 per violation per day.[37]

While the Clean Water Act addresses federal enforcement, the majority of actions taken to enforce the Act are undertaken by states, both because states issue the majority of permits to dischargers and because the federal government lacks the resources for day-to-day monitoring and enforcement.[38] However, EPA has ultimate oversight authority of state enforcement and retains the right to bring a direct action when it believes that a state has failed to take timely and appropriate action or when a state or local agency requests EPA involvement.[39]

b. Criminal Liability

Criminal liability under the Clean Water Act may be based on either negligent or knowing conduct. The only difference between the two Clean Water Act criminal provisions is the mental state required.

i. Negligent Violations

With respect to *negligent* violations, the Clean Water Act provides:

> Any person who ... negligently violates section 1311, 1312, 1316, 1317, 1318, 1321(b)(3), 1328 or 1345 ... shall be punished by a fine or not less than $2,500 nor more than $32,500 per day of violation, or imprisonment for not more than 1 year, or by both. . . . [40]

The statute does not define "negligently" but the courts have held that the statute requires only ordinary—as opposed to gross—negligence.[41] However, courts also have held that a defendant may be convicted only on the basis of his own negligent conduct, and not the negligence of others.[42]

ii. Knowing Violations

With respect to *knowing* violations, the Act provides:

> Any person who ... knowingly violates section 1311, 1312, 1316, 1317, 1318, 1321(b)(3), 1328 or 1345 ... shall be punished by a fine of not less than $5,000 nor more than $50,000 per day of violation, or by imprisonment for not more than 3 years, or by both.[43]

> **"Knowingly" means only that the defendant was aware of its conduct, and not that it was aware that its conduct was in violation of the law.**

"Knowingly" means only that the defendant was aware of its conduct, and not that it was aware that its conduct was in violation of the law.[44] Courts have held that the "knowingly" element requires the government to prove the defendant's awareness of engaging in the activities at issue (e.g., discharging); the factual nature of any legally relevant substance; and the lack of a required permit.[45]

Knowledge also can be proven circumstantially. Outside of the environmental context, courts have allowed the government to prove a statutory requirement of knowledge by showing that the defendant was willfully blind to the reality of the situation.[46] In the environmental context, at least one court has noted the applicability of the willful blindness doctrine to a prosecution under a different environmental statute.[47] In addition, corporate criminal liability can be imposed based on the "collective knowledge" doctrine, in which aggregate knowledge of the corporation's employees and agents is imputed to the organization.[48]

c. Citizen Enforcement

In addition to enforcement by the federal or state governments, a citizen may bring a lawsuit against any person who is alleged to be in violation of the Act.[49] For example, in *Natural Resources Defense Council v. Southwest Marine, Inc.*,[50] environmental organizations successfully brought a citizen suit against a shipyard operator, claiming that the operator was discharging unlawful amounts of pollutants into the ocean and had failed to prepare and implement the environmental compliance and monitoring plans required by the Clean Water Act.

B. Ocean Dumping Act (Marine Protection, Research, and Sanctuaries Act of 1972)/London Convention

1. Overview of Statute

Due to concern over the related ecological, health, and economic costs of continued unregulated dumping of waste materials into the oceans, Congress enacted the Marine Protection, Research, and Sanctuaries Act of 1972, or the Ocean Dumping Act. The Ocean Dumping Act implements the London Convention, which is discussed in Section II.B.3, below.

The Ocean Dumping Act applies to, among other things, the transportation by any person of material from the United States for the purpose of dumping the material into ocean waters. "Ocean waters" means the "waters of the open seas lying seaward of the base line from which the territorial sea is measured," or beyond three miles from the shore.[51] Section 101(a) of the Ocean Dumping Act requires a permit for any dumping into ocean waters when the material is transported from the United States or on an American vessel or aircraft.[52]

The dumping of sewage sludge and industrial waste in particular was further restricted by amendment in the Ocean Dumping Ban Act of 1988, or the Dumping Ban Act. The amendment prohibited the issuance of new dumping permits and phased out all sewage sludge and industrial waste dumping by 1991.[53]

2. Ocean Dumping Permits

The Ocean Dumping Act prohibits most forms of ocean dumping unless authorized by a permit issued by the EPA or, in the case of dredged materials, by the Secretary of the Army Corps of Engineers (Corps).[54]

The definitions of "dumping" and "material" are key issues in determining the applicability of the Ocean Dumping Act. For example, the Ocean Dumping Act defines the term "dumping" simply as "a disposition of material."[55] Thus, the Ocean Dumping Act appears to cover incidental activities in addition to deliberate dumping.

The term "material" is defined in the Ocean Dumping Act very broadly to include

> matter of any kind or description, including, but not limited to, dredged material, solid waste, incinerator residue, garbage, sewage, sewage sludge, munitions, radiological, chemical, and biological warfare agents, radioactive materials, chemicals, biological and laboratory waste, wreck or discarded equipment, rock, sand, excavation debris, and industrial, municipal, agricultural, and other waste; but such term does not mean sewage from vessels within the meaning of [Section 312 of the Clean Water Act].[56]

Despite this broad definition, the Act expressly excludes sewage. The Act has been interpreted to apply to ocean incineration.[57] In addition, Title III of the Ocean Dumping Act addresses the dumping of medical waste by public vessels at sea,[58] which Congress passed to confront the growing problem of potentially infectious medical waste washing ashore.[59]

Under the Ocean Dumping Act, the EPA may issue two types of permits: short-term "research" permits, or "special" commercial operating permits.[60] The Act requires the EPA to promulgate regulations for reviewing and evaluating applications for ocean dumping permits, which must include consideration of specific environmental factors as well as alternatives to ocean dumping and incineration.[61] The factors are nearly identical to those required for ocean discharges. The EPA may issue a permit only after it determines that: (1) there are no practical technological improvements that will reduce adverse impacts, and (2) there are no practical alternatives available that have less adverse environmental impact or potential risk.[62]

In addition to the EPA's criteria, the Corps, in evaluating the disposal of dredged material, is also required to consider the effect of the project on "navigation, economic and industrial development, and foreign and domestic commerce of the United States."[63] In determining the appropriate location for the ocean dumping, the Act provides that the Corps shall "to the extent feasible, utilize the recommended sites designated" by the EPA.[64]

3. London Convention

The Ocean Dumping Act implements the London Convention of 1972, to which the United States is a contracting party. The objective of the London Convention is to promote the effective control of all sources of marine pollution. At present, there are eighty-two countries that are parties to the London Convention. Countries that are members of the Convention are required to take effective measures to prevent pollution of the marine environment caused by dumping at sea.[65]

Under the London Convention, wastes are placed onto a "black" or "grey" list. The categories determine whether the wastes can be considered for disposal at sea based on the hazard they present to the environment. Dumping of wastes in the black-list category is prohibited. Dumping of the grey-listed materials requires a special permit from a designated national authority. The permits should be strictly controlled and require that certain conditions are met. All other materials or substances can be dumped after a general permit has been issued.[66]

4. Enforcement

The Ocean Dumping Act provides for injunctive relief to prevent the issuance of permits by the EPA or the Corps.[67] The plaintiff bears the burden of proof to establish irreparable harm based on actual or threatened injury to the physical, chemical, and biological balance at the dump site.[68] In addition, the Act contains civil and criminal enforcement provisions.

a. Civil Liability

Under the Act, the EPA may impose civil penalties on any person who illegally dumps sewage sludge or industrial waste.[69] The maximum civil penalty for each sewage sludge or industrial waste violation is $55,000, unless the violation involves the dumping of medical waste, in which case the maximum civil penalty for each violation is increased to $137,500.[70]

b. Criminal Penalties

The Ocean Dumping Act also imposes criminal penalties for knowing violations of the statute:

> (1) any person who knowingly violates any provision of this subchapter, any regulation promulgated under this subchapter, or a permit issued under this subchapter, shall be fined under Title 18 or imprisoned for not more than 5 years, or both; and

> (2) any person who is convicted of such a violation pursuant to paragraph (1) shall forfeit to the United States—

>> (A) any property constituting or derived from any proceeds that the person obtained, directly or indirectly, as a result of such violation; and

>> (B) any of the property of the person which was used, or intended to be used in any matter or part, to commit or to facilitate the commission of the violation.[71]

c. In rem and Seizure of Vessels

The Ocean Dumping Act contains a provision to allow for vessels used in a violation, except public vessels, to be liable in rem for any civil penalty or criminal fine imposed.[72] However, it must be shown that one or more of the vessel owners was a consenting party or aware of the violation when it occurred.[73]

d. *Private Right of Action*

The Ocean Dumping Act also authorizes private citizens who have suffered an actual injury to bring a private citizen suit against any person, including the United States and government agencies.[74] Like the Clean Water Act, the statute requires sixty days' notice to the EPA and the alleged violator and prevents the commencement of an action if the United States is "diligently prosecuting" a violation.[75]

e. *London Convention Enforcement*

The provisions for enforcement of the London Convention are addressed in Article VII of the Convention. Article VII requires each member country to take appropriate measures to prevent and punish conduct in violation of the Convention. In addition, Article VII requires cooperation among the countries to ensure the development of procedures for the effective application of the Convention on the high seas. This includes procedures for the reporting of vessels and aircraft observed dumping in contravention of the Convention.[76]

The basic intent of Article VII is to impose on each country a duty to enforce the Convention within its jurisdiction. As noted above, the United States has enacted the Ocean Dumping Act to fulfill that duty. Therefore, based on the Ocean Dumping Act, the United States has jurisdiction over all dumping activities within "waters of the open seas lying seaward of the base line from which the territorial sea is measured," or beyond three miles.[77]

Responsibility for enforcement on the high seas[78] lies primarily with the country where the dumping vessel is registered. Each country is required to verify that no illegal dumping operations are carried out and that conditions set out in dumping permits are met, including that the waste is dumped at the approved site. The United States government refers illegal dumping outside of U.S. waters by foreign-flag ships to the country where the ship is registered.[79]

C. Act to Prevent Pollution from Ships/MARPOL

1. Overview

The Act to Prevent Pollution from Ships[80] was enacted to implement the International Convention for the Prevention of Pollution from Ships (MARPOL)[81] and its 1978 Protocol[82] (collectively known as "MARPOL 73/78"). The purpose of MARPOL is to eliminate completely the intentional pollution of the marine environment by oil and other harmful substances and to minimize the accidental discharge of such substances.[83]

> **The purpose of MARPOL is to eliminate completely the intentional pollution of the marine environment by oil and other harmful substances.**

The Coast Guard has credited the adoption of MARPOL for reducing oil tanker operational pollution by eighty-five percent since 1973.[84] MARPOL 73/78 is not self-executing, and signatory nations must enact laws to execute the treaty. Approximately 144 countries, whose fleets comprise over ninety-eight percent of global shipping tonnage, have ratified the Convention.[85]

2. MARPOL Provisions

MARPOL 73/78 essentially covers all of the technical aspects of pollution from ships, except the disposal of waste into the sea by dumping.[86] The 1973 convention includes five annexes, regulating pollution with respect to oil (Annex I); noxious liquid substances (Annex II); harmful goods in packaged form (Annex III); sewage (Annex IV); and garbage (Annex V). The first two of these annexes were mandatory, meaning that countries that ratified MARPOL (including the United States) were required to accept them.

The Act to Prevent Pollution from Ships provisions apply only to seagoing ships. Regulations implementing Annex I and II limit discharges of oil and noxious substances, set forth reporting requirements for discharges, and establish specific requirements for monitoring equipment and record-keeping aboard vessels. Such vessels are required to keep oil record books detailing all discharges, disposal, and transfers of oil.[87]

The remaining three MARPOL 73/78 Annexes are optional, and before one of the optional Annexes can take effect, it must be adopted by at least fifteen nations with a combined fleet representing fifty percent of world tonnage. Annex V relating to garbage[88] went into force in 1988 and Annex III, addressing hazardous substances carried in packaged form,[89] entered into force in 1991. Annex IV, addressing sewage, entered into force on September 27, 2003.[90] To date, the United States has adopted only two of the three optional Annexes.

3. Regulation of Sewage Discharges Under MARPOL

Annex IV to MARPOL 73/78 exclusively addresses sewage. It is generally considered that, on the high seas, the oceans are capable of assimilating and dealing with raw sewage through natural bacterial action and, therefore, the regulations in Annex IV prohibit ships only from discharging sewage within four miles of the nearest land, unless they have in operation an approved treatment plant. Between four and twenty-three miles from land, sewage must be comminuted and disinfected before discharge. Ships must be equipped with one of three types of approved sewage treatment systems: a sewage treatment plant, a sewage comminuting and disinfecting system for the temporary storage of sewage when the ship is less than three nautical miles from the nearest land, or a holding tank for the retention of all sewage.

Upon ratification, the sewage regulations were immediately effective, in the 117 countries that have ratified Annex IV, to ships on international voyages.[91] Many countries already have imposed regulations that are in line with the requirements of Annex IV on ships visiting their coastlines. And, as a practical matter, all cruise ships and large passenger ships already have sewage treatment plants on board.

The regulations also apply immediately to "new" ships (built after September 27, 2003) of 400 gross tonnage and above, and to new ships of less than 400 gross tonnage that are certified to carry more than fifteen persons. Existing ships (built before

September 27, 2003) of 400 gross tonnage or above and of less than 400 gross tonnage that are certified to carry more than fifteen persons have until September 27, 2008, to comply. The United States has not ratified Annex IV and has no plans to do so, because the administration regards Section 312 of the Clean Water Act as more stringent.

4. Plastics and Other Garbage

Annex V of MARPOL includes a complete ban on the dumping of plastic. In 1987, Congress amended the Act to Prevent Pollution from Ships to implement the Marine Plastic Pollution Research and Control Act to implement Annex V.[92] This Act prohibits the dumping of plastics in all U.S. waters and applies to almost all watercraft—from the smallest recreational boat to the largest commercial ship. In addition, marinas are required to maintain adequate facilities for the disposal of refuse regulated under the Act.[93]

Vessels included under the Marine Plastic Pollution Research and Control Act are

- A ship of United States registry or nationality, or one operated under the authority of the United States, wherever located; and
- Any other ship while in the navigable waters or the exclusive economic zone of the United States.[94]

Excluded vessels under the Marine Plastic Pollution Research and Control Act include

- A warship, naval auxiliary, or other ship owned or operated by the United States when engaged in noncommercial service; or
- Any other ship specifically excluded by the MARPOL Protocol or the Antarctic Protocol.[95]

Although the statute's primary emphasis is on plastics, it also restricts the disposal of other garbage according to a vessel's distance from shore, as follows:

- Within U.S. lakes, rivers, bays, sounds, and within three nautical miles of shore, it is illegal to dump plastic, paper, rags, glass, metal, crockery, dunnage (lining and packing material, nets, lines, etc.), and food.
- Between three and twelve nautical miles from shore, it is illegal to dump plastic and any other garbage that is greater than one inch in size.
- Between twelve and twenty-five nautical miles from shore, it is illegal to dump plastic and dunnage.
- Beyond twenty-five nautical miles, it is illegal to dump plastic.[96]

These dumping restrictions apply to all vessels operating in all navigable waters of the United States and the 200-mile Exclusive Economic Zone (EEZ). All vessels greater than twenty-six feet must display a MARPOL placard outlining the garbage dumping restrictions. All vessels over forty feet must also have a written waste management plan on board.[97]

Under the Marine Plastic Pollution Research and Control Act, ports and terminals, including recreational marinas, must have adequate and convenient "reception facilities" for their regular customers. That is, marinas must be capable of receiving garbage from vessels that normally do business with them, including transients.[98]

5. Enforcement

a. Jurisdiction

Under the general enforcement regime, any violation of the MARPOL 73/78 Convention within the jurisdiction of any party to the Convention is punishable either under the law of that party or under the law of the flag state. Violations outside territorial waters should be referred by coastal states to the foreign-flag states that have the primary responsibility to enforce MARPOL.[99] A flag state must investigate once it has received notice or evidence of a violation by one of its ships. If sufficient evidence of a violation is obtained, an action must be brought against the vessel. The flag state must also notify the party who reported the violation on the action taken.[100]

In the United States, the Act to Prevent Pollution from Ships applies to all U.S. flag ships operating in U.S. navigable waters, while at a port or terminal under U.S. jurisdiction, or in foreign waters.

Further, under the Act to Prevent Pollution from Ships, the United States has concurrent jurisdiction with the foreign-flag state over all foreign-flag vessels operating in U.S. navigable waters or while at a port or terminal under U.S. jurisdiction.[101] If the violation occurs outside the navigable waters of the United States, MARPOL and the Act to Prevent Pollution from Ships require violations in foreign waters to be referred to the flag-state where the vessel is registered for investigation and prosecution.[102]

The Coast Guard and EPA are the primary agencies responsible for the enforcement of the Act to Prevent Pollution from Ships.

b. Civil Liability

A person who violates MARPOL 73/78, the Marine Plastic Pollution Research and Control Act, or the Coast Guard regulations is liable for a civil penalty of up to $32,500 for each violation, as provided by 33 U.S.C. § 1908(b)(1) (adjusted for inflation by 33 C.F.R. § 27.3). Each day of a continuing violation constitutes a separate violation.[103]

A person who makes a false or fictitious statement or a fraudulent representation in any matter in which a statement or representation is required to be made to the Coast Guard under MARPOL 73/78, the Act, or the regulations of this subpart, is liable for a civil penalty of up to $6,500 for each statement or representation, as provided by 33 U.S.C. § 1908(b)(2) (adjusted for inflation by 33 C.F.R. § 27.3).[104]

Further, the ship that was operated in violation of the Act to Prevent Pollution from Ships can be liable in rem for any criminal sanction or civil penalty assessed.[105]

c. Criminal Liability

i. The Act to Prevent Pollution from Ships

The Act to Prevent Pollution from Ships specifies that a person who knowingly violates the provisions of the Act or its regulations commits a class D felony.[106] In the discretion of the court, an amount equal to not more than one-half of the fine may be paid to the person giving information leading to conviction.[107]

ii. False Statements Act

One of the MARPOL requirements is that ships must maintain an Oil Record Book in which entries of activities relating to oil discharges are to be entered.[108] The Oil Record Book is subject to inspection by Coast Guard officials.

To prevent foreign-flag vessels from escaping liability in lax enforcement regimes, the United States has successfully used false entries in the Oil Record Book as a basis to prosecute foreign-flag vessels in U.S. courts under the False Statements Act.[109] A violation of the False Statements Act occurs when the captain presents an Oil Record Book that omits an illegal discharge to the Coast Guard. To prove a violation, the following elements must be met: (1) a statement, (2) falsity, (3) materiality, (4) specific intent, and (5) agency jurisdiction.

A federal district court has rejected the argument that if the United States lacks jurisdiction to prosecute under the Act to Prevent Pollution from Ships due to the location of the violation or the flag-state of the vessel, then the United States cannot prosecute under 18 U.S.C. § 1001.[110] The court held that the act of presenting a materially false Oil Record Book to a government agent constitutes a separate, actionable crime under the False Statements Act.[111]

d. Law of the Flag Defense

Although the law of the flag is customary international law recognized within the courts of the United States and the world, it is generally not a defense to U.S. jurisdiction for violations of the Act to Prevent Pollution from Ships violations in U.S. territorial waters by foreign-flag vessels. The law of the flag was explained by the United States Supreme Court in *Lauritzen v. Larsen*:[112]

> The law of the flag supersedes the territorial principle, even for purposes of criminal jurisdiction of personnel of a merchant ship, because . . . [the ship] "is deemed to be a part of the territory of the sovereignty [whose flag it flies], and not to lose that character when in navigable waters within the territorial limits of another sovereignty.

However, courts have held that the law of the flag applies only to jurisdiction over the aboard activities of ships and their personnel.[113] If the pollution occurred within the territorial boundaries of the United States, jurisdiction properly lies with the United States.[114]

D. Refuse Act

1. Background

The Refuse Act was enacted as part of the Rivers and Harbors Act of 1899 and bans the deposit of refuse into navigable waters of the United States.[115] The Refuse Act bans dumping or discharge of any refuse or matter except as permitted by the Secretary of the Army Corps of Engineers (other than that flowing from sewers and streets in a liquid state) into navigable waters or tributaries of navigable waters, and bans placing any material on the bank of a navigable water where the material may be washed into a water body.[116]

2. Enforcement

The Refuse Act provides that knowing or negligent violations are a misdemeanor, punishable by a fine of up to $25,000 per day or by imprisonment for a minimum of thirty days and a maximum of one year.[117] The Refuse Act also permits the court to award one-half of any fines imposed under the Act to the person or persons who provides information leading to conviction.[118] Legislation introduced in 2005 would have increased certain criminal penalties,[119] but the legislation did not pass the House and no further legislation has been introduced.

Because of the Refuse Act's use of a negligence standard, criminal charges have recently become more common in combination with charges for violations of other environmental laws. For example, following the *Exxon Valdez* spill, Exxon Corporation was charged with violating Sections 407 and 411 of the Refuse Act.[120]

III. Emerging and Unresolved Issues

A. Ballast Water Discharge Regulation

1. Background

The Clean Water Act prohibits "discharges of pollutants," which presumably would include ballast water discharges. However, EPA implemented 40 C.F.R. § 122.3(a), which exempts ballast water from the NPDES program and allows for the unregulated discharge of pollutants if the discharge is "incidental to the normal operation of the vessel."

The term "ballast water" refers to the water taken on, from, or discharged into the water body surrounding a vessel to accommodate changes in the vessel's weight and trim as it loads and unloads cargo and/or passengers. Although this is necessary in order to maintain the balance, maneuverability and safety of the vessel, the historic and current methods of ballast water exchange have resulted in "one of the most serious, yet least appreciated, environmental threats of the twenty-first century" due to the tendency of ballast discharges to contain aquatic invasive species.[121]

2. Ballast Water Management to Minimize Invasive Species Introductions

Ballast water management involves the various measures aimed to prevent the invasion of aquatic invasive species into U.S. waters from foreign ports. The most widely used ballast water management method is ballast water exchange, which requires the vessel to release the lower salinity coastal water it brought aboard and replace it with higher salinity water before reaching port. However, this technique is less than completely effective in removing all dangerous organisms because they can either survive any level of salinity or are unable to be pumped out as they settle to the bottom of the residual water during the exchange.[122]

Other methods and options for ballast water management that are being researched and considered are mechanical treatment methods such as filtration and separation; physical treatment methods such as sterilization by ozone, ultraviolet light, electric currents and heat treatment; and chemical treatment methods such as adding biocide, chlorine, or hydrogen peroxide to ballast water to kill organisms.

As described in the following section, the Coast Guard has implemented programs to encourage the installation, testing, and improved technology of ballast water treatment aboard vessels. Aside from the more traditional systems aforementioned, vessel owners can now apply for acceptance of any experimental ballast water treatment systems that they have installed and tested aboard their ships.

3. Statutory and Regulatory Developments

In recent years, the federal government has taken a number of actions to address the issue of ballast water discharge. The enactment of the Nonindigenous Aquatic Nuisance Prevention and Control Act of 1990, or NANPCA,[123] was the first such attempt to address the concern of ballast water and invasive species concern in the United States. It was enacted in response to the invasion of species from ballast water discharge in the Great Lakes region. The NANPCA established a program to control the entry and spread of invasive species in the Great Lakes via the Coast Guard's issuance of voluntary guidelines for ballast water exchange.

In recent years, the federal government has taken a number of actions to address the issue of ballast water discharge.

In 1996, Congress enacted the National Invasive Species Act of 1996.[124] The National Invasive Species Act reauthorized and modified a number of the ballast management programs and provisions identified in the NANPCA and extended the ballast water exchange requirements to include the Hudson River region. It directed the establishment of record keeping, reporting procedures and sampling techniques, and enforced the monitoring of vessels for compliance with the voluntary guidelines issued by the Coast Guard. Despite having significant room for improvement, the regulatory standards developed under these two statutes have demonstrated some success and positive evolution over the past decade.

Of greater importance and impact was the Coast Guard's shift from voluntary ballast water management guidelines to more mandatory regulatory standards. Due to the ineffectiveness of the voluntary guidelines, in 2003 the Coast Guard proposed its "Mandatory Ballast Water Management Program for U.S. Waters," which required a mandatory ballast water management program for all vessels equipped with ballast water tanks that were entering U.S. navigable waters. Requirements for those entering the Great Lakes and Hudson River from outside the EEZ would remain the same.[125]

In 2004, the Coast Guard, under the authority of the NANPCA and the National Invasive Species Act, further established national mandatory ballast water management requirements for vessels equipped with ballast water tanks that are bound for ports or places within the United States.[126] There are three general objectives for vessels operating outside of the EEZ: (1) each vessel must engage in a specific ballast water management practice of either midocean exchange of ballast water (i.e., complete ballast water exchange in an area no less than two hundred nautical miles from any shore); retaining the ballast water onboard; or using a Coast Guard–approved alternative management method to midocean exchange; (2) each vessel must develop and maintain a ballast water management plan that any appropriate ship's officer can understand and follow while serving on that vessel; and (3) vessels that operate within U.S. waters are required to conduct ballast water management practices to minimize the movement of nonindigenous species.[127]

The rulemaking also created penalties for ships headed to the United States that fail to submit a ballast water management reporting form, as well as vessels that fail to comply with mandatory requirements found in 33 C.F.R. part 151. The final rule also broadened the applicability of the reporting and recordkeeping requirements to all vessels bound for ports or places within the United States. The Coast Guard may now impose a civil penalty of up to $27,500 per day or a Class C felony charge against vessels failing to abide by the mandatory ballast water management guidelines.[128]

Furthermore, in 2005, the Coast Guard announced its policy on "Ballast Water Management for Vessels Entering the Great Lakes That Declare No Ballast Onboard."[129] By encouraging vessels to discharge their ballast prior to entering the Great Lakes, the policy seeks to prevent the introduction of aquatic nonindigenous species from vessels entering the Great Lakes and establishes best management practices for residual ballast water and sediment management to be followed by "no ballast onboard" vessels.

Also in 2005, the National Oceanic and Atmospheric Administration (NOAA) and the U.S. Fish and Wildlife Service (FWS) announced the solicitation of proposals to develop a cooperative agreement to establish a ballast water technology research and development facility in the Great Lakes.[130] NOAA projected $950,000 in funds for startup grants, and up to $50,000 in future facilities development. The NOAA Great Lakes Environmental Research Laboratory continues to fund and conduct research regarding invasive species and the development of technologies aimed at limiting the impact of ballast water discharges on the region.[131]

Finally, the National Aquatic Invasive Species Act of 2005 bill was introduced in April 2005 in both the Senate[132] and the House of Representatives[133] to amend the NANPCA, as amended by the National Invasive Species Act, and to reauthorize and reinforce the Acts. The objective behind the bill was to strengthen the current mandatory National Ballast Water Management Programs directed by the U.S. Coast Guard for all ships operating in waters of the United States. The legislation aimed to establish minimum requirements and limitation periods for compliance for all ships. It required that ships meet performance standards issued by the Coast Guard and the EPA by using one of the recommended programs: either the Ballast Water Exchange program, under which ninety-five percent of ballast water should be purged in the high seas, or the Ballast Water Treatment Program, which incorporates environmentally safe treatment to the ballast water. The bill would have also required the U.S. Coast Guard to periodically review and revise, in concurrence with EPA, the ballast water management regulations, including the list of best performing technologies. It also contained provisions to prevent invasive species introductions from other pathways; support state management plans; screen live aquatic organisms intentionally brought into the United States for the very first time commercially; authorize rapid response funds; create education and outreach programs; conduct research on invasion pathways, early detection and prevention and control technologies; and strengthen the Great Lakes current ballast water management program. The bill was referred to the House subcommittee, but neither the House nor the Senate moved it forward.[134]

4. Judicial Developments

The environmental community and others have been pushing for more mandatory and strictly enforced regulation for ballast water discharge that apply to all vessels by repudiating the EPA's exception to the NPDES permit program. This fight to require that all vessels obtain NPDES permits found its way in the federal district court in Northern California in 2003.

In *Northwest Environmental Advocates v. EPA*,[135] plaintiffs brought a challenge to EPA's denial of a petition to rescind the agency's exclusion of ballast water from NPDES requirements and repeal 40 C.F.R. § 122.3(a) because it exceeds EPA's authority under the Clean Water Act.[136]

The district court agreed with the plaintiffs that the regulation exempting vessel discharges was contrary to the plain requirements of the Clean Water Act. The court later granted the plaintiffs' request for injunctive relief and ordered EPA to vacate the regulation (to the extent it provides an exemption for vessel discharges from the Clean Water Act) by September 30, 2008.[137] In so holding, the court emphasized its belief that this timeframe gave EPA sufficient time to promulgate rules that create a general permit or other "flexible approach" towards regulating vessel discharges. The court expressly rejected EPA's request to limit the relief to only ballast water discharges, and, therefore, the case has implications for the other types of vessel discharges discussed herein. EPA has appealed the decision to the Ninth Circuit, but has begun the process of developing a permit program for discharges incidental to the normal operation of vessels.[138] The parties argued the case in August 2007 but, as of the time of publication, the Ninth Circuit had yet to issue a ruling.

B. Cruise Ship Discharges

1. Introduction: The Cruise Ship Problem

The cruise ship industry presents unique environmental issues. There currently are 250 cruise ships worldwide, and both the number and size of cruise ships increase each year, as cruise lines compete to create larger vessels. In 2004, Carnival Corporation, the leading cruise operator, launched the world's largest passenger ship, *Queen Mary 2*, which stretches the length of four football fields. In response, two years later, Carnival's rival, Royal Caribbean, sailed an even larger ship, *Freedom of the Seas*. These megaships come fully equipped with luxurious amenities, such as mall-sized promenades and ice skating rinks, and are said to be the industry's response to the growing demands of the increasing number of passengers.[139] Today, the industry transports approximately ten million passengers per year, seventy percent of whom are handled by the United States. Between 1996 and 2006, the number of North Americans taking cruises increased from five million to ten million, and in the last five years, there has been a forty-seven percent increase in cruise ship passengers worldwide.[140]

The size and growth of the cruise ship industry raises unique environmental concerns. Like all vessels, cruise ships generate many different types of wastes, including blackwater (sewage), graywater (from sinks, showers and laundry), solid waste, and ballast water. Cruise ships also may generate hazardous waste from dry-cleaning, photo processing, and paint. It has been estimated that during a typical one-week voyage, a large cruise ship (carrying 3,000 passengers and crew) is apt to generate 210,000 gallons of sewage, one million gallons of graywater (from sinks, showers, and laundries), over 130 gallons of hazardous wastes, eight tons of solid waste, and 25,000 gallons of oily bilge water.[141] As the size of the industry grows, greater pollution problems are inevitable, and many argue that the measures currently in place are inadequate to regulate cruise ship discharges.

> **During a typical one-week voyage, a large cruise ship is apt to generate 210,000 gallons of sewage.**

In recent years, cruise ships have been attracting the attention of environmental groups and regulators because of both legal and illegal discharges. According to a 2000 report of the General Accounting Office (GAO), cruise ships have been implicated in more than eighty-seven illegal discharge cases between 1993 and 1998.[142] Environmental groups have reported that U.S. cruise lines paid approximately $50 million in fines for illegal dumping between 1995 and 1999, and an additional $25 million between 2000 and 2005.[143] The nature of the offenses giving rise to these fines ranges from oil discharges to the dumping of plastic, garbage, hazardous waste, toxic chemicals, sewage, and ballast water.[144] In one notable case, Carnival Cruise Lines pled guilty to six felony counts and paid $18 million in fines for dumping oil discharges into the waters off Florida and the Caribbean.[145] Another case involved Norwegian Cruise Line, which paid the EPA $1 million in fines in December 1997 after admitting to having lied repeatedly to the Coast Guard for several years about the discharge of its oil-contaminated bilge waste.[146]

Unregulated, but currently legal, cruise ship discharges are drawing attention as well. For example, in August 2003 the *Crystal Harmony*, a luxury cruise liner, disposed of 36,400 gallons of wastewater fourteen miles offshore of Monterey, California.[147] Residents and officials of Monterey were outraged, and the *Crystal Harmony* subsequently was banished from the town, but the discharge was legal because it occurred fourteen miles offshore.[148]

The Monterey incident highlights one of the primary environmental concerns regarding the cruise ship industry—it is insufficiently regulated. This concern prompted a coalition of fifty-three environmental advocacy groups to petition the EPA in 2000 to take regulatory action to address cruise ship discharges.[149]

2. Applicability of Clean Water Act, Refuse Act, and Ocean Dumping Act to Cruise Ship Discharges

Cruise ships are not currently subject to the Clean Water Act's permitting requirement for several reasons.[150] First, NPDES permits are required only for point source discharges of pollutants into "navigable waters," and the term "navigable waters" is defined as waters within three miles of the shore.[151] Thus, discharges from vessels beyond the three-mile limit of territorial seas are exempt from NPDES permit requirements. Furthermore, the statute's definition of "pollutant" specifically excludes the discharge of sewage from vessels.[152] EPA regulations are even broader, exempting both ordinary sewage *and* graywater discharges that are incidental to the operation of a vessel from the NPDES permit requirement.[153]

This means that the Clean Water Act's marine sanitation device requirement does not apply beyond three miles from shore.[154] Similarly, states are unable to establish "no discharge zones" more than three miles from shore.[155]

Other federal statutes that address waste disposal also fall short of covering most cruise ship discharges. For example, the Refuse Act[156] makes the discharge of "refuse" into navigable waters illegal. However, *ordinary* graywater discharges are unlikely to be regulated under the Act because graywater is unlikely to qualify as "refuse."[157] The Ocean Dumping Act[158] applies only to territorial seas, the contiguous zone, and waters of the open ocean, not "navigable waters" within three miles of shore. Moreover, the Ocean Dumping Act does not cover graywater.[159]

At the international level, as discussed above, Annex IV of the International Convention for the Prevention of Pollution from Ships (MARPOL) does regulate sewage discharges from ships. The Annex IV regulations prohibit ships from discharging sewage within four miles of the shoreline, unless they are equipped with an approved treatment plant. The MARPOL treaty also requires sewage to be comminuted and disinfected before being discharged, if discharge occurs within four and twenty-three miles of the shoreline.[160] Annex IV applies to ships on international voyage that enter waters of any of the 110 countries that have ratified the treaty. As noted above, however, the United States does not plan to ratify Annex IV, because Section 312 of the Clean Water Act is regarded as more stringent.[161]

3. Federal Initiatives to Govern Cruise Ship Discharges

a. Federal Legislation Governing Cruise Ship Discharge in Alaska—Title XIV

In 2000, Congress passed Title XIV—Certain Alaskan Cruise Ship Operations to regulate the discharge of blackwater and graywater from cruise ships (carrying more than five hundred passengers) that operate in the Alexander Archipelago and navigable waters of Alaska.[162] This legislation was enacted in response to controversy surrounding allegations that some cruise ships were discharging untreated blackwater and graywater into areas within three miles of the Alaskan shore. The significance of this legislation is that it establishes operational and end-of-pipe requirements for blackwater and graywater discharges into Alaskan waters. It also authorizes the EPA and the Coast Guard to develop regulations for implementing the statute. The Coast Guard has developed regulations that largely restate the requirements of the statute.[163]

b. EPA Survey Regarding Alaska Discharges

In 2004, the EPA published notice of its intent to collect information for developing regulations to control cruise ship discharges of graywater and sewage, pursuant to Title XIV. As part of its information collection efforts, EPA sampled wastewater from four cruise ships operating in Alaska, in order to characterize sewage and graywater generated on the ships, and to evaluate the effectiveness of various advanced treatment systems. EPA also distributed questionnaires to all cruise ships authorized to carry five hundred or more passengers in Alaska, seeking information on sources of graywater and sewage, shipboard plumbing systems, data on the effectiveness of sewage and graywater treatment systems in removing pollutants, and costs of these systems.[164] EPA has stated that it intends to use the responses to the survey, along with the sampling results and other relevant information, to conduct environmental, economic, and engineering analyses to determine the need for, scope, and substance of any additional standards.[165]

c. The Clean Cruise Ship Act

The Clean Cruise Ship Act was introduced in both the Senate and the House of Representatives in 2005.[166] The bill was designed to establish national standards for cruise ship discharges, to remedy the gaps in federal legislation that currently allow certain cruise ship discharges, and to eliminate the discharge of pollutants from sewage and graywater in U.S. waters by 2015. However, the bill was unsuccessful and no efforts have been made to reintroduce the bill, or anything similar, in Congress.[167]

4. State Initiatives to Regulate Cruise Ship Discharges

a. Alaska

Alaska has also enacted statutes and promulgated regulations similar to Title XIV described above.[168] The regulations are enforced by the Coast Guard.[169] The Alaska statute prohibits the discharge of untreated sewage from any commercial passenger vessel in state marine waters.[170] The statute also prohibits the discharge of sewage, graywater, or other waste matter from cruise ships that exceed the discharge limits set by the state.[171] However, the statute does allow large cruise ships to discharge blackwater and graywater in Alaska while under way, and allows for the continuous discharge of blackwater and graywater that meet very stringent requirements, by means of a certification process.[172] Ships approved by the Coast Guard to discharge continuously are also required to submit samples of their wastewater twice per month.[173]

The combined federal and state regulation initiatives in Alaska generally have been hailed as a success; however, some Alaskan environmental groups prepared an initiative for the November 2006 ballot that would require cruise ships to obtain wastewater discharge permits to operate in Alaska.[174] The measure, which also calls for an Ocean Ranger program to ensure compliance with the permit requirement, passed, and in March 2007, the Alaska Department of Environmental Conservation published *Commercial Passenger Vessel Environmental Compliance Program Technical Assistance,*[175] an implementation guidance document for the ballot measure.

b. Washington State

The cruise industry is one of the fastest growing business sectors in the Port of Seattle. In an effort to protect the port's marine environment, Seattle joined forces with the Washington Department of Ecology (the agency responsible for enforcing water quality regulations in the State of Washington) and the Northwest Cruise Ship Association to develop a Memorandum of Understanding on April 20, 2004. This agreement provides protection for Washington's marine waters that are described as the strongest in the industry.[176] However, the Memorandum of Understanding applies only to members of the Northwest Cruise Ship Association, which currently is comprised of nine cruise lines.[177]

The Memorandum of Understanding prohibits the discharge of untreated blackwater and graywater in the waters of Washington State. The discharge of sludge in waters within twelve miles of the shoreline is also prohibited, and the discharge of solid waste is completely banned.[178] Further, only wastewater that has been treated by advanced wastewater treatment systems, capable of removing all bacteria and solids from waste and leaving it nontoxic and harmless to humans, may be discharged.[179]

The Memorandum of Understanding was amended in 2005 by (1) changing the language to clarify that the restrictions placed on wastewater discharges applied to all ports in Washington State, not just Seattle; (2) requiring all ships calling at ports in Washington to file discharge compliance reports with the state's Department of Ecology, even if the ships do not discharge wastewater while in Washington; and (3) adding that all cruise ships subject to the Memorandum of Understanding are also subject to the pollutant limits set in Alaska.[180] Ships also must obtain approval from the Department of Energy before discharging wastewater using an advanced wastewater treatment system.[181]

c. California

The outrage that followed *Crystal Harmony*'s August 2003 wastewater discharge fourteen miles off the coast of Monterey propelled California lawmakers to introduce legislation designed to protect the state's waters.[182] In 2004, California enacted three statutes to regulate cruise ship discharges in the state's waters. One prohibits the discharge of treated waste from cruise ships while in California waters (Assembly Bill

2672). Another bars ships from releasing graywater (Assembly Bill 2093), and the third prohibits the operation of waste incinerators on cruise ships (Assembly Bill 471).[183] Combined, the three bills ban all discharges within three miles of the state's coastline.

In addition, in 2003, the California legislature passed a law banning the discharge of sewage sludge and oil bilge water from cruise ships (Assembly Bill 121). The legislature also enacted a bill prohibiting vessels from discharging hazardous wastes from photo processing and dry-cleaning into the state's waters (Assembly Bill 906).[184]

Unlike Alaska's recent legislation, which requires cruise ships to update their wastewater treatment system to comply with federal effluent standards, the California legislation simply imposes a ban on *all* wastewater, including treated sewage and graywater, within three miles of California's shoreline.[185]

> **The California legislation imposes a ban on *all* wastewater, including treated sewage and graywater, within three miles of California's shoreline.**

d. Maine

Maine enacted legislation to govern discharges of graywater, or any combination of graywater and blackwater, into the state's waters.[186] The statute became effective on January 1, 2006, and it bars ships from entering state waters unless they have advanced wastewater treatment systems and comply with the discharge and reporting requirements set out in Title XIV. Ships also must acquire a permit from the state's Department of Environmental Protection.[187] Additionally, under the statute, the state is required to apply to the EPA for the designation of up to fifty No Discharge Zones, so that Maine may obtain federal authorization to ban blackwater discharges into the state's waters. The law applies only to large cruise ships having overnight accommodations for 250 or more passengers.[188]

e. Florida

In 2001, Florida entered into an agreement with the cruise ship industry through the International Council of Cruise Lines and other related organizations. Under the agreement, cruise ships are prohibited from discharging wastewater within four miles of the Florida Coast, and are required to report the amount of hazardous waste discharged by each ship in the United States on an annual basis.[189] Cruise ships also are required to submit to environmental inspections conducted by the Coast Guard.[190]

5. Voluntary Initiatives Taken by the Cruise Ship Industry

In addition to the statutory and regulatory measures taken by the federal and state governments, described above, the cruise ship industry has taken voluntary steps to reduce the impact from its discharges. In 2001, the International Council of Cruise Lines, which is comprised of fifteen of the world's largest cruise lines, adopted waste management standards for international operations, supplementing regulations of the International Maritime Organization and the EPA.[191] The standards require graywater and blackwater to be discharged only while a ship is under way and at minimum four miles from shore. They also require hazardous waste to be disposed of or recycled in accordance with applicable regulations. In December of 2003 the International Council of Cruise Lines joined forces with the environmental group Conservation International to form the Ocean Conservation and Tourism Alliance, which aims to protect biodiversity in cruise destinations and promote industry practices that minimize the industry's environmental impact.[192]

6. EPA Development of NPDES Permit Program

In June 2007, EPA published a notice of intent and request for comments and information in the *Federal Register*.[193] The agency's decision to undertake this initial gathering of information and program development is in reaction to the district court's decision in *Northwest Environmental Advocates*, in which the court found that the regulatory exemption at 40 C.F.R. § 122.3 exceeds the Agency's statutory authority.[194] The decision could potentially affect all vessels, both commercial and recreational, that have discharges incidental to their normal operation, such as deck runoff and graywater. The court's order will vacate the current regulatory exclusion at 40 C.F.R. § 122.3(a) as of September 30, 2008. EPA notes throughout its *Federal Register* notice that it disagrees with the court's finding and has appealed the ruling to the Ninth Circuit. However, EPA states that "it is prudent to initiate responsive action now rather than await the outcome of that appeal."[195]

Importantly, the 2007 notice does not establish any regulatory requirements. Rather, it is designed to provide the public with early notice of EPA's intent to begin the development of NPDES permits for discharges incidental to the normal operation of vessels, to provide an explanation of the *Northwest Environmental Advocates* opinion, to describe the status of that litigation,[196] and to request comments and technical input on matters associated with the development of such permits.[197]

IV. Conclusion

The regulation of ocean dumping and discharges creates domestic and international regulatory challenges. As science develops further regarding the condition of the world's oceans, the existing programs will need to respond, and new approaches to governance probably will be needed. Ultimately, and particularly due to the increasing public scrutiny being applied to this issue, the statutes, regulations, and other guidance addressing ocean dumping and discharges could change significantly in the not-too-distant future.

Notes

1. M. Collie & J. Russo, *NOAA's Underwater Research Program—In the Spotlight: Deep-Sea Biodiversity and the Impacts of Ocean Dumping* (June 30, 2000), http://www.nurp.noaa.gov/Spotlight/OceanDumping.htm (world population is forecasted to double from five billion to ten billion in the next century).

2. *Id.*; MarineBio, *Ocean Dumping Grounds*, http://marinebio.org/Oceans/OceanDumping
   .asp.
3. In fact, there is a growing movement in the scientific community advocating for an overhaul of international ocean governance to ensure that policies reflect science and are less
   reactionary and more precautionary. *See, e.g.*, L. B. Crowder et al., *Resolving Mismatches
   in U.S. Ocean Governance*, 313(5787) SCIENCE 617–18 (Aug. 4, 2006) (urging a zoning
   regulatory approach to ocean use and the overhaul and coordination of regulatory programs); Collie & Russo, *supra* note 1.
4. UNEP's UN-Oceans is an interagency coordination entity focusing on ocean and coastal issues. More information is available through the UN-Oceans Web site, http://www
   .oceansatlas.org/www.un-oceans.org/Index.htm.
5. *See, e.g.*, UN-Oceans, http://www.oceansatlas.org/www.un-oceans.org.
6. *See, e.g.*, WASH. REV. CODE § 77.120; MD. CODE. ANN. [Nat. Res.] tit. 8, subtit. 7.
7. 72 Fed. Reg. 34,241 (June 21, 2007).
8. 33 U.S.C. §§ 1251–1387.
9. *Id.* § 1251.
10. *Id.* § 1311(a).
11. *Id.* § 1362(12).
12. *Id.* §§ 1362(7), (8).
13. *Id.* § 1362(9); Contiguous Zone of the United States, Proclamation No. 7219, 64 Fed.
    Reg. 48,701 (Aug. 2, 1999).
14. *Id.* § 1362(10); *see also* Proclamation No. 5030, 48 Fed. Reg. 10,605 (Mar. 10, 1983)
    (declaring the two-hundred-mile zone an Exclusive Economic Zone (EEZ) for all pur-
    poses, stating that within the EEZ, the United States, to the extent permitted by interna-
    tional law, held "sovereign rights for the purpose of exploring, exploiting, conserving and
    managing natural resources"); Wash. State Charterboat Ass'n v. Baldrige, 702 F.2d 820,
    824–25 (9th Cir. 1983), *cert. denied*, 464 U.S. 1053 (1984) (noting that the Magnuson-
    Stevens Fishery Conservation and Management Act extended an exclusive fisheries zone
    of the United States from twelve to two hundred miles off the coast and provided for
    management of fishing within the two-hundred-mile zone); H.R. REP. No. 94-445, at 21
    (1975), *as reprinted in* 1976 U.S.C.C.A.N. 593, 593–94.
15. *See* Chevron U.S.A., Inc. v. Hammond, 726 F.2d 483, 489 (9th Cir. 1984), *cert. denied*,
    471 U.S. 1140 (1985) ("The federal marine environmental protection scheme establishes
    a three-mile demarcation for states' authority over ocean pollution, and for most pur-
    poses—including pollution from vessels—the CWA applies only to the ocean within three
    miles of shore.").
16. 33 U.S.C. § 1342(a)(1). Most states are authorized to implement NPDES permitting pro-
    grams in lieu of the EPA. *Id.* § 1342(b). Given the Act's definition of "navigable waters"
    at 33 U.S.C. 1362(7), however, a state has NPDES permitting authority only within three
    miles of its coast.
17. *Id.* § 1362(6).
18. *Id.*
19. 40 C.F.R. § 122.3(a).
20. *Id.*
21. These developments are discussed in detail in Section III.A.4 below. EPA's Notice of Intent
    is available at 72 Fed. Reg. 34,241 (June 21, 2007).
22. Congress added the definition of "discharge incidental to the normal operation of a vessel
    to Clean Water Act section 312" in 1996. It works in concert with a change to the statu-
    tory definition of pollutant (discussed above) to exempt a variety of military vessel dis-
    charges (including graywater) from the Clean Water Act's permitting requirements.
23. 33 U.S.C. § 1362(6).
24. 40 C.F.R. § 122.3(a).
25. In dicta, the Ninth Circuit Court of Appeals stated: "Sewage from vessels is one of two
    specific exemptions from the permit system of the Clean Water Act. 33 U.S.C. § 1362(6).

Sewage from vessels is exclusively regulated under 33 U.S.C. § 1322." *Chevron U.S.A., Inc. v. Hammond, supra* note 15, 726 F.2d at 493 n.13.

26. 33 U.S.C. § 1322(b)(1); 40 C.F.R. § 122.2 (Sewage from vessels is defined as: "human body wastes and the wastes from toilets and other receptacles intended to receive or retain body wastes that are discharged from vessels and *regulated* under Section 312 of [the Clean Water Act]. . . .") (emphasis added).

27. *Id.* § 1322(b)(l), (k).

28. The precise requirements for any vessel would depend on when the vessel was built, whether it had an existing marine sanitation device, and in certain cases whether the vessel is operated in a "no discharge" zone. *See* 40 C.F.R. § 140.3 (EPA); 33 C.F.R. § 159.7(a)–(c) (Coast Guard).

29. 33 C.F.R. § 159.3; *see also id.* § 159.53(b).

30. *Id.* § 159.53(b).

31. 33 U.S.C. § 1362(6).

32. 40 C.F.R. § 122.3(a).

33. Nw. Envtl. Advocates v. U.S. EPA, 2006 WL 2669042 (N.D. Cal. 2006).

34. 33 U.S.C. § 1343(c).

35. 40 C.F.R. § 125.122.

36. *Id.* § 125.123.

37. 33 U.S.C. § 1319; 28 U.S.C § 2461 note; 40 C.F.R. § 19.4.

38. *See* David L. Markell, *The Role of Deterrence-Based Enforcement in a "Reinvented" State/Federal Relationship: The Divide Between Theory and Reality,* 33 Harv. Envtl. L. Rev. 1, 32 (2000) (citing state officials for statement that eighty to ninety percent of all enforcement actions are taken by states).

39. 33 U.S.C. § 1319(a)(1).

40. *Id.* § 1319(c)(1); 28 U.S.C. § 2461.

41. United States v. Hanousek, 176 F.3d 1116, 1120–22 (9th Cir. 1999) (holding that the use of an ordinary negligence standard does not violate due process because violation of the Clean Water Act is a public welfare offense and because the defendant knew the facts that would alert a person to the probability of strict regulation).

42. *Id.*

43. *Id.* § 1319(c)(2); 28 U.S.C. § 2461.

44. *See, e.g.,* United States v. Weitzenhoff, 35 F.3d 1275 (9th Cir. 1993), *cert. denied,* 513 U.S. 1128 (1995).

45. *See, e.g.,* United States v. Wilson, 133 F.3d 251 (4th Cir. 1997) (holding that government must prove defendant's knowledge of (1) discharging a substance, (2) "the method of instrumentality" used to discharge it, and (3) lack of permit, and distinguishing such knowledge of permit status from knowledge that permit is required); United States v. Ahmad, 101 F.3d 386 (5th Cir. 1996) (holding that the government was required to establish "knowledge" for each element of the Clean Water Act offense, and reversing defendant's conviction because the defendant claimed that he thought he was discharging water, not gasoline).

46. *See, e.g.,* United States v. Jewell, 532 F.2d 697 (9th Cir. 1976) (en banc).

47. *See, e.g.,* United States v. Pac. Hide & Fur Depot, 768 F.2d 1096, 1098–99 (9th Cir. 1985) (to prove willful blindness, the government must present evidence indicating that defendant purposely contrived to have a defense in the event of subsequent prosecution); United States v. Wasserson, 418 F.3d 225 (3d Cir. 2005) (willful blindness as to handling of hazardous waste sufficient for conviction on aiding and abetting theory under the Resource Conservation and Recovery Act, 42 U.S.C. § 6923 (d)(2)(A) ("knowing" standard)); United States v. Hopkins, 53 F.3d 533, 542 (2d Cir. 1995) (finding "conscious-avoidance" jury instruction appropriate for proving the mental state of "knowingly" under 33 U.S.C. § 1319(c)(4)), *cert. denied,* 516 U.S. 1072 (1996).

48. United States v. Bank of New England, 821 F.2d 844, 856 (1st Cir. 1987).

49. 33 U.S.C. § 1365.

50. Natural Res. Def. Council v. Sw. Marine, Inc., 236 F.3d 985 (9th Cir. 2000).

51. 33 U.S.C. § 1402(b).

52. *Id.* § 1411(a).

53. *Id.* § 1414b(a)(1)(B),(2).

54. *Id.* § 1402(b)–(c),(e).

55. *Id.* § 1402(f).

56. *Id.* § 1402(c).

57. *See* Seaburn Inc. v. EPA, 712 F. Supp. 218, 218 (D.D.C. 1989).

58. 33 U.S.C. §§ 2501 *et seq.*

59. *Id.* § 2501(1). "Public vessel" is defined as any type of vessel (including hydrofoils, air-cushion vehicles, submersibles, floating craft whether propelled or not, and fixed or floating platforms) that is owned or demise chartered and operated by the United States Government, and is not engaged in commercial service. *Id.* § 2502(2). Public vessels are prohibited from disposing of potentially infectious medical waste into ocean waters except in certain limited circumstances, including: if the health or safety of individuals on board the vessel is threatened; during war or a declared national emergency; or if the disposal occurs more than fifty nautical miles from the nearest land and is sterilized, properly packaged, and sufficiently weighted to prevent the waste from washing ashore. *Id.* § 2503.

60. *Seaburn,* 712 F. Supp. at 219.

61. *Id.*

62. 40 C.F.R. § 227.16(a)(1),(2).

63. *Id.*

64. 33 U.S.C. § 1413(b).

65. *Convention on the Prevention of Marine Pollution by Dumping Wastes and Other Matters (London Convention),* Dec. 29, 1972, arts. I–II, 26 U.S.T. 2403, 2406–07, 1046 U.N.T.S. 120 (entered into force on Aug. 30, 1975).

66. *Id.* at art. IV.

67. 33 U.S.C. § 1415(g)(1).

68. Town of Huntington v. Marsh, 884 F.2d 648, 654 (2d Cir. 1989).

69. 33 U.S.C. § 1414b(d)(1).

70. *Id.* § 1415(a); 40 C.F.R. § 19.4; 28 U.S.C. § 2461.

71. 33 U.S.C. § 1415(b).

72. *Id.* § 1415(e).

73. *Id.*

74. 33 U.S.C. § 1415(g)(1).

75. *Id.* § 1415(g)(2).

76. *See* Article VII, sec. 3.

77. 33 U.S.C. § 1402(b).

78. The "high seas" consist of those areas outside of a nations territorial seas "which are international waters not subject to the dominion of any single nation," with the territorial seas being those within twelve miles of shore. United States v. Louisiana, 394 U.S. 11, 22–23 (1969); *In re* Crash off Long Island, New York, on July 17, 1996, 209 F.3d 200, 205–06 (2d Cir. 2000).

79. 33 U.S.C. § 1419.

80. 33 U.S.C. §§ 1901 *et seq.*

81. *Reprinted in* 12 I.L.M. 1319 (1973).

82. *Reprinted in* 17 I.L.M. 546 (1978).

83. MARPOL 73, Preface, at 1319.

84. Andrew Griffin, *MARPOL 73/78 and Vessel Pollution: A Glass Half Full or Half Empty,* 1 IND. J. GLOBAL LEGAL STUD. 489, 503 (1994).

85. *See* International Maritime Organization, *Summary of Conventions as at 31 May 2007,* http://www.imo.org/conventions/mainframe.asp?topic_id=247 (accessed July 19, 2007) [hereinafter IMO Web site].

86. *See* MARPOL 73/78, art. 2(3)(b) (excluding "dumping" from the definition of "discharge").

87. *See* 33 C.F.R. §§ 151.25, .51–.57, .66–.73.
88. Annex V deals with different types of garbage and specifies the distances from land and the manner in which they may be disposed of. Annex V includes a complete ban on the dumping of all forms of plastic. *See* MARPOL 73/78, Annex V.
89. Annex III applies to "harmful substances" in packaged forms, or in freight tankers, portable tanks, or road and rail tank wagons. *See* MARPOL 73/78, Annex III, Reg. 1. Annex III requires countries to issue detailed requirements on things such as marking, packaging, and labeling such substances. "Harmful substance" means "any substance which, if introduced into the sea, is liable to create hazards to human health, to harm living resources and marine life, to damage amenities or to interfere with other legitimate uses of the sea, and includes any substance subject to control" by MARPOL 73/78. MARPOL 73/78, art.2. Annex III is actually implemented in the United States through the Hazardous Materials Transportation Act, 49 U.S.C. §§ 5101 *et seq.*
90. *See* IMO Web site, *supra* note 85.
91. *Id.*
92. *See* Title II, Plastic Pollution Research and Control, Pub. L. 100-220. For a detailed discussion of the regulation of plastics and other forms of marine debris, *see* Baur and Iudicello, *Stemming the Tide of Marine Debris Pollution: Putting Domestic and International Control Authorities to Work*, 17 ECOLOGY L.Q. 71 (1990).
93. 33 U.S.C. §§ 1901–1915.
94. *Id.* § 1902.
95. *Id.*
96. 33 C.F.R. §§ 151.66–.73.
97. *Id.* §§ 151.51–.59 (2006).
98. 33 U.S.C. § 1905; 33 C.F.R. §§ 158.100 *et seq.*
99. *See id.* § 1907(c)(2); MARPOL, Article 6(4).
100. 33 U.S.C. § 1907(b).
101. *See id.* §§ 1902(a), 1907(c); MARPOL, Article 9.3.
102. 33 U.S.C. § 1907(c)(2); MARPOL, Article 6(2).
103. 33 C.F.R. § 151.04(a).
104. *Id.* § 151.04(b); 28 U.S.C. § 2461.
105. 33 U.S.C. § 1908(d).
106. *Id.* § 1908(a); *See* 18 U.S.C. §§ 3551 *et seq.*
107. 33 U.S.C. § 1908 (a); 33 C.F.R. § 151.04(c).
108. *See* MARPOL Regulation 20 of Annex 1.
109. 18 U.S.C. § 1001.
110. United States v. Royal Caribbean Cruises Ltd., 11 F. Supp. 2d 1358, 1363 (S.D. Fla. 1998).
111. *Id.* at 1368.
112. Lauritzen v. Larsen, 345 U.S. 571, 584 (1953).
113. United States v. Royal Caribbean Cruises Ltd., 24 F. Supp. 2d 155, 160 (D.P.R. 1997).
114. *Id.*
115. 33 U.S.C. §§ 411 *et seq.*
116. *Id.* § 407.
117. *Id.* § 411.
118. *Id.*
119. H.R. 757, 109th Cong. (2005).
120. *In re* the Exxon Valdez, 296 F. Supp. 2d 1071 (D. Alaska 2004).
121. United States General Accounting Office, *Invasive Species: Obstacles Hinder Federal Rapid Response to Growing Threat* (July 2001).
122. *See generally* Eugene H. Buck, *Ballast Water Management to Combat Invasive Species*, Congressional Research Service Report for Congress (Apr. 8, 2004) [hereinafter CRS Report].
123. 16 U.S.C. § 4701.

124. Pub. L. No. 104-332 (NISA).

125. 68 Fed. Reg. 44,691 (July 30, 2003).

126. *Id.* at 32,864 (June 14, 2004); 33 C.F.R. § 151.2035.

127. 33 C.F.R. § 151.2035.

128. 68 Fed. Reg. 32,864 (June 14, 2004).

129. 70 Fed. Reg. 51,831 (Aug. 31, 2005).

130. *Id.* at 37,766 (June 30, 2005).

131. *See generally* NOAA, *Aquatic Invasive Species,* http://www.glerl.noaa.gov/res/Programs/ais/.

132. S. 770, 109th Cong. (2005).

133. H.R. 1591, 109th Cong. (2005).

134. The issue continues to reappear, however, as the Great Lakes Collaboration Implementation Act of 2006, H.R. 5100, 109th Cong. (2006), S. 2545, 109th Cong. (2006), and most recently as the Great Lakes Collaboration Implementation Act of 2007, S. 791, 110th Cong. (2007).

135. 2005 WL 756614 (N.D. Cal. 2005).

136. *Id.*

137. Northwest Envtl. Advocates v. EPA, 2006 WL 2669042 (N.D. Cal. 2006).

138. 72 Fed. Reg. 34,241 (June 21, 2007).

139. John Pain, *Bigger Cruise Ships Causing Some Trouble,* ASSOCIATED PRESS, Aug. 19, 2005.

140. Bluewater Network, *Cruise Ships: More Ships, More Passenger, More Pollution,* 2006, *available at* http://www.bluewaternetwork.org/reports/cv/Cruiseship_MiniReport_06.pdf [hereinafter *Cruise Ships*].

141. *Id.* at 2.

142. U.S. General Accounting Office, *Marine Pollution: Progress Made to Reduce Marine Pollution by Cruise Ships, but Important Issues Remain,* GAO, Washington, D.C., GAO/RCED-00-48, Feb. 2000. 70 pp, http://www.epa.gov/owow/oceans/cruise_ships/gaofeb00.pdf.

143. *Cruise Ships, supra* note 140, at 1.

144. *Id.*

145. KAHEA, *Our Ocean is Not a Dump,* at 6, http://www.kahea.org/ocean/Cruise_Ship_Brochure.pdf.

146. *Id.*

147. Kenneth Weiss, *Cruise Line Pollution Prompts Legislation,* L.A. TIMES, Aug. 18, 2003.

148. As noted above, the Clean Water Act only regulates discharges within three miles from the shoreline. *See* CRS Report, *supra* note 122, at 9.

149. Bluewater Network, Petition to the Administrator, U.S. Environmental Protection Agency, Mar. 17, 2000.

150. *Id.*

151. 33 U.S.C. §§ 1362(7), (8).

152. *Id.* § 1362(6).

153. 40 C.F.R. § 122.3 (a). As noted above, recent EPA actions in response to *Northwest Envtl. Advocates v. EPA,* 2006 WL 2669042 (N.D. Cal. 2006), indicate that permitting requirements may soon tighten.

154. As discussed above, the Clean Water Act requires cruise ships with installed toilets to have marine sanitation devices, which are used to prevent the discharge of untreated sewage. CRS Report, *supra* note 122, at 9.

155. Under that section, within three miles from shore, states may establish "no-discharge zones" to prevent the discharge of both treated and untreated sewage from ships into either a portion, or all, of the water over which they have jurisdiction. To create a no-discharge zone, a state must apply to the EPA under one of three categories. The first is based on a need for greater environmental protection. For this category, states have to demonstrate that they have adequate and readily available pumpout facilities to

accommodate the sanitary removal and treatment of sewage from ships. The second category is for special waters, found to have significant environmental importance (for example, sensitive areas, such as coral reefs or shellfish beds). For this category, states need not show pumpout availability. Examples of no-discharge zones in this group include the Florida Keys National Marine Sanctuary and the Boundary Waters Canoe area in Minnesota. Finally, the third category is for barring the discharge of sewage into waters designated as drinking water intake zones. As in the second category, states do not have to demonstrate pumpout availability. An example of such a designated zone is a portion of the Hudson River in New York. *Id.* at 10.

156. 33 U.S.C. §§ 401 *et seq.*

157. 33 U.S.C. § 407.

158. 33 U.S.C. §§ 1401 *et seq.*

159. Similarly, graywater discharges are not governed by the corresponding international treaty, the Convention on Prevention of Marine Pollution by Dumping of Wastes and Other Matter, Dec. 29, 1972, 26 U.S.T. 2403, 1046, U.N.T.S. 120 (London Dumping Act). *See* Aaron Courtney, Eric Fjelstad & Sloane Anders Wildman, *Multijurisdictional Regulation of Cruise Ship Discharges,* NAT. RES. & ENV'T, Summer 2004, at 50, 51.

160. *Id.* at 53.

161. CRS Report, *supra* note 122, at 10.

162. Pub. L. No. 106-554, 114 Stat. 2763.

163. 66 Fed. Reg. 38,926, 33 C.F.R. §§ 159.300–.321.

164. EPA, Sewage and Gray Water Standards Development, www.epa.gov/owow/oceans/cruise_ships/sewage_gray.html.

165. *Id.*

166. S. 793, 109th Cong. (2005); H.R. 1636, 109th Cong. (2005).

167. *Id.*

168. *See* ALASKA STAT. §§ 46.03.460–.490; 18 ALASKA ADMIN. CODE tit. 18, § 69 (2002).

169. State Environmental Resource Center, *Innovative State Legislation: Cruise Ship Pollution,* June 3, 2004, http://www.serconline.org/cruiseShipPollution.html.

170. ALASKA STAT. § 46.03.463 (a).

171. ALASKA STAT. § 46.03.463 (b)–(d).

172. *State News in Brief: Washington Cruise Ship Agreement Amended,* 36 ENV'T REP. (BNA) 28 (July 15, 2005), at 9.

173. *Id.*

174. *Id.*

175. Alaska Department of Environmental Conservation. *Commercial Passenger Vessel Environmental Compliance Program Technical Assistance* (Mar. 7, 2007), *available at* http://www.dec.state.ak.us/water/cruise_ships/pdfs/ADEC%20Report_OR_implementation_7Marchl.pdf.

176. Port of Seattle, *Environmental Practices* (Feb. 9, 2006), *available at* http://www.portseattle.org/downloads/seaport/WACruise%20MOUFinal.pdf. The Memorandum of Understanding can be found at http://www.ecy.wa.gov/programs/wq/wastewater/cruise_mou/index.html.

177. Washington State Department of Ecology, *2005 Assessment of Cruise Ship Environmental Effects in Washington,* Pub. No. 06-10-003 (Jan. 2006), at 4 [hereinafter *2005 Assessment*].

178. *Id.* at 9.

179. *Id.*

180. The MOU was most recently amended in May 2007, and is available at http://www.ecy.wa.gov/programs/wq/wastewater/cruise_mou/MOU%203rd%20Amendment%205-25-07%20final.pdf.

181. 2005 Assessment, *supra* note 177.

182. *Id.*

183. *Id.*

184. CRS Report, *supra* note 122, at 18.
185. *Id.*
186. Maine LD. 1158; CRS Report, *supra* note 122, at 18.
187. *Id.*
188. *Id.*
189. The 2001 MOU can be found at http://www.dep.state.fl.us/legal/Operating_Agreement/
    agreements/Cruise%20Line/cruiselineMOU12-06-01.pdf.
190. *Id.*
191. CRS Report, *supra* note 122, at 19.
192. *Id.*
193. EPA, *Notice of Intent; Request for Comments and Information. Development of Clean
    Water Act National Pollutant Discharge Elimination System Permits for Discharges Inci-
    dental to the Normal Operation of Vessels.*
194. Northwest Envtl. Advocates v. U.S. EPA, 2006 WL 2669042 (N.D. Cal. 2006).
195. 72 Fed. Reg. 34,241 (June 21, 2007).
196. The notices states that "[b]ecause the Government respectfully disagrees with the District
    Court's decision, on November 16, 2006, we filed an appeal in the U.S. Court of Appeals
    for the Ninth Circuit. Oral argument is expected in mid-August of 2007." 72 Fed. Reg.
    34,241, 34,244 (June 21, 2007).
197. 72 Fed. Reg. 34,241, 34,245 (June 21, 2007).

chapter nine

Domestic Fishery Management

Josh Eagle

I. Introduction

The purpose of this chapter is to explain how the federal government manages fisheries within U.S. marine waters.[1] The chapter is divided into three parts. The first part lays out the jurisdictional boundaries of federal authority over ocean fishing.[2] The second part of the chapter focuses on the nation's most important federal fishery management law,[3] the Magnuson-Stevens Fishery Conservation and Management Act,[4] and on the institutions responsible for implementing it, the National Marine Fisheries Service (NMFS),[5] and the Regional Fishery Management Councils (councils). The last section highlights some recent court decisions interpreting key provisions of the Magnuson-Stevens Act.

II. Federal Authority

As a general rule, the federal government has sole responsibility for managing those fishing activities that take place from three to two hundred miles from the coasts of the United States. This rule—the exceptions to which are discussed below—is a product of two historical legal developments. In 1953, Congress enacted a statute giving coastal states authority to regulate fishing activities within three miles from shore.[6] At

The author wishes to thank Mike Sutton and Sarah Chasis for their helpful comments and insights.

that time, the three-mile line defined the extent of the United States' fishery jurisdiction under international law.[7] In 1976, Congress passed the law that is now known as the Magnuson-Stevens Act.[8] The Act established a Fishery Conservation Zone stretching from the shores of the United States to a distance of two hundred miles as well as a set of rules and institutions for managing fishing activities within that zone.[9] In 1983, President Reagan formalized the United States' claim to sovereign rights over living marine resources within two hundred miles from shore through a Presidential Proclamation.[10] This proclamation mirrored the rights given coastal nations under Part VI of the United Nations Convention on the Law of the Sea.[11]

While the general rule is that the federal government, acting through NMFS, manages fishing activities within the three- to two-hundred-mile area ("federal waters"), there are many qualifications to this rule.

A. Federal Management Authority over Fisheries in State Waters

There are a multitude of ways in which the federal government can exercise authority over fishing activities that take place within three miles of shore (within "state waters"). First, Congress has, and absent a constitutional amendment always will have, the power to repeal or modify the Submerged Lands Act. Second, Congress can preempt state fishery management law through specific federal laws. Thus, for example, the Magnuson-Stevens Act provides that if a fishery "covered by a fishery management plan implemented under this Act . . . is engaged in predominately within" federal waters, and that state management of that fishery in state waters "will substantially and adversely affect the carrying out of such fishery management plan," then NMFS may exercise regulatory authority over fishing activities in state waters.[12] Other examples of federal statutes that limit state authority within state waters include the Marine Mammal Protection Act,[13] the Endangered Species Act,[14] the Clean Water Act,[15] and the Atlantic Coastal Fisheries Cooperative Management Act.[16]

In addition to these statutory limits, federal obligations to Indian tribes pursuant to treaties between the federal government and tribes also limit state power within state waters. So, for example, in *United States v. Washington*,[17] the court held that treaty rights granted to fourteen tribes under the so-called "Stevens treaties" limited the kinds of fishery regulation the State of Washington could lawfully impose on those tribes.[18]

B. State Management Authority over Fisheries in Federal Waters

While all state management authority is ultimately subject to preemption, states can exercise some degree of control over fishing activities in federal waters. Some of the states' power to regulate such activities is rooted in federal law.

Under the Magnuson-Stevens Act, for example, states may regulate a vessel's fishing activities outside state waters if

(A) The fishing vessel is registered under the law of that State, and

(i) there is no fishery management plan or other applicable Federal fishing regulations for the fishery in which the vessel is operating; or

(ii) the State's laws and regulations are consistent with the fishery management plan and applicable Federal fishing regulations for the fishery in which the vessel is operating;

or

(B) The fishery management plan for the fishery in which the fishing vessel is operating delegates management of the fishery to a State and the State's laws and regulations are consistent with such fishery management plan.[19]

Under the Coastal Zone Management Act, there are administrative and judicial procedures available to a coastal state convinced that proposed federal, or federally permitted, activities will "affect[] any land or water use or natural resource" in a way that it is inconsistent with the "enforceable policies" of a state's coastal zone management plan.[20] Although these procedures apply to fishing permitted under a federal fishery management plan,[21] there are no reported court decisions along these lines.[22]

Under the aforementioned Atlantic Coastal Fisheries Cooperative Management Act, fishery management plans developed by the Atlantic States Marine Fisheries Commission,[23] an interstate body, may cover fishing in federal waters.[24]

In addition to these direct federal grants of power to the states, states may, where not preempted by federal law, regulate fishing activities that take place beyond state waters by regulating landings.[25] For example, a state could effectively prohibit the use of particular fishing gear in federal waters through a ban on landing fish at its ports caught with that gear.

C. International Law Limits on Federal Management Authority over Fisheries in Federal Waters

Although the United States is not a party to the United Nations Convention on the Law of the Sea, its claims of jurisdictional benefits consistent with that treaty, e.g., a Territorial Sea and an Exclusive Economic Zone, probably mean that it is also responsible for obligations arising under the treaty.[26] Thus, domestic fishery management should be consistent with, for example, the provisions of Articles 61 and 62 in the Law of the Sea regarding management and utilization of living marine resources.[27]

In addition, the United States is a party to a number of other fishing treaties and "soft law" agreements, such as the International Convention for the Conservation of Atlantic Tuna[28] and the FAO Code of Conduct for Responsible Fisheries.[29] These agreements impose both restrictions and affirmative duties on the United States in its management of domestic fisheries.

III. The Council Realm and the Condition of Domestic Fisheries

At the center of Congress's approach to domestic fisheries management are eight Regional Fishery Management Councils, each of which is responsible for managing fisheries within a sizable fraction of federal waters.[30] The size of the area managed by each council varies. The Western Pacific Fishery Management Council has the largest spatial jurisdiction, covering nearly 1.5 million square miles, while the North Pacific Council manages an area of about 900,000 square miles.[31] Some of the councils manage only a few hundred thousand square miles.[32]

The number of members on each council varies as well, although the numerical size of each council is not proportional to the size of the area it manages.[33] Rather, it is based on the number of states and U.S. territories bordering the managed area.[34] Thus, the largest council in terms of membership is the Mid-Atlantic Council, with twenty-one voting members; the Caribbean Council has only seven.[35]

The voting membership of each council is comprised of two groups. The first group consists of what are known as "mandatory" members.[36] These are state and federal officials: the head of each coastal state or territory's marine fisheries agency and the NOAA Regional Administrator from that region of the country.[37] The second group of voting members is comprised of "appointed" members.[38] These members are citizens who have been nominated by coastal state governors and then appointed to the council by the Secretary of Commerce.[39] Traditionally, governors draw heavily from fishing or fishing-related industries in nominating citizens for council membership.[40] Over the past twenty years, industry representatives have filled, on average, about eighty percent of appointed seats.[41] Each council also has a number of nonvoting members, including representatives of the Coast Guard, the State Department, and the United States Fish and Wildlife Service.[42]

The Magnuson-Stevens Act requires each council to establish two advisory committees: a scientific and statistical committee "to assist it in the development, collection, evaluation, and peer review of such statistical, biological, economic, social, and other scientific information as is relevant,"[43] and a fishing industry advisory committee to "provide information and recommendations on, and assist in the development of, fishery management plans and amendments to such plans."[44]

Under the provisions of the Magnuson-Stevens Act, the councils have discretion to decide which fisheries within their respective jurisdictions need "conservation and management."[45] Until a council makes such a determination regarding a particular fishery, the fishery is not subject to federal regulation, and may not be subject to any regulation at all.[46]

Once a council makes the determination that management is needed, the Act requires it to develop a Fishery Management Plan (FMP).[47] Discussed in greater detail below, FMPs must establish "management measures necessary and appropriate . . . to prevent overfishing and rebuild overfished stocks, and to protect, restore and promote the long-term health and stability of the fishery.[48]

Currently, the councils together manage nearly seven hundred distinct populations, or stocks, of fish under forty-five Fishery Management Plans.[49] NMFS classifies 252 of these 700 fish stocks as "major" stocks; taken together these 252 major stocks account for about ninety-nine percent of all commercially caught fish landed at U.S. ports each year.[50]

According to NMFS's 2004 fisheries status report, the councils' success in managing both major and minor stocks is mixed. The report indicates that about twenty percent of major stocks—and twenty-eight percent of all stocks—could be classified as "overfished," that is, below a "prescribed biomass threshold."[51] It also reveals that twenty-one percent of major stocks—and nineteen percent of all stocks—could be characterized as being in a state of "overfishing," that is subject to "harvesting at a rate above a prescribed fishing mortality threshold."[52]

About twenty percent of major stocks—and twenty-eight percent of all stocks—could be classified as "overfished."

The NMFS report does not provide information on the economic and ecological ramifications of these facts: How many more fishing jobs would be provided if all stocks were in healthy condition? How much less would consumers have to pay for seafood if fish were more plentiful? What are the impacts of too much fishing on other important components of ocean ecosystems and those systems as a whole? There have been some recent efforts in the scientific community to answer the latter question.[53] The conclusion of those studies is that the impacts have been dramatic and strongly negative. As to the question of economic impacts, a 1999 NOAA study indicated that U.S. landings were at that time about thirty to forty percent less than could be produced by healthy fisheries.[54] These unnecessary shortfalls reduce the number of potentially available fishing jobs and increase the cost of fish for consumers.

The reports of the United States Commission on Ocean Policy and the Pew Oceans Commission have opened the question of ocean governance reform.[55] In this context, accurate assessments of council performance are particularly important. Unfortunately, the annual NMFS status report is at best a crude tool for measuring the performance of the council system.

First, the report indicates that NMFS lacks sufficient information to assess the population status of more than half the species under council management.[56] The percentage of "unknown" major stocks is lower (about twenty percent), but still large enough to warrant concern, given the importance of these species.[57]

Moreover, there are significant problems with the methodology and data used to determine how many of the "known" stocks are overfished or subject to overfishing. First, the great bulk of the data used are derived from fishery landings and not from independent scientific investigations.[58] Data collected in this way are characterized by a variety of infirmities, from collection biases to reporting problems.[59] Second, the councils themselves are responsible for writing the criteria by which management "success" is measured.[60] Whether or not a particular species appears as "overfished" or "not overfished" in NMFS's "Status of United States Fisheries" report depends in large part on the technical definition of "overfished" adopted for that species by the relevant council.[61]

Perhaps the most significant problem in evaluating the council system through the status reports is that the "overfished" and "overfishing" criteria provide a very limited perspective on management "success" or "failure." Taking a broader view of the proper role of fisheries management institutions, other possible criteria would include economic measures of success (whether a fishery is being managed optimally, taking into account the costs of fishing effort) and ecological measures (whether a fishery is being conducted in a manner consistent with a healthy ocean ecosystem).

A. Implementing the Magnuson-Stevens Act

Using these kinds of additional criteria would be more consistent with the goals expressed in the current version of the Magnuson-Stevens Act. This section will spell out the goals of the Act, the management tools available to the councils in attempting to carry out those goals, and the procedures that the councils must follow in writing FMPs and implementing regulations.

1. The Substance of Management

In its original form, the Magnuson-Stevens Act was primarily an industry-regulation law.[62] In other words, it was less focused on achieving harmony between the fishing industry and the marine environment than it was on ensuring that fish stocks continued to provide business opportunities for the fishing industry.[63] To this end, the original Act allowed the councils a great deal of discretion in order to meet the short-term needs of the industry.[64] For example, while it limited catches to "optimum" levels, it defined those as the "maximum sustainable yield from the fishery, as modified by any relevant social, economic, or ecological factor."[65] The "as modified by" language in the original Act permitted the councils to sacrifice the health of fisheries for the short-term well-being of commercial and recreational fishermen.[66]

Reacting to a steady stream of bad news about the condition of the nation's fisheries, and at the urging of marine conservation organizations, Congress in 1996 passed the Sustainable Fisheries Act.[67] The law, as amended, requires the councils to make conservation of fish stocks their top priority.[68]

Ten years later, in response to continued problems, Congress again significantly amended the law.[69] The most important changes made in 2006 include a greater role for scientific advice in council decision-making processes,[70] language meant to bring about an immediate end to overfishing,[71] and provisions to encourage wider use of market-based tools in fishery management.[72]

Under the current Magnuson-Stevens Act, each FMP must be consistent with ten "national standards" of fishery management.[73] Although these standards are somewhat vague, they are the clearest expression of Congress's objectives found in the Act.

National Standard One requires the councils to achieve optimum yield from each fishery, to prevent overfishing, and to rebuild those stocks that are in overfished condition.[74] National Standard Two mandates that, in managing stocks, the councils make use of the "best available scientific information."[75] National Standard Three encourages the councils and NMFS to coordinate their efforts in managing stocks that span multiple jurisdictions.[76] National Standard Four establishes a policy of fair allocation of fishing privileges among fishermen.[77] National Standard Five expresses Congress's view that efficiency should be one—but only one—consideration in fishery management.[78]

National Standard Six requires the councils to take into account the possibility of future environmental and economic change in making management decisions.[79]

National Standard Seven is the "Paperwork Reduction Act" of the national standards,[80] mandating that the councils "minimize costs," presumably administrative costs, and "avoid unnecessary duplication."[81] National Standard Eight requires the councils to take into account the needs of fishing communities in managing fisheries and to minimize economic impacts on those communities.[82] National Standard Nine requires the councils to manage so as to minimize bycatch (fish caught incidentally by fishermen that cannot or will not be landed) in fisheries; the "requirement" is tempered by language stating that councils must do this only "to the extent practicable."[83] National Standard Ten states that the councils should attempt to manage fisheries so as to promote the safety of human life, but again "only to the extent practicable."[84]

a. Mandatory Components of the FMP

A council must meet all of these objectives in each FMP, amended FMP, or interim regulation that it adopts.[85] Furthermore, the Act sets out a list of items and provisions that must be included in each FMP.[86] These items and provisions fall into three categories: basic information, management objectives, and required measures. Each FMP must include basic economic information about the fishery as well as biological and ecological information about the "targeted" fish species.[87] Required economic information includes historic landings, the kinds of fishermen (commercial, recreational, tribal, and foreign) involved in the fishery, the number of vessels used by these fishermen, the types of fishing gear used, and the actual and potential revenues of the fishery.[88] Biological and ecological information includes a description of the species' geographic range, the areas within that range considered to be essential for "spawning, breeding, feeding or growth to maturity," and the steps that might be taken to conserve and enhance that habitat.[89] After providing this basic economic and scientific information, a council must describe the kinds of information it will continue to collect in the future, and the methods it will use to collect these data.[90] Although the kinds of data to be collected by a council are not limited, it must demonstrate a plan to acquire certain information, including data on fishermen, catches, the location of catches, the kinds of fishing gear used by fishermen in the fishery, and fish processing.[91] The council must also establish "a standardized reporting methodology" for bycatch and a plan to measure, in recreational fisheries, catch-and-release mortality rates.[92]

The plan must also include a council's management objectives and the standards it will use in later assessing whether or not it is meeting those objectives. For example, in order to show that the FMP is consistent with National Standard One, the council must give its best estimate of the fishery's maximum sustainable and optimum yield.[93] Along the same lines, and as noted above, the council must also establish "objective and measurable criteria" that can be used to determine whether or not the fishery is, or has become, overfished.[94] The council must support this "overfished" definition with an explicit description of its scientific basis.[95]

In addition to those measures "necessary and appropriate for the conservation and management of the fishery," the FMP must include three specific kinds of management measures. First, the FMP must contain measures that, "to the extent practicable," minimize the impacts of fishing and fishing gear on "essential fish habitat."[96] Second, the FMP must contain measures that, "to the extent practicable," minimize bycatch and bycatch mortality.[97] Although the strength of these two required elements is obviously tempered by inclusion of the word "practicable," the councils should take them very seriously, given that they were added by Congress in the 1996 amendments in order to address identified shortcomings in past council management actions.[98] Third, where a fishery is overfished or nearly overfished, the FMP must establish a specific plan "to prevent overfishing or end overfishing and rebuild the fishery."[99]

As discussed further in Section IV of this chapter, each of these three "action items" has spawned controversy (and litigation) in the course of implementation. As noted, the practicability language in the bycatch and essential fish habitat provisions creates opportunities for NMFS and the councils to avoid gear restrictions or area closures that would be unpopular among members of the fishing community, whether such measures might be "practicable" or not.[100] As to the rebuilding provisions added in 1996, NMFS interpreted the statute's language so as to allow extremely long rebuilding periods.[101] And, while statutory language regarding "preventing overfishing" has always been clear, the uncertain science of fisheries management has allowed NMFS and the councils to choose the degree of certainty with which they would "end" overfishing.[102] For example, in the events that led to the Daley case, NMFS determined that a management measure with an eighteen percent probability of ending overfishing satisfied National Standard One's "shall prevent overfishing" mandate.[103]

Congress, perhaps wisely, chose not to wrestle with the "probability problem."

It is possible, although not certain, that changes made in 2006 will help remedy this last problem. Congress, perhaps wisely, chose not to wrestle with the "probability problem." Instead, it chose two other means of encouraging NMFS and the councils to take strong, quick action to end overfishing. First, as noted, Congress in 2006 added language emphasizing that NMFS and the councils are, beginning in 2009, to take steps to end overfishing "immediately."[104] Second, Congress added Section 1853(a)(15), which provides that each plan must

> establish a mechanism for specifying annual catch limits in the plan (including a multiyear plan), implementing regulations, or annual specifications, at a level such that overfishing does not occur in the fishery, *including measures to ensure accountability.*[105]

The Magnuson-Stevens Act does not specify what these accountability measures might be. One possibility would be for plans to provide that, if catches were to exceed target levels, then future quotas would be reduced accordingly.[106]

b. Discretionary Components of the FMP

Beyond these mandatory features, a council may include any of a range of discretionary provisions in its FMP.[107] A council may require fishermen to obtain a permit for fishing, either free of charge or for a fee;[108] create a "limited entry" system for the fishery, setting a cap on the number of vessels eligible to participate;[109] create temporary or permanent marine protected areas, designating "zones where, and periods when, fishing shall be limited, or shall not be permitted, or shall be permitted only by specified types of fishing vessels or with specified types and quantities of fishing gear";[110] and, in order to collect better data on a fishery, require vessels in the fishery to carry onboard observers or require fish processors to report purchases.[111]

If it chooses, a council may also include a Limited Access Privilege Program (LAPP) in an FMP.[112] Under a LAPP, the council allocates individual fishermen (or vessel owners) the privilege of catching a percentage share of the total amount of fish made available to the fishery each year.[113] These privileges are permits, not property, with a maximum duration of ten years.[114] Thus, the government may revoke or modify them without compensating the holder.[115]

LAPPs must promote safety and conservation; provide economic benefits; prohibit share ownership by other than U.S. citizens, corporations, partnerships, or permanent resident aliens;[116] require that all fish caught under the program be processed on vessels of the United States or on U.S. soil; provide for regular and detailed review by the relevant council and NMFS; include an effective monitoring and enforcement system, such as onboard observers or electronic vessel monitoring; provide an appeals process for contesting the initial allocation of shares; and contain mechanisms for ensuring that federal antitrust laws are not violated by shareholders.[117]

Before it adopts a LAPP for an overfished fishery, a council must demonstrate that the program will "assist in rebuilding."[118] In an overcapitalized fishery, it must be shown that the LAPP will "contribute to reducing capacity."[119]

For a variety of reasons, the initial allocation of shares in LAPP-like systems is always controversial: The allocation process distributes valuable fishing rights, necessarily excludes some fishermen, and, may benefit some industry members, e.g., vessel owners, at the expense of others, e.g., crew.[120] The Act attempts to provide guidelines for "fair and equitable initial allocations."[121] The law requires that councils consider, and that they may employ, "an auction system or other program to collect royalties" for the initial allocation of LAPP shares.[122]

Another controversial aspect of quota share systems is that, where shares are transferable, there is a possibility that share ownership may eventually become concentrated in one or a few participants.[123] In the Act, Congress has expressed the policy that the councils ought to prevent "excessive" concentration.[124] The law does not, however, precisely indicate what would or would not constitute "excessive" concentration.

In every LAPP, a council must have system in place to collect data on management and must "provide for a program of fees paid by" shareholders in order to finance both data collection and enforcement.[125]

2. The Process of Management

Analogous to a National Forest Plan or Land Management Plan, the Fishery Management Plan contains broad-scale, long-term management goals and strategies.[126] The council is required to amend the FMP as "necessary from time to time."[127] Year-to-year (or season-to-season) management of fisheries is frequently accomplished not through FMPs or amendments, but through regularly issued fisheries rules or "specifications" that are consistent with the overall plan.[128]

The process by which FMPs, amendments, and specifications are developed and adopted is dictated by procedural requirements found in the Magnuson-Stevens Act.[129] The councils are also bound by some of the statutes generally applicable to agency decision making, such as the National Environmental Policy Act[130] and the Administrative Procedure Act.[131] At the same time, they are specifically exempted from compliance with other federal laws, namely the Federal Advisory Committee Act and conflict of interest laws otherwise applicable to federal employees.[132]

The 2006 Reauthorization Act added an important new limit on council decision making. Section 1852(h) of the Magnuson-Stevens Act now provides that the councils must "develop annual catch limits for each of its managed fisheries that may not exceed the fishing level recommendations of its scientific and statistical committee or the peer review process. . . ."[133] This provision mirrors the long-standing practice of the North Pacific Council.[134]

The councils typically meet four times each year, once each season.[135] Except in very limited circumstances, these meetings must be open to the public, and the council must provide timely notice of upcoming meetings in local newspapers and in the *Federal Register*.[136] Notices of meeting shall not only include the time and place of the meeting, but must contain an agenda of the matters to be discussed and decided.[137]

Once a council has finished drafting an FMP (or FMP amendment), it transmits the document to NMFS for review and approval.[138] The standard of review is "consistency" with the National Standards and other provisions of the Magnuson-Stevens Act.[139] NMFS must begin review of the plan as soon as it is received, and at the same time file a notice in the *Federal Register* advising the public that the plan is available and that written comments will be accepted for sixty days.[140] Once the sixty-day review and comment period has expired, NMFS has thirty days to "approve, disapprove, or partially approve" the plan.[141] If NMFS does not act within this thirty-day period, the plan takes affect as submitted.[142] If NMFS "disapproves" the plan in full or in part, the agency must explain to the council exactly how the plan is inconsistent with applicable law, and must provide the council with recommendations as to how the plan can be altered so as to conform.[143] The council then has a second opportunity to submit an acceptable plan.[144]

Critics have pointed to two flaws in this system of review. First, councils have no, or very little, incentive to submit acceptable plans or to move quickly to revise disapproved plans. In fact, the councils have every incentive to drag the process out for as long as possible.[145] After all, most new or revised plans contain stricter conservation measures that are very unpopular with fisheries interests. Where a council prefers not to adopt these measures, or to delay their implementation, it may draw out the approval process through repeated bites at the review apple. The second flaw in the review system is that NMFS appears to provide very lax review of council plans. One study found that, over a twenty-year period, NMFS disapproved about one in every 10,000 council management measures it reviewed.[146] This high level of deference is problematic, especially if agency review is meant to serve as a check on decisions made by industry-heavy councils.

Beyond its review authority, NMFS has certain other limited powers over fisheries within the councils' jurisdiction. The agency may take over management of a fishery otherwise subject to council management if the council either fails to develop a plan (and the agency has made a determination that the fishery is in need of conservation and management), or if the council fails to submit a revised plan after its initial submission has been disapproved.[147] (In no case may NMFS use these powers to limit entry to a fishery.[148]) NMFS may also write and implement an FMP in cases where it has notified a council that a fishery is overfished and the council fails to submit a rebuilding plan within one year.[149] In practice, NMFS has rarely, if ever, utilized these powers.[150] The agency also has the power, under the Magnuson-Stevens Act, to issue emergency regulations for a fishery.[151] Again, it has rarely used this power.[152] It is worth noting that in no case may NMFS unilaterally repeal or revoke a previously approved FMP.[153]

B. Judicial Review of Council Actions

Citizens may challenge the legality of FMPs, amendments, or regulations in federal court. Such suits must be filed within thirty days of the publication of the final rule in the *Federal Register*.[154] The standard of review applied by courts in these cases is the "arbitrary and capricious" standard contained in the Administrative Procedure Act.[155] In order to prevail in such a case, a citizen must prove that a council "relied on factors Congress has not intended it to consider, entirely failed to consider an important aspect of the problem, offered an explanation for its decision that runs counter to the evidence before [it], or is so implausible that it could not be ascribed to a difference in view or the product of agency expertise."[156] The high level of deference afforded to agency decision-makers under this standard means that it is very difficult for citizens to prevail in Magnuson-Stevens Act court challenges.[157] Despite this fact, the number of suits filed against NMFS and the councils has increased significantly over the past decade.[158]

IV. Emerging and Unresolved Issues

The 1996 amendments to the Magnuson-Stevens Act attempted to narrow the range of management strategies available to the councils, for example, by tightening the definition of "optimum yield," while at the same time creating significant new council responsibilities—assessing economic impacts, rebuilding overfished fisheries, protecting essential fish habitat, and minimizing bycatch.[159] These changes created what must be considered a more conservation-minded statute. At the same time, Congress grafted the 1996 amendments onto what had fundamentally been an industry-regulation statute, and attempted to balance new, enhanced conservation provisions with language

> **Despite greater specificity than its predecessor, the post-1996 Magnuson-Stevens Act remains both ambiguous and internally conflicted.**

aimed at protecting the fishing industry from "excessive" conservation. One symptom of this effort is that, despite greater specificity than its predecessor, the post-1996 Act remains both ambiguous and internally conflicted.[160] Litigation by both industry groups and environmental groups has attempted to resolve these uncertainties, and to produce a judicially refined version of the statute more favorable to their own interests.[161] This section highlights some of the cases in which they have succeeded and failed.[162]

A. National Standard One

National Standard One provides that "[c]onservation and management measures shall prevent overfishing while achieving, on a continuing basis, the optimum yield from each fishery for the United States fishing industry."[163] Two questions have arisen with respect to the phrase "shall prevent overfishing." The first is whether the word "shall" means that a council must end overfishing immediately or, in the alternative, whether it permits a council to comply with the law simply by adopting a plan to end overfishing. In *Oceana, Inc. v. Evans*,[164] a marine conservation group challenged Amendment 13 to the Northeast Multispecies FMP on the ground that it did not immediately end overfishing of depleted stocks. In Amendment 13, the New England Council had adopted, and NMFS had approved, a plan to reduce overfishing gradually, phasing in stricter fishing limits over the course of a rebuilding plan. The court upheld the council's action, noting that although it did not end overfishing immediately, it "enabl[ed] more fishermen to remain in business while stocks rebuild."[165]

This holding represents a judicially crafted compromise between the strict conservation language of the statute ("shall") and the perception that a literal interpretation of the statute would have strong short-term economic effects on the fishing industry. Courts have crafted similar compromises in the context of other Magnuson-Stevens Act provisions.[166]

Such holdings are, in part, a product of the hybrid nature of the statute. Despite its clear emphasis on conservation, the post-1996 Magnuson-Stevens Act includes a substantial amount of language expressing Congress's desire to protect the fishing industry from unnecessary economic shocks. National Standard Eight, discussed further below, is the best example of this.[167] While the language of particular provisions is clear, the statute as a whole delivers a mixed message.

> **Twenty-five years of lax regulation meant that, by 1996, many fisheries were severely overfished and that probably even more were overcapitalized.**

Court-crafted compromises probably also reflect the fact that the 1996 amendments represented a dramatic departure from the prior law in terms of conservation. Twenty-five years of lax regulation meant that, by 1996, many fisheries were severely overfished and that probably even more were overcapitalized. The combination of the strict restrictions necessary for rebuilding and the thin profit margins characteristic of overcapitalized fisheries is not a recipe for pain-less transition. Their decisions seem to indicate that courts recognize the existence of this situation.

The second question that has arisen regarding National Standard One relates to the certainty that a council must have regarding the likely effectiveness of actions to end overfishing. In the context of significant scientific uncertainty, which is a part of all fishery stock assessments, the only way to be one hundred percent certain that overfishing will cease is to ban fishing entirely. Councils are obviously reluctant to take this step. On the other hand, even the least stringent measures may have some small chance of accomplishing the goal. How much certainty is required as a matter of law? In *Natural Resources Defense Council v. Daley*,[168] the D.C. Circuit established the rule that council management measures, in order to comply with the law, must have a greater than fifty percent chance of succeeding.

This result, although better than the one urged by the government, i.e., that an eighteen percent chance of success was sufficient,[169] seems inconsistent with the con-servation objectives of the statute. After all, it means that conservation measures may have a forty-nine percent chance of failing. It is difficult, though, to imagine how the court could have reached a different result, once it had decided that an 18 percent probability was not enough. It is also hard to imagine how Congress might go about fixing this problem through an adjustment to the language of the statute. A require-ment that a management measure have a seventy percent chance of success would not guarantee conservation. Furthermore, and more important, there is always uncer-tainty about the level of uncertainty in a scientific assessment.[170] Such a statutory pro-vision would simply change the subject of the debate to that second-order problem.

B. National Standard Two

National Standard Two provides that "conservation and management measures shall be based upon the best scientific information available."[171] Alleged violations of National Standard Two have been among the most frequently stated causes of action in complaints filed under the Magnuson-Stevens Act.[172] In these cases, courts have required plaintiffs to demonstrate, consistent with the holding in *Motor Vehicles Manufacturers Association*,[173] that there was no scientific basis whatsoever for the decision in question.

This is obviously a high burden to overcome. Plaintiffs have, however, occasion-ally prevailed. There are a few cases in which courts have admonished councils for making decisions based not on science, but on "pure political compromise."[174] For example, in *Hadaja, Inc. v. Evans*,[175] the Mid-Atlantic Council included in the Tilefish Fishery Management a provision allocating full- and part-time permits to some forty-six vessels, based on their historic landings of tilefish. The plaintiff alleged that the council's method of determining permit eligibility was not based on scientific infor-mation, but was simply the result of a "hallway compromise" among vessel own-ers.[176] The council conceded that the compromise formed the basis of the decision, but argued that scientific information collected after the compromise had been reached justified the result.[177] The court rejected this argument, finding the council's scientific justification "conclusory."[178] This case, along with *Midwater Trawlers Cooperative v. Department of Commerce*,[179] stands for the proposition that in order to comply with the requirements of National Standard Two, councils must provide a scientific rationale for both conservation and allocation decisions.

C. Conflicting National Standards

As noted above, the Magnuson-Stevens Act is internally conflicted. The relative priority of National Standards has thus also been the subject of important litigation. While National Standard One requires councils to meet certain conservation obligations, National Standard Eight requires them to "minimize adverse economic impacts on" fishing communities.[180]

In the district court decision in the above-cited *Natural Resources Defense Council v. Daley* case, the court found that NMFS had acted properly in balancing National Standards One and Eight and approving a rebuilding plan for summer flounder with a very low probability (eighteen percent chance) of success.[181] The court's view was that Congress had delegated broad authority to NMFS and the councils that allowed them to interpret "the construction of the [Magnuson Stevens Act] given the multitude of variables and interests."[182] This decision was overturned by the D.C. Circuit, which rejected "the District Court's suggestion that there is a conflict between the Fishery Act's expressed commitments to conservation and to mitigating adverse economic impacts. . . . [U]nder the Fishery Act, the Service must give priority to conservation measures."[183]

That holding is consistent with the language of the statute: National Standard Eight provides that "[c]onservation and management measures shall . . . take into account the importance of fishery resources to fishing communities," but only to the extent that this can be done without sacrificing "the conservation requirements of this Act (including the prevention of overfishing and rebuilding of overfished stocks)."[184] It should be stressed, however, that a holding that National Standard One takes priority over National Standard Eight neither represents a clear triumph of conservation over the short-term economic needs of the industry, nor guarantees conservation results in federal fishery management. Even with the priority issue settled, the "fifty-one percent rule" derived from the case means that lawful conservation measures will in many instances have a significant chance of not accomplishing their objective.

D. National Standard Nine

Because it combines a clear directive with what some might call "wiggle words," litigation of National Standard Nine was to be expected. While requiring the councils to minimize bycatch, the standard qualifies this requirement by providing that the councils need only do so "to the extent practicable."[185] Although the language of the standard implies that Congress had the substantive goal of bycatch reduction in mind, courts have given the standard a procedural flavor.

For example, in *Pacific Marine Conservation Council v. Evans*,[186] the court found that the Pacific Council had failed to meet the requirements of National Standard Nine in amending its Pacific Coast Groundfish FMP. The root of the violation, according to the court, was that the council failed to *"fully consider* the practicability of the more comprehensive observer program necessary to administer vessel incentives or discard caps. . . . [and that the council] engaged in *unreasoned decision-making* in dismissing these two potential bycatch reduction measures."[187] In other words, had the council carefully considered the bycatch reduction measures, it would have then been free to dismiss the measures as impracticable. It is unlikely that future courts will be eager to inject themselves into the question of whether a particular bycatch reduction measure is, or is not, practicable.

E. Essential Fish Habitat

Under the Magnuson-Stevens Act as amended, the councils are required to take several steps with respect to "essential fish habitat," that is, "those waters and substrate necessary to fish for spawning, breeding, feeding or growth to maturity."[188] First, the councils are required to "describe and identify essential fish habitat for the fishery."[189] Once they identify the habitat, they are required to take steps to "minimize to the extent practicable adverse effects on such habitat caused by fishing, and identify other actions to encourage the conservation and enhancement of such habitat."[190] Thus, the essential fish habitat requirements can be separated into procedural or informational requirements and action requirements.

Due to the nature of these mandates, as well as the way in which they were written, it is predictable that courts will be more interested in policing compliance with the former than with the latter. It is relatively straightforward to review the administrative record and determine whether or not a council has met its obligation to gather and consider scientific information on fish habitats within its jurisdiction. On the other hand, and as with the bycatch provisions, courts will probably not be inclined to review a council's practicability (or impracticability) determination. Such a review would be difficult because the limits of practicability are not defined in the statute. Congress did not specify whether these limits ought to be based on cost, efficiency, or any other factor.

The cases support the hypotheses regarding the kinds of supervision courts are likely to apply. In *Conservation Law Foundation v. Evans*,[191] for example, the plaintiffs challenged the New England Council's decision not to close four areas to fishing in order to protect essential fish habitat (EFH), arguing that the "decision was irreconcilable with record evidence that the closures would be beneficial with respect to EFH and bycatch."[192] The court rejected this argument:

> [T]he plaintiffs essentially call for an interpretation of the statute that equates "practicability" with "possibility," requiring NMFS to implement virtually any measure that addresses EFH and bycatch concerns so long as it is feasible. Although the distinction between the two may sometimes be fine, there

is indeed a distinction. The closer one gets to the plaintiffs' interpretation, the less weighing and balancing is permitted. We think by using the term "practicable" Congress intended rather to allow for the application of agency expertise and discretion in determining how best to manage fishery resources.[193]

On the other hand, in *American Oceans Campaign v. Daley*,[194] the court found a procedural violation where several councils had failed to properly "describe and identify" essential fish habitat: The councils "only discussed fish habitats in general terms, describing the types of EFHs that should be protected, but not specifying which EFHs needed protection and why."[195] The court noted that while "neither the statute nor the regulation requires the Councils to affirmatively conduct research to better identify EFHs and the adverse effects of fishing on them," the councils were obligated to include a "substantive discussion of [known impacts, such as] how fishing practices and gear may damage corals, disrupt fish habitat, and destroy benthic life that helps support healthy fish populations.[196]

F. Rebuilding Requirements

As noted above, the 1996 amendments require that the councils rebuild overfished fisheries. Congress had at least two objectives in adding Section 1854(e) to the Magnuson-Stevens Act.[197] The first was to fill an obvious void in the statute. Prior to the 1996 amendments, while National Standard One provided that councils were to prevent overfishing, the Act did not specify what the councils were to do once a stock became overfished. A stock could linger in this status indefinitely. The second objective of the rebuilding provisions was to set enforceable limits on the amount of time the councils could take in rebuilding stocks to the point where they could once again provide "the greatest overall benefit to the nation."[198]

While it is clear that Congress wanted overfished stocks rebuilt, and that it wanted to set a time limit on the rebuilding process, the language of the "rebuilding period" provisions is not clear; Section 1854 supplies yet another example of the tension in the Act between the two policies of conservation and short-term cost avoidance. First, the statute provides that rebuilding horizons should be "as short as possible."[199] Then, it defines "as short as possible" as a time period that does "not exceed ten years."[200] Finally, it adds an exception to this ten-year limit: The councils may craft rebuilding plans exceeding ten years "where the biology of the stock of fish, other environmental conditions, or management measures under an international agreement in which the United States participates dictate otherwise."[201]

As noted above, this language leaves open the question of whether there are any time limits on rebuilding once a council makes the determination that, even if fishing were to cease completely, the stock could not be rebuilt within ten years.[202]

The language in Section 1854(e)(4)(A) might be interpreted in several ways. The most conservative interpretation would be that if the stock cannot be rebuilt within ten years, due to the biology of the species or environmental conditions, the councils must halt all fishing for the species so that the stock can be rebuilt within as short a time as possible. At the other end of the spectrum, the provision could be interpreted to mean that if a stock cannot be rebuilt within ten years, the councils are free—after considering the available scientific information—to set the rebuilding horizon wherever they deem appropriate.

In the 2005 case of *Natural Resources Defense Council v. NMFS,*[203] plaintiff marine conservation group challenged a NMFS regulation that interpreted Section 1854(e)(4)(A) in a relatively nonconservative manner.[204] The NMFS regulation provided that, if a stock could not be rebuilt within ten years, then a council could set the rebuilding horizon at a date determined "by adding the shortest possible time to rebuild plus 'one mean generation time . . . based on the species' life-history characteristics.'"[205] In the case at hand, this regulation meant that the Pacific Council could lawfully establish a *forty-seven-year* rebuilding period for darkblotched rockfish.[206]

The plaintiff argued that this interpretation was impermissible, pursuant to the standard established by the Supreme Court in *Chevron,*[207] because it was inconsistent with the conservation objectives of the Magnuson-Stevens Act. As it had in *Natural Resources Defense Council v. Daley,*[208] the government argued that the Act contained two equal objectives, conservation and short-term cost avoidance, and that Congress had empowered the councils and NMFS to balance these in interpreting ambiguous language in the Act.[209]

Echoing the D.C. Circuit's conclusion in *Daley,* the Ninth Circuit agreed with the plaintiff that the two goals were not equal.[210] The court found that NMFS's interpretation did not reflect the purpose of the Act, which is "clearly to give conservation of fisheries priority over short-term economic interests."[211] Furthermore, the court found that the regulation could not be reconciled with Congress's intent as manifested in the "as short as possible" language of Section 1854(e)(4)(A)(i).[212]

While the court found NMFS's interpretation of the statute unreasonable, it did not concur with plaintiff's argument that the only reasonable interpretation of the statute was that if a stock cannot be rebuilt within ten years, then all fishing for the species must cease. The court stated that

> Although [Natural Resources Defense Council's] interpretation of the statute is reasonable, it is not the only reasonable one. It is also reasonable to conclude that the needs of fishing communities may still be taken into account even when the biology of the fish dictates exceeding the 10-year cap—so long as the weight given is proportionate to the weight the Agency might give to such needs in rebuilding periods under 10 years. This interpretation would allow the Agency's rebuilding periods to account for short-term concerns such as bycatch in the same manner whether the rebuilding period exceeds 10 years or not.[213]

Thus, although helpful to conservation, the Ninth Circuit's decision did not supply clear guidance to councils in future decisions regarding "10-plus" rebuilding horizons. Furthermore, as of December of 2006, NMFS had not yet proposed a replacement regulation.

The Pacific Council's recent proposal to amend the FMP for darkblotched rock-fish, written in direct response to the Ninth Circuit's decision in *Natural Resources Defense Council v. NMFS*, provides some insight into how the councils might interpret Section 1854(e)(4) in the absence of new regulatory guidance.[214] The Pacific Council reads the court's decision to mean that rebuilding periods must be as short as possible; however, the rebuilding horizon may be extended if necessary to "avoid disastrous short-term consequences for fishing communities."[215] The council does not identify a maximum time limit for these economically based rebuilding extensions.

V. Conclusion

From 1976 to 1996, the flexible language of Magnuson-Stevens Act permitted NMFS and the councils to avoid making difficult decisions. Rather than face the ire of the fishing industry, the councils often chose to defer conservation.[216] Sadly, and ironically, putting off conservation is not in the best long-term interests of the fishing industry. This is true for two reasons. First, and most obviously, the long-term health of the industry depends on the existence of healthy fish stocks and healthy oceans. Second, the effect of deferring difficult choices is to make them ever more difficult. Whereas conservation in the early stages of overfishing would mean relatively small cutbacks, rebuilding an overfished stock might require closing a fishery entirely.

Thus it was not surprising that, after twenty years of putting off hard choices, the councils and NMFS have not taken an aggressive approach to implementing the 1996 amendments. *Natural Resources Defense Council v. Daley*[217] and *Natural Resources Defense Council v. NMFS*[218] illustrate that these institutions continue to make efforts to further defer difficult decisions. In the former case, the Mid-Atlantic Council and NMFS attempted to avoid actually ending overfishing by choosing a quota that had very little chance of actually doing that.[219] In the latter, NMFS interpreted the rebuilding provisions of the Act in a way that allowed the councils to put off rebuilding for very long periods of time. The agency could have just as easily interpreted the law to mean that fisheries that could not be rebuilt within ten years had to be closed.[220]

The courts' decisions in these two cases indicate that courts, too, are not inclined to impose drastic cutbacks on the industry. In *Daley*, the court opted to read "shall end overfishing" to mean "have at least a 51% chance of ending overfishing"; in *NMFS*, the court left open the possibility that rebuilding periods could stretch beyond ten years if necessary to avoid "disastrous" impacts on the industry.

The leap from the current state of U.S. fisheries to a sustainable state will—because of past neglect—be a big one.

The ultimate problem is one of transition. The leap from the current state of U.S. fisheries to a sustainable state will—because of past neglect—be a big one, and will in fact involve some disastrous short-term consequences for the industry. While it is important that the Magnuson-Stevens Act continue to emphasize conservation, it is perhaps more important that Congress (and NMFS and the councils) think creatively about how to structure and finance the transition to sustainable fisheries.

The 1996 amendments to the Act added a range of possibilities, including buybacks and individual fishing quotas, for doing exactly this. To date, these mechanisms have not been widely used. The 2006 Reauthorization Act has increased the number of tools in the "transition kit." In addition to the new Limited Access Privilege Program provisions, the 2006 amendments include the creation of a Fisheries Conservation and Management Fund. To a limited extent, this fund can be used to aid in the transition to sustainability, by "providing financial assistance to fishermen to offset the costs of modifying fishing practices and gear to meet the requirements of this Act."[221] Without a greater focus on mitigating and equitably distributing the costs of transition, it is likely that the industry, the councils, NMFS, and courts will continue to struggle with the difficult choices necessary to achieve sustainable fisheries.

Notes

1. The United States' marine waters consist, for fishery management purposes, of those waters within two hundred nautical miles of shore. A nautical mile is 1.15 miles. Throughout the rest of this chapter, the word "mile" refers to a nautical mile. The United Nations Convention on the Law of the Sea [hereinafter Law of the Sea], Art. 62, Dec. 10, 1982, 21 I.L.M. 1261, 1281; 1833 U.N.T.S. 397, 421 established two hundred-mile Exclusive Economic Zones for coastal nations. The United States has not yet ratified this treaty. However, the United States has claimed an Exclusive Economic Zone, presumably under the theory that such rights at some point became customary international law. Presidential Proclamation No. 5030, 3 C.F.R. 22 (1984).
2. Unless otherwise noted, the word "fishing," as used in this chapter, includes both commercial and recreational fishing activities.
3. The term "fishery" refers to the people and equipment involved in catching fish in a defined area, as well as the fish that are pursued. While "fishery management" is aimed at conserving fish and the marine environment, fishery management laws can only regulate the people who fish and the fishing equipment they use.
4. 16 U.S.C. §§ 1801–1883 (2000) [hereinafter Magnuson-Stevens Act]. About one year before publication of this book, Congress passed the Magnuson-Stevens Fishery Conservation and Management Reauthorization Act of 2006, H.R. 5946, 109th Cong. (2006) [hereinafter 2006 Reauthorization Act]. That Act amended some important provisions of the law. Those changes are noted, where appropriate, in this chapter. Discussion of important Magnuson-Stevens Act cases, in Section IV of this chapter, should be read in the context of the law prior to the passage of the Reauthorization Act.
5. The National Marine Fisheries Service is a subagency of the National Oceanic and Atmospheric Administration (NOAA). NOAA is an agency within the United States Department of Commerce. For an organizational chart, *see* http://www.commerce.gov/organization.html (last visited Dec. 7, 2006).
6. 43 U.S.C. §§ 1301–1315 (2000), commonly known as the Submerged Lands Act of 1953. *See* 43 U.S.C. § 1311(a)(2). The exceptions to the general three-mile limit of state waters are the west coast of Florida and the coast of Texas, where the limits are three leagues, or nine nautical miles. United States v. Florida, 363 U.S. 121 (1960); United States v. Louisiana, 363 U.S. 1 (1960).
7. United States v. California, 332 U.S. 19 (1947).
8. 94 Pub. L. No. 265, 90 Stat. 331. The law was originally known simply as the Fishery Conservation and Management Act. In 1980, Congress re-named it the Magnuson Fishery Conservation and Management Act; in 1996, it became the Magnuson-Stevens

Fishery Conservation and Management Act. 96 Pub. L. No. 561, 94 Stat. 3275; 104 Pub. L. No. 208, 110 Stat. 3009.

9. 16 U.S.C. §§ 1801–1883.

10. 3 C.F.R. 22 (1984).

11. 21 I.L.M. 1261, 1285; 1833 U.N.T.S. 397, 428.

12. 16 U.S.C. § 1856(b).

13. *Id.* §§ 1361–1421 (2000). *See* 16 U.S.C. § 1362(15)(A); 16 U.S.C. § 1372.

14. *Id.* §§ 1531–1544 (2000). *See* 16 U.S.C. § 1538(a)(1)(B).

15. 33 U.S.C. §§ 1251–1387 (2000). *See* 33 U.S.C. § 1362(7), 1362(8).

16. 16 U.S.C. §§ 5101–5108 (2000). *See* 16 U.S.C. § 5106(c).

17. 384 F. Supp. 312 (W.D. Wash. 1974).

18. The court in that case held that state fishery management laws must:

> a. Not discriminate against the Treaty Tribe's reserved right to fish; b. Meet appropriate standards of substantive and procedural due process; and c. Be shown by the State to be both reasonable and necessary to preserve and maintain the resource.

> *Id.* at 407.

19. 16 U.S.C. § 1853 (a)(3). Congress has granted Alaska unique powers in managing fisheries in federal waters off the state's coast: In certain circumstances, the state may regulate vessels registered in other states as well as vessels registered under Alaska law. 16 U.S.C. § 1853(a)(3)(C). *See* John Winn, *Alaska v. F/V Baranof: State Regulation Beyond the Territorial Sea after the Magnuson Act*, 13 B.C. Envtl. Aff. L. Rev. 281 (1986).

20. 16 U.S.C. § 1456(c).

21. *See* Ocean Conservancy v. Evans, 2003 U.S. Dist. LEXIS 24888 (M.D. Fla. 2003).

22. There are reported decisions of state challenges to the "consistency" of, for example, federally permitted oil and gas exploration activities. *See, e.g.*, California v. Norton, 311 F.2d 1162 (9th Cir. 2002).

23. There are two other such commissions, the Gulf States Marine Fisheries Commission and the Pacific States Marine Fisheries Commission. Unlike the Atlantic States Marine Fisheries Commission, the other two commissions do not regulate fisheries, but do provide a forum for member-states to discuss issues and pursue research projects of mutual interest. For information, *see* Gulf States Marine Fisheries Comm'n, http://www.gsmfc.org/, and Pac. States Marine Fisheries Comm'n, http://www.psmfc.org/ (last visited Dec. 7, 2006).

24. 16 U.S.C. § 5103(b)(1). For a description of how the commission operates, *see* Joseph A. Farside, Jr., *Atlantic States Marine Fisheries Commission: Getting a Grip on Slippery Fisheries Management*, 11 Roger Williams U. L. Rev. 231 (2005).

25. 16 U.S.C. § 1856(a); People v. Weeren, 26 Cal. 3d 654, 607 P.2d 1279 (1980); *but see* Vietnamese Fishermen Ass'n of Am. v. Cal. Dep't of Fish & Game, 816 F. Supp. 1468 (N.D. Cal. 1993).

26. *See* Sections II and V of The Law of the Sea, 21 I.L.M. 1272, 1279; 1833 U.N.T.S. 400, 418; Martin Lishexian, *The Interrelation Between the Law of the Sea and Customary International Law*, 7 San Diego Int'l L.J. 405 (2006).

27. 21 I.L.M. 1281, 1833 U.N.T.S. 420, 421. Article 61 of the Law of the Sea requires that coastal nations ensure that "the maintenance of the living resources in the exclusive economic zone is not endangered by over exploitation," that conservation and management measures "shall . . . be designed to maintain or restore populations of harvested species at levels which can produce the maximum sustainable yield," and that such measures "take into consideration the effects on species associated with or dependent upon harvested species with a view to maintaining or restoring populations of such associated or dependent species above levels at which their reproduction may become seriously threatened." *Id.* Article 62 requires that coastal nations "[do] not have the capacity to harvest the entire allowable catch" of particular species, they shall "give other States

access to the surplus of the allowable catch," giving priority in access to underdeveloped and landlocked nations. *Id.*

28. May 14, 1966, 6 I.L.M. 293.

29. http://www.fao.org/figis/servlet/static?dom=org&xml=CCRF_prog.xml (last visited Dec. 7, 2006).

30. 16 U.S.C. § 1852(a). NMFS directly regulates Atlantic and Gulf of Mexico fisheries for "highly migratory species" such as sharks, tunas, and swordfish. 16 U.S.C. § 1854(g).

31. N. Pac. Fishery Mgmt. Council, http://www.fakr.noaa.gov/npfmc/ (last visited Dec. 7, 2006); W. Pac. Reg'l Fishery Mgmt. Council, http://www.wpcouncil.org/ (last visited Dec. 7, 2006).

32. *See, e.g.,* New Eng. Fishery Mgmt. Council, http://www.nefmc.org/ (last visited Dec. 7, 2006).

33. 16 U.S.C. § 1852(a).

34. The Magnuson-Stevens Act generally mandates that councils be composed of members from states bordering the marine area under management. There are several exceptions to this rule. First, the law mandates that the North Pacific Council include representatives from Oregon and Washington, which do not physically border on the marine area managed by the council. 16 U.S.C. § 1852(a)(1)(G). Second, the law provides that Idaho, a landlocked state, have a seat on the Pacific Council, owing to its interest in salmon management. 16 U.S.C. § 1852(a)(1)(F). Finally, the Magnuson-Stevens Act requires that the Pacific Council include one member of "an Indian tribe with Federally recognized fishing rights from California, Oregon, Washington, or Idaho." 16 U.S.C. § 1852(a)(1)(F).

35. 16 U.S.C. § 1852(a).

36. *Id.* § 1852(b)(1)(A).

37. *Id.*

38. *Id.* § 1852(b)(2)(A).

39. *Id.* The 2006 Reauthorization Act added a requirement that NMFS train new council members in the basic science and economics of fishery management. 16 U.S.C. § 1852(k).

40. Josh Eagle et al., Taking Stock of the Regional Fishery Management Councils (2003); Thomas A. Okey, *Membership of the Eight Regional Fishery Management Councils in the United States: Are Special Interests Over-Represented?*, 27 Marine Pol'y 193 (2003).

   In this chapter, the word "industry" refers to commercial and recreational fishing, as well as fish processing. Although those groups and their subgroups, e.g., commercial line and trawl fishermen, often have conflicting interests, they generally share important common interests: the maintenance of high catch levels and the minimization of restrictions on fishing.

   The 2006 Reauthorization Act added a requirement that, with respect to the Gulf of Mexico Council only, governors must include the name of one nonindustry person on nomination lists submitted to the Secretary of Commerce. 16 U.S.C. § 1852(b)(2)(D).

41. Eagle et al., *supra* note 40, at 24.

42. 16 U.S.C. § 1852(c).

43. *Id.* § 1852(g)(1). The members of the scientific and statistical committee are appointed by the councils, and must be "Federal employees, State employees, academicians, or independent experts" with "strong scientific or technical credentials and experience." 16 U.S.C. § 1852(g)(1)(C). Members of these committees are subject to the same conflict-of-interest disclosure rules as council members. 16 U.S.C. § 1852(g)(1)(D).

44. *Id.* § 1852(g)(3).

45. *Id.* § 1852(h).

46. There is no information available regarding the number of unregulated fisheries currently being prosecuted in federal waters.

47. 16 U.S.C. § 1852(h).

48. *Id.* § 1853(a)(1).

49. Nat'l Oceanic & Atmospheric Admin., Status of United States Fisheries (2004), http://www.nmfs.noaa.gov/sfa/domes_fish/StatusoFisheries/StatusReport2004.pdf (last visited Dec. 7, 2006).

50. *Id.* at 10.

51. *Id.* at 3, 10.

52. *Id.* at 3, 10.

53. *See, e.g.,* Jeremy B.C. Jackson et al., *Historical Overfishing and the Recent Collapse of Coastal Ecosystems*, 293 Science 629, 636 (2001) ("[O]ur analysis demonstrates that overfishing fundamentally altered coastal marine ecosystems during each of the cultural periods we examined."); Daniel Pauly et al., *Fishing Down Marine Food Webs*, 279 Science 860 (1998) ("[L]andings from global fisheries have shifted in the last 45 years from large piscivorous fishes toward smaller invertebrates and planktivorous fishes, especially in the Northern Hemisphere. This may imply major changes in the structure of marine food webs.").

54. Nat'l Oceanic & Atmospheric Admin., Our Living Oceans 8 (1999).

55. U.S. Comm'n on Ocean Policy, An Ocean Blueprint for the 21st Century: Final Report of the U.S. Commission on Ocean Policy (2004) [hereinafter USCOP Report], *available at* http://www.oceancommission.gov/documents/full_color_rpt/000_ocean_full_report.pdf (last visited Dec. 8, 2006); Pew Oceans Comm'n, America's Living Oceans: Charting a Course for Sea Change (2003), *available at* http://www.pewtrusts.org/pdf/env_pew_oceans_final_report.pdf (last visited Dec. 8, 2006).

56. Nat'l Oceanic & Atmospheric Admin., *supra* note 49, at 10.

57. *Id.*

58. Nat'l Academy of Science, Improving Fish Stock Assessments 13–25 (1998).

59. *Id.* at 36.

60. 16 U.S.C. § 1853(a)(10).

61. Marine Fish Conservation Network, Shell Game: How the Federal Government Is Hiding Mismanagement of Our Nation's Fisheries (2006), *available at* http://www.conservefish.org/site/pubs/network_reports/ (last visited Dec. 8, 2006).

62. Michael L. Weber, From Abundance to Scarcity: A History of U.S. Marine Fisheries Policy 173–93 (2002). Weber's argument is that the pre-1996 Magnuson-Stevens Act could have been interpreted and implemented in a conservation-oriented manner, but that NMFS and the councils chose not to do this. *Id.* at 174.

63. *Id.* at 182–85.

64. *Id.* at 174–77.

65. 94 Pub. L. No. 265 § 3(18)(B); 90 Stat. 331, 335.

66. Weber, *supra* note 62, at 189.

67. *Id.* at 187–90.

68. *Id.* at 190–92.

69. *See supra* note 4.

70. 16 U.S.C. § 302(h)(6).

71. 16 U.S.C. §§ 302(a)(10), 304(e)(3).

72. 16 U.S.C. § 303A.

73. 16 U.S.C. § 1851.

74. *Id.* § 1851(a)(1).

75. *Id.* § 1851(a)(2).

76. *Id.* § 1851(a)(3).

77. *Id.* § 1851(a)(4).

78. *Id.* § 1851(a)(5).

79. *Id.* § 1851(a)(6).

80. Paperwork Reduction Act, 44 U.S.C. §§ 3501–3520 (1990). The Act was intended, in part, to "ensure the greatest possible public benefit from and maximize the utility of information created . . . by or for the Federal Government." *Id.* § 3501.

81. 16 U.S.C. § 1851(a)(7).

82. 16 U.S.C. § 1851(a)(8).
83. 16 U.S.C. § 1851(a)(9).
84. 16 U.S.C. § 1851(a)(10).
85. *Id.* § 1854(a)(1)(A).
86. *Id.* § 1853(a).
87. A "targeted" species is one purposefully pursued by fishermen. Fishermen often catch species they did not intend to catch. If these "nontargeted" fish have enough value, and there are no regulations to the contrary, fishermen will land and sell them. Otherwise, the "nontargeted" fish will be discarded as "bycatch."
88. 16 U.S.C. § 1853(a)(2),(13).
89. *Id.* § 1853(a)(2),(7).
90. *Id.* § 1853(a)(5).
91. *Id.*
92. *Id.* § 1853(a)(11),(12).
93. *Id.* § 1853(a)(3).
94. *Id.* § 1853(a)(10).
95. *Id.*
96. *Id.* § 1853(a)(7).
97. *Id.* § 1853(a)(11).
98. 104 Pub. L. No. 297, 110 Stat. 3591. *See* Lee Benaka and Dennis Nixon, *Essential Fish Habitat and Coastal Zone Management: Business as Usual Under the Magnuson-Stevens Act?*, 30 Golden Gate U.L. Rev. 969, 973–82 (2000); Frank M. Sprtel, *Essential Fish Habitat's Role in Fisheries Management of Pacific Coast Groundfish*, 15 J. Envtl. L. & Litig. 67, 69–72 (2000).
99. 16 U.S.C. § 1853(a)(10).
100. *See, e.g.,* Pacific Marine Conservation Council v. Evans, 200 F. Supp. 2d 1194 (N.D. Cal. 2002) and discussion at Section IV.D, *infra.*
101. *See, e.g.,* Natural Res. Def. Council v. Nat'l Marine Fisheries Serv., 421 F.3d 872 (9th Cir. 2005) and discussion at Section IV.F, *infra.*
102. *See, e.g.,* Natural Res. Def. Council v. Daley, 62 F. Supp. 2d 102 (D.D.C. 1999) and discussion at Section IV.C, *infra.*
103. *Id.*
104. 16 U.S.C. § 1854(e)(3)(A).
105. *Id.* § 1853(a)(15) (emphasis added).
106. This kind of "penalty" provision was in at least one earlier version of the final 2006 Reauthorization Act. *See* Magnuson-Stevens Fishery Conservation and Management Reauthorization Act of 2005, S. 2012, 109th Cong., § 104 (2005).
107. 16 U.S.C. § 1853(b).
108. *Id.* § 1853(b)(1).
109. *Id.* § 1853(b)(4).
110. *Id.* § 1853(b)(2).
111. *Id.* § 1853(b)(8).
112. *Id.* § 1853A. Prior to 2006, limited access privileges were known in the statute as "individual fishing quotas."

    The law provides that a council may began the process of adopting a LAPP on its own initiative or if "the Secretary has certified [a] petition" signed by a certain percentage of fishery participants. 16 U.S.C. § 1853A(c)(6)(A). However, a certified petition does not mean that a council must adopt a LAPP.

    The law limits the power of two councils, the Gulf of Mexico Council and the New England Council, to adopt LAPPs. In these regions, any proposed LAPP program must pass a referendum vote before the council may submit it to NMFS for approval. 16 U.S.C. § 1853A(c)(6)(D).
113. For examples of such programs, *see* Suzanne Iudicello et al., Fish, Markets, Fishermen 89-159 (1999). There are currently three such programs in federally managed

fisheries: surf clam and ocean quahog (Mid-Atlantic), Pacific halibut and sablefish (North Pacific), and wreckfish (South Atlantic). These existing programs are not affected by the LAPP provisions added in 2006. 2006 Reauthorization Act, § 106(a).

114. 16 U.S.C. § 1853A(b)(1),(4); *Id.* § 1853A(f).
115. *Id.* § 1853A(b)(3).
116. "Fishing communities" and "regional fishery associations" may hold LAPP shares. 16 U.S.C. § 1853A(c)(3),(c)(4).
117. 16 U.S.C. § 1853A(c)(1).
118. *Id.*
119. *Id.*
120. Iudicello et al., *supra* note 113, at 83-85. *See* Dallas DeLuca, *One for Me and One for You: An Analysis of the Initial Allocation of Fishing Quotas*, 13 N.Y.U. Envtl. L. J. 723 (2005).
121. *Id.* § 1853A(c)(5).
122. *Id.* § 1853A(d).
123. From the perspective of efficiency, concentration is not bad: It simply means that those who can fish most cheaply are catching the fish. (There may be monopoly problems if the fishery becomes too concentrated.) From a political perspective, concentrated ownership is controversial because, among other things, it reduces the number of fishing jobs and changes the relative bargaining power of fishermen and fish processors.
124. *Id.*
125. 16 U.S.C. § 1853A(e).
126. These plans are written pursuant to, respectively, the National Forest Management Act (16 U.S.C. §§ 1600–1687 (2000)), and the Federal Land Policy and Management Act (43 U.S.C. §§ 1701–1782 (2000)).
127. 16 U.S.C. § 1852(h)(1)(B).
128. *Id.* § 1853(c).
129. *Id.* §§ 1852(i), 1854(a), (b).
130. 42 U.S.C. §§ 4321–4370f (2006). The 2006 Reauthorization Act directs the Council on Environmental Quality to develop new procedures for streamlining NMFS and fishery management council compliance with the National Environmental Policy Act. 2006 Reauthorization Act, § 107.
131. *See, e.g.,* Natural Res. Def. Council v. Evans, 243 F. Supp. 2d 1046 (N.D. Cal. 2003); 5 U.S.C. §§ 501–596; 16 U.S.C. § 1855(f).
132. 16 U.S.C. § 1852(i), (j). For a discussion of the conflict-of-interest issue, *see* Eagle et al., *supra* note 40.
133. 16 U.S.C. § 1852(h)(6). The creation of a peer review process is optional. 16 U.S.C. § 1852(g)(1)(E).
134. North Pacific Fishery Management Council, Responsible Fisheries Management into the 21st Century (2002), http://www.fakr.noaa.gov/npfmc/summary_reports/ResponsibleManagement.pdf (last visited Dec. 13, 2006).
135. *See, e.g.,* Mid-Atlantic Fishery Mgmt. Council, Council Meetings, http://www.mafmc.org/mid-atlantic/meetings/meetings.htm (last visited Dec. 7, 2006).
136. 16 U.S.C. § 1852(i).
137. *Id.* § 1852(i)(2)(C).
138. *Id.* § 1854(a)(1). Similar rules apply to specifications implementing FMPs.
139. *Id.* § 1854(a)(1)(A).
140. *Id.* § 1854(a)(1)(B).
141. *Id.* § 1854(a)(3).
142. *Id.*
143. *Id.*
144. *Id.* § 1854(a)(4).
145. USCOP Report, *supra* note 55, at 279–80.
146. Eagle et al., *supra* note 40, at 32.

147. 16 U.S.C. § 1854(c)(1).

148. *Id.* § 1854(c)(3).

149. *Id.* § 1854(e)(5).

150. Eagle et al., *supra* note 40, at 33.

151. 16 U.S.C. § 1855(c).

152. A search of the *Federal Register* reveals that NMFS has issued emergency regulations under § 1855(c) fewer than ten times since 1980.

153. 16 U.S.C. § 1854(h).

154. *Id.* § 1855(f).

155. *Id.*

156. Motor Vehicle Mfrs. Ass'n v. State Farm Mut. Auto. Ins. Co., 463 U.S. 29, 43–44 (1983).

157. *See* Vic Sher, *Breaking Out of the Box: Toxic Risk, Government Actions, and Constitutional Rights*, 13 J. Envtl. L. & Litig. 145, 147–48 (1998) ("[T]he APA requires that conflicts among experts always be resolved in favor of the government. Always means that, even if you have one hundred experts holding an opinion in your favor while only one expert supports the government, you still lose.").

158. The number of cases filed per year increased from about three per year prior to 1997 to about thirty per year in 2001. Nat'l Academy of Public Admin., Courts, Congress, and Constituencies: Managing Fisheries by Default 13–16 (2002).

159. 16 U.S.C. §§ 1851(a)(8), (9); 1853(a)(7),(10).

160. These conflicts were not wholly eliminated by the 2006 amendments, although Congress did continue the trend, begun in 1996, of shifting the statute's balance toward conservation.

161. Nat'l Academy of Public Admin., *supra* note 158, at 17–28.

162. For another, longer summary of recent cases, *see* Marian Macpherson and Mariam McCall, *Judicial Remedies in Fisheries Litigation: Pros, Cons, and Prestidigitation?*, 9 Ocean & Coastal L.J. 1 (2003).

163. 16 U.S.C. § 1851(a)(1).

164. 2005 U.S. Dist. LEXIS 3959 (D.D.C. Mar. 9, 2005).

165. *Id.* at *34. This issue might be resolved differently after the 2006 Reauthorization Act, which added language clarifying that the councils have two years to end overfishing. 16 U.S.C. § 1854(e)(3).

166. *See* discussion of *Natural Res. Def. Council v. Nat'l Marine Fisheries Serv.*, 421 F.3d 872 (9th Cir. 2005), *infra.*

167. 16 U.S.C. § 1851(a)(8).

168. 209 F.3d 747 (D.C. Cir. 2000).

169. *Id.* at 751.

170. *See* Thomas Nilsen and Terje Aven, *Models and Model Uncertainty in the Context of Risk Analysis*, 79 Reliability Engineering and System Safety 309 (2003).

171. 16 U.S.C. § 1851(a)(2).

172. Nat'l Academy of Public Admin., *supra* note 158, at 18.

173. 463 U.S. 29 (1983).

174. Midwater Trawlers Coop. v. Dept. of Commerce, 282 F.3d 710, 720–21 (9th Cir. 2002). For a critique of the decision in this case, *see* Sarah McCarthy, *Midwater Trawlers Cooperative v. Department of Commerce: A Troublesome Dichotomy of Science and Policy*, 8 Ocean & Coastal L.J. 127 (2002).

175. 263 F. Supp. 2d 346 (D.R.I. 2003).

176. *Id.* at 353.

177. *Id.*

178. *Id.* at 354.

179. 282 F.3d 710 (9th Cir. 2002).

180. 16 U.S.C. § 1851(a)(1),(8).

181. Natural Res. Def. Council v. Daley, 62 F. Supp. 2d 102, 109 (D.D.C. 1999).

182. *Id.* at 108.
183. Natural Res. Def. Council v. Daley, 209 F.3d 747, 753 (D.C. Cir. 2000).
184. 16 U.S.C. § 1851(a)(8).
185. *Id.* § 1851(a)(9).
186. 200 F. Supp. 2d 1194 (N.D. Cal. 2002).
187. *Id.* at 1203.
188. 16 U.S.C. § 1802(10).
189. *Id.* § 1853(a)(7).
190. *Id.*
191. 360 F.3d 21 (1st Cir. 2004).
192. *Id.* at 28.
193. *Id.*
194. 183 F. Supp. 2d 1 (D.D.C. 2000).
195. *Id.* at 21.
196. *Id.* at 13, 20.
197. *Improving Fisheries Management in the Magnuson Act: Hearing Before the Subcomm. on Fisheries, Wildlife, and Oceans of the H. Comm. on Resources*, 104th Cong., 18–19 (1995) (Testimony of Roland A. Schmitten, Asst. Admin. for Fisheries, National Marine Fisheries Service, NOAA, U.S. Dept. of Commerce); Roger Fleming, Peter Shelley, and Patricia M. Brooks, *Changing Tides in Ocean Management: Twenty-Eight Years and Counting: Can the Magnuson-Stevens Act Deliver on its Conservation Promise?*, 28 Vt. L. Rev. 579, 585–89 (2004).
198. 16 U.S.C. § 1802(28)(A).
199. *Id.* § 1854(e)(4)(A)(i).
200. *Id.* § 1854(e)(4)(A)(ii).
201. *Id.*
202. The reference to extending rebuilding periods because of international agreements is clear. Regarding some fisheries, such as Atlantic bluefin tuna, Congress has elsewhere ordered NMFS to adhere to catch levels that are set by treaty organizations. *See, e.g.*, Atlantic Tunas Convention Act, 16 U.S.C. § 971d(c)(3)(2000). Congress wanted to be clear that the Magnuson-Stevens Act would not supersede such statutes: Rebuilding periods established by the International Commission for the Conservation of Atlantic Tuna, for example, would govern even if they were longer than ten years.
203. 421 F.3d 872 (9th Cir. 2005).
204. 50 C.F.R. § 600.310(e)(4)(ii)(B).
205. *Id.* at 875, citing to 162 Fed. Reg. 67,610, 67,608, 67,609–10 (Dec. 29, 1997).
206. *Id.* at 876.
207. Chevron U.S.A. Inc. v. Natural Res. Def. Council, 467 U.S. 837 (1984). Under *Chevron*, agencies must interpret an ambiguous provision in a statute in a manner consistent with the overall purpose of the statute. *Id.*
208. Natural Res. Def. Council v. Daley, 62 F. Supp. 2d 102, 108 (D.D.C. 1999).
209. 421 F.3d 872, 875–76 (9th Cir. 2005). The District Court agreed with the government's view: "In light of MSA's dual conservationist and commercial objectives, an interpretation that accommodates both objectives, rather than selecting one to the exclusion of the other, is permissible." 280 F. Supp. 2d 1007, 1014 (N.D. Cal. 2003).
210. "As an initial matter, we reject the District Court's suggestion that there is a conflict between the Fishery Act's expressed commitments to conservation and to mitigating adverse economic impacts." Natural Res. Def. Council v. Daley, 209 F.3d 747, 753 (2000).
211. Natural Res. Def. Council v. Nat'l Marine Fisheries Serv., 421 F.3d at 879.
212. *Id.* at 879–80.
213. *Id.* at 881.
214. 71 Fed. Reg. 189, 57,764 (Sept. 29, 2006).
215. *Id.* at 57,766.
216. Weber, *supra* note 62, at 173–93.

217. 209 F.3d 747 (D.C. Cir. 2000).
218. 421 F.3d 872 (9th Cir. 2005).
219. In fact, the council chose a measure with a *three* percent chance of ending overfishing. *Daley*, 209 F.3d at 750–51.
220. The Ninth Circuit stated that this interpretation of Section 1854(e)(4), unlike the interpretation offered by NMFS, would have been reasonable and thus, legal.
221. 2006 Reauthorization Act, § 208. The fund is to be managed by the Secretary of Commerce and to be funded by "quota set-asides," future congressional appropriations, and funds donated by states and non-governmental organizations. *Id.*

chapter ten

International Fisheries Management

Suzanne Iudicello

I. Introduction

For centuries, customary international law and practice embraced the concept of *mare liberum,* freedom of the seas. Many assumptions that flowed from this principle continued until as recently as the 1980s and 1990s: Anyone possessing the wherewithal to ply the seas and cast nets was free to fish; anyone wanting to impose restrictions on fishing bore the burden of proof to demonstrate the activity was harmful; fish, like wildlife, belonged to the state, which was the decision-maker on issues of access and other rights in the living resources of the sea.

This chapter examines fishery management in an international context through a detailed look at several important agreements that changed the traditional freedom of seas approach to fisheries and led to the emergence of the precautionary principle. These agreements include the fishing provisions of the 1982 United Nations Convention on the Law of the Sea (UNCLOS),[1] the so-called U.N. Convention on Straddling and Highly Migratory Fish Stocks (Fish Stocks Agreement),[2] and the U.N. Food and Agricultural Organization Code of Conduct for Responsible Fisheries (Code of Conduct, or Code).[3] Also briefly summarized are a number of other important international and regional agreements that govern fisheries, including the Convention on the Conservation of Antarctic Marine Living Resources,[4] the International Convention for the Conservation of Atlantic Tunas,[5] the Convention for the Conservation and

Management of Highly Migratory Fish Stocks in the Western and Central Pacific Ocean,[6] and the North Atlantic Fisheries Organization (NAFO).[7]

The role of regional fishery management organizations (RFMOs) is explored as a tool for managing resources that cross jurisdictions. Amendments to U.S. laws are also examined that provide substantial new authority to foster RFMOs, push adoption of programs comparable to those of the United States for reducing bycatch of protected species in fishing operations, and address illegal, unregulated, and unreported (IUU) fishing in international waters. Finally, the chapter identifies remaining gaps in international fishery management, particularly high seas fishing and ecosystem approaches to fishery management.

II. The Current State of the Law[8]

A. Historical Background

For most of human history, people have seen the ocean as a frontier to be explored or a limitless and unchangeable source of fish. Hugo Grotius first expressed the philosophy of freedom of the seas in an anonymously published essay in November 1608 in defense of the rights of the Dutch East India Company to trade in waters claimed by Spain or Portugal.[9] Historically, fishing fleets took advantage of access to the richest fishing grounds—relatively shallow areas on the continental shelf—no matter where they were. It was not until after World War II that within their own waters, states exercised control over who fished and how much they caught. Beyond the territorial sea, access to fisheries continued to remain open and subject only to such regulations as their flag state imposed.[10] In the early nineteenth century, increased exploitation of fisheries led several coastal states to enter explicit bilateral and multilateral agreements to conserve and manage fisheries.[11] However, even where a multilateral institution was created by such agreements, the fishing nations and the coastal states generally were not willing to confer on such institutions the authority needed to enforce the rules. Therefore, few of the world's fisheries were subjected to meaningful management.[12]

It was not until after World War II, as world population and food demands increased, and technology increased the distance to which nations could send their fleets in search of fish, that coastal states became concerned that foreign vessels were exploiting fish off their shores. According to commentators, the idea of extending fisheries jurisdiction was fueled not only by the increased capacity of distant water fleets to take amounts of fish viewed by coastal states as excessive, but also by their unwillingness to enter into agreements with coastal states to regulate catch and effort.[13]

It was not until after World War II that coastal states became concerned that foreign vessels were exploiting fish off their shores.

The first push out of coastal state jurisdiction was the 1945 Truman Proclamation, asserting U.S. exclusive jurisdiction and control over the natural resources of the continental shelves "in those areas of the high seas contiguous to the coast of the United States."[14] The Truman Proclamation recognized the pressing need for conservation and protection of fishery resources, and established fishery "conservation zones," subject to U.S. regulation and control.[15] Shortly thereafter, Chile, Peru, and Ecuador followed suit. Even with these claims, however, the principle of freedom of fishing on the high seas was the prevalent doctrine for the next two decades, modified only by such multilateral arrangements as fishing and coastal nations were able to conclude.[16] Although some disputed the limits of extended jurisdiction, most nations accepted the concept of a fishery zone, where a coastal state could claim exclusive jurisdiction independent of its territorial sea.

During this period, a number of agreements were concluded that created international fishery regulatory bodies such as the Inter-American Tropical Tuna Commission,[17] International Pacific Halibut Commission,[18] and the International North Pacific Fisheries Commission.[19] While these bodies, and the conventions and treaties that established them, had conservation as their objective, commentators have noted these shortcomings: The scope of their authority did not reach to all the places the fish were found; the regulatory measures they recommended were not binding without legislative action; and there was no enforcement mechanism or authority other than the flag state.[20] In the period from the 1960s to 1970s, more and more nations extended their fisheries jurisdictions, and numerous states adopted two-hundred-mile fishery zones. The trend toward enlarged national jurisdiction was fueled in part by concerns by coastal states over access to fishing, and by late in the decade the notion that a separate fishery zone, wider than the territorial sea, was widely accepted.[21]

Attempts at widespread international agreement on fishery management were unsuccessful until the 1982 United Nations Conference on the Law of the Sea (UNCLOS).[22] With it came recognition of the extension of coastal state jurisdiction to two-hundred-mile Exclusive Economic Zones (EEZs). In addition to reaffirming the right of coastal states to manage the living marine resources within their two-hundred-mile EEZs, for the first time UNCLOS placed qualifications on the rights of distant water fishing fleets fishing on the high seas.[23]

These international fishery regimes, however, have not solved the problems facing the world's fisheries. Seventy-five percent of fish stocks are now fished at or above sustainable levels, and global production from capture fisheries has remained relatively flat since the 1980s, excluding China.[24]

B. UNCLOS: Fishery Management Provisions of the Law of the Sea Treaty

The 1982 U.N. Convention on the Law of the Sea is the overarching body of law covering every aspect of marine endeavor from transportation to pollution to military issues to scientific research. In its sections on protection of living marine resources, UNCLOS sets out the rights and responsibilities of coastal states and flag states with regard to fishing. While UNCLOS conferred economic rights over resources to coastal states, it preserved the traditional notion of freedom of fishing on the high seas. Although it only entered into force in 1994, "by the time UNCLOS was signed its provisions already constituted customary international law in the eyes of most countries."[25]

UNCLOS gives coastal states sovereign rights over resources out to two hundred miles for "the purpose of exploring and exploiting, conserving and managing the natural resources, whether living or non-living."[26] The coastal nation must ensure, using best scientific information available and conservation and management measures, that the living resources of the EEZ are not threatened by overexploitation.[27] UNCLOS adopts the concept of maximum sustainable yield (MSY) as the goal for maintaining or restoring exploited populations.[28] The costal state is to collect, contribute, and exchange scientific information, catch, and effort statistics with other concerned states.[29] Access to the EEZ by foreign fleets is solely within coastal state discretion and subject to its laws and regulations, including requirements for licensing, observers, and other conservation measures; compliance with conservation and management measures is required.[30] UNCLOS directs states to seek coordinated measures necessary to conserve stocks that occur within the EEZs of two or more coastal states, or adjacent to their zones.[31]

With regard to highly migratory species, UNCLOS calls for cooperation through international organizations and, where none exists, for the establishment of such organizations "with a view to ensuring conservation and promoting the objective of optimum utilization of such species throughout the region, both within and beyond the exclusive economic zone."[32] UNCLOS even imposes new obligations on high seas fishing states. While freedom of fishing on the high seas continues in principle, UNCLOS can be read as imposing a dual responsibility on fishing nations: conservation and cooperation with coastal states.[33]

Even though the 1982 Convention provided a new framework for better fisheries management, the extended jurisdiction of coastal states to two hundred miles was insufficient to protect ocean fisheries. As fleets, technology, and the demand for fish and fishery products grew, it became clear by the late 1980s that the world's fish populations could not withstand continuing rapid and often uncontrolled exploitation and development.[34] Reports of violence, confrontations between fishing nations, uncontrolled fishing on the high seas, and—for the first time in history—several consecutive years of declines in world catches led to a series of meetings and conferences where fishery experts called for action to control high seas fishing. In 1991, the Committee on Fisheries (COFI)[35] called for the development of new concepts to foster responsible, sustainable fisheries. This was followed by an International Conference on Responsible Fishing in Cancun, Mexico, in 1992, where participants adopted a Declaration stating that "States should cooperate . . . to establish, reinforce and implement effective means and mechanisms to ensure responsible fishing on the high seas."[36] These efforts culminated in the 1992 U.N. Conference on Environment and Development in Rio de Janeiro (UNCED).[37]

UNCED, or the "Earth Summit," adopted a list of recommendations, including a chapter on the marine environment. Specifically, Chapter 17.C of Agenda 21 called for the United Nations to find ways to conserve fish populations and prevent international conflicts over fishing on the high seas, consistent with the provisions of the Law of the Sea.[38] Ten years later, at the World Summit on Sustainable Development,

191 nations agreed to a series of targets and timetables to restore depleted fish stocks, manage fishing capacity, prevent IUU fishing, and create marine protected areas.[39]

C. FAO Code of Conduct for Responsible Fisheries

The U.N. Food and Agricultural Organization (FAO) recognized the need for norms for international fisheries and in 1995 unanimously recommended "the formulation of a global Code of Conduct for Responsible Fisheries which would . . . establish principles and standards applicable to the conservation, management and development of all fisheries."[40] In its twelve Articles, the Code of Conduct covers both policy and technical matters including fisheries management, fishing operations, aquaculture, coastal area development, research, and trade.

The Code is voluntary, but some provisions are binding because of their relation to other legal instruments.[41] The Code is directed toward all persons concerned with conservation, management, or development of fisheries, processing, marketing, or any "users of the aquatic environment in relation to fisheries."[42] It provides principles and standards for every aspect of fisheries from aquaculture to capture, from research to fishing operations, from processing to trade.[43]

For the first time, the Code attaches an obligation to the freedom to fish, and calls for users of living marine resources to use them "in a responsible manner so as to ensure effective conservation and management."[44] Intergenerational equity appears in the fishery context for the first time, as well, with the call for maintaining the diversity of fishery resources for "present and future generations" as well as for "food security, poverty alleviation and sustainable development."[45] The Code urges effort controls, ecosystem management, the precautionary approach, selective fishing gear, habitat protection, and use of the best scientific information.[46] It calls for not only monitoring and control of flag state vessels, but also cooperation at all levels and among jurisdictions, and cooperation to prevent disputes.[47]

In procedural recommendations, as well as substantive ones, the Code is far ahead of traditional fishery agreements. States are urged to conduct transparent decision-making processes, provide education and training, provide safe and fair working conditions, and recognize and protect the rights of subsistence, small-scale, and artisanal fishers.[48] Articles 7 through 12 provide specific guidance to states and interested parties on operational and technical matters. These have been further elaborated by a series of technical guidelines from the FAO. Many of the provisions provide further detail on the principles by setting out how, for example, application of the precautionary approach would occur in fishery management measures.[49]

Management objectives include maintaining or restoring stocks to maximum sustainable yield,[50] avoiding excess fishing capacity, protecting biodiversity and endangered species, assessing and mitigating adverse impacts from human activities, and minimizing pollution, waste, discards, ghost fishing,[51] and bycatch.[52] The Code recommends assessment of whole ecosystems and interrelationships, and directs states to consider the whole stock unit over its entire area of distribution.[53]

At the same time the FAO was developing the Code of Conduct for Responsible Fisheries, it was responding to growing concerns, highlighted during the Earth Summit, about incursions on coastal states' EEZs, confrontations between distant water fleets and coastal states, violations of fishing agreements, reflagging to avoid compliance with applicable rules, and general dissatisfaction with increasing fishing pressure on the high seas that was likely to affect stocks or fishing fleets in adjacent EEZs. In November 1993, the parties to the FAO Conference 27th Session adopted the Agreement to Promote Compliance with International Conservation and Management Measures by Fishing Vessels on the High Seas (Compliance Agreement).[54] The parties made clear that the provisions of the agreement were to be made part of the Code, where the Compliance Agreement is referenced as one of the exceptions to the voluntary nature of the Code.[55]

The Compliance Agreement applies to all fishing vessels on the high seas, with a few exceptions for small vessels. Flag states are called upon to ensure that vessels flying their flag do not engage in activity that undermines the effectiveness of international conservation and management measures. The Agreement requires a party to authorize the use of its flag by fishing vessels, and parties may not authorize vessels unless they can exercise control over them, nor may they authorize vessels with previous compliance problems. Significantly, the authorization to fly the flag constitutes an authorization to fish on the high seas, and can be withdrawn: "Where a fishing vessel that has been authorized to be used for fishing on the high seas by a Party ceases to be entitled to fly the flag of that Party, the authorization to fish on the high seas shall be deemed to have been canceled."[56] Parties are required to ensure that vessels are clearly marked, that they can be identified, and that they fulfill record keeping and information sharing obligations. Parties are required to take enforcement measures against vessels acting in contravention to the Agreement, and are urged to use serious sanctions "of sufficient gravity as to be effective in securing compliance . . . and to deprive offenders of the benefits accruing from their illegal activities."[57] Parties are also directed to urge nonparties to adopt consistent measures, and to exchange information about nonparties whose activities undermine the effectiveness of international conservation and management measures.[58]

D. U.N. Convention on Straddling and Highly Migratory Fish Stocks

The most significant outcome of the fishery management directives of Agenda 21 at the Earth Summit was the Agreement for the Implementation of the Provisions of the United Nations Convention on the Law of the Sea Relating to the Conservation and Management of Straddling Fish Stocks and Highly Migratory Fish (Fish Stocks Agreement).[59] The Fish Stocks Agreement, which prescribes "generally recommended international minimum standards" for conservation,[60] has been called a "sea change" in international fishery management.[61]

Following a conference to address the problems of high seas fishing convened on April 19, 1993, delegates met six times in negotiating sessions over the next two years, concluding a document that was open for signing on December 4, 1995. As of April 2007, sixty-six states and the European Community had become parties.[62]

The Fish Stocks Agreement establishes detailed minimum international standards for the conservation and management of straddling fish stocks and highly migratory fish stocks.[63] It calls for compatible measures and effective high seas compliance and enforcement. It was the first time an international fishing agreement shifted focus from producing maximum food for humans to sustainable fishing, ecosystem protection, conservation of biodiversity, and the precautionary approach to fishery management.[64] It also is the first agreement to produce an actual methodology for the precautionary approach, setting up reference points, targets, and limits.[65] Most significantly, it denies (for party nations) unqualified access to fish on the high seas.[66]

The Fish Stocks Agreement does all this without creating a new international structure, relying instead on existing regional agreements and organizations, and calling for mechanisms to strengthen them. Where such agreements or organizations do not exist, it directs states to create them.[67] It also elaborates on the fundamental principle, established in UNCLOS, that states should cooperate to ensure conservation and promote the objective of the optimum utilization of fisheries resources both within and beyond the exclusive economic zone.[68]

The Fish Stocks Agreement provided for subsequent conferences to assess the adequacy of the provisions and propose ways to strengthen its implementation. These conferences have resulted in declaration of additional objectives such as considering the regional, subregional, and global implementation. Informal consultations of state parties have met annually to continue review and oversight of the implementation of the Fish Stocks Agreement.[69]

E. U.N. Resolution Prohibiting Large-Scale Pelagic Driftnet Fishing

Large-scale, high seas driftnets were recognized in the 1980s as a significant cause of incidental take of marine mammals, birds, turtles, and nontarget fish species. This gear was finally banned internationally by United Nations resolution in 1990.[70]

Until they were outlawed, driftnets were used in the North Pacific and on the high seas where single vessels were capable of deploying driftnets ranging from up to forty miles in length. In the North Pacific from 1976 to 1989, two million miles (3.2 million km) of net were set per season.[71] With more than enough netting set each night to encircle the earth, not only were target fish caught (squid, tuna, and billfish) but approximately 100,000 dolphins and porpoises, and hundreds of thousands of seabirds, sharks, sea turtles, and salmon.

Single vessels were capable of deploying driftnets ranging from up to forty miles in length.

Although the driftnet fleet operated under requirements set by a multinational agreement relating to salmon fishing, that agreement did not address incidental take of birds and marine mammals.[72] Additionally, the fleets were frequently found by U.S. enforcement to be catching salmon and steelhead in violation of the provisions of the governing treaty. In 1987, due to continued compliance problems with Japan, Korea, and Taiwan, the U.S. Congress passed the Driftnet Impact Monitoring, Assessment, and Control Act (Driftnet Act), calling for negotiations with the nations driftnetting in the North Pacific to establish monitoring and enforcement agreements by June 29, 1989.[73] If these nations refused to come to the bargaining table, they risked trade sanctions.[74] The Driftnet Act required further research into the nature and extent of driftnet fishing to facilitate the development of effective solutions to the problem.[75]

The Driftnet Act also addressed the control of driftnet debris. Congress assigned the Secretary of Commerce with three responsibilities: establishment of controls for marking, registry, and identification of foreign driftnets so that the original vessel can be identified if its gear is lost, abandoned, or discarded; development of alternative materials for making driftnets "for the purpose of increasing the rate of decomposition"; and the implementation of a bounty system, so that people who find, retrieve, and return to the Secretary of Commerce lost, abandoned, or discarded driftnets and other plastic fishing materials may receive payment.[76]

Driftnetting had also become a major concern in the South Pacific. After several nations had banned driftnet fishing in their waters, twenty nations in the South Pacific negotiated and signed the Convention for the Prohibition of Fishing with Long Driftnets in the South Pacific (The Wellington Convention).[77] The Wellington Convention endorsed a ban on driftnets as of May 1991, prevented the violators from crossing their waters, and denied access to food, fuel, and facilities of the signing nations. The Wellington Convention set the stage for international efforts to end driftnetting.

On December 22, 1989, the United Nations General Assembly passed Resolution 44/225, promoted by the United States and New Zealand, calling for an end to driftnetting by June 30, 1992, and an end in the South Pacific by 1991.[78] Although Resolution 44/225 is nonbinding under international law, its strength lies in the fact that it demonstrates a global consensus on the issue. Its weakness, however, is that South Korea and Taiwan are not Member States of the United Nations and use driftnets frequently. Moreover, the Resolution carries neither sanctions nor any mechanisms for monitoring driftnet operations.

Conflicts continued between driftnet fishing nations and nations opposed to the practice. Reports surfaced of the introduction of driftnets into new areas such as the Caribbean, and in 1990 the United Nations passed Resolution 45/197 restating concern about the practice of driftnetting and calling for a report on driftnetting.[79]

In June 1991, the observer data from two previous years of driftnetting were compiled and experts met in British Columbia to discuss the results. The numbers confirmed fears of massive numbers of marine mammals, sea birds, and nontarget fish being killed by the driftnet fishery. Armed with the new data, the United States submitted a report to the United Nations condemning the use of large-scale pelagic driftnets, and soon thereafter introduced a resolution mandating a ban on their use by June 1992. Japan introduced a resolution to study the problem further, again suggesting that there may be 'effective management measures' available to continue the fishery. However, the U.N. General Assembly passed Resolution 46/215, which stated, without exceptions, that large-scale high seas driftnetting end by December 31, 1992.[80] The deadline affects the high seas. But it should be noted that much driftnetting continues within the EEZs of many nations, including the United States, with only slightly smaller nets.

The United Nations reaffirmed its stance on driftnets in 1995, particularly in the context of unauthorized fishing in national zones, of the effects of driftnets on bycatch mortality, and in the adoption of the FAO Code of Conduct for Responsible Fisheries. The General Assembly resolution reaffirms the global moratorium on high seas driftnet fishing, urges nations to take greater enforcement responsibility and to impose sanctions, refers to the Compliance Agreement and states' responsibilities under that convention, and makes a high priority of improvement of monitoring and enforcement.[81]

F. Convention on International Trade in Endangered Species of Wild Fauna and Flora

The Convention on International Trade in Endangered Species (CITES) is a multilateral treaty regarding the export, import, and transit of certain species of wild animals and plants—trade that poses a threat to their continued survival.[82] The goal of CITES is to prevent overexploitation of listed species whose survival is jeopardized.[83]

CITES entered into force July 1, 1975, and contains Appendices that list species based on a set of criteria. Parties to CITES may not trade in species listed in the Appendices of the Convention, except as prescribed.[84] Appendix I lists species threatened with extinction, Appendix II lists species that may become threatened with extinction unless trade is subject to regulation, and Appendix III lists species that are protected by individual state parties. Commercial trade is generally prohibited for Appendix I species.[85] Commercial trade in Appendix II species requires an export permit verifying that trade will not be detrimental to the survival of the species.[86] "CITES allows the imposition of bans against the export of listed species to any signatory nation in order to diminish the economic incentives for continued taking" of the species.[87]

The Conference of the Parties (CoP) is the decision-making body of CITES, made up of all its member states. It has adopted a set of biological and trade criteria to help determine whether a species should be included in Appendices I or II. At each regular meeting of the CoP, parties submit proposals based on those criteria to amend these two Appendices. Those amendment proposals are discussed and then submitted to a vote. Although only nine species of marine fishes are listed on CITES appendices, assessment of marine species has become a priority of the International Union for the Conservation of Nature (IUCN), which began a comprehensive regional assessment of marine species groups in 2006. The IUCN publishes the Red List of Threatened Species, which in 2006 included 1,372 species of fish (both marine and freshwater).[88]

G. Regional Fishery Management Organizations and Agreements

Although regional fishery management organizations (RFMOs) have existed since the 1940s and earlier, their importance has increased significantly with the adoption of treaties such as the Fish Stocks Agreement, which call for creation of such bodies. In its Oceans Atlas, FAO editors point out that "under existing international law, and within the current paradigm for the governance of high seas fisheries to regulate straddling, highly migratory and high seas fish stocks, [Regional Fishery Management Organizations] provide the only realistic mechanism for the enhanced international cooperation in their conservation and management."[89]

Table 10.1
Regional Fishery Management Organizations

Commission for the Conservation of Antarctic Marine Living Resources

Commission for the Conservation of Southern Bluefin Tuna

Commission for Inland Fisheries of Latin America

Fishery Committee for the Eastern Central Atlantic

Forum Fisheries Agency

General Fisheries Commission for the Mediterranean

Indian Ocean Tuna Commission

Inter-American Tropical Tuna Commission

International Baltic Sea Fishery Commission

International Commission for the Conservation of Atlantic Tunas

International Pacific Halibut Commission

International Whaling Commission

North Atlantic Salmon Conservation Organization

Northeast Atlantic Fisheries Commission

Northwest Atlantic Fisheries Organization

North Atlantic Salmon Conservation Organization

North East Atlantic Fisheries Commission

As of 2006, there were forty-four regional fishery bodies including RFMOs, advisory bodies, and scientific bodies. These organizations' responsibilities include collecting and distributing fishery statistics, stock assessments, setting catch quotas, limiting vessels allowed in the fishery, regulating gear, allocation, research oversight, monitoring, and enforcement.[90]

Although the implementation of many of the regional agreements hinges on the effectiveness of the relevant RFMO, the success of these organizations has been the exception rather than the rule. The RFMOs are only as strong as the members make them, and rely on flag state enforcement of their provisions. Criticisms and shortcomings of these bodies include inconsistent authority; failure of key fishing interests to join the RFMO or participate by its rules; illegal, unreported, and unregulated fishing; lack of equity and disparate interests between developed states and developing states; conflicts of interest among parties; lack of funding; and lack of political will.[91] A number of innovations have been suggested to make RFMOs more effective including audits, performance review, improvements through neutral bodies such as the FAO, a stronger role for port state enforcement, the use of technology such as vessel monitoring systems to track fishing, and modifying incentives for membership to ensure participation by all interested parties.[92]

This section describes major regional agreements creating RFMOs in the North Atlantic, South Atlantic, North Pacific, South Pacific, Indian, and Southern Ocean regions. Additional agreements in the ocean regions are listed in the tables. These regional agreements are representative of both the older, pre-Fish Stocks Agreement conventions and the newer, more precautionary regimes that provide additional authority for coastal and port states to take action against distant water fleets fishing in their regions. It has been argued that even though the RFMOs have not had much time to prove their mettle, it is time to consider a more structured framework international management organization with nations as "beneficial owners."[93] Rather than relying on cooperation among RFMOs, the governance structure would call for a right to share in the net wealth generated from sustainable harvest of high seas fisheries. In contrast, those who want to preserve the rights of individual states argue that RFMOs should be strengthened in order to enhance compliance and performance of their member flag states. At a 2006 meeting of the parties to the Fish Stocks Agreement, other recommendations to improve RFMO performance included accountability underscored by performance measures, self-assessments, independent external performance review, and an international panel of experts to conduct such review.[94]

1. North Atlantic Ocean

The Convention on Future Multilateral Cooperation in the Northwest Atlantic Fisheries established the Northwest Atlantic Fisheries Organization (NAFO).[95] Although the Convention applies to the whole of the northwest Atlantic, the regulatory powers of NAFO include only the high seas beyond the EEZs of its members.[96] This regulatory area is divided into six subareas. NAFO's members are Bulgaria, Canada, Cuba, Denmark, European Union, France (in respect of St. Pierre et Miquelon), Iceland, Japan, Korea, Norway, Russia, and the United States.[97]

A general council oversees the organization and coordinates the legal, financial, and administrative affairs of NAFO.[98] A scientific council serves as a forum for analysis and consultation among scientists from the member states.[99] The Fisheries Commission decides on management and conservation measures, with the purpose of ensuring consistency in the EEZs of member states.[100]

NAFO has jurisdiction over all fishes in the Regulatory Area with the exception of salmon, tunas, marlin, and the sedentary species of the continental shelf.[101] NAFO currently provides for the conservation and management of stocks of American plaice, yellowtail flounder, cod, witch flounder, redfish, Greenland halibut, capelin, and squid. Stocks that straddle the Regulatory Area and Canada's EEZ, such as cod, American plaice, redfish, flounder, and Greenland halibut, are regular objects of diplomatic tension.[102] Conflicts also have arisen with the vessels of nonparties, including Chile,

Malta, Mauritania, Mexico, Panama, St. Vincent and the Grenadines, and Venezuela. Some of these vessels have reflagged from member states of NAFO to nonmember states.[103]

2. South Atlantic Ocean

a. The Southeast Atlantic Convention

Until the late 1990s, there were no regional management regimes for fisheries in the Southeast Atlantic. Angola, Namibia, and South Africa had formed the Southern Africa Development Community (SADC), which includes a Marine Fisheries Policy and Strategy. These three coastal states of the southeast Atlantic negotiated access agreements with distant water fleets. In the late 1990s, Namibia, South Africa, and the United Kingdom began talks on the formation of a new fisheries organization, called the Southeast Atlantic Fisheries Organization, for the conservation and management of deepwater straddling stocks. Eventually Angola, the European Community, Iceland, Namibia, Norway, Republic of Korea, South Africa, United Kingdom (on behalf of St. Helena and its dependencies of Tristan da Cunha and Ascension Islands), and the United States signed the Convention on the Conservation and Management of Fishery Resources in the Southeast Atlantic Ocean (Southeast Atlantic Convention).[104] States that have participated in the negotiations but have not signed the Convention are Japan, Russian Federation, and Ukraine.

Table 10.2
Atlantic Ocean Agreements and Organizations

Convention for Fisheries and Conservation of Living Resources of the Black Sea

Convention on Conduct of Fishing Operations in the North Atlantic

Convention on Future Multilateral Cooperation in the Northeast Atlantic Fisheries

EU Fisheries Agreement (Common Fisheries Policy)

General Fisheries Council for the Mediterranean

International Convention for the Conservation of Atlantic Tunas

International Convention for the Northwest Atlantic Fisheries

International Council for the Exploration of the Sea

The Southeast Atlantic Convention is one of the first regional fisheries agreements negotiated since the adoption of the U.N. Fish Stocks Agreement, and closely follows that model.[105] It seeks to ensure the conservation and sustainable management of the fishery resources of the Southeast Atlantic, and establishes the South-East Atlantic Fisheries Commission (Commission) as the RFMO to implement the Convention.[106]

The Southeast Atlantic Convention sets long-term conservation and sustainable use as a goal. Articles 2, 3, and 7 set out principals such as the precautionary approach, ecosystem management, protection of biological diversity, and protection of the marine ecosystem. Recognition of the special position of developing states is taken in Articles 12 and 21. Species covered in Article 1 are all but sedentary species within the coastal states' jurisdiction. The geographic coverage of the convention is roughly FAO Statistical Area 47.

The Commission defines fishing broadly, taking in such activities as support operations, mother ships, transshipment, and similar activities.[107] The responsibilities of the Commission include setting quotas, allocating fishing rights, determining participants in the fishery, and other management duties. The Convention also creates a Scientific Committee and a Compliance Committee.[108] Flag states are responsible for authorizing their vessels to fish in the Convention area, for keeping a record of such authorizations, for reporting catches, and monitoring compliance. In addition, port states are authorized to develop control measures, conduct inspections, and deploy observers.

b. International Convention for the Conservation of Atlantic Tunas

Management regimes for the conservation of highly migratory species, such as salmon and tuna, which cross national boundaries, require international cooperation. In the Atlantic Ocean, the organization with responsibility for large ocean species is the International Convention for the Conservation of Atlantic Tunas (ICCAT).[109] ICCAT was established to respond to concern about the dramatic decline of bluefin and other tunas.[110] Although it entered into force in 1969, the first measures to restrict catch were not adopted until the 1975 fishing season. Its efficacy as a conservation and management agreement has been controversial since its inception.[111]

ICCAT's efficacy as a conservation and management agreement has been controversial since its inception.

ICCAT established the International Commission for the Conservation of Atlantic Tunas (Commission), which has ocean-wide responsibility for nearly all species of tuna, swordfish, and billfishes, as well as fishes exploited in tuna fishing if these are not under investigation by another international organization.[112] The principal goal of ICCAT is to maintain populations at levels that will permit maximum sustainable catch for food and other purposes.[113] The Commission may, on the basis of scientific evidence, make regulatory recommendations.[114] It does not explicitly provide for allocation, but that has become a large part of its activity. It has been observed that one of ICCAT's failures is that it is unable to prevent excess effort, and therefore cannot achieve a management objective of allocating benefits.[115] "In the case of ICCAT, if its recommended regulations have in fact improved the fishery, this has not been reflected in member states' willingness to support the agency."[116]

Commissioners set management policy.[117] They meet annually to review findings by the Standing Committee on Research and Science (SCRS). Unlike the Secretariat of the Inter-American Tropical Tuna Commission (IATTC), which has its own scientific staff, the ICCAT Secretariat depends on member-country scientists, and the Commissioners have no independent source of scientific advice.[118] Scientists from several countries comprise the scientific committee that compiles catch statistics and models population trends. With the decline in some large pelagic populations in the Atlantic Ocean, discussion and decisions among Commissioners and within the scientific committee have become highly politicized.[119]

Although the Commissioners adopt management measures such as size limits and quotas, ICCAT has no authority to implement or enforce its recommendations, and relies on member nations to implement them. In its earlier years, ICCAT could not take action against nonmembers.[120] Since the late 1990s, ICCAT has had quota compliance rules on the books that allow for the imposition of penalties, including trade sanctions, against members for quota overharvests in the swordfish and bluefin tuna fisheries.[121] Sanctions have been applied to a member under the quota compliance rules once. In 2003, ICCAT adopted a comprehensive trade measures resolution that covers both members and nonmembers.[122] The trade measures resolution has not yet been applied against an ICCAT member although several nonmembers have had sanctions placed against them under the 2003 measure and its predecessors.[123]

According to conservation advocates, management under ICCAT has resulted in a decline in Western Atlantic bluefin tuna, and until recently, substantial overexploitation of swordfish.[124] The history of ICCAT decisions on bluefin tuna and swordfish illustrates a continued practice of setting catch levels in response to demands of fishing nations, regardless of recommendations of its scientific committee.[125] Even under the Atlantic Tunas Convention Act (ATCA), the U.S. legislation that implements the Convention domestically, the U.S. government cannot alter a U.S. quota allocation adopted by ICCAT—even if the quota level agreed by ICCAT has been set at an unsustainable level.[126]

At the Commission's 2006 meeting, marking the forty-year anniversary of ICCAT, incoming chairman Dr. William Hogarth of the United States described bluefin fishing in the eastern Atlantic as "out of control." In comments after the meeting, Dr. Hogarth said:

> I am very disappointed that the international fishing community was unable to agree to a plan to halt the severe over-harvest of eastern Atlantic and Mediterranean bluefin tuna . . . Ignoring advice from ICCAT's own scientific advisory committee, the EU recommendation did not incorporate a suggested three-year quota reduction, did not address over-harvest in past years, and did not include provisions to reduce harvest in future years if over-harvesting continues.[127]

The scientific analysis by ICCAT's Standing Committee for Research and Statistics (SCRS) presented at the meeting in Croatia found the current fishing mortality rate three times the level necessary to stabilize the bluefin tuna stock, according to reports of the meeting. A member of the U.S. delegation said, "Dire warnings from ICCAT's scientific panel, unprecedented public scrutiny in Europe and elsewhere, and unusually outspoken criticism from other ICCAT members; all were not enough" to achieve cutbacks in the catch quota for bluefin tuna.[128] Although the U.S. delegation pressed the body to heed the SCRS scientific findings of impending eastern collapse, delegates did not vote to cut catches back to the recommended level.[129]

It has been suggested that ICCAT needs to be updated to reflect the more recent policy standards of the Fish Stocks Agreement and the precautionary approach.[130] Neither the treaty establishing ICCAT nor its implementation reflects the precautionary approach.[131] Indeed, ICCAT members have successfully resisted consideration of changes necessary to bring ICCAT into consistency with Fish Stocks Agreement requirements such as binding regulations, enforcement, collection of scientific and catch information, precautionary reference points, and rebuilding requirements.[132]

The ICCAT Commission itself may recognize that it is time for an update. In a PowerPoint presentation on the ICCAT Web site, the Commission discusses considerations apparent in "adapting a 40-year-old convention to modern instruments," including the requirements of the Fish Stocks Agreement, flag state requirements, port state measures, more effective reference points, bycatch, and ecosystem-based approaches to management.[133]

With Dr. Hogarth taking the helm at ICCAT, the organization faces the potential of an activist role by the United States from within and without—through the mandates of recent amendments to the Magnuson Stevens Act calling for better compliance from high seas and international fisheries.[134]

3. North Pacific

Intense fishing for pollock occurs in an area of the North Pacific that is outside the EEZs of the United States and the Russian Federation.[135] Concerns about the impact of this fishing on pollock stocks within the EEZs of the United States and the Russian Federation led to a series of negotiations that began in 1991 and concluded in February 1994 with the Convention on the Conservation and Management of Pollock Resources in the Central Bering Sea (Bering Sea Convention) among China, South Korea, Poland, the Russian Federation, and the United States.[136] (Because of its diplomatic dispute with China, Taiwan is not a signatory.) The Bering Sea Convention's objectives are conservation, management, optimum utilization of Bering Sea pollock, restoration of pollock to levels that will produce maximum sustainable yield, and cooperation in data gathering.

Rather than establishing a separate Secretariat, the Bering Sea Convention calls for annual meetings of the member states, between which the governments of the member states are to perform many of the functions of a Secretariat.[137] The only "internationalized" administrative structure is the Scientific and Technical Committee (STC), which is composed of at least one representative from each member state.[138] The STC provides the annual meeting of the member states with the assessments of Aleutian Basin pollock that are the basis for the harvest levels.

Principal functions of the annual meeting include setting the allowable harvest level for pollock in the area covered by the Convention and allocating this quota among the member states.[139] The annual meeting also is to adopt other conservation and management measures, to establish terms and conditions for any trial fishing operations, to discuss cooperative enforcement measures, to review an observer program established by the member states, and to discuss scientific research in the region.

Table 10.3
Pacific Ocean Agreements and Organizations

Asia Pacific Fishery Commission

Asia-Pacific Economic Cooperation

Convention for a North Pacific Marine Science Organization

Convention for the Conservation of Anadromous Stocks in the North Pacific Ocean

Convention for the Prohibition of Fishing with Long Driftnets in the South Pacific Ocean

Convention on the Conservation and Management of Highly Migratory Fish Stocks in the Western and Central Pacific

Eastern Pacific Ocean Tuna Fishing Agreement

Inter-American Tropical Tuna Commission

International Convention for the High Seas Fisheries of the North Pacific Ocean

International Pacific Halibut Commission

Latin American Organization for Fisheries Development

North Pacific Anadromous Fisheries Convention

Pacific Salmon Treaty

All decisions of substance must be taken by consensus. If a member state considers a matter to be of substance, then it is to be voted on in that way. Other decisions are taken by simple majority vote.

4. South Pacific

The Convention for the Establishment of an Inter-American Tropical Tuna Commission (IATTC)[140] defines its area of competence as the Eastern Pacific Ocean, but does not further define the area. The IATTC focuses on skipjack tuna, yellowfin tuna, and fish used as bait, although it has studied bigeye tuna, black skipjack, bluefin tuna, albacore tuna, and billfishes, as well as dolphins, turtles, and sharks. Members are Costa Rica, Ecuador, El Salvador, France, Guatemala, Japan, Mexico, Nicaragua, Panama, Peru, Republic of Korea, the United States, Vanuatu, and Venezuela. Belize, Canada, China, Cook Islands, the European Union, Honduras, and Chinese Taipei are Cooperating Non Parties or Cooperating Fishing Entities.[141]

Unlike other tuna management regimes, the IATTC maintains an independent scientific staff that collects catch and other information and prepares recommendations for the member governments.

The IATTC is authorized to make recommendations to its members regarding measures that will maintain the fishes covered by the Convention at levels that will permit maximum sustained catch. The Convention also calls for the Commission to collect, analyze, and disseminate information regarding the catches and operations of vessels in the fishery. Unlike other tuna management regimes, the IATTC maintains an independent scientific staff that collects catch and other information and prepares recommendations for the member governments. IATTC has also carried out a program to estimate bycatch of nontarget fishes and dolphins in the fishery.

At a September 1990 meeting in Costa Rica, representatives of Chile, Colombia, Costa Rica, Ecuador, El Salvador, France, Honduras, Japan, Mexico, Nicaragua, Panama, Spain, the United States, Vanuatu, and Venezuela agreed that the IATTC was the appropriate body to coordinate technical aspects of the program to reduce the incidental capture and mortality of dolphins in their EEZs and the adjacent high seas during purse seine operations. At a 1995 meeting, the member countries of the IATTC adopted a Declaration on Strengthening the Objectives and Operation of the IATTC, which called for implementing the Fish Stocks Agreement.

Another agreement in the Pacific, the Convention on the Conservation and Management of Highly Migratory Fish Stocks in the Western and Central Pacific Ocean,[142] was one of the first treaties developed after the Fish Stocks Agreement. It was the culmination of complex negotiations among twenty-five nations including small island nations and developed countries with active distant water fleets. As of November 2004, Australia, China, Cook Islands, Federated States of Micronesia, Fiji Islands, Korea, Kiribati, Marshall Islands, Nauru, New Zealand, Niue, Papua New Guinea, Samoa, Solomon Islands, Tonga, and Tuvalu had ratified or acceded to the Convention.[143]

5. Indian Ocean

The Convention for the Conservation of Southern Bluefin Tuna (CCSBT)[144] arose from annual trilateral meetings among Australia, Japan, and New Zealand. The three countries had operated under a voluntary management agreement, but negotiated the formal convention in response to continued heavy fishing that had resulted in significant declines of mature fish throughout the 1980s.[145]

Table 10.4
Indian Ocean Organizations

Indian Ocean Fishery Commission
Indian Ocean Tuna Commission
Southwest Indian Ocean Fisheries Commission

Concerned that activity of nonparty nations in the fishery was reducing the effectiveness of members' conservation and management measures, the parties in 1996 asked Taiwan, South Korea, and Indonesia to become parties. On October 17, 2001, the Republic of Korea joined the membership. The Fishing Entity of Taiwan's membership of the Extended Commission became effective on August 30, 2002.[146]

In 2003, the CCSBT allowed countries with an interest in the fishery to participate in its activities as formal cooperating nonmembers. These parties must comply with the management and conservation objectives and agreed catch limits of the Convention and may participate in discussions, but cannot vote. The Philippines was accepted as a formal cooperating nonmember in 2004, and parties continue discussions with Indonesia and South Africa.[147]

The CCSBT goal is conservation and optimum utilization of bluefin tuna.[148] Though the scope of the Convention limits its attention to bluefin tuna, definitions include consideration of all "ecologically related species."[149] The CCSBT covers not just fishing activity, but support operations as well. State parties are required to enforce the provisions of the Convention, provide information including scientific and catch statistics and effort data, exchange scientific and fishing information, and report fishing by nonparties. Member countries are legally bound by decisions on total allowable catch and other conservation and management measures. Enforcement is by the parties on their flag vessels. Significantly, the CCSBT requires parties to take action to prevent vessels from transferring registration to avoid compliance with CCSBT Commission decisions.[150] Member countries also must act to deter nonparties from activities that undermine the objectives of the Convention. The measures adopted by the CCSBT are not limited to the high seas, but apply to the EEZs of all member countries.

CCSBT Commission duties include gathering and disseminating scientific information, statistical data, and legal information. It adopts regulations, sets catch limits, allocates catch, and operates a monitoring system.[151] All decisions are by unanimous vote.[152] The CCSBT created a Scientific Committee, and allows both nonparty and NGO observers at meetings.

6. Southern Ocean

The principal instrument for management of fisheries in the Southern Ocean is the 1980 Convention on the Conservation of Antarctic Marine Living Resources (CCAMLR).[153] By the time it came into force, CCAMLR had inherited significantly damaged fish stocks—twelve of thirteen assessed fish stocks were considered depleted.[154]

> **By the time CCAMLR came into force, twelve of thirteen assessed fish stocks were considered depleted.**

The purpose of CCAMLR is to ensure conservation of Antarctic marine living resources in the high seas within the Antarctic.[155] Unlike most other conventions on fisheries, CCAMLR requires rational use in accordance with the following ecosystem-based conservation principles:

- Prevention of decreases in the size of any harvested population to levels below those which ensure stable recruitment;
- Maintenance of ecological relationships among harvested, dependent, and related populations of Antarctic marine living resources and the restoration of depleted populations; and
- Prevention of changes or minimization of the risk of changes in the marine ecosystems that are not potentially reversible over two to three decades.[156]

The CCAMLR Commission coordinates research, gathers and analyzes catch and effort statistics, identifies and evaluates conservation measures, adopts conservation measures based on the best scientific evidence, and implements observer and inspection programs.[157] The Commission, not state parties, places observers on fishing vessels. Commission membership is open to the original participants in the negotiations and to countries who have acceded to the convention, on approval of an application and indication of willingness to abide by conservation measures that are in force under the Convention.[158]

The Commission may designate open and closed seasons, set quotas, and regulate gear.[159] Decisions on matters of substance require a consensus. Observers from nonmember countries and nongovernmental organizations may attend most meetings with few restrictions, and may submit reports and views.

The Antarctic Scientific Committee includes representatives from countries that are members of the Commission. The Committee regularly assesses the status and trends of Antarctic marine living resources and the effectiveness of conservation measures, and has established programs such as developing precautionary measures for krill exploitation, ecosystem monitoring, and acquiring catch and effort data.[160]

In design, CCAMLR is considered one of the most advanced of fisheries conservation regimes in the world.[161] It is consistent in many respects with the Fish Stocks Agreement. Besides a conservation-based management goal, CCAMLR also includes significant elements of the precautionary approach, including conservation controls over exploratory and new fisheries.[162] CCAMLR's observer and inspection programs are considered among the most developed in international fisheries management organizations. For example, members may board vessels of other members for the purposes of inspection; if a breach of CCAMLR rules is detected, the flag state must inform CCAMLR of the action it has taken against the offender.[163] CCAMLR also requires flag states to maintain an accessible registry of vessels, to ensure that vessels are properly marked, and to report catch and other information in a timely fashion.[164]

H. Magnuson-Stevens Fishery Conservation and Management Act 2006 Amendments

In 2006 the Congress reauthorized the Magnuson-Stevens Fishery Conservation and Management Act (MSA Reauthorization),[165] the law governing how the United States manages fisheries within its EEZ. The reauthorization directed substantial attention to fishing issues outside U.S. waters, particularly illegal, unregulated, and unreported (IUU) fishing and bycatch in high seas fisheries. New provisions are aimed primarily at strengthening U.S. leadership in international conservation and management of fisheries to level the playing field between the U.S. fleet and those of other nations.[166] The law also provides for implementation of the Western and Central Pacific Fisheries Convention.[167]

Section 207 of the Reauthorization creates an international title authorizing the Secretary of Commerce to promote improved monitoring and compliance for high seas fisheries or fisheries governed by international or regional fishery management agreements.[168] Among other provisions, the section calls for improved communication and information exchange among law enforcement organizations, an international monitoring network, an international vessel registry, expansion of remote sensing technology, technical assistance to developing countries, and support of a global vessel monitoring system for large vessels by the end of 2008.[169]

The international provisions of the Reauthorization are designed to "strengthen the ability of international fishery management organizations, and the United States, to ensure appropriate enforcement and compliance with conservation and management measures in high seas fisheries," particularly with regard to IUU fishing, expanding fleets, and high bycatch levels.[170]

Section 207 also establishes an international compliance and monitoring program, authorizing the Secretary of Commerce to promote improved monitoring and compliance for high seas fisheries or fisheries governed by international or regional fishery management agreements. Authorized activities include information sharing including real-time reporting, an international monitoring network, registry of fishing vessels, enhanced enforcement capability including use of remote sensing technology, technical assistance to developing countries, and a requirement for VMS systems on all large-scale vessels operating on the high seas by the end of 2008.[171]

Section 403 of the Reauthorization's international provisions amends the High Seas Driftnet Fisheries Enforcement Act[172] by adding four new sections: a requirement for a biennial report on international compliance; action to strengthen regional fishery management organizations; identification and listing of nations whose vessels participate in IUU fishing; and identification and listing of nations that "fail to end or reduce bycatch of protected living marine resources by using regulatory measures that are comparable to those of the United States, taking into account different conditions."[173] "Protected living marine resource" are defined as nontarget fish, sea turtles, or marine mammals that are protected under U.S. law or international agreement.[174]

In cases where regional or international fishery management organizations or the nation in question are unable to stop IUU fishing, amendments to the High Seas Driftnet Fisheries Enforcement Act allow for the use of sanctions to enforce compliance.[175] The steps include identification, listing, and certification prior to sanction.

The listing provisions are very comparable to certification under the Pelly and Packwood amendments.[176] The Secretary of Commerce determines whether a nation has taken appropriate corrective action in response to illegal fishing, gives the offending party notice and opportunity for comment, and then certifies to Congress whether it has provided documentary evidence of corrective action.[177]

A listing is required if vessels of that nation have engaged in IUU fishing within the past year, the relevant International Fishery Management Organization (IFMO) has not implemented measures to end IUU fishing by that nation's vessels or the nation is not party to an IFMO, or no relevant IFMO exists.

Once a nation is listed, the Secretary of the Treasury is required to withhold or revoke the clearance of any vessels of the identified nation and deny them entry into the navigable waters or any port of the United States; prohibit the importation of fish, fish products, or sport fishing gear from that nation; and impose other economic sanctions if denial of clearance and import bans are not successful in stopping the violation.[178]

A similar procedure is required for bycatch of protected living marine resources in international waters or of a protected resource shared by the United States. The certification must demonstrate that

- the vessels have had bycatch in the prior year;
- the relevant organization has failed to implement measures to reduce such bycatch;
- the nation is not a party to a relevant organization; or
- the nation has not adopted a bycatch reduction program comparable to that of the United States.[179]

After a notification and consultation process that gives the international community time to respond under relevant agreements, amend existing treaties or develop new instruments, the list of certified nations is provided to Congress and the sanctions of the Driftnet Enforcement Act may be applied.[180] An alternative procedure allows for certification on a shipment-by-shipment or shipper-by-shipper basis of fish or fish products. The measure calls for the Secretary of Commerce and Secretary of State to provide assistance to nations or organizations to help them develop gear and management plans that will reduce bycatch.[181]

III. Emerging and Unresolved Issues

Though some international fishery agreements are celebrating anniversaries in multiple decades, there is a growing consensus that traditional forms of management and governance are still not doing the job. Even the Fish Stocks Agreement, held out by many as the model for the future of precautionary fishery management, has critical gaps.[182] IUU fishing, fisheries targeting deep sea species in international waters, compliance with existing agreements, and approaches to ecosystem-based management in large marine systems all remain outside the reach of existing international law and practice. Even fisheries that are managed or that fall within national, international, or regional agreements suffer from overexploitation because of excess capacity issues. None of the existing agreements, including those examined here, get at what many experts argue is the heart of the matter: rights, privileges, access, and allocation.

None of the existing agreements get at what many experts argue is the heart of the matter: rights, privileges, access, and allocation.

Allocation is of increasing national and international interest to those involved in fisheries management. At a conference in Australia in early 2006, presenters tackled the issue of "Sharing the Fish" from legal, economic, social, governance, and biological perspectives.[183] Whether governance takes the form of an international framework, shoring up the authority of RFMOs, application of rights-based systems in the international realm, market solutions, or trading fisheries commission quotas among states, experts and practitioners seem to agree that the next frontier should be an examination of some new principles of resource sharing.[184]

The problem of IUU fishing has been a topic in the U.S. Congress, at the United Nations, and at meetings of RFMOs. The United Nations considers IUU fishing one of the most severe problems facing global fisheries.[185] IUU fishing undermines sustainable fishery efforts and robs the poorest nations of more than $1 billion worth of fish per year.[186] Noncompliance with management regimes by both members and nonmembers has a significant effect on undermining any conservation benefit of the rules agreed to and implemented by member nations. The far-reaching effects of IUU fishing were part of the impetus for passage in the United States of legislation providing significant new authority to reach out to nations fishing on the high seas to compel compliance with generally accepted practices.[187]

In addition to these unilateral efforts by the United States, the parties reviewing implementation of the Fish Stocks Agreement have discussed strategies to reduce IUU fishing. In a May 2006 conference to review the agreement, members proposed increased controls over ports and fishing vessels to reduce illegal fishing.[188] Other recommendations included satellite tracking systems of fishing vessels, a stronger system of controls on vessels flying flags of convenience, and steps that would make it more difficult to offload illegal fish catches in ports. Norway proposed, and the United States, Australia, and the European Community supported, the idea of a global binding instrument among all port states, agreeing to mandatory obligations such as inspection of documents, fishing gears, and catch on board—all measures already included in the Fish Stocks Agreement.[189] Canadian representatives encouraged fishing nations to join the relevant RFMO and obey its management rules or abstain from fishing. Canada also called for concerted international action to address fishing vessels operating under flags of convenience, and urged the Conference to endorse strong sanctions to address noncompliant behavior.[190]

Finally, the last frontiers of open access, unregulated fishing are the deep sea fisheries on the high seas. The Fish Stocks Agreement does not apply to these operations that target discreet stocks of fish, and few RFMOs have legal competence or authority to manage them.[191] Several options have been suggested for the short term: a U.N. General Assembly Resolution, a U.N. General Assembly Declaration of Principles and Action Plan, direct state action to control its vessels and citizens, state action to protect the sedentary species of the continental shelf, direct action by RFMOs, and development of FAO guidelines. Longer-term suggestions explored development of legally binding agreements, revision of the Fish Stocks agreement to apply to all high seas fish stocks including deep sea fishes, a new global agreement, amendments to UNCLOS, improving RFMO performance, and development of a deep sea biodiversity agreement.[192]

IV. Conclusion

The oceans are no longer a frontier to be conquered or a limitless source of protein. World fish production has leveled off and most fish stocks are fished at or above sustainable levels. If ocean fisheries are to be managed for future generations, effective institutions are needed to manage common ocean resources. UNCLOS took an important step by limiting some traditional freedoms of the seas and establishing duties for conserving living resources both within and beyond national jurisdictions. Although UNCLOS generally provides a framework for addressing the world fish crisis, it cannot by itself prevent the chief causes of fishery declines: national overfishing, destructive fishing practices, IUU fishing, and habitat destruction.

Measures for responsible international fishing were promoted at the Earth Summit, the FAO Code of Conduct, the World Summit on Sustainable Development, and U.N. Resolutions banning destructive fishing practices such as high seas driftnets. What continue to be needed however, are effective enforcement and implementation mechanisms. The U.N. Fish Stocks Agreement, which has been described as effecting a sea change in international fishery management, contains some innovations such as minimum standards for the conservation and management of fish stocks, the precautionary approach, new compliance mechanisms, and reliance on Regional Fishery Management Organizations.

RFMOs, however, are only as effective as their members allow, and flag state enforcement and IUU fishing are still major hurdles to sustainable international fisheries. If RFMOs are the wave of the future, further innovations will be needed and nations must also step up conservation within their own EEZs. The 2006 reauthorization of the MSA addresses some of these international challenges such as IUU fishing, bycatch, monitoring, and compliance with international fishery agreements. It is a step in the right direction, one of many that will be needed to put the management of world fisheries on a sustainable path.

Notes

1. The Third United Nations Convention on the Law of the Sea, Dec. 10, 1982, 21 I.L.M. 1245 (entered into force Nov. 16, 1994) [hereinafter UNCLOS].
2. The Agreement for the Implementation of the Provisions of the United Nations Convention on the Law of the Sea of 10 December 1982 Relating to the Conservation and Management of Straddling Fish Stocks and Highly Migratory Fish Stocks, U.N. Doc. A/Conf./164/37 [hereinafter Fish Stocks Agreement].
3. United Nations Food and Agriculture Organization, Code of Conduct for Responsible Fisheries (1995) [hereinafter FAO Code of Conduct].
4. Convention on the Conservation of Antarctic Marine Living Resources, May 20, 1980, 33 U.S.T. 3476 [hereinafter CCAMLR].
5. International Convention for the Conservation of Atlantic Tunas, May 14, 1966, 20 U.S.T. 2887 [hereinafter ICCAT].
6. Convention for the Conservation and Management of Highly Migratory Fish Stocks in the Western and Central Pacific Ocean, Sept. 5, 2000 [hereinafter Fish Stocks Convention], *available at* http://www.wcpfc.int/ (last visited Nov. 17, 2006).

7. The Convention on Future Multilateral Cooperation in the Northwest Atlantic Fisheries, Oct. 24, 1978, Senate Executive Treaty Series 96th Cong. 1st Sess. (entered into force Jan. 1, 1979) [hereinafter Multilateral Cooperation Convention].

8. Portions of Section II adapted from Suzanne Iudicello & Margaret Lytle, *Marine Biodiversity and International Law: Instruments and Institutions That Can Be Used to Conserve Marine Biological Diversity Internationally*, 8 TUL. ENVTL. L.J. 123, 129–134 (1994).

9. HUGO GROTIUS, MARE LIBERUM OR THE FREEDOM OF THE SEAS OR THE RIGHT WHICH BELONGS TO THE DUTCH TO TAKE PART IN THE EAST INDIAN TRADE (Oxford Univ. Press 1916).

10. WILLIAM BURKE, THE NEW INTERNATIONAL LAW OF FISHERIES 2–6 (Clarendon Press 1994).

11. LOUIS B. SOHN & KRISTEN GUSTAFSON, THE LAW OF THE SEA 115 (1984).

12. William Burke, Remarks at University of Washington on Fisheries Law, at 3-1 (1992) (transcript on file with author), cited in Iudicello, *supra* note 8, at 129.

13. *Id.* Burke at 3-2, Iudicello at 130.

14. Truman Proclamation No 2667, 10 Fed. Reg. 12,303 (1945).

15. Burke, *supra* note 12, at 3-2; Iudicello, *supra* note 8, at 130.

16. *Id.* Burke at 3-1, Iudicello at 130–31.

17. The Convention for the Establishment of an Inter-American Tropical Tuna Commission, May 31, 1949, 1 U.S.T. 230, T.I.A.S. 2044 (entered into force Mar. 3, 1950) [hereinafter IATTC].

18. Preservation of the Halibut Fishery of the Northern Pacific Ocean and Bering Sea Convention, Mar. 2, 1953, U.S.-Can., 5 U.S.T. 5.

19. International Convention for the High Seas Fisheries of the North Pacific Ocean, May 9, 1952, 4 U.S.T. 380.

20. Burke, *supra* note 12, at 3-6 to 3-7; Iudicello, *supra* note 8, at 135.

21. *Id.* Burke at 3-21, 3-27; Iudicello at 135.

22. UNCLOS, *supra* note 1.

23. UNCLOS, *supra* note 1, pt. VII, sec. 2.

24. FAO, *The State of World Fisheries and Aquaculture 2004*, *available at* http://www.fao .org/sof/sofia/index_en.htm (last visited May 9, 2006). *See also* Reg Watson & Daniel Pauly, *Systematic Distortions in World Fisheries Catch Trends*, NATURE, Nov. 29, 2001, at 534–36. China remains the largest producer by far and in 2002 produced 16.6 and 27.7 million tons from capture fisheries and aquaculture respectively. The top ten countries producing supply from capture fisheries in 2002 (in addition to China) were Peru, the United States, Indonesia, Japan, Chile, India, Russian Federation, Thailand, and Norway. This group has not changed since 1992. *Id., FAO.*

25. DAVID HUNTER, JAMES SALZMAN & DURWOOD ZAELKE, INTERNATIONAL ENVIRONMENTAL LAW AND POLICY 659 (Foundation Press 2002).

26. UNCLOS, *supra* note 1, art. 56.

27. *Id.* art. 61(2).

28. *Id.* art. 61(3). "The concept of maximum sustainable yield recognizes that fisheries must be managed so that fish stocks can be sustainably caught year after year without causing the population of fish stocks to decline. 50 C.F.R. 602.11(d)(1). . . . Scientists assume that population levels at 40% of unfished abundance (or biomass) are close to MSY, and that populations are overfished when levels fall below half the MSY level, roughly 20% of unfished abundance." However, MSY does not necessarily signify healthy fish populations, and should be viewed as a minimum target used in conjunction with precautionary and ecosystem management approaches. *See* Tim Eichenberg & Mitchell Shapson, *The Promise of Johannesburg: Fisheries and the World Summit on Sustainable Development*, 34 GOLDEN GATE U.L. REV. 587, 624–26 (2004).

29. UNCLOS, *supra* note 1, art. 61(5).

30. *Id.* art. 62.

31. *Id.* art. 63.

32. *Id.* art. 64.

33. SOHN & GUSTAFSON, *supra* note 11. UNCLOS imposes duties on all states to take "such measures for their respective nationals as may be necessary for the conservation of the living resources of the high seas," art. 117; to cooperate "in the conservation and management of living resources" of the high seas, art. 118; and to "maintain or restore populations of harvested species at levels which can produce maximum sustainable yield," art. 119.

34. FAO, *The State of World Fisheries and Aquaculture 2004, supra* note 24, preface.

35. "The Committee on Fisheries (COFI), a subsidiary body of the FAO Council, was established by the FAO Conference at its Thirteenth Session in 1965. The Committee presently constitutes the only global inter-governmental forum where major international fisheries and aquaculture problems and issues are examined and recommendations addressed to governments, regional fishery bodies, NGOs, fishworkers, FAO, and international community, periodically on a worldwide basis. COFI has also been used as a forum in which global agreements and non-binding instruments were negotiated." *Available at* http://www.fao.org/fi/body/cofi/cofi.asp (last visited May 3, 2007).

36. International Conference on Responsible Fishing, Declaration of Cancun, May 8, 1992.

37. United Nations Conference on Environment and Development (1992). UNCED, or the Earth Summit, produced an action plan for sustainable development worldwide, Agenda 21. The two weeks of negotiation produced what was called at the time the most comprehensive program ever sanctioned by the international community. Its emphasis on integration of environmental considerations into economic decisions has influenced all subsequent UN conferences. Information on the conference is available online at http://www.un.org/geninfo/bp/enviro.html (last visited Feb. 10, 2008).

38. Agenda 21, UN Doc. A/CONF.151/26 (vols. I–III).

39. *See generally* http://www.johannesburgsummit.org; *Report of the World Summit on Sustainable Development, available at* http://www.un.org/jsummit/html/documents/documents.html. Although the WSSD set a number of ambitious fishery timetables, it generally fell short of expectations and mechanisms to ensure the timetables are met. *See* Eichenberg & Shapson, *supra* note 28, at 588, 624–36.

40. FAO Code of Conduct, *supra* note 3.

41. *Id.* art. I, 1.

42. *Id.* art. II, 2.

43. *Id.* art. I, 3.

44. *Id.* art. VI, 1.

45. *Id.* art. VI, 2.

46. *Id.* art. VI, 3–8.

47. *Id.* arts. VI, 10–12; VI, 15.

48. *Id.* arts. VI, 13; VI, 16–18.

49. *Id.* art. VI, 5. *See infra* notes 64–65 and accompanying text for further explanation of the precautionary approach.

50. For an explanation of MSY see *supra* note 28.

51. Capture of fish in the water by lost or abandoned fishing gear. Angela Somma, Nat'l Marine Fisheries Serv., *The Environmental Consequences and Economic Costs of Depleting the World's Oceans* (2003), *available at* http://usinfo.state.gov/journals/ites/0103/ijee/somma.htm (last visited May 3, 2007).

52. Fish or other fauna (e.g., birds or marine mammals) that are caught during fishing, but that are not sold or kept for personal use. In commercial fishing these include both fish discarded for economic reasons (economic discards) and because regulations require it (regulatory discards). Organisation for Economic Co-operation and Development, Glossary of Statistical Terms, 2001, http://stats.oecd.org/glossary/detail.asp?ID=252 (last visited May 3, 2007).

53. FAO Code of Conduct, *supra* note 3, arts. II, VIII.

54. Food and Agriculture Organization of the United Nations. Agreement to Promote Compliance with International Conservation and Management Measure by Fishing Vessels on the High Seas (1993) [hereinafter Compliance Agreement].

55. FAO Code of Conduct, *supra* note 3, art. I, 1.

56. Compliance Agreement, *supra* note 54, art. III, 4.

57. *Id.* art. III, 8.

58. *Id.* art. V, 1.

59. Fish Stocks Agreement, *supra* note 2. The Fish Stocks Agreement is also described in detail in this book in Chapter 12, "The 1982 United Nations Convention on the Law of the Sea."

60. Fish Stocks Agreement, *supra* note 2, art. V(b).

61. David Freestone, Address at Tulane Law School Symposium: International Fisheries Law: Who is Leading Whom?; The Magnuson Stevens Act: Sustainable Fisheries for the 21st Century?, Sept. 7–9, 1997.

62. UN, Chronological List of Ratifications. Apr. 2007, *available at* http://www.un.org/Depts/los/reference_files/chronological_lists_of_ratifications.htm (last visited May 3, 2007).

63. In general, highly migratory species have a "wide geographic distribution, both inside and outside the 200-mile zone, and . . . undertake migrations on significant but variable distances across oceans for feeding or reproduction. They are pelagic species (do not live on the sea floor). . . ." UNCLOS annex I "includes 11 tuna, 12 billfish species, pomfrets, 4 species of sauries, dolphinfish (Coryphaena spp.), oceanic sharks and cetaceans (both small and large)." FAO, Fisheries and Aquaculture Dept., Highly Migratory Species Fact Sheet, *available at* http://www.fao.org/fi/website/FIRetrieveAction.do?dom=topic&fid=13686 (last visited May 3, 2007). *See also* UNCLOS, *supra* note 1, annex 1 and art. 64.

64. The precautionary approach includes these general features: identifying precautionary reference points for each stock, identifying in advance what measures will be adopted if reference points are exceeded, adopting cautious management for developing fisheries, monitoring impact on nontarget species, and adopting emergency measures if continued fishing would increase the risk of depletion caused by a natural event. Freestone, *supra* note 61.

65. Fish Stocks Agreement, *supra* note 2, art. 6, annex II. The precautionary approach is described in more detail in Chapter 12.

66. *Id.* art. VVIII.

67. *Id.* art. VIII, 5.

68. United Nations website, *available at* http://www.un.org/Depts/los/convention_agreements/convention_overview_fish_stocks.htm (last visited May 3, 2007). Despite its many innovations, the Fish Stocks Agreement still suffers some of the limitations similar to other international fishery agreements such as the absence of major fishing nations and reliance on flag state enforcement. Eichenberg & Shapson, *supra* note 28, at 610.

69. *See, e.g.* Resolutions, Report of 2006 conference, ICSP5/UNFSA/REP/INF.1. Apr. 26, 2006, *available at* http://www.un.org/Depts/los/convention_agreements/fishstocksmeetings/icsp5report.pdf.

70. UN Resolution A/RES/45/197, Dec. 21, 1990. *See also* UN Resolution A/RES/44/225 (Dec. 22, 1989).

71. Simon P. Northridge with the United Nations Environment Programme, *Driftnet Fisheries and Their Impacts on Non-Target Species: A Worldwide Review* (FAO 1991).

72. Pacific Salmon Treaty, Mar. 18, 1985, U.S.-Can., 99 Stat. 7.

73. 16 U.S.C.A. § 1822.

74. 16 U.S.C.A. § 1826 (f) relating to 22 U.S.C.A. § 1978 authorizing, inter alia, the banning of the import of fish products from offending nations.

75. 16 U.S.C.A. § 1826 (b)(3), (4).

76. 16 U.S.C.A. § 1822 note, Pub. L. No. 100-220, 1987 H.R. 3674 Sec 4007 (b), (c).

77. The Wellington Convention, May 17, 1991, *available at* http://www.oceanlaw.net/texts/summaries/wellington.htm (last visited May 3, 2007).

78. UN Resolution A/RES/44/225 (Dec. 22, 1989).

79. UN Resolution A/RES/45/197 (Dec. 21, 1990).

80. UN Resolution A/RES/46/215 (Dec. 21, 1992).

81. UN Resolution A/RES/50/25 (Jan. 4, 1996).

82. Convention on International Trade in Endangered Species of Wild Fauna and Flora, Mar. 3, 1973, 27 U.S.T. 1087, T.I.A.S. 8249 (entered into force July 1, 1975).

83. *Id.* art. II.

84. *Id.*

85. *Id.* art. III, 2.

86. *Id.* art. IV, 2–6.

87. Global Marine Biological Diversity: A Strategy for Building Conservation into Diversity 209 (Elliot A. Norse ed., 1993).

88. International Union for the Conservation of Nature, Red List of Threatened Species, *available at* http://www.iucn.org/themes/ssc/biodiversity_assessments/indexgmsa.htm (last visited May 4, 2007).

89. Regional Fishery Organizations, Oceans Atlas USES: Fisheries and Aquaculture, http://www.oceansatlas.com/servlet/CDSServlet?status=ND0yOTQ (updated Aug. 25, 2000; last visited May 8, 2006).

90. P. L. Devaney, *Regional Fisheries Management Organizations: Bringing Order to Disorder*, in XIV Papers on International Environmental Negotiation 4 (L. E. Susskind & W. R. Moomaw eds., 2005). *See also* FAO Oceans Atlas, Regional Fishery Organizations, http://www.oceansatlas.com/servlet/CDSServlet?status=ND0yOTQ (last visited May 8, 2006.

91. *Id.* at 5–6. *See also* Eichenberg & Shapson, *supra* note 28, at 611–16.

92. *Id.* at 7–12.

93. G.T. Crothers & L. Nelson, *High Seas Fisheries Governance: a Framework for the Future?* Papers collected at Sharing the Fish 2006, Mar. 2006, Perth, Australia, *available at* http://www.fishallocation.com/speakers/index.html (last visited Mar. 31, 2007).

94. Earth Negotiations Bulletin, International Institute for Sustainable Development (IISD) vol. 7, no. 58 (May 24, 2006).

95. Multilateral Cooperation Convention, *supra* note 7.

96. *Id.* art. I.

97. Estonia, Latvia, Lithuania, Poland, Portugal, Spain, and Germany were contracting parties, but acceded to the European Union. Romania withdrew from the convention. NAFO Web site at http://www.nafo.int/about/frames/about.html (last visited May 4, 2007).

98. Multilateral Cooperation Convention, *supra* note 7, art. II (a).

99. *Id.* art. II (b), VI.

100. *Id.* art. XI.

101. *Id.* art. I (4).

102. Kwame Mfodwo, *Summaries and Evaluations of Selected Regional Fisheries Management Regimes* (Feb. 1998) (unpublished manuscript prepared for the Pew Charitable Trusts, on file with author).

103. *Id.*

104. Convention on the Conservation and Management of Fishery Resources in the Southeast Atlantic Ocean, Apr. 20, 2001 (entered into force Apr. 2003) [hereinafter Southeast Atlantic Convention], *available at* http://www.seafo.org.

105. C. Hedley, *The South-East Atlantic Fisheries Organization (SEAFO) Convention: an initial review* (OceanLaw On-Line Paper No. 2, Apr. 2001); Internet Guide to International Fisheries Law, http://www.intfish.net/ops/papers/2.htm (last visited May 4, 2007).

106. Southeast Atlantic Convention, *supra* note 104, art. 5.

107. *Id.* art. 1(h).

108. *Id.* art. 10.

109. ICCAT, *supra* note 5.

110. Ellen Peel & Michael L. Weber. No Place to Hide: Highly Migratory Fish in the Atlantic Ocean, Fishery Management and Status. (Center for Marine Conservation, Washington, D.C., 1995).

111. Burke, *supra* note 10, at 250.

112. ICCAT, *supra* note 5, art. IV(1).

113. *Id.* art. IV (2)(b).

114. ICCAT, *supra* note 5, art. VII.

115. Burke, *supra* note 10, at 241.

116. *Id.* at 250.

117. ICCAT, *supra* note 5, art. VIII.

118. Michael L. Weber & Frances Spivy-Weber, *Proposed Elements for International Regimes to Conserve Living Marine Resources.* Report in fulfillment of Marine Mammal Commission Contract No. T30916119. NTIS, Springfield, VA, Oct., 1995. For more information on IATTC, see *infra* notes 140–141 and accompanying text.

119. Carl Safina, *North Atlantic Fishery Resources at Risk* (Dec. 1998) (unpublished manuscript prepared for the Pew Charitable Trusts). *See also* Carl Safina, Song for the Blue Ocean 92–99 (Henry Holt 1997) (describing difficulties of getting ICCAT members, especially Japan and Canada, to reduce quotas for bluefin tuna in 1992 despite fifteen years of consecutive declining stocks and a ninety percent drop in population).

120. *Id.*

121. Resolution 94-9 by ICCAT on Compliance with the ICCAT Conservation and Management Measures (including Addendum). (Transmitted to Contracting Parties: Jan. 23, 1995).

122. Resolution 03-15 by ICCAT Concerning Trade Measures. (Transmitted to Contracting Parties: Dec. 19, 2003).

123. Author communication with Mark Wildman, NOAA Office of International Affairs, Mar. 2007.

124. Peel & Weber, *supra* note 110, at xi; *see also* Michael Leech. *Comments at the Atlantic Highly Migratory Species Advisory Panel* (Silver Springs, Md., Feb. 9–11, 2004). Transcript at 117–20.

125. Peel & Weber, *id.*

126. The exact ATCA wording is "[N]o regulation promulgated under this section may have the effect of increasing or decreasing any allocation or quota of fish or fishing mortality level to the United States agreed to pursuant to a recommendation of the Commission." 16 U.S.C.A. § 971d(c)(3).

127. William Hogarth, Letter to the Editor, *Tuna Talks Frustrating,* Nat'l Fisherman, Feb. 2007, at 13.

128. Kenneth Hinman, *quoted in The Two Faces of ICCAT: Bluefin Breakdown Overshadows Progress on Other Species,* NCMC Bull, Winter 2007.

129. Author communication with Michael Sutton, Monterey Bay Aquarium, 2007.

130. Elizabeth deLone, *Improving the Management of the Atlantic Tuna: The Duty to Strengthen the ICCAT in Light of the 1995 Straddling Stocks Agreement,* 6 N.Y.U. Envtl. L.J. 656 (1998).

131. Safina 1997, *supra* note 119.

132. DeLone, *supra* note 130.

133. ICCAT Overview at slide 31, *available at* http://www.iccat.es/Documents/Other/ICCAT .ppt (last visited May 4, 2007).

134. *See infra,* notes 165–181 and accompanying text.

135. Suzanne Iudicello, *Background Paper: Major Fisheries at Risk in the North Pacific Ocean* (Dec. 1997) (unpublished manuscript prepared for the Pew Charitable Trusts, on file with author).

136. Convention on the Conservation and Management of Pollock Resources in the Central Bering, June 16, 1995, U.S. Treaty Document 103-27 (entered into force Dec. 8, 1995).

137. Mfodwo, *supra* note 102.

138. *Id.*

139. Iudicello, *supra* note 135.

140. IATTC, *supra* note 17.

141. IATTC Web site at http://www.iattc.org/HomeENG.htm (last visited Nov. 17, 2006).

142. Fish Stocks Convention, *supra* note 6.

143. *Id.*

144. Convention for the Conservation of Southern Bluefin Tuna, May 1993 (entered into force May 20, 1994) [hereinafter CCSBT].

145. Commission for the Conservation of Southern Bluefin Tuna Web site, http://www.ccsbt .org/docs/about.html (last visited Feb. 10, 2008).

146. CCSBT, *supra* note 144.

147. *Id.*

148. *Id.* art. III.

149. *Id.* art. II.

150. Mfodwo, *supra* note 102.

151. CCSBT, *supra* note 144, art. VIII.

152. *Id.* art. 7.

153. CCAMLR, *supra* note 4. Current members are Argentina, Australia, Belgium, Brazil, Chile, the European Union, France, Germany, India, Italy, Japan, Namibia, Republic of Korea, Norway, New Zealand, Poland, Russian Federation, South Africa, Spain, Sweden, Ukraine, United Kingdom, United States, and Uruguay. Bulgaria, Canada, Cook Islands, Finland, Greece, Mauritius, Netherlands, Peru, and Vanuatu acceded to the Convention and are also parties.

154. Mfodwo, *supra* note 102.

155. CCAMLR, *supra* note 4, art. I, II.

156. *Id.* art. II (3).

157. *Id.* art. X.

158. *Id.* Web site at http://www.ccamlr.org (last visited May 3, 2007).

159. *Id.* art. IX(2).

160. *Id.* arts. XIV, XV.

161. Mfodwo, *supra* note 102.

162. CCAMLR, *supra* note 4, art. IX.

163. *Id.* art. XXIV.

164. *Id.* art. XX.

165. 16 U.S.C. §§ 1801–1882 (1976), Pub. L. No. 94-265, as amended by H.R. 5946, Dec. 2006. Signed into law Jan 12, 2007 [hereinafter MSA Reauthorization].

166. *Report of the Committee on Commerce, Science & Transportation on S.2012, Magnuson-Stevens Fishery Conservation and Management Act Reauthorization Act of 2005*, Apr. 4, 2006, S. Rep. 109-229 [hereinafter *Senate Report*]. The Senate Report notes that restrictions placed on U.S. vessels to protect endangered or protected species "disadvantage U.S. fleets and fail to address the problem" because the harmful fishing practices continue by other fleets in high seas fisheries. *Senate Report* at 43.

167. Fish Stocks Convention, *supra* note 6.

168. MSA Reauthorization, *supra* note 165, sec. 207(a).

169. *Id.* sec. 207(b) (1)–(7).

170. *Senate Report, supra* note 166, at 12. For more on IUU fishing see *infra* notes 185–187 and accompanying text. FAO, International Plan of Action to Prevent, Deter and Eliminate Illegal, Unreported and Unregulated Fishing, http://www.fao.org/fi/website/FIRetrieve Action.do?dom=org&xml=ipoa_IUU.xml (last visited May 15, 2007).

171. MSA Reauthorization, *supra* note 165, sec. 401 amending 16 U.S.C.A. §§ 1821 *et seq.*

172. *Id.* sec. 403 amending 16 U.S.C. §§ 1826 *et seq.*

173. *Senate Report, supra* note 166, at 45; MSA Reauthorization, *supra* note 165, sec. 609.

174. MSA Reauthorization, *supra* note 165, sec. 610(e).

175. *Id.* sec. 403.

176. 22 U.S.C.A. § 1978(a); 16 U.S.C.A. § 1371(a).

177. MSA Reauthorization, *supra* note 165, sec. 609.

178. 16 U.S.C.A. § 1825(b).

179. MSA Reauthorization, *supra* note 165, sec. 610(a)(1)–(3).

180. *Id.* sec. 610(c)(5).

181. *Senate Report, supra* note 166, at 12.

182. *See* Eichenberg & Shapson, *supra* note 28, at 610.

183. The Western Australian Department of Fisheries presented the conference in cooperation with the Food and Agriculture Organization of the United Nations and with support by the Australian Government Department of Agriculture, Fisheries and Forestry and the New Zealand Ministry of Fisheries.

184. *See, e.g.,* A. Serdy, *Fishery Commission Quota Trading Under International Law;* G.R. Munro, *International Allocation Issues and the High Seas, an Economist's Perspective;* Nienke van der Burgt, *The Role of Fisheries Agreements in Promoting Equity within Resource Allocation;* Q. Hanich & M. Tsamenyi, *Exclusive Economic Zones, Distant Water Fishing Nations and Pacific Small Island Developing States: Who Really Gets all the Fish?;* and G. T. Crothers & L. Nelson, *High Seas Fisheries Governance: A Framework for the Future?* Papers collected at Sharing the Fish 2006, Mar. 2006, Perth, Australia, *available at* http://www.fishallocation.com/speakers/index.html (last visited Mar. 31, 2007).

185. The Secretary-General, *Report of the Secretary-General on Oceans and the Law of the Sea, delivered to the General Assembly,* U.N., Doc. A/55/61, at 26 (2000); *see also* FAO, International Plan of Action to Prevent, Deter and Eliminate Illegal, Unreported and Unregulated Fishing (2002), *available at* http://www.fao.org/fi/website/FIRetrieveAction .do?dom=org&xml=ipoa_IUU.xml (last visited May 15, 2007).

186. David Freestone, *Protecting Our Oceans: New Challenges, New Solutions. An Overview of this Issue,* VII(1) Sustainable Dev. L.& Pol'y 3 (Fall 2006).

187. *Senate Report, supra* note 166, at 43.

188. U.N. News E-mail release. "UN Conference Considers Measures to Limit Illegal Fishing," New York, May 24, 2006, 8 p.m. From: UNNews@un.org To: news4@list.un.org Date: 5/24/2006 6:55:27 PM.

189. *Id.*

190. Earth Negotiations Bulletin, International Institute for Sustainable Development (IISD) vol. 7, no. 58 (May 24, 2006).

191. Kristina M. Gjerde & David Freestone, *Unfinished Business: Deep-Sea Fisheries and the Conservation of Marine Biodiversity Beyond National Jurisdiction,* 19(3) Int'l J. Marine & Coastal L., 209–22 (2004).

192. *Id.*

chapter eleven

Trade in Fish and Fisheries Products

David K. Schorr

I. Introduction

The world's oceans have an ancient and storied connection with international trade. Crisscrossed by trade routes and trade winds, the sea not only provides transportation beyond horizons, but has itself long been a rich source of tradable wealth. In fact, archeological evidence suggests that trade in marine resources accompanied the rise of human civilization.[1]

Of all commerce in marine products, trade in fish is by far the most important in its economic, social, and environmental dimensions. International trade in fish—even narrowly defined (as discussed below)—amounts to more than $71 billion per year, with approximately thirty-eight percent of fish (by live weight) entering international commerce.[2] For developing countries—which account for ninety-seven percent of the estimated 41.4 million people directly employed in fishing and fish farming worldwide[3]—this trade is particularly important. Developing countries produced nearly half of all fish products traded on international markets, bringing in net hard currency earnings worth more than what these countries gain through the export of coffee, rubber, cocoa, bananas, meat, tea, and sugar combined.[4] Meanwhile, developed countries see nearly seventy-five percent of their fish production sold internationally.[5]

While trade in most marine products is governed by ordinary trade law, the legal regime controlling trade in fish reflects the sector's unusual combination of economic

The author would like to thank Marc Allain, Kevern Cochrane, Beatrice Gorez, Roman Grynberg, Elizabeth Havice, Rich Lincoln, Cathy Roheim, and Rolf Willmann for their extensive contributions to this chapter. All opinions and errors contained in this chapter nevertheless remain entirely those of the author.

importance, global geography, relationship to food security, and high environmental sensitivity.[6] Where fishing affects other forms of ocean life—and especially charismatic (i.e., culturally and environmentally important) species such as marine mammals and sea turtles—additional legal complexities can arise.

This chapter gives an overview of the main legal issues relating to international trade in fish and fish products. Even within this relatively narrow field, however, students often confront a bewildering array of specific topics and potential sources of law. Additional complexity arises from the high state of flux evident in much of the prevailing legal system. Given the limitations of space, this chapter will concentrate mainly on global trade rules administered by the World Trade Organization (WTO) and relevant U.S. domestic law.

A. The Basic Context: Dwindling Stocks, Bloated Fleets, and Uneven Development

Three central challenges characterize the context surrounding fisheries and fish traders today: First, the world's fisheries are facing a profound crisis of depletion. Dramatic improvements in fishing technology, matched with rising demand for fish products and aggressive government efforts to develop fishing industries, have resulted in the deepest and most widespread reduction in fish stocks known to recorded history. The U.N. Food and Agriculture Organization conservatively estimates that more than three-quarters of the world's fisheries are overexploited, fully exploited, significantly depleted, or recovering from overexploitation.[7] According to other leading analyses, the biomass of large predatory fish (i.e., many of the world's most commercially valuable species) has dropped by ninety percent since the onset of industrial fishing.[8] A recent study published in *Science Magazine* reached the dramatic (and controversial) conclusion that current trends could lead to "the global collapse of all taxa currently fished" by the middle of this century.[9]

> **The FAO conservatively estimates that more than three-quarters of the world's fisheries are overexploited, fully exploited, significantly depleted, or recovering from overexploitation.**

Second, among the factors underlying fisheries depletion is the grossly overcapitalized condition of many of the world's fishing fleets. Excess fishing capacity—mainly but not exclusively in a handful of major economic powers—creates significant economic and social pressures on fisheries and on the governments seeking to manage them. Fishing fleets worldwide are now estimated to be from 30 percent to as much as 250 percent larger than needed for sustainable levels of fishing.[10] This overcapacity has intensified competition among fishers, and has led to the dependence of some major fleets on a steady stream of government subsidies. The economic impacts of overcapacity are further compounded by the extraordinary price volatility of international fish markets, and by the rapid expansion of competition from aquaculture. The social adjustments necessary to retire unsustainable capacity continue to pose difficult political challenges to regulators and elected officials.

Third, even as global fishing capacity is too high in the aggregate, the fishing industries of many developing countries remain underdeveloped. While a very few have emerged as major fishing powers,[11] many lack the capacity to exploit the fisheries resources adjacent to their own coasts or to join the international race to catch fish on the high seas. Meanwhile, rural poverty remains an often intractable problem in coastal developing states, with fisheries providing a "livelihood of last resort" for millions of people. Yet the real terms of trade for developing countries often let them enjoy only a fraction of the rents extracted from their coastal fishing grounds.

These three basic characteristics of the fisheries sector have a direct impact on (and in turn stand to be shaped by) the operation of international fisheries trade law. The regulation of fisheries trade cannot be adequately understood without reference to them.

B. Fish in the Context of Trade Law

Before looking into a few details relating to fisheries, it is well to recall two facts about the overarching system of international trade law itself. First, it has not much attended explicitly to the fisheries sector. Since the close of the Second World War, the multilateral trading system—first under the General Agreement on Tariffs and Trade (GATT), and now under its successor, the WTO—has aimed for a comprehensive set of rules to encourage liberalized trade across all sectors. Of course, some particularly "sensitive" sectors—such as agriculture and (until recently) textiles—have escaped this homogenizing urge, and instead have enjoyed carve-outs for special treatment within the trade system. Fisheries products, however, have been left within the general category of industrial goods to which the main body of multilateral rules applies. This is not accidental. During the Uruguay Round (the 1986–1993 global negotiations that produced the WTO), negotiators specifically excluded fish from the special WTO rules applicable to agriculture, the result (according to some observers) of "unresolved issues pertaining to access to resources."[12]

Second, despite the sometimes unavoidable links between fisheries policy and trade law discussed below, the prevailing myth of the multilateral trade system is that it is policy-neutral with regard to "nontrade" issues. But trade laws help allocate markets (and thus wealth), and express a clear tendency towards favoring economic "efficiency" over other possible elements of public welfare. In the context of fish, as will be seen, trade laws can also have a direct bearing on the allocation of access to productive resources (i.e., fisheries). What is more, where a common natural resource like fish is concerned, access to production cannot be separated from access to trade, and resource management policies cannot be separated from production and trade. In short, the fishery sector is one in which the impossibility of "policy-neutral" trade law is especially stark.

C. Uncertainty at the WTO: The Doha Round Negotiations

As noted above, this chapter focuses in part on international rules promulgated by the World Trade Organization. Those rules, always evolving, are in a particularly uncertain condition today due to the difficulties surrounding the so-called Doha Round of global trade negotiations.[13] Like the eight previous rounds of global trade talks since

WWII, the Doha Round was intended to last roughly half a decade, and to result in a single comprehensive package of new trade liberalizing measures, including reductions in tariffs, quotas, subsidies, and other barriers to trade. In late July of 2006, however, the Doha Round talks were officially suspended in the face of an impasse among leading WTO delegations over proposed cuts in agricultural subsidies and industrial tariffs. As this book went to press, the talks had been formally resumed at a technical level, but without the political breakthroughs considered necessary for a successful conclusion to the round. How and when the talks will end remained unknown.

As discussed below, the Doha Round agenda includes several topics with potentially significant consequences for trade in fisheries products. Most prominently, a portion of the talks have aimed directly at crafting new WTO rules to reduce subsidies associated with overcapacity and overfishing. In addition, WTO members have been discussing proposals for the elimination tariffs on fish products, and for reconciling potential conflicts between WTO rules and multilateral environmental agreements including fisheries management treaties. The immediate future of WTO law on these issues has been left in limbo by the uncertainties of the Round.

It is important, however, not to exaggerate the impact of WTO rulemaking on trade in fish products. Topics discussed at the WTO, including tariffs, are often the subject of bilateral and regional trade deals that can effectively supersede the WTO. Other important topics, such as rules of origin and ecolabeling standards for fish products, are also actively being discussed in these "subglobal" trade fora, as well as in nontrade fora such as the United Nations Food and Agriculture Organization. Regardless of the outcome of the Doha Round, it is clear that the international law governing fisheries trade will remain in a state of relatively rapid evolution for the foreseeable future.

II. The Current State of the Law

A. The Law of the Sea: Allocating Basic Rights and Expectations

In fundamental legal terms, before there can be international trade there must be ownership and nationality. For fish swimming wild in the sea, however, both of these basic concepts bring unusual difficulties. As discussed at length in Chapter 12, the U.N. Convention on the Law of the Sea (UNCLOS or U.N. Law of the Sea) currently provides the basic international framework for apportioning jurisdiction over marine resources, including fish.[14] UNCLOS divides the world's oceans into four basic jurisdictional categories:

- *Internal* or *inland* waters are, loosely speaking, those contained within a country's terrestrial landscape, such as rivers, lakes, and estuaries;[15]
- Waters of a nation's *territorial sea* are those immediately adjacent to its coastline, up to a distance of twelve nautical miles;[16]
- Beyond the twelve-mile limit, nations enjoy an *Exclusive Economic Zone* (EEZ) extending out to two hundred nautical miles from shore;[17] and
- Beyond two hundred nautical miles from any coast lie the *high seas*.

UNCLOS is essentially silent with regard to a country's sovereignty over resources within its internal waters and territorial sea. Legal control over those resources—at least arguably—remains equivalent to that over terrestrial resources.[18] There is little doubt that fish found within these waters are effectively "owned" by national (or in some cases subnational) governments.[19] A similar analysis can be applied to fish found on the high seas: Until they are caught, they are the property of no nation, and form a valuable part of the global commons.[20]

Things get more complicated in the case of EEZ fisheries. There, UNCLOS grants coastal nations "sovereign rights for the purpose of exploring and exploiting, conserving and managing" natural resources, including fish. But UNCLOS also imposes specific duties on coastal states to manage and conserve their EEZ fisheries, and to allow foreign fishers access to any "surplus" stocks that nationals of a coastal state do not exploit.[21] EEZ fisheries resources thus have a hybrid status somewhere between national patrimony and property of the global commons.[22]

Unsurprisingly, national policymakers often focus more on the rights granted by UNCLOS than on the duties it imposes, and so tend to view EEZ fisheries as national resources. It would also seem consistent with the policies underlying UNCLOS to consider fish caught in one country's EEZ and sold in the markets of another to have entered the stream of international commerce. As we will see, however, trade law treats the ownership of fish—and the definition of fish "trade"—somewhat differently.

B. Rules of Origin—Old Laws with New Consequences?

In both technical and popular terms, "trade" is usually understood as the movement of goods, capital, or services across international borders. But a substantial percentage of cross-border commerce in fish products falls outside the legal definition of "trade"—a fact that arises out of a set of trade regulations known as "rules of origin."

Narrowly speaking, rules of origin are the rules by which customs agents determine the national origin of imported products as they arrive at the border. Since the application of tariffs, quotas, and in some cases even health and safety standards can vary greatly depending on the country of origin, rules of origin are a mainstay of international trade law. For many years, for example, products entering the United States from communist countries were subjected to prohibitively high tariff rates. Today, the "most favored nation" (MFN) principle enshrined in many WTO rules—which generally requires WTO members to afford each other equal treatment—has helped reduce trade law distinctions based national origin. But MFN does not wholly remove the question of nationality. Some WTO rules (such as "sanitary and phytosanitary standards," discussed below) require equal treatment only of goods from countries "where identical or similar conditions prevail."[23] Other WTO rules provide for special treatment of goods originating in developing countries. And the proliferation of preferential trading arrangements—such as NAFTA—has given rules of origin continuing relevance.[24]

> **A substantial percentage of cross-border commerce in fish products falls outside the legal definition of "trade."**

In the case of most tradable goods, rules of origin treat products as "originating" where they are produced. Where production (or, in the case of primary products, harvest or extraction) takes place in a single country, the products are usually treated as "wholly obtained or produced" in that country. Where a product undergoes processing in a third country prior to final importation and sale, the most commonly applied rule of origin is the rule of "last substantial transformation"—i.e., the product is considered to originate in the last country where it underwent sufficient processing to create "a new and different article."[25]

The rule of "last substantial transformation" is emerging as an international norm—WTO members have agreed to make its application obligatory upon completion of a new WTO code harmonizing national rules of origin.[26] But the negotiations towards that code (which predate and are separate from the Doha Round negotiations) have yet to conclude, despite an original target date at the end of 2001.[27] Still, even in the absence of a multilateral obligation, the "last substantial transformation" rule is widely applied, including by the United States[28] and the EU[29]—at least for most products.[30]

In the case of fish products, however, the normal rules of origin do not apply. Rather, they are subject to at least one special twist, and sometimes two. Long-standing international law holds that the nationality of a vessel at sea is determined by the identity of the country in which it is registered, and whose flag it flies.[31] By extension, wild fish are generally considered to share the nationality of the vessel that catches them, whether the fish are caught in a vessel's domestic waters, on the high seas, or even within the waters of another nation.[32] This "flag state" rule is applied without regard to the nationality of the real parties in interest who control or benefit from the fishing at issue.[33] The flag state rule dates from well before the extension of coastal state jurisdiction out to two hundred nautical miles, and thus is from a time when a much larger share of valuable marine fisheries were found in unregulated international waters.

In accordance with the flag state rule, then, the physical transfer of fish across borders is not per se considered an act of "trade"—either legally[34] or for the purpose of compiling most international fish trade statistics.[35] Indeed, some major fish-consuming countries obtain large portions of their "domestic" supply of fish from foreign fisheries. For example, the EU has reported that it obtains about forty percent of its fish supplies from its distant-water fleets operating outside of EU waters.[36]

Beyond the "flag state" rule, the rules of origin applicable to fish products are at times subject to another twist: Some major consumer countries decline to apply the rule of "last substantial transformation" where this would extend preferential market access to fish processing industries in developing countries. This is most evident in the case of the EU's imports from its former colonial territories (known in EU parlance as the Africa, Caribbean, and Pacific, or ACP, countries). Trade between the EU and its former colonies has been governed by the 2000 Cotonou Agreement (successor to the Lomé Conventions), which granted non-reciprocal preferential (often duty-free) access to EU markets for ACP exports.[37] However, this preferential trading regime was designed to end on January 31, 2007, upon the expiration of a WTO waiver allowing the arrangement as a derogation from the WTO's normal "most favored nation" rules.[38] In place of this generalized system, the EC has been negotiating a new generation of "Economic Partnership Agreements" (EPAs) with its ACP partners, on a region-by-region basis.[39] Since EPAs had not been fully negotiated by the January 31 deadline, however, the EU has entered into a series of "interim EPAs," even as broader EPA negotiations continue.[40]

While the Cotonou Agreement does cover primary products from fish caught by ACP fishers, it sharply restricts the preferential access granted to the land-based fish processing industries (such as tuna canners) in ACP countries.

Specifically, EU regulations will not treat processed fish products as originating from ACP countries even if the products would normally qualify under the "last substantial transformation" rule.[41] Instead, EU regulations require that all fish contained in processed imports from ACP countries be caught either within EU or ACP territorial seas[42] or by EU or ACP vessels. Moreover, EU regulations also depart from the traditional flag state rule. To be considered an ACP or EU fishing vessel for purposes of the Cotonou Agreement, not only must the vessel be flagged in the EU or in an ACP state, but a majority of both its owners and its crew must be EU or ACP nationals.[43]

These departures from standard rules of origin prevent ACP countries from using fish landed by non-ACP (other than EU) vessels as inputs to processed goods destined for the EU market. In other words, an ACP country that wishes to extract the most benefit from its EEZ fisheries by exporting its fish duty-free to the EU market, but that lacks the fleet capacity to exploit its resources fully, cannot invite low-cost competitors to EU fishing fleets to provide raw materials for its value-added fish processing industry. A number of ACP countries see significant missed export opportunities as a result of this rule,[44] which they also find inconsistent with the intention of the Law of the Sea.[45] The EU, for its part, has agreed to contemplate changes to these rules to broaden access for ACP processors,[46] possibly to include removing the national crew requirement.[47] In November 2007, the EU took its first concrete step towards such reforms by including revised rules of origin for processed tuna in an "Interim Economic Partnership Agreement" that it signed with Fiji and Papua New Guinea.[48] This agreement for the first time would apply normal "last substantial transformation" rules for Fijian and Papuan fish products.[49] As of February 2008, however, such reforms had not been extended beyond this single agreement.

Beyond the EU, both Japan and the United States also depart (albeit to a lesser extent) from the rule of "last substantial transformation" to restrict the preferential market access available to fish processors in developing countries. Like the EU, Japan's basic rules granting preferential market access to developing countries require qualifying fish processors to source unprocessed fish from their own (or Japanese) vessels.[50] The United States, which depends much less on distant-water fleets than either the EU or Japan, does not require processed fish to be caught on U.S. or beneficiary country vessels. Still, the United States departs from the "last substantial transformation" rule in its "generalized system of preferences" for developing countries by requiring any product (including processed fish) not "wholly obtained" in beneficiary countries to have at least thirty-five percent of its value come from domestic materials and other inputs.[51] Neither the United States nor Japan derogates directly from the "flag state" rule in the manner of current EU practice.

It should be noted that changes to the rules of origin contained in preferential trading arrangements are among the topics under discussion in the Doha Round[52]—and so the EU is not alone in floating the suggestion that these rules may change in ways favorable to developing countries. But the situation will remain complex; new preferential access granted to one developing country may, for example, work to the detriment of another.[53] Nevertheless, distant-water fleets are a major element of international commerce that escape the standard definitions of "trade"—a fact that will not be altered by moves towards more evenhanded use of the last substantial transformation rule.

C. Access Arrangements: Trade by Another Name

As discussed above, a significant portion of the fish landed by domestic fleets in their home ports is taken from foreign EEZs. Except where these fish are taken illegally (or in the complete absence of national regulation, if such cases still exist), the associated fishing activities are governed by some kind of formal agreement with the host coastal state. In a growing number of cases, these access agreements are executed directly between host governments and private fishing interests, without a formal access agreement between the host coastal state and the government of the so-called distant-water-fleet nation (DWF nation). Still, the majority of access arrangements do include formal or informal international arrangements between the host country and the DWF nation. Even where the formal terms of the access are concluded between private fishing interests and coastal governments, diplomatic and other interventions by the DWF nation can play a crucial role.

The legal and financial terms of these access agreements are varied and sometimes quite complex.[54] They may involve government-to-government payments in return for fishing rights, "tied aid" (foreign aid donated to the host government with formal or informal strings attached), the exchange of reciprocal fishing rights (mutual EEZ access), and/or payments directly from private fishing enterprises to host governments. As discussed below, they are also often associated with subsidies granted by the DWF nation to its domestic fleets.

The right—and very likely the obligation—to grant access to EEZ fisheries is enshrined in Article 62.2 of the U.N. Convention on the Law of the Sea. At first glance, this right/obligation appears to apply only to fisheries resources that are underexploited, or to what UNCLOS calls the "surplus of the allowable catch" that the EEZ state "does not have the capacity to harvest." In truth, however, the situation is less clear. First, a close reading of UNCLOS suggests that coastal states may under some circumstances set "total allowable catch" at levels that allow at least some degree of overexploitation.[55] Moreover, in practice access arrangements are often concluded in the absence of careful assessment of resource conditions or of limits on the amount of DWF fishing they allow.

Overall, the extent to which these access agreements return net benefits to EEZ host states or their fisheries is a matter of significant international debate. Clearly, the answer depends on the facts of each specific case. But some generalizations about access agreements can be made, both positive and negative:

- For some host countries (especially small island states), access agreements are vitally important sources of hard currency income, and in a few cases may amount to a significant percentage of GNP. In some cases access payments provide government revenue earmarked for fisheries management.

- For some smaller developing countries, access agreements may be an essential part of economic development strategies that depend more on establishing onshore processing facilities than on developing the catching and trading capacities of domestic fishing fleets. Such countries might, for example, seek access agreements under which DWFs agree to land fish in the host state for processing, and may even seek tied investments from DWFs (or their governments) in onshore processing facilities.

- Nevertheless, the terms of access agreements generally reflect the very uneven negotiating power of developing country host and developed country DWF states, allocating the lion's share of rents to DWFs.

- And in a significant number of cases, access agreements have been associated with overfishing of coastal resources and with detrimental impacts on the coastal fishing industries and fishing communities of host states.[56]

If similar access arrangements were made to allow land-based mining or the cultivation of forest products by foreign enterprises on the soil of a host nation, traditional trade law would likely treat the foreign involvement in extraction as foreign investment or as the export of extraction services, and then treat the resulting transfer of goods as the export of natural products from the host countries. But just as the flag state rule of maritime law prevents recognizing domestic landings by distant-water-fishing fleets as "trade," the Law of the Sea discourages viewing distant-water-fishing-activities as the exportation of services. The result is that trade law has little or nothing to say about the regulation of international commerce based on fisheries access agreements.[57]

Yet fisheries access agreements are doubtless part and parcel of the trade policies of both DWF nations and coastal host countries.[58] For example, U.S. law has clearly reflected an expectation that access agreements would be granted as a matter of right, and in an economically reciprocal fashion. Just as UNCLOS was being negotiated, Congress adopted a law that provided for embargos on imports of fish products from any country that, among other possible offenses, refuses to grant U.S. vessels access to its fisheries pursuant to an access agreement.[59]

D. Limiting Trade: Tariffs and Quotas

As a general matter, the most basic national measures used to restrict trade flows—tariffs and quotas—no longer pose a serious impediment to the majority of trade in fisheries products. Developed countries have committed themselves to MFN bound tariff rates[60] that average 4.5 percent for all fisheries products, with actual applied

Trade today may more often be hindered by reduced fishing quotas due to stock depletion than by import quotas or duties.

tariffs often somewhat lower.[61] Moreover, developing countries widely benefit from duty-free access to developed country fish markets under a series of preferential trading arrangements.[62] The use of import quotas—once a mainstay of the fisheries policy of postwar Japan, for example—has similarly declined sharply over recent decades, leaving the bulk of fish trade free from quantitative restrictions.[63] Indeed, trade today may more often be hindered by reduced fishing quotas due to stock depletion than by import quotas or duties.

But this does not mean that tariffs and import quotas on fish products have become irrelevant to traders or to policymakers. Although tariff rates on fish products in developed countries are low on average, they are not uniformly so. Many developed countries still maintain "tariff peaks"—highly protective tariffs—and some quotas on a few products of special interest to their national fishing industries. In addition, developed countries often maintain higher tariffs on processed fish products than on raw (fresh or frozen) fish—a practice known as "tariff escalation" that is designed to give domestic processing industries access to cheap raw materials and protection from foreign manufacturers.[64]

It should also be noted that the United States, among others, makes regular use of "fair trade" laws such as antidumping rules to create ad hoc tariff peaks on specific fisheries products. U.S. antidumping legislation[65] provides for the mandatory imposition of additional duties (beyond applicable tariff rates) on any imported products being sold (or found likely to be sold) in the United States "at less than its fair value" in a manner that causes material injury to a U.S. industry. Antidumping constitutes a highly technical and specific (not to mention controversial) area of trade law practice that has little direct overlap with fisheries law or policy, apart from its occasional use in competitive contests over particular products. Still, a true assessment of the openness of the U.S. market to fish trade cannot overlook the impact of antidumping law. Among the fisheries products that have recently been subject to U.S. antidumping duties are shrimp,[66] catfish,[67] and salmon.[68] The EU has similarly imposed antidumping duties on Norwegian salmon. A number of these antidumping actions have been challenged at the WTO, although all on the basis of arcane points of antidumping law unrelated to the fisheries context out of which the cases arise.[69]

Meanwhile, many developing countries maintain significant import restrictions on fish products across the board. The Cote d'Ivoire, for example, has a "special tax" on imported fish of twenty percent.[70] Ghana routinely closes its markets to imported fish (other than canned fish) from May to October of each year.[71] Similarly, many developing countries control fish imports through tariffs[72] or strict licensing requirements, which can function as ad hoc quantitative restrictions.[73] Trade barriers such as these have particular relevance as the amount of so-called "south-south" fish trade increases.

Overall, the tariffs and quotas still applied to fish products have enough commercial importance that export-oriented governments repeatedly demand their reduction or elimination. In the context of the Doha Round, the fisheries sector has been specifically identified as a priority for tariff negotiations, and a coalition of *demandeurs* has proposed "zeroing out" tariffs on all fish products.[74]

These proposals to eliminate tariffs on fish trade have drawn the usual resistance from businesses that currently enjoy tariff protection. But beyond such routine reactions, the proposals have sparked debate over their possible impacts on developing countries, and on efforts to combat overfishing.

Concerns about the impacts of tariff liberalization on developing countries have been raised from two general perspectives. First, some developing country stakeholders argue that reducing their tariffs would damage their rural economies, retard the development of their "infant industries," reduce their policy flexibility, and threaten national food security by increasing dependence on protein imports.[75] But some developing countries have also been concerned about proposed reductions in "first world" tariffs, fearing that their fisheries export sectors will lose the advantages they enjoy as a result of the preferential tariff treatment widely granted to them by the United States, Europe, and Japan. This fear of "preference erosion" arises despite the ability of many developing country producers to offer low-cost competition to first-world fleets, for several reasons: First, developing country producers continue to face significant problems with the costs of transportation and meeting first-world sanitary standards; second, developing country producers continue to face stiff price competition from heavily subsidized DWFs; and, third, commercial realities now include growing "south-south" competition between developing country producers.

Whatever the merits of these arguments, the role of fish tariff policies in the economic strategies of developing and developed countries alike remains complex. It is clear, for example, that without protective tariffs, developing country producers can sometimes face tough competition from foreign fleets in their own local markets. But since in some cases the competitive imports are actually being fished by distant-water fleets from the coastal waters of the "importing" country itself, the issue may involve questions of EEZ access as well as tariff policy. Meanwhile, other cases suggest that the reorientation of developing country fishers towards exports may reduce supplies of fish available in the domestic market, leaving the local population with less locally produced fish at higher prices.[76]

In addition to these "developmental" concerns, some governmental and nongovernmental stakeholders have argued that lowering tariffs on fish products will provide additional incentives to fish already overtaxed resources. Greenpeace, for example, has said:

> [W]hen fish trade is liberalized in a context of deficient management, or worse, no management at all, it quickly leads to overexploitation of fisheries resources, and results in social harm and environmental degradation.
>
> In the context of extremely weak fisheries management systems in most countries of the world today, the consequences of this are patently clear.[77]

This view is echoed in the negotiating positions of several governments.[78]

The extent to which reduced tariffs can cause additional overfishing remains an understudied question. The Organisation for Economic Cooperation and Development (OECD) recently issued a report suggesting that "there is scope for further market liberalisation in the fishery sector" but cautioning that the effectiveness of fisheries management is a "determining factor" that may distinguish between positive and negative outcomes.[79] Meanwhile, the claims of Greenpeace and other environmental NGOs rest on logical arguments about the relationship between consumer demand and fishing pressure, but no one has yet produced a solid technical demonstration that marginal differences in tariff levels could really have a significant impact on incentives to fish. Indeed, with the price of fish rising around the world—and with demand predicted to continue rising sharply for years to come—it seems unlikely that changes in tariff levels will be a major factor affecting the total amount of fishing worldwide.

Still, it is possible that specific changes in tariff levels could have significant impacts on particular fisheries. Accordingly, some stakeholders have called for case-by-case evaluation of proposed reductions in tariffs on fish products.[80] Such calls seek to balance the possibility that tariff changes can have real impacts on the sustainability of fisheries with the view that high tariffs are not ultimately the best method for avoiding depletion.[81]

E. Controlling Government Investment: Disciplining Fisheries Subsidies

One of the hottest area of current international debate over the links between trade law and fisheries policy is the problem of government subsidies to the fisheries sector. Not only are subsidies a classical focus of international trade law—ranking just behind tariffs and quotas on the target list of the multilateral trade system—but inappropriate subsidies have now been identified as a critical factor contributing to the global fisheries crisis.

Although largely hidden from public view, government payments to the fishing industry total at least $15 billion per year worldwide,[82] with some estimates ranging to more than twice that amount.[83] With the annual value of the fish catches hovering around $85 billion,[84] subsidies are thus equivalent to a substantial portion of industry revenue. These subsidies come in many forms, such as grants, low-cost loans, guarantees, tax breaks, price supports, and the direct provision of goods and services. And they are granted for a variety of purposes, such as vessel construction, fishing gear, fuel, bait, ice, income supports, housing, construction of port facilities, transfer of rights for access to foreign fisheries, research and development, and conservation measures, among others. The great majority are granted by a handful of major industrialized countries, with Japan and the EU leading the pack.[85]

> **Although largely hidden from public view, government payments to the fishing industry total at least $15 billion per year worldwide.**

While fisheries subsidies that support conservation and improved fisheries management can clearly have a positive impact on the sustainability of fisheries, governments now widely agree that many fisheries subsidies actively contribute to the twin problems of overcapacity and depleted fish stocks. In 2002, heads of state at the Johannesburg World Summit on Sustainable Development identified the elimination of harmful subsidies as one of the top priorities for achieving sustainable fisheries.[86]

Moreover, governments have recognized the potential for international trade law to play a direct role in confronting unsustainable fisheries subsidies. In fact, most fisheries subsidies already fall within the scope of the current WTO Agreement on Subsidies and Countervailing Duties (ASCM). But current WTO subsidies rules have proved ineffective against harmful fisheries subsidies for several reasons:

- Even the most obviously harmful fisheries subsidies are not prohibited, because current WTO rules impose an outright ban only on subsidies that directly promote or prevent exports;
- WTO rules for challenging nonprohibited subsidies generally require proof that export markets have been distorted, and thus offer little redress to fishermen whose ability to catch fish, and only indirectly to sell it, has been reduced by foreign subsidies;
- Current rules make no distinction between subsidies applied in well-managed fisheries and those applied where management is substandard, despite the widely acknowledged link between the adequacy of fisheries management and the impact of fishery subsidies;
- ASCM rules requiring governments to disclose information about subsidy programs are famously weak; they lack enforcement mechanisms and do not require the disclosure of information critical to evaluating fisheries subsidies, such as the identity of fisheries affected by subsidy programs.

In order to address these weaknesses, a coalition of governments (with leading participation by the United States[87]) successfully argued to include fisheries subsidies among the core issues on the negotiating agenda for the Doha Round.[88] As a result, for the first time in the history of modern trade diplomacy, a significant element of a global trade negotiation is directly aimed at helping conserve a vital natural resource while simultaneously reducing trade distortions.

Moreover, despite the difficulties at the heart of the broader Doha Round talks (see Section I.C, above), the fisheries subsidies talks have made steady progress. At a ministerial meeting in Hong Kong in December 2005—amidst failures to progress on other aspects of the Doha Round—WTO governments achieved a breakthrough on fisheries subsidies: they agreed in principle to adopt a new WTO prohibition on "certain forms of fisheries subsidies that contribute to overcapacity and over-fishing." While only an "agreement to agree," the Hong Kong mandate made front-page news around the world[89] and solidified a high level of environmental ambition for the fisheries subsidies talks. The ministerial decision further emphasized the need for rules that address transparency, enforceability, and the "appropriate and effective special and differential treatment" of developing countries.[90]

Even after the formal suspension of political level Doha Round talks in July 2006, technical discussions on fisheries subsidies continued to move forward.[91] As a result, in late November 2007, the chair of the WTO Negotiating Group on Rules issued the first draft of formal legal text for the new fisheries subsidies rules.[92] The Chair's draft proposed a broad prohibition on many of the most dangerous classes of fisheries subsidies, along with innovative provisions for conditioning non-prohibited subsidies on various sustainability criteria meant to ensure that subsidies are not employed where minimum standards of fisheries management are not met.[93]

As of this writing (February 2008), WTO members were engaged in what was widely regarded as a last-ditch effort to end the impasse over agricultural subsidies and industrial tariffs, in order to conclude the Round by early 2009. With the talks thus entering a highly political phase—and with the EU continuing to lead an effort to gut the proposed fisheries subsidies rules—the ultimate fate of the fisheries subsidies text remained difficult to predict. A "low ambition" outcome to the Round as a whole could lead to a substantially weakened result. On the other hand, the steady momentum within the fisheries subsidies talks themselves continued to hold out the hope for substantial new disciplines, including an international ban on at least some important fisheries subsidies.

The legal innovations that will be required to achieve strong fisheries subsidies rules pose some interesting challenges for the WTO trade regime. First, robust rules will require expanding the legally cognizable harms addressed by the ASCM to include economic distortions at the level of production rather than only at the level of international sale. In political terms, this means expanding WTO subsidy rules to protect the interests of some producers, and not merely those of exporters. This is not a small step for a code that until now has carefully guarded the rights of governments to grant "production subsidies" so long as these do not cause measurable (and thus more or less immediate) export market distortions.

Second, as the chair's draft reflects, new rules on fisheries subsidies will require integrating some basic environmental norms into the ASCM. But integrating environmental considerations into WTO rules is a delicate task, given the strong desire on the part of both trade policymakers and environmental stakeholders to keep the WTO from an entanglement with issues beyond its trade-related mandate. To solve this problem, negotiators and civil-society stakeholders have been exploring ways to make use of what might be called baseline fisheries management norms—that is, tests of sustainable management that are universally accepted and easily verified. The Chair's draft would look to the U.N. Code of Conduct for Responsible Fishing for elements of minimally acceptable management.[94] The Chair's draft also proposes a direct role for the FAO in helping determine whether such management criteria have been met[95]—an idea that could be modeled in part upon the FAO-CITES arrangement discussed below. WWF has also suggested that governments wishing to subsidize fishing should first comply with voluntary U.N. codes such as the International Plan of Action for the Management of Fishing Capacity.[96] Rules such as these would create an unprecedented degree of coordination between fisheries management policies and international trade laws.

Finally, as noted above, effective rules will depend on whether the WTO can oblige governments to open their books on fisheries subsidies. Here again, the Chair's draft proposes attaching real legal consequences to notification failures, and would require governments to disclose information about the fisheries affected by subsidy programs. Both of these proposals, however, pose significant tests to the political will of the governments involved in the negotiations.

The halting character of the Doha Round negotiations has obviously cast doubt on the future of the legal innovations discussed above. But the progress towards new rules at the WTO has been unusual and encouraging. Moreover, the high priority now being given to the elimination of harmful fisheries subsidies suggests that this issue will remain on the international agenda even if the Doha Round fails.

F. Protecting Consumers: Sanitary Standards and Labeling Requirements

1. Health and Food Safety Standards

From the perspective of fish merchants and their legal counsel, the trade rules most frequently encountered in daily commerce are the health and food safety standards routinely applied to imports of fisheries products. These standards—known technically as "sanitary and phytosanitary standards" (SPS)—are technically intricate, highly specialized to the fisheries trade, and variable from country to country despite growing international efforts at harmonization. The details of these regulations are far beyond the scope of this chapter, and practitioners will know to consult the extensive technical literature that is available.[97] Instead, this chapter will briefly review the international framework governing SPS rules on fisheries products, and note a few of the most salient policy issues now under discussion in this field.

The principal international legal framework governing how governments apply SPS standards is the WTO SPS Agreement.[98] The goal of the SPS Agreement is to allow effective national SPS standards while avoiding undue hindrances to trade. Thus, the Agreement reaffirms the right of countries to adopt strong SPS measures, so long as those measures are based on a risk assessment and on scientific principles, are nondiscriminatory among WTO members, and are not more trade-restrictive than necessary.[99]

The SPS agreement also seeks to support harmonization and the application of international standards, including by holding that SPS measures that conform to international "standards, guidelines or recommendations" shall be deemed "necessary to protect human, animal or plant life or health."[100] In the case of food products, including both fisheries and agricultural goods, the principal source of the international SPS standards on which the WTO relies is the Codex Alimentarius Commission. This Commission was created by the U.N. Food and Agriculture Organization and the World Health Organization to develop standards and guidelines aimed at protecting the health of consumers, ensuring fair trade practices in the food trade, and promoting harmonization.[101]

The Codex Alimentarius has issued a Code of Practice that provides a basic guide to food safety standards in the fisheries sector.[102] This code adopts the Hazard Analysis and Critical Control Point (HACCP) approach to food safety procedures. HACCP procedures set out the essential elements of a food safety system that monitors the condition of the product through the entire chain of production. This system includes hazard analysis, establishment of "critical limits," establishment of a monitoring and control system, setting procedures for corrective action when necessary, and establishing a documentation regime.[103] The United States, like many other jurisdictions, has adopted sanitary standards for fish imports based on the HACCP approach.[104] The widespread adoption of HACCP-based standards has not, however, resulted in effective harmonization of standards. On the contrary, a 2005 report by the FAO found that the HACCP-based systems of the United States, EU, Canada, and Japan varied substantially, with significant negative results for the "free flow of trade" in fisheries products.[105]

SPS standards on fish products result in hundreds of shipment-specific enforcement actions at border control points each year.[106] However, these actions rise to the level of international trade law disputes infrequently, mainly when they are seen as disguised forms of protectionism.[107] These disputes, in turn, rarely have a direct bearing on the three overarching policy issues—stock depletion, fleet overcapacity, and uneven development—identified at the outset of this chapter. They are, in essence, run-of-the-mill SPS trade law cases, and thus fall mainly beyond the scope of this chapter.

Of greater relevance to the regulation of oceans and coasts—and particularly to the "north-south" issue of uneven fishing industry development—is the legal policy trend in fish product SPS requirements in many developed countries. Here, some importing nations (led by the EU) are increasingly turning away from import controls based on "end product" quality inspections performed at the border, and towards "quality assurance" or "prevention at source" approaches that shift the locus of responsibility for compliance more directly onto the exporting producers and their governments.[108] These more process-oriented approaches look to the handling and processing procedures in place from the time of capture to the time of importation, and are thought to reduce border control problems while raising the overall likelihood of compliance with end product standards. However, many developing country exporters find it difficult to adapt their production and handling systems to achieve the "mutual recognition" and precertification of enterprises they need to gain access to first world markets. This is especially a challenge for coastal developing countries with small scale rural fishing enterprises that hope to gain access to international markets.

2. Labeling for Consumer Protection

Alongside sanitary and food safety standards, a parallel set of labeling requirements generally applies to fish products. As with the substantive quality standards, these labeling requirements can be specific to fish trade, although they share little of the same arcane technical complexity. The principal trade law framework for the regulation of labeling standards is the WTO Agreement on Technical Barriers to Trade (TBT). Like the SPS agreement, the TBT code seeks to allow governments to impose standards on products, so long as they do so in a nondiscriminatory fashion and without undue interference with trade.[109] An example of the issues that can arise under the

TBT code with regard to labeling of fish can be found in a 2001 WTO case in which Peru challenged the use of the commercial name "sardines" affixed to labels of certain exports from the EU.[110]

The labeling of fisheries products does not currently raise issues of trade law beyond what is routine to TBT practice generally, and thus is of little special interest from the perspective of oceans and coasts law. Once again, however, emerging trends in national regulation may be of greater relevance. In particular, regulations in the EU now require all fish products sold in EU markets to bear labels stating the kind of fish (according to mandatory correlations between commercial and scientific names), their marine geographic origin (ocean region), and whether they are wild-caught or farmed.[111] Although these steps may seem modest, they form part of an increasingly rigorous EU regime requiring "traceability" of fish products (see next section). As businesses and consumers become ever more interested in the "sustainability" of the fish products they sell and purchase, the new EU regulations mark a significant move toward publication of information derived from compulsory "chain of custody" documentation, and may represent an emerging trend in national regulation more broadly (see further discussion of ecolabeling, below).

3. Traceability

Increasingly, governments, businesses, and consumers are interested in knowing the specific origins of the wild-capture fish that are brought to market. This growing emphasis on traceability is rooted in a variety of intersecting policy goals. For the sake of consumer protection, governments may wish to help prevent the fraudulent labeling of fish products as to their type (is that really sole, and not flounder?), geographic origin (is that really "Maryland" blue crab?), or even production method (is this truly "wild caught" salmon?). For health and safety reasons—and even to prevent bio-terrorism—governments may want to know the handling history of fish products back to the ship's deck. To combat pirate fishing, port inspectors may want to be sure that fish were caught by properly licensed vessels. And to encourage sustainable fishing, producers and retailers may want to ensure that only fish from properly certified fisheries bear valuable ecolabels.

Increasingly, governments, businesses, and consumers are interested in knowing the specific origins of the wild-capture fish that are brought to market.

Ultimately, such goals imply the need for product traceability from fisherman to the ultimate consumer. But no government yet mandates complete traceability for all imports of fisheries products.[112] The most comprehensive legal requirements currently in place are EU regulations that came into force at the beginning of 2005.[113] These regulations mandate traceability from fishing vessels onward for all domestic EU fish products and for products landed directly in the EU by foreign vessels, but stop short of having full extraterritorial effect.[114] Still, the pressure for all suppliers to conform to the EU requirements is strong.[115] Meanwhile, in the United States, the Public Health

Security and Bioterrorism Preparedness and Response Act of 2002 also creates what the FAO has called a de facto chain of custody requirement for food products,[116] but the regulations implementing the Act explicitly exempt most fishing vessels from its terms.[117]

G. Trade Measures for Environmental Purposes

The use of trade restrictions in support of environmental policies has been a growing practice—and a source of controversy—since at least the 1970s. Whether imposed unilaterally or pursuant to cooperative international action, these trade-related environmental measures (TREMs) have generated substantial legal and political debate. While TREMs may be found wherever international commerce and environmental concerns intersect, they have become particularly common in the fisheries sector. Indeed, some of the best-known trade law cases relating to TREMs have involved fisheries products. This comparative frequency of TREMs in the fisheries sector is likely a reflection of the transnational nature of fisheries resources, and of the incomplete authority of international institutions charged with managing them. Put another way, few spheres of economic activity more clearly illustrate a continuing tragedy of the commons than the race for fish. As governments have sought ways to confront this reality through international regulation, and to prevent uncooperative states from acting as free riders, TREMs have repeatedly been seen as a tool of choice.

1. Tuna, Shrimp, TREMs, and PPMs—Unilateralism at Issue

The field of legal study and practice known as "trade and environment" is often said to have originated with the seminal "Tuna-Dolphin" dispute that was litigated under the General Agreement on Tariffs and Trade (GATT) in the early 1990s. That dispute—and the subsequent "Shrimp-Turtle" case at the WTO—contain the two leading discussions by international trade tribunals to date of the limits imposed on the unilateral use of TREMs. More specifically, these cases focus on whether international trade law allows unilateral trade restrictions based on how a product is produced, even in cases where the sale and consumption of the product itself poses no immediate environmental danger.[118] Often known as the PPM (process and production method) problem, this question is one of the core concerns at the heart of the trade and environment legal debate. As will be seen, the tribunals in the *Tuna-Dolphin* and *Shrimp-Turtle* cases offered very different answers.

The Tuna-Dolphin dispute has a long and intricate history, which has yet to be laid entirely to rest. Its details provide an instructive illustration of the scientific, commercial, and political complexities of a dispute over the governance of an international fishery (see next section). Legally, however, the long and short of it is this: In 1988, the United States adopted legislation that in effect imposed a ban on imports of tuna products harvested in the Eastern Tropical Pacific Ocean (ETP) using a fishing method known as "dolphin encirclement." Two years later, the United States also passed a law forbidding the labeling of ETP tuna products caught through dolphin encirclement as "dolphin safe." These laws, which essentially closed the U.S. market to tuna producers from Mexico, Venezuela, and other Latin American countries, remained in effect even after cooperative international action succeeded in sharply reducing dolphin mortality in the ETP.

The U.S. Tuna-Dolphin embargo was challenged twice before the GATT—once by Mexico, and subsequently by the EU.[119] In both instances, the United States lost, with the GATT panels enunciating a clear "anti-PPM" rule. As the second panel put it:

> [T]he import embargoes distinguished between tuna products according to harvesting practices and tuna import policies of the exporting countries; that the measures imposed by the United States in respect of domestic tuna similarly distinguished between tuna and tuna products according to tuna harvesting methods; and that none of these practices, policies and methods could have any impact on the inherent character of tuna as a product.[120]

The previous panel had gone on to suggest that allowing such unilateral PPM-based TREMs would spell the undoing of the multilateral trade system:

> The Panel considered that if the broad interpretation . . . suggested by the United States were accepted, each [GATT] contracting party could unilaterally determine the life or health protection policies from which other contracting parties could not deviate without jeopardizing their rights under the General Agreement. The General Agreement would then no longer constitute a multilateral framework for trade among all contracting parties. . . . [121]

Many governments and civil-society stakeholders outside the United States (and especially in developing countries) applauded these rulings, which they saw as a bulwark against unilateral bullying by the major economic powers. But environmentalists in the United States and Europe saw the matter otherwise, focusing on the need for limits on "process and production methods" as a fundamental element of environmental regulation. As will be seen below, the urgent international fight against illegal fishing activities increasingly depends on the use of PPM-based trade measures. It is small wonder that the *Tuna-Dolphin* rulings drew substantial international attention.

Despite their fame, however, the *Tuna-Dolphin* rulings never took formal legal effect,[122] and even if they had, the panel opinions theoretically had no precedential weight. The starkly different ruling later handed down by the WTO Appellate Body in the *Shrimp-Turtle* case is thus likely to be far more influential.

The *Shrimp-Turtle* case once again saw a challenge to a unilateral PPM-based embargo imposed by the United States—this time against imports of shrimp products from any country not requiring the use of turtle excluder devices to prevent endangered sea turtles from drowning in shrimp nets. But, unlike in the *Tuna-Dolphin* case, the United States undertook significant international action (in the form of both diplomacy and foreign aid) to promote cooperative solutions consistent with U.S. policy.

This more internationalist approach of the United States—most likely combined with a more mature judicial view of the political and legal context surrounding the newly born WTO—helped the Appellate Body reach a conclusion that appears to endorse the potential legality of unilateral PPM-based TREMs. The Appellate Body found that several of the enumerated legal exceptions to GATT's rules against nondiscrimination allow "conditioning access to a Member's domestic market on whether exporting Members comply with, or adopt, a policy or policies unilaterally prescribed by the importing Member."[123]

But while the United States seems thus to have won much of the PPM war, it nevertheless lost the *Shrimp-Turtle* battle. The Appellate Body found that although the Shrimp-Turtle embargo was not per se illegal, the United States had not afforded the complainants (Malaysia, Pakistan, and Thailand) equal opportunity to enter into international agreements that would have avoided the need for unilateral U.S. action.[124] In addition, the Appellate Body found that the U.S. certification process for determining which countries could import shrimp products into the United States was insufficiently transparent or predictable to avoid "arbitrary discrimination."[125]

The Appellate Body thus appears to have opened the door to unilateral PPM-based TREMs, so long as they are accompanied by even-handed efforts to achieve cooperative solutions, and are administered with scrupulous fairness. Presumably, the PPM-based TREMs applied in support of policies adopted by regional fisheries management organizations—discussed next—would tend to be facially valid under the *Shrimp-Turtle* rule. But the diplomacy surrounding them, and their specific implementation at national borders, could still come under WTO scrutiny.

Given its importance in the history of the international law of trade and environment and of fisheries-related trade law, the next section provides an overview of the history of the *Tuna-Dolphin* case.

2. *Tuna-Dolphin*—A Case Study

For reasons still not understood by biologists, mature yellowfin tuna in the Eastern Tropical Pacific Ocean (ETP)[126] often swim closely in association with schools of dolphins. Since the 1950s, fishermen in the ETP have used the visibility of dolphins to locate tuna, which they then surround with huge purse seine nets. Up through the late 1960s, this form of fishing was done without regard for the ensuing dolphin deaths, which at times rose to more than 700,000 animals per year.[127]

This wholesale slaughter contributed to the depletion of several ETP dolphin species. It also led to an outcry from thousands of U.S. schoolchildren—many raised on a popular TV show about a dolphin named Flipper—who joined in a nationwide campaign calling for an end to dolphin encirclement.[128] U.S. tuna producers quickly responded, shifting their tuna sourcing to waters outside the ETP where the tuna-dolphin association is less prevalent and labeling their canned tuna "dolphin safe."[129] The U.S. Congress followed suit, amending the Marine Mammal Protection Act in 1988 effectively banning imports of ETP tuna caught through dolphin encirclement,[130] and then, in 1990, prohibiting use of the "dolphin safe" label on any tuna produced through dolphin encirclement.[131]

Fishermen from Mexico, Venezuela, and other Latin American countries—who had increased their fishing in the ETP after the departure of the U.S. fleet—also responded. With their cooperation, governments party to the Inter-American Tropical Tuna Commission (IATTC) put in place the International Dolphin Conservation Program,[132] which included

- Teaching fishermen how to release dolphins prior to hauling in their nets;
- Setting mandatory vessel-by-vessel dolphin mortality limits, to be progressively reduced each year with the goal of achieving levels approaching zero;
- Requiring an observer aboard each tuna vessel to track dolphin deaths; and
- Monitoring and enforcing compliance with dolphin mortality limits.

The IATTC program quickly became one of the most rigorous (and expensive) regional fisheries management regimes operating anywhere in the world, leading to significant declines in dolphin mortality. But even as Mexico and other countries were building the strength of the IATTC program, they challenged the U.S. embargo, arguing that U.S. dolphin-safe requirements violated U.S. obligations under the GATT. In 1991, a GATT panel ruled against the United States,[133] as did a second panel in a similar case brought three years later by the EU.[134] Neither ruling, however, was ever given formal legal effect[135]—and in any case, the U.S. embargo and labeling laws were left in place.

By 1995, international pressure against the U.S. tuna embargo had mounted even further. In Geneva, the WTO replaced the GATT, bringing the prospect of unavoidable trade sanctions should the United States lose another international challenge. In the ETP, Latin American fishermen continued to produce sharp reductions in dolphin mortality, achieving levels of fewer than 2,000 animals annually—an average of around 0.5 dolphin deaths per encirclement in place of the hundreds per "set" in previous years.[136] And in Washington, some environmental groups concluded that continuation of the U.S. embargo was not environmentally justified, and could erode the success of the IATTC dolphin protection program.

Accordingly, with the support of these environmental groups,[137] the United States, Mexico, and half a dozen other Latin American countries issued a declaration aimed at resolving the *Tuna-Dolphin* dispute. The Declaration of Panama,[138] as it was known, included a promise by Latin governments to strengthen the IATTC dolphin conservation program and to accept its terms in a binding and permanent international treaty. In return, the United States was to lift its embargo and change the definition of "dolphin safe" to include tuna from the ETP if it was (1) caught in compliance with the strengthened IATTC program and (2) caught with zero actual dolphin deaths as certified by a neutral onboard observer.

The Declaration of Panama included a promise by Latin governments to strengthen the IATTC dolphin conservation program.

Several steps were subsequently taken toward implementing the Panama Declaration. In 1997, the U.S. Congress passed the International Dolphin Conservation Program Act (IDCPA),[139] laying the legal groundwork for lifting the embargo[140] and adjusting the definition of "dolphin safe" for use on commercial labels,[141] but conditioning the latter action on a regulatory finding by the Secretary of Commerce that continued encirclement would not have "a significant adverse impact on any depleted dolphin stock."[142] A year and a half later, the relevant Latin American countries joined the United States in a new treaty incorporating the commitments promised in the Panama Declaration.[143] And, also in 1999, the Secretary of Commerce issued an "initial finding" of no "significant adverse impact" of continued encirclement.[144] In early January of 2000, the U.S. tuna embargo was formally lifted, and steps towards adjusting the "dolphin safe" labeling regulation were initiated.[145]

But the Panama Declaration and its implementation under the IDCPA were bitterly opposed by a number of environmental and animal rights groups on the grounds that continued encirclement disrupts dolphin reproduction, causes unobserved mortality, and is inhumane.[146] These groups brought legal action to block the change in the "dolphin safe" labeling regulation—and they prevailed. In successive rulings in 2000[147] and 2004,[148] a federal district court set aside initial and final findings by the Secretary of Commerce of no "significant adverse impact." In strongly worded opinions, the court ruled that the Secretary had unlawfully ignored scientific reports generated by his own department, failed to carry out congressionally mandated research, and based his findings in part on unauthorized considerations of diplomacy and trade policy. The court's final order, which was confirmed by the U.S. Court of Appeals for the Ninth Circuit,[149] took the unusual step of barring the Secretary from taking any corrective action, which (if the order stands) would appear to disallow further implementation of the Panama Declaration unless Congress legislates anew.

3. Trade Measures Against "Pirate Fishing"

The *Tuna-Dolphin* and *Shrimp-Turtle* cases both relate to the relatively rare unilateral use of trade-related environmental measures to protect so-called charismatic nonfish species. Of perhaps greater importance, however, is the growing use of TREMs to combat illegal, unregulated, or unreported (IUU) fishing.

Pirate fishing—as IUU fishing is commonly called—is a critical problem. It is estimated that nearly twenty percent of catches from wild capture marine fisheries may be the results of IUU activities.[150] For some major stocks, according to the FAO, the figure may be as high as thirty percent.[151] Pirate fishing is thought to be particularly prevalent on the high seas and in the waters of developing countries, where governmental resources for monitoring and enforcement at sea are unfortunately thin. As stock depletion has intensified the race for fish, the need to confront IUU fishing has emerged as a top priority of international ocean policymakers. (See Chapter 10.)

Given the high proportion of fish products that enter international commerce, it is little wonder that policymakers have noted the potential utility of barriers to trade in IUU fisheries products. Members of the U.N. FAO have adopted a voluntary International Plan of Action on IUU fishing that, among other things, calls on all governments to "take all steps necessary, consistent with international law, to prevent fish caught by vessels identified by the relevant regional fisheries management organization to have been engaged in IUU fishing being traded or imported into their territories."[152]

In legislation signed into law in early 2007, the United States appears to have become the first country to mandate the unilateral use of TREMs against IUU fishing. The Magnuson-Stevens Fishery Conservation and Management Reauthorization Act of 2006[153] requires the United States to ban imports of fish, fish products, and sports fishing equipment from any nation identified by the Secretary of Commerce as having nationals engaged in IUU fishing on the high seas.[154]

This threat of unilateral action against IUU fishing by the United States comes in the context of a broad international trend. Increasingly, regional fisheries management organizations (RFMOs) are adopting rules that encourage or require the use of TREMs to combat fishing activities that contravene their management programs.[155] To date, trade measures to combat IUU fishing have been specifically promoted by at least five major RFMOs: the Commission for the Conservation of Southern Bluefin Tuna (CCSBT),[156] the Convention for the Conservation of Antarctic Marine Living Resources (CCAMLR),[157] the Inter-American Tropical Tuna Commission (IATTC),[158] the International Commission for the Conservation of Atlantic Tunas (ICCAT),[159] the North Eastern Atlantic Fisheries Commission (NEAFC),[160] and the Northwest Atlantic Fisheries Organization (NAFO).[161]

These anti-IUU trade measures are of several types. The most elemental measures are prohibitions on landing and transshipment of fish from vessels associated with IUU fishing. In some cases, such vessels are identified simply by their flag—such as when vessels from "noncooperating states" are discovered within waters regulated by an RFMO. In other cases, RFMOs keep lists of vessels authorized to fish under their authority, with other vessels barred from off-loading in ports of member states. (Note that these anti-IUU landing restriction measures are not often applied by the United States, principally because U.S. law generally prohibits foreign fishing vessels from landing fish in U.S. ports.[162])

Despite the growing use of anti-IUU landing restrictions, however, their legal status under international trade law remains unclear, as evident in a dispute that arose between Chile and the EU over swordfish. While that case involved landing restrictions applied by Chile unilaterally (there was and still is no RFMO with jurisdiction over the fishery in question), the EU's legal arguments against the restrictions suggest potential questions about the legality of even RFMO-sanctioned measures, at least when applied to nonmembers.[163] The Chile-EU swordfish case—which simmered for a decade and is still not entirely resolved—focused on a prohibition imposed by Chile in 1991 against the landing of swordfish from Spanish vessels fishing in the South-East Pacific just beyond Chile's EEZ. The Spanish fleet had begun taking swordfish in those waters only a year earlier,[164] and sought to land the fish in Chile for transshipment to new export markets elsewhere in the Americas. Chile justified the closure of its ports on the grounds that the Spanish fleet was threatening a stock long vital to Chile through fishing activities that contravened basic international fisheries conservation norms.

Years of diplomatic wrangling came to a head in late 2000, when the disputants initiated simultaneous proceedings against one another in the WTO (EU complaining)[165] and under UNCLOS (Chile complaining).[166] Both might well have been groundbreaking cases,[167] and their parallel progress was certain to raise novel and important questions about jurisdiction over fisheries (and fish trade) within the patchwork system of global governance.[168]

But while both cases are still officially pending, the disputes have been on hold since just weeks after their formal inception—the result of a compromise reached in January 2001.[169] Chile agreed to open its ports to four Spanish vessels, ostensibly for purposes of "scientific research fishing" to collect data about the thinly studied South-East Pacific swordfish stocks, but with rights to transship product for commercial export. The EU agreed to participate in a bilateral commission to study the fishery, and to work towards creation of an RFMO for its multilateral governance. In July 2007, the parties met to discuss a permanent resolution to the dispute, having agreed that the interim arrangements should not extend beyond 2008. As of this writing, the parties were discussing a settlement proposal tabeled by Chile.[170]

A second category of anti-IUU trade measures consists of catch documentation schemes, which are coupled with the use of import permits and sometimes with mandatory labeling requirements.[171] Part of the rising emphasis on traceability of fish products (see Section II.F.3, above), these measures are seen by the FAO as a basic step towards confronting IUU fishing, and a prerequisite to the use of internationally agreed anti-IUU trade barriers.[172] Catch documentation schemes aim to require the collection and maintenance of information including the identity of fishing vessels, the kind and quantity of fish landed, the location of the fishing activities, the date and location of capture and of landing, and of any transshipment at sea.[173] Perhaps the earliest RFMO catch documentation scheme to come into force was adopted by ICCAT in 1992 to cover frozen bluefin tuna products.[174] Now expanded to cover all major products from ICCAT fisheries,[175] ICCAT's statistical documents program (along with a similar program established by the IATTC for bigeye tuna in the Eastern Tropical Pacific[176]) is implemented under U.S. law as mandatory procedure for U.S. fishermen and a prerequisite for the import of affected tuna products.[177] (Regarding the relationship between the ICCAT program and debate within the Convention on International Trade in Endangered Species, see note 184 and accompanying text).

A particularly sophisticated catch documentation scheme is the one implemented by CCAMLR to combat illegal fishing for Patagonian toothfish.[178, 179] The CCAMLR scheme works hand in hand with other CCAMLR rules that require marking of fishing vessels and gear, licensing and inspection of vessels, and mandatory use of satellite-based vessel monitoring systems.[180] Regulations implementing the CCAMLR documentation requirements in the United States were put in place in 2000, shortly after the establishment of the scheme.[181] Along with related management efforts, the CCAMLR scheme appears to have substantially reduced illegal toothfish fishing.[182]

The third, and ultimate, class of anti-IUU trade measures consists of direct bans on importation of IUU tainted products. These bans differ from prohibitions on landing (discussed above) in two ways. First, they apply to all acts of importation, and not only landings by fishermen (which may or may not be associated with importation).

Second, in some cases they are imposed in a quasi-punitive manner on a country-by-country basis, and not merely on imports associated with specific pirate vessels. In both of these respects, anti-IUU import bans affect commerce undertaken by enterprises that may be some distance from the IUU fishing that the measures ultimately target. Moreover, import bans are a direct interference with the core activity that international trade law is principally intended to promote. In short, they are the most severe and potentially controversial of anti-IUU TREMs.

4. When Does a Fish Look Like a Rhinoceros? CITES and Fish Trade

Since 1975, the Convention on International Trade in Endangered Species (CITES) has been the principal global instrument for limiting trade in goods derived from animals and plants at risk of extinction. Probably most famous for its trade bans on elephant ivory and rhino horn, CITES has only recently been invoked to regulate trade in depleted species of commercial fish.

Even an introductory review of CITES law and practice is mainly beyond the scope of this chapter. It suffices here to point out that CITES imposes trade controls by listing species on one of three CITES appendices, as follows:

- Appendix I lists species that are "threatened with extinction"; trade in Appendix I species is effectively banned, except under exceptional circumstances.
- Appendix II lists species that are likely to become threatened with extinction in the absence of trade controls; trade in Appendix II species is allowed, but only subject to strict permitting requirements (usually determined by the exporting country) that limit exports and imports to products subject to protective management.
- Appendix III lists species that are protected by at least one country, and regarding which individual member governments are seeking international cooperation in support of domestic management and protection efforts.

Appendices I and II are thus the core of CITES's multilateral activity, with a two-thirds vote by CITES members needed to add species to (or remove them from) either list. As of this writing, there were 892 species listed on CITES Appendix I, and 33,033 species listed on Appendix II.[183] Only a few of these (15 on Appendix I and 71 on Appendix II) were fish, of which few were species of major commercial value.

Still, the application of CITES to commercial fish species has been under discussion since at least the early 1990s, when conservation groups frustrated with the poor performance of some regional fisheries management organizations first turned to the Convention as an alternative forum to limit trade in overexploited stocks. A leading example was the 1991 proposal to list Atlantic bluefin tuna on CITES Appendix II.[184] This effort was part of a campaign by some NGOs and governments to pressure ICCAT into more aggressive steps to manage the bluefin stock in the face of rising trade pressures. Although the proposal's sponsor, Sweden, ultimately withdrew its request, the specter of a CITES listing contributed to the adoption of ICCAT's catch documentation scheme in 1992, discussed above.

In the late 1990s, efforts to list commercial fish species on CITES Appendix II gained significant momentum and international support. But even proponents were concerned that CITES might be ill-equipped to deal with fisheries issues. The result was an unusual interinstitutional dialogue between CITES and the FAO, in which the FAO reviewed the existing criteria and formulated recommendations for amendments and additions that would make them more applicable to commercial fish species. CITES had also been undertaking a general review of the listing criteria and, in 2004, formally adopted revised criteria that included the most important of the FAO recommendations. At the same time, in order to improve the scientific review process for proposals dealing with commercial fish species, the FAO created an ad hoc expert panel to provide advice to CITES on specific listing proposals. The cooperative relationship between CITES and FAO was formalized through a Memorandum of Understanding signed in October 2006.[185] As of March 2008, FAO-CITES panels had been convened twice, on the occasions of the thirteenth and fourteenth meetings of the CITES Conference of Parties (in 2005 and 2007, respectively).[186] Although the panels have brought a strong measure of objective science to the process, the CITES listing procedure remains subject to other influences, as is evident in the reluctance of the CITES Secretariat and its member states to follow the expert panel advice in some cases.[187]

But as CITES seems poised to move further into the regulation of fisheries trade, its role remains somewhat controversial. Some protagonists argue that CITES is intended to control trade only where the true extinction of a species is at issue. Others argue that CITES should help encourage the sustainable use of commercial species as a tool of active management to safeguard both biological and economic values. The trend seems to be with the latter camp, as proposals to list commercial fish species on CITES Appendix II appear to be growing. In any case, the use of CITES in "forum shopping" tactics such as those that surrounded Atlantic bluefin tuna more than a dozen years ago are still a visible part of the policy debate over fisheries trade and fisheries management today.[188]

As CITES seems poised to move further into the regulation of fisheries trade, its role remains somewhat controversial.

5. TREMS and MEAs—The WTO Debate Continues

The trade-related environmental measures sanctioned under CITES, like those adopted by RFMOs to combat IUU fishing, obviously enjoy significant international political support. Nevertheless, as the earlier discussion of the *Tuna-Dolphin* and *Shrimp-Turtle* cases implies, the WTO law surrounding these measures remains uncertain. Since the WTO appellate body appears to have opened the door to unilateral national use of TREMs (at least provided certain procedural conditions are met), the WTO legality of TREMs imposed under the terms of international treaties would seem relatively secure.

But the potential for WTO challenge even against TREMS associated with multilateral environmental agreements (MEAs) remains real—enough so that an effort to clarify the relationship between MEAs and the WTO is meant to be part of the Doha Round negotiations.[189] Among the legal questions still in need of clarification are

- Do WTO members accept that environmental PPMs can be legitimate under some circumstances, as the Appellate Body has held?
- Should priority of any kind between WTO and MEA provisions be established, or should the legal relationships between MEAs and the WTO generally remain subject to the standard rules of treat interpretation, such as those enshrined in the 1969 Vienna Convention on the Law of Treaties?
- To what extent can the WTO review the implementation of TREMs applied under an MEA? Must, for example, their implementation pass a WTO "least restrictive to trade" test?
- To qualify as an MEA-sanctioned TREM, how specifically must the measure be contemplated by the MEA text? Must the MEA make application of the TREMs obligatory?
- How should the WTO treat the application of TREMs to states nonparty to the MEAs under which the TREMs are applied?

There is, however, little hope that questions such as these will receive significant answers in the context of the Doha Round. To start with, the Doha mandate on MEAs is narrow and effectively excludes consideration of the last two questions listed above. But even within the remaining scope of the MEA talks, there has been little or no visible progress at the negotiating table. For the foreseeable future, the law surrounding WTO-MEA relationship looks likely to remain largely in the hands of dispute resolution panels and the WTO Appellate Body.

III. An Important Emerging Issue: Ecolabeling

The ecolabeling of fish products is a growing phenomenon that has received substantial attention from fisheries policymakers, and has generated both hope and controversy around the world. For some stakeholders, ecolabeling represents a critical opportunity to harness market forces in favor of sustainable fishing; for others, it raises the threat of market barriers and of private sector intrusion into the province of public fisheries policy. Efforts to develop ecolabels—and to control them—are thus important and growing parts of the normative framework surrounding trade in fish products, even if (as will be seen) little hard law has yet to be brought to bear on the subject.

The ecolabeling of fish products dates back at least to the promotion of "dolphin safe" tuna by U.S. and European producers in the late 1980s, discussed above. This kind of single-issue labeling, however, is quite distinct from the broader effort to promote sustainable fisheries management that a decade later motivated ecolabeling efforts such as the Marine Stewardship Council (MSC).[190] Today, the MSC remains the leading entity involved in ecolabeling fish,[191] although a number of other more localized or issue-specific efforts have been considered.[192]

Although trends in just the past few years suggest a burgeoning interest by major fish retailers in Europe and the United States, ecolabeled products today still represent only a small fraction of the market. This likely explains why laws specifically regulating the ecolabeling of fish have yet to appear. (In this regard, a comparison might be drawn to "organic" food labeling in the United States, which became a subject of regulatory attention only after significant market penetration by claimed "organic" products.) For the legal practitioner, then, it is the process of norm-building more than the weight of existing law that is of interest here. Among the key developments to note and track are:

- FAO Guidelines on Ecolabelling of Fish and Fishery Products—Formally adopted by the FAO in March 2005,[193] these nonbinding norms were the result of lengthy technical consultations and negotiations. In general, they resemble many of the criteria adopted by the MSC, but do not yet reach the same level of detail; further elaboration by the FAO may be in the works.[194] Although they have yet to be applied in practice, these guidelines have real potential to influence the future of ecolabeling (and relevant regulation) in the fishery sector.

- Possible EU legislation—In June 2005 the EC Commission issued a formal communication to launch a process to launch "a debate on a Community approach towards eco-labelling schemes for fisheries products."[195] The Commission subsequently conducted an expert consultation process, but as of this writing had not brought forward further reports or recommendations. According to the original communication, the Commission believes that some action to regulate fishery ecolabels is necessary, but that establishment of a government-controlled labeling scheme is not an attractive option. If this process does move forward, the direction seems to be toward a regulatory definition of minimum requirements for voluntary ecolabeling of fishery products.

- Ecolabels in the WTO—The fear that ecolabels may pose discriminatory de jure or de facto market barriers persists, particularly among some developing country stakeholders. The *Tuna-Dolphin* experience has also left lingering fears that ecolabels can be associated with regulatory trade restrictions—a concern compounded by the direct interest of some governments in creating government-sponsored ecolabels.[196] To date, however, there have been no direct challenges to the use of ecolabels (other than in the *Tuna-Dolphin* context) under WTO law. Still, ecolabels remain a regular topic of WTO debate, and the Doha Round negotiating mandate calls on WTO members to explore the need to clarify the WTO rules in regard to them.[197] As with the Doha negotiations on MEAs, however, there seems little prospect that a final Doha package will include significant language on ecolabels.

For the time being, ecolabels for fishery products remain a growing experiment, bounded only by the routine commercial laws governing advertisement and consumer information generally. Moreover, the ability of ecolabels to generate significant change in the behaviors of producers, merchants, and consumers is just beginning to be tested seriously. If the experiment succeeds, a more mature regulatory infrastructure may begin to emerge.

IV. Conclusions

The discussion in this chapter reveals that the international legal framework surrounding trade in wild-capture fish and fish products is complex and in a significant state of flux. Overall, the trends in the law seem to be moving—albeit unevenly—toward more purposeful support for policies encouraging conservation of fishery resources and international equity in access to fisheries-based livelihoods.

But the positive trends in the law are still offset by disturbing economic and environmental realities in fisheries and fishing communities around the world. Even as trade law edges towards a more coherent and sustainable future, fisheries trade itself continues to bring mixed blessings to its practitioners. The negative impacts of export-driven growth on resource husbandry and food security in some developing countries is now clear, and yet export-led development remains very much in vogue. Meanwhile, oversized first-world fishing fleets continue to benefit from subsidies and other trade policies that run counter to the professed intention of governments to reduce global fishing capacity and to encourage responsible management and poverty alleviation.

The shifting balance among these trends and realities will affect the lives of hundreds of million of people around the world in the decades ahead. Meanwhile, between fish dinners, students of the law will have plenty of food for study and thought.

Notes

1. *See generally* R. D. BALLARD, MYSTERY OF THE ANCIENT SEAFARERS: EARLY MARITIME CIVILIZATIONS (Nat'l Geographic 2004). Fish were among the cargoes archeologists have discovered were transported across ancient seas. *See, e.g., id.* at 74, 80.
2. FAO, THE STATE OF WORLD FISHERIES AND AQUACULTURE 2006 (2007) [hereinafter FAO SOFIA 2006] at 41, 44. The $71 billion figure represents export values for 2004.
3. *Id.* at 23.
4. *Id.* at 45.
5. *Id.* at 44. The FAO points out that some of this trade may be in the form of re-exports.
6. While there may also be unique features to the laws affecting ocean products other than fish, these tend more often to focus on the legal treatment of ownership, management, and extraction of ocean-based resources than on trade per se.
7. FAO SOFIA 2006, *supra* note 2, at 29.
8. D. Pauly & R. Watson, *Counting the Last Fish*, SCI. AM., July 2003, at 43, 47.
9. B. Worm et al., *Impacts of Biodiversity Loss on Ocean Ecosystem Services*, 314 SCI. MAG. 787 (Nov. 3, 2006).
10. G. PORTER, ESTIMATING OVERCAPACITY IN THE GLOBAL FISHING FLEET (WWF 1998).
11. China and Peru are most often cited in this regard, being the two leading catchers of fish (by live weight) and respectively responsible for eighteen percent and ten percent of total world wild capture fisheries production. FAO SOFIA 2006, *supra* note 2, tbl. 1 & fig. 4. Still, neither government would accept that their fishing industries are like those of major industrialized countries such as the EU, Japan, or the United States. Peru in particular might argue that the great majority of its production is in low-value fish exported for fish meal, and that its national capacity to fish for higher-value stocks remains underdeveloped.
12. M. Ahmed, *Market Access and Liberalisation in Fish Trade* (paper presented at Untangling Fisheries and Trade: Towards Priorities for Action, a symposium organized by the

International Centre for Trade and Sustainable Development, May 9–10, 2005, Geneva, Switzerland), at 2.

13. The Doha Round was launched in December 2001 and takes its name from the Qatari capital in which WTO ministers met to agree on a negotiating agenda.

14. United Nations Convention on the Law of the Sea, U.N. Document A/CONF.62/122 (as corrected by Corr. 1 and Corr. 8), 21 I.L.M. 1261 (1982). The U.N. Law of the Sea was concluded in 1982 and entered into force in 1995. As of February 2008, UNCLOS had been ratified by 155 members of the United Nations. *Table recapitulating the status of the Convention and of the related Agreements, as at 1 February 2008, available at* http://www.un.org/Depts/los/reference_files/status2007.pdf. It has been signed by the United States (by President Clinton in 1994), but not ratified by the Senate. Still, the terms of the Convention are treated by U.S. courts, among others, as expressing customary international law. *See, e.g.,* Sarei v. Rio Tinto, PLC, 456 F.3d 1069, 1078 (9th Cir. 2006), and citations therein. Although legal disputes—including about sovereign rights over marine fisheries—may arise at the margins of argument over the Convention's status, this chapter will treat UNCLOS as prevailing international law.

15. Technically, UNCLOS defines "internal waters" as "waters on the landward side of the baseline of the territorial sea." UNCLOS art. 8.1.

16. This limit, and other boundaries established by UNCLOS, are slightly modified and expanded in the case of "archipelagic" states. *See* UNCLOS art. 47.

17. UNCLOS art. 57.

18. When it comes to navigation, however, UNCLOS does distinguish between internal waters and territorial seas, granting foreign vessels rights of "innocent passage" through the latter. *See* UNCLOS art. 17; *see also* art. 8.

19. This does not mean, however, that other countries are completely devoid of legal interests in fish found within another's internal or territorial waters. Customary international environmental law recognizes certain rights and obligations of states regarding the transboundary effects of resource use. *See, e.g.,* Restatement (Third) of Foreign Relations Law of the United States §601 (State Obligations with Respect to Environment of Other States and the Common Environment). Fishing in particular can have transboundary effects, since fish found within internal or territorial waters may straddle or migrate across international borders. Even "inland" fisheries can have this characteristic, such as Atlantic and Pacific salmon, Nile perch in Lake Victoria, and catfish in the Amazon. *See* WWF, The Best of Texts, The Worst of Texts 6–7 (2006).

20. Over recent years, efforts have been increasing through international treaties and regional fisheries management organizations (RFMOs) to allocate fishing rights on the high seas. At least so far, however, it seems unlikely that these rights could amount to an ownership interest in wildly swimming fish themselves.

21. UNCLOS art. 62.2. UNCLOS also recognizes the need for international management of stocks that straddle or migrate across boundaries between multiple EEZs or between EEZs and the high seas. UNCLOS art. 63. But the Convention requires only that the implicated states "shall seek to agree" on arrangements for international management, and leaves apparently undiminished the right of each coastal state to exploit fish within its EEZ. A subsequent treaty, known colloquially as the U.N. Fish Stocks Agreement, seeks to elaborate the UNCLOS obligations regarding these transboundary stocks, but still does not diminish coastal rights of exploitation. *See* Agreement for the Implementation of the Provisions of the United Nations Convention on the Law of the Sea of 10 December 1982 Relating to the Conservation and Management of Straddling Fish Stocks and Highly Migratory Fish Stocks, UN Doc. A/CONF.164/37, 34 I.L.M. 1542 (1995), art. 4 ("Nothing in this Agreement shall prejudice the rights, jurisdiction and duties of States under the Convention").

22. For an interesting discussion of this hybrid status by a U.S. federal court, see Koru N. Am. v. United States, 12 Ct. Int'l Trade 1120, 1123–24 (1988).

23. Agreement on the Application of Sanitary and Phytosanitary Measures, art. 2.3.

24. *See, e.g., infra* note 53.

25. As a general matter, any transformation that changes a product's classification under applicable tariff headings will meet this test. For a discussion of various legal tests used to define a "substantial transformation" *see* Koru N. Am. v. United States, 12 Ct. Int'l Trade 1120 701 F. Supp. (1988) 229, 234 & n.9.

26. WTO Agreement on Rules of Origin (1994), art. 3(b). This "agreement to agree" was adopted as part of the Uruguay Round, along soft provisions intended to govern the use of rules of origin pending adoption of a harmonized approach.

27. An effort to complete the talks in 2007—*see* WTO Committee on Rules of Origin, *Twelfth Annual Review of the Implementation and Operation of the Agreement on Rules of Origin, Note by the Secretariat*, WTO Doc. No. G/RO/63 (Nov. 3, 2006)—appears to have run aground amidst numerous disagreements over technical issues. See *Thirteenth Annual Review of the Implementation and Operation of the Agreement on Rules of Origin, Note by the Secretariat*, WTO Doc. No. G/RO/65 (30 November 2007) ¶ 3.4.

28. This rule is codified in the United States under 19 C.F.R. § 134.1(b); *see also* Target Sportswear v. United States, 19 Ct. Int'l Trade 65, 72 (1995) ("it has long been a basic tenet of Customs Law, as judicially and administratively articulated . . . that an imported article's country of origin is the country of place where it last underwent a 'substantial transformation,' that is, the last location where a new and different article emerged" (citations omitted)).

29. *See* Council Regulation (EEC) No 2913/92 of Oct. 12, 1992, as amended, art. 24.

30. The "last substantial transformation" rule is not always applied where it would run counter to sensitive national economic interests. For example, it is not applied where it would unduly increase the product coverage of a free trade agreement. *See, e.g.,* NAFTA arts. 401–415, setting out complex rules for determining "origin" from one of the three NAFTA countries. Similarly, the normal rule is sometimes eschewed where its application would risk undesirable levels of imports in specially protected sectors. *See, e.g.,* 19 C.F.R. § 102.21 (setting out elaborate rules of origin for most textile imports into the United States) (note—these are now largely made moot by the expiration on Jan. 1, 2005, of the Multi-Fiber Arrangement, which had been the principle carve-out from core WTO obligations that had existed for textile trade).

31. UNCLOS art. 91:1; Lauritzen v. Larsen, 345 U.S. 571, 585 (1953) (quoting United States v. Flores, 289 U.S. 137, 155–59 (1933)).

32. *See, e.g.,* Procter & Gamble Mfg. v. United States, 60 Treas. Dec. 356, T.D. 45,099 (1931), *aff'd,* 19 C.C.P.A. 415, C.A.D. 3488, *cert. denied,* 287 U.S. 629 (1932).

33. *See, e.g.,* Koru N. Am. v. United States, 12 Ct. Int'l Trade 1120 701 F. Supp. 229 (1988) (fish caught aboard vessels registered in the Soviet Union originated in the Soviet Union even though fish were caught in the EEZ of New Zealand by vessels chartered and controlled by a New Zealand company and licensed to fish under New Zealand laws, were landed in New Zealand, and ultimately traded by the New Zealand company).

34. *See, e.g.,* 19 C.F.R. § 10.78(a).

35. *See, e.g.,* FAO, Notes for Fisheries Commodities Production and Trade Dataset, associated with the downloadable Fishstat statistical software and database (version downloaded Nov. 2006) (explaining inter alia that "[i]n accordance with the internationally recommended practice, import statistics include fish caught by foreign fishing craft, whether or not processed on board, landed in domestic ports; export statistics include fish caught by domestic fishing craft, whether or not processed on board, landed in foreign ports").

36. European Comm'n, European Distant Water Fishing Fleet (2001), *available at* http://ec.europa.eu/fisheries/publications/facts/peche_en.pdf.

37. *See generally* European Comm'n, *The Cotonou Agreement,* http://ec.europa.eu/development/body/cotonou/index_en.htm (last visited Mar. 15, 2007).

38. *See* European Communities, The ACP-EC Partnership Agreement (Ministerial Decision of 14 November 2001), WTO Doc. No. WT/MIN(01)/15 (2001), art. 1. *See also* Cotonou Agreement arts. 36.3 & 37.1 and Annex V, art. 1(d).

39. *See generally* official information about the EPAs on the EC website, http://ec.europa .eu/trade.

40. *See* EC Directorate General for Trade, *Update: Interim Economic Partnership Agreements* (13 December 2007).

41. A good overview of the EU rules of origin applicable to fisheries products can be found in L. Campling, et al., Pacific Island Countries, The Global Tuna Industry and The International Trade Regime—A Guidebook ch. 6 (Forum Fisheries Agency, 2007). This 450-page treatise based on primary research provides an unusually comprehensive analysis available of trade relations in a specific fisheries subsector.

42. Cotonou Agreement art. 4. The EC has also made clear that for purposes of this rule it will recognize territorial seas only out to the twelve-nautical-mile limit set by UNCLOS. Cotonou Agreement—Final Act, Declaration XXXVIII.

43. Cotonou Agreement annex V, art. 1:2. Under some circumstances, and with the permission of the ACP-EU Customs Cooperation Committee, an exception can be made to the ownership provision. *See id.* art. 1:3.

44. *See* C. Greenidge, *Overview of the Main Challenges in ACP-EU Fisheries Relations: An ACP Perspective* (paper presented at ACP EU Fisheries Relations—Maximising Socioeconomic Benefits for the ACP Fisheries Communities expert meeting, Brussels, Dec. 13–14, 2004; Technical Centre for Agricultural and Rural Cooperation 2004).

45. *See* Cotonou Agreement—Final Act, Declaration XXXIX ("ACP Declaration relating to Protocol 1 of Annex V on the origin of fishery products").

46. The Cotonou Agreement foresees the negotiation of new "economic partnership agreements" between the EU and ACP countries, and states that in negotiating these "EPAs" the EU will "aim at improving current market access for the ACP countries through inter alia, a review of the rules of origin." *Id.* art. 37.7.

47. *See* European Comm'n Communication, The Rules of Origin in Preferential Trade Arrangements: Orientations for the Future, COM (2005) 100 final, (Mar. 16, 2005), at 8–9; *see also* International Centre for Trade and Sustainable Development, *EU to Modify Rules of Origin for Trade Preference Schemes*, 9 Bridges Wkly. Trade News Dig. 10 (Mar. 23, 2005).

48. Interim Partnership Agreement Between Pacific States, on the One Part, and the European Community, on the Other Part Joint Text Initialed on 23 November 2007 in Brussels, *available at* http://www.bilaterals.org.

49. *See* L. Campling, *FFA Fisheries Trade Briefing*, Vol 1:1 (December 2007), *available at* http://www.ffa.int.

50. *See* "Japan" in *List of Processed Products for Which the Condition for Origin Country Acknowledgement is Specified* (app. The Administrative Rule for Enforcement of the Temporary Tariff Measures Law), H.S. Heading chs. 3 & 16, *available at* http:// www.mofa.go.jp/policy/economy/gsp/explain.html, *reproduced in* UNCTAD, Generalized System of Preferences: Handbook on the Scheme of Japan (United Nations 2006), annex 6. The Japanese rule gives preference only to products "originating" from beneficiary countries—thus requiring them to source fish from their own vessels (or Japanese flag vessels, in accordance with the "use of materials imported from Japan" rule—*see* UNCTAD at 13). Since there is no ownership or crew nationality requirement, this rule is in one sense broader than the EU rule.

51. 19 C.F.R. 10.176(a)(1).

52. *See* WTO, Doha Work Programme: Ministerial Declaration, ¶ 47, WT/MIN(05)/DEC, Dec. 22 , 2005 [hereinafter Hong Kong Ministerial Declaration]. *See also Least-Developed Countries' Proposal on Rules of Origin: Communication from Zambia on behalf of the LDC Group*, WTO Doc. No. TN/MA/W/74 (June 12, 2006).

53. For example, the proposed Thai-U.S. free trade agreement may offer favorable terms (including rules of origin) to the Thai tuna processing industry (and the U.S. companies invested therein), to the detriment of the Philippine tuna industry. *See* Prix. D. Banzon, *Thailand Bilateral Free Trade with US Alarms Tuna Industry Key Players*, Bilaterals. org, Mar. 21, 2007, http://www.bilaterals.org/article.php3?id_article=7541.

54. For an overview of different approaches to access agreements, *see* S. Mwikya, Fisheries Access Agreements: Trade and Development Issues 3–8 (ICTSD 2006). For a discussion of a "model" access agreement aimed at enhancing resource conservation and sustainable development, *see* W. Martin et al., A Handbook for Negotiating Fishing Access Agreements (WWF 2001).

55. Here, "overexploitation" is understood to mean fishing beyond "maximum sustainable yield"—that is, the maximum extraction of biomass that can be biologically sustained indefinitely. UNCLOS requires coastal states to manage their EEZ fisheries resources to achieve MSY, as qualified by "relevant environmental and economic factors." UNCLOS art. 61.3. The "economic factors" in question specifically include "the special requirements of developing States," a reference that some have interpreted to mean that economic expediency can legitimately trump biological conservation objectives.

56. *See generally* Mwikya| supra note 54.

57. It should be noted, however, that some observers see—and fear—the possibility that fisheries access could come to be treated as the exportation of services, and thus subject to mandatory liberalization under future adjustments to the WTO General Agreement on Trade in Services (GATS). *See* A. Wijeratna, Taking the Fish: Fishing Communities Lose Out to Big Trawlers in Pakistan 6 *et seq.* (ActionAid International 2007).

58. *See id; see also* T. Bostock et al., Policy Research—Implications of Liberalization of Fish Trade for Developing Countries 21 (University of Greenwich 2004), box 1.

59. Pub. L. No. 94-265 (Apr. 13, 1976), 16 U.S.C.. § 1825. The author is not aware of any instance in which the "no access" provision of § 1825 has been applied, although the United States did impose sanctions under adjacent language in that section against Canada in retaliation for its seizure of U.S. fishing vessels within its then-contested two-hundred-mile EEZ. *See* Dunoff, *Reconciling International Trade with Preservation of the Global Commons: Can We Prosper and Protect?*, 49 Wash & Lee L. Rev. 1407, 1446–47 & nn.244–45 (1992).

60. The "MFN bound tariff rate" is the maximum tariff WTO members are allowed to apply to one another in accordance with their commitment to offer each other "most favored nation" tariff treatment. The "applied" tariffs actually imposed may be lower than the MFN bound rate, so long as the lower rate is offered on an MFN basis.

61. OECD, Liberalizing Fisheries Markets: Scope and Effects 80–81 (2003). Note, however, that in some significant cases, tariffs on fish products remain "unbound" under current WTO agreements. Korea, for example, has declined to bind tariff rates on most of its fish products. U.S. Trade Rep., *2006 National Trade Estimate Report on Foreign Trade Barriers* [hereinafter *U.S. 2006 NTE*], at 394.

62. UNCTAD, *Promoting Participation of Developing Countries in Dynamic and New Sectors of World Trade: Fishery Products*, UNCTAD Doc. No. TD/B/COM.1/EM.28/3 (1 September 2005), ¶ 21.

63. Japan does still maintain absolute quantitative limits on imports of some fisheries products (including pollock, surimi, pollock roe, herring, Pacific cod, mackerel, whiting, squid, and sardines), but appears to be the only OECD country to do so. OECD, Liberalizing Fisheries Markets: Scope And Effects 32 (2003); *U.S. 2006 NTE, supra* note 61, at 355. Other countries continue to impose some "tariff-rate quotas" that limit the quantity of imports benefiting from lenient tariff treatment. There is, for example, a U.S. tariff rate quota on imports of canned tuna. Harmonized Tariff System of the United States (HTSUS), subheadings 1604.14.20–22.

64. The U.S. tariff-rate quota on canned tuna is a classic example of tariff escalation. Still, some observers consider that the level of tariff escalation in fisheries products is "very moderate." *See* C. Roheim, *Trade Liberalization in Fish Products: Impacts on Sustainability of International Markets and Fish Resources, in* A. Aksoy & J. Beghin, Global Agricultural Trade and Developing Countries (World Bank 2004). The importance of tariff escalation may be declining in part as the percentage of fish trade in fresh and frozen products increases. Nevertheless, escalation remains significant in some subsectors (such as tuna trade) and to some exporters. Some advocacy groups continue to treat tariff escalation on

fish products as a priority target for policy reform. *See* GREENPEACE, TRADING AWAY OUR OCEANS: WHY TRADE LIBERALIZATION OF FISHERIES MUST BE ABANDONED 33 *et seq.* (2007).

65. 19 U.S.C. §§ 1673 *et seq.*

66. U.S. antidumping duties have been imposed in recent years on shrimp products from China, Vietnam, Brazil, Ecuador, India, and Thailand. *See, e.g.*, 69 Fed. Reg. 70,997 (Dec. 8, 2004), as amended by 70 Fed. Reg. 5149 (Feb. 1, 2005) (imposing antidumping duties of up to 112 percent on certain shrimp products from China); *see also* 72 Fed. Reg. 2857 (Jan. 23, 2007) and rulings cited therein.

67. *See, e.g.,* Certain Frozen Fish Fillets from the Socialist Republic of Vietnam: Final Results of the Second Administrative Review, 72 Fed. Reg. 13,242 (Mar. 21, 2007) (imposing duties of up to eighty percent on certain catfish imports from Vietnam).

68. *See* 56 Fed. Reg. 7661 (Feb. 25, 1991) (imposing duties of up to thirty-one percent on certain salmon products from Norway). These antidumping duties have been maintained in one form or another since 1991. For the most recent regulatory action in this case (Case No. A 403-801), *see* 72 Fed. Reg. 15,650 (Apr. 2, 2007) (notifying annual review process).

69. A few examples: In 2007, a WTO panel found against the United States in a challenge brought by Ecuador to certain U.S. antidumping duties on shrimp. Panel Report, *United States—Anti-Dumping Measure on Shrimp from Ecuador,* WTO Doc. No. WT/DS335/R (Jan. 30, 2007). The United States lost the case on a technicality involving the method it used to calculate dumping margins. A 2004 case in which Thailand (subsequently joined by Japan, Brazil, the European Communities, China, India, and Ecuador) has requested consultations on the same basic issues is still pending. *See United States—Provisional Anti-Dumping Measures on Shrimp from Thailand,* WTO Doc. Nos. WT/DS324/1 *et seq.* A second shrimp case in which Thailand requested consultations in 2006 is also pending. *United States—Final Anti-Dumping Measures on Shrimp from Thailand,* WTO Doc. Nos. WT/DS343/1 *et seq.* Regarding the EC-Norway salmon dispute, *see European Communities—Anti-Dumping Measure on Farmed Salmon from Norway,* WTO Doc. Nos. WT/DS337/1 (2006) *et seq.*

70. *U.S. 2006 NTE, supra* note 61, at 184.

71. *Id.* at 279.

72. UNCTAD 2005, *supra* note 62, ¶ 21.

73. *See e.g.,* Philippines Fisheries Code § 61(c), *available at* http://www.internationalwidelife law.org/PhilFisheriesAct.pdf. The United States has identified Namibia and Russia as other countries whose special license requirements pose an impediment to U.S. fish exports. *See U.S. 2006 NTE, supra* note 61, at 522, 550, & 583.

74. *See Liberalisation of Trade in Fish and Fish Products: Communication from Canada, Iceland, New Zealand, Norway, Singapore and Thailand,* WTO Doc. No. TN/MA/W/63 (Oct. 18, 2005).

75. *See, e.g.,* Tambuyog Development Center, *Fisheries Trade Liberalization and Food Insecurity* (Sept. 2003) published online at http://www.focusweb.org/philippines/content/view/16/4.

76. *See, e.g.,* O. Ndiaye, *International Fish Trade and Food Security—Case of Senegal, in* FAO, REPORT OF THE EXPERT CONSULTATION ON INTERNATIONAL FISH TRADE AND FOOD SECURITY (2003).

77. GREENPEACE, *supra* note 64, at 58.

78. *See, e.g., Communication from Japan: Addendum,* WTO Doc. No. TN/MA/W/15/Add.11 (Jan. 6, 2003); *Comments on the Sectoral Tariff Elimination of Fishery Products Communication from the Separate Customs Territory of Taiwan,* WTO Doc. No. TN/MA/W/19/Add.2 (July 7, 2003); *Korea's View on Fisheries-Related Issues in DDA Negotiations: Addendum,* WTO Doc. No. TN/MA/W/6/Add.3 (July 15, 2003).

79. OECD, LIBERALISING FISHERIES MARKETS SCOPE AND EFFECTS 37 (2003). *See also* HANNESSON, EFFECTS OF LIBERALIZING TRADE IN FISH, FISHING SERVICES AND INVESTMENT IN FISHING VESSELS (OECD 2001).

80. *See, e.g.,* WWF, Clarification of WWF's Position on Liberalisation of Tariffs in the Fisheries Sector (statement at the WTO Hong Kong ministerial, Dec. 17, 2005), *available at* http://www.panda.org/about_wwf/what_we_do/policy/trade_and_investment/news/index.cfm?uNewsID=54540.

81. These calls are also consistent with commitments made by the United States, the EU, and others to carry out "environmental impact assessments" of proposed trade policies to help improve "policy coherence." To date, however, these assessments have not had a significant influence on policy in practice. One reason for this apparent ineffectiveness (apart from insufficient political will) is that assessments are usually conducted at a level of generality that fails to capture significant local impacts. The case of tariff liberalization on fish products illustrates this point. In the aggregate, tariffs reductions may have little or no significant impact on global levels of fish production or consumption. It is likely, however, that specific fisheries could suffer important impacts as a result of particular tariff changes. Unless trade policy impact assessments are conducted with an eye toward identifying and evaluating such cases, they are likely to remain fairly sterile econometric exercises.

82. WWF, HARD FACTS, HIDDEN PROBLEMS: A REVIEW OF CURRENT DATA ON FISHING SUBSIDIES (2001).

83. R. SUMAILA & D. PAULY, CATCHING MORE BAIT: A BOTTOM-UP RE-ESTIMATION OF GLOBAL FISHERIES SUBSIDIES (Fisheries Centre, University of British Columbia, 2006) (estimating total subsidies of $30 billion to $34 billion).

84. The FAO estimates that the total value of wild-capture fish in 2004 was $84.9 billion. FAO SOFIA 2006, *supra* note 2, at 5.

85. WWF 2001, *supra* note 82.

86. United Nations, "World Summit on Sustainable Development Plan of Implementation," in *Report of the World Summit on Sustainable Development,* ¶ 31(f), U.N. Doc. A/CONF.199/20 (2002).

87. *See, e.g., Environmental and Trade Benefits of Removing Subsidies in the Fisheries Sector: Submission by the United States,* WTO Doc. No. WT/CTE/W/51 (May 19, 1997); *Preparations for the 1999 Ministerial Conference—Fisheries Subsidies: Communication from Australia, Iceland, New Zealand, Norway, Peru, Philippines and United States,* WTO Doc. No. WT/GC/W/303 (Aug. 6, 1999).

88. Ministerial Declaration—Adopted on 14 November 2001. Ministerial Conference, Fourth Session, November 9–14, 2001, Doha, ¶ 28, WTO Doc. No. WT/MIN(01)/DEC/1 (Nov. 20, 2001) [hereinafter Doha Declaration].

89. *See, e.g.,* K. Bradsher, *Collective stance at WTO: Activists ally with nations on fishing aid,* INTERNATIONAL HERALD TRIBUNE (Dec. 15, 2005), lead story, 1.

90. *Hong Kong Ministerial Declaration,* annex D, ¶1.9, WTO Doc. No. WT/MIN(05)/DEC (Dec. 22, 2005).

91. For a review of some of the issues that dominated the technical discussions in this period, *see* WWF, BEST OF TEXTS, WORST OF TEXTS (WWF 2006).

92. WTO Doc. No. TN/RL/W/213 (30 Nov 2007), Annex VIII [hereafter "Chair's draft"].

93. For a review of some of the technical issues raised by the Chair's draft, *see* WWF, "Fisheries Subsidies: Preliminary Review of the Chairman's Draft" (11 December 2007).

94. Chair's draft, *supra* note 92, arts. III.3, IV.1, & V.1. For a relevant earlier negotiating proposal, *see Fisheries Subsidies: Special and Differential Treatment: Paper from Argentina (Revision),* WTO Doc. No. TN/RL/GEN/138/Rev.1 (Jan. 26, 2007).

95. Chair's draft, *supra* note 92, arts. III.2(b)(3), & V.1. For an earlier relevant proposal, *see, e.g., Possible Disciplines on Fisheries Subsidies: Paper from Brazil (Revision),* WTO Doc. No. TN/RL/GEN/79/Rev.3 (June 2,2006), at 4 n.8.

96. WWF, HEALTHY FISHERIES, SUSTAINABLE TRADE 73 n.244 & 67 ¶ V.C.5(c)(iv) (2004).

97. *See, e.g.,* FISH INSPECTION, QUALITY CONTROL, AND HACCP: A GLOBAL FOCUS (Roy Martin ed., CRC Press 1998) (now somewhat outdated).

98. WTO, Agreement on the Application of Sanitary and Phytosanitary Measures.

99. *Id.* art. 2.

100. *Id.* art. 3.2.

101. *See generally* Codex Alimentarius Comm'n, http://www.codexalimentarius.net.

102. Codex Alimentarius Comm'n, *Code of Practice for Fish and Fishery Products*, Doc. No. CAC/RCP 52-2003, Rev. 2-2005.

103. *See generally* Codex Alimentarius Comm'n, Basic Texts on Food Hygiene 31 *et seq.* (3d ed.).

104. *See* U.S. Dept. of Health & Human Services regulations on fish and fishery products for human consumption, 21 C.F.R. pt. 123.12.

105. L. Ababouch et al., *Detentions and Rejections in International Fish Trade*, FAO Fisheries Technical Paper No. 473 (FAO 2005).

106. *See id* § 3.

107. One leading example was the WTO case successfully brought by Canada against quarantine restrictions imposed on salmon imports by Australia. *See Australia—Measures Affecting Importation of Salmon* (Report of the Appellate Body), WTO Doc. No. WT/DS18/AB/R (Oct. 20, 1998).

108. Ababouch et al., *supra* note 105, § 3.6.1. The United States has not embraced such an approach. *See* U.S. GAO, *FDA's Imported Seafood Safety Program Shows Some Progress, but Further Improvements Are Needed*, GAO Report. No. GAO-04-246 (Jan. 2004), at 18–19.

109. WTO Agreement on Technical Barriers to Trade, art. 2.2.

110. *See European Communities—Trade Description of Sardines*, WTO Doc. No. WT/DS231/R (Panel Report, May 29, 2002); WTO Doc. No. WT/DS231/AB/R (Appellate Body Report, Sept. 26, 2002).

111. EC, Council Regulation (EC) No. 104/2000 of 17 December 1999, art. 4. In the United States, fish products must bear country of origin information, but information about processing method and catch are not required. *See* 7 U.S.C. § 1638 and associated regulations embodying the U.S. Country of Origin Labeling (COOL) requirements at 7 C.F.R. §§ 60.101 *et seq.*

112. For an overview discussion of traceability, including brief descriptions of relevant regulations in the EU and the United States, *see* FAO, *Traceability and Labelling in Fish Trade*, background document prepared for the Tenth Session of the FAO Committee on Fisheries, Subcommittee on Fish Trade, May 30 to June 2, 2006, FAO Doc. No. COFI:FT/X/2006/6.

113. *See* Regulation (EC) No. 178/2002; the traceability requirements of this regulation are supplemented by the detailed food safety regulations of Regulation (EC) Nos. 853/2004 and 854/2004.

114. *See* U.K., *EC General Food Law Regulation 178/2002: Guidance Notes on the Food Safety Act 1990 (Amendment) Regulations 2004 and the General Food Regulations 2004*, *available at* http://www.food.gov.uk/multimedia/pdfs/generalfoodsafetyguide2.pdf, at 11.

115. *See, e.g.,* the advice of the Dutch government in Centre for the Promotion of Imports from Developing Countries (CBI), *European Market Access Requirement: Supply Chain Management and Traceability for Fish* (Ministry of Foreign Affairs of The Netherlands 2005), *available at* http://www.cbi.nl/, at 1. *See also* EAN-UCC, Traceability of Fish Guidelines (2002), at 19 (including vessel identity and catch date as recommended but optional data elements on chain of custody documents for fish products). EAN-UCC, now renamed GS1, is a leading international organization dedicated to promoting "global standards and solutions" for international chains of custody. *See* http://www.gs1.org/about/overview.html.

116. FAO, *Traceability and Labelling in Fish Trade*, *supra* note 112, ¶ 20.

117. 21 C.F.R. § 1.327(c). Note, however that vessels engaged in processing other than "solely to prepare fish for holding on board a harvest vessel" (presumably "factory ships" or other vessels undertaking value added processing at sea) are subject to the Act's documentation rules.

118. These cases are thus distinguished from situations involving trade in immediately dangerous products such as toxic wastes or ozone-depleting products.

119. The U.S. "dolphin-safe" labeling law was challenged on much narrower grounds, due to its voluntary nature, and was found to be GATT-consistent. Panel Report, *United States—Restrictions on Imports of Tuna*, ¶ 5.41–.44, GATT Doc. No. DS21/R-39S/155 (Sept. 3, 1991). But given the insistence of U.S. canners and consumers on dolphin-safe tuna, the labeling requirement obstructs imports with much the same effect as the embargo itself. As discussed above, today the Tuna-Dolphin embargo has been formally lifted, but the labeling rule against dolphin encirclement remains in place.

120. Panel Report, *United States—Restrictions on Imports of Tuna*, ¶ 5.9, GATT Doc. No. DS29/R (June 16, 1994). A similar view had been articulated by the first panel. Panel Report, *United States—Restrictions on Imports of Tuna*, ¶ 5.14, GATT Doc. No. DS21/R-39S/155 (Sept. 3, 1991).

121. Panel Report, *United States—Restrictions on Imports of Tuna*, ¶ 5.27, GATT Doc. No. DS21/R-39S/155 (Sept. 3, 1991).

122. *See infra* note 135.

123. *United States—Import Prohibition of Certain Shrimp and Shrimp Products*, ¶ 121, WTO Doc. No. WT/DS58/AB/R (Oct. 12, 1998).

124. The Appellate Body found that the United States had "negotiated seriously with some, but not with other Members," *id.* ¶ 172, noting in particular the successful conclusion of an Inter-American Convention on sea turtles, *id.* ¶¶ 169 ff.

125. *Id.* ¶¶ 177 *et seq.*

126. The ETP extends from Southern California to Peru, and as far west as Hawaii. *See* NOAA Southwest Fisheries Science Center Web site at http://swfsc.noaa.gov/textblock.aspx?id=1053&ParentMenuId=111.

127. *Id.* at http://swfsc.noaa.gov/textblock.aspx?Division=PRD&ParentMenuId=248&id=1408.

128. *See* T. Hall, *How Youths Rallied To Dolphins' Cause*, N.Y. TIMES, Apr. 18, 1990, at C1.

129. The U.S. tuna fleet had already begun abandoning the ETP as a result of a variety of factors, including the decision by Mexico in 1980 to begin enforcing the exclusion of U.S. tuna vessels from its EEZ. *See* M. Kurlansky, *U.S., Mexico talk fishing rights as the tuna market ebbs*, THE SAN DIEGO UNION-TRIBUNE, at C-4 (op-ed, May 13, 1984) (available on Nexis).

130. Pub. L. No. 100-711 (Nov. 23, 1988). The 1988 law did not directly prohibit all imports of dolphin-encircled tuna, but rather created standards for imported tuna based on U.S. practices and annual dolphin mortality rates. The precise legal formula for the ban (which based mortality limits for foreign vessels on mortality rates for U.S. vessels for the same season) meant that the limits for foreign vessels could not be accurately known until after the close of a fishing season. *See id.* § 4(a)(2)(B) (then codified at 16 U.S.C. § 1371(a)(2)(B), subsequently deleted by the 1997 amendments, and now appearing in 16 U.S.C. § 1371 n.3). The retroactive nature of this cap was later noted as problematic by the first GATT panel, but was not decisive due to the more general finding that the "PPM" focus of the ban was GATT-illegal. *See* Panel Report, *United States—Restrictions on Imports of Tuna*, ¶ 5.16, GATT Doc. No. DS21/R-39S/155 (Sept. 3, 1991) [hereinafter *Tuna-Dolphin I*]. In any case, the practical effect of the law was simply to ban imports of all dolphin-encircled tuna.

131. Pub. L. No. 100-627 (Nov. 28, 1990), Title IX (Dolphin Protection Consumer Information Act) (originally codified in 16 U.S.C. § 1385(d), subsequently amended in 1997, and now appearing at 16 U.S.C. § 1385 n.2).

132. The International Dolphin Conservation Program grew out of a nonbinding international accord known as the "La Jolla Agreement." *See* U.S. NOAA, *The Tuna-Dolphin Issue*, http://swfsc.noaa.gov/textblock.aspx?Division=PRD&ParentMenuId=248&id=1408 [hereinafter NOAA Tuna-Dolphin History]; *see also* IATTC Resolution on the La Jolla Agreement (Apr. 1992), *available at* http://www.iattc.org/PDFFiles2/IATTC-Resolution-on-LJ-Agreement-Apr-1992.pdf.

133. *Tuna-Dolphin I, supra* note 130.

134. Panel Report, *United States—Restrictions on Imports of Tuna,* GATT Doc. No. (DS29/R) (June 16, 1994).

135. A principal weakness of the GATT (corrected under the WTO) was the procedural requirement that dispute resolution rulings be adopted by consensus among all of the GATT's Contracting Parties, including the party against whom a ruling had issued. With the United States likely prepared to block adoption of the Tuna-Dolphin panel report, and with the United States and Mexico then actively engaged in concluding the North American Free Trade Agreement, Mexico declined to place the Tuna-Dolphin report before the GATT Contracting Parties for adoption. The EU pressed for adoption of the report in its case, but was effectively blocked by the United States, which declined to join a consensus decision to adopt the report. *See* WTO case synopsis at http://www.wto.org/English/tratop_e/envir_e/edis04_e.htm.

136. By 2002 there were 1,513 observed deaths in 12,433 sets—fewer than one death for every eight sets. *Estimated Numbers of Sets on Fish Associated with Dolphins, and Mortalities of Dolphins Due to the Fishery* (IATTC 2006), (http://www.iattc.org/PDFFiles2/Dolphin%20mortalities%20table.pdf).

137. US environmental groups supporting the change in U.S. policy included the Center for Marine Conservation (now known as Ocean Conservancy), Environmental Defense Fund (now known as Environmental Defense), Greenpeace, National Wildlife Federation, and WWF (World Wildlife Fund). These groups argued in favor of lifting the U.S. tuna embargo on the grounds that the IATTC program was an adequate and effective dolphin conservation program, that the ban on encirclement was causing other ecosystem impacts in the ETP fishery (such as high levels of bycatch from alternative fishing techniques), and that the IATTC program would likely be weakened or destroyed if the United States continued to maintain punitive sanctions against IATTC other members. (For the sake of transparency, the author notes that he worked for WWF at the time of these events.)

138. Declaration of Panama, Oct. 4, 1995 (executed by the governments of Belize, Columbia, Costa Rica, Ecuador, France, Honduras, Mexico, Panama, Spain, United States, Vanuatu, and Venezuela) (facsimile of signed text available at http://www.iattc.org/IDCPDocuments ENG.htm).

139. Pub. L. No. 105-42 (Aug. 15, 1997).

140. *Id.* §4 (c odified at 16 U.S.C. §1371(a)(2).

141. *Id.* §5(a) (c odified at 16 U.S.C. §1385(d) & esp. §1385(d)(2).

142. *Id.* §5(c) (c odified at 16 U.S.C. §1385 & esp. §1385(h)(2).

143. Agreement on the International Dolphin Conservation Program, Feb. 15, 1999, *available at* http://www.iattc.org/PDFFiles2/AIDCP-(amended-Jun-2006).pdf (as amended through June 2006).

144. 64 Fed. Reg. 24,590 (May 7, 1999).

145. 65 Fed. Reg. 30, 48 (Jan. 3, 2000) (revising 50 C.F.R. §216.24).

146. *See, e.g.,* Earth Island Institute, Questions and Answers About Earth Island Institute's Dolphin Safe Tuna Program, http://www.earthisland.org/immp/QandAdolphinSafe.html.

147. Brower v. Daley, 93 F. Supp. 2d 1071 (N.D. Cal. 2000) (Henderson, USDJ), *aff'd,* Brower v. Evans, 257 F.3d 1058 (9th Cir. 2001).

148. Earth Island Inst. v. Evans, 2004 U.S. Dist. LEXIS 15729, 34 Envtl. L. Rep. (Envtl. Law Inst.) 20,069 (N.D. Cal. 2004) (Henderson, USDJ).

149. Earth Island Inst. v. Hogarth, 484 F.3d 1123, 2007 U.S. App. LEXIS 9572 (9th Cir. Cal. 2007). The U.S. declined to seek review by the Supreme Court.

150. Marine Resources Assessment Group, Review of IUU Fishing and Developing Countries 8 (2005).

151. D. Doulman, *A General Overview of Some Aspects of Illegal, Unreported and Unregulated Fishing, in* FAO, Report of and Papers Presented at the Expert Consultation on Illegal, Unreported and Unregulated Fishing, ¶ 8, FAO Fisheries Report No. 666 (2001).

152. FAO, International Plan of Action to Prevent, Deter and Eliminate Illegal, Unreported and Unregulated Fishing ¶ 66 (2001) [hereinafter IPOA-IUU].

153. Pub. L. No. 109-479 (Jan. 12, 2007).

154. *Id.* § 206a(b), 16 U.S.C. § 1826a.(b). The language of the Act appears to make both the requisite finding by the Secretary of Commerce and the imposition of sanctions (failing resolution of the issue through international consultations) nondiscretionary. The Act further provides for automatic triggering of the U.S. Pelly Amendment (22 U.S.C. § 1978) (opening a discretionary process that allows imposition of broader trade sanctions) if the initial sanctions are not effective. 16 U.S.C. § 1826a(b)(4)(C).

155. *See generally* C. Roheim & J. Sutinen, Trade and Marketplace Measures to Promote Sustainable Fishing Practices (ICTSD 2006); B. Le Gallic, *Using Trade Measures in the Fight Against IUU Fishing: Opportunities and Challenges* (paper presented at Twelfth Biennial Conference of the International Institute of Fisheries Economics & Trade (IIFET), July 20–30, 2004, Tokyo, Japan), *available at* http://www.oecd.org/dataoecd/31/44/34227035.pdf); L. Chavez, *Illegal, Unreported and Unregulated Fishing: WTO-Consistent Trade Related Measures to Address IUU Fishing, in* FAO, Report of and Papers Presented at the Expert Consultation on Illegal, Unreported and Unregulated Fishing (FAO 2001).

156. CCSBT, Action Plan (adopted at the CCBST Sixth Annual Meeting—Second Part; Mar. 21–23, 2000), ¶ 6 (authorizing the Commission "to impose trade-restrictive measures consistent with Members' international obligations" on southern bluefin products from non-cooperating non-members).

157. *See, e.g.,* CCAMLR Conservation Measure 10-05 (2006), ¶ 10 (prohibiting imports, exports, and reexports of toothfish not bearing CCAMLR-required catch documents).

158. IATTC, Adoption of Trade Measures to Promote Compliance, Res. No. C-05-06 (2006).

159. *See* ICCAT, Resolution by ICCAT Concerning Trade Measures, Resolution No. 03-15 (2003); *see also* Recommendation Regarding Compliance in the Bluefin Tuna and North Atlantic Swordfish Fisheries (adopted Nov. 1996, entered into force Aug. 1997), ¶ 3 (stating that the Commission may recommend "trade restrictive measures . . . on the subject species . . . consistent with each Party's international obligations" to be imposed on any Party exceeding catch limits); this measure was extended to cover swordfish in the southern Atlantic in 1998.

160. NEAFC, Scheme of Control and Enforcement, art. 46.3 (adopted Nov. 15, 2006; entered into force May 1, 2007) (authorizing NEAFC parties "to adopt appropriate multilaterally agreed non-discriminatory trade related measures, consistent with the World Trade Organisation").

161. NAFO, *Conservation and Enforcement Measures,* NAFO/FC Doc. 07/1, art. 50(h).

162. 46 U.S.C. § 55114 (current codification of language which, in the main, dates back to the Nicholson Act of 1950 (64 Stat. 577)); *see also* U.S. Customs and Border Protection, Frequently Asked Questions: Inbound Vessel Only—Trade Act of 2002 Final Rule (revised Mar. 15, 2006) (http://www.cbp.gov/linkhandler/cgov/import/communications_to_trade/advance_info/vessel_faq.ctt/vessel_faq.doc). Some exceptions are made for vessels from Canada, Guam, and the U.S. Virgin Islands.

163. Such landing restrictions are almost certain to be found facially inconsistent with Article V of the GATT, which provides for the freedom of transit of goods and vessels through the territories of WTO members, without discrimination based on "the flag of vessels, the place of origin, departure, entry, exit or destination, or on any circumstances relating to the ownership of goods, of vessels or of other means of transport." The question then arises whether such measures could be justified under GATT art. XX(g)—the same enumerated exception for trade restrictions "relating to the conservation of exhaustible natural resources" as was at issue in the *Tuna-Dolphin* and *Shrimp-Turtle* cases. As noted above, the *Shrimp-Turtle* ruling has at least opened the door to the acceptance of unilateral TREMs under WTO law, but the limits and implications of that ruling in cases such as the EU-Chile swordfish dispute are far from clear.

164. D. Hervé Espejo & X. Fuentes Torijo, *El caso del pez espada,* 37:145 Estudios Interna-cionales 83 (Universidad de Chile 2004).

165. *Chile: Measures Affecting the Transit and Importation of Swordfish,* WTO Doc. No. WT/DS193/1 (Apr. 26, 2000).

166. ITLOS Order 2000/3 of Dec. 20, 2000. Although the EU denied ITLOS had jurisdiction over the matter, it agreed to allow the formation of a "special chamber" under the aus-pices of the Tribunal to hear the case.

167. In particular, the ITLOS case would likely have tested Chile's novel theories about the rights of coastal states with regard to straddling or migratory stocks in waters just beyond EEZ boundaries, and could also have raised interesting questions about the status under customary international law of emerging international norms regarding fishing on the high seas; the WTO case, in turn, represented the first challenge brought by a developed country against a trade-related environmental measure imposed by a developing country, and would likely have extended the WTO's jurisprudence on unilateral TREMs beyond the holdings of the *Shrimp-Turtle* case (see above notes 115–18 and accompanying text).

168. For a thorough treatment of the issues (in Spanish), *see* Hervé Espejo & Fuentes Torijo, *El caso del pez espada: una controversia de jurisdiccion y de derecho sustantivo, y los di-versos argumentos para inclinar la balanza,* 145 Estudios Internacionales 83 (Univer-sidad de Chile, Instituto de Estudios Internacionales, 2004) (available on LEXIS); *see also* M. Orellana, *The Swordfish in Peril: The EU Challenges Chilean Port Access Restrictions at the WTO,* 4:6 Bridges 11 (ICTSD, Aug. 2000).

169. *See* Press Release, EU, EU and Chile Settle WTO/ITLOS Swordfish Dispute (Brussels, Jan. 24, 2001), http://www.europa-eu-un.org/articles/en/article_2230_en.htm#top.

170. *See* EC Directorate General for Trade, *General Overview of Active WTO Dispute Settle-ment Cases Involving the EC as Complainant or Defendant and of Active Cases Under the Trade Barriers Regulation* (Brussels 16 Jan. 2008), at 23–24.

171. *See generally* Roheim & Sutinen, *supra* note 155, at 2; Le Gallic, *supra* note 155, at 7; FAO, *Report of the Expert Consultation of Regional Fisheries Management Bodies on Harmonization of Catch Certification—La Jolla, United States of America, 9–11 January 2002,* FAO Fisheries Report No. 697 (2002).

172. FAO, *Implementation of the International Plan of Action to Prevent, Deter and Eliminate Illegal, Unreported and Unregulated Fishing,* FAO Technical Guidelines for Responsible Fisheries No. 9 (Rome, FAO. 2002), at 48.

173. *See* FAO 2002, *supra* note 171, at 9 (Table 1); Roheim & Sutinen, *supra* note 155, at 2 (citing M. Lack & G. Sant, *Patagonian Toothfish: Are Conservation and Trade Measures Working?,* 19:1 Traffic Bull.).

174. *See* Recommendation by ICCAT Concerning the ICCAT Bluefin Tuna Statistical Docu-ment Program, ICCAT Rec. No. 92-1, *available at* http://www.iccat.es/Documents/Recs/compendiopdf-e/1992–01-e.pdf.

175. *See Compendium: Management Recommendations and Resolutions Adopted by ICCAT for the Conservation of Atlantic Tunas and Tuna-Like Species,* Doc. No. PLE-012/2006 (ICCAT 2006), at 142–84.

176. IATTC Resolution No. C-03-01 (Resolution on IATTC Bigeye Tuna Statistical Document Program, approved June 24, 2003).

177. *See* 16 U.S.C.S. § 971d and 50 C.F.R. pt. 300, subpt. M (and especially § 300.184).

178. Patagonian toothfish—also known in the United States as "Chilean sea bass"—are cov-eted in the restaurant trade of the United States and Japan for their rich flavor. These large, slow-growing fish flourish on the shoulders of underwater sea mounts across the Southern Ocean, and have been especially devastated by IUU fishing. *See generally* WWF, *Last Chance Saloon?,* WWF Newsroom, Oct. 23, 2002, http://www.panda.org/news_facts/newsroom/index.cfm?uNewsID=4142&uLangID=1; Chilean Sea Bass Frequently Asked Questions, joint Fact Sheet by the U.S. Departments of Commerce and State (Mar. 2002), http://www.state.gov/g/oes/rls/fs/2002/8989.htm. Toothfish are principally caught by bot-tom trawling, which has been especially harmful due to the long reproductive cycle of the species and the scarcity and fragility of sea mount habitats. *See generally* T. Morato &

D. Pauly, eds., *Seamounts: Biodiversity and Fisheries,* 12(5) Fisheries Centre Research Rep. (2004).

179. The CCAMLR catch documentation scheme was established in 2000. *See* CCAMLR Conservation Measure 170/XIX (Catch Documentation Scheme for *Dissostichus* spp.) in *Schedule of Conservation Measures in Force—2000/01 Season* (CCAMLR 2000). The current version of the scheme, with some strengthening amendments, is found in CCAMLR Conservation Measure 10-05 (2006). This scheme has been called one of the strongest in the world. *See, e.g.,* High Seas Task Force, Closing the net: Stopping Illegal Fishing on the High Seas 29 (Task Force on IUU Fishing on the High Seas 2006).

180. Chavez, *supra* note 155.

181. 16 U.S.C. §§ 2431 *et seq.* and 50 C.F.R. pt. 300, subpt. G (and especially § 300.107).

182. NOAA, "International Commission Sees Large Drop in Illegal Fishing for Chilean Sea Bass" (Press Release No. 2004-107 (Nov. 9, 2004) (http://www.publicaffairs.noaa.gov/ releases2004/nov04/noaa04-107.html).

183. CITES, The CITES Species, http://www.cites.org/eng/disc/species.shtml (last visited Feb. 11, 2008).

184. *See generally* C. Safina, *Bluefin Tuna in the West Atlantic: Negligent Management and the Making of an Endangered Species,* 7 Conservation Biology, 229–34 (1993).

185. *See* Press Release, FAO, FAO-CITES Agreement Promotes Sustainable Fish Trade: Collaborative Relationship Formalized in MoU (Oct. 3, 2006), http://www.fao.org/newsroom/ en/news/2006/1000410/index.html.

186. *See,* FAO, *Report of the FAO Ad Hoc Expert Advisory Panel for the Assessment of Proposals to Amend Appendices I and II of CITES Concerning Commercially-Exploited Aquatic Species (Rome, 13–16 July 2004),* FAO Fisheries Report. No. 748. (2004); FAO, *Report of the Second FAO Ad Hoc Expert Advisory Panel for the Assessment of Proposals to Amend Appendices I and II of CITES Concerning Commercially-Exploited Aquatic Species (Rome, 26–30 March 2007),* FAO Fisheries Report. No. 833. (2007). NB—The first panel was convened prior to the formal conclusion of the FAO-CITES MOU. Documents relating to CITES COPs can be found at http://www.cites.org/eng/cop/ index.shtml.

187. *See, e.g.,* exchange of letters between Ichiro Nomura (FAO Assistant Director-General for Fisheries and Aquaculture) and Willem Wijnstekers (Secretary-General of CITES), CITES.

188. *See, e.g.,* Press Release, Oceana, Oceana Urges Spain to Support the Regulation of Trade for Two Imperiled Shark Species (Dec. 14, 2006), http://www.oceana.org/?id=327& nocache=1&tx_pressrelease_pi1[pointer]=0&tx_pressrelease_pi1[showUid]=559 (regarding current efforts to protect shark species in the Atlantic, and noting, "lack of action by ICCAT leaves conservationists looking to the Convention on International Trade in Endangered Species (CITES) to protect the endangered shark species caught in ICCAT fisheries").

189. *See* Doha Declaration, *supra* note 88, ¶ 31(i).

190. Founded in 1997, the non-governmental MSC grew originally out of a partnership between the conservation group WWF and the UK-based transnational corporation Unilever, then one of the world's leading producers and retailers of processed fish products. After developing policies and criteria for certification and labeling through a multi-year international stakeholder process, the MSC began certifying individual fisheries in 2000. By October 2007, the MSC had certified twenty-four fisheries (with more than twenty others in the pipeline), resulting in the sale of a thousand different MSC labeled products, with a worldwide retail value of over $500 million. *See* MSC Web site (http://www.msc .org) and *Marine Stewardship Council Annual Report 2005/06.*

191. Ecolabels are sometimes broadly categorized as taking either "single issue" or "life-cycle" approaches to product evaluation, with the latter seeking to evaluate the total environmental impacts of a product from production through use and disposal. In fact, ecolabeling of fish products tends to rest between these extremes, focusing broadly on the environmental aspects of fish production (such as the adequacy of management), but taking little

or no account of the environmental consequences of the processing, distribution, or use of fish products.

192. *See, e.g.*, Nordic Technical Working Group on Fisheries Ecolabelling Criteria, *An Arrangement for the Voluntary Certification of Products of Sustainable Fishing—Final Report* (June 21, 2000), *available at* http://www.globefish.org/filedownload.php?fileId=44.

193. FAO, *Guidelines for the Ecolabelling of Fish and Fishery Products from Marine Capture Fisheries* (Rome, 2005); formal adoption of the Guidelines is reported in *Report of the Twenty-Sixth Session of the Committee on Fisheries* (Rome, Mar. 7–11, 2005), FAO Fisheries Report No. 780 (2005), at xv.

194. *See Report of the Twenty-Seventh Session of the Committee on Fisheries* (Rome, Mar. 5–9, 2007), FAO Fisheries Report No. 830 (2007), ¶ 36.

195. *Communication from the Commission to the Council, the European Parliament and the European Economic and Social Committee,* COM (2005) 275 final (June 29, 2005).

196. The Nordic Swan, for example, is a quasi-official ecolabel (not restricted to fish products) created by the Nordic Council of Ministers and administered by a government-owned company in Sweden. the Nordic Swan website *at* http://www.sismab.se/. For a somewhat outdated list of governmental and quasi-governmental ecolabels, *see* U.S. EPA, *Environmental Labeling Issues, Policies, and Practices Worldwide* (1998), Appendix A.

197. Doha Declaration, *supra* note 88, ¶ 32(iii).

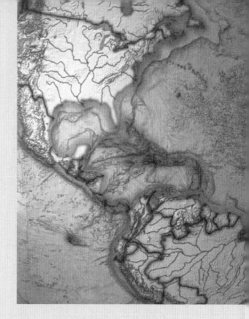

chapter twelve

The 1982 United Nations Convention on the Law of the Sea

Jon M. Van Dyke

I. Introduction

The oceans have served historically as a "commons" to be used by the people of all nations. Hugo Grotius wrote in the 1600s that the seas must be free for navigation and fishing because natural law forbids the ownership of things that seem "to have been created by nature for common use."[1] He argued that because the use of the seas for navigation by one nation does not diminish the potential for the same use by others, and "because it is so limitless that it cannot become a possession of one,"[2] the inherent nature of the ocean is that of a common space or shared resource. In Grotius's time the fish in the ocean also seemed limitless. But we have seen in our time that with high-technology fishing methods the fish of the oceans are definitely exhaustible and that overfishing by one nation can have a grave impact on the ability of other nations to harvest "their share" of the resource. These technological developments have required us to reconsider the functional meaning of "freedom" of the seas.

Should ships be free to move freely in all parts of the oceans? Even if they are warships carrying nuclear weapons? Even if they are carrying ultrahazardous radioactive cargoes that impose risks on coastal populations? What law applies when vessels collide? Or when a crime takes place on a vessel sailing on the high seas or other waters off the coast of a foreign state? Should fishing vessels be free to harvest fish wherever they can be found, or should the people living near the sea have priority over, or even ownership of, the fish that live near their coasts? Should a different approach be taken regarding fish that "straddle" adjacent fishing nations or a fishing nation and the high seas? Who should own the petroleum and mineral resources found under the sea? Can scientific research been done freely in all parts of the ocean, or in certain parts only with permission of an adjacent country? How should ocean boundaries be drawn?[3]

Many of these questions are now answered in the 1982 United Nations Convention on the Law of the Sea,[4] which is described by many as the "constitution of the oceans." This multinational treaty is a comprehensive document that provides rules to govern most ocean activities and procedures for resolving competing and overlapping uses. It was drafted after more than a decade of preparatory meetings and formal negotiations that involved countries from all parts of the globe. It is a monumental achievement and (as of February 2008) has been ratified by 155 of the 192 members of the United Nations.[5] But it has not yet reached universal adherence. Key nations such as the United States, Turkey, Iran, and Thailand are still withholding ratification. The United States says that most of the substantive provisions of the Convention reflect customary international law, and thus are binding on all countries whether they have ratified or not. But those countries that have not ratified the Convention cannot utilize the dispute-resolution mechanisms of the Convention, and many disputes over interpretation continue to fester.

II. The Current State of the Law

A. Background—Negotiation of the 1982 Law of the Sea Convention

1. Early Efforts at Codification

The need for a comprehensive treaty governing the exploitation of ocean resources and other maritime activities became clear after World War II, when technological advances permitted countries to operate in ocean areas previously unreachable and countries started making claims to offshore resources. The first formal claim to an extended maritime zone was made by the United States in the 1945 Truman Proclamation, when it claimed sovereign rights and jurisdiction over the nonliving resources on its "continental shelf."[6] This claim was designed primarily to allow the United States to drill for oil and natural gas in the gently sloping continental shelf extending off of the U.S. coast in the Gulf of Mexico. In making this claim, the United States sought to protect its navigational freedoms by distinguishing between the ability to claim resources on the one hand, and the ability to regulate navigation on the other, adding: "The character of the waters above the continental shelf and the right to their free and unimpeded navigation are in no way thus affected."[7] But other countries ignored this distinction and responded to the U.S. action by making a bewildering array of claims to the resources near their coasts. Countries without gradually sloping continental shelves off their coasts, such as those on the west coast of Latin America, for instance, sought to make a comparable claim with respect to living resources. They claimed territorial seas that extended two hundred nautical miles from their coasts and claimed sovereign rights over all the fish in that zone.[8]

2. The 1958 Geneva Conventions

In an effort to resolve these competing claims, the international community met in Geneva in 1958 and negotiated four treaties at the First U.N. Conference on the Law of the Sea, which reasserted traditional freedoms of fishing and navigation but accepted coastal state jurisdiction over the continental shelf: the Convention on the Territorial Sea and Contiguous Zone;[9] the Convention on the High Seas;[10] the Convention on Fishing and Conservation of Living Resources of the High Seas;[11] and the Convention on the Continental Shelf.[12] These treaties allowed coastal states to extend maritime zones and adopt fishery conservation measures over adjacent waters, but they did not define the permissible limits of the territorial sea or fisheries jurisdiction. In addition, because countries could ratify some of the treaties, but not others, a patchwork of treaty law emerged. In 1960, a second conference on the law of the sea was held in Geneva to determine the width of the territorial sea, but it ended in failure.

> **Because countries could ratify some of the treaties, but not others, a patchwork of treaty law emerged.**

3. Arvid Pardo's Speech on Polymetallic Nodules

The nations of the world renewed their effort to develop a comprehensive treaty to govern the oceans after the discovery of polymetallic nodules on the ocean floor, which were thought by some to be a source of future wealth. In 1967, Ambassador Arvid Pardo of Malta told the U.N. General Assembly that vast riches lay scattered across the floor of the deep seabed in the form of exploitable softball-sized rocks and offered the "Pardo proposal" urging that they be viewed as the "common heritage" of humankind.[13] Within three years of Ambassador Pardo's speech, an international consensus developed that these nodules should be viewed as a "common heritage" resource, that national claims of exclusive rights to seabed resources must be prohibited, that exploitation should take place pursuant to an international legal regime, and that developing nations should share genuine benefits from seabed exploitation. The key international document was the U.N. General Assembly's 1970 Declaration of Principles Governing the Seabed and the Ocean Floor, and the Subsoil Thereof, Beyond the Limits of National Jurisdiction.[14]

Whether these nodules will ever be commercially exploitable is still uncertain, but some countries are actively experimenting with techniques to bring up the nodules from the deep ocean and process them into valuable metals. In any event, the creation of an acceptable international legal regime to govern their exploitation has proven to be challenging.

4. The Third United Nations Conference on the Law of the Sea (1974–1982)

The Third United Nations Conference on the Law of the Sea began in 1974 in Caracas, Venezuela, amid great fanfare and high expectations. The delegations gathered to negotiate a comprehensive treaty that would clarify and bring certainty to the many ocean issues that had divided nations over the years. Eight years later, after long negotiating sessions that alternated between New York and Geneva, the Law of the Sea Convention was completed, and on December 10, 1982, 119 nations signed the document in Montego Bay, Jamaica. The Convention came into force in July 1994 after a sufficient number of countries had formally ratified the treaty.[15]

The central disputes among the countries negotiating this treaty concerned the width of the territorial sea, coastal state control of adjacent offshore resources, and the navigational rights of commercial and military vessels to pass through straits and through island archipelagoes. The United States initially resisted efforts to allow countries to claim extended fisheries zones, because it was concerned that such a zone could limit navigational freedoms. The United States was particularly concerned about its continuing ability to navigate its warships, including submerged submarines, through key international straits such as the Strait of Gibraltar (into the Mediterranean Sea), the Strait of Hormuz (into the Persian/Arabian Gulf), the Strait of Bab el Mandeb (into the Red Sea), the Strait of Malacca (connecting the Indian Ocean with the Pacific), the Dover Strait (through the English Channel), the Bering Strait (in the Arctic), and the Strait of Lombok (through the Indonesian archipelago). The U.S. worried that if countries were allowed to extend their territorial seas from three to twelve nautical miles, no high-seas corridors would remain in these narrow straits, and control over passage might fall under the control of the countries bordering these key waterways. The United States maintained that free movement through these straits was essential to its national security, and protested claims of expanding territorial seas.[16]

The compromise that emerged consisted of (1) allowing coastal states to extend their territorial seas to twelve nautical miles, (2) recognizing the right to transit passage through international straits, and (3) allowing countries to establish an "exclusive economic zone" (EEZ) out to a distance of two hundred nautical miles from its coast. The right of "transit passage through international straits" is nonsuspendable and applies to all vessels and also to airplanes. Submarines are allowed to remain submerged when they exercise this right of transit passage. In the newly created EEZ, the adjacent or coastal state has sovereign rights over the living and nonliving resources and can exercise certain forms of jurisdiction to protect the marine environment, regulate scientific research, and govern artificial structures. Coastal states must also exercise "due regard to the rights and duties of other States" under Article 56(2) and must permit navigational passage, but debates continue regarding the types of restrictions that can be imposed upon the movement of ships.

The EEZ was designed to balance carefully the interests of both the coastal and the maritime states. Maritime countries contend that they have the same navigational freedoms in the EEZs of other countries as they have on the high seas, but a number of coastal countries, including some of the maritime powers, have imposed restrictions on navigation in their EEZs in order to protect coastal resources and coastal populations. Disputes continue regarding the nature of military activities one country can engage in while its vessels are in the EEZ of another country, and disputes also exist regarding whether hydrographic surveying by one country is permitted in the EEZ of another country.[17] Countries cannot engage in marine scientific research in the EEZs of other countries without permission, but coastal countries are encouraged to grant permission when it is requested.[18]

5. Failure of the United States to Ratify the Convention

Although the United States had the largest delegation by far in Caracas and played a leading role in negotiating the Convention, President Ronald Reagan refused to allow the U.S. delegation to sign the treaty in 1982. When Reagan became President in January 1981, he reassigned or fired most of the U.S. diplomats who had been conducting negotiations at the Third U.N. Law of the Sea Conference, and ordered his aides to undertake a year-long review of the Draft Convention. Two negotiating sessions were held that year, but no serious talks took place because the United States refused to participate in substantive discussions.

In early 1982, President Reagan said the United States would return to the Conference, but would insist on specific changes before it would sign the treaty. His statement of January 29, 1982, explained the position of the United States:

> Serious questions had been raised in the United States about parts of the draft convention and, last March, I announced that my Administration would undertake a thorough review of the current draft and the degree to which it met U.S. interests in the navigation, overflight, fisheries, environmental, deep seabed mining, and other areas covered by that convention. We recognize that the last two sessions of the conference have been difficult, pending the completion of our review. At the same time, we consider it important that a Law of the Sea treaty be such that the United States can join in and support it. Our review has concluded that while most provisions of the draft convention are acceptable and consistent with U.S. interests, some major elements of the deep seabed mining regime are not acceptable.
>
> I am announcing today that the United States will return to those negotiations and work with other countries to achieve an acceptable treaty. In the deep seabed mining area, we will seek changes necessary to correct those unacceptable elements and to achieve the goal of a treaty that:
>
> - Will not deter development of any deep seabed mineral resources to meet national and world demand;
> - Will assure national access to these resources by current and future qualified entities to enhance U.S. security of supply, to avoid monopolization of the resources by the operating arm of the international Authority, and to promote the economic development of the resources;

- Will provide a decisionmaking role in the deep seabed regime that fairly reflects and effectively protects the political and economic interests and financial contributions of participating states;
- Will not allow for amendments to come into force without approval of the participating states, including in our case the advice and consent of the Senate;
- Will not set other undesirable precedents for international organizations; and
- Will be likely to receive the advice and consent of the Senate. In this regard, the convention should not contain provisions for the mandatory transfer of private technology and participation by and funding for national liberation movements.

The United States remains committed to the multilateral treaty process for reaching agreement on law of the sea. If working together at the conference we can find ways to fulfill these key objectives, my Administration will support ratification.

I have instructed the Secretary of State and my Special Representative for the Law of the Sea Conference, in coordination with other responsible agencies, to embark immediately on the necessary consultations with other countries and to undertake further preparations for our participation in the conference.[19]

During the spring 1982 session, intense negotiations were held in an effort to bridge the gap between the United States and the nations of the developing world. The United States was given a virtually guaranteed seat on the governing body of the International Seabed Authority (Article 161(1)(a)), and a resolution was passed protecting the investments already made by the mining consortia interested in deep seabed mining and guaranteeing to them access to the polymetallic nodules of the deep seabed.

These actions did not satisfy the Reagan Administration, however, and on April 30, 1982, the U.S. Ambassador to the Conference insisted that a vote be taken on the Convention as a whole. 130 nations voted for the Convention, four voted against (Israel, Turkey, the United States, and Venezuela), and seventeen abstained. The abstaining nations included the Eastern European nations, who thought the United States had been given too much in the spring 1982 negotiating session, plus several Western European nations.

On July 9, 1982, President Reagan announced that the United States would not sign the Convention, citing the following problems as forming the basis for this decision:

- Provisions that would actually deter future development of deep seabed mineral resources, when such development should serve the interest of all countries;
- A decision-making process that would not give the United States or others a role that fairly reflects and protects their interests;
- Provisions that would allow amendments to enter into force for the United States without its approval; this is clearly incompatible with the U.S. approach to such treaties;

- Stipulations relating to mandatory transfer of private technology and the possibility of national liberation movements sharing in benefits; and
- The absence of assured access for future qualified deep seabed miners to promote the development of these resources.[20]

On March 10, 1983, President Reagan issued a Proclamation establishing an exclusive economic zone for the United States and an Oceans Policy Statement announcing U.S. policy on related oceans issues.[21] Then on December 27, 1988, President Reagan issued another proclamation extending the U.S. territorial sea from three to twelve nautical miles.[22]

6. The Convention as Customary International Law

Finally, after certain provisions of the Convention had been revised by the "Part XI Agreement," described below, President William Clinton signed the Agreement, and submitted the Convention to the Senate for advice and consent to ratification on October 7, 1994.[23] As of the date of this publication, however, the U.S. Senate has not yet provided the necessary advice and consent. Nonetheless, the United States adheres to almost all provisions of the Convention and considers most of its provisions to be a reflection of binding customary international law.[24]

> **The United States adheres to almost all provisions of the Convention and considers most of its provisions to be a reflection of binding customary international law.**

U.S. courts have referred to the Convention as reflecting customary international law. In *U.S. v. Royal Caribbean Cruises*, the court stated that "[a]lthough the . . . convention is currently pending ratification before the Senate, it nevertheless carries the weight of law from the date of its submission by the President to the Senate," because such submission "expresses to the international community the United States' ultimate intention to be bound by the pact."[25] Other U.S. courts have also recognized the central role that the Convention plays in governing ocean affairs.[26] The U.N. Convention on the Law of the Sea entered into force November 16, 1994, without U.S. accession, after the sixtieth nation submitted its ratification.

B. The Innovative Provisions of the Convention

What does the Convention contain, and why has it been controversial in the United States? Some articles repeat language from earlier treaties, and many of the articles are based on longstanding norms of customary international law. Other sections were new and innovative in 1982, and their status as customary international law remains uncertain.

1. Archipelagic States

Articles 46–49 of the Convention describe the concept of "archipelagic waters." These provisions specify that countries that are made up exclusively of islands and that have a water-to-land ratio of between 1:1 and 9:1 can become "archipelagic states" and exercise unique jurisdiction over the waters within their islands. These provisions apply to countries such as the Bahamas, Fiji, Indonesia, Papua New Guinea, the Philippines, the Solomon Islands, and Vanuatu. Other countries can exercise the right of innocent passage through archipelagic waters and can exercise "archipelagic sea lanes passage" in "archipelagic sea lanes," which is a right of nonsuspendable passage applicable to all vessels and planes, like the right of transit passage through international straits.

2. The Exclusive Economic Zone

The recognition of exclusive economic zones (EEZs) in the Law of the Sea Convention transferred most of the productive fishing areas from the high seas, where fishing freedoms have traditionally been recognized, to the exclusive jurisdiction of the adjacent coastal or island community. This transfer was based on the views, recognized in the *Anglo-Norwegian Fisheries Case*,[27] that coastal communities tend to have an economic dependence on their nearby fisheries and that they are more likely to manage these resources carefully to protect them for future generations.

Management under this new regime has not always been enlightened or orderly, however, and new disputes have arisen, particularly when fish stocks overlap or "straddle" between an EEZ and its adjacent high seas zone. In areas such as the productive fisheries off the east coast of Canada, European fishing vessels have harvested just outside the two hundred-nautical-mile EEZ in a way that has impacted the stocks within the EEZ. This activity has led to disputes and also led in 1995 to the creation of an innovative new treaty designed to reduce such conflicts, the Straddling and Migratory Fish Stocks Agreement.[28]

3. Application to the International Law of Fisheries

How do the principles of international law designed to protect the environment apply to the international law of fisheries? The provisions of the 1982 U.N. Convention on the Law of the Sea are general in nature but nonetheless clearly articulate an overarching duty to cooperate in all situations involving shared fisheries. Article 56 gives the coastal state sovereignty over the living resources in the two hundred-nautical-mile EEZ, but Articles 61, 62, 69, and 70 require the coastal state (1) to cooperate with international organizations to ensure that species are not endangered by overexploitation, (2) to manage species in a manner that protects "associated or dependent species" from overexploitation, (3) to exchange data with international organizations and other nations that fish in its EEZ, and (4) to allow other states (particularly developing, landlocked, and geographically disadvantaged states) to harvest the surplus stocks in its EEZ. Article 63 addresses stocks (or stocks of associated species) that "straddle" adjacent EEZs, or an EEZ and an adjacent high seas area, and requires the states concerned to agree either directly or through an organization on the measures necessary to ensure the conservation of such stocks. Article 64 requires coastal states and distant-water-fishing states that harvest highly migratory stocks such as tuna to cooperate either directly or through an organization to ensure the conservation and optimum utilization of such stocks. Article 65 contains strong language requiring nations to "work through the appropriate international organization" to conserve, manage, and study whales and dolphins. Article 66 gives the states of origin primary responsibility for anadromous stocks (e.g., salmon), but requires the states of origin to cooperate with other states whose nationals have traditionally harvested such stocks and states whose waters these fish migrate through.

On the high seas, Articles 118 and 119 require states to cooperate with other states whose nationals exploit identical or associated species. Article 118 recognizes mandatory duties by stating that nations "shall enter into negotiations with a view to taking the measures necessary for the conservation of the living resources concerned," and advocates creating regional fisheries organizations. Article 120 states that the provisions of Article 65 on marine mammals also apply on the high seas.

These provisions reinforce the duty to cooperate, which has always existed in customary international law. Because they were not specific enough to resolve conflicts that have arisen as species have been overexploited, however, the 1995 Straddling and Migratory Fish Stocks Agreement was negotiated.[29] This treaty, discussed in more detail below, requires countries to cooperate with each other directly and through regional fishery organizations, to utilize the precautionary approach with regard to fishery regulation, to collect and share data, and to assess carefully the health of each fish stock. It expands enforcement powers and authorizes countries to utilize the dispute-resolution procedures established in the Law of the Sea Convention for fishery disputes involving the straddling and migratory fish stocks.

4. Standards Governing the Marine Environment

The environmental provisions in Part XII of the Convention use broad, general language but confirm the importance of protecting the marine environment for its own sake. The simple, direct, and elegant language of Article 192 articulates the importance of human stewardship of the ocean: "States have the obligation to protect and preserve the marine environment." Each word in this sentence has importance and power. The operative word "obligation" makes it clear that countries have positive duties and responsibilities and must take action. The verbs "protect" and "preserve" reinforce each other, to emphasize that countries must respect the natural processes of the ocean and must act in a manner that understands these processes and ensures that they continue for future generations. The "marine environment" is a purposively comprehensive concept covering all aspects of the ocean world—the water itself, its resources, the air above, and the seabed below—and it covers all jurisdictional zones—internal waters, territorial seas, contiguous zones, exclusive economic zones, continental shelves, archipelagic waters, and high seas. Article 192 thus recognizes the responsibility that all countries have to govern the oceans in a manner that respects the marine creatures that inhabit them. The marine environment must be preserved for the benefit of those who will come later to exploit its resources, to study its mysteries, and to enjoy the many pleasures that the oceans offer us.

5. Deep Seabed Mining and the International Seabed Authority

Part XI of the Law of the Sea Convention regulates seabed mining on the sea floor in the area beyond the exclusive economic zones of coastal countries. As explained above, the primary resource thought to be of potential value is the softball-size polymetallic nodules on the sea floor, particularly in the Pacific and Indian Oceans, which contain nickel, manganese, cobalt, copper and trace amounts of other metals.

The Convention declared this resource to be "the common heritage" of humankind and established an International Seabed Authority, based in Jamaica, to regulate it.[30] The structure of this Authority was one of the major reasons the Reagan Administration refused to sign the Convention in 1982 and refused to participate in the Preparatory Commission to establish the details of the international regime to govern exploitation of the polymetallic nodules. The dispute over these resources was based in part on a disagreement regarding whether the concept of the "freedom of the seas," which protects navigational freedoms and fishing activities on the high seas, also includes the ability to harvest mineral resources.[31] Because the nodules are on the floor of the abyssal plains in the deep seabed, they have never been exploited historically, and the question was not addressed in earlier agreements.

The Clinton Administration worked with the international community to modify the provisions of Part XI of the Law of the Sea Convention to address the concerns that had been identified during the Reagan Administration. The modifications made to the regime governing the nonliving resources of the deep seabed are dramatic and reveal a new approach to international decision making and resource sharing. The detailed provisions of Part XI of the 1982 Law of the Sea Convention have been simplified through an agreement signed on July 29, 1994, generally referred to as the "Part XI Agreement."[32] Some of the provisions of Part XI are put on hold for the time being, and others are scaled down or altered to meet new perceptions of the economic potential of the seabed minerals and the greater acceptance of free market principles by the world community.[33] The Agreement is effectively an amendment to the Law of the Sea Convention, although its creation was not in compliance with the Convention's provisions on amendments, reservations, or modifying agreements.

Perhaps the most significant change for the United States concerned decision making within the International Seabed Authority. Article 161 of the Convention established a sophisticated decision-making procedure calling for different levels of enhanced majorities depending on the type of decision being made. Section 3 of the Part XI Agreement restructured this procedure by establishing a system of "chambered voting" within the Seabed Authority's governing Council, to protect minority interests. This approach was originally advocated by the Nixon Administration in 1970 when it outlined a system of decision making for the body that eventually became the International Seabed Authority.

As modified in 1994, the Council, which is the main decision-making body of the International Seabed Authority, consists of thirty-five members and has four distinct "chambers" of nations representing different interest groups. One chamber consists of four of the nations with the world's largest economies, with a specific seat allocated to the United States and one reserved for an Eastern European nation. The second chamber consists of four of the nations that have made the largest investments in deep seabed mining. The third chamber includes four of the nations that are net exporters of the minerals to be mined from the sea floor, including at least two developing countries that rely heavily on the income from these minerals. And the fourth chamber consists of all the other developing nations that are elected to the Council.

All questions of substance must be adopted by a two-thirds majority of the entire Council and cannot be opposed by a majority in any of the chambers. In other words, each chamber can veto any decision and block action. Certain key decisions can be made only if there is "consensus" of the entire Council.

Another change affecting decision making is the establishment of a Finance Committee, made up of representatives of fifteen countries, which has the power to control the budget of the International Seabed Authority. The United States, if it ratifies the Convention, would have a guaranteed seat on the Finance Committee as one of the five largest financial contributors to the Authority automatically elected to the Committee. Because decisions of the Committee on substance must be made by consensus, the United States (along with the other members of the Committee) will effectively have a veto on the budget of the International Seabed Authority. This change was important in the Clinton Administration's decision to support ratification of the 1982 Convention.

Other changes of importance concerned the articles on transfer of technology, the Review Conference, production policies, and the financial terms of contracts. With regard to the mandatory provisions on these topics in the 1982 Law of the Sea Convention, the 1994 Agreement says simply that the text of the Convention "shall not apply."[34]

Pioneer investors who registered their claims were protected under the Part XI Agreement, and they had thirty-six months from the entry into force of the Convention to submit their plan of work of exploration.[35] Mining consortia licensed under U.S. law would also have been eligible to attain pioneer investor status on the basis of terms and conditions "similar to and no less favorable than" those granted to companies registered with the Preparatory Commission. Fees owed by pioneer investors may also be waived for a period of time under this new scheme. It should also be emphasized that the fundamental principle that the resources of the seabed are the common heritage of humankind, first established in 1970, remains unchanged, and that the obligation to share these resources, particularly with the least developed nations, remains firm.

The fundamental principle that the resources of the seabed are the common heritage of humankind remains unchanged.

6. The Dispute Resolution Procedures

The dispute-resolution provisions in Part XV of the Law of the Sea Convention are innovative and are carefully crafted to maintain the Convention's delicate balances between competing interests. Article 287 instructs each ratifying nation to pick from among four possible means of settling disputes over the interpretation of the Convention: (1) the International Tribunal for the Law of the Sea (ITLOS) (a twenty-one-judge court located in Hamburg, Germany, established according to Annex VI); (2) the International Court of Justice (in The Hague, Netherlands); (3) an arbitral tribunal established pursuant to Annex VII; or (4) a special arbitral tribunal established pursuant to Annex VIII to deal with specialized scientific issues. If the disputing countries have picked different procedures and cannot agree on a procedure, their dispute will be resolved through an Annex VII arbitration.

According to Article 297, controversies subject to mandatory dispute-resolution procedures include those involving coastal state environmental regulations that limit navigation (Article 297(1)(a) & (b)), allegations that a coastal state is violating internationally established environmental regulations (Article 297(1)(c)), and allegations that a coastal state has improperly seized a vessel flying the flag of another country (Article 292). Coastal states are not required to submit to these dispute-resolution procedures their decisions regarding marine scientific research on their continental shelf and exclusive economic zone (Article 297(2)), and their decisions regarding management of their EEZ fisheries and the allocation of their surplus catch (Article 297(3)). Ratifying countries have the option of withdrawing from mandatory dispute resolution disagreements over maritime boundaries (Article 298(1)(a)), disputes concerning military activities (Article 298(1)(b)), and disputes that are pending before the U.N. Security Council (Article 298(1)(c)). Disputes relating to deep seabed mining are subject to a special regime, and the Seabed Disputes Chamber of ITLOS will deal with most of these controversies.

7. The International Tribunal for the Law of the Sea and Its Jurisprudence[36]

When the Law of the Sea Convention came into force in 1994, twenty-one distinguished experts were elected to be judges on the International Tribunal for the Law of the Sea (ITLOS). In its first case, *The M/V Saiga*,[37] the Tribunal was presented with a dispute that could have been perceived as having an environmental dimension, but instead was argued more narrowly by the coastal state (Guinea) based on its claim to be able to exercise customs and fiscal authority over vessels selling and transferring fuel to fishing boats in the EEZ. Refueling in a resource-rich area presents environmental risks, and Guinea might have contended that its power to regulate refueling was linked to its authority to regulate fishing in the EEZ. But Guinea argued only that it was being deprived of tax revenue by not being able to extend its customs laws to the foreign-flag vessel.

Voting 18–2 on most questions (with Judges Warioba and Ndiaye dissenting), the Tribunal issued a strong opinion in favor of the flag state (Saint Vincent and the Grenadines), ruling that Guinea could not apply its custom laws to sales made in its EEZ except "in respect of artificial islands, installations and structures."[38] It also rejected the Guinean claims that its "public interest," "self-protection," or "state of necessity" justified extending its jurisdiction over an area not authorized by the Convention.[39]

The decision confirmed and protected maritime freedoms in the exclusive economic zone, but because Guinea did not claim that its actions were taken to protect its marine resources and coastal environment, the Tribunal did not address the important issue of how to balance navigational freedoms with resource and environmental protection. If that issue had been presented to it, the Tribunal might have concluded that because the coastal state could regulate the harvesting of resources in this zone, it could also regulate the refueling of fishing vessels engaged in the harvesting. It may be possible for coastal states to regulate this activity in the future by conditioning fishing licenses on agreements to buy fuel from within the coastal country or to pay tax on the fuel.

In the *Southern Bluefin Tuna Case*,[40] the Tribunal used its power under Article 290 of the Convention to prescribe "provisional measures" pending final outcome, whenever "appropriate under the circumstances to preserve the respective rights of the parties to the *dispute or to prevent serious harm to the marine environment*" (emphasis added). The Tribunal ordered Japan to "refrain from conducting an experimental fishing programme involving the taking of a catch of southern bluefin tuna," unless the catch from such a program is deducted from Japan's annual national allocation as agreed upon with Australia and New Zealand. But the second stage of this case was most unfortunate, because an ad hoc arbitral tribunal established under Annex VII of the Convention declared that both it and the Tribunal lacked jurisdiction over the case because of conflicting dispute-resolution provisions in the relevant treaties.

Despite the inconclusive ending of this case, the provisional measures issued by ITLOS may still be important for future disputes. The Tribunal tried to freeze the status quo, and ordered Japan to stop its unilateral "experimental fishing" in order to give the bluefin tuna a chance to recover while the countries developed new management arrangements. In its Order, the Tribunal used the following language:

> [P]arties should in the circumstances act with prudence and caution to ensure that effective conservation measures are taken to prevent serious harm to the stock of southern bluefin tuna . . .
>
> . . . [Although there is] scientific uncertainty regarding measures to be taken to conserve the stock of southern bluefin tuna and. . . . although the Tribunal cannot conclusively assess the scientific evidence presented by the parties, it finds that measures should be taken as a matter of urgency to preserve the rights of the parties and to avert further deterioration.[41]

Judge Alexander Yankov, referring to this language, wrote later that "there are some statements of the Tribunal in the Order which appear to reveal its stand in favor of essential elements of the precautionary approach."[42] Judge Tullio Treves added in his concurring opinion that, although he "understood the reluctance of the Tribunal in taking a position as to whether the precautionary approach is a binding principle of customary international law," nonetheless "a precautionary approach seems to me inherent in the very notions of provisional measures."[43] "These provisional measures remained in place for one year, yielding great benefits in environmental protection."[44]

In the *MOX Plant Case*,[45] the Tribunal issued another important provisional-measures ruling, stating that the duty to cooperate required Ireland and the United Kingdom to exchange information concerning the risks created by the expansion of the Sellafield nuclear facility in the United Kingdom, to monitor the effects of this plant on the marine environment in the Irish Sea, and to work together to reduce these risks. This case—a dispute between two members of the European Union—also faced procedural obstacles in its second phase, and was later addressed in European tribunals.

In December 2002, the Tribunal addressed in *The Volga Case*[46] the nature of the bond that can be required by a coastal country before it is obliged to release a vessel accused of fishing illegally in the coastal state's EEZ. The Tribunal said that the bond could be set by Australia at the full value of the vessel, fuel, lubricants, and fishing equipment, which came to AU$1,920,000.[47] But it rejected Australia's effort to charge another AU$1,000,000 as a "good behavior bond" to ensure that the vessel carried a fully operational vessel monitoring system (VMS), and recognized the conservation measures of the Convention for the Conservation of Antarctic Marine Living Resources (CCAMLR).[48] The Tribunal said that it "understands the international concerns about illegal, unregulated and unreported fishing and appreciates the objectives behind the measures taken by States, including the States Parties to CCAMLR, to deal with the problem."[49] But it nonetheless gave a narrow textual ruling, saying that the "bond or other security" allowed in Article 73(2) must be reasonable in light of its purpose, which "is to provide the flag State with a mechanism for obtaining the prompt release of a vessel and crew . . . by posting a security of a financial nature whose reasonableness can be assessed in financial terms."[50]

These early cases demonstrate that the Tribunal recognizes the challenges presented by overfishing and marine pollution. And the orders issued in the *Southern Bluefin Tuna* and the *MOX Plant* cases indicate that the Tribunal is prepared to issue preliminary measures to protect the marine environment from dangers.

III. Emerging and Unresolved Issues

A. Straddling and Migratory Fish Stocks[51]

To deal with the thorny issue of fish stocks that overlap or straddle the EEZ and high seas, the nations of the world negotiated an important treaty in 1995 with the cumbersome title of "Agreement for the Implementation of the Provisions of the United Nations Convention on the Law of the Sea of 10 December 1982 Relating to the Conservation and Management of Straddling Fish Stocks and Highly Migratory Fish Stocks" (1995 Agreement).[52] It builds on existing provisions in the 1982 United Nations Convention on the Law of the Sea described above, but it also introduces a number of new strategies and obligations, which have been requiring fishers to alter their operations in a number of significant ways. In addition to strengthening the role of regional organizations, as explained below, it also promotes peaceful dispute resolution by applying the dispute-resolution procedures of the Law of the Sea Convention to disputes involving straddling and migratory stocks. Ratifications of the 1995 Agreement have been steady, but many important countries have not become contracting parties. As of February 2008, sixty-eight countries had ratified the Agreement including most European countries, the United States, Japan, South Korea, India, and Liberia, but key fishing countries like South Korea, China, and most of the Latin American and African countries, and many of the countries providing flags of convenience had not yet ratified the Agreement.[53]

Professor Rosemary Rayfuse has recently suggested that "even in the absence of . . . wider ratification, it is arguable that certain principles embodied in the [Straddling and Migratory Fish Stocks Agreement] and the [FAO] Compliance Agreement may be binding on all states as a matter of customary international law."[54] Her primary example of a provision that has become obligatory through state practice is "the obligation to co-operate in respect of high seas fisheries through the medium of RFMOs or other co-operative arrangements."[55]

1. The Duty to Cooperate

The guiding principle that governs the 1995 Agreement is the duty to cooperate. This core concept is given specific new meaning, and the coastal nations and distant-water-fishing nations of each region are now required to share data and manage the straddling fisheries together. Article 7(2) requires that "[c]onservation and management measures established for the high seas and those adopted for areas under national jurisdiction *shall be compatible* in order to ensure conservation and management of the straddling fish stocks and highly migratory fish stocks in their entirety" (emphasis added). This duty gives the coastal state a leadership role in determining the allowable catch to be taken from a stock that is found both within and outside its exclusive economic zone, as evidenced by the requirement in Article 7(2)(a) that contracting parties "take into account" the conservation measures established by the coastal state under Article 61 of the Law of the Sea Convention for its EEZ "and ensure that measures established in respect of such stocks for the high seas do not undermine the effectiveness of such measures." This polite diplomatic language indicates clearly that catch rates outside a two hundred-nautical-mile exclusive economic zone cannot differ significantly from those within the EEZ.

2. The Duty to Work Through an Existing or New Fisheries Organization

The 1995 Agreement requires coastal and island nations to work together with distant-water-fishing nations in an organization or arrangement to manage shared fisheries. Article 8(3) provides that coastal and island nations must cooperate with the distant-water-fishing nations fishing in adjacent high seas areas either by allowing them into an existing fishery management organization or by creating a new one that all can join. All states "having a real interest" in the shared fishery stock must be allowed into the organization. Only those states that join a regional organization or agree to

The 1995 Agreement requires coastal and island nations to work together with distant-water-fishing nations to manage shared fisheries.

observe its management regulations can fish in a regional fishery (Articles 8(4) and 17(1)). Article 13 requires existing fisheries management organizations to "improve their effectiveness in establishing and implementing conservation and management measures."

Article 11 addresses the difficult question whether *new* distant-water-fishing nations must be allowed into such an organization once established. Do the nations that have established fishing activities in the region have to allow new entrants? The language of Article 11 does not give a clear answer to this question, but it seems to indicate that some new entrants could be excluded if the current fishing nations have developed a dependency on the shared fish stock in question. Furthermore, developing nations from the region would appear to have a greater right to enter the fishery than would developed nations from outside the region. "Article 25(1)(b), implies some degree of preference for developing countries that are new members, by requiring states to 'facilitate access [to high seas fisheries] . . . subject to articles 5 and 11."[56] The 1995 Agreement emphasizes the need to cooperate, and it requires the coastal and island nations to cooperate with the distant-water-fishing nations operating in the adjacent high-seas areas to the same extent that the distant-water-fishing nations must cooperate with the coastal and island nations.

3. The Precautionary Principle

The "precautionary principle" (called the "precautionary approach" by some) has gained almost universal acceptance during the past decade as the basic rule that should govern activities that affect the ocean environment.[57] This principle requires users of the ocean to exercise caution by undertaking relevant research, developing nonpolluting technologies, and avoiding activities that present uncertain risks to the marine ecosystem. It requires policy makers to be alert to risks of environmental damage, and reflects the view that the "greater the possible harm, the more rigorous the requirements of alertness, precaution and effort."[58] It rejects the notion that the oceans have an infinite or even a measurable ability to assimilate wastes or support living resources, and it instead recognizes that our knowledge about the ocean's ecosystems may remain incomplete and that policy makers must err on the side of protecting the environment. It certainly means at a minimum that a thorough evaluation of the environmental impacts must precede actions that may affect the marine environment. All agree that it requires a vigorous pursuit of a research agenda in order to overcome the uncertainties that exist.

The precautionary principle is given center stage as the primary basis for decision making in the new Straddling and Migratory Stocks Agreement. Article 5(c) of the 1995 Agreement lists the "precautionary approach" among the principles that govern conservation and management of shared fish stocks, and Article 6 elaborates on this requirement in some detail, focusing on data collection and monitoring. States are required to improve their data collection, and to share their information widely with others. When "information is uncertain, unreliable or inadequate," states must be "more cautious" (Article 6 (2)) and they must take "uncertainties" into account when establishing management goals (Article 6(3)(c)). Species thought to be under stress shall be subjected to "enhanced monitoring in order to review their status and the efficacy of conservation and management measures" (Article 6(5)). If "new or exploratory fisheries" are opened, precautionary conservation measures must be established "as soon as possible" (Article 6(6)).

In Annex II, the Agreement identifies a specific procedure that must be used to control exploitation and monitor the effects of the management plan. For each harvested species, a "conservation" or "limit" reference point as well as a "management" or "target" reference must be determined. If stock populations go below the agreed-upon conservation/limit reference point, then "conservation and management action should be initiated to facilitate stock recovery" (Annex II(5)). Overfished stocks must be managed to ensure that they can recover to the level at which they can produce the maximum sustainable yield (Annex II(7)). The continued use of the maximum sustainable yield approach indicates that the Agreement has not broken free from the approaches that have led to the rapid decline in the world's fisheries,[59] but the hope is that the conservation/limit reference points will lead to early warnings of trouble that will be taken more seriously.

4. The Duty to Assess and to Collect and Share Data

Article 5(d) reaffirms the duty to "assess the impacts of fishing, other human activities and environmental factors" of stocks, and Articles 14 and 18(3)(e) explain the data collection requirements necessary to facilitate such assessments. Article 14 requires contracting parties to require fishing vessels flying their flags to collect data "in sufficient detail to facilitate effective stock assessment" (Article 14(1)(b)). Annex I then explains the specific information that must be collected, which includes the amount of fish caught by species, the amount of fish discarded, the types of fishing methods used, and the locations of the fishing vessels (Annex I, art. 3(1)). In order to permit stock assessment, each nation must also provide to the regional fishery organization data on the size, weight, length, age, and distribution of its catch, plus "other relevant research, including surveys of abundance, biomass surveys, hydro-acoustic surveys, research on environmental factors affecting stock abundance, and oceanographic and ecological studies" (Annex I, art. 3(2)).

These requirements, if taken seriously, will revolutionize the fishing industry, where the competitive nature of the quest for fish has encouraged each nation to hide its activities from others to the extent possible. The data collected "must be shared with other flag States and relevant coastal States through appropriate subregional or regional fisheries management organizations or arrangements" in a "timely manner," although the "confidentiality of nonaggregated data" should be maintained (Annex I, art. 7). Decision making at regional fishery organizations must now be "transparent" under Article 12, and international and nongovernmental organizations must be allowed to participate in meetings and to observe the basis for decisions.

B. Methods of Enforcement

Article 18 of the 1995 Agreement further requires contracting parties to establish "national inspection schemes," "national observer programmes," and "vessel monitoring systems, including, as appropriate, satellite transmitter systems" to manage their flag fishing vessels with some rigor. Article 21(1) gives these requirements teeth by authorizing the ships of a nation that is party to a regional fisheries agreement to board and inspect on the high seas any ship flying the flag of any other nation that is a party to the same agreement.[60] If the boarded vessel is found to have committed a "serious violation," it can be brought into the "nearest appropriate port" for further inspection (Article 21(8)). The term "serious violation" is defined in Article 21(11) to include using prohibited fishing gear, having improper markings or identification, fishing without a license or in violation of an established quota, and failing to maintain accurate records or tampering with evidence needed for an investigation.

1. Dispute-Resolution

Part VIII of the 1995 Agreement requires contracting parties to settle their disputes peacefully, and extends the dispute-resolution mechanisms of the Law of the Sea Convention to disputes arising under this new Agreement. These procedures are complicated and somewhat untested, but should provide flexible and sophisticated mechanisms to allow nations to resolve their differences in an orderly fashion.

2. Recognition of the Special Needs of Developing Nations

The 1995 Agreement recognizes in Articles 24–26 that the burden of conservation may affect the coastal fisheries that many communities rely upon for subsistence. These articles state that developing states should not be required to shoulder a "disproportionate burden of the conservation action" (Art. 24(2)(c)), and they call for increased technical and financial aid to developing countries to allow them to meet their duties of data collection and dissemination.

3. The 2000 Honolulu Convention

The Pacific Island and distant-water-fishing nations with an interest in the Pacific met in Honolulu every six months for several years in the late 1990s to draft an important new treaty governing the migratory fish stocks of the Pacific Ocean. Formally called "The Convention on the Conservation and Management of Highly Migratory Fish Stocks in the Western and Central Pacific Ocean"[61] and signed in Honolulu in September 2000, this treaty creates the regional organization anticipated by Article 64 of the 1982 Law of the Sea Convention[62] and by the 1995 Straddling and Migratory Stocks Agreement.[63]

The 2000 Honolulu Convention is breathtakingly innovative in a number of significant respects.

The 2000 Honolulu Convention is breathtakingly innovative in a number of significant respects. It is huge in its geographical scope, covering much of the vast Pacific Ocean and governing territorial seas and exclusive economic zones as well as high seas areas. It creates a Commission with authority to set catch limits and allocate catch quotas to fishing nations both within and outside the exclusive economic zones of coastal and island nations. The Commission can also regulate vessel types, fish size, and gear, and can establish area and time limitations. Decision making is by consensus for the central issues—such as allocation of fish to contracting parties—and by chambered voting on others, requiring a majority of support from the two chambers—one consisting of the ten distant-water-fishing nations and the other consisting of the sixteen island nations—thus carefully protecting both groups. Decisions of the Commission can be reviewed by an arbitral review panel to ensure consistency and protect against discrimination.

This new treaty requires fishing of migratory species in the high seas to be compatible with the regulations that apply within adjacent exclusive economic zones. It relies on the precautionary approach as its basic foundation throughout. It reinforces the importance of the duty to cooperate. It allows Taiwan to participate in decision making (as "Chinese Taipei"), it allows non-self-governing territories to participate (pursuant to rules to be adopted), and nongovernmental organizations can also participate in appropriate ways. Compliance will be through flag-state and port-state enforcement, boarding and inspection rights, obligatory transponders on all high-seas fisheries, and regional observers on the vessels. President George W. Bush recommended ratification in May 2005,[64] and the Senate Foreign Relations Committee held a hearing on it on September 29, 2005.[65] The United States formally deposited its instrument of ratification to this treaty on July 27, 2007.

C. Military Activities in the EEZ[66]

Can countries engage in military exercises and maneuvers, including the firing of weapons, in the exclusive economic zone of another country? The text of the 1982 United Nations Law of the Sea Convention addresses freedoms in the EEZ in Article 58 (1):

> In the exclusive economic zone, all States, whether coastal or landlocked, enjoy, subject to the relevant provisions of this Convention, the freedoms referred to in article 87 of navigation and overflight and of the laying of submarine cables and pipelines, and other internationally lawful uses of the sea related to these freedoms such as those associated with the operation of ships, aircraft and submarine cables and pipelines, and compatible with the other provisions of this Convention.

Article 87 recognizes the freedom of navigation for all states in the high seas, and Article 58(1) thus confirms that this same right also exists in the exclusive economic zone, subject, however, to the qualifications found in Article 58(3):

> In exercising their rights and performing their duties under this Convention in the exclusive economic zone, States shall have due regard to the rights and duties of the coastal State and shall comply with the laws and regulations adopted by the coastal State in accordance with the provisions of this Convention and other rules of international law in so far as they are not incompatible with this Part.

When Brazil signed the Convention on December 10, 1982, it issued a Declaration containing the following language:

> (3) The Brazilian Government understands that the provisions of Article 301, which prohibits "any threat or use of force against the territorial integrity or political independence of any State, or in any other manner inconsistent with the principles of international law embodied in the Charter of the United Nations," apply, in particular, to the maritime areas under the sovereignty or the jurisdiction of the coastal State.
>
> (4) The Brazilian Government understands that the provisions of the Convention do not authorize other States to carry out in the exclusive economic zone military exercises or manoeuvres, in particular those that imply the use of weapons or explosives, without the consent of the coastal State.

Is Brazil's "understanding" of the Convention correct?[67] Similar declarations have been filed by Cape Verde, India, Malaysia, Pakistan, and Uruguay, and sharply opposing declarations have been filed by Germany, Italy, the Netherlands, and the United Kingdom.[68] What is the effect of these "declarations" and "understandings"? Article 309 of the Convention prohibits ratifying countries from filing reservations that would have the effect of opting out of any of the Convention's obligation, but Article 310 does permit states to make declarations explaining the relationship of the Convention's provisions to their own laws "provided that such declarations or statements do not purport to exclude or to modify the legal effect of the provisions of this Convention in their application to that State."

Also relevant to the analysis of what military activities are permissible near the coasts of other countries is Article 2(4) of the United Nations Charter,[69] which says: "All members shall refrain in their international relations from the threat or use of force against the territorial integrity or political independence of any state, or in any other manner inconsistent with the Purposes of the United Nations."[70] This limitation is reinforced by Article 88 of the Law of the Sea Convention, which says that "[t]he high seas shall be reserved for peaceful purposes," and which explicitly applies to the exclusive economic zone pursuant to Article 58(2).[71]

Are there some military activities in the coastal areas that would be viewed as inherently threatening? Are there some that would threaten the marine environment and offshore resources in the exclusive economic zone, which the coastal state is obliged to protect and authorized to exploit? Could a coastal state rightly require that it be notified prior to military maneuvers occurring in its EEZ pursuant to the over-arching international-law obligation to consult with affected states prior to engaging in activities that might threaten their interests?[72]

During the negotiations, some countries expressed strong opposition to military activities in the exclusive economic zone, because of the threats such activities present to coastal communities and marine resources. Delegates focused particularly on military activities that involved the use of weapons, the launching of aircraft, espionage, interference with coastal communications, and propaganda aimed at the coastal communities. Among the nations that expressed concern were Peru, Brazil, Albania, the Khmer Republic (Cambodia), North Korea, Costa Rica, Ecuador, El Salvador, Pakistan, the Philippines, Portugal, Senegal, Somalia, and Uruguay.[73] The delegate from China said that "freedom of scientific research in the past has meant espionage" and sought clarification about what activity would be considered legitimate scientific research in the EEZ.[74] The United States took the consistent position during these negotiations that military activities on the high seas and in the EEZ were consistent with the "peaceful purpose" requirement if they were conducted in a nonthreatening fashion in order to prepare for legitimate self-defense.[75]

Governing principles of international law emerge from multilateral treaties and from state practices undertaken with a sense of legal obligation which provide evidence of an international consensus that certain behavior is required. Where the text of a governing treaty leaves certain matters ambiguous or unresolved, the subsequent practices of states become particularly important to determine the proper interpretation of the treaty's provisions.[76] One commentator has concluded that "[i]n the case of military exercises in the exclusive economic zone no prevailing orientation or trend can be inferred from present States practice."[77]

D. Balancing Navigational Freedom with Environmental and Security Concerns

1. The San Onofre Nuclear Reactor

In what may be seen as a defining moment in the tension between navigational freedom and the right of coastal states to restrict the movement of ships through their exclusive economic zones based on the nature of the ship and its cargo, the United States announced February 3, 2004, that it was abandoning its plan to ship the 770-ton decommissioned nuclear reactor from the San Onofre nuclear plant in Southern California around Cape Horn at the tip of South America to South Carolina for burial.[78] The plan, which had previously been approved by the U.S. Department of Transportation despite conflicting views within the U.S. government, was to put the reactor on a barge that would make a ninety-day journey around South America. This journey would thus include the transiting of Drake's Passage at the continent's tip, which is one of the world's most dangerous nautical passages, where gale force winds blow two hundred days each year. Although logic would have favored burial in California, or Hanford, Washington, or transporting the reactor across the United States by train, these options had all been rejected because of U.S. laws governing the disposal of nuclear wastes and because of liability concerns.

The first hurdle faced by the proposed shipment concerned Chile's "Law for Nuclear Safety," which had been modified in October 2002 to require prior authorization for any transport of "nuclear substances" and "radioactive materials" through Chile's exclusive economic zone.[79] The law explained that such authorization would be granted only if the transporter establishes that the shipment will "keep[] the environment free of contamination" and only after information has been provided regarding the date and route of the shipment, the "characteristics of the load," and the "safety and contingency measures" that are being utilized.[80]

The U.S. State Department had originally instructed Southern California Edison that it "should not apply for Chilean authorization for the passage because it was concerned that our doing so would set an unfavorable precedent for future shipments."[81] Subsequently, however, the U.S. Transportation Department indicated that it thought consultations with Chile would be logical because of the potential risks and the advantages of having emergency contingency plans in place.[82] The Department of Transportation also urged Southern California Edison to develop more realistic plans for salvage in the case of a sinking.[83]

These concerns seemed to have resonated in the State Department because two weeks later the State Department said that "a number of significant issues" needed to be resolved before the reactor could be shipped, and stated specifically that Southern California Edison should consider another route around South America, explain in detail its salvage contingency plans, and show that it has adequate liability insurance.[84] Finally, however, the Department of Transportation did issue a permit for the shipment on December 1, 2003. Southern California Edison said that "the ocean journey will be made in international shipping lanes hundreds of miles off the coasts of Central and South America."[85] It was never clear whether the vessel was going to try to avoid passing through Chile's EEZ altogether by staying more than two hundred nautical miles from the Chilean coast.

A second hurdle was presented by a January 2004 court decision in Argentina, which prohibited the passage of the reactor through Argentina's EEZ.[86] This decision, issued by Argentine federal judge Jorge Pfleger, cited the Basel Convention on the Control of Trans-Boundary Movements of Hazardous Wastes and Their Disposal as authorizing coastal countries to block such shipments.[87] After this decision, Argentine officials stated that if the shipment passed through Argentina's exclusive economic zone, "the load will be intercepted by the military and escorted out of the nation's territorial waters."[88] This important decision set the stage for a significant international incident if the shipment had taken place and had transited within two hundred nautical miles of Argentina's coast. A conflict was avoided, however, when the United States cancelled the voyage.

2. Opposition to Nuclear Cargoes from Other Countries

The decision to abandon the effort to ship the reactor by sea, and thus to leave it in place in Southern California, avoided confrontations, and also reinforced the view that countries can act to protect their coastal populations and coastal resources by preventing passage of particularly dangerous cargoes and unseaworthy ships through their coastal waters. Numerous states have previously declared that the shipments of ultrahazardous nuclear cargoes should not transit through their EEZs. In 1992, for instance, South Africa and Portugal explicitly requested that Japan's shipment of plutonium stay out of their EEZs, and in response to an inquiry from Australia, Japan stated that "in principle" the ship would stay outside the two hundred-nautical-mile zone of all nations.[89] In 1995, Brazil, Argentina, Chile, South Africa, Nauru, and Kiribati all expressly banned the British nuclear cargo ship *Pacific Pintail* from their EEZs, and Chile sent its ships and aircraft to force the ship out of its EEZ.[90] In 1999, New Zealand issued a strong statement protesting these shipments and stating that they should not be permitted through New Zealand's EEZ because of the "'precautionary principle' enshrined in the Rio Declaration."[91]

3. European Restrictions on Navigational Freedoms

Perhaps even more significantly, the maritime states of Europe have also begun to restrict passage based on the nature of the cargo and the ship. The breakup of the oil tanker *Prestige* off the coast of Spain in November 2002 provided another defining moment that appears to have changed perceptions and the governing law. Spain refused to permit the crippled tanker to come into a Spanish port for "safe haven," and when the vessel was towed out into the open ocean it broke apart, causing a dramatic and destructive spillage of its cargo. After huge amounts of oil washed up along the beautiful and resource-rich coasts of Spain, Portugal, and France, France and Spain issued a decree that said:

The maritime states of Europe have begun to restrict passage based on the nature of the cargo and the ship.

> A. All oil tankers traveling through these two countries' EEZs will have to provide advance notice to the coastal countries about their cargo, destination, flag, and operators.
>
> B. All single-hulled tankers more than 15 years old traveling through the EEZs of Spain and France will be subject to spot inspections by coastal maritime authorities while in the adjacent EEZs and will be expelled from the EEZs if they are determined, after inspection, to be not seaworthy.[92]

Shortly after the Spanish-French decree, Portugal announced that it would also take the same position on this issue.[93] And then Morocco announced that single-hull oil tankers more than fifteen years old carrying heavy fuel, tar, asphaltic bitumen, or heavy crude oil would be subject to the requirement that they provide prior notification and adhere to strict safety regulations.[94]

Also in the spring of 2003, the European Union banned large single-hulled tankers carrying heavy-grade oil from coming into any European ports, and on April 3, 2003, the French National Assembly unanimously adopted a new law asserting the right to intercept ships out to a distance ninety miles from its Mediterranean coast that release polluting ballast waters and also imposing stricter controls on transient oil tankers.[95] Captains of vessels violating these new French rules can be sentenced to up to four years in prison and fined up to $600,000.[96] About this same time, Spain, France, and Portugal were joined by Belgium and the United Kingdom in submitting a petition to the International Maritime Organization (IMO) to declare virtually their entire EEZs to be "particularly sensitive sea areas" that would be completely off-limits for single-hulled oil tankers and other cargo vessels transporting dangerous cargoes.[97] Although the IMO has not yet approved this initiative, this effort by five maritime countries to protect their own coastal resources provides strong support for the view that it is legitimate to restrict maritime freedom in order to protect the resources of the EEZ.

4. U.S. Restrictions on Navigational Freedoms

Even the United States has imposed some restrictions on navigational freedoms to protect its environmental and security interests. In December 1998, for instance, the International Maritime Organization (IMO) approved a U.S. proposal to require ships transiting through the northeast and southeast coasts of the United States to report their locations and travel plans in order to protect the northern right whale from being hit by ships.[98] This whale species was hunted almost to extinction because of its oil, and is now thought to be the rarest whale species in the world. This mandatory ship reporting area joins nine others that have been established by IMO to protect other fragile environmental areas.[99]

Although it is not yet clear how all these conflicts will be sorted out, it seems that we are in a period of reassessment and transition regarding how to strike the balance between navigational freedoms and the right of coastal states to limit navigation to protect their environment and security. The law of the sea has always been created through the give-and-take process of states making conflicting claims, which are ultimately resolved through negotiation, a decision rendered by a tribunal or international organization, military force, or a pattern of practice that emerges and is accepted as obligatory by those concerned about the issue.[100] We are in a particularly active law-making period at present regarding navigational rights and responsibilities, and it appears that the law that will emerge will be different than the law that had existed previously.

E. Use of Low Frequency Sonar[101]

On July 15, 2002, the U.S. National Marine Fisheries Service (NMFS) exempted the U.S. Navy's Low Frequency Active Sonar (LFAS) program from the requirements of the Marine Mammal Protection Act after determining that its operation would have a "negligible impact" on any species.[102] NMFS thus authorized the Navy to use two ships to transmit low frequency active sonar in about seventy-five percent of the world's oceans (exempting the polar extremes). Ten weeks later, in late September 2002, fifteen Cuvier's beaked whales beached on the Canary Islands at the same time the U.S. destroyer *Mahan* was maneuvering in the area with ships from nine other members of the North Atlantic Treaty Organization.[103] Autopsies of the whales revealed brain damage consistent with an acoustic impact. This mass stranding followed similar incidents near the Bahamas in March 2000,[104] near Greece in 1996,[105] and in the Canaries between 1985 and 1989.[106]

The U.S. Navy's Surveillance Towed Array Sensor System (SURTASS) Low Frequency Active Sonar (LFAS) will employ very loud low-frequency sounds (less than 500 Hz with intensity levels as great as 230 dB re: 1μPa at 1 m), posing a significant threat to the safety and welfare of marine mammals, and possibly to other forms of marine life as well.[107] The transmitted sound will be about 215 dB at its source, arrayed in a manner to have "an effective source level" of 230–240 dB.[108] According to the Navy's environmental impact statement (EIS), the sound would be at the 180 dB level one kilometer from the source, at 173 dB two kilometers from the source, about 165 dB 40 nautical miles from the source, at the 150–160 dB level up to 100 miles from the source, and some 140 dB 400 miles from the source vessel.[109] (Decibel levels are logarithmic in nature, so that a sound of 180 dB is ten times as intense as one of 170 dB.) The sounds are not transmitted uniformly in all directions from the source, but travel in a beam that is a few hundred feet in width.[110] These sounds are the loudest ever put into the world's oceans by humans, with the possible exception of underground explosions. They are designed to travel great distances and are audible by humans 1,000 kilometers away without any signal processing.

In October 2002, federal Magistrate Judge Elizabeth D. LaPorte determined that the Navy's use of low frequency active sonar was likely to violate four U.S. statutes and to cause irreparable injury to ocean creatures, and she thus issued a preliminary injunction restricting the Navy's actions, but allowing further testing and training of personnel regarding this system.[111] The court explained: "It is undisputed that marine mammals, many of whom depend on sensitive hearing for essential activities like finding food and mates and avoiding predators, and some of whom are endangered species, will at a minimum be harassed by the extremely loud and far traveling LFA sonar."[112] The subsequent agreement between the parties allowed the Navy to test its sonar in an area of the Western Pacific extending from Saipan, in the Commonwealth of the Northern Mariana Islands, to Japan's Bonin Islands, south of Tokyo, pending the hearing for a preliminary injunction.[113] About the same time, another federal judge in Northern California issued a temporary restraining order blocking geographers from the National Science Foundation, Columbia University, and the Georgia Institute of Technology from mapping the sea floor with 220 dB sound blasts that had killed at least two beaked whales.[114]

In January 2003, U.S. District Judge Samuel Conti of the Northern District of California made an additional ruling against sonar use, blocking experiments (authorized by NMFS) that were to be conducted by Woods Hole Oceanographic Institution scientist Dr. Peter Tyack to determine the effect of the sound on the gray whales migrating along the West Coast of California to their winter grounds along the coast of Mexico.[115] Judge Conti ruled that because the permits involved "major amendments" to the original project, which had generated "public controversy," it was necessary to conduct a proper environmental impact assessment under the National Environmental Policy Act before undertaking the experiments. In the process of "balancing" the "harms" to determine whether to issue an injunction, Judge Conti noted that the population of gray whales had been dropping since 1984 (from 21,942 individuals to 17,414) and that "Dr. Tyack's proposed experiments might inflict unacceptable levels of harm on the gray whales."[116]

If U.S. judges eventually allow the Navy and other researchers to proceed with this powerful new sonar, this activity is sure to be challenged at the international level.

The unusually loud sounds emitted in the LFAS process would certainly be considered "pollution" under Article 1(1)(4) of the Law of the Sea Convention, which is defined as:

> the introduction by man, directly or indirectly, of substances or *energy* into the marine environment, including estuaries, which *results or is likely to result* in such *deleterious effects* as *harm to living resources and marine life*, hazards to human health, hindrance to marine activities, including fishing and other legitimate uses of the sea, impairment of quality for use of sea water and reduction of amenities. (Emphasis added).

Sound is a "form of energy manifested by small pressure and/or particle velocity variations in a continuous medium."[117] It has been observed that "while the definition of [pollution in the Law of the Sea Convention] was . . . not drafted with acoustic pollution in mind, the inclusion of 'energy' implies that noise can be a form of pollution under the terms of the LOS Convention."[118] Although the U.S. Navy did prepare an EIS, the scientific tests it relied upon were woefully inadequate because they did not test the effects above 155 dB; even so, these tests demonstrated that LFAS will have significant negative impacts on marine mammals.[119]

IV. Conclusion

The 1982 Law of the Sea Convention has served to regulate ocean activities for a quarter of a century and should continue to be the primary international authority to guide conduct and resolve disputes. This carefully crafted treaty includes many compromises and leaves some issues unresolved or ambiguous. But it will be the starting point that officials and scholars turn to when conflicts arise. It has brought substantial stability and has allowed countries to utilize ocean resources cooperatively. It will be viewed in coming generations as one of the international community's crowning achievements.

Notes

1. HUGO GROTIUS, MARE LIBERUM [THE FREEDOM OF THE SEAS] 28 (James B. Scott ed. & Ralph Van Deman Magoffin trans., 1916) (originally published in 1633).
2. *Id.*
3. *See generally* FREEDOM FOR THE SEAS FOR THE 21ST CENTURY 72 (Jon M. Van Dyke, Durwood Zaelke & Grant Hewison eds., 1993).
4. United Nations Convention on the Law of the Sea, Dec. 10, 1982, U.N. Doc. A/CONF.62/122, *reprinted in* 21 I.L.M. 1261 (1982) and *The Law of the Sea: Official Text of the United Nations Convention on the Law of the Sea* with Annexes and Index, UN Sales No. E.83.V.5 (1983).
5. http://www.un.org/Depts/los/reference_files/chronological_lists_of_ratifications.htm.
6. Presidential Proclamation No. 2667, 10 Fed. Reg. 12,303 (1945), 4 DIG. INT'L L. 756–58 (Margery Whiteman ed., 1965); *see* 2 FOREIGN RELATIONS OF THE UNITED STATES, 1945, at 1502.
7. *Id.* President Truman issued a second proclamation asserting "fishery conservation zones" subject to the regulation and control of the United States. Presidential Proclamation 2668, 10 Fed. Reg. 12,304 (Oct. 2, 1945).

8. By 1958 nearly twenty nations had claimed legal jurisdiction and control over their continental shelves. Freedom for the Seas, *supra* note 3, at 78–79.

9. 516 U.N.T.S. 205, 15 U.S.T. 1606.

10. 450 U.N.T.S. 82, 13 U.S.T. 2312.

11. 17 U.S.T. 138, 599 U.N.T.S. 285.

12. 499 U.N.T.S. 311, 15 U.S.T. 471.

13. This idea was also developed in John Mero, The Mineral Resources of the Sea (1965).

14. U.N. General Assembly's 1970 Declaration of Principles Governing the Seabed and the Ocean Floor, and the Subsoil Thereof, Beyond the Limits of National Jurisdiction, G.A. Res. 2749 (XXV), 25 U.N. GAOR, Supp. No. 28, at 24, U.N. Doc. A/8028 (1970).

15. Law of the Sea Convention, *supra* note 4.

16. George Galdorisi, *The United States and the Law of the Sea: Decade of Decision, in* The United States and the 1982 Law of the Sea Convention: The Cases Pro and Con 7, 16–17 (George Galdorisi, Doug Bandow & M. Casey Jarman eds., Law of the Sea Institute Occasional Paper No. 38, 1994).

17. *See, e.g.,* Jon M. Van Dyke, *The Disappearing Right to Navigational Freedom in the Exclusive Economic Zone,* 29 Marine Pol'y 107–21 (2005).

18. Law of the Sea Convention, *supra* note 4, Article 246.

19. Statement of President Ronald Reagan, Jan. 29, 1982, *reprinted in* U.S. Department of State Bureau of Public Affairs, Current Policy No. 371.

20. Statement of President Ronald Reagan, July 9, 1982, *reprinted in* U.S. State Department Bureau of Public Affairs Current Policy No. 416. Articles that explain the dynamics of how the decision not to sign was reached include Leigh Ratiner, *The Law of the Sea: A Crossroads for American Foreign Policy,* 60(5) Foreign Aff. 1006 (1982); Nossiter, *Underwater Treaty: The Fascinating Story of How the Law of the Sea Was Sunk,* Barron's 10 (July 26, 1982).

21. The Exclusive Economic Zone of the United States of America, Proclamation No. 5030 (Mar. 10, 1983), 48 Fed. Reg. 10,605 (Mar. 14, 1983).

22. The Territorial Sea of the United States of America, Proclamation No. 5928 (Dec. 27, 1988), 54 Fed. Reg. 777 (Jan. 9, 1989). The twelve-mile territorial sea proclaimed by the United States was the maximum consistent with Art. 3. Convention on the Law of the Sea, *supra* note 4. The Proclamation stated that it extended the territorial sea for purposes of international law only, and did not alter existing domestic federal or state law.

23. Letter by President William J. Clinton, Transmittal Letter to the U.S. Senate, Washington, D.C., Oct. 6, 1994. In *United States: President's Transmittal of the United Nations Convention on the Law of the Sea and the Agreement Relating to the Implementation of Part XI to the U.S. Senate with Commentary,* Oct. 7, 1994. U.S. Department of State Dispatch Supplement, vol. 6, supp. no. 1 (Feb. 1995).

24. *See, e.g.,* R.M.S. Titanic, Inc. v. Haver, 171 F.3d 943, 965 n.3 (4th Cir.1999).

25. United States v. Royal Caribbean Cruises, 24 F. Supp. 2d 155, 159 (D.P.R.1997).

26. *See, e.g.,* United States v. Alaska, 503 U.S. 569, 588 n.10 (1992) ("The United States has not ratified [the Law of the Sea Convention], but has recognized that its baseline provisions reflect customary international law."); Mayaguezanos por la Salud y el Ambiente v. United States, 198 F.3d 297, 305 n. 14 (1st Cir. 1999) (noting that because it had signed the Convention, even though it had not yet ratified it, the United States "is obliged to refrain from acts that would defeat the object and purpose of the agreement"); Mansel v. Baker Hughes, Inc., 203 F. Supp. 2d 745, 746 n.1 (S.D. Texas 2002) (same); Sarei v. Rio Tinto PLC, 221 F. Supp. 2d 1116, 1161, 1162 (C.D. Cal. 2002) (explaining that because the Convention has been ratified by so many nations and signed by the United States, it "thus appears to represent the law of nations," and because it "reflects customary international law, plaintiffs may base an ATCA [Alien Tort Claims Act, 28 U.S.C. § 1350] claim upon it").

27. *Fisheries Case (United Kingdom v. Norway),* 1951 I.C.J. 116 (Dec. 18).

28. Agreement for the Implementation of the Provisions of the United Nations Convention on the Law of the Sea of 10 December 1982 Relating to the Conservation and Management

of Straddling Fish Stocks and Highly Migratory Fish Stocks, UN Doc. A/CONF.164/37, 34 I.L.M. 1542 (1995) [hereinafter Straddling Fish Stocks Treaty, described in more detail *infra* notes 29 & 51–60 and accompanying text].

29. *Id.*
30. Law of the Sea Convention, *supra* note 4, pt. XI.
31. *See generally* Jon Van Dyke & Christopher Yuen, *"Common Heritage" v. "Freedom of the High Seas": Which Governs the Seabed?*, 19 SAN DIEGO L. REV. 493–551 (1982); also published in THE LAW OF THE SEA AND OCEAN DEVELOPMENT ISSUES IN THE PACIFIC BASIN, 206–76 (E. Miles & S. Allen eds., Law of the Sea Institute 1983).
32. Agreement Relating to the Implementation of Part XI of the United Nations Convention of the Law of the Sea of 10 December 1982, U.N. G.A. Res. 48/263 (28 July 1994).
33. Section 1 of the Annex to the Part XI Agreement says, for instance, that "all organs and subsidiary bodies to be established under the Convention and this Agreement shall be cost-effective" and that the creation of such organs "shall be based on an evolutionary approach." Section 2(3) states that "[t]he obligation of States Parties to fund one mine site of the Enterprise . . . shall not apply." Other provisions in the Annex state that the provisions of Articles 151(1–7) and (9), 155(1) and (3–4), 161(1), 161(8)(b) and (c), 162(2)(j) and (q), 165(2)(n), and Annex III, Articles 5, 6(5), and 7 of the Law of the Sea Convention "shall not apply."
34. *Id.*
35. Part XI Agreement, *supra* note 32, annex, sec. 1(6)(ii).
36. Some of the material that follows is updated from Jon M. Van Dyke, *Giving Teeth to the Environmental Obligations in the LOS Convention*, in OCEANS MANAGEMENT IN THE 21ST CENTURY: INSTITUTIONAL FRAMEWORKS AND RESPONSES 167–86 (A. G. Oude Elferink & D. R. Rothwell eds., 2004).
37. *The M/V Saiga Case (Saint Vincent and the Grenadines v. Guinea)* (ITLOS July 1, 1999), http://www.un.org/Depts/los/ITLOS/Saiga_cases.htm (Mar. 22, 2000).
38. *Id.* paras. 127 & 129 (citing art. 60(2) of the Convention).
39. *Id.* para. 131.
40. *Southern Bluefin Tuna Case (Australia and New Zealand v. Japan)*, Provisional Measures Order (ITLOS Aug. 27, 1999), http://www.itlos.org/start2_en.html; Award on Jurisdiction and Admissibility, Aug. 4, 2000, http://www.worldbank.org/icsid/bluefintuna/award080400.pdf.
41. *Id.* ITLOS Provisional Order, paras. 77, 79, 80 (emphasis added).
42. Alexander Yankov, *Irregularities in Fishing Activities and the Role of the International Tribunal for the Law of the Sea*, in NISUKE ANDO, EDWARD MCWHINNEY & RUDIGER WOLFRUM (EDS.), LIBER AMICORUM JUDGE SHIGERU ODA (Kluwer Law International, The Hague, 2002).
43. *Southern Bluefin Tuna Case, supra* note 40, Separate Opinion of Judge Treves, para. 9; *see also* Separate Opinion of Judge Shearer ("the measures ordered by the Tribunal are rightly based upon considerations deriving from a precautionary approach").
44. Leah Sturtz, *Southern Bluefin Tuna Case: Australia and New Zealand v. Japan*, 28 ECOLOGY L.Q. 455, 459 (2001); *see generally* Tom Placheck, *Experimental Catches and the Precautionary Approach: The Southern Bluefin Tuna Dispute*, 26 MARINE POL'Y 283–94 (2002).
45. *The MOX Plant Case (Ireland v. U.K.)* (ITLOS Dec. 3, 2001), 41 I.L.M. 405 (2002).
46. *The Volga Case (Russian Federation v. Australia)* (ITLOS Dec. 23, 2002), http://www.itlos.org/start2_en.html (May 23, 2003).
47. *Id.* para. 73.
48. *Id.* para. 77. Australia had also sought to obtain, as a condition of the release of the vessel, the "particulars about the owner and ultimate beneficial owners of the ship," but the Tribunal ruled that obtaining such information was not a proper function of the bonding process. *See id.* para. 75.
49. *Id.* para. 68.

50. *Id.* paras. 77, 80. Judge David Anderson and Ad Hoc Judge Ivan Shearer dissented from this ruling. Judge Anderson explained that "the duty of the coastal State to ensure the conservation of the living resources of the EEZ contained in article 61 of the Convention, as well as the obligations of Contracting Parties to CCAMLR to protect the Antarctic ecosystem" justified the good behavior bond, particularly in light of the "clear risk of the *Volga* re-joining this fleet [fishing in the Antarctic region] immediately or shortly after its release." *Id.* para. 2 & 22(b).

51. Some of the material in this section is adapted and updated from Jon M. Van Dyke, *The Straddling and Migratory Stocks Agreement and the Pacific,* 11 Int'l J. Marine & Coastal L. 406 (1996).

52. Straddling Fish Stocks Treaty, *supra* note 28. *See generally* Jameson E. Colburn, Comment, *Turbot Wars: Straddling Stocks, Regime Theory, and a New U.N. Agreement,* 6 J. Transnat'l L. & Pol'y 323 (1997); Derrick M. Kedziora, *Gunboat Diplomacy in the Northwest Atlantic: The 1995 Canada-EU Fishing Dispute and the United Nations Agreement on Straddling and Migratory Fish Stocks,* 17 Nw. J. Int'l L. & Bus. 1132 (1996–97); Moritaka Hayashi, *The 1995 Agreement on the Conservation and Management of Straddling and Highly Migratory Fish Stocks: Significance for the Law of the Sea Convention,* 29 Ocean & Coastal Mgmt. 51 (1996); Moritaka Hayashi, *Enforcement by Non-Flag States on the High Seas Under the 1995 Agreement on Straddling and Highly Migratory Fish Stocks,* 9 Geo. Int'l Envtl. L. Rev. 1 (1996); David A. Balton, *Strengthening the Law of the Sea: The New Agreement on Straddling Fish Stocks and Highly Migratory Fish Stocks,* 27 Ocean Dev. & Int'l L. 125 (1996); Julie R. Mack, Comment, *International Fisheries Management: How the U.S. Conference on Straddling and Highly Migratory Fish Stocks Changes the Law of Fishing on the High Seas,* 26 Cal. W. Int'l L. J. 313 (1996); Mark Christopherson, Note, *Toward a Rational Harvest: The United Nations Agreement on Straddling Fish Stocks and Highly Migratory Species,* 5 Minn. J. Global Trade 357 (1996).

53. http://www.un.org/Depts/los/convention_agreements/convention_overview_fish_stocks.htm. (last visited Dec. 3, 2006).

54. Rosemary Rayfuse, *To Our Children's Children's Children: From Promoting to Achieving Compliance in High Seas Fisheries,* 20 Int'l J. Marine & Coastal L. 509, 525 (2005).

55. *Id.*

56. Michael W. Lodge & Satya N. Nandan, *Some Suggestions Towards Better Implementation of the United Nations Agreement on Straddling Fish Stocks and Highly Migratory Fish Stocks of 1995,* 20 Int'l J. Marine & Coastal L. 345, 374 (2005).

57. *See generally* Jon M. Van Dyke, *The Evolution and International Acceptance of the Precautionary Principle,* in Bringing New Law to Ocean Waters 357–79 (David D. Caron & Harry N. Scheiber eds., 2004).

58. David Freestone, *The Precautionary Principle,* in International Law and Global Climate Change 21, 36 (Robin Churchill & David Freestone eds., 1991).

59. Fishing to attain the maximum sustainable yield inevitably means reducing the abundance of a stock, sometimes by one-half or two-thirds. This reduction can threaten the stock in unforeseeable ways and also will impact on other species in the ecosystem.

60. Nations already have the power to board, inspect, and arrest vessels violating laws established to "control and manage the living resources in the exclusive economic zone." Law of the Sea Convention, *supra* note 4, art. 73(1).

61. The Convention on the Conservation and Management of Highly Migratory Fish Stocks in the Western and Central Pacific Ocean, Honolulu, Sept. 4, 2000, http://www.wcpfc.int; *see generally* Violanda Botet, *Filling in One of the Last Pieces of the Ocean: Regulating Tuna in the Western and Central Pacific Ocean,* 41 Va. J. Int'l L. 787–813 (2001).

62. Law of the Sea Convention, *supra* note 4, art. 64; *see generally* Jon Van Dyke & Susan Heftel, *Tuna Management in the Pacific: An Analysis of the South Pacific Forum Fisheries Agency,* 3 U. Haw. L. Rev. 1, 11–17 (1981).

63. Straddling Fish Stocks Treaty, *supra* note 28.

64. Press Release, President George W. Bush, Message to the United States Senate Regarding WCPF Convention (May 16, 2005), available at http://www.whitehouse.gov/news/releases/2005/05/20050516-7.html (visited Sept. 4, 2005).

65. 151 CONG. REC. S D990 (daily ed. Sept. 29, 2005).

66. Some of the material that follows is updated from Jon M. Van Dyke, *Military Ships and Planes Operating in the Exclusive Economic Zone of Another Country*, 28 MARINE POL'Y 29–39 (2004).

67. In November 1990, a Brazilian judge ordered a U.S. submarine out of Brazil's EEZ, ruling that it posed environmental danger because it was nuclear powered. *Judge Orders US Sub Out of Brazilian Waters*, HONOLULU ADVERTISER, Nov. 5, 1990, at D1.

68. When Germany ratified the Convention in 1994, it filed the following declaration: "According to the Convention, the coastal State does not enjoy residual rights in the exclusive economic zone. In particular, the rights and jurisdiction of the coastal States in such zone do not include the right to obtain notification of military exercises or maneoeuvres or to authorize them." Italy, the Netherlands, and the U.K. filed similar declarations.

69. Charter of the United Nations, June 26, 1945, 59 Stat. 1031, T.S. No. 993, 3 Bevans 1153.

70. Article 103 of the U.N. Charter says that if a country's obligations under the U.N. Charter are inconsistent with its obligations under any other treaty, the "obligations under the present Charter shall prevail."

71. Also relevant is Article 301 of the Law of the Sea Convention, which says that: "In exercising their rights and performing their duties under this Convention, State Parties shall refrain from any threat or use of force against the territorial integrity or political independence of any State, or in any other manner inconsistent with principles of international law embodied in the Charter of the United Nations."

72. The duty to consult is a seminal principle of international law found, for instance, in Principle 19 of the Rio Declaration on Environment and Development, June 14, 1992, U.N. Doc. A/CONF.151/5/Rev.1 (1992), 31 I.L.M. 874 (1992), which says: "States shall provide prior and timely notification and relevant information to potentially affected States on Activities that may have a significant adverse transboundary environmental effect and shall consult with those States at an early stage and in good faith." *See also Lac Lanoux Arbitration*, 24 I.L.R. 101 (1957) (requiring France to consult in good faith with Spain over riparian rights); *MOX Plant Case (Ireland v. United Kingdom)* (ITLOS Dec. 2001) (requiring the United Kingdom to consult in good faith with Ireland over the pollution issues created by the Sellafield nuclear reprocessing plant, including the exchange of information about the risks, monitoring the emissions and their effect on the marine environment of the Irish Sea, and working together to reduce these risks).

73. *See* Michele Wallace, *The Right of Warships to Operate in the Exclusive Economic Zone as Perceived by Delegates to the Third United Nations Law of the Sea Convention*, in INTERNATIONAL NAVIGATION: ROCKS AND SHOALS AHEAD? 345, 346–47 (Jon M. Van Dyke, Lewis M. Alexander & Joseph R. Morgan eds., 1988).

74. *Id.* at 347 (citing Third United Nations Conference on the Law of the Sea, 2 OR (3d Sess. Geneva) (30th mtg.) 28 (1975)).

75. *See, e.g., id.* (quoting U.S. delegate T. Vincent Learson, who said "[t]he term 'peaceful purposes' did not, of course, preclude military activities generally. The United States had consistently held that the conduct of military activities for peaceful purposes was in full accord with the Charter of the United Nations and with principles of international law." Third United Nations Conference on the Law of the Sea. 5 OR (4th Sess. New York) (67th mtg.) 62 (1976)).

76. *See, e.g.,* Vienna Convention on the Law of Treaties, May 23, 1969, U.N. Doc. A/CONF. 39/27, art. 31(3)(b), recognizing the importance of "any subsequent practice in the application of the treaty which establishes the agreement of the parties regarding its interpretation."

77. TULLIO SCOVAZZI, THE EVOLUTION OF INTERNATIONAL LAW OF THE SEA: NEW ISSUES, NEW CHALLENGES 162, 163–64 (The Hague: Martinus Nijhoff Publishers 2001) (reprinted from Volume 286 of Recueil des Cours).

78. SAN DIEGO UNION TRIB., Feb. 3, 2004, http://www.signonsandiego.com/news/northcounty/20040203-1311-nuclear.html.

79. Chile's Law for Nuclear Safety, Law No. 18.302, art. 4, originally promulgated Apr. 16, 1984, and amended pursuant to Law No. 19.825 on Oct. 1, 2002.

80. *Id.* art. 4(II).

81. Associated Press, *Nuke Waste Move Plan Hits Snag,* CBSNEWS.COM, Nov. 5, 2003.

82. *Id.* "Although we recognize that advance notification of coastal states is not required, we consider it to be an important element in preparation for contingencies," Robert A. McGuire, the U.S. Department of Transportation associate administrator for hazardous materials, wrote in an Oct. 17, 2003, letter. "It may be necessary to seek shelter in waters of a coastal state." McGuire's letter also noted that Southern California Edison had made no arrangements for emergency equipment, such as cranes, backup tugs, or salvage vessels.

83. *Id.* (quoting McGuire's Oct. 17, 2003, letter as saying: "Given that your transport is entirely over open ocean, your proposal to salvage only in water up to 300 feet appears insufficient.").

84. *"Significant" Issues Delay Reactor's Move,* SAN DIEGO UNION TRIB., Nov. 21, 2003; referring to letter of John A. Dooley, Acting Director, Office of Nuclear Energy Affairs, U.S. Dept. of State, to Robert A. McGuire, Associate Administrator for Hazardous Material Safety, Research & Special Programs Administration, U.S. Dept. of Transportation, Nov. 4, 2003.

85. H. G. Reza, *Edison Cleared to Ship San Onofre Reactor,* L.A. TIMES, Dec. 3, 2003.

86. Dan Weikel & Hector Tobar, *Argentina Limits Reactor Route,* L.A. TIMES, Jan. 16, 2004.

87. Basel Convention on the Control of Transboundary Movements of Hazardous Wastes and Their Disposal, signed at Basel Mar. 22, 1989, UNEP Doc. T/BSL/000, 28 I.L.M. 657 (1989) (entered into force May 5, 1992). For a discussion of the applicability of the Basel Convention to radioactive wastes, *see* Jon M. Van Dyke, *Applying the Precautionary Principle to Ocean Shipments of Radioactive Materials,* 38 OCEAN DEV. & INT'L L. 379, 383–85 (1996).

88. Weikel & Tobar, *supra* note 86.

89. Statement of Toichi Sakata, Director of the Japanese Science & Technology Agency's Nuclear Fuel Division, to participants in the Asia-Pacific Forum on Sea Shipments of Japanese Plutonium, Tokyo (Oct. 6, 1992).

90. *See* Van Dyke, *Precautionary Principle, supra* note 87, at 386–87.

91. Letter from Don McKinnon, New Zealand Minister of Foreign Affairs & Trade, to Michael Szabo, July 7, 1999 (on file with author).

92. *See, e.g.,* Emma Daly, *After Oil Spill, Spain and France Impose Strict Tanker Inspections,* N.Y. TIMES, Nov. 27, 2002, at A5, col. 3. Earlier, France had banned vessels over 1,600 tons from coming within seven nautical miles of the coast around Cherbourg and Brest, to protect the fragile coastal environment. Robert Nadelson, *After MOX: The Contemporary Shipment of Radioactive Substances in the Law of the Sea,* 15 INT'L J. MARINE & COASTAL L.193, 224 n. 189 (2000) (citing Joint Prefectorial Decree 326 Cherbourg/18/81 Brest of May 13, 1981).

93. Interview with Kristina Gjerde, High Seas Policy Advisor to IUCN, Paris, Nov. 12, 2003.

94. Press release from Government of Morocco, Jan. 23, 2003.

95. Marlise Simons, *France Clamps Down on Shipping Pollution,* N.Y. TIMES, Apr. 7, 2003, at A8.

96. *Id.*

97. Interview with Kristina Gjerde, *supra* note 93.

98. IMO Resolution MSC.85(70) (Dec. 3, 1998), *discussed in* Lt. Rachel Cantry (U.S. Coast Guard), *The Coast Guard and Environmental Protection,* 52:4 NAVAL WAR C. REV. 77 (Autumn 1999).

99. IMO Resolution MSC 52(66) (May 30, 1996) (Torres Strait between Australia and Papua New Guinea, the inner route of Australia's Great Barrier Reef, and the area adjacent to France's Ouessant (Ushant) islet); IMO Resolution MSC.63(67) (Dec. 3, 1996) (Denmark's Great Belt Traffic Area, the Strait of Gibraltar, and the area off of Finisterre on

the Spanish coast); IMO Resolution MSC.73(69)(May 29, 1998) (the Strait of Bonifacio between Corsica (France) and Sardinia (Italy) and also through the Straits of Malacca and Singapore); IMO Resolution MSC.85(70) (Dec. 3, 1998) (the Strait of Dover/Pas de Calais).

100. *See, e.g.,* Myres McDougal & Norbert Schlei, *The Hydrogen Bomb Tests in Perspective: Lawful Measures for Security,* 64 YALE L.J. 648, 659–60 (1955).

101. Some of the material that follows is updated from Jon M. Van Dyke, *Balancing Navigational Freedom with Environmental and Security Concerns,* 15 COLO. J. ENVTL. L. & POL'Y 2003 Y.B. 19–28 (2004).

102. Kenneth R. Weiss & Tony Perry, *Navy's Use of Sonar OK'd Despite Risk to Whales,* L.A. TIMES, July 16, 2002, at A1; Marc Kaufman, *Navy Cleared to Use a Sonar Despite Fears of Injuring Whales,* WASH. POST, July 16, 2002, at A3; 2002 WL 23853879.

103. Nine Cuvier's beaked whales were found dead on Sept. 24–25, 2002, on the Canary Islands of Fuerteventura and Lanzarote. Six beached whales were pushed back into the sea, and another two were seen floating lifeless in coastal waters. Ships from Belgium, Canada, France, Germany, Greece, Norway, Portugal, Turkey, the United Kingdom, and the United States were conducting a multinational exercise known as Neo Tapon 2002 designed to practice securing the Strait of Gibraltar. The Cuvier's beaked whale is a toothed cetacean that ranges from five to eight meters in length. Jerome Socolovsky, *Investigation Points to NATO Exercise in Mass Whale Beaching,* ASSOCIATED PRESS, Oct. 10, 2002, http://www .enn.com/news/wire-stories/2002/10/10102002/ap_4866.

104. Seventeen whales of four different species, including Cuvier's beaked whales and two minke whales, and a dolphin were stranded in the Bahamas in March 2000 as a result of tactical mid-frequency sonar transmitted from U.S. Navy vessels, which were thought to have reached the whales at the 165 decibel level. Scientists found hemorrhaging around the brain and ear bones of the beached cetaceans, injuries consistent with exposure to extremely loud sounds. The U.S. Navy admitted that these strandings "were most likely caused by its [mid-range] sonar transmissions." *Center for Biological Diversity v. National Science Foundation,* No. C02-5065, 2002 WL 31548073 (N.D. Cal. Temporary Restraining Order, 30 Oct. 2002), slip op. at 8.

105. Twelve Cuvier's beaked whales were stranded in the Mediterranean near Greece at a time that coincided temporally and geographically with "sound detecting system trials" of LFAS by the NATO research vessel *Alliance.* The whales were exposed to sound transmitted from at least 25 kilometers away, which was determined to have reached them at the level of 150–160 decibels after 238 four-second pings of sound were released, which caused severe tissue damage to their ear cavities. U.S. Dept. of Commerce and Secretary of the Navy, *Joint Interim Report Bahamas Marine Mammal Stranding Event of 15–16 March 2000* (Dec. 2001), http://www.nmfs.noaa.gov/prot_res/overview/Interim_Bahamas_ Report.pdf.

106. M. P. Simmonds & L. F. Lopez-Jurado, *Whales and the Military,* 351 NATURE 448 (June 6, 1991).

107. Although the Navy refuses to release the maximum source level of SURTASS LFA, claiming it to be classified information, reports indicate the maximum source level to be 230 dB re: 1μPa at 1 m, *Quiet Please. Whales Navigating,* ECONOMIST, Mar. 7, 1998, at 85; Alexandros Frantis, *Does Military Testing Strand Whales?* 352 NATURE 29 (Mar. 5, 1998).

108. Because of the way sound is measured and the different speed that sound travels through water, as compared to land, it is estimated that "underwater sound pressure levels numerically are about 61.5 dB greater than sound pressure levels in air for an equal intensity." Robert C. Gisiner, Proceedings, Workshop on the Effects of Anthropogenic Noise in the Marine Environment, 10–12 Feb. 1998 (Marine Mammal Science Program, Office of Naval Research, 1988) 24. In other words, sound measured at 131 dB in water would have the same pressure impact as sound measured at 70 dB on land. 60 dB on land is the sound

generated by freeway traffic. Continuous exposure above 85 dB (on land) is likely to degrade the hearing of most humans. "Deafening" noise (on land) begins at 110 dB, with 120 dB measuring a hard rock band, 130 dB being the point at which pain is registered, and 140 dB being the point adjacent to a jet engine. The 180 dB (in water) figure said by the Navy to be "safe" for cetaceans would thus affect them at about the same extent as human hearing would be affected by standing next to a hard rock band at a rock concert, if we can assume that the hearing system of cetaceans is roughly comparable to ours.

109. *See* Natural Res. Def. Council v. Evans, 232 F. Supp. 2d 1003, 1021, 1033–34 (N.D. Cal. 2002) (Opinion and Order Granting Plaintiffs' Motion for a Preliminary Injunction).

110. *Id.* at 1033–34.

111. *Natural Res. Def. Council v. Evans,* 232 F. Supp. 2d at 1053. The four statutes are the Marine Mammal Protection Act of 1972, 16 U.S.C. § 1361 (2003); the National Environmental Protection Act of 1969, 42 U.S.C. § 4332 (2003); the Endangered Species Act of 1973, 16 U.S.C. § 1531 (2003); and the Administrative Procedure Act of 1940, 5 U.S.C. § 551 (2003).

112. *Id.* Although Magistrate Judge LaPorte found that the Navy's activities violated four federal statute, she accepted the testimony of the NMFS experts regarding the impact of LFAS on marine mammals over the sharply conflicting testimony presented by the Natural Resources Defense Counsel. Judge LaPorte wrote, "The law is clear . . . that when qualified experts on both sides reach carefully reasoned but different conclusions, the Court must defer to the agency's experts . . ." *Id.* at 1017. Other U.S. courts dealing with ocean environmental issues have taken a more skeptical view of the scientific opinions offered by U.S. agencies. *See, e.g.,* Natural Res. Def. Counsel v. Daley, 209 F.3d 747, 755, 754 (D.C. Cir. 2000) (explaining that courts "do not hear cases merely to rubber stamp agency actions" and criticizing the agency's scientific conclusions as ones that could only be correct in "Superman Comics' Bizarro world, where reality is turned upside down"); Greenpeace v. Nat'l Marine Fisheries Serv., 106 F. Supp. 2d 1066 (W.D. Wash. 2000) (where the court treated the views of the two sides' experts as having equal credibility and issued the injunction sought by plaintiffs despite the contrary testimony of the agency's experts).

113. David Kravets, *U.S. Navy Agrees to Temporarily Limit Testing of New Sonar System amid Marine Life Concerns,* ASSOCIATED PRESS, Nov. 18, 2002.

114. *Court Order Blocks Whale Killing in Gulf of California* (Oct. 29, 2002), http://www.endangeredearth.org/alerts/result.asp?index=1210 (Nov. 2, 2002) (summarizing issuance of temporary restraining order by Magistrate Judge James Larson in the case of *Center for Biological Diversity v. National Science Foundation,* No. C2-5065 JL (N.D. Cal. Oct. 31, 2002)).

115. Haw. County Green Party v. Evans, No. C-03-0078-SC (N.D. Cal., Order Granting Permanent Injunction, Jan. 24, 2003).

116. *Id.* slip op. at 24.

117. W. J. RICHARDSON ET AL., MARINE MAMMALS AND NOISE 544 (1995).

118. H. M. Dotinga & A. G. Oude Elferink, *Acoustic Pollution in the Oceans: The Search for Legal Standards,* 31 OCEAN DEV. & INT'L L. 151, 158 (2000).

119. *See* Christopher W. Clark, Peter Tyack, & William T. Ellison, *Quicklook, Low-Frequency Sound Scientific Research Program, Phase I: Responses of Blue and Fin Whales to SURTASS LFA, Southern California Bight,* 5 September–21 October, 1997 at 30–31 (Feb. 27, 1998), fig. 28; Peter Tyack & Christopher Clark, *Quicklook Phase II, Playback of Low-Frequency Sound to Gray Whales Migrating Past the Central California Coast,* Jan. 1998 at 22–25 (June 23, 1998).

chapter thirteen

Offshore Energy Development

Milo C. Mason

I. Introduction

The Outer Continental Shelf Lands Act of 1953 (OCSLA),[1] as variously and some-times quite extensively amended, constitutes the basis of U.S. ocean energy law. Pres-idential policy preferences have, since 1945 when President Truman declared that the Outer Continental Shelf (OCS) belonged to the United States, influenced—if not largely formed—the basis of U.S. ocean energy policy, while coastal states and envi-ronmental groups have tempered and, in some instances and areas, fully thwarted efforts at equitably balanced or aggressive federal offshore oil and gas programs.

A number of significant events have played a role in shaping the manner in which those policies have been carried out. The Santa Barbara Channel oil spill off the Cali-fornia shore in 1969 galvanized considerable opposition to offshore oil and gas devel-opment and resulted eventually in the process-laden and environmentally focused 1978 amendments to the OCSLA and the Coastal Zone Management Act (CZMA). The oil embargo of 1973 added to the scope and pace of lease sale plans contained in the 1978 amendments. The *Exxon Valdez* oil spill of 1989 provided a new impetus for offshore environmental safeguards and for coastal states' increased voice in fed-eral offshore lease sales.

The author expresses his appreciation to Emily Morris for invaluable legal research, Sylvia Murphy for editing, and Darryl Francois for searching MMS sources. Any errors or omissions are solely the fault of the author. The views and opinions herein are the author's only and not in any way necessarily reflect or represent the position of the Office of the Solicitor, the Depart-ment of the Interior, or the Minerals Management Service.

This chapter briefly surveys the major components and processes of the evolving OCSLA and presents the current status of its regulatory regime and its scope in the context of past litigation, presidential policy history, and congressional budget actions. Lastly, it proposes a possible solution to the existing failures of the OCSLA to achieve one of its stated purposes—that of balanced, equitable, and expeditious exploration and development among all the oil- and gas-bearing regions of the OCS.

II. The Current State of the Law

A. The Evolution of the OCSLA

After President Truman proclaimed the U.S. continental shelf, its seabed, and its resources subject to national jurisdiction and dominion, and after the Supreme Court in several cases brought by Truman's Attorney General on behalf of the United States held that paramount rights in the continental shelf and its valuable resources rested with the national government and not with any adjacent state,[2] coastal state rights became an issue in the 1952 presidential election. What later emerged from Congress were two companion laws that President Eisenhower signed in 1953—the Submerged Lands Act (SLA)[3] and the OCSLA.[4] Those two laws initiated the U.S. ocean energy program. As Chapter 1 more fully spells out, the SLA gave the first three miles of continental shelf (that of the traditional territorial sea of the time) to the coastal states; the remaining continental shelf, the "outer" continental shelf, remained within the national dominion. The OCSLA lodged the management of the OCS with the Secretary of the Department of the Interior (Secretary) and directed the Secretary to offer for lease the minerals contained in it, with the revenues generated going to the U.S. treasury. The law stated in its policy goal that "[i]n order to meet the urgent need for further exploration and development of the oil and gas deposits of the submerged lands of the outer continental shelf, the secretary is authorized to [manage and lease it]."

The only explicitly stated environmental standard in the 1953 statute was that exploration activities were to be conducted "without undue harm to the environment." Lease sales occurred at a somewhat leisurely pace from 1954 to 1973—almost annually in the Gulf of Mexico, except for 1956, 1957, and 1958, and just occasionally offshore California and in two other areas in the 1960s. The oil embargo of 1973 changed much of the thinking behind that leisurely pace, and yet the earlier 1969 Santa Barbara oil spill publicized the potential risks of offshore drilling and the shortcomings of the 1953 general delegation of almost unfettered discretionary authority to the Secretary.

After over five years of hearings and drafting, Congress enacted and President Carter signed the 1978 amendments to the OCSLA. These amendments changed the delegation to the Secretary in several important ways without changing the overall approach of federal management of private sector development for the benefit of the federal treasury. The newly revised OCSLA declared that "the Outer continental shelf is a vital national resource held by the federal government for the public, which should be made available for expeditious and orderly development, subject to environmental safeguards, in a manner consistent with the maintenance of competition and other national needs."[5] It authorized new bidding systems and lease terms and profit sharing arrangements. It mandated a planning process in five-year chunks for lease sales that gave considerable notice and comment opportunities to coastal states and the public. The 1978 amendments provided lease cancellation and buy-back criteria and authorization for both producing and nonproducing leases. The new law also separated exploration from development by staged reviews and explicitly layered into the planning and approval schemes all other applicable federal laws, especially the environmental ones.

Other features of the 1978 amendments included increased civil and criminal penalties for violations of its provisions and secretarial orders issued under it; citizen suits; authorization for coastal states to have a greater voice in the planning and leasing process (Sections 18 and 19) and in the approval process (through the CZMA[6]) and a financial stake in the second three miles of continental shelf to account for any drainage of state resources (Section 8(g)); and a prohibition on the export of OCS oil and gas.[7] Important regulatory measures included an allowance for royalty in kind; required government access to company geologic and geophysical data; conservation and diligence standards; and an oil-spill liability fund and a fisherman's contingency fund. Finally, the 1978 amendments authorized environmental studies, mandated best available and safest technology (BAST), and sought expeditious, balanced, and equitable exploration and development throughout the entire U.S. OCS. As discussed later in this chapter, this last goal of the OCSLA has yet to be realized.

While the equitable sharing of risks posed by offshore oil and gas development appears set aside by current congressional moratoria and Presidential withdrawals under Section 12 of the OCSLA,[8] expeditious development has occurred at least in the central and western Gulf of Mexico. The Gulf now provides about thirty percent of our nation's oil and twenty-five percent of its natural gas. This ocean energy production generates about $8 billion a year to the federal treasury and to states and coastal communities through their share of the Section 8(g) revenue and a portion of the land and water conservation fund which, when appropriated by Congress, gets distributed throughout the nation. Both the East and West Coasts of the United States are currently off limits to OCS leasing and development by both congressional moratoria and Presidential withdrawal.

The Gulf of Mexico now provides about thirty percent of our nation's oil and twenty-five percent of its natural gas.

B. OCSLA Nuts and Bolts

The Secretary of the Interior has considerable discretion and many duties under the OCSLA. The Secretary oversees the OCS oil and gas program and must balance orderly resource development with protection of the human, marine, and coastal environments while simultaneously ensuring that the public receives an equitable return for these resources and that free market competition is maintained. The Secretary must prepare a five-year oil and gas leasing program and may offer leases only in areas included in the five-year plan. The five-year program must go through an elaborate four-stage public notice process that must result from consideration of almost every aspect of the offshore environment and the risks posed by the proposed program.[9] The planned lease sales are held only after further National Environmental Policy Act (NEPA), CZMA, and affected state reviews of a proposed notice of sale, which is announced in the *Federal Register* and indicates what tracts or "blocks" (no more than 5,260 acres or three miles square) are available for lease. The final notice of sale contains the terms and conditions for the lease sale and any lease issued as a result of the sale. The lease sale is by competitive, sealed bidding.[10] Each bid is opened and announced in public. The high bid on each tract offered is reviewed for sufficiency and rejected if found not to provide fair value. Bidders must provide twenty percent of their cash bonus bid upfront by electronic transfer and provide information on the geological and geophysical data on which their bid relied. If the bid is considered sufficient, the bidder must transfer the remaining eighty percent of the bid amount, and the lease is issued usually for a five-year time period in shallow water, ten years in deep water or frontier areas, and thereafter as long as paying production occurs, subject to the terms and conditions specified in the sale notice and "all applicable laws now and hereinafter in effect." While the OCSLA authorizes several bidding systems and royalty arrangements, the prevalent and now almost routine method is by cash bonus bid and a fixed royalty rate (normally 16.67 percent for shallow water leases and 12.5 percent for deeper water but recently raised to 16.7 in 2007). OCS leases specify a minimum (usually fixed but sometimes escalating) annual rental until production begins.

The Secretary has delegated most offshore management matters to the Minerals Management Service (MMS), a secretarially created bureau at Interior. In its ministerial role, MMS has three core objectives: safe offshore operations, environmental protection, and fair value for the lease rights conveyed.[11]

1. Five-Year Program

Section 18 of the OCSLA states that the Secretary must prepare and maintain an OCS leasing program schedule "which he determines will best meet national energy needs for the five-year period following its approval or reapproval,"[12] and that

> Management of the outer Continental Shelf shall be conducted in a manner which considers economic, social, and environmental values of the renewable and nonrenewable resources contained in the outer Continental Shelf, and the potential impact of oil and gas exploration on the other resource values of the outer Continental Shelf, and the marine, coastal, and human environments.[13]

Section 18 lists eight considerations and three balancing calculations for determining the size, timing, and location for the scheduled lease sales.[14] These considerations and calculations outnumber the six specified congressional policy declarations announced in the beginning of the OCSLA.[15] In all, they convey that the OCSLA intends a careful and detailed analysis at least every five years, which rationally weighs the relative merits of our nation's energy needs and the potential benefit versus harm from OCS oil and gas development amongst all the nation's OCS areas and that the OCSLA intends an expeditious and orderly inventory and development with equitable sharing of the risks posed for the benefits gained among all the OCS regions. No lease sale may be held and no lease issued unless the lease area was included in the five-year program.[16]

The Secretary must review the five-year program at least yearly.[17] This yearly review requires the Secretary to redetermine if the program still meets the specified goals set forth in the OCSLA.

The first three five-year programs were challenged in court; the three thereafter escaped any litigation.[18] While the program may be challenged in the Court of Appeals for the District of Columbia only,[19] and reviewed solely on the record made before the Secretary, the program may not be enjoined,[20] and will be upheld if the Secretary's factual findings were based on substantial evidence on the record as a whole[21] and the policy choices are rational. In *California v. Watt* (the Secretary Watt proposal),[22] the court transformed the statutory "substantial evidence" standard for the five-year program basically into an Administrative Procedure Act "arbitrary and capricious" standard for the policy choices during the first legal challenge to a five-year program. For the most part, the Court of Appeals has deferred to the Secretaries' findings, as demonstrated by *California v. Watt* (the Secretary Andrus proposal)[23] and *California v. Watt* (the Secretary Watt proposal).[24] The five-year programs have scheduled as many as thirty-seven lease sales in twenty-two of the twenty-six planning areas and as few as sixteen sales in eight planning areas. The 2007–2012 program includes twenty-one sales in eight areas.[25]

2. Prelease Sale Process

a. Generally

The MMS publishes a Call for Information and the Notice of Intent to Prepare an Environmental Impact Statement (EIS) in the *Federal Register.* NEPA scoping for what issues to address in the EIS and what alternatives and mitigation measures should be considered occurs both formally and informally through public meetings, newspaper notices, mailings, and on the Internet. MMS solicits federal, state, and local agencies and any other interested parties to send comments on what should be considered for a lease sale or series of lease sales. Because of the same area, similar nature, and nearly identical resources, MMS started in the mid-1990s to consider and publish multisale EISs for the central and western Gulf of Mexico. The NEPA process for subsequent annual lease sales then may be more able to focus on and address in more depth any changes in resources or impacts resulting from the same or nearly same proposed lease sale of the remaining tracts in the area-wide sale.[26]

MMS conducts early coordination with appropriate federal and state agencies and other interest groups to meet and discuss the proposed lease sales. Key agencies and organizations include the National Oceanic and Atmospheric Administration's

National Marine Fisheries Service (NOAA Fisheries), U.S. Fish and Wildlife Service (FWS), the U.S. Department of Defense (DOD), U.S. Coast Guard (USCG), U.S. Environmental Protection Agency (EPA), state governors' offices, and citizen and industry groups. An area decision then occurs and describes the geographical areas of the proposed action and any alternatives to it, as well as mitigation measures and issues for analysis in the NEPA consideration documents.

The publication of the Draft EIS initiates a normally sixty-day public review and comment period. A Notice of Availability is published in the *Federal Register*, mailed out, and posted on the MMS website. Copies of the Draft EIS are sent to federal, state, and local agencies; libraries; industry; special interest groups; and private individuals. Formal public hearings on the Draft EIS and the proposed actions are held in the affected coastal states during the comment period. Written or electronic comments are accepted until the close of the comment period. MMS must consider the comments and usually revises the Draft EIS accordingly. The publication of a Final EIS initiates a thirty-day comment period. After the end of that comment period, the Department reviews the Final EIS and all comments received on both the Draft and Final EISs. The Assistant Secretary of the Interior for Land and Minerals then decides which proposed alternative to implement.

At the same time as the preparation of the Final EIS for the lease sale, MMS does a consistency review under the CZMA and prepares a Consistency Determination (CD). This OCS sale CD requirement came about when Congress chose to overrule the Supreme Court's decision that lease sales, by themselves, did not directly affect coastal zones of states under the 1972 CZMA.[27] For presale consistency determinations, MMS reviews each affected state's coastal zone management program, analyzes the potential impacts to the coastal zone management program, and makes an assessment of consistency with the policies of each state's program identified by the state as enforceable. If a state disagrees with MMS's CD, the CZMA requires the state to do the following: (1) indicate how the MMS presale proposal is inconsistent with their coastal program; (2) suggest alternative measures to bring the MMS proposal into consistency with their coastal program; or (3) describe the need for additional information that would allow a determination of consistency. Unlike the consistency process for specific OCS plans and permits, no procedure exists for an administrative appeal to the Secretary of Commerce for federal agency consistency determinations for federal presale activities. Either MMS or the state may request mediation. Mediation is voluntary, and the Department of Commerce would serve as the mediator. Whether there is mediation or not, the final consistency determination is made by the Department of the Interior and is the final administrative action for the presale consistency process.[28]

A Final Notice of Sale is published in the *Federal Register* at least thirty days prior to the scheduled lease sale. The Final Notice announces the deadline to submit bids and the time and place of bid opening, and identifies the terms, stipulations, and conditions of the leases offered and the specific configuration of the proposed sale. Lease sale stipulations and specific royalty terms or tract-specific conditions, considered a normal part of an OCS lessee's duties and the OCS operating regime, provide a more nimble and geographically focused manner to regulate lease conduct than the C.F.R. regulations. Compliance with lease stipulations, terms, and conditions is mandatory and a part of the lease.

Once bids are opened and read in public, MMS reviews only the valid high bid for each tract. All bidders must submit with their bid information the seismic geological and geophysical data they used or possess in determining their bid. Access to, and knowledge of, this seismic information helps MMS determine whether the bid constitutes fair market value for the resources of the lease.[29]

b. Geological and Geophysical Activities

Any party wanting to conduct geological or geophysical exploration or scientific research on unleased OCS lands or on lands under lease to a third party must obtain a geological and geophysical (G&G) permit from MMS.[30] This allows geological investigations including various seafloor sampling techniques to determine the geochemical, geotechnical, or engineering properties of the sediments. Seismic surveys obtain information on surface and near-surface geology and on subsurface geologic formations through low-energy, high-resolution surveys. These surveys collect data on surface geology used to identify potential shallow geologic or manmade hazards (e.g., faults or pipelines) for engineering and site planning for seabed-placed structures and to identify environmental and archaeological resources such as low-relief, live-bottom areas, pinnacles, chemosynthetic community habitat, and shipwrecks. High-energy, deep-penetration, common-depthpoint seismic surveys obtain data about geologic formations thousands of feet below the seafloor to map structural features of stratigraphically important horizons to identify potential hydrocarbon traps. Recent seismic gathering technology accompanied by sophisticated computer software provides accurate three-dimensional depictions of what lies below the seabed.

3. Post Sale Process, Reviews, and Enforcement

a. Exploration and Development Plans

Lessees must submit formal exploration and development plans with supporting information for review and approval by MMS before a lessee's operator may begin exploration, development, or production activities on any lease.[31] Supporting environmental information, archaeological reports, biological reports (monitoring and/or live-bottom survey), and other environmental data determined to be necessary must be submitted with the OCS plan for approval by MMS. This information provides the basis for an analysis of both offshore and onshore impacts that may occur from the activities. The MMS may require additional and more specific supporting information to help in evaluating the potential environmental impacts of the proposed activities.[32] The MMS can disapprove or require amendment of a submitted OCS plan based on inadequate or inaccurate supporting information. The plans are reviewed by geologists, geophysicists, engineers, biologists, archaeologists, air quality specialists, oil-spill specialists, and other technical experts. MMS evaluates the plans and accompanying

Lessees must submit formal exploration and development plans for review and approval before beginning exploration, development, or production activities on any lease.

information to determine whether any seafloor or drilling hazards are present; whether air and water quality issues are addressed appropriately; whether plans for hydrocarbon resource conservation, development, and drainage are adequate; whether environmental issues and potential impacts have been properly evaluated and are aptly mitigated; and that the proposed action complies with NEPA, MMS operating regulations, and any other federal requirements. Federal agencies, including FWS, NOAA Fisheries, the EPA, the U.S. Navy, the U.S. Air Force, and the USCG, may be consulted if the proposal has the potential to impact areas under their jurisdiction.

b. Exploration Plans

An exploration plan (EP) must be submitted to MMS for review and approval before any exploration activities, except for basic preliminary activities, can begin on a lease. The EP must fully describe the exploration activities, the type of drilling rig or vessel proposed, all proposed drilling and well-testing operations, environmental monitoring plans, and any other relevant information, and must include a proposed timeline for the exploration activities.[33] After receiving an EP, MMS performs both technical and environmental reviews. MMS evaluates the proposed exploration activities for potential impacts on or concerning geohazards and manmade hazards (including existing pipelines), archaeological resources, endangered species,[34] sensitive biological features, water and air quality, oil-spill response, and other uses (e.g., military operations). The proposed EP is also reviewed for compliance with all applicable federal laws and regulations.

MMS prepares a categorical exclusion review (CER), EA, and/or EIS in support of the NEPA environmental review of the EP. The CER, EA, and/or EIS is based on all the available information, which may include the geophysical report (for determining the potential for the presence of deepwater benthic communities); archaeological report; air emissions data; live-bottom survey and report; biological monitoring plan; and recommendations by the affected state(s), DOD, FWS (for selected plans under provisions of a DOI agreement), NOAA Fisheries, and/or any other internal DOI or MMS offices. As part of the review process, most EPs and analyzed environmental impacts and information are sent to the affected state(s) for consistency certification review and determination under the approved CZMA programs.

Even after EP approval and prior to conducting drilling operations, the operator is required to submit and obtain approval for an Application for Permit to Drill (APD). The APD requires more detailed information—including project layout at a scale of 24,000:1, design criteria for well control and casing, specifications for blowout preventers, a mud program, cementing program, and direction drilling plans—to allow evaluation of operational safety and pollution-prevention measures. The APD is reviewed for conformance with the engineering requirements and other technical considerations.

c. Production Plans

After a lessee has explored and found economically feasible and recoverable hydro-carbons, a production plan must then be submitted to MMS for review and approval before any development operations may begin on a lease. Also known as a Development Operations Coordination Document (DOCD) in the Gulf of Mexico, the produc-tion plan must describe all the proposed development activities, specific drilling activi-ties, platforms or other fixed facilities, proposed production operations, environmen-tal monitoring plans, and other relevant information, and include a proposed timeline of development and production activities.[35] Again, MMS performs the technical and environmental reviews and evaluates the proposed development activity for poten-tial impacts on or concerning geohazards and manmade hazards (including existing pipelines), archaeological resources, endangered species, sensitive biological features, water and air quality, oil-spill response, and other uses (e.g., military operations). Just as with the EP, the DOCD or Development and Production Plan is reviewed for compliance with all applicable federal laws and regulations. And again, NEPA review occurs. If the Production Plan is the first in a planning area, the OCSLA mandates that an EIS be done.[36] MMS must review the potential environmental impacts and the recommendations by any affected state(s), DOD, FWS, NOAA Fisheries, and/or any other internal DOI or MMS offices. As part of the review process, the DOCD and any analyzed environmental impacts and information will be sent to the affected state(s) for consistency certification review and determination under the approved CZMA programs. The OCSLA provides for this coordi-nation and consultation with the affected state and local governments.[37]

One of MMS's primary responsibilities is to ensure development of economically producible reservoirs accord-ing to sound conservation, engineering, and economic practices. MMS has established requirements for the sub-mission of conservation information for production activi-ties. Conservation reviews are performed to ensure that economic reserves are fully developed and produced.[38]

One of MMS's primary responsibilities is to ensure development of economically producible reservoirs according to sound conservation, engineering, and economic practices.

4. Cradle to Grave Regulatory Oversight

For the Secretary to accomplish fully all the responsibilities and mandates contained in the OCSLA, MMS employs hundreds of employees—engineers, analysts, economists, inspectors, and managers—in its headquarters and three regional offices. Their duties and roles vary in carrying out the OCSLA regulatory regime. Besides the matters mentioned previously, the OCSLA requires both annual and unannounced inspections of all OCS facilities,[39] an enforcement regime with both civil and criminal penalties,[40] BAST,[41] and a host of actions appropriate to protecting the marine environment, the safety of OCS workers, and the federal financial interests.[42]

MMS's comprehensive regulations rely on both design criteria and performance-based standards.[43] MMS conducts project-specific engineering safety reviews to ensure that the equipment proposed for use is designed to withstand the operational and environmental condition in which it will operate. When an OCS operator proposes the use of technology or procedures not specifically addressed in established MMS regulations, the operations are evaluated for alternative compliance or departure approval. Any new technologies or equipment that represent an alternative compliance or departure from existing MMS regulation must be fully described and justified before approval for use. For MMS to grant alternative compliance or departure approval, the operator must demonstrate an equivalent or improved degree of protection.[44]

MMS must keep close track of the thousands of production platforms and wells, and the production therefrom, both for royalty collection purposes and pollution prevention. The statutorily required annual inspection examines all safety equipment designed to prevent blowouts, fires, spills, or other major accidents. These annual inspections involve the inspection for the installation and performance of all platform safety system components. The random and unannounced inspections may focus on any aspect of the OCSLA regulatory regime or it may be a follow-up from an annual inspection. MMS administers an active civil penalties program.[45] A civil penalty in the form of substantial monetary fines ($100,000 per day per violation) may be issued against any operator that commits a violation that may constitute a threat of serious, irreparable, or immediate harm or damage to life, property, or the environment. MMS may make recommendations for criminal penalties if a willful violation occurs. In addition, the regulations authorize suspension of any operation in the Gulf of Mexico region if the lessee has failed to comply with a provision of *any* applicable law, regulation, or order or provision of a lease or permit.[46] Furthermore, the Secretary may invoke his authority[47] to cancel a lease.

MMS's responsibilities include assuring that absolutely no oil spills occur and if they do, they are promptly addressed and cleaned up. After the *Exxon Valdez* spill, Congress passed the Oil Pollution Act of 1990 (OPA 90), which added new vigor to the MMS efforts offshore to keep any spills from occurring as a result of OCS drilling and production activities. MMS's duties include spill prevention in federal and state offshore waters, review and approval of oil-spill response plans (OSRPs), inspection of oil-spill containment and cleanup equipment, and ensuring oil-spill financial responsibility.

The MMS regulations require that all owners and operators of oil handling, storage, or transportation facilities located seaward of the coastline submit an OSRP for approval.[48] The regulations require that an OSRP must be submitted and approved before an operator can use a facility, or the operator must certify in writing to the MMS that it is capable of responding to a "worst-case" spill or the substantial threat of such a spill.[49] The facility must be operated in compliance with the approved OSRP or the MMS-accepted "worst-case" spill certification. Owners or operators of offshore pipelines are required to submit an OSRP for any pipeline that carries oil, condensate, or gas with condensate; pipelines carrying essentially dry gas do not require an OSRP. The OSRP describes how an operator intends to respond to an oil spill. The OSRP may be site-specific or regional.

The Emergency Response Action Plan within the OSRP outlines the availability of spill containment and cleanup equipment and trained personnel. It must ensure that full-response capability can be deployed during an oil-spill incident. The OSRP includes an inventory of appropriate equipment and materials, their availability, and the time needed for deployment. All MMS-approved OSRPs must be reviewed at least every two years and all resulting modifications must be submitted to MMS within fifteen days whenever (1) a change occurs that appreciably reduces an owner/operator's response capabilities; (2) a substantial change occurs in the worst-case discharge scenario or in the type of oil being handled, stored, or transported at the facility; (3) there is a change in the name(s) or capabilities of the oil-spill removal organizations cited in the OSRP; or (4) there is a change in the applicable Area Contingency Plans.

The responsible party for every covered offshore facility must demonstrate oil-spill financial responsibility (OSFR),[50] as required by OPA 90. A covered offshore facility is any structure and all of its components, equipment, pipelines, or devices (other than a vessel or other than a pipeline or deepwater port licensed under the Deepwater Port Act of 1974) used for exploring, drilling, or producing oil, or for transporting oil from such facilities. MMS must ensure that each responsible party has sufficient funds for removal costs and damages resulting from any accidental release of hydrocarbons into the environment for which the responsible party is liable.

MMS also has responsibility for regulatory oversight of the design, installation, and maintenance of OCS oil and gas pipelines. The MMS operating regulations for pipelines[51] are intended to provide safe and pollution-free transportation of fluids in a manner that does not interfere with other users of the OCS. Pipeline applications are usually submitted and reviewed separately from development and production plans. Pipeline applications may be for on-lease pipelines or rights-of-way for pipelines that cross other lessees' leases or unleased areas of the OCS. Pipeline permit applications to MMS must include the pipeline location drawing, profile drawing, safety schematic drawing, pipe design data to scale, a shallow hazard survey report, and an archaeological report.

Almost no aspect of the OCS operations may go unaccounted for by MMS—air emissions, effluent discharges, archeological resources, Endangered Species Act fauna and flora, Marine Mammal Protection Act mammals, shut down and emergency evacuation procedures, drilling fluid requirements,[52] pollution control,[53] blow-out preventers,[54] production safety,[55] production rates,[56] safety training for personnel, and a myriad of other specific requirements.[57]

After an operator has relinquished the lease, it must perform the appropriate plugging, abandonment, and site clearance duties, as required, within one year of relinquishment,[58] unless approval is obtained to maintain the structure to conduct other activities.[59] Permanent lease abandonment includes the isolation of zones in the open wellbore, plugging of perforated intervals, plugging the annular space between casings (if they are open), setting a surface plug, and cutting and retrieving the casing at least fifteen feet below the seabed mudline. All plugs must be tested in accordance with the regulations.

While there are no routine surveys of permanently abandoned well locations, if a plugged well were found to be leaking, MMS would require the last operator of record to repair the leak. If a well is just temporarily abandoned at the seafloor, an operator must provide MMS with an annual report summarizing plans to abandon the well permanently or to bring the well into production. Part of the annual report for a temporarily abandoned well is a survey of the well location to ensure the temporary abandonment is intact and adequately restricting any reservoir fluids from migrating out of the well. All equipment such as wellheads, production trees, casing, manifolds, etc., must be designed to withstand the pressures of the deepwater areas. These designs are verified by MMS through multiple levels of engineering safety reviews prior to the equipment being placed into service.

MMS makes sure the workmanship of the abandonment meets industry standards and all equipment removed and well pipes and platform legs have been cut off at least fifteen feet below the seabed[60] where the remains of the OCS activities must rest.

In MMS's efforts to continue updating BAST, the regulations often incorporate by reference recommended practices of the industry's American Petroleum Institute as the minimum requirements for operations.[61] MMS maintains a database of past accidents and their cause and continually reviews any need to change its regulations, current technology, or recommended practices. MMS conducts periodic safety and technology workshops with industry and others to keep abreast of the evolving needs and challenges of the offshore environment.

5. OCS Litigation and Case Law

Ocean energy law litigation may be grouped into five categories: (1) litigation over the meaning and scope of the Secretary's authority to lease, manage, and enforce under the OCSLA; (2) litigation over the state/federal relationship and balance; (3) cases involving lease royalty terms and royalty collection; (4) litigation challenging OCSLA matters and actions based on another statute—NEPA, CZMA, Clean Air Act, Endangered Species Act, etc.; and (5) litigation combining elements of these litigation bases.

Little, if any, OCSLA litigation occurred before NEPA or the Santa Barbara oil spill. The Secretary sought successfully to suspend leases for environmental concerns[62] and impose new environmental requirements[63] shortly after the 1969 spill. The first EIS for an OCS lease sale—all twenty pages of it—escaped challenge, but many over the years did not. Litigation completely derailed only one final proposed lease sale—the second Georges Bank Sale in 1983.[64] The first three proffered five-year programs were challenged in court; the three thereafter were not. The D.C. Court of Appeals with original jurisdiction in five-year program litigation helped define the extent and scope of the Secretary's analysis and discretion pursuant to Section 18, but basically deferred to and upheld the Secretary's choices and analysis.[65]

CZMA consistency certification administrative litigation (appeals to the Secretary of Commerce from a state's decision to deny consistency) has a more speckled history of success. Of the thousands of consistency certifications submitted by industry to states, only fifteen were appealed to the Secretary of Commerce. Seven were upheld, seven reversed. California's challenge to the Secretary's view of lease sales not directly affecting the state's coastal zone and thus not triggering a consistency determination under the CZMA failed in the Supreme Court,[66] but won on the Hill as a result of OPA 90. Alabama challenged the Secretary's position that the cooperative development dictates of Section 5(j)[67] for common hydrocarbon bearing areas did not grant a unilateral veto by states of resource production by the federal government. The Eleventh Circuit sided with the Secretary.[68] California currently has expanded its view of the CZMA in that it requires consistency determinations before the Secretary may suspend leases.[69] The most recent litigation flurry involves royalty relief,[70] Arctic seismic and exploration plans, and the meaning and scope of Section 4 of the OCSLA.

Industry plaintiffs have been successful in arguing that suspensions of their leases in offshore North Carolina during the pendency of environmental analysis imposed by the Outer Banks Protection Act caused a breach of those leases.[71] Quite recently, industry continued its successful litigation by convincing the Fifth Circuit Court of Appeals that the Deep Water Royalty Relief Act provided royalty relief in the millions of barrels specified in that Act to each lease, rather than groups of leases overlying fields of hydrocarbons, despite the fact that the statute referred to "leases" rather than "lease."[72]

If a lack of litigation against OCSLA lease sales and the OCSLA five-year programs signified consensus in the nation on OCS ocean energy policy, then the first twenty years of the OCSLA and mostly the last fifteen years can be viewed as having basically achieved that consensus. Yet, if it merely indicates a truce amongst competing users seeking benefits from ocean resources during periods of our nation's energy picture being relative calm and plentiful, then a renewed and robust competition may soon occur between those who seek to preserve the status quo off our shores and those who think the value of the oil and gas or offshore renewable energy should outweigh our nation's complacency about the risk of imported oil tanker spills, Middle East oil dependency, and OPEC politics with its concomitant military presence.

C. Presidential Policy Preferences

President Truman proclaimed the seabed off our shores as our national arena to exploit for its energy resources to the exclusion of the coastal states and vigorously challenged state claims to the contrary. President Eisenhower viewed the national interest a bit differently: he endorsed and signed the 1953 Submerged Lands Act (SLA), which, despite consistent losses by states to their claims seaward of their high-tide line in the Supreme Court, gave coastal states an enormously valuable area in the first three miles off their coastlines for their own, and not the nation's, benefit.

The OCSLA, which Eisenhower also endorsed and signed, stated the need for OCS oil and gas exploration and development as "urgent" for our nation, and proceeded with federal development. Until the Santa Barbara oil spill on the eighth day of President Nixon's presidency, the OCS energy policy quietly carried on in DOI with little notice by the public. Nixon sought and gained more environmental regulation of offshore activities as well as more OCS development activities to help domestic production make up for the OPEC Oil Embargo of 1973. He pledged additional offshore resources—one million more acres of OCS by 1975. President Ford continued this approach and, in a 1975 speech in Cincinnati to open an EPA environmental center, promised more offshore oil and gas leasing and development to meet our nation's energy needs.[73]

President Carter sought more environmental safeguards, signed the 1978 amendments to the OCSLA, and still pledged even more OCS development to meet our nation's energy needs. His Secretary of the Interior, Cecil Andrus, proceeded with a rather vigorous five-year leasing program. It was challenged in court by a multitude of interests. While that challenge was pending, President Reagan's Secretary James Watt chose to redo Secretary Andrus's five-year program and expand it to more areas and to include area-wide leasing rather than the more focused, preselected tracts to offer for lease. Secretary Watt's proposals seemed overly aggressive to many and Congress chose, through the budget process by prohibiting federal funding for prelease activities, to place leasing moratoria on selected offshore planning areas where coastal states and their congressional members opposed OCS leasing.

> **Secretary Watt's proposals seemed overly aggressive to many; Congress chose, through the budget process, to place leasing moratoria on selected offshore planning areas.**

President George H.W. Bush chose to withdraw areas from leasing for a definite period of time beyond the yearly budget moratoria imposed by Congress. Many observers at the time viewed his action as seeking to defuse growing efforts toward more permanent moratoria by Congress and to lessen discontent over offshore development in coastal states seen important to his reelection. The announced withdrawal and subsequent suspension of existing leases in the areas prompted the so-called buy-back litigation of the 1990s. All but two companies with leases offshore North Carolina, and some areas off Alaska, Florida, and California, settled by having the government pay a discounted value for their leases.[74] The two companies that pursued the full amount paid for their leases plus interest eventually won in the Supreme Court on the grounds that the Outer Banks Protection Act breached their leases.[75]

President Clinton, some may say reading a similar political playbook as his predecessor, expanded and lengthened in time the withdrawals of OCS areas for leasing initiated by the previous President. These withdrawals had the practical effect of not only removing the areas from potential OCS lease sales, but also removing the areas from any need to analyze them in the upcoming five-year programs' public notice, government fact gathering, and comparative analysis. Any efforts by DOI toward five-year program efforts in those areas would be statutorily futile, a waste of government resources, and seen as arousing unnecessary concern to those fearful of offshore oil development off their state's coast. The Department has taken the position that withdrawals, under Section 12, trump the requirements of Section 18 analysis.[76]

III. Emerging and Unresolved Issues

A. Section 1333(a)—Defining the Scope of Federal Jurisdiction over the OCS Seabed and Natural Resources

What specific legal regime applies to the OCS seabed? What laws determine use conflicts between energy and mineral development matters and nonenergy and mineral matters? Use conflicts will likely increase in the next fifty to one hundred years as more and more use of the coastal ocean and its seabed resources occurs. DOI faces these questions and potential conflicts in any proposed Energy Policy Act of 2005 rulemaking on alternative energy siting matters. Also as a practical matter, DOI or some "appropriate officer" of the federal government must determine or regulate who can do what and where on or about the seabed and its resources. Section 4 of the OCSLA[77] largely provides the framework for answering those questions. Thus, to shed light on how to address those important future issues warrants a full analysis of Section 4.

Section 4 sets forth the laws and regulations that govern the OCS. Described as the heart of the OCSLA during the debate on the Senate floor,[78] Section 4 presents several important ongoing and basic issues still over fifty years later: its meaning, its application, and its directive to the President. In particular, Section 1333(a) states:

> (1) The Constitution and laws and civil and political jurisdiction of the United States are hereby extended to the subsoil and seabed of the outer Continental Shelf and to all artificial islands, and all installations and other devices permanently or temporarily attached to the seabed, which may be erected thereon for the purpose of exploring for, developing, or producing resources therefrom, or any such installation or other device (other than a ship or vessel) for the purpose of transporting such resources, to the same extent as if the outer Continental Shelf were an area of exclusive Federal jurisdiction located within a State: Provided, however, That mineral leases on the outer Continental Shelf shall be maintained or issued only under the provisions of this Act.

> (2) (A) To the extent that they are applicable and not inconsistent with this Act or with other Federal laws and regulations of the Secretary now in effect or hereafter adopted, the civil and criminal laws of each adjacent State now in effect or hereafter adopted, amended, or repealed are hereby declared to be the law of the United States for that portion of the subsoil and seabed of the outer Continental Shelf, and artificial islands and fixed structures erected thereon, which would be within the area of the State if its boundaries were extended seaward to the outer margin of the outer Continental Shelf, and the President shall determine and publish in the Federal Register such projected lines extending seaward and defining each such area. All of such applicable laws shall be administered and enforced by the appropriate officers and courts of the United States. State taxation laws shall not apply to the outer Continental Shelf. . . . [79]

The language of Section 1333(a) is not as clear as a reader's first impression and has created questions. First, does the United States have jurisdiction over artificial islands and other installations that touch the subsoil or seabed of the OCS but that are not involved with natural resource exploration, transportation, or production? Second, what laws apply to civil or criminal actions committed on the seabed that are not related to the exploration, transportation, or production of natural resources? Third, what laws are applicable to fauna and flora, e.g., coral reefs, which touch or are attached to the OCS seabed? Fourth, what effect does Section 1333 have on the possible future construction of windmill or other motion energy plants on the OCS?

1. Federal Jurisdiction over Artificial Islands Whether or Not Energy Related or Dealing with Natural Resource Exploration, Production, or Transportation

Although the First Circuit has recognized that the language of Section 1333(a)(1) is ambiguous, the courts have resolved that Section 1333(a) extends the jurisdiction and the laws of the United States to the *entire* OCS and structures attached to it, regardless of their purpose.[80] Thus, United States jurisdiction, as set forth in the OCSLA, is not limited to those structures just engaged in the exploitation of the OCS's natural resources.

Section 1333(a) extends the civil and political jurisdiction of the United States to the OCS's subsoil and seabed "and to *all* artificial islands, and *all* installations and other devices permanently or temporarily attached to the seabed."[81] The next dependent clause provides an example of such structures. Although this dependent clause can be read to limit the scope of delegation—i.e., the jurisdiction of the United States is extended to all installations and devices, which may be erected for the purpose of exploring—the clause has been interpreted to be one of example only. In other words, the OCS "extends to all 'artificial islands, installations, and other devices located on the seabed, to the seaward limit of the [OCS],' including, but not limited to, those that '*may be*' used to explore for, develop, or produce resources."[82]

For the court, the legislative history was determinative for resolving this ambiguity. In the original version of Senate Bill 1901, Section 3 provided that it was the "policy of the United States that *the natural resources of the subsoil and seabed of the outer Continental Shelf appertain to the United States and are subject to its jurisdiction, control, and power of disposition.*"[83] However, the phrase "the natural resources" was removed from the language during the Senate Committee's consideration of the bill.[84] The Committee proceeded to explain that "[t]he deletion of the limitation to 'natural resources' carries out the committee's intent to extend the jurisdiction of the United States to the seabed and subsoil as such."[85] Obviously, by deleting that phrase Congress intended to claim jurisdiction in the entire seabed and subsoil of the OCS and not simply the natural resources contained therein.

Section 3 of Senate Bill 1901 set forth the United States' claim of jurisdiction over the OCS.[86] The legislative history of the 1978 OCSLA Amendments indicates that Congress did not intend to change the substance of the original Section 3; instead,

Congress sought to make it into a "declaration of national policy."[87] Indeed, Section 1332 currently states, in part:

It is hereby declared to be the policy of the United States that—

(1) *the subsoil and seabed of the outer Continental Shelf appertain to the United States and are subject to its jurisdiction, control, and power of disposition as provided in this Act;*

(2) this Act shall be construed in such a manner that the character of the waters above the outer Continental Shelf as high seas and the right to navigation and fishing therein shall not be affected;

(3) the outer Continental Shelf is a vital national resource reserve held by the Federal Government for the public, which should be made available for expeditious and orderly development, subject to environmental safeguards, in a manner which is consistent with the maintenance of competition and other national needs. . . . [88]

Thus, Congress carried over Section 3 of the original OCSLA with virtually identical language in Section 202. The subsequent amendment of Section 1332, therefore, did not reflect a change in congressional intent; Congress still asserted jurisdiction over the entire subsoil and seabed of the OCS.

While the removal of the phrase "natural resources" from Section 1332 provides congressional intent that the United States was claiming jurisdiction over more than just the natural resources contained in the OCS, numerous other instances in the legislative history support that understanding as well. Perhaps the most persuasive piece of legislative history is the evolution of Section 4 of Senate Bill 1901, which later became Section 1333 of OCSLA. Section 4, as introduced, would have extended United States jurisdiction only over structures located on the OCS involved in the extraction of natural resources.[89] However, the Senate Committee removed that language "because the committee determined to extend jurisdiction *over the whole of the seabed and the subsoil, as well as to the operational structures.*"[90] Thus, Congress wanted to extend jurisdiction to the entire OCS and not simply structures constructed to remove natural resources.[91]

None of the subsequent amendments to the OCSLA have altered that intent. The 1975 amendments were minor.[92] By contrast, the OCSLA Amendments enacted in 1978 were substantive and wide-reaching. However, as described in the context of Section 3, the OCSLA Amendments did not presume to change the legislative intent that existed in 1953; instead, the 1978 Congress recognized the focus of the amendments were to regulate oil and gas leasing on the OCS.[93]

In addition, the House of Representatives noted that in amending the OCSLA, it was doing so under Article IV

Congress specified that the subsoil and seabed of the OCS, not just its natural resources, belonged to the United States.

of the Constitution.[94] Thus, Congress recognized that the subsoil and seabed of the OCS, not just its natural resources, belonged to the United States. Furthermore, the House stated:

> The OCS *lands and the resources of those lands are public property,* which the Federal Government holds in behalf of the people of the United States. Therefore, the Government has a duty to properly and carefully manage this vital natural resource reserve, so as to obtain fair value for the resources, protect competition, preserve the environment, and generally reflect the public interest.[95]

The Conference Report for the OCSLA Amendments provides that "[t]he existing authority of the Corps of Engineers, in [Section 1333(e)], applies to all artificial islands and fixed structures on the [OCS], whether or not they are erected for the purpose of exploring for, developing, removing, and transporting resources therefrom."[96] The Conference Report continues: "It is not the intention of the conferees to limit the authority of the Corps of Engineers as to structures used for the exploration, development, removal, and transportation of resources."[97]

Thus, the primary focus of the OCSLA Amendments was to regulate and manage oil and gas leases that were, at that time, the bulk of the development on the OCS. It did not presume to limit the United States' control over the other facets of the development of the OCS. Thus, with the passage of the OCSLA in 1953, Congress specified that the United States had jurisdiction over the entire subsoil and seabed of the OCS, not simply the natural resources contained in the OCS, and the later amendments did not alter that intent.

There is some conflicting authority for the proposition that the United States has jurisdiction and control of the OCS for purposes other than natural resource exploitation. The OCSLA does not exist in a vacuum. Several years after the OCSLA was enacted, the international community agreed on the governance of the continental shelves worldwide. The United States signed the Geneva Convention on the Continental Shelf (Geneva Convention) on April 29, 1958, and the treaty entered into force on June 10, 1964.[98] Article 2 of the Convention states "[t]he coastal [nation] exercises over the continental shelf sovereign rights for the purpose of exploring it and exploiting its natural resources."[99] Thus, by its language, the Geneva Convention only addresses the sovereign rights of countries over the exploitation of natural resources of the OCS.

When there is a federal statute and a self-executing treaty on the same topic, courts will attempt to construe them so no conflict exists.[100] However, if there is a true conflict between the treaty and the statute, the "one last in date will control the other."[101] Thus, the Geneva Convention could be interpreted to limit the broad expression of United States control as stated in the OCSLA. Although Congress reaffirmed the OCSLA in 1978, after the Geneva Convention went into effect, there is a rule of interpretation that a treaty "will not be deemed to have been abrogated or modified by a later statute unless such purpose on the part of Congress has been clearly expressed."[102] Legislative silence has been regarded as insufficient to repeal a treaty.[103]

In 1980, the Solicitor of the Department of the Interior issued an opinion that limited the Department's authority over cultural resources on the OCS to activities and structures engaged in the exploration or exploitation of mineral resources.[104] That opinion was correct in that the OCSLA only provides, in Section 5, regulatory authority over mineral matters to the Secretary of the Interior. However, the Solicitor's Opinion was based in part on an analysis of the Geneva Convention and *Treasure Salvors, Inc. v. Unidentified Wrecked & Abandoned Sailing Vessel*,[105] which the Solicitor viewed at the time as holding that the OCSLA "extended the sovereignty of the United States to the exploitation of the mineral resources of the OCS, but not for other purposes."[106]

Both the 1980 Solicitor's Opinion and the Fifth Circuit's view appear unduly narrow. There is another way to reconcile the Geneva Convention and the OCSLA, while giving the United States control over the OCS and structures attached to it. Simply, the Geneva Convention gives nations sovereign power over the OCS for natural resource exploitation and prevents nations from extending those rights to the high seas or the skies above the OCS. It is, for the most part, silent on the amount of sovereignty nations have over the OCS for purposes other than natural resource exploitation.[107] It does not specifically prevent a nation from claiming those rights as long as it does not interfere with navigation.[108] Of course, the OCSLA gives the United States authority to prevent obstruction to navigation, thus complying with Article 5 of the Geneva Convention.

Additionally, several court decisions have minimized the impact of the Geneva Convention on the OCSLA. Neither *Alliance to Protect Nantucket Sound v. U.S. Department of the Army*[109] nor *Ten Taxpayer Citizens Group v. Cape Wind Associates*[110] mentions the Geneva Convention when discussing the United States' authority to regulate the entire OCS. The Fifth Circuit in *United States v. Ray*[111] stated, in dictum, that "there is nothing in the pertinent language of the Geneva Convention on the Continental Shelf which detracts from or is inconsistent with the [OCSLA]." Thus, the Geneva Convention did not restrict the pertinent sections of Section 1333 with respect to whether a nation has control and jurisdiction over other aspects of the OCS.

After reviewing the plain language and legislative history, the OCSLA on its face has asserted United States' authority and its laws over the entire seabed and subsoil of the OCS without limitation. The language in Section 1333(a)(1) that extends federal jurisdiction to the subsoil, seabed, and all artificial islands that attached to the subsoil or seabed of the OCS is not limited to artificial islands engaged in the production, exploration, or transportation of natural resources. Thus, any artificial island on the OCS adjacent to the United States, whether or not it is engaged in natural resource exploration, is subject to the jurisdiction and control of the United States to the same extent as a structure engaged in natural resource extraction. What "other officers" means in Section 4 remains a question for the Executive Branch executing regulatory and enforcement matters. As competing ocean uses multiply or intensify, that question will inevitably and eventually be answered. Until Congress becomes more specific or the President issues a directive or delegates to the officers, Section 4 will remain either largely dormant or a source of continuing litigation to discover its original or inherent meaning.

2. Federal Laws Apply to Incidents Whether Energy-Development Related or Not That Occur on the Seabed of the OCS

Assuming that the United States has jurisdiction and control of the OCS regardless of the extraction of natural resources, federal laws would apply to any civil or criminal incident or activity that occurs on the seabed of the OCS, pursuant to Section 1333(a). For example, federal law would apply to any action that occurs on the OCS seabed, subsoil, or a structure, temporarily or permanently, attached to the seabed or subsoil. However, determining what federal law applies is problematic.

Basically, two issues need resolution to understand what federal laws would apply to an incident that occurred on the OCS. First, if the incident did not happen in the context of the exploration, transportation, or production of natural resources, is the OCSLA even applicable? For all of the reasons mentioned above regarding the applicability of the OCSLA on artificial islands that are constructed for non-mineral-extraction purposes, the United States has extended its jurisdiction to the entire seabed. Thus, the OCSLA would apply to any incident occurring on the OCS or an OCS structure. Next, since the OCSLA is applicable, would state or federal laws govern litigation arising out of an incident or activity on the OCS or an OCS structure?

Section 1333(a)(1) extends "[t]he Constitution and laws and civil and political jurisdiction of the United States" to the seabed. Section 1333(a)(2)(A) states:

> [t]o the extent that they are applicable and not inconsistent with this sub-chapter or with other Federal laws and regulations of the Secretary now in effect or hereafter adopted, the civil and criminal laws of each adjacent State, now in effect or hereafter adopted, amended, or repealed *are hereby declared to be the law of the United States for that portion of the subsoil and seabed of the [OCS], and artificial islands and fixed structures erected thereon. . . .* [112]

The United States has, thus, adopted the state laws of coastal states, which do not conflict with federal laws, as federal law in the absence of federal law for the purpose of the OCS for any activity on the seabed.

Federal courts have specified that state law pursuant to Section 1333(a)(2)(A) fills in the gaps of federal law.[113] Indeed, the application of federal law, with the assimilation of state law, became the cornerstone of the original OCSLA.[114] As such, a large part of the legislative history focuses on the decision regarding what law to apply to the OCS.

The original version of Section 4 in Senate Bill 1901 would have treated structures erected on the OCS as vessels, thus applying federal maritime law.[115] However, a faction in Congress preferred that, at least initially, only state law should apply to the OCS.[116] As mentioned earlier, the Senate changed the language in Section 4 so as to broaden the United States' jurisdiction over the entire OCS and not just structures constructed atop it.[117] But that reason alone does not explain the scheme of applying federal law to the OCS and adopting state law as federal law, when needed to fill a gap in federal law.

Section 4 in the original OCSLA caused considerable, if not the most, debate. Senator Cordon explained on the Senate Floor that the committee was divided on the adoption of state law.[118] In summary, Senator Cordon noted that for the United States Constitution to be applicable to the OCS, Congress needed to include a specific provision.[119] The committee next "determined to make applicable the whole body of Federal law which applies today to those areas inside States owned by the Federal Government under exclusive Federal jurisdiction."[120] The committee decided "that the laws of abutting States should become a part of Federal law."[121] Senator Cordon expressed reservations about adopting state law.[122] He stated:

> Personally, I am not at all certain that the adoption of [Section 4] will not create more problems than it will solve. . . . On the other hand, I must concede that I recognize that in the absence of the adoption of State law, there would also be some very difficult problems to be faced in the operations in the area.
>
> Speaking only for myself, I would have preferred to apply to the [OCS] the body of Federal law to the extent that it applies to Federal areas within exclusive Federal jurisdiction and within any one of the several states, and thereafter to meet the need for additional law as the need arose.[123]

House Bill 5134 took a slightly different approach to the application of state versus federal law.[124] Specifically, House Bill 5134 stated:

> Except to the extent that they are inconsistent with applicable Federal laws not in effect or hereafter enacted, or such regulations as the Secretary may adopt, the laws of each coastal state *which so provide* shall be applicable to that portion of the [OCS] which would be within the area of the State if its boundaries were extended seaward to the outer margin of the [OCS]. . . . [125]

After the Senate dropped the federal maritime jurisdiction, the state supplement to federal law gained the most support. In the Senate Report following the amendment of Senate Bill 1901, the committee explained that state taxation laws would specifically be excluded from applying to the OCS.[126] Furthermore, the committee envisioned that state and federal authorities would cooperate in the operation of conservation laws.[127]

The conclusion that state law only supplements the gaps in federal law conflicts with some of the other bills introduced at about the same time to regulate the OCS. For example, the report accompanying House Bill 4195 noted that in that bill the police power of each state would be made applicable to the area that the state would have controlled as long as it was not inconsistent with applicable federal laws.[128] Attached to the report for House Bill 4195 is the report for a similar bill before the previous

Congress.[129] In that report, the committee explained that the police powers the states would exercise over the OCS would include "the power of taxation, conservation, and control of the manner of conducting geophysical explorations. . . . Criminal statutes, workmen's compensation laws, and other police powers should be applicable to Continental Shelf operations."[130] These suggestions did not become law.

Nothing in the 1978 amendments to the OCSLA have affected the substance of the original Section 4.[131] The Senate Report states that "[t]he 1953 Act reflects this emphasis on jurisdictional questions. Its 'bare bones' leasing authority with essentially no statutory standards or guidelines also reflects the relative lack of basic knowledge concerning, and interest in, development of the resources of the Shelf at that time."[132] All Senate Bill 9 purported to do to Section 4(a) of the original OCSLA was to make a few technical changes to the wording.[133] Indeed, the Conference Report for the OCSLA Amendments specified that Congress did not intend to alter the legislative intent that existed in 1953; instead, the Congress in 1977–78 was focusing on improvement in oil and gas leasing on the OCS.[134] Thus, the OCSLA Amendments did not indicate a change in congressional intent about the underlying scope of Section 4.

A review of the extensive legislative history shows that the OCSLA adopted state law as federal law to fill in gaps in federal law. Congress, when passing the OCSLA, wanted courts to treat the OCS as a federal enclave.[135] By analogy, the "federal Assimilative Crimes Act (ACA)[18 U.S.C. §13(a)] assimilates into federal law, and thereby makes applicable on federal enclaves such as Army bases, certain criminal laws of the State in which the enclave is located."[136]

> **A review of the extensive legislative history shows that the OCSLA adopted state law as federal law to fill in gaps in federal law.**

The Supreme Court has held that the ACA did "not make the state provision part of federal law."[137] Specifically, just like the OCSLA, the Court found that "[t]he ACA's basic purpose is one of borrowing state law to fill gaps in the federal criminal law that applies on federal enclaves."[138]

3. Federal Law, as Supplemented by State Law, Applies to OCS Coral Reefs and Other Marine Animal and Plant Life

Coral reefs are universally acknowledged as important habitat to innumerable species in the oceans. They face potential harm from a variety of sources, including energy development, unless they are located in a protected area. Because they are natural resources located on the OCS seabed, the law applicable to them is directed by the OCSLA and Section 1333(a), which applies federal law and adopts consistent state law to supplement any gaps. A district court has held that "reefs and their coral and piscatorial inhabitants are natural resources not only as that term is understood by the general public, but as defined by [the OCSLA]."[139] On appeal, the Fifth Circuit agreed, concluding that "the United States has the exclusive right for purposes of exploration and exploitation of the reefs."[140] The court based this finding on several factors. First, the reefs were completely submerged at mean high water.[141] Thus, "the reefs are contemplated within the definition of the [OCSLA] and the Geneva Convention on the Continental Shelf."[142] The court also looked at the common definition of seabed as "lands underlying the sea."[143] The SLA supports this understanding by providing some of the applicable definitions for the OCSLA.[144]

Likewise, the Geneva Convention includes both living and nonliving resources in its definition of "natural resources."[145] The Fifth Circuit recognized the important interest the United States has in coral reefs when it stated:

> The evidence overwhelmingly shows that the Government has a vital interest, from a practical as well as an aesthetic viewpoint, in preserving the reefs for public use and enjoyment. The protective underwater crannies of the reefs serve as a haven and spawning ground for myriad species of tropical and game fish. The unique and spectacular formations of the submerged coral deposits attract scores of water sports enthusiasts, skin divers, nature students, and marine researchers. Certain organisms living on the reefs contain substances useful in pharmacology. The reefs protect the inland waters from the heavy wave action of the open sea, thus making the area conducive to boating and other water sports. . . . [146]

Thus, coral reefs have been determined to be part of the seabed. Coral reefs and "other marine animal and plant life" that are part of the seabed are covered by the OCSLA, and federal law, which adopts state law to fill gaps, would apply to anything that happened on the reef, to the in-place marine animal and plant life, or to any artificial island, installation, or device that is permanently or temporarily attached to the coral reef or seabed.

Section 4's broad reach and imposition of all federal laws and adjacent state law in the absence of federal law does not tap the Secretary of the Interior to administer those laws. It merely states: "All of such applicable laws shall be administered and enforced by the appropriate officers and courts of the United States."[147] Congress, other than in a few matters, e.g., liquefied natural gas facilities, alternative energy, and mineral leasing, has not specified or directly delegated to those officers who are appropriate. Presumably, that question is left to the President or the Attorney General.

4. Section 4's Presidential Directive to Determine Lateral Boundaries of States for Choice of Law Questions

Since 1953, Section 4 has stated "the President shall determine and publish in the Federal Register such projected lines extending seaward and defining each such [adjacent state] area." The OCSLA provides no deadline for determining the projected lines.

The only explanation of why, more than fifty years later, nothing has been done by any president to carry out this directive is that no pressing need has existed to do so and some states may perhaps feel slighted if the projected state lateral boundaries based on equal distance principles lessen their perception of influence. Courts have taken a case-by-case approach to finding which state is the adjacent state for choice of law issues in cases that have arisen thus far. Most times it is obvious. As more and more ocean uses, facilities, and activities occur further out from the coastal states, the need for more definite adjacent state boundary areas increases. Recently, the Secretary of the Interior established administrative lines based on equal distance principles for OCS leasing area process purposes only.[148]

B. Energy Policy Act of 2005

Congress passed the Energy Policy Act of 2005 and mandated that MMS administer several new aspects of the OCSLA, including conducting a comprehensive new OCS assessment of the inventory of potential oil and gas, and provided explicit authority for MMS to review and permit renewable/alternative energy facilities on the OCS. It mandated incentives for ultra-deep gas wells, and required the Secretary of the Interior to consider incentives for gas hydrates and carbon dioxide injections. It provided $250 million annually for distribution to coastal states with federal OCS production seaward of their coastlines. MMS is currently in the process of implementing the provisions of the Energy Policy Act, largely through regulations now under development. Recently, the Department chose to defer action on incentives for gas hydrates and carbon dioxide injections. In November 2007, MMS issued a final programmatic EIS for alternative energy siting.[149]

> **As more and more ocean uses, facilities, and activities occur further out from the coastal states, the need for more definite adjacent state boundary areas increases.**

The Energy Policy Act of 2005 provided for the Coastal Impact Assistance Program (CIAP) by amending Section 31 of the OCSLA.[150] The Secretary has the authority and responsibility for managing CIAP. The Secretary delegated this authority and responsibility to MMS.

Under Section 384 of the Act, MMS must disburse $250 million for each fiscal year 2007 through 2010 to eligible producing states and Coastal Political Subdivisions (CPSs). The MMS must determine CIAP funding allocations to states and is using the formulas mandated by Section 31(b), which requires a minimum annual allocation of one percent to each state and provides that thirty-five percent of each state's share shall be allocated directly to its CPSs. The funds allocated to each state are based on the proportion of qualified OCS revenues offshore of the individual state to total qualified OCS revenues to all states.[151]

Section 31(d)(1) stipulates that a state or CPS shall use CIAP funds only for one or more of the following authorized uses:

1. Projects and activities for the conservation, protection, or restoration of coastal areas, including wetlands;
2. Mitigation of damage to fish, wildlife, or natural resources;
3. Planning assistance and the administrative costs of complying with CIAP;
4. Implementation of a federally approved marine, coastal, or comprehensive conservation management plan; and
5. Mitigation of the impact of OCS activities through funding of onshore infrastructure projects and public service needs.

State agencies and CPSs responsible for preparing the CIAP grant applications and managing the subsequent CIAP funding are subject to the Federal consistency guidelines under Subpart F of the CZMA regulations.[152] Under Subpart F, each state's coastal agency must review the application for federal assistance (i.e., the grant application) to determine whether the application is consistent with its Coastal Zone Management Program.

To receive CIAP funds, states must submit a coastal impact assistance plan that MMS has to approve before disbursing any funds, and all funds must be disbursed through a grant process. Pursuant to the Act, a state must submit its plan no later than July 1, 2008.

C. Gulf of Mexico Energy Security Act of 2006

While considerable debate occurred in Congress in 2006 about changing OCS moratoria and areas available for drilling, only one law emerged, which President Bush signed on December 20, 2006: the Gulf of Mexico Energy Security Act of 2006 (GOMESA). GOMESA makes available two new areas in the Gulf for leasing, places a moratorium until 2022 on other areas in the Gulf, allows for exchange of some previously leased blocks close to Florida for bidding or royalty credits, and increases the distribution of offshore oil and gas revenues to coastal states.[153]

Prior to GOMESA, affected states received recurring annual disbursements of 27 percent of royalty, rent, and bonus revenues received only within the state's 8(g) zone. Beginning in fiscal year 2007, and thereafter, Gulf producing states (i.e., Texas, Louisiana, Mississippi, and Alabama) will receive 37.5 percent of revenue from new leases issued in the 181 Area and 181 South Area. Beginning in fiscal year 2016, and thereafter, Gulf producing states will receive 37.5 percent of the annual revenues from leases issued after 2006, subject to an annual cap, in the existing areas available for leasing. The remaining 50 percent and 12.5 percent of the total revenues will be distributed to the U.S. Treasury and the Land and Water Conservation Fund, respectively.

IV. Conclusion and Recommendations

Now more than fifty years old, federal ocean energy law presents the same basic issues, with new issues continuing to emerge. Many coastal states view OCS development as placing an unfair risk on their state interests. Other states without any offshore development feel pressure as energy petroleum prices rise. The current situation of OCS management by congressional budget moratoria and presidential withdrawals is at least a political answer and may not be the best way to address all of the important considerations enumerated in Section 18 for a balanced and equitable OCS ocean energy program. Our national ocean energy policy may continue with a standoff between those wanting more domestic OCS oil and gas production and those happy with the status quo. There are a variety of reasons for more domestic OCS production—national security and environmental. Many positive environmental reasons exist for OCS development; the record supports the fact that foreign oil-laden supertankers pulling into our coastal waters may pose far more risk to our nation's coastlines and coastal zones than U.S. offshore drilling does. Since 1969, our OCS exploration and development uses the best technology in the world and has an unrivaled environmental record. Mounting price pressure on U.S. petroleum needs and supplies from the Middle East has started a new impetus toward more OCS exploration and production. Congress has already considered and has several possible proposals under consideration to change the status quo. Several bills the last few years have been introduced to change the duration and extent of the current moratoria, to expand OCS development (including gas-only leasing), and to generate more revenue for coastal states. A flurry of legislative proposals were considered in 2006, almost all of which gave greater say or money to coastal states.

Foreign oil-laden supertankers may pose far more risk to our nation's coastlines and coastal zones than U.S. offshore drilling does.

To address the current OCS energy issues, a two-part proposal is suggested. The first part would change a few words in the OCSLA to allow the Secretary to lease natural-gas-only leases in areas potentially sensitive to oil spills—i.e., the East and West Coasts and offshore Florida. While many oil companies active in the U.S. OCS would not like this "half a loaf" approach, it may, with sufficient outreach and education of the public and stakeholders in the coastal areas, be the best chance of any energy development in the areas currently under moratoria. Natural gas exploration and production causes virtually no oil spills. A local natural gas supply makes energy cheaper to consumers by avoiding long-distance transportation charges. Current natural gas transportation charges from Canada or the Gulf of Mexico to the East Coast or West Coast now increase its cost to consumers. Over two-thirds of the natural gas wells are dry gas only, with no oil or liquid condensate of any note. They can be developed with almost zero risk of any oil or liquid spills.

If oil were found by a lessee with a gas-only lease, what would happen? It gets noted, and capped. It just becomes oil in the proverbial bank for national security purposes that we never use or use only after a national emergency need or, say, the Strategic Petroleum Reserve has been completely drained. If both oil and gas were found and extracting only the gas would leave the oil unextractable, the recommended law would mandate that the both the oil and gas remain in place.

The legislation to allow dry-natural-gas-only leasing would and could make it nearly impossible (just like the current moratoria) to drill for and produce oil with its concomitant small risk of an oil spill. While some companies may not like having to cap and abandon an oil discovery, all they bid for (and adjusted their bidding strategy accordingly) and received would be a dry natural gas lease. The legislation could provide a right of first refusal to companies if oil drilling were ever allowed in the area. Those who think additional public or industry pressure would lead policy makers to try to produce the oil found from such natural gas drilling could have their fears allayed by the legislation. Congress could enact the highest hurdle known to congressional action: Only two or more consecutive Presidential certifications of national need a year apart and two successive congressional votes two years apart could lift an oil moratorium in the areas off limits to oil drilling.

The second part of the proposal would give another large windfall to coastal states: The federal government would convey all the twelve-mile territorial sea submerged lands to the coastal states. This territorial sea zone was three miles in 1953; now, by the Presidential Proclamation of 1988 and current international law as codified in the Convention on the Law of the Sea, it comprises twelve miles. Louisiana, for example, receives almost $1 billion a year in revenue from its current 1953 federally quit-claimed three-mile belt of submerged lands. Thus, expanding state submerged land title to twelve miles and providing that all revenues go to the coastal states would create state incentives to promote properly sited and environmentally sound energy development. (Existing federal leases could be grandfathered so the impact to our federal treasury receipts would be less severe.)

Finally, states should be allowed to veto all activities on, or provide half of all revenue from, OCS development of the next twelve miles—the currently mapped contiguous zone established in 1999.[154] The coastal states then could choose to develop oil and gas, or natural gas only, in their twelve-mile area or not; and have the say in whether federal leases should occur in the next twelve miles. This would localize most new development choices to the states with the concomitant benefit (or not) to its state citizens. (Viewed from the shoreline, a large platform twelve miles offshore is about the size of a dime; any facility sited beyond fifteen miles is literally over the horizon and beyond human sight perception from the shore.) Industry would, just as it does now in the first three miles of coastal producing states (California has over 150 oil wells producing in its waters and providing almost $0.5 billion a year to the citizens of California), deal directly with the states. If an East or West Coast coastal state wanted natural gas development, or oil and gas development, and the potential revenue and energy derived from it, it could lease or grant leasing of the offshore tracts and regulate them (or seek MMS's assistance in regulating them). This relatively simple proposal of dry-gas-only leasing with all coastal states having a new source of say and revenue with a stakehold out to twenty-four miles may not solve the nation's energy needs or issues, but it could help considerably.

In his 1980 State of the Union speech, President Carter announced that if Soviet involvement in Afghanistan at the time were a first step or ploy to take over the Middle East oil fields of OPEC, then the United States would oppose that takeover with all the force available to the United States. At the time, I had recently read the DOI's EIS and risk analysis of the threat of oil spills from potential OCS drilling in the Atlantic Ocean Georgia's Bank to the fish and lobster populations there and what measures that industry would or could take to protect them. I vividly recall thinking at the time about the worst case scenarios and that a few oiled lobsters might be better than a world of mostly radioactive lobster and also that, if the United States could gain energy independence from OPEC through a rational and balanced national energy policy of domestic production and conservation, perhaps we could avoid nuclear strife in the Middle East and the massive cost and transfer of wealth from our country to OPEC. (That peaceful transfer of wealth at the time (and

The transfer of U.S. dollars to OPEC and strife in the Middle East continues today with its concomitant high cost.

now) has no known precedent in the history of the world.) The transfer of U.S. dollars to OPEC and strife in the Middle East continues today with its concomitant high cost.

We face better choices for our nation, our OCS, our coastal areas, and the ocean. Since 1969, our nation's OCS oil and gas extraction activities, mandated to use the best and safest technology in the world, pose little risk to our coastal areas compared to that of oil tankers loaded with foreign oil. The true conflict today may not be between offshore OCS development and pristine coastal areas, but between those areas and imported oil tankering. Back in 1992, MMS Director S. Scott Sewell stated that "U.S. [OCS] natural gas could, if fully tapped and distributed, defang OPEC, help save the environment, and fuel an economic renaissance." That may still hold true in 2008.

Notes

1. 43 U.S.C. §§ 1331 *et seq.*
2. *See* United States v. California, 332 U.S. 19 (1947); United States v. Louisiana, 340 U.S. 899 (1950); United States v. Texas, 339 U.S. 707 (1950).
3. Pub. L. No. 83-31, 67 Stat. 29, 43 U.S.C. §§ 1301–1315, May 22, 1953.
4. Pub. L. No. 83-212, 67 Stat. 462, 43 U.S.C. §§ 1331–1343, Aug. 7, 1953.
5. 43 U.S.C. § 1332.
6. 16 U.S.C. § 1456.
7. 43 U.S.C. § 1354.
8. *Id.* § 1341. This section authorizes the president to "from time to time withdraw from disposition any of the unleased lands of the outer Continental Shelf." President Eisenhower withdrew the first OCS area from leasing for the Key Largo Coral Reef Preserve. *See* Proclamation No. 3339, 25 Fed. Reg. 2352 (Mar. 17, 1960).
9. *Id.* § 1343.
10. *Id.* § 1337.
11. The regulations governing the pre-sale process and leasing of the submerged lands are found at 30 C.F.R. pt. 256. The operational regulatory regime for leases is contained in the regulations codified at 30 C.F.R. pt. 250. The seismic exploration permitting regulations are found at 30 C.F.R. pt. 251; royalty terms and matters at 30 C.F.R. pts. 203 and 260. The entire regulatory regime, much of its history, and all current and pending MMS OCS regulatory matters can be viewed at MMS's Web site, http://www.mms.gov.
12. *Id.* § 1344(a).
13. *Id.* § 1344(a)(1).
14. *Id.* § 1344(a)(2) & (3).
15. *Id.* § 1332.
16. *Id.* § 1344(d)(3).
17. *Id.* § 1344(e). *See also* Solicitor's Opinion M-36983 (1996), *available at* www.Doi.gov/sol/M36983.pdf.
18. The first three proposals were robust, followed Section 18's directive for an equitable program, and preceded the Congressional moratoria. The three thereafter five-year programs chose to exclude from consideration those areas off limits to leasing via Section 12's Presidential withdrawals. The latest five-year program includes small areas previously off-limits. Because of the short time span of congressional budget moratoria on spending any funds for leasing, Section 18's five-year leasing process outlives and thus does not trump, arguably, annual congressional moratoria. *See* text *infra* at note 75.
19. 43 U.S.C. § 1349(c)(1).
20. *Id.* § 1344(d)(3).
21. *Id.* § 1349(c)(6).
22. 712 F.2d 584 (1983).
23. 668 F.2d 1290 (1981).

24. 712 F.2d 584 (1983); *See also* Natural Res. Def. Council v. Hodel, 865 F.2d 288 (D.C. Cir. 1988).

25. *See* Outer Continental Shelf Five Year Program 2007–2012, *available at* www.mms.gov/5-year/. This five-year program has been challenged by several plaintiffs in two consolidated D.C. circuit cases: Center for Biological Diversity v. DOI, No. 07-1247 and Native Village of Point Hope, Alaska Wilderness League, Pacific Environment v. DOI, No. 07-1344 (D.C. Cir.)

26. This process was challenged in *Blanco v. Burton*, Civ. Action No. 06-3813 (2006 E.D. La.). While a preliminary injunction motion failed by the state, the court viewed tiering off a 2002 EIS to examine impacts of an OCS sale after Hurricane Katrina to be suspect. The case on the merits, which involved NEPA, CZMA, and OCSLA claims, was settled on October 24, 2006.

27. Sec'y of the Interior v. California, 464 U.S. 312 (1984).

28. 16 U.S.C. § 1456. The only redress at that point is an Administrative Procedures Act challenge to the Secretary's decision.

29. 43 U.S.C. § 1352.

30. 30 C.F.R. § 251.4.

31. *Id.* §§ 250.201 and 250.202. Preliminary site review exploration activities may occur to analyze the best approach for and impacts of an exploration plan. 30 C.F.R. § 250.207.

32. *Id.* § 250.201(b).

33. *Id.* §§ 250.211 and 250.212.

34. On April 13, 2007, MMS finalized updated comprehensive regulations for protected species. 72 Fed. Reg. 18,578 (Apr. 13, 2007).

35. *Id.* C.F.R. §§ 250.241 and 250.242.

36. 43 U.S.C. § 1351(e).

37. *Id.* § 1345(a) through (d) and 43 U.S.C. § 1351(a)(3).

38. 30 C.F.R. § 250.1101.

39. 43 U.S.C. § 1348(c).

40. *Id.* 1350.

41. *Id.* 1347(b).

42. These include personnel training and education; emergency and evacuation plans; structural removal and site clearance; oil-spill response plans; pollution prevention; operator financial responsibility; pipeline rights-of-way; pipeline design, safety, and inspection; resource evaluations; environmental studies; technical assessment and research; and the proverbial "all other matters and needs as they arise."

43. *See, e.g.,* 30 C.F.R. §§ 250.107(a) and 250.1002.

44. *Id.* § 250.141 to .143.

45. *Id.* § 250, subpt. N.

46. *Id.* § 250.173(a).

47. 43 U.S.C. § 1337 and 30 C.F.R. § 250.181 to .185.

48. 30 C.F.R. § 254.

49. *Id.* § 254.2.

50. *Id.* § pt. 253.

51. *Id.* § 250, subpt. J.

52. *Id.* § 250.455.

53. *Id.* § 250.300.

54. *Id.* §§ 440 to 451; 515–516; 615–616; and 1610 to 1612.

55. *Id.* § 250.800.

56. *Id.* § 250.1100.

57. It is beyond the scope of this chapter to expound on all of these matters in any detail. For more information, the MMS Web site, http://www.mms.gov, provides a thorough updated overview of the responsibilities, regulations, and ongoing OCS program matters.

58. 30 C.F.R. §§ 250.902 and 250.1700-.1754.

59. *Id.* § 250.1725(a), .1730.

60. *Id.* § 250.1728.
61. *See, e.g., id.* § 250.900(g), .901.
62. Gulf Oil Corp. v. Morton, 493 F.2d 141 (9th Cir. 1974).
63. Union Oil Co. of Cal. v. Morton, 512 F.2d 743 (9th Cir. 1975).
64. Conservation Law Found. v. Watt, 560 F. Supp. 561 (D. Mass.), *aff'd,* Massachusetts v. Watt, 716 F. 2d 946 (1st Cir. 1983).
65. *See* California v. Watt (the Secretary Andrus proposal), 668 F.2d 1290 (D.C. Cir. 1981); California v. Watt (the Secretary Watt proposal), 712 F.2d 584 (D.C. Cir. 1983); Natural Res. Def. Council v. Hodel, 865 F.2d 288 (D.C. Cir. 1988).
66. Sec'y of the Interior v. California, 464 U.S. 312 (1984).
67. 43 U.S.C. § 1337(j).
68. Alabama v. U.S. Dep't of the Interior, 84 F.3d 410 (11th Cir. 1996).
69. California v. Norton, 311 F.3d 1162 (9th Cir. 2002).
70. *See* Santa Fe Snyder Corp. v. Norton, 385 F. 3d 884 (5th Cir. 2004); Kerr-McGee Oil & Gas Corp. v. Burton, No. 06-CV0439 LC (W.D. La. Mar. 17, 2006).
71. Marathon Oil Corp. v. United States, 530 U.S. 604 (1999).
72. *Santa Fe Snyder Corp,* 385 F. 3d 884.
73. Gerald R. Ford's Remarks at Dedication Ceremonies for the National Environmental Research Center, Cincinnati, Ohio, July 3, 1975, http://www.fordlibrarymuseum.gov/library/speeches/750373.htm.
74. *See Marathon Oil,* 530 U.S. 604.
75. *Id.*
76. 43 U.S.C. §§ 1337 and 1344.
77. 43 U.S.C. 1333.
78. 99 CONG. REC. 6963 (1953).
79. 43 U.S.C. § 1333(a)(2005).
80. The First Circuit upheld the district court's opinion in *Alliance to Protect Nantucket Sound v. U.S. Department of the Army,* 398 F.3d 105 (1st Cir. 2005). The First Circuit determined the "which may be" language in § 1333(a)(1) was ambiguous, but that there was no need to invoke *Chevron* deference because the "legislative history reveals, with exceptional clarity, Congress's intent that Section 4 authority under OCSLA not be restricted to structures related to mineral extraction." *Id.* at 109.
81. 43 U.S.C. § 1333(a)(1) (emphasis added).
82. Alliance to Protect Nantucket Sound, Inc. v. U.S. Army Corps of Eng'rs, 288 F. Supp. 2d 64 (D. Mass. 2003) (footnotes omitted) (holding that the language of § 1333(a) did not limit the United States' jurisdiction to artificial islands and installations related to natural resources) (emphasis added).
83. S. 1901, 83d Cong. (1st Sess. 1953) (as introduced) (emphasis added). That language tracks that in Presidential Proclamation Number 2667 described above.
84. *See* S. REP. NO. 83-411, at 15.
85. *Id.* at 23.
86. S. 1901, 83d Cong. (1st Sess. 1953). Section 3 was codified as 43 U.S.C. § 1332, but the entire section was replaced by the 1978 amendments to the OCSLA. *See* Outer Continental Shelf Lands Act Amendments of 1978 ("OCSLA Amendments"), Pub. L. No. 95-372, § 202, 92 Stat. 629, 634–35 (1978).
87. H.R. REP. NO. 95-590, at 127 (1977); H.R. CONF. REP. NO. 95-1474, at 79 (1978) ("The original provisions of section 3, providing that the subsoil and seabed of the OCS belong to the United States and that all existing rights of navigation and fishing in OCS waters are to be continued, are restated").
88. 43 U.S.C. § 1332 (emphasis added).
89. S. 1901, 83d Cong. (1st Sess. 1953) (as introduced). To read the entire text of section 4 as introduced, *see infra* 115.
90. S. REP. NO. 83-411, at 23 (emphasis added).
91. Additional examples of Congressional intent to assert jurisdiction over the entire OCS abound. *See* S. REP. NO. 83-411, at 2 ("The purpose of S. 1901, as amended, is to assert

the exclusive jurisdiction and control of the Federal Government . . . over the seabed and subsoil of the outer Continental Shelf, and to provide for the development of its vast mineral resources." (emphasis added)); 99 CONG. REC. 6962 (Senator Cordon: "I call to the attention of the Members of the Senate the fact that the jurisdiction declared embraces the seabed and subsoil as an entity, and is not merely asserted over the natural resources of that seabed and subsoil, as was provided in the proclamation of September 28, 1945. . . ." (emphasis added)); 99 CONG. REC. 6964 (Senator Cordon: "There is a recognition, from cover to cover, in the bill, of the sole jurisdiction and control of seabed and subsoil by the Federal Government, but no change in the character of the waters nor with respect to fishing or navigation in them.").

92. *See* Deepwater Port Act of 1974, 88 Stat. 2127.

93. *See* H.R. CONF. REP. NO. 35-1474, at 75; *see also Alliance to Protect Nantucket Sound,* 288 F. Supp. 2d at 75 n.83 ("[T]he 1978 amendments to the OCSLA did not materially amend the key modifying phrase in *section 1333(a).* . . . It is, therefore, the case that if the Corps had the authority to issue a permit for the placement of a structure unrelated to mineral extraction on the OCS prior to 1978 (and both parties agree that it had that authority), then the 1978 amendments should have had no effect on that power."); *Alliance to Protect Nantucket Sound,* 288 F. Supp. 2d at 75 ("Congress has, thus, made crystal clear its intention that the Corps exert jurisdiction over *both extractive and non-extractive structures on the OCS.*" (emphasis added)).

94. H.R. REP. NO. 95-590, at 54 ("Congress has a special constitutional responsibility to make all needful rules and regulations respecting the territory or other property belonging to the United States. (U.S. Constitution, art. IV, sec. 3. clause 2).").

95. *Id.* at 122 (emphasis added).

96. H.R. CONF. REP. NO. 95-1474, at 82.

97. *Id.* As provided in its regulations, a Corps of Engineers' Section 10 permit does not confer property rights on the recipient. *See Alliance to Protect Nantucket Sound,* 398 F.3d at 110. Although the First Circuit has determined that additional authorization other than a Section 10 permit is not needed when the structure involved is temporary and minor, its opinion cast serious doubt as to whether a Section 10 permit alone could serve as a sufficient authorization to construct anything other than an insignificant structure on the OCS. With reference to a large-scale wind energy plant proposed for the OCS within Nantucket Sound, the First Circuit stated:

> Whether, and under what circumstances, additional authorization is necessary before a developer infringes on the federal government's rights in the OCS is a thorny issue, one that is unnecessary to delve into in the instant case. The data tower at issue here involves no real infringement on federal interests in the OCS lands. To start, the structure is temporary, of five years' duration, more than two of which have now passed. . . . It is inconceivable to us that permission to erect a single, temporary scientific device, like this, which gives the federal government information it requires, could be an infringement on any federal property ownership interest in the OCS. . . . We do not here evaluate whether congressional authorization is necessary for construction of Cape Wind's proposed wind energy plant, a structure vastly larger in scale, complexity, and duration, which is not at issue in the present action.

Id. at 114. The need for clear legal authority to develop renewable energy projects on the OCS that would vest authority in the Secretary of the Interior, rather than the Corps, led to the enactment of Section 388 of the EPA of 2005, codified at 43 U.S.C. § 1337(p) (2007). Under Section 388, the Secretary of the Department of the Interior, in consultation with the USCG and other agencies, must first grant a lease, easement, or right-of-way to develop alternate energy facilities on the OCS. That decision must take into account a number of factors, including, inter alia: safety; protection of the environment; prevention of waste; conservation of the natural resources of the outer Continental Shelf; coordination with relevant federal agencies; protection of national security interests of the United

States; a fair return to the United States for any lease, easement, or right-of-way under this subsection; prevention of interference with reasonable uses (as determined by the Secretary) of the exclusive economic zone, the high seas, and the territorial seas; and other factors.

98. Convention on the Continental Shelf, art. 2, Apr. 29, 1958, 15 U.S.T.S. 471.

99. *Id.*

100. Whitney v. Robertson, 124 U.S. 190, 194 (1888).

101. *Id.*

102. Cook v. United States, 288 U.S. 102, 120 (1933).

103. *See* Weinberger v. Rossi, 456 U.S. 25, 32 (1982).

104. 87 I.D. 593, M-36928 (Nov. 24, 1980).

105. 569 F.2d 330 (5th Cir. 1978).

106. *Id.*

107. Some remarks made in the context of the Geneva Convention indicate that nations do not have sovereignty over other specific aspects that touch the OCS, e.g., shipwrecks.

108. In reference to the Geneva Convention, the International Law Commission stated:

> Commission accepted the idea that the coastal State may exercise control and jurisdiction over the continental shelf, with the proviso that such control and jurisdiction shall be exercised solely for the purpose of exploiting its resources; and *it rejected any claim to sovereignty or jurisdiction over the superjacent waters.*

U.N. General Assembly Official Records, Eleventh Session, supp. no. 9 (A/3159), p. 40 (emphasis added). The real concern of the International Law Commission appears to be the claims of nations to the high seas above the OCS.

109. 288 F. Supp. 2d 64 (D. Mass. 2003).

110. 373 F.3d 183 (1st Cir. 2004).

111. 423 F.2d 16, 21 (5th Cir. 1970).

112. 43 U.S.C. § 1333(a)(2)(A) (emphasis added).

113. *See* Gulf Offshore Co. v. Mobil Oil Corp., 453 U.S. 473, 480 (1981) ("All law applicable to the Outer Continental Shelf is federal law, but to fill the substantial 'gaps' in the coverage of federal law, OCSLA borrows the 'applicable and not inconsistent' laws of the adjacent States as surrogate federal law."); Rodrigue v. Aetna Cas. & Sur. Co., 395 U.S. 352, 357 (1969) ("Since federal law, because of its limited function in a federal system, might be inadequate to cope with the full range of potential legal problems, the Act supplemented gaps in the federal law with state law through the "adoption of State law as the law of the United States."); *see also Ten Taxpayer,* 373 F.3d at 193 ("Federal law is interstitial by its nature, and no other body of law applies on the outer Continental Shelf. So rather than legislate for every conceivable circumstance that might arise, Congress simply incorporated state law, thereby simultaneously retaining federal control over the outer Continental Shelf and ensuring that a comprehensive body of substantive law will be available to resolve disputes.").

114. *See* S. REP. No. 83-411, at 6 ("The primary policy question before the committee in its consideration of S. 1901 has been not a question of State versus Federal rights, but whether, and how far, the Federal Government should make use of already existing State laws and State facilities, backed by state experience and knowledge, in providing for administration of the area. The argument was that the States already were on the job, that they had a governmental system in operation which was effective for the purpose, and that no real need existed for Congress to enact new law, in an area of activity new to the Federal Government."); 99 CONG. REC. 4884 (Congressman Brooks: "I can say that section 9 [which became § 4] is the heart of the whole bill.); 99 CONG. REC. 6963 (Senator Cordon: "Section 4 might be said to be the heart of the bill legislatively and administratively.").

115. S. 1901, 83d Cong. (1st Sess. 1953) (as introduced). Specifically, the original version of Senate Bill 1901 stated:

> (a) All acts occurring and all offenses committed on any structure (other than a vessel), which is located on the outer Continental Shelf or on the waters above the outer Continental Shelf for the purpose of exploring for, developing, or removing

the natural resources of the subsoil or seabed of such outer Continental Shelf, shall be deemed to have occurred or been committed aboard a vessel of the United States on the high seas and shall be adjudicated and determined or adjudged and punished according to the laws relating to such acts or offenses occurring on vessels of the United States on the high seas.

S. 1901, 83d Cong. (1st Sess. 1953) (as introduced).

116. *See* 99 CONG. REC. 4882–83 (Congressman Willis: "[Applying federal law116] is a brand new approach to the problem. I repeat that this approach was never before contained in any bill introduced in Congress. . . . Heretofore the bills provided that begin with, the laws and police power of the States would apply, until such time at least as Congress and committees of Congress studied the question of the adequacy and applicability of Federal laws to the Continental Shelf."); *see also* Letter from J. Lee Rankin, Assistant Attorney General, Office of Legal Council (May 26, 1953), *reprinted in* S. REP. NO. 83-411, at 33 (disapproving of the state law supplement to federal law because "[i]t raises a serious constitutional question of delegation of legislative power. This is a Federal area, outside State boundaries, and to give the States a sort of extraterritorial jurisdiction over it is unnecessary and undesirable. The situation is not comparable to that of federally owned areas within a State, as to which State law has some measure of applicability.").

117. *See* S. REP. NO. 83-411, at 23.

118. 99 CONG. REC. 6963–64. Indeed, in 1948, a bill was introduced in the House that would have given states exclusive control over the OCS. *See* H.R. 5992, 80th Cong. (1948); *see also* H.R. REP. NO. 80-1778 (1948).

119. *Id.* at 6963.

120. *Id.*

121. *Id.* Interestingly and by design, the original Section 4 adopted only those state laws in effect at the time the bill was passed in 1953 as federal law. OCSLA, Pub. L. No. 83-212, § 4, 67 Stat. 462 (1953) ("To the extent that they are applicable and not inconsistent with this Act or with other Federal laws and regulations of the Secretary now in effect or hereafter adopted, the civil and criminal laws of each adjacent State *as of the effective date of this Act* are hereby declared to be the law of the United States. . . ." (emphasis added)); *see* 99 CONG. REC. 6963–64. Congress changed that provision during the 1975 Amendment. Deepwater Port Act of 1974, Pub. L. No. 93-627, § 19(f), 88 Stat. 2126, 2146 (1975) (striking "as of the effective date of this Act" and inserting "now in effect or hereafter adopted, amended, or repealed").

122. *Id.* at 6964.

123. *Id.*

124. *See* H.R. 5134, 83d Cong. (1st Sess. 1953) (as introduced).

125. *Id.* (emphasis added).

126. S. REP. NO. 83-411, at 3.

127. *Id.*

128. H.R. REP. NO. 83-215, at 7–8 (1953).

129. H.R. REP. NO. 82-695 (1951), *reprinted at* H.R. REP. NO. 83-215, at 11.

130. *Id.* at 23.

131. *See* S. REP. NO. 95-284, at 48 (1977).

132. *Id.*

133. *See* S. 9, 95th Cong. § 203 (1st Sess. 1977); S. REP. NO. 95-284, at 6, 72. Specifically, Senate Bill 9 changed the wording in section 4(a)(1) by replacing "fixed structures" with "all installations and other devices permanently or temporarily attached to the seabed" and changing "removing, and transporting resources therefrom" to "or producing resources therefrom, or any such installation or other device (other than a ship or vessel) for the purpose of transporting such resources." S. 9, 95th Cong. § 203 (1st Sess. 1977). As to Section 4(a)(2) of the OCSLA, all Senate Bill 9 did was to add a time limit for resolving international boundary disputes. The committee helpfully noted that "Section 203 amends section 4 of the OCS Act. The intent is clear." S. REP. NO. 95-284, at 72.

134. H.R. Conf. Rep. No. 35-1474, at 75, 80 ("The intent of the managers in amending section 4(a) of the 1953 OCS Act is technical and perfecting and is meant to restate and clarify and not change existing law. Under the conference report language, Federal law is to be applicable to all activities on all devices in contact with the seabed for exploration, development, and production.").

135. *See* 43 U.S.C. § 1333(a)(1) ("The Constitution and laws and civil and political jurisdiction of the United States are hereby extended to the subsoil and seabed of the [OCS] . . . to the same extent as if the [OCS] were an area of exclusive Federal jurisdiction located within a State. . . .").

136. United States v. Lewis, 523 U.S. 155, 158 (1998).

137. *Id.*

138. *Id.* at 160.

139. United States v. Ray, 294 F. Supp. 532, 539 (S.D. Fla. 1969).

140. *Ray,* 423 F.2d at 22.

141. *Id.* at 20.

142. *Id.* In the OCSLA, the OCS is defined as "all submerged lands lying seaward and outside of the area of lands beneath navigable waters . . . and of which the subsoil and seabed appertain to the United States and are subject to its jurisdiction and control." In the Geneva Convention on the Continental Shelf, the OCS is defined as "(a) . . . the seabed and subsoil of the submarine areas adjacent to the coast but outside the area of the territorial sea, to a depth of 200 metres or, beyond that limit, to where the depth of the superjacent waters admits of the exploitation of the natural resources of the said areas; (b) to the seabed and subsoil of similar submarine areas adjacent to the coasts of islands." Geneva Convention on the Continental Shelf, Article 1, Apr. 29, 1958, 15 U.S.T. 471.

143. *Id.*

144. *See* 43 U.S.C. § 1301(e) (The term "natural resources" is defined as including "oil, gas, *and all other minerals,* and fish, shrimp, oysters, clams, crabs, lobsters, sponges, kelp, *and other marine animal and plant life."* (emphasis added)).

145. Geneva Convention on the Continental Shelf, Article 2, ¶ 4, Apr. 29, 1958, 15 U.S.T.S. 471.

146. *Ray,* 423 F.2d at 22–23.

147. 43 U.S.C. § 1333(a)(2)(A).

148. *See* 71 Fed. Reg. 127 (Jan. 3, 2006).

149. *See* OCS Alternative Energy and Alternate Use Programmatic EIS Information Center, http://ocsenergy.anl.gov.

150. 43 U.S.C. 1356a.

151. States eligible to receive funding are Alabama (Baldwin and Mobile counties), Alaska, California, Louisiana (Assumption, Calcasieu, Cameron, Iberia, Jefferson, Lafourche, Livingston, Orleans, Plaquemines, St. Bernard, St. Charles, St. James, St. John the Baptist, St. Martin, St. Mary, St. Tammany, Tangipahoa, Terrebonne, and Vermilion parishes), Mississippi (Hancock, Harrison, and Jackson counties), and Texas (Aransas, Brazoria, Calhoun, Cameron, Chambers, Galveston, Harris, Jackson, Jefferson, Kenedy, Kleberg, Matagorda, Nueces, Orange, Refugio, San Patricio, Victoria, and Willacy counties). A total of 67 CPSs are eligible to receive CIAP funding.

152. Consistency for Federal Assistance to State and Local Governments (15 C.F.R. § 930.90–930.101).

153. Pub. L. No. 109-432.

154. Proclamation No. 7219, 64 Fed. Reg. 48,701 (Aug. 2, 1999).

chapter fourteen

Emerging Ocean Uses

Ann Powers
Odin Smith

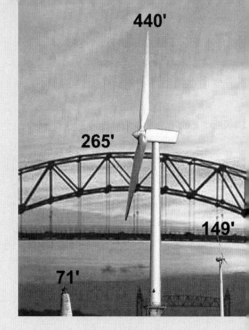

I. Introduction

Although a broad array of issues that currently affect our oceans are outlined in this book, there are numerous others that are either of current concern, or may be in the near future. Special cognizance should be taken of the challenges presented by new technologies and emerging uses. Some of the challenges are similar, involving uncertain jurisdictions, unknown impacts, and lack of comprehensive governance. In this chapter we outline problems from the quasi-traditional aquaculture activities conducted in a new ocean context, to energy production and the questions attendant on the development of alternative sources such as wind, wave, and current power, to cutting edge bioprospecting related activities. Other potential uses not treated in these materials also merit continued attention such as harvesting microorganisms for food or other uses, encouraging algal blooms through chemical means, proposals to sequester carbon in ocean plants, the production of methane hydrates, the impact of nanotechnology produced materials on ocean biota, and the exploitation of Antarctic resources.

II. The Current State of the Law

One of the salient characteristics of the current state of ocean law in general is that it is not comprehensive. The recent reports of both the U.S. Commission on Ocean

---

The views expressed in this chapter are those of the authors and do not necessarily reflect those of NOAA or the U.S. Department of Commerce.

Policy and the Pew Oceans Commission have noted that ocean law is currently a mélange of resource- and activity-specific statutes and regulatory programs that have been established as particular needs have developed.[1] Given this, it is not surprising that the current state of the law regarding emerging ocean uses is best characterized as nascent, and still in flux. Emerging and unresolved issues have precipitated the use of existing authorities in new ways, as well as the establishment of entirely new authorities. For example, the first proposed offshore wind energy project in the United States, the Cape Wind project in Nantucket Sound, initially began regulatory review under the authority of Section 10 of the Rivers and Harbors Act of 1899, with the U.S. Army Corps of Engineers as the lead federal regulatory agency.[2] Since then, however, the Minerals Management Service (MMS) has assumed the lead federal agency role for the Cape Wind project under the authority of the amendments to the Outer Continental Shelf Lands Act enacted in the Energy Policy Act of 2005.[3] As a further example, jurisdiction over offshore hydrokinetic energy projects is not yet fully resolved between the MMS's authority under the recently enacted Energy Policy Act, and the Federal Energy Regulatory Commission's authority under the venerable Federal Power Act.[4] Notably, the ongoing resolution of these emerging issues in ocean law continues the established pattern of resource- and activity-specific responses to new demands, rather than a truly comprehensive approach to ocean governance.

III. Emerging and Unresolved Issues

A. Marine Aquaculture (Mariculture)

1. Status of the Industry

Aquaculture, the cultivation of aquatic organisms, particularly fish for human consumption, is hardly a new activity. Chinese cultivation may date back as much as four thousand years, and Egyptian hieroglyphics indicate that some type of aquaculture was practiced. Even biblical references to such activities can be found.[5] Over time, capturing and impounding fish has been practiced on a small scale in many societies, as has the propagation of shellfish. Because of the modest level at which these activities were carried out, there was generally little negative impact on the local environment.

In the late 1800s formal hatchery programs were developed in Europe and the United States, aimed primarily at stocking streams for recreational fisheries.[6] Over time the focus of many of the noncommercial hatchery programs shifted from merely stocking programs to propagation of threatened or endangered species.[7] It was not until after World War II that farming fish for commercial purposes was undertaken on any substantial scale. In the United States, the chosen species was primarily catfish, and the farming typically was done by small aquaculturists in freshwater ponds created for that purpose. Although environmental problems might be associated with these facilities, they usually did not destroy significant habitats or create extensive pollution. But as the world's population has increased and as countries have become more affluent, world demand for protein in the form of fish also has increased. As a result both freshwater and marine aquaculture (mariculture) has been expanding, at the same time that capture fisheries have remained stable or have declined.[8]

In 2005 almost 48 million metric tons of fish were farmed, the bulk by China.[9] The United States produces only a small proportion of the world's aquaculture harvest, but its share is growing, with increasing attention to marine species. Moreover, the United States is a major consumer of fish products, and thus has a substantial trade imbalance for these products. In 1999 the U.S. Department of Commerce issued its Aquaculture Policy with the vision of developing "a highly competitive, sustainable aquaculture industry," which would increase domestic production at least fivefold by 2025 to offset the annual trade deficit in seafood.[10]

2. Environmental Issues

With the growth of aquaculture in the United States have come increased problems, both social and environmental. This is especially true for marine aquaculture. Because most facilities are in near-shore waters they may be placed in fragile coastal habitats, and may raise community concerns about siting. These facilities can lead to destruction of habitats and alterations to local ecosystems,[11] impairment of water quality, along with the potential for introduced diseases. In addition, escapees from aquaculture operations may pose genetic threats to wild species.[12]

With the growth of aquaculture in the United States have come increased problems, both social and environmental.

Marine aquaculture poses additional concerns in the United States because it has focused largely on the production of high-end species, mostly salmon and shrimp. Both of these species are carnivorous, and require feeds made from other fish. By contrast, freshwater catfish are herbivores and so can be fed meals made from vegetable crops such as soybeans. Shellfish, such as oysters, provide an even greater contrast, since they require no feed but instead filter their food from the water column, a process that has the ancillary benefit of improving water quality. While it might seem that fish farming adds to the amount of fish mass, it is not true for carnivorous varieties.[13] Indeed, producing a pound of salmon may require two pounds or more of forage fish such as anchovy or menhaden. The commercial capture of such forage species not only depletes the stock, but may also upset the ecological balance of the fishing area and deprive wild predator fish, including the native varieties of farmed fish, of adequate food.[14] As we increasingly use biotechnology to genetically alter organisms in order to produce fish particularly suited for aquaculture, such genetically modified or transgenic fish may pose additional threats for wild populations.[15] For these reasons some states have banned or are considering stringent controls on offshore fish farming.[16]

Most marine species are raised in net pen systems located in near-shore waters, and in the United States appropriate sites are limited. Accordingly, there is increasing commercial interest in establishing facilities further offshore, within the exclusive economic zone (EEZ) of the United States,[17] although the technology remains experimental and costly.[18] An additional barrier to the expansion of aquaculture into the EEZ is the unclear regulatory structure for such operations.[19]

3. Regulatory Issues

In the United States, aquaculture falls within the purview of a number of federal departments and agencies, implementing a myriad of federal laws. The agencies include the U.S. Departments of Agriculture and the Interior (U.S. Fish & Wildlife Service); the U.S. Coast Guard; the U.S. Army Corps of Engineers;[20] the Food and Drug Administration;[21] and most important for offshore aquaculture, the National Oceanic and Atmospheric Administration's (NOAA) National Marine Fisheries Service (NMFS) in the Department of Commerce,[22] and the Environmental Protection Agency.[23] In addition, the states play a significant role in regulating aquaculture activities within their coastal jurisdictions.[24]

Reports produced by the Pew Oceans Commission in 2003 and the U.S. Commission on Ocean Policy in 2004 both noted the fragmented regulatory system and recommended a comprehensive and environmentally sound regulatory program for offshore aquaculture.[25] Subsequently, the Bush Administration issued the U.S. Ocean Action Plan, which tasked NOAA with developing a regulatory scheme for offshore projects that resulted in the introduction in Congress of the National Offshore Aquaculture Act of 2005.[26] The bill languished in Committee and was reintroduced in substantially similar form in 2007.[27] The proposed Act does not supersede other authorities, but grants to the Secretary of Commerce the authority to establish a permit program for aquaculture in the United States' EEZ and calls for coordination among agencies.[28] The permit program would in essence lease federal offshore submerged lands for use as aquaculture sites. The regulation of the facilities would, however, be subject to the Clean Water Act and its wastewater-permitting provisions.

The Environmental Protection Agency is entrusted with implementation of the Clean Water Act.[29] Section 318 of the Act[30] directs the Administrator to issue procedures and guidelines for permitting aquaculture projects, and provides for the states to establish their own programs, with EPA's approval.[31] EPA issued regulations under the National Pollutant Discharge Elimination System (NPDES),[32] defining as point sources concentrated aquatic animal production (CAAP) facilities,[33] and in 2004 established categorical effluent guidelines for the industry.[34] The guidelines apply to commercial and noncommercial fish farms, hatcheries, reserves and other aquaculture facilities that meet the definition of CAAP and produce 100,000 pounds or more of aquatic animals per year in flow-through, recirculating, net pen, or submerged cage systems.[35] Flow-through and recirculating are land-based systems and thus have different characteristics and problems than net pen systems, which are located in open water and are of primary interest for offshore aquaculture.[36]

Net pens are typically anchored in open water, and depend on the tides and currents to bring fresh oxygenated water to the facility and remove wastes. Net pen facilities can release high levels of solids and biological oxygen demanding wastes, primarily from fish feces and uneaten feeds,[37] as well as antibiotics and pesticides, which are used to protect the health of the farmed animals.[38] In addition, metals and other contaminants may leach from the structures and associated equipment themselves.[39] These substances can pollute the water and sediments, and may negatively affect the benthic community in the area of the pens. Because EPA believes that treating wastewater is not generally realistic, regulation of net pens under the Clean Water Act's NPDES system focuses on management practices that minimize the release of pollutants, including proper practices for feed management,[40] storage of drugs and pesticides to avoid spilling, and disposal of feed bags, nets, and other materials, as well as minimizing the discharge of dead animals or animal parts.[41] Regular inspection and maintenance are also key.[42] The standards for new and existing facilities are the same, although the Agency stresses the importance of siting in evaluating new facilities.[43] The Agency emphasizes the potential for growth of offshore production and notes that these facilities will be subject to NPDES permitting and new source requirements for net pens.[44]

Regulation of aquaculture facilities under the Clean Water Act has been challenged on at least two occasions, in both instances by citizens. In *U.S. Public Interest Research Group v. Atlantic Salmon of Maine,* the court found that a net pen facility was subject to the Clean Water Act and that the operators had discharged various pollutants without a permit, including salmon feces and urine, uneaten feed, chemicals to combat infection and lice, and copper flakes from the pens.[45] The nonnative salmon that escaped were also found to be pollutants whose discharge was prohibited, and the court enjoined the company from stocking nonnative fish.[46] In *Association to Protect Hammersley, Eld, and Totten Inlets v. Taylor Resources, Inc.,* a group of coastal residents sued a company raising and harvesting mussels on floating rafts, without a permit under the Clean Water Act.[47] The mussels were grown without using feed or chemicals, but cultivated in a natural state. As a consequence, the court found that the feces and shells from the mussels were not pollutants since they did not result from a transformative human process. Thus the facility did not run afoul of the Act's prohibitions.[48] The court also determined that the rafts were not point sources because EPA's regulations defining concentrated aquatic animal production facilities exempts entities that feed less than a specified amount of food.[49] Both cases affirm EPA's generally authority to regulate aquaculture facilities.

4. International Issues

As a major consumer of aquaculture products, the United States is in a position to encourage progressive and sustainable practices at a global level. The Pew Oceans Commission noted that the United States had prevailed before a World Trade Organization panel when a U.S. prohibition on the importation of shrimp that were not harvested using turtle excluder devices was challenged.[50] The Commission suggested that the United States, after adopting appropriate measures for its own aquaculture industry, might then use the measures as a model to negotiate trade agreements with other countries, which would encourage similar measures on their part.[51] Because most mariculture will be carried out within national territorial waters, or at least within countries' EEZs, global commons questions are not likely to arise. However, the mariculture activities of one nation may have transboundary effects on its neighbors. The United Nation's Food and Agriculture Organization has adopted a Code of Conduct for Responsible Fisheries that includes a section on aquaculture development.[52] Although the code is voluntary, some aspects of it, such as the admonition to avoid impacts on other nations, may be international law due to treaties or custom. The Code seeks to protect transboundary aquatic ecosystems and encourages states to consult with their neighboring states before introducing nonnative or genetically altered species into transboundary aquatic ecosystems.[53] The Code also calls for a variety of other actions and safeguards, both to assure the ecological soundness of mariculture activities and to prevent damage by one state to the fisheries and ecosystems of others.[54]

5. The Future

With the NPDES regulations in place, and the proposed National Offshore Aquaculture Act under consideration by Congress, the United States is beginning to establish a regulatory framework that could address some of the major concerns about the management of the U.S. aquaculture industry and the fragmented federal responsibilities. At present, however, there is no way to determine the final shape any legislation may take. If enacted in its present form, pending federal legislation leaves other statutes in place and may not substantially reduce the regulatory hurdles for an entity seeking to establish an offshore facility. Nor does it adequately address public participation or environmental issues. Much will depend on the degree to which enforcement under the Clean Water Act assures that any offshore facilities constructed are operated in a manner that not only advances the fishery but also protects the environment.

B. Liquefied Natural Gas

1. Status of the Industry

The United States is the world's largest consumer of natural gas, using roughly 23 trillion cubic feet of gas a year, almost a quarter of the world's production.[55] Although the United States is also a major natural gas producer, primarily from the Gulf of Mexico region, consumption outstrips production. As a consequence the United States imports over 4 trillion cubic feet a year, mostly by pipeline from Canada. A small amount is imported in liquefied form by ship to the United States, to be vaporized at U.S. facilities and fed into pipelines servicing various regions of the country.[56] Liquefied natural gas (LNG) is primarily methane (CH_4), and has been converted from its normal gaseous state by refrigeration in a liquefaction plant, typically to −260 degrees Fahrenheit. This process reduces the volume of the gas by a ratio of 1:610 of its original state, making shipping and large-scale storage practical.[57] Unlike liquefied petroleum gas (LPG), primarily propane and butane, LNG is not pressurized.[58] The reduction in volume is caused by refrigeration, not pressurization. But the LNG is volatile, and does require special double-walled cryogenic containers that maintain the liquid at the requisite temperature.[59] A typical LNG tanker is over 900 feet long, with as many as five tanks, each holding 6.5 million gallons.[60]

The market for natural gas has varied in the past, but it appears that the demand for gas will rise as the cost of oil increases and the search for cleaner forms of fuel becomes more serious, especially for electric utilities. However, the United States has barely three percent of the world's natural gas reserves,[61] and must look to other sources. At the present time the bulk of the LNG derives from Trinidad and Tobago, with most of the balance from a variety of other countries.[62] Although LNG presently accounts for only a small percentage of U.S. gas consumption, imports are increasing and could rise to as high as twenty percent by 2025. The Department of Energy forecasts that net LNG imports will increase from the present 0.76 trillion to 4.53 trillion cubic feet by that date.[63] This has stimulated interest on the part of the industry in building new LNG facilities to service increased imports. The interest was encouraged by former Federal Reserve Chairman Alan Greenspan, who envisioned a major expansion of LNG imports to meet U.S. demand for natural gas, which would require substantially increased terminal import capacity.[64]

The Department of Energy forecasts that net liquefied natural gas imports will increase to 6.4 trillion cubic feet by 2025.

Until recently, there were only four LNG import facilities in the United States, all built over twenty years ago and all onshore.[65] Because onshore plants often face vigorous community opposition, to meet future import demands industry is planning offshore construction of facilities to convert the liquefied gas back to vapor and transport the gas to shore by pipeline. Since changes were made in 2002 to establish a permitting system under the Deepwater Port Act,[66] numerous applications to construct such offshore terminals have been filed.[67] One application resulted in the first offshore LNG receiving facility, Gulf Gateway, which was constructed by Excelerate Energy Limited Partnership in the Gulf of Mexico[68] and began operation in 2005, 116 miles off the coast of Louisiana. As of January 2008 permits for roughly two dozen additional offshore facilities have been approved, and there are formal permit applications pending, or preapplication feasibility studies underway, for another dozen locations.[69] The sites are primarily in the Gulf of Mexico or off the coast of the Northeastern United States, with a few off the Pacific coast.[70] The permitting process for these facilities involves numerous federal agencies and state authorities, but is now relatively settled, as detailed below.

The system used by Excelerate Energy at its Gulf Gateway terminal employs a swiveling loading buoy anchored to the sea floor, connected to a subsea pipeline. The buoy is submerged when not in use. The tanker, called an Energy Bridge Regasification Vessel, connects to the buoy during unloading. The vaporization occurs on the vessel, and there are no stationary storage tanks. According to Excelerate, the technology has been employed safely in areas such as the North Sea.[71]

2. Health, Safety, and Environmental Issues

Like other petroleum products and thousands of chemicals in current use, there are risks to humans and the environment associated with the transportation, storage, and processing of liquefied natural gas. Hazards include damage from routine discharges and emissions, spillage, fire and explosion, and now terrorism.[72] These hazards can be associated with both onshore and offshore facilities, since both have tanker traffic, pipelines, and possibly storage facilities. Thus both coastal and ocean waters may be subject to substantial risk. Onshore and near-shore facilities could be especially problematic for sensitive coastal areas, but more remote offshore facilities can also threaten important ocean and coastal resources.

Of substantial concern is the potential for spills or other accidents. Spilled LNG does not present the same pollution picture that oil does, since it will generally either vaporize or burn,[73] and the liquid will not spread, as oil will, to foul waters and beaches over many miles. Instead the major danger appears to be to populations in the vicinity of a facility or vessel from explosion, fire, or asphyxiation. The likelihood of these events is relatively small, and the safety record of LNG production and shipment is considered relatively good, but the potential for extensive damage does exist.[74] Studies have reached different conclusions about the substantiality of the threat, but four major areas of risk have been identified: vapor cloud explosions; fires of pools of LNG; the formation of flammable vapor clouds; and potential rapid phase transition (RPT) accidents (the spontaneous and explosive boiling that could occur when super-cooled LNG mixes with warmer sea water).[75] Of the four, pool fires are regarded by some as the most severe threat. A pool fire would occur if spilled LNG was ignited, and would burn over the pool of LNG as it vaporized, spreading the fire as the pool of gas spreads. It burns so intensely that it cannot be extinguished, and thermal damage can occur a substantial distance from the fire itself.[76] A pool fire on the water could be more severe than on land because the liquid could spread more rapidly, and the warmth of the sea water could cause more rapid volatilization than on land.[77]

Like other energy facilities, there exists the possibility that LNG vessels or facilities could be the target of a terrorist attack, and extensive damage could result from an explosion or fire. But this holds true for thousands of other types of facilities that store or process petroleum products and other hazardous chemicals.[78] It does seem likely that if terrorists were choosing an LNG facility to target, it would be one onshore, in a densely populated area, rather than an isolated offshore location. Nonetheless, the threat to offshore facilities should not be discounted.[79]

Safety requirements, both for accidents and terrorism, are addressed by Department of Transportation regulations that require specific training, equipment, and safety zones. Those zones are imposed around both the facility and the tankers.[80] A terminal proposed in Long Island Sound by the Broadwater company will likely have a traffic-free zone of five hundred meters around the fixed facility;[81] a similar zone might apply to ships using the terminal, raising concerns that the main entrance to the Sound might have to be closed to other vessel traffic each time one of the estimated 100 to 150 LNG tankers a year passed through.[82]

Other localized environmental impacts could result from the use of seawater in the regasification process. In order to vaporize the liquid, some onshore regasification facilities use a portion of the transported gas as a heat source. The four existing U.S. facilities employ this method, and several of the planned facilities propose to use it as well. This is costly, so some offshore facilities use, or prefer to use, a system that pumps seawater through a heat exchange structure to warm the liquid gas. This is referred to as an open-loop system, or open rack vaporization, and would both discharge seawater chilled by twenty degrees and pose the threat of entrainment and destruction of aquatic organisms that pass through the structure.[83] Biocides used to prevent fouling by marine organisms in the exchange system would also be discharged.[84] The Gulf Gateway terminal now operating 116 miles offshore in the Gulf of Mexico is using an open-loop system licensed to pump up to 76 million gallons of water a day, 248 days a year.[85] Shell Oil has received approval to build a facility thirty-eight miles offshore that would use 136 million gallons of seawater a day.[86] These open-loop systems in the Gulf have been strenuously opposed by commercial and recreational fishing interests, as well as resource professionals. Of primary concern is the impact on the larval stages of red drum, a fishery that has been seriously depleted.[87] An environmental impact study for Shell's proposed Gulf Landing terminal estimated that the project could cause the loss of a million pounds of redfish a year, although that number was disputed by industry and was not used in the final environmental impact statement for the project.[88]

A number of other LNG facilities are being proposed for the Gulf, raising concerns that the cumulative impact could be even more significant.[89] The Shell facility was approved nonetheless, but with monitoring provisions that will eventually allow its impact on the biota to be accurately assessed. A group of environmental and fishing organizations filed a petition for review in the U.S. Court of Appeals for the Fifth Circuit challenging the issuance of the permit, asserting harmful impacts to critical Louisiana fisheries, including redfish.[90] The groups charge that the government's failure to adequately analyze the cumulative impacts to fisheries from the seven facilities proposed for the Gulf region violates the National Environmental Policy Act. The suit also charges violation of the Deep Water Ports Act, arguing that the open-loop system is not the "best available technology" for regasification, as required by the statute.[91]

The possibility of entrainment of aquatic organisms has also been raised in connection with ballast water operations. After discharging their cargoes, LNG ships will take on ballast water in the area of the LNG terminal. That water may contain local aquatic organisms, although the actual impact as the result of frequent loadings is not clear. There is no obvious threat of invasive species being discharged at the terminal, but there could be at the liquefaction plant where the tanker eventually discharges the ballast water in order to take on more cargo.[92]

Other potential environmental impacts from an offshore facility including disruption of bird or fish life by noise and light from the facility at night, interference with marine mammal populations, and destruction of habitat due to pipeline construction from the offshore unloading facility to the onshore storage and distribution point.[93]

Depending on the location and configuration of the import terminal there may be the potential for spills from accidents, collisions, or storm events. Excelerate noted that discharge operations at the Gulf Gateway terminal continued without incident in 2005 during Hurricane Katrina, which passed two hundred miles from the terminal. There were no discharge operations in progress when Hurricane Rita shortly thereafter passed twenty-five miles from the terminal. According to the company there was no damage to the subsea components of the terminal and only slight cosmetic damage to a metering platform.[94] However, across the Gulf there were reports of at least one hundred production platforms destroyed, and others set adrift.[95]

3. Regulatory Issues

There are a number of agencies involved in approving and overseeing LNG facilities, and a variety of statutes come into play. In many respects LNG is subject to the same regulatory scheme as natural gas and gas synthesized from petroleum (LPG).[96] The Natural Gas Act of 1938 (NGA) prohibits the importation or exportation of natural gas without the authorization of Federal Energy Regulatory Commission (FERC), and gives the Commission the responsibility for evaluating and licensing natural gas processing, storage and transportation facilities, including pipelines.[97] In carrying out these responsibilities FERC applies safety standards for siting, design, construction, and operation established by the Department of Transportation.[98]

Until recently the only offshore port facility of any type was the Louisiana Offshore Oil Port[99] regulated by the U.S. Department of Transportation under the Deepwater Port Act of 1974 (DPA), which applied only to oil terminals.[100] All LNG import terminals in the United States were onshore. Increasing interest in importing LNG through offshore terminals led Congress, when enacting the Maritime Transportation Security Act of 2002,[101] to amend the Deepwater Port Act to include offshore structures and facilities intended for importation of natural gas.[102] FERC retains jurisdiction over onshore facilities and facilities within the territorial limits of the states for natural gas, including LNG,[103] but with these amendments the responsibility for licensing offshore LNG terminals beyond the territorial limits of the states was shifted from FERC to the Department of Transportation.[104] That responsibility was delegated to two agencies within the Department, the Maritime Administration (MARAD) and the U.S. Coast Guard. MARAD is primarily responsible for processing and issuing the permit, while the Coast Guard manages the environmental review[105] and has responsibility for security. When the Coast Guard was transferred to the Department of Homeland Security, it maintained its responsibilities regarding licensing.[106]

The federal resource agencies, including the EPA and NOAA's National Marine Fisheries Service, play an important consultative role in the permit issuance and environmental review process. However, the ultimate permit decision remains with MARAD and the Coast Guard.

Coastal states also play a role in the siting and licensing process under the Deepwater Port Act. Section 9(b)(1) provides that the Secretary of Transportation "shall not issue a license without the approval of the Governor of each adjacent coastal state."[107] By contrast, the Energy Policy Act of 2005 amended the Natural Gas Act to give exclusive authority over siting and construction of an onshore facility to FERC.[108] This legislation ended an attempt by the State of California to assert jurisdiction over a proposed LNG terminal in the Port of Long Beach that the state contended was not in interstate commerce, and thus not covered by the Natural Gas Act, since it only imported gas for shipment and use within California.[109]

Under the Natural Gas Act, for both onshore and offshore facilities there must be compliance with other applicable statutes, including the Clean Water Act, the Clean Air Act, and the Coastal Zone Management Act.[110] The Clean Water Act's state certification requirement provides a potent tool to the state in the siting and construction of a facility onshore or within the state's territorial waters. An applicant for a permit to construct a facility must obtain from the state a certification that the proposed activity will not interfere with the attainment of the state's water quality standards. The state may refuse certification, or may place conditions on the license sufficient to protect the water body at issue.[111] The state's decision is generally controlling, and may not be rejected by the federal agency.[112] A similar provision is found in Section 307 of the Coastal Zone Management Act, which requires that any federal or federally permitted activity that may impact the state's coastal zone must be consistent with the state's coastal zone management plan.[113] However, it is the permit applicant that certifies consistency, and even if the state objects, the Secretary of Commerce may overrule the objection.[114]

A seemingly unanswered question is the extent to which a National Pollutant Discharge Elimination System permit under Section 402 of the Clean Water Act[115] will be required for terminals. Section 403 extends the permit program to ocean discharges, and Section 316 requires that the thermal component of a discharge not interfere with fish and wildlife in the receiving water.[116] The only offshore facility licensed as of January 2008 is Execlerate's Gulf Gateway terminal. Shell Oil has also applied for a permit for its Gulf Landing terminal.[117] The EPA determined that an NPDES permit would be required "for the proposed facility's operational discharges, including discharges of non-contact warming water associated with the regasification process, hydrostatic test water, deck drainage, and sanitary and domestic wastewater."[118]

4. International Issues

The primary legal issues involving LNG are domestic in nature, and as discussed below regarding renewable energy, the siting of facilities within the US's EEZ is consonant with international law. If regasification plants were to be located close to borders with either Canada or Mexico, then the United States would have a duty under international law not to cause harm to the territory or citizens of those countries. The transportation of LNG on the high seas and through other national jurisdictions would not seem to raise concerns different from those that normally pertain in international commerce.

5. The Future

Natural gas is an attractive option for meeting future consumption, from both an environmental and economic viewpoint, and imports of LNG to meet U.S. domestic demands plainly will increase. Like other fuels, it poses serious risks in transportation and storage that must be taken into consideration when siting a terminal or other facility. Offshore facilities, where the LNG can be regasified and transferred to shore via a pipeline, appear to be a good choice from the point of view of protecting the populace. However, open-loop systems can have serious adverse environmental effects, and the cumulative impacts of numerous plants in close proximity could be substantial. Accordingly, licensing authorities must be rigorous in assessing the hazards posed by a proposed facility and carefully analyze the potential impacts on the local environment.

C. Renewable Energy Uses

1. Status of the Industry

As interest in alternative energy sources has increased, and technology has evolved, the development of offshore renewable energy resources has gained prominence as an emerging ocean use.[119] Offshore wind energy has generated particular interest, although wave and current projects have also been proposed.[120] Wind energy has the environmental benefit of producing none of the harmful emissions associated with the combustion of fossil fuels. However, objections raised to offshore wind energy include the impacts to migratory birds, incompatibility with existing uses, aesthetics, and, until recently, the lack of a clear regulatory framework.[121] Although offshore wind energy plants have been in operation in Europe for many years, it was only in 2001 that a federal permit application was submitted for what could eventually be the nation's first offshore wind energy project, the Cape Wind project in federal waters of Nantucket Sound.[122] Other offshore wind energy projects, such as the Long Island Power Authority (LIPA) project in federal waters off of Long Island,[123] have since been proposed, but the Cape Wind project has by far been the most controversial, resulting in litigation regarding the regulatory authority for the use of federal offshore alternative energy resources.[124] More recently, wind energy projects have also been proposed in state coastal waters, where state and federal regulatory authority is not in question.[125]

> **Wind energy has the environmental benefit of producing none of the harmful emissions associated with the combustion of fossil fuels.**

2. Regulatory Issues and the Energy Policy Act of 2005

Initially, proposals for offshore wind energy projects began proceeding under the U.S. Army Corps of Engineers' regulatory process for authorizing obstructions to navigation under Section 10 of the Rivers and Harbors Act of 1899,[126] as extended to the outer continental shelf (OCS)[127] by the Outer Continental Shelf Lands Act (OCSLA).[128] This regulatory approach was strongly criticized as inadequate by opponents of the controversial Cape Wind project, and the Corps's jurisdiction to authorize structures on the OCS unrelated to oil and gas development was challenged in the context of a Section 10 permit issued by the Corps to the Cape Wind developer for the construction of a preliminary data collection tower in federal waters of Nantucket Sound.[129]

In *Alliance to Protect Nantucket Sound, Inc. v. Dep't of the Army*,[130] the First Circuit ruled that the OCSLA extends the authority of the Corps of Engineers to the OCS for all structures, regardless of purpose, and upheld the jurisdiction of the

Corps to issue a Section 10 permit for the data tower at issue.[131] The court, however, declined to rule on whether a Corps permit would be sufficient to authorize the actual construction of a wind energy project on the OCS.[132] As distinguished from the proposed wind energy plant itself—"a structure vastly larger in scale, complexity, and duration" (and not directly at issue in the litigation)—the preliminary data-collection tower at issue was but a single tower, temporarily authorized for only five years. The use and collected data from this tower would be made available to the federal government and others, and the Corps's public interest review resulted in a finding of "negligible impact" on property interests.[133] As such, the court ruled only that the data tower at issue did not involve any real infringement on any federal property interest in OCS lands.[134] The "thorny issue" of what additional authorization from Congress might be necessary to develop a wind energy project on the OCS was left unanswered, but the clear implication of the court's opinion was that large-scale, long-term uses of the OCS cannot be approved under Section 10.[135]

Additional questions of regulatory jurisdiction exist in the context of other offshore renewable energy resources, such as wave and current energy. In 2003, the Federal Energy Regulatory Commission (FERC) asserted jurisdiction over a wave energy project proposed to be located just over three miles (originally just under two miles) from shore in the Olympic Coast National Marine Sanctuary.[136] FERC dismissed arguments that the proposed wave energy project was not a conventional hydropower facility, holding that a license under the Federal Power Act (FPA)[137] is required for any project located in navigable waters or on federal public lands or reservations that utilizes water power to produce electricity. FERC also discounted the significance of the project location shifting from approximately two miles to over three miles from the coast, asserting that its jurisdiction over "navigable waters" encompasses coastal waters to twelve nautical miles from the coast, the breadth of the territorial sea claimed by the United States since 1988. In addition, FERC concluded that an independent basis for jurisdiction lay in the location of project structures on federal public lands or reservations, since the wave buoys were located within the Olympic Coast National Marine Sanctuary, and connected across state submerged lands to onshore facilities on the federal Makah Indian Reservation. FERC's assertion of jurisdiction under the FPA, therefore, potentially extends to offshore wave and current energy projects located anywhere on the OCS or within state coastal waters. A number of tidal energy projects in state coastal waters are currently proceeding under FERC review.[138]

This regulatory uncertainty has now been considerably alleviated by the Energy Policy Act of 2005,[139] which establishes clear authority for alternative energy uses of the OCS. Section 388 of the Act evolved from similar legislation introduced in the 107th Congress, and subsequently incorporated into the omnibus energy bill.[140] It also was essentially identical to legislation proposed by the Department of the Interior's Minerals Management Service (MMS) in response to the questions of regulatory jurisdiction raised by the Cape Wind proposal.[141]

Section 388 of the Act amends the OCSLA to authorize the Secretary of the Interior (Secretary) to grant a lease, easement, or right-of-way on the OCS for activities that, among other things, "produce or support production, transportation, or transmission of energy from sources other than oil and gas."[142] The Act thus addresses one of the major legal objections to the regulatory scheme under Section 10 of the Rivers and Harbors Act, as arguably extended to the OCS by Section 4(e) of the OCSLA:[143] the lack of a clear and unambiguous authorization to use and occupy OCS lands for activities unrelated to mineral exploitation.[144]

The Act also provides that the Secretary "shall establish royalties, fees, rentals, bonuses, or other payments to ensure a fair return to the United States for any lease, easement, or right-of-way granted,"[145] thus addressing one of the major policy objections to the regulatory scheme under Section 10: the lack of any mechanism to ensure a fair return to the federal government for the use of federal public resources. For projects located at least partially within three nautical miles of state submerged lands, the Act further provides for the sharing of twenty-seven percent of revenues received among coastal states that have a coastline within fifteen miles of the geographic center of the project.[146]

More importantly, the Act provides for a comprehensive regulatory framework by setting forth general requirements for the activities authorized and by requiring the Secretary to promulgate "any necessary regulations" within 270 days of the date of enactment of the Act.[147] Activities authorized under the Act must be carried out in a manner that provides for safety; protection of the environment; prevention of waste; conservation of natural resources; coordination with relevant Federal agencies; protection of national security interests and correlative rights in the OCS; fair return to the United States; prevention of interference with reasonable uses (as determined by the Secretary) of the exclusive economic zone, the high seas, and the territorial seas; consideration of other uses of the OCS, including fisheries, sealanes, potential deepwater port sites, navigation, or other leases, easements, or right-of-ways; public notice and comment on proposals for leases, easements, or right-of-ways; and oversight, inspection, research, monitoring, enforcement relating to a lease, easement, or right-of-way.[148] This laundry list of general requirements will presumably be further developed in the required rulemaking, due to be completed in May 2006, but now considerably delayed.

In addition, the Act provides for leases, easements, or rights-of-way to be issued on a competitive basis, unless there is no competitive interest;[149] that the Secretary provide for the duration, issuance, transfer, renewal, suspension, and cancellation of leases, easements, or rights-of-way;[150] and that holders of leases, easements, or rights-of-way furnish a surety bond or other form of security, and provide for the restoration of the leases, easements, or rights-of-way.[151] The Secretary must consult with relevant federal agencies and must provide for coordination and consultation with the Governor of any State or the executive of any local government that may be affected by a lease, easement, or right-of-way.[152] Leases, easements, or rights-of-way may not be granted in any area of the OCS within the boundaries of any unit of the National Park System, National Wildlife Refuge System, or National Marine Sanctuary System, or any National Monument.[153] The Act also mandates the Secretary establish an interagency comprehensive digital mapping initiative for the OCS to assist in decision making relating to the new activities authorized by the Act.[154]

Finally, the Act includes a savings provision clearly directed at the two proposed offshore wind farm projects that had substantially begun the regulatory approval process under the Section 10 regulatory scheme—the Cape Wind project in Nantucket Sound and the LIPA project off of Long Island.[155] The savings provision exempts any project for which "an offshore test facility has been constructed" (referring to the data tower erected in Nantucket Sound by Cape Wind), or for which "a request for a proposal has been issued by a public authority" (referring to the LIPA request for proposals), from "the resubmittal of any document that was previously submitted or the reauthorization of any action that was previously authorized."[156] Presumably, this provision was intended to have the effect of transferring the permit applications being reviewed by the U.S. Army Corps of Engineers under Section 10 of the Rivers and Harbors Act to the Minerals Management Service (MMS), the Department of the Interior bureau designated with the administration of the OCSLA, as lead agency,[157] and of exempting the Cape Wind test tower from any requirement to secure an after-the-fact authorization under the Act. In addition, the projects are authorized, but not required, to be issued a lease, easement, or right-of-way on a noncompetitive basis.[158] MMS has since issued Notices of Intent to prepare Environmental Impact Statements for the Cape Wind and LIPA projects.[159] MMS anticipates a Record of Decision on the Cape Wind project in winter 2007.[160]

After passage of the Act, in October 2005, MMS launched a Web site for its new OCS Renewable Energy and Alternative Uses Program.[161] MMS states that its near-term objective is to assume oversight of existing offshore renewable energy projects, including the Cape Wind and LIPA projects, and its longer term objective is to judiciously integrate new and existing uses of offshore resources.[162] MMS apparently has no plans to issue any leases, easements, or rights-of-way under the Act prior to completing the required rulemaking.

Shortly after, in December 2005, MMS issued an Advance Notice of Proposed Rulemaking (ANPR) seeking comments on the development of a regulatory program to implement Section 388 of the Act.[163] The ANPR specifically sought comments on five areas integral to the development of the new program for alternate energy-related uses of the OCS: access to OCS lands and resources; environmental information, management, and compliance; operational activities; payments and revenues; and coordination and consultation.[164] Within these five program areas, the ANPR sought comments on thirty-two general issues and thirty-six specific questions.[165] The ANPR also sought comments on alternate uses of existing facilities, including offshore aquaculture, research, education, recreation, support for offshore operations and facilities, and telecommunications.[166]

In May 2006, MMS issued a Notice of Intent (NOI) to prepare a Programmatic Environmental Impact Statement (PEIS) under the National Environmental Policy Act (NEPA) to analyze the potential environmental effects of implementing the National Offshore Alternate Energy-Related Use Program, and associated rulemaking.[167] The

NOI also announced a series of scoping meetings to be held in several coastal states.[168] MMS estimates that the PEIS process will be completed in about eighteen months.[169] The Department of the Interior's Bureau of Land Management (BLM) has already completed a PEIS for onshore wind energy development on federal public lands that could serve as a model for this effort.[170] Various commentators have also suggested proposals for a comprehensive regulatory program for wind and other renewable energy resources offshore.[171] The rulemaking and PEIS processes will constitute a key opportunity for stakeholders to participate in the development of a comprehensive regulatory scheme for the development of offshore alternative energy resources.

More recently, in March 2007, MMS issued the draft PEIS and announced a series of public hearings.[172] The draft PEIS focuses on the general impacts of a generic regulatory program and regulations (not yet drafted) for activities projected for each industry sector for the next five to seven years, and identifies issues for subsequent, site-specific NEPA analyses that may tier-off of the PEIS.[173] However, the draft PEIS does not evaluate specific areas of the OCS for their suitability for alternative energy uses.[174] MMS expects to issue the final PEIS in August 2007 and publish a Record of Decision in September 2007.[175] MMS anticipates that the Notice of Proposed Rule-making will be issued at the end of June 2007 and that the Final Rule will be promulgated in 2008.[176]

Finally, as noted above, FERC's assertion to jurisdiction over wave and current energy projects potentially extends to the entire OCS.[177] In response to this potential overlap in jurisdictions, FERC and MMS are currently discussing a Memorandum of Understanding to clarify their respective jurisdictions over wave and current energy projects on the OCS.[178]

3. International Issues

It is worth noting that this emerging regulatory scheme is consonant with international law. Under Article 56 of the 1982 United Nations Convention on the Law of the Sea (UNCLOS), within the two-hundred-nautical-mile Exclusive Economic Zone (EEZ), coastal States have sovereign rights "for the purpose of exploring and exploiting, conserving and managing the natural resources, whether living or non-living, of the waters superjacent to the seabed and of the seabed and its subsoil, and with regard to other activities for the economic exploitation and exploration of the zone, *such as the production of energy from the water, currents and winds.*"[179] Under Article 60, coastal states have the exclusive right within the EEZ to construct and to authorize and regulate the construction, operation, and use of artificial islands, installations, and structures for such purposes.[180] The regulatory framework established by Section 388, therefore, fits easily within the existing framework of international law.[181]

4. The Future

The provisions of the Energy Policy Act of 2005 regarding alternate energy-related uses on the OCS are the most significant recent development in the emerging offshore renewable energy industry. The Act provides clear authorization for such activities, establishes a mechanism for the conveyance of property interests in OCS lands, requires fair compensation to the federal government for the use of federal public resources, and sets forth general standards to guide a lead agency in the development of the regulations necessary to implement these new authorities and mandates. Although the Act is not nearly as detailed as comparable resource management statutes, such as the OCSLA, the Minerals Management Service rulemaking should provide a key opportunity for stakeholders to participate in the development of a comprehensive regulatory program for renewable energy uses of the OCS.

D. Bioprospecting and Exploitation of Deep Sea Resources

1. Status of the Industry

Humans have used biologically derived products since time immemorial. Like mariculture, bioprospecting on both the land and in the oceans is a traditional activity. Although there is no official definition, bioprospecting is generally regarded as the gathering of wild genetic resources and the subsequent development of commercial products.[182] Typically, bioprospecting is employed to harvest biological materials, which are then used to manufacture products, or to create synthetic substances. To add clarity, a division is sometimes suggested between biodiscovery, the search for new materials, and bioprospecting, the gathering of materials for production purposes.[183] Attempts are also made to distinguish between "marine scientific research" and bioprospecting, but the distinction seldom seems useful, since the lines are easily blurred.[184]

Bioprospecting in the oceans has already yielded commercial products for industry and agriculture, including new pharmaceuticals.[185] The AIDS medication AZT is derived from marine sponges, and other marine organisms have been the source of a class of antibiotics.[186] Just recently, a painkiller 1,000 times more powerful than morphine, but not addictive, became available in Britain. It was derived from the venom of a sea snail.[187] Moreover, industry enthusiasm to pursue bioprospecting activities appears to be high. The U.N. Secretary General, in his 2005 report on oceans, noted that the biotechnology sector is one of the most dynamic research areas, with increasing prospects for growth and profitability.[188] In the words of a trade organization, "Recent exploratory research demonstrates the great potential for unitizing the biochemical capabilities of marine organisms to provide models for new classes of pharmaceuticals, polymers, enzymes, other chemical products, and industrial processes, as well as for development of vaccines, diagnostic and analytical reagents."[189] However, adequate mechanisms for protecting the resources are not in place.

2. Environmental Issues

In spite of the substantial amount of both scientific and commercial exploration, the ocean remains relatively unexplored and little understood. As humans been able to pierce into deep ocean reaches, unsuspected worlds of incredible diversity have been revealed. Many thoughtful individuals now fear that the impact of these human

In spite of the substantial amount of both scientific and commercial exploration, the ocean remains relatively unexplored and little understood. activities may have serious deleterious consequences, long before they become obvious. The deep seabed, seamounts, ocean ridges, and hydrothermal vents are some of the entities that are already being touched, and perhaps transformed, by humans. Thus, in addition to serious depletion of fishery resources, the oceans face damage to unique and fragile ecosystems and the unregulated exploitation of genetic resources.

While there is a tendency to think of the ocean as deep and flat, the terrain of the ocean bottom is often highly varied just as might be encountered on dry land, with deep trenches, plateaus, hills, ridges, and mountains. Seamounts vary substantially in location and height, but are generally defined as areas that protrude 1,000 meters above the seafloor, although lower "hills" and knolls" are often included.[190] They are especially rich in species, and typically have a high rate of endemism—organisms found in no or few other areas. Seamounts are under dual threat: They are being destroyed by bottom trawling for commercial fish species, and they may be the subject of marine scientific research and bioprospecting that could interfere with delicate ecosystems.[191] Hydrothermal vents, deep sea hot springs generally found at mid-ocean ridges and the continental shelves of some countries, contain an astonishing array of species in unusual ocean communities.[192] Like seamounts, they may be threatened by research and bioprospecting activities, as well as mining activities.

3. Regulatory Issues

There is no recognized definition of the "deep seabed." While it might geologically fall either within or outside of national jurisdictions, the term is generally used to refer to the deep ocean floor found beyond the limits of national jurisdiction, as described by UNCLOS.[193] To the extent that the seabed and its resources are located within national jurisdictions, then the laws of the state control the use of the resources. If they are located within the exclusive economic zone of a nation, then the provisions of UNCLOS apply. While the nature of the organism, sedentary or nonsedentary, may determine the obligation of the state to conserve and share the resource, for the most part the legal scheme is clear. But for the deep sea and seabed, as with mariculture, wind, wave, and geothermal energy, bioprospecting is unregulated.

Bioprospecting regulations in U.S. waters are limited to state fishing licenses and limits on the removal of sensitive species such as corals. Research permits are required in marine protected areas such as national marine sanctuaries. But bioprospecting is virtually unregulated in areas outside state waters and marine sanctuaries unless protected species are affected.

4. International Issues

A number of international legal agreements and instruments do or could play a role in the management of marine bioprospecting. The two most notable are the United

Nations Convention on the Law of the Sea (UNCLOS), and the Convention on Biodiversity. In addition, the intellectual property regimes may bear on the management of biological resources and bioprospecting.[194]

a. UNCLOS

UNCLOS contains no explicit reference to biodiversity, but concerns itself instead with resources in general, both living and nonliving.[195] The extent of protection afforded by UNCLOS varies with the location of the resource. In its territorial waters a coastal state is sovereign, but beyond the territorial sea certain limitations apply. For living resources of the Exclusive Economic Zone the coastal state has a duty to conserve and manage the resources.[196] A coastal state also has rights over nonliving resources of the continental shelf, and sedentary living resources.[197] For sedentary species, however, there is no specific duty of conservation, other than the general "obligation to protect and preserve the marine environment."[198] In the EEZ and on the continental shelf other states have the right to engage in marine scientific research, subject to the consent of the coastal state, which should, in normal circumstances, grant consent.[199] However, if the coastal state determines that the research being conducted "is of direct significance for the exploration and *exploitation*" of either living or nonliving resources, it may withhold its consent.[200] This presents a fine question as to what "direct significance" and "exploitation" mean in the context of marine scientific research, since much of such research, even by academic institutions, ultimately results in commercial products.[201]

More problematic, however, is the lack of any provisions addressing bioprospecting beyond national jurisdictions. Traditional freedoms of the high seas include freedom to fish, and freedom of scientific research.[202] But these freedoms are tempered by the obligation of signatory states to conserve high seas living resources.[203] The seabed and subsoils below the high seas are designated as "The Area,"[204] and the Area and its mineral resources are declared the common heritage of mankind,[205] and subject to the International Seabed Authority established under UNCLOS.[206] But the jurisdiction of the Authority does not appear to extend to the living resources of the deep seabed.[207] Accordingly, UNCLOS provides scant basis for the management of bioprospecting activities.

b. Convention on Biological Diversity[208]

The Convention on Biological Diversity (CBD) was established with the primary objectives of conserving biological diversity and providing for sustainable use of biological resources, while assuring access to genetic resources and "the fair and equitable sharing of the benefits arising out of" their utilization.[209] Article Fifteen (Access to Genetic Resources) recognizes the sovereignty of states over their resources, but imposes an obligation to facilitate access to genetic resources "and not to impose restrictions that run counter to the objectives of the Convention."[210] The thrust of the agreement is to encourage states to conserve their own biological resources, and to allow access to others, with prior informed consent and on mutually agreed-on terms, in return for an equitable share of the benefits.[211] Article Sixteen encourages the transfer of technology among parties, but recognizes that patent and other national intellectual property legislation may impede implementation of the CBD. It binds parties to cooperate in assuring that such legislation does not interfere with the objectives of the treaty.[212] Article Nineteen also requires each country to promote access, especially for developing countries, to the benefits that result from the exploitation of a source country's genetic resources.[213] In light of these and other provisions, the CBD provides incentives for the protection of biological resources, and a rough framework in which bioprospecting might begin to be addressed.[214] But, it applies only to areas under national jurisdiction, and not to the high seas or deep seabed beyond national jurisdiction, a profound gap.[215]

c. Intellectual Property Issues

Many countries have patent and other intellectual property schemes that would cover pharmaceuticals and other derivatives of genetic materials, so long as there is some innovative human activity involved. Such regimes might make it difficult to enforce Convention requirements against entities that have obtained legitimate rights to a product under national law. Complicating the picture are the efforts to strengthen international protection of intellectual property rights, as reflected in the Trade Related Aspects of Intellectual Property Agreement (TRIPS) administered by the World Trade Organization.[216] The TRIPS Agreement mandates uniform minimum national standards, and it has been suggested that these are likely to lead to the enforcement of patents on pharmaceuticals and other commercial products derived from marine genetic resources,[217] although at this point the actual impact remains speculative.

5. The Future

Obviously the problems surrounding marine biological resources and bioprospecting will not be easily solved. Various proposals have been made, including extending the authority of the International Seabed Authority to regulate bioprospecting, giving regional fisheries organizations authority to regulate bioprospecting, and developing a protocol to the Convention on Biological Diversity to address the issue. One scholar has proposed the development of marine protected areas in the high seas,[218] and at least one environmental organization has suggested that a new UNCLOS implementing agreement be devised.[219] An international working group is exploring the development of a voluntary code of conduct for sustainable use of hydrothermal vents.[220] Perhaps a more significant development is the establishment by the U.N. General Assembly of an ad hoc working group that might ultimately lead to a further protocol to UNCLOS.[221] Whether any of these proposals comes to fruition is difficult to foresee.

IV. Conclusion

This chapter addresses new and emerging uses of the ocean related to marine aquaculture, liquefied natural gas, renewable energy uses, bioprospecting, and the exploitation of deep sea resources. However, the potential uses of our oceans and ocean resources are as extensive as the human imagination, and cannot easily be catalogued. Likewise, the potential for abuse is substantial. Current activities of commerce, recreation, and defense can cause not only chemical pollution, but light and acoustic pollution.[222] Deep sea exploration and research may itself alter ecosystems. Similarly, essential activities such as the construction of desalination plants may transform local ecosystems. New uses of the oceans may present even more severe problems. There already exist a number of fisheries for krill, organisms essential to certain species of whales, and harvesting of krill appears likely to increase substantially as it becomes a favored feed for fish farming.[223] Others propose to seed ocean waters with iron to increase algal growth for harvesting.[224] Increasing marine plankton could also serve to sequester atmospheric gases, thus reducing the buildup of carbon dioxide in the environment, which threatens the global climate.[225] Researchers suggest that algae and other marine organisms may one day be used as a source of hydrogen, to replace fossil fuels.[226] Also suggested as a source of energy are methane hydrates, deposits of which are located throughout the Arctic and Antarctic and along most continental shelves, even though mining such deposits could be extremely hazardous.[227] In summary, all of these activities or proposed activities raise concerns for their impact on fragile ecosystems and should be examined further as they develop.

Notes

1. *See* U.S. COMM'N ON OCEAN POLICY, AN OCEAN BLUEPRINT FOR THE 21ST CENTURY Appendix 6 Review of U.S. Ocean and Coastal Law 2–3 (2004) [hereinafter OCEAN BLUEPRINT]; PEW OCEANS COMMISSION, AMERICAN'S LIVING OCEANS: CHARTING A COURSE FOR SEA CHANGE 26 (2003) [hereinafter America's Living Oceans].
2. *See infra,* notes 126–178 and accompanying text.
3. *Id.*
4. *Id.*
5. LADON SWANN, ILLINOIS-INDIANA SEA GRANT PROGRAM, TECHNICAL BULLETIN SERIES # 102, A BASIC OVERVIEW OF AQUACULTURE 1 (1992).
6. OFFICE OF WATER, U.S. EPA, EPA-821-R-04-012, TECHNICAL DEVELOPMENT DOCUMENT FOR THE FINAL EFFLUENT LIMITATIONS GUIDELINES AND NEW SOURCE PERFORMANCE STANDARDS FOR THE CONCENTRATED AQUATIC ANIMAL PRODUCTION POINT SOURCE CATEGORY 4-1 (2004) [hereinafter CAAP TECHNICAL DOCUMENT], available at http://www.epa.gov/guide/aquaculture/tdd/final.htm.
7. *Id.* at 4-2. Public fish hatcheries typically focus on protecting the "wild" quality of the target species, while commercial hatcheries are interested in maximizing economic return. The latter seek to enhance genetic traits for rapid growth and adaptability to hatchery conditions.
8. One-third of the 304 U.S. fish populations that have been assessed are overfished or are being fished at unsustainable rates. The status of 655 fish populations are unknown and may show even greater declines. AMERICAN'S LIVING OCEANS, *supra* note 1 at 33–34.
9. FISHERIES DEP'T, U.N. FOOD & AGRIC. ORG, THE STATE OF WORLD FISHERIES AND AQUACULTURE 2006, *available at* ftp://ftp.fao.org/docrep/fao/009/a0699e/a0699e01.pdf (preliminary estimate). Other countries are expanding their aquaculture efforts. Vietnam, for example, has extensive shrimp farms supplying a substantial part of the world market. Unfortunately these enterprises are often minimally or completely unregulated.
10. U.S. Dep't of Commerce, Aquaculture Policy (1999), *available at* http://www.lib.noaa.gov/docaqua/docaquapolicy.htm. Production at the time was valued at $900 million annually, which the Department seeks to increase to $5 billion. For a recent description of

the status of aquaculture in several regions see Paul Greenberg, *Green to the Gills*, N.Y. TIMES, June 18, 2006, *available at* http://www.nytimes.com/2006/06/18/magazine/18fish .html?pagewanted=print.

11. Aquaculture activities in many parts of the world have destroyed hundreds of thousands of hectares of mangrove forests and other coastal wetlands. Rosamond L. Naylor et al., *Effects of Aquaculture on World Fish Supplies*, 8 ISSUES IN ECOLOGY (2001), at 6, *available at* http://www.esa.org/science/Issues/FileEnglish/issue8.pdf. In the United States, regulation of coastal areas has prevented substantial degradation of this nature.

12. *See* OCEAN BLUEPRINT *supra* note 1; NATIONAL RESEARCH COUNCIL, GENETIC STATUS OF ATLANTIC SALMON IN MAINE: INTERIM REPORT FROM THE COMMITTEE ON ATLANTIC SALMON IN MAINE 21 (2002). As a result of a storm, over 100,000 salmon escaped from a fish farm in Maine. That is roughly 1,000 times the number of wild adult salmon in Maine. Beth Daley, *Escaped Farm Salmon Raise Alarm in Maine*, BOSTON GLOBE, Feb. 23, 2001, *available at* http://www.biotech-info.net/escape.html.

13. Naylor, *supra* note 11, at 1–2.

14. *Id.* at 1, 3–5.

15. REBECCA J. GOLDBURG ET AL., PEW OCEANS COMM'N, MARINE AQUACULTURE IN THE UNITED STATES 7–9 (2001) [hereinafter PEW AQUACULTURE REPORT]. *See also* NOAA, Aquaculture Policy 6 (1998) (biotechnology important to development of U.S. aquaculture), *available at* http://swr.ucsd.edu/fmd/bill/aquapol.htm.

16. Alaska banned all ocean fish farming in 1990. ALASKA STAT. §16.40.210. California banned ocean farming of salmon, genetically modified and nonnative species in 2003, CAL. FISH & GAME CODE § 15007, and enacted legislation to establish strong environmental standards on ocean farming of native fish populations. SB 201 (2006). Cal. Fish & Game Code §§ 15008, 15400, 15405, 15406, 15406.5, 15409; Cal. Pub. Res. Code § 30411.

17. *See* The National Offshore Aquaculture Act of 2007, H.R. 2010, 110th Cong. § 3(c) (2007) (defining The EEZ).

18. CAAP TECHNICAL DOCUMENT, *supra* note 6, at 4-101. In the Agency's estimation offshore aquaculture is not likely to be developed until the cost of importing salmon from other countries rises. *Id. See also* PEW AQUACULTURE REPORT, *supra* note 15, at 4-5.

19. PEW AQUACULTURE REPORT, *supra* note 15, at 5; OCEAN BLUEPRINT, *supra* note 12, at 101 (describing the overlapping agency responsibilities for approval of an offshore facility).

20. The Corps of Engineers issues permits under Section 10 of the Rivers and Harbors Act, 33 U.S.C. § 403 (2006), for placement of obstructions in navigable waters, which includes the Outer Continental Shelf. Outer Continental Shelf Lands Act (OCSLA), 43 U.S.C. § 1333 (e). *See* Alliance to Protect Nantucket Sound v. U.S. Dep't of the Army, 288 F. Supp. 2d 64, 72–74 (D. Mass. 2003). The Corps also has authority to issue "dredge & fill" permits pursuant to § 404 of the Clean Water Act, 33 U.S.C. § 1344 (2006). On its face the Act appears to limit jurisdiction to navigable waters, defined as within three miles of the coast. *See* CWA § 502(7) (defining navigable waters to include territorial seas); § 507(8) (limiting territorial seas to three miles). However, Sections 301 and 502(12)(B) prohibit "any addition of any pollutant to the waters of the contiguous zone or the ocean from any point source other than a vessel or other floating craft." Since dredged spoil is a pollutant, § 502(6), to the extent that construction of an aquaculture facility would involve the placement of fill material, including posts or piers, a § 404 permit would be required.

21. A variety of veterinary drugs may be employed to prevent disease in confined fish populations.

22. NMFS has regulatory responsibilities under the Magnuson-Stevens Fishery Conservation and Management Act, 16 U.S.C. § 1885 (2006).

23. For an extensive list of potentially applicable statutes see Jeremy Firestone et al., *Regulating Offshore Wind Power and Aquaculture: Messages from Land and Sea*| 14 CORNELL J.L. & PUB. POL'Y 71, 79 (2005).

24. State sovereignty over coastal waters and submerged lands extends three miles. Submerged Lands Act (SLA), 43 U.S.C. § 1301 (2006), further for Texas and for Florida in

the Gulf of Mexico. States also have authority under § 307(c)(3)(A) of the Coastal Zone Management Act (CZMA), 16 U.S.C. § 1456(c)(3)(A), and § 401 of the Clean Water Act, 33 U.S.C. § 1341, to affect federal and federally permitted activities. Section 307(c)(3)(A) of the CZMA requires federally permitted activities that might have an impact on a state's coastal zone to be consistent with the state's coastal zone management plan. For more information on the CZMA federal consistency provisions, see Chapter 5, "Managing Coastal Development." Activities beyond the state's coastal waters might still have an onshore impact. Clean Water Act § 401 requires that an applicant for a federal permit that would result in a discharge to navigable waters to secure a certification by the state where the discharge would originate that it would not adversely impact the quality of the receiving water. This section would apply to activities carried out in the state's coastal waters, but not to offshore activities since the pollution would not originate in the state. For more information on § 401 of the Clean Water Act, *see* 7, "Coastal Water Quality Protection."

25. *See* America's Living Oceans, *supra* note 1, at 78–79 (2003); Ocean Blueprint, *supra* note 1, at 333–36. This fragmentation of authority and interest is demonstrated by the broad membership of the U.S. Joint Subcommittee on Aquaculture (13 agencies), which was established by the National Aquaculture Act of 1980 to serve as a federal interagency coordinating group. 16 U.S.C. § 2801(6)(a) (2006). *See* U.S. Joint Subcomm. on Aquaculture Web site at http://aquanic.org/jsa/mission.htm and *Sustainable Marine Aquaculture: Fulfilling the Promise; Managing the Risks*, Report of the Marine Aquaculture Task Force, January 2007, available at http://www.whoisedu/sbl/liteSite.do?litesiteid=2790&articleID=4439.

26. S. 1195, 109th Cong. (2005).

27. H.R. 2010, 110th Cong. (2007). The Act would extend to all forms of marine life except marine mammals and birds. *Id.* § 3(e). The House Subcommittee on Fisheries, Wildlife and Oceans of the House Committee on Natural Resources conducted hearings in July 2007, the last major action on the bill. The legislation remains under consideration. Its status of the legislation may be found at http://thomas.loc.gov.

28. Environmental organizations and other groups have expressed concern about, among other things, the lack of strong environmental standards; the broad discretion given to NOAA to establish the permit program; the lack of a clear process for participation by state governments and by the public; and the lack of restrictions on genetically modified and nonnative species that might negatively affect native fish. Letter from the Institute for Fisheries Resources, et al. to Representative Madeline Z. Bordallo, April 24, 2007. Letter from the Ocean Conservancy to Senators Ted Stevens and Daniel Inouye, Nov. 1, 2005. *See also* Marian Burros, *Plan Would Expand Ocean Fish Farming*, N.Y. Times, June 6, 2005, at A17.

29. Clean Water Act § 101(d), 33 U.S.C. § 1251(d).

30. 33 U.S.C. § 1328 (2006).

31. 33 U.S.C. § 1328(c) (2006).

32. CWA § 402, 33 U.S.C. § 1342 (2006).

33. 40 C.F.R. § 122.24 & app. C (2007).

34. 40 C.F.R., pt. 451 (2007). The preamble to the regulations explains the factors which the Agency considered in formulating the regulations. *See* 69 Fed. Reg. 51,892 (Aug. 23, 2006).

35. 40 C.F.R. § 451.1 (2007). The animals produced by these facilities are species intended for human consumption, animal food, capture fisheries, and other uses.

36. 40 C.F.R. § 451.2(j) (2007). Net pen system is defined as "a stationary, suspended or floating system of nets, screens, or cages in open waters of the United States. Net pen systems typically are located along a shore or pier or may be anchored and floating offshore." *See also* CAAP Technical Document, *supra* note 6, at 4-11 to 4-12.

37. According to one researcher, a salmon farm of 200,000 fish releases an amount of fecal matter roughly equivalent to that in the untreated sewage from 65,000 people. R.W. Hardy, *Urban Legends and Fish Nutrition*, 26(6) Aquaculture Mag.

38. 69 Fed. Reg. at 51,899. The drugs used in these aquaculture processes may be experimental, or may not have been approved for the particular use. 69 Fed. Reg. at 51,899–903.

39. 69 Fed. Reg. at 51,920 (e.g., copper-based antifouling paint may be used on net pens). In December 2005 the U.S. Department of the Interior issued an advance notice of proposed rulemaking for alternative uses of the Outer Continental Shelf pursuant to Section 388 of the Energy Policy Act of 2005. It is not seeking authority over aquaculture, "but only the decision to allow platforms to be converted to such uses, if the appropriate agency approves the underlying activity." 70 Fed. Reg. 77,345, 77,346 (2005). One proposal to convert a disused offshore oil and gas platform complex in the Gulf of Mexico to aquaculture resulted in extended litigation, with the research institute that proposed the facility eventually prevailing. *Sea Farming 7 Year Lawsuit Win*, GROWFISH, http://www.growfish.com.au/content.asp?ContentId=5549.

40. Active feed management techniques are required, which may include the use of real-time camera monitoring to detect excess feed and assess the condition of the water and the bottom. 40 C.F.R. § 451.21(a) (2007). Although such monitoring is not mandated, many facilities already use this technology. 69 Fed. Reg. at 51,892, 51,910–11 (Aug. 23, 2004).

41. 40 C.F.R. § 451.21 (2007).

42. *Id.* § 451.21(f).

43. 69 Fed. Reg. at 51,911.

44. 69 Fed. Reg. at 51,912. Net pen technology is used primarily for anadromous species, typically salmonids. CAAP TECHNICAL DOCUMENT, *supra* note 6, at 4-12.

45. 339 F.3d 23, 28 (1st Cir. 2003).

46. *Id.* at 27.

47. 299 F.3d 1007 (9th Cir. 2002).

48. *Id.* at 1017–18.

49. *Id.* at 1018; 40 C.F.R. Pt. 122, App. C(a). The court seemed to reject the notion that live organisms could be pollutants, but did cite with seeming approval *National Wildlife Fed'n v. Consumers Power Co.*, 862 F.2d 580, 583 (6th Cir. 1988) to the effect that live fish could be pollutants. *Id.* at 1017.

50. Report of the Appellate Body on U.S. Import Prohibition of Certain Shrimp and Shrimp Products, Recourse to article 21.5 by Malaysia (WT/DS58/RW (Oct. 22, 2001), 2001 WL 1261572 (W.T.O.).

51. AMERICA'S LIVING OCEANS, *supra* note 1, at 79.

52. UN FAO Code of Conduct for Responsible Fisheries and Law of the Sea, Art. 9, Aquaculture Development, *available at* http://www.fao.org/DOCREP/005/v9878e/v9878e00.htm#9.

53. Art. 9.2, 9.3.

54. For a recent examination of the law and policy issues that must be addressed in achieving effective regulation of aquaculture activities, see DAVID VANDERZWAAG & GLORIA CHAO, AQUACULTURE LAW AND POLICY: TOWARDS PRINCIPLED ACCESS AND OPERATIONS (2006).

55. *See* Energy Info. Admin., U.S. Dep't of Energy, *International Energy Annual 2005* (posted June–July 2007), at http://www.eia.doe.gov/emeu/iea/ng.html; *id.* Table 1.3, *World Dry Natural Gas Consumption, 1980–2005* (posted June 21, 2007), *at h*ttp://www.eia.doe.gov/emeu/iea/ng.html; Table 2.4, *World Dry Natural Gas Production, 1980–2005*, http://www.eia.doe.gov/pub/international/iealf/table24.xls (posted June 21, 2007).

56. ENERGY INFO. ADMIN., U.S. DEP'T OF ENERGY, RPT. NO. DOE/EIA-0384, ANNUAL ENERGY REVIEW 2006, Tables 6.1, 6.3 [hereinafter EIA ANNUAL ENERGY REVIEW 2006], *available at* http://www.eia.doe.gov/emeu/aer/contents.html. *See also* Suedeen G. Kelly, *Address to the Environmental Regulation, Energy, and Market Entry Symposium*, 15 DUKE ENVTL. L. & POL'Y F. 251, 251–52 (2005). For current market information see Energy Info. Admin., U.S. Dep't of Energy, *Natural Gas Weekly Update*, http://tonto.eia.doe.gov/oog/info/ngs/ngs.html.

57. Energy Info. Admin., U.S. Dep't of Energy, Rep. No. DOE/EIA-0637|éThe Global Liquefied Natural Gas Market: Status and Outlook (2003), *What Is Liquefied Natural Gas?* [hereinafter EIA Global Liquefied Natural Gas Market: Status and Outlook (2003)], *available at* http://www.eia.doe.gov/oiaf/analysispaper/global/index.html. *See also* Broadwater, *What is LNG?*, http://www.broadwaterenergy.com/index.php?page=info_what_is_LNG; Energy Info. Admin., U.S. Dep't. of Energy, *LNG Markets and Uses: June 2004 Update*, at http://www.eia.doe.gov/pub/oil_gas/natural_gas/feature_articles/2004/lng/lng2004.pdf.

58. Liquefied petroleum gas (LPG) is gas synthesized from petroleum or natural gas, and typically liquefied and stored using pressure.

59. The containers were described by one industry source as "like a giant Thermos bottle." Judy Benson, *Afloat in the Sound*, The Day (New London, Ct.) (Nov. 6, 2005), at A1, *available at* http://www.theday.com/eng/web.

60. Jerry Havens, *Ready to Blow?*, Bull. of Atomic Scientists (July/Aug. 2003), *available at* http://www.wildcalifornia.org/pages/page_109. *See also* Al Rogers, *First Open Loop NLG Terminal Launched*, RodnReel.com, Mar. 17, 2005, http://rodnreel.com/articles/articles.asp?cmd=view&StoryID=782 (first tanker at new Gulf of Mexico facility was 908 feet carrying 3 billion cubic feet (138,000 cubic meters) of LNG). Natural gas is measured by volume in its gaseous state, and by weight as a liquid. For conversions of cubic feet, cubic meters, and metric tons, see EIA Global Liquefied Natural Gas Market: Status and Outlook (2003), *supra* note 57, app. A;. Natural gas data in million cubic meters can be converted to million cubic feet by multiplying by 35.315. Energy Info. Admin., U.S. Dep't of Energy, *International Natural Gas Information*, at http://www.eia.doe.gov/emeu/iea/tablec1.html (May–July, 2006).

61. Energy Info. Admin., U.S. Dep't of Energy, Rpt. No. DOE/EIA-0484, International Energy Outlook 2005, Table 8, *World Natural Gas Reserves by Country as of January 1, 2007, available at* http://www.eia.doe.gov/oiaf/ieo/pdf.nat_gas.pdf. *See also* Kelly, *supra* note 56, at 252.

62. EIA Annual Energy Review 2006, *supra* note 56, Table 6.3, *Natural Gas Imports, Exports, and Net Imports, 1949–2006, available at* http://www.eia.doe.gov/emeu/aer/txt/ptb0603.html. *See also* Paul W. Parfomak & Aaron M. Flynn, Congressional Research Service, CRS Rpt. RL32205, Liquefied Natural Gas (LNG) Import Terminals: Siting, Safety and Regulation 2 (updated Apr. 20, 2005) [hereinafter CRS LNG Siting, Safety and Regulation], *available at* http://www.ncseonline.org/NLE/CRSreports/05apr/RL32205.pdf. The balance of the imported LNG not supplied by Trinidad and Tobago traditionally came from Algeria, but substantial supplies now also come from Egypt. *See* Energy Info. Admin., U.S. Dep't of Energy, U.S. Energy Natural Gas Monthly, Summary of U.S. Natural Gas Imports and Exports, 2000–2004, *available at* http://www.eia.doe.gov/oil_gas/natural_gas/data_publications/natural_gas_monthly/ngm.html.

63. Energy Info. Admin., U.S. Dep't of Energy, Rep. No. DOE/EIA-0383, Annual Energy Outlook 2007, *Oil and Natural Gas Projections*, Table 13, *available at* http://www.eia.doe.gov/oiaf/aeo/index.html. *See also* CRS LNG Siting, Safety and Regulation, *supra* note 62, at 2–3.

64. *Natural Gas Supply and Demand Issues: Hearing Before the H. Energy and Commerce Comm.*, 108th Cong. 91, 98–99, 105 (2003) (testimony of Alan Greenspan, Chairman of the U.S. Fed. Reserve Bd.), *available at* http://energycommerce.house.gov/reparchives/108/Hearings/06102003hearing944/print.htm. Greenspan did not waver in his push for increased capacity. *See The Economic Outlook: Hearing Before the H. Joint Economic Comm.*, 109th Cong. (Nov. 3, 2005) (statement of Alan Greenspan, Chairman of the U.S. Fed. Reserve Bd.), *available at* http://www.bulk.resource.org/gpo.gov/hearings/1108h/88422.pdf.

65. The four locations are Everett, Massachusetts; Cove Point, Maryland; Elba Island, Georgia; and Lake Charles, Louisiana. Office of Energy Projects, Fed. Energy Regulatory Comm'n,

Existing and Proposed North American LNG Terminals (last visited Jan. 14, 2008), http://www.ferc.gov/industries/lng/indus-act/terminals/exist-prop-lng.pdf (a facility in Kenai, Alaska, exports, rather than imports). An additional terminal is located in Puerto Rico, which receives gas for a nearby electric utility. *LNG Markets and Uses: June 2004 Update, supra* note 57, at 3 n.3.

66. Maritime Transportation Security Act of 2002, Pub. L. No. 107-295, § 106, 116 Stat. 2064, 2086–87 (2002) (codified as amended at 46 U.S.C. § 2101 (2006).

67. The first application apparently was filed within hours of the passage of the amendment. Al Rogers, *Collateral Damage,* RODNREEL.COM, Jan. 28, 2005, http://rodnreel.com/articles/articles.asp?cmd=view&StoryID=760.

68. Office of Energy Projects, Fed. Energy Regulatory Comm'n, *Existing and Proposed North American LNG Terminals, supra* note 65.

69. *Id.*

70. *Id.* These areas are logically preferred because of proximity to both the primary source of LNG, Trinidad-Tobago, and to pipeline facilities and population centers.

71. Excelerate Energy Limited Partnership, http://www.excelerateenergy.com/gulfgateway .html (last visited Feb. 11, 2008). Because this facility services two pipelines it also includes a stationary metering tower, a structure which would not be present at other similar facilities. *Id.*

72. *See* CRS LNG SITING, SAFETY AND REGULATION, *supra* note 62, at 20–21. Unlike most facilities that handle hazardous chemicals, the federal government, rather than local or state officials, is the primary regulatory authority. *Id.* at 23.

73. LNG has a narrow range for ignition, since if the concentration of LNG to air is below 5 percent, there will not be sufficient oxygen to support combustion; if it is over 15 percent, it will have sufficiently vaporized in open air. Marine Firefighting, Inc., Newsletter #19, *Liquid Natural Gas (LNG),* http://www.marinefirefighting.com/Pages/Newsletters/Newsletter.htm.

74. CRS LNG SITING, SAFETY AND REGULATION, *supra* note 62, at 6; MIKE HIGHTOWER, ET AL., SANDIA NATIONAL LABORATORIES, SAND2004–6258, GUIDANCE ON RISK ANALYSIS AND SAFETY IMPLICATIONS OF A LARGE LIQUEFIED NATURAL GAS (LNG) SPILL OVER WATER (2004), *available at* http://www.fossil.energy.gov/programs/oilgas/storage/lng/ sandia_lng_1204.pdf.

75. CRS LNG SITING, SAFETY AND REGULATION, *supra* note 62, at 5, 18; Havens, *supra* note 60.

76. Havens, *supra note* 60.

77. CAL. ENERGY COMM'N, PUB. NO. 700-03-005, LIQUEFIED NATURAL GAS IN CALIFORNIA: HISTORY, RISKS, AND SITING 3 (2003), *available at* http://www.energy.ca.gov/reports/2003 -07-17_700-03-005.pdf. *See also* CH-IV INTERNATIONAL, TECH. DOC. TD-02109, SAFETY HISTORY OF INTERNATIONAL LNG OPERATIONS 5 (2006) (safety history of international LNG operations). The most serious accident in the US occurred in 1944 in Cleveland, OH, when improperly constructed tanks failed, releasing their contents. Fires resulted, which killed 128 people and devastated about 30 acres. A summary of this incident is available at http://www.ch-iv.com/links/history.html. The report maintains that the current tank construction requirements would have prevented the tragedy.

78. CRS LNG SITING, SAFETY AND REGULATION, *supra* note 62, at 20–21.

79. For further examination of security issues see PAUL W. PARFOMAK, CONGRESSIONAL RESEARCH SERVICE, CRS RPT. RL32073, LIQUEFIED NATURAL GAS (LNG) INFRASTRUCTURE SECURITY: ISSUES FOR CONGRESS (updated Mar. 16, 2005), *available at* http://www .ncseonline.org/nle/crsreports/05mar/RL32073.pdf.

80. *See* 49 C.F.R. §§ 193.2057, 2059 (2007) (requiring exclusion zones to protect against thermal radiation and flammable vapor-gas).

81. Broadwater, *Broadwater Project Description* 16 (undated), *available at* http://broad waterenergy.com/pdf/Full_Profile.pdf. *See also* Final Environmental Impact Statement re: Broadwater LNG FEIS Project under CP06-54, ES 3-4, *available at* http://elibrary.ferc.gov/ idmws/file_list.asp?accession_num=2008011-4001 *and* http://broadwaterenergy.com/pdf/ Broadwater_PEIS_Executive_Summary.pdf; CAL. ENERGY COMM'N, *supra* note 77, at 6.

82. Benson, *supra* note 59. *See generally* Laurie Nadel, *Coast Guard Assesses Risks of Gas Plant*, N.Y. TIMES, June 5, 2005, at CT3. For a detailed review of the safely related statutes and regulations *see* CRS LNG SITING, SAFETY AND REGULATION, *supra* note 62, at 7–11.

83. There are other ways to regasify LNG, which avoid or minimize the volume of seawater used (and thus the impingement and entrainment), while lessening the costs incurred by the burning of a small percentage of the LNG. C.C. Yang & Zupeng Huang, *Lower Emission LNG Vaporization*, LNG JOURNAL (Nov./Dec. 2004), *available at* http://www.fwc .com/publications/tech_papers/files/Lower%20Emission%20LNG%20Vap.pdf.

84. Broadwater, *Broadwater Project Description, supra* note 81, at 31.

85. Rogers, *First Open Loop NLG Terminal Launched, supra* note 60. The facility also has the option of operating as a closed loop facility. *Id.* Excelerate Energy has committed that its proposed Northeast Gateway Project off the coast of Massachusetts would operate only in the closed-loop mode. Northeast Gateway, Excelerate Energy, *Seawater Protection, at* http://www.northeastgateway.com/overview/benefits.php (last visited Feb. 13, 2008).

86. Gulf Landing LLC Liquefied Natural Gas Deepwater Port License Application, Final Environmental Impact Statement 4-5 (Nov. 2004), *available at* http://dmses.dot.gov/docimages/ pdf90/307025_web.pdf. The facility is referred to as Gulf Landing. The application and related materials for this and other facilities can be found on the U.S. Coast Guard docket at http://www.uscg.mil/hq/g-m/mso/mso5.htm.

87. Rogers, *Collateral Damage, supra* note 67.

88. Letter from Larry B. Simpson, Exec. Dir. Gulf States Marine Fisheries Commission to James L. Connaughton, Chairman, Council on Environmental Quality (Jan. 28, 2005), *available at* http://dmses.dot.gov/docimages/pdf91/315674_web.pdf. *See also* Rogers, *Collateral Damage, supra* note 67.

89. Final Environmental Impact Statement for the Gulf Landing LLC Deepwater Port License Application, DOT Docket No. USCG-2004-16860; Al Rogers, *Gulf Landing May Be Only Tip of an LNG Iceberg*, RODNREEL.COM, Mar. 17, 2005, http://rodnreel.com/ articles/ articles.asp?cmd=view&StoryID=781.

90. Gulf Restoration Network v. United States Dep't of Transp., No 05-60321 (5th Cir. filed Oct. 10, 2005).

91. *Id.* Similar concerns about the open loop system are being raised in other areas on the Gulf. *See, e.g.,* Laura Elder, *Groups to Speak Out Against LNG Terminal*, DAILY NEWS-GALVESTON COUNTY, June 29, 2005, *available at* http://galvestondailynews.com/story .lasso?ewcd=a4d5c5676284967e (terminal proposed 40 miles offshore from Galveston, TX); Al Rogers, *LNG Proposal Stalls*, RODNREEL.COM, May 17, 2005, *available at* http:// www.rodnreel.com/articles/articles.asp?cmd=view&StoryID=810 (terminal proposed near Dauphin Island, AL); Cain Burdeau, *Exxon Mobil Faces Opposition Over Its LNG Terminal*, STATE.COM (South Carolina), May 2, 2005, http://www.thestate.com/mld/thestate/ business/11546543.htm (proposed terminal near Shell's Gulf Landing site off Louisiana coast).

92. CAL. ENERGY COMM'N, *supra* note 77, at 15–16.

93. *See generally* Broadwater, *Broadwater Project Description, supra* note 81, at 30–34.

94. Northeast Gateway, Excelerate Energy, http://www.northeastgateway.com/overview/ overview.php (last visited Feb. 13, 2008). As noted above, the need for a metering tower is unique to this site. *Supra* note 71.

95. Jennifer Nist & M.E. Rolle, American Bar Association, Section of Environment, Energy, and Resources, *Oil and Gas on the Louisiana Coast: After the Hurricanes*, TRENDS, Mar./ Apr. 2006, at 10.

96. The principal regulatory statute is the Natural Gas Act of 1938 (NGA), 15 U.S.C. § 717 (2006). LNG is natural gas within the meaning of the Act, although not specifically mentioned in the statutory definition. NGA § 2(5), 15 U.S.C. § 717a(5) (2006) (means either natural gas unmixed, or any mixture of natural of artificial gas). The Deepwater Port Act, 33 U.S.C. § 1502(9) (2006), specifically includes compressed or liquefied natural gas in the definition.

97. NGA §§3, 7, 15 U.S.C. §§717 b, 717f (2006). The implementing regulations are found at 18 C.F.R. pt. 153 (2007). When the NGA was enacted, the only international natural gas imports and exports were with Canada and Mexico by pipeline. Two subsequent Executive Orders dealt with border facilities, requiring authorization by FERC, after approval by the Secretaries of State and Defense, through issuance of a "Presidential Permit" analogous to a Section 3 permit. Exec. Order No. 10,485, 18 Fed. Reg. 5397 (Sept. 3, 1953); Exec. Order No. 12,038, 43 Fed. Reg. 4957 (Feb. 7, 1978). Because these orders do not apply to the border between the U.S. and international waters, Presidential Permits are not required for marine LNG terminals. *Phillips Petroleum Co.*, 37 F.P.C. 777 (1967). For a short summary of FERC's past regulatory policies see Gearold L. Knowles, *Liquefied Natural Gas: Regulation in a Competitive Natural Gas Market*, 24 ENERGY L.J. 293, 305 (2003).

98. Pipeline Safety Act, 49 U.S.C. §§60103, 60112, 60117 (2006). Regulations are found at 49 C.F.R. §§191–199 (2006). *See also* Fed. Energy Regulatory Comm'n. *Memorandum of Understanding Between the Department of Transportation and the Federal Energy Regulatory Commission Regarding Liquefied Natural Gas Transportation Facilities*, 31 F.E.R.C. 61,232 (1985), *available at* Office of Pipeline Safety, http://ops.dot.gov/library/mous/1985_DOT_FERC.pdf (note that in appropriate circumstances FERC may impose more stringent regulations than DOT prescribes). The regulations incorporate internationally recognized standards developed by the independent National Fire Protection Association. NAT'L FIRE PROTECTION ASS'N, NFPA 59A: STANDARD FOR THE PRODUCTION, STORAGE, AND HANDLING OF LIQUEFIED NATURAL GAS (2005), *available at* http://www.nfpa.org/aboutthecodes/AboutTheCodes.asp?DocNum=59A. Note that the DOT regulations make reference to the 2001 version of the standard. *See* 49 C.F.R. pt. 193 (2007).

99. Ken Kusano, U.S. Coast Guard, *The Deepwater Port Act: Understanding the Licensing Process* 3, http://www.slc.ca.gov/Division_Pages/MFD/Prevention_First/Documents/2004/LNG%20ON%20THE%20WEST%20COAST/Kusano%20paper.pdf.

100. 33 U.S.C. §1501 (2006).

101. Maritime Transportation Security Act of 2002, Pub. L. No. 107-295, §1a, 116 Stat. 2064 (2002) (codified as amended at 46 U.S.C. §2101 (2006)).

102. *Id.* §106(a)(1), 116 Stat. 1086 (codified as amended at 33 U.S.C. §1501. As amended, "deepwater port" is defined related to natural gas as structures "located seaward of the high water mark." DPA §3(9)(C), 33 U.S.C. §1502(9)(C)(2006). For other products, deepwater ports facilities are those "beyond State seaward boundaries." *Id.* §3(9)(A), §1502(9)(A).

103. *Memorandum of Understanding Related to the Licensing of Deepwater Ports Licensing* 5, May 20, 2004 (Depts. of Army, Commerce, Defense, Energy, Homeland Security, Interior, State, Transportation; U.S. EPA, Federal Energy Regulatory Commission, Council on Environmental Quality), *available at* http://www.uscg.mil/hq/g-m/mso/docs/dwp_white_house_task_force_energy_streamlining.pdf. The memorandum's discussion of FERC's jurisdiction was superseded by the Energy Policy Act of 2005.

104. 33 U.S.C. §1503 (2006).

105. *See* Kusano, *supra* note 99, at 4: CRS LNG SITING, SAFETY AND REGULATION, supra note 62, at 27. The Deepwater Port Act specifies that the environmental review must be in accordance with the recommendations of the Administrators of EPA and NOAA, and consistent with NEPA. DPA §6, 33 U.S.C. §1505 (2006).

106. Homeland Security Act of 2002, Pub. L. No. 107-296, §§888, 1512(d) 116 Stat. 2135 (2002) (codified as amended at 6 U.S.C. §§468, 552(d) (2006)).

107. 33 U.S.C. §1508(b)(1)(2006).

108. Energy Policy Act of 2005, Pub. L. No. 109-58, §311(e) (codified as amended at 15 U.S.C. §717b(e) (2006)). The Energy Policy Act established a strict timetable for the Secretary to approve or deny a permit. 15 U.S.C. §717n (2006) The Energy Policy Act did not alter the governors' role under the Deep Water Ports Act, so the governor of an adjacent coastal state still can veto a project outside of the states territorial waters.

109. *See* Sound Energy Solutions, Docket No. CP04-58-001, 107 F.E.R.C. ¶ 61263 (2004). For an analysis of the Commerce Clause issues involved in the dispute, see Monica Berry, *Liquefied Natural Gas Import Terminals: Jurisdiction over Siting, Construction, and Operation in the Context of Commerce Clause Jurisprudence*, 26 ENERGY L.J. 135 (2005). For background on the various jurisdictional conflicts see AARON M. FLYNN, CONGRESSIONAL RESEARCH SERVICE, CRS RPT. RL32575, LIQUEFIED NATURAL GAS (LNG): JURISDICTION CONFLICTS IN SITING APPROVAL (updated Sept. 10, 2004), *available at* http://www.ncseonline.org/NLE/CRSreports/04Sep/RL32575.pdf.

110. *See* NGA § 3(d), 15 U.S.C. § 717b(d) (2006). Although the Deepwater Port Act does not contain a similar explicit provision, there is nothing to the contrary.

111. Clean Water Act § 401, 33 U.S.C. § 1341 (2006). For more information on § 401, see Chapter 7, "Coastal Water Quality Protection."

112. *See* American Rivers, Inc. v. FERC, 129 (F.3d 99 (2d Cir. 1997). *See also* Escondido Mut. Water Co. v. La Jolla, Rincon, San Pasqual, Pauma & Pala Band of Mission Indians, 466 U.S. 765 (1984).

113. 16 U.S.C. § 1456 (2006).

114. 16 U.S.C. § 307 (c)(3)(A) (2006). For more information on the CZMA, see Chapter 5, "Managing Coastal Development."

115. 33 U.S.C. § 1342 (2006).

116. 33 U.S.C. § 1326 (2006).

117. *See* Letter from Robert D. Lawrence, Senior Policy Advisor for Energy Issues, U.S. EPA 6, to Mark A. Prescott, Dep't of Homeland Security, *Shell's Gulf Landing LNG Proposed Facility* (Dec. 21, 2004), DOT Docket No. USCG-2004-16860-87, U.S. Dep't of Transportation, Document Management System, http://dmses.dot.gov/docimages/pdf91/314616_web.pdf.

118. Letter from Robert D. Lawrence, Senior Policy Advisor for Energy Issues, U.S. EPA 6, to Mark A. Prescott, Dep't of Homeland Security (Apr. 18, 2004), *EPA Authority Over Construction and Operation: Shell's Gulf Landing Deepwater Port Act Project*, DOT Docket No. USCG-2004-16860-23, U.S. Dep't of Transportation, Document Management System, http://dmses.dot.gov/docimages/pdf89/277447_web.pdf.

119. *See generally* OCEAN BLUEPRINT, *supra* note 1.

120. *Id.* at 365–67.

121. *See generally* Victoria Sutton and Nicole Tomich, *Harnessing Wind Is Not (by Nature) Environmentally Friendly*, 22 PACE ENVTL. L. REV. 91 (2005); Jeremy Firestone *et al.*, *Regulating Offshore Wind Power and Aquaculture: Messages from Land and Sea*, 35 ENVTL. L. REP. 10,289 (2005).

122. *See generally* Thomas Arthur Utzinger, *Federal Permitting Issues Related to Offshore Wind Energy, Using the Cape Wind Project in Massachusetts as an Illustration*, 34 ENVTL. L. REP. 10,794 (2004).

123. *See* LIPA, Long Island Offshore Wind Park Web site, http://www.lipower.org/cei/offshore.html (last visited Nov. 5, 2005).

124. *See generally* Utzinger, *supra* note 122.

125. *See, e.g.*, Steven Mufson & Juliet Eilperin, *Offshore Wind Farm Is Approved: Plant off Texas Coast to Be Biggest of Its Kind in U.S.*, WASH. POST (May 12, 2006).

126. 33 U.S.C. § 403.

127. The term "OCS" refers to federal lands extending seaward of the generally three-nautical-mile grant of coastal lands made to the states in the Submerged Lands Act, 43 U.S.C. § 1301 *et seq.* 43 U.S.C. § 1331(a). It has been suggested that wind energy developers have avoided siting offshore wind energy projects in state waters to minimize regulatory oversight. *See* Guy R. Martin & Odin A. Smith, *The World's Largest Wind Energy Facility in Nantucket Sound? Deficiencies in the Current Regulatory Process for Offshore Wind Energy Development*, 31 B.C. ENVTL. AFF. L. REV. 285 (2004); *but see* Dina Cappiello, *Wind Farm May Yield Windfall for Texans*, HOUSTON CHRON. (Oct. 23, 2005) (reporting that Texas recently issued the nation's first lease of offshore lands for a wind energy

project projected to begin operations sometime between 2010 and 2012), *available at* http://www.chron.com/content/archive/index.mpl (last visited Nov. 5, 2005).

128. 43 U.S.C. § 1331 *et seq.*; §1333(e).

129. *See generally* Martin and Smith, *supra* note 127; Donald C. Baur & Jena A. MacLean, *The "Degreening" of Wind Energy: Alternative Energy v. Ocean Governance*, 19 NAT. RES. & ENV'T 44 (Summer 2004).

130. 398 F.3d 105 (1st Cir. 2005).

131. *Id.* at 110–11.

132. *Id.* at 113–14.

133. *Id.* at 114.

134. *Id.*

135. *Id.*

136. *In re* AquaEnergy Group, Ltd., 102 F.E.R.C. ¶ 61,242 (Feb. 28, 2003) (Order Denying Rehearing).

137. 16 U.S.C. §§ 791a *et seq.*

138. *See, e.g.,* Stephanie Ebbert & Beth Daley, *As Some Talk Wind Farms, Others Want to Harness the Tides: Nantucket Sound Considered as Site*, BOSTON GLOBE (June 13, 2006).

139. Pub. L. No. 109-58 (Aug. 8, 2005).

140. H.R. 5156 (July 18, 2002).

141. *See* Letter from Rebecca W. Watson, Assistant Sec'y of the Interior for Land and Minerals Management, to the Honorable Richard B. Cheney, President of the Senate 1 (June 20, 2002) (discussing the lack of federal regulations regarding the utilization of the Outer Continental Shelf (OCS) for non-oil and gas related activities) (on file with author); *Administration Legislation on Energy Related Uses of the OCS: Hearing on H.R. 5156 Before the House Subcomm. on Energy and Mineral Res., Comm. on Res.*, 107th Cong. 4 (2002) (statement of Johnnie Burton, Director, Minerals Mgmt. Serv.), *available at* http://www.mms.gov/ooc/newweb/congressionalaffairs/testimony72502.htm (last visited Jan. 23, 2004).

142. Pub. L. No. 109-58, § 388(a), codified at 43 U.S.C. §1337(p)(1), (p)(1)(C). Leases, easements, or right-of-ways are also authorized for activities that support oil and gas activities, or utilize oil and gas-related facilities. *Id.*

143. 43 U.S.C. § 1333(e).

144. The Act technically authorizes leases, easements, or right-of-ways on the OCS "for activities not otherwise authorized in [the OCSLA] . . . or other applicable law." Pub. L. No. 109-58, § 388(a), codified at 43 U.S.C. § 1337(p)(1). Nonetheless, there does not appear to be any inclination on the part of offshore wind energy project proponents or the Corps of Engineers to continue to argue that non-oil and gas activities on the OCS are authorized under Section 10 of the Rivers and Harbors Act of 1899, as extended to the OCS by the OCSLA.

145. Pub. L. No. 109-58, § 388(a), codified at 43 U.S.C. § 1337(p)(2)(A).

146. Pub. L. No. 109-58, § 388(a), codified at 43 U.S.C. § 1337(p)(2)(B).

147. Pub. L. No. 109-58, § 388(a), codified at 43 U.S.C. § 1337(p)(4), (8).

148. Pub. L. No. 109-58, § 388(a), codified at 43 U.S.C. § 1337(p)(3).

149. Pub. L. No. 109-58, § 388(a), codified at 43 U.S.C. § 1337(p)(4), (8).

150. Pub. L. No. 109-58, § 388(a), codified at 43 U.S.C. § 1337(p)(5).

151. Pub. L. No. 109-58, § 388(a), codified at 43 U.S.C. § 1337(p)(6).

152. Pub. L. No. 109-58, § 388(a), codified at 43 U.S.C. § 1337(p)(1), (7).

153. Pub. L. No. 109-58, § 388(a), codified at 43 U.S.C. § 1337(p)(10).

154. Pub. L. No. 109-58, § 388(b).

155. Pub. L. No. 109-58, § 388(d).

156. Pub. L. No. 109-58, § 388(d).

157. *See* Press Release, MMS, MMS Launches OCS Renewable Energy & Alternative Use Website (Oct. 6, 2005), *available at* http://www.mms.gov/ooc/press/2005/press1006a.htm (last visited Nov. 4, 2005); Kevin Dennehy and David Schoetz, *Interior Will Rule on*

Wind Project, Cape Cod Times, Oct. 14, 2005, *available at* http://www.capecodonline
.com/special/windfarm/interiorrule14.htm (last visited Nov. 4, 2005).

158. Pub. L. No. 109-58, § 388(a), codified at 43 U.S.C. §1337(p)(3) (lease, easement, or right-of-way to be issued on a competitive basis unless no competitive basis is determined).

159. 71 Fed. Reg. 30,693 (May 30, 2006); 71 Fed. Reg. 35,293 (June 19, 2006).

160. Press Release, MMS, MMS to Extend Comment Period on Cape Wind Energy Project Notice of Intent (July 13, 2006), *available at* http://www.mms.gov/ooc/press/2006/press0713
.htm (last visited July 31, 2006).

161. MMS, Renewable Energy & Alternative Uses Web site, http://www.mms.gov/offshore/
RenewableEnergy/RenewableEnergyMain.htm (last visited Nov. 4, 2005).

162. MMS, *OCS Renewable Energy & Alternative Uses* 1, *available at* http://www.mms
.gov/offshore/RenewableEnergy/OCSRenewableEnergyAndAlternateUses.pdf (last visited
Nov. 4, 2005).

163. 70 Fed. Reg. 77,345 (Dec. 30, 2005).

164. *Id.* at 77,346.

165. *Id.* at 77,345–48.

166. *Id.* at 77,346.

167. 71 Fed. Reg. 26,559 (May 5, 2006).

168. *Id.* at 26,560.

169. Press Release, MMS, Minerals Management Service Schedules Public Meetings on Renewable Energy and Alternate Use on America's Outer Continental Shelf (May 5, 2006), *available at* http://www.mms.gov/ooc/press/2006/press0505.htm (last visited July 31, 2006).

170. Bureau of Land Management, Wind Energy Development Programmatic EIS Web site, *available at* http://windeis.anl.gov/ (last visited Nov. 4, 2005).

171. *See, e.g.,* Jeremy Firestone *et al.*, *Regulating Offshore Wind Power and Aquaculture: Messages from Land and Sea,* 35 Envtl L. Rep. 10,289 (2005); Martin and Smith, *supra* note 127; Baur and MacLean, *supra* note 129.

172. 72 Fed. Reg. 13,307 (Mar. 21, 2007).

173. *Id.*; MMS, *Draft Programmatic Environmental Impact Statement for Alternative Energy Development and Production and Alternative Use of Facilities on the Outer Continental Shelf* (Mar. 2007), at 2-1, 2-2 [hereinafter DPEIS], *available at* http://ocsenergy.anl.gov/
documents/dpeis/index.cfm (last visited July 10, 2007).

174. DPEIS at 2-4.

175. Press Release, MMS, MMS Publishes OCS Alternative Energy and Alternative Use Program Draft Environmental Impact Statement (Mar. 21, 2007), *available at* http://www
.mms.gov/ooc/press/2007/press0320.htm (last visited July 10, 2007).

176. *Id.*

177. *See* note 136–138, *supra,* and accompanying text.

178. *See Opportunities, Issues and Implementation of Section 388 of the Energy Policy Act of 2005: Hearing Before the Senate Comm. on Energy and Natural Resources,* 110th Cong. (June 7, 2007) (statements of C. Stephen Allred, Asst. Sec'y of the Interior for Land and Minerals Management, and J. Mark Robinson, Director, FERC Office of Energy Projects), *available at* http://energy.senate.gov/public/index.cfm?FuseAction=Hearings
.Hearing&Hearing_ID=1636 (last visited July 10, 2007).

179. Art. 56(1) (emphasis added). For more information, see Chapter 12, "The 1982 United Nations Convention on the Law of the Sea."

180. *Id.*; Art. 60(1).

181. The regulatory framework established by Section 388, however, applies to the outer continental shelf, which may extend beyond the two-hundred-nautical mile EEZ. Pub. L. No. 109-58 § 388(a); UNCLOS Art. 76. On the continental shelf, Article 80 provides that Article 60 applies, *mutatis mutandis,* to artificial islands, installations, and structures. The sovereign rights of coastal states on the continental shelf, however, extend only to its natural resources, which are defined as "the mineral and other non-living resources of the

seabed and subsoil together with [sedentary living organisms]." Art. 77(1), (4). Nonetheless, given the impracticability of developing renewable energy resources more than 200 nautical miles from the coast, this difference in scope of sovereign rights is unlikely to result in any actual conflict with international law.

182. United Nations Univ., Inst. of Advanced Studies Rep., Bioprospecting of Genetic Resources in the Deep Seabed: Scientific, Legal and Policy Aspects 7 (2005).

183. *Id.* at 15 n.79.

184. *Id.* at 7, 15.

185. Donald K. Anton, *Law for the Sea's Biological Diversity,* 36 Colum. J. Transnat'l L. 341, 348 (1997).

186. *Id.;* Rita R. Colwell, *Fulfilling the Promise of Biotechnology* 20 Biotechnology Advances 215 (2002).

187. Nigel Hawkes, *The Deadly Sea Snail Venom That Will Take Away Your Pain,* Times Online, July 10, 2006, http://www.timesonline.co.uk/article/0,,8122-2262948.html.

188. Oceans and the Law of the Sea, Report of the Secretary General, A/60/63/Add.1, Para. 77 (July 15, 2005), *available at* http://www.un.org/Depts/los/general_assembly/general_assembly_reports.htm.

189. Press Release, Biotechnology Industry Organization (BIO), Hawaii Summit to Highlight Marine Biotechnology Discoveries, Benefits (Jan. 6, 2006), *available at* http://www.bio.org/news/newsitem.asp?id=2006_0106_01. *See also* D. K. Leary, *Bioprospecting and the Genetic Resources of Hydrothermal Vents on the High Seas: What Is the Existing Legal Position, Where Are We Heading and What Are Our Options?,* 1 Macquarie J. Int'l & Comp. Envtl. L. 137, 143 (2004) (table of biotechnology companies involved in hydrothermal vent research and development).

190. Gregory S. Stone et al., *Seamount Biodiversity, Exploitation and Conservation, in* Defying Ocean's End: An Agenda for Action 44 (Linda K. Glover & Sylvia A. Earle eds., 2005).

191. *See generally* Matthew Gianni, *High Seas Bottom Trawl Fisheries and Their Impacts on the Biodiversity of Vulnerable Deep-Sea Ecosystems,* Report prepared for IUCN/the World Conservation Union, Natural Resources Defense Council, WWF International, Conservation International (June 2004), at http://info.greenpeace.ch/de/arten/attachments/seamounts.pdf.

192. Article 76(3) of UNCLOS excludes oceanic ridges, where most hydrothermal vents are found, from the definition of continental shelves.

193. This definition describes the "Area," which is "the sea-bed and ocean floor and subsoil thereof beyond the limits of national jurisdiction." UNCLOS Art. 1, 1(1).

194. For a detailed examination of both the technical and legal aspects of deep sea genetic resources, see Horst Korn, Susanne Friedrich & Ute Feit, Fed. Agency for Nature Conservation [Germany], Deep Sea Genetic Resources in the Context of the Convention on Biological Diversity and the United Nations Convention on the Law of the Sea (2003).

195. *See, e.g.,* UNCLOS Arts. 61, 133, 156.

196. Arts. 51(1)(b)(iii), 61.

197. Art. 77.

198. Art. 192.

199. Art. 246, para. 3. To protect a vent community within its EEZ, Canada established a Marine Protected Area. David Leary, *Law Reaches New Depths: The Endeavour Hydrothermal Vents Marine Protected Area, in* Aquatic Protected Areas: What Works Best and How Do We Know? (World Congress on Aquatic Protected Areas, J. P. Beumer et al. eds., 2002).

200. Art. 246, para. 5(a) (emphasis added).

201. An additional issue arises when a state's continental shelf extends beyond its two-hundred-mile EEZ. In this region the provisions of Part VI, Continental Shelf, apply, but not Part

V, EEZ. Thus the coastal state has jurisdiction only over the nonliving resources and *sedentary* living species. Sedentary species are those that "at the harvestable stage, either are immobile on or under the sea-bed or are unable to move except in constant physical contact with the sea-bed or the subsoil." Art 77(4). But most of the species that might be found in sea mounts or vents are not species that have a harvestable stage. And they may be mobile in some stages of their development, and sedentary in others. This issue is discussed in detail in Leary, *supra* note 189.

202. Art. 87, paras. 1(e), (f), 116.

203. Art. 117.

204. Art. 1, para. 1(1).

205. Arts. 133, 136.

206. Art. 156. The United States is not a party to UNCLOS, primarily because of the deep seabed provisions, and has established its own regime for regulating United States citizens or corporations who wish to engage in deep sea mining. Deep Seabed Hard Mineral Resources Act, 30 U.S.C. §§1401–1473 (2006). Nevertheless, there remains the possibility that the U.S. Congress will in the future ratify the treaty.

207. There is some argument that Art. 145, Protection of the Marine Environment, vests a general power in the Authority to protect the marine environment. This is problematic since the language of the provision must be construed in the context of Part XI which deals only with minerals in the Area.

208. Convention on Biological Diversity, U.N. Conference on Environment and Development, June 5, 1992, reprinted in 31 I.L.M. 818 (1992) (entered into force Dec. 29, 1993) (the United States signed but has not ratified the Convention).

209. Art. 1.

210. Art. 15, para. 1, 2.

211. Art. 15, paras. 1, 4, 5, 7. The United States has not ratified the CBD, but it has been suggested that if it were to do so, government institutions might be in violation of the Convention since they would be barred from entering into royalty agreements for sample collection and testing. Julia Jabour Green, *Report of the Workshop on Bioprospecting in the High Seas* 3, University of Otago, Dunedin, NZ, Nov. 28–29, 2003.

212. Art. 16, para. 5.

213. Art. 19, para. 2.

214. *See generally* Christopher J. Hunter, *Sustainable Bioprospecting: Using Private Contracts and International Legal Principles and Policies to Conserve Raw Medicinal Materials,* 25 B.C. ENVTL. AFF. L. REV. 129, 148 (1997).

215. The CBD also obligates states to regulate the conduct of their own citizens beyond national jurisdiction, but so far none have done so.

216. Richard J. McLaughlin, *Managing Foreign Access to Marine Genetic Materials: Moving From Capture to Cooperation, in* BRINGING NEW LAW TO OCEAN WATERS 257, 264–65 (David D. Caron & Harry N. Scheiber eds. 2004); Curtis M. Horton, *Protecting Biodiversity and Cultural Diversity Under Intellectual Property Law: Toward a New International System,* 10 J. ENVTL. L. & LITIG. 1, 25 (1995).

217. McLaughlin, *supra* note 216, at 264–65.

218. Leary, *supra* note 199 at 143.

219. Greenpeace International, *Bioprospecting in the Deep Sea,* Nov. 2005.

220. World Conservation Union (IUCN) Bulletin, World Conservation, "International Marine Law: From Hindsight to Foresight" (Jan. 2004), at 27.

221. Ad Hoc Open-ended Informal Working Group to study issues relating to the conservation and sustainable use of marine biological diversity beyond areas of national jurisdiction, http://www.un.org/Depts/los/biodiversityworkinggroup/biodiversityworkinggroup.htm.

222. UNU-IAS Report, *supra* note 182, at 22 & n.137 (2005), *available at* http://www.ony.unu.edu/09June2005.html.

223. Stephen Nicol, Yoshinari Endo, *Krill Fisheries: Development, Management and Ecosystem Implications,* 12 Aquatic Living Resources (1999), *available at* http://www.edpsciences.org/articles/alr/pdf/1999/02/alr9230.pdf?access=ok.

224. *Iron Fertilization,* NPR, Living on Earth, at http://www.loe.org/series/iron_fertilization (last visited Feb. 13, 2008).

225. This is a two-edged sword since increasing ocean absorption of CO_2 has already resulted in acidification, and consequent damage to ecosystems. Envtl. Law Inst., *Politics Pushing Policies of Inaction,* ENVTL. F. 18 (May/June 2006).

226. Press Release, Biotechnology Industry Organization (BIO), Algae May Hold Key to Hydrogen Economy; Hawaii Summit to Highlight Marine Biotechnology Discoveries, Benefits (Jan. 6, 2006), *available at* http://www.bio.org/news/newsitem.asp?id=2006_0106_01.

227. Edith Allison, "Gas Hydrates: A Future Ocean Resource," presentation at the fifth meeting of the UN Open-ended Informal Consultative Process on Oceans and the Law of the Sea (June 2004), *at* http://www.un.org/Depts/los/consultative_process/documents/5e_allisson.pdf.

chapter fifteen

The Law of Marine Mammal Conservation

Donald C. Baur
Michael L. Gosliner
Nina M. Young

I. Introduction

"Once destroyed, biological capital cannot be recreated." With these words, John Dingell opened the floor to debate in 1971 over the first attempt by Congress to design a comprehensive program to conserve a broad array of wildlife species.[1] The topic was how to fashion a law to protect marine mammals; a law that would govern human conduct to allow the marine ecosystem of which such mammals are a part to remain healthy and function according to the "laws of nature."[2]

The ambitious nature of this effort is evident in Chairman Dingell's opening remarks, in which he recognized: (1) the wide array of mammals to be covered— "whales, seals, walruses, sea otters, polar bears, and the sea cows"; (2) that these animals "are found on the high seas, in territorial waters, and on U.S. lands"; (3) that Congress would have to address problems of overlapping jurisdiction and the lack of consistency in the degree of protection afforded each species; and (4) that the legislation would have to be developed in spite of the fact that "hard evidence" that would lead to clear solutions was too often lacking.[3]

During the course of these and other hearings, lawmakers heard from state officials, environmental groups, animal welfare groups, commercial fishing industry representatives, businesses and trade associations, Alaska Native organizations, zoological

The authors express their appreciation to Rebecca Brezenoff, Emily Plette-Miyake, and Jennifer L. Schorr, all of Perkins Coie, for their extensive contributions to this chapter.

parks and aquariums, and many concerned individuals. In crafting the law that would emerge from these hearings, the Marine Mammal Protection Act of 1972 (MMPA),[4] Congress also relied extensively on the advice of biologists and other experts from the field of conservation.

The members of Congress harbored no illusions that sufficient information existed about marine mammals to guide the law-making process. As the House Merchant Marine and Fisheries Committee declared in its report on the proposed 1971 marine mammal bills:

> In the teeth of this lack of knowledge of specific causes, and of the certain knowledge that these animals are almost all threatened in some way, it seems elementary common sense to the Committee that legislation should be adopted to require that we act conservatively—that no steps should be taken regarding these animals that might prove to be adverse or even irreversible in their effects until more is known. As far as could be done, we have endeavored to build such a conservative bias into the legislation here presented.[5]

Attaining the goals of the Act in the face of scientific uncertainty remains as challenging today as it was in 1971. Although more is now known about marine mammals and their habitat, the task of developing solutions to the threats to the species and their habitat is in many cases more complex than it was at the time of MMPA's original enactment.

This chapter discusses this innovative and enduring law. While a variety of other domestic legal authorities (e.g., the Endangered Species Act (ESA), the Magnuson-Stevens Fishery Conservation and Management Act, the Animal Welfare Act, the laws governing habitat in marine protected areas) and international agreements (e.g., the International Convention for the Regulation of Whaling, the Agreement on the Conservation of Polar Bears, the Convention on International Trade in Endangered Species of Flora and Fauna) also apply to these species, the MMPA remains the centerpiece in the marine mammal conservation effort. As described in this chapter, although the MMPA has evolved through twists and turns over its thirty-five years of existence, it has remained true to its central principles and has proven to be an effective piece of species-conservation legislation.

II. The Current State of the Law—Marine Mammal Conservation

A. The Marine Mammal Protection Act—Principles for Conservation

In examining the need for marine mammal protection, four themes emerged on the congressional and public agendas. First was concern over the fate of species. Second was the call for broader protection of marine ecosystems. Third was the recognition that little information existed about marine mammals and their status. Finally, all participants in the debate recognized the need for greater international cooperation.

1. Species of Special Concern

Several high-profile ecological disputes and catastrophes involving marine mammals coincided with congressional efforts to protect the environment in the early 1970s.

One of these was the commercial harvest of seals, including the annual harvest of newborn harp seals and hooded seals off Canada's east coast.

At the same time, there was strong concern over the decline of most whale stocks. Whaling was still a significant commercial enterprise for many nations, including the United States, and the International Whaling Commission, charged with conserving the stocks, had been ineffective at this task. Indeed, in 1970 eight species of great whales were listed under the then-existing ESA as endangered or threatened with extinction, heightening the call for improved protection.

Meanwhile, in the eastern tropical Pacific Ocean, the U.S. tuna fleet was exploiting an unusual bond between yellowfin tuna and various species of dolphins to deploy large purse seine nets around schools of dolphins, thereby trapping the fish swimming below. The disastrous result was that by 1971 an estimated five million dolphins had perished in the tuna purse seine fishery. At the time of the 1971 congressional hearings, more than 400,000 dolphins were being killed every year.[6] The public outcry over this fishing practice grew throughout the consideration of the legislation, and it had become a major issue by the time the MMPA was enacted in 1972.

At the time of the 1971 congressional hearings, more than 400,000 dolphins were being killed every year.

Other marine mammal species also received considerable attention. These included, for example, polar bears, thought by some to be threatened as a result of overhunting; West Indian manatees, which had previously been overhunted and at the time were being killed by motorboats and losing important feeding habitat; and the California population of sea otters, driven to the brink of extinction by hunting and threatened by incidental take in fishing activities, oil-spill risks, and habitat loss.

All these species received special consideration. But as Congress suspected, and as research conducted in subsequent years has borne out, other marine mammals were at risk. As the House Merchant Marine and Fisheries Committee summed up in its 1971 report on the Act:

> Recent history indicates that man's impact upon marine mammals has ranged from what might be termed malign neglect to virtual genocide. These animals, including whales, porpoises, seals, sea otters, polar bears, manatees and others, have only rarely benefitted from our interest; they have been shot, blown up, clubbed to death, run down by boats, poisoned, and exposed to a multitude of other indignities, all in the interest of profit or recreation, with little or no consideration of the potential impact of these activities on the animal populations involved.[7]

The result was a law that Congress intended would ensure that "future generations will be able to enjoy a world populated by all species of marine mammals."[8]

To advance this goal, Congress developed two innovative legal features that would be incorporated into subsequent wildlife legislation: (1) building in a conservative bias in favor of the species, and (2) assigning the burden of proof to the party seeking an authorization to take or import the species. The first feature was a mandate for a risk-averse approach: in cases of doubt or ambiguity, decisions would favor marine mammals. The House Merchant Marine and Fisheries Committee made clear its intent to "build such a conservative bias into the legislation here presented."[9] The Senate expressed a similar view. "Scientists generally will state that our level of knowledge of marine mammals is very low. . . . Barring better and more information, it would therefore appear to be wise to adopt a cautious attitude toward the exploitation of marine mammals."[10]

In keeping with this principle, the courts generally have given the interests of marine mammals priority over the interests of other parties, such as commercial fisheries and tour boat operators, who may take marine mammals directly or indirectly in their economic pursuits. In *Committee for Humane Legislation, Inc. v. Richardson,* one of the first court decisions to interpret the MMPA, Judge Charles Richey held that the Act should be interpreted "for [the benefit of the protected species] and not for the benefit of commercial exploitation."[11] Similarly, in *Kokechik Fishermen's Ass'n v. Secretary of Commerce,* the District of Columbia Circuit Court of Appeals declared that, when balancing commercial and conservation interests under the Act, "the interest in maintaining healthy populations of marine mammals comes first."[12]

The second legal principle inherent in the MMPA is that any party wishing to exploit marine mammals should have the burden of proof that such activity will be consistent with the Act's overall goals and not disadvantage the species or stock involved. As stated in the House Merchant Marine and Fisheries Committee report:

> If that burden is not carried—and it is by no means a light burden—the permit may not be issued. The effect of this set of requirements is to insist that the management of the animal populations be carried out with the interests of the animals as the prime consideration.[13]

The presumption favors protection. Activities that disturb, capture, injure, or kill marine mammals will be authorized only if the requesting party sufficiently demonstrates that its activities will not disadvantage the species, harm the marine ecosystem, or result in avoidable pain to the animal. As stated by Judge Richey in *Committee for Humane Legislation,* the Act's mandate is "to proceed knowledgeably and cautiously."[14]

2. Ecosystem Protection

Interspersed throughout the testimony of witnesses and the statements made by members of Congress during the original consideration of the MMPA were expressions of concern over the health of the marine environment as a whole and the ecosystem of which marine mammals are a part. The result was a strong and unified expression of the need for action to protect marine ecosystems. The Act, however, did not contain explicit provisions for accomplishing this goal.

In the section-by-section analysis included in the 1972 report on the original Senate bill, the Commerce Committee noted that the Act's finding regarding the importance of marine mammals as functioning parts of their ecosystems was meant to emphasize "the need to protect those geographic areas of significance for each species of marine mammals from adverse activities."[15] The Committee observed that "[a]ll of these animals are a part of the ocean biomass and are important in maintaining an ecological balance."[16]

From this consideration emerged the ecosystem conservation goal of the Act, that all marine mammals should be brought to and maintained at their optimum sustainable population (OSP) level, provided that efforts to do so are consistent with maintaining the overall health and stability of the marine environment.

3. Research

Congress was clear about its intent to make research a key element of the Act. For all of the high-minded goals, principles, and concepts reflected in the MMPA, the law would be ineffective without more information about the species and their habitats. Congress recognized the need for studies on nutrition and diseases, effects of contaminants, life history, and population dynamics.[17] Congress also acknowledged the role of science as immensely important and declared a goal of the Act to be nothing short of making it possible for "science [to] make an adequate interpretation of the entire marine environment to predict what will happen to marine mammals under different management programs and increasing utilization of marine resources by society and industry."[18]

4. International Cooperation

Members of Congress, federal officials, and others involved in drafting the MMPA agreed that, for many species, the application of stringent laws to U.S. waters and U.S. citizens would not be enough. Because of the migratory nature of many marine mammal species, and the fact that the activities of foreign citizens posed some of the most severe threats, cooperative international efforts would be needed. Among the species especially in need of international protection efforts were most whales, many species of dolphins, harp seals, fur seals, polar bears, and dugongs.

In addressing this need, Congress directed the State Department and other federal agencies to pursue protective treaties and agreements. To reduce the incentive for killing marine mammals in foreign countries, Congress adopted a moratorium on the importation of marine mammals and their products. Congress also recognized the need to give the United States some leverage against foreign nations that were undermining international conservation efforts. This was to be achieved through the economic pressure of trade sanctions, authorized by the Act and other measures, such as the Pelly and Packwood-Magnuson Amendments to the Fishermen's Protective Act.[19]

B. Implementing the Principles of Protection

With these four principles in mind, Congress fashioned the provisions that became the MMPA of 1972. The final product was a compromise between two fundamentally

The law that emerged from the congressional debate was protectionist in tone, but stopped short of a full ban on taking marine mammals.

different points of view as reflected in more than forty introduced bills.[20] The legislative compromise ultimately reached resulted in the adoption of broad and somewhat ambiguous policy goals. The law that emerged from the congressional debate was protectionist in tone, but stopped short of a full ban on taking marine mammals.

1. Policies of the Act

In Section 2 of the MMPA, Congress set forth six "findings" that have endured throughout the Act's history and that serve as the foundation for the law's substantive requirements.

First, Congress recognized that certain species and populations were or may be in danger of extinction as a result of human activities.[21]

Second, species and stocks "should not be permitted to diminish beyond the point at which they cease to be a significant functioning element in the ecosystem of which they are a part, and, consistent with this major objective, they should not be permitted to diminish below their optimum sustainable population level."[22] Immediate action, Congress directed, should be taken to encourage recovery of stocks that have fallen below this level, and particular efforts should be made to protect essential habitats.

Third, Congress found that there is inadequate information on the ecology and biology of marine mammals.[23] Although much has certainly been learned, the need for more information about these species remains as critical as when the law was enacted.

Fourth, Congress issued a finding calling for international efforts to encourage research on, and conservation of, all marine mammals.[24]

Fifth, Congress recognized the economic importance of marine mammals by noting that they either "move in interstate commerce" or "affect the balance of marine ecosystems in a manner which is important to other animals and animal products which move in interstate commerce." This focus, however, may have had more to do with exercising jurisdiction over marine mammal issues under the Commerce Clause of the U.S. Constitution than with a broad concern about interstate commerce.

Congress listed last the foremost goal of the MMPA. As set forth in Section 2(6):

[M]arine mammals have proven themselves to be resources of great international significance, esthetic and recreational as well as economic, and it is the sense of the Congress that they should be protected and encouraged to develop to the greatest extent feasible commensurate with sound policies of resource management and that the primary objective of their management should be to maintain the health and stability of the marine ecosystem. Whenever consistent with this primary objective, it should be the goal to obtain an optimum sustainable population keeping in mind the carrying capacity of the habitat.

Thus, Congress declared that the primary goal of the MMPA is maintaining the health and stability of the marine ecosystem.

2. Requirements of the MMPA

As its name implies, the Act provides protection to all marine mammals. It applies to "any mammal which (A) is morphologically adapted to the marine environment (including sea otters and members of the orders Sirenia, Pinnipedia and Cetacea), or (B) primarily inhabits the marine environment (such as the polar bear)."[25] The Act also covers "any part of any such marine mammal, including its raw, dressed or dyed fur or skin."[26]

As specified in Section 3(12), jurisdiction over marine mammals is divided between two federal agencies. The Secretary of Commerce, through the National Oceanic and Atmospheric Administration and its component agency, the National Marine Fisheries Service (NMFS, also known as NOAA Fisheries), has responsibility for cetaceans and all pinnipeds except the walrus, and the Secretary of the Interior has responsibility for all other marine mammals (e.g., sea otters, marine otters, manatees, dugongs, walruses, and polar bears).[27] Within the Department of the Interior, marine mammal research is undertaken by the U.S. Geological Survey and regulatory and management actions are taken by the U.S. Fish and Wildlife Service (FWS).

Title II of the Act establishes the independent Marine Mammal Commission, an oversight commission of three members appointed by the President, with the advice and consent of the Senate.[28] In carrying out its duties, the Commission is required to consult with its nine-member Committee of Scientific Advisors on Marine Mammals.[29]

a. Federal Preemption

As noted above, one of the central concerns of the drafters of the MMPA was the large number of federal and state government agencies and conflicting laws involved in marine mammal management. To bring some order, Congress consolidated the marine mammal program in the hands of the federal government. Using its "constitutional power . . . to regulate traffic in these animals and their products, deeply involved as they are in interstate and foreign commerce," Congress provided through Section 109(a) that "[n]o State may enforce or attempt to enforce, any State law or regulation relating to the taking of any species . . . of marine mammal within the States."[30] Federal preemption also applies to the importation of marine mammals.[31] This sweeping step of replacing all state regulation with federal control was controversial and strongly opposed by state fish and wildlife agencies. Nevertheless, Congress felt that such action was necessary because marine mammal protection varied so greatly from state to state, resulting in inadequate measures to achieve the desired conservation goals.[32]

In contrast to the MMPA, the ESA authorizes states to supplement the taking prohibition for listed species. Specifically, Section 6(f) of the ESA provides that "[a]ny State law or regulation respecting the taking of an endangered or threatened species may be more restrictive than the exemptions or permits provided for in this [Act] or in any regulation which implements this [Act] but not less restrictive than the prohibitions so defined."[33] Section 17 of the ESA provides that, except as specified in the

Act, "no provision of [the ESA] shall take precedence over any more restrictive conflicting provision of the Marine Mammal Protection Act."[34] The legislative history of the 1981 amendments to the MMPA suggested that the opposite was also true—that more restrictive provisions of the ESA took precedence over conflicting provisions of the MMPA. Relying on these provisions and statements of legislative intent, many believed that the best reconciliation of the preemption provisions of the ESA and MMPA was that states could regulate the taking of endangered and threatened marine mammals, but not unlisted species. This thesis was put to the test in a recent federal district court case.[35]

Hawaii had adopted a law that prohibited parasailing in certain waters around Maui between December 15 and May 15 of each year.[36] These dates coincide with the presence of humpback whales in Hawaiian waters. UFO Chuting, a parasailing company, successfully challenged this law as being preempted by Section 109(a) of the MMPA. While an appeal was pending, Congress enacted legislation to overturn the lower court ruling. The legislation itself pertained only to the specific fact at issue under the challenged Hawaiian law.[37] Of greater interest in resolving the general issue of how best to reconcile the seemingly inconsistent preemption provisions of the ESA and MMPA for listed marine mammal species is the legislative history accompanying that provision. The Senate report explains that the new law "does not affect 16 U.S.C. § 1535(f), which allows States to enforce laws and regulations more restrictive than Federal laws and regulations for endangered or threatened species, including humpback whales."[38]

Congress also set in place provisions that would allow states to apply for and obtain return of management authority. Under these provisions, in the mid-1970s, Alaska sought the return of management for ten marine mammal species. The state achieved a transfer of management for Pacific walrus,[39] but lost its authority as a result of a lawsuit filed by Alaska Natives, who challenged the Secretary's determination that the Act's Native take exemption terminated upon the transfer. In *People of Togiak v. United States*,[40] the court determined that the Native take exemption survived the return of management. As a result, Alaska elected not to pursue a return of management for any marine mammal species or stock, and the request was withdrawn.[41]

In response to this decision, Congress amended Section 109 in 1981 to clarify the process of returning management to the states. These new procedures, which remain in effect, require the Secretary to determine whether the state involved has a program that is consistent with the Act and includes a process for determining the population status of the affected stocks and whether and to what extent taking may be allowed.[42] If the required findings are made, the Secretary may transfer management authority to the state,[43] but no taking may be allowed until the state conducts adjudicatory hearings to determine if the species or stock involved is within its OSP range and how many animals may be taken without reducing the species or stock below that level.[44] To date, no state has sought a transfer of management under the Section 109 procedures as revised in 1981.

b. Optimum Sustainable Population

Section 2(6) of the Act provides that, whenever consistent with the primary objective of maintaining the health and stability of the marine ecosystem, "it should be the goal to obtain an optimum sustainable population keeping in mind the carrying capacity of the environment."[45] This is the species or stock conservation goal of the Act. OSP is defined in Section 3(9) to mean "with respect to any population stock, the number of animals which will result in the maximum productivity of the population of the species keeping in mind the carrying capacity of the habitat and the health of the ecosystem of which they form a constituent element."[46]

FWS and NMFS share a common regulatory definition of the term, which recognizes OSP as a population size that falls "within a range from the population level of a given species or stock which is the largest supportable within the ecosystem to the population level that results in maximum net productivity."[47] Because the maximum net productivity level is the lower bound of the OSP range, it has been the focal point, or target, of conservation efforts under the Act. "Maximum net productivity level" is defined to mean "the greatest net annual increment in population numbers or biomass resulting from additions to the population due to reproduction and/or growth less losses due to natural mortality."[48] As applied in numerous Commerce Department rulemaking proceedings on small cetacean stocks, the term has been generally interpreted for some species to mean a population size that represents sixty percent of the species' or stock's carrying capacity.[49] Any species or stock that is below its OSP is considered "depleted" under the Act.[50]

The OSP standard has considerable legal significance under the MMPA. In addition to serving as the conservation objective of the Act, OSP establishes a threshold for determining when certain activities are to be prohibited or restricted. The Act provides, for example, that a waiver of the moratorium on taking or importing marine mammals cannot be granted for species or stocks below their OSP levels (depleted).[51] Public display permits cannot be issued for depleted marine mammals, and additional requirements are applicable to some types of scientific research involving depleted marine mammals.[52] Regulations limiting hunting areas and seasons used by Alaska Natives to take marine mammals for subsistence or handicraft purposes, or even prohibiting takes altogether, may be established for species that are below their OSP levels.[53] However, such regulations are to be rescinded once the need for their imposition has disappeared. After a transfer of management, no take may be authorized by a state for a species or stock that is below its OSP level.[54]

In the late 1980s, the problems associated with the rigidity of the OSP requirement for incidental take authorizations came into focus. On January 26, 1988, NMFS announced its intention to prepare an Environmental Impact Statement (EIS) on the proposed reissuance of domestic general permits that authorized commercial fishermen, primarily in West Coast waters, to take marine mammals incidental to commercial fishing operations.[55] The existing general permits and two small-take exemptions were scheduled to expire on December 31, 1988. In preparing the draft EIS, NMFS determined that it had insufficient information to determine whether most of the marine mammal stocks that interacted with commercial fishing were within their OSP, and that collecting the necessary data to determine OSP would require many years and the commitment of large amounts of resources.[56]

The significance of the problem became clear when, in the 1988 *Kokechik* decision,[57] the D.C. Circuit indicated that the lack of adequate information on many affected marine mammal species made it unlikely that any general permits could meet the MMPA's requirements. Without the information necessary to support OSP determinations, for all species taken in a fishery, the agency could not make the findings required to promulgate regulations authorizing the incidental take of marine mammals. The implication of this interpretation of the MMPA, as set forth in the *Kokechik* decision, was to render "de facto depleted" status for all marine mammals for which population determinations have not been made.[58]

As a result, Congress enacted amendments in 1988 and 1994 which changed the role that OSP plays in authorizing the taking of marine mammals incidental to commercial fishing operations under the Act. Under an interim exemption adopted in 1988 and a long-term provision enacted in 1994, OSP and maximum net productivity standards are no longer the thresholds for permitting incidental take in most commercial fisheries. Instead, Congress established a complex regulatory regime with different biological goals, as discussed in Section II.B.2.d.ii., *infra*. The 1994 amendments reaffirmed the goals and objectives of the MMPA, including the goals to maintain or restore marine mammal stocks to their OSP levels and to reduce incidental death and serious injury of marine mammals to insignificant levels approaching a zero rate, known as the zero mortality rate goal (ZMRG), but instituted an alternative mechanism for achieving OSP, the potential biological removal level.[59] Thus, while OSP remains the MMPA species/stock conservation goal and retains important regulatory significance under several provisions of the Act (as discussed previously), since 1988 it has not served as the threshold for authorizing incidental take of marine mammals in domestic commercial fisheries.

c. The Moratorium on Taking and Its Exceptions

The centerpiece of the MMPA is the moratorium on taking set forth in Section 101(a).[60] The moratorium establishes a general ban on the taking of marine mammals throughout areas subject to U.S. jurisdiction and by any person, vessel, or conveyance subject to the jurisdiction of the United States on the high seas.[61]

"Take" is defined under Section 3(13) of the Act to mean "to harass, hunt, capture, or kill, or attempt to harass, hunt, capture, or kill any marine mammal."[62] This definition has been expanded by regulation. FWS defines the term to mean:

> to harass, hunt, capture, collect, or kill, or attempt to harass, hunt, capture, collect, or kill any marine mammals, including, without limitation, any of the following: the collection of dead animals or parts thereof; the restraint or detention of a marine mammal, no matter how temporary; tagging a marine mammal; or the negligent or intentional operation of an aircraft or vessel, or

the doing of any other negligent or intentional act which results in the disturbing or molesting of a marine mammal.[63]

NMFS uses the same definition, with one difference, added in 1991, specifically prohibiting "feeding or attempting to feed a marine mammal in the wild."[64] NMFS expanded the take definition to prohibit commercial tour boat operators and their passengers from feeding wild dolphins for the purpose of luring them nearer to vessels for viewing, a regulation that was upheld in *Strong v. United States*.[65]

Neither the original Act nor its implementing regulations defined the term "harass." However, concerned that emerging judicial interpretations were off the mark and in an effort to streamline the scientific permitting process, Congress amended the Act in 1994 to add a statutory definition of the term. Section 3(18)(A) defines the term "harassment" to mean "any act of pursuit, torment, or annoyance which (i) has the potential to injure a marine mammal or marine mammal stock in the wild; or (ii) has the potential to disturb a marine mammal or marine mammal stock in the wild by causing disruption of behavioral patterns, including, but not limited to, migration, breathing, nursing, breeding, feeding, or sheltering."[66] Harassment that has the potential to injure a marine mammal is considered Level A harassment; other forms of harassment are classified as Level B.[67]

Sections 101(a), (b), (c), and (d) of the Act allow for the taking of marine mammals in specific situations.[68] These are taking (1) for scientific research; (2) for public display; (3) during photography for educational or commercial purposes; (4) to enhance the survival or recovery of a species or stock; (5) of endangered or threatened marine mammals incidental to commercial fishing operations; (6) by citizens of the United States of small numbers of marine mammals incidental to a specified activity other than commercial fishing within a specified geographical area over a period of not more than five consecutive years, or, if by harassment only, over a one-year period;[69] (7) by any Indian, Aleut, or Eskimo who resides in Alaska and who dwells on the coast of the North Pacific Ocean or the Arctic Ocean if such taking is for subsistence or handicraft purposes and is not accomplished in a wasteful manner; (8) by nonlethal means to protect personal safety, private property, or fishing gear or catch; (9) for purposes of self-defense or to save the life of a person in immediate danger; (10) to free a marine mammal entangled in fishing gear or debris; and (11) under a catchall waiver provision applicable to a variety of situations, including culling and commercial exploitation.

Section 104(b)(2)(B) of the Act specifies that any take authorized by permit issued for purposes (1) through (4) in the preceding paragraph must be "humane."[70] Under Section 3(4), humane is defined as that "method of taking which involves the least possible degree of pain and suffering practicable to the mammal involved."[71] In accordance with Section 104(d)(3), the take must also be consistent with the purposes of the Act.[72]

As noted above, Section 101(a)(3)(A) of the Act allows the Secretary of Commerce to waive the moratorium in certain circumstances.[73] A waiver can be obtained only after notice and opportunity for on-the-record rulemaking.[74] The waiver must be "compatible" with the purposes of the Act and in accord with "sound principles of resource protection and conservation."[75] More specifically, a waiver may not be granted for any depleted species or stock.[76] Any waiver must accord "due regard to the distribution, abundance, breeding habits, and times and lines of migratory movements of such marine mammals."[77]

Finally, under Section 109(h) a federal, state, or local government official, or person formally designated under the Act for such purpose, may take a marine mammal "in the course of his or her duties" as an official or designee, if such taking is for the protection of the animal, the protection of the public health or welfare, or the nonlethal removal of nuisance animals.[78]

Violations of the Act are subject to potentially severe penalties. Civil penalties can result in fines up to $10,000 for each violation. Any person who knowingly violates the Act is subject to a fine of up to $100,000 for each violation and as much as one year of imprisonment.[79] Vessels involved in unlawful taking are subject to seizure and forfeiture of cargo, a fine of up to $25,000, and imposition of a lien against the vessel.[80]

d. Fisheries Incidental Take

One of the most significant problems of marine mammal protection is incidental take in commercial fishing operations. Indeed, the incidental take of small cetaceans in the tuna purse seine fishery was one of the principal factors leading to enactment of the MMPA. Numerous other fishery-related takes have had major impacts on marine mammal populations: the take of sea otters in California set net fisheries; Dall's porpoises and other marine mammals in high-seas driftnet fisheries; vaquitas in Gulf of California gillnet fisheries; harbor porpoises in salmon gillnet, and cod trap, herring weir, and demersal sink gillnet fisheries.

i. General Permits—Tuna/Dolphin, Dall's Porpoise, and the Interim Exemption for U.S. Fisheries

As first enacted, the MMPA provided only one method for issuing permits to take marine mammals incidental to commercial fishing operations—a permit under Section 101(a)(2). To obtain a permit, referred to as a "general permit," the applicant had to satisfy the requirements of Section 103, which involved an adjudicatory process including an on-the-record rulemaking with sworn testimony before a federal administrative law judge. Due to their complexity, however, these rigorous requirements found application to only two fisheries, the eastern tropical Pacific yellowfin tuna fishery and the Japanese high-seas fisheries for salmon in the North Pacific, which occurred partially in U.S. waters.

A general permit is obtained through a procedure[81] distinguished by the following elements: (1) the permit is based on regulations, developed after notice and opportunity for comment and an on-the-record hearing before an administrative law judge;[82] (2) the permit applicant (e.g., the fishery) and the agency proposing to issue the permit and regulations carries the burden of proof;[83] (3) the applicant/agency must demonstrate that the take level authorized will not disadvantage the species or be inconsistent with MMPA purposes and policies (e.g., the population is within its OSP range), known as "the disadvantage test";[84] (4) the permit is to be based on the best scientific information available;[85] (5) all relevant factors are given full consideration (including population levels, treaty obligations, marine ecosystem and related considerations, the conservation, development and utilization of fishery resources, and the economic and technological feasibility of implementation);[86] and (6) when applying these factors, a conservative bias in favor of marine mammals applies.[87] If the applicant meets this burden, the Secretary issues a general permit to take marine mammals in the course of commercial fishing under Sections 101(a)(2) and 104, based on regulations under Section 103.[88] The economic and technological feasibility of implementing the permit are factors to be considered, but they are secondary to the interests of the marine mammals. And, as specified in Section 101(a)(2), an "immediate goal" of the taking authorization is to achieve the ZMRG—to reduce the incidental kill and serious injury rate "to insignificant levels approaching a zero mortality and serious injury rate."[89]

This permitting procedure became one of the hallmarks of the MMPA. During the 1970s, the U.S. tuna fleet sought a series of permits under Section 101(a)(2). These permit proceedings brought together many of the Act's key provisions and principles. The adjudicatory hearings under Section 103 proved to be the essence of what the drafters of the Act had in mind to ensure that a protective regime remained in place. Permit proceedings before an administrative law judge occurred in 1974, 1975, 1976–77, and 1980 for the tuna fleet's incidental take permit. They also took place in 1981 and 1986 for the Japanese high seas salmon driftnet permit.

The results were generally favorable for marine mammals, resulting in quotas on allowable takes and forced reductions in the numbers of marine mammals taken through commercial fisheries. In each case, the general permits and associated regulations set quotas that pushed the allowed take levels lower and lower, required improved gear and fishing techniques, ordered research, placed observers on fishing vessels, and required the permit holders to return to the same proceeding within a few years to obtain a new permit and once again meet their burden of proof and satisfy the Act's requirements. Through this procedure, the take of dolphins incidental to the U.S. tuna fishery dropped from an estimated 368,600 dolphins in 1972 to an estimated 15,305 in 1980, due in large part to the use of fishing gear and procedures that reduced dolphin mortality.[90]

Congress began to retreat from the adjudicatory process in the 1984 MMPA amendments. The U.S. tuna fleet's general permit was up for renewal, and the industry sought to avoid another contentious and costly adjudicatory proceeding. In addition, at least two stocks of dolphins were thought to be depleted (i.e., below OSP), and hence incidental take could not be authorized under the existing law. To address these concerns, the tuna fleet in essence negotiated a new permit with environmental groups, and Congress amended the MMPA to reflect that agreement. In doing so,

Congress took a dramatic step away from the concepts underlying the Act as first enacted. No longer did the permit applicant for the tuna fishery have to meet a burden of proof to obtain authorization to take; neither did the agencies have the discretion to fashion permit terms based on the best available science. Instead, Congress dictated what should be required of the fishery. One of the most significant steps taken by Congress was to extend the then-existing allowable take level, thereby setting a mortality limit of 20,500 dolphins per year.

Adjudicatory proceedings for a general permit also took place in 1981 and 1986 for the Japanese high seas salmon driftnet permit. In these proceedings, a similar pattern emerged in the effort to reduce the incidental take of Dall's porpoises and other marine mammals in the Japanese high seas salmon driftnet fishery. Under international treaty, the Japanese were permitted to fish at certain times for salmon inside the U.S. two-hundred-nautical-mile exclusive economic zone (EEZ).

In a general permit issued under the MMPA in 1981, the Japanese fleet received a three-year general permit with an annual quota of up to 5,500 Dall's porpoises, 450 northern fur seals, and twenty-five Steller sea lions for the portion of the fishery within the U.S. EEZ. This permit also required observers and gear research and innovation.[91]

Congress legislatively renewed the permit in 1982, and it was not until 1986 that the Section 103 adjudicatory process for authorizing incidental take came into application again for this fishery. After a lengthy and contested general permit proceeding before an administrative law judge, the Under Secretary of Commerce for Oceans and Atmosphere issued the permit, limiting the aggregate Dall's porpoise take over the three-year permit term to 5,250 from the North Pacific Ocean stock (1,750 average annual take) and 789 from the Bering Sea stock (263 average annual take).[92] Based on the failure of the Federation of Japanese Salmon Fisheries Cooperative Association (Federation) to meet its burden of proof[93] and show that other species were within their OSP range and would not be disadvantaged, he denied the permit request to take northern fur seals and Steller sea lions.[94] In this regard, the Under Secretary observed that one stock of fur seals involved had been designated as depleted.[95]

Shortly after fishery operations began in 1987, Alaska Native and environmental groups challenged the general permit.[96] The court enjoined the Japanese fishery on the grounds that, because the Federation had not met its burden of proof to show that the inevitable take of fur seals would meet MMPA standards, no fishing could be authorized.[97] In *Kokechik Fishermen's Ass'n v. Secretary of Commerce*, the D.C. Circuit upheld this decision, invalidating the permit and prohibiting the Japanese fleet from operating within U.S. waters.[98] Specifically, the court stated that the Secretary of Commerce has no authority to disregard incidental takings of certain species or stocks without first determining whether the population of each species was at the OSP level, even if the impact on the population would be negligible, in issuing a permit that authorizes the take of another species or stock.[99] This decision meant that NMFS could not issue general permits in the absence of definitive findings that the take of *all* marine mammals expected to occur in a particular fishery would pass the "will not disadvantage the species" and "consistency with MMPA purposes and policies" tests of Section 103.[100] Of particular significance was the court's conclusion that the agency could not issue a permit for one species if it would also result in the take of a depleted species.[101] Finally, the court stated that "the MMPA does not allow for a Solomonic balancing of the animals' and fisheries' interest such as the Secretary attempted."[102]

The *Kokechik* decision meant that NMFS could not issue general permits for many other commercial fisheries because it was certain that they would take marine mammals that either were depleted, and therefore outside the scope of Section 103, or were not known to be above their maximum net productivity level and thus within the OSP range, rendering it impossible to make the required no-disadvantage finding.[103] This holding had significant implications for U.S. fisheries other than the tuna fleet. Although many of these fisheries caused incidental take of marine mammals (albeit on a less significant level than the tuna fleets), none had applied for a general permit prior to the ruling. Thus, under the *Kokechik* decision, these fisheries were subject to closure because of the unauthorized take of marine mammals.

Rather than run the risk that many commercial fisheries would be shut down as a result of their inability to obtain a general permit, Congress amended the MMPA in 1988 to establish a five-year exemption from the moratorium, allowing the incidental take of marine mammals for most domestic commercial fisheries.[104] During this interim exemption period, the Secretary of Commerce, through NMFS, and based on recommended guidelines developed by the Marine Mammal Commission, was to develop a long-term program to govern incidental take, once the interim exemption expired, and to collect information on the species and numbers of marine mammals taken in the various fisheries. This program was to be submitted to Congress in the form of recommended amendments to the Act to address the *Kokechik* problem.

The proposal subsequently developed by the Secretary was not entirely acceptable to the affected interest groups. This prompted commercial fishing and environmental groups to develop their own joint proposal after extensive negotiations. That proposal borrowed some of the key concepts of the NMFS program and became the basis for congressional action in 1994 to develop an alternative approach to regulate incidental take in domestic commercial fisheries under new Sections 117 and 118, instead of the general permit requirements of Sections 101(a)(2) and 103.

ii. The Post-Kokechik Domestic Fisheries Incidental Take Program

Under the 1994 amendments, participants in a fishery no longer need to obtain an incidental take permit and no longer have the burden of demonstrating that a marine mammal stock is within its OSP range and would not be disadvantaged by any authorized take. Instead, participants in domestic commercial fisheries are allowed to take marine mammals incidental to their operations by registering their vessels and abiding by certain requirements. Although monitoring and reporting requirements are applicable across broad categories of fisheries, the Secretary is authorized to establish fishery-specific limits on incidental mortality and serious injury or to impose time, area, gear, or other restrictions where necessary to reduce such taking to less than the potential biological removal level (PBR) calculated for the stock. PBR is defined as the maximum number of animals that can be removed from a stock, in addition to natural mortality, without compromising the ability of the stock to achieve OSP.[105]

With the 1994 amendments, one of the most notable features of the Act during its first twenty years—the fact-intensive, contested general permit proceeding before an administrative law judge in which the party seeking to exploit the marine mammal stock had to prove it was entitled to do so—had been replaced for all domestic fisheries. Although the general permit requirement ostensibly applies to foreign fisheries operating within the U.S. EEZ under some authority other than a permit issued under Section 204(b) of the Magnuson-Stevens Fishery Conservation and Management Act, there are currently no such fisheries and no application has been submitted since the 1986 Dall's porpoise request.

The new program governing incidental take for commercial fisheries is quite detailed, comprising ten pages of text in the United States Code Annotated. The major elements, described below, add three new Sections to the MMPA: Section 117, requiring stock assessments, status determinations, and calculation of each stock's PBR level; Section 118, setting out the requirements for fishery participants, modeled somewhat after the interim exemption; and Section 120, establishing a process whereby states and NMFS can address interactions between pinnipeds and certain fishery resources.[106]

Stock assessments form the underpinning of the new regime. The 1994 amendments direct the Secretaries of Commerce and the Interior to prepare stock assessments under Section 117 of the Act for each marine mammal population that occurs in U.S. waters.[107] These stock assessments, which are updated periodically, serve as the basis for determining permissible take levels and for identifying those fisheries that are subject to take reduction plan requirements and, ultimately, regulation.

Stocks that are listed as endangered or threatened under the ESA, that are designated as depleted under the MMPA, or for which estimated human-caused mortality and serious injury equals or exceeds the PBR are categorized as strategic stocks.[108] Stock assessments are noticed for public review and comment.[109] The Secretaries are to prepare assessments annually for strategic stocks and for those stocks for which significant new information is available, and every three years for other stocks.[110]

The Section 118 regulatory regime[111] follows from the information developed under the Section 117 stock assessments. Actions required to implement the new incidental take regime are the responsibility of the Secretary of Commerce. The amendments require, however, that the Secretary of Commerce consult with the Secretary of the Interior before taking any action or making any determination that affects or relates to marine mammal stocks under the jurisdiction of the Department of the Interior.[112]

The new regime established under Section 118 retains, and attempted to strengthen, the Act's ZMRG, by setting a deadline by which it was to be achieved: April 30, 2001.[113] Additionally, Section 118 requires the Secretary to conduct an interim review of progress made by each fishery toward achieving the ZMRG.[114] Fisheries that keep mortality and injury to insignificant levels are not required to reduce their interactions further.

The dates by which the interim analyses of progress to meet the ZMRG were to be completed and the goal was to be achieved passed without any such analyses and without meeting this goal. Therefore, in August 2002, several environmental organizations filed suit against NMFS alleging that the agency had failed to satisfy these requirements of MMPA Section 118. These organizations and NMFS negotiated a settlement agreement which required, among other things, that NMFS define (quantify) the ZMRG through regulations and submit to Congress the report on fisheries' progress toward meeting the ZMRG as required by MMPA Section 118(b)(3).[115]

Section 118 directs NMFS to categorize fisheries according to whether they frequently (category I), occasionally (category II), or rarely (category III) kill or injure marine mammals. Vessels participating in category I or category II fisheries are required to register to obtain authorization to take marine mammals.[116] Section 118 prohibits the take of marine mammals in a category I or category II fishery without the required authorization.[117] Authorized vessels must display a decal, report takes, comply with take reduction plans and emergency regulations, and accept observers when requested.[118] The Secretary is required to suspend or revoke an authorization to take marine mammals if the vessel owner fails to comply with the reporting and observer requirements and may suspend or revoke an authorization for noncompliance with the other requirements.[119]

The 1994 Amendments also require the Secretary to develop and implement an incidental take reduction plan[120] for each strategic stock that interacts with a category I or category II fishery. Under Section 118, the Secretary may also develop take reduction plans for other marine mammal stocks that interact with a category I fishery if it is determined, after public notice and comment, that the fishery is responsible for high levels of mortality and serious injury for a number of marine mammal stocks.[121]

The immediate goal of a take reduction plan is to reduce incidental mortality or serious injury to levels less than the PBR for each affected stock within six months. The long-term goal of the plan is to reduce incidental mortality and serious injury to insignificant levels approaching a zero rate within five years, taking into account the economics of the fishery, existing technology, and applicable state or regional fishery management plans.[122] Take reduction plans are to include, among other things, recommended regulatory or voluntary measures designed to reduce incidental mortality and serious injury, and recommended dates for achieving the plan's objectives. The plans are to be developed by take reduction teams composed of representatives of federal agencies, coastal states, regional fishery management councils, interstate fisheries commissions, academic and scientific institutions, environmental groups, commercial and recreational fisheries groups, Alaska Native or Indian tribal organizations, and others.[123]

Finally, if the Secretary determines that incidental mortality and serious injury of marine mammals resulting from commercial fisheries is having, or is likely to have, an immediate and significant adverse effect on a species or stock, Section 118 requires emergency regulations to reduce the level of take.[124] The provision mandates adoption of emergency regulations, amendments to take reduction plans, or expedited approval and implementation of plans to address such adverse impacts.[125] The Secretary must also undertake development of a plan to mitigate adverse impacts, where one does not exist or is not being developed, if a fishery, even one categorized as rarely interacting with marine mammals, is contributing to such adverse impacts.[126]

The Section 118 incidental take regime does not apply to marine mammals that are listed as endangered or threatened under the ESA. This authority is found in Section 101(a)(5)(E), added to the MMPA in the 1994 amendments, which enables the Secretary to authorize such taking if it would have a negligible impact on the species or stock, a recovery plan for the species has been or is being developed, and, where required under Section 118, a monitoring program has been established, the vessels are registered, and a take reduction plan has been, or is being, developed. Such authorizations are limited to a three-year period and apply only to vessels of the United States or foreign vessels permitted to fish under Section 204(b) of the Magnuson-Stevens Fishery Conservation and Management Act.[127]

Despite difficulties in balancing both the need to reduce marine mammal deaths and serious injuries and to minimize economic impacts on fisheries, the take reduction team process has produced consensus take reduction plans from five of the eight take reduction teams,[128] and has succeeded in establishing better working relationships among the different interest groups. Dialogue that would otherwise not have taken place has resulted in the development of research recommendations and strategies to reduce marine mammal entanglement in fishing gear. Thus, while losing the more rigorous procedural and substantive requirements of the formal rulemaking process previously used to authorize incidental take in commercial fisheries, the 1994 amendments established a workable substitute that has, in most cases, proven to be well suited to many of the commercial fisheries that incidentally take marine mammals. The general permit process, geared more toward major fisheries with large take numbers, would have been unworkable for the many smaller fisheries with lower take numbers.

iii. The Tuna-Dolphin Issue, 1988 to the Present

While Congress developed a special program for domestic fisheries following the *Kokechik* decision, it still needed to address the continuing controversy over the tuna-dolphin incidental take problem. This controversy heightened in the mid-1980s when it became known that extremely high numbers of dolphins were being killed in foreign tuna fishery activities. In fact, at a time when dolphin mortality in the domestic tuna fishery had declined from 368,000 (1971) to 20,692 (1986), evidence became available that 112,482 dolphins had been killed in 1986 alone by foreign tuna fisheries.[129]

Congress first took action to reduce foreign incidental take rates in 1984 when it amended the MMPA to make more effective use of trade sanctions. In these amendments, Congress required each nation exporting tuna to the United States to demonstrate, through documentary evidence, that it had adopted a regulatory program to control incidental take that was "comparable" to that of the United States and that its take rate was "comparable" to that of the U.S. fleet.[130] Failure to meet the comparability test would result in a ban on the importation of tuna products from that country under Section 101(a)(2).

When NMFS failed to implement these requirements rigorously and in a timely manner, Congress amended the Act again in 1988 to mandate the specific regulatory measures foreign nations would have to take to avoid an importation ban.[131] Congress also defined the incidental take rates that must be achieved by foreign fleets and even required a ban on the importation of tuna from intermediary nations unless proof could be provided that the exporting nation had ensured that it also had prohibited the importation of tuna from nations subject to the MMPA embargo.

When NMFS was slow to implement the 1988 embargo requirements, environmental groups sued and obtained a mandatory embargo against five violating nations, which went into effect on September 6, 1990 (1990 Embargo).[132] In a second round of litigation, environmental groups secured a ruling that all tuna from intermediary nations must be embargoed if that nation did not make the necessary showing that it was enforcing MMPA requirements.[133] This ruling resulted in embargoes on tuna imports from twenty intermediary nations. Action by the embargoed nations, along with a change to the embargo mandate to require proof for only the six-month period preceding the importation, caused the intermediary nation trade ban to remain in place for only three countries by 1994.

In response to the 1990 Embargo, Mexico initiated a legal action against the United States before a panel established under the international treaty, the General Agreement on Tariffs and Trade (GATT). The GATT's foremost policy objective was to avoid discrimination among foreign nations engaged in international trade.[134] This prohibition on discrimination is reflected in the principle that the GATT would not accommodate the use of import barriers to affect production and consumption activities outside of the country that imposed those barriers. Citing to the articles implementing this principle, Mexico argued that the embargo violated the terms of the GATT because it allowed the United States to use trade as a mechanism to enforce its environmental standards on actions occurring under the authority of another country. On September 3, 1991, the GATT Panel ruled in Mexico's favor and determined that both the direct and the intermediary embargoes were inconsistent with nondiscriminatory trade practices.[135] In 1994, a subsequent GATT Panel ruled against the intermediary nation embargo in response to a separate challenge filed by the European Community and the Netherlands.[136]

Neither of these rulings took effect, however. Under GATT rules, a Panel Report must be adopted by the governing GATT Council before it becomes enforceable. The tuna embargo rulings never reached this stage. After the issuance of the 1991 GATT Panel decision, the United States entered into negotiations with the embargoed nations. As a result, neither party took the necessary actions to refer the Panel decision to the GATT Council. These negotiations led to the 1992 MMPA amendments, described below. Similarly, the 1994 Panel decision was not referred to the Council because of negotiations and legislative actions by the United States.

Activity was also occurring in ways that affected not only whether, but how, tuna could be marketed in the United States. Following enactment of the 1988 amendments, environmental groups began to organize a consumer boycott of tuna caught by encircling dolphins. In response, the three largest U.S. tuna canners announced in 1990 that they would no longer purchase tuna caught in association with dolphins. This policy prompted additional amendments to the MMPA establishing standards for labeling tuna marketed in the United States as being "dolphin safe."[137] Tuna caught in the eastern tropical Pacific could carry the dolphin-safe label only if harvested by a vessel that is too small to engage in dolphin-sets or by a vessel that had refrained from setting on dolphins for the entirety of its fishing trip.

The first GATT Panel decision and the dolphin-safe label campaign led to the 1992 MMPA amendments, which took a decidedly different tack for addressing the tuna-dolphin issue. Rather than merely trying to reduce dolphin mortality, Congress sought ways to eliminate it entirely. The amendments, referred to as the International Dolphin Conservation Act, established the framework for a five-year, global moratorium on the practice of setting on dolphins to catch tuna. Any country agreeing to abide by such a moratorium beginning in March 1994 would not be subject to U.S. tuna embargoes in the interim. For the moratorium to enter into force, however, at least one other tuna-fishing nation would have to agree to it, a condition that was never met. Thus, Congress sought to address the GATT Panel decision by creating the impetus for an international treaty, the existence of which would avoid the effect of a unilateral U.S. embargo. The 1992 amendments also tightened the requirements applicable to the U.S. tuna fleet. They lowered the longstanding annual domestic mortality limit from 20,500 to 1,000 and mandated further reductions in subsequent years, proscribed making sets on eastern spinner and coastal spotted dolphins (two stocks believed to be depleted), and prohibited the purchase or sale in the United States of any tuna that was not dolphin safe after June 1, 1994.[138]

Action to reduce dolphin mortality further was also being pursued internationally by the nations participating in the eastern tropical Pacific tuna fishery, in an effort to provide an alternative to the moratorium codified in the 1992 amendments, which none of these nations endorsed. These nations entered into a nonbinding agreement (called the La Jolla Agreement) that established international dolphin mortality limits to cap allowable mortality at 19,500 in 1993, with annual reductions down to 5,000 by 1999. The key feature of the La Jolla Agreement was the assignment of individual dolphin mortality limits to the vessels participating in the fishery. Once its limit was reached, a vessel would have to refrain from setting on dolphins for the remainder of the year. By linking a vessel's regulatory fate directly to its performance, dolphin mortality tumbled further. By 1993, the first year of implementation of the La Jolla Agreement, dolphin mortality dropped below the target of 5,000 set for 1999.[139]

Even though dolphin mortality had been reduced to levels that many thought to be no longer biologically significant, the U.S. embargo remained in place for tuna that did not qualify as dolphin safe. This prompted several of the parties to the La Jolla

Agreement to call on the United States to lift the embargo. They contended, among other things, that dolphin-safe fishing methods, although better for dolphin conservation, resulted in more unmarketable juvenile tuna being caught and in higher bycatch of nontarget species other than dolphins.

The United States responded to these concerns in 1995 by signing the Declaration of Panama, an agreement with eleven other nations under which the La Jolla Agreement would be formalized and strengthened contingent on certain changes to U.S. law. The Declaration envisioned changes to U.S. law which, with one exception, were made to the MMPA through the International Dolphin Conservation Program Act,[140] calling for: (1) lifting the embargoes of tuna caught in compliance with the La Jolla Agreement, as it would be modified under the Declaration of Panama; (2) allowing access to the U.S. market for all tuna, whether dolphin safe or not, caught in compliance with applicable international agreements;[141] and (3) redefining the term "dolphin safe" to include any tuna caught in the eastern tropical Pacific by a purse seine vessel in a set in which no dolphin mortality or serious injury was observed. This last proposed change proved to be the crucial one. As long as tuna caught by setting on dolphins could be readily differentiated from other tuna, an effective consumer boycott could be instituted. The corollary, from the perspective of the fishing nations, was that regaining access to the U.S. marketplace would be of little value if many consumers would nevertheless spurn the product.

The proposed changes sparked considerable debate in Congress. Ultimately, Congress enacted the changes called for under the Declaration of Panama, but with one notable exception. Congress responded to concerns expressed by some environmental groups that repeatedly chasing and encircling schools of dolphins was causing postrelease deaths of dolphins and sublethal, but significant, effects on the recovery of depleted dolphin stocks that were not reflected in the reported mortality figures. Thus, rather than changing the definition of dolphin-safe tuna outright, the International Dolphin Conservation Program Act made such a change contingent on the results of a mandated research program that would examine the effects of chase and encirclement. The definition of dolphin-safe tuna would be changed as called for under the Declaration of Panama unless the research indicated that chase and encirclement are having significant adverse impacts on depleted dolphin stocks.

NMFS completed the research program in 2002 and, despite not achieving meaningful sample sizes for some crucial studies, issued a finding that chase and encirclement were not having significant adverse effects. This finding was immediately challenged by environmental organizations and soon vacated.[142] The reviewing district court believed that the agency had improperly relied on factors other than those set forth in the International Dolphin Conservation Program Act in reaching its conclusion.[143] The court observed that the best available science indicated that some dolphin stocks remained severely depleted and were not recovering as expected in light of the observed levels of mortality, that some factor appeared to be acting to suppress recovery, and that, based on the research that had been conducted, the most plausible explanation was indirect effects of the tuna fishery.[144] Consistent with this opinion, the court enjoined NMFS from implementing the new definition of dolphin-safe tuna.[145]

As a result, upon publication of this chapter, the dolphin-safe label still applied only to tuna caught without setting on dolphins for the entirety of a fishing trip, and ten countries[146] remained subject to embargo for failure to meet the requirements of the 1997 MMPA amendments.[147] While the continued use of the dolphin-safe label as linked to the prohibition on sets on dolphin remained in dispute as of the publication of this chapter, the question of what constitutes comparability with U.S. practices and take rates has been largely resolved. Today, the embargoes have less to do with take rates, but are mostly the result of failure to join the Inter-American Tropical Tuna Commission, pay the required dues, or comply with all of the conservation and management measures.

e. Small Take Authorization

"Small takes" of marine mammals incidental to all activities other than commercial fishing are addressed under Section 101(a)(5).[148] Congress added this provision in 1981 to establish a more streamlined procedure than the waiver requirement when the likely impact on marine mammal stocks will be negligible.

There are two categories of take authorization for non-fishing activities. The first covers takes that may be lethal. A take may be authorized only when requested by a citizen of the United States.[149] Before issuing an authorization, the Secretary must find that the proposed take will have a negligible impact on the species or stock and will not have an unmitigable adverse impact on the use of the species for subsistence purposes by Alaska Natives, as specified in Section 101(a)(5)(A). The Secretary also must publish regulations setting forth the permissible methods of taking and other requirements pertaining to habitat protection, reporting and monitoring. Such an authorization is valid for no more than five consecutive years.[150] Specific activities are authorized under the regulations through letters of authorization.

In 1994, Congress established an even more simplified mechanism for authorizing the take of small numbers of marine mammals incidental to activities other than commercial fishing when taking only by harassment is involved. Such authorizations are to be issued for periods of up to one year if the Secretary determines, after notice and opportunity for public comment, that the taking will have a negligible impact on the marine mammal species or stock and will not have unmitigable adverse impacts on the availability of the marine mammals for subsistence use by Alaska Natives.[151]

Finally, incidental take of ESA-listed species may be authorized for U.S. commercial fishing activities for up to three consecutive years if, after notice and comment, the Secretary determines that the take will have a negligible impact, an ESA recovery plan has been developed, and any necessary mentoring program is in place.[152]

f. The Moratorium on Importation and Its Exceptions

The moratorium under Section 101(a) of the MMPA also applies to the importation of marine mammals and marine mammal products.[153] As with the moratorium on taking, the moratorium on importing marine mammals may be waived, provided that certain determinations are made in the course of a formal rulemaking.[154] In addition, permits authorizing imports for purposes of scientific research, public display, and enhancement of the species can be issued under the same conditions as for taking and, as a result of the 1994 amendments, permits are available to import polar bear trophies from some Canadian populations.[155] Also, the 1994 amendments created exceptions to allow the importation of marine mammal products that are (1) legally possessed and exported by a U.S. citizen for purposes of foreign travel if reimported by the same person; (2) acquired outside the United States as part of a cultural exchange by an Alaska Native; or (3) owned by a Native inhabitant of Russia, Canada, or Greenland and imported for noncommercial purposes in conjunction with travel inside the United States or as part of a cultural exchange with an Alaska Native.[156]

Except for purposes of scientific research or species enhancement, Section 102(b) specifies that no authorization may be granted for the importation of a marine mammal that was pregnant or nursing at the time of taking or less than eight months old; taken from a depleted species or stock; or taken in an inhumane manner.[157] An exception to these general prohibitions allows importation if necessary for the protection or welfare of the animal. No marine mammal taken in violation of the Act or the law of a foreign nation may be imported for any reason.[158] Both the taking and importation prohibitions do not apply to animals taken or imported before enactment of the Act.[159] Marine mammals also may be imported by the Secretary or a designee "if . . . necessary to render medical treatment that is otherwise not available."[160]

The 1994 amendments added an export prohibition to the Act. Section 102(a)(4) prohibits the unauthorized export or attempted export of a marine mammal or marine mammal product. This section also prohibits transporting, purchasing, selling, exporting, or attempting to engage in such activities if the marine mammal or marine mammal product was taken in violation of the MMPA, or if such activities are for any purpose other than public display, scientific research, or enhancing the survival of a species or stock authorized under Section 104(c).[161]

g. Habitat Protection

In its findings and declaration of policy, the MMPA emphasizes habitat and ecosystem protection. The habitat and ecosystem goals set forth in Section 2 of the Act include

1. Management of marine mammals to ensure they do not cease to be a significant functioning element of the ecosystem of which they are a part;[162]
2. Protection of essential habitats, including rookeries, mating grounds, and areas of similar significance "from the adverse effect of man's actions";[163]
3. Recognition that marine mammals "affect the balance of marine ecosystems in a manner that is important to other animals and animal products" and that marine mammals should therefore be protected and conserved;[164] and
4. the primary objective of maintaining "the health and stability of the marine ecosystem."[165]

The Act also refers to habitat in the definition of *conservation* and *management*.[166] Those terms are defined to include "habitat acquisition and improvement."

Without referring specifically to habitat protection or other measures, Section 112 authorizes the Secretary to "prescribe such regulations as are necessary and appropriate to carry out the purposes of the Marine Mammal Protection Act."[167] This authority, although general, arguably may be used to promulgate regulations to protect specific habitat or advance the Act's ecosystem heath and stability goal. In the legislative history of the 1994 amendments, Congress made it clear that Section 112 includes such authority. As stated by the House Merchant Marine and Fisheries Committee, it added the phrase "essential habitats" to Section 2(2) in order to underscore that "[t]he Committee believes that the Secretary currently has the authority to protect marine mammals and their habitats under the general rulemaking authority of Section 112 of the Act."[168] The Committee noted that this authority would permit the Secretary, for example, "to protect polar bear denning, feeding, and migration routes in order to fully comply with the United States obligations under Article II of the Agreement on the Conservation of Polar Bears."[169]

h. Research

As discussed previously, the MMPA places a high priority on research. In Section 2(3), Congress set forth the finding and declaration of policy that "there is inadequate knowledge of the ecology and population dynamics of such marine mammals and of the factors which bear upon their ability to reproduce themselves successfully."[170] Congress also declared that "negotiations should be undertaken immediately to encourage the development of international arrangements for research on, and conservation of, all marine mammals."[171] The definition of the terms *conservation* and *management* includes "the entire scope of activities that constitute a modern scientific resource program, including, but not limited to, research, census" and other activities.[172]

Under the MMPA and its implementing regulations, NMFS may issue permits for the taking, importing, and exporting[173] of marine mammals, including threatened or endangered species, for scientific purposes or to enhance the propagation or survival of such species;[174] and the taking, import, or export of marine mammals for purposes of scientific research, public display, enhancing the survival or recovery of a species or stock, or the taking of marine mammals by no more than Level B harassment for photography for commercial or educational purposes.[175] Waivers of the moratorium and permits authorizing the taking of marine mammals must be based on "the best scientific evidence available."[176]

The 1994 amendments to the MMPA provided for the general authorization (GA) of scientific research for activities involving only Level B Harassment of marine mammals.[177] This is a simplified process where researchers submit a letter of intent that contains detailed information such that NMFS or FWS can accurately determine whether the research is bona fide and the impacts of the activities are limited to Level B Harassment. If the Service determines that the project is eligible, based on the information provided by the applicant, no public comment period is necessary. Rather, the researcher receives a letter of confirmation that he or she is covered under the GA and may commence research activities immediately.[178]

A scientific research permit is required for any proposed research activity that involves "take" with the exception of those activities covered by the GA. Any research involving ESA-listed species also requires a permit under that statute and, as such, a permit is still required for research that otherwise would qualify for a GA. Prior to permit issuance, applications undergo a thirty-day public comment period and are reviewed by experts from NMFS/FWS, the Marine Mammal Commission, and other appropriate federal agencies.

In Section 110, the Act provides for grants or other forms of financial assistance to qualified entities or persons "to undertake research in subjects which are relevant to the protection and conservation of marine mammals."[179]

Although the MMPA recognizes the importance of research on marine mammals and related ecosystem components, the authorized funding levels, particularly in recent years, have been too low to undertake comprehensive research programs. This problem has been exacerbated by the addition of new research-intensive responsibilities, such as the preparation of stock assessments. Nevertheless, some research projects have received specific congressional attention and have resulted in the authorization of supplemental funding. For example, amendments enacted in 1984 specifically authorized $4 million to be appropriated for a program to monitor the indices of abundance and trends of dolphin stocks affected by the eastern tropical Pacific tuna fishery.[180] Amendments enacted in August 1997 authorized appropriations of $12 million over a four-year period to conduct abundance surveys and stress studies to assess the status of dolphin stocks and examine the effects on dolphins of chase and encirclement by tuna seiners.[181] More often, however, funding decisions for marine mammal research are made as part of annual appropriations legislation. For example, funding for Steller sea lion research spiked in 2001 and 2002 to about $40 million per year, which amounted to about a tenfold increase in the budget for this species and effectively doubled the appropriations for NMFS marine mammal research as a whole. Although using appropriations bills to establish research funding levels allows legislators to respond more quickly to specific issues, annual swings in available funding undercut the agency's ability to fund long-term studies or engage in long-term planning. Still, the MMPA lacks a dedicated extramural research program with established research priorities to answer critical scientific questions related to emerging threats to marine mammals and their habitat.

Although the MMPA recognizes the importance of research on marine mammals, funding levels have been too low to undertake comprehensive programs.

i. International Cooperation

The Act's international program is set forth in Section 108.[182] It requires the Secretary of Commerce or the Secretary of the Interior, working through the Secretary of State, to "initiate negotiations as soon as possible for the development of bilateral or multinational agreements with other nations for the protection and conservation of all marine mammals."[183] It also directs the federal government to encourage other agreements to protect specific ocean and land regions "which are of special significance to the health and stability of marine mammals,"[184] and to amend any existing treaty to make it consistent with the purposes and policies of the Act.[185]

In 1994, Congress took specific note of concerns that had been raised over the effectiveness of the Agreement on the Conservation of Polar Bears by amending Section 113 of the Act to require two reviews of the treaty.[186] First, Congress directed the Secretary of the Interior, in consultation with the Secretary of State and the Marine Mammal Commission, to review the effectiveness of U.S. implementation, particularly with respect to the Agreement's habitat protection mandates.[187] Second, the Secretary of the Interior, in consultation with other parties to the Agreement, was to initiate a review of its effectiveness and establish a process for conducting similar reviews in the future. Although responses from most other parties have been received, one party never responded officially. As such, the initial review has never been completed.

In addition, Section 113 directed the Secretary of the Interior, acting through the Secretary of State and in consultation with the Marine Mammal Commission and the State of Alaska, to consult with appropriate officials of the Russian Federation on the development of enhanced cooperative research and management programs for the conservation of polar bears in Russia and Alaska.[188] Even before this requirement, FWS had begun discussions with Russian officials on the need for a bilateral polar bear treaty to protect the population of polar bears shared by the two countries. Following several rounds of negotiations, the two countries concluded in October 2000 the Agreement between the Government of the United States of America and the Government of the Russian Federation on the Conservation and Management of the Alaska-Chukotka Polar Bear Population. Among other things, the agreement specifies that subsistence hunting by Native residents of Alaska and Chukotka is to be the only consumptive use of polar bears from the stock and includes standards and procedures for establishing annual hunting limits. The U.S. Senate provided its advice and consent to the Agreement in July 2003. Congress passed needed implementing legislation for the Agreement on the final day of its 2006 session. That legislation is part of Public Law 109-479, signed into law on January 12, 2007.

j. Pinniped-Fishery Interactions

In 1994, Congress amended the Act to address interactions between pinnipeds and fisheries in Section 120, as provided for under Sections 117 and 118. The amendments established a special procedure to address the problem of sea lion predation of certain salmon stocks off the northwestern coast of the United States.[189] The process to authorize a lethal take or removal of pinnipeds is triggered when a state applies to the Secretary of Commerce for authorization to intentionally and lethally take individually identifiable pinnipeds that are causing a significant negative impact on the decline or recovery of salmonid fishery stocks which have been listed as endangered or threatened, or are approaching threatened or endangered species status under the ESA, or which migrate through the Ballard Locks at Seattle, Washington.[190] The state's application must include a means of identifying individual pinnipeds causing the problem, a detailed description of the interaction problem, and the expected benefits of the taking.[191] Once filed, an application triggers a detailed administrative process that includes the formation of a "pinniped-fishery interaction" task force to investigate the problem and take action on the request. This provision has been applied only for pinniped-salmonid conflicts involving California sea lions and winter steelhead that migrate through the Ballard Locks,[192] although in late 2006 Washington, Oregon, and Idaho applied for authority to remove California sea lions feeding on salmon in the Columbia River.

k. Marine Mammal Health and Stranding Amendments

Large numbers of bottlenose dolphin strandings that resulted in unusual levels of mortality in 1987–88 led to enactment of special provisions for addressing such events, as set forth in title IV of the Act.[193] Added to the MMPA in 1992, Title IV requires the Secretary to establish a health and stranding response program. The purpose of the program is to facilitate the collection and dissemination of reference data on marine mammal health and health trends, correlate marine mammals' health with data on physical, chemical, and biological environmental parameters, and coordinate effective responses to unusual mortality events by developing a response process within the Department of Commerce. Title IV directs the Secretary of Commerce to monitor strandings, collect information on procedures for rescuing and rehabilitating stranded marine mammals, collect marine mammal tissues for analysis, and develop objective criteria for deciding when a rehabilitated marine mammal is releasable to the wild. It also allows the Secretary to enter into agreements with persons to take marine mammals in response to a stranding.[194] Title IV also requires the Secretary to establish a marine mammal unusual-mortality-event working group to develop contingency plans for responding to these events.[195]

From 1991 to 2004, NMFS documented twenty-eight unusual mortality events for marine mammals. The causes of some of these events have been identified as disease, harmful algal bloom toxins, and human interactions; however, the cause for twenty-five percent of the events remains undetermined. These events may be increasing in frequency and severity, suggesting that they will continue to be a threat to marine mammal health and well-being.

C. The Exemption for Military Activities

Interactions between some marine mammals and sonar used by the U.S. Navy have become increasingly controversial in recent years. Midfrequency sonars have been implicated in several strandings of beaked whales and other cetaceans, and litigation has prevented the Navy from obtaining incidental taking authorization to deploy low frequency active sonar (SURTASS) capable of detecting submarines at greater distances than is possible with other technologies on a broad-scale basis. This controversy prompted the Department of Defense to seek amendments to the MMPA during MMPA authorization and appropriations legislation in 2003.

The National Defense Authorization Act for Fiscal Year 2004[196] included amendments responding to the Department's concerns. First, Congress amended the definition of the term "harassment" as it pertains to "military readiness" activities and marine mammal research undertaken by or on behalf of any federal agency.[197] For such activities, harassment is defined as any act that (1) "injures or has the significant potential to injure a marine mammal or marine mammal stock in the wild" or (2) "disturbs or is likely to disturb a marine mammal or marine mammal stock in the wild by causing disruption of natural behavioral patterns, including, but not limited to, migration, surfacing, nursing, breeding, feeding, or sheltering, to a point where such behavioral patterns are abandoned or significantly altered."[198] Congress intended this new definition to exclude activities that have only a low potential to injure marine mammals, or that may disturb marine mammals but only in insignificant ways, and to clear up some of the ambiguities in the generally applicable definition. Although some of the previous ambiguities were eliminated, new ones were created. That is, it is not clear how significant the potential for injury must be or how significant alteration of marine mammal behavior must be to constitute harassment under the new definition. To date, neither NMFS nor FWS has issued any guidance on making these determinations.

Second, certain requirements of the Section 101(a)(5) small-take provisions that had been at issue in the SURTASS case were eliminated. Last, and most sweeping, the amendments added Section 101(f) to the MMPA to enable the Secretary of Defense, after conferring with the Secretary of Commerce and/or the Secretary of the Interior, as appropriate, to exempt any action or category of actions by the Department of Defense or its components from compliance with the requirements of the MMPA if "necessary for national defense." Such an exemption may be established for up to two years at a time.[199]

The exemption is at the heart of *NRDC v. Winters*, in which environmental organizations and the California Coastal Commission challenged the use of mid-frequency active (MFA) sonar in Navy training exercises off the coast of southern California water. The Pentagon invoked the MMPA exemption on January 23, 2007, and the plaintiffs responded with litigation under the National Environmental Policy Act and the Coastal Zone Management Act. After a Ninth Circuit order on November 13, 2007, that the Navy could not use MFA in certain activities, district court on remand determined that there is "scientific consensus on the correlation between the use of MFA sonar and mass whale strandings" and imposed restrictions on the Navy to protect marine mammals. The Bush Administration responded with Council on Environmental Quality "alternative arrangements" for NEPA compliance, issued on January 15, 2008, and a Presidential exemption from the CEMA on January 16, 2008. These actions were invalidated by the district court on February 4, 2008, setting up a major confrontation between the Executive and Judiciary branches.[200]

III. Emerging and Unresolved Issues

Since enactment of the MMPA in 1972, the issues involving marine mammals have grown more complicated. While significant progress has been made in some areas, for example in the tuna-dolphin dispute, marine mammal conservation problems have emerged in new areas and several old problems remain unresolved. Anthropogenic sound, climatic regime shifts, and persistent pollutants do not lend themselves to simple strategies addressed through the MMPA's take prohibition.

A. Implementation of Take Reduction Teams

The commercial fisheries take reduction process is at a critical juncture. Many problems have plagued the process, most notably NMFS's failure to meet the statutory deadlines for finalizing and implementing take reduction plan regulations and lack of resources to enforce the regulations, conduct necessary research to improve the plan, and reconvene take reduction teams to track progress in meeting the ZMRG. Through its interpretation of a plan developed by a take reduction team or during translation into implementing regulations, NMFS has significantly changed some elements of consensus plans, thereby undermining the process. If the take reduction team process is to be successful, NMFS needs to adopt the view that this process is a high-priority partnership among itself and all of the various stakeholders.

NMFS should be adequately represented on the take reduction team by individuals with the ability to evaluate and effectively interpret the plan being developed from a variety of perspectives and with the authority to commit the agency to that consensus at the time the plan is being negotiated. Sufficiently senior officials providing the perspective of regional, legal, and enforcement offices need to participate actively in the negotiating process. These officials should be responsible for advising the team as to whether the recommendations can be effectively implemented and enforced, and whether the research recommendations are achievable. Without such advice, team members may conclude the negotiation process believing the consensus plan will be implemented as drafted, only to discover, upon publication of a proposed implementing rule, that NMFS has significantly changed some elements of the plan or its intent.

Further, NMFS needs to do a better job of meeting statutory timeframes established under the MMPA for convening take reduction teams, developing and implementing take reduction plans, and, ultimately, achieving the ZMRG. To do this, the agency will need to be provided with sufficient resources to achieve adequate levels of observer coverage to carry out the research essential for developing and evaluating take reduction strategies and to enforce applicable regulations. It is frustrating for team participants and the constituencies they represent

> **NMFS needs to do a better job of meeting statutory timeframes established under the MMPA for developing and implementing take reduction plans.**

to see a take reduction plan fail to meet the Act's mandates because the agency does not enforce its provisions. These concerns highlight the need not only for greater resources to implement the take reduction plans, but for a greater commitment on the part of NMFS to the process and the resulting plans.

B. Sound

Within the last twenty to thirty years, several high-visibility projects that proposed to use sound either in scientific research or military operations have sparked controversy. These include the Heard Island Feasibility Study,[201] the Acoustic Thermometry of Ocean Climate (ATOC) experiment,[202] the proposed Surveillance Towed Array Sensor System Low Frequency Active (SURTASS LFA), and the southern California Naval MFA exercises.[203] These projects were instrumental in bringing the issue of the impact of sound on marine mammals to the forefront of marine wildlife conservation issues. High intensity, discrete sound sources such as the ATOC signal and SURTASS LFA are now recognized as being only a small component of anthropogenic sounds in the marine environment. There also is increasing concern related to the larger and more pervasive sources of sound, such as commercial shipping, oil and gas exploration and production, construction, and military sonar.

The effects of anthropogenic sound on marine mammals were not a recognized threat upon enactment of the MMPA in 1972. But today it is clear that anthropogenic sound is a concern that is likely to grow as sound levels in the ocean increase. The National Academy of Sciences (NAS) reviewed certain aspects of this issue in 1994, 2000, 2003, and 2005.[204] In its reports, the NAS recommended continued dedicated research and a coordinated response and regulatory strategy to protect marine mammals. While several federal agencies fund and conduct research to improve understanding of the effects of sound on marine mammals, current information is still insufficient to assess or evaluate the risks accurately. Consequently, the uncertainty about the effects of sound on marine mammals confounds management efforts. Managers need improved, widely accepted risk assessment approaches designed to protect marine mammals and their ecosystem, while avoiding unnecessary burdens on sound produces.

C. Environmental Contaminants

Environmental contaminants, biotoxins, pharmaceuticals, industrial spills, and wastes are a growing and widespread threat to marine mammals. Scientists have demonstrated that contaminants such as organohalogenated compounds (DDT, DDE, DDD), polychlorinated biphenyls (PCBs), polycyclic aromatic hydrocarbons, and trace metals (mercury, lead, selenium, and cadmium) can cause organ anomalies, impair reproduction, and suppress immune function.[205] An overarching problem is that the direct cause and effect relationship between an environmental contaminant and an observed health problem has rarely been demonstrated. In addition, new chemicals are being produced, used, and released into the oceans daily through point and nonpoint sources. These chemicals include flame retardants, household chemicals, pesticides from lawns, fields, orchards, and gardens, engine exhausts, and urban and agricultural runoff.[206]

Prey is the most significant proximate source of environmental contaminants for many marine mammals. These chemicals tend to concentrate, especially in fatty tissue, and bioaccumulate as they move up the food chain. Consequently, PCB and DDT levels are higher in transient killer whales and polar bears that consume marine mammals, than in fish-eating or plankton-eating seals and whales.[207] PCBs may be responsible for impaired reproduction in harbor seals, gray seals, California sea lions, and beluga whales. High concentrations of PCBs and DDT may result in tumors, digestive tract and mammary gland lesions, colonic ulcers, and uterine tumors. Immune suppression associated with environmental contaminants likely have aggravated and made marine mammals more susceptible to die-offs.[208] Finally, some nations such as Russia, Japan, and Norway consume marine mammals, and in some cases contamination has led to advisories regarding the consumption of certain tissues. This is also a matter of concern for some Alaska Natives, whose diets may include considerable amounts of marine mammals.[209]

Pollution often occurs as a mixture of chemical compounds; therefore, it is often difficult to attribute an effect to a single source. Without this evidence, it becomes difficult for managers to take precautionary management measures. Considerable basic research, rigorous diagnostic procedures, and credible risk assessment models are needed to determine the extent to which contaminants are impairing the health, reproduction, and immune systems of marine mammals. At this point, the most the MMPA can provide is the mechanism to support the needed research and to coordinate such efforts across agencies. Until the science is improved and the management tools developed, managers should employ a precautionary approach to reduce the risk of exposure.

D. Climate Change

The use of ozone-depleting chemicals and hydrocarbons and large-scale deforestation and desertification have all contributed to climate change. Scientists predict that over the next 100 years, temperatures will rise by 1.0° to 3.5° C and that sea level will rise by 15 to 95 cm. Global climate change is an emerging issue for marine mammals, the effects of which will likely be felt most acutely by ice-associated animals such as Arctic and Antarctic seals, walruses, and polar bears. These marine mammals are dependent on ice for resting, giving birth, or in the case of polar bears, hunting.[210] As global warming causes changes to the thickness, extent, and duration of ice cover, these species will lose important habitat.[211] For example, as the amount and thickness of sea ice changes, ringed seals become harder for polar bears to find. This reduced availability of prey can be expected to translate into reduced breeding success.[212] In response to this problem, FWS has proposed to list polar bears as a threatened species under the ESA.[213]

In addition, scientists expect changes in the frequency and velocity of storms and more extreme changes in seasonal weather patterns such as the El Niño Southern

Climate-driven changes will lead to the loss of important feeding or breeding habitats and distributional changes for many marine mammals.

Oscillation. Climate-driven changes in primary productivity will lead to the loss of important feeding or breeding habitats and distributional changes for many marine mammals. For example, El Niño events often result in reduced pup production for both Galapagos fur seals and California sea lions due to starvation.[214] Finally, scientists believe that there will be an increased occurrence of epizootics among seals and sea lions because disease transmission will increase with increased haul-out behavior. Similarly, marine mammals are expected to face increasing exposure to new epizootics as they expand their ranges into warming polar waters.

The MMPA is currently not well-equipped to address these global issues that result in broad scale changes in the habitat use and distribution of marine mammals. Although the legislative history of the amendments indicates that the rulemaking authority of Section 112(a) can be used to address habitat-related issues,[215] the MMPA is not well-equipped to serve as the regulatory vehicle for a problem as complex as climate change. It can, however, provide support through research mandates and stock assessments to determine long-term changes in the overall health and distribution of marine mammals and to identify the causes. In addition, the MMPA and other laws can be used to reduce impacts from other, more controllable activities, to help compensate for the negative effects that are being caused by climate change.

E. International Issues

According to the U.S. Ocean Commission, the "biggest threat to marine mammals worldwide is their accidental capture or entanglement in fishing gear (bycatch), which kills hundreds of thousands of them each year."[216] Bycatch is a serious and widespread threat to marine mammals and there is an urgent international need to develop alternative fishing gear and practices, and at the same time put into place effective regional agreements that can mandate mitigation measures ranging from temporal and spatial closures to deterrents. As already discussed, environmental contaminants, noise pollution, habitat degradation, and climate change are global environmental threats that can best be addressed through international mechanisms.

The MMPA provides the tools necessary to address some of these international threats. Specifically, the MMPA requires the Secretary of Commerce, working through the Secretary of State, to initiate negotiations "as soon as possible" for the development of bilateral or multilateral agreements for the protection and conservation of all marine mammals covered by the MMPA.[217] These provisions are particularly focused in the area of bycatch, calling on the Secretary of State to initiate negotiations with all foreign governments engaged in commercial fishing found to be unduly harmful to any species or population stock of marine mammal to develop bilateral and multilateral treaties with such countries to protect marine mammals.[218]

Section 108 also provides an avenue to protect important marine mammal habitat by explicitly calling for the Secretary of State to pursue other agreements for the protection of ocean and land regions of special significance to the health and stability of marine mammals.[219] The final two provisions of Section 108(a) call on the Secretary of State to seek to amend any existing international treaty for the protection and conservation of any species of marine mammal to which the United States is a party, to make such treaties consistent with the purposes and policies of the MMPA. The Secretary was also to seek an international ministerial meeting on marine mammals by July 1, 1973, to negotiate a binding international convention for the protection and conservation of all marine mammals.[220]

With the exception of the provisions associated with the Agreement on the International Dolphin Conservation Program, these provisions have rarely been used and have never been fully implemented to reduce bycatch or protect ecosystems abroad. The MMPA provides the United States with the tools that enable it to take a leadership role in reducing bycatch. Reducing marine mammal bycatch will require an international commitment, implemented through regional agreements to target areas of high risk and/or an international treaty to tackle the global threats to marine mammals.

F. Ecosystem-Based Management

The U.S. Ocean Commission recognized that it is essential to establish a program for ecosystem-based management of coastal and ocean resources. Ecosystem-based management is a term frequently used, but rarely defined. The Commission's report makes the case that the health of the oceans and their resources is degraded and in decline, that this is the result of the failure to integrate multiple uses of the oceans and coastal environments in a sustainable way, and that a new era of integrated, ecosystem-based management must be science-based and adaptive.[221]

One central element of ecosystem-based management is consideration of biodiversity on species, genetic, and ecosystem levels, because an ecosystem's survival is intimately linked to species survival. Ecosystem-based management requires greater knowledge, increased capacity, and improved integration, interpretation, and application of complex information in decision-making processes. The initiation, conduct, application, and coordination and integration of the science required for ecosystem-based management represents a challenge for the future. The requirements of ecosystem-based management, as articulated by the Ocean Commission, have never been fully met, even on a local scale, much less on regional, national, or international scales.[222]

As stated previously in this chapter, the MMPA contains directives to consider and conserve the marine ecosystem. Similarly, the Magnuson-Stevens Fishery Conservation and Management Act, ESA and NEPA, also contain provisions that could be helpful in promoting ecosystem-based management. Yet, to date, these and other U.S. laws concerning natural resource issues have produced management regimes that focus largely on single species or species complexes, or discrete areas, such as the Northwest Hawaiian Islands. Further, while some of these statutes, such as the MMPA, emphasize protection and recovery, others, such as the Magnuson-Stevens Fishery Conservation and Management Act, emphasize utilization. When protected species, such as marine mammals, sea turtles, or migratory birds, encounter fishing operations, conflicts arise. In the face of such conflicts, the response is often to attack the underlying statutory protection. An effective ecosystem-based management regime could be a solution to these conflicts. Recommendations on how to grapple with this problem are set forth in Chapter 19 of this book.

IV. Conclusion

The problems facing marine mammals are becoming more complex and difficult to resolve. They encompass competition with commercial fisheries, habitat degradation associated with sound production and pollution, and long-term chronic threats such as global climate change. Increasing populations of both humans and some marine mammals along the nation's coasts have brought about not only competition for space on boats, docks, and beaches, but have given rise to conflicts between a public that wants to feed, swim with, and get close to these wild creatures, and wildlife management policy that argues against such interactions. When all of these threats cumulatively contribute to the decline of a marine mammal species or several species, conventional marine conservation and management statutes that focus on single species management offer few remedies.

Implementation of, and further amendments to, the MMPA must move in the direction of conserving and managing marine mammals while taking into consideration the relationships among all ecosystem components, including humans and nonhuman species and the environments in which they live. Applying the Act's ecosystem principles will require defining relevant geographic management areas based on ecosystems, rather than on political boundaries. It will also require an ecosystem-based management system that looks at all the links among living and nonliving resources, rather than considering single issues in isolation, and that is science-based and adaptive.

There is no telling to what degree humans have already "reset" the system by reducing carrying capacity for marine mammals, fish, birds and other wildlife through increased human population and activities that impact the oceans and coastal areas (e.g., coastal development, pollution, global climate change, and a host of other anthropogenic effects). It is time to find ways to bridge living marine resource laws to create a legal regime for marine mammal and marine resource conservation and management that is multispecies and ecosystem-based.

Notes

1. *Marine Mammals: Hearings Before the Subcommittee on Fisheries and Wildlife Conservation of the House Committee on Merchant Marine and Fisheries*, 92d Cong. 2 (Sept. 9, 1971) (statement of Rep. Dingell).
2. *Id.* at 4.
3. *Id.* at 1–2.
4. 16 U.S.C. §§ 1361 *et seq.*
5. H.R. Rep. No. 92-707, at 15 (1971).
6. *Id.* at 13.

7. *Id.* at 11–12.

8. S. Rep. No. 92-863, at 11 (1972).

9. H.R. Rep. No. 92-707, *supra* note 5, at 24.

10. 118 Cong. Rec. S15680 (daily ed. Oct. 4, 1971) (statement of Sen. Packwood).

11. 414 F. Supp. 297, 307 n.24 (D.D.C. 1976) (quoting a House Committee Report on H.R. 10420), *aff'd,* 540 F.2d 1141, 1148 (D.C. Cir. 1976).

12. 839 F.2d 795, 802 (D.C. Cir. 1988), *cert. denied sub nom.,* Verity v. Center for Envtl. Educ., 488 U.S. 1004 (1989).

13. H.R. Rep. No. 92-707, *supra* note 5, at 18.

14. Comm. for Humane Legislation v. Richardson, *supra* note 11, at n.29.

15. S. Rep. No. 92-863, *supra* note 8, at 11.

16. *Id.* at 10.

17. *Id.* at 20.

18. *Id.* at 10.

19. The Pelly Amendment authorizes the President to impose a ban on the importation of goods from countries that undertake actions which diminish the effectiveness of international fishery conservation efforts. 22 U.S.C. § 1978. The Packwood-Magnuson Amendment requires the reduction of foreign fishery allocations in U.S. waters for countries certified for actions diminishing the effectiveness of the International Convention for the Regulation of Whaling. *Id.* § 1978(a)(3), 16 U.S.C. § 1821(e)(2).

20. Michael J. Bean & Melanie Rowland, The Evolution of National Wildlife Law 109–11 (3d ed., Praeger Publishers 1997).

21. 16 U.S.C. § 1361(1).

22. *Id.* § 1361(2).

23. *Id.* § 1361(3).

24. *Id.* § 1361(4).

25. *Id.* § 1362(6).

26. *Id.*

27. *Id.* § 1362(12)(A)(ii).

28. *Id.* § 1401(b)(1).

29. *Id.* § 1403. Federal agencies are required by the Act to respond to all Commission recommendations. Detailed written explanations must be provided to the Commission by an agency that declines to follow its recommendations. *Id.* § 1402(a),(d).

30. *Id.* § 1379(a).

31. Fouke Company v. Mandel, 386 F. Supp. 1341 (D. Md. 1974).

32. Ironically, Section 109 also had the effect of preempting state laws (except in cases where special cooperative agreements are in place or the state has obtained return of management) that would be more protective of marine mammals than the Act.

33. 16 U.S.C. § 1535(f).

34. *Id.* § 1543.

35. UFO Chuting of Haw., Inc. v. Young, 327 F. Supp. 2d 1220 (D. Haw. 2004).

36. Haw. Rev. Stat. § 200-37(I).

37. Section 213 of the Fiscal Year 2005 Omnibus Appropriations Act, Pub. L. No. 108-447, 118 Stat. 2809 (2004), states that "[h]ereafter, notwithstanding any other Federal law related to the conservation and management of marine mammals, the State of Hawaii may enforce any State law or regulation with respect to the operation in State waters of recreational or commercial vessels, for the purpose of conservation and management of humpback whales, to the extent that such law or regulation is no less restrictive than Federal law." Based on enactment of this provision, the district court vacated its previous order. UFO Chuting of Haw. v. Young, 380 F. Supp. 2d 1166 (D. Haw. 2005).

38. S. Rep. No. 108-344, at 120 (2004).

39. 40 Fed. Reg. 54,959 (1975).

40. 470 F. Supp. 423, 428 (D.D.C. 1979).

41. 44 Fed. Reg. 45,565 (1979).

42. 16 U.S.C. § 1379(b)(1).
43. *Id.* § 1379(b)(2).
44. *Id.* § 1379(c).
45. *Id.* § 1361(6).
46. *Id.* § 1362(9).
47. 50 C.F.R. § 216.3 (NMFS); 44 Fed. Reg. 2540, 2541–42 (1979) (FWS).
48. 16 U.S.C. § 1362(9).
49. 42 Fed. Reg. 64,548 (1977); 45 Fed. Reg. 72,178 (1980).
50. 16 U.S.C. § 1362(1).
51. *Id.* § 1371(a)(3)(A).
52. *Id.* §§ 1371(a)(1) and 1374(c)(3)(B).
53. *Id.* § 1371(b).
54. *Id.* § 1379(b)(1) and (e).
55. 53 Fed. Reg. 2069 (1988).
56. *Id.*
57. *Kokechik Fishermen's Ass'n, supra* note 12, 839 F.2d 795. *See* additional discussion on this case in text accompanying notes 96–104.
58. H.R. Rep. No. 100-970, at 17–19 (1988).
59. Potential biological removal level is discussed *infra,* in Section II.B.2.d.ii.
60. The moratorium also applies to importing marine mammals. The moratorium on imports is discussed *infra* in Section II.B.2.f.
61. 16 U.S.C. § 1371(a) (moratorium); § 1372(a) (prohibition). This means any person in U.S. waters (including the U.S. Exclusive Economic Zone), or U.S. citizens on the high seas. It does not apply to U.S. citizens in foreign countries. *See* United States v. Mitchell, 553 F.2d 996 (5th Cir. 1977).
62. *Id.* § 1362(13).
63. 50 C.F.R. § 18.3.
64. *Id.* § 216.4.
65. Strong v. United States, 5 F.3d 905 (5th Cir. 1993).
66. 16 U.S.C. § 1362(18)(A)(i),(ii).
67. *Id.* § 1362(18)(A)–(C). *See* United States v. Hayashi, 22 F.3d 859, 864 (9th Cir. 1993) (shooting in the direction of dolphins to protect fishing gear and catch determined not to be harassment because it did not involve "direct and significant intrusions upon the normal, life-sustaining activities of a marine mammal"). This definition does not apply to military readiness activities or federal agency research.
68. 16 U.S.C. § 1371(a)–(d).
69. Although authorizations for taking by harassment are of shorter duration, they are subject to less extensive procedural requirements. If an authorization is needed for more than one year, the applicant has the option of seeking multiple one-year authorizations or a single multiyear authorization, which would be subject to rulemaking.
70. *Id.* § 1374(b)(2)(B).
71. *Id.* § 1362(4).
72. *Id.* § 1374(d)(3).
73. *Id.* § 1371(a)(3)(A).
74. *Id.* § 1374(d).
75. *Id.* § 1371(a)(3)(A) and 1374(a).
76. *Id.* § 1371(a)(3)(B).
77. *Id.* The complexity of the waiver process has caused parties to avoid using it. Indeed, only three waivers have been formally requested: (1) to import fur seal pelts from South Africa (1975); (2) to return management to the state of Alaska (1975); and (3) a pending request filed in 2005 by the Makah Tribe of Indians in Washington to hunt gray whales. Although the first two waivers were initially granted, neither ultimately succeeded. The fur seal import waiver was invalidated because the harvest exceeded the permissible quota and because some skins came from animals that were less than eight months old or that were still nursing in contravention of the Act's import provisions. As discussed previously, the

Secretary of the Interior's determination that the Native take exemption did not survive a transfer of management was invalidated in court, and Alaska therefore decided not to pursue the waiver further. *People of Togiak, supra* note 40, 470 F. Supp. 423. As of the date of publication of this chapter, the request of the Makah Tribe was making its way through the waiver process.

78. *Id.* § 1379(h)(1).
79. *Id.* § 1375.
80. *Id.* § 1376.
81. The general permit procedure, although providing a mechanism to allow takes in commercial fisheries, reaffirms the Act's goal to reduce incidental take to "insignificant levels approaching [a] zero . . . rate." *Id.* §§ 1374 (d)(3), 1374(h).
82. *Id.* § 1373(d).
83. *Id.* § 1374(d)(3).
84. *Id.* § 1373(d)(2).
85. *Id.* § 1373(a).
86. *Id.* § 1373(b)(1)–(5).
87. *Id.* § 1373(d)–(f). *See* discussion of *Committee for Humane Legislation, supra.*
88. *Id.* § 1374.
89. *Id.* § 1371(a)(2).
90. Marine Mammal Commission, 1991 Annual Report to Congress 94 (1992).
91. *Id.* The take of Dall's porpoises before permit issuance is not known, but it is estimated to have been about 5,900 in 1980. Under the 1981 general permit, the estimated take for the 1981, 1982, and 1983 fishing seasons covered by the permit was 1,850, 4,187, and 2,906, respectively. (The 1981 level was low because of reduced fishing effort.)
92. *See* 52 Fed. Reg. 19,874 (1987).
93. Marine Mammal Commission, 1987 Annual Report to Congress 145–46 (1988). The Federation failed to demonstrate that the affected stocks were within their OSP levels and that the projected levels of take would not be to the disadvantage of those stocks.
94. *See supra* note 12.
95. *Id.*
96. Federation of Japan Salmon Fisheries v. Baldrige, 679 F. Supp. 37 (D.D.C. 1987).
97. *Id.* at 46, 49.
98. *Kokechik Fishermen's Ass'n, supra* note 12, 839 F.2d 795.
99. *Id.* at 802–03.
100. *Id.* at 802–03.
101. *Id.* at 802.
102. *Id.* at 802. *See also* Mary M. Sauer, *Balancing Marine Mammal Protection Against Commercial Fishing: The Zero Mortality Goal, Quotas, and the Gulf of Maine Harbor Porpoise,* 45 Me. L. Rev. 419 (1993).
103. S. Rep. No. 100-592, at 4-5 (1985).
104. 16 U.S.C. § 1383(a).
105. *Id.* § 1362(20).
106. *Id.* § 1387.
107. *Id.* § 1386(a).
108. *Id.* § 1362(19).
109. *Id.* § 1386(b)(1).
110. *Id.* § 1386(c).
111. The new regime does not apply to commercial fishing takes of endangered marine mammals, dolphins taken incidental to purse seine fishing in the Eastern Pacific Ocean tuna fishery, or California sea otters. *Id.* § 1387(a)(2)–(4) (1994).
112. *Id.* § 1387(k).
113. *Id.* §§ 1387(a)(1), 1387(b).
114. *Id.* § 1387(b)(3).
115. Center for Biological Diversity v. Nat'l Marine Fisheries Serv., No. C-02-3901-SC (N.D. Cal. April 30, 2003) (Stipulated Settlement Agreement).

116. 16 U.S.C. § 1387(c).
117. Although not reflected in the prohibitions set forth in the implementing regulations published by NMFS (50 C.F.R. § 229.3), it is also a violation of the Act to engage in a category I or II fishery without registering, whether or not any marine mammal is taken. 16 U.S.C. § 1379(c)(3)(C).
118. *Id.* § 1387(c)(3).
119. *Id.* § 1387(c)(4).
120. The goal of take reduction plans are to "assist in the recovery or prevent the depletion of each strategic stock which interacts with a [listed] commercial fishery. . . ." *Id.* § 1387(f)(1).
121. *Id.*
122. *Id.* §1387(f)(2).
123. *Id.* §1387(f)(6)(C). As of August 2006, the following take reduction teams had been established:

The Atlantic large whale take reduction team covers the incidental serious injury and mortality of right, humpback, fin, and minke whales in the South Atlantic shark gillnet fishery, the Gulf of Maine and Mid-Atlantic lobster trap/pot fishery, the Mid-Atlantic gillnet fishery, and the Northeast sink gillnet fishery. This team did not submit a consensus take reduction plan. The broad gear modifications and time-area closures it recommended have been modified more than a half-dozen times. Mortality and serious injury of humpback and right whales remains above PBR.

The Atlantic offshore cetacean take reduction team addresses the incidental serious injury and mortality of right whales, humpback whales, sperm whales, beaked whales, pilot whales, common dolphins, bottlenose dolphins, and spotted dolphins in the Atlantic pelagic driftnet, pelagic longline, and pair trawl fisheries. The team submitted a consensus plan, but two years later NMFS closed the pelagic driftnet fishery for swordfish and target catch and bycatch regulations, and changed the nature of the longline fisheries, so NMFS disbanded the Team in August 2001.

The bottlenose dolphin take reduction team addresses serious injuries and deaths of western North Atlantic coastal bottlenose dolphins incidental to several East Coast fisheries including the North Carolina inshore gillnet, Southeast Atlantic gillnet, Southeastern U.S. shark gillnet, U.S. Mid-Atlantic coastal gillnet, Atlantic blue crab trap/pot, Mid-Atlantic haul/beach seine, North Carolina long haul seine, North Carolina roe mullet stop net, and Virginia pound net. NMFS is currently implementing the gear restrictions and the time/area closures called for in the team's plan.

The Gulf of Maine harbor porpoise take reduction team covers the incidental serious injury and mortality of harbor porpoise in the Gulf of Maine groundfish sink gillnet fishery. The team's consensus plan and its revisions called for closures and the use of acoustic deterrent devices (pingers) to reduce harbor porpoise bycatch. Initially, the plan was effective with harbor porpoise takes being reduced below PBR and approaching ZMRG. In recent years, harbor porpoise bycatch has increased.

The Mid-Atlantic harbor porpoise take reduction team concerns incidental serious injury and mortality of harbor porpoise in coastal gillnet fisheries. Implementation of the team's plan has significantly reduced harbor porpoise bycatch.

The Pacific offshore cetacean take reduction team addresses incidental serious injury and mortality of beaked, pilot, pygmy sperm, sperm, and humpback whales in the California/Oregon swordfish drift gillnet fishery. The draft consensus take reduction plan required gear modifications, the use of pingers on all nets, educational workshops on marine mammals, and the take reduction plan.

The pelagic longline take reduction team addresses the incidental mortality and serious injury of long-finned pilot whales and short-finned pilot whales in the mid-Atlantic region of the Atlantic pelagic longline fishery. The team submitted its plan to NMFS in July 2006 and implementation of the plan is ongoing.

The Atlantic trawl gear take reduction team is charged with developing a take reduction plan to reduce bycatch of pilot whales, common dolphins, and white-sided dolphins in Atlantic trawl fisheries (Northeast bottom trawl, Northeast mid-water trawl (including pair trawl), mid-Atlantic mid-water trawl (including pair trawl), and mid-Atlantic bottom trawl fisheries).

124. *Id.* § 1387(g).

125. *Id.* § 1387(g)(1)(A)–(B).

126. *Id.* § 1387(g)(1)(C). Arguably, this applies to any category III fishery with any incidental mortality or serious injury of the affected species.

127. *Id.* § 1371(a)(5)(E).

128. The Atlantic Offshore Cetacean, Bottlenose Dolphin, Gulf of Maine Harbor Porpoise, Pacific Offshore Cetacean, and Pelagic Longline take reduction teams all submitted consensus take reduction plans.

129. MARINE MAMMAL COMMISSION, 2005 ANNUAL REPORT TO CONGRESS 116 (2006).

130. Pub. L. No. 98-364, § 101(a)(2), 98 Stat. 440 (1984) (codified at 16 U.S.C. § 1371(a)(2)).

131. Pub. L. No. 100-711, § 114, 102 Stat. 4759 (1988) (codified at 16 U.S.C. § 1371(a)(2)).

132. Earth Island Inst. v. Mosbacher, 746 F. Supp. 964 (N.D. Cal. 1990), *aff'd*, 929 F.2d 1449 (9th Cir. 1991). The five countries were Mexico, Venezuela, Vanuatu, Panama, and Ecuador.

133. Earth Island Inst. v. Mosbacher, 785 F. Supp. 826, 836 (N.D. Cal. 1992). The Ninth Circuit later reversed this decision on the grounds that the case should have been filed in the Court of International Trade. Earth Island Inst. v. Brown, 28 F.3d 76 (9th Cir. 1994).

134. Established after World War II, GATT had been the central world trade institution since its creation, providing a forum for trade negotiations and a set of rules governing trade between member countries. The last round of talks under GATT, known as the Uruguay Round, resulted in an agreement creating the World Trade Organization (WTO), effective January 1, 1995. The new rules under the WTO are broader than those under GATT, and the organization has more significant powers than did its predecessor.

135. GATT, *United States—Restrictions on Imports of Tuna*, 4–49 (Sept. 3, 1991) (Panel Report No. DS21/E).

136. GATT, *United States—Restrictions on Imports of Tuna*, 889–92 (June 1994), 33 I.L.M. (1994). This challenge was against the 1992 20-nation embargo.

137. The Dolphin Protection Consumer Information Act, Pub. L. No. 101-627, § 901, codified at 16 U.S.C. § 1385.

138. Pub. L. No. 102-523, § 2(c), 106 Stat. 3425 (1992) (codified at various sections of 16 U.S.C. §§ 1361 *et seq.*).

139. MARINE MAMMAL COMMISSION, 2005 ANNUAL REPORT TO CONGRESS 116 (2006).

140. 16 U.S.C. §§ 1411 *et seq.*

141. The amendments set forth standards that would be made for this comparability finding. NMFS successfully defended its regulations implementing these requirements in 2001 in *Defenders of Wildlife v. Hogarth*, a case heard before the Court of International Trade, 177 F. Supp. 2d 1336 (2001), *aff'd*, 330 F.3d 1358 (Fed. Cir. 2003). This resulted in lifting embargoes on three countries (Mexico, Ecuador, El Salvador) and leaving embargoes in place for eleven.

142. Earth Island Inst. v. Evans, No. C 03-00072004, 2004 WL 1774221 (N.D. Cal. Aug. 9, 2004).

143. *Id.* at *31.

144. *Id.* at *24–25.

145. *Id.* at *32. This ruling is on appeal as of the publication of this chapter.

146. Belize, Bolivia, Colombia, Guatemala, Honduras, Nicaragua, Panama, Vanuatu, Venezuela, Peru. There are currently no intermediary nation embargoes.

147. NMFS, Tuna/Dolphin Embargo Status Update, http://swr.nmfs.noaa.gov/psd/embargo2.htm.

148. Separate authority formerly existed in Section 101(a)(4) to authorize small takes of marine mammals incidental to domestic commercial fishing. 16 U.S.C. § 1374(a)(4). This take authority served as a more streamlined process than the general permit process when the incidental take levels were small and the impacts negligible. This authority has been

supplanted primarily by the Section 118 process and Section 101(a)(4) has been revised to allow for the non-lethal deterrence of marine mammals in certain instances. This procedure has been used to authorize incidental take of marine mammals for a large variety of activities, ranging from harassment of harbor seals incidental to the demolition and reconstruction of a dock in Puget Sound by the Washington Department of Corrections, to harassment of harbor seals, California sea lions, and elephant seals incidental to launches of space vehicles from Vandenberg Air Force Base in California, to harassment of walruses and polar bears incidental to oil and gas activities in the Chukchi Sea and ringed and bearded seals in the Beaufort Sea. One of the most controversial applications of the small take provision was the Navy's proposed worldwide deployment of its SURTASS low-frequency active sonar program to detect quiet submarines. *See* NMFS, Taking Marine Mammals Incidental to Navy Operations of Surveillance Towed Array Sensor System Low Frequency Active Sonar, Proposed Rules, 66 Fed. Reg. 15,375 (Mar. 19, 2001). *See also* M. Jasny, *Sounding the Depths: Supertankers, Sonar, and the Rise of Undersea Noise* (Natural Res. Def. Council 1999); E.M. McCarthy, *International Regulation of Transboundary Pollutants: The Emerging Challenge of Ocean Noise*, 6 OCEAN & COASTAL L.J. 257 (2001).

149. *Id.* § 1371(a)(5)(A). The term "citizens of the United States" is defined by regulation at 50 C.F.R. §§ 18.27(c) and 216.03 and includes corporations or similar entities organized under the laws of the United States.

150. *Id.* § 1371(a)(5)(A)(i).

151. *Id.* § 1371(a)(5)(D).

152. *Id.* § 1371(E)(i).

153. 16 U.S.C. § 1371(a)(1)(moratorium), § 1372(b) (prohibition).

154. *Id.* § 1371(a)(3).

155. The 1994 amendments established an exception under Section 104(c)(5)(A) to allow the issuance of permits for the importation of certain polar bear trophies legally taken in sport hunts in Canada. *Id.* § 1374(c)(5)(A). In 1997, Congress amended the Act to allow the issuance of import permits for all polar bear trophies legally taken in Canada before the enactment of the 1994 amendment, regardless of the status of the population or the adequacy of Canada's management program. This "grandfathering" of polar bear trophies was further extended under a 2003 amendment to cover all polar bears legally taken in Canada prior to February 18, 1997. (This is the date on which FWS published a final rule identifying those Canadian management units from which imports would be allowed. *See* Pub. L. No. 101-108, Title I, § 149.)

156. *Id.* § 1371(b).

157. *Id.* § 1372(a)(6).

158. *Id.* § 1372(c).

159. *Id.* §§ 1372(a),(e).

160. *Id.* § 1379(h)(2).

161. *Id.* § 1372(a)(4).

162. *Id.* § 1361(2).

163. *Id.*

164. *Id.* § 1361(5).

165. *Id.* § 1361(6).

166. *Id.* § 1362(2).

167. *Id.* § 1382(a).

168. H.R. REP. NO. 103-439, at 29 (1994).

169. *Id.* To date, neither FWS nor NMFS has relied exclusively on this authority to protect marine mammal habitat. Prior to the 1994 amendments, both agencies were concerned that Section 112 of the Act alone did not provide sufficient authority to protect habitat. Section 112 has been used in conjunction with the ESA, however, to protect marine mammal habitat. For example, FWS, in cooperation with the state of Florida, designated motorboat speed zones in the Crystal River area to protect manatees. 50 C.F.R. §§ 17.100–17.108. Also, the MMPA, the ESA, and the National Park Service Organic Act were jointly used

as authority to designate zones in Glacier Bay National Park to protect humpback whales from disturbance by cruise ships and other vessels. 36 C.F.R. § 13.65(b). More recently, NMFS has indicated a willingness to consider using this rulemaking authority to protect habitat used by spinner dolphins in Hawaii. *See* Advance Notice of Proposed Rulemaking, 70 Fed. Reg. 73,426 (Dec. 12, 2005).

170. 16 U.S.C. § 1361(3).

171. *Id.* § 1361(4).

172. *Id.* § 1362(2).

173. Although applicable NMFS regulations (*see, e.g.,* 50 C.F.R. § 216.33(b)) suggest that permits may be issued to authorize the export of marine mammals, Section 104(a) of the MMPA authorizes the agency to issue permits only for the taking or importation of marine mammals.

174. 50 C.F.R. §§ 216, 217–222.

175. *Id.* § 216.

176. 16 U.S.C. §§ 1371(a)(3), 1373(a).

177. The GA applies to all marine mammals, but because an ESA permit is still required for endangered and threatened and species, permit applicants generally seek permits under both the MMPA and ESA. See 50 C.F.R. § 216.45(a)(1) and (2).

178. *Id.* § 1374(3)(C).

179. *Id.* § 1380(a).

180. Pub. L. No. 98-364, § 102(3)(D), 98 Stat. 440 (1984).

181. 16 U.S.C. § 1414a(a).

182. *Id.* § 1378.

183. *Id.* § 1378(a)(1).

184. *Id.* § 1378(a)(3).

185. *Id.* § 1378(a)(4).

186. *Id.* § 1383(b).

187. The Marine Mammal Commission had previously prepared a legal analysis of this issue. *See* D. Baur, *Reconciling Polar Bear Protection Under United States Laws and the International Agreement for the Conservation of Polar Bears*, 2 ANIMAL LAW 9–99 (1996).

188. 16 U.S.C. § 1383(d).

189. *Id.* § 1389.

190. *Id.* § 1389(b)(1). Ballard Locks was identified specifically to allow the Secretary to consider a request from Washington State to address the predation of steelhead at that location without having to determine that the fish stock merited listing under the ESA.

191. *Id.* § 1389(b)(2)(1994).

192. As the winter steelhead population began to decline during the 1980s, concerns about sea lion predation increased. By 1994, the winter steelhead population had dropped to an all-time low of 70 spawners (down from 2,500 spawning fish in the mid-1980s). Although other factors such as freshwater and ocean survival may have contributed to the declining status of the steelhead population, lethal removal authority was granted. This action was not used when nonlethal alternatives proved effective. By 1997, the Lake Washington winter steelhead run had increased to 610 fish returning to spawn.

193. 16 U.S.C. §§ 1421–1421h.

194. *Id.* §§ 1421–1421b.

195. *Id.*

196. Pub. L. No. 108-136, 117 Stat. 1723 (2003).

197. 16 U.S.C. § 1362(18)(B).

198. 16 U.S.C. § 1362(18)(B).

199. *Id.* § 1371(f).

200. The complete history of this case is summarized in the district court decision invalidating the Executive Branch exemptions. 2008 WL 314192 (E.D. Cal. Feb. 4, 2008).

201. The Heard Island Feasibility Test was an experiment based in the southern Indian Ocean during which acoustic sources suspended below a ship transmitted acoustic signals to receivers around the globe. Heard Island was selected because signals transmitted from that

location can reach both coasts of North America. The project showed that underwater acoustic signals could be received worldwide and serve as a method for measuring global warming. A. B. Baggeroer & W. H. Munk, *The Heard Island Feasibility Test*, 45(9) Physics Today 22–30 (1992).

202. Acoustic Thermometry of Ocean Climate, or ATOC, is an international program involving eleven institutions in seven nations. It was designed as a 30-month "proof-of-concept" project to measure large-scale changes in ocean temperature and heat content to provide data and test climate models to assess global climate change.

203. The SURTASS LFA sonar system is a long-range, low-frequency (between 100 and 500 Hertz) sonar that has both active and passive components. The sonar's detection capability does not rely on noise generated by the target, but rather on the use of active sounds or pulses originating from the system. The purpose of SURTASS LFA sonar is to provide the Navy with a reliable and dependable system for long-range detection of quieter, harder-to-find submarines.

204. Nat'l Res. Council, Ocean Noise and Marine Mammals (Nat'l Academy Press 2003); Nat'l Res. Council, Marine Mammals and Low-Frequency Sound: Progress Since 1994 (Nat'l Academy Press 2000).

205. T. M. O'Hara & T. J. O'Shea, *Assess Impacts of Environmental Contaminants, in* J. E. Reynolds, W. F. Perrin, R. R. Reeves, S. Montgomery & T. J. Ragen (eds.), Marine Mammal Research Conservation Beyond Crisis 63 (Johns Hopkins Univ. Press 2005).

206. *Id.* at 64.

207. *Id.* at 68–70.

208. P. J. H. Reijnders & A. Aguilar, *Pollution and Marine Mammals, in* Encyclopedia of Marine Mammals 952 (W. F. Perrin, B. Wursig, and J. G. M. Thewissen eds., Academic Press 2002).

209. *Supra* note 205, at 74.

210. S. E. Moore, *Long Term Environmental Change and Marine Mammals, in* J. E. Reynolds, W. F. Perrin, R. R. Reeves, S. Montgomery & T. J. Ragen (eds.), Marine Mammal Research Conservation Beyond Crisis 142 (Johns Hopkins Univ. Press 2005).

211. *Id.*

212. *Id.*

213. 72 Fed. Reg. 1064 (Jan. 9, 2007).

214. C. B. Heath, *California, Galapagos, and Japanese Sea Lions, in* Encyclopedia of Marine Mammals 185 (W. F. Perrin, B. Wursig, and J. G. M. Thewissen eds., Academic Press 2002).

215. H.R. Rep. No. 103-439, at 29 (1994).

216. U.S. Comm'n on Ocean Policy, An Ocean Blueprint for the 21st Century: Final Report. Washington DC, 2004 ISBN#0-9759462-0-X, at 306.

217. 16 U.S.C. § 1378(a).

218. *Id.* § 1378 (a)(2).

219. *Id.* § 1378 (a)(3).

220. *Id.* § 1378 (a)(4) and (5).

221. U.S. Comm'n on Ocean Policy, An Ocean Blueprint for the 21st Century: Final Report 63, *available at* http://oceancommission.gov/documents/full_color_rpt/welcome.html.

222. *Id.* at 65.

chapter sixteen

The Endangered Species Act and Marine Species

Wm. Robert Irvin
Michael J. Bean

I. Introduction

In 1741, Commander Vitus Bering and his crew of Russian sailors were shipwrecked in what are now called the Commander Islands in the Bering Sea. Forced to subsist on whatever food they could find, the marooned sailors were fortunate to find a large sirenian, closely related to dugongs and manatees, living in the shallow waters surrounding the islands. The animal was later named Steller's sea cow, after Bering's shipboard naturalist, Georg Wilhelm Steller. Steller's sea cows were rich in fatty meat and oil, ideal as food and useful for lamp fuel. Although Bering died of scurvy in the islands, Steller and other members of the crew survived, eventually returning to Russia, where they reported their fortuitous discovery. Subsequently, Russian sealers returned to the islands to kill fur seals, sea lions, sea otters, and Steller's sea cows. By 1768, from a population estimated to have originally numbered around 1,500, not a single Steller's sea cow remained.[1]

The story of the extinction of Steller's sea cow is often used as the "paradigm of anthropogenic extinction."[2] More than that, however, it is a cautionary tale reminding us that, despite the seeming abundance of life in the sea, species extinction can take place in the oceans as well as on land. Furthermore, the list of endangered marine species is not restricted to large marine mammals hunted for their meat, oil, or fur. Today, species of marine and anadromous fish, marine mammals, marine turtles, a

The authors wish to express their thanks to Vermont Law School students James Kyle, Melissa Gibbons, Christine Roberts, and Jennifer DeHart for their contributions to this chapter.

marine invertebrate, white abalone, and even a marine plant, Johnson's sea grass, are listed by the United States as threatened or endangered species.[3]

Like threatened and endangered species on land, threatened and endangered species in the ocean are protected by the Endangered Species Act of 1973 (ESA).[4] This chapter provides an overview of the ESA and discusses its specific application to marine species. While much of the application of the ESA is the same on land or in the sea, there are some areas in which the law's application has developed approaches unique to the protection of threatened and endangered marine species. These include the listing of distinct population segments of anadromous fish species, the relationship of the ESA to other marine conservation laws such as the Marine Mammal Protection Act of 1972[5] and the Magnuson-Stevens Fisheries Conservation and Management Act of 1976,[6] and the extraterritorial application of the ESA to the high seas. This chapter will explore these issues and focus on regulatory and case law that is unique to the conservation of threatened and endangered marine species.

II. The Current State of the Law— Overview of the Endangered Species Act[7]

The ESA was signed into law by President Richard M. Nixon on December 28, 1973.[8] In enacting the law, Congress found that "various species of fish, wildlife, and plants in the United States have been rendered extinct as a consequence of economic growth and development untempered by adequate concern and conservation."[9] In addition, Congress found that "other species of fish, wildlife, and plants have been so depleted in numbers that they are in danger of or threatened with extinction,[10] and "these species of fish, wildlife, and plants are of aesthetic, ecological, educational, historical, recreational, and scientific value to the Nation and its people."[11] Congress further found that "the United States has pledged itself as a sovereign state in the international community to conserve to the extent practicable the various species of fish or wildlife and plants facing extinction,"[12] including the International Convention for the Northwest Atlantic Fisheries[13] and the International Convention for the High Seas Fisheries of the North Pacific Ocean.[14] Consequently, Congress declared that the purposes of the ESA are to "provide a means whereby the ecosystems upon which endangered species and threatened species depend may be conserved, to provide a program for the conservation of such endangered species and threatened species, and to take such steps as may be appropriate to achieve the purposes of the treaties and conventions" for conservation of threatened and endangered species.[15]

The extraordinary power of the ESA was recognized early on, when the U.S. Supreme Court ruled in *Tennessee Valley Authority v. Hill*[16] that a nearly completed multimillion-dollar dam must yield to the protection of an endangered minnow, the snail darter, only three inches in length. The Court declared, "One would be hard pressed to find a statutory provision whose terms were any plainer than those" of the ESA.[17] Accordingly, the Court found that "examination of the language, history, and structure of the [ESA] indicates beyond doubt that Congress intended endangered species to be afforded the highest of priorities."[18] In subsequent years, while implementation of the ESA has waxed and, more recently, waned in an age of shrinking federal budgets and increasing criticism of the ESA, the law remains one of our strongest environmental laws.

The power of the ESA was recognized early on, when the Court ruled that a multimillion-dollar dam must yield to the protection of an endangered minnow.

The ESA is administered jointly by the Secretary of the Interior, acting through the U.S. Fish and Wildlife Service, and the Secretary of Commerce, acting through the National Oceanic and Atmospheric Administration's National Marine Fisheries Service (NMFS).[19] In general, the Secretary of the Interior is responsible for avian, terrestrial, and freshwater species, while the Secretary of Commerce is responsible for marine and anadromous species. There are exceptions, however. The Secretary of Commerce is responsible for marine turtles when they are in the ocean; the Secretary of the Interior manages them when they are on their nesting beaches. The Secretary of the Interior manages sea otters.[20]

For a species to be protected under the ESA, it first must be listed as threatened or endangered. The Secretary of the Interior administers the list, but the Secretary of Commerce determines, for the marine and anadromous species under his or her jurisdiction, whether a species should be listed or removed from the list.[21] Listing (and delisting) may be initiated by nonfederal parties petitioning the Secretary of the Interior or Secretary of Commerce, or by one of the Secretaries on his or her own initiative.[22] There are precise deadlines for the Secretary to respond to petitions and reach listing decisions. Listing decisions must be based on five criteria:

1. The present or threatened destruction, modification, or curtailment of the species' habitat or range;
2. Overutilization of the species for commercial, recreational, scientific, or educational purposes;
3. Disease or predation;
4. The inadequacy of existing regulatory mechanisms; or
5. Other natural or manmade factors affecting the species' continued existence.[23]

Critical habitat is defined as the specific geographic areas that contain the physical and biological features essential to the species' conservation and that may require special management or protection.[24] The Secretary (of the Interior or Commerce, as appropriate) is required to designate critical habitat for species at the time of listing, or within one year of listing if critical habitat is not determinable at the time of listing. The Secretary may decline to designate critical habitat if he or she determines that it is not prudent to designate it; that is, if the benefit to the species of designating critical habitat is outweighed by the potential harm to the species of identifying its habitat, such as where designating critical habitat would lead to overexploitation of the species. The Secretary may also exclude areas from critical habitat if he or she determines that the economic and social costs of designating critical habitat outweigh the benefit to the species, so long as failure to designate critical habitat will not result in the species' extinction.[25]

Once a species is listed, the goal of the ESA is to conserve the species, defined as bringing the species back to the point where the protection of the ESA is no longer required, that is, recovery of the species.[26] The ESA provides various methods for accomplishing this.

First, the Secretary is required to develop and implement recovery plans unless he or she determines that a plan will not promote the conservation of the species.[27] Recovery plans generally are detailed and identify actions to be taken by various parties over an extended period of time. Both the U.S. Fish and Wildlife Service and NMFS have developed detailed policies and procedures for recovery planning.[28] The obligation to implement recovery plans rests with the Secretary; thus, agencies within the Department of the Interior and the Department of Commerce are obligated to implement recovery plans or to provide an explanation why implementation is not appropriate. For other federal agencies, recovery plans are advisory, not mandatory.[29]

Second, the ESA encourages cooperation between the federal government and the states to conserve listed species. The Secretary is authorized under Section 6 of the ESA to enter into cooperative agreements with states that establish "adequate and active" programs for the conservation of listed species and to provide funding for such programs.[30] A state that enters into a cooperative agreement is eligible to receive federal financial assistance to help in the administration of the state's own program. Congress anticipated that the prospect of such federal financial assistance would serve as an incentive to the states to develop their own complementary conservation programs.[31] In practice, however, that expectation was largely unfulfilled, as Congress provided only modest and irregular amounts of funding. That fact, and the further fact that there were few listed marine species in the early years of the ESA, meant that NMFS initially paid little attention to Section 6. Although the Fish and Wildlife Service entered into Section 6 cooperative agreements with nearly all of the states within a few years of the ESA's enactment, NMFS did not enter into its first such agreement until 1984, eleven years after the ESA became law. Ironically, although cooperative agreements between NMFS and eleven states are in effect today, they do not include any Pacific coast states, where most of today's listed marine species occur.[32] During the period 2003–2005, NMFS's very modest Section 6 grants program to the states was administered for it by the National Fish and Wildlife Foundation. In fiscal year 2006, NMFS resumed administering the grants itself.[33]

Third, endangered animal species are protected against take within the United States, in its territorial sea, and upon the high seas (i.e., take on the high seas is prohibited if done by persons subject to the jurisdiction of the United States).[34] "Take" is defined by the ESA as "to harass, harm, pursue, hunt, shoot, wound, kill, trap, capture, or collect, or to attempt to engage in any such conduct."[35] It may include significant habitat destruction that actually kills or injures an endangered species.[36] Threatened species are protected to the extent that the Secretary deems "necessary and advisable" through the issuance of special regulations pursuant to Section 4(d) of the ESA.[37] The Secretary of the Interior has issued a regulation applying the same protection generally to threatened species that endangered species receive under the ESA, unless special regulations are issued for particular threatened species. The Secretary of Commerce issues special regulations for each threatened species, although those regulations generally provide threatened species with the same protection as endangered species.[38] In addition to the prohibition against take, Section 9 of the ESA also prohibits transport and commerce in endangered species.[39]

Fourth, federal agencies have a special obligation to conserve listed species. Section 7(a)(1) of the ESA directs federal agencies, in consultation with the Secretary, to carry out programs for the conservation of threatened and endangered species.[40] Section 7(a)(2) requires all federal agencies to consult with the Secretary of the Interior or Commerce, as appropriate, to ensure that "any action authorized, funded, or carried out" by the agency "is not likely to jeopardize the continued existence of any endangered species or threatened species or result in the adverse modification or destruction" of critical habitat.[41]

This process, known as Section 7 consultation, is the real strength of the ESA as a conservation tool and sets it apart from all other wildlife conservation laws. If an agency determines that a proposed action may affect a listed species or critical habitat, it must prepare a biological assessment of the action's impacts and obtain the concurrence of the Secretary in that assessment.[42] If, as a result of the biological assessment or at the Secretary's request, an agency determines that the proposed action may adversely affect a listed species or critical habitat, it must formally consult with the Secretary.[43] In formal consultation, the Secretary prepares a biological opinion on the impacts of the proposed action on listed species or critical habitat. If the Secretary concludes that the action is likely to jeopardize a listed species or adversely modify or destroy critical habitat, he or she will suggest available reasonable and prudent alternatives to the proposed action. If the Secretary concludes that the action, while not likely to jeopardize a listed species, will result in incidental take of the species, the Secretary will provide the agency with an incidental take statement, authorizing a certain level of take provided that specific reasonable and prudent measures to minimize the take are implemented by the agency. The Secretary may also suggest conservation recommendations to minimize the impacts of the action.[44] The action agency is free to reject the Secretary's determination of jeopardy or adverse modification or destruction of critical habitat and, indeed, has an independent obligation to determine whether its action will result in jeopardy to a listed species or adverse modification or destruction of critical habitat.[45] If an agency rejects the Secretary's determination, however, it must then seek an exemption from the Cabinet-level Endangered Species Committee, a rarely invoked procedure.[46]

In addition to exemptions granted by the Endangered Species Committee, other exemptions from the take prohibition are available. The Secretary may issue permits allowing the take of listed species for scientific purposes or to enhance the propagation and survival of the species.[47] The Secretary may also issue permits allowing incidental take of listed species, provided that the applicant for the permit has developed a conservation plan that minimizes and mitigates the impact of the taking on the species and the Secretary concludes that the taking will not appreciably reduce the likelihood of survival and recovery of the species in the wild.[48] These plans have come to be known as habitat conservation plans.[49] There are also exemptions for subsistence taking of listed species by Alaska Natives and nonnative permanent residents of Alaska native villages,[50] and for articles over one hundred years old that are composed of listed species.[51]

The ESA also provides special rules for experimental populations established to restore extirpated species to the wild. Experimental populations must be wholly separate geographically from nonexperimental populations of the same species. Experimental populations are generally treated as threatened species. However, the Secretary must also designate an experimental population as either essential or nonessential. Nonessential experimental populations are treated as species proposed to be listed, except when they occur within national wildlife refuges or national parks.[52] Thus, for nonessential experimental populations occurring outside national parks or national wildlife refuges, federal agencies need only confer with the Secretary on the impacts of any proposed action on such populations.[53]

The prohibitions of the ESA may be enforced by the federal government or by citizen suits. The government may seek injunctive relief against ESA violations, and civil or criminal penalties. Only injunctive relief is available in citizen suits.[54]

III. Emerging and Unresolved Issues

A. Listing of Evolutionarily Significant Units and Distinct Population Segments

While the ESA provides for the listing of species as threatened or endangered, it defines species broadly to include subspecies and any distinct population segment of vertebrate fish and wildlife that interbreeds when mature.[55] Application of the distinct population segment provision to listing of salmon and other marine species has proven particularly complicated.

Salmon and other anadromous fish hatch in freshwater streams where they grow to juvenile size, then migrate to the ocean where they live for one to several years, finally returning to their natal streams to spawn and die.[56] Fish that return to a particular area at a particular season are usually thought of as a distinct population segment. Thus, for example, Chinook salmon may be comprised of Sacramento River winter-run Chinook, Snake River spring- and summer-run Chinook, and Deschutes Rivers summer- and fall-run Chinook, to name a few.[57]

In 1991, NMFS issued guidance on how it would determine whether a particular run of salmon or steelhead trout constituted a distinct population segment eligible for listing under the ESA.[58] NMFS decided that a run must constitute an "evolutionarily significant unit" (ESU) to qualify as a distinct population segment. An ESU had to be substantially reproductively isolated from other salmon in the same streams and represent an important component in the evolutionary legacy of the species.[59] In adopting this policy, NMFS was attempting to determine whether a particular run is physically or reproductively isolated from other runs and whether the run was unique genetically or ecologically.

Applying the ESU policy, NMFS listed, albeit reluctantly, Oregon coast coho salmon as a threatened species.[60] In listing Oregon coast coho salmon, NMFS excluded from the listing substantial numbers of hatchery-spawned coho salmon. That decision, and the underlying ESU policy, was challenged in *Alsea Valley Alliance v. Evans*.[61] Plaintiffs argued that, in making its listing decision, NMFS should have considered both hatchery-spawned and naturally spawned coho as the distinct population segment. The federal district court upheld NMFS's creation of the ESU policy as a permissible interpretation of the meaning of distinct population segment under the ESA. However, the court also held that excluding hatchery-spawned fish from the ESU was arbitrary and capricious. According to the court, listing distinctions below distinct population segments are not allowed under the ESA. Since hatchery-spawned fish mix freely with naturally spawned fish, the court found that there was no basis for NMFS to exclude them from the ESU and thus the distinct population segment.[62] The court noted that, while preservation of genetic attributes of naturally spawning fish might be a worthy goal, the ESA does not allow NMFS to further divide distinct population segments for purposes of listing in order to achieve that goal.[63]

The impact of the *Alsea Valley Alliance* decision reached far beyond the listing of Oregon coast coho salmon. Since virtually all Pacific salmon stocks are comprised of both natural- and hatchery-spawned fish, with the latter far outnumbering the former, the validity of nearly every listing of Pacific salmon runs as threatened or endangered was thrown into doubt. Compounding the uncertainty, the Bush administration declined to appeal the district court's decision in *Alsea Valley Alliance*, opting instead to adopt a new policy to reconsider all Pacific salmon listing decisions.[64]

The impact of the *Alsea Valley Alliance* decision reached far beyond the listing of Oregon coast coho salmon.

The inclusion of hatchery-spawned fish to determine whether a distinct population segment should be listed was again challenged, with the opposite result, in *Trout Unlimited. v. National Marine Fisheries Service*.[65] In that case, plaintiffs challenged a decision by NMFS to change the status of Upper Columbia River steelhead from endangered to threatened. Specifically, plaintiffs challenged the application by NMFS of its Hatchery Listing Policy, developed in the wake of the *Alsea Valley Alliance* decision. The federal district court held that the purpose of the ESA is to promote naturally self-sustaining populations of a species. The court held that the inclusion of hatchery-spawned fish to determine the listing status of a distinct population segment was contrary to that purpose. Consequently, the court held that considering the number of hatchery-spawned fish together with naturally spawned fish pursuant to the Hatchery Listing Policy rendered the decision to change the status of Upper Columbia River steelhead to threatened was arbitrary and capricious.[66]

While the ESU policy applies only to Pacific salmon and steelhead, the application of a similar policy on what constitutes a distinct population segment applicable to other wildlife, which was jointly developed by NMFS and the U.S. Fish and Wildlife Service (FWS) in 1996, was at issue in *Center for Biological Diversity v. Lohn*.[67] In *Lohn*, plaintiffs challenged NMFS's decision not to list the southern resident population of orcas, commonly called killer whales, found in the waters of Puget Sound, Washington. The distinct population segment policy adopted by NMFS and FWS provides that three factors be considered in deciding whether a distinct population segment exists: (1) the discreteness of the population in relation to the species as a whole; (2) the significance of the population to the entire species; and (3) whether the population, if treated as a species, would warrant listing.[68] Applying these factors, NMFS decided that the southern resident population of orcas failed to meet the second requirement, significance. Plaintiffs challenged both the determination and the underlying policy, arguing that Congress did not authorize the agencies to add a significance requirement to the determination of what constitutes a distinct population segment. The court rejected this argument, however, finding that the distinct population segment policy, including the requirement for a showing of significance, was a reasonable interpretation of an ambiguous phrase in the ESA.[69] The court went on to hold, however, that, in light of abundant evidence that lumping all orcas into a single taxon was not supported by science, NMFS had not used the best available science to determine that the southern resident population of orcas should not be listed.[70]

In both *Alsea Valley* and *Lohn*, courts upheld the underlying policies for determining what constitutes a distinct population segment in marine species. In both cases, however, the courts found fault with the application of those policies by NMFS. In *Alsea Valley*, the court found that splitting hatchery-spawned and naturally spawned salmon went beyond congressional authority in allowing the listing of distinct population segments, while in *Lohn*, the court found that lumping the southern resident population of orcas with other orcas was not as discriminating as Congress intended. The principal difference in the two outcomes was that in *Alsea Valley*, the fish were not geographically or reproductively separate from one another, while in *Lohn*, there was a clear physical separation of orca populations. Similarly, in *Trout Unlimited*, the court did not find fault with the underlying policies for determining a distinct population segment; instead, the court found that, in applying those policies, the conflation of hatchery-spawned and naturally spawned fish was inconsistent with the ESA's purpose of promoting naturally self-sustaining populations.

B. ESA Listing and Designation of Depleted Populations Under the Marine Mammal Protection Act

Just as birds listed as threatened or endangered under the ESA are also protected by the Migratory Bird Treaty Act,[71] marine mammals listed as threatened or endangered also receive protection under another law, the Marine Mammal Protection Act of 1972 (MMPA).[72] While take of whales, dolphins, sea lions, seals, sea otters, and other marine mammals under the MMPA is generally prohibited, subsistence take of some of these creatures by Alaska Natives is permitted. If, however, a marine mammal is designated as depleted, even subsistence take can be prohibited or limited.[73] A marine mammal can be designated as depleted if it is listed as threatened or endangered under the ESA or it is below its optimum sustainable population as defined by the MMPA.[74] Unlike the ESA, though, the MMPA does not require designation and protection of critical habitat or consultation by federal agencies with NMFS on proposed actions.

The relationship between designation of a marine mammal as depleted under the MMPA and listing under the ESA was explored in *Cook Inlet Beluga Whale v. Daley*.[75] In that case, NMFS opted to designate the Cook Inlet beluga whale, a distinct population segment, as depleted under the MMPA, while declining to list it under the ESA. Indeed, NMFS relied on its decision to designate the population as depleted as an excuse not to list under the ESA, concluding that regulation of Alaska Native take of the whales under the MMPA obviated the need for protection under the ESA. Plaintiff environmental organizations challenged that decision, arguing that the same factor that justified designation of the population as depleted, declining population resulting from Native take, warranted its listing under the ESA.[76]

The district court rejected plaintiffs' argument. While the court recognized that some limited take of whales would continue under the MMPA, it noted that plaintiffs had not shown that the population would continue to decline. Moreover, the court concluded that, in the event of a continuing decline in the population, it could be listed at a later date under the ESA.[77] Thus, designation of a marine mammal as depleted under the MMPA does not automatically mean that the species should be listed under the ESA and, indeed, such designation may be used as a reason not to list under the ESA.[78]

C. Critical Habitat and Essential Fish Habitat

Critical habitat has been designated for a number of marine species, including twenty-five Pacific salmon and steelhead ESUs,[79] Hawaiian monk seal, northern right whale, Steller sea lion,[80] West Indian manatee, spectacled eider, Steller's eider, marbled murrelet, green sea turtle, hawksbill sea turtle, leatherback sea turtle, Gulf sturgeon, and Johnson's seagrass.[81] Under Section 7 of the ESA, federal agencies are required to consult with NMFS or FWS to ensure that their actions are not likely to adversely modify or destroy critical habitat.[82]

Critical habitat designations for marine species have, in general, been less controversial than for terrestrial species. Although critical habitat affects private landowners only indirectly, through Section 7 consultation on federal permits, the designation of private land as critical habitat has proven contentious, giving rise to claims that restrictions on activities on private land amount to takings of private property for public use requiring compensation under the Fifth Amendment to the U.S. Constitution.[83] Since the ocean and seabed are publicly owned, and uses of those public resources are subject to licenses from federal and state authorities, there is even less basis for such claims resulting from designation of critical habitat in marine environments.

In addition to critical habitat protection under the ESA, marine species[84] may also have essential fish habitat designated pursuant to the Magnuson-Stevens Fishery Conservation and Management Act of 1976 (FCMA).[85] Under the FCMA, essential fish habitat is defined as "those waters and substrate necessary to fish for spawning, breeding, feeding or growth to maturity."[86] Regional fishery management councils and the Secretary of Commerce are required in fishery management plans to identify and designate essential fish habitat, minimize adverse effects from fishing on essential fish habitat, and identify other actions to encourage the conservation and enhancement of essential fish habitat.[87]

As with critical habitat, once essential fish habitat has been designated, federal agencies are required to consult with NMFS with respect to any action authorized, funded, or carried out by the agency that may adversely affect essential fish habitat.[88] In addition, a regional fishery management council may provide its views on the proposed action to the agency proposing it as well as NMFS. Unlike with critical habitat, however, the agency proposing the action has no obligation to ensure that the action will not adversely affect essential fish habitat. Instead, if NMFS determines that the proposed action will adversely affect essential fish habitat, it will suggest measures to conserve essential fish habitat. The agency proposing the action then has thirty days in which to respond by adopting the recommendations, proposing alternative measures to avoid, mitigate, or offset adverse impacts, or explain why such measures will not be adopted.[89]

Clearly, critical habitat designation provides more stringent habitat protection for threatened and endangered marine species than that provided by designation of essential fish habitat. However, essential fish habitat designation may provide some protection for threatened and endangered marine species for which critical habitat has not been designated. In addition, while areas may be excluded from critical habitat where the Secretary determines that economic or other costs outweigh the benefits to the species,[90] no such balancing is required for the designation of essential fish habitat. Thus, designation of essential fish habitat may be more biologically based than critical habitat designation and, as a result of the less stringent protection for essential fish habitat, less controversial.

D. Technological Solutions and Marine Species

While habitat destruction is a substantial threat to endangered marine species, exploitation of those species, through either direct take or indirect take as bycatch in commercial fishing, is also a significant and somewhat unique threat. As one writer has put it, ocean fishing is the "last buffalo hunt . . . on the rolling blue prairies of the oceans."[91] Consequently, technological solutions, in the form of fishing gear devices or modifications, often are key to conservation of marine species.

Perhaps the best example of a technological fix to an endangered marine species problem is the use of turtle excluder devices (TEDs) to prevent the drowning of sea turtles in fishing nets. As detailed in *State of Louisiana ex rel. Guste v. Verity*,[92] bycatch of threatened and endangered sea turtles in shrimp nets posed the single greatest

Technological solutions, in the form of fishing gear devices or modifications, often are key to conservation of marine species.

threat to their continued survival. The use of TEDs, a gridlike device that, when placed in shrimp nets, prevents sea turtles from being caught in the net while allowing shrimp to be caught, reduced sea turtle mortality by ninety-seven percent. The required use of TEDs was challenged by the State of Louisiana, arguing that the effectiveness of TEDs had not been adequately demonstrated and the cost to Louisiana's shrimp fishermen outweighed the benefits to sea turtles. The Fifth Circuit rejected both arguments, finding that NMFS had reasonably concluded that TEDs were necessary to protect sea turtles and that Congress had already struck the balance of equities in favor of conservation of endangered species.[93]

E. Extraterritorial Application of Section 7 Consultation and Marine Species

Application of ESA Section 7 consultation requirements is largely the same whether the species at issue is terrestrial or marine. One issue that is unique to marine species, however, is the extraterritorial application of Section 7 consultation requirements. Regulations implementing Section 7 specify that federal actions which occur in the United States or upon the high seas are subject to consultation.[94] A related question is whether federal actions occurring within the territorial seas of another nation are subject to consultation.

This question was posed in *Natural Resources Defense Council v. U.S. Department of the Navy,*[95] a suit challenging the Navy's conduct of underwater sonar tests, which have been associated with injury to endangered whales. In arguing against the need to conduct Section 7 consultation, the Navy suggested that if some of the testing was conducted in the territorial seas of another nation, Section 7 would not apply. The court found, however, that there was no evidence that tests were conducted anyplace other than the territorial seas of the United States and on the high seas. Since regulations implementing Section 7 specify that federal agency actions within the United States or on the high seas are subject to consultation,[96] the court rejected the Navy's argument.[97]

F. Role of the States in Conservation of Threatened and Endangered Marine Species

States have an important role to play in the conservation of threatened and endangered species on land or at sea. States often have principal authority over streams and rivers in which anadromous species reproduce and grow. Bays and estuaries that provide critical breeding and nursery habitat for fish, shellfish, shorebirds, and other wildlife are often under state jurisdiction. Even beyond the three-mile limit that generally marks state waters, fishing vessels licensed by the states cast their nets or set their hooks.

The importance of state marine resource management to overall conservation of threatened and endangered species was illustrated in *Strahan v. Coxe.*[98] In that case, the plaintiff argued that, by licensing gillnet and lobster pot fishing in state waters, the State of Massachusetts Division of Marine Resources was liable for illegal takes of endangered northern right whales that drowned after becoming entangled in fishing gear. Massachusetts asserted in its defense that merely granting fishing licenses did not result in right whale takes, rather, the intervening acts of the fishermen themselves were responsible for the takes. The court rejected this argument, finding that the issuance of licenses by the state was a proximate cause of the right whale takes and, therefore, a violation of Section 9's prohibition against take of listed species.[99] Massachusetts also argued that principal responsibility for protecting right whales rested with the federal government, specifically NMFS, and the state could not be compelled to carry out conservation measures that were federal responsibilities. The court concluded, however, that holding the state liable for illegal take resulting from its action in licensing fishing was different from requiring the state to act affirmatively to conserve right whales.[100] Thus, the court implicitly recognized both the importance of state regulation of marine resources and its role in conserving threatened and endangered species within state waters.

State management of declining salmon populations has also been used by the Secretary of Commerce to justify not listing those populations as threatened species. In *Oregon Natural Resources Council v. Daley,*[101] the Secretary declined to list Oregon coast coho salmon on the grounds that a salmon conservation plan adopted by the State of Oregon promised to provide adequate regulatory protection for the fish. The court overturned this decision, however, noting that the ESA requires that regulatory mechanisms must actually be in place, not just promised, in order to justify relying on them as adequate existing regulatory mechanisms obviating the need for listing.[102]

IV. Conclusion

As the number of imperiled marine species grows, threatened by overexploitation, habitat destruction, invasive species, climate change, and other causes, the Endangered Species Act has become an increasingly vital tool in the effort to conserve these species. While there are many similarities in the ESA's application to marine and terrestrial species, there are also important differences. The smaller number of listed species, public ownership and management of the oceans, and the availability of technological solutions to reduce threats to marine life offer important opportunities to use the ESA's provisions to effectively conserve marine species. At the same time, overlapping statutory authorities for management of marine species, and the movement of those species between state, federal, and international waters, as well as freshwater, terrestrial, and marine environments, can create conflict and confusion. Navigating these shoals requires creativity on the part of federal agencies implementing the ESA as well as practitioners representing clients seeking to comply with, or enforce, the ESA if it is to be an effective tool in conserving the oceans on which life on earth depends.

Notes

1. RICHARD ELLIS, NO TURNING BACK: THE LIFE AND DEATH OF ANIMAL SPECIES 132–34 (2004).
2. *Id.* at xix.
3. As of July 2007, there were 61 marine species listed as threatened or endangered. *See* NMFS, Office of Protected Species, Species Under the Endangered Species Act, http://www.nmfs.noaa.gov/pr/species/esa_species.htm (last visited July 2, 2007).
4. *Id.* §§ 1531 *et seq.*
5. *Id.* §§ 1361 *et seq.*
6. *Id.* §§ 1801 *et seq.*
7. *See generally* Donald C. Baur & William Robert Irvin, *Overview, in* ENDANGERED SPECIES ACT: LAW, POLICY AND PERSPECTIVES xi–xix (Donald C. Baur & Wm. Robert Irvin eds., 2002). *See also* MICHAEL J. BEAN & MELANIE J. ROWLAND, THE EVOLUTION OF NATIONAL WILDLIFE LAW 193–282 (3rd ed. 1997).
8. Pub. L. No. 93-205, 87 Stat. 884 (1973) (current version at 16 U.S.C. §§ 1531–1543).
9. 16 U.S.C. § 1531(a)(1).
10. *Id.* § 1531(a)(2).
11. *Id.*
12. 16 U.S.C. § 1531(a)(4).
13. International Convention for the Northwest Atlantic Fisheries, Feb. 8, 1949, 1 U.S.T. 477.
14. International Convention Between the U.S., Can. and Japan for the High Seas Fisheries of the N. Pacific Ocean, U.S.-Can.-Japan, May 9, 1952, 1955 U.N.T.S. 80 (*replaced by* Convention for the Conservation of Anadromous Stocks in the North Pacific Ocean, Feb. 11, 1992, 1992 WL 602605 (Int'l Envtl. L.)).
15. 16 U.S.C. § 1531(b).
16. 437 U.S. 153 (1978).
17. *Id.* at 173.
18. *Id.* at 174. *But see* Nat'l Ass'n of Home Builders v. Defenders of Wildlife, 551 U.S.___, 2007 WL 1801745 (June 25, 2007) ("Today the Court turns its back on our decision in *Hill* and places a great number of endangered species in jeopardy. . . ." (Stevens, J., dissenting)).
19. 50 C.F.R. § 402.01(b).
20. *Id.* § 17.11.
21. 16 U.S.C. § 1533(a)(2).
22. *Id.* § 1533(b).
23. *Id.* § 1533(a).
24. *Id.* § 1532(5).
25. *Id.* § 1533(b)(2).
26. *Id.* § 1532(3).
27. *Id.* § 1533(f).
28. *See* U.S. Fish & Wildlife Serv., Endangered Species Program, http://www.fws.gov/endangered/recovery/index.html (last visited Feb. 8, 2006), and NMFS, Office of Protected Res., Recovery of Species Under the Endangered Species Act, http://www.nmfs.noaa.gov/pr/recovery/ (last visited Feb. 8, 2006).
29. John M. Volkman, *Recovery Planning, in* ENDANGERED SPECIES ACT: LAW, POLICY AND PERSPECTIVES, *supra* note 7, at 80–81.
30. 16 U.S.C. § 1535.
31. In Section 2 of the ESA, 16 U.S.C. § 1531(1)(5), Congress declared that "encouraging the States . . . through Federal financial assistance . . . to develop and maintain programs which meet national and international standards is a key to . . . better safeguarding . . . the Nation's heritage in fish, wildlife, and plants."

32. A list of states with cooperative agreements with NMFS, and the dates of those agreements, can be found at NMFS, Office of Protected Res., Cooperation with States: ESA Section 6 Program, http://www.nmfs.noaa.gov/pr/conservation/states/ (last visited Mar. 24, 2006).

33. *See* NMFS, Office of Protected Res., Protected Species Cooperative Conservation: ESA Section 6 Grants, http://www.nmfs.noaa.gov/pr/conservation/states/grant.htm (last visited Mar. 24, 2006).

34. 16 U.S.C. § 1538(a).

35. *Id.* § 1532(19).

36. 50 C.F.R. § 17.3. *See also* Babbitt v. Sweet Home Chapter of Cmties. for a Great Or., 515 U.S. 687 (1995).

37. 16 U.S.C. 1533(d).

38. *Compare* 50 C.F.R. § 17.31 *with* 50 C.F.R. §§ 223.101 *et seq.*

39. 16 U.S.C. § 1538(a).

40. *Id.* § 1536(a)(1).

41. *Id.* § 1536(a)(2). The obligation to consult does not apply to nondiscretionary actions by federal agencies. *See* Nat'l Ass'n of Home Builders et al. v. Defenders of Wildlife, 551 U.S.___, 2007 WL1801745 (June 25, 2007) (decision by U.S. Environmental Protection Agency to transfer Clean Water Act permitting authority to State of Arizona is nondiscretionary and, therefore, pursuant to 50 C.F.R. § 402.03, not subject to ESA Section 7's consultation requirement).

42. 50 C.F.R. § 402.12(j).

43. 50 C.F.R. § 402.14(a). If the affected species has been proposed for listing, but is not yet listed, an agency must informally confer with the Secretary on the proposed action's impacts on the candidate species. The results of this Section 7 conference are not binding on the action agency. 16 U.S.C. § 1536(a)(1)(A); 50 C.F.R. § 402.14(g)(4).

44. 50 C.F.R. § 402.14.

45. *See* Pyramid Lake Paiute Tribe of Indians v. U.S. Dep't of the Navy, 898 F.2d 1410, 1415 (9th Cir. 1990) (Navy cannot rely solely on Secretary's biological opinion to satisfy its substantive obligation under Section 7).

46. 16 U.S.C. § 1536(e)–(p).

47. *Id.* § 1539(a)(1)(A).

48. *Id.* § 1539(a)(1)(B)–(2)(C).

49. Conservation plans under Section 10(a)(1)(B) for marine species differ from habitat conservation plans for terrestrial species. Since habitat for marine species is generally publicly owned, setting aside, restoring, or creating habitat to mitigate adverse effects on marine habitat is generally not an option, as it is for terrestrial species found on private land.

50. 16 U.S.C. § 1539(e).

51. *Id.* § 1539(h).

52. *Id.* § 1539(j).

53. Section 10(j) was used to designate an experimental population of southern sea otters off the coast of California. A special law governing the translocation provided that formal Section 7 consultation would occur within a designated area where sea otters were translocated, while only informal consultation would be required in an area outside the translocation area, designated as an otter-free zone. *See* Mimi S. Wolok, *Experimenting with Experimental Populations, in* ENDANGERED SPECIES ACT: LAW, POLICY AND PERSPECTIVES, *supra* note 7, at 370–71 n.18.

54. 16 U.S.C. § 1540.

55. *Id.* § 1532(16).

56. Pacific salmon return only once to spawn. Atlantic salmon may return to their natal stream several times during their life to spawn. CHARLES H. W. FOSTER, YANKEE SALMON: THE ATLANTIC SALMON OF THE CONNECTICUT RIVER 4 (1991).

57. *See* NMFS, Nw. Reg'l Office, Chinook Salmon, http://www.nwr.noaa.gov/ESA-Salmon-Listings/Salmon-Populations/Chinook/ (last visited Feb. 17, 2006).

58. Policy on Applying the Definition of Species Under the Endangered Species Act to Pacific Salmon, 56 Fed. Reg. 58,612 (Nov. 20, 1991).

59. *Id.* at 58,618.

60. *See* Oregon Nat. Res. Council v. Daley, 6 F. Supp. 2d 1139 (D. Or. 1998) (NMFS's refusal to list Oregon coastal coho salmon based on promises of future conservation steps by the State of Oregon was arbitrary and capricious). *See also* Fed'n of Fly Fishers v. Daley, 131 F. Supp. 2d 1158 (N.D. Cal. 2000) (NMFS could not rely on promises of future conservation action by states as basis for not listing Klamath Mountains province ESU of steelhead as threatened).

61. 161 F. Supp. 2d 1154 (D. Or. 2001).

62. *Id.* 1162–63.

63. *Id.* 1163.

64. *See* Alsea Valley Alliance v. Dep't of Commerce, 358 F.3d 1181, 1183–84 (9th Cir. 2004). In June 2005, NMFS determined that listing of 16 ESUs of Pacific salmon continued to be appropriate and delayed decision on another 11 ESUs. 70 Fed. Reg. 37,160 (June 28, 2005). In January 2006, NMFS affirmed the previous listing of 10 of the remaining 11 ESUs. 71 Fed. Reg. 834 (Jan. 5, 2006). Only the proposed listing of Oregon coho salmon was withdrawn, based on a determination that conservation actions by the State of Oregon were sufficient to obviate the need for listing. 71 Fed. Reg. 3033 (Jan. 19, 2006).

65. ___ F. Supp. 2d ___, 2007 WL 1795036 (W.D. Wash. June 13, 2007).

66. The court in *Trout Unlimited* expressly recognized that its decision conflicted squarely with *Alsea Valley Alliance,* noting, "To the extent that this Court's order can be read to conflict with *Alsea,* perhaps this will have the happy result of instigating needed appellate review." 2007 WL 1795036.

67. 296 F. Supp. 2d 1223 (W.D. Wash. 2003).

68. *Id.* 1229–30. *See* 61 Fed. Reg. 4722, 4725 (Feb. 7, 1996).

69. 296 F. Supp. 2d 1223, 1235–36.

70. *Id.* 1239–40. The court remanded the decision to NMFS and the southern resident population of orcas was listed as an endangered species. 70 Fed. Reg. 69,903 (Nov. 18, 2005). NMFS subsequently designated more than 2,500 square miles of Puget Sound as critical habitat for the whales. 50 C.F.R. § 226.206.

71. 16 U.S.C. §§ 703 *et seq.*

72. *Id.* §§ 1361 *et seq.* For a full discussion of the MMPA, see Chapter 15.

73. *Id.* § 1371(b).

74. *Id.* § 1362.

75. 156 F. Supp. 2d 16 (D.D.C. 2001).

76. *Id.* at 20.

77. *Id.* at 20–21.

78. Despite the designation of the Cook Inlet beluga whale as depleted under the MMPA, the population has continued to decline. On April 20, 2007, NMFS proposed listing the Cook Inlet beluga whale as an endangered species. 72 Fed. Reg. 19,854 (Apr. 20, 2007).

79. NMFS, Nw. Reg'l Office, Critical Habitat Redesignations, http://www.nwr.noaa.gov/Salmon-Habitat/Critical-Habitat/Redesignations/Index.cfm (last visited Mar. 3, 2006).

80. NMFS, Office of Protected Res., Critical Habitat, http://www.nmfs.noaa.gov/pr/species/habitat.htm (last visited Mar. 3, 2006).

81. 50 C.F.R. § 17.95. Critical habitat for marine species may include terrestrial and freshwater habitat as well as marine habitat. *See, e.g.,* 50 C.F.R. §§ 226.201–226.214.

82. 16 U.S.C. § 1536(a)(2).

83. U.S. Const. amend. V. Despite the oft-repeated claim that ESA restrictions take private property, in fact only one case has resulted in a successful claim of a Fifth Amendment taking under the ESA. *See* Tulare Lake Basin Water Storage District v. United States, 49 Fed. Cl. 313 (2001).

84. Under the Magnuson-Stevens Fishery Conservation and Management Act (FCMA), "fish" are defined as "finfish, mollusks, crustaceans, and all other forms of marine and animal

plant life other than marine mammals and birds." 16 U.S.C. § 1802(12). Thus, threatened and endangered sea turtles as well as threatened Johnson's sea grass are treated as "fish" under the FCMA.

85. 16 U.S.C. §§ 1801 *et seq.* For a full discussion of the FCMA, see Chapter 9. For a discussion of the essential fish habitat provisions of the FCMA, see Donald C. Baur, Wm. Robert Irvin & Darren Misenko, *Putting "Protection" into Marine Protected Areas*, 28 Vt. L. Rev. 497, 546–49 (2004).

86. 16 U.S.C. § 1802(10).

87. 16 U.S.C. § 1853(a)(7).

88. 16 U.S.C. § 1855(b)(2).

89. 16 U.S.C. §§ 1855(b)(3),(b)(4).

90. 16 U.S.C. § 1533(b)(2). Areas may be excluded from critical habitat unless to do so would lead to the extinction of the species. *Id.*

91. Carl Safina, Song for the Blue Ocean xiv (1997).

92. 853 F.2d 322 (5th Cir. 1988). By contrast, conservationists were unsuccessful in challenging a technological fix, in the form of trucking and barging juvenile salmon around massive hydroelectric dams on the Columbia River, in order to save them from being killed in dam turbines or eaten by predatory fish in slow-moving reservoirs. *See* Am. Rivers v. NMFS, 109 F.3d 1484 (9th Cir. 1997).

93. *Id.* at 327–31.

94. 50 C.F.R. § 402.02.

95. 2002 WL 32095131 (C.D. Calif. 2002).

96. 50 C.F.R. § 402.02.

97. *Id. See also* Turtle Island Restoration Network v. NMFS, 340 F.3d 969, 974 (9th Cir. 2003). The question of whether federal agencies must consult on actions occurring on foreign soil remains unsettled, *see* Defenders of Wildlife v. Lujan, 504 U.S. 555 (1992), although as a practical matter, such consultations do not occur.

98. 127 F.3d 155 (1st Cir. 1997), *cert. denied*, 525 U.S. 830 (1998), and *cert. denied sub nom. Coates v. Strahan*, 525 U.S. 978 (1998).

99. 127 F.3d at 163–64.

100. *Id.* 164.

101. 6 F. Supp. 2d 1139 (D. Or. 1998).

102. *Id.* 1152.

chapter seventeen

Marine Protected Areas

Kim Diana Connolly
Jennifer L. Schorr
Darren Misenko

I. Introduction

Oceans cover more than seventy percent of the Earth's surface.[1] A variety of legal measures provide differing levels of protection to these marine ecosystems, but there is no single or coherent system to protect such ecosystems.[2] That being said, this chapter describes the basic legal requirements of the principal ocean, coastal, and land-based laws used to provide certain protections to areas of the marine environment.

Many of these laws involve the establishment of what have come to be called marine protected areas (MPAs).[3] It is important to note at the outset that there is no agreed-upon definition of what constitutes an MPA.[4] MPAs serve many different purposes, are established for a variety of reasons, and provide varying levels of protection and levels of use under a variety of management schemes. Stakeholders affected by or interested in MPAs have varying perceptions on their use and value.[5] Accordingly, the authorities covered here do not and cannot represent an exhaustive list of the laws governing all marine ecosystems but instead focus on the legal mechanisms currently playing the most significant roles. This area of ocean law and policy should, and likely will, be evolving in the near future.

A. Definition of Marine Ecosystem

Ecosystems have been defined as "integrated system[s] of living species, their habitat, and the processes that affect them."[6] Because ecosystems "have no apparent boundaries and lack the sort of clear objective or purpose that can be ascribed to other, more tractable, biological or ecological entities (e.g., cell, individual or population),"[7] they are difficult to define with precision.

Marine ecosystems are even harder to define, which is in part why they are so difficult to regulate. The National Research Council has described them as

> large, complex interactive systems in which organisms, habitats, and external influences act together to regulate both the abundance and distribution of species. Species interactions and the effects of variability in ocean climate on those interactions occur at spatial scales ranging from centimeters to hundreds of kilometers and on temporal scales ranging from minutes to decades. Human activities also act at various scales and may act selectively on certain components of an ecosystem (e.g., higher trophic levels), although such activities can have cascading effects throughout marine ecosystems. These disparate spatial and temporal scales make it difficult to measure the processes affecting marine ecosystems and to monitor ecosystem structure and functioning.[8]

One subset of marine ecosystems has received discrete attention: large marine ecosystems (LMEs). They are "natural regions of ocean space encompassing coastal waters from river basins and estuaries to the seaward boundary of continental shelves and the outer margins of coastal currents."[9] LMEs are relatively large regions of 200,000 square kilometers or more with their natural boundaries based on four ecological criteria: bathymetry, hydrography, productivity, and trophically related populations.[10]

B. Definition of Marine Protected Area and Marine Reserve

Despite numerous attempts to develop definitions for MPAs and marine reserves, confusion over the meaning of the term continues to exist.[11] The most commonly used definition of MPA is "an area of land and/or sea especially dedicated to the protection and maintenance of biological diversity and of natural and associated cultural resources, and managed through legal or other effective means."[12] In the United States, MPAs are defined as "any area of the marine environment that has been reserved by federal, state, territorial, tribal or local laws or regulations to provide lasting protection for part or all of the natural or cultural resources therein."[13] As described above, MPAs provide varying degrees of protection and permit or prohibit different uses. Most MPAs permit certain human recreational or commercial activities and some extractive activities such as fishing or shellfish harvesting, while many MPAs prohibit certain extractive activities such as oil and gas drilling.[14]

Marine reserves are a more restrictive type of MPA, and generally ban all or most extractive activities and other human disturbances. Fully protected marine reserves are defined as "areas of the ocean completely protected from all extractive activities" and explicitly prohibit the removal or disturbance of all living or nonliving marine resources, except as required for monitoring or research to evaluate reserve effectiveness.[15]

C. Benefits of MPAs and Marine Reserves

Experts increasingly recognize MPAs and particularly marine reserves as effective tools for protecting and conserving valuable ocean resources. Potential benefits of marine reserves include enhancing the reproductive potential of marine species, maintaining species diversity, preserving habitat, preserving ecosystem functions, and supporting fisheries production.[16] Designation of MPAs may also motivate coastal communities to increase conservation efforts by implementing pollution controls and stricter land-use policies in order to protect marine resources.[17]

Potential benefits of marine reserves include enhancing the reproductive potential of marine species, maintaining species diversity, preserving habitat, preserving ecosystem functions, and supporting fisheries production.

Marine reserves are recognized as providing greater benefits than multiuse MPAs, and recent studies have led to growing support of reserves by the scientific community. In 2001, 161 marine scientists signed the Scientific Consensus Statement on Marine Reserves (the Statement). The Statement included the following conclusions based on the review of the evidence surrounding the effectiveness of marine reserves: (1) reserve status results in long-lasting and often rapid increases in the abundance, diversity, and productivity of marine organisms; (2) such changes are due to decreased mortality, less habitat destruction, and indirect ecosystem effects; (3) reserves decrease the probability of extinction for marine species present within them; (4) even small reserves have these positive effects, but larger reserve size results in increased benefits; and (5) full marine reserve status—as opposed to multiuse MPA status—is critical to maximize the full range of benefits from MPAs.[18] A follow-up scientific consensus statement on ecosystem-based management was issued in 2005 and additional signatories have been added since.[19] Entitled "Scientific Consensus Statement on Marine Ecosystem-Based Management," the 2005 statement has the following executive summary: "The current state of the oceans requires immediate action and attention. Solutions based on an integrated ecosystem approach hold the greatest promise for delivering desired results. From a scientific perspective, we now know enough to improve dramatically the conservation and management of marine systems through the implementation of ecosystem-based approaches."[20]

Other recent studies have also found that marine reserves are effective in conserving habitat and supporting the recovery of overexploited species.[21] Marine scientists acknowledge that marine reserves have a significant positive impact on marine ecosystems, and that they often generate those benefits quickly. For example, a review of 112 independent measurements of eighty different marine reserves found that they contained higher average values of population density, biomass, average organism size, and species diversity within as early as one year after marine reserve status designation.[22] However, despite these benefits, currently less than one percent of MPAs in the United States are no-take marine reserves.[23]

MPAs, particularly larger MPAs, are often managed through the use of zoning regulations that permit different uses in different areas of the MPA. For example, an MPA may provide a core marine reserve where only nonconsumptive uses are permitted, with multiple use zones permitting a variety of uses surrounding the core marine reserve.[24] The primary objectives of zoning plans are typically to segregate conflicting human uses and to provide protection for critical or representative habitats, ecosystems, and ecological processes.[25]

II. The Current State of the Law

While most legal protections for marine ecosystems are provided by federal law, some coastal state laws and certain international protections may apply. The following sections provide an overview of some of these federal, state, and international protections.

A. Federal Coastal, Ocean, and Land-Based Legal Authorities

The following section describes the legal mechanisms used to designate and manage marine ecosystems under federal laws, including Executive Order 13,158, the National Marine Sanctuaries Act, Magnuson-Stevens Fishery Conservation and Management Act, Coastal Zone Management Act, Clean Water Act, Outer Continental Shelf Lands Act, Coastal Barrier Resources Act, National Park Service Organic Act, National Wildlife Refuge System Administration Act of 1966, and National Wildlife Refuge System Improvement Act of 1977.

1. Executive Order 13,158

In an effort to help protect natural and cultural resources within the marine environment, Executive Order 13,158 (the Order) was promulgated on May 26, 2000, to "strengthen the management, protection, and conservation of existing marine protected areas and establish new or expanded MPAs."[26] Furthermore, the Order was intended to "develop a scientifically based, comprehensive national system of MPAs representing diverse U.S. marine ecosystems, and the Nation's natural and cultural resources" and to "avoid causing harm to MPAs through federally conducted, approved, or funded activities."[27] To fulfill these objectives, the Departments of the Interior and Commerce (agencies) were charged with beginning a process for developing a national system of MPAs.[28]

The Order defines an MPA as "any area of the marine environment that has been reserved by Federal, State, territorial, tribal or local laws or regulations to provide lasting protection for part or all of the natural and cultural resources therein."[29] The Order further defines "marine environment" to mean "those areas of coastal and ocean waters, the Great Lakes and their connecting waters, and submerged lands thereunder, over which the United States exercises jurisdiction, consistent with international law."[30] In addition, there are other tools besides MPAs being used to conserve natural and cultural marine heritage pursuant to the Order. For example, the term

"Marine Managed Area" (MMA) denotes a broader set of areas under a spectrum of place-based management.[31] As stated by the federal advisory committee created to implement the Order, MPAs "allow populations of organisms within their borders to recover from damage, provide focal points for comprehensive protection from most major threats, provide reference sites for measuring the effectiveness of management and for separating the effects of natural phenomena from human effects, and raise awareness of natural and cultural resources by creating a sense of place."[32] To that end, the advisory committee recommended a national system of MPAs to "provide a variety of synergistic benefits beyond those realized by the current array of individual MPAs."[33]

The primary action-forcing provisions of the Order are found in Sections 3, 4, and 5. Section 3 calls for the establishment, protection, and management of MPAs. Section 4 calls for a national system of MPAs. Section 5 requires federal agencies to avoid harm to the resources protected by those MPAs identified under the Order. According to Section 3, agencies who have authority to establish or manage MPAs shall take actions aimed at providing greater protection to existing MPAs and establishing or recommending new MPAs. Under Section 4, the agencies involved with establishing and managing MPAs are called on to take actions to develop a national system of MPAs. In developing a national system, agencies are first tasked with managing an MPA Web site that includes a current list of MPAs and other information to assist government agencies and interested parties as they implement the Order.[34] The Order asks agencies to "coordinate and share information, tools, and strategies" as they work toward the common goal of enhancing and expanding protection of existing MPAs and establishing or recommending new sites for protection.[35]

The agencies have begun an administrative process for creating the official list of MPAs called for in the Order. The agencies' first step has been to compile an inventory of MMAs.[36] This MMA inventory represents an "initial pool of sites" that will be considered for inclusion on the MPA list.[37] The agencies found the definition of MPA in the Order too broad to provide criteria or characteristics to determine which sites should be included in the ultimate list of MPAs.[38] Because of this finding, the agencies proposed a list of specific criteria and data fields to be used in the development of the MMA inventory.[39]

As noted above, the Order called on the Department of Commerce (DOC) to develop a "Marine Protected Area Federal Advisory Committee" made up of "non-Federal scientists, resource managers, and other interested persons and organizations" to provide "expert advice and recommendations" in developing a national system of MPAs.[40] The Advisory Committee has been formed and consists of twenty-six non-federal members appointed by the Secretary of Commerce, in consultation with the Secretary of the Interior.[41] These members represent stakeholder groups such as scientists, resource managers, conservationists, and representatives from interest groups such as fishing, boating, and diving.[42] The Advisory Committee's advice and recommendations are based on materials and information developed by subcommittees and scientific working groups.[43]

The Order also directed the DOC to establish a "Marine Protected Area Center" to "develop a framework for a national system of MPAs, and to provide Federal, State, territorial, tribal, and local governments with the information, technologies, and strategies to support the system."[44] The MPA Center has been established and is managed by a small staff within the Ocean Services Office of the National Oceanic and Atmospheric Administration (NOAA) and is supported by the MPA Science Institute.[45] In addition to managing the Web site called for in the Order and developing the framework for the national system of MPAs, the responsibilities of the MPA Center include supporting the Advisory Committee; conducting outreach and education; and overseeing the collection of data for the MMA inventory.[46]

Section 4 of the Order charges the EPA with using its Clean Water Act authority to provide better protection to "beaches, coasts, and the marine environment from pollution."[47] The Order specifically calls on the EPA to propose new science-based regulations toward this end.[48] The Order states that "[s]uch regulations may include the identification of areas that warrant additional pollution protections and the enhancement of marine water quality standards."[49]

Rounding out the primary action provisions, Section 5 establishes agency responsibilities to "avoid harm" to areas identified by the list of MPAs called for in Section 4.[50] Under this section, federal agencies must first identify actions that affect the natural or cultural resources protected by an MPA.[51] Federal agencies taking actions that affect MPAs must then, "[t]o the extent permitted by law and to the maximum extent practicable . . . avoid harm to the natural and cultural resources that are protected by an MPA."[52] In early 2008, the Federal Advisory Committee published an updated report entitled "Toward a National System of Marine Protected Areas: A Report by the MPA Federal Advisory Committee, Recommendations from 2006–2007."[53] The Committee will continue its work throughout 2008 and beyond.

2. National Marine Sanctuaries Act

The most prominent federal authority for establishing and protecting MPAs is the National Marine Sanctuaries Program (NMSP) established by the National Marine Sanctuaries Act (NMSA), enacted in 1972.[54] The NMSP represents, in part, a framework for protecting marine areas of special national, and sometimes international, significance.[55] The general purpose of the NMSP is to create a system for identifying and designating special marine areas as national marine sanctuaries, and managing and protecting such areas for the long-term benefit and enjoyment of the public.[56] There are currently thirteen national marine sanctuaries encompassing approximately 18,000 square miles of ocean and coastal area, managed to accommodate multiple uses.[57]

> **There are currently thirteen national marine sanctuaries encompassing approximately 18,000 square miles of ocean and coastal area, managed to accommodate multiple uses.**

The Secretary of Commerce, with presidential approval, may designate as a national marine sanctuary "any discrete area of the marine environment" having "special national significance."[58] An act of Congress may also be used to designate such areas.[59] When making determinations and findings regarding a potential sanctuary designation, the Secretary must consult with interested parties and Congress may reject a designation or any of its terms by adopting a concurrent resolution during a forty-five day review period.[60] Furthermore, if any portion of the proposed sanctuary is within state waters, the governor of the state may declare the designation or any of its parts unacceptable as applied to state waters.[61]

Designation of a national marine sanctuary is a complex and lengthy process that requires extensive environmental impact studies, consideration of multiple factors, and public comment.[62] The NMSA calls for the Secretary of Commerce to consult with other federal and state agencies and officials; appropriate officials of a Regional Fishery Management Council that may be affected by the proposed designation, and other "interested persons."[63] Prior to designating a national marine sanctuary, a draft environmental impact statement is prepared by NOAA, which permits for public comment on the required draft management plan, draft regulations, and the proposed designation.[64] In addition, a public hearing is required in the area(s) that will be most affected by the designation.[65]

The NMSA does not proscribe use of a designated area. The legislative history of the NMSA suggests that Congress intended to create a system to protect significant marine areas, not by prohibiting all uses, but rather by recognizing the "values of the site and manag[ing] compatible human uses."[66] The NMSA does prohibit certain activities within any designated national marine sanctuary. First, it is unlawful to "destroy, cause the loss of, or injure any sanctuary resource managed under law or regulations for that sanctuary."[67] Likewise, it is unlawful to "possess, sell, offer for sale, purchase, import, export, deliver, carry, transport, or ship by any means any sanctuary resource taken in violation of this section."[68] Violators of these provisions are liable for the sum of the response costs and damages resulting from any violation(s), plus interest.[69]

Under the NMSA, the Department of Commerce may allow certain activities within the sanctuaries through special use permits. Special use permits may be issued if it is determined that the authorization is necessary "to establish conditions of access to and use of any sanctuary resource" or "to promote public use and understanding of a sanctuary resource."[70] Each permit is limited by certain terms established by the NMSA.[71] For example, permitted activities must be "compatible with the purposes for which the sanctuary is designated and with protection of sanctuary resources,"[72] and they must be "carried out . . . in a manner that does not destroy, cause the loss of, or injure sanctuary resources."[73] The NMSA also establishes a five-year time limit for all permitted activities unless the Secretary renews the authorization for such activities.[74] Violation of a permit term or condition may result in the permit being revoked or suspended with the possible imposition of a civil penalty.[75]

The Administrator of NOAA has been delegated the authority to implement the NMSA.[76] The Administrator in turn has promulgated regulations regarding the general implementation of the NMSP, as well as site-specific regulations dealing with each individual sanctuary.[77]

The first NMSA regulation that applies generally to all national marine sanctuaries requires implementation of a sanctuary management plan and other regulations to carry out activities such as surveillance, enforcement, research, monitoring, evaluation, and education.[78] The regulations also generally allow activities such as fishing, boating, diving, research, and education within sanctuaries unless prohibited or regulated by the sanctuary-specific regulations or specific restrictions imposed by other valid authorities.[79] If leases, permits, licenses, or rights of use or access existed on the date of the sanctuary's designation, the regulations direct that they are to be upheld.[80] The regulations also allow activities that would be generally prohibited, so long as they comply with a national marine sanctuary permit, or other federal, state, or local leases, permits, licenses, or other authorizations issued after the designation date of the sanctuary.[81]

Under NMSA, NOAA has also promulgated sanctuary-specific regulations to protect resource values of particular ecosystems. Each sanctuary is responsible for its own independent zoning and each is operated under its own designation document, so that the management and zoning of each sanctuary depends on the type of ecosystem and the type(s) of human activities in that individual sanctuary.[82] Some specific regulations are commonly applied in many of the sanctuaries, while others are tailored to protect the particular resources found in individual sanctuaries. For example, many of the sanctuary-specific regulations prohibit activities that alter the seabed[83] or are related to developing oil, gas, or minerals.[84] Other common regulations prohibit the removal or injury of historical resources,[85] or the taking of any marine mammal, sea turtle, or seabird.[86] Less common regulations may prohibit activities such as operating personal watercraft[87] or vessels carrying cargo.[88] Some sanctuary-specific regulations prohibit activities such as attracting white sharks,[89] diving of any type,[90] coming within one hundred yards of a humpback whale,[91] or removing, injuring, or possessing coral or live rock.[92]

3. Magnuson-Stevens Fishery Conservation and Management Act

Under the Magnuson-Stevens Fishery Conservation and Management Act (Magnuson-Stevens Act),[93] eight regional fishery management councils[94] prepare fishery management plans (FMPs) to establish time and area closures, where fishing is prohibited or limited to certain size vessels or certain gear types.[95] Plans may also limit or require the use of certain types of vessels for fishing.[96] These provisions may provide significant protection for marine habitats. For example, bottom trawling, which can be destructive to rock and reef habitats used for spawning or feeding areas, may be prohibited in certain areas.[97]

The 1996 amendments to the Magnuson-Stevens Act provided for the first time direct protection for marine habitat through the requirement that fishery management plans "describe and identify essential fish habitat" (EFH), minimize adverse effects on EFH from fishing, and identify other actions to encourage the conservation and enhancement of EFH.[98] EFH is defined as "those waters and substrate necessary to fish for spawning, breeding, feeding or growth to maturity."[99] Once EFH has been designated, each federal agency must consult with the Secretary of Commerce, acting through the National Marine Fisheries Service, with respect to any action authorized, funded, or undertaken that may adversely affect EFH.[100] Fishery management councils may provide comments on such actions to the Secretary of Commerce and the agency proposing the action.[101] If the Secretary determines that an action would adversely affect EFH, the Secretary will provide EFH conservation recommendations to the agency proposing the action.[102] The agency must respond within thirty days, proposing measures to avoid, mitigate, or offset adverse impacts to EFH, or explaining why it will not follow the Secretary's recommendations.[103] Thus, in contrast to critical habitat under the Endangered Species Act (ESA), there is no requirement that federal agencies ensure that their actions will not harm EFH. Agencies must only consider the recommendations of the Secretary for avoiding or mitigating such harm.

Habitat areas of particular concern (HAPC) are subsets of EFH. FMPs identify specific types or areas of habitat within EFH as HAPCs. HAPCs are based on one or more of the following considerations:

1. The importance of the ecological function provided by the habitat.
2. The extent to which the habitat is sensitive to human-induced environmental degradation.
3. Whether, and to what extent, development activities are, or will be, stressing the habitat type.
4. The rarity of the habitat type.[104]

FMPs have been used, although not frequently, to establish fully protected zones or marine reserves. For example, in 2006 the FMP for Groundfish of the Bering Sea and Aleutian Islands Management Area was amended to designate HAPCs and close fishing in Alaska seamount habitat protection areas and Aleutian Island coral habitat protection areas.[105] The Pacific Fishery Management Council (PFMC) has also used marine reserves in order to address the continuing decline of the groundfish fishery in their region.[106] The PFMC plan defines marine reserves as "[z]oning that precludes fishing activity on some or all species to protect critical habitat, rebuild stocks (long term, but not necessarily permanent closure), provide insurance against overfishing, or enhance fishery yield."[107] The PFMC has established two marine reserves and initiated the process for considering additional reserves in their region.[108] The existing marine reserves cover an area of 4,700 square miles and prohibit fishing for the groundfish species listed under the FMP.[109]

The South Atlantic Fishery Management Council (SAFMC) has also developed a plan for MPAs (Amendment 14). The SAFMC plan allows for the use of MPAs to prohibit harvest of certain long-lived deepwater snapper grouper species.[110] Deepwater species are vulnerable to overfishing because of their complex life histories and the depths at which these fish are found; thus all of the MPA candidate sites prohibit fishing for these deepwater species, while at the same time allowing trolling for pelagics such as tuna, dolphin and sailfish.[111] The SAFMC approved Amendment 14 in March 2007; on approval by the Secretary, Amendment 14 will create a series of eight deepwater MPAs off the coasts of Florida, Georgia, and the Carolinas.[112]

4. Coastal Zone Management Act of 1972

The Coastal Zone Management Act of 1972 (CZMA)[113] provides additional mechanisms related to the protection of coastal and marine resources. First, the CZMA establishes a coastal zone management program to provide incentives for eligible states and territories to implement coastal management plans that protect coastal resources. As part of this incentive system, the Act makes federal grants available for those states and territories that implement coastal management programs adhering to specific guidelines set forth by the Act.[114]

In addition to the federal grants providing support for states to develop and implement coastal management programs, Section 309 of the CZMA also makes federal grants available for state programs aimed at developing greater protections for coastal and ocean resources.[115] These grants, known as coastal zone enhancement grants, are available for state programs designed to provide increased protection to both land-based and marine resources.[116] For instance, with regard to land-based resources, Section 309 allocates federal assistance to state programs that seek to address the impacts of coastal growth and development.[117] This section also provides federal grants for state programs that plan "for the use of ocean resources."[118]

The federal consistency provision under Section 307 of the CZMA is additional incentive for states to participate in the coastal management program and protect coastal and marine areas within their borders. Under this provision, federal actions within or affecting a state's coastal uses or resources must be "consistent to the maximum extent practicable" with the federally approved state coastal management program.[119] This requirement provides an incentive by assuring the states that federal activities impacting their coastal resources will not be allowed unless they are consistent with the state management plan.

The CZMA contains a second mechanism to research and protect certain coastal estuarine areas by establishing a system of reserves. This system, known as the National Estuarine Research Reserve System (NERRS), encourages the protection and study of estuarine areas through a network of individual national estuarine reserves.[120] Upon designation of a national estuarine reserve, the federal government assists local communities and regional groups in managing the reserve and conducting research.[121] The federal government also assists local communities in addressing "issues such as non-point source pollution, habitat restoration, and invasive species."[122] There are currently twenty-seven individual national estuarine reserves covering more than 1.3 million acres of estuarine habitat.[123]

Further, Section 315 of the CZMA gives the Secretary of Commerce (Secretary) the authority to designate national estuarine reserves that coastal state governors nominate for designation.[124] One requirement of particular relevance is that the law of the nominating coastal state must provide "long-term protection for reserve resources to ensure a stable environment for research."[125]

Upon designation of a national estuarine reserve, the financial assistance provision of Section 315 authorizes the Secretary to provide federal grants to the nominating coastal state for acquiring "lands and waters . . . as are necessary to ensure the appropriate long-term management" of the national estuarine reserve.[126] The Act further requires the Secretary to provide financial assistance for operating or managing the reserve, constructing facilities, or conducting educational, research, or monitoring activities.[127] Although Section 315 of the CZMA fails to include any specific protective provisions, the availability of federal grants under NERRS is an incentive for coastal states to enact laws that protect estuarine areas.

5. Antiquities Act

The Antiquities Act authorizes the President, in his or her discretion, to declare historic landmarks, historic and prehistoric structures, and other objects of historic or scientific interest situated on lands owned or controlled by the United States national monuments.[128] The lands reserved as national monuments must be "confined to the smallest area compatible with the proper care and management of the objects to be protected."[129] Designation as a national monument under the Antiquities Act means that the lengthy designation process required for a national marine sanctuary designated under the NMSA, including the requirements for an environmental impact study and public comment, are not required.

On June 15, 2006 President George W. Bush issued a proclamation using the Antiquities Act establishing what would come to be called the Papahānaumokuākea Marine National Monument[130] in Hawaii.[131] The single largest conservation area in the United States, the Papahānaumokuākea Marine National Monument is also the largest marine conservation area in the world.[132] It is home to more than 7,000 marine species, more than half of which are native to Hawaii. It is also a center of cultural significance for the Hawaiian people.[133] The monument encompasses close to 140,000 square miles, including ten islands and atolls spanning approximately 1,400 miles in length.[134]

The Papahānaumokuākea Marine National Monument is managed under a fairly restrictive regime, and extractive activities are either prohibited or regulated by permitting procedures. Activities that are prohibited in this monument include exploring for or producing oil, gas, or minerals; using or attempting to use poisons, explosives, or electrical charges in the harvest or collection of resources; introducing or otherwise releasing introduced species; and vessel anchoring on any living or dead coral.[135] Regulated activities include removing or moving any living or nonliving monument resource, vessel activities and discharge from vessels, swimming or snorkeling in certain areas, and possessing fishing gear.[136]

Under the proclamation the Secretary of Commerce, through NOAA, has primary responsibility for managing marine areas in consultation with the Secretary of the

Interior. The Secretary of the Interior, through the Fish and Wildlife Service, has sole responsibility for managing certain terrestrial areas of the national monument.[137]

6. Clean Water Act

The Federal Water Pollution Control Act of 1972, commonly known as the Clean Water Act (CWA),[138] also provides legal authority for establishing MPAs. One mechanism is the National Estuary Program (NEP) established by Section 320 of the CWA.[139] Section 320 provides for states to designate estuarine areas within their borders and calls for the development of a management plan for restoration and protection of such areas.[140] This section directs the Environmental Protection Agency (EPA) to work collectively with state and local entities to develop the management plans.[141] This section also authorizes the EPA to provide financial assistance for developing these management plans.[142] The protective measures provided under Section 320 include assessing impacts on estuarine areas and developing plans to address pollution, maintain water quality, and protect designated uses.[143] A collective group of federal, state, and local government officials along with members of affected industries, educational institutions, and members of the public carry out these protective measures.[144] There are currently twenty-eight estuarine areas designated under the NEP.[145]

Another CWA mechanism involves Section 403, the Ocean Discharge Criteria title, which protects coastal and ocean areas by requiring a permit for certain discharges into all ocean waters.[146] This section requires the EPA to promulgate regulations for implementing the permit process and criteria for ocean discharges.[147] EPA is currently undergoing a proposed rulemaking process to revise its regulations in response to the mandate of Executive Order 13,158. This Order requires the EPA to ensure the protection of MPAs through methods including the "identification of areas that warrant additional pollution protections."[148]

In response to this mandate, the EPA has proposed to define MPAs, known as "Special Ocean Sites," as "specific areas within ocean waters that have significant outstanding ecological, environmental, recreational, scientific, or esthetic value."[149] The EPA proposes to designate four Special Ocean Sites and to establish a process for designating additional sites.[150] In identifying and establishing areas for designation, the proposed regulations allow petitioning parties to identify sites.[151] However, the EPA will likely still have to follow a rulemaking process before any proposed sites can be considered for designation. The proposed process for managing Special Ocean Sites prohibits new discharges within the area.[152] In addition, existing permits will be revoked if they increase pollutant loadings beyond a certain limit.[153]

7. Outer Continental Shelf Lands Act

In 1953, Congress passed the Outer Continental Shelf Lands Act (OCSLA) to establish a system for managing the development of oil and gas resources in the outer continental shelf (OCS).[154] In general, OCSLA established federal jurisdiction of submerged lands of the OCS seaward of state territorial waters.[155] Furthermore, OCSLA provided the Secretary of the Interior with the authority to grant leases for the development of energy resources within the OCS.[156]

OCSLA includes specific provisions related to the protection of ocean areas. For example, the Secretary of the Interior must balance the economic benefits and environmental impacts of developing various regions of the OCS.[157] The Secretary must also consider "environmental sensitivity and marine productivity" of areas when determining whether such areas will be open for development.[158] Under this provision, the Secretary may set aside particular areas or regions of the OCS where leasing is not allowed, thereby protecting such areas from development.

Another provision of OCSLA gives the Secretary the authority to ensure that the development of the OCS is conducted in an environmentally sound manner by allowing the cancellation or suspension of leases where activities threaten the marine, coastal, or human environment or otherwise damage fish and aquatic life.[159] In effect, these OCSLA powers can create de facto MPAs protected from oil and gas activities.

8. Coastal Barrier Resources Act

Congress enacted the Coastal Barrier Resources Act (CBRA) in 1982 to protect undeveloped coastal barriers and related areas.[160] Congress sought to protect coastal barriers because they provide important habitat for marine and coastal wildlife,[161] as well as buffers against storms.[162] The main objectives of the CBRA are to minimize the loss of human life, decrease wasteful expenditures of federal funds, and prevent damage to fish, wildlife, and other natural resources.[163]

In order to protect undeveloped coastal barriers, the CBRA eliminates federal financial assistance for developing coastal barrier areas that are a part of the Coastal Barrier Resources System as designated by the Act.[164] Under this provision, no new federal financial assistance may be used to support actions within designated areas, including such actions as the construction or purchase of any structure, road, airport, boat landing, bridge, or the nonemergency stabilization of shoreline areas.[165] The CBRA contains certain limited exceptions where federal funding may be available for certain projects. For example, one provision funds facilities for the development of energy resources, or certain road and navigational channel maintenance.[166] Projects involving the study, management, and protection of fish and wildlife resources and habitats may also receive funding along with projects involving nonstructural restoration for purposes of shoreline stabilization.[167]

9. National Park Service Organic Act

a. General Legal Authority

The centerpiece of the legal framework governing the Park System is the so-called "National Park Service Organic Act."[168] Enacted in 1916 and amended on several occasions, the Organic Act created the National Park Service (NPS), defined the resource management goals to be met by that agency, and established some of the management tools to be used.

The unifying theme of NPS's legal mandate, as defined by Section 1 of the Organic Act, is to "promote and regulate the use" of the Park System so as to "conserve the scenery and the natural and historic objects and the wild life therein and to provide for the enjoyment of the same in such manner and by such means as will leave them unimpaired for the enjoyment of future generations."[169] The legislative history of Section 1 and a long line of administrative and congressional interpretations make it clear that resource protection is the foremost goal to be promoted by NPS; however, public use of NPS-administered areas should be consistent with that goal.

In formulating the Section 1 mandate, Congress in 1916 explained that, unlike national forests, which are established to promote multiple use values, units of the Park System are intended to address "the question of the preservation of nature as it exists."[170] Congress reiterated this theme in 1980 when, in passing the Alaska National Interest Lands Conservation Act (ANILCA),[171] it declared that the guiding principle for NPS management actions are to "strive to maintain the natural abundance, behavior, diversity, and ecological integrity of native animals as part of their ecosystem."[172]

Section 1a-1 of the Organic Act provides that the "promotion and regulation" of park system units should be guided by "the purpose established by section 1."[173] Section 1a-1 further provides that "[t]he authorization of activities . . . shall not be exercised in derogation of the values and purposes" set forth in Section 1 and the statutory provisions governing a given unit of the System "except as may have been or shall be directly and specifically provided by Congress."[174] Section 1c of the Organic Act reinforces this formula by applying Section 1 and other provisions of the Organic Act to all Park System units, regardless of the classification of the area (e.g., park, monument, recreation area, lakeshore). It also directs that each unit shall be administered "in accordance with the provisions of any statute made specifically applicable to that area."[175]

Thus, to determine what activities are permissible in a particular NPS unit, it is necessary to look to Section 1 and the other provisions of the Organic Act that govern all areas, as well as to the laws applicable to each area individually. If permission to conduct an activity is not found in either of these authorities, and it would be contrary to the Section 1 mandate or the values and purposes of the unit, then that action is presumed to be prohibited.

b. Unit-Specific Enabling Authorities

The statutory provisions individually applicable to each Park System area define permissible uses of the unit, while also helping to define the activities that are prohibited generally in the Park System.

Congress's express authorization of certain consumptive-use activities in some units creates a presumption that such activities are prohibited in all other units where such authorization does not exist. For example, because Congress gave express approval to commercial fishing in certain areas,[176] the absence of such an authorization in other areas is understood to mean that commercial fishing is "in derogation" of unit-specific purposes and values and hence prohibited in such areas.[177] Authorizations for consumptive uses of park resources are rare exceptions to the rule that Park System units are to be administered to allow nature to follow its course without human manipulation, interference, or exploitation.

Generally, national parks and monuments are given the strongest protection since their purposes and values call for adherence to a stringent preservation mandate. National recreation areas, lakeshores, and seashores are established, in most instances, with a greater emphasis on public use and recreation. Hence, the enabling legislation for these areas usually provides more management flexibility and allows for a wider range of activities.

Like marine sanctuaries under the NMSA, the Secretary of the Interior supplements Park System statutory requirements with regulations promulgated under the authority of Section 3 of the Organic Act.[178] The regulations set forth general requirements applicable to all units of the System,[179] and area-specific regulations that are tailored to the unique resource management needs of particular units.[180] In addition, there are regulations for particular types of activities, such as boating and water use activities,[181] motor vehicle use,[182] rights-of-way,[183] and others.[184] Special regulations apply to Park System units in Alaska.[185]

10. National Wildlife Refuge System

More than six decades after the designation of the first national wildlife refuge (Pelican Island, 1903), a uniform set of management principles to govern the Refuge System was created under the National Wildlife Refuge System Administration Act of 1966 (Refuge Administration Act).[186] The Refuge Administration Act, which serves as an organic act for the National Wildlife Refuge System, has itself undergone a series of amendments with the most recent changes occurring under the National Wildlife Refuge System Improvement Act of 1997 (Refuge Improvement Act).[187]

a. National Wildlife Refuge System Administration Act of 1966

The Refuge Administration Act authorizes the Secretary of the Interior by regulation to "permit the use of any area within the System for any purpose, including but not limited to hunting, fishing, public recreation and accommodations, and access whenever he determines that such uses are compatible with the major purposes for which such areas were established."[188] The U.S. Fish and Wildlife Service (FWS) administers all units of the Refuge System.[189] One court construed this delegation as imposing a duty to manage the refuge "by regulating human access in order to conserve the entire spectrum of wildlife" found there.[190]

Unlike the National Park System, where units are designated by federal statutes,[191] national wildlife refuges are established by an act of Congress, presidential or secretarial order,[192] donation from private parties, or transfer from other agencies.[193] Some of these authorities, such as acts of Congress, provide clearly stated purposes against which the compatibility standard can be measured.[194] In the case of areas incorporated through transfer or donation, however, frequently there is no statement of purpose for the area, and it is necessary to look to the transferring statute to determine what activities are compatible. Acquisition pursuant to the ESA, for example, would dictate that activities occurring on the refuge must be consistent with the goal of conserving the endangered or threatened species found there.[195]

b. National Wildlife Refuge System Improvement Act of 1997

The National Wildlife Refuge System Improvement Act of 1997[196] provides further guidance regarding how the overall refuge system should be managed. For example, the 1997 amendments established a new process for determining compatible uses of refuges.[197] These amendments also adopted an overall mission of the Refuge System to conserve fish, wildlife, plants, and their habitats.[198] Furthermore, the amendments dictate that all human uses of the refuge must be compatible with this overall mission.[199] The highest-priority human uses, known as "wildlife-dependent recreational uses," include consumptive uses such as hunting and fishing, as well as nonconsumptive uses such as wildlife observation and photography.[200] In managing such uses, FWS is required to issue a "comprehensive conservation plan," which includes a determination of the compatibility of wildlife-dependent recreational uses.[201]

While the purposes of protecting and enhancing wildlife and wildlife habitat have primacy, FWS allows a wide variety of secondary uses ranging from recreational activities, such as boating, hiking, and hunting, to commercial uses, such as timber harvesting and oil and gas production. Refuge managers have considerable discretion in making compatibility determinations.

c. Other Statutes Defining Permissible Uses of Refuge System Lands

Several statutes define activities that are permissible on Refuge System lands, provided that such activities satisfy the compatibility test. The Refuge Recreation Act, for example, authorizes the Secretary to allow public recreation as a secondary use, but only "to the extent that is practicable and not inconsistent with . . . the primary objectives for which each particular area is established."[202]

While not authorizing activities, the Refuge Revenue Sharing Act indicates which secondary uses may be permissible by requiring that "net receipts" resulting from those activities be shared with the counties in which the refuge is located.[203] Funds come "from the sale or other disposition of animals, . . . timber, hay, grass, or other products of the soil, minerals, shells, sands, or gravel" from refuge lands.[204]

Clearly defined statements of purposes and authorizations for permissible activities in Alaska refuges are set forth in ANILCA.[205] Primary purposes of Alaska refuges are conserving the natural abundance and diversity of fish and wildlife populations and their habitats, and protecting refuge water resources and water quality.[206] In addition to these general purposes, individual refuges in Alaska have their own purposes.[207]

Pursuant to authority granted by the Refuge Administration Act and the Refuge Recreation Act, FWS has promulgated regulations to govern the Refuge Systems. These regulations include public use and access restrictions for the entire Refuge System,[208] as well as for certain refuges.[209] They spell out prohibited acts,[210] such as harming wildlife.[211] The regulations govern the issuance of rights-of-way,[212] mineral activities,[213] range and wildlife management,[214] hunting,[215] and sport fishing.[216] There are special regulations for refuges in Alaska.[217]

B. State Requirements

Many states have established legal mechanisms governing MPAs within their waters. All such laws are, however, limited by the reach of state jurisdiction over coastal and ocean waters.[218] A few examples of such laws are provided below.

1. California Marine Life Protection Act

One example of a law that provides a legal mechanism for managing a state's system of MPAs is California's Marine Life Protection Act (MLPA).[219] The MLPA requires the California Department of Fish and Game (CDFG) to take certain steps to more effectively manage the existing MPAs in California waters. In developing a more effective management scheme for MPAs, CDFG must consider no-take reserves or "marine life reserves" as an essential component of a more effective MPA system.[220]

The MLPA was introduced to more effectively protect California's marine life, habitat, and ecosystems. The definition of MPAs provided in the MLPA recognizes a broad array of areas subject to varying degrees of protection. Included within this definition are areas that allow commercial and recreational activities, such as fishing for certain species and kelp harvesting.[221] The most restrictive subset of MPAs, recognized by the MLPA, is the marine life reserve, which prohibits "all extractive activities, including the taking of marine species, and . . . other activities that upset the natural ecological functions of the area."[222] The MLPA further provides such areas shall "to the extent feasible . . . be open to the public for managed enjoyment and study" while also being "maintained to the extent practicable in an undisturbed and unpolluted state."[223]

In order to increase the coherence and effectiveness of California's MPA system, the MLPA requires the California Fish and Game Commission (the Commission) to take two measures aimed at improving the design and management of the MPA system. First, the Commission must adopt a "Marine Life Protection Program," which establishes a framework for managing California's MPA system.[224] The program must comply with an established set of goals that focus on "conservation of biological diversity and health of marine ecosystems; recovery of wildlife populations; improving recreational and educational opportunities consistent with biodiversity conservation; protection of representative and unique habitats for their intrinsic value; ensuring that MPAs have defined objectives, effective management, and enforcement; are designed on sound science; and are managed, to the extent possible, as a network."[225] The program must also include certain elements such as (1) an improved marine life reserve component; (2) specific objectives, and management and enforcement measures; and (3) provisions for monitoring, research, evaluation, and educating the public.[226] Finally, the program must include the involvement of interested parties in a process for "the establishment, modification, or abolishment of existing MPAs or new MPAs."[227] The above goals and elements are the framework for modifying California's MPA system to increase its coherence and effectiveness.

Second, the MLPA requires the Commission to adopt a "master plan" to guide the establishment and implementation of the Marine Life Protection Program.[228] The master plan provides guidance for "decisions regarding the siting of new MPAs and major modifications of existing MPAs."[229] The CDFG is charged with developing the master plan, which must be based on the "best readily available science" and in accordance with the advice and assistance of a "master plan team."[230] The master plan team must contain some members with expertise in marine life protection, including knowledge about the use of protected areas as a marine ecosystem management tool.[231] In carrying out the master plan, the CDFG must consider relevant information from local communities, along with comments and advice from other interested parties.[232] The master plan, issued in 2007, sets forth the framework for the development of alternative proposals of MPAs statewide and includes specific recommendations for MPAs in each region.[233]

On August 16, 2006, the California Fish and Game Commission took its first major step to implement the MLPA by voting to designate a comprehensive network of marine reserves.[234] The network encompasses twenty-nine individual MPAs along California's central coast from Santa Barbara north to Santa Cruz, encompassing approximately 204 square miles.[235] The network encompasses different central coast habitats including kelp forests, nearshore reefs, and submarine canyons. The Commission adopted regulations to create the MPAs in April 2007, adopting all twenty-nine MPAs including eighty-five square miles designated as no-take state marine reserves.[236]

2. Massachusetts Ocean and Sanctuaries Act

Another example of a state legal mechanism governing MPAs is the Massachusetts Ocean Sanctuaries Act (MOSA)[237] and the Ocean Sanctuaries regulations administered by the Massachusetts Department of Environmental Management (DEM).[238]

Currently, there are five areas in Massachusetts waters designated as ocean sanctuaries including Cape Cod, Cape Cod Bay, Cape and Islands, North Shore, and South Essex.[239] The primary goal of the MOSA is to prohibit activities that may significantly alter or endanger the ecology or appearance of the ocean, seabed, or subsoil of areas designated as ocean sanctuaries.[240] To achieve this goal, the MOSA prohibits (1) building structures on or under the seabed; (2) construction or operation of offshore or floating electrical generating stations; drilling or removal of sand, gravel (except of the purposes of beach nourishment), other minerals, gases, or oils; (3) dumping or discharge of commercial, municipal, domestic or industrial wastes; (4) commercial advertising; and (5) incineration of solid waste or refuse on vessels within sanctuary boundaries.[241] These prohibitions may be waived if the proposed project or activity is found to have a "public necessity and convenience."[242]

The regulatory body under the MOSA, the DEM, does not issue any licenses or permits but acts through the regulatory process of other agencies.[243] For example, the DEM comments on Massachusetts Environmental Policy Act (MEPA) filings by other Massachusetts agencies and on Massachusetts Department of Environmental Protection Chapter 91 license applications. Proposals that are below MEPA thresholds are presumed to comply with the Ocean Sanctuaries Act, and also a project that receives a Chapter 91 License is likewise presumed to comply with the Ocean Sanctuaries Act.

C. International

1. United Nations Convention on the Law of the Sea

The first United Nations Conference on the Law of the Sea was held in Geneva in 1958 following a draft report from the International Law Commission related to the high sea and territorial seas.[244] Four conventions were adopted as a result of the conference: the Convention on the Territorial Sea and the Contiguous Zone; the Convention on High Seas; the Convention on the Continental Shelf; and the Convention on Fishing and Conservation of the Living Resources of the High Seas.[245] The United States became a party to all four of the conventions in 1961.[246] A second conference was held in 1960 to address the failure by earlier conferences to determine the breadth of the territorial sea, an effort that was not successful. The third Conference began in 1973, prompted by an effort to analyze issues related to the deep sea bed.[247] Following several years of work and a series of negotiating texts, the U.N. Convention on the Law of the Sea (UNCLOS) was adopted on April 30, 1982, and was opened for signature for two years. UNCLOS entered into force on November 16, 1994, following the sixtieth ratification.[248] Currently 143 parties have joined the Convention.[249]

UNCLOS has been described as having a substantive range broader than any other lawmaking treaty.[250] It is meant to provide a framework for international ocean law and provide universal standards for all States. To further this goal, under Article 309 reservations or exception by party States are not permitted except where expressly allowed.

The United States, along with several other developed countries, did not sign UNCLOS in 1982.[251] The United States objected primarily to the provisions in Part XI regarding a regime for the deep sea bed. In 1994 President Clinton sent UNCLOS to the Senate requesting advice and consent, but the Senate did not pursue accession.[252] No Administration since has opposed Senate advice and counsel or accession to the treaty.[253] The Bush Administration has stated that it is "strongly committed to U.S.

The United States did not sign UNCLOS, objecting primarily to the provisions regarding a regime for the deep sea bed.

accession to the UN Convention on the Law of the Sea" but there has been no recent activity towards accession to UNCLOS.[254] The United States did become a party to the Convention relating to the Conservation and Management of Straddling Fish Stocks and Highly Migratory Fish Stocks of 1995 (Straddling Stock Agreement) in 1996.

UNCLOS provides a much-needed framework for protecting highly sensitive or critical marine ecosystems. Article 194(5) includes measures necessary to prevent, reduce, and control pollution in rare or fragile ecosystems or in the habitat of depleted, threatened, or endangered species. Article 211(6) provides that a coastal State may prescribe special mandatory measures for the prevention of vessel pollution in certain special clearly defined areas where the international rules and standards are not stringent enough to protect the ecosystem. This provides Parties with the ability to put in place additional protections for areas considered critical to biodiversity, or habitat for endangered or threatened species.

2. Agenda 21, the Convention on Biological Diversity, and the Jakarta Mandate on Marine and Coastal Biological Diversity

At the 1992 Earth Summit in Rio de Janeiro, many of the participants adopted Agenda 21, a global program intended to foster global sustainable developments.[255] Chapter 17 of Agenda 21 is related to "the protection of oceans, all kinds of seas, including enclosed and semienclosed seas, and coastal areas." Chapter 17 explicitly calls for Coastal States, with the support of international organizations, to undertake measures to maintain biological diversity and productivity of marine species and habitats under national jurisdiction.[256] These measures include the establishment and management of ocean and coastal protected areas.

One of the key agreements adopted at the 1992 Earth Summit was the Convention on Biological Diversity (CBD) related to sustainable development. The three primary goals of the CBD are the conservation of biological diversity, the sustainable use of its components, and the fair and equitable sharing of the benefits from the use of genetic resources.[257] The CBD sets forth commitments to maintaining biological diversity in cooperation with economic development. Article 8 of the CBD specifically requires the Parties to "[e]stablish a system of protected areas or areas where special measures need to be taken to conserve biological diversity."[258] The United States signed the CBD in 1993, but has not yet ratified the agreement.[259]

The Jakarta Mandate on Marine and Coastal Biological Diversity (Jakarta Mandate) was adopted in 1995 by the Parties to the CBD. The Conference of Parties agreed that the primary goal for efforts related to Marine and Coastal Protected Areas (MCPAs) under the Convention should be the "establishment and maintenance of MCPAs that are effectively managed, ecologically based, and contribute to a global network of MCPAs, building on national and regional systems, and including a range of levels of protection."[260] The Conference of Parties has adopted the goal of developing such national and regional systems by the year 2012. The Secretariat of the CBD has also published a document providing technical advice on the establishment and management of a national system of MPAs.[261]

3. International Coral Reef Initiative

The International Coral Reef Initiative (ICRI) was announced at the First Conference of the Parties under the Biodiversity Convention in 1994.[262] The ICRI was established to implement Chapter 17 of Agenda 21 through protection of coral reefs and related ecosystems through a partnership between governments, international organizations, and nongovernmental organizations.[263] The partnership was originally entered into by Australia, France, Japan, Jamaica, the Philippines, Sweden, the United Kingdom, and the United States.[264] In 1995, the Global Coral Reef Monitoring Network (GCRMN) was established as one of the operating units of ICRI to increase research and monitoring of reefs to provide data necessary for effective management.[265]

III. Emerging Issues and Hot Topics

A. Implementation of Executive Order 13,158

Although Executive Order 13,158 represents an important step toward creating a national and coordinated system of MPAs in the United States, implementation of the Order has been extremely slow and the Order has been criticized as containing a number of weaknesses that make implementation of the national system of MPAs uncertain.[266] For example, the Order does not establish specific mechanisms to create a national representative system of MPAs, such as policy or legal instruments. The Order lacks a specific mandate for federal or state governments to implement and enforce its measures protecting MPAs, and does not alter any existing authority at the state, local, tribal, or treaty level regarding the establishment or management of MPAs. State and local government participation in the development of the national system is completely voluntary, so local governments have the discretion to decide not to participate in the development of the national system.[267] In addition, the Order does not specify appropriations to carry out the Order, giving the current executive branch the discretion to choose not to fund actions to implement the Order.[268] Sites designated as MMAs that are currently at risk therefore continue to lack meaningful protection, because such sites will not be subject to the protective measures of the Order until after the list of MPAs has been prepared and the site is added to the list.[269]

There are also indications that the agencies charged with developing and implementing the national system are interpreting the Order as applying protection to MPAs only once the national system has been established, meaning that areas currently protected but not yet included in the national system are subject to harm from federal actions. In a June 2002 letter regarding a request that the Order be invoked to protect Nantucket Sound from the negative impacts of a proposed offshore wind farm, the Assistant Secretary for Land and Minerals Management (the development arm of the Department of the Interior) stated that without the formal designation of a marine area under the Order, "the 'Harm' provisions of the Executive Order do not apply."[270] By its terms, however, the harm avoidance requirement in Section 5 is applicable now. The provision is not limited to MPAs actively included on the MPA list.

Instead, Section 5 simply provides that "[i]n implementing this section, each Federal agency shall refer" to the MPA list.[271] This provision is obviously intended to help guide agency identification of MPAs, but it is not a prerequisite to protective measures (e.g., it does not say "in implementing this section, each Federal agency shall comply with this requirement only for those areas identified under subsection 4(d) of this Order"). Thus, federal agencies should be abiding by this provision for all areas that meet the definition of an MPA.

In addition to the weaknesses in the Order, implementation of the Order's requirements has proceeded at a very slow pace. Although the Order was issued in 2000, as of the end of 2007 the inventory of MMAs was not complete.[272] In July 2006, after several years of stakeholder meetings and comments, the MPA Center issued a Draft Framework for Developing the National System of Marine Protected Areas (Draft Framework). The Draft Framework defines the key terms in the definition of MPA provided in the Order, and sets forth three goals of the national system: (1) to advance comprehensive conservation and management of the nation's significant natural and cultural heritage and sustainable production marine reserves through ecosystem-based approaches; (2) to increase the effectiveness of the national system of MPAs and promote sound stewardship; and (3) to enhance effective coordination and integration among MPAs in the national system and within the broader ecosystem-based management context.[273] The Draft Framework describes the objectives for each of these three goals.[274]

> **In addition to the weaknesses in Executive Order 13,158, implementation of its requirements has proceeded at a very slow pace.**

The Draft Framework also sets forth the process for developing the national system of MPAs called for in the Order. Development of the national system will occur in two phases: (1) building and supporting the initial national system of MPAs and (2) identifying national system gaps and future conservation priorities.[275] Phase 1 requires identifying and nominating candidate national system MPAs by reviewing the sites in the MMA Inventory to determine whether the MMA meets the definitions of MPA and the key terms, as well as the national system MPA criteria.[276] For those sites that meet the criteria, the MPA Center will send a letter to the managing authority, following which the managing authority will review the MPA and decide whether to nominate it to the national system.[277] Candidate sites will be reviewed and public comment solicited prior to the MPA Center's adding approved sites to the official National System List of MPAs (List of MPAs).[278]

Although the Draft Framework is an important step in developing the national system of MPAs, there are still many questions regarding the timing, implementation, and effectiveness of the national system. The Draft Framework does not provide any deadlines or timelines for establishing the List of MPAs. In addition to the fact that participation by state, local, and tribal governments is voluntary, the Draft Framework provides that an MPA may be removed from the List of MPAs at any time at the written request of the managing agency(ies) if the MPA ceases to exist or the managing authority requests removal.[279] These and other limitations mean that implementation and enforcement of the national system of MPAs may lack regulatory effectiveness.

B. Ecosystem-Based Fisheries Management Movement

The concept of ecosystem-based management has become popular over the past decade or so.[280] Some form of ecosystem-based fisheries management appears likely, since the United States Congress, the National Marine Fisheries Service (NMFS or NOAA Fisheries) of the National Oceanic and Atmospheric Administration, the Department of Commerce, top fisheries scientists, and other leaders seem committed to such a transition.[281] However, what such management actually will look like is far from clear.

As the Pew Institute for Ocean Science defines it, ecosystem-based fisheries management is

> a new approach that reverses the usual order of management priorities so that ecosystems, rather than single species, are paramount. [Ecosystem-based fisheries management] is an improvement over single species management because it integrates ecosystem impacts into the management of fisheries. Thus, habitat, predators, and prey of the target species, as well as other ecosystem components and interactions, are taken into account in managing fisheries. This approach both ensures that ecosystems will be sustained, and provides the foundation for long-term sustainability of fisheries.[282]

Ecosystem-based management takes into account the richness, diversity, interactivity, and chaos of true ecological systems, acknowledging the constant flux and adaptation of the real environment.[283] Ecosystem-based management, however, is not a part of the governance systems of most environmental laws, including those laws governing fisheries.[284] However, during the 1996 reauthorization of the Magnuson-Stevens Act,[285] Congress and NMFS began demonstrating the intent to shift to an ecosystem-based management approach for fisheries. As a result of congressional directives in 1996, an Ecosystem Principles Advisory Board was convened, which issued a report in 1998 entitled *Ecosystem-Based Fishery Management*.[286] The report indicates an expectation that "ecosystem-based fishery management will contribute to the stability of employment and economic activity in the fishing industry and to the protection of marine biodiversity on which fisheries depend."[287]

C. Comprehensive Ocean Management—Proposed Changes to Ocean Policy

1. Commission Reports (U.S. Commission and Pew)

Two commissions, the U.S. Commission on Ocean Policy and the Pew Oceans Commission, have recently issued reports regarding the current conditions of the oceans and recommendations for significant changes in ocean policy. If the changes suggested by these reports are implemented, the United States will move a long way toward a comprehensive system of ocean management and ecosystem protection and a national system of MPAs, including marine reserves.

In 2004, the U.S. Commission on Ocean Policy released its final report (Ocean Policy Report).[288] The Ocean Policy Report generally called for a new national ocean policy framework, including establishment of a new National Ocean Council within the Executive Office of the President.[289] The Ocean Policy Report also discussed employing MPAs as a management tool and contained two recommendations related to MPAs regarding national coordination of MPAs.

Recommendation 6-3 provides that the National Ocean Council should develop national goals and guidelines "leading to a uniform process for the effective design, implementation, and evaluation of" MPAs. The Ocean Policy Report recognized that design of MPAs should recognize important national interests such as international trade including freedom of navigation, national security, recreation, clean energy, economic development, and scientific research.[290] Specifically, the U.S. Commission on Ocean Policy recommended that this process contain the following steps: (1) MPA designations based on the best available science to ensure that an area is appropriate for its intended purpose; (2) periodic assessment, monitoring, and modification to ensure continuing ecological and socioeconomic effectiveness of MPAs; and (3) design and implementation processes that consider issues of national importance such as freedom of navigation, and are conducted based on an ecosystem-based comprehensive offshore management regime.[291]

In addition, the Ocean Policy Report recognized that the wide variety of stakeholders and their relevant interests create controversy regarding the designation and implementation of MPAs. Recommendation 6-4 emphasized the importance of cooperation among regional ocean councils and appropriate federal, regional, state, and local entities in MPA designation, implementation, and evaluation.[292] The Ocean Policy Report recommended that MPA planners follow the process created by the National Ocean Council and actively solicit stakeholder input and participation in these processes.

The Pew Oceans Commission released its report and recommendations for a new ocean policy in 2003.[293] The Pew Commission Report (Pew Report), like the U.S. Commission on Ocean Policy's report, calls for ecosystem-based management by a new national oceans agency. The Pew Report also calls for creation of a national system of MPAs: this latter recommendation is one of the five key recommendations in the Pew Report and is targeted specifically towards creation of a national system of no-take reserves.[294]

The Pew Report calls for Congress to provide a mandate and authority for designating a national system of marine reserves, using proposed regional ocean ecosystem councils to designate areas of regional importance as individual reserves or networks of reserves.[295] The Pew Report also calls for Congress to directly designate areas of special national significance as marine reserves and to direct the national oceans agency, in coordination with the regional councils, to establish an inventory of potential reserves and to nominate specific areas for Congress to consider including in the national reserve system.[296] The Pew Report recommends that the national oceans agency should be granted authority to manage the national system, including the development, implementation, and management of reserves created in federal waters pursuant to the new authority, and for coordination of federal agencies currently managing marine reserves and for coordination of management of reserves that contain both federal and state waters. Finally, the Pew Report recommends that the national system of reserves encompass significant portions of ecosystems and a variety of habitats, including benthic and pelagic elements.[297]

The Pew Report recommends that the national system of reserves encompass significant portions of ecosystems and a variety of habitats, including benthic and pelagic elements.

In response to the Ocean Policy Report, in December 2004 President Bush established a Cabinet-level Committee on Ocean Policy (COP) by Executive Order.[298] The purpose of the COP is to coordinate the ocean-related activities of executive branch departments and agencies and to facilitate coordination and consultation on ocean-related matters among federal, state, local, and tribal governments as well as the private sector, foreign governments, and international organizations.[299] Several subsidiary bodies were created to establish an ocean governance structure that coordinates with the existing ocean governance framework.[300] Also in December 2004, President Bush submitted to Congress his formal response to the Ocean Policy Report to identify immediate, short-term actions that provide direction for ocean policy and address additional long-term actions for the future.[301] Action highlights include developing an ocean research priorities plan and implementation strategy,[302] supporting accession to the UN Convention on the Law of the Sea, and implementing coral reef local action strategies.[303]

2. Proposed Legislation and Amendments to Various Legislation

New legislation regarding protection and management of marine ecosystems has been introduced in recent years that, if adopted, would help make progress towards ecosystem management and conservation. In 2007, the Oceans Conservation, Education, and National Strategy for the 21st Century Act was introduced to specify a national oceans policy, establish a Committee on Ocean Policy, and strengthen NOAA.[304] The Act would establish national standards to require any federal agency or federally funded activities that impact U.S. ocean waters or resources to be conducted in a manner that protects and maintains healthy marine ecosystems or in some circumstances restores degraded ecosystems.[305] The House Natural Resources Committee's Subcommittee on Fisheries, Wildlife, and Oceans held a hearing on the proposed legislation in 2007.[306] A proposed Marine Debris Research, Prevention, and Reduction Act would have established a marine debris prevention and removal program within NOAA in order to reduce and prevent the occurrence and adverse impacts of marine debris on the environment and on navigation safety, but it was not reintroduced in the 110th Congress.[307]

The Coral Reef Conservation Amendments Act of 2007 passed the United States House of Representatives in late 2007.[308] This Act amends the Coral Reef

Conservation Act of 2000 to extend the award of remaining coral reef conservation program grant funds for appropriate projects, in addition to authorizing projects addressing emerging priorities or threats and revising the criteria for project approval. The 2000 Act provides support for marine protected areas.[309]

In addition, a bill was proposed to expand the boundaries of the Gulf of the Farallones National Marine Sanctuary and the Cordell Bank National Marine Sanctuary, and to prohibit the "leasing, exploration, development, production, or transporting by pipeline of minerals or hydrocarbons"; the conduct of aquaculture, including within Monterey Bay National Marine Sanctuary (with certain exceptions); and the discharge of materials or a change in the salinity level within the two sanctuaries.[310]

IV. Conclusion

Although the United States is making progress toward ecosystem-level protection and management of marine resources, establishment and management of MPAs currently remain uncoordinated and disjointed. As impacts to ocean and coastal areas increase, and as the threats to specific marine ecosystems grow, coordinated efforts to designate and manage MPAs on an ecosystem and national scale become more critical.

Establishment of a coordinated national system of MPAs, as required by Executive Order 13,158, will greatly assist in moving toward adequate protection of marine ecosystems. The United States should actively participate in international marine conservation and protection efforts and should accede to the UNCLOS. Finally, adoption of recommendations to move towards comprehensive ocean management approaches, including ecosystem-based fisheries management, should also proceed as quickly as possible in order to ensure adequate marine ecosystem protection.

Notes

1. Scott D. Woodruff et al., *A Comprehensive Ocean-Atmosphere Data Set*, 68 Bull. Am. Meteorological Soc'y 10 (1987).
2. *See, e.g.*, Donald C. Baur, Wm. Robert Irvin & Darren R. Misenko, *Putting "Protection" Into Marine Protected Areas*, 26 Vt. L. Rev. 497 (2004); Robin Kundis Craig, *Protecting International Marine Biodiversity: International Treaties and National Systems of Marine Protected Areas*, 20 J. Land Use & Envtl. L. 333 (2005).
3. *See generally* Protecting America's Marine Environment: A report of the Marine Protected Areas Federal Advisory Committee on Establishing and Managing a National System of Marine Protected Areas, *available at* http://mpa.gov/fac/pdf/mpafac_report_06_05.pdf (last visited July 16, 2007).
4. U.S. Dep't of Commerce, Nat'l Oceanic & Atmospheric Admin. & U.S. Dep't of Interior, What Is a Marine Protected Area? Definition and Common Terminology, *available at* http://www.mpa.gov/helpful_resources/archives/what_is_mpa.html#varying (last visited July 16, 2007).
5. *See generally* U.S. Dep't of Commerce, Nat'l Oceanic & Atmospheric Admin. & U.S. Dep't of Interior, Marine Protected Areas of the United States, http://mpa.gov/ (last visited July 16, 2007).
6. Nat'l Res. Council, Marine Protected Areas: Tools for Sustaining Ocean Ecosystem 215 (Academy Press 2001) [hereinafter MPAs: Tools for Sustaining Ocean Ecosystems].

7. Philippe Cury, Lynne Shannon & Yunne-Jai Shin, *The Functioning of Marine Ecosystems*, http://marine.rutgers.edu/courses/expl_oceans/07Cury.PDF (last visited July 16, 2007).

8. National Research Council, A Century of Ecosystem Science: Planning Long-Term Research in the Gulf of Alaska (2002), citations omitted.

9. Working Group, ICES/BSRP/HELCOM/UNEP Regional Seas Workshop, Background Paper: Indicators of Changing States of Large Marine Ecosystems, *available at* http://sea.helcom.fi/dps/docs/documents/Baltic%20Sea%20Regional%20Project%20(BSRP)/Indicators-LME%20by%20K.%20Sherman%20&%20J.%20Thulin.pdf (last visited July 16, 2007).

10. *Id.*

11. Baur, Irvin & Misenko, *supra* note 2, at 506.

12. Tundi Agardy et al., *Dangerous Targets? Unresolved Issues and Ideological Clashes Around Marine Protected Areas*, 13 Aquatic Conservation: Marine & Freshwater Ecosystems 353, 355 (2003).

13. Exec. Order No. 13,158, 65 Fed. Reg. 34,909 (May 26, 2000), *reprinted in* 16 U.S.C. § 1431 (2000).

14. *See* Jane Lubchenco et al, *Plugging a Hole in the Ocean: The Emerging Science of Marine Reserves*, 13 Ecological Applications 1 (2003).

15. *Id.* at S3.

16. Lydia K. Bergen & Mark H. Carr, *Establishing Marine Reserves: How Can Science Best Inform Policy?*, Environment, Mar. 2003, at 10.

17. MPAs: Tools for Sustaining Ocean Ecosystems, *supra* note 6, at xi.

18. Scientific Consensus Statement on Marine Reserves, *available at* http://www.nceas.ucsb.edu/consensus/ (last visited Feb. 15, 2008)

19. Scientific Consensus Statement of Marine Ecosystem-Based Management, *available at* http://www.compassonline.org/pdf_files/EBM_Consensus_Statement_v12.pdf.

20. *Id.* at 1.

21. *Supra* note 18 at 175.

22. Benjamin S. Halpern & Robert R. Warner, *Marine Reserves Have Rapid and Lasting Effects*, 5 Ecology Letters 361 (2002).

23. Nat'l MPA Center, *Draft Framework for Developing the National System of Marine Protected Areas* iv (2006).

24. Jennifer L. Schorr, *The Australian National Representative System of Marine Protected Areas and the Marine Zoning System: A Model for the United States?* 13 Pac. Rim & Pol'y J. 673, 680 (2004).

25. Jon C. Day, *Zoning—Lessons from the Great Barrier Reef Marine Park*, 45 Ocean & Coastal Mgmt. 139, 141 (2002).

26. Exec. Order No. 13,158, *supra* note 13, § 1.

27. *Id.*

28. *Id.* § 1, 4.

29. *Id.* § 2.

30. *Id.*

31. Nat'l Ocean Serv., Final Criteria and Data Fields for an Inventory of Existing Marine Managed Areas and Response to Comments, 70 Fed. Reg. 3512 (Jan. 25, 2005); *see also* Inventory of Marine Managed Areas in the United States, *available at* http://www.mpa.gov/helpful_resources/inventory.html (last visited July 18, 2007).

32. Protecting America's Marine Environment: A Report of the Marine Protected Areas Federal Advisory Committee on Establishing and Managing a National System of Marine Protected Areas 2, *available at* http://mpa.gov/fac/pdf/mpafac_report_06_05.pdf (last visited July 16, 2007).

33. *Id.*

34. Exec. Order No. 13,158, *supra* note 13, § 4.

35. *Id.* § 4.

36. Marine Protected Areas and an Inventory of Existing Marine Managed Areas, 68 Fed. Reg. 43, 495 (July 23, 2003).

37. *Id.*

38. *Id.* at 43,496.

39. The criteria for inclusion in the MMA inventory require that an MPA be an area with legally defined geographical boundaries; marine (ocean or coastal waters or an area of the Great Lakes or their connecting waters); reserved (established by and currently subject to federal, state, commonwealth, territorial, local, or tribal law or regulation); lasting; and subject to existing protection. The criteria also include a definition for the term "cultural resources" used in the Executive Order. 70 Fed. Reg. 3512, *supra* note 31.

40. Exec. Order No. 13,158, *supra* note 13, § 4(8)(c).

41. Nat'l Oceanic & Atmospheric Admin., MPA Federal Advisory Committee Charter, *available at* http://mpa.gov/pdf/fac/final_mpafac_charter111906.pdf (revised Nov. 19, 2006) (last visited July 18, 2007).

42. *Id.*

43. *Id.*

44. Exec. Order No. 13,158, *supra* note 13, § 4(8)(e).

45. Nat'l Oceanic & Atmospheric Admin., About the MPA Center, *available at* http://mpa .gov/mpa_center/about_mpa_center.html (last visited July 18, 2007).

46. *Id.*

47. Exec. Order No. 13,158, *supra* note 13, § 4(8)(f).

48. *Id.*

49. *Id..*

50. *Id.* § 5.

51. *Id.*

52. *Id.*

53. See http://mpa.gov/pdf/fac/fac_recmd_06_07.pdf, 6–7. The Executive Summary provides the following concepts and recommendations: Chapter 2, "Marine Protected Areas: Fundamental Tools for Ecosystem-Based Management," was produced in response to inconsistencies within the federal government regarding the relationship between MPAs and ecosystem approaches to ocean management being developed by NOAA and other agencies. Chapter 3, "Management Criteria, Priority Objectives, and Categories for the National System of Marine Protected Areas," addressed questions posed by the National MPA Center regarding the process for developing a National System of MPAs in order to address public comments on the draft Framework for Developing a National System of Marine Protected Areas, the MPA Center document that will guide the implementation of the national system. Chapter 4, "Process for Determining Which Existing MPA Sites Will Constitute the Initial National System of MPAs," outlines a two-step process for, first, filtering over 1,600 existing Marine Managed Areas in the United States to a set of eligible MPAs, whose managers will be invited to join the National System of MPAs, and second, completing the nomination process, thereby creating the initial National System of MPAs composed of sites already in existence. Chapter 5, " Developing Plans for Effective MPA Management: A Model," outlines an ideal management plan for MPAs, with the intention that all U.S. MPAs ultimately operate under well-structured and adaptive plans. Chapter 6, "Incentives for Participation in the National System of Marine Protected Areas," addresses in detail the important issue of why the managers of any MPA or MPA system would want to join the National System of MPAs, offering eight explicit recommendations and potential sources of funding for such incentives. Chapter 7, "Regional Approaches to Planning and Coordination of Marine Protected Areas," provides how-to guidance regarding cooperative management of MPAs based on ten relevant case studies, which are thoroughly documented.

54. National Marine Sanctuaries Act, 16 U.S.C. §§ 1431–1445c-1 (2000).

55. 15 C.F.R. § 922.2 (2003).

56. *Id.*

57. Only roughly fifteen percent of the nation's marine conservation areas are under the jurisdiction of the federal government. Nat'l MPA Center, Draft Framework for Developing the National System of Marine Protected Areas iii (July 2006).

58. 16 U.S.C. § 1433(a). The NMSA specifies that "special national significance" is determined by the proposed areas' "conservation, recreational, ecological, historical, scientific, cultural, archaeological, educational, or esthetic qualities; . . . the communities of living marine resources it harbors; . . . or its resource or human-use values." *Id.* § 1433(a)(2)(A)–(C).

59. For example, the Florida Keys National Marine Sanctuary and Protection Act established the Florida Keys National Marine Sanctuary. Pub. L. No. 101-605, 104 Stat. 3089 (1990).

60. 16 U.S.C. § 1434(b)(1).

61. *Id.*

62. 16 U.S.C. § 1433.

63. *Id.*

64. 16 U.S.C. § 1434.

65. *Id.* § (a)(3).

66. John Epting, *National Marine Sanctuary Program: Balancing Resource Protection with Multiple Use,* 18 Hous. L. Rev. 1037, 1038 (1981).

67. 16 U.S.C. § 1436(1).

68. *Id.* § 1436(2).

69. *Id.* § 1443(a)(1)(A)–(B).

70. *Id.* § 1441(a)(1)–(2).

71. *Id.* § (c).

72. *Id.* § (c)(1).

73. *Id.* § (c)(3).

74. *Id.* § (c)(2).

75. *Id.* § 1441(e).

76. *Id.* § 1439.

77. Baur, Irvin & Misenko, *supra* note 2, at 511.

78. 15 C.F.R. § 922.30(a)(2003).

79. *Id.* § 922.42.

80. *Id.* § 922.47.

81. *Id.* §§ 922.48–922.49.

82. Schorr, *supra* note 24, at 694.

83. 15 C.F.R. §§ 922.91(a)(1), 922.102(a)(5), 922.122(a)(4), 922.132(a)(4), 922.142(a)(3), 922.163(a)(3), 922.193(a)(2) (subsections preventing alteration of the seabed).

84. *Id.* §§ 922.71(a)(1), 922.82(a)(1), 922.111(a)(3), 922.122(a)(1), 922.132(a)(1) (subsections preventing exploration of oil, gas, and minerals).

85. *Id.* §§ 922.132(a)(3), 922.142(a)(4), 922.152(a)(3), 922.163(a)(9) (subsections preventing removal and injury of a sanctuary historical resource).

86. *Id.* §§ 922.122(a)(6), 922.132(a)(5), 922.142(a)(5), 922.152(a)(5), 922.163(a)(10) (subsections preventing the taking of mammals, sea turtles, and seabirds).

87. *Id.* §§ 922.82(a)(7), 922.132(a)(7) (prohibiting the operation of personal watercraft).

88. *Id.* §§ 922.71(a)(4), 922.82(a)(4) (prohibiting operation of cargo vessels).

89. *Id.* § 922.132(a)(10).

90. *Id.* § 922.61(c).

91. *Id.* § 922.184(a)(1).

92. *Id.* § 922.163(a)(2).

93. 16 U.S.C. 1801–1882 (1997) (as amended by Sustainable Fisheries Act, Pub. L. No. 104-297, 1996 U.S.C.C.A.N. (110 Stat. 3559 (1996)).

94. *See* Fishery Management Councils, http://www.nmfs.noaa.gov/councils/ (last visited Nov. 10, 2005).

95. 16 U.S.C. § 1853(b)(2).

96. *Id.* § 1853(b)(4).

97. *Id.* § 1853(b)(2).

98. Magnuson-Stevens Fishery Conservation and Management Act, 16 U.S.C. § 1853(a)(7) (2000). Since the 1996 amendments to the FCMA, fishery management councils have identified EFH for sixty species. Nat'l Oceanic & Atmospheric Admin., Guide to Essential

Fish Habitat Descriptions, *at* http://www.nero.noaa.gov/ro/doc/list.htm (last visited Apr. 12, 2004).

99. 16 U.S.C. § 1802(10). Under the FCMA, "fish" includes "finfish, mollusks, crustaceans, and all other forms of marine animal and plant life other than marine mammals and birds." *Id.* § 1802(12).

100. *Id.* § 1855(b)(2). In the first three years of EFH requirements, the Secretary of Commerce consulted on more than 5,000 federal actions that may have adversely affected EFH. Tanya Dobrzynski, *Essential Fish Habitat (EFH) Update: Progress and Available Resources,* 22 Coastal Soc'y Bull. 1 (2000).

101. 16 U.S.C. § 1855(b)(3).

102. *Id.* § 1855(b)(4)(A).

103. *Id.* § 1855(b)(4)(B).

104. 50 C.F.R. § 600.815(a)(8).

105. Fisheries of the Exclusive Economic Zone Off Alaska: Groundfish, Crab, Salmon, and Scallop Fisheries off the Bering Sea and Aleutian Islands Management Area and Gulf of Alaska, 71 Fed. Reg. 36,694 (June 28, 2006).

106. Dr. Richard Parrish et al., Pac. Fishery Mgmt. Council, Marine Reserves to Supplement Management of West Coast Groundfish Resources: Phase I Technical Analysis ES-1 (Feb. 2001), *available at* http://www.pcouncil.org/reserves/recent/phase1 analysis.pdf (last visited July 16, 2007).

107. Pac. Fishery Mgmt. Council, Fishery Management Background: Marine Reserves (citing the National Research Council Ocean Studies Board definition of "fishery reserve"), *available at* http://www.pcouncil.org/reserves/reservesback.html (last visited July 16, 2007).

108. *Id.*

109. *Id.*

110. S. Atl. Fishery Mgmt. Council, Public Hearing Summary on Snapper Group Amendment 14, *available at* http://www.safmc.net/portals/6/meetings/Council/BriefingBook/Sept2006/SG14%20PH%20Summary%208-30-06.pdf (last visited July 19, 2007).

111. Snapper Group Amendment 14—MPAs, *available at* http://www.safmc.net/MPAInformationPage/tabid/469/Default.aspx (last visited July 19, 2007).

112. Amendment 14 was approved with the stipulation that a transit provision be included to allow commercial fishermen to cross areas with fish onboard but with all gear stowed. *Id.*

113. Coastal Zone Management Act of 1972, 16 U.S.C. §§ 1451–1465 (2000).

114. *Id.* § 1455(b).

115. *Id.* § 1456b(a)(5).

116. *Id.*

117. *Id.*

118. *Id.* § 1456b(a)(7).

119. *Id.* § 1456(c)(1)(A).

120. Nat'l Oceanic & Atmospheric Admin., National Estuarine Research Reserve System: An Overview of the Reserve System, *available at* http://nerrs.noaa.gov/Background_Overview.html (last visited July 16, 2007).

121. *Id.*

122. *Id.*

123. Nat'l Oceanic & Atmospheric Admin., National Estuarine Research Reserves: Strategic Plan 2005–2010, *available at* http://nerrs.noaa.gov/Background_StrategicPlan.html (last visited July 16, 2007).

124. 16 U.S.C. § 1461(b)(1).

125. *Id.* § 1461(b)(2)(B).

126. *Id.* § 1461(e)(1)(A)(i).

127. *Id.* § 1461(e)(1)(A).

128. 16 U.S.C. § 431.

129. *Id.*

130. Proclamation 8031, 71 Fed. Reg. 35,443 (June 15, 2006). The monument was originally called the Northwestern Hawaiian Islands Marine National Monument. It was renamed in honor of native Hawaiian culture. Department of the Interior, Fish and Wildlife Service, Department of Commerce, National Oceanic and Atmospheric Administration, Papahānaumokuākea Marine National Monument, Hawaii; Monument Management Plan 72 Fed. Reg. 16328 (Apr. 4, 2007), *available at* http://www.epa.gov/fedrgstr/EPA-IMPACT/2007/April/Day-04/i1652.htm. *See also Papahānaumokuākea: A Sacred Name, A Sacred Place The Meaning, Pronunciation and Significance of Our Name*, http://hawaiireef.noaa.gov/about/Name.html.

131. *See generally* http://hawaiireef.noaa.gov/welcome.html.

132. *Aloha! Welcome to the Papahānaumokuākea Marine National Monument*, http://hawaiireef.noaa.gov/about/welcome.html.

133. *See* Governor Linda Lingle, *Papahānaumokuākea Marine National Monument* (Radio Address, Mar. 2, 2007), http://hawaii.gov/gov/news/radioadd/2007/Document.2007-03-02.2903

134. The White House, *Fact Sheet: The Northwestern Hawaiian Islands Marine National Monument: A Commitment to Good Stewardship of Our Natural Resources* (June 15, 2006), *available at* http://www.whitehouse.gov/news/releases/2006/06/20060615-9.html.

135. 71 Fed. Reg. at 36,446.

136. *Id.*

137. These include Midway Atoll National Wildlife Refuge, the Battle of Midway National Memorial, and the Hawaiian Islands National Wildlife Refuge.

138. Federal Water Pollution Control (Clean Water) Act of 1972, 33 U.S.C. §§ 1251–1387 (2000).

139. *Id.* § 1330. In 1987, Congress amended the CWA and established the NEP to provide for greater protection of estuarine areas.

140. *Id.* § 1330(a)(1).

141. *Id.* § 1330(c).

142. *Id.* § 1330(g)(1)–(2).

143. *Id.* § 1330(b)(1), 1330(b)(4).

144. *Id.* § 1330(c)(1)–(5).

145. U.S. EPA, National Estuary Program: Which Estuaries are in the NEP?, *at* http://www.epa.gov/owow/estuaries/find.htm (last updated Mar. 9, 2005).

146. 33 U.S.C. § 1343(a).

147. *Id.* § 1343(c)(1).

148. Exec. Order No. 13,158, 3 C.F.R. 274, 276 (2001), *reprinted in* 16 U.S.C. § 1431 (2000).

149. Robin Kundis Craig & Sarah Miller, *Ocean Discharge Criteria and Marine Protected Areas: Ocean Water Quality Protection Under the Clean Water Act*, 29 B.C. Envtl. Aff. L. Rev. 1, 28 (2001).

150. Press Release, U.S. EPA, EPA Proposes Special Ocean Sites (Jan. 19, 2001), *available at* http://yosemite.epa.gov/opa/admpress.nsf/a16b318fd6d8e076852572a000650bff/e5e2e383ff959439852569d9006db3fb!OpenDocument (last visited July 16, 2007).

151. *Id.*

152. *Id.*

153. *Id.*

154. Outer Continental Shelf Lands Act, Pub. L. No. 95-372, 67 Stat. 462 (codified at 43 U.S.C. § 1332 (2000)).

155. See 43 U.S.C. § 1333(a)(1)–(2)(A) (extending the United States Constitution and the laws of the adjacent states to the subsoil and seabed of the Outer Continental Shelf).

156. *Id.* § 1334(a).

157. *Id.* § 1344(a)(3).

158. *Id.* § 1344(a)(2)(G); *see also id.* § 1344(f)(1) (requiring regulations to establish procedures for "receipt and consideration of nominations for any area to be offered for lease or to

be excluded from leasing"); § 1345a (allowing state and local governments to recommend areas suitable for leasing).

159. *Id.* § 1334(a)(1)(B), 1334(a)(2)(A)(i).
160. Coastal Barrier Resources Act § 2, Pub. L. No. 97-348, 96 Stat. 1653 (codified at 16 U.S.C. §§ 3501 *et seq.* (2000)).
161. 16 U.S.C. § 3501(a)(1).
162. *Id.* § 3501(a)(3).
163. *Id.* § 3501(b).
164. *Id.* §§ 3503(a), 3504(a).
165. *Id.* § 3504(a)(1)–(3).
166. *Id.* § 3505(a)(1)–(3).
167. *Id.* § 3505(a)(6)(A), (G).
168. National Park Service Organic Act, 16 U.S.C. §§ 1–460 (2000) (originally enacted as Act of August 25, 1916, ch. 408, 39 Stat. 535 (1916)).
169. *Id.* § 1.
170. H.R. Rep. No. 64-700, at 3 (1916). *See also* Nat'l Rifle Ass'n of Am. v. Potter, 628 F. Supp. 903, 910 (D.D.C. 1986) (citing this legislative history in support of the "protectionist" goal of wildlife management in units of the Park System); Organized Fishermen of Fla. v. Watt, 590 F. Supp. 805, 812–13 (S.D. Fla. 1984) (upholding the Secretary of the Interior's power to close Everglades to fishing).
171. Alaska National Interest Lands Conservation Act, Pub. L. No. 96-487, 94 Stat. 2371 (1980) (codified in scattered sections of the U.S.C.).
172. S. Rep. No. 96-413, at 171 (1979).
173. 16 U.S.C. § 1–1a.
174. *Id.*
175. *Id.* § 1c(b).
176. For example, commercial fishing is expressly authorized in the Cape Hatteras National Seashore, 16 U.S.C. § 459a-1, and portions of the Glacier Bay National Preserve, § 410hh-4. See 36 C.F.R. § 2.3(d)(4) (2003) (prohibiting commercial fishing unless authorized by Congress).
177. See 16 U.S.C. § 1a-1.
178. *Id.* § 3.
179. 36 C.F.R. pts. 1–2 (2003). Included in Part 1 are general requirements to guide NPS's administration of the system. *Id.* § 1.2. Part 2 contains regulations for a host of activities ranging from hunting and trapping, § 2.2, to collecting scientific research specimens, § 2.5, to conducting a political demonstration, § 2.51.
180. *Id.* §§ 7.1–7.100.
181. *Id.* §§ 3.1–3.24.
182. *Id.* §§ 4.1–4.31.
183. *Id.* §§ 14.1–14.96.
184. *See id.* §§ 5.1–5.14, 9.1–10.4 (discussing commercial activities, minerals management, and disposal of wild animals).
185. *Id.* § 13.1–13.87.
186. National Wildlife Refuge System Administration Act of 1966, 16 U.S.C. §§ 668dd–668ee (2000).
187. National Wildlife Refuge System Improvement Act of 1997, Pub. L. No. 105-57, 111 Stat. 1252 (1997) (codified at 16 U.S.C. §§ 668dd–668ee (2000)).
188. 16 U.S.C. § 668dd(d)(1)(A).
189. *Id.* § 668dd(a)(1).
190. Trustees for Alaska v. Watt, 524 F. Supp. 1303, 1309 (D. Alaska 1981), *aff'd*, 690 F.2d 1279 (9th Cir. 1982).
191. *See, e.g.,* Antiquities Act of 1906, 16 U.S.C. §§ 431–433 (2000) (allowing Presidents to establish national monuments by proclamation).
192. Secretarial authority to create refuges is derived from numerous statutes, the most significant of which are in the Endangered Species Act of 1973 (ESA), 16 U.S.C. § 1533(b)(2) (2000), and the Migratory Bird Conservation Act, 16 U.S.C. § 715d (2000).

193. Authority to incorporate donated and transferred lands into the Refuge System comes from several statutes, including the ESA, 16 U.S.C. § 1534(a)(2), the National Wildlife Refuge System Administration Act, 16 U.S.C. § 668dd(a)(6), the Fish and Wildlife Improvement Act, 16 U.S.C. §§ 715d, 742f(b) (2000), and the Fish and Wildlife Conservation Act of 1980, 16 U.S.C. § 2901(b)(2) (2000).

194. In the case of the Charles M. Russell National Wildlife Refuge in Montana, where there was some question as to whether there was a dual wildlife management and grazing purpose, the Ninth Circuit held that grazing must be given secondary consideration. Schwenke v. Sec'y of the Interior, 720 F.2d 571, 572, 574–75, 577–78 (9th Cir. 1983).

195. The purposes of each refuge are listed in Appendix B of the 1988 FWS Draft EIS on Refuge System Administration. B-3 to B-54.

196. Pub. L. No. 105-57, 111 Stat. 1252 (1997) (codified at 16 USC §§ 668dd-668ee (2000).

197. 16 U.S.C. § 668dd(a)(3)(A)–(D).

198. *Id.* § (a)(2).

199. *Id.* § 668ee(1).

200. *Id.* § (2).

201. *Id.* § 668dd(e)(2).

202. Refuge Recreation Act, 16 U.S.C. § 460k (2000).

203. *Id.* § 715s(c)(1)(C).

204. *Id.* § (a).

205. Alaska National Interest Lands Conservation Act, Pub. L. No. 96-487 § 302(B), 94 Stat. 2384 (1980) (codified at 16 U.S.C. § 668dd (2000)).

206. *Id.*

207. *Id.* § 302.

208. 50 C.F.R. §§ 26.11–26.33 (2003).

209. *Id.* § 26.34.

210. *Id.* §§ 27.11–27.97.

211. *Id.* § 27.51.

212. *Id.* § 29.21.

213. *Id.* §§ 29.31–29.32.

214. *Id.* §§ 30.1–31.17.

215. *Id.* §§ 32.1–32.2.

216. *Id.*

217. *Id.* §§ 36.1–36.42.

218. See Submerged Lands Act, 43 U.S.C. §§ 1301–1356a (2000) (establishing the boundary limit of state jurisdiction over tidewaters and submerged lands). According to the Act, state jurisdiction is generally limited to three geographic miles from the coastline. *Id.* § 1301(a)(2). In the Gulf of Mexico, the Florida and Texas boundaries extend out three leagues (approximately nine miles) from the coastline. *Id.* § 1301(b).

219. Cal. Fish & Game Code §§ 2850–2863 (West Supp. 2004).

220. *Id.* § 2853(c)(1).

221. *Id.* § 2852(c).

222. *Id.* § 2852(d).

223. *Id.*

224. *Id.* § 2853.

225. California Dep't of Fish and Game, Master Plan for Marine Protected Areas ii (2007), *available at* http://www.dfg.ca.gov/mlpa/masterplan.asp (last visited July 19, 2007) [hereinafter Master Plan].

226. Cal. Fish & Game Code § 2853(c)(1)–(4).

227. *Id.* § 2853(c)(5).

228. *Id.* § 2855(a).

229. *Id.*

230. *Id.* § 2855(a), (b)(1).

231. *Id.* § 2855(b)(2).

232. *Id.* § 2855(c).

233. Master Plan, *supra* note 225, at i.

234. Roddy Scheer, *California Establishes Major Marine Reserve Network*, L.A. TIMES, August 22, 2006.

235. Press Release, Cal. Dep't. of Fish & Game, Fish and Game Commission Moves Forward with Proposal to Create Network of Marine Protected Areas Along Central Coast, *available at* http://www.dfg.ca.gov/news/news06/com06004.html (last visited July 19, 2007).

236. Commission Gives Final Approval for Central Coast Marine Protected Areas, *available at* http://www.dfg.ca.gov/mlpa/ccmpas.asp (last visited July 19, 2007).

237. Massachusetts Ocean Sanctuaries Act, MASS. ANN. LAWS ch. 132A, §§ 12A-16F (Law. Co-op. 2001).

238. 302 MASS. CODE REGS. 5.00 (Ocean Sanctuaries).

239. *Id.* at §13.

240. MASS. ANN. LAWS ch. 132A, § 14.

241. *Id.* at §15.

242. *Id.* at §16.

243. 302 MASS. CODE REGS. 5.09(1).

244. R.R. CHURCHILL & A.V. LOWE, THE LAW OF THE SEA 15 (Juris 1999) (1983). See *id.* at 13–22 for a detailed discussion of the history and development of UNCLOS III.

245. *Id.*

246. *Id.* app. II at 480.

247. *Id.* at 15–16.

248. Article 308 provides the process for entry into force.

249. *Law of the Sea Treaty: Hearing on the Law of the Sea Convention before the Senate Foreign Relations Comm.*, 108th Cong. (2003) [hereinafter *Hearing*].

250. Bernard H. Oxman, *Complementary Agreements and Compulsory Jurisdiction*, 95 AM. J. INT'L L. 277, 278 (2001).

251. Fact Sheet: U.S. Oceans Policy and the Law of the Sea Convention, U.S. Dep't of State Dispatch Vol. 7, No. 11 (1996).

252. Message from the President Transmitting the 1982 United Nations Convention on the Law of the Sea and the Agreement Relating to the Implementation of Part XI of the Convention, S. TREATY DOC. No. 39, 103d Cong., 2d Sess. (1994).

253. *Hearing, supra* note 249 (statement of John Norton Moore, Professor, University of Virginia School of Law).

254. U.S. OCEAN ACTION PLAN: THE BUSH ADMINISTRATION'S RESPONSE TO THE U.S. COMMISSION ON OCEAN POLICY, *available at* http://ocean.ceq.gov/actionplan.pdf (last visited July 18, 2007).

255. Agenda 21: Programme of Action for Sustainable Development, United Nations Conference on Environment and Development, 3–14 June 1992, Rio de Janiero, Brazil, *available at* http://www.un.org/esa/sustdev/documents/agenda21/english/agenda21toc.htm (last visited July 16, 2007).

256. *Id.* at ch. 17.7.

257. Article 1 of the Convention on Biological Diversity, *available at* http://www.cbd.int/convention/convention.shtml (last visited Feb. 15, 2008).

258. *Id.* at Article 8.

259. The Convention on Biological Diversity Around the World, *available at* http://www.cbd.int/countries/?ctr=us (last visited July 16, 2007).

260. Jakarta Mandate on Marine and Coastal Biodiversity—Marine and Coastal Protected Areas, *available at* http://www.cdb.int/programmes/areas/marine/documents.aspx.

261. *Technical Advice on the Establishment and Management of a National System of Marine and Coastal Protected Areas*, CBD Technical Series No. 13, *available at* http://www.biodiv.org/doc/publications/cbd-ts-13.pdf (last visited July 16, 2007).

262. The International Coral Reef Initiative, *available at* http://www.icriforum.org/router.cfm?show=secretariat/sec_home.html (last visited July 16, 2007).

263. *Id.*

264. What is ICRA?, *available at* http://www.icriforum.org/router.cfm?show=secretariat/about_ICRI.html (last visited July 16, 2007).

265. Global Coral Reef Monitoring Network: About, *available at* http://www.gcrmn.org/about.aspx (last visited July 16, 2007).

266. Baur, Irvin & Misenko, *supra* note 2, at 554–55; Schorr, *supra* note 24, at 695–97.

267. Nat'l MPA Center, Draft Framework for Developing the National System of Marine Protected Areas 9 (July 2006).

268. Baur, Irvin & Misenko, *supra* note 2, at 545.

269. *Id.* at 554–55.

270. *Id.* at 502.

271. Exec. Order No. 13,158, *supra* note 13, at § 5.

272. The MMA inventory was expected to be completed in 2006, although as of February 2008 it was still incomplete. Inventory of Sites—Status of the Inventory, *available at* http://www3.mpa.gov/exploreinv/status.aspx (last visited Feb. 22, 2008).

273. Nat'l MPA Center, Draft Framework for Developing the National System of Marine Protected Areas 17 (July 2006).

274. *Id.* at 17–21 (July 2006).

275. *Id.* at 23.

276. *Id.* at 24–25.

277. *Id.* at 25. Any federal, state, local, or tribal managing agency may also nominate an eligible site as a candidate site for the national system. *Id.*

278. *Id.* at 26.

279. *Id.* at 33–34.

280. *See, e.g.*, STEVEN L. YAFFEE ET AL, ECOSYSTEM MANAGEMENT IN THE UNITED STATES (1996); R. Edward Grumbine, *Reflections on "What Is Ecosystem Management,"* 11 CONSERVATION BIOLOGY 41 (1997); Rebecca W. Thompson, *Ecosystem Management: Great Idea, But What Is It, Will It Work, and Who Will Pay,* 9 NAT. RES. & ENV'T 42 (1995); and George Frampton, *Beyond the Balance of Nature: Environmental Law Faces the New Ecology: Ecosystem Management in the Clinton Administration,* 7 DUKE ENVTL. L. & POL'Y F. 39 (1996).

281. *See, e.g., Ecosystem-Based Fishery Management and the Reauthorization of the Magnuson-Stevens Fishery Conservation and Management Act, Oversight Hearing before the Subcomm. on Fisheries Conservation, Wildlife & Oceans of the House Comm. on Res.,* 107th Cong. (2001); Ecosystem Approach Task Force, Strategic Guidance for Implementing an Ecosystem-based Approach to Fisheries Management (May 2003); Jason S. Link, *Ecological Considerations in Fisheries Management: When Does It Matter?,* FISHERIES, Apr. 2002; R.W. Zabel et al., *Ecologically Sustainable Yield,* 91 AM. SCIENTIST 150 (Mar.-Apr. 2003); Food & Agriculture Org. of the U. N. Technical Guidelines for Responsible Fisheries, *Fisheries Management: The Ecosystem Approach to Fisheries* (No. 4 Supp. 2 2003); and PEW OCEANS COMM., AMERICA'S LIVING OCEANS: CHARTING A COURSE FOR SEA CHANGE (May 2003).

282. Pew Institute for Ocean Science, Ecosystem-Based Fishery Management (EBFM), http://www.pewoceanscience.org/projects/Ecosystem_Based/intro.php (last visited Nov. 10, 2005).

283. *See* J. B. Ruhl, *Thinking of Environmental Law as a Complex Adaptive System: How to Clean Up the Environment by Making a Mess of Environmental Law,* 34 HOUS. L. REV. 933 (1997).

284. Interagency Ecosystem Management Task Force Report, *The Ecosystem Approach: Healthy Ecosystems and Sustainable Economies* (June 1995); Marian Macpherson, *Integrating Ecosystem Management Approaches into Federal Fishery Management Through the Magnuson-Stevens Fishery Conservation and Management Act,* 6 OCEAN & COASTAL L.J. 1 (2001).

285. Through the Sustainable Fisheries Act, Pub. L. No. 104-297, 110 Stat. 3559 (1996).

286. Ecosystem-Based Fishery Management, *at* http://www.nmfs.noaa.gov/sfa/EPAPrpt.pdf (last visited July 18, 2007).

287. *Id.* at v.

288. U.S. COMM'N ON OCEAN POL'Y, AN OCEAN BLUEPRINT FOR THE 21ST CENTURY: FINAL REPORT (2004).

289. See Chapter 20 for a more detailed discussion of a new appraoch to oceans management.
290. *Id.* at 105.
291. *Id.*
292. *Id.* at 106.
293. Pew Oceans Commission, America's Living Oceans: Charting a Course for Sea Change (May 2003).
294. *Id.* at 34. The Pew Report defines "marine reserve" as "a type of marine protected area in which all extractive, additive, or ecologically destructive human activities are prohibited on a lasting basis, except as necessary for evaluation of reserve effectiveness and appropriate research. Destructive human activities include, but are not limited to, those that alter habitats, harm or kill organisms, or change the dynamics of the ecosystem." *Id.* at 106.
295. *Id.* at 106.
296. *Id.*
297. *Id.*
298. Executive Order 13,336 (Dec. 17, 2004).
299. About the Committee on Ocean Policy, *available at* http://ocean.ceq.gov/about/welcome.html (last visited July 18, 2007). Members of the COP include the Secretaries of State, Defense, the Interior, Agriculture, Health and Human Services, Commerce, Labor, Transportation, Energy, Homeland Security, and the Attorney General as well as others. *Id.*
300. These include the Interagency Committee on Ocean Science and Resource Management Integration, National Science and Technology Council Joint Subcommittee on Ocean Science and Technology, Subcommittee on Integrated Management of Ocean Resources, National Security Council Policy Coordinating Committee, and an expanded Ocean Research Advisory Panel. *Id.*
301. U.S. Ocean Action Plan: The Bush Administration's Response to the U.S. Commission on Ocean Policy, *available at* http://ocean.ceq.gov/actionplan.pdf (last visited July 18, 2007).
302. The National Science and Technology Council Joint Subcommittee on Ocean Science and Technology (JSOST) published an Ocean Priorities Framework in April 2005. Ocean Priorities Framework, *available at* http://ocean.ceq.gov/about/docs/JSOST_Priorities_040505.pdf (last visited July 19, 2007). In 2007, JSOST issued Charting the Course for Ocean Science for the United States for the Next Decade: An Ocean Research Priorities Plan and Implementation Strategy, *available at* http://ocean.ceq.gov/about/docs/orppfinal.pdf (last visited July 19, 2007).
303. U.S. Ocean Action Plan, *supra* note 301, at 4–5.
304. H.R. 21, 110th Cong. (2007).
305. *Id.*
306. *See* http://resourcescommittee.house.gov/index.php?option=com_jcalpro&Itemid=32&extmode-=view&extid=44.
307. S. 362, H.R. 3692, 109th Cong. (2005). The bill was referred to House subcommittee on Sept. 26, 2005.
308. GovTrack.us, H.R. 1205: Coral Reef Conservation Admendments Act of 2007, http://www.govtrack.us/congress/bill.xpd?bill=h110-1205.
309. Department of Commerce, *Administration Releases: Coral Reef Ecosystem Conservation Amendments Act (CRECAA) of 2007,* http://www.coralreef.noaa.gov/crca.html.
310. S. 880, H.R. 1712, 109th Cong. (2005).

chapter eighteen

Climate Change and the Marine Environment

Christophe A. G. Tulou
Michael L. Goo
Patrick A. Parenteau
John Costenbader

I. Introduction

The environmental stresses our oceans now face are numerous and diverse. They include coastal development, ocean dumping, marine pollution, overfishing, exploitation of undersea resources, depletion of marine species, and the deterioration and collapse of marine ecosystems. These stresses alone severely threaten the vitality of our oceans and marine biological resources. However, these stresses are magnified substantially when considered in connection with the worldwide threat of global warming, caused by the buildup of human-generated emissions of greenhouse gases resulting in sea level rise, warming of the oceans, and ocean acidification. As discussed in this chapter, global warming as an exacerbating factor itself is arguably among the greatest threats ever to ocean stability and health. Although perhaps the principal focus has been on the impact of the warming of the earth on terrestrial systems and ice sheets, ocean warming and ocean acidification may pose greater and more immediate risks.

Environmental law is built on the premise that all elements of the natural world are interconnected. Nowhere is this more apparent than in the relationship between the atmosphere, the ocean, and global warming. Although global warming pollutants are emitted into the atmosphere and are not directly discharged into the ocean, the

The authors express their appreciation to Emily K. Merolli, an associate with Perkins Coie, for her contribution to this chapter.

effects of these pollutants on the health and sustainability of life in the ocean are direct and pervasive. In combination with other stresses already affecting the ocean, the reality of climate change and its consequences of ocean warming and acidification put our already imperiled marine ecosystems at serious risk.

If U.S. environmental laws are to preserve the quality of the human environment and maintain the links that hold together natural ecosystems, they need to be equipped to confront the challenge of climate change. After discussing the ways in which global warming affects coastal and ocean areas, this chapter analyzes the U.S. laws that can be used to combat climate change. While these laws have some application to climate change, they unfortunately are not equipped fully to grapple with the widespread and cumulative nature of the greenhouse gas emissions that are the cause of global warming. This chapter concludes with a discussion of new legal mechanisms that would be most effective in controlling greenhouse gas emissions.

II. Current State of the Law

A. Climate Change and the Marine Environment—Scope of the Problem

1. The Continued Health and Vitality of Oceans and Coasts Is Crucial to Public Health and Welfare

In 2003, it was estimated that 153 million Americans, or fifty-three percent of the U.S. population, lived in U.S. coastal counties.[1] The estimated socioeconomic value of global ocean and coastal ecosystems is $21 trillion per year through food production, recreation, nutrient recycling, climate regulation, and the oceans' influence over the chemical composition of the atmosphere.[2] In the United States, coastal watershed counties contribute over $4.5 trillion per year, half of the nation's gross domestic product, involving about 60 million jobs—many of which are tied to industries directly dependent on healthy coastal and ocean ecosystems and living resources, such as recreation, tourism, and fisheries. The United States has an extraordinary incentive to preserve and protect the population and industries of the coastal areas.

> **The United States has an extraordinary incentive to preserve and protect the population and industries of its coastal areas.**

Coastal fisheries and coastal-dependent industries in the United States are large economic contributors. The total value of U.S. commercial fisheries was over $3 billion in 2001.[3] California beaches alone generate $14 billion in direct revenues, contribute $73 billion to the national economy, generate $2.6 billion in direct federal taxes, generate $14 billion in indirect taxes, and provide over 883,000 jobs.[4] On average, a twelve-inch rise in sea level would inundate 100 feet of dry beach, greatly reducing the area and recreational amenities of many beaches. Increased storminess combined with direct, sea level inundation would reduce many Southern California recreational beaches to narrow, hazardous strips of sand with ocean waves on the seaward side and urban development on the inland side. Shore protection costs would escalate while beach recreation, tourism revenues, taxes, and jobs would plummet.

2. Human Activities Are Increasing Atmospheric Concentrations of Carbon Dioxide, Thereby Contributing to Changes in Climate and the Marine Environment

Carbon dioxide is the primary contributor among a suite of atmospheric gases that contribute to climate change. Present-day levels of about 380 parts per million are unprecedented over the past 650,000 years. Based on historical data (derived from Greenland and Antarctic ice cores), concentrations of carbon dioxide did not rise much above 280 parts per million prior to the industrial revolution. Over the past decade, carbon dioxide levels have increased at a rate of about 1.9 parts per million per year on average, with the primary sources being fossil fuel burning and land use changes, including tropical deforestation.[5]

a. Increased Carbon Dioxide Levels Are Affecting Atmospheric and Ocean Temperatures

The world's climate is warming; it is going to get much warmer; and humans are significantly responsible. The earth's surface, atmosphere, and at least the upper 3,000 meters of the oceans are warming. There is scientific consensus that the observed global surface warming over the past century—of 0.74°C (0.56 to 0.92°C)—is due to increases in greenhouse gas concentrations and that this warming has been particularly strong over the past twenty years. In fact, eleven of the last twelve years (1995–2006) rank among the 12 warmest since 1850. Global average temperatures will increase about 0.2°C per decade over the next two decades under business-as-usual emissions, and even if emissions remained at 2000 levels, temperatures would still increase by 0.1°C per decade. Depending on emissions projections, surface warming will increase anywhere from 1.8 to 4.0°C by the year 2099. This warming is occurring despite the fact that the ocean has absorbed more than 80 percent of the heat added to the climate system.[6]

b. Increased Carbon Dioxide Levels Are Creating a Fundamental and Detrimental Shift in Ocean Chemistry

Through the absorption of a substantial portion of the carbon dioxide emitted by human activities, the oceans are becoming more acidic, with dramatic consequences for organisms from corals to the planktonic foundation of marine food webs.

On timescales of several thousands of years, the oceans will ultimately absorb about ninety percent of the carbon dioxide in the atmosphere. However, because of slow mixing time, the ocean has only taken up about thirty percent of the carbon dioxide emitted in the past twenty years or so. From 1800 to 1994, the ocean absorbed about forty-eight percent of fossil fuel and cement-manufacturing emissions.[7]

Emissions of nitrogen and sulfur oxides also contribute to increasing ocean acidity, particularly in coastal areas near major pollution sources, where this contribution could amount to ten to fifty percent of the anthropogenic carbon-dioxide-driven changes.[8]

While this "ocean sponge" effect has certainly forestalled more pronounced climate change above the surface, it is lowering pH and saturation states of the carbonate minerals substantially, making survival increasingly difficult for the many major groups of marine organisms that use these minerals to build skeletons and shells—a process known as calcification. Assuming that carbon dioxide emissions continue at the current pace, surface water pH levels will decrease by 0.4 pH units relative to preindustrial levels by 2100, lower than they have been in millions of years.[9]

Calcifying organisms are sensitive to changes in ocean chemistry; even small changes will have large impacts, and it is clear that their ability to grow calcium carbonate shells and skeletons will decrease with increasing acidification. Extrapolations of laboratory experiments indicate that calcification rates will decrease up to sixty percent during the twenty-first century. Such a reduction will affect individual corals and the ability of reefs to maintain a positive balance between reef building and reef erosion, which is the process by which corals' calcium carbonate skeletons are rubbed, scraped, and chewed away by a combination of physical forces and reef fish.[10]

Basic chemistry dictates that as carbon dioxide levels in seawater increase, not only will calcification decrease, but, at some point, calcium carbonate skeletons will also dissolve. Although there are many questions about the particulars of organism survival and ecosystem effects, it is clear that at some threshold level of carbon dioxide, reef dissolution will exceed calcification—the reef equivalent of osteoporosis. Although that may occur at different times and in different ways from reef to reef, it will be yet another substantial blow to the prospects for reef survival.[11]

Deep-sea corals appear particularly vulnerable to these changes.[12] As atmospheric carbon dioxide concentrations increase, saturation levels for aragonite, the form of calcium carbonate used by these corals, is decreasing. By 2099, an estimated seventy percent of known scleractinian deep-water coral ecosystems will become undersaturated—making it unlikely they will be able to calcify and more likely that coral structures will dissolve, with potentially significant implications on the distribution of deep-sea coral reefs and the organisms that depend on them.[13]

A variety of planktonic organisms also build calcium carbonate shells, many of which form an important foundation of marine food webs. As with corals, there is clear evidence that elevated carbon dioxide levels reduce their ability to build shells through calcification. In fact, data suggest that in some plankton species, this is not a linear relationship as it is among corals, but rather that there may be a threshold value below which there will be sudden and large decreases in calcification rates.[14] And, as with corals, it is not yet known whether or how planktonic calcifiers can adapt to reduced calcification rates.[15] However, since calcification does confer advantages to these species, decreased calcification is likely to compromise their fitness and thus impact marine food webs, which would substantially alter the biodiversity and productivity of the ocean.[16]

3. Changes to the Ocean Environment Will Have Major Adverse Effects on Human Safety, the Economy, and the Natural Environment

Although a relatively slow process compared to the warming of the atmosphere, the warming of oceans is occurring by virtue of their interaction with the air above them.

Over the period from 1961 to 2003, the upper 700 meters of the ocean warmed by 0.1°C.[17] Temperatures at the sea surface, where hurricanes are spawned and corals live, have warmed 0.4 to 0.8°C since the late 1800s.[18] Numerous serious public health and welfare implications arise from this oceanic warming.

a. Sea Level Rise Will Have Negative Effects on the Health and Welfare of U.S. Populations in Coastal Areas

The changing climate causes sea level to rise in two basic ways: warmer ocean waters take up greater volume, and melting glaciers and ice fields increase water supply to the oceans.

Estimated sea level rise over the past century was 0.17 (0.12 to 0.22) meters, with an average rate of 1.7 ± 0.5 mm/year during that period. Satellite observations from 1993 to 2003 show a 3.1 ± 0.7 mm/year increase, and scientists are unsure whether the difference is due to decadal variability or represents an increase in the long-term trend.[19] There is a great deal of historical support for the conclusion that global warming has contributed substantially to these increases; the correlation among past changes in atmospheric carbon dioxide, global warming, and changes in global sea level is clearly shown in the geologic record.[20]

Based on climate change projections, sea levels will rise between 0.18 and 0.59 meters from the present (1980–1999) to the end of the century (2090–2099) at a projected rate of about 3.8 mm/year by century's end, with thermal expansion due to warming of the oceans adding about seventy to seventy-five percent of the total increase.[21]

Intergovernmental Panel on Climate Change (IPCC) scientists acknowledge that temperature increases could lead to increases in Greenland and Antarctic ice sheet flow, thus affecting these estimates, but those effects are impossible to estimate at this time.[22] Recent reports point to startling changes at the margins of the Greenland and Antarctic ice sheets, which indicate that projections of sea level rise may indeed need to be revised upward.[23] The collapse of the Larsen B Ice Shelf in 2002 was followed by an acceleration of its major tributary glaciers by two- to eightfold, contributing about 0.07 mm/year to sea level rise.[24] This process is also playing out along the Amundsen Coast of the Antarctic Peninsula.[25] The flow changes associated with the removal of ice shelves are long-lived, and have a long-term and irreversible impact on glaciers.[26] For some time, the West Antarctic Ice Sheet has been the subject of great scientific focus because it contains enough ice to raise sea levels by six meters and is relatively unstable.[27]

Similar warming-caused losses of glacier-restricting ice shelves along the coast of Greenland have led to increased contributions to sea level rise of up to 0.09 mm/year.[28] A net loss of ice mass on Greenland could occur at global average warming in the range of 1.9 to 4.6°C (in line with global surface atmospheric temperature projections by the end of this century). Interestingly, temperatures in the same range (3–5°C) during the last interglacial period (about 125,000 years ago) accompanied global sea levels about four to six meters higher than today. The Greenland and other Arctic ice sheets contributed no more than four meters to that rise, suggesting that Antarctica may also have contributed.[29] Sustained warming of Greenland over hundreds or thousands of years would eliminate its ice sheet, resulting in a seven-meter sea level rise.[30]

This warming and sea level rise will continue for more than a millennium, even if carbon dioxide concentrations are stabilized, due to the long time required to remove this gas from the atmosphere.[31]

b. Warming and Acidification of the Oceans Will Detrimentally Affect Marine Life

> **Immersed in warming oceans, sensitive marine organisms must adapt, alter their geographic distribution, or face extinction.**

Immersed in warming oceans, sensitive marine organisms must adapt, alter their geographic distribution (i.e., shift poleward), or face extinction. There is scientific evidence for all of these responses. Degradation of marine life will negatively affect U.S. and global populations by affecting potential food suppliers, coastal fisheries, marine biological diversity, and the economy.

Coral reefs are among the ecosystems most sensitive to climate change, and the most conservative estimates suggest that half of all reefs will be destroyed by 2030–2050.[32] Much more than their beauty and recreational value will be lost. Coral reefs buffer shorelines from storms and erosion and provide homes, food, and nurseries for tens of thousands of marine species. They provide an estimated $375 billion per year in goods and services worldwide, with approximately 500 million people dependent on them for food, materials, or income. Approximately half of all U.S.-managed commercial fish species depend on coral reefs for at least a portion of their life cycle.[33]

Extinction due to increases in sea-surface temperatures is a real prospect for shallow-water, tropical corals. It is clear that many corals are operating within very close margins of their thermal tolerance, with bleaching occurring for many species at about 1°C above mean summer maximum temperatures, and causing widespread concern as this threshold will be chronically exceeded as temperatures rise over the next fifty years.[34] There is evidence that at least some corals and their algal symbionts (called zooxanthellae), which provide nourishment and lend color to corals, may be able to adapt to increasing temperatures. Nonetheless, it is not clear whether either life form will be able to adapt quickly enough to keep pace with the accelerating rate of environmental change.[35]

Evidence from the field is not encouraging. About twenty percent of the world's coral reefs have been effectively destroyed as a result of increasing sea-surface temperatures and show no immediate prospects for recovery. Another twenty-four percent of the world's reefs are under imminent risk of collapse, and a further twenty-six percent are under a longer-term threat of collapse.[36] Caribbean reefs are in catastrophic decline, with two of the major reef-building coral species in this area—staghorn and elkhorn—recently listed as endangered under the U.S. Endangered Species Act.[37]

A major global bleaching event in 1998 destroyed sixteen percent of the world's coral reefs, with most of the damage in the Indian Ocean (fifty percent of Indian Ocean coral was destroyed) and the western Pacific. Unfortunately, what was then a once-in-a-thousand-years event will become a regular occurrence within fifty years, based on projections of tropical sea-surface temperature increases in the range of 1 to 3°C by 2100.[38]

There is a significant connection between increasing ocean temperatures and primary productivity, a link especially pronounced in the tropics and midlatitudes. There, warmer surface waters lead to water column stratification, inhibited mixing, and reduced nutrient flow into surface waters, with resulting reduction in net primary production.[39] These changes will affect the magnitude and distribution of carbon dioxide exchange, fishery yields, and large-scale biological regimes.[40] Changing ocean temperatures also correlate with altered fish growth rates. Increasing surface temperatures are reflected by enhanced growth rates among species found at less than 250 meters depth, while growth rates of deep-water species below 1,000 meters have slowed in step with long-term cooling at those depths.[41]

Ocean warming is having an impact on the distributions of other important species. A marine diatom, *Neodenticula seminae*, has made its first appearance in the North Atlantic in 800,000 years, likely in response to climate change-enabled circulation between the North Pacific and North Atlantic via the Arctic Ocean.[42] Warm-water populations of copepods, small marine organisms that form a vital link in the food web as a food source for the larvae of many commercial and noncommercial marine fish, have moved 1,000 kilometers northward in the northeast Atlantic over the past forty years, accompanied by retraction in the range of their cold-water cousins.[43] Similar shifts have been shown among marine snails, squid, corals, and fish.[44] The distribution of the Balearic shearwater, *Puffinus mauretanicus*, has rapidly shifted northward, correlating with a 0.6°C increase in sea surface temperatures and a corresponding northward shift in prey (anchovies and sardines) and plankton.[45] Some of these adjustments can be abrupt, affecting the survival of not only the adjusting species but also many others, with huge implications for commercial fisheries and the basic functioning of marine ecosystems.[46]

If species that otherwise depend on one another, for instance as predator and prey, respond differently to ocean warming, the consequences can be significant. There is evidence of warming-induced mismatches in the timing of the spawning of certain zooplankton, the arrival of fish larvae, and blooms of the phytoplankton they eat, thus jeopardizing the survival of fish species and potentially affecting commercial fisheries.[47]

Alteration of aquatic habitats and species distributions by warming temperatures also exacerbates problems with invasive species, making native populations more susceptible to invasion.[48]

c. Hurricane Intensity Will Increase Because of Warmer Oceans

There is growing evidence that the theoretical link between warming seas and hurricane intensity exists in fact, based on broad confluence of theory, modeling, and observations.[49] Nonetheless, this assertion remains controversial.[50] Tropical sea-surface temperatures have risen by about 0.6°C since measurements began and about 0.5°C of that increase has occurred since 1970.[51] Record sea-surface temperatures (0.9°C above the norm) in the area critical for hurricanes contributed to the most active North Atlantic hurricane season on record in 2005; about half of that temperature anomaly can be attributed to global warming.[52]

A careful review of global data confirms a trend toward more frequent intense (category 4 and 5) storms over the past thirty years, a trend directly linked to increases in sea-surface temperatures.[53]

Even if tropical storms do not change markedly in intensity, rising sea levels, beach and wetland erosion, and storm surges will ensure increased damage along increasingly developed shorelines.[54] Hurricanes are already the costliest natural events in the United States, accounting for a significant fraction of damage, injury, and loss of life from natural hazards.[55]

d. Increased Storm Damage Will Endanger U.S. Coastal Communities

Large swaths of low-lying coastal lands around the United States are extremely vulnerable to any increase in sea level. As Hurricane Katrina demonstrated, such areas are already vulnerable to erosion, flooding, storm surges, and tsunamis; and poor development planning has placed trillions of dollars worth of building and infrastructure directly in the path of these threats. Further, higher sea levels interact with tides and storms to create more destructive impacts, as extreme high water levels occur with more frequency.[56] Approximately 58,000 square kilometers of land along the Atlantic and Gulf of Mexico coasts of the United States lie below 1.5 meters above sea level. Louisiana, Florida, Texas, and North Carolina account for more than eighty percent of these low-lying areas. In fact, North Carolina alone has as much land within one meter of sea level as the Netherlands.[57]

In California, a thirty-centimeter (twelve-inch) rise in sea level would shift the 100-year storm-surge-induced flood event to once every ten years.[58] Even a small rise in sea level would be accompanied by large amounts of coastal flooding, inundation, and storm damage. Along the San Diego coast, model results demonstrate approximately ten extreme water level events between 2070 and 2100 if there is no increase in sea level. Over the same time period there would be approximately 330 extreme events with a rise in sea level of twenty centimeters, 2,300 extreme events with a rise of forty centimeters, and almost 19,000 events with a rise of eighty centimeters.[59]

For the eighty-five coastal counties from Massachusetts to Virginia, approximately 1,000 square miles of land area lies below three feet above current sea levels, which includes about seventy square miles of developed land, 3,000 miles of roads, and some 388,000 people.[60]

e. Erosion Will Increase in Coastal Areas

Each year, erosion along U.S. shorelines will claim about 1,500 homes and the property they occupy at a cost of about $530 million annually.[61] According to the Federal

Emergency Management Agency, by 2060, coastal erosion will have threatened nearly 87,000 homes in U.S. coastal areas.[62]

The nature and extent of human development has severely undermined the ability of natural coastal features, such as wetlands and mangrove forests, to survive increasing seas. Under normal circumstances, they can accrete sediment to keep pace with, and retreat in the face of, rising sea levels. However, dams and levees impede the flow and deposition of sediments, a situation played out with devastating consequences in the Mississippi delta in Louisiana. The delta has lost more than 1,000 square miles since 1950, and continues to lose twenty-five to thirty-five square miles per year through the combination of sea level rise, land subsidence, and erosion. At this pace, more that 630,000 acres of Louisiana wetlands will disappear by 2050.[63]

By 2060, coastal erosion will have threatened nearly 87,000 homes in U.S. coastal areas.

B. Legal Authorities

There are no coastal or ocean laws that specifically address climate change. Instead, laws of general applicability to the environment, such as the Clean Air Act, Endangered Species Act, and the National Environmental Policy Act, must be used to address the effect of various federal actions that result in greenhouse gas emissions. Some of these actions will affect marine ecosystems and resources.

1. Clean Air Act

The Clean Air Act[64] is the principal federal statute regulating emissions of air pollutants into the ambient air from sources such as power plants, cars, and industry. These sources and others also emit greenhouse gases that cause global warming. Although no comprehensive federal statutory program[65] yet exists for combating global warming or limiting the overall amount of greenhouse gas emissions into the atmosphere from such sources within the United States, there are numerous provisions under the Clean Air Act that could be used to reduce global warming pollution. Recent case law, most notably the decision of the Supreme Court of the United States in *Massachusetts v. EPA*,[66] confirms this point. In addition, there are substantial efforts currently underway in the U.S. Congress to enact a comprehensive federal global warming statute.

In *Massachusetts v. EPA*, the Supreme Court faced the question of whether the Environmental Protection Agency has the statutory authority under Section 202(a)(1) of the Clean Air Act to regulate greenhouse gas emissions from new motor vehicles and whether EPA's reasons for refusing to regulate such emissions are consistent with the statute.[67] In a 5–4 decision, the Supreme Court concluded that EPA has such authority and rejected EPA's reasons for declining to regulate. The Supreme Court did not direct EPA to move forward with regulation, but instead remanded the case to EPA with instructions to determine whether greenhouse gas emissions "can reasonably be anticipated to endanger public health and welfare." As of the date of publication of this chapter, EPA had not yet made such a determination.[68]

In reaching its decision that EPA has authority under the Clean Air Act to regulate greenhouse gas emissions, the Supreme Court found that carbon dioxide and other greenhouse gases are air pollutants as defined Section 302(g) of the Clean Air Act.[69] The Court based its holding on the "unambiguous" language of the definition. Specifically, the Court held that the Clean Air Act's definition of "air pollutant" includes "any air pollution agent or combination of such agents, including any physical, chemical . . . substance or matter which is emitted into or otherwise enters the ambient air. . . ." Carbon dioxide, methane, nitrous oxide, and hydrofluorocarbons are without a doubt "physical [and] chemical . . . substance[s] which [are] emitted into . . . the ambient air."[70] According to the Court, on this point "[t]he statute is unambiguous."[71]

Based on this finding, the Court went on to conclude that "because greenhouse gases fit well within the Clean Air Act's capacious definition of 'air pollutant,' we hold that EPA has the statutory authority to regulate the emission of such gases from new motor vehicles."[72]

The court also rejected EPA's arguments for declining to regulate greenhouse gas emissions from motor vehicles under Section 202, but stopped short of concluding that EPA must regulate such emissions. According to the Court, "[t]he alternative basis for EPA's decision—that even if it has authority to regulate greenhouse gases, it would be unwise to do so—rests on reasoning divorced from the statutory text."[73] The Court concluded that "[u]nder the clear terms of the Clean Air Act, EPA can avoid taking further action only if it determines that greenhouse gases do not contribute to climate change or if it provides some reasonable explanation as to why it cannot or will not exercise its discretion to determine if they do."[74]

As detailed more fully below, concluding that greenhouse gas emissions do not contribute to climate change or that they cannot be reasonably anticipated to endanger public health and welfare will be extremely difficult, even on the basis of the impacts on oceans alone. As the Court itself noted, "[t]he harms associated with climate change are serious and well recognized."[75] Moreover, "EPA does not dispute the existence of a causal connection between man-made greenhouse gas emissions and global warming." These considerations led the court to conclude that Massachusetts had standing to bring the case on the basis of an alleged loss of Massachusetts coastline resulting from sea level rise due to global warming. As of the time of this writing, EPA had not yet issued its endangerment finding.

Given that carbon dioxide is a pollutant under the Clean Air Act, numerous other provisions of this statute could be invoked to reduce greenhouse gas emissions. For instance, Section 165(a)(4) of the Clean Air Act requires that permits for proposed major sources include an emission limit reflecting the Best Available Control Technology (BACT) "for each pollutant subject to regulation" under the Act.[76] In light of the *Massachusetts v. EPA* decision, one can easily conclude that CO_2 is a pollutant "subject to regulation" under the Act.

In fact, not only is CO_2 "subject to regulation" under the Clean Air Act, it is actually a "regulated" pollutant under the Clean Air Act, pursuant to existing EPA regulations under Section 821 of the Clean Air Act, which requires utilities to report CO_2 emissions. Given the status of CO_2 as a pollutant that is already "regulated," as well as a pollutant that is "subject to regulation" under the Clean Air Act, Section 165 requires that an emission limitation be established for CO_2 at new coal-fired power plants, reflecting best available control technology (BACT). Emission limits for CO_2 are already effective in states such as California, Washington, and Wyoming that would require substantial carbon capture and geologic disposal for coal-fired power plants (or the use of energy sources other than coal).

In addition to requiring a BACT emission limitation for CO_2, the Clean Air Act can be used to address greenhouse gas emissions through Sections 165(a)(4) and 169(3), which require that EPA consider other environmental effects, as well as alternatives to reduce them, as it conducts its BACT analysis for conventional pollutants.[77] This requirement also obligates EPA to consider the impact of greenhouse gases, including CO_2, as it determines what is BACT for conventional pollutants (such as sulfur oxides and nitrogen oxides). Although few other environmental considerations could be more important, EPA has refused to undertake this critical analysis.[78]

Finally, under Section 165(a)(2), EPA must consider comments that are raised during the comment process including "the air quality impacts of such sources, alternatives thereto, control technology requirements, and other appropriate considerations."[79] Other provisions of the Clean Air Act that could be invoked on the basis that CO_2 is a pollutant include the provisions relating to National Ambient Air Quality Standards (Section 109) and standards for fuels regulation (Section 211).[80]

2. Endangered Species Act

Looming over all efforts to conserve endangered species, including marine species, and to arrest the accelerating rate of global extinctions already underway is the unprecedented threat of climate change. According to the latest projections of the IPCC, "[a]pproximately 20–30 percent of the plant and animal species assessed so far are likely to be at increased risk of extinction if increases in global average temperatures exceed 1.5–2.5° C.[81] Experts say that to hold temperatures below that range, carbon concentrations in the atmosphere, which are currently at 280 parts per million, must be stabilized between 450 and 550 parts per million by 2050.[82] This in turn will require an unprecedented reduction in carbon emissions across many economic sectors, chiefly energy and transportation, as well as changes in land use to conserve and expand "carbon sinks," especially the tropical rain forests in places like the Amazon Basin.[83] According to scientists, temperatures in the midrange projections for 2050 could result in over a million species being "committed to extinction."[84] As discussed above, corals are particularly at risk.

These problems have lead to the potential applicability of the Endangered Species Act (ESA) to addressing climate change. Application of the ESA starts with the listing of a species. In 2006, for example, the National Marine Fisheries Service (NMFS) listed two species of coral—elkhorn and staghorn—as threatened species on May 9, 2006.[85] This was the first listing under the ESA based on the effects of climate change. In explaining the basis for its decision, the National Oceanic and Atmospheric Administration (NOAA) cited both bleaching and acidification as major threats to these two species:

> Temperature-induced bleaching affects growth, maintenance, reproduction, and survival of these two species. As summarized in the status review report, bleaching has been documented as the source of extensive elkhorn and staghorn mortality in numerous locations throughout their ranges. The extent and impact of bleaching is a function of the magnitude and duration of the increase in temperature.
>
> Along with elevated sea surface temperature, atmospheric carbon dioxide levels have increased in the last century, and there is no apparent evidence the trend will not continue. As atmospheric carbon dioxide is dissolved in surface seawater, seawater becomes more acidic, shifting the balance of inorganic carbon away from carbon dioxide and carbonate toward bicarbonate. This shift decreases the ability of corals to calcify because corals are thought to use carbonate, not bicarbonate, to build their aragonite skeletons. Experiments have shown a reduction of coral calcification in response to elevated carbon dioxide levels; therefore, increased carbon dioxide levels in seawater may be contributing to the [threatened] status of the two species.[86]

In January 2007, the U.S. Fish and Wildlife Service (FWS) announced the proposed listing of the polar bear as a threatened species.[87] Though the statutory deadline for making a final listing decision expired on January 9, 2008, FWS Director Williams recently announced that the agency needs more time to complete its analysis.[88] As a "charismatic mega-fauna," the polar bear has quickly become the poster child for the effects of climate change on vulnerable ecosystems. The arctic is experiencing global warming at twice the average worldwide rate, in part due to feedback loops resulting from the melting of sea ice and the loss of the albedo effect, and to the release of methane, another greenhouse gas, resulting from the melting of the permafrost.[89]

As a "charismatic mega-fauna," the polar bear has quickly become the poster child for the effects of climate change on vulnerable ecosystems.

The listing of these species ushers in a whole new dimension to the ESA processes. The ESA provides several legal tools that can be used to address climate. Once a species is listed as endangered, it is subject to the take prohibition, which makes it illegal to "harass, harm, pursue, hunt, shoot, wound, kill, trap, capture, or collect," or attempt to do any of those things."[90] The prohibited act of "harm" has been defined by regulation to mean habitat modification that "actually kills or injures wildlife by significantly impairing essential behavioral patterns, including breeding, feeding or sheltering." The take prohibition can be extended to threatened species by regulation. Thus, if it can be established that a source of greenhouse gas emissions is causing a take (admittedly, a potentially difficult showing given the widespread and cumulative nature of the emissions that cause global warming), it would be prohibited under the ESA. In addition, even if an action does not cause emissions, the ESA take prohibition may still be helpful for addressing the effects of climate change on marine species. If, for example, a listed species alters its behavior because of climate change and is taken by a human activity, the ESA prohibition can be applied in an effort to help reduce threats to that species. Additionally, the provision may possibly improve a species' chances for surviving until the underlying causes of climate change are addressed through other legal authorities.

The ESA also will have application to marine species affected by global warming through the Section 7(a)(2) consultation process and jeopardy/adverse modification of critical habitat prohibitions. Under Section 7(a)(2), federal action agencies must engage in consultation with either the FWS or NMFS to determine whether a proposal is likely to cause jeopardy to a listed species or adversely modify or destroy critical habitat, in which case the action is prohibited unless modified through a reasonable and prudent alternative.[91]

This requirement can be useful in two ways. First, it requires all federal agencies to study the effects of their actions rigorously to determine how they impact listed species. This analysis must consider not only actions that contribute to climate change, but also how actions that do not cause greenhouse gas emissions nonetheless affect species that are being impacted by global warming.[92]

Second, the prohibition itself could cause activities to be halted or modified if they will, individually or cumulatively, jeopardize the species or adversely modify designated critical habitat. Such effects need not be related to climate change. If, for example, climate has caused a significant deterioration of habitat, such as the loss of sea ice, causing a species like the polar bear to alter its behavior or become vulnerable to other activities, then the prohibition can apply to actions that do not in and of themselves cause climate change but have a synergistic impact on listed species (for example, oil and gas leasing in polar bear habitat).

Finally, the ESA brings to bear the recovery plan process. Section 4(f) of the ESA requires FWS and NMFS to "develop and implement plans for the conservation and survival of endangered and threatened species . . . unless [FWS/NMFS] finds that such a plan will not promote the conservation of the species."[93] The agency must give priority to those species in conflict with construction or other development projects or specific forms of economic activity. These plans may not have the force of law, but they provide a helpful blueprint and measurable criteria for species recovery that could be particularly helpful in defining how climate change effects are considered under the ESA and addressed through a wide range of federal, state, local, and private activities affecting the species. Climate change impacts will also have a bearing on the risk analysis that underlies delisting decisions.[94]

3. National Environmental Policy Act

The National Environmental Policy Act (NEPA) requires federal agencies to assess the environmental impacts associated with major federal actions, projects, or decisions, such as issuing permits, spending federal funds, or approving actions that affect federal lands. Several states have similar planning laws that require state and local agencies to consider the environmental impacts of their decisions. Under these laws, federal and state administrators evaluate and approve or reject many diverse business and development proposals ranging from local land use developments to major energy projects.

Federal and state administrators are increasingly requiring greenhouse gas issues to be evaluated in the proposals they review. This heightened concern is likely driven by recent court rulings under environmental law such as NEPA, the Endangered Species Act, and the Clean Air Act requiring consideration and evaluation of climate change impact.

Under NEPA, federal agencies must consider and publicly disclose the environmental impacts of their decisions and explore and evaluate reasonable alternatives to a proposed action. Agencies perform an environmental assessment (EA) of a project to evaluate its expected impacts, potential alternatives, and mitigation strategies. For those projects not expected to have any measurably significant impact, the agencies will issue a "Finding of No Significant Impact." A more extensive "environmental impact statement" (EIS) is required for projects with significant impacts. Some project categories that generally require extensive NEPA analysis include timber sales, oil and gas development or other resource use on federal lands, permits for the construction and operation of dams, construction of transportation corridors, and some permits to discharge wastewater into navigable waters.

Federal courts have required agencies to evaluate greenhouse gas emissions from proposed projects under NEPA.[95] NEPA-based climate change litigation has recently intensified and now includes more focus on the federal government's role as project financier.[96]

Most recently, a federal agency's rulemaking was successfully challenged under NEPA. In the landmark decision in *Center for Biological Diversity v. National Highway Traffic Safety Administration*,[97] eleven states, the District of Columbia, the City of New York, and four public interest organizations petitioned for review of a rule issued by the National Highway Traffic Safety Administration (NHTSA) titled "Average Fuel Economy Standards for Light Trucks, Model Years 2008–2011." The rule set corporate average fuel economy (CAFE) standards for light trucks, defined by NHTSA to include many sport utility vehicles, minivans, and pickup trucks. In addition to challenges brought under the Energy Policy and Conservation Act of 1975, petitioners also challenged the rule under NEPA. Under NEPA, petitioners argued that NHTSA's EA was inadequate because it failed to take a "hard look" at the greenhouse gas implications of its rulemaking and failed to analyze a reasonable range of alternatives or examine the rule's cumulative impact. Petitioners further maintained that the agency was required to prepare an EIS. The Ninth Circuit agreed: "The impact of greenhouse gas emissions on climate change is precisely the kind of cumulative impacts analysis that NEPA requires agencies to conduct. Any given rule setting a CAFE standard might have an 'individually minor' effect on the environment, but these are collectively significant actions taking place over a period of time."[98]

In the wake of these and other lawsuits, some federal agencies have stepped up their own scrutiny of project decisions that may either directly or indirectly increase greenhouse gas emissions. For example, EPA recently questioned a draft EIS prepared by the U.S. Forest Service for failing to predict the amount of methane to be released and not adequately analyzing the capture and utilization of methane as an energy resource. EPA ranked the draft planning document as insufficient and emphasized that the missing information and analysis were substantial issues to be resolved and disclosed in the final EIS. The Department of Interior (DOI) has also signaled increased interest in the assessment of climate change impacts under NEPA. For example, DOI has created an internal task force on climate change to study climate science and land and water management, and to assess the implications of climate change for a range of documents the agency relies on to make its decisions. The Department of Energy has also issued internal guidance on how to address climate change under NEPA. It is likely that in the current political and legal atmosphere, more agencies will follow suit.

NEPA applies only to environmentally significant projects that have some sort of federal action, or federal "hook," involved. However, several states have their own environmental planning laws, often termed "little NEPAs," which apply to state and local environmental and land use decisions. Some of these states have also enacted significant laws to address climate change, and their state and local administrators have begun to take a hard look at the greenhouse gas emissions associated with the projects or plans they review. In California and Washington, general development plans for city and county planning and growth have been required to consider climate change impacts under state environmental planning laws, by courts, and by executive order.

As regulatory responses to climate change intensify, it is also important to recognize that past interpretations of the scope and requirements of well-established environmental planning laws like NEPA may also change to adapt to this emerging issue. Federal actions significantly affecting the marine environment will be among those that are required to take climate change into account, not only if the actions themselves contribute to global warming but also if the resources otherwise affected by the proposal are experiencing the effects of climate change and are, therefore, more vulnerable to harm. Clearly, climate change will become a significant factor to be evaluated in EISs in the years to come.

III. Emerging and Unresolved Issues

For global warming to be halted and reversed, it will be necessary to enact new international and U.S. legal authorities. Several important initiatives are already underway in each area.

A. International Climate Change Authorities

One hundred ninety-two countries are parties to the United Nations Framework Convention on Climate Change (UNFCCC), which was created at the United Nations Conference on Environment and Development in 1992 in Rio de Janeiro. The treaty was opened for signature in 1992 and came into force in 1994. The United States is a signatory to the treaty, whose objective is "stabilization of greenhouse gas concentrations in the atmosphere at a level that would prevent dangerous anthropogenic interference with the climate system."[99] The United States ratified the UNFCCC in 1994. The UNFCCC applies to both developed and developing nations, under the principle of "common but differentiated responsibilities."[100] The UNFCCC states that developing countries shall take the lead in reducing greenhouse gas emissions with a goal of reducing their emissions to 1990 levels by 2000.[101]

The UNFCCC treaty contemplates that additional negotiations under the treaty will result in further "Protocols" aimed at reducing greenhouse gas emissions. In 1997, at Kyoto, Japan, the Kyoto Protocol was created under the UNFCCC. This treaty created an initial "commitment period" for the years 2008 to 2012, designed to reduce industrialized countries' total emissions by at least five percent below their 1990 levels.[102] The United States budget called for a seven percent reduction below 1990 levels by the end of the first commitment period. Although the United States signed the Kyoto Protocol in 1998, unfortunately, the United States never ratified the treaty. In fact, President Clinton chose not to submit it to the Senate for approval, in the wake of the Senate's 95–0 vote in favor of S. Res. 98, the Byrd-Hagel resolution, which stated that no global warming treaty requiring action by developed countries should be ratified unless such a treaty also required developing countries to reduce their emissions. However, even though the United States is not a party to the Kyoto Protocol, 168 nations, including virtually all developed countries except the United States, have ratified or accepted the protocol and are moving forward to reduce emissions in accordance with its terms.

Virtually all developed countries have ratified or accepted the Kyoto Protocol and are moving to reduce emissions in accordance with its terms.

Both the Parties to the UNFCCC treaty and the Kyoto Protocol continue to negotiate regarding additional commitments for reductions in greenhouse gas emissions. At the latest Conference of the Parties in Bali, Indonesia, a "roadmap" was developed leading up to the next two Conferences to be held in Poznan, Poland, and Copenhagen, Denmark. This roadmap sets up a framework for future negotiations with the aim of developing an agreement governing the period after the end of the Kyoto Protocol's first "commitment period" in 2012. Although the United States was widely criticized at the Bali Conference for blocking progress and for eliminating language that would have called for scientifically based emission reduction goal, ultimately the United States was not entirely successful in preventing an agreement to begin the process of negotiating toward future commitments at the upcoming Poznan and Copenhagen Conferences of the Parties. Nevertheless, most observers believe that a key element for a successful set of negotiations under the UNFCCC treaty is the adoption by the United States of a set of binding limits for U.S. greenhouse gas emissions, a process that, as described below, is well underway within the U.S. Congress.

B. U.S. Legislative Proposals

In the 110th Congress there are numerous legislative proposals designed to create comprehensive "cap and trade" programs for capping carbon emissions. The leading legislative proposals include S. 309, the Sanders-Boxer bill; S. 1766, the Bingaman-Specter bill; and S. 2191, the Lieberman-Warner bill. Notable House proposals include the Waxman bill, H.R. 1590; the Gilchrest-Olver bill, H.R. 4067; and the Udall-Petri bill, H.R. 5042.

Each of these bills would create a comprehensive "cap and trade" system for limiting emissions of greenhouse gases to specific levels, requiring permits for each ton of emission, and allowing such permits to be freely traded. They vary substantially in terms of the level of required reductions.

For instance, the most stringent bills, the Sanders-Boxer bill and its House companion legislation, the Waxman Safe Climate Act, would require a reduction in greenhouse gas emissions of eighty percent from 1990 levels by 2050 and a return to 1990 emission levels (about a sixteen percent reduction from 2005 levels) by 2020. These levels are consistent with stabilization of greenhouse gases at 450 parts per million and are identical to the levels mandated in the California law, AB 32. At the other end of the spectrum, the Bingaman-Specter bill would require the United States to reduce its emissions to 2006 levels by 2020 and to 1990 levels by 2030. The principal and unique feature of the Bingaman-Specter bill is its so-called "safety valve," which caps the cost of carbon allowances at $12 per ton. The Lieberman-Warner bill, which was reported from the Environment and Public Works Committee in December 2007, represents a midrange proposal that would reduce U.S. emissions by approximately eighteen to twenty-five percent by 2020 and by sixty-three to sixty-six percent by 2050. The Gilchrest-Olver bill is a version of an earlier Senate bill, the McCain-Lieberman bill, and the Udall-Petri legislation includes some features that are similar to prior versions of the Bingaman bill.

A key feature of these bills is that by creating a cap-and-trade system, substantial amounts of revenue are generated through the granting and auctioning of permit to emit. The Congressional Budget Office has estimated these revenues could be as large as $300 billion per year.[103] A key issue in Congress is how to distribute these permits and the revenue generated from auctioning such permits. This funding stream could be used to help benefit or protect ocean resources.

Of particular note regarding oceans is the Lieberman-Warner bill, S. 2191. Sections 4101 and 4702 of the bill create an adaptation fund (funded through the auctioning of emission allowances) to be used consistent with a national strategy for "assisting fish and wildlife, fish and wildlife habitat, plants and associated ecological processes in becoming more resilient and adapting to the impacts of climate change and ocean acidification." In developing this strategy, the President is to consider the reports of the Pew Oceans Commission and the United States Commission on Ocean Policy. The national strategy is to include efforts to protect ocean and coastal species from the impacts of climate change and ocean acidification, adaptation strategies to address sea level rise and numerous other ocean-related impacts on fish and wildlife and their ocean, freshwater, and terrestrial habitats. If enacted, these provisions of the S. 2191 would create significant new ocean-related protection efforts and would provide substantial funding for such programs.

Finally, in recent years, several bills dealing specifically with ocean management and conservation have been introduced that include provisions dealing with climate change. In 2005, S.1224 (known as the National Oceans Protection Act, or NOPA) recognized climate change as a threat, as well as the linkages among oceans, atmospheric systems, and land, including climate change. NOPA identified climate change as a national priority for coordination of research and technology development, and assigned responsibility for monitoring and responding to climate change issues to a variety of actors, including the Council on Ocean Stewardship and a Presidential Panel of Advisors on Oceans and Climate. Also in 2005, H.R. 2939 (the Oceans Conservation, Education, and National Strategy for the 21st Century Act, or OCEANS-21) identified global climate change as a threat, and required the establishment of a network of regional ocean ecosystem resource information systems, based on the idea that information generated by various resource monitoring systems is more useful if fully integrated. OCEANS-21 was reintroduced as H.R. 21, and is currently pending before Congress.

C. Implementation of Existing Laws

As discussed in the previous section, several existing laws provide mechanisms for addressing the climate change problem, including the Clean Air Act, ESA, and NEPA. Currently, there are few regulatory initiatives being undertaken by the Executive Branch to implement these laws for purposes of addressing global warming. Consequently, it is likely that litigation will be the chosen vehicle for defining the extent to which these laws can be used for controlling climate change, generally, and the effects of global warming on the oceans, in particular. As this chapter goes to publication, numerous lawsuits seeking to force existing U.S. law into a proactive stance for addressing climate change have been initiated, and the courts are sure to play a leading role in determining the extent to which domestic laws can be applied for this purpose.

IV. Conclusion

Global changes due to human-caused alterations in climate are rapid, systemic, and global. In contrast, the laws and institutions on which we depend to respond and protect us are slow to change and limited in their issue focus and geographic application. As a nation, the United States faces a significant challenge in addressing the pace and scope of climate change, a challenge it has only begun to accept.

As observations and climate models point out with increasing clarity, neither the United States nor the rest of the world has the luxury of time to fully develop and digest science before acting. We are already passing ecosystem tipping points, and while global temperatures have risen about 0.75° C so far, we are guaranteed at least a doubling of that warming, ensuring that we will cross many significant ecological thresholds in short order. The survival of thousands, if not millions, of species is at stake. The nation's laws and institutions must evolve in parallel with the increasing pace of global change and our rapidly expanding understanding of this change and its implications.

Though by no means robustly, the legal system is responding. The courts are finding existing legal authorities in the Clean Air Act, the Endangered Species Act, and the National Environmental Policy Act that permit action to limit greenhouse gas emissions and protect species like corals and polar bears and their habitats. While the legal capacity to respond is demonstrated, action based on this understanding has yet to manifest in any of these cases. And the nation—while acknowledging the link of human activity and climate change—still awaits a comprehensive climate strategy and policy that links causes and effects and the need to integrate responses among all agencies at all levels of government with the private sector, the NGO community, academics, and the rest of society.

We see a similar evolution globally, complicated by significant regional and national variability in culpability as well as capacity to mitigate causes and adapt to global change. Given these circumstances, a post-Kyoto global strategy is all the more critical—one that makes substantial progress toward greenhouse gas emission reduction and carbon sequestration, while respecting the importance of poverty reduction and other measures to offset the adverse implications of climate change on the world's poor.

Notes

1. Kristen M. Crossett et al., Population Trends Along the Coastal United States: 1980–2008, at 1 (Nat'l Oceanic & Atmospheric Admin., Sept. 2004).
2. R. Costanza et al., *The Value of the World's Ecosystem Services and Natural Capital*, 387 Nature 253 (1997).
3. J. Kildow & C. Colgan, California's Ocean Economy: Report to the Resources Agency, State of California 35 (July 2005).
4. P. King, The Fiscal Impact of Beaches in California 3 (Pub.Research Inst., San Francisco State Univ., Sept. 1999).
5. *See* R. Alley et al., *Summary for Policymakers, in* Climate Change 2007: The Physical Science Basis 2 (S. Solomon, D. Qin, M. Manning, Z. Chen, M. Marquis, K.B. Averyt, M. Tignor & H.L. Miller eds., Cambridge Univ. Press 2007); J.R. Petit et al., *Climate and Atmospheric History of the Past 420,000 Years from the Vostok Ice Core, Antarctica*, 399 Nature 429, 433 (1999).
6. Climate Change 2007: The Physical Science Basis, *supra* note 5, at 5, 7, 10, 13.
7. C.L. Sabine et al., *The Oceanic Sink for Anthropogenic CO2*, 305 Science 367 (2004).
8. S.C. Doney et al., *Impact of Anthropogenic Atmospheric Nitrogen and Sulfur Deposition on Ocean Acidification and the Inorganic Carbon System*, 104 Proc. Nat'l Acad. Sci. USA 14,580, 14,583 (2007).
9. J.A. Kleypas, R.A. Feely, V.J. Fabry, C. Langdon, C.L. Sabine & L.L. Robbins, *Impacts of Ocean Acidification on Coral Reefs and Other Marine Calcifiers: A Guide for Future Research* 69 (report of a workshop held Apr. 18–20, 2005, in St. Petersburg, Fla., sponsored by NSF, NOAA & the U.S. Geological Survey) (2006); *see also* K. Caldeira & M.E. Wickett, *Anthropologic Carbon and Ocean pH*, 425 Nature 365 (2003).
10. Kleypas et al., *supra* note 9, at 1, 5.

11. *Id.* at 26–27; *see also* M. Fine & D. Tchernov, *Ocean Acidification and Scleractinian Corals—Response,* 317 SCIENCE 1032, 1033 (2007).

12. C.M. Turley, J.M. Roberts & J.M. Guinotte, *Corals in Deep Water: Will the Unseen Hand of Ocean Acidifi cation Destroy Cold-Water Ecosystems?* 26 CORAL REEFS 445, 446 (2007).

13. *Id.* at 447; J.M. Guinotte et al., *Will Human-Induced Changes in Seawater Chemistry Alter the Distribution of Deep-Sea Scleractinian Corals?* 4 ECOLOGICAL ENV'T 141, 142–143, 146 (2006).

14. Kleypas et al., *supra* note 9, at 30.

15. *Id.* at 31.

16. *Id.* at 69.

17. N.L. Bindoff et al., *Observations: Oceanic Climate Change and Sea Level, in* CLIMATE CHANGE 2007: THE PHYSICAL SCIENCE BASIS 387 (Cambridge Univ. Press 2007).

18. J.T. HOUGHTON ET AL., EDS., INTERGOVERNMENTAL PANEL ON CLIMATE CHANGE, CLIMATE CHANGE 2001: THE SCIENTIFIC BASIS, SUMMARY FOR POLICYMAKERS 35 (Cambridge Univ. Press, 2001), *available at* http://www.grida.no/climate/ipcc_tar/wg1/pdf/WG1_TAR -FRONT.PDF [hereinafter HOUGHTON ET AL.].

19. Bindoff et al., *supra* note 17, at 387; *see also* G.A. Nerem, E. Leuliette & A. Cazenave, *Present-Day Sea-Level Change: A Review,* 338 C.R. GEOSCIENCE 1077, 1078 (2006).

20. HOUGHTON ET AL., *supra* note 18, at 641, 643; *see also* R.B. Alley, P.U. Clark, P. Huybrechts & I. Joughin, *Ice-Sheet and Sea-Level Changes,* 310 SCIENCE 456 (2005).

21. G.A. Meehl et al., *Global Climate Projections, in* CLIMATE CHANGE 2007: THE PHYSICAL SCIENCE BASIS 750–751 (Cambridge Univ. Press 2007).

22. *Id.* at 821.

23. E. Rignot, *Changes in Ice Dynamics and Mass Balance of the Antarctic Ice Sheet,* 364 PHIL. TRANSACTIONS ROYAL SOC'Y A 1637, 1649 (2006).

24. Alley et al., *supra* note 20, at 458. Ice shelves act as dams, impeding the flow of glaciers into coastal waters.

25. *Id.*

26. Rignot, *supra* note 23, at 1649.

27. HOUGHTON ET AL., *supra* note 18, at 642.

28. I. Joughin, W. Abdalati & M. Fahnestock, *Large Fluctuations in Speed on Greenland's Jakobshavn Isbrae Glacier,* 432 NATURE 608 (2004); The loss of Arctic sea ice and snow cover may exacerbate the melting along Greenland by reducing reflection of incoming solar radiation and causing additional atmospheric and ocean warming. *See* H.D. Shindell, *Estimating the Potential for Twenty-First Century Sudden Climate Change,* 365 PHIL. TRANSACTIONS ROYAL SOC'Y A 2675, 2689 (2007).

29. CLIMATE CHANGE 2007: THE PHYSICAL SCIENCE BASIS, *supra* note 5, at 10.

30. *Id.* at 17; *see also* J.M. Gregory & P. Huybrechts, *Ice-Sheet Contributions to Future Sea-Level Change,* 364 PHIL. TRANSACTIONS ROYAL SOC'Y A 1709, 1728 (2006).

31. CLIMATE CHANGE 2007: THE PHYSICAL SCIENCE BASIS, *supra* note 5, at 17.

32. C. WILKINSON, ED., STATUS OF CORAL REEFS OF THE WORLD: 2004, at 25 (Australian Inst. Marine Sci. 2004).

33. U.S. COMM'N ON OCEAN POL'Y, AN OCEAN BLUEPRINT FOR THE 21ST CENTURY: FINAL REPORT 321–22 (2004); *available at* http://www.oceancommission.gov/documents/full_ color_rpt/welcome.html#full (last visited Feb. 11, 2008) [hereinafter USCOP FINAL REPORT].

34. T.P. Hughes et al., *Climate Change, Human Impacts, and the Resilience of Coral Reefs,* 301 SCIENCE 929, 930 (2003); *see also* S.D. Donner, T.R. Knutson & M. Oppenheimer, *Model-Based Assessment of the Role of Human-Induced Climate Change in the 2005 Caribbean Coral Bleaching Event,* 104 PROC. NAT'L ACAD. SCI. USA 5483, 5487 (2007).

35. Hughes et al., *supra* note 34, at 930; S.D. Donner, W.J. Skirving, C.M. Little, M. Oppenheimer & O. Hoegh-Guldberg, *Global Assessment of Coral Bleaching and Required Rates of Adaptation Under Climate Change,* 11 GLOBAL CHANGE BIOLOGY 2251, 2263 (2005).

36. Wilkinson, *supra* note 32, at 7.
37. *Id.* at 14; 71 Fed. Reg. 26,852 (May 9, 2006) (to be codified at 50 C.F.R. pt. 223).
38. Wilkinson, *supra* note 32, at 21.
39. S.C. Doney, *Plankton in a Warmer World,* 444 Nature 695, 696 (2006).
40. M.J. Behrenfeld et al., *Climate-Driven Trends in Contemporary Ocean Productivity,* 444 Nature 752, 754 (2006).
41. R.E. Thresher, J.A. Koslow, A.K. Morison & D.C. Smith, *Depth-Mediated Reversal of the Effects of Climate Change on Long-Term Growth Rates of Exploited Marine Fish,* 104 Proc. Nat'l Acad. Sci. USA 7461, 7461 (2007).
42. P.C. Reid, D.G. Johns, M. Edwards, M. Starr, M. Poulin & P. Snoeijs, *A Biological Consequence of Reducing Arctic Ice Cover: Arrival of the Pacific Diatom* Neodenticula seminae *in the North Atlantic for the First Time in 800,000 Years,* 13 Global Change Biology 1910, 1919 (2007).
43. G.C. Hays, A.J. Richardson & C. Robinson, *Climate Change and Marine Plankton,* 20 Trends Ecology & Evolution 337, 339 (2005).
44. C.D.G. Harley et al., *The Impacts of Climate Change in Coastal Marine Systems,* 9 Ecology Letters 228, 234 (2006); L.D. Zeidberg & B.H. Robison, *Invasive Range Expansion by the Humboldt Squid,* Dosidicus gigas, *in the Eastern North Pacific,* 104 Proc. Nat'l Acad. Sci. USA 12,948, 12,948 (2007).
45. R.B. Winn, S.A. Josey, A.P. Martin, D.G. Johns & P. Yésou, *Climate-Driven Range Expansion of a Critically Endangered Top Predator in Northeast Atlantic Waters,* 3 Biology Letters 529, 529–530 (2007).
46. Hays et al., *supra* note 43, at 340; G.A. McFarlane, J.R. King & R.J. Beamish, *Have There Been Recent Changes in Climate? Ask the Fish,* 47 Progress Oceanography 147 (2000).
47. Harley et al., *supra* note 44, at 232; Hays et al., *supra* note 43, at 342.
48. USCOP Final Report, *supra* note 33, at 253.
49. R.A. Anthes et al., *Hurricanes and Global Warming—Potential Linkages and Consequences,* 87 Bull. Am. Meteorological Soc'y 623 (2006); *see also* G.J. Holland & P.J. Webster, *Heightened Tropical Cyclone Activity in the North Atlantic: Natural Variability or Climate Trend?* 365 Phil. Transactions Royal Soc'y A 2695, 2713 (2007); T.R. Knutson & R.E. Tuleya, *Impact of CO2-Induced Warming on Simulated Hurricane Intensity and Precipitation: Sensitivity to the Choice of Climate Model and Convection Parameterization,* 17 J. Climate 3477 (2004); K. Trenberth, *Uncertainty in Hurricanes and Global Warming,* 308 Science 1753 (2005).
50. The debate involves questions about the possible underestimation of the intensity of historical tropical cyclones, thus making more recent storms appear stronger by comparison. In addition, accurate assessments of tropical cyclone intensity, based on satellite data, are relatively recent. There is also an argument that West African monsoons and the El Niño/Southern Oscillation (ENSO) might have been more important drivers of intense hurricane activity than sea surface temperatures over the past several millennia. *See* J.P. Donnelly & J.D. Woodruff, *Intense Hurricane Activity over the Past 5,000 Years Controlled by El Niño and the West African Monsoon,* 447 Nature 465, 467 (2007).
51. Anthes et al., *supra* note 49, at 624.
52. K.E. Trenberth & D.J. Shea, *Atlantic Hurricanes and Natural Variability in 2005,* 33 Geophysical Res. Letters L12704, doi:10.1029/2006GL026894 (2006).
53. P.J. Webster, G.J. Holland, J.A. Curry & H.R. Chang, *Changes in Tropical Cyclone Number, Duration, and Intensity in a Warming Environment,* 309 Science 1844 (2005); C.D. Hoyos, P.A. Agudelo, P.J. Webster & J.A. Curry, *Deconvolution of the Factors Contributing to the Increase in Global Hurricane Intensity,* 312 Science 94 (2006); K. Emanuel, *Increasing Destructiveness of Tropical Cyclones over the Past 30 Years,* 436 Nature 686 (2005). *See also* M.A. Saunders & A.S. Lea, *Large Contribution of Sea Surface Warming to Recent Increase in Atlantic Hurricane Activity,* 451 Nature 557–560 (2008), in which the authors found that local sea surface warming was responsible for about forty percent

of the rise in the number of storms between 1996 and 2005 (compared to the 1950–2000 average) in the North Atlantic.

54. COMM. ON THE SCIENCE OF CLIMATE CHANGE, NAT'L RESEARCH COUNCIL, NAT'L ACADEMY OF SCIENCES, CLIMATE CHANGE SCIENCE: AN ANALYSIS OF SOME KEY QUESTIONS 4 (National Academy Press, 2001), *available at* http://books.nap.edu/html/climatechange/climatechange.pdf; Anthes et al., *supra* note 49, at 624.

55. Emanuel, *supra* note 53, at 686.

56. D. CAYAN ET AL., PROJECTING FUTURE SEA LEVEL RISE: A REPORT FOR CALIFORNIA CLIMATE CHANGE CENTER 18 (Mar. 2006).

57. J.G. Titus & C. Richman, *Maps of Lands Vulnerable to Sea Level Rise: Modeled Elevations Along the US Atlantic and Gulf Coasts*, 18 CLIMATE RES. 205 (2001).

58. CAYAN ET AL., *supra* note 56, at 18.

59. *Id.* at 23–29.

60. S.Y. Wu, R. Najjar & J. Siewert, *Impact of Sea-Level Rise on the Mid- and Upper-Atlantic Coast* (Consortium for Atl. Reg'l Assessment 2005).

61. H.J. HEINZ III CTR. FOR SCI., ECON. & ENV'T, EVALUATION OF EROSION HAZARDS 2, Report Brief (2000).

62. Gary B. Griggs, *Coastal Cliff Erosion in San Diego County* (2002), *at* http://repositories.cdlib.org/cgi/viewcontent.cgi?article=1091&context=csgc (last visited Aug. 29, 2006).

63. PEW OCEANS COMM., AMERICA'S LIVING OCEANS: CHARTING A COURSE FOR SEA CHANGE 54 (2003).

64. 42 U.S.C. §§ 7401 *et seq.*

65. Numerous states, most notably California, have moved to legally limit emissions of greenhouse gases from sources within their borders. *See* California Global Warming Solutions Act of 2006, 2006 CAL. STAT. 488 (AB 32); *see also* California AB 2264 (Pavley) (proposing a minimum fuel economy standard for the purchase of state passenger vehicles and light trucks); California SB 1368 (Perata) (proposing long-term contracts for baseload generation to comply with state performance standards for greenhouse gas emissions). States limiting emissions (by executive order or other means) include Arizona, California, Connecticut, Florida, Illinois, Maine, Maryland, Massachusetts, New Jersey, New Mexico, New York, Oregon, Pennsylvania, Rhode Island, Vermont, and Washington. *See* Pew Center on Global Climate Change, States with Greenhouse Gas Emissions Targets, http://www.pewclimate.org/what_s_being_done/in_the_states/emissionstargets_map.cfm (last visited Feb. 4, 2008). *See also* DARREN SPRINGER, NAT'L GOVERNOR'S ASS'N, STATE AND REGIONAL GREENHOUSE GAS INITIATIVES (ENERGY SECTOR) (2006), http://www.nga.org/Files/pdf/0610greenhouse.pdf. American states have joined a number of regional climate programs as well, several of which include Canadian provinces. The more binding programs among these include the following: Northeast Regional Greenhouse Gas Initiative (RGGI) (ten states, agreeing to a regional program to cap-and-trade power plant emissions at approximately current levels between 2009 and 2015, and to subsequently reduce this level ten percent by 2019); New England Governors' Climate Change Action Plan (six states and five Canadian provinces, setting goals of achieving 1990 emission levels by 2010 and ten percent below 1990 levels by 2020, to be achieved in conjunction with RGGI and other programs); Midwestern Regional Greenhouse Gas Reduction Accord (six states and one Canadian province, establishing a long-term emissions reduction goal of sixty to eighty percent below current levels and a cap-and-trade system, to be fully implemented by mid-2009); Western Governors' Association Clean and Diversified Energy Initiative (five states, planning to meet 30,000 megawatts of clean energy by 2015 and a twenty percent improvement in energy efficiency by 2020); Western Regional Climate Action Initiative (six states and two Canadian provinces, with another six states, three Canadian provinces, and one Mexican state listed as "Observers," agreeing to a regional emissions limit of fifteen percent below 2005 levels by 2020 and a market-based system by Aug. 2008). *See generally* Pew Center on Global Climate Change, Regional Initiatives, http://www.pewclimate.org/what_s_being_done/in_the_states/regional_initiatives .cfm (last visited Feb. 20, 2008).

66. 127 S. Ct. 1438 (2007).

67. *Id.* at 1446.
68. On Dec. 19, 2007, EPA Administrator Stephen Johnson denied California's request for a waiver of preemption of motor vehicle greenhouse gas emission standards on the basis of California's inability to demonstrate "compelling and extraordinary conditions" as required under Clean Air Act § 209(b)(1)(B). *See* Letter to Governor Arnold Schwarzenegger from EPA Administrator Stephen Johnson Regarding California's Request for a Waiver of Pre-emption for Its Greenhouse-Gas Regulations, U.S. Envtl. Protection Agency, http://epa.gov/otaq/climate/20071219-slj.pdf (reasoning that climate change is a global concern and thus met best by a unified national approach rather than a patchwork of state regulations); *see also* Juliet Eilperin, *EPA Chief Denies Calif. Limit on Auto Emissions,* WASH. POST, Dec, 20, 2007, at A-1, *available at* http://www.washingtonpost.com/wp-dyn/content/article/2007/12/19/AR2007121902012.html. On Jan. 2, California filed suit in the Ninth Circuit Court of Appeals seeking reversal of the EPA waiver denial. *See* Press Release, Office of the Governor of California, Governor Schwarzenegger Announces EPA Suit Filed to Reverse Waiver Denial (Jan. 2, 2008) http://gov.ca.gov/press-release/8400/; *see also id.,* Text of Letter from Gov. Schwarzenegger and 13 Other Governors to EPA Administrator Stephen L. Johnson on California's Waiver Request Denial (Jan. 24, 2008) http://gov.ca.gov/press-release/8596/. This waiver would have given California the legal ability to implement its own greenhouse gas standard for motor vehicles and for sixteen additional states to adopt the California standard. EPA had delayed making a decision on the waiver in light of the ongoing litigation in *Massachusetts v. EPA.* California and other states have petitioned the D.C. Circuit for review of EPA's denial.
69. 42 U.S.C. § 7602(g).
70. 127 S. Ct. 1438, 1460 (2007).
71. *Id.*
72. *Id.* at 1462. In reaching its conclusion that EPA has such authority, the court also rejected EPA's argument that EPA lacks authority to regulate greenhouse gases from motor vehicles because doing so would constitute an implicit fuel economy standard that Congress has already assigned to DOT. The court concluded that an overlapping EPA greenhouse gas standard and a mileage standard set by DOT can be administered without inconsistency.
73. *Id.*
74. *Id.*
75. *Id.* at 1455.
76. 42 U.S.C.A. § 7475(a)(4).
77. *See* Gregory B. Foote, *Considering Alternatives: The Case for Limiting CO₂ Emissions from New Power Plants Through New Source Review,* 34 Envtl. L. Rep.10,642 (2004).
78. *See* Letter from Henry Waxman (D-Calif.), Chair of the House Committee on Oversight and Government Reform, to Stephen Johnson, EPA Administrator (Sept. 19, 2007), http://oversight.house.gov/documents/20070919110339.pdf (urging EPA to use its authority under Section 165(a)(4) to expand BACT determinations for coal-fired power plants to include carbon capture and sequestration technologies).
79. 42 U.S.C.A. § 7475(a)(2).
80. There are numerous other provisions in federal law relating to climate change on issues such as climate change research. *See, e.g.,* EPA Global Change Research Program, http://cfpub.epa.gov/gcrp/ (last visited Feb. 10, 2008), and development of "clean coal" technologies. In general, however, these programs are not regulatory programs aimed at reducing greenhouse gas emissions. However, in the recently enacted Energy Independence and Security Act of 2007, Congress did establish a renewable fuels standard that requires the production of specified volumes of renewable fuel meeting specific lifecycle greenhouse gas reduction targets. In addition, Congress passed a revised fuel economy standard program for vehicles that will have significant greenhouse gas reduction impacts. Energy Independence and Security Act of 2007, Pub. L. No. 110-140, 121 Stat. 1492 (codified as amended in scattered sections of 42 U.S.C.).
81. Intergovernmental Panel on Climate Change, *Summary for Policy Makers, in* CLIMATE CHANGE 2007: IMPACTS, ADAPTATION AND VULNERABILITY 6 (2007).

82. CLIMATE CHANGE 2007: THE PHYSICAL SCIENCE BASIS, *supra* note 5; SIR NICHOLAS STERN, STERN REVIEW REPORT ON THE ECONOMICS OF CLIMATE CHANGE (2006), *available at* http://www.hm-treasury.gov.uk/independent_reviews/stern_review_economics_climate_change/stern_review_report.cfm (last visited July 7, 2007).

83. STERN, *supra* note 82, at 610–12.

84. Chris D. Thomas et al., *Extinction Risk from Climate Change*, 427 NATURE 145, 145–46 (2007).

85. Endangered and Threatened Species Listings, Final Listing Determinations for Elkhorn Coral and Staghorn Coral, 71 Fed. Reg. 26,852 (May 9, 2006).

86. *Id.* at 26,858–59.

87. Endangered and Threatened Wildlife & Plants, 12-Month Petition Finding and Proposed Rule to List the Polar Bear (*Ursus maritimus*) as Threatened Throughout Its Range, 72 Fed. Reg. 1064, 1071–79 (Jan. 9, 2007). In announcing the proposed listing, Interior Secretary Kempthorne stated, "[W]e are concerned the polar bears' habitat may literally be melting." Press Release, U.S. Dep't of Interior, Interior Secretary Kempthorne Announces Proposal to List Polar Bears as Threatened Under Endangered Species Act (Dec. 27, 2006), http://www.doi.gov/news/06_News_Releases/061227.html (last visited July 7, 2007).

88. *See* News Release, U.S. Fish & Wildlife Service, Bulletin: Statement for Polar Bear Decision (Jan. 7, 2008), http://www.fws.gov/news/newsreleases/showNews.cfm?newsId=54D2A6BD-E928-94E6-6BA905F3F540B8F7 (last visited Feb. 15, 2008).

89. CLIMATE CHANGE 2007: IMPACTS, ADAPTATION AND VULNERABILITY, *supra* note 81, at 11 ("In the Polar Regions, the main projected biophysical effects are reductions in thickness and extent of glaciers and ice sheets, and changes in natural ecosystems with detrimental effects on many organisms including migratory birds, mammals and higher predators. In the Arctic, additional impacts include reductions in the extent of sea ice and permafrost, increased coastal erosion, and an increase in the depth of permafrost seasonal thawing.").

90. 16 U.S.C. §§ 1532(19) 1538(a)(1), 50 C.F.R. § 17.3.

91. *Id.* § 1536(a)(2).

92. *See* NRDC v. Kempthorne, 2007 WL 1577896 (E.D. Cal. May 25, 2007) (consultation on Central Valley Project must consider effects of project operations on hydraulic conditions needed by Delta smelt that have been impacted by global warming).

93. 16 U.S.C. § 1533(f)(1)(B).

94. For example, the delisting of the grizzly bear has been challenged on the grounds that climate change is causing the rapid decline of white bark pine beetles, one of the bear's four essential food sources. *See* Western Watersheds Project v. Servheen, No. 4:2007cv00243 (D. Ida. June 4, 2007).

95. *See, e.g.,* Border Power Plant Working Group v. Dep't of Energy, 206 F. Supp. 2d 997 (S.D. Cal. 2003) (federal agencies failed to perform proper NEPA analysis to disclose and evaluate potential environmental impacts of increased carbon dioxide emissions associated with proposed electricity transmission lines that would connect Mexican power plants to the Southern California power grid); Mid-State Coalition for Progress v. Surface Transp. Bd., 345 F.3d 520 (8th Cir. 2003) (court found increased coal consumption and associated carbon dioxide emissions a "reasonably foreseeable effect" of an agency's proposed approval of new rail lines to transport low-sulfur coal in Wyoming to plants in the Midwest, and held that such effects should be considered during a NEPA analysis).

96. Mont. Envtl. Info. Ctr. v. Johanns, No. 07-1311 (filed July 23, 2007, D.D.C.) (plaintiffs argued that a branch of the Department of Agriculture violated NEPA when it failed to consider the cumulative impact of greenhouse gases from its proposed funding of a coal-fired power plant in combination with seven other coal plants that sought funding from the agency).

97. Ctr. for Biological Diversity v. Nat'l Highway Traffic Safety Admin., 508 F.3d 508 (9th Cir. 2007).

98. *Id.* at 550.

99. United Nations, Framework Convention on Climate Change, art. 2, May 9, 1992, 31 I.L.M. 849, 854 (1992), *available at* http://unfccc.int/resource/docs/convkp/conveng.pdf.
100. *Id*. art. 3, para. 1.
101. *Id*. art. 4, para. 2(b), at 857.
102. Kyoto Protocol to the U.N. Framework Convention on Climate Change, Dec. 10, 1997, art. 3, para. 1, U.N. Doc. FCCC/CP/1997/L.7/Add.1, 37 I.L.M. 22 (1998), *available at* http://unfccc.int/kyoto_protocol/items/2830.php.
103. Approaches to Reducing Carbon Dioxide Emissions: Hearing Before the H. Comm. on the Budget, 110th Cong., 11–12 (Nov. 1, 2007) (statement of Peter Orszag, Director, Congressional Budget Office), *available at* https://www.cbo.gov/ftpdoc.cfm?index=8819&type=1.

chapter nineteen

Legal Authorities for Ecosystem-Based Management in U.S. Coastal and Ocean Areas

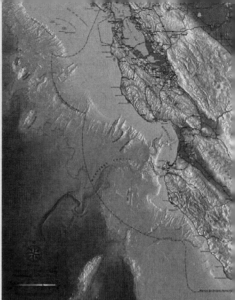

Patrick A. Parenteau
Donald C. Baur
Jennifer L. Schorr

I. Introduction

In 1981 and 1985, Congress held hearings on the ratification of a protocol among Canada, Japan, the United States, and the U.S.S.R. to extend the International Convention on the Conservation of the North Pacific Fur Seal.[1] This treaty drew opposition from some conservation groups because it subsidized the commercial harvest of fur seals on the Pribilof Islands.[2]

The authors express their appreciation to Rebecca Brezenoff and Emily Merolli of Perkins Coie and Jen Abdella, a third-year student at the Vermont Law School, for their assistance with this chapter. The authors also acknowledge and express their gratitude to the David and Lucile Packard Foundation for supporting the research and development of this chapter.

Both proponents and opponents of the Convention expressed concern over the decline of North Pacific fur seal stocks, which had been reduced from about 1.8 million animals in the Pribilof Islands in the 1950s to about 800,000 in the early 1980s.[3] At the same time, all of the parties agreed that, whatever role the commercial harvest may have played in the fur seal decline, other factors were adversely affecting the entire ecosystem of the Bering Sea and the North Pacific Ocean.

Alaska Native residents of the Pribilofs were the first to recognize the system-wide declines, and they sounded what proved to be a prophetic call about the onset of a serious ecosystem collapse. As Ilarion Merculieff, President of the Tanadgusix Native Corporation, testified in a 1985 hearing:

> For example, we know for a fact that seals, sea lions and two major Bering sea bird species are experiencing severe population distress. Sea lions in the eastern Bering Sea reached a population of approximately 60,000 in the late 60's. The population declined to an estimated 25,000 in the late seventies and is now down to 12,000. Murres and kittiwakes, two bird species, have been experiencing major reproductive failures in the past five years to the point that reproductivity of kittiwakes on St. Paul decreased 84% in a span of nine years between 1975 and 1984.
>
> Kittiwakes, normally fish eaters, have been observed eating tundra berries. Sea lions, normally fish eaters, have been observed eating fur seals. Fur seal pelts taken in 1984 have been reported by local Aleut experts as being thinner than ever in anyone's memory. All three types of observations indicate possible food stress although there is no scientific evidence available that addresses this possibility.[4]

Witnesses in the hearings agreed on the solution. They called for legal authority to study and manage the marine environment, in general, and the Bering Sea/North Pacific Ocean, in particular, under an ecosystem-based regimen. As stated by Alaska Governor Hammond in 1981:

> The issue which is brought to the fore is whether we are in fact attempting to achieve a systems management approach (as is desirable), including maintenance of healthy populations of those components affected by man, or whether we are pursuing mutually exclusive goals for different species or groups which will eventually have undesirable yet unnecessary consequences.[5]

A representative of the Center for Environmental Education (now The Ocean Conservancy) explained:

> With single species management, attention is focused on the dynamics of particular species or stocks without explicit regard to the interactions between those species or stocks and other components of the ecosystem. . . . The greatest problem facing policy makers is that presently we have insufficient information about the numerical and functional relationships between species.

Diligent acquisition of such information is of utmost importance if we are ever to be able to make conscientious resource management decisions.[6]

Unfortunately, no action was taken to establish a legal regime that would respond to these concerns.

While the federal government failed to respond to these, and other,[7] calls for an effective ecosystem-based program for the Bering Sea, the living marine resources of the region continued to decline at an alarming rate. Fur seals were not the only species affected, and within two decades of the Fur Seal Convention hearings, it became clear that a full-scale ecological catastrophe was underway:

- Steller sea lions in the Bering Sea and parts of the western and central Gulf of Alaska: eighty percent decline in the last thirty years; listed as threatened under the Endangered Species Act (ESA) in 1990;[8] populations west of 144° West longitude listed as endangered in 1997.[9]
- Harbor seals: ninety percent decline since the 1970s in the Gulf of Alaska, sixty percent decline in Bristol Bay since 1991.[10]
- Northern fur seals: sixty percent decline since 1950s in the breeding population on Pribilof Islands; pup numbers declining steadily since the 1970s;[11] listed as depleted under the Marine Mammal Protection Act of 1972 (MMPA).[12]
- Northern sea otters: ninety percent decline in the Aleutians during the 1990s;[13] listed as threatened under the ESA in 2005.[14]
- Common and thick-billed murres: colonies in the Pribilof Islands declined dramatically in the 1980s.[15]
- Black-legged kittiwakes: sharp declines in Pribilof Islands (Eastern Bering Sea) and northern Gulf of Alaska colonies.[16]
- Red-legged kittiwakes: declines of seventy-seven percent on St. Paul and fifty-eight percent on St. George in the Pribilof Islands. Bering Sea and Aleutian Island populations have declined more than fifty percent.[17]
- Short-tailed albatross: endangered and at perilously low numbers (1,300 birds).[18]
- Bering Sea spectacled eiders: ninety percent decline since the 1970s,[19] listed as threatened in 1993.[20]
- Gulf of Alaska pollock stocks: eighty percent decline since the mid-1980s.[21]
- Bering Sea Greenland turbot: sixty-five percent to eighty-five percent decline since the 1960s.[22]

The net effect of the system-wide biological collapse has not only been a serious threat to the viability of the Bering Sea/North Pacific Ocean ecosystem and the sustainability of the economic and subsistence economies dependent on these resources, it also has resulted in a more-than-decade-old legal and political controversy on how to respond. These biological declines are mirrored by extensive commercial fishery restrictions, fishery-area closures, and lawsuits to provide protection for species throughout the region.[23]

While the debate continues over how to arrest the species declines of the Bering Sea, the need for effective management responses has become apparent in other marine ecosystems as well. For example, the Beaufort Sea and Arctic Ocean are experiencing a notable loss of sea ice as a likely result of global warming, placing species such as the polar bear at risk.[24] Puget Sound, a marine ecosystem in Washington State, is so degraded and contaminated that Governor Gregoire recently proposed a two-year, $220 million program to implement a long-term effort to restore the health of the region by 2020.[25] In the Puget Sound/Georgia Basin eco-system, over sixty species have decreased so significantly that they are considered at risk by U.S. and Canadian agencies, including several that are listed as threatened or endangered.[26] In the Gulf of Maine, major ecosystem changes have occurred due to fishing pressure, including increases in introduced species that threaten native species.[27] Deep sea corals, which provide habitat for fish and invertebrate species, are threatened by bottom trawling off the coast of Florida, and large areas of deep sea coral habitat have been destroyed by fishing practices.[28] In California, critically important estuaries and nearshore ecosystems such as Morro Bay and Elkhorn Slough are declining and threatened by coastal development.[29] This is only a partial list of declining U.S. marine ecosystems, and the problem is even greater on an international scale.

In the Puget Sound/ Georgia Basin ecosystem, over sixty species have decreased so significantly that they are considered at risk.

As observed in a paper published in the November 2006 edition of the journal *Science,* the problem of marine ecosystem deterioration and the loss of biodiversity from these geographically large and taxonomically complex regions has become so severe that "business as usual would foreshadow serious threats to global food security, coastal water quality, and ecosystem stability, affecting current and future generations."[30] This trend is reversible, however, through "sustainable fisheries management, pollution control, maintenance of essential habitats, and the creation of marine reserves."[31]

To address this problem, the scientific community has been at the forefront of the call for ecosystem-based management (EBM). In 1989, for example, forty-one of the world's leading marine biologists testified jointly on the reauthorization of the Magnuson-Stevens Fishery Conservation and Management Act (FCMA), calling for a new regulatory approach to fisheries management.[32] Criticizing the single-species focus of the FCMA, the scientists stated that human activities "can and do have stabilizing or destabilizing influences on the natural variability and cause or accelerate severe shifts in the composite ecosystem."[33] Observing the effects of human intervention in fisheries around the world, the scientists called for a revision to the FCMA "to promote a total ecosystem perspective in managing the Nation's fish stocks, taking into account the protection of essential habitat, including the habitats essential to early life histories, and consideration of marine species neither harvested nor consumed."[34] While Congress amended the FCMA in 1996 to require an evaluation of the effect of agency actions on essential fish habitat,[35] nothing was done to make EBM an integral component of fisheries management.

The continued absence of effective system-wide management regimes for the marine environment led two national commissions studying U.S. ocean policy (Pew Oceans Commission and U.S. Commission on Ocean Policy (USCOP)) to recommend that a comprehensive, integrated ecosystem-based approach serve as the cornerstone of U.S. oceans law.[36] Echoing this recommendation, in March 2005 nearly 220 scientists and academicians issued a "Scientific Consensus Statement on Marine Ecosystem-Based Management."[37] Citing to the Commission reports and noting the current and ever-increasing threats to the marine environment, the signers of the Statement observed that solutions to these threats "based on an integrated ecosystem approach hold the greatest promise for delivering desired results."[38] The authors of the Statement declared that "[f]rom a scientific perspective, we now know enough to improve dramatically the conservation and management of marine systems through the implementation of ecosystem-based approaches."[39] The authors also observed: "A delay in implementing management based on an ecosystem approach will result in continued conflicts over resources, degradation of ocean ecosystems, disruption of fisheries, loss of recreational opportunities, health risks to humans and wildlife and loss of biodiversity."[40]

With the issuance of the Commission reports and the Scientific Consensus Statement, the policy and scientific justification for EBM is clear. Putting such an approach into place, however, remains a challenging and difficult task because of funding shortages and the need to reorient decades of fragmented ocean management and research programs, as well as the absence of legal directives that serve as the basis for EBM. The laws governing U.S. ocean management are themselves fragmented and have little or no connection to each other. Fish, birds, coral, marine mammals, oil and gas, minerals, renewable energy resources, wetlands, and other components of the marine environment are subject to discrete, and largely unrelated, legal authorities. Moreover, within each law, little attention is given to EBM.

While there is no substitute for statutory authority specifically directed to EBM, the realities of the current political environment make the prospect for such legislative reform uncertain. To fill the gap in authority to implement EBM in federal oceans management, this chapter makes recommendations on actions that can be taken under *existing federal law* to put in place the basic elements of an EBM legal regime. As this chapter demonstrates, existing U.S. law contains many large gaps for EBM that are not easily filled.[41] It is possible, however, to stitch together a legal program that is sufficient to achieve this goal.

Although the problem of declining marine ecosystems is international in scope, this chapter focuses on actions that can be taken under domestic U.S. laws. This chapter begins with a discussion of the key components for EBM, as defined by the Scientific Consensus Statement, discussed in the Commission reports, and addressed in the proposed federal legislation. It then analyzes current U.S. law to identify the legal mechanisms that are available for implementing EBM. The final section sets forth recommendations on how to carry out EBM under existing law.

II. Current State of the Law

A. The Principles of Ecosystem-Based Management

The starting place for a legal regime based on EBM is the definition of what this concept means and identification of the key elements that are necessary for its success. This task has been confronted by the two Commissions, the Scientific Consensus Statement, and literature from leading experts in the field.

Building upon the Pew Commission and USCOP Reports,[42] the 2005 Scientific Consensus Statement set forth a working definition of EBM as:

> [A]n integrated approach to management that considers the entire ecosystem, including humans. The goal of ecosystem-based management is to maintain an ecosystem in a healthy, productive and resilient condition so that it can provide the services humans want and need. Ecosystem-based management differs from current approaches that usually focus on a single species, sector, activity or concern; it considers the cumulative impacts of different sectors. Specifically, ecosystem-based management:
>
> - emphasizes the protection of ecosystem structure, functioning, and key processes;
>
> - is place-based in focusing on a specific ecosystem and the range of activities affecting it;
>
> - explicitly accounts for the interconnectedness within systems, recognizing the importance of interactions between many target species or key services and other non-target species;
>
> - acknowledges interconnectedness within systems, such as between air, land and sea; and
>
> - integrates ecological, social, economic, and institutional perspectives, recognizing their strong interdependences.[43]

With this definition in mind, general agreement has emerged on some of the management actions that should be taken to carry out EBM, as defined in the Scientific Consensus Statement.

In 1993, the Congressional Research Service (CRS) issued a report on the scientific basis for marine EBM.[44] The CRS Report acknowledged the wide range of threats confronting the marine environment. As the CRS Report observed: "Overexploitation (e.g., overfishing), habitat destruction, declining water quality, introduction of exotic species, and global climate change all threaten to degrade marine resources by affecting the biological, chemical, and physical foundation these resources share."[45] In addition to the harmful effects of these human influences, CRS observed that marine resources also "are susceptible to natural disturbances such as disease epidemics, predator infestations, hurricanes, and periodic climate shifts like El Niño events of the Pacific. These natural forces are key factors affecting the health of marine ecosystems, and their potential effects are magnified by the stresses from human impacts."[46]

The CRS Report explained that, while management systems exist to address many of the threats independently, the unanswered question is whether it is possible to respond to "several or all threats at once."[47] The answer to this question is especially difficult in the marine setting because "[d]iscrete geographic areas may have less relevance since much of the living resource is constantly moving"[48] and because "marine ecosystems are generally not as well defined as terrestrial ecosystems."[49] In addition, the CRS Report noted that "theoretical models for guiding comprehensive management planning are relatively scarce for marine resources," and "[t]he weak scientific base for more comprehensive ecosystem management in the marine realm, the meager experience with comprehensive approaches to management of terrestrial or marine ecosystems, and the prevailing common property attitudes for living marine resources will complicate the implementation of a comprehensive regime for managing marine resources."[50]

Experts on marine resources have discussed the complex nature of the threats confronting the oceans. As summarized by Dr. Elliott Norse, these problems include

> 1) accelerating loss of marine biodiversity; 2) sharply reduced abundance of species at higher trophic levels (large predators); 3) serial depletion of fisheries (moving from one abundant species or biomass-rich place to the next as each is depleted); 4) extensive elimination of benthic structure-forming species such as corals . . . ; 5) proliferation and spread of . . . non-native species . . . ; and 6) dramatic change in biogeochemical functioning.[51]

The growing recognition of the interrelated nature of these and other problems confronting the marine environment has led not only to the nearly unified call for an EBM regime, but also to the emergence of generally recognized principles that should serve as the foundation for such a program.

In his article *Regional Governance and Ecosystem-Based Management of Ocean and Coastal Resources: Can We Get There From Here?*, Professor Andrew Rosenberg identifies three important elements for EBM.[52] The first element is to "conserve ecosystem services, which are those processes and products provided by a fully functioning ecosystem that support human well-being."[53] As Rosenberg notes, "current management approaches to fisheries, water quality, coastal development, or energy development are basically focused on a single service or a small set of services, not an interlocking set."[54]

Rosenberg's second element is that EBM must be "cross-sectoral, meaning that management plans are comprehensive, with the goal of conserving ecosystem services, and inclusive of all types of human activity that may impact coastal and ocean resources."[55] According to Rosenberg, "[c]urrent management is fundamentally sectoral with weak interactions across sectors," and it is carried out principally through the National Environmental Policy Act (NEPA), which is diminished in its effectiveness because it calls only for an analysis of impacts with no clear goals or mandates.[56]

Finally, Rosenberg calls for a program that will "specifically address the cumulative impact of human activities on the ecosystem and, hence, ecosystem services."[57] It is necessary not only to look at cumulative impacts, but to do so across sectors. "Current management can only really look at cumulative impacts within a sector, and then the accumulation is probably only in a single dimension of the ecosystem, such as wetlands."[58] Cumulative impacts must not only be analyzed, as required under NEPA—they must also be managed.

> **Cumulative impacts must not only be analyzed, as required under NEPA—they must also be managed.**

To achieve these goals, Rosenberg recognizes, as do other experts in the field, the need to attack the problem on a regional basis.[59] An ambitious and "cross-sectoral" management regime must flow out of a national mandate under centralized decision authority, but governance itself should be on a regional scale. While it is possible, Rosenberg observes, to readily define ecosystems, such as salt-marsh or deep-water ecosystems, the challenge from a management perspective is "to find a workable scale for the consideration of a set of services and for the management of human activities [impacts]."[60]

To implement management on this regional scale, ten Large Marine Ecosystems (LMEs) have been identified for the United States.[61] LMEs involve the division of the ocean into large functional units based on shared bathymetry, hydrography, productivity, and populations. The LMEs start in coastal areas and extend offshore to the boundaries of continental shelves and major current systems.[62] Their design "take[s] into account the biological and physical components of the marine environment, as well as terrestrial features such as . . . estuaries that drain into" coastal areas.[63] The ten LMEs that have been identified for the United States are Chuckchi Sea, Beaufort Sea, Gulf of Alaska, Eastern Bering Sea, California Current, Insular Pacific-Hawaiian, Northeast U.S., Southeast U.S., Gulf of Mexico, and the Caribbean.[64]

The importance of adopting a regional approach for carrying out EBM is at the heart of the increasingly strong effort to establish a "place-based" or "zoning" approach to coastal and ocean management.[65] Elliott Norse advocates the adoption of such an approach to solve the problems that result from the "frontier mentality of governance" that characterizes U.S. coastal and ocean management.[66]

Norse observes that the oceans have historically been viewed as "an inexhaustible cornucopia" of natural resources and that viewpoint has led to management regimes based on the premise that "society, therefore, should give primacy to supporting consumptive users."[67] Treatment of the oceans as a frontier, generally open to exploitation under minimal controls, emerged as the consequence of the 1969 Stratton Commission[68] report on ocean management:

> Driven by the need to ensure "full and wise use of the marine environment," [the Stratton Commission of 1969] focused on oceans as a frontier with vast resources, and largely recommended policies to coordinate the development

of ocean resources. Reflecting the understanding and value of this earlier era, we have continued to approach our oceans with a frontier mentality.[69]

The result of this frontier approach to the ocean, expressed principally in the form of open access to resources, has led to the current plight confronting the marine environment, especially as a result of the overexploitation of fisheries. As Norse observes:

> [Sea]grass, birds, mangrove forests, kelp forests, coral reefs, estuaries, continental shelves, continental slopes, deep-sea coral forests, seamounts, and the oceanic pelagic zone are all suffering as elephantine user groups fight over resources.[70]

These adverse resource impacts, of course, eventually lead to economic consequences. Norse observes that "[e]conomic dislocation in fishing communities is increasing. The list of losers grows steadily. This almost universally unsatisfactory collective action dilemma has created the conditions that have people increasingly asking, could there be a better way of managing the sea?"[71]

Under a marine spatial management program, a matrix would be established that includes networks of reserves and other marine protected areas composed of sufficient size and connectivity to allow ecosystem processes (or ecosystem services, as defined by Rosenberg) to continue.[72] The matrix would designate other zones within which various commercial, recreational, subsistence and other human activities can be conducted.[73] As Norse observes, if properly implemented, marine spatial planning of "shipping lanes, oil production facilities, pot fishing, trawling alleys, and marine biodiversity reserves gives different interests the unprecedented opportunity of avoiding intersectoral competition within their zones."[74] The efficiency of such zones in achieving the desired goals can be best achieved if they are established, and enforced, on a large, regional scale, consistent with Rosenberg's recommendations. As noted by Norse, "[t]he kind of zones, their distribution in any zoning system, and their effectiveness will reflect the scientific understanding, economic principles, procedural efficiency, inclusiveness, transparency, fairness, and effectiveness of measures to ensure compliance."[75] In short, successful implementation of marine spatial planning will require "a broad range of interests . . . to decide—each for their own reasons—that having the opportunity to use and exert substantial control over a portion of the sea is better than fighting incessantly for all of it while its resources continue to disappear."[76]

For purposes of this article, we will address the manner in which existing domestic laws can be applied to implement spatial planning and EBM (as defined by the Scientific Consensus Statement) and advance the management principles articulated by the Commissions, the Scientific Consensus Statement, and others. Before doing so, however, we provide a summary of the measures recommended to implement EBM in the two Commission reports, the current U.S. Ocean Action Plan, and in legislation previously and currently introduced for this purpose.

B. Current Proposals to Implement Ecosystem-Based Management

1. Commission Reports

a. Pew Commission

In May 2003, the Pew Commission issued its recommendations for a new ocean policy in the report *America's Living Oceans: Charting a Course for Sea Change* (Pew Report).[77] The Pew Report focuses on the crisis facing America's oceans and the importance of establishing a "principled, unified national ocean policy" that would ensure healthy marine ecosystems and ecological sustainability.[78] In addition to the objective of a unified national ocean policy, the Pew Report called on the federal government to (1) "encourage comprehensive and coordinated governance of ocean resources and uses," including fisheries management on a regional scale; (2) "restructure fishery management institutions and reorient policy" to focus on and protect ecosystems; (3) "protect important habitat and manage coastal development"; and (4) "control sources of pollution."[79]

The Pew Report highlights the lack of adequate mechanisms for EBM, noting that over 140 federal laws and dozens of federal agencies are involved in ocean administration, leading to fragmented and ineffective management.[80] To address this problem, the Pew Report calls for mechanisms to protect and manage marine ecosystems by creating a coordinated approach among different levels of government. Recommendations for achieving EBM include enactment of a National Ocean Policy Act (NOPA) requiring protection, maintenance, and restoration of marine ecosystems; establishment of regional ecosystem councils under the NOPA; establishment of a national system of marine reserves to protect ecosystems; and establishment of an independent national oceans agency and a permanent interagency oceans council.[81]

> **Over 140 federal laws and dozens of federal agencies are involved in ocean administration, leading to fragmented and ineffective management.**

According to the Pew Report, NOPA should establish the framework to improve coordination for ecosystem management among different levels of government.[82] It also should establish strict standards to guide ocean governance and provide a strong implementation and compliance regime.[83] The regional ecosystem councils would be responsible for implementing EBM by developing and overseeing the implementation of comprehensive regional ocean governance plans, which would be based on science, and include discussion of threats to marine ecosystem health.[84] The regional ecosystem councils would include federal, state, and tribal authorities with jurisdiction over ocean and coastal areas and would use an advisory process to encourage stakeholder participation.[85] Regional ocean plans would be enforceable against all parties, and they would include consistency mechanisms similar to those in the Coastal Zone Management Act (CZMA).[86] The councils and the regional ocean governance plans, along with NOPA, would promote coordination among different levels of government and lead to an EBM approach.[87]

b. The United States Commission on Ocean Policy

The USCOP issued its final report in September 2004 (USCOP Report), setting forth proposals for the establishment of a comprehensive and coordinated ocean policy.[88] Like the Pew Commission, the USCOP noted that the lack of communication and coordination among governmental agencies was inhibiting effective ocean management.[89] To encourage an EBM approach, the USCOP Report also called for the use of regional ocean councils under a new National Ocean Policy Framework.[90] The Framework would be based on a voluntary "bottom-up" regional process.[91] This approach calls for the creation of a National Ocean Council within the Executive Office of the President, which would work with Congress, the President's Council of Advisors on Ocean Policy,[92] and state, territorial, local, and tribal leaders to create a flexible and voluntary process for decision making to be implemented through regional ocean councils.[93] The councils would correspond to LMEs or other ecosystem-based areas, and their "core functions" would include "[f]acilitating coordinated . . . responses to regional issues[,] [d]eveloping regional goals and priorities, [and] [c]ommunicating regional concerns to the National Ocean Council."[94]

The USCOP Report also encourages an EBM approach through the development of regional ecosystem assessments to establish baselines of ecosystem health, improve the environmental review process under NEPA, and evaluate cumulative impacts of proposed activities on ecosystems over time.[95] The Report makes detailed recommendations for moving toward an EBM approach for fisheries management, including changing the designation of essential fish habitat to an ecosystem approach, developing regional bycatch reduction plans to address ecosystem impacts, and expanding the National Marine Fisheries Service's (NMFS, also referred to as NOAA Fisheries) program in conservation engineering to help reduce the impacts of fishing practices on ecosystems.[96]

2. U.S. Ocean Action Plan

The Oceans Act of 2000 required submittal of the USCOP Report to the President and Congress, and provided that within ninety days the President was to issue a response to the recommendations.[97] The President issued the U.S. Ocean Action Plan in December 2004.[98] The Ocean Action Plan establishes the Committee on Ocean Policy, a Cabinet-level committee "to advise the President and, as appropriate, agency heads on the establishment and implementation of policies concerning ocean-related matters."[99] Established in December 2004 by Executive Order, the Committee functions under the leadership of the Chairman of the Council on Environmental Quality (CEQ).[100] The Ocean Action Plan also establishes two new subsidiary bodies: (1) the Interagency Committee on Ocean Science and Resource Management Integration, and (2) the Subcommittee on Integrated Management of Ocean Resources.[101] The Ocean Action Plan provides that the National Science and Technology Council's Joint Subcommittee on Oceans (now the Joint Subcommittee on Ocean Science and Technology) is to report directly to the Co-chairs of the new Interagency Committee.[102] Finally, the Ocean Action Plan expands the existing Ocean Research Advisory

Panel, which provides advice and guidance to the Interagency Committee, and calls for coordination with the National Security Council Policy Coordinating Committee.[103] Although the Ocean Action Plan takes steps towards fulfilling the USCOP's recommendations by creating a new Executive Office level structure for ocean policy, it makes only very limited references to ecosystem issues, and does not require any concrete or specific steps towards EBM.

3. Introduced Bills

In 2005, Congress began to consider legislation that would implement the recommendations of the two Commissions. Although the bills did not become law, they included provisions that would establish the administrative and legal framework to implement EBM in the marine environment. Congress began to consider additional legislation in 2007. These bills offer insight into how Congress would approach marine EBM implementation.

a. The National Oceans Protection Act of 2005, S. 1224

In June 2005, Sen. Boxer introduced S. 1224, the National Oceans Protection Act of 2005 (NOPA 2005).[104] This bill proposed a framework for EBM. The purpose of NOPA 2005 was "to secure, for present and future generations of people of the United States, the full range of environmental, economic, educational, social, cultural, nutritional, and recreational benefits of healthy marine ecosystems."[105] To implement this purpose, NOPA 2005 recognized that "ecosystem-based management of coastal lands, oceans, and marine resources to protect, maintain, and restore the health of marine ecosystems requires a partnership between Federal, State, local, and tribal governments."[106] NOPA 2005 focused on a coordinated ecosystem approach, noting that "EBM and a precautionary and adaptive approach" should be used "to ensure responsible and sustainable use of fishery resources and other ocean and coastal resources."[107]

NOPA 2005 would designate the National Oceanic and Atmospheric Administration (NOAA) as the agency responsible for providing "management, conservation, protection, and restoration of ocean resources including living marine resources, habitats and ocean ecosystems."[108] NOPA 2005 also called for establishment of the Council on Ocean Stewardship in the Executive Office of the President.[109] The Council was to be responsible for coordinating ocean activities among federal agencies and departments and "ensur[ing] that all federal agencies engaged in ocean and atmospheric activities adopt and implement the principle of ecosystem-based management and take necessary steps to improve regional coordination and delivery of services around common eco-regional boundaries."[110] Likewise, EBM would be a national priority for coordination.[111]

b. The Oceans Conservation, Education, and National Strategy for the 21st Century Act, H.R. 2939 (2005)

On June 16, 2005, Rep. Weldon introduced the Oceans Conservation, Education, and National Strategy for the 21st Century Act (OCEANS).[112] Like NOPA 2005, OCEANS was a response to the Pew and USCOP Reports and "the call for a more comprehensive and integrated [EBM] approach."[113] OCEANS proposed to establish a national oceans policy and regional ocean partnerships.[114] The national oceans policy, which was almost identical to the purpose set forth in NOPA 2005, would provide that "[t]he Congress declares that it is the continuing policy of the United States to protect, maintain, and restore the health of marine ecosystems in order to fulfill the ecological, economic, educational, social, cultural, nutritional, recreational, and other requirements of present and future generations of Americans."[115] OCEANS also proposed national standards, the first of which was that "covered actions affecting . . . ocean waters or ocean resources must be conducted in a manner . . . consistent with the protection and maintenance of healthy marine ecosystems.[116] OCEANS also would reestablish and strengthen NOAA.[117]

OCEANS proposed establishment of a National Oceans Advisor and a Committee on Ocean Policy, both within the Executive Office of the President, as well as a Council of Advisors on Oceans Policy.[118] OCEANS would implement EBM through the establishment of Regional Ocean Partnerships, which were to provide for regional ecosystem assessment and EBM.[119] The regions established in OCEANS were to include the coastal zone as defined in the CZMA, as well as watersheds that have a significant impact on coastal waters, seaward to the extent of the two-hundred-mile Exclusive Economic Zone.[120] The Partnerships were to create and implement a strategic plan for adaptive EBM within each region, under the guiding principles of protecting, maintaining, and restoring marine ecosystem health and providing for sustainable use and management of marine resources.[121] The Regional Ocean Partnerships would not supplant the functions or authorities of existing regional entities, but instead were directed to build upon such existing frameworks.[122]

c. The Oceans Conservation, Education, and National Strategy for the 21st Century Act, H.R. 21 (2007)

On January 4, 2007, Rep. Farr introduced the Oceans Conservation, Education, and National Strategy for the 21st Century Act (OCEANS-21).[123] Like the two bills introduced in 2005, OCEANS-21 would implement key recommendations of the Pew and USCOP reports.[124]

The purposes of OCEANS-21 are more detailed and focused on EBM than the 2005 bills. For example, OCEANS-21 has the goal of "secur[ing] for present and future generations of people of the United States, the full range of ecological, economic, educational, social, cultural, nutritional, and recreational benefits of healthy marine ecosystems."[125] It would do so in part by "promoting ecosystem-based approaches to management of ocean waters and resources."[126] OCEANS-21 also includes detailed definitions of EBM, "marine ecosystem health" and "health of marine ecosystems," and "healthy marine ecosystems."[127]

Like the 2005 bills, OCEANS-21 would establish NOAA as the agency with responsibility for oversight of all coastal, ocean, and Great Lakes waters and resources and coordination with other agencies and governments.[128] The bill also creates a National Oceans Advisor and a Committee on Ocean Policy, both in the Executive Office of the

President.[129] Like the 2005 version of OCEANS, the bill would implement EBM through the creation of Regional Ocean Partnerships and preparation of Regional Ocean Strategic Plans, based on the same regions as the earlier bill.[130] Finally, OCEANS-21 establishes an Ocean and Great Lakes Conservation Trust Fund, and establishes approval requirements for coastal states seeking to receive grants from the Fund.[131] On April 26, 2007, the House Subcommittee on Fisheries, Wildlife, and Oceans held a legislative hearing on OCEANS-21, beginning the bill's journey through the legislative process.

C. Application of Existing Laws to Implement Ecosystem-Based Management

As the Commission reports make clear, and the 2005 and 2007 ocean bills confirm, existing law in the United States does not provide any single or comprehensive source of authority for establishing an EBM program for the marine environment. When considered individually, however, existing statutes and other legal authorities contain many components of an EBM management approach. By analyzing each of these laws separately, the elements of a comprehensive EBM program can be identified based in existing law. When administered together, existing U.S. laws provide an adequate framework for marine environment EBM.

1. Marine Mammal Protection Act

The first statute to identify marine ecosystem management as a priority for federal action was the MMPA.[132] Although Congress passed the MMPA to deal with problems confronting certain marine mammal species and population stocks, as early as the 1971 hearings and committee reports the parties supporting an MMPA enactment recognized the critical importance of making ecosystem health and stability the primary focus of the law.[133]

References to the need for ecosystem protection are found throughout the MMPA legislative history. In 1972, the Senate Commerce Committee wrote, "[b]asic life history and population information ought to be obtained for each marine mammal of concern to the United States. . . . All of these animals are a part of the ocean biomass and are important in maintaining an ecological balance."[134]

In a letter to the Department of State about the proposed MMPA, Rep. Dingell stressed the importance of focusing on the marine ecosystem by stating:

> The disappearance or low population levels of certain species of marine mammals would clearly have implications for the ecosystems of which these mammals have been a significant part. Also, the level of pollution of the world's oceans will unquestionably have some effect upon them which might well be to increase the environmental stress limiting their growth and survival rates.[135]

The State Department replied:

> [T]he disappearance or serious reduction in the population levels of marine mammals can affect the stability and viability of marine ecosystems which in

turn can lead to a more generalized disruption of the marine environmental balance. If we are to preserve the oceans, and if their resources are to be preserved for mankind, programs must be developed that view the oceans and their flora and fauna as a totality. . . . [136]

Dr. G. Carleton Ray of the Marine Mammal Council suggested Congress use ecosystems to define marine mammal population goals:

> The concept of "sustainable yield" is important and it is clear that such a yield must not be calculated merely in economic terms. . . . What is "optimum" from the point of view of economic yield may not be optimum in terms of a species or population in its environment. A part of the difficulty in management practice is that it has been in terms of human needs, rather than in terms of the needs of ecological balance within a natural ecosystem.[137]

As Dr. Ray wrote to the Senate subcommittee, "[i]t must be apparent that man has already perturbed all the earth's ecosystems and it is now our clear duty, as conservationists, to protect the future health of these ecosystems by managing them wisely at an international level."[138]

In the Senate debates, Sen. Stevens noted, "[t]he well-being of the entire ecosystem must therefore be kept in mind. It also requires a judgment, not only on the maximum population of the species, but on the maximum total productivity of the environment including all constituent elements."[139]

Witnesses discussing the management approach that should be employed under the MMPA referred to the need for a comprehensive, ecosystem-based program. As Dr. Kenneth Norris of the Marine Mammal Council testified before the Senate subcommittee:

> The management should be based not only upon the biological health of the individual species, but upon the health of the ecosystem of which it is a part. . . . Such management must be based upon continuing reappraisal of the health of both animal and ecosystem. . . . Enlightened management today is no longer species management, it is instead ecosystem management.[140]

Howard Pollack, then Deputy Administrator of NOAA, expressed a similar sentiment when he testified that "any conservation program for a particular species must not only include studies of that species, but also other organisms which interact with that species in the marine environment, and indeed the environment itself."[141]

In response to these strong expressions of concern for the marine environment of which marine mammals are a part, Congress established the *primary goal* of the MMPA as being "to maintain the health and stability of the marine ecosystem."[142] Congress did not, however, provide specific authority to advance this primary goal. For example, no direct authority exists to protect marine mammal habitat or components of such habitat, including prey species. No research programs expressly address marine ecosystem health and stability or the relationship between marine mammals and other elements of the marine environment. Perhaps most importantly, no

No management or enforcement tools are available in the MMPA expressly for the purpose of managing marine ecosystems on a comprehensive basis.

management or enforcement tools are available in the MMPA expressly for the purpose of managing marine ecosystems on a comprehensive basis, recognizing the interrelated nature of all resources of the marine environment and the role that marine mammals play in the dynamics of each such ecosystem.

While recognizing the importance of marine ecosystem protection, the MMPA as enacted in 1972 did little to establish the basis for comprehensive management action on an ecosystem basis. Beginning in 1994, however, more substantive EBM authority began to make its way into the MMPA.

In 1994, Congress amended the MMPA to require the use of an EBM approach for scientific research in the Bering Sea.[143] At the same time, Congress required a "regional workshop for the Gulf of Maine to assess human-caused factors affecting the health and stability of that marine ecosystem of which marine mammals are a part."[144] The goal of the workshop was to be a recommended "program of research and management to restore or maintain that marine ecosystem and its key components."[145] Once again, Congress made "maintenance of the health and stability of the marine ecosystems" the "primary management objective."[146] These provisions were important because, for the first time, Congress acknowledged that ecosystem-based considerations, rather than single species population goals, should be the focal point of federal action under a law concerned with ocean resources.

Even more significant for future EBM actions was legislative history accompanying the 1994 amendments. Prior to the 1994 amendments and the accompanying legislative history, it was unclear what could be done under the MMPA to advance these habitat goals because the law's action-forcing provisions and enforcement authority only concerned "take" of marine mammals by means that did not include habitat modification.

In the 1994 legislative history, Congress took up the habitat protection issue with reference to the MMPA's general rulemaking authority set forth in Section 112, which authorizes the Secretary to "prescribe such regulations as are necessary and appropriate to carry out the purposes of [the MMPA]."[147]

This authority, although general, arguably can be used to promulgate regulations to protect specific habitat or advance the Act's ecosystem health and stability goal. In the legislative history of the 1994 amendments, Congress made it clear that Section 112 provides such authority. The House Merchant Marine and Fisheries Committee acknowledged that it added the phrase "essential habitats" to the congressional purposes in Section 2(2) to underscore that "[t]he Committee believes that the Secretary currently has the authority to . . . protect marine mammals and their habitats under the general rulemaking authority of Section 112 of the MMPA."[148] The Committee noted that this authority would allow the Secretary, for example, "to protect polar bear denning, feeding, and migration routes in order to fully comply with the United States' obligations under Article II of the Agreement on the Conservation of Polar Bears."[149]

This general authorizing provision of the MMPA therefore becomes quite important for efforts to fashion an EBM approach out of existing law. It empowers the Secretaries of the Interior and Commerce to "prescribe . . . regulations" to carry out MMPA purposes.[150] The foremost purpose of the MMPA is "marine ecosystem health and stability"[151] and, as Congress explained in 1994, this rulemaking authority can be used to protect marine mammal habitat and to achieve compliance with international treaty obligations. Considering the pervasive range of MMPA-protected species throughout U.S. coastal and ocean waters, Section 112 can be used as a central source of legal authority to promulgate regulations to protect the marine ecosystem. The manner in which this authority can be used in combination with other U.S. laws to fashion the legal basis for EBM in the marine environment is discussed in the final section of this chapter.

2. Endangered Species Act

a. The Relationship Between Species and Ecosystems

The ESA[152] is a remarkable law in many ways, not least because it represents a judgment that humans do not have the right consciously to extirpate other life forms, regardless of their perceived utilitarian value.[153] As Aldo Leopold, whom many consider the father of the modern conservation movement, once observed: "To keep every cog and wheel is the first precaution of intelligent tinkering."[154] For over three decades, the ESA has been hard at work trying to save every cog and wheel. Though its stated purpose is "to provide a means whereby the ecosystems upon which endangered . . . and threatened species depend may be conserved,"[155] the mechanisms of the Act focus on preservation of individual species, subspecies and even smaller taxonomic units called "distinct population segments."[156]

Critics argue that saving species one at a time is neither efficient nor effective.[157] In response, in the 1990s Interior Secretary Bruce Babbitt instituted a number of administrative "reforms,"[158] in part to stave off legislative attacks on the statute.[159] Babbitt genuinely believed that his reforms would improve the ESA and enhance recovery of imperiled species.[160] Babbitt championed an ecosystem-based approach to the ESA[161] and became the Clinton Administration's leading spokesperson on the issue.[162]

While a broader focus on ecosystems is undoubtedly the right way to go in managing human activities affecting the oceans, the needs of individual species have to be factored into any management plan. Ecosystems need species as much species need ecosystems. The scientific community has come to a broad consensus on many aspects of the relationship between biodiversity and ecosystem functioning, including many points relevant to the management of ecosystems. As stated in a recent Position Paper of the Ecological Society of America:

> Species' functional characteristics strongly influence ecosystem properties. Functional characteristics operate in a variety of contexts, including effects of dominant species, keystone species, ecological engineers, and interactions among species (*e.g.*, competition, facilitation, mutualism, disease, and

predation). Relative abundance alone is not always a good predictor of the ecosystem-level importance of a species, as even relatively rare species (*e.g.,* a keystone predator) can strongly influence pathways of energy and material flows.[163]

In short, biodiversity matters. Along with the structure, function, and processes of ecosystems, managers must also pay attention to the *composition* of species that make up the biological communities of ecosystems. More precisely, EBM plans and policies must ensure that, to the greatest extent possible, viable populations of indigenous species are maintained or restored if the biological integrity of marine ecosystems, and the services they provide, are to be sustained over time. The ESA can be used to help achieve this goal.

The ESA is jointly administered by the U.S. Fish and Wildlife Service (FWS) within the Department of Interior and NMFS within the Department of Commerce.[164] In general, FWS is responsible for terrestrial species, and NMFS is responsible for marine species.[165] Although the agencies derive their authority from the same statute, there are some important differences in the way that they each interpret and apply that authority, which will be pointed out below.

Species must be listed as either threatened or endangered[166] to receive the special protection afforded under the ESA. In general, species are listed one at a time through a very time-consuming rulemaking process.[167] In recent years, most of the listings have come in response to citizen petitions and lawsuits under the ESA's citizen suit provision.[168] Currently, there are approximately 1,300 domestic species of plants and animals on the list, of which approximately sixty are marine species under NOAA's jurisdiction.[169] FWS and NMFS also maintain lists of "candidate species" whose biological status warrants protection but whose listing must await the resources necessary to complete the administrative process.[170]

Though there has been no wholesale shift to an ecosystem approach under the ESA, there have been some notable steps in that direction. Spurred in part by the Babbitt reforms, and by the emergence of conservation biology as an influential body of applied science, a number of multispecies conservation plans and programs have been initiated in both the public and private sectors. Before turning to examples of these multispecies conservation efforts, background on the substantive standards and regulatory requirements of the ESA is in order to understand how the ESA can be used to further EBM in federal programs and activities.

b. Endangered Species Act Framework

Section 7(a)(2) directs each federal agency to "insure that any action authorized, funded, or carried out by such agency . . . is not likely to jeopardize the continued existence of any endangered species or threatened species or result in the destruction or adverse modification of any habitat which is determined by the Secretary . . . to be critical."[171] In the Tellico Dam case, the U.S. Supreme Court held that this statutory command "admits of no exception." [172] Species must be protected, said the Court, "whatever the cost."[173] The ESA strips the courts of their usual equitable balancing authority; once a violation of Section 7(a)(2) is found, an injunction is automatic.[174] Only the Endangered Species Exemption Committee (dubbed the "God Squad"), created under the 1978 amendments to the ESA, has the power to exempt actions from the strict mandates of the Act.[175]

Only the Endangered Species Exemption Committee (dubbed the "God Squad") has the power to exempt actions from the strict mandates of the ESA.

In addition to prohibiting actions that are likely to "jeopardize" species survival, Section 7(a)(2) prohibits federal agencies from taking actions that could result in the destruction or adverse modification of designated critical habitat.[176] The designation is one of the areas where the policies of FWS and NMFS differ significantly.[177] The adverse modification standard is the only provision in the Act that requires species recovery needs to be factored into decisions.[178] Since habitat fragmentation and the loss of ecosystem values is the leading cause of endangerment for listed species, the enhanced legal protection that comes with critical habitat designation is an important tool for recovery.[179]

Violations of the prohibitions on jeopardy and adverse modification of critical habitat can be avoided under the Section 7(a)(2) consultation process. Through these procedures, the federal action agency consults with FWS or NMFS to determine the effect of a proposed action on listed species. When an action may affect a species, FWS or NMFS will issue a biological opinion. If the opinion concludes that jeopardy or adverse modification of critical habitat will occur, reasonable and prudent alternatives must be specified that, if followed, will avoid violating the Section 7(a)(2) prohibitions.[180]

The other significant substantive provision of the ESA is Section 9, which broadly prohibits the "take" of any endangered animal.[181] By rule, FWS has extended the take prohibition to all threatened species, unless the agency opts to use a "special rule" under Section 4(d).[182] By contrast, NMFS has opted to use the Section 4(d) rules as the exclusive mechanism for regulating the take of threatened species. NMFS pioneered a new approach to Section 4(d) rules in the case of fourteen distinct units of salmon and steelhead in the Pacific Northwest.[183] This Section 4(d) rule approved certain existing state and local programs, and created a process whereby NMFS could approve additional programs meeting conservation standards.[184] Incorporating limits in Section 4(d) rules allows activities to be conducted while maintaining protection for threatened species and their habitats, relieving state agencies, government entities, tribes, and others from certain liability for takes.[185]

In response to concerns of private landowners engendered by the Ninth Circuit's decision in the *Palila* case,[186] which held that introduction of exotic sheep into the montane habitat of an endangered bird resulted in prohibited take, Congress amended the ESA in 1982 to provide for incidental take permits (ITP).[187] "Incidental take" is defined as take that occurs in pursuit of, "but is not the purpose of . . . an otherwise lawful activity."[188] Section 10(a) authorizes FWS and NMFS to issue permits for the incidental take of listed species under certain circumstances. To obtain an incidental take permit, the applicant must submit a habitat conservation plan (HCP).[189] Permits are required only for the take of federally listed species, but applicants are encouraged to include state-listed, proposed, candidate and rare species in their HCPs.[190] When take will occur under a federal action subject to Section 7(a)(2), the biological opinion can authorize incidental take under reasonable and prudent measures set forth in an incidental take statement in the biological opinion.[191]

c. Applying the Endangered Species Act to Ecosystem-Based Management

There are several aspects of the ESA that can be applied to implementation of an EBM approach. The most obvious of these are ESA authorities that apply to HCPs and the issuance of ITPs. Other provisions of the ESA of potential value to EBM include the take prohibition, critical habitat designation, 4(d) rules, and the ESA's broad rulemaking authority.

i. Habitat Conservation Plan

HCPs can be applied on a multispecies, or even ecosystem-based scale. The first significant multispecies HCP was the San Diego Multiple Species Conservation Program (SDMSCP) approved in 1996 by the California Fish and Game Department under the California Natural Community Conservation Planning Act (NCCP), and by FWS under the ESA.[192] The SDMSCP is a comprehensive habitat conservation program that addresses multiple species habitat needs and the preservation of native vegetation communities for a nine-hundred-square-mile planning area in southwestern San Diego County.[193] The SDMSCP provides for a preserve management program that actively maintains habitat quality and reduces threats to covered species and a subregional biological monitoring program to gauge the progress of the program towards meeting its biological objectives. Since the SDMSCP, there have been dozens of multispecies HCPs approved under the NCCP.[194] Taken together, the NCCP effectively establishes a regional HCP that covers an entire ecosystem for eighty-five terrestrial species.[195]

The Lower Colorado River Multi-Species Conservation Program (LCRMSCP) is an example of a programmatic approach to multispecies conservation entailing aquatic, although nonmarine, species.[196] The LCRMSCP was initiated in 1995 as a partnership providing ESA compliance for water and power resource management in southern California, Nevada, and Arizona.[197] The Bureau of Reclamation releases flows for various water users, including Los Angeles, San Diego, Las Vegas, and Phoenix. The goal is to meet public needs, avoid species jeopardy, and assist in recovery of species such as the bonytail chub, razorback sucker, southwestern willow flycatcher, and Yuma clapper rail.[198] But the LCRMSCP does more, by targeting at least ninety species in all of the habitats that comprise the riverine corridor of the lower Colorado River from Hoover Dam to the Mexican border, including aquatic, marsh, cottonwood-willow riparian, and mesquite habitats.[199] Nonlisted species that will benefit from the plan include the flannelmouth sucker, the yellow-billed cuckoo, and other neotropical migratory birds and bats that use riparian habitats.[200] A stakeholder process includes representatives from tribes, private landowners, irrigation districts, local communities, and other parties.[201]

The South Florida Multi Species Recovery Plan (SFMSRP) is an example of an ecosystem approach to recovery planning under the ESA.[202] Completed by the FWS in 1999, the SFMSRP covers recovery actions for sixty-eight species and applies to 26,002 square miles in south Florida. It embraces the ecology and restoration needs of twenty-three natural communities in the region.[203] This diverse array of "biomes" illustrates the complexity of designing EBM plans even at relatively modest regional scale.[204]

As these examples demonstrate, there are a variety of models that lead themselves to use in advancing ecosystem or habitat-based approaches. To date, no such plans have been developed solely within a marine environment setting. In part, this is because the moving force behind HCPs is where nonfederal lands and actions are involved and it is not possible to gain take authorization under Section 7(a)(2) through an incidental take statement. These circumstances do not arise after the marine environment setting. However, HCPs have been used to authorize activities under state law, which would be more than readily adaptable to state fishery and coastal zone programs. In fact, state agencies are subject to the Section 9 prohibition as a result of take by fishing industry participants in state-licensed fisheries; thus, there is good reason to consider HCPs for such programs.[205] In addition, HCPs have been used in cases where federal programs exist to cover large geographic areas and includes nonfederal participants, such as the LCRMSCP. And, of course, HCPs can be used to cover habitat important to marine species, such as anadromous fish, within large areas of privately owned land, such as tree farms for forest products companies. As a result, it is likely that HCPs could be used as a source of legal authority for implementing EBM in specific coastal and marine settings.

ii. The Take Prohibition

The ESA's take prohibition also could be used to implement EBM. As recognized by the Supreme Court in the *Sweet Home* case, Section 9 confers broad authority to prohibit or regulate activities that "actually kill or injure" threatened and endangered species through habitat modification that "significantly impairs essential behavioral patterns such as breeding feeding and sheltering."[206] For species listed as endangered, Section 9 automatically prohibits any take except as specifically authorized by an incidental take statement under Section 7[207] or an incidental take permit under Section 10.[208] Moreover, the prohibition on the take of endangered species of fish or wildlife extends to activities within the territorial sea of the United States or the "high seas."[209] For threatened species, Section 4(d) authorizes the agencies to adopt special rules that specify prohibited activities but also allow some exceptions. NMFS, in particular, has begun to make broader use of these authorities to manage activities within larger geographic areas.

An unresolved question is the extent to which Section 9 prohibits habitat modification that impairs species recovery without actually causing death or injury to identifiable animals.[210] In her concurring opinion in *Sweet Home*, Justice O'Connor observed: "To raze the last remaining ground on which the piping plover currently breeds, thereby making it impossible for any piping plovers to reproduce, would obviously injure the population (causing the species' extinction in a generation)."[211]

In *Bensman v. U.S. Forest Service*, the District Court for the Western District of Missouri ruled that "[h]abitat destruction that prevents the recovery of the species by affecting essential behavioral patters causes actual injury to the species and effects a taking under Section 9 of the Act."[212] As the law on this question evolves, agencies have an opportunity to articulate the connection between habitat loss and harm to the species to further the purpose of ESA to "provide a means whereby the ecosystems upon which endangered and threatened species depend may be conserved."

Recently, for example, NMFS proposed a rule setting a uniform mandatory vessel speed restriction of ten knots or less in locations along the East Coast during specified times to reduce the risk of collisions between ships and the critically endangered North Atlantic right whale.[213] Additionally, NMFS has sought to reroute ship traffic away from the areas where whales congregate. At NMFS's urging, the United States is seeking approval from the International Maritime Organization to reconfigure the Traffic Separation Scheme (TSS) for Boston.[214] Analysis by NMFS indicates that a slight shift in the northern leg of the TSS and narrowing the two traffic lanes by approximately one-half mile each would reduce the risk of ship strikes to right whales by fifty-eight percent, while also reducing ship strike risk to other endangered large whale species by eighty-one percent. This is an example of "zoning" within the marine environment using the authority of the ESA to protect both species and their habitat under Section 9. A similar approach was used to designate activities that constitute take of whales, in the Glacier Bay ecosystem, and manatees, in the Crystal River ecosystem.[215] Thus, by regulation, FWS and NMFS can implement sweeping activity restrictions throughout an ecosystem.

iii. Critical Habitat

The Steller sea lion provides a useful example of how critical habitat can be used to protect marine ecosystems. NMFS listed the Steller sea lion as a threatened species on April 5, 1990, due to substantial declines in the western portion of the range in the Gulf of Alaska and the Bering Sea.[216] It designated critical habitat on August 27, 1993, based on the location of terrestrial rookery and haulout sites, spatial extent of foraging trips, and availability of prey items.[217] NMFS designated two kinds of marine habitat as critical. First, areas around rookeries and haulout sites were chosen based on evidence that many foraging trips by lactating adult females in summer may be relatively short. Second, three large foraging areas were chosen based on (1) at-sea observations indicating that sea lions commonly used these areas for foraging, (2) records of animals killed incidentally in fisheries in the 1980s, (3) knowledge of sea lion prey and their life histories and distributions, and (4) foraging studies.

In designating critical habitat, NMFS adopted a "zonal" approach that closed some areas to commercial fishing altogether and sought to reduce the allowable catch of pollock and other groundfish in other areas, in order to maintain an adequate "carrying capacity" of forage fish to meet the nutritional needs of the Steller sea lion.[218]

Greenpeace and other conservation organizations challenged NMFS's approach and the issuance of biological opinions on the commercial fishery in litigation that lasted for over ten years and produced a number of key decisions and orders requiring a more comprehensive approach to fisheries management and recovery planning for the Steller sea lion within the North Pacific ecosystem.[219] The designation of critical habitat meant that NMFS would be held to a higher standard of ensuring that the groundfish fishery would not adversely modify the critical habitat by reducing the "carrying capacity" of forage fish (pollack and mackerel) to supply the nutritional needs of the Steller sea lion.[220] Thus, critical habitat designation can be applied throughout the ecosystem area of a listed species and implemented in zones based on the presence of activities that potentially harm the listed species.

iv. Rulemaking

Finally, as was true under the MMPA, the ESA imposes broad rulemaking authority.[221] Under this power, FWS and NMFS can fashion regulations that would implement EBM for species that occur throughout coastal and marine ecosystems. Such regulations could assure a particularly broad scope due to the ESA purpose of providing the means whereby the ecosystems on which listed species depend may be conserved.[222] In addition, Section 4(d) can be applied where threatened species are involved. As discussed above, Section 4(d) has been used in a wide variety of contexts to establish regional, or ecosystem-wide, conservation programs. Although this authority has not been applied in the marine environment setting, it is reasonably well-suited to such a purpose.

3. Magnuson-Stevens Fishery Conservation and Management Act

The FCMA is the principal legal authority for managing most fisheries within the Exclusive Economic Zone (EEZ). Management responsibility is held by NMFS, which acts upon recommendations from eight Regional Fishery Management Councils (Councils).[223] As originally enacted, the FCMA did not expressly provide for EBM or ecosystem considerations, and focused instead on management of individual species.[224] This management regimen has been criticized for failing to maintain or restore fish stocks, leading to overfishing and declining stocks.[225]

In 1996, Congress reauthorized the FCMA with the Sustainable Fisheries Act (SFA), making a number of major changes to address the shortfalls of single-species management.[226] The SFA provisions included a requirement that councils set harvest rates at or below maximum sustainable yields; determine the effects of fishing on the environment; and identify essential fish habitat and take measures to protect it.[227] The SFA was a shift toward an ecosystem perspective,[228] but it did not include any requirements for EBM or other ecosystem considerations. Under the SFA, Congress tasked NMFS with establishing the Ecosystem Principles Advisory Panel.[229] The Panel recommended that each council develop a Fisheries Ecosystem Plan (FEP) for the ecosystem(s) under its jurisdiction.[230] Each FEP is an "umbrella document containing information on the structure and function of the ecosystem in which fishing activities occur, so that managers can be aware of the effects their decisions have on the ecosystem, and the effects other components of the ecosystem may have on fisheries."[231]

To implement EBM, Councils may utilize the process for preparing proposed regulations implementing a fishery management plan (FMP). Proposed regulations necessary or appropriate for implementing an FMP or an FMP amendment must be submitted to the Secretary.[232] The Secretary reviews the FMP and associated regulations for consistency with the FCMA.[233] If they are consistent, the Secretary conducts rulemaking.[234] If a negative determination is made, the Secretary notifies the council and provides recommendations on how to make the proposed regulations consistent with the FMP and the FCMA.[235]

Despite the absence of direct authority or requirements for EBM in the FCMA, the councils have made a significant shift towards this management approach and are in the process of developing FEPs for many ecosystems. For example, the Western Pacific Regional Fishery Management Council (WPRFMC) has prepared five draft FEPs, including American Samoa Archipelago, Hawaii Archipelago, Mariana Archipelago, Pacific Pelagic Fisheries, and Pacific Remote Island Areas.[236] The WPRFMC prepared the first ecosystem-based plan for fisheries developed in the U.S. in 2001, with the FMP for Coral Reef Ecosystems in the Western Pacific.[237] In addition, in October 2005 NMFS issued a draft programmatic environmental impact statement (DPEIS) analyzing the impacts of implementing an ecosystem approach to fisheries management in the Western Pacific region, which was reissued in draft in March 2007.[238] The DPEIS represents the first step in the incremental process to develop and implement the FEPs for the region. Under the FEP, existing fishery regulations in the Council's current, species-based FMP regulations would be revised into geographically based FEP regulations, "with no substantive changes to current fishing regulations."[239] Other councils are also in the process of developing FEPs. For example, the North Pacific Fishery Management Council is developing an FEP for the Aleutian Islands ecosystem,[240] and the South Atlantic Fishery Management Council is also currently preparing an FEP and a draft environmental impact statement.[241]

On January 12, 2007, President Bush signed the Magnuson-Stevens Fishery Conservation and Management Reauthorization Act of 2006 (2006 Reauthorization).[242] The 2006 Reauthorization legislation requires a greater consideration of scientific recommendations, requiring councils to set an annual catch limit for each fishery so that optimum sustainable yield is not exceeded.[243] The Reauthorization also explicitly recognizes the efforts made by councils to move toward EBM, amending the FCMA to state that "[a] number of the Fishery Management Councils have demonstrated significant progress in integrating ecosystem considerations in fisheries management using the existing authorities provided under this Act."[244] Although the reauthorization does not specifically require EBM or create a framework for EBM, it supports the integration of EBM into fisheries management and the efforts by councils to shift towards EBM through development of FEPs. This policy objective, combined with the authority currently available to the Councils and the Secretary to establish FMPs, provides a basis under which EBM can be incorporated into fisheries management.

4. Outer Continental Shelf Lands Act

Congress enacted the Outer Continental Shelf Lands Act (OCSLA) in 1953 to manage offshore gas and oil development.[245] The Minerals Management Service (MMS) in the Department of the Interior is responsible for implementing the OCSLA. In 1978, Congress amended the OCSLA to include consideration of marine and coastal ecosystems and impacts from development.[246] While the OCSLA calls on the Secretary to balance economic, social, and environmental values in the development of offshore resources,[247] the law also expressly contemplates consideration of marine and coastal ecosystems in several places. As a starting point, the term "marine environment" is defined as

> the physical, atmospheric, and biological components, conditions, and factors which interactively determine the productivity, state, condition, and quality of the marine ecosystem, including the waters of the high seas, the contiguous zone, transitional and intertidal areas, salt marshes, and wetlands within the coastal zone and on the outer Continental Shelf.[248]

The definition of "coastal environment" includes the same biological and other components "which interactively determine the productivity, state, condition, and quality of the terrestrial ecosystem from the shoreline inward to the boundaries of the coastal zone."[249]

The congressional declaration of policy also includes provisions for protection of marine ecosystems by coastal states, providing that the development of offshore energy protection will have significant impacts on both coastal and noncoastal areas of states and that accordingly, in recognition

> 4) . . . of the national interest in the effective management of the marine, coastal, and human environment . . .

> 5) . . . the rights and responsibilities of all States and, where appropriate, local governments, to preserve and protect their marine, human, and coastal environments through such means as regulation of land, air, and water uses, of safety, and of related development and activity should be considered and recognized.[250]

The legislative history of the 1978 law also demonstrates that Congress intended to address environmental and ecosystem health by describing the amendment as containing "many provisions . . . for the protection of the marine, coastal, and human environment."[251]

Not only does the framework for the OCSLA authorize the Secretary and the states to consider ecosystem impacts and regulate on an ecosystem level, the law also provides the Secretary with the express authority to develop, approve, and review leases based partly on consideration of impacts to the marine and coastal environment. Section 18 provides that the Secretary shall prepare an oil and gas leasing program for the Outer Continental Shelf, consistent with the principle that management "shall be conducted in a manner which considers economic, social, and environmental values of the renewable and nonrenewable resources."[252] The leasing program is required to

Timing and location of leases are based in part on the environmental sensitivity and marine productivity of the affected areas.

"consist of a schedule of proposed lease sales indicating, as precisely as possible, the size, timing, and location of leasing activity which [the Secretary] determines will best meet national energy needs for the five-year period following its approval or reapproval."[253] The lease program are based on a consideration of, among other factors, the relative environmental sensitivity and marine productivity of the affected areas, and the leasing program must be reviewed at least once per year.[254]

Under the leasing regulations, MMS prepares a proposed area-wide leasing program and forwards a copy of the draft proposal to the Governor of each affected state for comment.[255] The Director of MMS recommends to the Secretary areas identified for environmental analysis and consideration for leasing. In making a recommendation, the Director is required to consider "all available environmental information" as well as comments received from states, local governments, and other interested parties.[256] In determining appropriate areas for leasing, the Director is required to evaluate fully "the potential effect of leasing on the human, marine and coastal environments, and develop measures to mitigate adverse impacts."[257] Tracts approved for leasing are offered by competitive sealed bidding and leases are issued for an initial period of five years, or up to ten years when additional time is necessary to encourage exploration and development due to adverse conditions such as unusually deep water.[258]

Pursuant to the 1978 amendments, the Secretary must conduct environmental studies of "any area or region included in an oil and gas lease sale or other lease to establish information for assessment and management of environmental impacts on the marine and coastal environments of the Outer Continental Shelf and coastal areas affected by development."[259] Following the leasing and development of any area, the Secretary conducts additional studies to monitor the marine and coastal environments and to identify significant changes to those environments.[260] The Secretary also must submit to Congress an assessment of cumulative impacts of activities conducted under the OCSLA on the human, marine, and coastal environments every three years.[261] This requirement arguably requires the Secretary to assess ecosystem-level impacts. The leasing provisions described above also provide the Secretary and the MMS with the clear authority to consider ecosystem concerns when selecting areas suitable for leasing, and permit the Secretary to set aside areas that are particularly sensitive or that perform a critical ecosystem function. Within this leasing program, there is ample flexibility to abide by any spatial planning or zones established to implement EBM.

In addition, the OCSLA contains provisions that authorize the Secretary to suspend or cancel any activity that threatens serious harm to the marine or coastal environment. The OCSLA directs that the Secretary promulgate regulations, including "provisions for the suspension or temporary prohibition of any operation or activity, including production," if there is a "threat of serious, irreparable, or immediate harm or damage to life (including fish or other aquatic life), to property, to any mineral deposits (in areas leased or not leased), or to the marine, coastal, or human environment."[262] After a hearing, the Secretary may cancel any existing lease or permit if the Secretary determines that continued activity under the lease or permit would "probably cause serious harm or damage to life (including fish and other aquatic life) . . . or to the marine [or] coastal . . . environment."[263] This authority would certainly cover ecosystem impacts.

5. Coastal Zone Management Act

The CZMA provides a framework for coastal states to participate in a partnership with the federal government to manage development and resource use in coastal areas.[264] The CZMA applies to the "coastal zone," which is defined as "the coastal waters (including the waters therein and thereunder) and the adjacent shorelands . . . strongly influenced by each other and in proximity to the shorelines of the several coastal states, and includes islands, transitional and inter-tidal areas, salt marshes, wetlands, and beaches."[265] The CZMA is based on a cooperative federalism approach and provides two primary incentives for state involvement: funding and the federal consistency requirement.

The CZM program is implemented by state-level coastal programs, with states preparing a coastal zone management plan (CMP), which is submitted to the Secretary for review and approval.[266] Each state with an approved CMP is eligible to receive grants from the Secretary of Commerce.[267] Under the consistency requirement, federal agency activities that have reasonably foreseeable effects on any land or water use or natural resource of the coastal zone must be consistent with the enforceable policies of a state's federally approved coastal management program (CMP) to the maximum extent practicable.[268]

Under Section 307 of the CZMA, federal agency activities that have reasonably foreseeable effects on any land or water use or natural resource of the coastal zone are required to be consistent to the maximum extent practicable with the enforceable policies of a federally approved CMP.[269] Federal license or permit activities, as well as federal financial assistance activities that have reasonably foreseeable effects, must be fully consistent with the state's enforceable policies.[270] A lead state agency conducts federal consistency reviews. Failure to obtain consistency with the state's enforceable policies means that a proposed project cannot proceed unless the Secretary of Commerce overrides the inconsistency determination.[271]

Neither the CZMA nor the regulations expressly require the consideration of ecosystem factors, nor do they provide for EBM. However, the legislative history of the 2000 amendments to the CZMA states that "[t]he program was designed to strike a balance between conserving and maintaining healthy coastal ecosystems and providing for the sustainable development and use of coastal resources."[272] In addition, the CZMA requires that the Secretary consult and cooperate with, and to the maximum extent practicable, coordinate with other federal agencies and requires consistency determinations by the state for federal activities.[273] Alternatively, coastal states could amend their CMPs to require EBM.

The most effective mechanism by which EBM can be addressed through the CZMA is under the federal consistency process. Although no coastal states appear to have integrated EBM into their approved CMPs to date, some states have other laws requiring EBM considerations for ocean and coastal resources. These states should amend or modify their CMPs to incorporate those requirements as enforceable policies.[274]

For example, Massachusetts's CMP (MCMP) is based solely on existing state statutory authority.[275] The MCMP sets forth program policies that are enforceable under state statute and regulations.[276] These statutes include the Massachusetts Ocean Sanctuaries Act (MOSA), which provides for ecosystem protection of sanctuaries as follows:

> All ocean sanctuaries as described in section thirteen shall be under the care, oversight and control of the department and shall be protected from any exploitation, development, or activity that would significantly alter or otherwise endanger the ecology or the appearance of the ocean, the seabed, or subsoil thereof, or the Cape Cod National Seashore.[277]

Although MOSA requires protection of the ecology of all sanctuaries, which arguably requires ecosystem protection, the current MCMP enforceable policies do not include any express requirement for EBM. This shortfall has been recognized by the Massachusetts Ocean Management Task Force, which noted the importance of EBM and recommended that Massachusetts "pursue ecosystem management of offshore waters through federal, regional, and state coordination and cooperation."[278] To implement EBM, the Task Force specifically recommended that the Commonwealth "review and revise the state's enforceable coastal policies, based on the passage of the proposed Comprehensive Ocean Resources Management Act or other state legislation, existing statutes, and formal approval by [NOAA]."[279]

California is another state with existing statutes related to marine and coastal management that specifically address EBM. The Marine Life Protection Act (MLPA) requires that the California Department of Fish and Game establish networks of MPAs in state waters.[280] Two of the goals of the MLPA specifically address marine ecosystems and EBM: (1) "to protect the natural diversity and abundance of marine life, and the structure, function, and integrity of marine ecosystems" and (2) "to improve recreational, educational, and study opportunities provided by marine ecosystems that are subject to minimal human disturbance, and to manage these uses in a manner consistent with protecting biodiversity."[281] In addition, California fisheries management laws require EBM. For example, the general policies for conservation and management of marine living resources include the objective to "support and promote scientific research on marine ecosystems and their components to develop better information on which to base marine living resource management decisions."[282] To comport with these existing laws, California's CMP could be amended to include EBM.

As these examples demonstrate, the CZMA is a potential tool for advancing EBM. To do so, however, coastal states need to incorporate EBM into their approved plans. As in the case of California and Massachusetts, there are existing state laws that provide the basis for doing so. Once incorporated into the CMP, under the federal consistency requirement, EBM would be considered during evaluation of effects caused by federal agency activities.

6. Pollution Laws

There are a number of federal pollution control statutes that could come into play for regulating activities that impact the marine environment,[283] but the laws with the greatest potential to support EBM are the Clean Water Act (CWA) and the Clean Air Act (CAA).

The objective of the CWA is "to restore and maintain the chemical, physical, and biological integrity of the Nation's waters."[284] The geographic jurisdiction of the CWA extends to all "navigable waters," defined as the "waters of the United States including the territorial seas."[285] Discharges of pollutants to navigable waters are regulated under Section 402.[286] Discharges beyond the territorial sea are regulated under Section 403. Section 403 authorizes EPA to establish "ocean discharge criteria" to regulate the discharge of pollutants into the territorial seas, the contiguous zone and the oceans"[287] This provision also authorizes EPA to adopt guidelines for determining the degradation of marine waters. The guidelines must assess the effects on marine life including "changes in marine ecosystems, diversity, productivity, and stability; and species and community population changes."[288]

> **The laws with the greatest potential to support ecosystem-based management are the Clean Water Act and the Clean Air Act.**

Under Section 404 of the CWA, the U.S. Army Corps of Engineers regulates the discharge of "dredge or fill material."[289] Many activities in coastal waters require Section 404 permits including piers and docks for marine terminals. Permits must meet ecological criteria known as the 404(b)(1) Guidelines developed by EPA and the Corps.[290] Among other things, these criteria prohibit the use of wetlands, estuaries, and other sensitive ecological resources as disposal sites unless there is no "practicable alternative." Thus, Section 404 can be used as part of a coordinated EBM program to preclude dredge and fill activities in areas necessary to protect for ecosystem purposes.

The CWA contains a number of "place-based" programs that take an ecosystem approach to protecting water quality and aquatic biota. Among the most significant of these programs are the Great Lakes,[291] Chesapeake Bay,[292] Long Island Sound[293] and Lake Champlain.[294]

The CWA's Total Maximum Daily Load (TMDL) program, authorized by Section 303(d),[295] is another tool to support EBM in coastal waters. This provision requires states to (1) identify and list waterbodies where state water quality standards[296] are not being met following the application of technology-based point source pollution controls,[297] and (2) establish TMDLs for these waters. A TMDL is the sum of the allowable loads of a single pollutant from all contributing point and nonpoint sources. The calculation must include a margin of safety and account for seasonal variation in water quality. The goal of a TMDL is the attainment of water quality standards. The TMDL implementation plan can identify the need for point source and nonpoint source controls. EPA must review and approve or disapprove state lists and TMDLs. If state actions are not adequate, EPA must prepare lists and TMDLs.[298] However, states have considerable latitude when it comes to the actual implementation of TMDLs, particularly for nonpoint source controls.[299]

Many of the problems affecting coastal waters, such as the "dead zone" in the Gulf of Mexico, originate in the headwaters of the nation's river systems. The Gulf of Mexico dead zone is an area of hypoxic (less than 2 PPM dissolved oxygen) waters at the mouth of the Mississippi River. Its area varies in size, but can cover up to 6,000–7,000 square miles. The zone occurs between the inner and midcontinental shelf in the northern Gulf of Mexico, beginning at the Mississippi River delta and extending westward to the upper Texas coast.

The dead zone is caused by nutrient enrichment from the Mississippi River, particularly nitrogen and phosphorous.[300] Watersheds within the Mississippi River Basin drain much of the United States, from Montana to Pennsylvania and extending southward along the Mississippi River. Most of the nitrogen input comes from major farming states in the Mississippi River Valley, including Minnesota, Iowa, Illinois, Wisconsin, Missouri, Tennessee, Arkansas, Mississippi, and Louisiana. Thus, protecting marine ecosystems like the Gulf sometimes can require regulatory upstream source of pollution under Section 402 and the TMDL program.

The Clean Air Act (CAA)[301] may seem an unlikely candidate for an EBM approach to marine conservation, but with the Supreme Court's decision in *Massachusetts v. EPA*[302] the CAA has assumed new prominence in the effort to stabilize anthropogenic greenhouse gas (GHG) emissions that are causing climate change. In *Massachusetts v. EPA,* the Court held that EPA has authority to regulate GHG emissions from new motor vehicles under Section 202(a) of the Act and determined that EPA had failed to provide a sufficient scientific basis for declining to regulate these emissions.[303]

The second issue addressed by the Court was whether EPA had provided a sufficient basis for declining to regulate GHG under Section 202, which provides that the Administrator "shall by regulation prescribe . . . standards applicable to the emission of any air pollutant from any class or classes of new motor vehicles or new motor vehicle engines, which in his judgment cause, or contribute to, air pollution which may reasonably be anticipated to endanger public health or welfare."[304] According to the Court, "EPA can avoid taking further action [under Section 202] only if it determines that greenhouse gases do not contribute to climate change or if it provides some reasonable explanation as to why it cannot or will not exercise its discretion to determine whether they do."[305] Because EPA had already conceded that GHGs contribute to climate change, the Agency must provide "some reasonable explanation as to why it cannot or will not exercise its discretion."[306] EPA had provided a number of reasons why it believed regulating GHG emissions from new vehicles was imprudent; however, the Court rejected all of these justifications, concluding that they were insufficient to avoid the mandate of Section 202 and directed EPA on remand to reconsider its decision and to provide an appropriate scientific basis if it should again decide not to regulate greenhouse gas emissions for new motor vehicles.[307]

In the wake of the Supreme Court's decision, President Bush signed an Executive Order directing EPA and the Departments of Transportation and Agriculture to take the first steps toward regulations that would cut gasoline consumption and GHG emissions from motor vehicles, using as a starting point his "Twenty in Ten" plan to reduce U.S. gasoline consumption by twenty percent over the next ten years.[308] The Order also addresses the need for regulations under the CAA and directs these agencies to complete their rulemaking by the end of 2008.

Although the CAA does not apply directly to the marine ecosystems, the pervasive effects of climate change in the oceans call for remediation through all available legal mechanisms.[309] Development of an EBM approach for any specific area therefore should take into account the degree to which the CAA is being used to effectively regulate GHG emissions.

7. Marine Protected Areas

The most obvious authority to implement EBM is found in the laws for designating and managing marine protected areas (MPAs). Ranging from national parks, refuges, and marine sanctuaries to locations set aside by state and local governments, MPAs consist of specific areas established for conservation purposes that are subject to their own legal controls. MPAs are subject to divergent management goals and requirements and constitute isolated areas of resource protection that are not integrated into a cohesive management structure. The challenge to using these areas for EBM is, therefore, to link them together in a coordinated system and ensure that they serve an appropriate role within any managed ecosystem.

a. Executive Order 13,158

In 2000, President Clinton issued Executive Order 13,158 to "strengthen the management, protection and conservation of existing marine protected areas and to establish new or expanded MPAs."[310] The Order represents the most comprehensive effort to date to unify the various classifications of MPAs into a "scientifically based, comprehensive national system . . . representing diverse U.S. marine ecosystems, and the Nation's natural and cultural resources."[311] It defines an MPA as "any area of the marine environment that has been reserved by Federal, State, territorial, tribal, or local laws or regulations to provide lasting protection for part or all of the natural and cultural resources therein."[312]

Under Section 3 of the Order, federal agencies are to take action aimed at providing greater protection to existing MPAs, or creating new areas or expanding existing ones.[313] Section 4 directs these agencies to "coordinate and share information, tools, and strategies" to develop a national system of MPAs, and Section 5 directs all federal agencies "to the extent permitted by law and the maximum extent practicable . . . [to] avoid harm to the natural and cultural resources that are protected by an MPA."[314] This directive is not limited to agencies managing MPAs, but applies to all federal agencies and therefore should cover not only actions occurring inside MPAs, but also actions that occur outside MPAs but would cause harm within their boundaries if the actions are undertaken by the government itself or by nonfederal entities approved or funded by those agencies.

Theoretically, the MPA Executive Order provides an ideal mechanism for carrying out EBM. Numerous provisions of the Order identify the importance of protecting marine ecosystems and basing federal actions on ecosystem functions.[315] In reality, however, the Order has not proven to be an effective conservation tool. Like all Executive Orders, it suffers the inherent weakness of not being enforceable.[316] In addition, implementation of the Order has been very slow, and little has been done to coordinate the efforts of the various federal agencies with jurisdiction over MPAs for purposes of (1) systematically emphasizing EBM within such MPAs, and (2) connecting the individual MPA conservation mandates and EBM objectives in a coordinated manner.

b. National Marine Sanctuaries

Under the National Marine Sanctuaries Act,[317] NOAA has the authority, with Presidential approval and after complying with complex procedures, to designate national marine sanctuaries.[318] Such designation can be used to advance EBM, as reflected in some of the larger sanctuaries designated to date.[319] The objectives of each sanctuary are enforced by means of regulations, which can be readily tailored to reflect ecosystem goals.[320]

c. National Parks

Some units of the National Park System include coastal and offshore waters.[321] These areas are managed by the National Park Service (NPS) within the Department of the Interior under the general mandate of the 1916 National Park Service Organic Act, which requires that areas within the National Park System be managed to "promote and regulate the use" of the Park System to "conserve the scenery and the natural and historic objects and the wild life therein and to provide for the enjoyment of the same in such manner and by such means as will leave them unimpaired for the enjoyment of future generations."[322] Considered with the Organic Act legislative history, this mandate is consistent with an EBM approach, as it is intended to address "the question of the preservation of nature as it exists."[323] In addition to this general authority, the enabling authorities for each unit of the National Park System specify additional goals and directives that can call for actions to meet EBM objectives. NPS has the power to promulgate regulations to meet its management objectives,[324] which, as noted above, can include EBM.

An NPS legal authority of particular utility for EBM in the marine environment is found in 16 U.S.C. § 1a-1. This provision applies to all actions taken under the authority of the Secretary of the Interior, not just NPS, including, for example, offshore oil and gas exploration and development decisions by MMS. Under Section 1a-1, the Secretary may not authorize activities that are "in derogation of the values and purposes" of a unit of the National Park System.[325] Thus, under this authority, any unit that is in a coastal area and includes EBM as an element of its "values and purposes" could extend those EBM principles to Secretarial-authorized activities occurring outside of the Park area boundaries.

d. National Wildlife Refuges

Numerous National Wildlife Refuges managed by FWS in the Department of the Interior are located in coastal areas. Refuges are administered under the National Wildlife Refuge Administration Act, which requires management actions for individual refuges to achieve the "major purposes" for which each such area was established.[326] This Act also defined the mission of the Refuge System generally to consist of conserving fish, wildlife, plants, "and their habitats," creating the basis for EBM to be applied to Refuge management.[327] Uses of refuges must be "compatible" with the major purposes, which in many cases could be determined by FWS to include ecosystem protection.[328] FWS has authority to promulgate regulations to govern areas included in the Refuge System.[329]

e. National Monuments

The Antiquities Act authorizes the President to designate "national monuments" for purposes of protecting "historic landmarks, historic and prehistoric structures, and other objects of historic or scientific interest" on federally owned lands.[330] In 2006, President Bush used this authority to establish the Northwestern Hawaiian Islands Marine National Monument.[331] The large scale of the Monument (140,000 square miles), and its purpose of preserving marine life confirm that Antiquities Act legal authority can be used to protect the "scientific interest" in ecosystem processes. Legal control over activities affecting monuments can take the form of regulation and restriction or prohibition imposed under the Act.[332]

f. Fisheries Zones

As discussed previously, the FCMA includes express authority for the designation of EFH. In addition, in specific FMPs, regional fishery management councils can prepare, and NMFS can adopt, the designation of "marine reserves" that are closed to some, or all forms, of fishing. Both of these actions provide extensive authority for implementing EBM management measures targeted at fish and fish habitat. Because those purposes do not identify ecosystem protection as a management goal, such action must be taken on the basis of a record supporting the need for marine reserve designation for fishery management reasons.

Fishery Management Councils have used their authority under the FCMA to establish marine reserves. For example, the Gulf of Mexico Fishery Management Council established the Tortugas marine reserve habitat area of particular concern, where fishing for any species and bottom anchoring by fishing vessels is prohibited,[333] as well as three marine reserves in the eastern Gulf of Mexico encompassing approximately 219 square nautical miles.[334] The North Pacific Fishery Management Council created the Sitka Pinnacles Marine Reserve, closing an area of 2.5 square nautical miles to fishing for groundfish and halibut and anchoring by vessels.[335] The Pacific Fishery Management Council has established two de facto marine reserves off southern California to help rebuild cowcod stocks.[336] These two reserves cover 4,700 square miles, and all fishing for federally managed groundfish species is prohibited.[337]

g. State Marine Protected Areas

States may establish MPAs within coastal waters under their jurisdiction. Such MPAs can be based on a desire to pursue an EBM approach to marine resource management. One example of such a law is the California MLPA, discussed previously in Section II.C.5.[338] This sweeping law authorizes the designation of MPAs, such as "marine life reserves," that would prohibit activities that "upset the natural ecological function of the area."[339] Pursuant to this authority, California has adopted a network of twenty-nine MPAs.[340] In addition, under the MLPA, the California Fish and Game Commission must develop a Marine Life Protection Program, which must have, among other goals, ecosystem protection.[341] To the extent states develop legal programs such as this, federal agencies must conform their actions to the state requirements under Executive Order 13,158.[342] If fully implemented, state EBM actions therefore should be extended by virtue of corresponding actions by federal agencies to ensure their actions do not impede state conservation efforts.

8. Public Trust

The public trust doctrine traces its roots to the Justinian Code and to the words of the Roman jurist Marcius: "By the law of nature these things are common to all mankind: the air, running water, the sea, and consequently the shores of the sea."[343] The "lodestar in American public trust law"[344] is the U.S. Supreme Court decision in *Illinois Central Railroad Co. v. Illinois,* where the Court ruled that the State of Illinois held title to the submerged lands of Lake Michigan and had no authority to relinquish it to a private party.[345] The Court articulated this principle of the public trust: "[t]he State can no more abdicate its trust over property in which the whole people are interested, like navigable waters and the soils under them, so as to leave them entirely under the use and control of private parties ... than it can abdicate its police powers in the administration of government and the preservation of peace."[346]

The earliest recognized uses of navigable waters and submerged lands were navigation, commerce, and fishing, but over time the scope of protected uses has steadily enlarged to include wildlife, water quality, public recreation, aesthetics, and ecological integrity.[347] Three basic principles derive from this body of public trust law. First, courts are critical of attempts by the sovereign to surrender valuable public resources to a private entity. Second, courts presume a violation of the public trust when the primary purpose of a legislative or executive grant is to benefit a private interest. Finally, courts will routinely invalidate any attempt by the sovereign to relinquish its power over a public trust resource.[348]

The U.S. Supreme Court has recognized the application of the public trust doctrine to tidal waters and lands since the mid-1800s.[349] In 1947, the Court rejected the State of California's claim to the oil and gas resources of the submerged lands within the territorial sea, stating, "[n]ational interests, responsibilities, and therefore national rights are paramount in waters lying to the seaward in the three-mile belt.[350] In 1953, Congress enacted the Submerged Lands Act (SLA).[351] With this act, Congress generally granted coastal states title to the waters and submerged lands lying beyond the coastline out to three nautical miles. In the same year Congress passed the SLA, it enacted the OCSLA. This law established federal dominion over the waters and submerged lands lying seaward of the coastal states SLA boundary. Thus, state waters constitute up to three nautical miles while federal waters are three to two hundred nautical miles. The federal-waters area is often referred to as the EEZ. The OCS refers to the seabed and subsoil of the submerged lands that lie seaward of the coastal state's SLA boundary. The OCS "either extends 200 miles from the coastline or beyond, depending upon the geographical composition of the coastal nation's submerged lands."[352] A good argument can be made that the public trust doctrine now extends to the full two-hundred-mile EEZ.[353]

The U.S. Supreme Court has recognized the application of the public trust doctrine to tidal waters and lands since the mid-1800s.

The Supreme Court has repeatedly stressed the government's fiduciary obligations under the public trust doctrine.[354] Although most public trust doctrine cases involve actions by state legislatures and agencies, courts have found it applicable to the federal government as well. For example, it has been ruled that when the federal government takes title to tidelands it does so subject to a public trust duty to retain control over the property to protect the public interest.[355] In another case, the court held that the United States, as a grantee of tidelands from the City of San Francisco, was a "co-trustee" and lacked authority to convey tidelands to private party.[356]

Courts and commentators have recognized that the public trust is a flexible doctrine.[357] It is certainly flexible enough to provide support for the use of EBM as a framework for protecting marine ecosystems. Of course, there are limitations to what the doctrine can do. For example, it does not establish a hierarchy of uses. However, it does provide legal support for the adoption of a variety of management techniques for avoiding or reducing ocean use conflicts through legislative and administrative implementation. These would include (1) multiple-use planning to identify potential conflicts; (2) separating the award of exploration and development rights to remove legal impediments to conflict avoidance; (3) using activity schedules, corridors, and buffer zones to avoid conflicts; (4) coordinating federal and state planning and permit processes to reduce conflicts; and (5) facilitating user-to-user compensation for unavoidable conflicts.[358] The public trust doctrine can also serve as an organizing principle for coastal states seeking to enter into agreements for joint management of regional coastal resources.

9. National Environmental Policy Act

In many ways, the National Environmental Policy Act (NEPA) is the quintessential ecosystem-based statute, advocating the goal of achieving a world "where man and nature can exist in productive harmony."[359] The language of NEPA speaks of an ecologically centered approach to government policies and programs. One of its stated purposes is to "enrich the understanding of the ecological systems and natural resources important to the Nation."[360] In Section 101, Congress declares it to be the "continuing responsibility of the Federal Government to use all practicable means . . . to improve and coordinate federal plans, functions and programs, and resources to the end that the Nation may . . . fulfill the responsibilities of each generation as trustee of the environment for succeeding generations; and assure for all Americans safe, healthful, productive and aesthetically pleasing surroundings."[361]

Section 102 contains the "action forcing" mechanisms, of which the environmental impact statement requirement in Section 102(2)(C) is the most familiar. But other procedures in Section 102 warrant consideration for implementing EBM. Section 102 calls for an interdisciplinary approach to decision making.[362] This approach, drawing on the full range of natural and social sciences, accommodates the integrated and ecosystem-based thinking that is now recognized as critical to sustaining environment quality.

NEPA's interdisciplinary approach helps balance and integrate competing goals by focusing on all the environmental, economic, and social factors affecting a single place. This is likewise the premise behind the ecosystem approach to management and planning. One of the most promising trends in government today is the collaborative efforts of federal, state, and local stakeholders in regional planning efforts. By working at the level of specific ecosystems, such as LMEs, and involving the planning goals of local and state agencies, federal agencies can make better decisions for an ecosystem and its surrounding communities.

The key to implementing an interdisciplinary place-based approach, and addressing the full range of cumulative effects, is obtaining adequate environmental data. Increased data improves federal decisions across the board. Prior to NEPA, the collection and analysis of data were inconsistent or nonexistent and management decisions were made without the benefit of environmental information. Under NEPA, environmental considerations in decision making are better integrated with economic and technical considerations. Today, agencies often use these data to discover adverse environmental impacts early on and then either modify the impacts or, in some cases, abandon proposals with unacceptable impacts.[363] Cumulative effects analysis is more challenging, primarily because of the difficulty in defining the geographical (spatial) and time (temporal) boundaries. For example, if the boundaries are set too broadly, the analysis becomes unwieldy; if they are set too narrowly, significant issues may be missed and decision makers will be incompletely informed about the consequences of their actions.

Experience with NEPA also has revealed the wisdom of the adaptive management approach to coping with the dynamic and often unpredictable nature of complex ecosystems. The old paradigm for environmental management was "predict, mitigate, and implement." A new paradigm has emerged: "predict, mitigate, implement, monitor, and adapt." The two latest threads—monitor and adapt—reflect the need to track the accuracy of predictions and allow enough flexibility for midcourse corrections. Adaptive management deals with this situation as a process of adjusting actions in light of new information about the ecosystem. It does so by recognizing the limits of knowledge and experience and moves iteratively toward goals in the face of uncertainty. Providing for flexibility in project implementation of this nature is especially valuable for EBM because of the need to account for a wide variety of activities and resources throughout a geographic region that are inherently difficult to manage based on a one-time decision. By making adaptive management part of the environmental impact review, NEPA can provide this needed flexibility.

Finally, the CEQ NEPA regulations, which have the force of law,[364] contain several provisions that can facilitate EBM. For example, the CEQ regulations require preparation of programmatic environmental impact statements (PEIS) for "broad Federal actions such as adoption of new agency programs or regulations."[365] Courts have interpreted these regulations to require a PEIS (1) for actions relating to broad program or regional planning, and (2) when there are cumulative or synergistic environmental impacts upon the environment from past, present, or reasonably foreseeable future actions.[366] In this regard, a PEIS serves as an analytical tool for regional planning and potential implementation of EBM for the various federal actions within LMEs.[367] For example, NEPA has been used to promote EBM through programmatic EISs under the FCMA, as discussed in Section II.C.3 of this chapter.

III. Emerging and Unresolved Issues

As discussed in Section II, there are numerous federal legal authorities that provide the basis for implementing EBM in the marine environment. While it is true that none of these authorities provides a comprehensive, self-contained basis for taking action to protect marine ecosystems from all threats or to govern the full-range of activities affecting an ecosystem area, it is nonetheless the case that essentially the same result can be achieved by using these existing legal authorities in a coordinated and complementary manner. Clearly, enactment of a tough and broad-based federal law specifically calling for EBM in the marine environment is the desired result. In the absence of such congressional action, however, the Executive Branch does have the legal wherewithal to move forward with EBM for the marine environment. When the legal authorities discussed in this chapter are viewed in their totality, there is ample authority to reach almost any problem, govern virtually every use, and provide for a wide-range of affirmative actions all designed to implement an EBM regime for the marine environment.

This section discusses how the federal government can develop and implement an EBM program under existing legal authorities. Before setting forth this prescription, however, the four principal obstacles to success must be acknowledged. These problems are, unfortunately, endemic to many federal natural resource management programs. To be successful, marine EBM under existing law must be achieved through

1. Strong and effective, if not creative, applications of regulatory and enforcement power to control agency and nonfederal stakeholder behavior;
2. Cooperative interagency coordination across multiple agencies and programs, where individual agency agendas must take a back seat to a general environmental goal;
3. A centralized source of authority to oversee, if not direct, such cooperation and coordination; and
4. Adequate funding.

The difficulty of overcoming the inherent reluctance within the Executive Branch to undertake bold measures calls into question how realistic it is to believe existing authorities can be used to pursue the universally lauded goal of marine EBM. At the very least, this chapter demonstrates that the lack of EBM in federal marine resources management programs cannot be blamed on the absence of legal authority. If the federal government can overcome its traditional reluctance to pursue cross-agency, intraprogram initiatives, the legal framework does exist to carry out EBM for coastal and ocean areas.

A. Executive Branch Mandate to Pursue Ecosystem-Based Management

The starting point for a comprehensive federal EBM program would ideally be a directive to require all federal agencies to use their authorities, resources, and funds for that purpose. Such a directive also should designate a lead decision-making entity, establish affirmative duties, and prohibit actions that are inconsistent with EBM.

In the absence of legislation, the most effective tool for this purpose would be an Executive Order. Such Orders have been used in recent years to require federal agencies to coordinate their actions and collaborate in applying their legal authorities to promote a general environmental goal. In the marine environment setting, the best example of such a directive is Executive Order 13,158 for MPAs issued by President Clinton in 2000. President Clinton issued a similar mandate in 2001 through Executive Order 13186 to require "[e]ach federal agency taking actions that have, or are likely to have, a measurable negative effect on migratory bird populations" to enter into a memorandum of understanding with FWS to "promote the conservation of migrating bird populations."[368] Providing a model for EBM, President Clinton based both of these orders on multiple federal laws, with eleven statutes invoked for MPAs and five statutes used as the basis for migratory bird protection.[369] President Bush used this power to direct agencies to use their diverse legal authorities to advance a uniform policy objective in Executive Order 13,352 for "cooperative conservation" designed to "implement laws relating to the environment and natural resources . . . with an emphasis on appropriate inclusion of local participation in Federal decision-making, in accordance with respective [specified federal] agency missions, policies, and regulations."[370]

Through an EBM Executive Order, the mission and mandate for a comprehensive federal program could be established. The foremost element of the Order should be the mandate to all federal agencies to use their authorities to implement EBM and to participate in a unified federal effort to establish and carry out an EBM program. Ideally, the Order also would provide for the creation of an administrative structure to implement EBM, define what that program should accomplish, and set forth federal agency duties, as well as prohibited acts.

1. Administrative Structure and Large Marine Ecosystem Plans

EBM in the marine environment must be pursued through a multiagency approach under a combination of legal authorities. Centralized management and decision making is necessary, especially in an area such as marine conservation and management where many agencies with divergent, if not conflicting, missions are involved.

One way to conceptualize an EBM administrative structure is through a federal decision-making apparatus and a stakeholder participation mechanism. For federal purposes, centralized management under an entity like CEQ is likely to be necessary. No individual department or agency is ideally situated to play the coordinating role. None of them has control over the resources necessary to carry out a comprehensive EBM program, and many of them have internally conflicting duties and missions that could interfere with a truly ecosystem-based regime.[371]

Ecosystem-based management in the marine environment must be pursued through a multiagency approach under a combination of legal authorities.

Under the management of a centralized federal authority, all federal agencies with responsibility for coastal and marine action should come together to develop an EBM program. As discussed previously, that program should adopt a regional approach, possibly relying on the ten LMEs described in the USCOP. An EBM plan should be developed for each of the LMEs.

To be successful, the federal administrative structure and the LME plans will need to be guided by stakeholder input, and carried out by stakeholder participation. As recommended in the USCOP Report, regional ocean councils should be used to facilitate improved coordination and collaboration.[372] Regional ocean councils could address a wide range of coastal and ocean issues, and membership in the councils should be broad and include a variety of stakeholders, including representatives of all appropriate levels of government, as well as nongovernmental stakeholders.[373]

Two models for stakeholder-involvement are found in existing law: under the FCMA through regional fishery management councils, and under the MMPA through take reduction teams.[374] Under both of these formats, the stakeholder teams play a formal role in developing recommended regulatory requirements to be implemented by the responsible federal agencies (NMFS or FWS).[375]

The authors of this chapter believe that stakeholder participation is crucial to successful EBM program development and implementation. Compared to fisheries under the FCMA and marine mammal/fisheries interactions under MMPA, however, the nature of the interests involved in EBM are far more diverse in any regional area. Whereas fishery councils and take reduction teams generally focus on a relatively well-defined set of issues that relate to commercial fishing and its impacts, EBM will be far broader and also cover, depending on location, shipping, recreation, subsistence use, energy development, seabed mining, national security, and other activities. The multiplicity of parties involved in these activities makes the use of the fisheries management council or marine mammal team models difficult and impractical. It would indeed be a tall order for such a stakeholder group to come to some degree of consensus on recommendations for regulatory actions. Consequently, while advisory groups should be established to make recommendations to the federal agencies responsible for developing each LME plan, that role should be limited to providing information and advice rather than developing recommended regulations that are expected to be implemented by the appropriate agencies, as is done by fishery management councils and take reduction teams.

One possible approach is to have regional EBM teams established in accordance with the Federal Advisory Committee Act.[376] These teams would be managed under an administrative framework coordinated by CEQ or other centralized coordinating agency and served by funds and staff assistance provided by the agencies with a principal stake in marine EBM (EPA, Departments of Commerce, Defense, Interior), which would also serve as a coordinating council. The teams would meet on a regularly scheduled basis and make recommendations to the EBM coordinating council. That council would then develop an overall EBM plan based on those recommendations. The resulting elements of the plan would be extended to individual federal agencies for implementation in accordance with the Executive Order.

2. Coordinated Legal Authority and Action-Forcing Mechanisms

It is beyond the scope of this chapter to discuss what the content of LME plans should be.[377] Once those plans are developed, however, adequate authority does exist for them to be implemented. As discussed in Section II, virtually every U.S. law that applies to the marine environment includes provisions that authorize, if not require, an EBM approach. Common law under the public trust doctrine provides an additional source of authority. Moreover, some of the laws with the strongest ecosystem mandate, such as the ESA and MMPA, are of the most potential value because their provisions apply to highly migratory, wide-ranging species that are found throughout most U.S. coastal and offshore waters and require ecosystem-wide conservation and management efforts. As a result, to the extent discretionary authorities, including rulemaking powers, are intended to advance ecosystem conservation and management goals, they can be used as the foundation for structuring multilayered legal regimes to achieve EBM goals.

The key to structuring the legal framework for carrying out EBM is to consolidate legal authorities from various statutes and administered by various agencies to provide a kind of legal "peg board" into which elements of an LME plan can be inserted for purposes of implementation. The ability to use this approach is enhanced by the fact that virtually all of the laws that are likely to be relevant to EBM implementation include broad rulemaking powers, which could be used in a consolidated manner by the action agencies to put into effect whatever regulations are called for by a specific LME.

B. Congressional Mandate to Pursue Ecosystem-Based Management

As discussed previously, Congress has already considered three bills to establish a comprehensive ocean conservation and management program. Each of these bills would make EBM a central component of that program. The bills would establish a significant new oceans management bureaucracy within the federal government and provide for the development of regional ecosystem plans.

Future legislation could build off of the many excellent ideas in the three bills. Developing regional plans for LMEs, as called for in the bills, is a critically important step. So too is the articulation in the bills of a national policy to protect, maintain, and restore the health of marine ecosystems and an action-forcing mechanism that applies that policy, as well as specific implementing standards, to federal agency actions. Most of the important laws that deal with marine resources provide a basis for EBM actions. The provisions in the bills for federal agencies to protect ocean ecosystems and to act consistently with regional EBM plans would prompt use of current EBM authorities, in furtherance of marine ecosystem health.

IV. Conclusion

The goal of adopting an EBM approach to managing marine resources is widely accepted and supported. From the early 1970s, with the enactment of the MMPA, to the bills introduced in Congress in 2005 and 2007, EBM has served as a common goal in coastal and ocean reform initiatives. Despite the frequent lip service accorded to EBM as a policy goal, however, very little has been done to implement the concept in ongoing marine resource programs.

One of the principal impediments to the practical application of EBM has been the mistaken assumption that legal authority does not exist to carry out EBM under existing laws and regulations. Instead, any effort to understand EBM on a comprehensive basis under federal programs has been set aside on the theory that new legal authority must first be enacted to empower, if not compel, such action.

As this chapter demonstrates, there is authority under existing law to establish an effective EBM regime using federal coastal and ocean programs. What is missing, however, is a strong directive from the President or the Congress to use that authority in a coordinated and effective way to further a clearly articulated goal, namely the protection, maintenance, and restoration of marine ecosystem health. The resulting improved management of the marine environment at a time of global environmental crisis is well worth the long-overdue effort.

Notes

1. *See* Marine Mammal Comm'n, 1988 Annual Report to Congress (1989).
2. See *id*. 45–46. In 1984, the four parties signed a Protocol to extend the Interim Convention, but the controversial nature of the harvest and concerns over the fur seal population

decline caused the Senate to refuse to ratify that Agreement. As a result, the commercial harvest came to an end, with a subsistence hunt regulated under the Marine Mammal Protection Act (MMPA).

3. *Id.* at 45.

4. *North Pacific Fur Seal Treaty: Hearings on Treaty Doc. 990-5 Before the Senate Committee on Foreign Relations*, 99th Cong., 1st Sess. 250–51 (1985) (statement of L. Merculieff).

5. Id. (quoted in testimony of L. Merculieff).

6. *Id.*

7. *See* Section II.C.1., *infra.*

8. Inforain, Fisheries and Wildlife Declines in the North Pacific, www.inforain.org/maparchive/declines.htm (last visited May 2, 2007); For 1990 listing, see Listing of Steller Sea Lions as Threatened Under the Endangered Species Act, 55 Fed. Reg. 49,204 (Nov. 26, 1990) (codified at 50 C.F.R. § 223.102).

9. Threatened Fish and Wildlife; Change in Listing Status of Steller Sea Lions Under the Endangered Species Act, 62 Fed. Reg. 24,345, 24,345 (May 5, 1997) (codified at 50 C.F.R. § 224.101).

10. Inforain, *supra* note 8.

11. *Id.*

12. Northern Pacific Fur Seal, Pribilof Island Population; Designated as Depleted, 53 Fed. Reg. 17,888, (May 18, 1988) (codified at 50 C.F.R. § 216.5).

13. Inforain, *supra* note 8.

14. Determination of Threatened Status for the Southwest Alaska Distinct Population Segment of the Northern Sea Otter, 70 Fed. Reg. 46,366 (Aug. 9, 2005) (codified at 50 C.F.R. § 17.11).

15. Inforain, *supra* note 8.

16. *Id.*

17. *Id.*

18. *Id.*

19. *Id.*

20. Endangered and Threatened Wildlife & Plants; Final Rule to List Spectacled Eider as Threatened, 58 Fed. Reg. 27,474 (May 10, 1993) (codified at 50 C.F.R. § 17.11).

21. Inforain, *supra* note 8.

22. *Id.*

23. *See, e.g.,* Nat'l Acad. of Sci., The Bering Sea Ecosystem (1996); Nat'l Acad. of Sci., The Decline of the Steller Sea Lion in Alaskan Waters: Untangling Food Webs and Fishing Nets (2003); NOAA Fisheries, Steller Sea Lions, *available at* http://www.fakr.noaa.gov/protectedresources/stellers.htm (last visited April 15, 2007) (contains a summary of research, management, and litigation related to the decline of the Steller sea lion).

24. *See, e.g.,* Endangered and Threatened Wildlife & Plants, 12-Month Petition Finding and Proposed Rule to List the Polar Bear (*Ursus maritmus*) as Threatened Throughout Its Range, 72 Fed. Reg. 1064–99 (Jan. 9, 2007).

25. Policy Brief, Gov. Chris Gregoire, Puget Sound: Protecting Our Health and Safety, *available at* http://www.pugetsoundpartnership.org/reports/GovGregoire_policy_brief12-1306.pdf (last visited July 7, 2007).

26. Nicholas Brown & Joseph Gaydos, Seadoc Soc'y, Listed Species of Concern Within the Puget Sound Georgia Basin Marine Ecosystem Including Changes from 2002 to 2004, *available at* http://www.epa.gov/region10/psgb/indicators/species_at_risk/what (last visited July 7, 2007).

27. Larry G. Harris & Megan C. Tyrell, *Changing Community States in the Gulf of Maine: Synergism Between Invaders, Overfishing and Climate Change*, 3 Biological Invasions 9 (2001).

28. Marine Conservation Biology Inst., Protecting U.S. Deep-Sea Corals Through Legislation, http://www.mcbi.org/what/coral_policy.htm (last visited July 7, 2007).

29. Army Corps of Eng'rs, Morro Bay Ecosystem Restoration Study, *summary available at* http://www.spl.usace.army.mil/cms/index.php?option=com_content&task=view&id= 82&Itemid=31 (last visited January 9, 2007); Elkhorn Slough Found. & Nature Conservancy, Elkhorn Slough Watershed Conservation Plan 1, *available at* http://www .elkhornslough.org/eswcp/watershedplan.htm (last visited January 9, 2007).

30. Boris Worm et al., *Impacts of Biodiversity Loss on Ocean Ecosystem Services,* 314 Science 787, 790 (2006).

31. *Id.* Agencies with management authority for ocean and coastal areas are also increasingly recognizing the importance of ecosystem research and management. For example, the National Oceanic and Atmospheric Administration's (NOAA) Ecosystem Research Program (ERP) conducts applied research. The charter for this program provides that the ERP is governed by existing statutes "that require NOAA to provide coastal managers with scientific knowledge, financial assistance, and other support to manage the coastal zone to support society's needs," and sets forth the authority for each relevant statute. Nat'l Oceanic & Atmospheric Admin., Ecosystem Research Program Charter 1, *available at* http://www.oarhq.noaa.gov/erp/documents/ERP-Charter-7-8-05.pdf (last visited July 7, 2007). Likewise, in 2006 federal and state agencies in Alaska entered into a Memorandum of Understanding to establish the Alaska Marine Ecosystem Forum, designed to enhance coordination in support of sustainable management of Alaska's marine ecosystems. Alaska Marine Ecosystem Forum Memorandum of Understanding (Sept. 18, 2006), *available at* http://www.fakr.noaa.gov/npfmc/current_issues/ecosystem/AMEF_MOU.pdf (last visited Feb. 22, 2007).

32. William F. Fox et al., Statement of Concerned Scientists on the Reauthorization of the Magnuson Fishery Conservation and Management Act (1989).

33. *Id.* at 3.

34. *Id.* at 4.

35. Sustainable Fisheries Act, Pub. L. No. 104-297, § 108, 110 Stat. 3559, 3574 (1996) (codified at 16 U.S.C. § 1853).

36. Pew Oceans Comm'n, America's Living Oceans: Charting a Course for Sea Change (2003), *available at* http://www.pewtrusts.org/uploadedFiles/wwwpewtrustorg/ Reports/Protecting_ocean_life/env_pew_oceans_final_report.pdf (last visited July 7, 2007); U.S. Comm'n on Ocean Pol'y, An Ocean Blueprint for the 21st Century: Final Report (2004); *available at* http://www.oceancommission.gov/documents/full_color_rpt/ welcome.html#full (last visited July 7, 2007) [hereinafter USCOP Final Report].

37. Scientific Consensus Statement on Marine Ecosystem-Based Management (Mar. 21, 2005), *available at* http://www.compassonline.org/pdf_files/EBM_consensus_statement_v12.pdf (last visited July 7, 2007) [hereinafter Scientific Consensus Statement].

38. *Id.* at 1.

39. *Id.*

40. *Id.* at 2.

41. *See also* Josh Eagle, *Regional Ocean Governance: The Perils of Multiple-Use Management and the Promise of Agency Diversity,* 16 Duke Envtl. L. & Pol'y F. 143 (2006); Donna Christie, *Living Marine Resources Management: A Proposal for Integration of United States Management Regimes,* 34 Envtl. L. 107 (2004); Martin H. Belsky, *The Ecosystem Model Mandate for a Comprehensive United States Ocean Policy and Law of the Sea,* 26 San Diego L. Rev. 417 (1989).

42. *See* Section II.B.1. *infra.*

43. Scientific Consensus Statement, *supra* note 37, at 1.

44. Eugene H. Buck, Cong. Research Serv., CRS Report for Congress: Marine Ecosystem Management (1993).

45. *Id.* at 5.

46. *Id.* at 7.

47. *Id.*

48. *Id.* at 8.

49. *Id.* at 3.

50. *Id.* at 9.

51. Elliott A. Norse, *A Zoning Approach to Managing Marine Ecosystems, in* Workshop on Improving Regional Ocean Governance in the United States 53–57, at 53 (Biliana Cicin-Sain, Charles Ehler and Kevin Goldstein eds., 2003); *available at* http://www.ocean.udel.edu/cmp/pdf/RegionalProceedings.pdf [hereinafter Norse, *Zoning Approach*] (internal citations omitted).

52. 16 Duke Envtl. L. & Pol'y F. 179 (2006).

53. *Id.* at 180. Citing the Millennium Ecosystem Assessment, Rosenberg identifies these ecosystem services as: "(1) provisioning services (food and fresh water), (2) regulating services (climate and flood regulations), (3) cultural services (spiritual and aesthetic values), and (4) supporting services (nutrient cycling and primary production)." *Id.*

54. *Id.*

55. *Id.* at 181.

56. *Id.*

57. *Id.*

58. *Id.*

59. *Id.* at 183–85.

60. *Id.* at 184.

61. USCOP Final Report, *supra* note 36, at 64.

62. *Id.*

63. *Id.*

64. *Id.*

65. *See generally* Norse, *Zoning Approach, supra* note 51.

66. *See* Norse, *Zoning Approach, supra* note 51, at 53.

67. Elliot A. Norse, *Ending the Range Wars on the Last Frontier: Zoning the Sea, in* Marine Conservation Biology: The Science of Maintaining the Sea's Biodiversity 422, 423 (Elliot A. Norse and Larry B. Crowder eds., 2005) [hereinafter Norse, *Last Frontier*].

68. Appointed in 1967, the Commission on Marine Science, Engineering and Resources (Stratton Commission) found that conflicting laws and regulations and a lack of coordination compromised the ability to protect ocean and coastal resources, and set forth a plan for national action. Comm'n on Marine Sci., Eng'g & Res., Our Nation and the Sea: A Plan for National Action 8 (1969) available at http://www.lib.noaa.gov/edocs/stratton/title.html (last visited July 7, 2007).

69. Norse, *Last Frontier, supra* note 67, at 424 (quoting the Pew Report).

70. *Id.* at 429.

71. *Id.*

72. *Id.* at 433.

73. *Id.* at 434.

74. *Id.*

75. *Id.* at 435.

76. *Id.* In an effort to analyze and document best practices of marine spatial planning, the Intergovernmental Oceanographic Commission and UNESCO's Division of Ecological and Earth Sciences organized a three-day International Workshop on Ecosystem-based, Sea Use Management/Marine Spatial Planning held in Paris in November 2006. The papers presented at the workshop, as well as conclusions drawn from the workshop, are available at http://ioc3.unesco.org/marinesp/ (last visited July 7, 2007).

77. Pew Oceans Comm'n, *supra* note 36. The mission of the Pew Commission was to "identify policies and practices necessary to restore and protect living marine resources in U.S. waters and the ocean and coastal habitats on which they depend." *Id.* at ix. For a detailed discussion of this report, see Chapter 20.

78. *Id.* at v–x.

79. *Id.* at x.

80. *Id.* at 26.

81. *Id.* at 33–34.

82. *Id.* at 102.

83. *Id.* at 102–03.
84. *Id.* at 103–04. Regional plans would also require the approval of a national ocean agency created by NOPA. *Id.*
85. *Id.*
86. States could hold federal actions to consistency with regional ocean governance plans and could appeal federal actions not in compliance with a plan and/or seek injunctive relief in federal court. *Id.* at 104. The federal government could also preempt state actions not in compliance with a plan, and third parties could utilize citizens suits under NOPA. *Id.* For a detailed discussion of the CZMA, *see* Chapter 5.
87. The Pew Commission's proposals for EBM have been criticized due to the creation of an enforceable regional governance structure that states might perceive as a significant infringement on state sovereignty. *See* Donna R. Christie, *Implementing an Ecosystem Approach to Ocean Management: An Assessment of Current Regional Governance Models,* 16 Duke Envtl. L. & Pol'y F. 117 (2006).
88. USCOP Final Report, *supra* note 36. The Commission was created by the Oceans Act of 2000 and appointed by President Bush in 2001, and consists of sixteen Commissioners. *Id.* at 3. For a detailed discussion of this report, see Chapter 20.
89. *Id.* at 77.
90. *Id.* at 87.
91. *Id.*
92. Along with the National Ocean Council, the President's Council of Advisors on Ocean Policy would be at the executive office level and consist of nonfederal parties appointed by the President. *Id.* at 81.
93. *Id.* at 87.
94. *Id.* at 91.
95. *Id.* at 96.
96. *Id.* at 298–99.
97. Oceans Act of 2000, Pub. L. No. 106-256 §§ 3–4, 114 Stat. 644, 647–48 (codified at 33 U.S.C. § 857.19).
98. U.S. Ocean Action Plan: The Bush Administration's Response to the U.S. Commission on Ocean Policy (2004), *available at* http://ocean.ceq.gov/actionplan.pdf (last visited January 14, 2007) [hereinafter Ocean Action Plan].
99. *Id.* at 6–7.
100. Exec. Order No. 13,366, 3 C.F.R. 244 (2005).
101. Ocean Action Plan, supra note 98, at 7–8. The NSTC subcommittee was established as the Joint Subcommittee on Oceans in 2003; the Ocean Action Plan alters the name to include Science and Technology. *Id.*
102. *Id.* at 8.
103. *Id.* at 9.
104. National Oceans Protection Act of 2005, S. 1224, 109th Cong. (2005).
105. *Id.* § 3.
106. *Id.* § 2 (10).
107. *Id.* § 103(4).
108. *Id.* §§ 111–112. The bill provides that the NOAA established by the NOPA succeeds the current NOAA established in 1970 and "shall continue the activities of that agency as it was in existence on the day before the effective date of [the NOPA]." *Id.* § 111.
109. *Id.* § 131. The Council is composed of between three and five "exceptionally well qualified" members appointed by the President. *Id.* at § 132.
110. *Id.* § 133(1),(3).
111. *Id.* § 134.
112. Oceans Conservation, Education, and National Strategy for the 21st Century Act, H.R. 2939, 109th Cong. (2005).
113. *Id.* § 401.
114. *Id.* §§ 401–402.
115. *Id.* § 101(a).

116. *Id.* § 111(a).

117. *Id.* § 201.

118. *Id.* §§ 301, 311, 321.

119. *Id.* § 402. The following ocean regions are designated in OCEANS: (1) North Pacific Ocean Region; (2) Pacific Ocean Region; (3) Western Pacific Ocean Region; (4) Gulf of Mexico Ocean Region; (5) Caribbean Ocean Region; (6) Southeast Atlantic Ocean Region; (7) Northeast Atlantic Ocean Region; and (8) Great Lakes Region. *Id.*

120. *Id.* § 402(f) (referring to the definition of coastal zone in 16 U.S.C. § 1453 and the Exclusive Economic Zone as set out in Proclamation No. 5030, 48 Fed. Reg. 10605 (Mar. 10, 1983)).

121. *Id.* § 402(a–b).

122. *Id.* § 402(e).

123. Oceans Conservation, Education, and National Strategy for the 21st Century Act, H.R. 21, 110th Cong. (2007).

124. *Id.* § 2.

125. *Id.* § 3.

126. *Id.* § 3(6).

127. *Id.* § 4(12–13) (defining all three terms in reference to the ability of the marine ecosystem "to support and maintain a productive and resilient community of organisms, having a species composition, diversity, and functional organization resulting from the natural habitat of the region, such that it provides a complete range of benefits.").

128. *Id.* § 201.

129. *Id.* §§ 301, 302.

130. *Id.* § 402.

131. *Id.* §§ 501–507.

132. Marine Mammal Protection Act of 1972, Pub. L. No. 92-522, 86 State 1027 (codified at 16 U.S.C. §§ 1361–1421). For a detailed discussion of the MMPA, see Chapter 15.

133. *See, e.g.,* H.R. Rep. No. 92-707 § 2 (1971), *as reprinted in* 1972 U.S.C.C.A.N. 4144, 4155 (declaring the "primary objective of [marine mammal] management . . . to be to maintain the health and stability of the marine ecosystem").

134. S. Rep. No. 92-863, at 10 (1972).

135. Letter from John Dingell, Chairman of the House Subcomm. on Fisheries & Wildlife Conservation, to Christian Herter, Special Asst. to the Sec'y for Envtl. Affairs, Dep't of State (Aug. 17, 1971), *reprinted in Marine Mammals: Hearings before the Subcomm. on Fisheries and Wildlife Conservation of the H. Comm. on Merchant Marine and Fisheries,* 92d Cong. 200 (1971) [hereinafter *House Hearings*].

136. Letter from Harrison M. Symmes, Acting Asst. Sec'y of State for Cong. Relations, to John Dingell, Chairman of the House Subcomm. on Fisheries & Wildlife Conservation (not dated), *reprinted in House Hearings,* at 200–01.

137. Statement of Dr. G. Carleton Ray, Program Director, William E. Schevill, and Dr. Kenneth S. Norris, Marine Mammal Council (Sept. 23, 1971), *reprinted in House Hearings,* at 401–02.

138. *Ocean Mammal Protection: Hearings on S. 685, et al., Before the Subcomm. on Oceans & Atmosphere of the Senate Comm. on Commerce,* 92d Cong., 2d Sess. 836 (1972) [hereinafter *Senate Hearings*].

139. 118 Cong. Rec. 25,258 (1972).

140. *Senate Hearings, supra* note 138, at 359–60.

141. *Id.* at 426.

142. MMPA, 16 U.S.C. § 1361(6) (2000). Other provisions of the MMPA refer to ecosystem management. Section 2(2) provides that "[certain] species and population stocks should not be permitted to diminish beyond the point at which they cease to be a significant functioning element in the ecosystem of which they are a part." *Id.* § 1361(2). Congress also found, in Section 2(5)(B), that "marine mammals and marine mammal products. . . . affect the balance of marine ecosystems in a manner which is important to other animals and animal products which move in interstate commerce." *Id.* § 1361(5)(B). The MMPA

defines optimum sustainable population (OSP) as "the number of animals which will result in the maximum productivity of the population or the species, keeping in mind the carrying capacity of the habitat and the health of the ecosystem of which they form a constituent element." *Id.* § 1362(9). Similarly, the Secretary may issue a general taking or importation permit, provided that in issuing the regulations governing such a situation, "the Secretary shall give full consideration to . . . the marine ecosystem and related environmental considerations." *Id.* § 1373(b)(3). Finally, in a recent addition to the MMPA, the "Marine Mammal Health and Stranding Response Act," Congress focused attention on the impacts that pollutants in the marine environment are having on the health of marine mammals. Marine Mammal Health and Stranding Response Act, Pub. L. No. 102-587, Title III, 106 Stat. 5039, 5059–67 (1992) (codified as amended at 16 U.S.C. §§ 1421, 1421(a)). One purpose of the program established by this Act is to "correlate the health of marine mammals and marine mammal populations, in the wild with available data on physical, chemical, and biological environmental parameters." *Id.* § 3003, 106 Stat. at 5061 (codified at 16 U.S.C. § 1421). This amendment, passed partly in response to die-offs of bottlenose dolphins on the East Coast in the late 1980s, constitutes legislative recognition of the dependence of the health of marine mammals on the health of their environment.

143. Marine Mammal Protection Act Amendments of 1994, Pub. L. No. 103-238, § 20, 108 Stat. 532, 561 (codified at 16 U.S.C. § 1380(d)(1)). The program was to "utilize, where appropriate, traditional local knowledge" and involve Alaska Native organizations. *Id.* § 1380(d)(2). Unfortunately, this amendment has not been implemented.

144. *Id.* § 1380(c).

145. *Id.*

146. *Id.* § 1380(c)(1)(B).

147. Marine Mammal Protection Act Amendments of 1994, Pub. L. No. 103-238, § 7, 108 Stat 532, 541 (1994) (adding 16 U.S.C. § 1382(a), which allows for habitat protection).

148. H.R. Rep. No. 103-439, §§ 2–3 (1994).

149. *Id.* As discussed later in this chapter, this authority has been used, in part, for manatee protection zones in Florida, 50 C.F.R. § 17.100–.108, and humpback/vessel regulations in Glacier Bay, Alaska, 36 C.F.R. § 13.1174 (2007) NMFS has indicated a willingness to consider using this rulemaking authority to protect habitat used by spinner dolphins in Hawaii. *See* Advance Notice of Proposed Rulemaking: Protecting Spinner Dolphins in the Main Hawaiian Islands from Human Activities that Cause "Take," 70 Fed. Reg. 73,426 (Dec. 12, 2005).

150. 16 U.S.C. § 1382(a).

151. *Id.* § 1361(6).

152. Endangered Species Act of 1973, Pub. L. No. 93-205, 87 Stat. 884 (codified as amended at 16 U.S.C. § 1531 et seq.). For a detailed discussion of the ESA, see Chapter 16.

153. *See generally* Bryan G. Norton, ed., The Preservation of Species: The Value of Biological Diversity (1986); Edward O. Wilson, The Creation: An Appeal to Save Life on Earth (2006).

154. Aldo Leopold, Round River 145–46 (Oxford University Press 1993).

155. 16 U.S.C. § 1531(b).

156. The Act defines "species" to include "any subspecies of fish or wildlife or plants, and any distinct population segment of any species of vertebrate fish or wildlife which interbreeds when mature." *Id.* § 1532(16). FWS has adopted a Distinct Population Segment Policy. Policy Regarding the Recognition of Distinct Vertebrate Population Segments Under the Endangered Species Act, 61 Fed. Reg. 4722 (Feb. 7, 1996). Under this policy, a population must meet two criteria: (1) it must be substantially reproductively isolated from other nonspecific population units; and (2) it must represent an important component in the evolutionary legacy of the species. *Id.* at 4722. NOAA has adopted an Evolutionarily Significant Unit Policy for Pacific Salmonids. Policy on Applying the Definition of Species Under the Endangered Species Act to Pacific Salmon, 56 Fed. Reg. 58,612 (Nov. 20, 1991). Such a unit is a Pacific salmon population or group of populations that is "substantially

reproductively isolated from other conspecific units" and that "represents an important component in the evolutionary legacy of the species." *Id.* at 58,612.

157. *See generally* NAT'L RESEARCH COUNCIL, SCIENCE AND THE ENDANGERED SPECIES ACT (1995): CONG. RESEARCH SERV., THE ENDANGERED SPECIES ACT AND SOUND SCIENCE (RS 21264) (2002).

158. *See Making the ESA Work Better,* 20 ENDANGERED SPECIES BULL. (1993) (listing ten principles announced by Secretary Babbitt to "improve ESA implementation"), *available at* http://www.fws.gov/endangered/esb/95/10points.html (last visited July 7, 2007).

159. *See, e.g.,* Robert W. Hahn, Sheila M. Olmstead, & Robert N. Stavins, *Environmental Regulation in the 1990s: A Retrospective Analysis,* 27 HARV. ENVTL. L. REV. 377 (2003).

160. *See Making the ESA Work Better,* supra note 158.

161. J. B. Ruhl, *Endangered Species Act Innovations in the Post-Babbittonian Era—Are There Any?,* 14 DUKE ENVTL. L. & POL'Y F. 419, 430 (2004) (describing Babbitt's ESA innovations, which included "a greater emphasis on ecosystem-level management of habitat and other resources").

162. *See, e.g., id.* 434–38.

163. D. U. HOOPER ET AL., ECOLOGICAL SOC'Y OF AM., EFFECTS OF BIODIVERSITY ON ECOSYSTEM PROCESSES: IMPLICATIONS FOR ECOSYSTEM MANAGEMENT (2005), *reprinted in* D. U. Hooper et al., *Ecosystem Functioning: A Consensus of Current Knowledge,* 75 ECOLOGICAL MONOGRAPHS 3, 4 (2005), *available at* http://www.npwrc.usgs.gov/pdf/npwrc1436 .pdf (last visited July 7, 2007).

164. 16 U.S.C. § 1533 (2000); 50 C.F.R. § 402.01(b) (2007).

165. 50 C.F.R. §§ 17.2, 17.11 (2007). For certain species, such as the Atlantic salmon and sea turtles, there is joint management. *See, e.g.,* 50 C.F.R. § 223.102 (noting that NOAA's jurisdiction for sea turtles is limited to when they are in water).

166. The Act defines an endangered species to mean "any species which is in danger of extinction throughout all or any significant portion of its range." 16 U.S.C. § 1532(6). A threatened species is "any species which is likely to become an endangered species within the foreseeable future throughout all or any significant portion of its range." 16 U.S.C. § 1532(20). For current lists of threatened and endangered species, see 50 C.F.R. § 17.11– .12; 50 C.F.R. pts. 223 and 224.

167. 16 U.S.C. § 1533(a).

168. *Id.* § 1540(g) (authorizing citizen suits under the ESA).

169. NOAA Fisheries, Species Under the Endangered Species Act, http://www.nmfs.noaa.gov/ pr/species/esa/ (last visited Jun. 5, 2007).

170. 16 U.S.C. § 1533(b)(3)(B)(iii) (2000) (requiring the FWS to take action on petitions for listing species or make the finding that the "petition action is warranted, but that . . . immediate . . . [action] is precluded by pending proposals."). For a list of "candidate species" maintained by FWS, see U.S. Fish & Wildlife Serv., Candidate Conservation Program, *available at* http://www.fws.gov/Endangered/candidates/index.html (click on "List of Current Candidates") (last visited Feb. 7, 2008). For NOAA's "candidate species" list, see http://www.nmfs.noaa.gov/pr/species/concern/ (last visited May 27, 2007).

171. 16 U.S.C. § 1536(a)(2) (2000). "The Secretary" refers to either the Secretary of the Interior or the Secretary of Commerce, depending on which species is involved. *Id.* § 1532(15). The term "jeopardize the continued existence" is defined by rule to mean "to engage in an action that reasonably would be expected, directly or indirectly, to reduce appreciably the likelihood of both the survival and recovery of a listed species in the wild by reducing the reproduction, in numbers, or distribution of that species." 50 C.F.R. § 402.02.

172. Tennessee Valley Auth. v. Hill, 437 U.S. 153, 173 (1978).

173. *Id.* at 184.

174. *Id.* at 187–88, 193–94 ("Congress has spoken in the plainest of words, making it abundantly clear that the balance has been struck in favor of affording endangered species

the highest of priorities. . . ."). The automatic injunction rule has been extended by the lower courts to include procedural as well as substantive violations of Section 7. *See, e.g.,* Thomas v. Peterson, 753 F.2d 754, 764–65 (9th Cir. 1985).

175. 16 U.S.C.§ 1536 (g)–(p) (2000). The exemption process has rarely been invoked and only two exemptions have been granted, one of which was subsequently withdrawn. *See* Patrick A. Parenteau, *The Exemption Process and the God Squad, in* THE ENDANGERED SPECIES ACT: LAW, POLICY AND PERSPECTIVES 131, 143–51 (Donald C. Baur & Wm. Robert Irvin eds., 2002).

176. 16 U.S.C. § 1536(a)(2). Critical habitat is generally defined as habitat "essential to the conservation of a species." *Id.* § 1532(5)(A)(i) (2000). The term "conservation" is defined as the "use of all methods and procedures necessary to bring [species] to the point at which the measures provided pursuant to this chapter are no longer necessary." *Id.* § 1532(3). The courts have regarded this definition to be synonymous with recovery. Sierra Club v. U.S. Fish & Wildlife Serv., 245 F.3d 434, 444–45 (5th Cir. 2001).

177. *See* Patrick Parenteau, *An Empirical Assessment of the Impact Critical Habitat Litigation on the Administration of the Endangered Species Act, in* VT. L. SCH. FAC. PAPERS NO. 1, at 2, *available at* http://lsr.nellco.org/vermontlaw/vlsfp/Faculty/1 (noting that only seven of the thirty CH designations completed by NMFS since 1990 were forced by litigation compared to many more by FWS) (last visited July 7, 2007).

178. Center for Biological Diversity v. Norton, 240 F. Supp. 2d 1090, 1103 (D. Ariz. 2003) ("FWS has long held the policy position that 'CHDs [Critical Habitat Designations] are unhelpful, duplicative, and unnecessary.' . . . 'Perhaps it is time for FWS to reassess its long held policy position' ").

179. Critics of the ESA sometimes point to the fact that so few species have been delisted as evidence that "the Act isn't working." This criticism ignores the fact that reversing significant habitat losses—in some cases ninety percent of a species historic range—is incredibly difficult and will take decades of concerted effort, not to mention substantial investments in land acquisition and restoration of degraded ecosystems.

180. 16 U.S.C. § 1535(a)(2).

181. *Id.* § 1538(a) (2000). The term "take" means "to harass, harm, pursue, hunt, shoot, wound, kill, trap, capture, or collect, or to attempt to engage in any such conduct." *Id.* § 1532(19). The term "harass" has been defined by rule to include "an intentional or negligent act or omission which creates the likelihood of injury to wildlife by annoying it to such as extent as to significantly disrupt normal behavior patterns." 50 C.F.R. § 17.3 (2007). "Harm" means "an act which actually kills or injures wildlife," including through "significant habitat modification or degradation [that] significantly impair[s] essential behavioral patterns, including breeding, feeding, or sheltering." *Id.* In Babbitt v. Sweet Home Chapter of Cmtys. for a Great Or., 515 U.S. 687 (1995), the Supreme Court upheld the "harm rule" as a valid exercise of the Secretary's authority under the Act. The lower courts have generally required proof of a "reasonable likelihood of injury" to an identifiable individual animal before enjoining a prospective take. *Cf.* Nat'l Wildlife Fed'n v. Burlington N. RR, 23 F.3d 1508, 1512–13 (9th Cir. 1994).

182. 50 C.F.R. pt. 17.

183. Endangered and Threatened Species; Final Rule Governing Take of 14 Threatened Salmon and Steelhead Evolutionarily Significant Units, 65 Fed. Reg. 42,422 (July 1, 2000).

184. *Id.* at 42,423.

185. *Id.*

186. Palila v. Haw. Dep't Nat. Res., 639 F.2d 495 (9th Cir. 1981).

187. 16 U.S.C. § 1539(a)(1)(B)(2000).

188. 50 C.F.R. § 17.3(2007).

189. 16 U.S.C. § 1539(a)(2).

190. U.S. FISH & WILDLIFE SERV. & NAT'L OCEANIC & ATMOSPHERIC ADMIN., HABITAT CONSERVATION PLANNING AND INCIDENTAL TAKE PERMIT PROCESSING HANDBOOK 4-1(1996),

available at http://www.fws.gov/endangered/hcp/hcpbook.html (last visited July 7, 2007). FWS and NOAA published this handbook to establish guidelines for HCP development.

191. 16 U.S.C. § 1536(o).

192. The Web site for the NCCP is available at http://www.dfg.ca.gov/habcon/ (last visited July 7, 2007).

193. Final Multi-Species Conservation Program Plan 1-1 (1998), *available at* http://www.sandiego.gov/planning/mscp (last visited July 7, 2007).

194. California Dept. of Fish & Game, Status of NCCP Planning Efforts, *available at* http://www.dfg.ca.gov/habcon/ (last visited Jun. 5, 2007).

195. *See generally, e.g.*, William Vogel & Lorin Hicks, *Multi Species HCPs: Experiments with an Ecosystems Approach*, 25 Endangered Species Bull. 20 (2000), *available at* http://www.fws.gov/Endangered/esb/2000/07-08/20-22.pdf (describing HCPs in Washington) (last visited July 7, 2007).

196. U.S. Dept. of Interior, Bureau of Reclamation, Lower Colorado River Multi-Species Conservation Program, *available at* http://www.lcrmscp.gov/ (last visited Jun. 5, 2007).

197. *Id.*

198. 2 Lower Colo. River Multi-Species Conservation Prog., Final Habitat Conservation Plan 1-3, 4-31-4-46 (2004), *available at* http://www.lcrmscp.gov/publications/VolumeII.pdf (last visited July 7, 2007).

199. *Id.* at 3-10-3-18, 4-13-4-25.

200. *Id.* at 4-31-4-82.

201. *Id.* at 1-13.

202. U.S. Fish & Wildlife Serv., S. Fla. Ecological Serv. Office, Multi-Species Recovery Plan, *available at* http://www.fws.gov/verobeach/index.cfm?Method=programs&NavProgramCategoryID=3&programID=107&ProgramCategoryID=3 (last visited June 5, 2007). Recovery plans are required under Section 4 (f). 16 U.S.C. § 1533(f) (2000). The plans must address each of the five listing criteria set forth in § 1533(a)(1), and must contain "site-specific management actions" and "objective, measurable criteria" that will achieve recovery goals. Fund for Animals v. Babbitt, 903 F. Supp. 96, 110–11 (D.D.C. 1995).

203. U.S. Fish & Wildlife Serv., South Florida Multi-Species Recovery Plan: A Species Plan . . . An Ecosystem Approach ix (1999), *available at* http://myfwc.com/critters/panther/Panther%20section%20from%20multi-species%20recovery%20plan.pdf (last visited July 7, 2007).

204. Multispecies HCPs and recovery plans are not without their critics. In a critical review of twenty-two multispecies HCPs approved between 1994 and 2004 by FWS Region 1, which includes California and accounts for eighty-five percent of the approved multispecies plans nationwide, the authors found that the HCPs included "a large number of species not known to be present in the planning area." In a similar vein, a number of distinguished conservation biologists analyzed the effectiveness of recovery plans against four hypotheses, one of which was that "multi-species plans would be more effective than single-species plans." While acknowledging that such an approach made "intuitive sense," the authors found that the data did not support the hypothesis; they concluded that "species covered under multi-species plans were almost four times less likely to exhibit improving status trends than were species covered by single-species plans." The authors added that "[t]hese results do not necessarily mean that multispecies and ecosystem plans are inherently ineffective" and recommended that "as multispecies and ecosystem plans are developed, careful attention must be paid to ensure that efficiency is not achieved at the expense of thoroughness or explicit science." *Id.* at 647–48.

205. Strahan v. Coxe, 137 F.3d 155 (1st Cir. 1997), *cert. denied*, 525 U.S. 830 (1995) (Massachusetts Department of Fisheries liable for take of night whales in state-authorized gill net and lobster pot fisheries).

206. 515 U.S. 687; *see supra* note 181.

207. 16 U.S.C. § 1536(4).

208. *Id.* § 1539(a)(1)(B).

209. *Id.* § 1538(a)(1). Under the Law of the Sea Convention, the term "high seas" means "all waters seaward of the territorial sea of the United States, except waters officially recognized by the United States as the territorial sea of another country, under international law." 50 C.F.R. 17.21.

210. *See, e.g.,* Steven Davison, *The Aftermath of Sweet Home Chapter: Modification of Wildlife Habitat as a Prohibited Taking in Violation of the Endangered Species Act,* 27 WM. & MARY ENVTL. L. & POL'Y REV. 541 (2003); James R. Rasband, *Priority, Probability, and Proximate Cause: Lessons from Tort Law About Imposing ESA Responsibility for Wildlife Harm on Water Users and Other Joint Habitat Modifiers,* 33 ENVTL. LAW 595 (2003).

211. 515 U.S. at 709–10.

212. 984 F. Supp. 1242, 1248 (W.D. Mo. 1997); *but see* Am. Bald Eagle v. Bhatti, 9 F.3d 163, 165 (1st Cir. 1993) (requiring proof of "actual" injury to identifiable individual animals).

213. *See* Endangered Fish and Wildlife; Proposed Rule to Implement Speed Restrictions to Reduce the Threat of Ship Collisions with North Atlantic Right Whales, 71 Fed. Reg. 36,299 (2006). North Atlantic right whales are among the most depleted of all large whales, worldwide. Only about 300 exist, and the population is not recovering. Collisions with ships are the greatest threat. Typically, one or two known ship-strike deaths occur each year—likely more deaths go undetected or unreported. Additional information available at http://www.nmfs.noaa.gov/pr/shipstrike/ (last visited Oct. 9, 2007).

214. *See* http://www.nmfs.noaa.gov/pr/pdfs/shipstrike/imo_proposal_tss.pdf (last visited Oct. 9, 2007).

215. *See* Glacier Bay National Park, Vessel Management Plan Regulations, 71 Fed. Reg. 69,328 (Nov. 30, 2006); Endangered and Threatened Wildlife and Plants; Final Rule to Establish Thirteen Additional Manatee Protection Areas in Florida, 67 Fed. Reg. 68,450 (Nov. 8, 2002); U.S.. Fish & Wildlife Serv., N. Fla. Field Office, Florida Manatee Protection, http://www.fws.gov/northflorida/Manatee/federal-manatee-protection-areas.htm.

216. Listing of Steller Sea Lions as Threatened Under Endangered Species Act with Protective Regulations, 55 Fed. Reg. 12,645 (Apr. 5, 1990).

217. Designated Critical Habitat; Steller Sea Lion, 58 Fed. Reg. 45,269 (Aug. 27, 1993).

218. Information available at NOAA Fisheries, Steller Sea Lions, http://stellersealions.noaa .gov/ (last visited Oct. 9, 2007).

219. *See* Greenpeace Action v. Franklin, 14 F.3d 1324 (9th Cir. 1992).

220. Greenpeace v. NMFS, 237 F. Supp. 2d 1181, 1203 (W.D. Wash., 2002).

221. 16 U.S.C. § 1540(f).

222. *Id.* § 1531(b).

223. Fishery Conservation and Management Act, Pub. L. No. 94-265, 90 Stat. 331 (1976) (codified at 16 U.S.C. §§ 1801 *et seq.*). For a detailed discussion of the FCMA, see Chapter 9.

224. *Id.*

225. *See, e.g.,* Christie, *supra* note 41, at 120, 135.

226. Sustainable Fisheries Act, Pub. L. No. 104-297, 110 Stat. 3559 (1996).

227. *Id.* at §§ 102(7), 108(3)(a)(3), 110 Stat. 3561, 3575 (codified at 16 U.S.C. §§ 1802, 1853).

228. *See* Marian Macpherson, *Integrating Ecosystem Management Approaches into Federal Fishery Management Through the Magnuson-Stevens Fishery Conservation and Management Act,* 6 OCEAN & COASTAL L.J. 1, 12 (2001).

229. ECOSYSTEM PRINCIPLES ADVISORY PANEL, ECOSYSTEM-BASED FISHERY MANAGEMENT: A REPORT TO CONGRESS (1998), *available at* http://www.nmfs.noaa.gov/sfa/EPAPrpt.pdf (last visited July 7, 2007).

230. *Id.* at 27.

231. *Id.* at 3.

232. 16 U.S.C. § 1853(c).

233. *Id.* § 1854(a–b).

234. *Id.* § 1854(b).

235. *Id.*

236. Western Pacific Regional Fishery Management Council, *available at* http://www
.wpcouncil.org/ (last visited Feb. 9, 2007).

237. Press Release, NOAA Releases Draft Environmental Impact Statement for the Fishery
Management Plan for Coral Reef Ecosystems (Jan. 30, 2001), *available at* http://www
.publicaffairs.noaa.gov/releases2001/jan01/noaa01r103.html (last visited July 7, 2007).

238. Nat'l Marine Fisheries Serv., Towards an Ecosystem Approach for the Western
Pacific Region: From Species-Based Fishery Management Plans to Place-Based
Fishery Ecosystem Plans (2005, reissued 2007), *available at* http://www.wpcouncil
.org/documents/DPEIS.pdf (last visited July 7, 2007).

239. *Id.* at i.

240. N. Pac. Fishery Mgmt. Council, Information on Ecosystem-Based Management, *available
at* http://www.fakr.noaa.gov/npfmc/current_issues/ecosystem/Ecosystem.htm (last visited
Feb. 9, 2007).

241. Fisheries of the Caribbean, Gulf of Mexico, and South Atlantic; Comprehensive Amendment for the Fishery Ecosystem Plan, 70 Fed. Reg. 29,482 (May 23, 2005); S. Atl. Fishery Mgmt. Council, Moving Toward Ecosystem Management, http://www.safmc.net/
ecosystem/Home/EcosystemHome/tabid/435/Default.aspx (last visited Feb. 9, 2007). For
an overview of efforts to move towards EBM in fisheries in 2005, *see* Amy Mathews
Amos, Moving Forward: A Snapshot of U.S. Activities in Ecosystem-Based Fisheries Management, *available at* http://www.safmc.net/Portals/0/EMHome/Moving
_Forward_EBFM_Final2-7-05.pdf (last visited July 7, 2007).

242. Magnuson-Stevens Fishery Conservation and Management Reauthorization Act of 2006,
Pub. L. No. 109-479, 120 Stat. 3575 (2007).

243. *Id.* § 3(a) (codified at 16 U.S.C. § 1801(a)).

244. *Id.*

245. Outer Continental Shelf Lands Act, ch. 345, 67 Stat. 462 (1953) (codified as amended at
43 U.S.C. §§ 1331 *et seq.*). For a detailed discussion of the OCSLA, see Chapter 13.

246. Outer Continental Shelf Lands Act Amendments of 1978, Pub. L. No. 95-372, § 201,
92 Stat. 629 (codified at 43 U.S.C. § 1331(g–h); H.R. Rep. No. 95-590 at 125 (1978),
reprinted in 1978 U.S.C.C.A.N. 1450, 1531.

247. *See, e.g.,* 43 U.S.C. § 1344(a)(3) (requiring the Secretary to "select the timing and location
of leasing . . . so as to obtain a proper balance between the potential for environmental
damage, the potential for the discovery of oil and gas, and the potential for adverse impact
on the coastal zone").

248. 43 U.S.C. § 1331(g).

249. *Id.* § 1331(h). Under the OCSLA, each coastal state identifies the inward boundaries of its
coastal zone. *Id.* § 1331(e).

250. *Id.* § 1332(4–5).

251. H.R. Rep. No. 95-590, at 51, 1978 U.S.C.C.A.N. 1450, 1458.

252. 43 U.S.C. § 1344(a).

253. *Id.*

254. *Id.* § 1344(a)(2)(g), (e).

255. 30 C.F.R. § 256.17(a)(1).

256. *Id.* § 256.26.

257. *Id.* § 256.26.

258. *Id.* § 256.32, 256.37.

259. 16 U.S.C. § 1346(a)(1).

260. *Id.* § 1346(b).

261. *Id.* § 1346(e).

262. *Id.* § 1334(a)(1).

263. *Id.* § 1334(a)(2).

264. 16 U.S.C. §§ 1451 *et seq.* For a detailed discussion of the CZMA, see Chapter 5.

265. *Id.* § 1453(1). The zone extends seaward to the outer limit of state title and ownership (generally three nautical miles offshore) and inland to the "extent necessary to control shorelands, the uses of which have a direct and significant impact on the coastal waters, and to control those geographical areas which are likely to be affected by or vulnerable to sea rise." *Id.* This definition creates significant variations in the extent of the coastal zone between states, or even within states.

266. *Id.* §§ 1454–1455.

267. *Id.* §§ 1455–1455a.

268. *Id.* § 1456.

269. *Id.* § 1456(c). *See generally* U.S. Dep't of Commerce, Nat'l Oceanic & Atmospheric Admin., Federal Consistency Overview, *available at* http://coastalmanagement.noaa.gov/consistency/welcome.html (last visited April 2, 2007).

270. *Id.*

271. *Id.*

272. S. Rep. No. 106-412, 1–2.

273. 16 U.S.C. § 1456.

274. For coastal states to amend CMPs to implement EBM as enforceable polices, they must comply with the complex amendment process and deal with the cost and political constraints that accompany such an effort.

275. 301 Mass. Code Regs. 20.02(3).

276. *Id.* § 21.05. The MCMP also includes "management principles," which "do not have authority based on existing state environmental statute or regulation, and are therefore not enforceable under existing state law, but which provide guidance to proponents of activities in the Coastal Zone." *Id.*

277. Mass. Gen. Laws ch. 132A, § 14; 301 Mass. Code Regs. § 21.98(12).

278. Mass. Ocean Mgmt. Taskforce, Waves of Change (2004), available at http://www.mass.gov/czm/oceanmanagement/waves_of_change/pdf/wavesofchange.pdf (last visited July 7, 2007). The Massachusetts Ocean Management Task Force released final reports and recommendations in March 2004. Mass. Office of Coastal Zone Mgmt., The Massachusetts Ocean Management Task Force Reports and Recommendations, *available at* http://www.mass.gov/czm/oceanmanagement/waves_of_change/index.htm (last visited March 8, 2007).

279. *Id.*

280. Cal. Fish & Game Code § 2053.

281. *Id.* § 2853(b)(1, 3).

282. *Id.* § 7050(b)(5).

283. For a detailed discussion of these laws, see Chapters 4 (wetlands), 7 (coastal water quality), and 8 (ocean dumping and marine pollution).

284. 33 U.S.C. § 1251(a). In Riverside Bayview Homes, Inc. v. U.S. Army Corps of Eng'rs, 474 U.S. 121, 132 (1985), the U.S. Supreme Court interpreted this statutory objective to "[incorporate] a broad systemic view of the goal of maintaining and improving water quality." The Court cited the 1972 House Report defining the word "integrity" as referring to a "condition in which the natural structure and function of ecosystems [are] maintained." *Id.* The Court concluded, "Protection of aquatic ecosystems, Congress recognized, demanded broad federal authority to control pollution, 'for water moves in hydrologic cycles and it is essential that discharge of pollutants be controlled at the source.'" *Id.* at 133.

285. 33 U.S.C. § 1602(7).

286. *Id.* § 1342. This is the NPDES permit program, which is the central mechanism under the CWA for achieving its water quality objectives. The NPDES permit program is administered by EPA or by the states under delegation agreements. Forty-five states have received full or partial authority to issue NPDES permits. Information available at http://www.epa.gov/npdes/images/State_NPDES_Prog_Auth.pdf (last visited July 7, 2007).

287. *Id.* § 1343(a). Ocean dumping permits are issued by the Corps of Engineers under the Marine Protection and Sanctuaries Act.

288. *Id.* § 1343(c)(1)(A).

289. *Id.* § 1344. Regulations defining what constitutes the discharge of dredge or fill material are at 33 C.F.R. pt. 323.

290. *See* 40 C.F.R. pt. 232.

291. 33 U.S.C. § 1268. EPA's Great Lakes National Program Office (GLNPO), located in Chicago, Illinois, has a staff of forty-six and a budget of almost $15 million. GLNPO brings together federal, state, tribal, local, and industry partners in an integrated, ecosystem approach to protect, maintain, and restore the chemical, biological, and physical integrity of the Great Lakes.

292. *Id.* § 1267. In May 2003, the EPA Region III issued guidance entitled *Ambient Water Quality Criteria for Dissolved Oxygen, Water Clarity and Chlorophyll-a for the Chesapeake Bay and Its Tidal Tributaries.* This is a basin-wide approach to restoring the aquatic ecosystem of the nation's premier estuary under the 2000 Chesapeake Bay agreement signed by the states of Virginia, Maryland, and Pennsylvania and the District of Columbia, the Chesapeake Bay Commission, and EPA. The agreement commits the parties "to identify the essential elements of habitat and environmental quality necessary to support the living resources of the Bay." More information is available at http://www.chesapeakebay.net/agreement.htm (last visited July 7, 2007).

293. 33 U.S.C. § 1269. In 1994, the states of Connecticut and New York and EPA approved the Comprehensive Conservation and Management Plan for Long Island Sound. Developed by the Long Island Sound Study, the Plan identifies the specific commitments and recommendations for actions to improve water quality, protect habitat and living resources, educate and involve the public, improve the long-term understanding of how to manage the Sound, monitor progress, and redirect management efforts. More information is available at Long Island Sound Study, http://www.longislandsoundstudy.net/ (last visited July 7, 2007).

294. 33 U.S.C. § 1270. The Lake Champlain Basin Program works in partnership with government agencies from New York, Vermont, and Quebec, private organizations, local communities, and individuals to coordinate and fund efforts that benefit the Lake Champlain Basin's water quality, fisheries, wetlands, wildlife, recreation, and cultural resources. More information is available at Lake Champlain Basin Program, http://www.lcbp.org/.

295. 33 U.S.C. § 1313(d).

296. Water quality standards are set by states, territories, and tribes. They identify the uses for each water body—for example, drinking water supply, contact recreation (swimming), and aquatic life support (fishing)—and the scientific criteria to support that use. 40 C.F.R. pt. 131.

297. 33 U.S.C. §§ 1311(b), 1314(b).

298. 40 C.F.R. § 130.7; *see also* O. H. HOUCK, THE CLEAN WATER ACT TMDL PROGRAM: LAW, POLICY & IMPLEMENTATION (2d ed., Envtl. Law Inst. 2002).

299. Pronsolino v. Nastri, 291 F.3d 1123, 1140 (9th Cir. 2002), *cert. denied,* 539 U.S. 926 (2002).

300. The NOAA Web site on the dead zone is at http://oceanservice.noaa.gov/products/pubs_hypox.html (last visited July 7, 2007).

301. 42 U.S.C. §§ 74001 to 7671(q). The 1970 Act established national ambient air quality standards (NAAQS) to protect public health and welfare. Section 302 of the Act defines "welfare" to include "effects on soils, water . . . vegetation . . . wildlife . . . and climate." *Id.* § 7602 (h). The 1977 amendments to the Act established the Prevention of Significant Deterioration (PSD) program, which protects "clean air" areas including National Parks and other priceless natural resources. *Id.* § 7470(2). The 1990 amendments to the Act added two provisions with particular application to ecosystem protection. The first is the acid rain control program, which sought to halt and reverse the ecological damage to alpine lakes and forests through a "cap and trade" program under which sulfur dioxide emissions from power plants and major industrial sources have been greatly reduced in a cost-effective manner. The other provisions added in 1990 pertain to stratospheric ozone depletion and measures to protect ozone and implement the U.S. obligations under the

Montreal Protocol. They require that EPA establish a program for controlling ozone-depleting chemicals such as chlorofluorocarbons and hydroflurocarbons.

302. 127 S. Ct. 1438 (2007).
303. *Id.* at 1460–61, 1463.
304. 42 U.S.C. § 7521(a)(1).
305. 127 S. Ct. at 1462.
306. *Id.* at 1463.
307. The Court noted, "We need not and do not reach the question whether on remand EPA must make an endangerment finding, or whether policy concerns can inform EPA's actions in the event that it makes such a finding." *Id.*
308. Exec. Order No. 13,432, 72 Fed. Reg. 27,715 (May 16, 2007). The order, entitled "Cooperation Among Agencies in Protecting the Environment with Respect to Greenhouse Gas Emissions From Motor Vehicles, Nonroad Vehicles, and Nonroad Engines" was signed by President Bush on May 14, 2007.
309. For a detailed discussion of climate change and the oceans, see Chapter 18.
310. Exec. Order No. 13,158, 3 C.F.R. 273, 273–74 (2001). The Bush Administration reaffirmed the Order on June 4, 2001. Nominations for Federal Advisory Committee on Marine Protected Areas, 66 Fed. Reg. 42,204, 42,204 (Aug. 10, 2001). For a detailed discussion on MPAs, see Chapter 17.
311. *Id.*
312. *Id.*
313. Exec. Order No. 13,158, § 3, 65 Fed. Reg. 34,909 (May 31, 2000).
314. *Id.* §§ 4–5.
315. *See id.* §§ 3, 4(a), 5.
316. Donald C. Baur, Robert W. Irvin, & Darren R. Misenko, *Putting "Protection" into Marine Protected Areas*, 28 Vt. L. Rev., 497, 499–500 (2004). In fact, agencies appear to be flaunting the Section 5 directive and proceeding with actions that cause direct harm to MPAs. One of the most notable instances is the consideration by the U.S. Army Corps of Engineers and the MMS of authorization for the Cape Wind energy plant in federal waters in Nantucket Sound, even though the project would significantly harm the surrounding Massachusetts State sanctuary waters. *See* T. Agardy, *Ocean Zoning Is Coming! Ocean Zoning Is Coming! Music to Some Ears, A Fearsome Sound to Others*, W2o Observer, *available at* http://auei.auburn.edu/pdf/w2o.pdf (last visited July 7, 2007).
317. 16 U.S.C. §§ 1431–1445c-1.
318. *Id.* §§ 1433–1434.
319. For example, marine zoning has been implemented as a management tool at the 2,800-square-nautical-mile Florida Keys National Marine Sanctuary. The Sanctuary contains several different types of zones, including the Existing Management Areas in the Keys (national wildlife refuges, state parks, etc.), Wildlife Management Areas, Ecological Reserves, Sanctuary Preservation Areas, and Special-Use Areas. Florida Keys National Marine Sanctuary, Marine Resource Protection, *available at* http://floridakeys.noaa.gov/resource_protection/welcome.html#zoning (last visited May 16, 2007). Likewise, NOAA's Center for Coastal Monitoring and Assessment is evaluating different boundary adjustment alternatives for the Channel Islands National Marine Sanctuary based on a biogeographic assessment of the distribution of organisms and habitats from Point Sal to the U.S./Mexico border. Center for Coastal Monitoring and Assessment, Biogeographic Assessment of the Channel Islands National Marine Sanctuary to Support Boundary Alternative Assessments, *available at* http://ccma.nos.noaa.gov/ecosystems/sanctuaries/chanisl_nms.html (last visited Mar. 11, 2007).
320. 16 U.S.C. §§ 1433–1434.
321. For example, units of the National Park System such as Cape Hatteras National Seashore, Olympic National Park, Glacier Bay National Park, and Everglades National Park, to name a few, have boundaries that include coastal waters.
322. National Park Service Organic Act, ch. 408, 39 Stat. 535 (1916) (codified at 16 U.S.C. § 1).

323. H.R. Rep. No. 64-700, at 3 (1916). When it enacted the Alaska National Interest Lands Conservation Act in 1980, Congress shed further light on the meaning of the guiding management principles for the National Park System when it stated that such areas should be managed "to maintain the natural abundance, behavior, diversity, and ecological integrity of native animals as a part of their ecosystem." S. Rep. No. 96-413, at 171 (1979).

324. 16 U.S.C. § 3.

325. *Id.* § 1a-1.

326. *Id.* § 668 dd(d)(1)(A).

327. *Id.* § 668 dd(a)(2).

328. *Id.* § 668 dd(d)(1)(A).

329. The National Wildlife Refuge System Administration Act of 1966, *id.* § 668dd(b)(5); The National Wildlife Refuge System Improvement Act of 1997, Pub. L. No. 105-57 § 6(3)(B).

330. 16 U.S.C. § 431. For a detailed discussion of the Antiquities Act, *see* Mark Squillace, *The Monumental Legacy of the Antiquities Act of 1906*, Ga. L. Rev. 473 (2003).

331. Proclamation No. 8031, 71 Fed. Reg. 36,443 (Jun. 26, 2006). The marine national monument was renamed the Papahānaumokuākea Marine National Monument in 2007. Papahānaumokuākea Marine National Monument, Management, http://www.hawaiireef .noaa.gov/management (last visited May 16, 2007).

332. 16 U.S.C. § 432 (providing that the Secretaries of the Interior, Agriculture, and the Army shall make and publish uniform rules and regulations for the purpose of carrying out the provisions of Sections 431–433 of the Antiquities Act). *See, e.g.,* 50 C.F.R. pt. 404 (regulations for the Northwestern Hawaiian Islands Marine National Monument). Monuments included within the National Park System are covered by the legal authorities for such units, including the U.S.C. §§ 1, 1a-1, 3, discussed previously.

333. Fisheries of the Caribbean, Gulf of Mexico, and South Atlantic; Gulf of Mexico Essential Fish Habitat Amendment, 70 Fed Reg. 76216 (Dec. 23, 2005).

334. Fisheries of the Caribbean, Gulf of Mexico, and South Atlantic; Reef Fish Fishery of the Gulf of Mexico; Extension of Marine Reserves, Final Rule, 69 Fed. Reg. 24532 (May 4, 2004).

335. Fisheries of the Exclusive Economic Zone off Alaska; Sitka Pinnacles Marine Reserve, Final Rule, 65 Fed. Reg. 67305 (Nov. 9, 2000).

336. The PFMC began a formal two-phase process to consider marine reserves to manage groundfish in 1999; although the first technical analysis phase was completed in 2000, the second phase of developing options for the design and location of marine reserves has been stalled by lack of funding. Marine Reserves, *available at* http://www.pcouncil .org/reserves/reservesback.html (last visited Mar. 11, 2007).

337. *Id.*

338. Cal. Fish & Game Code §§ 2850–2863 (West 2007).

339. *Id.* § 2852(d).

340. Commission Gives Final Approval for Central Coast Marine Protected Areas, *available at* http://www.dfg.ca.gov/mlpa/ccmpas.asp (last visited Nov. 7, 2007).

341. *Id.* § 2853(b).

342. *See* Section II.C.7.b., *supra.*

343. For a detailed discussion of the public trust doctrine, see Chapter 2.

344. *See* Joseph Sax, *The Public Trust Doctrine in Natural Resources Law: Effective Judicial Intervention*, 68 Mich. L. Rev. 471, 489 (1970).

345. Ill. Central R.R. Co. v. Illinois, 146 U.S. 387 (1892).

346. *Id.* at 453.

347. *See* Joseph Sax, *Liberating the Public Trust Doctrine From its Historical Shackles*, 14 U.C. Davis L. Rev. 185 (1980).

348. *See* Lake Mich. Fed'n v. U.S. Army Corps of Eng'rs, 742 F. Supp. 441, 444 (N.D. Ill. 1990).

349. Pollard's Lessee v. Hagan, 44 U.S. (3 How.) 212, 217 (1845) ("all the navigable waters of the U.S. are the public property of the nation, and subject to all requisite legislation by Congress"). Federal power over these areas stems from the Property and Supremacy Clauses of the Constitution. Shively v. Bowlby, 152 U.S. 1, 14 (1894). The federal government has a trust obligation over all tidal lands. The doctrine extends to protection of the biological resources associated with tidal waters. Martin v. Waddell, 41 U.S. (16 Pet.) 367 (1842).

350. United States v. California, 332 U.S. 19, 39–40 (1947) ("The ocean, even its three-mile belt, is thus of vital consequence to the nation in its desire to engage in commerce and to live in peace with the world; it also becomes of crucial importance should it ever again become impossible to preserve that peace."); *see also* Alabama v. Texas, 347 U.S. 272, 273–74 (1954) ("The power over the public land thus entrusted to Congress is without limitations. And it is not for the courts to say how that trust shall be administered. That is for Congress to determine.").

351. 43 U.S.C. §§ 1301 *et seq.* The Gulf of Mexico coasts of Florida and Texas have a three-marine-league SLA boundary. *Id.* § 1301(b).

352. Laura K. Welles, Aaron M. Flynn & Eugene H. Buck, *Federal-State Maritime Boundary Issues,* CRS Report RL32912, at 4. n.18. *See also* UNCLOS III art. 76(1).

353. Casey Jarman, *The Public Trust Doctrine in the Exclusive Economic Zone,* 65 Or. L. Rev. 1, 2 (1986); W. K. Ris Jr. & V. P. Nanda, *The Public Trust Doctrine: A Viable Approach to International Environmental Protection,* 5 Ecology L.Q. 291–319 (1976).

354. Light v. United States, 220 U.S. 523, 537 (1911) ("The public lands are held in trust for the people of the whole country and the government is charged with the duty and clothed with the power to take control of public lands."); *see also* Knight v. U.S. Land Ass'n, 142 U.S. 161, 181 (1891) (federal government is "the guardian of the people of the United States over the public lands"); United States v. Trinidad Coal Co., 137 U.S. 160, 170 (1890).

355. United States v. 1.58 acres of Land, 523 F. Supp. 120, 124–25 (D. Mass. 1981) ("[T]he federal government is as restricted as the [states] in [their] ability to abdicate to private individuals its sovereign *jus publicum* in the land.").

356. City of Alameda v. Todd Shipyards, 632 F. Supp. 333, 339 (N.D. Calif. 1986), *but see* United States v. 11.037 Acres of Land, 685 F. Supp. 214, 216 (N.D. Calif. 1988) (U.S. condemnation of coastal property extinguishes public trust easement under the Supremacy Clause).

357. Marks v. Whitney, 6 Cal. 3d 251, 259, 491 P.2d 374, 380 (Cal. 1971); Richard G. Hildreth, *The Public Trust Doctrine and Coastal and Ocean Resources Management,* 8 J. Envtl. L. & Litig. 221, 230 (1993); Jack H. Archer and M. Casey Jarman, *Sovereign Rights and Responsibilities: Applying Public Trust Principles to the Management of EEZ Space and Resources,* 17 Ocean & Coastal Mgmt. 253–71 (1992), and M. Casey Jarman, *The Use of the Public Trust Doctrine for Resource-Based Area-Wide Management,* 4 Alb. L.J. Sci. & Tech. 7 (1994).

358. Richard Hildreth, *The Public Trust in Ocean and Coastal Resource Management,* available at http://www.ecy.wa.gov/programs/sea/pubs/93-53/resource.html (last visited July 7, 2007).

359. 42 U.S.C. § 4331(a). For a detailed discussion of NEPA, see Chapter 6.

360. *Id.* § 4321.

361. *Id.* § 4331(c).

362. Section 102 provides: "the Federal Government shall . . . (A) utilize a systematic, interdisciplinary approach which will ensure the integrated use of the natural and social sciences and the environmental design arts in planning and decision-making which may have an impact on man's environment; (B) identify and develop methods and procedures . . . which will insure that presently unquantified environmental amenities and values may be given appropriate consideration along with economic and technical considerations. . . ." *Id.* § 4332(A).

363. CEQ, *The National Environmental Policy Act: A Study of Its Effectiveness* at 25–27, Executive Office of the President (Jan. 1997).

364. Andrus v. Sierra Club, 442 U.S. 347, 358–9 (1979).

365. 40 C.F.R. § 1502.4(b) ("Agencies shall prepare statements on broad actions so that they are relevant to policy and are timed to coincide with meaningful points in agency planning and decision making.").

366. *See* Daniel L. Mandelker, NEPA Law and Litigation § 9:9 (2d ed., 2006).

367. *See, e.g.,* Bryant, *NEPA Compliance in Fisheries Management: The Programmatic Supplemental Environmental Impact Statement on Alaskan Groundfish Fisheries and Implications for NEPA Reform,* 30 Harv. Envtl. L Rev. 441.

368. Exec. Order No. 13,158, 65 Fed. Reg. 34,909 (June 26, 2000); Exec. Order No. 13,186, 66 Fed. Reg. 3,853 (Jan. 17, 2001).

369. *Id.*

370. Exec. Order No. 13,352, 69 Fed. Reg. 52,989 (Aug. 30, 2004).

371. For example, NOAA within the Department of Commerce has responsibility both for conservation programs, such as marine endangered species, marine mammals, and marine sanctuaries, and for resource development programs, like commercial fisheries management. The same is true for the Department of the Interior, which must conserve ESA-listed species and protect marine mammals, national parks, and national wildlife refuges, and develop the Outer Continental Shelf for energy purposes.

372. USCOP Final Report, *supra* note 36, at 90.

373. *Id.* at 91.

374. For a detailed discussion of Fishery Management Councils, see Chapter 9. Take reduction teams are discussed in Chapter 15.

375. A detailed proposal for using regional management teams for EBM purposes, following an approach somewhat similar to fishery management councils and take reduction teams, is described in Christie, *supra* note 41, at 171–72. Prof. Christie calls for the development of ecosystem management plans for living marine resources by NMFS based on the recommendations of Ecosystem Management Committees, the membership of which would be modeled on MMPA take reduction teams and cover a broad representation of interests, including Native Alaskan entities and Indian Tribes.

376. FWS is currently following this approach to establish a committee of stakeholders to make recommendations on the development of wind energy projects based upon the impacts such facilities have on birds. Establishment of Wind Turbine Guidelines Advisory Committee: Notice of Establishment and Call for Nominations, 72 Fed. Reg. 11,373 (Mar. 13, 2007); *see also* Interim Guidelines to Avoid and Minimize Wildlife Impacts From Wind Turbines, http://www.fws.gov/habitatconservation/wind.pdf.

377. *See, e.g.,* Christie, *supra* note 41, at 169.

chapter twenty

Ocean Commissions Issue an Urgent Call for Action to Reform U.S. Ocean Policy and Law

Sarah Chasis

I. Introduction

As the previous chapters in this book amply demonstrate, major improvements are needed in oceans and coastal law and policy to meet the challenges of the twenty-first century. Some of these improvements may be implemented with improved, more effective and creative uses of existing laws and programs. Others require changes to and strengthening of current law.

The recommendations made in this book echo the far-reaching and visionary blueprints for ocean and coastal policy reform in the two national oceans commission reports that are the subject of this chapter. These commissions issued an urgent call for reform of U.S. ocean policy and law. To appreciate the nature and extent of the changes called for, it is worth reviewing the detailed recommendations of the two commissions. It is important to note that, already four and five years after their issuance (in 2003 and 2004), the reforms are only just beginning to be implemented.

II. Background

In response to the growing concern about the serious decline of the oceans, two national commissions, the independent Pew Oceans Commission and the congressionally established U.S. Commission on Ocean Policy, conducted comprehensive reviews of current U.S. law and policy. Each commission spent approximately three years doing in-depth research and analysis and holding public hearings and meetings around the country. The Pew Oceans Commission's eighteen members included public officials (two sitting governors, one former governor, a former member of Congress, and one mayor), academics, and leaders of fishing groups and environmental organizations. It was chaired by the Honorable Leon E. Panetta, a former long-time member of Congress, who also served as Director of the Office of Management and Budget and then Chief of Staff to President Clinton. The U.S. Commission, which was created by the Oceans Act of 2000, had sixteen members that were appointed by President Bush, with congressional input, and were drawn from academia, industry, the military, and public life (including the first Administrator of the U.S. EPA). The U.S. Commission was chaired by Admiral James D. Watkins, USN (Ret.), a former Chief of Naval Operations during the Reagan Administration and Secretary of Energy during the George H.W. Bush Administration.

The Pew Oceans Commission focused on ocean life and ocean health, addressing primarily fishing, pollution, coastal development, and governance issues. The U.S. Commission covered these issues as well as a number of others, including shipping, offshore energy development, monitoring, and ocean exploration.

The Pew Oceans Commission released its report, *America's Living Oceans, Charting a Course for Sea Change,* in June 2003.[1] The U.S. Commission on Ocean Policy issued its report, *An Ocean Blueprint for the 21st* Century, in September 2004.[2] These were the first comprehensive reviews of ocean policy in thirty-five years, since the release in 1969 of *Our Nation and the Sea: A Plan for National Action.*[3]

Despite their differing compositions and mandates, both commissions reached similar conclusions. They found that the oceans were in serious trouble and there was an urgent need for a more coordinated and accountable system of ocean governance, a significant increase in the national investment in ocean stewardship, and a shift to an ecosystem-based approach to ocean management. Both called for an overhaul of U.S. ocean law and policy to achieve these objectives.

In response, the Administration issued its Ocean Action Plan,[4] Members of Congress introduced oceans legislation, and several coastal states enacted new laws. To accelerate the pace of change in U.S. ocean law and policy, commissioners from the two commissions formed the Joint Ocean Commission Initiative (JOCI),[5] an effort led by Adm. Watkins and Mr. Panetta, the former commission chairs.

Despite these steps, the pace of implementation of the two commission reports has been frustratingly slow, as reflected in the overall grade of "C minus" given in the most recent oceans report card issued by the Joint Ocean Commission Initiative (JOCI).[6] However, as the report card points out, there are some hopeful signs of progress, including action at the state and regional levels—for example, oceans initiatives in California, New York, the West Coast Governors' Agreement, and the Gulf of Mexico Alliance—as well as at the federal level with Congress's passage of the Magnuson-Stevens Fishery Conservation and Management Reauthorization Act of 2006 and the President's creation of the Northwestern Hawaiian Islands Marine National Monument, the world's largest marine protected area.

This chapter discusses the overriding themes of the two commission reports and focuses on the findings and recommendations in four key areas that both commissions addressed: governance, fisheries, pollution, and coastal development. The chapter also discusses responses to the commission reports, including the Administration's Ocean Action Plan, oceans legislation in Congress, state and regional efforts, and the work of the Joint Ocean Commission Initiative.

III. Commissions' Findings and Recommendation

A. Overarching Themes

The fundamental conclusion of the Pew Oceans Commission is that "the nation needs to ensure healthy, productive, and resilient marine ecosystems for present and future generations."[7] In the long term, economic sustainability depends on ecological sustainability. To achieve and maintain healthy ecosystems, the commission found that we must extend an ethic of stewardship toward the oceans and treat our oceans as a public trust. National ocean policy and governance must be realigned to reflect and apply principles of ecosystem health, integrity, sustainability, and precaution. We must redefine our relationship with the ocean to reflect an understanding of the land-sea connection and organize institutions and forums capable of managing on an ecosystem basis.

> **The fundamental conclusion of the Pew Oceans Commission: "the nation needs to ensure healthy, productive, and resilient marine ecosystems for present and future generations."**

To embrace these reforms, the Pew Oceans Commission recommended that the nation realize five priority objectives:

- Declare a principled, unified national ocean policy based on protecting ecosystem health and requiring sustainable use of ocean resources;
- Encourage comprehensive and coordinated governance of ocean resources and uses appropriate to the problems to be solved (on a large marine ecosystems scale for fisheries management and governance generally, on a watershed level for coastal development and pollution control);

- Restructure fishery management institutions and reorient fisheries policy to protect and sustain ecosystems on which fisheries depend;
- Control sources of pollution, particularly nutrients, that are harming marine ecosystems; and
- Protect important habitat and manage coastal development to minimize habitat damage and water quality impairment.[8]

The U.S. Commission agreed that existing management approaches have not been updated to reflect new scientific findings that demonstrate the complexity and interconnectedness of natural systems, with responsibilities remaining dispersed among a confusing array of agencies at the federal, state, and local levels. It also concluded that there had been decades of underinvestment in the study, exploration, protection, and management of our oceans, coasts, and Great Lakes. The Commission emphasized the need for improved and timely access to reliable data and solid scientific information that is translated into timely and useful results and products for decision makers and for enhancement of ocean-related education so that all citizens recognize the role of the oceans, coasts, and Great Lakes in their own lives, and the impacts they themselves have on these environments.[9]

The U.S. Commission identified the following "critical actions" to meet these needs: improved governance; *doubling* the nation's investment in ocean research; launching a new era of ocean exploration; implementing the national Integrated Ocean Observing System and a national monitoring network; improving ocean education; strengthening coastal and watershed management and the links between them; setting measurable goals for reducing water pollution, particularly from nonpoint sources, and strengthening incentives, technical assistance, enforcement, and other management tools to achieve those goals; reforming fisheries management by separating assessment and allocation, improving the Regional Fishery Management Council system, and exploring the use of dedicated access privileges; acceding to the United Nations Convention on the Law of the Sea; and establishing an Ocean Policy Trust Fund dedicated to supporting improved ocean and coastal management at federal and state levels.[10]

B. Ocean Governance

Both Commissions found that a key reason that our oceans are in trouble is a vastly inadequate governance regime. The U.S. Commission on Ocean Policy (USCOP) found:

> [T]he nation is not now sufficiently organized legally or administratively to make decisions, set priorities, resolve conflicts, and articulate clear and consistent policies that respond to the wealth of problems and opportunities ocean users face.[11]

The Pew Oceans Commission sounded a similar theme:

[W]e have continued to approach our oceans with a frontier mentality. The result is a hodgepodge of ocean laws and programs that do not provide unified, clearly stated goals and measurable objectives. Authority over marine resources is fragmented geographically and institutionally. Principles of ecosystem health and integrity, sustainability, and precaution have been lost in the fray. Furthermore, the nation has substantially underinvested in understanding and managing our oceans. The information we do have in hand is often underutilized. Plagued with systemic problems, U.S. ocean governance is in disarray.[12]

Both Commissions called for major reform. The U.S. Commission called for a new "National Ocean Policy Framework" to improve decision making, promote effective coordination, and move toward an ecosystem-based approach to management.[13] The proposed Framework has four major elements. First, at the federal level, there would be a National Ocean Council (NOC) within the Executive Office of the President, chaired by an Assistant to the President and composed of cabinet secretaries of departments or administrators of independent agencies with relevant ocean- and coastal-related responsibilities. The NOC would provide high-level attention to ocean, coastal, and Great Lakes issues; develop and guide the implementation of appropriate national policies; and coordinate the many federal departments and agencies with ocean and coastal responsibilities. A President's Council of Advisors on Ocean Policy would be established to ensure nonfederal input to the NOC and the President on ocean and coastal policy matters. A small Office of Ocean Policy would provide staff support to the Council, the Assistant to the President, and the Council of Advisors.

Second, at the regional level, states would be encouraged to form, on a voluntary basis, regional ocean councils to respond to issues that cross jurisdictional boundaries and to address large-scale connections and conflicts among watershed, coastal, and offshore uses. To complement this effort, federal agencies would be directed to improve their regional coordination.

Third, in light of the increasing number of economic uses being proposed for federal waters, a comprehensive *offshore management regime* would be established. As part of this regime, a lead federal agency for each offshore activity would be designated.

Fourth, the existing charter for the National Oceanic and Atmospheric Administration (NOAA) would be codified in legislation. (NOAA's existence now depends solely on Executive Order 11,564, which was issued in 1970 by President Nixon.) There would be a follow-up process to determine if additional ocean-related responsibilities should be consolidated into NOAA or whether some other form of reorganization should occur.

The Pew Oceans Commission recommended that Congress enact a National Ocean Policy Act (NOPA) that would establish a national policy to protect, maintain, and restore the health of marine ecosystems and require that marine resources be used in an ecologically sustainable manner.[14] The Act would require that federal agencies conduct their activities in a manner consistent with that national policy and with national standards that implement that policy. (Like the Pew Oceans Commission, the U.S. Commission also articulated the need for a national ocean policy. However, it put the onus on the NOC to make recommendations to Congress for establishing such a policy and for other legislative fixes, such as an organic act for NOAA and proposals for the reorganization of agencies and programs.)

A new independent national ocean agency would be created outside of the Department of Commerce that would be tasked with helping implement the National Ocean Policy Act. Its authority would include reviewing federal actions for consistency with the policy and standards of the Act. However, ultimate compliance with the Act would be up to each federal agency. The new independent oceans agency would consist of NOAA combined with various programs from other federal agencies (for example, the ocean minerals program from Interior, marine mammal and seabird jurisdiction from the U.S. Fish and Wildlife Service, the National Estuary Programs from EPA, aquaculture programs for marine species from the U.S. Department of Agriculture, and shoreline protection programs from the U.S. Army Corps of Engineers).

There would also be a National Ocean Council within the Executive Office of the President to coordinate interagency action on ocean issues and, among other things, ensure that all agencies are complying with the National Ocean Policy Act.

At the regional level, the Pew Oceans Commission recommended the formation of regional ocean ecosystem councils that would consist of appropriate state, federal, and tribal representatives. The councils would develop regional ocean governance plans that would establish clear and measurable management and restoration goals for marine ecosystem health. Once approved for consistency with the policies and standards of NOPA, states and federal agencies would be required to act consistently with these plans. Substantial federal funding would be provided for development and implementation of these plans.

The Pew Oceans Commission recommended that Congress provide a mandate and authority for designating a national system of marine reserves. Marine reserves were defined as a type of marine protected area in which all extractive, additive, or ecologically destructive human activities are prohibited on a lasting basis, except as necessary for evaluation of reserve effectiveness or for appropriate research. The regional ocean ecosystem councils would be empowered to designate marine reserves or networks of reserves of regional importance; additionally, the national oceans agency would inventory and nominate to Congress areas of special national significance, which Congress then could designate for inclusion in a national reserve system. The U.S. Commission did not address marine reserves specifically, but recognized marine protected areas as an effective tool for ecosystem-based management and called on the National Ocean Council to create a process for the effective design, implementation, and evaluation of such areas.[15]

C. Sustainable Fisheries

The U.S. Commission found the following with respect to the current fishery management process:

> While the current regime has many positive features, such as an emphasis on local participation, the pairing of science and management, and regional flexibility, it has also allowed overexploitation of many fish stocks, degradation of habitats, and negative impacts on many ecosystems and fishing communities.[16]

The U.S. Commission made a number of important recommendations to strengthen the link between science and fisheries management. Most significantly, the Commission recommended that the regional fishery management councils not be allowed to approve harvest levels that exceed the allowable biological catch levels recommended by their Scientific and Statistical Committees (SSC). Because of their importance in the process, the SSC members should be appointed by the Administrator of NOAA, rather than the councils, and their credentials and potential conflicts of interest should be vetted by an external organization. There should be a process for independent review of the scientific information relied on by the SSCs.

The U.S. Commission recommended that the regional fishery management councils not be allowed to approve harvest levels that exceed allowable biological catch levels recommended by their SSC.

The Commission recommended that the membership of the regional councils be diversified, with the goal of creating councils that are knowledgeable and fair and that reflect a broad range of interests.

To reverse existing incentives that create an unsustainable "race for fish," the Commission recommended that fishery managers explore the adoption of dedicated access privileges to promote conservation and help reduce capitalization. Congress, it said, should amend the Magnuson-Stevens Fishery Conservation and Management Act to affirm the councils' authority to institute these privileges, subject to meeting national guidelines, and fishery management bodies should consider the benefits of adopting such programs. In addition, Congress should address overcapitalization directly by revising federal programs that subsidize this practice, as well as working with NOAA to develop programs that permanently reduce overcapitalization in fisheries.

Consistent with one of the major themes of the report, the Commission recommended a move toward an ecosystem-based approach, noting that such an approach would be particularly helpful in protection essential fish habitat and reducing the impacts of bycatch (the incidental catch of fish and other marine life in fishing operations).

The Pew Oceans Commission found the three following fundamental problems with the current fisheries management regime under the Magnuson-Stevens Act:

> First, its management regime emphasizes short-term commodity production, revenues, and employment rather than sustaining natural systems that support

and enhance wild fish populations. . . . Second, the management structure and process suffer from regulatory capture, a state of affairs in which government regulators (in this case, fisheries managers) have come to believe that their role is to defend the interests of the regulated community rather than promote the public interest. . . . Third, the law codified an open access, laissez-faire approach. This fosters a reactive management philosophy that focuses more on day-to-day fishing needs than on restoring and maintaining sustainable resources for the future.[17]

The Pew Oceans Commission said that the principal objective of fishery policy should be the long-term health and viability of fisheries by protecting the marine ecosystems on which they depend. Without healthy ecosystems, there can be no healthy fisheries. Fishery management plans should be based on consideration of how the entire ecosystem will be affected by fishing. There should be no fishing without an approved fishery management plan that addresses core problems, such as bycatch, habitat damage, and overcapacity. The Commission also recommended a clear separation between conservation and allocation decisions, with conservation decisions being made by the National Marine Fisheries Service (NMFS), based on the recommendations of regional science and technical teams, and allocation decisions—who gets what proportion of the catch, when and where—made by the regional fishery management councils.

To provide independent scientific oversight, the Commission recommended that a Marine Fisheries Oversight Commission be established, modeled on the Marine Mammal Commission, or that periodic audits be conducted by the National Academy of Sciences, or both. The Commission strongly recommended the prohibition of mobile bottom fishing gear in habitats known to be especially sensitive to disturbance from such gear, including coral-reef and deepwater corals, rocky bottoms, seamounts, kelp forests, seagrass beds and sponge habitats.

To address overcapacity, the Commission recommended requiring comprehensive access and allocation planning as a condition of fishing, including limiting access and entry to all fisheries to match the size of the fleet to the health of the targeted fish population and the health of the overall ecosystem. The Commission found that individual or community fishing quotas were among the more effective allocation mechanisms and recommended national standards to guide their implementation and evaluate their performance. The Commission recommended the establishment of a Fishery Conservation and Management Fund to be used for research, data collection, management, enforcement, and habitat restoration. The Fund would be financed through fees collected from fines and other penalties and royalty payments generated by quota allocation programs.

D. Pollution

The U.S. Commission found that

> Over the last few decades, great strides have been made in controlling water pollution from point sources, although further improvements could be real-

ized through increased funding, strengthened enforcement, and promotion of innovative approaches such as market-based incentives. However, substantial enhancement of coastal water quality will require significant reductions in nonpoint source pollution—a technical and political challenge. Establishing measurable pollution reduction goals for coastal areas is needed, as is coordination of the many related agencies and program to effectively target the various laws, programs, funds, training, technical assistance, incentives, disincentives, and other management tools to address nonpoint source pollution of coastal waters.[18]

To address nonpoint sources of pollution, the Commission recommended that

- The National Ocean Council, working with states, should establish reduction of nonpoint source pollution in coastal watersheds as a national goal, with particular emphasis on impaired watersheds. The Council should then set specific, measurable objectives to meet human health-based and ecosystem-based water quality standards and ensure that all federal nonpoint source pollution programs are coordinated to attain those objectives.
- The Council should also review nonpoint programs established under Section 6217 of the Coastal Zone Act Reauthorization Amendments and under Section 319 of the Clean Water Act and make recommendations for improvements in these programs, including their possible consolidation.
- Congress should provide federal agencies with authority under the Clean Water Act and other laws to establish enforceable management measures for nonpoint sources of pollution and to impose financial disincentives if a state does not make meaningful progress toward meeting water quality standards on its own.
- EPA, working with state and local governments, should strengthen implementation of stormwater programs.[19]

The U.S. Commission also made recommendations related to other sources of pollution, including recommending that EPA and the states require advanced nutrient removal for wastewater treatment plant discharges into nutrient-impaired waters and that Congress amend the Clean Water Act to establish a new national regime for managing wastewater discharges from cruise ships. It also said that Congress should significantly increase the Clean Water and Drinking Water Revolving Funds.

Like the USCOP Report, the Pew Report focused on nonpoint source pollution: "Today, nonpoint sources present the greatest pollution threat to our oceans and coasts." Yet, "[t]he current legal framework is ill equipped to address this issue."[20]

The Commission noted a National Research Council study that found that the same amount of oil released by the *Exxon Valdez* oil spill—over 10 million gallons—washes off our coastal lands and into the surrounding waters every eight months.[21]

The Pew Oceans Commission found that one of the major sources of nonpoint pollution is nitrogen. Although nitrogen is essential to life, in excess it can significantly damage and alter ecosystems. In fact, as the Pew Report noted, *scientists now believe that nutrients are the primary pollution threat to living marine resources.*[22]

Most nitrogen in the oceans arrives from nonpoint sources, including stormwater runoff from roads and agricultural fields, and airborne nitrogen emitted from power plants and car tailpipes.[23]

The Pew Report recommends that to strengthen controls on nonpoint sources, the Clean Water Act should be revised to require the use of best management practices for agriculture and development. Compliance with the Clean Water Act should be a condition for receipt of federal funds for agriculture and transportation since these activities contribute significantly to polluted runoff. For example, the implementation of best management practices to control polluted runoff should be a condition of receipt of federal agricultural subsidies for farms and animal feeding operations over a certain size. Progress toward compliance with the Clean Water Act should be a condition for state eligibility for federal transportation funds, just as under the Clean Air Act progress towards compliance is now a condition for receipt of federal transportation funds. All states should establish water quality standards for nutrients, and these standards should be numeric standards (as opposed to just narrative standards) wherever possible.

In addition to nonpoint source pollution, the Pew Report discusses and makes recommendations regarding other pollution sources: unabated point sources of pollution (such as confined animal feeding operations), toxic pollution, cruise ship pollution, sound pollution, and invasive species.[24] It also recommends that Congress enact legislation to regulate ballast water discharges and to require ballast water treatment for all vessels carrying ballast water in U.S. waters.

E. Coastal Development

According to the U.S. Commission:

> Poorly planned growth reduces and fragments fish and wildlife habitat and can alter sedimentation rates and flows. It is also well understood that growth in coastal areas contributes to water pollution, with impacts on fishing, swimming, and many other recreational and economic activities. . . . Some evidence indicates that ecosystem health may be seriously impaired when the impervious area in a watershed reaches 10 percent, particularly in the absence of mitigating factors, such as a high percentage of wetlands or forest cover in a watershed, or urban stormwater best management practices such as riparian buffers along streams. If current coastal growth trends continue, many more watersheds will cross the 10 percent threshold over the next twenty-five years.[25]

The USCOP Report recommends reauthorization of the federal Coastal Zone Management Act (CZMA) to strengthen the planning and coordination capabilities of states and to enable them to incorporate a coastal watershed focus and more effectively manage growth. Amendments to the CZMA should include requirements for resource assessments; the development of measurable goals and performance measures; improved program evaluations; incentives for good performance and disincentives for inactions; and expanded boundaries that include coastal watersheds.[26]

To provide for more coordinated management, the USCOP Report recommends that Congress bring together area-based coastal management programs in a strengthened NOAA, including the CZM program, Marine Sanctuaries, the National Estuarine Research Reserve System (programs currently housed in NOAA), and the area-based coastal programs of other agencies, including the National Estuary Program, the Coastal Barrier Resources System, and the U.S. Fish and Wildlife Service Coastal Program.[27] The National Ocean Council should recommend changes to federal funding and infrastructure programs to discourage inappropriate growth in fragile or hazard-prone coastal areas and ensure consistency with national, regional, and state goals aimed at achieving economically and environmentally sustainable development.[28]

In the USCOP Report chapter on coastal hazards, there is an eerily accurate assessment of what could happen to New Orleans if the levees were to fail.[29] To avert such hazards, the report calls for the following:

- The U.S. Army Corps of Engineers, with guidance from the National Ocean Council, should ensure valid, peer-reviewed cost-benefit analyses of coastal projects, provide greater transparency to the public, enforce requirements for mitigating the impacts and coordinate such projects with broader coastal planning efforts;
- The National Ocean Council should establish a task force to improve collection and use of hazard-related data[30] and FEMA should enhance the technical assistance to state and local governments for developing or improving their hazard mitigation plans.[31]
- The National Ocean Council should recommend changes in the National Flood Insurance Program to reduce incentives for development in high-hazard areas.[32]

To better conserve and restore coastal habitat, the U.S. Commission recommends

- The CZMA should be amended to create a dedicated funding program for coastal and estuarine land conservation.[33]
- The regional ocean councils should assess regional needs and set goals and priorities for ocean and coastal habitat conservation and restoration efforts. The National Ocean Council should develop national goals.
- The U.S. Fish and Wildlife Service should complete, digitize, and periodically update the National Wetlands Inventory.
- The National Ocean Council should coordinate development of a comprehensive wetlands protection framework that is linked to coastal habitat and watershed management efforts and should make recommendations for integration of the Clean Water Act Section 404 wetlands permitting process into that broader management approach.[34]

The Pew Oceans Commission found that

We are fundamentally changing the natural ecosystems that attract us to the coasts. In some areas, we have converted expansive wetlands into cities, protected on all sides by levees. In others, we have converted sand dunes into irrigated gold courses and subdivisions.[35]

Government programs have contributed to the degradation of coastal ecosystems:

Government programs have contributed to the degradation of coastal ecosystems.

Government projects have dramatically altered our rivers and coastal waterways. . . . Habitats, species, and whole ecosystems are threatened by the elimination of wetlands, the channelization and damming of rivers, and the stabilization of inherently unstable beaches and barrier islands.[36]

To address the threats to coastal habitat, the Pew Report recommends use of a watershed approach to controlling the impact of development, particularly on water quality; supporting the development and implementation of state comprehensive habitat protection programs; and the redirecting of government programs and subsidies away from harmful coastal development and toward beneficial activities such as restoration.[37]

IV. The Administration Response

Under the Oceans Act of 2000, the Administration was required to issue a response to the U.S. Commission report. On December 17, 2004, the White House issued a forty-page "Ocean Action Plan"[38] in response to the U.S. Commission on Ocean Policy report, and President Bush established by Executive Order 13,366 a Cabinet-level Committee on Ocean Policy to coordinate the activities of executive branch departments and agencies regarding ocean-related matters in an integrated and effective manner. The Chairman of the Council on Environmental Quality (CEQ), James L. Connaughton, serves as Chairman of this Committee.

Among other things, the Ocean Action Plan called for setting federal research priorities, building a network of buoys to observe ocean and atmospheric conditions, working with local officials to protect coral reefs, and giving some fishermen an ownership stake in their fishing grounds as incentive to catch fish in a more sustainable way.

The Northwestern Hawaiian Islands Marine National Monument, consisting of approximately 139,793 square miles, is the largest marine protected area in the world.

Since release of the Ocean Action Plan, other steps have been taken, including, most notably, President Bush's Proclamation establishing the Northwestern Hawaiian Islands Marine National Monument, which was issued on June 15, 2006. The monument, consisting of approximately 139,793 square miles, is the largest marine protected area in the world. Another important step was the signing into law of the Magnuson-Stevens Fishery Conservation and Management Reauthorization Act of 2006, discussed below, which sets clear deadlines for ending overfishing.

On January 29, 2007, the Administration released *Charting the Course for Ocean Science in the United States: An Ocean Research Priorities Plan and Implementation Strategy,* which outlines twenty critical ocean research priorities for the United States for the next decade.[39] It also released an *Ocean Action Plan Update* that reviewed the steps taken to implement the USCOP Report recommendations and the additional actions that are being planned.[40]

V. The Legislative Response

A. Fisheries Conservation Legislation

On January 12, 2007, President Bush signed into law the Magnuson-Stevens Fishery Conservation and Management Reauthorization Act of 2006.[41] The legislation (1) preserves the strong conservation provisions already included in the Act; (2) preserves the applicability of the National Environmental Policy Act to the fishery management process; (3) sets a firm deadline for ending overfishing; (4) requires that annual catch levels be set such that overfishing does not occur and requires accountability measures to enforce those catch levels; (5) requires that regional fishery management councils set catch levels that do not exceed those recommended by the Science and Statistical Committees; (6) sets standards for Limited Access Privilege Program; and (7) requires the imposition of trade sections on countries whose vessels engage in illegal, unreported or unregulated fishing in international waters. Several of these provisions reflect the input and recommendations of the two national commissions, including those requiring a stronger role for science in establishing sustainable harvest levels, setting a clear deadline for ending overfishing, authorizing the use of market-based approaches in fisheries management, and providing stronger tools for addressing illegal, unregulated, and unreported fishing in international waters. However, many of the Commissions' recommendations were not adopted, including those dealing with reform of the council system, broadening representation of the councils beyond fishing interests, and separating conservation and allocation decisions.

B. Ocean Governance Legislation

On January 4, 2007, Rep. Sam Farr, along with Reps. Allen, Gilchrest, and Saxton, introduced the Oceans Conservation, Education, and National Strategy for the 21st Century Act, better known as OCEANS-21.[42] This bill, which is a streamlined version of legislation that was introduced in the 108th and 109th Congresses, focuses on ocean governance reform and contains many of the principles articulated in the two commission reports. It does the following: (1) establishes a comprehensive national oceans policy to guide federal management of U.S. coasts, oceans, and Great Lakes; (2) codifies NOAA, strengthening its mission and functions; (3) codifies the Committee on Ocean Policy; (4) promotes ecosystem-based, regional ocean partnerships; (5) enhances responsible ocean stewardship through education, information collection, and citizen involvement; and (6) establishes an Oceans and Great Lakes Conservation

Trust Fund. A hearing on this legislation was held in April 2007 by the Subcommittee on Fisheries, Wildlife, and Oceans of the House Committee on Natural Resources. Representatives of the Administration, the coastal states, fishing and environmental interests, and a member of the U.S. Commission testified.

Two other bills were introduced in the 108th and 109th Congresses that also addressed ocean governance:

- National Oceans Protection Act,[43] introduced in June 2005 by Sens. Boxer (D-CA) and Lautenberg (D-NJ), with. Sen. Dodd (D-CT) as a co-sponsor; and
- National Ocean Policy and Leadership Act,[44] introduced in July 2004 by Sen. Hollings (D-SC) and co-sponsored by Sens. Akaka (D-HI), Boxer (D-CA), Breaux (D-LA), Carper (D-DE), Gregg (R-NH), Inouye (D-HI), and Lautenberg.

In 2006, a NOAA Organic Act[45] passed the U.S. House of Representatives. This legislation codified the mission and structure of NOAA, but did not address the agency's resource management responsibilities.

As of the final writing of this book, no bill to reform ocean governance has yet been enacted into law.

VI. State and Regional Responses

The two commission reports have already spurred action in a number of coastal states. For example, in response to the commission reports, California passed the California Ocean Protection Act[46] and joined with the states of Washington and Oregon to form the West Coast Governors' Agreement on Ocean Health.[47] New York passed the New York Ocean and Great Lakes Ecosystem Conservation Act[48] and launched an Oceans and Great Lakes Initiative. Florida created the Florida Oceans and Coastal Resources Council.[49] Massachusetts is considering adopting an Ocean Act that would call for the development and implementation of a comprehensive ocean management plan for the commonwealth's waters. The Gulf of Mexico Alliance[50] and the Northeast Regional Ocean Council have been formed to promote cooperation around a set of priority issues among coastal states (and in the case of the Northeast council, the Eastern Canadian Premiers as well) in those regions. These are just some of the efforts under way by states acting individually or in partnership with other states.

VII. The Joint Ocean Commission Initiative

The Joint Ocean Commission Initiative (JOCI), the ongoing effort by commissioners from the two ocean commissions led by Adm. Watkins and Mr. Panetta, has issued two annual report cards grading the nation on its progress in implementing the recommendations of the two commissions. The most recent report card, released on January 30, 2007, gave the nation an overall grade of "C minus," due to the overall lack of significant progress in ocean policy reform.[51] Individual grades were given in six subjects as follows:

- C– on National Ocean Governance Reform;
- A– for Regional and State Ocean Governance Reform;
- D– for International Leadership;
- D+ for Research, Science, and Education
- B+ for Fisheries Management Reform;
- F for New Funding for Ocean Policy and Programs.

The Joint Initiative plans to continue pursuing governance reform, science, and funding initiatives identified in its June 2006 report to Congress, *From Sea to Shining Sea*.[52] This report identifies ten top actions that need to be taken by Congress, including an increase in base funding for core ocean and coastal programs on the order of an additional $750 million per year above fiscal year 2006 levels. By shining a public spotlight on the progress being made—or not made—in implementing the commissions' recommendations, the Joint Initiative is seeking to generate support for action.

VIII. Conclusion

The burgeoning state and regional ocean initiatives and the somewhat heightened congressional interest in oceans provide some hope for the future. These efforts need to be carefully nourished and supported. State initiatives and regional partnerships, by providing more effective management of ocean waters under their jurisdiction, can provide valuable models for the nation and spur federal action. Ultimately, federal action and leadership are essential. The federal responsibility for managing the U.S. Exclusive Economic Zone, an area larger than the county's entire land mass, and the important role the U.S. government plays in international ocean issues make federal leadership imperative.

Some of the issues that cry out for action in the near term include U.S. accession to the United Nations Convention on the Law of the Sea; enactment of legislation establishing a national ocean policy to protect, maintain, and restore health to ocean ecosystems and coordinating federal agency action to implement that policy; significantly increased funding for ocean programs and research; effective implementation of the Magnuson-Stevens Fishery Conservation and Management Reauthorization Act of 2006; and action to address the impacts of climate change and ocean acidification on ocean ecosystems. These and the other actions recommended both by many of the authors of this book and by the two national ocean commissions must be taken if we are to preserve and restore the health and productivity of the ocean on which the well-being of this and future generations depends.

Notes

1. *Available at* http://www.pewoceans.org [hereinafter Pew Report].
2. *Available at* http://www.oceancommission.gov [hereinafter USCOP Report].
3. Also known as the Stratton Commission report after the commission's chair, Jay Stratton, a former president of MIT and Chairman of the Ford Foundation; *available at* http://www.lib.noaa.gov/edocs/stratton/.

4. Dec. 2004, *available at* http://ocean.ceq.gov/actionplan.pdf.
5. For information, see http://www.jointoceancommission.org.
6. Jan. 2007, *available at* http://www.jointoceancommission.org/resource-center/2-Report
   -Cards/2007-01-01_2006_Ocean_Policy_Report_Card.pdf.
7. Pew Report, *supra* note 1, at ix.
8. *Id.* at x.
9. USCOP Report, *supra* note 2, at 4.
10. *Id.* at 25.
11. *Id.* at 55.
12. Pew Report, *supra* note 1, at viii.
13. USCOP Report, *supra* note 2, at 5–11.
14. Pew Report, *supra* note 1, at 102–108.
15. USCOP Report, *supra* note 2, at 104–106.
16. *Id.* at 20.
17. Pew Report, *supra* note 1, at 44–45.
18. USCOP Report, *supra* note 2, at 204.
19. *Id.* at 217–222.
20. Pew Report, *supra* note 1, at 60.
21. Nat'l Res. Council, Oil in the Sea III: Inputs, Fates, and Effects (Nat'l Acad. of Sci.
    Press 2002).
22. Nat'l Res. Council, Clean Coastal Waters: Understanding and Reducing the
    Effects of Nutrient Pollution (Nat'l Acad. Sci. 2000) (emphasis added).
23. Pew Report, *supra* note 1, at 60.
24. *Id.* at 122–125.
25. USCOP Report, *supra* note 2, at 151 (citations omitted).
26. *Id.* at 154.
27. *Id.* at 156.
28. *Id.* at 157.
29. *Id.* at 165.
30. *Id.* at 166.
31. *Id.* at 169.
32. *Id.* at 168.
33. *Id.* at 172.
34. *Id.* at 172–179.
35. *Id.* at 172–179.
36. Pew Report, *supra* note 1, at 53.
37. *Id.* at 57–58.
38. *Available at* http://ocean.ceq.gov/actionplan.pdf.
39. *Available at* http://ocean.ceq.gov/about/sup_jsost_prioritiesplan.html.
40. *Available at* http://ocean.ceq.gov/oap_update012207.pdf.
41. H.R. 5946, 109th Cong. (2006).
42. H.R. 21, 110th Cong. (2007).
43. S. 1224, 109th Cong. (2005).
44. S. 2647, 108th Cong. (2004).
45. H.R. 5450.
46. *Available at* http://www.resources.ca.gov/copc/documents.html.
47. *Available at* http://westcoastoceans.gov/.
48. New York Environmental Conservation Law Article 14–0101–14–0113.
49. *Available at* http://www.dep.state.fl.us/oceanscouncil.
50. For further information, see http://www2.nos.noaa.gov/gomex/upcoming/welcome.html.
51. *Supra* note 6.
52. *Available at* http://jointoceancommission.org/resource-center/I-Reports/2006-06-13_Sea_
    to_Shining_Sea_Report_to_Senate.pdf.

Table of Cases

Earth Island Inst. v. Evans, No. C 03-00072004, 2004 WL 1774221 (N.D. Cal. Aug. 9, 2004), 515 n.142

Earth Island Inst. v. Mosbacher, 746 F. Supp. 964 (N.D. Cal. 1990), *aff'd,* 929 F.2d 1449 (9th Cir. 1991), 515 n.132

Earth Island Inst. v. Mosbacher, 785 F. Supp. 826 (N.D. Cal. 1992), 515 n.133

Eastlake Cmty. Council v. City of Seattle, 823 P.2d 1132 (Wash. Ct. App. 1992), 176 n.119

11.037 Acres of Land; United States v., 685 F. Supp. 214 (N.D. Calif. 1988), 653 n.356

Enewetak, People of v. Laird, 353 F. Supp. 811 (D. Haw. 1973), 200 n.82

Environmental Def. Ctr., Inc. v. EPA, 344 F.3d 832 (9th Cir. 2003), 235 n.109

Escondido Mut. Water Co. v. La Jolla, Rincon, San Pasqual, Pauma & Pala Band of Mission Indians, 466 U.S. 765 (1984), 471 n.112

Esplanade Properties v. City of Seattle, 307 F.3d 978 (9th Cir. 2002), *cert. denied,* 123 S. Ct. 2574 (2003), 47, 48

Exxon Valdez, *In re,* 296 F. Supp. 2d 1071 (D. Alaska 2004), 270 n.120

Fanning v. Oregon Div. of State Lands, 151 Or. App. 609, 950 P.2d 353 (1997), 172 n.13

Federation of Fly Fishers v. Daley, 131 F. Supp. 2d 1158 (N.D. Cal. 2000), 533 n.60

First English Evangelical Lutheran Church v. County of Los Angeles, 482 U.S. 304 (1987), 62 n.50

Fisheries Case (United Kingdom v. Norway), 1951 I.C.J. 116 (Dec. 18), 401 n.27

Flores; United States v., 289 U.S. 137 (1933), 363 n.31

Florida; United States v., 363 U.S. 121 (1960), 82 n.10, 293 n.6

Florida Rock, 21 Cl. Ct. 161 (1990), 144 n.499

Forest Properties, Inc. v. United States, 177 F.3d 1360 (Fed. Cir.), *cert. denied,* 528 U.S. 951 (1999), 144 n.499

Fouke Company v. Mandel, 386 F. Supp. 1341 (D. Md. 1974), 511 n.31

Frezzo Bros.; United States v., 642 F.2d 59 (3d Cir. 1981), 234 n.108

Georgia v. South Carolina, 497 U.S. 376 (1990), 12, 32 n.80

Gerke Excavating, Inc.; United States v., 464 F.3d 723 (7th Cir., 2006), 127 n.173, 174

Gibbons v. Ogden, 22 U.S. 1 (1824), 118 n.50

Gillis v. Louisiana, 294 F.3d 755 (5th Cir. 2002), 172 n.13

Greater Yellowstone Coalition v. Flowers, 359 F.3d 1257 (10th Cir. 2004), 197 n.22, 198 n.43

Greenfield Mills, Inc. v. Macklin, 361 F.3d 934 (7th Cir. 2004), 128 n.183, 184

Greenpeace USA v. Stone, 748 F. Supp. 749 (D. Haw. 1990), *dismissed as moot,* 986 F.2d 175 (9th Cir. 1991), 200 n.83

Greenpeace v. NMFS, 55 F. Supp. 2d 1248 (W.D. Wash. 1999), 195, 199 n.58

Gulf Offshore Co. v. Mobil Oil Corp., 453 U.S. 473 (1981), 440 n.113

Gulf Oil Corp. v. Morton, 493 F.2d 141 (9th Cir. 1974), 438 n.62

Guste, State of Louisiana *ex rel.* v. Verity, 853 F.2d 322 (5th Cir. 1988), 528–529

Gwathmey v. North Carolina, 464 S.E.2d 674 (N.C. 1995), 52, 62 n.35

Hadaja, Inc. v. Evans, 263 F. Supp. 2d 346 (D.R.I. 2003), 287

Hanousek; United States v., 176 F.3d 1116 (9th Cir. 1999), 268 n.41

Hanson v. United States, 710 F. Supp. 1105 (E.D. Tex. 1989), 129 n.206

Hawaii, State of, v. Zimring, 479 P.2d 202 (Haw. 1970), 51

Hayashi; United States v., 22 F.3d 859 (9th Cir. 1993), 512 n.67

Hayden v. Noyes, 5 Conn. 391 (1824), 82 n.26

National Ass'n of Homebuilders v. Defenders of Wildlife, 551 U.S. ___, 2007 WL1801745 (June 25, 2007), 84 n.84, 87, 531 n.18, 532 n.41

National Ass'n of Home Builders v. U.S. Army Corps of Eng'rs, Civ. No. 00-379 (D.D.C., Sept. 29, 2006), 133 n.274, 277, 278

National Ass'n of Home Builders v. U.S. Army Corps of Eng'rs, 311 F. Supp. 2d 91 (D.D.C. 2004), 99, 131 n.242

National Ass'n of Home Builders v. U.S. Army Corps of Eng'rs, 440 F.3d 459 (D.C. Cir. 2006), 131 n.244

National Ass'n of Home Builders v. U.S. Army Corps of Eng'rs, 2007 U.S. Dist. LEXIS 6366 (Jan. 30, 2007), 131 n.245

National Mining Association v. U.S. Army Corps of Eng'rs, 145 F.3d 1399 (D.C. Cir. 1998), 97–98, 130 n.227

National Parks & Conservation Assoc. v. Babbitt, 241 F.3d 722 (9th Cir. 2001), 197 n.21

National Wildlife Fed'n v. Consumers Power Co., 862 F.2d 580 (6th Cir. 1988), 466 n.49

Natural Res. Def. Council, Inc. v. EPA, 22 F.3d 1125 (D.C. Cir. 1987), 234 n.108

Natural Res. Def. Council, Inc. v. EPA, 656 F.2d 768 (D.C. Cir. 1981), 230 n.37, 232 n.61

Natural Res. Def. Council, Inc. v. EPA, 863 F.2d 1420 (9th Cir. 1988), 230 n.31, 231 n.41, 54, 237 n.164

Natural Res. Def. Council, Inc. v. Train, 396 F. Supp. 1393, 1396–97 (D.D.C. 1975), *aff'd sub nom.* Natural Res. Def. Council, Inc. v. Costle, 568 F.2d 1369 (D.C. Cir. 1977), 234 n.108

Natural Res. Def. Council v. Daley, 62 F. Supp. 2d 102 (D.D.C. 1999), 291, 297 n.102, 299 n.181, 300 n.208

Natural Res. Def. Council v. Daley, 209 F.3d 747 (D.C. Cir. 2000), 287, 300 n.183, 301 n.219

Natural Res. Def. Council v. Evans, 232 F. Supp. 2d 1003 (N.D. Cal. 2002), 407 n.109–112

Natural Res. Def. Council v. Evans, 243 F. Supp. 2d 1046 (N.D. Cal. 2003), 298 n.131

Natural Res. Def. Council v. Hodel, 865 F.2d 288 (D.C. Cir. 1988), 437 n.24, 438 n.65

Natural Res. Def. Council v. NMFS, 280 F. Supp. 2d 1007 (N.D. Cal. 2003), 200 n.84

Natural Res. Def. Council v. NMFS, 421 F.3d 872 (9th Cir. 2005), 291, 297 n.101, 298 n.166, 300 n.211

Natural Res. Def. Council v. Nuclear Regulatory Comm'n, 647 F.2d 1345 (D.C. Cir. 1981), 200 n.83

Natural Res. Def. Council v. Sw. Marine, Inc., 236 F.3d 985 (9th Cir. 2000), 249, 268 n.50

Natural Res. Def. Council v. U.S. Dep't of the Navy, 2002 WL 32095131 (C.D. Cal. 2002), 200 n.85, 529

Needham, *In re*, 354 F.3d 340 (5th Cir. 2003), 124 n.143

New Hampshire v. Maine, 426 U.S. 363 (1976), 12, 32 n.78

New Jersey Dep't of Envtl. Protection & Energy v. Long Island Power Auth., 30 F.3d 403 (3d Cir. 1994), 239 n.205

New Jersey Dep't of Envtl. Protection v. Jersey Central Power & Light Co., 308 A.2d 671 (N.J. Super. Ct. Law Div. 1973), *aff'd*, 336 A.2d 750 (N.J. Super. Ct. App. Div. 1975), *rev'd on other grounds*, 351 A.2d 337 (N.J. 1976), 64 n.119

Nollan v. California Coastal Commission, 483 U.S. 825 (1987), 49, 165, 177 n.131

Norfolk v. U.S. Army Corps of Eng'rs, 968 F.2d 1438 (1st Cir. 1992), 137 n.334

North Carolina Wildlife Federation v. Tulloch, No. C90-713-CIV-5-BO (E.D.N.C. 1992), 98

Northern Cal. River Watch v. City of Healdsburg, 457 F.3d 1023 (9th Cir. 2006), 127 n.172

North Hempstead, Town of v. Village of North Hills, 482 F. Supp. 900 (E.D.N.Y. 1979), 175 n.91

Northwest Envtl. Advocates v. EPA, 2005 WL 756614, at *1 (N.D. Cal. Aug. 19, 2005), 237 n.148, 260, 266

Tabb Lakes v. United States, 715 F. Supp. 726 (E.D. Va. 1988), *aff'd without opinion*, 885 F.2d 866 (4th Cir. 989), 124 n.138

Target Sportswear v. United States, 19 Ct. Int'l Trade 65 (1995), 363 n.28

Tennessee Valley Authority v. Hill, 437 U.S. 153 (1978), 520–521

Ten Taxpayer Citizens Group v. Cape Wind Associates, 373 F.3d 183 (1st Cir. 2004), 427, 440 n.113

Texas; United States v., 339 U.S. 707 (1950), 436 n.2

Texas Boundary Case, 394 U.S. 1 (1969), 35 n.144

Texas Landowners Rights Ass'n v. Harris, 453 F. Supp. 1025 (D.D.C. 1978), 177 n.141

Texas v. Louisiana, 426 U.S. 465 (1976), 12, 32 n.79

Thornton, State *ex rel.* v. Hay, 462 P.2d 671 (Or. 1969), 64 n.97

Togiak, People of v. United States, 470 F. Supp. 423 (D.D.C. 1979), 484

Toomer v. Witsell, 334 U.S. 385 (1948), 32 n.74, 35 n.147

Town of Huntington v. Marsh, 884 F.2d 648 (2d Cir. 1989), 269 n.68

Town of North Hempstead v. Village of North Hills, 482 F. Supp. 900 (E.D.N.Y. 1979), 175 n.91

Treacy v. Newdunn Assocs. LLP, 344 F.3d 407 (4th Cir. 2003), 125 n.142

Treasure Salvors, Inc. v. Unidentified Wrecked & Abandoned Sailing Vessel, 569 F.2d 330 (5th Cir. 1978), 427

Trinidad Coal Co.; United States v., 137 U.S. 160 (1890), 653 n.354

Trout Unlimited v. National Marine Fisheries Service, ___ F. Supp. 2d ___, 2007 WL 1795036 (W.D. Wash. June 13, 2007), 525, 526

Trustees of Brookhaven v. Strong, 60 N.Y. 56 (1875), 82 n.26

Tulare Lake Basin Water Storage District v. United States, 49 Fed. Cl. 313 (2001), 533 n.83

Turtle Island Restoration Network v. NMFS, 340 F.3d 969 (9th Cir. 2003), 534 n.97

UFO Chuting of Haw., Inc. v. Young, 327 F. Supp. 2d 1220 (D. Haw. 2004), 511 n.35

Union Oil Co. of Cal. v. Morton, 512 F.2d 743 (9th Cir. 1975), 438 n.63

United Kingdom v. Norway (Fisheries Case), 1951 I.C.J. 116 (Dec. 18), 401 n.27

United States Public Interest Research Group v. Atlantic Salmon of Maine, 257 F. Supp. 2d 407 (D. Me. 2003), 119 n.59

United States Public Interest Research Group v. Atlantic Salmon of Maine, 339 F.3d 23 (1st Cir. 2003), 447

United States v. *See Name of opposing party*

Utah Div. of State Lands v. United States, 482 U.S. 193 (1987), 30 n.30, 66 n.173

Ventura County Commercial Fishermen's Ass'n v. California Fish & Game Comm'n, 2004 WL 293565 (Cal. Ct. App. 2d Div., Feb. 17, 2004), 65 n.127

Verity v. Center for Envtl. Educ., 488 U.S. 1004 (1989), 510 n.12

Vermont Yankee Nuclear Power Corp. v. NRDC, 435 U.S. 519 (1978), 198 n.31

Vietnamese Fishermen Ass'n of Am. v. Cal. Dep't of Fish & Game, 816 F. Supp. 1468 (N.D. Cal. 1993), 294 n.25

Virginia Beach, City of v. Brown, 858 F. Supp. 585 (E.D. Va. 1994), 175 n.92

Vujnovich v. La. Wildlife & Fisheries Comm'n, 376 So. 2d 330 (La. App. 1979), 172 n.13

Washington; United States v., 384 F. Supp. 312 (W.D. Wash. 1974), 276

Washington State Charterboat Ass'n v. Baldrige, 702 F.2d 820 (9th Cir. 1983), *cert. denied*, 464 U.S. 1053 (1984), 267 n.14

Wasserson; United States v., 418 F.3d 225 (3d Cir. 2005), 268 n.47

Index

Convention on Wetlands of International Importance Especially as Waterfowl Habitat, 88
Cooperate, duty to, 389
COP (Committee on Ocean Policy), 190, 558–559, 609, 610, 666, 667
Corals and coral reefs, 430–431, 554, 574, 576, 582, 600–601
Cordell Bank National Marine Sanctuary, 559
Corps of Engineers
  aquaculture, 446
  artificial islands, 426
  beach renourishment and shore armoring programs, 148
  Civil Works water resource development activities, 89
  coastal hazards, 665
  divisions and districts, 89
  dredge and fill activities, 70
  harborworks permits, 22
  ocean dumping permits, 250–250
  OCS authority, 26
  Regulatory Guidance Letters, 91
  regulatory staff, 116 n.30
  Rivers and Harbors Act implementation and enforcement, 90
  Section 406 implementation and enforcement, 91–99, 110
  Tulloch Rule, 98
  wetlands, 88–89, 90, 100–110, 112
  wind energy projects, 444, 454–455
  See also Ocean Dumping Act (ODA) (1988)
Cotonou Agreement, 338–339
Council on Environmental Quality (CEQ), 103, 183, 184, 187, 193, 607
Council on Environmental Quality (CEQ) NEPA Task Force, 189, 633
Council on Ocean Stewardship in the Executive Office of the President, 608
CPSs (Coastal Political Subdivisions), 432–433
Critical habitat, under ESA, 521–522, 527–528, 618–619
Cruise ship discharges, 260–266, 663
Cumulative impact, 164, 185
CWA. See Clean Water Act (CWA)
CZARA (Coastal Zone Act Reauthorization Amendments) (1990), 206, 222, 223

CZMA. See Coastal Zone Management Act (CZMA) (1972)
CZM (coastal zone management) program, 149–150, 151, 665

D

Dall's porpoises, 490
Data collection, UNCLOS straddling and migratory fish stocks agreement, 391
Data towers, 26
DDT, 506
Dead zones, 626
Declaration of Panama, 497
Deep sea exploration, 459–462, 463
Deepwater Port Act (DPA) (1974), 449, 451, 452
Defense Department, 217, 414
De Jure Maris (Hale), 40–41
Developing countries
  access arrangements, 340
  fishing industry and employment, 333, 335
  Fish Stocks Agreement, 390, 392
  greenhouse gas emissions reduction, 586
  import restrictions, 342
  special treatment of goods from, 337, 338–339, 341
  tariff liberalization impact, 342–343
  technical assistance under Magnuson-Stevens Reauthorization, 322
  UNCLOS, 392
Development Operations Coordination Document (DOCD), 417
Dingell, John, 477
Discharges
  of ballast water, 80, 246, 257–260, 664
  from cruise ships, 260–266, 663
  of dredged or filled material, 96–99
  of graywater, 245, 262
  from military vessels, 216–217
  no-discharge zones, 218, 264–265
  of sewage, 216–218, 246, 250, 253–254, 262
Dispute resolution procedures, under UNCLOS, 385–386, 392
Distinct population segments, 524–526
District of Columbia, Chesapeake Bay Program, 77
DOCD (Development Operations Coordination Document), 417

and ecosystem-based management, 630–631

energy resource management, 52–53, 56–57

evolution and scope of, 42–45

Exclusive Economic Zone, 57–60, 631

fisheries management, 52, 54–55

government's fiduciary obligations, 631

introduction to, 39–42

origins of, 40–41

takings and coastal development, 45–48

unresolved issues, 53–60

Puerto Rico, 69, 150

Puffinus mauretanicus, 577

Puget Sound, 600

Q

Quotas and tariffs, 341–344

R

Ramsar Convention on Wetlands, 88

Ray, G. Carleton, 611

Rayfuse, 389

Reagan administration

EEZ establishment, 27, 28, 57

Fishery Conservation Zone, 276

OCS policy, 422

territorial sea extension, 25

UNCLOS, 379–381

Reauthorization Act (2006), 284, 293

Recreational activities, 49–50, 206

Refuge Recreation Act, 550

Refuge Revenue Sharing Act, 550

Refuse Act, 256–257, 262

Regional fishery management councils, 76–78, 277–285, 541, 542–543, 629–630, 661

Regional fishery management organizations (RFMOs), 304, 311–321, 324, 325, 355

Regional Greenhouse Gas Initiative (RGGI), 592 n.65

Regional ocean councils, 659, 660, 665

Regional Oceans Partnerships, 609

Renewable/alternative energy, 432, 444, 454–459, 463

Research

ecosystem-based management, 602–603

Ecosystem Research Program, 639 n.31

high seas, 10

marine protected areas, 74, 481, 500–501

National Estuarine Research Reserve System, 152, 544–545, 665

polar bears, 502

RFMOs (regional fishery management organizations), 304, 311–321, 324, 325, 355

Rhode Island

no-discharge zones, 218

Public Trust Doctrine, 43

Rivers, 4–5, 32 n.72, 44

Rivers and Harbors Act (1899), 27, 88, 89–90, 256, 444

Rock awash, 15–16

Rocks, defined, 19–20

Romans, 40

Rosenberg, Andrew, 603–604

Rules of origin, 337–339

Russia

Commander Island shipwreck, 519

Northwest Atlantic Fisheries Organization membership, 313–314

polar bears, 502

pollock management, 317

S

SADC (Southern Africa Development Community), 314

SAFMC (South Atlantic Fishery Management Council), 543

Salmon, 78, 342, 502–503, 524–526, 530

Salmon farming, 55–56, 445

Sanctuaries, marine, 168, 540–542, 559, 628

Sanders-Boxer bill, 587

San Diego Multiple Species Conservation Program (SDMSCP), 616

Sand rights, 54

Sanitary and phytosanitary standards (SPS), 347–348

San Onofre Nuclear Reactor, 395–396

Santa Barbara oil spill, 421

Sax, Joseph, 40, 42

Schofield, Clive, 8, 19

Science Magazine, 334, 600

Scientific and Statistical Committees (SSCs), 661

Scientific research. See Research

Scientists, support for marine reserves, 537

SCRS (Standing Committee on Research and Science), 315, 316

World Trade Organization
(WTO) *(continued)*
rules of origin, 337–338
trade-related environmental measures,
358–359
WPRFMC (Western Pacific Regional Fishery
Management Council), 277–278, 620

Z

Zero mortality rate goal (ZMRG), 486, 489,
493, 505

Zones of jurisdiction
"Area," 10–11
contiguous zone, 8
continental shelf, 9–10, 25–28
diagram of, 7
exclusive economic zone, 8–9, 11, 19, 27
high seas, 10
internal waters, 3–7, 11
issues and disputes, 13–25
territorial sea, 7–8, 25